BUSINESSES AND ORGANIZATIONS CITED IN THIS BOOK

3M Dental Products Division

ADAC Laboratories
Allied Signal
Amazon.com
American Electric Power
American Express
American National Standards Institute
American Parkinson's Disease Association
American Red Cross
American Society for Quality
Ames Rubber Corporation
Analog Devices, Inc.
Apple Computer
Armstrong Building Products Operations
AT&T
Australian Quality Council
Avis

Baxter Healthcare International
Bell System
BI
Big Bear Stores
Bloomfield Tool Company
Black & Decker
Boeing Airlift and Tanker
Boise Cascade
Bose Corporation
Branch-Smith Printing Division

CapStar Health Systems
Cargill, Inc.
Caterpillar, Inc.
Center for Quality of Management
Chase Manhattan Bank
Chemical Workers Association
Child Focus, Inc.
Cincinnati Water Works
Clarke American Checks
CNH Capital
Coca-Cola Company
Continental Airlines
Convergys Corporation
Coors Brewing Company
Copeland Companies
Corryville Foundry Company
CRI Star
Crystal Silicon
Custom Research Inc.

Daimler-Chrysler
Dana Corporation
Deer Valley Resort
Defense Supply Center Philadelphia

Dell Computer
Disney Corporation
Domino's Pizza
Douglas Aircraft

Eastman Chemical Company
European Foundation for Quality
    Management
Excelsior Inn

Fanuc Ltd.
Federal Quality Institute
FedEx
Fidelity Investments
First National Bank of Chicago
Florida Power and Light
Ford Motor Company
Federal Quality Institute
Froedtert Memorial Lutheran Hospital

General Electric
The Gap
General Motors Powertrain Division
GeoOrb Polymers, North America
Gold Star Chili, Inc.
Granite Rock Company
GTE Directories Corporation

Herend Porcelain Manufacturing
Hershey Foods Corporation
Hewlett Packard
Hillerich & Bradby Co.
Hilton Hotels
Honeywell, Inc.
Honeywell International
Hydraulic Lift Company
Hyundai Motor Co.

IBM Rochester
Ina Tile Company
Institute for Healthcare Improvement
Internal Revenue Service
International Organization for
    Standardization
ITT

Janson Medical Clinic
Joint Commission on Accreditation of
    Healthcare Organizations
Jim's SteakHouse
Johnson & Johnson
Johnson Controls, Inc.
Juran Institute

continued on next page

JUSE (Union of Japanese Scientists and Engineers)

KARLEE Company
Kelly's Seafood Restaurant
Koalaty Kid

La Ventana Window Company
LaRosa's, Inc.
Legal Sea Foods
L.L. Bean
Los Alamos National Bank
Lucas Suminomo Brakes, Inc.

Magnivision
Marlow Industries
Master Black Belts
McDonald's
McDonnell Douglas
Merrill Lynch Credit Corporation
Microsoft Corporation
Middletown Regional Hospital
Midwest Express Airlines
Mitsubishi
Motorola, Inc.
Murphy Trucking, Inc.

National Cash Register Company
National Committee for Quality Assurance
National Furniture
National Institute of Standards and Technology
National Labor Relations Board
National Quality Institute (Canada)
National Quality Program
Nationwide Insurance
NCR Corporation
Nissan
Nordstrom
Nucor Corporation

Operational Management International, Inc.

Palmer Sausage Co.
Pal's Sudden Service
Penn State University
PepsiCo
PIMS Associates
Polaroid
Procter & Gamble
Prudential Insurance Company

Rath & Strong
Raytheon

Readilunch Restaurant
Red Cross
The Ritz-Carlton Hotel Company
Rotor Clip Company, Inc.
Royal Mail (UK)
Rubbermaid

Samsung Electronics Co.
SAS Institute, Inc.
Selit Corp.
Semco S/A
Shure, Inc.
Siemens Energy and Automation
Solar Turbines, Inc.
Solectron Corporation
Southwest Airlines
Southwest Louisiana Regional Medical Center
Starbucks
STMicroelectronics
Stuart Injection Molding Co.
Sun Microsystems
Sundaram-Clayton
Sunny Fresh Foods
Sunset Manufacturing, Inc.
Superquinn

TD Industries
Techneglas
TecSmart Electronics
Texas Instruments (TI)
Texas Nameplate Company
Torque Traction Technologies, Inc.
Toyota Motor Corporation
Trident Precision Manufacturing, Inc.
TVS Partnership Proprietary, LTD

Ultra-Productivity Fasteners Company
Unison Industries, Inc.

W. Edward Deming Institute
Wainwright Industries
Wal-Mart
Walt Disney Company
Westel Mobile Telecommunications Co. Ltd.
Westerfield Construction
Western Electric Company
Whirlpool
Wilson Sporting Goods

Xerox Corporation Business Services

For more information, go to
http://www.evans.swlearning.com

THE MANAGEMENT AND CONTROL OF QUALITY

SIXTH EDITION

JAMES R. EVANS
UNIVERSITY OF CINCINNATI

WILLIAM M. LINDSAY
NORTHERN KENTUCKY UNIVERSITY

THOMSON
™
SOUTH-WESTERN

Australia · Canada · Mexico · Singapore · Spain · United Kingdom · United States

THOMSON

SOUTH-WESTERN

The Management and Control of Quality, 6e
James R. Evans and William M. Lindsay

VP/Editorial Director:
Jack W. Calhoun

VP/Editor-in-Chief:
George Werthman

Acquisitions Editor:
Charles E. McCormick, Jr.

Developmental Editor:
Alice C. Denny

Marketing Manager:
Larry Qualls

Production Editor:
Chris Sears

Manufacturing Coordinator:
Diane Lohman

Technology Project Editor:
Christine A. Wittmer

Media Editor:
Amy Wilson

Design Project Manager:
Bethany Casey

Production House:
Trejo Production

Cover Designer:
Bethany Casey

Cover Image:
PhotoDisc, Inc.

Internal Designer:
Jennifer Lambert, Jen2 Design

Printer:
Thomson-West
Eagan, MN

For permission to use material from
this text or product, submit a
request online at
http://www.thomsonrights.com.
Any additional questions about per-
missions can be submitted by email
to thomsonrights@thomson.com.

For more information
contact South-Western,
5191 Natorp Boulevard,
Mason, Ohio, 45040.
Or you can visit our Internet site at:
http://www.swlearning.com

Brief Contents

CONTENTS

PREFACE

"Why is quality still so bad?" laments Scott Paton, editor-in-chief of *Quality Digest*, a major trade publication for the quality profession, in his April 2002 editorial. Although he notes that the quality of U.S. products as a whole is better now than it was in 1972, it is worse than it was in 1992 (when quality was *the* buzzword among businesses). And it's not just in manufacturing. Paton states, "If you've had a truly high-quality experience on a recent flight or with your loan application or buying a car or with your hospital, you're in the minority." He places the blame squarely on senior management, who fail to see the simple but essential relationship between customers' needs and expectations and designing, building, and delivering great products and services.

We agree completely—the war for better quality must continue—which is why we continue to update and improve this book. Today's business and not-for-profit organizations need to capitalize on the knowledge and "lessons learned" that excellent organizations have acquired. One of the best ways of obtaining such knowledge is from the national role models that have emerged from the Malcolm Baldrige National Quality Award in the United States and similar programs throughout the world. The expansion of Baldrige to nonprofit education and health care—along with recent winners—has generated a high level of interest among these sectors. Thus in this new edition, we continue to use Baldrige as the fundamental framework for organizing and presenting key issues of performance excellence.

Six Sigma* has taken the corporate world by storm and represents the thrust of many efforts to improve products, services, and processes. Moreover, Six Sigma is grounded in the fundamental principles of total quality that have defined the concept for several decades. Hence, the most significant revision to this edition of the book is a comprehensive focus on Six Sigma and its relationships with fundamental quality principles and the Baldrige categories.

CHANGES IN THE SIXTH EDITION

The sixth edition of *The Management and Control of Quality* continues to embrace the fundamental principles and historical foundations of total quality and to promote

---

* Six Sigma is a federally registered trademark and service mark of Motorola, Inc.

high-performance management practices that are reflected in the Baldrige Criteria, while providing a foundation for understanding and applying Six Sigma. The significant changes for the new edition include:

- Revised, integrated, and more comprehensive coverage of Six Sigma philosophy, concepts, and techniques, and new chapters on Principles of Six Sigma and Design for Six Sigma.
- Contrasts and comparisons of Baldrige, ISO 9000, and Six Sigma in the managerial chapters of the book.
- New internal layout highlighting important concepts to improve readability.
- A new "Bonus Materials" folder on the CD-ROM that includes additional cases, summaries of key points and terminology, and supplementary topics for each chapter.
- Text coverage of most of the body of knowledge (BOK) required for ASQ certification as a Certified Quality Manager.

As in the previous edition, Part 1 introduces fundamentals, and Part 2 concentrates on the management system. However, Part 3 has been refocused around Six Sigma and basic technical topics. The chapters in this section have been revised significantly, and new chapters on Six Sigma Principles and Design for Six Sigma have been added. This organization provides the instructor with considerable flexibility in focusing on both managerial and technical topics, for audiences ranging from undergraduate students, MBA students, or executives.

We have updated every chapter to reflect current thinking and practice, including many new and interesting *Quality in Practice* cases. Cases and a wide variety of examples from organizations around the world emphasize the importance of quality in the global economy.

New Organization and Focus on Six Sigma

Part 1 provides an introduction to quality management principles.

- Chapter 1 introduces the notion of quality, its history and importance, definitions, basic principles, and its impact on competitive advantage and financial return.
- Chapter 2 explores the role of total quality in all key economic sectors: manufacturing, service, health care, education, and the public sector.
- Chapter 3 presents the philosophical perspectives supporting total quality, chiefly those of Deming, Juran, and Crosby, as well as quality management frameworks defined by the Malcolm Baldrige National Quality Award and the Criteria for Performance Excellence, ISO 9000, and Six Sigma.

Part 2 focuses on the management system, which is concerned with planning to meet customers' needs, arranging to meet those needs through leadership and strategic planning, and accomplishing goals through the actions of people and work processes. All of these activities are done with an eye toward continuous improvement and using data and information to guide the decision-making process. Each of Chapters 4 through 8 summarizes the key relationships and importance of the topics to Baldrige, Six Sigma, and ISO 9000.

- In Chapter 4, the focus is on understanding customers and their needs, and practices to achieve customer satisfaction.
- Chapter 5 covers the important role of total quality in leadership and strategic planning.

- Chapter 6 deals with human resource practices, specifically the design of high-performance work systems and HR management in a total quality environment.
- Chapter 7 outlines the scope of process management activities for value creation and support processes, the philosophy of continuous improvement, and the role of project management in Six Sigma and other quality improvement efforts.
- In Chapter 8, the focus is on the use of data and information to measure and manage organizational performance. This chapter includes discussion of balanced scorecards and recent approaches to knowledge management.
- The final chapter in this part, Chapter 9, deals with building and sustaining quality organizations. Coverage includes building a quality infrastructure, organizational culture, and new sections on self-assessment and change management.

Part 3 includes basic technical issues, tools, and techniques that underpin Six Sigma.

- Chapter 10 is new and provides an overview of the principles of Six Sigma, its problem-solving orientation and methodology, and synergy with lean production.
- Chapter 11 provides a general introduction to statistical thinking and the role of statistical tools and methodology in quality and Six Sigma.
- Chapter 12 is also new and addresses tools that support the concept of design for Six Sigma (DFSS), including concept development, design development, design optimization, and design verification.
- Chapter 13 focuses on quality improvement, including process improvement paradigms, basic tools, and new material on engaging the workforce.
- Finally, Chapter 14 provides a comprehensive introduction to statistical process control.

Features and Pedagogy to Enhance Learning

The sixth edition of *The Management and Control of Quality* contains a new internal design to make it more "reader-friendly." Each chapter begins with a single-page *Quality Profile* of two role-model organizations. Significant points of learning and emphasis are now highlighted in distinctive boxes. Quality Spotlight icons in the margin identify examples of specific organizational actions, and CD icons in the margin indicate that extensive supplementary materials may be found on the accompanying Student CD-ROM.

The *Quality Profile* presented at the beginning of each chapter provides background, important practices, and results for organizations that embrace total quality principles. Most of these organizations are Baldrige winners. In each chapter, *Quality in Practice* case studies describe real applications of the chapter material. They reinforce the chapter concepts and provide opportunities for discussion and more practical understanding. Many of the case studies are drawn from real, published, or personal experiences of the authors.

End-of-chapter materials for each chapter include Review Questions, which are designed to help students check their understanding of the key concepts presented in the chapter. All the chapters in Parts 1 and 2 also have Discussion Questions that are open-ended or experiential in nature, and designed to help students expand their thinking or tie practical experiences to abstract concepts. Chapter 8 and those in Part 3 include Problems designed to help students develop and practice quantitative skills.

Most chapters have a section entitled Projects, Etc. that provides projects involving field investigation or other types of research. Finally, each chapter includes several Cases, which encourage critical thinking to apply the concepts to unstructured or more comprehensive situations.

Student CD-ROM

The CD-ROM that comes with new copies of the text contains extensive Bonus Materials, including the following:

- Summaries of key points and terminology for each chapter
- Additional readings that support and extend the presentations in the chapters
- Baldrige criteria and case studies,
- Multimedia cases (indicated with an icon in the textbook) with digital videos
- Additional cases for instruction and discussion
- Microsoft® Excel templates for quantitative analysis
- Web links to key organizations cited in the book
- A Glossary of terms from the textbook
- The Quality Gamebox™, developed by PQ Systems in Dayton, Ohio, which is a collection of simulations for teaching concepts of variability

InfoTrac® College Edition

InfoTrac provides students with complete online access to full-text articles from thousands of scholarly and popular periodicals. Research possibilities are unlimited. New copies of the sixth edition textbook include a passcode that provides unlimited access for four months.

Web Site

The URL for the Web site for new edition of *The Management and Control of Quality* is **http://www.evans.swlearning.com**. Among other resources on the site, the Web links for organizations mentioned in the text are given in the Internet Resources. The lists are organized by chapter for convenience and may be used to access the information about the organization. A listing of general Web links on quality is also included.

Note on Company References and Citations

In today's ever-changing business environment, many companies and divisions are sold, merged, divested, or declared bankruptcy, resulting in name changes. For example, Texas Instruments Defense Systems & Electronics Group was sold to Raytheon and is now part of Raytheon Systems Company, and AT&T Universal Card Services was bought by CitiBank (which is now CitiGroup). Although we have made efforts to note these changes in the book, others will undoubtedly occur after publication. In citing applications of total quality in these companies, we have generally preserved their original names to clarify that the practices and results cited occurred under their original corporate identities.

SUPPORT MATERIALS FOR INSTRUCTORS

The following support material is available from **http://www.swlearning.com** or the Thomson Learning Academic Resource Center at 800-423-0563. All instructor ancillaries are combined in the **Instructor's Resource CD** (ISBN: 0-324-20226-1).

- The **Instructors' Manual**—Prepared by author William Lindsay, contains teaching suggestions and answers to all end-of-chapter questions, exercises, problems, and cases.
- **Power Point™ presentation slides**—Prepared by author Jim Evans for use in lectures. New in this edition are Solved Problems in PowerPoint format to illustrate quantitative techniques, prepared by author William Lindsay.
- **Test Bank**—Prepared by Darrell Radson of John Carroll University, the Test Bank includes true/false, multiple-choice, and short answer questions for each chapter. ExamView® computerized testing software allows instructors to create, edit, store, and print exams. ExamView also allows online test delivery.

Possible Course Outlines

Because the textbook material is comprehensive, it normally cannot be covered fully in one course. The textbook is designed to be flexible in meeting instructor needs. We have used it in both undergraduate courses and in managerially oriented MBA electives.

We believe that undergraduate majors in industrial or operations management are best served by developing hands-on knowledge that they will be able to use in their entry-level jobs. Thus a typical course for these undergraduate students might emphasize the material in Parts 1 and 3, with some overview of the topics in Part 2. For MBAs, coverage of most of the first 9 chapters would be more appropriate for a quarter-long course, while much of Part 3 can be included in a semester-long course. At the University of Cincinnati, for example, we offer a 10-week MBA course that covers Chapters 1–9, and a shorter, 5-week course focused on the remaining chapters and Six Sigma.

ACKNOWLEDGMENTS

We are extremely grateful to all the quality professionals, professors, reviewers, and students who have provided valuable ideas and comments during the development of this and previous editions. For this sixth edition of *The Management and Control of Quality*, we received excellent feedback and suggestions from colleagues who participated in a focused survey. Our thanks and appreciation go to:

Richard Benedetto, Merrimack College
Victor L. Berardi, Kent State University, Stark
Greg Blundell, Kent State University, Stark
Gary Bragar, Bloomfield College
Jon Burch, Trevecca Nazarene University
Brenda J. Condrick, Western International University
Deborah F. Cook, Virginia Polytechnic Institute and State University
Robert A. Cornesky, Southern Wesleyan University
Christine L. Corum, Purdue School of Technology
Kazem Darbandi, California State Polytechnic University, Pomona
David Doll, California State University, Hayward
Craig G. Downing, Southeast Missouri State University
Ellen J. Dumond, California State University, Fullerton
Ahmad Elshennawy, University of Central Florida
Robert F. Grant, Carthage College
Marilyn M. Helms, Dalton State College

Anil Jambekar, Michigan Technological University
William "Coty" Keller, St. Joseph's College, New York
Henry W. Kraebber, Purdue University
Frances Kubicek, Kalamazoo Valley Community College
David Lewis, University of Massachusetts, Lowell
Kevin Linderman, University of Minnesota
Debra P. Maddox, Barry University
Sara McComb, University Massachusetts, Amherst
Jalane M. Meloun, Kent State University
Muhammad Obeidat, Southern Polytechnic State University
K. Praveen Parboteeah, University of Wisconsin, Whitewater
Jim Pesek, Clarion University of Pennsylvania
Darrell Radson, John Carroll University
J. M. Thom, Purdue University
John Todd, University of Arkansas
Chiang Wang, California State University, Sacramento
Don Wardell, University of Utah
Geoff Willis, University of Central Oklahoma

Many people deserve special thanks for their contributions to development and production of the book. Our regards go to senior acquisitions editor Charles McCormick, Jr., senior developmental editor Alice Denny, production editor Chris Sears, and designer Bethany Casey at Thomson Business and Professional Publishing, and Richard Fenton, Mary Schiller, and Esther Craig, our previous editors at West Educational Publishing.

Quality expert Joseph Juran was asked in an interview in 2002 what advice he would give to someone just starting out in quality today. He replied, "I would start out by saying 'Are you lucky!' Because I think the best is yet to be. In this current century, we are going to see a lot of growth in quality because the scope has expanded so much . . . away from manufacturing to all the other industries, including the giants: health care, education, and government."

We will continue to do our best to improve this book in our quest for quality and to spread what we truly believe is a fundamentally important message to future generations of business leaders. We encourage you to contact us at our e-mail addresses with any comments or improvement suggestions you may have.

Please recall that instructor ancillaries may be requested from your Thomson publisher's representative, from http://evans.swlearning.com, or by calling the Academic Resource Center at 800-423-0563 in the United States.

James R. Evans (james.evans@uc.edu)
William M. Lindsay (lindsay@nku.edu)

PART 1

THE QUALITY SYSTEM

Today, we generally do not hear about quality in business, except when things go wrong. Here is one example: "Spend $25,000 on a car that doesn't run the way you expect it to, and you get pretty angry. Spend $50,000 or $100,000, and you get really angry. Just listen to the anguished howls of Mercedes-Benz owners on Web sites . . . as they vent about the latest mishap to afflict their Benzes. Depending on the model, the complaints range from faulty key fobs and leaky sunroofs to balky electronics that leave drivers and their passengers stranded. Regardless of the severity, a single sentiment runs through the gripes: this shouldn't be happening to a Mercedes." Stories of successful organizations generally end up in publications dedicated to quality professionals, which basically "preach to the choir."

We believe that less attention is paid to quality today as the result of two forces— a "good-news, bad-news" type of story. The good news is that the principles of quality that were new to many organizations in the early 1980s have become a common part of routine management practice; in other words, quality is so ingrained in the cultures of many organizations that managers and employees need not consciously think about it. As Mercedes' longtime CEO noted, "Quality is part of our heritage, one of our core values." The bad news is that without a conscious focus on it, it is easy for quality to slip by the wayside, as apparently happened at Mercedes. For many other organizations, quality is viewed as a short-term fix; when the hype and rhetoric passes, so do their quality efforts. Quality often still takes a backseat to economic pressures.

Nevertheless, quality has not faded away, and will not fade away, simply because it works, with clear evidence that it improves the bottom line. Quality efforts are alive and well, perhaps under a different moniker in some organizations, and will remain an important part of a continual quest for improving performance across the globe. Joseph Juran, one of the most respected leaders of quality in the twentieth century, suggested that the past century will be defined by historians as the century of productivity. He also stated that the current century has to be the century of quality. "We've made dependence on the quality of our technology a part of life."[1] As a member of the emerging generation of business leaders, you have an opportunity and a responsibility to improve the quality of your company and society, not just for products and services, but in everything you say and do.

Part 1 introduces the basic concepts of quality. Chapter 1 discusses the history, definition, basic principles of quality, and the impact of quality on competitive advantage and business results. Chapter 2 describes the role of total quality in different types of organizations—manufacturing, service, health care, education, and government—and stresses the importance of taking a systems perspective of quality throughout an organization. Chapter 3 introduces the management philosophies on which modern concepts of quality are based, and managerial frameworks—the Malcolm Baldrige Criteria for Performance Excellence, ISO 9000, and Six Sigma—that guide today's organizational approaches to quality improvement and performance excellence. These topics provide the foundation for the key quality principles and practices that are the subject of the remainder of the book.

ENDNOTES

1. Alex Taylor III, "Mercedes Hits a Pothole," *Fortune*, October 27, 2003, 140–146.

2. Thomas A. Stewart, "A Conversation with Joseph Juran," *Fortune*, January 11, 1999, 168–169.

CHAPTER 1

INTRODUCTION TO QUALITY

Quality is by no means a new concept in modern business. In October 1887, William Cooper Procter, grandson of the founder of Procter & Gamble, told his employees, "The first job we have is to turn out quality merchandise that consumers will buy and keep on buying. If we produce it efficiently and economically, we will earn a profit, in which you will share." Procter's statement addresses three issues that are critical to managers of manufacturing and service organizations: *productivity, cost,* and *quality.* Productivity (the measure of efficiency defined as the amount of output achieved per unit of input), the cost of operations, and the quality of the goods and services that create customer satisfaction all contribute to profitability. Of these three determinants of profitability, the most significant factor in determining the long-run success or failure of any organization is quality. High-quality goods and services can provide an organization with a competitive edge. High quality reduces costs due to returns, rework, and scrap. It increases productivity, profits, and other measures of success. Most importantly, high quality generates satisfied customers, who reward the organization with continued patronage and favorable word-of-mouth advertising.

To better understand the relationship among these factors, just consider Ford Motor Company. During the 1980s, Ford fought its way from the bottom of Detroit's Big Three automakers to the top of the pack through a concerted effort to improve quality and better meet customer needs and expectations. It quickly became a highly profitable business. However, on January 12, 2002, a newspaper headline read, "Ford to cut 35,000 jobs, close 5 plants." CEO William Ford is cited as stating "We strayed from what got us to the top of the mountain, and it cost us greatly. . . . We may have underestimated the growing strength of our competitors. There were some strategies that were poorly conceived, and we just didn't execute on the basics of our business." The article goes on to observe that Ford "has been dogged by quality problems that forced the recall of several new models, including the Explorer, one of the top money-makers."[1] One of the key elements of Ford's 2002 Revitalization Plan was to "Continue Quality Improvements." In fact, the top *two* "vital few priorities" set by Ford's president for North America are "Improve quality" and "Improve quality"! If it were an easy task, there would be little need for this book. The mandate for focusing on quality is clear. In working with Chrysler Corporation (now Daimler-Chrysler) to improve quality, a vice president of the United Auto Workers (UAW) succinctly stated the importance of quality: "No quality, no sales. No sales, no profit. No profit, no jobs."

> *Building—and maintaining—quality into an organization's goods and services, and more importantly, into the infrastructure of the organization itself, is not an easy task.*

In this chapter we examine the notion of quality. We discuss its history, its importance in business, and its role in building and sustaining competitive advantage. At the beginning of each chapter we profile two leading companies that have developed exemplary quality management practices (see the *Quality Profiles* on page 5). These examples will help you understand some of the key cultural issues that comprise the foundation of high-performing organizations.

THE HISTORY AND IMPORTANCE OF QUALITY

In a broad sense, **quality assurance** refers to any planned and systematic activity directed toward providing consumers with products (goods and services) of appropriate quality, along with the confidence that products meet consumers' requirements. Quality assurance, usually associated with some form of measurement and inspection activity, has been an important aspect of production operations throughout history.[2] Egyptian wall paintings circa 1450 B.C. show evidence of measurement and inspection. Stones for the pyramids were cut so precisely that even today it is impossible to put a knife blade between the blocks. The Egyptians' success was due to the consistent use of well-developed methods and procedures and precise measuring devices.

The Age of Craftsmanship

During the Middle Ages in Europe, the skilled craftsperson served both as manufacturer and inspector. "Manufacturers" who dealt directly with the customer took considerable pride in workmanship. Craft guilds, consisting of masters, journeymen,

QUALITY PROFILES

CLARKE AMERICAN CHECKS, INC., AND MOTOROLA, INC.

CLARKE AMERICAN CHECKS, INC.

Headquartered in San Antonio, Texas, Clarke American supplies personalized checks, checking account and bill-paying accessories, financial forms, and a growing portfolio of services to more than 4,000 financial institutions in the United States. In the early 1990s, when an excess manufacturing capacity in check printing triggered aggressive price competition, Clarke American elected to distinguish itself through service. Company leaders made an all-out commitment to ramp up the firm's First in Service® (FIS) approach to business excellence. Comprehensive in scope, systematic in execution, the FIS approach defines how Clarke American conducts business and how all company associates are expected to act to fulfill the company's commitment to superior service and quality performance.

From orientation and onward, associates are steeped in the company's culture and values: customer first, integrity and mutual respect, knowledge sharing, measurement, quality workplace, recognition, responsiveness, and teamwork. They are schooled regularly in the application of standardized quality tools, performance measurement, use of new technology, team disciplines, and specialized skills. Individual initiative and innovation are expected. Associates are encouraged to contribute improvement ideas under Clarke American's S.T.A.R.—suggestions, teams, actions, results— program. In 2001, more than 20,000 process improvement ideas saved the company an estimated $10 million.

Motorola, Inc., is among the largest U.S. industrial corporations. Its principal product lines include communication systems and semiconductors, and it distributes its products through direct sales and service operations. Motorola was a leader in the U.S. quality revolution during the 1980s and was one of the initial group of companies to receive the Malcolm Baldrige National Quality Award in 1988. Two key beliefs guide the culture of the firm: respect for people and uncompromising integrity. Motorola's goals are to increase its global market share and to become the best in its class in all aspects—people, marketing, technology, product, manufacturing, and service. In terms of people, its objective is to be recognized worldwide as a company for which anyone would want to work.

Motorola was a pioneer in continual reduction of defects and cycle times in all the company's processes, from design, order entry, manufacturing, and marketing, to administrative functions. Employees in every function of the business note defects and use statistical techniques to analyze the results. Products that once took weeks to make are now completed in less than an hour. Even the time needed for closing the financial books has been reduced. What used to take a month now requires only four days.

Although the corporation has had its share of difficulties in tough competitive markets and the economic environment that technology companies have encountered, Motorola's focus on quality has not waned. In 2002, the Commercial, Government, and Industrial Solutions Sector (CGISS) was recognized as a Baldrige Award recipient. CGISS is the leading worldwide supplier of two-way radio communications and products and is recognized around the world for its environmental, health, and safety efforts. Customers report high levels of satisfaction, and the division demonstrates strong financial, product quality, cycle time, and productivity performance. These results stem from exceptional practices in managing human assets, sharing data and information with employees, customers, and suppliers, and aligning all its business processes with key organizational objectives.

and apprentices, emerged to ensure that craftspeople were adequately trained. Quality assurance was informal; every effort was made to ensure that quality was built into the final product by the people who produced it. These themes, which were lost with the advent of the Industrial Revolution, are important foundations of modern quality assurance efforts.

During the middle of the eighteenth century, a French gunsmith, Honoré Le Blanc, developed a system for manufacturing muskets to a standard pattern using interchangeable parts. Thomas Jefferson brought the idea to America, and in 1798 the new U.S. government awarded Eli Whitney a two-year contract to supply 10,000 muskets to its armed forces. The use of interchangeable parts necessitated careful control of quality. Whereas a customized product built by a craftsperson can be tweaked and hammered to fit and work correctly, random matching of mating parts provides no such assurance. The parts must be produced according to a carefully designed standard. Whitney designed special machine tools and trained unskilled workers to make parts following a fixed design, which were then measured and compared to a model. He underestimated the effect of variation in production processes, however (an obstacle that continues to plague companies to this day). Because of the resulting problems, Whitney needed more than 10 years to complete the project. Nonetheless, the value of the concept of interchangeable parts was recognized, and it eventually led to the Industrial Revolution, making quality assurance a critical component of the production process.

The Early Twentieth Century

In the early 1900s the work of Frederick W. Taylor, often called the "father of scientific management," led to a new philosophy of production. Taylor's philosophy was to separate the planning function from the execution function. Managers and engineers were given the task of planning; supervisors and workers took on the task of execution. This approach worked well at the turn of the century, when workers lacked the education needed for doing planning. By segmenting a job into specific work tasks and focusing on increasing efficiency, quality assurance fell into the hands of inspectors. Manufacturers were able to ship good-quality products, but at great costs. Defects were present, but were removed by inspection. Plants employed hundreds, even thousands, of inspectors. Inspection was thus the primary means of quality control during the first half of the twentieth century.

Eventually, production organizations created separate quality departments. This artificial separation of production workers from responsibility for quality assurance led to indifference to quality among both workers and their managers. Concluding that quality was the responsibility of the quality department, many upper managers turned their attention to output quantity and efficiency. Because they had delegated so much responsibility for quality to others, upper managers gained little knowledge about quality, and when the quality crisis hit, they were ill-prepared to deal with it.

Ironically, one of the leaders of the second Industrial Revolution, Henry Ford, Sr., developed many of the fundamentals of what we now call "total quality practices" in the early 1900s. This discovery was made when Ford executives visited Japan in 1982 to study Japanese management practices. As the story goes, one Japanese executive referred repeatedly to "the book," which the Ford people learned was a Japanese translation of *My Life and Work*, written by Henry Ford and Samuel Crowther in 1926 (New York: Garden City Publishing Co.). "The book" had become Japan's industrial bible and helped Ford Motor Company realize how it had strayed from its principles over the years. The Ford executives had to go to a used bookstore to find a copy when they returned to the United States.

The Bell System was the leader in the early modern history of industrial quality assurance.[3] It created an inspection department in its Western Electric Company in the early 1900s to support the Bell operating companies. Although the Bell System achieved its noteworthy quality through massive inspection efforts, the importance of quality in providing telephone service across the nation led it to research and develop new approaches. In the 1920s, employees of Western Electric's inspection department were transferred to Bell Telephone Laboratories. The duties of this group included the development of new theories and methods of inspection for improving and maintaining quality. The early pioneers of quality assurance—Walter Shewhart, Harold Dodge, George Edwards, and others, including W. Edwards Deming—were members of this group. These pioneers not only coined the term *quality assurance,* they also developed many useful techniques for improving quality and solving quality problems. Thus, quality became a technical discipline of its own.

The Western Electric group, led by Walter Shewhart, ushered in the era of statistical quality control (SQC), the application of statistical methods for controlling quality. SQC goes beyond inspection to focus on identifying and eliminating the problems that cause defects. Shewhart is credited with developing control charts, which became a popular means of identifying quality problems in production processes and ensuring consistency of output. Others in the group developed many other useful statistical techniques and approaches.

During World War II the United States military began using statistical sampling procedures and imposing stringent standards on suppliers. The War Production Board offered free training courses in the statistical methods developed within the Bell System. The impact on wartime production was minimal, but the effort developed quality specialists, who began to use and extend these tools within their organizations. Thus, statistical quality control became widely known and gradually adopted throughout manufacturing industries. Sampling tables labeled MIL-STD, for military standard, were developed and are still widely used today. The discipline's first professional journal, *Industrial Quality Control,* was published in 1944, and professional societies—notably the American Society for Quality Control (now called the American Society for Quality, http://www.asq.org)—were founded soon after to develop, promote, and apply quality concepts.

Post–World War II

After the war, during the late 1940s and early 1950s, the shortage of civilian goods in the United States made production a top priority. In most companies, quality remained the province of the specialist. Quality was not a priority of top managers, who delegated this responsibility to quality managers. Top management showed little interest in quality improvement or the prevention of defects and errors, relying instead on mass inspection.

During this time, two U.S. consultants, Dr. Joseph Juran and Dr. W. Edwards Deming, introduced statistical quality control techniques to the Japanese to aid them in their rebuilding efforts. A significant part of their educational activity was focused on upper management, rather than quality specialists alone. With the support of top managers, the Japanese integrated quality throughout their organizations and developed a culture of continuous improvement (sometimes referred to by the Japanese term *kaizen,* pronounced kī-zen). Back in 1951, the Union of Japanese Scientists and Engineers (JUSE) instituted the Deming Prize (see Chapter 3) to reward individuals and companies who meet stringent criteria for quality management practice.

Improvements in Japanese quality were slow and steady; some 20 years passed before the quality of Japanese products exceeded that of Western manufacturers. By the 1970s, primarily due to the higher quality levels of their products, Japanese companies' penetration into Western markets was significant. Hewlett-Packard reported one of the more startling facts in 1980. In testing 300,000 16K RAM chips from three U.S. and three Japanese manufacturers, Hewlett-Packard found that the Japanese chips had an incoming failure rate of zero failures per 1,000 compared to rates of 11 and 19 for the U.S. chips. After 1,000 hours of use, the failure rate of the U.S. chips was up to 27 times higher. In a few short years, the Japanese made major inroads into a market previously dominated by American companies. The automobile industry is another, more publicized, example. The June 8, 1987, *Business Week* special report on quality noted that the number of problems reported per 100 domestic models (1987) in the first 60 to 90 days of ownership averaged between 162 and 180. Comparable figures for Japanese and German automobiles were 129 and 152, respectively. The U.S. steel, consumer electronics, and even banking industries also were victims of global competition. U.S. business recognized the crisis.

The U.S. "Quality Revolution"

The decade of the 1980s was a period of remarkable change and growing awareness of quality by consumers, industry, and government. During the 1950s and 1960s, when "made in Japan" was associated with inferior products, U.S. consumers purchased domestic goods and accepted their quality without question. During the 1970s, however, increased global competition and the appearance of higher-quality foreign products on the market led U.S. consumers to consider their purchasing decisions more carefully. They began to notice differences in quality between Japanese- and U.S.-made products, and consequently began to expect and demand high quality and reliability in goods and services at a fair price. Consumers expected products to function properly and not to break or fail under reasonable use, and courts of law supported them. Extensive product recalls mandated by the Consumer Product Safety Commission in the early 1980s and the intensive media coverage of the *Challenger* space shuttle disaster in 1986, in which the *Challenger* exploded shortly after takeoff killing all seven astronauts, increased awareness of the importance of quality. Consequently, consumers are more apt than ever before to compare, evaluate, and choose products critically for total value—quality, price, and serviceability. Magazines such as *Consumer Reports* and newspaper reviews make this task much easier.

Obviously, the more technologically complex a product, the more likely that something will go wrong with it. Government safety regulations, product recalls, and the rapid increase in product-liability judgments have changed society's attitude from "let the buyer beware" to "let the producer beware." Businesses now see increased attentiveness to quality as vital to their survival. Xerox, for instance, discovered that its Japanese competitors were selling small copiers for what it cost Xerox to make them at the time, and as a consequence, initiated a corporate-wide quality improvement focus to meet the challenge. Xerox, and its former CEO David Kearns, who led their "Leadership Through Quality" initiative, were a major influence in the promotion of quality among U.S. corporations. In the five years of continuous improvement culminating in the firm's winning the Malcolm Baldrige National Quality Award in 1989, defects per 100 machines were decreased by 78 percent, unscheduled maintenance was decreased by 40 percent, manufacturing costs dropped 20 percent, product development time decreased by 60 percent, overall product quality improved 93 percent, service response time was improved by 27 percent, and the company recaptured much of the market it had lost. The company experienced strong growth during the 1990s. However, like Ford Motor Company discussed earlier in this chapter, Xerox lost focus on quality as a key business driver, much of it due to short-sightedness on the part of former top management. Fortunately, new corporate leadership recognized the crisis and renewed its focus and commitment to quality (see the *Quality in Practice* case at the end of this chapter).

A Westinghouse (now CBS) vice president of corporate productivity and quality summed up the situation by quoting Dr. Samuel Johnson's remark: "Nothing concentrates a man's mind so wonderfully as the prospect of being hanged in the morning." Quality excellence became recognized as a key to worldwide competitiveness and was heavily promoted throughout industry.[4] Most major U.S. companies instituted extensive quality improvement campaigns, directed not only at improving internal operations, but also toward satisfying external customers.

One of the most influential individuals in the quality revolution was W. Edwards Deming. In 1980 NBC televised a special program entitled "If Japan Can . . . Why Can't We?" The widely viewed program revealed Deming's key role in the development of Japanese quality, and his name was soon a household word among corporate executives. Although Deming had helped to transform Japanese industry three decades earlier, it was only after the television program that U.S. companies asked for his help. From 1980 until his death in 1993, his leadership and expertise helped many U.S. companies to revolutionize their approach to quality.

Early Successes

As business and industry began to focus on quality, the government recognized how critical quality is to the nation's economic health. In 1984 the U.S. government designated October as National Quality Month. In 1985 NASA announced an Excellence Award for Quality and Productivity. In 1987 the Malcolm Baldrige National Quality Award (see Chapter 3), a statement of national intent to provide quality leadership, was established by an act of Congress. The Baldrige Award became the most influential instrument for creating quality awareness among U.S. businesses. In 1988 President Reagan established the Federal Quality Prototype Award and the President's Award for governmental agencies.

From the late 1980s and through the 1990s, interest in quality grew at an unprecedented rate, fueled in part by publicity from the Malcolm Baldrige National Quality Award. Companies made significant strides in improving quality. In the automobile industry, for example, improvement efforts by Chrysler, General Motors, and Ford reduced the number of problems reported per 100 domestic cars in the first 60 to 90 days of ownership from about 170 in 1987 to 136 in 1991. The gaps between Japanese and U.S. quality began to narrow, and U.S. firms regained much of the ground they had lost.

In 1989 Florida Power and Light was the first non-Japanese company to be awarded Japan's coveted Deming Prize for quality; AT&T Power Systems was the second in 1994. Quality practices expanded into the service sector and into such non-profit organizations as schools and hospitals. By 1990, quality drove nearly every organization's quest for success. By the mid-1990s thousands of professional books had been written, and quality-related consulting and training had blossomed into an industry. Companies began to share their knowledge and experience through formal and informal networking. New quality awards were established by the federal government under the Clinton administration. The majority of states in the United States developed award programs for recognizing quality achievements in business, education, not-for-profits, and government. In 1999, Congress added nonprofit education and health care sectors to the Baldrige Award.

From Product Quality to Performance Excellence

Although quality initiatives focused initially on reducing defects and errors in products and services through the use of measurement, statistics, and other problem-solving tools, organizations began to recognize that lasting improvement could not be accomplished without significant attention to the quality of the management practices used on a daily basis. Managers began to realize that the approaches they use to listen to customers and develop long-term relationships, develop strategy, measure performance and analyze data, reward and train employees, design and deliver products and services, and act as leaders in their organizations are the true enablers of quality, customer satisfaction, and business results. In other words, they recognized that the "quality of management" is as important as the "management of quality." Many began to use the term **Big Q** to contrast the difference between managing for quality in all organizational processes as opposed to focusing solely on manufacturing quality **(Little Q)**. As organizations began to integrate quality principles into their management systems, the notion of **total quality management**, or **TQM**, became popular. Quality took on a new meaning of organization-wide performance excellence rather than a narrow engineering- or production-based technical discipline and permeated every aspect of running an organization.

Today, the term *TQM* has virtually disappeared from business vernacular; however, the underlying principles of quality management are recognized as the foundation of high-performance management systems and an important factor for competitive success. Many organizations have integrated quality principles so tightly with daily work activities that they no longer view quality as something special. In contrast, many other organizations have barely begun.

Disappointments and Criticism

Unfortunately, with all the hype and rhetoric (and the unfortunate three-letter-acronym, TQM), companies scrambled to institute quality programs. In their haste, many failed, leading to very disappointing results. Consequently, TQM met some harsh criticism. In reference to Douglas Aircraft, a troubled subsidiary of McDonnell Douglas Corporation (since merged with the Boeing Corporation), *Newsweek* stated, "The aircraft maker three years ago embraced 'Total Quality Management,' a Japanese import that had become the American business cult of the 1980s. . . . At

> *While quality initiatives can lead to business success, they cannot guarantee it, and one must not infer that business failures or stock price dives are the result of poor quality.*

Douglas, TQM appeared to be just one more hothouse Japanese flower never meant to grow on rocky ground."[5] Other articles in *The Wall Street Journal* ("Quality Programs Show Shoddy Results," May 14, 1992) and the *New York Times* ("The Lemmings Who Love Total Quality," May 3, 1992) suggested that total quality approaches were passing fads and inherently flawed. *Business Week* commentator John Byrne even pronounced TQM "as dead as a pet rock" (June 23, 1997, p. 47). However, reasons for TQM failures usually are rooted in poor organizational approaches and management systems, such as poor quality strategies or good strategies that were poorly executed, and not in the foundation principles of quality management. In fact, *Business Week*'s Byrne went on to say that today's most popular management ideas focus on "good old-fashioned, strategic planning" and customer satisfaction, which are generic to the quality management philosophy.

As the editor of *Quality Digest* put it: "No, TQM isn't dead. TQM failures just prove that bad management is still alive and kicking." A poor major business decision such as an inappropriate merger or acquisition, a weak global economy, or a change in top management can easily undo years of effort to build a quality-focused organization. This possibility is evident in what happened at Ford and Xerox. For example, in June 2003, the Securities and Exchange Commission fined six former top Xerox executives, including two former CEOs who followed David Kearns, to settle allegations of financial fraud—clearly executive attention was diverted to Wall Street rather than quality.

In recent years, a new interest in fundamental quality principles emerged in corporate boardrooms under the concept of *Six Sigma*, a customer-focused and results-oriented approach to business improvement. Six Sigma integrates many quality tools and techniques that have been tested and validated over the years, with a bottom-line orientation that appeals to senior managers. Xerox's new quality focus, for example, is based on Six Sigma principles. We will discuss the concepts of Six Sigma as they relate to the topics in many chapters of this book and delve into it in more depth in Part III.

Current and Future Challenges

The real challenge today is to ensure that managers do not lose sight of the basic principles on which quality management and performance excellence are based. As former Xerox president David Kearns observed, quality is "a race without a finish line." The global marketplace and domestic and international competition have made organizations around the world realize that their survival depends on high quality.[6] Many countries, such as Korea and India, are mounting national efforts to increase quality awareness, including conferences, seminars, radio shows, school essay contests, and pamphlet distribution. Spain and Brazil are encouraging the publication of quality books in their native language to make them more accessible (this book has been translated into Spanish and Chinese). These trends will only increase the level of competition in the future. New approaches, such as Six Sigma, require increased levels of training and education for managers and front-line employees alike, as well as the development of technical staff. Thus, a key challenge is to allocate the necessary resources to maintain a focus on quality, particularly in times of economic downturns. However, businesses will require an economic justification for quality initiatives: quality must deliver bottom-line results.

In 1999, the American Society for Quality identified eight key forces that will influence the future of quality in this new century:[7]

- *Partnering*: Superior products and services will be delivered through partnering in all forms, including partnerships with competitors.
- *Learning systems*: Education systems for improved transfer of knowledge and skills will better equip individuals and organizations to compete.
- *Adaptability and speed of change*: Adaptability and flexibility will be essential to compete and keep pace with the increasing velocity of change.
- *Environmental sustainability*: Environmental sustainability and accountability will be required to prevent the collapse of the global ecosystem.
- *Globalization*: Globalization will continue to shape the economic and social environment.
- *Knowledge focus*: Knowledge will be the prime factor in competition and the creation of wealth.
- *Customization and differentiation*: Customization (lot size of one) and differentiation (quality of experience) will determine superior products and services.
- *Shifting demographics*: Shifting demographics (age and ethnicity) will continue to change societal values.

A number of implications arise out of these forces. Organizations must reinterpret work to provide learning experiences for workers and use quality tools at all levels because they provide a common language and the means by which people work together. Fewer professionals will be dedicated strictly to quality; the main function of quality professionals will be to train others in cutting-edge tools. Business leaders must also take responsibility and be held accountable for the quality outcomes of their work processes.

In addition, the growth of the Internet continues to shape the business landscape. For example, consumers accustomed to the speed, efficiency, and superior customer service of e-commerce will demand the same in retail transactions. Tom Engibous, president and chief executive officer of Texas Instruments, commented on the present and future importance of quality in 1997: "Quality will have to be everywhere, integrated into all aspects of a winning organization." Companies such as Ford and Xerox recognized that the process is not easy; true quality requires persistence, discipline, and steadfast leadership committed to excellence.

DEFINING QUALITY

Quality can be a confusing concept, partly because people view quality in relation to differing criteria based on their individual roles in the production-marketing value chain. In addition, the meaning of quality continues to evolve as the quality profession grows and matures. Neither consultants nor business professionals agree on a universal definition. A study that asked managers of 86 firms in the eastern United States to define quality produced several dozen different responses, including the following:

1. Perfection
2. Consistency
3. Eliminating waste
4. Speed of delivery
5. Compliance with policies and procedures
6. Providing a good, usable product
7. Doing it right the first time
8. Delighting or pleasing customers
9. Total customer service and satisfaction[8]

Thus, it is important to understand the various perspectives from which quality is viewed in order to fully appreciate the role it plays in the many parts of a business organization.[9]

Judgmental Perspective

One common notion of quality, often used by consumers, is that it is synonymous with superiority or excellence. In 1931 Walter Shewhart first defined quality as the goodness of a product. This view is referred to as the *transcendent* (*transcend*, "to rise above or extend notably beyond ordinary limits") definition of quality. In this sense, quality is "both absolute and universally recognizable, a mark of uncompromising standards and high achievement."[10] As such, it cannot be defined precisely—you just know it when you see it. It is often loosely related to a comparison of features and characteristics of products and promulgated by marketing efforts aimed at developing quality as an image variable in the minds of consumers. Common examples of products attributed with this image are Rolex watches and BMW and Lexus automobiles.

Excellence is abstract and subjective, however, and standards of excellence may vary considerably among individuals. Hence, the transcendent definition is of little practical value to managers. It does not provide a means by which quality can be measured or assessed as a basis for decision making.

Product-Based Perspective

Another definition of quality is that it is a function of a specific, measurable variable and that differences in quality reflect differences in quantity of some product attribute, such as in the number of stitches per inch on a shirt or in the number of cylinders in an engine. This assessment implies that higher levels or amounts of product characteristics are equivalent to higher quality. As a result, quality is often mistakenly assumed to be related to price: the higher the price, the higher the quality. Just consider the case of a Florida man who purchased a $262,000 Lamborghini only to find a leaky roof, a battery that quit without notice, a sunroof that detached when the car hit a bump, and doors that jammed![11] However, a *product*—a term used in this book to refer to either a manufactured good or a service—need not be expensive to be considered a quality product by consumers. Also, as with the notion of excellence, the assessment of product attributes may vary considerably among individuals.

User-Based Perspective

A third definition of quality is based on the presumption that quality is determined by what a customer wants. Individuals have different wants and needs and, hence, different quality standards, which leads to a user-based definition: quality is defined as *fitness for intended use*, or how well the product performs its intended function. Both a Cadillac sedan and a Jeep Cherokee are fit for use, for example, but they serve different needs and different groups of customers. If you want a highway-touring vehicle with luxury amenities, then a Cadillac may better satisfy your needs. If you want a vehicle for camping, fishing, or skiing trips, a Jeep might be viewed as having better quality.

Nissan Motor Car Company Limited's experience provides an example of applying the fitness-for-use concept.[12] Nissan, which produced a line of vehicles called Datsun (stemming from the company's historical roots), tested the U.S. market in 1960. Not wanting to put the Nissan name on a very risky venture, they decided to use the name Datsun on all cars and trucks sold in North America. Although the car was economical to own, U.S. drivers found it to be slow, hard to drive, low-powered, and not very comfortable. In essence, it lacked most of the qualities that North American drivers expected. The U.S. representative, Mr. Katayama, kept asking questions and sending the answers back to Tokyo. For some time, his company refused to believe that U.S. tastes were different from its own. After many years of nagging, Mr. Katayama finally got a product that Americans liked, the sporty 1970 240Z. Eventually, the Nissan brand name replaced Datsun. Car enthusiasts will know that Nissan reintroduced a modern version of this classic vehicle in 2002.

A second example comes from a U.S. appliance company whose stoves and refrigerators were admired by Japanese buyers. Unfortunately, the smaller living quarters of the typical Japanese home lack enough space to accommodate the U.S. models. Some could not even pass through the narrow doors of Japanese kitchens. Although the products' performance characteristics were high, the products were simply not fit for use in Japan.

Value-Based Perspective

A fourth approach to defining quality is based on *value*; that is, the relationship of usefulness or satisfaction to price. From this perspective, a quality product is one that is as useful as competing products and is sold at a lower price, or one that offers greater usefulness or satisfaction at a comparable price. Thus, one might purchase a generic product, rather than a brand name one, if it performs as well as the brand-name product at a lower price. An example of this perspective in practice is evident in a comparison of the U.S. and Japanese automobile markets. A Chrysler marketing executive noted "One of the main reasons that the leading Japanese brands—Toyota and Honda—don't offer the huge incentives of the Big Three (General Motors, Ford, and Chrysler) is that they have a much better reputation for long-term durability." In essence, incentives and rebates are payments to customers to compensate for lower quality.[13]

Competing on the basis of value became a key business strategy in the early 1990s. Procter & Gamble, for example, instituted a concept it calls *value pricing*—offering products at "everyday" low prices in an attempt to counter the common consumer practice of buying whatever brand happens to be on special. In this way, P&G hoped to attain consumer brand loyalty and more consistent sales, which would provide significant advantages for its manufacturing system. Competition demands that businesses seek to satisfy consumers' needs at lower prices. The value approach to quality incorporates a firm's goal of balancing product characteristics (the customer side of quality) with internal efficiencies (the operations side).

Manufacturing-Based Perspective

A fifth view of quality is manufacturing-based and defines quality as the desirable outcome of engineering and manufacturing practice, or *conformance to specifications*. **Specifications** are targets and tolerances determined by designers of products and services. Targets are the ideal values for which production is to strive; tolerances are specified because designers recognize that it is impossible to meet targets all of the time in manufacturing. For example, a part dimension might be specified as "0.236 ± 0.003 cm." These measurements would mean that the target, or ideal value, is 0.236 centimeters, and that the allowable variation is 0.003 centimeters from the target (a tolerance of 0.006 cm.). Thus, any dimension in the range 0.233 to 0.239 centimeters is deemed acceptable and is said to conform to specifications. Likewise, in services, "on-time arrival" for an airplane might be specified as within 15 minutes of the scheduled arrival time. The target is the scheduled time, and the tolerance is specified to be 15 minutes.

For the Coca-Cola Company, for example, quality is "about manufacturing a product that people can depend on every time they reach for it," according to Donald R. Keough, former president and chief operations officer. Through rigorous quality and packaging standards, the company strives to ensure that its products will taste the same anywhere in the world a consumer might buy them. Even service organizations strive for consistency in performance; The Ritz-Carlton Hotel Company, which we discuss further in Chapter 2, seeks to ensure that its customers will have the same quality experience at any of their properties around the world. Conformance to specifications is a key definition of quality, because it provides a means of measuring quality. Specifications are meaningless, however, if they do not reflect attributes that are deemed important to the consumer.

Integrating Perspectives on Quality

Although product quality should be important to all individuals throughout the value chain, how quality is viewed may depend on one's position in the value chain, that is, whether one is the designer, manufacturer or service provider, distributor, or customer. To understand this concept more clearly from a manufacturing perspective, examine Figure 1.1. The customer is the driving force for the production of goods and services, and customers generally view quality from either the transcendent or the product-based perspective. The goods and services produced should meet customers' needs; indeed, business organizations' existences depend upon meeting customer needs. It is the role of the marketing function to determine these needs. A product that meets customer needs can rightly be described as a quality product. Hence, the user-based definition of quality is meaningful to people who work in marketing.

The manufacturer must translate customer requirements into detailed product and process specifications. Making this translation is the role of research and development, product design, and engineering. Product specifications might address such attributes as size, form, finish, taste, dimensions, tolerances, materials, operational characteristics, and safety features. Process specifications indicate the types of equipment, tools, and facilities to be used in production. Product designers must balance performance and cost to meet marketing objectives; thus, the value-based definition of quality is most useful at this stage.

A great deal of variation can occur during manufacturing operations. Machine settings can fall out of adjustment; operators and assemblers can make mistakes; materials can be defective. Even in the most closely controlled process, specific variations in product output are inevitable and unpredictable. The manufacturing function is responsible for guaranteeing that design specifications are adhered to during produc-

Figure 1.1 Quality Perspectives in the Value Chain

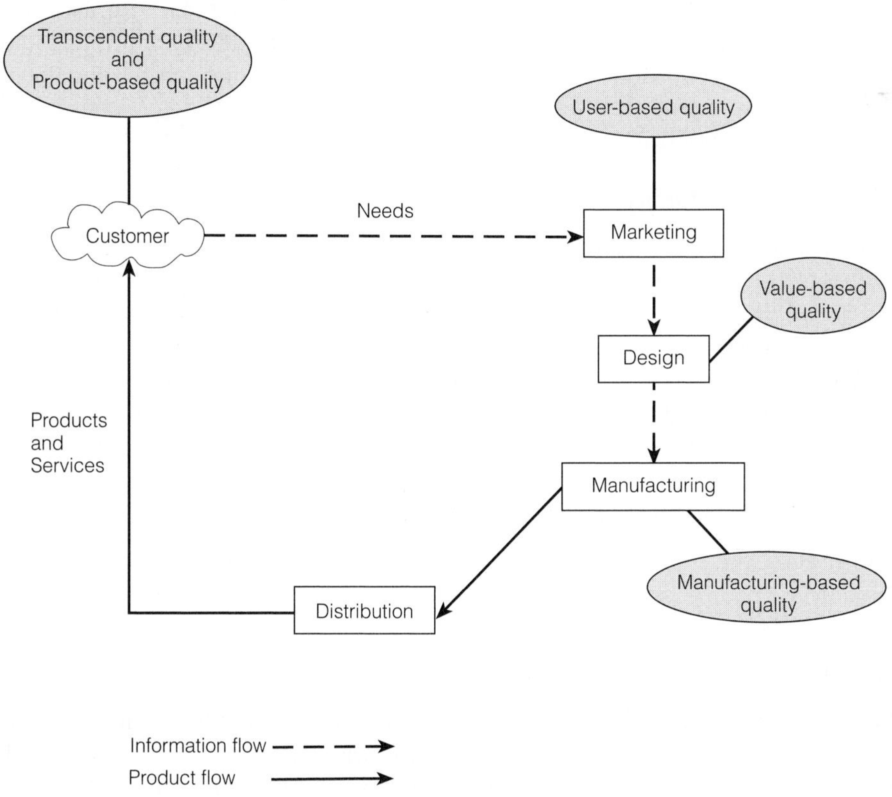

Information flow — — — →
Product flow ————→

tion and that the final product performs as intended. Thus, for production personnel, quality is described by the manufacturing-based definition. Conformance to product specifications is their goal.

The production-distribution cycle is completed when the product has been moved from the manufacturing plant, perhaps through wholesale and retail outlets, to the customer. Distribution does not end the customer's relationship with the manufacturer, however. The customer may need various services such as installation, user information, and special training. Such services are part of the product and cannot be ignored in quality management.

Hospital care offers a good illustration of how different views of quality can affect a single product in a service context. The transcendent definition of quality applies to the hospital's need to promote and maintain an image of excellence by ensuring the competency of its medical staff, the availability of treatments for rare or complicated disorders, or the presence of advanced medical technology. Patients and third-party organizations make subjective judgments about this kind of quality. Those who audit hospital efficiency and monitor treatment consistency and resource consumption define quality according to product-based dimensions. This view of quality is predominant among government and health care accrediting agencies.

> *Because individuals in different business functions speak different "languages," the need for different views of what constitutes quality at different points inside and outside an organization is necessary to create products of true quality that will satisfy customers' needs.*

Patients' perceptions of health care quality are focused on product-based and user-based criteria, and their expectations are high because of widely publicized improvements in medical care, advances in therapeutic drug treatments, and innovative surgery. These expectations increase the pressure on hospitals to provide a variety of services to meet these expectations. As demand for flawless service increases, the medical staff and ancillary services must turn their attention to a manufacturing-based definition of quality. This view of accrediting agencies and the medical profession mandates conformance to various practices and determines licensing requirements for practice.

Customer-Driven Quality

The American National Standards Institute (ANSI) and the American Society for Quality (ASQ) standardized official definitions of quality terminology in 1978.[14] These groups defined quality as "the totality of features and characteristics of a product or service that bears on its ability to satisfy given needs." This definition draws heavily on the product- and user-based approaches and is driven by the need to contribute value to customers and thus to influence satisfaction and preference. By the end of the 1980s, many companies had begun using a simpler, yet powerful, customer-driven definition of quality that remains popular today:

> *Quality is meeting or exceeding customer expectations.*

To understand this definition, one must first understand the meanings of "customer." Most people think of a customer as the ultimate purchaser of a product or service; for instance, the person who buys an automobile for personal use or the guest who registers at a hotel is considered an ultimate purchaser. These customers are more precisely referred to as **consumers**. Clearly, meeting the expectations of consumers is the ultimate goal of any business. Before a product reaches consumers, however, it may flow through a chain of many firms or departments, each of which adds some value to the product. For example, an automobile engine plant may purchase steel from a steel company, produce engines, and then transport the engines to an assembly plant. The steel company is a supplier to the engine plant; the engine plant is a supplier to the assembly plant. The engine plant is thus a customer of the steel company, and the assembly plant is a customer of the engine plant. These customers are called **external customers**.

Every employee in a company also has **internal customers** who receive goods or services from suppliers within the company. An assembly department, for example, is an internal customer of the machining department, and managers are internal customers of the secretarial pool. Most businesses consist of many such "chains of customers." Thus, the job of an employee is not simply to please his or her supervisor; it is to satisfy the needs of particular internal and external customers. Failure to meet the needs and expectations of internal customers can result in a poor-quality product. For example, a poor design for a computerized hotel reservation system makes it difficult for reservation clerks to do their job, and consequently affects consumers' satisfaction. Identifying who one's customers are and understanding their expectations are fundamental to achieving customer satisfaction. This focus is a radical departure from traditional ways of thinking in a functionally oriented organization. It allows workers to understand their place in the larger system and their contribution to the final product. (Who are the customers of a university, its instructors, and its students?)

Customer-driven quality is fundamental to high-performing organizations. The president and CEO of Fujitsu Network Transmission Systems, a U.S. subsidiary of Fujitsu, Ltd., stated, "Our customers are intelligent; they expect us to continuously evolve to meet their ever-changing needs. They can't afford to have a thousand mediocre suppliers in today's competitive environment. They want a few exceptional ones."

QUALITY AS A MANAGEMENT FRAMEWORK

In the 1970s a General Electric task force studied consumer perceptions of the quality of various GE product lines.[15] Lines with relatively poor reputations for quality were found to deemphasize the customer's viewpoint, regard quality as synonymous with tight tolerance and conformance to specifications, tie quality objectives to manufacturing flow, express quality objectives as the number of defects per unit, and use formal quality control systems only in manufacturing. In contrast, product lines that received customer praise were found to emphasize satisfying customer expectations, determine customer needs through market research, use customer-based quality performance measures, and have formalized quality control systems in place for all business functions, not just for manufacturing. The task force concluded that quality must not be viewed solely as a technical discipline, but rather as a management discipline. That is, quality issues permeate all aspects of business enterprise: design, marketing, manufacturing, human resource management, supplier relations, and financial management, to name just a few.

As companies came to recognize the broad scope of quality, the concept of **total quality (TQ)** emerged. A definition of total quality was endorsed in 1992 by the chairs and CEOs of nine major U.S. corporations in cooperation with deans of business and engineering departments of major universities, and recognized consultants:

> *Total Quality (TQ) is a people-focused management system that aims at continual increase in customer satisfaction at continually lower real cost. TQ is a total system approach (not a separate area or program) and an integral part of high-level strategy; it works horizontally across functions and departments, involves all employees, top to bottom, and extends backward and forward to*

include the supply chain and the customer chain. TQ stresses learning and adaptation to continual change as keys to organizational success.

The foundation of total quality is philosophical: the scientific method. TQ includes systems, methods, and tools. The systems permit change; the philosophy stays the same. TQ is anchored in values that stress the dignity of the individual and the power of community action.[16]

Procter & Gamble uses a concise definition: Total quality is the unyielding and continually improving effort by everyone in an organization to understand, meet, and exceed the expectations of customers.

Actually, the concept of TQ has been around for some time. A. V. Feigenbaum recognized the importance of a comprehensive approach to quality in the 1950s and coined the term **total quality control.**[17] Feigenbaum observed that the quality of products and services is directly influenced by what he terms the 9 Ms: markets, money, management, men and women, motivation, materials, machines and mechanization, modern information methods, and mounting product requirements. Although he developed his ideas from an engineering perspective, his concepts apply more broadly to general management.

The Japanese adopted Feigenbaum's concept and renamed it **companywide quality control.** Wayne S. Reiker listed five aspects of total quality control practiced in Japan.[18]

1. Quality emphasis extends through market analysis, design, and customer service rather than only the production stages of making a product.
2. Quality emphasis is directed toward operations in every department from executives to clerical personnel.
3. Quality is the responsibility of the individual and the work group, not some other group, such as inspection.
4. The two types of quality characteristics as viewed by customers are those that satisfy and those that motivate. Only the latter are strongly related to repeat sales and a "quality" image.
5. The first customer for a part or piece of information is usually the next department in the production process.

The term *total quality management* was developed by the Naval Air Systems Command to describe its Japanese-style approach to quality improvement and became popular with businesses in the United States during the 1980s. As we noted earlier, TQM has fallen out of favor, and many people simply use TQ, which we will do in this book.

Principles of Total Quality

Whatever the language, total quality is based on three fundamental principles:

1. A focus on customers and stakeholders
2. Participation and teamwork by everyone in the organization
3. A process focus supported by continuous improvement and learning

Despite their obvious simplicity, these principles are quite different from traditional management practices. Historically, companies did little to understand external customer requirements, much less those of internal customers. Managers and specialists controlled and directed production systems; workers were told what to do and how to do it, and rarely were asked for their input. Teamwork was virtually nonexistent. A certain amount of waste and error was tolerable and was controlled by postproduction inspection. Improvements in quality generally resulted from technological break-throughs instead of a relentless mindset of continuous improvement. With total quality, an organization actively seeks to identify customer needs and expectations, to build quality into work processes by tapping the knowledge and experience of its workforce, and to continually improve every facet of the organization.

Customer and Stakeholder Focus The customer is the principal judge of quality. Perceptions of value and satisfaction are influenced by many factors throughout the customer's overall purchase, ownership, and service experiences. To accomplish this task, a company's efforts need to extend well beyond merely meeting specifications, reducing defects and errors, or resolving complaints. They must include both designing new products that truly delight the customer and responding rapidly to changing consumer and market demands. A company close to its customer knows what the customer wants, how the customer uses its products, and anticipates needs that the customer may not even be able to express. It also continually develops new ways of enhancing customer relationships.

To meet or exceed customer expectations, organizations must fully understand all product and service attributes that contribute to customer value and lead to satisfaction and loyalty.

A firm also must recognize that internal customers are as important in assuring quality as are external customers who purchase the product. Employees who view themselves as both customers of and suppliers to other employees understand how their work links to the final product. After all, the responsibility of any supplier is to understand and meet customer requirements in the most efficient and effective way possible.

Customer focus extends beyond the consumer and internal customer relationships, however. Employees and society represent important stakeholders. An organization's success depends on the knowledge, skills, creativity, and motivation of its employees and partners. Therefore, a TQ organization must demonstrate commitment to employees, provide opportunities for development and growth, provide recognition beyond normal compensation systems, share knowledge, and encourage risk taking. Viewing society as a stakeholder is an attribute of a world-class organization. Business ethics, public health and safety, the environment, and community and professional support are necessary activities that fall under *social responsibility*.

Participation and Teamwork Joseph Juran credited Japanese managers' full use of the knowledge and creativity of the entire workforce as one of the reasons for Japan's rapid quality achievements. When managers give employees the tools to make good decisions and the freedom and encouragement to make contributions, they virtually guarantee that better quality products and production processes will result. Employees who are allowed to participate—both individually and in teams—in decisions that affect their jobs and the customer can make substantial contributions to quality.

In any organization, the person who best understands his or her job and how to improve both the product and the process is the one performing it.

This attitude represents a profound shift in the typical philosophy of senior management; the traditional view was that the workforce should be "managed"—or to put it less formally, the workforce should leave their brains at the door. Good intentions alone are not enough to encourage employee involvement. Management's task includes formulating the systems and procedures and then putting them in place to ensure that participation becomes a part of the culture.

Empowering employees to make decisions that satisfy customers without constraining them with bureaucratic rules shows the highest level of trust. Marriott and Nordstrom are examples of two companies that empower and reward their employees for service quality. Marriott calls its customer service representatives "associates." Associates are permitted wide discretion to call on any part of the company to help customers and can earn lush bonuses for extraordinary work. Nordstrom's customer service stories are legendary, and include employees who have ironed a new shirt for a customer who needed it that afternoon, one who warmed customers' cars in winter while they shopped, and even one who refunded money for a set of tire chains, even though Nordstrom does not sell them![19]

Another important element of total quality is teamwork, which focuses attention on customer-supplier relationships and encourages the involvement of the total workforce in attacking systemic problems, particularly those that cross functional boundaries. Ironically, although problem-solving teams were introduced in the United States in the 1940s to help solve problems on the factory floor, they failed, primarily because of management resistance to workers' suggestions. The Japanese, however, began widespread implementation of similar teams, called quality circles, in 1962 with dramatic results. Eventually, the concept returned to the United States. Today, the use of self-managed teams that combine teamwork and empowerment is a powerful method of employee involvement.

Traditionally, organizations were integrated vertically by linking all the levels of management in a hierarchical fashion (consider the traditional organization chart). TQ requires horizontal coordination between organizational units, such as between design and engineering, engineering and manufacturing, manufacturing and shipping, shipping and sales. Cross-functional teams provide this focus.

Partnerships with unions, customers, suppliers, and education organizations also promote teamwork and permit the blending of an organization's core competencies and capabilities with the complementary strengths of partners, creating mutual benefits. For example, many companies seek suppliers that share their own values. They often educate them in methods of improvement. If suppliers improve, then so will the company. For instance, Motorola requires suppliers to take courses in customer satisfaction and cycle time reduction at Motorola University. It also established a 15-member council of suppliers to rate Motorola's own practices and offer suggestions for improvement.[20]

Process Focus and Continuous Improvement The traditional way of viewing an organization is by surveying the vertical dimension—by keeping an eye on an organization chart. However, work gets done (or fails to get done) horizontally or cross-functionally, not hierarchically.

According to AT&T, a process is how work creates value for customers.[21] We typically think of processes in the context of production: the collection of activities and operations involved in

*A **process** is a sequence of activities that is intended to achieve some result.*

transforming *inputs* (physical facilities, materials, capital, equipment, people, and energy) into *outputs* (products and services). Common types of production processes include machining, mixing, assembly, filling orders, or approving loans. However, nearly every major activity within an organization involves a process that crosses traditional organizational boundaries. For example, an order fulfillment process might involve a salesperson placing the order; a marketing representative entering it on the company's computer system; a credit check by finance; picking, packaging, and shipping by distribution and logistics personnel; invoicing by finance; and installation by field service engineers. This process is illustrated in Figure 1.2. A process perspective links together all necessary activities and increases one's understanding of the entire system, rather than focusing on only a small part. Many of the greatest opportunities for improving organizational performance lie in the organizational interfaces—those spaces between the boxes on an organization chart.

Continuous improvement refers to both incremental changes, which are small and gradual, and breakthrough, or large and rapid, improvements. These improvements may take any one of several forms:

1. Enhancing value to the customer through new and improved products and services
2. Reducing errors, defects, waste, and their related costs
3. Increasing productivity and effectiveness in the use of all resources
4. Improving responsiveness and cycle time performance for such processes as resolving customer complaints or new product introduction

Thus, response time, quality, and productivity objectives should be considered together. A process focus supports continuous improvement efforts by helping to understand these synergies and to recognize the true sources of problems.

In 1950, when W. Edwards Deming was helping Japan with its postwar rebuilding effort, he emphasized the importance of continuous improvement. While presenting to a group of Japanese industrialists (collectively representing about 80 percent of the nation's capital), he drew the diagram shown in Figure 1.3. This diagram depicts not only the relationships among inputs, processes, and outputs, but also the roles of consumers and suppliers, the interdependency of organizational processes, the usefulness of consumer research, and the importance of continuous

Major improvements in response time may require significant simplification of work processes and often drive simultaneous improvements in quality and productivity.

Figure 1.2 Process Versus Function

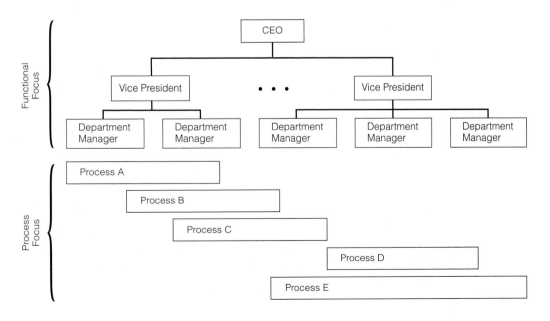

Figure 1.3 Deming's View of a Production System

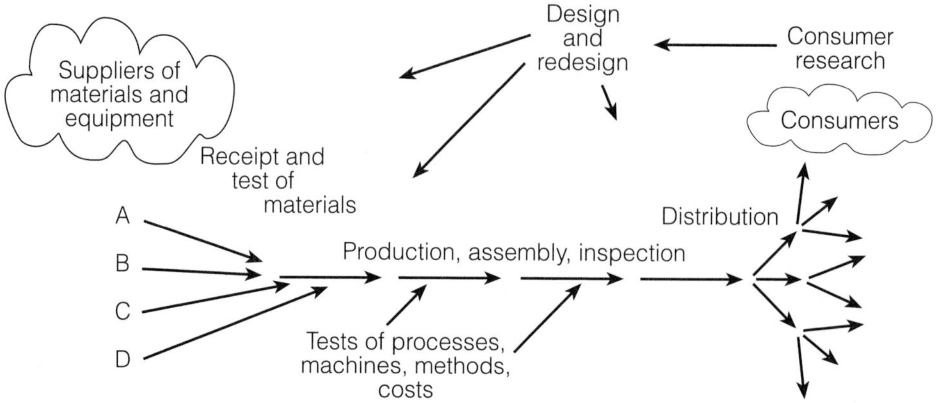

Source: Reprinted from *Out of the Crisis,* p. 5, by W. Edwards Deming, by permission of MIT Press and the W. Edwards Deming Institute. © 1986 by The W. Edwards Deming Institute.

improvement of all elements of the production system. Deming told the Japanese that understanding customers and suppliers was crucial to planning for quality. He advised them that continuous improvement of both products and production processes through better understanding of customer requirements is the key to capturing world markets. Deming predicted that within five years Japanese manufacturers would be making products of the highest quality in the world and would have gained a large share of the world market. He was wrong. By applying these ideas, the Japanese penetrated several global markets in less than four years!

Real improvement depends on *learning,* which means understanding why changes are successful through feedback between practices and results, leading to new goals and approaches. A **learning cycle** consists of four stages:

1. Planning
2. Execution of plans
3. Assessment of progress
4. Revision of plans based upon assessment findings

The concept of organizational learning is not new. It has its roots in general systems theory[22] and systems dynamics[23] developed in the 1950s and 1960s, as well as theories of learning from organizational psychology. Peter Senge, a professor at the Massachusetts Institute of Technology (MIT), has become the major advocate of the learning organization movement. He defines the learning organization as

> . . . an organization that is continually expanding its capacity to create its future. For such an organization, it is not enough merely to survive. "Survival learning" or what is more often termed "adaptive learning" is important— indeed it is necessary. But for a learning organization, "adaptive learning" must be joined by "generative learning," learning that enhances our capacity to create.[24]

The conceptual framework behind this definition requires an understanding and integration of many of the concepts and principles that are part of the total quality philosophy. Senge repeatedly points out, "Over the long run, superior performance depends on superior learning." Continuous improvement and learning should be a regular part of daily work, practiced at personal, work unit, and organizational levels, driven by opportunities to affect significant change, and focused on sharing throughout the organization.

Infrastructure, Practices, and Tools

The three principles of total quality need to be supported by an integrated organizational infrastructure, a set of management practices, and a set of tools and techniques, which all must work together as suggested in Figure 1.4. **Infrastructure** refers to the basic management systems necessary to function effectively and carry out the principles of TQ. It includes the following elements:

1. Customer relationship management
2. Leadership and strategic planning
3. Human resources management
4. Process management
5. Information and knowledge management

Practices are those activities that occur within each element of the infrastructure to achieve high-performance objectives. For example, reviewing company performance is a leadership practice; training and determining employee satisfaction are human resources management practices; and coordinating design and production/delivery processes to ensure trouble-free introduction and delivery of products and services is a process management practice. **Tools** include a wide variety of graphical and statistical methods to plan work activities, collect data, analyze results, monitor progress, and solve problems. For instance, a chart showing trends in manufacturing defects as workers progress through a training program is a simple tool to monitor the effectiveness of the training; the statistical technique of experimental design is often used in product development activities. The relationships among infrastructure, practices, and tools are illustrated in Figure 1.5.

This section gives a brief overview of the major elements of a total quality infrastructure. We will expand on these topics and describe specific practices and tools in

Figure 1.4 The Scope of Total Quality

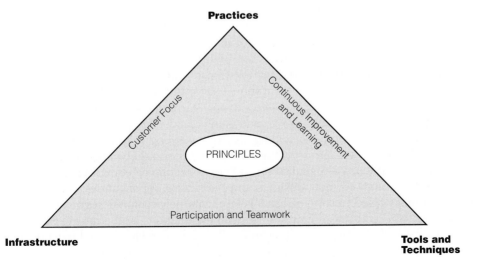

Figure 1.5 Relationships Among Infrastructure, Practices, and Tools

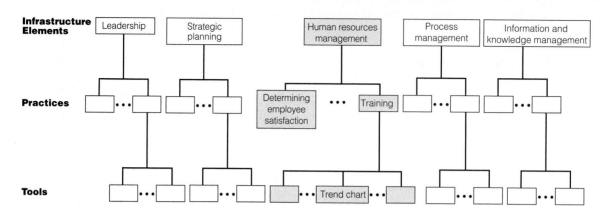

subsequent chapters. It is important to realize that quality management practices and helpful tools continually evolve and improve. Therefore, discussion of each and every useful practice or tool is not possible within the scope of this book.

Customer Relationship Management Understanding customer needs, both current and future, and keeping pace with changing markets requires effective strategies for listening to and learning from customers, measuring their satisfaction relative to competitors, and building relationships. Customer needs—particularly differences among key customer groups—must be linked closely to an organization's strategic planning, product design, process improvement, and workforce training activities. Satisfaction and dissatisfaction information are important because understanding them leads to the right improvements that can create satisfied customers who reward the company with loyalty, repeat business, and positive referrals. Creating satisfied customers includes prompt and effective response and solutions to their needs and desires as well as building and maintaining good relationships. These issues will be discussed in Chapter 4.

Leadership and Strategic Planning The success of any organization depends on the performance of the workers at the bottom of the pyramid. Ross Perot, the Texas billionaire and founder of a large software consulting firm, once said that inventories can be managed, but people must be led. All managers, ideally starting with the CEO, must act as the organization's leaders for quality. Their task is to create clear values and high expectations for performance excellence, and then build these into the company's processes. Senior management should serve as role models to inspire and motivate the workforce and encourage involvement, learning, innovation, and creativity.

The pursuit of sustainable growth and market leadership through quality requires a strong future orientation and willingness to make long-term commitments to customers and stakeholders. Strategic business planning should be the driver for quality excellence throughout the organization and needs to anticipate many changes, such as customers' expectations, new business and partnering opportunities, the global and electronic marketplace, technological developments, new customer segments, evolving regulatory requirements, community/societal expectations, and strategic changes by competitors. Plans, strategies, and resource allocations need to reflect these influences. Leadership and strategic planning are addressed further in Chapter 5.

Human Resource Management Meeting the company's quality and performance goals requires a fully committed, well-trained, and involved workforce. Front-line workers need the skills to listen to customers; manufacturing workers need specific skills in developing technologies; and all employees need to understand how to use data and information to drive continuous improvement. These can only be achieved through the design and management of appropriate work systems, reward and recognition approaches, education and training approaches, and a healthful, safe, and motivating work environment. Major challenges in this area include the integration of human resource practices and the alignment of human resource management with business directions and strategic change processes. Addressing these challenges requires effective use and understanding of employee-related data on knowledge, skills, satisfaction, motivation, safety, and well-being. These issues are discussed further in Chapter 6.

Process Management Process management involves the design of processes to develop and deliver products and services that meet the needs of customers, daily control so that they perform as required, and their continual improvement. Process management activities place a strong emphasis on prevention and organizational learning, as the costs of preventing problems at the design stage are much lower than costs of correcting problems that occur "downstream." Also, success in globally competitive markets demands creating a capacity for rapid change and flexibility, such as shorter product introduction cycles and faster and more flexible response to customers. Keeping pace with competition often requires simplification of processes and the ability to make rapid changeovers from one process to another. Process management activities involve not only an organization's core capabilities that create direct value for customers, but also those support processes that facilitate value creation. Process management is the subject of Chapter 7.

Information and Knowledge Management Modern businesses depend on data and information to support performance measurement, management, and improvement. Such measurements should derive from an organization's strategy and provide critical information about key processes, outputs, and results. The measures and indicators used should best represent the factors that lead to improved customer, operational, and financial performance. A comprehensive and balanced set of leading and lagging measures and indicators tied to customer and organization performance requirements represents a clear basis for aligning all activities with the organization's goals. These data must be supported by effective analysis capabilities to extract useful information to support evaluation, comparisons with competitor and best practices benchmarks, decision making, and operational improvement. In addition, information must be reliable, accurate, and timely. Disseminating and sharing organizational knowledge is critical to an effective management system. We will discuss these issues further in Chapter 8.

QUALITY AND COMPETITIVE ADVANTAGE

Competitive advantage denotes a firm's ability to achieve market superiority. In the long run, a sustainable competitive advantage provides above-average performance. S. C. Wheelwright identified six characteristics of a strong competitive advantage:[25]

1. It is driven by customer wants and needs. A company provides value to its customers that competitors do not.

2. It makes a significant contribution to the success of the business.
3. It matches the organization's unique resources with opportunities in the environment. No two companies have the same resources; a good strategy uses the firm's particular resources effectively.
4. It is durable and lasting, and difficult for competitors to copy. A superior research and development department, for example, can consistently develop new products or processes that enable the firm to remain ahead of competitors.
5. It provides a basis for further improvement.
6. It provides direction and motivation to the entire organization.

Each of these characteristics relates to quality, suggesting that quality is an important source of competitive advantage.

The importance of quality in achieving competitive advantage was demonstrated by several research studies during the 1980s. PIMS Associates, Inc., a subsidiary of the Strategic Planning Institute, maintains a database of 1,200 companies and studies the impact of product quality on corporate performance.[26] PIMS researchers found the following:

1. Product quality is an important determinant of business profitability.
2. Businesses that offer premium-quality products and services usually have large market shares and were early entrants into their markets.
3. Quality is positively and significantly related to a higher return on investment for almost all kinds of products and market situations. (PIMS studies showed that firms whose products were perceived as having superior quality earned more than three times the return on sales of firms whose products were perceived as having inferior quality.)
4. Instituting a strategy of quality improvement usually leads to increased market share, but at the cost of reduced short-run profitability.
5. High-quality producers can usually charge premium prices.

These findings are summarized in Figure 1.6. A product's value in the marketplace is influenced by the quality of its design. Improvements in design will differentiate the product from its competitors, improve a firm's quality reputation, and improve the perceived value of the product. These factors allow the company to command higher prices as well as to achieve a greater market share, which in turn leads to increased revenues that offset the costs of improving the design.

Figure 1.6 Quality and Profitability

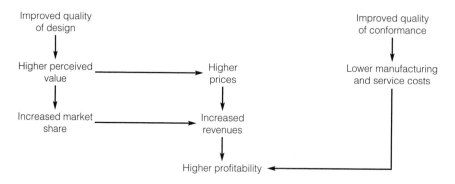

Improved conformance in production or service delivery leads to lower costs through savings in rework, scrap, resolution of errors, and warranty expenses. Philip Crosby popularized this viewpoint in his book *Quality Is Free.*[27] Crosby states:

> *Quality is not only free, it is an honest-to-everything profit maker. Every penny you don't spend on doing things wrong, over, or instead of, becomes half a penny right on the bottom line. In these days of "who knows what is going to happen to our business tomorrow," there aren't many ways left to make a profit improvement. If you concentrate on making quality certain, you can probably increase your profit by an amount equal to 5 percent to 10 percent of your sales. That is a lot of money for free.*

The net effect of improved quality of design and conformance is increased profits.

It is vital to focus quality improvement efforts on *both* design and conformance. Many organizations simply confine their quality efforts to one dimension; for example, they might focus on defect elimination but fail to design products that customers really want, or they design great products that are plagued with defects and service errors. In today's global marketplace, high conformance is considered "entry into the game," rather than a source of competitive advantage. Quality is simply the foundation for achieving competitive advantage. Competitive success in today's market depends on such attributes as the speed of new product development, flexibility in production and delivery, and extraordinary customer service. For example, *Business Week* reported in 1998 that several wireless communications providers had replaced products from Motorola—a long-time quality leader—with other companies' technologies. A BellSouth spokesman said the products did not pass its "shake and bake test." After Qualcomm, Inc., released digital phones the size of cigarette packs, Motorola was nearly a year behind, and as a result, was quickly losing market share.[28] However, within a year, Motorola's wireless communications returned to profitability, including making a $1 billion, 10-year pact with Sun Microsystems to build wireless telecom equipment for the Internet with a 99.999 percent reliability. Only the most agile companies could make such a quick turnaround.

Quality and Business Results

As an old saying goes, "The proof is in the pudding." Companies that invest in quality management efforts experience outstanding returns and improvements in performance. Various research studies show that quality-focused companies achieved better employee participation and relations, improved product and service quality, higher productivity, greater customer satisfaction, increased market share, and improved profitability.[29].

Considerable evidence exists that quality initiatives positively impact bottom-line results.

The Commerce Department annually evaluates the results of a hypothetical investment of $1,000 in common stock in each publicly traded company that won the Malcolm Baldrige National Quality Award (or a proportional investment in winning subsidiaries of larger companies). The stock performance of these companies has outperformed the Standard & Poor's (S&P) 500 stock index by a substantial margin in eight of the first nine years the study was conducted. The fictitious stock fund fell behind the S&P for the first time in 2003, primarily because technology stocks are a significant component of the portfolio, indicating that a poor economy can impact organizations no matter how good their management and quality practices may be. (The results of the current study can be found on the Baldrige Web site, http://www.baldrige.org.)

Kevin Hendricks and Vinod Singhal published one of the most celebrated studies in 1997.[30] Based on objective data and rigorous statistical analysis, the study showed that when implemented effectively, total quality management approaches improve financial performance dramatically. Using a sample of about 600 publicly traded companies that won quality awards either from their customers (such as automotive manufacturers) or through Baldrige and state and local quality award programs, Hendricks and Singhal examined performance results from six years before to four years after winning their first quality award. The primary performance measure tracked was the percent change in operating income and a variety of measures that might affect operating income: percent change in sales, total assets, number of employees, return on sales, and return on assets. These results were compared to a set of control firms that were similar in size to the award winners and in the same industry. The analysis revealed significant differences between the sample and the control group. Specifically, the growth in operating income of winners averaged 91 percent versus 43 percent for the control group. Winners also experienced a 69 percent jump in sales (compared to 32 percent for the control group), a 79 percent increase in total assets (compared to 37 percent), a 23 percent increase in the number of employees (compared to 7 percent), an 8 percent improvement in return on sales (compared to 0 percent), and a 9 percent improvement in return on assets (compared to 6 percent). Small companies actually outperformed large companies, and over a five-year period, the portfolio of winners beat the S&P 500 index by 34 percent.

A sample of specific operational and financial results achieved by recent Baldrige winners includes:

1. Among associates at Clarke American, overall satisfaction improved from 72 percent in 1996 to 84 percent in 2000. Rising associate satisfaction correlates with the 84 percent increase in revenue earned per associate since 1995. Annual growth in company revenues increased from a rate of 4.2 percent in 1996 to 16 percent in 2000, compared to the industry's average annual growth rate of less than 1 percent over the five-year period.

2. The Spicer Driveshaft Division of Dana Corporation lowered internal defect rates by more than 75 percent. Employee turnover is below 1 percent, and economic value added increased from $15 million to $35 million in two years.

3. Texas Nameplate Company increased its national market share from less than 3 percent in 1994 to 5 percent in 1997, reduced its defects from 3.65 percent to about 1 percent of billings, and increased on-time delivery from 95 to 98 percent.

4. Region Americas of STMicroelectronics, Inc., reduced lost-day injuries from 1.01 per 100 workers in 1996 to 0.65 in 1999, which is 74 percent below the industry average, and employee satisfaction levels in 1999 exceeded the industry composite in 8 of 10 categories.

5. Pal's Sudden Service, a privately owned quick-service restaurant chain in eastern Tennessee, garnered customer quality scores averaging 95.8 percent in 2001, compared with 84.1 percent for its best competitor, and improved order delivery speed by more than 30 percent since 1995.

6. Parent satisfaction at Pearl River School District increased from 62 percent in 1996 to 96 percent in 2001.

7. KARLEE, a contract manufacturer of precision sheet metal and machined components, reduced waste from 1.5 percent of sales to less than 0.5 percent of sales while nearly doubling productivity from 1995 to 2000.

8. SSM Health Care's share of the St. Louis market increased substantially while three of its five competitors lost market share. They achieved a AA credit rating

by Standard and Poor's for four consecutive years, a rating attained by fewer than 1 percent of U.S. hospitals.

THREE LEVELS OF QUALITY[31]

At the organizational level, quality concerns center on meeting external customer requirements. An organization must seek customer input on a regular basis. Questions such as the following help to define quality at the organizational level:

1. Which products and services meet your expectations?
2. Which do not?
3. What products or services do you need that you are not receiving?
4. Are you receiving products or services that you do not need?

An organization that is committed to total quality must apply it at three levels: the organizational level, the process level, and the performer/job level.

Customer-driven performance standards should be used as bases for goal setting, problem solving, performance appraisal, incentive compensation, nonfinancial rewards, and resource allocation.

At the process level, organizational units are classified as functions or departments, such as marketing, design, product development, operations, finance, purchasing, billing, and so on. Because most processes are cross-functional, the danger exists that managers of particular organizational units will try to optimize the activities under their control, which can suboptimize activities for the organization as a whole. At this level, managers must ask questions such as the folllowing:

1. What products or services are most important to the (external) customer?
2. What processes produce those products and services?
3. What are the key inputs to the process?
4. Which processes have the most significant effect on the organization's customer-driven performance standards?
5. Who are my internal customers and what are their needs?

At the performer level (sometimes called the job level or the task-design level), standards for output must be based on quality and customer-service requirements that originate at the organizational and process levels. These standards include requirements for such things as accuracy, completeness, innovation, timeliness, and cost. For each output of an individual's job, one must ask:

1. What is required by the customer, both internal and external?
2. How can the requirements be measured?
3. What is the specific standard for each measure?

Viewing an organization from this perspective clarifies the roles and responsibilities of all employees in pursuing quality. Top managers must focus attention at the organizational level; middle managers and supervisors at the process level; and all employees must understand quality at the performer level. Getting everyone involved is the foundation of TQ.

QUALITY AND PERSONAL VALUES

Today, companies are asking employees to take more responsibility for acting as the point of contact between the organization and the customer, to be team players, and to provide more effective and efficient customer service. Rath & Strong, a Lexington, Massachusetts-based management consulting firm, polled almost 200 executives from *Fortune* 500 companies about activities that foster superior performance results for an organization.[32] The survey revealed that *personal initiative*, when combined with a customer orientation, resulted in a positive impact on business success and sales growth rate. However, although 79 percent of all respondents indicated that employees are increasingly expected to take initiative to bring about change in the company, 40 percent of the respondents replied that most people in their company do not believe that they can make a personal contribution to the company's success. Alan Frohman, a senior associate with Rath & Strong, stated, "These results are significant because they suggest that although people are being expected to take personal initiative, most organizations have not figured out how to translate those expectations into positive behaviors."

Such behaviors reflect the personal values and attitudes of individuals. Employees who embrace quality as a personal value often go beyond what they're asked or normally expected to do in order to reach a difficult goal or provide extraordinary service to a customer. A good

> *Unless quality is internalized at the personal level, it will never become rooted in the culture of an organization. Thus, quality must begin at a personal level (and that means you!).*

example involved a young girl who laid her dental retainer on a picnic table at Disney World while eating lunch.[33] She forgot about it until later in the day. The family returned to the spot, found the table cleaned up, and were at a loss to know what to do. They spotted a custodian, told him the problem, and the custodian sought permission from his supervisor to have the garbage bags searched by the night crew that evening! Two weeks later, the family received a letter from the supervisor explaining that, despite their best efforts, they had been unable to locate the retainer.

The concept of "personal quality" has been promoted by Harry V. Roberts, professor emeritus at the University of Chicago's Graduate School of Business, and Bernard F. Sergesketter, vice president of the Central Region of AT&T.[34] Personal quality may be thought of as personal empowerment; it is implemented by systematically keeping personal checklists for quality improvement. Roberts and Sergesketter developed the idea of a personal quality checklist to keep track of personal shortcomings, or defects, in personal work processes. The authors defended the use of a checklist to keep track of defects:

> The word "defect" has a negative connotation for some people who would like to keep track of the times we do things right rather than times we do things wrong. Fortunately, most of us do things right much more than we do things wrong, so it is easier in practice to count the defects. Moreover, we can get positive satisfaction from avoiding defects—witness accident prevention programs that count days without accidents.

An example of a personal quality checklist developed to improve professorial activities is provided in Figure 1.7. It can be used as a starting point for developing a personal quality checklist (see the project later in the chapter). Note that each item on the checklist has a desired result, a way to measure each type of defect, and a time frame. Both work and personal defect categories are listed on the sheet.

Sergesketter plotted defects that he observed during the first 18 months of his use of his own personal quality checklist on a run chart as shown in Figure 1.8. Many of the results were surprising.[35] For instance, he was surprised at the extent to which he was not returning phone calls the same day. He discovered that he had no way to

Figure 1.7 An Example of a Personal TQ Checklist

Week of: _____

Defect Category	M	T	W	TH	F	S	SU	Total
Search for something misplaced or lost, over 20 minutes								
Failure to discard incoming junk by end of day								
Putting a small task on the "hold" pile, over 2 hours								
Failure to respond to letter or phone call in 24 hours								
Lack of clarity in setting requirements/deadlines								
Excessive "general interest" reading; over 30 minutes/weekday								
Failure to provide weekly opportunity for feedback from a class								
Less than two hours of writing per day, 4 days/week								
Less than 8 hours of sleep on a weeknight								
Less than 3 exercise periods/week								
Take wife out for fewer than 1 meal/week								
Less than 0.5 hour meditation per weekday								

count defects related to correspondence. As a result, he started to date stamp correspondence when it arrived and date stamp the file copy of the response. None of the items he measured were in the "four-minute mile" category, and yet he started out at a rate of 100 defects per month, but dropped drastically simply because he was aware of them. He also observed that when a person shares a defect list with others, they can help in reducing defects. Sergesketter noted, "I encourage and challenge you to start counting defects. It is impossible to reduce defects if we don't count them, and we can't reasonably ask our associates to count defects if we don't! I really believe that if several thousand of us here in the Central Region start counting defects, we will reduce them and differentiate ourselves from our competitors in a significant way."

In the daily attempt to bring about change in the individual parts of the organizational universe, managers, employees, professors, and students can find that personal quality is the key to unlock the door to a wider understanding of what the concept really is all about.

Personal quality is an essential ingredient to make quality happen in the workplace, yet most companies have neglected it for a long time. Perhaps management, in particular, operates under the idea that promoting quality is something that companies do *to* employees, rather than something they do *with* employees.

Figure 1.8 Chart of Number of Defects/Month

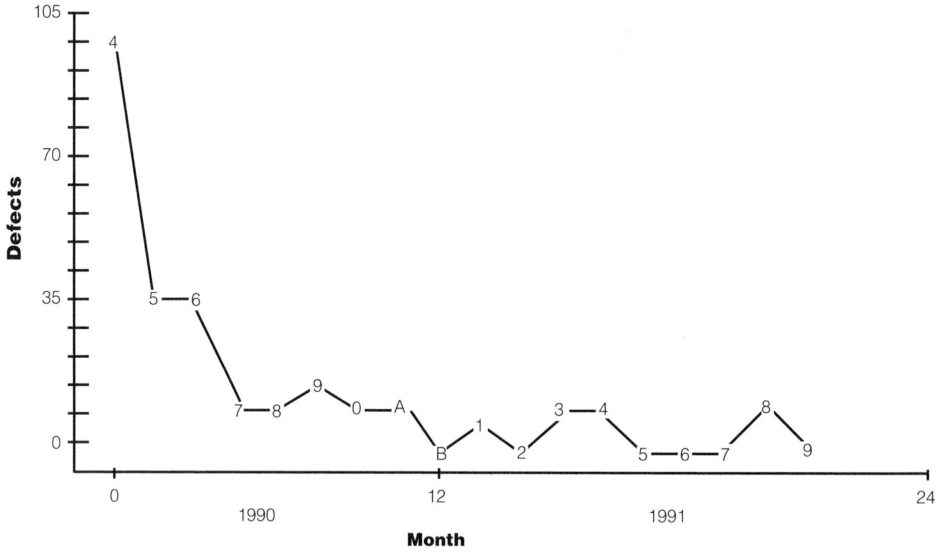

QUALITY IN PRACTICE

THE EVOLUTION OF QUALITY AT XEROX: FROM LEADERSHIP THROUGH QUALITY TO LEAN SIX SIGMA[36]

The Xerox 914, the first plain-paper copier, was introduced in 1959. Regarded by many people as the most successful business product ever introduced, it created a new industry. During the 1960s Xerox grew rapidly, selling all it could produce, and reached $1 billion in revenue in record-setting time. By the mid-1970s its return on assets was in the low 20 percent range. Its competitive advantage was due to strong patents, a growing market, and little competition. In such an environment management was not pressed to focus on customers.

Facing a Competitive Crisis

During the 1970s, however, IBM and Kodak entered the high-volume copier business—Xerox's principal market. Several Japanese companies introduced high-quality low-volume copiers, a market that Xerox had virtually ignored, and established a foundation for moving into the high-volume market. In addition, the Federal Trade Commission accused Xerox of illegally monopolizing the copier business. After negotiations, Xerox agreed to open approximately 1,700 patents to competitors. Xerox was soon losing market share to Japanese competitors, and by the early 1980s it faced a serious competitive threat from copy machine manufacturers in Japan; Xerox's market share had fallen to less than 50 percent. Some people even predicted that the company would not survive. Rework, scrap, excessive inspection, lost business, and other problems were estimated to be costing Xerox more than 20 percent of revenue, which in 1983 amounted to nearly $2 billion. Both the company and its primary union, the Amalgamated Clothing and Textile Workers, were concerned. In comparing itself with its competition, Xerox discovered that it had nine times as many suppliers, twice as many employees, cycle times that were twice as long, 10 times as many rejects, and seven times as many manufacturing defects in finished products. It was clear that radical changes were required.

Leadership Through Quality

In 1983 company president David T. Kearns became convinced that Xerox needed a long-range, comprehensive quality strategy as well as a change in its traditional management culture (see Figure 1.9). Kearns was aware of Japanese subsidiary Fuji Xerox's success in implementing quality-management practices and was approached by several Xerox employees about instituting total quality management. He commissioned a team to outline a quality strategy for Xerox. The team's report stated that instituting it would require changes in behav-

iors and attitudes throughout the company as well as operational changes in the company's business practices. Kearns determined that Xerox would initiate a total quality management approach, that they would take the time to "design it right the first time," and that the effort would involve all employees. Kearns and the company's top 25 managers wrote the Xerox Quality Policy, which states:

> *Xerox is a quality company. Quality is the basic business principle for Xerox. Quality means providing our external and internal customers with innovative products and services that fully satisfy their requirements. Quality improvement is the job of every Xerox employee.*

This policy led to a process called Leadership Through Quality, which had three objectives:

1. To instill quality as the basic business principle in Xerox, and to ensure that quality improvement becomes the job of every Xerox person.
2. To ensure that Xerox people, individually and collectively, provide our external and

---

Figure 1.9 Origin of the 1983 Xerox Quality Imperative

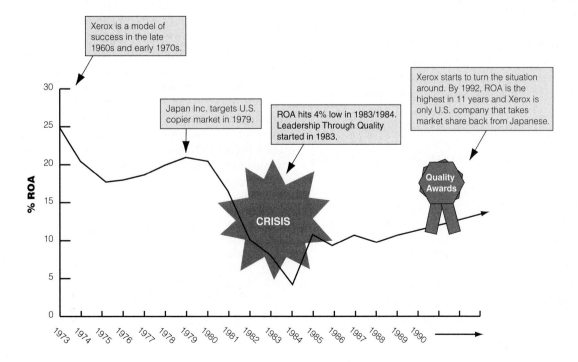

internal customers with innovative products and services that fully satisfy their existing and latent requirements.

3. To establish, as a way of life, management and work processes that enable all Xerox people to continuously pursue quality improvement in meeting customer requirements.

In addition, Leadership Through Quality was directed at achieving four goals in all Xerox activities:

- *Customer Goal:* To become an organization with whom customers are eager to do business.
- *Employee Goal:* To create an environment where everyone can take pride in the organization and feel responsible for its success.
- *Business Goal:* To increase profits and presence at a rate faster than the markets in which Xerox competes.
- *Process Goal:* To use Leadership Through Quality principles in all Xerox does.

Leadership Through Quality radically changed the way Xerox did business. All activities, such as product planning, distribution, and establishing unit objectives, began with a focus on customer requirements. Benchmarking—identifying and studying the companies and organizations that best perform critical business functions and then incorporating those organizations' ideas into the firm's operations—became an important component of Xerox's quality efforts. Xerox benchmarked more than 200 processes with those of noncompetitive companies. For instance, ideas for improving production scheduling came from Cummins Engine Company, ideas for improving the distribution system came from L.L. Bean, and ideas for improving billing processes came from American Express.

Measuring customer satisfaction and training were important components of the program. Every month, 40,000 surveys were mailed to customers, seeking feedback on equipment performance, sales, service, and administrative support. Any reported dissatisfaction was dealt with immediately and was usually resolved in a matter of days. When the program was instituted, every Xerox employee worldwide, and at all levels of the company, received the same training in quality principles. This training began with top management and filtered down through each level of the

firm. Five years, 4 million labor-hours, and more than $125 million later, all employees had received quality-related training. In 1988 about 79 percent of Xerox employees were involved in quality improvement teams.

Several other steps were taken. Xerox worked with suppliers to improve their processes, implement statistical methods and a total quality process, and to support a just-in-time inventory concept. Suppliers that joined in these efforts were involved in the earliest phases of new product designs and rewarded with long-term contracts.

Employee involvement and participation was also an important effort. Xerox had always had good relationships with its unions. In 1980 the company signed a contract with its principal union, the Amalgamated Clothing and Textile Workers, encouraging union members' participation in quality improvement processes. It was the first program in the company that linked managers with employees in a mutual problem-solving approach and served as a model for other corporations. A subsequent contract included the provision that "every employee shall support the concept of continuous quality improvement while reducing quality costs through teamwork."

Most important, management became the role model for the new way of doing business. Managers were required to practice quality in their daily activities and to promote Leadership Through Quality among their peers and subordinates. Reward and recognition systems were modified to focus on teamwork and quality results. Managers became coaches, involving their employees in the act of running the business on a routine basis.

From the initiation of Leadership Through Quality until the point at which Xerox's Business Products and Systems organization won the Malcolm Baldrige National Quality Award in 1989, some of the most obvious impacts of the Leadership Through Quality program included the following:

1. Reject rates on the assembly line fell from 10,000 parts per million to 300 parts per million.
2. Ninety-five percent of supplied parts no longer needed inspection; in 1989, 30 U.S. suppliers went the entire year defect-free.
3. The number of suppliers was cut from 5,000 to fewer than 500.

4. The cost of purchased parts was reduced by 45 percent.
5. Despite inflation, manufacturing costs dropped 20 percent.
6. Product development time decreased by 60 percent.
7. Overall product quality improved 93 percent.

Xerox learned that customer satisfaction plus employee motivation and satisfaction resulted in increased market share and improved return on assets. In 1989 president David Kearns observed that quality is "a race without a finish line."

Crisis and Quality Renewal

Throughout the 1990s, Xerox grew at a steady rate. However, at the turn of the century, the technology downturn, coupled with a decreased focus on quality by top corporate management, resulted in a significant stock price drop and a new crisis (see Figure 1.10). A top management shake-up, resulting in new corporate leadership, renewed the company's focus on quality, beginning with "New Quality" in 2001 and leading to the current "Lean Six Sigma" initiative.

The New Quality philosophy built on the quality legacy established in the 1983 Leadership Through Quality process. Soon afterward, as Six Sigma became more popular across the United States, this approach was refined around a structured, Six Sigma–based improvement process with more emphasis on behaviors and leadership to achieve performance excellence. The new thrust, established in 2003 and called "Lean Six Sigma" (see Chapter 10 for a detailed discussion), includes a dedicated infrastructure and resource commitment to focus on key business issues: critical customer opportunities, significant training of employees and "black belt" improvement specialists, a value-driven project selection process, and an increased customer focus with a clear linkage to business strategy and objectives. The basic principles support the core value "We Deliver Quality and Excellence in All We Do" and are stated as:

- Customer-focused employees, accountable for business results, are fundamental to our success.
- Our work environment enables participation, speed, and teamwork based on trust, learning, and recognition.
- Everyone at Xerox has business objectives aligned to the Xerox direction. A disciplined process is used to assess progress towards delivery of results.

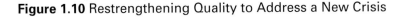

Figure 1.10 Restrengthening Quality to Address a New Crisis

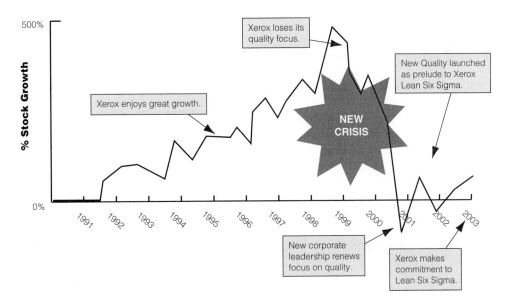

- Customer-focused work processes, supported by disciplined use of quality tools, enable rapid changes and yield predictable business results.
- Everyone takes responsibility to communicate and act on benchmarks and knowledge that enable rapid change in the best interests of customers and shareholders.

The key components of Xerox's Lean Six Sigma are as follows:

1. Performance excellence process
   - Supports clearer, simpler alignment of corporate direction to individual objectives
   - Emphasizes ongoing inspection/assessment of business priorities
   - Clear links to market trends, benchmarking, and Lean Six Sigma
   - Supports a simplified "Baldrige-type" business assessment model
2. DMAIC (define, measure, analyze, improve, control) process
   - Based on industry-proven Six Sigma approach with speed and focus
   - Four steps support improvement projects, set goals
   - Used to proactively capture opportunities or solve problems
   - Full set of lean and Six Sigma tools
3. Market trends and benchmarking
   - Reinforces market focus and encourages external view
   - Disciplined approach to benchmarking
   - Establishes a common four-step approach to benchmarking
   - Encourages all employees to be aware of changing markets
   - Strong linkage to performance excellence process and DMAIC
4. Behaviors and leadership
   - Reinforces customer focus
   - Expands interactive skills to include more team effectiveness
   - Promotes faster decision making and introduces new meeting tool
   - Supports leadership skills required for transition and change

The heart of Xerox's Lean Six Sigma is the performance excellence process, illustrated in Figure 1.11. It consists of three phases: setting direction, deploying direction, and delivering and inspecting results. It starts at the top of the organization—even the chair and CEO, Anne Mulcahy, has an individual performance excellence plan with objectives that are aligned with organization goals and measures and targets for assessment. This approach provides clear communication of direction and accountability for objectives. A structured approach is used to prioritize and select projects that have high benefits relative to the effort involved in accomplishing them. Statistical methods, lean work flow methods, and other process management skills are used to drive

Figure 1.11 Xerox Performance Excellence Process

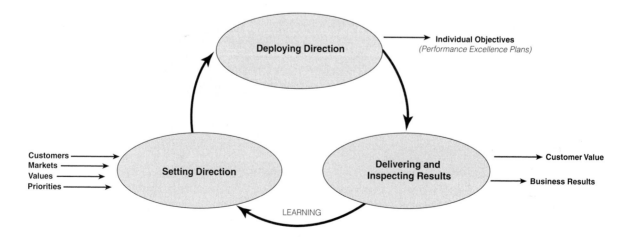

improvement from a factual, objective basis, driven by the DMAIC methodology.

Market trends and benchmarking help provide an external perspective required to lead the market with innovative products, services, and solutions and add value to the customer experience. This component encourages all people to share information and knowledge that enables changes in the best interest of customers and shareholders. Finally, behaviors and leadership reinforce customer-focused behaviors, based on the principle that "Quality is the responsibility of every Xerox employee."

In 2003, Xerox trained more than 1,000 senior leaders across the company and communicated this business approach, the key differences from their quality legacy, and expectations to every employee, and is rapidly moving Lean Six Sigma concepts from manufacturing and supply chain into all business areas. They recognize that full

leadership commitment is the key ingredient. As Anne Mulcahy noted, "What I worry most about is how to return Xerox to greatness. . . . Lean Six Sigma is not the only answer, but it's a significant part of the equation."

Key Issues for Discussion

1. Contrast Leadership for Quality and Lean Six Sigma as quality initiatives for Xerox. How did their motivations differ? What differences or similarities are evident in the principles behind these initiatives and the way in which they were implemented?
2. What lessons might this experience—particularly in responding to the new crisis—have for other organizations?
3. Discuss the meaning of "Quality is a race without a finish line." What is its significance to Xerox, or to any organization?

QUALITY IN PRACTICE
BRINGING TOTAL QUALITY PRINCIPLES TO LIFE AT KARLEE[37]

KARLEE is a contract manufacturer of precision sheet metal and machined components for telecommunications, semiconductor, and medical equipment industries, located in Garland, Texas. KARLEE provides a vertically integrated range of services that support customers from initial component design to a finished, assembled product. Their services include:

- Advanced design engineering support
- Prototype production
- Manufacture and assembly of precision machined and sheet metal fabricated products
- Product finishing (painting, silk screening, plating)
- Value-added assembly integration (cabling, power supply and back plane installation, and electrical testing)

KARLEE exemplifies the principles of total quality that we introduced in this chapter in a number of ways, which are discussed next.

Customer and Stakeholder Focus

KARLEE made a strategic decision to carefully select customers that support their values, which include a systematic approach to business and performance management, a desire for long-term partnerships, and being a global leader. Senior executives work with each customer to establish current requirements and future needs, and each customer is assigned a two-person customer service team that is on call 24 hours a day for day-to-day production issues. One member is an estimator who provides quotes for the customer. The second member is a customer service representative (CSR) who provides liaison support in communicating delivery, scheduling, order entry, and other requested information. The customer service representatives for three of KARLEE's primary customers provide on-site support, spending two to three days a week to full time at the customer site. KARLEE uses a mobile phone system that includes voice-mail, e-mail, and radio communications to make CSRs accessible whenever they are away from their office. In the event they are unavailable, a private voice-mail can be left for any team member. Home phone numbers of customer service representatives are given to customers as well.

KARLEE develops and ensures customer loyalty by providing a full range of manufacturing, engineering, and customer support services, maintaining a committed "can do" attitude, and being able to rapidly meet changing requirements. Their ability to vertically integrate processes and provide engineering support from design conception through production strengthens the bond they have with customers and ensures continued relationships. Additional methods of building and sustaining long-term relationships with customers include the following:

- Learning customers' business challenges and using this information to seek opportunities to better support their performance
- Providing proactive cost management solutions, remaining responsive and flexible to schedule changes, and maintaining capacity and resources to adjust to customer growth requirements
- Maintaining open communications at each business level
- Supporting major customer initiatives, such as lean manufacturing
- Sharing detailed cost information to assist customers in joint cost reductions

Participation and Teamwork

The entire workforce is organized into operational, administrative, and support teams to encourage decision making at the individual and team levels. A management team leader (MTL) or an operational team leader (OTL) leads each team. OTLs are charged with daily coaching and mentoring of team members while balancing customer needs such as quality and delivery, with corporate needs such as lowering scrap and rework. Team members are empowered to take initiative and contribute in many ways, including setting performance targets and monitoring and improving their processes.

Production and delivery processes are designed around teams of manufacturing cells. Each cell is responsible for knowing their customer's requirements and for producing products to meet those requirements. KARLEE promotes cross-training and job rotation to foster flexibility and learning and to enable rapid response to changing customer demands. These concepts are deployed throughout all teams. For example, accounting team members rotate to train in different accounting positions after mastering their primary job responsibilities. Job rotation provides a flexible response to peak loads in a work area, while enhancing job diversity and skill knowledge.

KARLEE helps team members to develop and utilize their full potential by creating an environment of empowerment and opportunity for growth. Team members are empowered to take ownership of, and are held accountable for, the processes within their work area. During strategic planning, objectives and targets are developed for the operational, administrative, and support teams across the company. Each team is empowered to change its recommended targets and request additional measures if they believe it will help them achieve higher performance. Team members plan and execute their own improvement activities to meet those targets. Teams are empowered to schedule work, manage inventory, and design the layout of their work areas. Any team member can stop production if the process is not performing to customer requirements or process specification. KARLEE fosters a team culture based on genuine caring and support among leaders and team members.

KARLEE stresses the importance of mutual trust, honesty, respect, and team member well-being. The support climate is also enhanced through the following means:

- The KARLEE Cares Team, which members formed to meet catastrophic needs of their fellow workers and the community
- The Cultural Advisory Committee, which recommends ways to better fulfill company values, vision, and mission
- The "KARLEE Super Kids" and scholarship programs, which recognize and reward the students of team members for scholastic achievement
- Team Resources, which provides a *Welcome Bag* to all new team members and sponsors social activities such as holiday lunches, picnics, and parties on a regular basis

Process Focus and Continuous Improvement

Processes such as prototype development, scheduling, production setup, fabrication, assembly, and delivery have process owners responsible for maintaining the process to customer requirements. The key steps for each process are clearly documented and measures are used to ensure that process requirements are met. A quality assurance team member works with manufacturing teams to create process documentation. For example, the process of generating a production quote consists of three steps: reviewing specifications, defining shop floor routing, and estimating materials and labor. Response time is a key requirement of this process, and is measured by customer satisfaction with the quote response time. This process focus extends to support processes that include maintenance, accounting, information systems, and training.

Teams use a structured approach to evaluate and improve their processes, document them, and present a status report of improvements to senior leaders and the KARLEE Steering Committee (KSC). Teams analyze defect data, customer-reported problems, and control charts generated during production to identify problems and opportunities for improvement. Teams benchmark competitors, "best practice" companies, and customers to learn from others. Manufacturing teams use benchmarking to focus on improved technologies, cell layout, process flow, and process procedures and identify methods to reduce cycle time and improve capacity. Examples of recent improvements include the addition of robotic brakes and welding equipment, upgrades in CAD/CAM software to support customer design requirements, and the replacement of their business computer system.

The KSC uses a cost/benefit approach for assessing and approving improvements. For example, the social committee budget and the annual selection of insurance benefits are evaluated against the perceived value of the benefits. Capital purchase requests, especially for machining and sheet metal equipment, are closely evaluated to ensure adequate cost justification. Every business goal and project has defined methods for measurement, and senior leaders meet weekly to review company performance and ensure alignment with directions and plans.

KARLEE's focus on continuous improvement extends to all its managerial activities, including its leadership processes. For example, KARLEE utilizes input from seven sources to improve leadership effectiveness and management skills:

- Annual team member surveys include questions regarding the leadership effectiveness.
- Senior executives perform peer reviews annually.
- Senior executives perform self-assessments annually.
- The SELs perform an assessment of the KSC during strategic planning.
- Senior executives assess organizational leadership against the MBNQA criteria.
- An annual strategic planning questionnaire includes questions about the effectiveness of KARLEE's mission, vision, and values.
- Leadership and quality consultants evaluate KARLEE's leadership effectiveness.

KARLEE was recognized for its business achievements by receiving a Baldrige Award in 2000.

Key Issues for Discussion

1. From the information presented in this case, how are the various definitions of quality that we discussed in this chapter reflected in KARLEE's practices?
2. A current trend in the industries that KARLEE serves (and in most high-tech industries) is toward mergers and acquisitions. However, with the small customer base that KARLEE has, this trend represents a high level of risk. What types of practices in the total quality infrastructure described in this chapter might KARLEE engage in to address this risk?

REVIEW QUESTIONS

1. Briefly summarize the history of quality before and since the industrial revolution. What caused the most significant changes?
2. What factors have contributed to the increased awareness of quality in modern business?
3. Explain the various definitions of quality. Can a single definition suffice? Why?
4. Distinguish among consumers, external customers, and internal customers. Illustrate how these concepts apply to a McDonald's restaurant, a Pizza Hut, or a similar franchise.
5. What is the concept of total quality? What does it mean for the way an organization is managed?
6. Describe the three fundamental principles of total quality.
7. What is a process? How does a process focus differ from a traditional organization?
8. List some examples of the types of improvements an organization can make.
9. What is the difference between improvement and learning?
10. What are the important elements of a total quality infrastructure?
11. Explain the relationship among infrastructure, practices, and tools.
12. How does quality support the achievement of competitive advantage?
13. What did Philip Crosby mean by "Quality is free"?
14. Explain the role of quality in improving a firm's profitability.
15. What evidence exists to counter the claim that "Quality does not pay"?
16. Explain the three levels of quality and the key issues that must be addressed at each level.
17. Why is it important to personalize quality principles?

DISCUSSION QUESTIONS

1. Discuss how either good or poor quality affects you personally as a consumer. For instance, describe experiences in which your expectations were met, exceeded, or not met when you purchased goods or services. Did your experience change your regard for the company and/or its product? How?
2. Discuss the importance of quality to the national interest of any country in the world.
3. How might the definitions of quality apply to your college or university? Provide examples of its customers and ways in which their expectations can be met or exceeded.
4. Think of a product or a service that you are considering purchasing. Develop a list of fitness-for-use criteria that are meaningful to you.
5. Select a service activity with which you are familiar. If you were the manager of this activity, what "conformance to specifications" criteria would you use to monitor it?
6. Choose a product or service (such as the hospital example on page 16 in this chapter) to illustrate how several definitions of quality can apply simultaneously.
7. What definition of quality is implied by the following consumer advertisements?
   a. A Tiffany & Co. ad for timepieces entitled "The Business Gift." In describing the gift, the ad suggests that "It must honor the recipient. It must express

your gratitude. It must reflect well upon you and your firm. It is packaged neatly, securely, elegantly. It arrives on time every time. It is an honest design. Original and timeless."

    b. An ad for Certified Preowned Ford vehicles that describes how it has been quality checked by a rigorous 115-point bumper-to-bumper inspection.

    c. A picture of a luxury automobile with the caption "Wish granted."

    d. A Land Rover ad that states, "Polished walnut and select leather combined with Electronic Air Suspension and a 460-watt, 12-speaker audio system make the best of even the worst conditions. As do permanent four-wheel-drive and four-wheel Electronic Traction Control."

    e. A Xerox ad that explains that its printer is three times faster than one produced by Hewlett-Packard, with the caption "Xerox color printers exceed all speed limits."

    f. A Lands' End ad that states, "The $68 down jacket that turns winter inside out," and explains how it is packed with goose down—the warmest insulation on earth.

8. How might quality management practices differ between a firm that might be characterized as "market-driven" and one that might be called "marketing-driven"?

9. Do you feel that your college or university is applying the principles of total quality? Why or why not?

10. What are some processes that you personally perform? What opportunities can you think of for improving them?

11. Choose some organization that you have read about or with which you have personal experience and describe their sources of competitive advantage. For each, state whether you believe that quality supports their strategy or does not support it.

12. Explain how the "three levels of quality" might apply to a college or university.

 ## PROJECTS, ETC.

1. Develop a portfolio of advertisements from newspapers and magazines and illustrate how quality is used in promoting these products. Do the ads suggest any of the different definitions of quality?

2. Visit the Malcolm Baldrige National Quality Award Web site at http://www.baldrige.org and summarize the key results of winners for the past two years. In addition, investigate the latest report on stock performance of Baldrige-winning companies.

3. Prepare a *Quality in Practice* case similar to the KARLEE and Xerox cases using sources such as business periodicals, personal interviews, and so on. Focus your discussion on how their approach to total quality supports their competitive strategy.

4. Examine the annual reports of one company over a period of years. Summarize how quality is discussed or implied in the company's statements and philosophy. Are any changes in the perspectives of quality evident over time?

5. Many countries around the world have professional organizations similar to the American Society for Quality; however, each has its own unique history and offers exclusive activities to its corporate and individual members. They include Excellence Finland, Excellence Ireland, German Society for Quality,

Hong Kong Society for Quality, Instituto Profesional Argentino para la Calidad y la Excelencia, Israel Society for Quality, Union of Japanese Scientists and Engineers (JUSE), National Quality Institute (Canada), Programa Gaucho da Qualidade e Produtividade (Brazil), Singapore Quality Institute, and the Spanish Association for Quality. Conduct some research on several of these societies and contrast their similarities and differences.

6. Develop your own personal quality checklist and analyze the results over an extended period of time. After you have gathered data for a week or two, review the data for the purposes of analysis and improvement. Use charts to plot and analyze weekly results. Use the following guidelines.
   • Each participant should initiate a personal quality improvement project and maintain and improve it during the rest of the study period.
   • Consistent effort, rather than elegant precision in pursuing the project will be rewarded; that is, individual benefit, rather than "a grade," or perfection, is to be the major objective.
   • The personal quality checklist in Figure 1.7 will provide a starting point for the project. Other tools and techniques may be incorporated at a later time.
   • Eight to ten items for personal tracking and improvement should be chosen. The listing of possible checklist standards in Table 1.1 may be useful. However, participants are not required to use only items from this list. Whatever is meaningful to you may be tracked.

Table 1.1 Suggested Standards for a Personal Quality Checklist

- Review class notes after each class
- Limit phone calls to ten minutes, where possible
- No more than 10 hours of TV per week
- Get up promptly—no snooze alarm
- Complete all reading assignments as due
- Plan by using a brief outline of what is to be accomplished daily
- Refer to daily plan each day
- Use stairs instead of elevator
- Follow up on job contacts within 24 hours
- Work in library (or other quiet place) to avoid interruptions
- Stick to one subject at a time while studying
- Don't doggedly persist in trying to clear up a confusing point (or "bug" in a computer program) when stuck; set it aside and return later; for example, no more than 10 minutes after searching for a problem
- Don't spend too much time on routine activities; for example, no more than 15 minutes for breakfast, decrease grooming time to no more than 20 minutes
- Remember names of people to whom you have been introduced
- In bed every night before midnight
- Good housekeeping standards around house, apartment, dorm room, by the end of the day
- Prompt payment of bills, before their due date
- Various dietary standards—eat vegetables, avoid fats (be specific!)
- Limit beer and/or cigarette consumption (be specific!)

Source: Adapted with the permission of The Free Press, a Division of Simon & Schuster Adult Publishing Group from *Quality Is Personal: A Foundation for Total Quality Management* by Harry V. Roberts and Bernard F. Sergesketter. Copyright © 1993 by Harry V. Roberts and Bernard F. Sergesketter, p. 35. All Rights reserved.

- After a week's data are gathered, plot a simple graph to determine the level of "defects" encountered.
- A suggested practice is that you share your personal checklist items and goals with your instructor, a colleague, spouse, or friend. Have that person ask you about your progress every week or so. If you are making regular progress, you should be happy to discuss it, and to show your charts and graphs. Even if your progress is uneven, you should be able to show that you've improved on one or two items, which is progress. Don't be too self-critical!
- An intermediate progress report should be built into the process around the middle of the pilot study period. The final report on the pilot project should be made at the end of the study period. Consideration should be given to making personal quality a permanent part of your personal planning and improvement process.

After completing the project, answer these questions:

a. What did your analysis reveal?

b. Did you experience the same thing that Sergesketter did when he found that certain items disappeared as problems in a short period of time, simply because he began to measure them?

c. How did you feel about discussing your "defects" with others?

d. How does the personal quality process tie into processes in a work environment?

 CASES

Additional cases are available in the Bonus Materials Folder on the CD-ROM.

I. SKILLED CARE PHARMACY[38]

Skilled Care Pharmacy, located in Mason, Ohio, is a $25 million dollar privately held regional provider of pharmaceutical products delivered within the long-term care, assisted living, hospice, and group home environments. The following products are included within this service:

- Medications and related billing services
- Medical records
- Information systems
- Continuing education
- Consulting services to include pharmacy, nursing, dietary, and social services

The key customer groups that Skilled Care provides services to include the senior population housed within the extended and long-term care environments. Customers within this sector depend on Skilled Care to provide their daily pharmaceutical needs at a competitive rate.

Because of the high risk factor of its business, these needs require that the right drug be delivered to the right patient at the right time. Moreover, depending on the environment being served, different medication dispensing methods may be used such as vials, multidose packaging, or unit dose boxes. Also, depending on the customer type, specific delivery requirements may be implemented to better serve the end user.

Skilled Care's dedication and commitment to continuous quality improvement is evident throughout its internal and external operations. By reflecting on the principles needed to attain quality success across all levels of customers, Skilled Care adopted the quality policy statement shown in Figure 1.12.

Skilled Care's employee population includes 176 culturally diverse associates committed to a substance-free workplace. The team includes associates with all levels of educational training representing many of the following disciplines: pharmacists, pharmacy technicians, medical data entry, accountants, billing specialists, nurses, human resources, sales/marketing, purchasing, administrative and administrative assistance, delivery, customer service representatives, and IT certified personnel. At times, multifaceted work teams are formed through cross-functional approaches to complete the task(s) at hand.

Skilled Care's deliverables are generated from its sole 24,000-square foot location in Mason, Ohio. The pharmacy, which is open 24 hours a day, 365 days a year is secured by a Honeywell alarm system. The company's primary technology rests within its pharmacy software, Rescot. This system enables Skilled Care to process, bill, and generate pertinent data critical to the overall operations of the company. Other partnerships have also been established within Skilled Care's multidosed packaging capabilities and wholesaler purchasing interface.

SCP utilizes the Internet for publishing pertinent information and news as well as hosts a Web-enabled customer service application called Track-It to report specific information about customer issues for companywide resolution. Advantages of e-commerce include quicker customer service response time for all areas of service including placing the order, pharmacist's review, delivery, and billing of the product.

Skilled Care Pharmacy faces key strategic challenges from the rapidly evolving financial structure of health care, a shortage of licensed pharmacist personnel, the constant evolution of medical practice, and employee retention at all levels. These as well as future challenges are always balanced with the responsibility to the stakeholders.

Discussion Questions

1. How might the various definitions of quality apply to Skilled Care?
2. How are the principles of total quality reflected in Skilled Care's policy and operations?
3. Given the nature of Skilled Care's operations and the challenges it faces, discuss how a total quality approach can help the company meet these challenges and improve its ability to provide the services its customers need.

Figure 1.12 Skilled Care Quality Policy

Our Quality Policy

S	Services and products that meet or exceed both our internal and external customers' expectations
C	**Leading to** Complete customer satisfaction
P	**Resulting in** People working together to enhance the lives of those served

II. A Tale of Two Restaurants[39]

Tim Kelley founded Kelley's Seafood Restaurant about 15 years ago. The restaurant is very profitable because of its excellent quality of food, but lately has been having problems with consistency because of numerous suppliers. The restaurant operations are divided into front-end (servers) and back-end (kitchen). The kitchen has Post-It notes to boost employee morale, employees are cross-trained in all areas, and the kitchen staff continually seeks improvements in cooking. Servers, however, have few perks and minimal wages, and turnover is a bit of a problem. Tim's primary criterion for selecting servers is their ability to show up on time. Little communication takes place between the front-end and back-end operations, other than fulfilling orders. Tim makes sure that the servers refer any complaints to him immediately.

The restaurant uses no automation, because Tim believes it would get in the way of customers' special requests. "This is the way we've done it for the past 15 years and how we will continue to do it," was his response to a suggestion of using a computerized system to speed up orders and eliminate delays. Tim formerly held staff meetings regularly, but recently went from one each week to one every five or six months. Most of his time is spent focusing on negative behavior, and he can often be heard to say, "You can't find good people anymore."

Jim's SteakHouse is a family-owned restaurant in the same state. Jim uses only the freshest meats and ingredients from the best suppliers and gives extra large portions of food to customers so they feel they are getting their money's worth. Jim pays

his cooks high wages to attract quality employees. Servers get 70 percent of tips, bussers 20 percent, and the kitchen staff 10 percent to foster teamwork. Many new hires come from referrals from current employees. Jim interviews all potential employees and asks them many pointed questions relating to courtesy, responsibility, and creativity. The restaurant sponsors bowling nights, golf outings, picnics, and holiday parties for its employees. At Jim's, birthday customers receive a free dinner, children are welcomed with balloons, candy, and crayons, and big screen TVs cater to sports fans. Jim walks around and constantly solicits customer feedback. Jim visits many other restaurants to study their operations and learn new techniques. As a result of these visits, Jim installed computers to schedule reservations and enter orders to the kitchen.

Discussion Questions

1. Contrast these two restaurants from the perspective of TQ. How do they exhibit or not exhibit the fundamental principles of TQ?
2. What advice would you recommend to the owners?

III. A Total Quality Business Model[40]

Two young entrepreneurs, Rob and Diane, were contemplating an idea of developing a new type of take-out restaurant with limited dining facilities that would provide a wider variety of home-cooked cuisines than found in currently available businesses. In developing their business model, they realized that a TQ-focused management infrastructure would be vital to success. Here are some of the ideas they arrived at.

Customer Relationship Management

Rob and Diane realized that they must focus on the customers' perceived quality of both the product and service. They believe they must provide unexpected value to their customers and go beyond customer expectations to create lifetime customers. As part of training, employees will focus on "moment of truths"—the many instances that a customer forms an impression of the company, either through its products or interactions with its employees. These moments include a

friendly greeting to each customer on arrival, recognizing repeat customers, offering samples of different items, answering questions, serving the products, and a genuine thank-you on leaving. Another way to exceed expectations would be to accommodate any reasonable request. Employees would have the authority to do whatever it takes to satisfy the customer. When a complaint is raised, the employee should act immediately to solve to the problem, listen attentively to the customer, and apologize. No matter what, the customer should always be thanked for bringing the complaint to the staff's attention.

To evaluate the customer's experience, the company would require shift managers to be the first customer on each shift, starting from the parking lot to check its cleanliness. In addition, they would use technology to track service times and complaints, and "mystery shoppers" each month throughout the system. Every quarter, all regional store and shift managers would meet to discuss their experiences and seek improvements.

Leadership and Strategic Planning

The leadership system would consist of regional vice presidents responsible for all of the stores in a geographical area, regional managers in charge of about a dozen stores within a region, store managers responsible for the day-to-day operations, and shift managers to manage the employees on each shift. This "cascading" structure would allow communications to be disseminated rapidly throughout the company, both top-down and bottom-up. A manager training and development program would ensure that each level of manager obtained the necessary skills for their job responsibilities. This training would not only address the needs of entry-level managers, but also those who move up the career ladder in the firm into higher leadership positions.

The company's vision would be simple: to be the consumer's choice for all varieties of fresh convenience meals. The strategy would be based on product quality (variety, freshness, value) and outstanding customer service. Rob and Diane realized that every employee needed to understand the company strategy, which would be conveyed during the employee orientation and management training and development programs. Managers would be responsible for ensuring that all hourly employees focus on these two goals through daily meetings, written quality check sheets that must be completed on every shift, and an employee stock-option program that would be tied to meeting these goals as well as profit targets.

Human Resource Management

All managers would be trained in several positions in order to gain a solid understanding of the duties and requirements of all employees, to be able to cover certain positions if needed, to train hourly employees, and to gain credibility with them. The training program for a new manager would be designed to be somewhat self-directed. The manager trainee would be given a skill checklist that includes each skill he or she should learn. Experienced trainers would be available to answer any questions and assist the manager trainee with any difficulties. Trainees would be given short evaluative tests and feedback from the trainer. Before their first day of work, all hourly employees would attend an orientation session focused on making them feel welcome in their new work environment. The session would include a history of the company, mission, policies, and training procedures. To keep good people, the compensation program would need to be competitive in the industry. Managers would be required to visit local competitors to identify their compensation structure and compare them.

Job performance of all hourly employees would be reviewed periodically using performance appraisals by the store manager after the first 30, 90, and 180 days of employment, followed by annual appraisals. The appraisal would cover such topics as customer focus, quality of work, teamwork, and responsibility. It would also require the employee to identify future goals and objectives and plans for improving performance.

Process Management

All food production processes would be carefully documented so that all employees are aware of what specifications must be met, particularly those health and safety requirements that regulated temperature of food and proper storage. Managers would be responsible for taking periodic measurements and observations to ensure that all employees are following procedures. Managers would also be responsible for their relationships with food suppliers. Rob and Diane are thinking of identifying one large supplier for most of their food supplies.

Information and Knowledge Management

All key data and information, such as inventories, financial reports and projections, customer feedback, employee and operational performance, would be collected and displayed in the kitchen area, so all employees can understand the results of their efforts. Information from all stores would be consolidated at corporate headquarters for evaluation and analysis.

Discussion Questions

1. What advice might you give Rob and Diane about the management practices they are proposing within each element of the TQ infrastructure? What additional practices might you suggest?
2. How might viewing the organization from the "Three Levels of Quality" discussed in the chapter help improve their business plan?

ENDNOTES

1. *The Cincinnati Enquirer*, January 12, 2002, pp. A1, A9.

2. Early history is reported in Delmer C. Dague, "Quality—Historical Perspective," *Quality Control in Manufacturing* (Warrendale, PA: Society of Automotive Engineers, 1981); and L. P. Provost and C. L. Norman, "Variation through the Ages," *Quality Progress* 23, no. 12 (December 1990), 39–44. Modern events are discussed in Nancy Karabatsos, "Quality in Transition, Part One: Account of the '80s," *Quality Progress* 22, no. 12 (December 1989), 22–26; and Joseph M. Juran, "The Upcoming Century of Quality," address to the ASQC Annual Quality Congress, Las Vegas, May 24, 1994. A comprehensive historical account may be found in J. M. Juran, *A History of Managing for Quality* (Milwaukee, WI: ASQC Quality Press, 1995).

3. M. D. Fagan (ed.), *A History of Engineering and Science in the Bell System: The Early Years, 1875–1925* (New York: Bell Telephone Laboratories, 1974).

4. "Manufacturing Tops List of Concerns Among Executives," *Industrial Engineering* 22, no. 6 (June 1990), 8.

5. "The Cost of Quality," *Newsweek*, September 7, 1992, 48–49.

6. Lori L. Silverman with Annabeth L. Propst, "Quality Today: Recognizing the Critical SHIFT," *Quality Progress*, February 1999, 53–60.

7. American Society for Quality: "Foresight 2020: The American Society for Quality Considers the Future," undated report.

8. Nabil Tamimi and Rose Sebastianelli, "How Firms Define and Measure Quality," *Production and Inventory Management Journal* 37, no. 3 (Third Quarter, 1996), 34–39.

9. Four comprehensive reviews of the concept and definition of quality are David A. Garvin, "What Does Product Quality Really Mean?" *Sloan Management Review,* 26, no. 1 (1984), 25–43; Gerald F. Smith, "The Meaning of Quality," Total Quality Management 4, no. 3 (1993), 235–244; Carol A. Reeves and David A. Bednar, "Defining Quality: Alternatives and Implications," *Academy of Management Review* 19, no. 3 (1994), 419–445; and Kristie W. Seawright and Scott T. Young, "A Quality Definition Continuum," *Interfaces* 26, 3 (May–June 1996), 107–113.

10. Garvin (see note 7), 25.

11. "Lamborghini owner says he got $262,000 lemon," *Cincinnati Enquirer*, June 23, 1998, B5.

12. Gregory M. Seal, "1990s—Years of Promise, Years of Peril for U.S. Manufacturers," *Industrial Engineering* 22, no. 1 (January 1990), 18-21. We also thank Ben Valentin for providing some historical facts about Nissan and Datsun.

13. Alex Taylor III, "Detroit's Used-Car Blues," *Fortune*, September 16, 2002, 147–150.

14. *ANSI/ASQC A3-1978, Quality Systems Terminology* (Milwaukee, WI: American Society for Quality Control, 1978).

15. Lawrence Utzig, "Quality Reputation—Precious Asset," *ASQC Technical Conference Transactions*, Atlanta, 1980, 145–154.

16. Procter & Gamble, *Report to the Total Quality Leadership Steering Committee and Working Councils* (Cincinnati, OH: Procter & Gamble, 1992).

17. A. V. Feigenbaum, *Total Quality Control*, 3rd ed., rev. (New York: McGraw-Hill, 1991), 77, 78.

18. Wayne S. Reiker, "Integrating the Pieces for Total Quality Control," *The Quality Circles Journal* (now *The Journal for Quality and Participation*) 6, no. 4 (December 1983), 14–20.

19. Ron Zemke and Dick Schaaf, *The Service Edge* (New York: New American Library, 1989), 352–355; William Davidow and Bro Utall, *Total Customer Service* (New York: Harper & Row, 1989), 86–87.

20. Myron Magnet, "The New Golden Rule of Business," *Fortune*, February 21, 1994, 60–64.

21. *AT&T's Total Quality Approach*, AT&T Corporate Quality Office (1992), 6.

22. L. von Bertalanffy, "The Theory of Open Systems in Physics and Biology," *Science*, 111 (1950), 23–29.

23. J. W. Forrester, *Industrial Dynamics* (New York: John Wiley & Sons, 1961).

24. Peter M. Senge, *The Fifth Discipline: The Art and Practice of the Learning Organization* (New York: Doubleday Currency, 1990), 14.

25. S. C. Wheelwright, "Competing through Manufacturing," in Ray Wild (ed.), *International Handbook of Production and Operations Management* (London: Cassell Educational, Ltd., 1989), 15–32.

26. *The PIMS Letter on Business Strategy*, no. 4 (Cambridge, MA: Strategic Planning Institute, 1986).

27. Philip Crosby, *Quality Is Free* (New York: McGraw-Hill, 1979).

28. Roger O. Crockett, Peter Elstrom, and Gary McWilliams, "Wireless Goes Haywire at Motorola," *Business Week*, March 9, 1998, 32.

29. U.S. General Accounting Office, "Management Practices: U.S. Companies Improve Performance Through Quality Efforts," GA/NSIAD-91-190 (May 1991); "Progress on the Quality Road," *Incentive*, April 1995, 7.

30. Kevin B. Hendricks and Vinod R. Singhal, "Does Implementing an Effective TQM Program Actually Improve Operating Performance? Empirical Evidence from Firms That Have Won Quality Awards," *Management Science* 43, 9 (September 1997), 1258–1274. The results of this study appeared in extensive business and trade publications such as *Business Week*, *Fortune*, and others.

48

48

48   Part 1   Foundations of Quality Management

31. Adapted from Alan P. Brache and Geary A. Rummler, "The Three Levels of Quality," *Quality Progress* 21, no. 10 (October 1988), 46–51.

32. Rath & Strong Executive Panel, Winter 1994 Survey on Personal Initiative, Summary of Findings.

33. David Armstrong, *Management by Storying Around* (New York: Doubleday Currency, 1992), 117–119.

34. Harry V. Roberts and Bernard F. Sergesketter, *Quality Is Personal: A Foundation for Total Quality Management* (New York: The Free Press, 1993).

35. Roberts and Sergesketter (see note 30), 13–14.

36. Information for this case was obtained from "Xerox Quest for Quality and the Malcolm Baldrige National Quality Award" presentation script; Norman E. Rickard, Jr., "The Quest for Quality: A Race without a Finish Line," *Industrial Engineering,* January 1991, 25–27; Howard S. Gitlow and Elvira N. Loredo, "Total Quality Management at Xerox: A Case Study," *Quality Engineering* 5, no. 3 (1993), 403–432; *Xerox Quality Solutions, A World of Quality* (Milwaukee, WI: ASQC Quality Press, 1993); and "Restrengthening Xerox: Our Lean Six Sigma Journey," Presentation slides, May 2003. Courtesy of Xerox Corporation. Our thanks go to George Maszle of Xerox Corporation for providing the information on current Six Sigma initiatives.

37. Adapted from KARLEE 2000 Malcolm Baldrige Application Summary, National Institute of Standards and Technology, U.S. Department of Commerce.

38. Appreciation for materials in this case is expressed to Nancy Mlinarik, VP of Quality, Skilled Care, Inc.

39. Based on a student project prepared by Stacey Bizzell, Suzanne Lee, and Kenneth Shircliff. We gratefully acknowledge their contribution.

40. Based on research conducted by Michael Judge, Melanie Landthaler, Pamela Stermer, and April Urso. We gratefully acknowledge their contribution.

BIBLIOGRAPHY

Bauer, John E., Grace L. Duffy, and Russell T. Wescott (eds.). *The Quality Improvement Handbook.* Milwaukee, WI: ASQ Quality Press, 2002.

Freund, Richard A. "Definitions and Basic Quality Concepts." *Journal of Quality Technology*, January 1985, 50–56.

Garvin, David A. *Managing Quality.* New York: The Free Press, 1988.

Hayes, Glenn E. "Quality: Quandary and Quest." *Quality*, 22, no. 7 (July 1983), 18.

Hiam, Alexander. *Closing the Quality Gap: Lessons from America's Leading Companies.* Englewood Cliffs, NJ: Prentice-Hall, 1992.

Hunt, V. Daniel. *Managing for Quality: Integrating Quality and Business Strategy.* Homewood, IL: Business One Irwin, 1993.

Page, Harold S. "A Quality Strategy for the '80s." *Quality Progress*, 16, no. 11 (November 1983), 16-21.

Schmidt, Warren H., and Jerome P. Finnigan. *The Race without a Finish Line.* San Francisco: Jossey-Bass, 1992.

Stewart, Tom. *The Wealth of Knowledge: Intellectual Capital and the Twenty First Century Organization.* New York: Currency, Inc., 2001.

Van Gigch, John P. "Quality—Producer and Consumer Views." *Quality Progress* 10, no. 4 (April 1977), 30–33.

Wachniak, Ray. "World-Class Quality: An American Response to the Challenge." In M. Sepehri (ed.), *Quest for Quality: Managing the Total System.* Norcross, GA: Institute of Industrial Engineers, 1987.

CHAPTER 2

TOTAL QUALITY IN ORGANIZATIONS

Although Hyundai Motor Co. dominated the Korean car market, it had a poor reputation for quality overseas, with doors that didn't fit properly, frames that rattled, and engines that delivered puny acceleration. And the company was losing money. When Chung Mong Koo became CEO in 1999, he visited Hyundai's plant at Ulsan. To the shock of his employees, who had rarely set eyes on a CEO, Chung strode onto the factory floor and demanded a peek under the hood of a Sonata sedan. He didn't like what he saw: loose wires, tangled hoses, bolts painted four different colors – the kind of sloppiness you'd never see in a Japanese car. On the spot, he instructed the plant chief to paint all bolts and screws black and ordered workers not to release a car unless all was orderly under the hood. "You've got to get back to basics. The only way we can survive is to raise our quality to Toyota's level," he fumed. The next year, U.S. sales rose by 42 percent. One of the keys, in addition to investing heavily in research and development, was creating a quality control czar, who studied quality manuals of U.S. and Japanese automakers and developed their own, making it clear who is responsible for each manufacturing step, what outcome is required, and who checks and confirms performance levels.[1]

As noted in Chapter 1, modern quality management in the United States began in the manufacturing sector, and in many nations, such as Korea, where quality management is still in the early stages, the principal focus is on manufacturing. By the 1990s, many manufacturers began to pay increased attention to service quality. They discovered that service quality is as critical to retaining customers as the tangible products they buy, and turned attention to such support processes as order entry, delivery, and complaint response. Pure service companies began to think in terms of "zero defections" and to explore new ways of developing customer loyalty. A hospital in Detroit, for example, promises to attend to its emergency room patients in 20 minutes or less. If it is unable to keep this promise, the care will be free.[2] Slogans such as "Whatever It Takes" and service guarantees are the norm in today's competitive environment. Nevertheless, many service industries struggle with quality. In the airline industry, for example, the number of consumer complaints rose from 1.08 per 100,000 passengers in 1998 to 2.48 in 1999, and the number of complaints about the top 10 airlines soared 89 percent in the first quarter 2000 from the previous year, and all prior to the cost cutting that airlines experienced since September 11, 2001. It's not that airlines are ignoring the problems. Delta Airlines, for example, is spending millions in service enhancements: trying to respond to e-mail within 48 hours and mail complaints within two weeks against a two-month industry standard, and using technology to identify vulnerable passengers—unaccompanied children, wheelchair travelers, and connecting passengers—when flights must be cancelled for weather problems. But *USA Today* noted that most of the promises are aimed at better communication with customers, not problem-free flights.[3]

Today, the concept of quality has moved far beyond its manufacturing roots. The *Quality Profiles* on the following page provide two examples of quality management in education and health care.

For all types of organizations, quality is absolutely vital to keep customers, sustain profitability, and gain market share. This chapter explores the role of quality in manufacturing and service organizations, large and small, including education, health care, not-for-profit, and government. We begin with the importance of

As consumer expectations have risen, a focus on quality has permeated other key sectors of the economy, most notably health care, education, not-for-profits, and government.

viewing all organizations as systems, and focus on the role that each component of an organization plays in achieving high quality. We then present a variety of examples of quality efforts in these organizations.

QUALITY AND SYSTEMS THINKING

A production system is composed of many smaller, interacting subsystems. For example, a McDonald's restaurant is a system that includes the order-taker/cashier subsystem, grill and food preparation subsystem, drive-through subsystem, purchasing subsystem, and training subsystem. These subsystems are linked together as internal customers and suppliers. Likewise, every organization is composed of many individual functions, which are often seen as separate units on an organization chart. However, managers need to view

*A **system** is a set of functions or activities within an organization that work together for the aim of the organization.*

the organization as a whole and concentrate on the important organizational linkages among these functions. For example, consider the infrastructure elements of a total quality system that we discussed in Chapter 1: customer relationship management,

QUALITY PROFILES

CHUGACH SCHOOL DISTRICT AND SSM HEALTH CARE

CHUGACH SCHOOL DISTRICT
SSM HEALTH CARE

Chugach School District and SSM Health Care are highly innovative organizations that apply the principles of TQ in managing their organizations. Chugach School District (CSD) is not your typical school district. It encompasses 22,000 square miles in south central Alaska, including much of the Prince William Sound coastline. Most of its 214 students live in remote areas, accessible only by aircraft. Teachers must be adept at a variety of subjects, including wilderness and cold-water safety and how to respond in the event of a tsunami or an encounter with a bear.

CSD has pioneered a standards-based system of "whole child education" that emphasizes real-life learning situations. After securing a waiver from the Alaska Department of Education, the district replaced credit hours and grade levels—hallmarks of traditional schooling—with an individualized, student-centered approach. This approach aims for measurable—and demonstrable—proficiency in 10 areas of performance, from basic academic and career development skills to cultural awareness and character skills. With the aim of helping students reach their full potential as individuals and as members of their communities, CSD created a continuum of standards for 10 content areas. Demonstrable proficiency in each area—and not the number of credit hours earned—was set as the essential condition for graduation. CSD proceeded to implement and refine an innovative standards-based system that provides the flexibility to accommodate the personal learning styles and speeds of all students. Expectations are clear and progress toward meeting them is documented in a running record of assessments completed in all content areas. Teachers, children, and parents regularly consult these student assessment binders. Upon graduation, students are given their assessment binders, which serve as proof of skill mastery. Students' results on the California Achievement Test rose dramatically—in reading, from the 28th percentile in 1995 to the 71st in 1999; in math, from 54th to 78th; and in language arts, from 26th to 72nd.

Based in St. Louis, Missouri, SSM Health Care (SSMHC) is a not-for-profit Catholic health system providing primary, secondary, and tertiary health care services. The system owns, manages, and is affiliated with 21 acute care hospitals and three nursing homes in four states: Missouri, Illinois, Wisconsin, and Oklahoma. Nearly 5,000 affiliated physicians and 22,200 employees work together to provide a wide range of services, including emergency, medical/surgical, oncology, mental health, obstetric, cardiology, orthopedic, pediatric, and rehabilitative care.

Every three years, during the strategic, financial, and human resource planning process, environmental scanning is used to identify and plan for potential customers, customers of competitors, and future markets. The scan includes market research, analysis of market share by product line, population trends, and an inventory of competitors, which includes their market share trends and competitive positions. In addition, data from annual medical staff surveys, patient satisfaction surveys, physician contacts, literature searches, telephone surveys, and focus groups of competitors' customers are used. As part of SSMHC's "Clinical Collaborative" process, physicians work with other caregivers, administrators, and staff to make rapid improvements in clinical outcomes. Selection of clinical collaboratives occurs in alignment with system goals, such as improving patient outcomes, satisfaction, and safety. SSMHC has undertaken six collaboratives, involving 85 teams in 2002, up from 14 teams in 1999. The results for SSMHC's clinical collaboratives for patients with congestive heart failure and ischemic heart disease demonstrate levels that approach or exceed national benchmarks. SSMHC's share of the market in the St. Louis area increased to 18 percent in 2002, while three of its five competitors lost market share.

Source: Baldrige Award Recipient Profiles, National Institute of Standards and Technology, U.S. Department of Commerce.

leadership and strategic planning, human resources management, process management, and information and knowledge management. Senior leaders need to focus on strategic directions and on customers; strategies need to be linked to human resource plans and key processes in order to effectively align resources; human resources issues such as training and work system design must support the processes that manufacture products or deliver services; and information and knowledge management provide the means for obtaining useful feedback to better understand the relationship between strategy and execution, and a means for improvement.

Russell Ackoff, a noted authority in **systems thinking**, explained the importance of systems thinking in the following way:

> . . . a combination of the best practices by each part of a system taken separately does not yield the best system. We may not even get a good one. A company that has 12 facilities, each producing the same variations of the same type of beverage, had broken the production process down into 15 steps. It produced a table showing each factory (a column) and each of the 15 steps (rows). The company then carried out a study to determine the cost of each step at each factory (a costly study), which identified for each step the factory with the lowest cost. At each factory, the company tried to replace each of its steps that was not the lowest cost with the one used in the factory that had the lowest cost. Had this succeeded, each factory would be producing with steps that had each attained the lowest cost in any factory. It did not work! The lowest-cost steps did not fit together. The result was only a few insignificant cosmetic changes that did not justify the cost of the exercise.[4]

Ackoff concluded that management should focus on the interactions of parts and of the system with other systems, rather than the actions of parts taken separately.

As we discuss quality in manufacturing, service, and other sectors, think about how important a systems perspective is in achieving quality.

Successful management relies on a systems perspective, one of the most important elements of total quality.

QUALITY IN MANUFACTURING

Well-developed quality assurance systems have existed in manufacturing for some time. The transition to a customer-driven organization has caused fundamental changes in manufacturing practices, changes that are particularly evident in areas such as product design, human resource management, and supplier relations. Product design activities, for example, now closely integrate marketing, engineering, and manufacturing operations (see Chapters 7 and 11). Human resource practices concentrate on empowering workers to collect and analyze data, make critical operations decisions, and take responsibility for continuous improvements, thereby moving the responsibility for quality from the quality control department onto the factory floor.

Suppliers have become partners in product design and manufacturing efforts. Many of these efforts were stimulated by the automobile industry as Ford, GM, and Chrysler forced their network of suppliers to improve quality during the 1980s. As they did so, quality efforts were pushed down the automotive supply chain.

Traditional quality assurance systems in manufacturing focus primarily on technical issues such as equipment reliability, inspection, defect measurement, and process control.

Exemplary quality leaders in the manufacturing sector include large companies such as Armstrong World Industries, AT&T, Boeing Airlift and Tanker Programs, Corning, Eastman Chemical Company, Motorola, and Solar Turbines Incorporated; and small companies such as Granite

Rock Company, Inc., Sunny Fresh Foods, KARLEE, Texas Nameplate Company, Trident Precision Manufacturing, and Wainwright Industries. Leading practices of these and other outstanding manufacturing companies are featured throughout this book.

Manufacturing Systems

Figure 2.1 illustrates a typical manufacturing system and the key relationships among its functions. The quality concerns of each component of the system are described next.

Marketing and Sales Milton Hershey, the founder of Hershey Foods Corporation, understood the relationship between quality and sales. He used to say, "Give them quality. That's the best advertising in the world." For the first 68 years it was in business, Hershey Foods did not see a need to advertise its products in the mass media.[5] Marketing and sales involve much more than advertising and selling. Today, marketing and sales employees have important responsibilities for quality. These responsibilities include learning the products and product features that consumers want, and knowing the prices that consumers are willing to pay for them. This information enables a firm to define products that are fit for use and capable of being produced within the technological and budgetary constraints of the organization. Effective market research and active solicitation of customer feedback are necessary for developing quality products. Salespeople can help to obtain feedback on product performance from customers and convey this information to

Marketing and sales personnel are responsible for determining the needs and expectations of consumers.

Figure 2.1 Functional Relationships in a Typical Manufacturing System

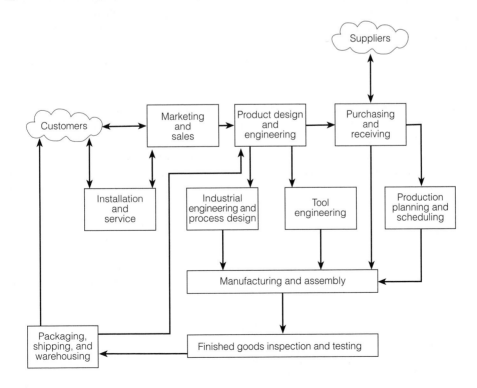

product designers and engineers. They should also help to ensure that customers receive adequate assistance and are completely satisfied.

Ames Rubber Corporation, based in Hamburg, New Jersey, produces rubber rollers used to feed paper, transfer toner, and fuse toner to paper in office machines such as copiers, printers, and typewriters. All products are made to order to customer design and specification. Its warranties are among the best in the industry and include a refund of the customer's portion of development costs for prototype parts if Ames fails to achieve the specifications. Sales representatives take special note of such things as the volume of work a customer or prospective customer expects, the product features the customer seeks, and the customer's cost, service, and delivery requirements. Ames's sales department also conducts quarterly customer satisfaction surveys and monthly customer contact surveys. Customer satisfaction surveys collect data in the areas of products, service, information, and relationships. Customer contact surveys, which take the form of informal conversations, explore quality, cost, delivery, and service. The company uses all of this information to improve customer satisfaction. Chapter 4 explores customer focus and the marketing function further.

Product Design and Engineering Underengineered products will fail in the marketplace because they will not meet customer needs. Products that are overengineered, those that exceed the customer requirements, may not find a profitable market. Japanese automakers, for instance, discovered in the early 1990s that

> *Product design and engineering functions develop technical specifications for products and production processes to meet the requirements determined by the marketing function.*

many consumers were unwilling to pay for some luxury features they had designed into their cars as standard features. Overengineering can also create a complacency that leads to poor quality. Poorly designed manufacturing processes result in poor quality or higher costs. Good design can help to prevent manufacturing defects and service errors and to reduce the need for the non-value-adding inspection practices that have dominated much of U.S. industry.

Motorola, which we profiled in Chapter 1, places considerable emphasis on improving manufacturing quality through its product and process design activities. Motorola sets an ambitious goal of six sigma quality—a level of quality representing no more than 3.4 defects per million opportunities—for every process in the company. To reach this goal, Motorola knows that before it manufactures a product it must first determine the product characteristics that will satisfy customers (marketing's role); decide whether these characteristics can be achieved through the product's design, the manufacturing process, or the materials used; develop design tolerances that will assure successful product performance; conduct measurements to determine process variations from existing specifications; and then hone the product design, manufacturing process, or both, in order to achieve the desired results. Quality in product and process design is considered further in Chapter 7.

Purchasing and Receiving The quality of purchased parts and services and the timeliness of their delivery are critical. The purchasing department can help a firm achieve quality by:

- Selecting quality-conscious suppliers
- Ensuring that purchase orders clearly define the quality requirements specified by product design and engineering
- Bringing together technical staffs from both the buyer's and suppliers' companies to design products and solve technical problems

- Establishing long-term supplier relationships based on trust
- Providing quality-improvement training to suppliers
- Informing suppliers of any problems encountered with their goods
- Maintaining good communication with suppliers as quality requirements and design changes occur

A purchasing agent should not simply be responsible for low-cost procurement, but should maintain a clear focus on the quality of purchased goods and materials.

An example of the quality consciousness of Japanese customers was related to a college class by the manager of a U.S. plant that was supplying stock to a Japanese manufacturer of semiconductor devices for electronics applications. The U.S. manager was justifiably proud of having the best-quality material of this type available from any U.S. supplier, which was why his company had been chosen as a supplier. However, when the Japanese firm tested the first shipment of 9 million parts, it was quite upset with the lack of quality and informed the U.S. firm that it would have to do better or face being replaced by a Japanese supplier. The incoming inspection had detected five bad parts in the total shipment!

The receiving department is the link between purchasing and production. It must ensure that the delivered items are of the quality specified by the purchase contract, which it does through various inspection and testing policies. If the incoming material is of high quality, extensive inspection and testing is not necessary. Many companies now require that their suppliers provide proof that their processes can consistently turn out products of specified quality and give preferential treatment to those that can.

The quality of incoming materials and parts becomes more critical as the use of flexible automation increases. Many U.S. firms have implemented the Japanese management concept of just-in-time (JIT) scheduling. JIT requires that inventories be reduced to the barest minimum. To maintain production, the quality of materials must be high because no buffer inventories are available to take up the slack. Motorola, for example, provides extensive assistance and training to its suppliers to improve their capabilities and quality and expects results in return. Suppliers are evaluated on the quality of delivered product and the timeliness of deliveries. Only those suppliers that meet the company's expectations for superior quality are retained.

Production Planning and Scheduling A production plan specifies long-term and short-term production requirements for filling customer orders and meeting anticipated demand. The correct materials, tools, and equipment must be available at the proper time and in the proper places in order to maintain a smooth flow of production. Modern concepts of production planning and scheduling, such as JIT, have been shown to lead to quality improvements and cost savings.

Poor quality often results from time pressures caused by insufficient planning and scheduling.

Manufacturing and Assembly The role of manufacturing and assembly in producing quality is to ensure that the product is made correctly. The linkage to design and process engineering, as noted earlier, is obvious; manufacturing cannot do its job without a good product design and good process technology. Once in production, however, no defects should be acceptable. If and when they do occur, every effort must be made to identify their causes and eliminate them. Inspecting-out already defective items is costly and wasteful.

Ames Rubber Corporation, for example, produces more than 17,000 custom parts by means of a wide range of manufacturing operations such as casting, extrusion, spraying, and molding. Each operation requires appropriate

Both technology and people are essential to high-quality manufacturing.

measuring methods and devices that can closely monitor the manufacturing process. Sophisticated measuring and testing equipment, such as laser-measuring devices, ensure in-line process control. All Ames manufacturing staff understand the importance and use of statistics in controlling processes. At each production step, operators, inspectors, and supervisors collect and evaluate performance data. This practice allows Ames to detect deviations from the processes immediately and to make the necessary adjustments.

Tool Engineering The tool engineering function is responsible for designing and maintaining the tools used in manufacturing and inspection. Worn manufacturing tools result in defective parts, and improperly calibrated inspection gauges give misleading information. These and other tool problems lead to poor quality and inefficiency. Engineers at Ames Rubber use statistical techniques to evaluate tooling and equipment and conduct periodic studies to ensure that Ames continues to meet or exceed product requirements. If they cannot, the result is excessive scrap, waste, and higher costs.

Industrial Engineering and Process Design The job of industrial engineers and process designers is to work with product design engineers to develop realistic specifications. In addition, they must select appropriate technologies, equipment, and work methods for producing quality products. For example, Nissan Motor Manufacturing has a fully automated paint system in which robots are programmed to move along with cars. Because the robots always know where the body

Manufacturing processes must be capable of producing output that meets specifications consistently.

is, the robot will stop if the line stops but continue the paint cycle until finished as a means of keeping paint quality consistent.[6] Industrial engineers also work on designing facilities and arranging equipment to achieve a smooth production flow and to reduce the opportunities for product damage. Recently, industrial engineering as a profession has been incorporating the types of activities more often taught in business schools.

Finished Goods Inspection and Testing If quality is built into the product properly, inspection should be unnecessary except for auditing purposes and functional testing. Electronic components, for example, are subjected to extensive "burn-in" tests that ensure proper operation and eliminate short-life items. In any case, inspection should be used as a means of gathering information that can be used to improve quality, not simply to remove defective items.

The purposes of final product inspection are to judge the quality of manufacturing, to discover and help to resolve production problems that may arise, and to ensure that no defective items reach the customer.

Packaging, Shipping, and Warehousing Even good-quality items that leave the plant floor can be incorrectly labeled or damaged in transit. Packaging, shipping, and warehousing—often termed *logistics activities*—are the functions that protect quality after goods are produced. Accurate coding and expiration dating of products is important for traceability (often for legal requirements) and for customers.

Installation and Service Products must be used correctly in order to benefit the customer. Users must understand a product and have adequate instructions for proper installation and operation. Should any problem occur, customer satisfaction depends on good after-the-sale service. At one company, truck drivers saw the opportunity to do more than merely deliver materials to receiving docks. Where labor relations permit, they make deliveries to specific locations within plants and assist with unloading, stocking, and inventory counts. Many companies specify standards for customer service similar to the dimensions and tolerances prescribed for manufactured goods. For example, associates are expected to arrive for all appointments on time and to return customer phone calls within a prescribed time period. They are also responsible for knowing and observing their respective customers' rules and regulations, especially those that concern safety procedures.

Service after the sale is one of the most important factors in establishing customer perception of quality and customer loyalty.

In addition to the functions directly related to manufacturing the product, certain business support activities are necessary for achieving quality. Some of these activities are discussed here.

Finance and Accounting The finance function is responsible for obtaining funds, controlling their use, analyzing investment opportunities, and ensuring that the firm operates cost-effectively and—ideally—profitably. Financial decisions affect manufacturing equipment purchases, cost-control policies, price-volume decisions, and nearly all facets of the organization. Finance must authorize sufficient budgeting for equipment, training, and other means of assuring quality. Financial studies can help to expose the costs of poor quality and opportunities for reducing it. Accounting data are useful in identifying areas for quality improvement and tracking the progress of quality improvement programs. Furthermore, inappropriate accounting approaches can hide poor quality.

In many organizations, quality is seldom considered in financial analysis and decision making.

Financial and accounting personnel who have contacts with customers can directly influence the service their company provides. At many companies, for example, employees chart invoice accuracy, the time needed to process invoices, and the time needed to pay bills. In addition, they can apply quality improvement techniques to improve their own operations. Financial personnel at Motorola, for example, were able to reduce the time needed to close the books from one month to four days.

Quality Assurance Because some managers lack the technical expertise required for performing needed statistical tests or data analyses, technical specialists—usually in the "quality assurance department"—assist the managers in these tasks. Quality assurance specialists perform special statistical studies and analyses and may be assigned to work with any of the manufacturing or business support functions. It must be remembered that a firm's quality assurance department cannot assure quality in the organization. Its proper role is to provide guidance and support for the firm's total effort toward this goal.

Every manager is responsible for studying and improving the quality of the process for which he or she is responsible; thus, every manager is a quality manager.

Legal Services A firm's legal department attempts to guarantee that the firm complies with laws and regulations regarding such things as product labeling, packaging, safety, and transportation; designs and words its warranties properly; satisfies its contractual requirements; and has proper procedures and documentation in place in the event of liability claims against it. The rapid increase in liability suits has made legal services an important aspect of quality assurance.

We see that manufacturing is a rather complex system that can be viewed as a "chain of customers." This approach suggests that a customer-driven quality focus must involve everyone in the organization. Quality is indeed everyone's responsibility.

QUALITY IN SERVICES

A service might be as simple as handling a complaint or as complex as approving a home mortgage. The North American Industry Classification System (NAICS) describes service organizations as those

> *Service can be defined as "any primary or complementary activity that does not directly produce a physical product—that is, the non-goods part of the transaction between buyer (customer) and seller (provider)."[7]*

> . . . primarily engaged in providing a wide variety of services for individuals, business and government establishments, and other organizations. Hotels and other lodging places, establishments providing personal, business, repair, and amusement services; health, legal, engineering, and other professional services; educational institutions, membership organizations, and other miscellaneous services are included.

This classification of service organizations includes all nonmanufacturing organizations except such industries as agriculture, mining, and construction. Also usually included in this category are real estate, financial services, retailers, transportation, and public utilities.

Pure service businesses deliver intangible products. Examples would include a law firm, whose product is legal advice, and a health care facility, whose product is comfort and better health. However, service is a key element for many traditional manufacturing companies. For instance, manufacturers such as IBM and Xerox provide extensive maintenance and consulting services, which may be more important to the customer than its tangible products.

The service sector grew rapidly in the second half of the twentieth century. In 1945, 22.99 million people were employed by service-producing industries, and 18.5 million were employed by goods-producing industries. By the middle of 1997, 97.66 million people were employed by service-producing industries, while the number of people employed by goods-producing industries had only grown to 24.71 million. Today more than 80 percent of the non-farm employees in the United States are working in services. More information about current labor statistics of this type can be found on the Bureau of Labor Statistics Web pages at http://evans.swlearning.com.

The service sector began to recognize the importance of quality several years after manufacturing had done so. This lag can be attributed to the fact that service industries had not confronted the same aggressive foreign competition that manufacturing faced. Another factor is the high turnover rate in service industry jobs, which typically pay less than manufacturing jobs. Constantly changing personnel makes establishing a culture for continuous improvement more difficult. Also, the very nature of quality changed from a focus on product defects to achieving customer satisfaction.

Companies nationally prominent in the service industry for their quality efforts include large organizations such as BI, Merrill Lynch Credit Corporation, FedEx, GTE Directories Corporation, and The Ritz-Carlton Hotel Company; and small companies such as Custom Research Inc. and Pal's Sudden Service. These companies will be featured throughout this book.

The American Management Association estimates that the average company loses as many as 35 percent of its customers each year, and that about two-thirds of these are lost because of poor customer service.

The importance of quality in services cannot be overestimated. Studies show that companies can boost their profits by almost 100 percent by retaining just 5 percent more of their customers than their competitors retain.[8] This drastic difference is because the cost of acquiring new customers is much higher than the costs associated with retaining customers. Companies with loyal, long-time customers—even with higher unit costs and smaller market share—can financially outperform competitors with higher customer turnover.

The definitions of quality that apply to manufactured products apply equally to service products. The very nature of service implies that it must respond to the needs of the customer; that is, the service must "meet or exceed customer expectations." These expectations must be translated into performance standards and specifications similar to standards of conformance that direct manufacturing activities. For example, a quick-service restaurant might be expected to serve a complete dinner within 5 minutes. In a fine restaurant, however, one might expect to have 10 to 15 minutes between courses, and might regard the service as poor if the time between courses is too short.

Contrasts with Manufacturing

The production of services differs from manufacturing in many ways, and these differences carry important implications for quality management. The most critical differences are described here.

1. Customer needs and performance standards are often difficult to identify and measure, primarily because the customers define what they are, and each customer is different.
2. The production of services typically requires a higher degree of customization than does manufacturing. Doctors, lawyers, insurance salespeople, and food-service employees must tailor their services to individual customers. In manufacturing, the goal is uniformity.
3. The output of many service systems is intangible, whereas manufacturing produces tangible, visible products. Manufacturing quality can be assessed against firm design specifications (for example, the depth of cut should be 0.125 inch), but service quality can only be assessed against customers' subjective, nebulous expectations and past experiences. (What is a "good" sales experience?) Also, the customer can "have and hold" a manufactured product, but can only remember a service. Manufactured goods can be recalled or replaced by the manufacturer, but poor service can only be followed up by apologies and reparations.
4. Services are produced and consumed simultaneously, whereas manufactured goods are produced prior to consumption. In addition, many services must be performed at the convenience of the customer. Therefore, services cannot be stored, inventoried, or inspected prior to delivery as manufactured goods are. Much more attention must therefore be paid to training and building quality into the service as a means of quality assurance.
5. Customers often are involved in the service process and are present while it is being performed, whereas manufacturing is performed away from the customer. For example, customers of a quick-service restaurant place their own orders, carry their food to the table, and are expected to clear the table when they have finished eating.

6. Services are generally labor intensive, whereas manufacturing is more capital intensive. The quality of human interaction is a vital factor for services that involve human contact. For example, the quality of hospital care depends heavily on interactions among the patients, nurses, doctors, and other medical staff. Banks have found that tellers' friendliness is a key factor in retaining depositors. Hence, the behavior and morale of service employees is critical in delivering a quality service experience.

7. Many service organizations must handle large numbers of customer transactions. For example, on a given business day, the Royal Bank of Canada might process more than 5.5 million transactions for 7.5 million customers through 1,600 branches and more than 3,500 banking machines, and FedEx might handle several million shipments across the globe each day. Such large volumes increase the opportunity for error.

The results of a survey conducted in the mid-1990s found that most smaller service firms had no TQ initiative, and many respondents believed that the unique characteristics of service as described were contrary to the ability to define quality and measure it clearly, and that understanding and fulfilling customer expectations are difficult because service customers usually do not complete a formal specification of the type, amount, and quality of service required.[9] These beliefs suggest that many service firms have not made the effort to fully understand the nature of TQ and its potential benefits, and ways in which it can be implemented effectively.

> *These differences make it difficult for many service organizations to apply total quality principles, and foster misguided perceptions that quality management cannot be effectively accomplished in services.*

Components of Service System Quality

Many service organizations such as airlines, banks, and hotels have well-developed quality systems. These systems begin with a commitment to the customers. For example, Amazon.com has pioneered a number of innovative approaches to improve customer satisfaction, ranging from easy-to-use Web site design to fast order fulfillment. Professor Claes Fornell, developer of the American Customer Satisfaction Index (see Chapter 4) stated:

> *Amazon.com continues to show remarkably high levels of customer satisfaction. With a score of 88 (up 5%), it is generating satisfaction at a level unheard of in the service industry. At the same time, however, Amazon is followed very closely by Barnes and Noble (87, up 6%). This might make one believe that the task of book selling online has now been mastered. Perhaps so, but Amazon has branched out far beyond books and is now selling myriad other products on its way to becoming the first online department store. Can customer satisfaction for Amazon climb more? The latest ACSI data suggest that it is indeed possible. Both service and the value proposition offered by Amazon have increased at a steep rate.*[10]

Service quality may be viewed from a manufacturing analogy, for instance, technical standards such as the components of a properly made-up guest room for a hotel, service transaction speed, or accuracy of information. However, managing intangible quality characteristics is more difficult, because they usually depend on employee performance and behavior. This dependence does not imply that

> *Two key components of service system quality are **employees** and **information technology**.*

these factors are not important in manufacturing, of course, but they have special significance in services—just as engineering technology might have in manufacturing.

Employees   Customers evaluate a service primarily by the quality of the human contact. A *Wall Street Journal* survey found that Americans' biggest complaints about service employees are of delivery people or salespeople who fail to show up when you have stayed home at a scheduled time for them; salespeople who are poorly informed; and salesclerks who talk on the phone while waiting on you, say "It's not my department," talk down to you, or cannot describe how a product works.

Researchers have repeatedly demonstrated that when service employee job satisfaction is high, customer satisfaction is high, and that when job satisfaction is low, customer satisfaction is low.[11]

Quality Spotlight
FedEx

Many service companies act on the motto "If we take care of our employees, they will take care of our customers." At FedEx, for instance, the company credo is stated simply as People, Service, Profits. All potential decisions in the company are evaluated on their effects on the employees (people), on their customers (service), and the company's financial performance (profits), in that order. FedEx has a "no layoff" philosophy, and its "guaranteed fair treatment procedure" for handling employee grievances is used by firms in many industries as a model. Employees are encouraged to be innovative and to make decisions that advance quality and customer satisfaction goals. Front-line workers can qualify for promotion to management positions, and the company has a well-developed recognition program for team and individual contributions to company performance. FedEx management continually sets higher goals for quality performance and customer satisfaction, investing heavily in state-of-the-art technology, and building on its reputation as an excellent employer.

In many companies, unfortunately, the front-line employees—salesclerks, receptionists, delivery personnel, and so on, who have the most contact with customers—receive the lowest pay, minimal training, little decision-making authority, and little responsibility (what is termed *empowerment*). High-quality service employees require reward systems that recognize customer satisfaction results and customer-focused behaviors, appropriate skills and abilities for performing the job, and supervisors who act more as coaches and mentors than as administrators. Training is particularly important, because service employees need to be skilled in handling every customer interaction, from greeting customers to asking the right questions.

Quality Spotlight
The Ritz-Carlton
Hotel Company

The Ritz-Carlton Hotel Company (see the *Quality in Practice* case at the end of this chapter) is one service company with an exemplary focus on its people.[12] The Ritz-Carlton motto is "We Are Ladies and Gentlemen Serving Ladies and Gentlemen," and all employees are treated as guests would be treated. The company's focus is to develop a "skilled and empowered workforce operating with pride and joy" by ensuring that everyone knows what they are supposed to do, how well they are doing, and have the authority to make changes as necessary. For example, the role of the housekeeper is not simply to make beds, but to create a memorable experience for the customer. Each hotel has a director of human resources and a training manager, who are assisted by the hotel's quality leader. Each work area has a departmental trainer who is responsible for training and certifying new employees in his or her unit. The Ritz-Carlton uses a highly predictive "character-trait recruiting" instrument for determining candidates' fitness for each of 120 job positions. New employees receive two days' orientation in which senior executives personally demonstrate Ritz-Carlton methods and instill Ritz-Carlton values. Three weeks later, managers monitor the effectiveness of the instruction and then conduct a follow-up training session. Later, new employees must pass written and skill-demonstration tests in order to become certified in their work areas. Every day, in each work area, each shift supervisor conducts a quality line-up meeting and briefing session. Employees receive continuous teaching and coaching to refresh skills and improve their performance, reinforce their purpose on the job, and receive recognition for achievements. Through these and other mechanisms, employees receive more than 100 hours of quality education aimed at fostering a commitment to premium service, solving problems, setting goals, and generating new ideas. Employees are empowered to "move heaven and earth to satisfy a customer," to enlist the aid of other employees to resolve a problem swiftly, to spend up to $2,000 to satisfy a guest, to decide the business terms of a sale, to be involved in setting plans for their particular work area, and to speak with anyone in the company regarding any problem. The Ritz-Carlton has decreased the turnover rate of employees steadily since 1989 to about 30% by 1999, well below industry averages.

Information Technology Information technology incorporates computing, communication, data processing, and various other means of converting data into useful information. Intelligent use of information technology not only leads to improved quality and productivity, but

Information technology is essential for quality in modern service organizations because of the high volumes of information they must process and because customers demand service at ever-increasing speeds.

also to competitive advantage, particularly when technology is used to better serve the customer and to make it easier for customers to do business with the company.

Many service industries exploit information technology to improve customer service. Restaurants, for example, use handheld order-entry computer terminals to speed up the ordering process. An order is instantaneously transmitted to the kitchen or bar, where it is displayed and the guest check is printed. In addition to saving time, such systems improve accuracy by standardizing the order-taking, billing, and inventory procedures and reducing the need for handwriting. Credit authorizations, which once took several minutes by telephone, are now accomplished in seconds through computerized authorization systems. FedEx's handheld "SuperTracker" scans packages' bar codes every time packages change hands between pickup and delivery.

The Ritz-Carlton Hotel Company exploits information technology to remember each of its 800,000+ customers. Knowledge of individual customer preferences, previous difficulties, family and personal interests, and preferred credit cards is stored in a database accessible to every hotel. This guest-profiling system allows each customer to be treated individually, by giving front-desk employees immediate access to such information as whether the guest smokes, whether he or she prefers scented or unscented soap, and what kind of pillow he or she prefers.

Another example is provided by Fidelity Investments.[13] Fidelity receives about 200,000 telephone calls each day, more than two-thirds of which are handled by a computer system without human intervention. A computer switching system monitors the call loads at Fidelity's four telephone centers and distributes calls among its more than 2,000 representatives. Fidelity developed a "workstation of the future" that allows its representatives to call up any customer's account on their terminal screen. Using this capability, Fidelity will be able to offer its customers up-to-the-second, personalized information and service while improving internal productivity.

Without a doubt, the largest impact of information technology for service has been in e-commerce. Customers can shop for almost any product; configure, price, and order computer systems; and take virtual test drives of automobiles and select from thousands of possible combinations of options on the Internet in the convenience of their homes. Information technology can be used to develop and enhance customer relationships. Amazon.com, from which many readers have probably ordered, has been extremely successful at this. They provide extensive information about products, such as reader reviews to help customers evaluate books, search used bookstores for out-of-print books, and even provide e-mail thank you letters a month or so after purchase. However, while information technology reduces labor intensity and increases the speed of service, it can have adverse effects on other dimensions of quality. Some people, including some customers, will argue that customer satisfaction is decreased when less personal interaction takes place. (Have you ever gotten irritated when wading through multiple menus on an automated telephone answering system?) Thus, service providers must balance conflicting quality concerns.

QUALITY IN HEALTH CARE

One service industry that faces continuing pressure to improve quality—and one with the fastest-growing interest in quality—is health care. Quality has been a focus for the industry for some time. In 1910, Ernest Codman, M.D., proposed the "end result system of hospital standardization." Under this system, a hospital would track every patient it treated long enough to determine whether the treatment was effective. If the treatment was not effective, the hospital would then attempt to determine why, so that similar cases could be treated successfully in the future. The American College of Surgeons (ACS) developed Minimum Standards for Hospitals in 1917 and began inspections the following year. The Joint Commission on Accreditation of Healthcare Organizations (JCAHO)—the principal accreditation agency for health care—was created in 1951 through a collaboration of ACS and several other agencies to provide voluntary accreditation. Its mission is "to continuously improve the safety and quality of care provided to the public through the provision of health care accreditation and related services that support performance improvement in health care organizations." By 1970, accreditation standards were recast to represent optimal achievable levels of quality, rather than minimum essential levels of quality. JCAHO issued new standards in 1992 requiring all hospital CEOs to educate themselves on CQI (*continuous quality improvement*—the term used in the health care profession to denote quality initiatives) methods.[14] The new standards emphasize performance improvement concepts and incorporate quality improvement principles more fully in areas such as surgical case review, blood usage evaluation, and drug usage evaluation. Further information about the Joint Commission may be found at its Web site at http://evans.swlearning.com.

Similar to the Joint Commission, the National Committee for Quality Assurance (NCQA) is a private, not-for-profit organization dedicated to improving the quality of health care.[15] The organization's primary activities are assessing and reporting on the quality of the nation's managed care plans, work that has led to partnerships and collaborative efforts with many states, the federal government, employer and consumer groups, and many of the nation's leading corporations and business coalitions. NCQA's mission is to provide information that enables purchasers and consumers of managed health care to distinguish among plans based on quality, thereby allowing them to make more informed health care purchasing decisions. This greater information encourages plans to compete based on quality and value, rather than on price and provider network. Efforts are organized around two activities, accreditation and performance measurement, which are complementary strategies for producing information to guide choice. These activities are integrated under NCQA's Accreditation program, which includes selected performance measures in such key areas as member satisfaction, quality of care, access, and service.

NCQA began accrediting managed care organizations (MCOs) in 1991 in response to the need for standardized, objective information about the quality of these organizations. Although the MCO accreditation program is voluntary and rigorous, it has been well received by the managed care industry, and almost half the HMOs in the nation, covering three-quarters of all HMO enrollees, are currently involved in the NCQA Accreditation process. For an organization to become accredited by NCQA, it must undergo a survey and meet certain standards designed to evaluate the health plan's clinical and administrative systems. In particular, NCQA's Accreditation surveys look at a health plan's efforts to continuously improve the quality of care and service it delivers.

Other organizations, such as the Institute for Healthcare Improvement (IHI), have emerged to support quality improvement in health care. IHI's goals are improved health status, better clinical outcomes, reduced costs that do not compromise quality, greater access to care, an easier-to-use health care system, and improved satisfaction to patients and communities. IHI focuses on fostering collaboration, rather than competition, among health care organizations, and promotes the use of quality control tools that have proven to be beneficial in manufacturing. One early pilot project driven by IHI at 37 intensive care units resulted in huge drops in pneumonia and other complications, shorter patient stays, and cost reductions of up to 30 percent.

Despite accreditation and collaborative efforts aimed at quality, the industry faces considerable challenges. A 1998 study by the President's Advisory Commission on Consumer Protection and Quality in the Health Care Industry entitled *Quality First: Better Health Care for All Americans*, noted several types of quality problems in health care.[16] They include:

1. *Avoidable errors.* Too many Americans are injured during the course of their treatment, and some die prematurely as a result. For example, a study of injuries to patients treated in hospitals in New York State found that 3.7 percent experienced adverse events, of which 13.6 percent led to death and 2.6 percent to permanent disability, and that about one-fourth of these adverse events were due to negligence. A national study found that from 1983 to 1993, deaths due to medication errors rose more than twofold, with 7,391 deaths attributed to medication errors in 1993 alone.

2. *Underutilization of services.* Millions of people do not receive necessary care and suffer needless complications that add to health care costs and reduce productivity. For example, a study of Medicare patients with myocardial infraction found that only 21 percent of eligible patients received beta blockers, and that the mortality rate among recipients was 43 percent less than that for nonrecipients. An estimated 18,000 people die each year from heart attacks because they did not receive effective interventions.

3. *Overuse of services.* Millions of Americans receive health care services that are unnecessary, increase costs, and often endanger their health. For example, an analysis of hysterectomies performed by seven health plans estimated that one in six was inappropriate.

4. *Variation in services.* A continuing pattern of wide variation continues in health care practice, including regional variations and small-area variations. This pattern clearly indicates that the practice of health care has not caught up with the science of health care to ensure evidence-based practice in the United States.

The Commission's report included more than 50 recommendations to address these issues. These recommendations, which include the use of measurements, stakeholder participation, error prevention, and continuous improvement, support the underlying philosophy of total quality that we described in Chapter 1. Details can be found in the CD-ROM Bonus Materials folder.

Although the national health care system as a whole may need a sweeping overhaul, many individual providers have turned toward quality as a means of achieving better performance and customer satisfaction.

In 1990, SSM Health Care, profiled at the beginning of this chapter, became one of the first health care organizations in the United States to implement CQI throughout its entire system. Five years later, after visiting manufacturing winners of the Baldrige Award and learning about their practices, SSM instituted a new leadership plan, improved strategic and financial planning processes, a new conference to share best practices among its hospitals, and an improved CQI model that permits rapid identification and correction of potential problems. In 2002, SSM became the first health care winner of the Baldrige Award. Other examples include Boston's New England Deaconess Hospital, where teams identify problems that add unnecessary days to hospital stays, achieving a 10 percent overall decrease in length of hospital stay in two years; and Nash General Hospital in Rocky Mount, North Carolina, which examined processes within the emergency department and was able to reduce the length of stay by more than 50 percent.[17]

As another example, the Virginia Beach Ambulatory Surgery Center (VBASC) built a new outpatient surgical facility using the principles of total quality.[18] The center engaged employees in writing a policy and procedure manual. It continues to ask their opinions on the quality of their work as individuals and the organization as a whole, to encourage and support professional development, to empower employees to develop and manage innovative programs, to listen to customers and act on their suggestions, to view surgeons and their office staff as key customers, to demonstrate a strong internal customer focus, to measure and objectively assess everything it does, and to hold monthly CQI meetings.

Although many health care organizations notice measurable improvements from their quality initiatives, they primarily occur in the areas of cost reduction and increased efficiency. A difficult challenge that most face is getting physicians involved in the quality process. Many are requiring their participation on teams and steering committees, creating a liaison role between management and physicians, using physicians as champions, and targeting training.[19]

QUALITY IN EDUCATION

Education represents one of the most interesting and challenging areas for quality improvement. Attacks on the quality of education in the United States, from kindergarten through the 12th grade (K–12) and at colleges and universities provided a rallying cry for education reform during the last decade.[20] One of the earliest and most widely publicized stories of the successful use of quality in education is that of Mt. Edgecumbe High School in Sitka, Alaska.[21] Mt. Edgecumbe is a public boarding school with some 200 students, often from problem homes in rural Alaska. Many are Native Americans, who are struggling to keep their culture alive while learning to live and work in American society. David Langford, a teacher, brought the quality concepts to Mt. Edgecumbe after hearing about them at a meeting at McDonnell-Douglas Helicopter Company. After reading many books by quality gurus such as

Deming, Juran, and Crosby, Langford took some students in a computer club on a trip to Gilbert (Arizona) High School. There, they observed how Delores Christiansen taught continuous improvement in her business classes. They also visited companies in the Phoenix area that were using quality principles. The students, with the coaching of Langford, began to use quality concepts to improve school processes. For example, the students tackled the problem of too many tardy classmates. By investigating the reasons for tardiness, the students persuaded the administration to drop the punishment for tardy students, and were able to reduce the average number of late occurrences per week from 35 to 5.

As an even more radical change, the school dropped the traditional grading system. Instead, students use statistical techniques to keep track of their own progress. No assignment is considered finished until it is perfect. Eliminating grades has had a positive effect. One student, James Penemarl reported, "I found myself learning a lot more. It's not the teacher having to check my progress, it's me having to check my progress. See, however much I learn is up to me, and if I want to learn, I'm going to go out and learn." What they call CIP, or the continuous improvement process, has been an obvious success (approximately 50 percent of students now go on to college), yet the messages that David Langford stresses in interviews about the school are (1) it takes time, effort, and persistence—it's not a "quick fix," and (2) there's always room for improvement. Current information, experiences of teachers and students, and articles on applying TQ in secondary education can be obtained at Mt. Edgecumbe's Web site, which may be accessed from http://evans.swlearning.com.

Many other K–12 school districts have implemented TQ initiatives. For example, the Conroe Independent School District just north of Houston, Texas, adopted a forward-looking strategic plan back in 1993 that included the following vision:

> *The school district in 2007 is a learning community united in its commitment to ensuring that all students graduate with confidence and competence. The schools and communities work together to provide performance standards that can be applied to the real world. This is achieved through the implementation of quality in instruction, operations, and leadership.*

The process developed to achieve this vision included a TQ implementation plan that relied heavily on training and teams. Initial projects included improving team teaching processes, accuracy in reporting data, purchasing processes, and communications and teamwork within the custodial department.[22] In 2001, two K–12 schools were among the first Baldrige Education winners: Chugach School District in Alaska, and Pearl River School District in New York.

In general, educators, educational institutions, political groups and leaders, and even the public have been slow to attack the problem of educational decline on a systematic basis. However, in 2002, President Bush signed into law the No Child Left Behind Act, which demanded accountability for results, tracking each student's accomplishments, and emphasizing teaching methods that have been proven to work. Essentially, states and districts will be given an annual report card to measure school performance and rate progress. In addition, some encouraging evidence shows that educators at the K–12 level are beginning to recognize the need for quality improvement efforts. A national survey of 401 public school principals by Harris Interactive and sponsored by the American Society for Quality, found that U.S. elementary schools are more advanced than secondary schools in their use of quality tools and approaches.[23] The majority of the principals surveyed (70 percent) believe that U.S. schools will be more likely to adopt quality improvement programs in the future.

Some highlights of the research include the following:

- In 2002, approximately 58 percent of U.S. public schools had a formalized quality improvement approach in place; however, 63 percent of elementary schools had such a program. One explanation for this difference may be because of greater parental involvement at the elementary level.
- Nearly all principals (95 percent) report that their school has a school improvement plan that includes measurable outcomes.
- Eight in ten principals (81 percent) believe that improving standardized test score performance is extremely or very important.
- Nearly all of these schools (98 percent) measure their efforts in this area by regularly gathering quantifiable data.

Despite these findings, "principals are not as likely to measure their efforts in other areas that are important to them," according to ASQ president Dr. Kenneth Case. "For example," Case continued, "the study showed that although 85 percent of principals believe that improving teacher satisfaction and morale is extremely or very important, only 71 percent of these schools are regularly gathering quantifiable data about their efforts in this area."

Koalaty Kid

The American Society for Quality (ASQ) has long promoted quality in elementary education through a program entitled *Koalaty Kid*.[24] It was an outgrowth of activities at Frederick C. Carder Elementary School in Corning, New York, where Fred the Koala appears throughout the school on bulletin boards, at assemblies, in the cafeteria, and in the classrooms. In the 1980s, several teachers and the principal at Carder identified factors they deemed most important to student success and areas where they felt their students needed improvement. First, they believed that reading was the key to all other learning, and observed that students did not read much beyond what was required in the classroom. Second, they found that all too often, students were handing in homework with numerous errors. When asked to correct them, students could do so easily. They knew how to do it, but simply didn't habitually do it right the first time. Third, they observed that the most successful students were those who felt confident of their abilities and comfortable with themselves.

Quality Spotlight
Carder Elementary School

Having identified these critical issues, they developed a plan to bring about change throughout the whole school. Reading became a primary focus. Students were invited to read books of their own choosing. Reading at home was encouraged with a system of contracts. Students demonstrated that they understood what they read through book reports, and each book was recorded. Students who met their contracts were recognized at assemblies, and incentives helped to encourage the habit. Second, the teachers communicated the standard of work they expected in homework—best work the first time. When students handed in papers, they were asked to assess in their own minds, "Is this your best work?" Excellent papers were displayed on bulletin boards, and students were recognized for "Koalaty work." Third, teachers established schoolwide expectations for behavior, and made a point of "catching" students being good. This combination of efforts became known as "Koalaty Kid," and students eagerly strove to become "Koalaty Kids" to read more, do their best work the first time, and treat others with courtesy and respect.

In 1988, two ASQ members from Corning, Incorporated visited the school and learned about Koalaty Kid. They immediately saw the parallels to total quality: critical issues had been identified, a plan for improvement was developed and implemented, clear expectations were communicated, a measurement system was put in place, and a consistent system of recognition and reward reinforced student success. Excited by what they saw in Carder School, the businesspeople brought the Carder model to the attention of ASQ headquarters. The Society invested in a pilot program, providing incentives for reading and tracked increases in 26 pilot schools over two years. A Koalaty Kid steering committee, including educators, sponsors, and ASQ members, was formed to oversee the effort, and Koalaty Kid began to emphasize a broader and more rigorous use of total quality in schools. More than 800 U.S. schools and many overseas have adopted Koalaty Kid.

Because Koalaty Kid is an approach, not a prescribed program, schools can utilize it to achieve their own objectives.

> *The four key factors that make Koality Kid work are active involvement of the whole school community, committed leadership, a system for continuous improvement, and an environment that celebrates successes.*

Active Involvement School administrators, teachers, sponsors, parents, and the students themselves work together on teams that are empowered to make decisions and implement change. This system does not mean that Koalaty Kid gives away the authority to run the schools. Rather, it means that everyone who is ultimately affected by a school has an opportunity to influence its success. Together, they represent a larger resource than the school's paid staff. And because they represent all constituencies, they can often create change more swiftly and lastingly. Teams might manage some of the school's ongoing operations. They might identify and tackle tough issues. Or they might help the schools and students in any number of creative ways. It's up to the school leadership and the teams themselves to decide how they can best work toward achieving the school's goals.

Outside sponsoring organizations are vitally important to the success of Koalaty Kid schools. These businesses, institutions, community organizations, or ASQ sections participate on the school-based team. They may help the school in a variety of ways, depending on their own capabilities and the school's needs. Some provide funds for quality training, while others become a source of help for important school activities, expertise in troubleshooting quality processes, or enrichment for academic areas. Most important, their perspective as future employers or community representatives with a stake in the school's "output" helps to bring the school and its community closer together.

Parent involvement is critical to the success of Koalaty Kid schools. Parents work closely with their own children, monitoring homework assignments, reading aloud, identifying trouble spots, and communicating with students, teachers, and administrators about any factors that affect their children's success. In addition, they often serve as the core of the school's volunteer base. As volunteers, they may help the school in a variety of ways—supplementing the work of classroom teachers with one-on-one tutoring, raising funds for needed equipment, and participating actively in decision making on the school's teams.

Committed Leadership Schools can change only if their designated leaders are committed to improvement. Change occurs quickly if these administrators are also capable of inspiring the faculty, students, parents, sponsors, and other administrators to work with them. Because of their positions, these individuals can allocate resources, call meetings, and generally "make things happen." However, leadership from others can also be effective, provided it is accepted and endorsed by those with ultimate decision-making authority. Leaders inspire others in the school community because of the depth and sincerity of their belief and commitment. Part of their ability to persuade others also comes from articulating their own clear understanding of where they are headed and the process they will use to get there. They constantly listen and learn, and they draw others with skill and ideas into the process. School leaders often find that undertaking the Koalaty Kid process inspires them to new levels of their own professional growth and a more profound understanding of their own roles as leaders.

A System for Continuous Improvement Koalaty Kid uses total quality principles—establishing consistent standards of excellence, setting and communicating clear expectations, continuous improvement (as opposed to finding fault and blaming), looking at a work task as a process, involving all who have a stake in the outcome in the improvement process, measuring results, and recognizing and rewarding success—for bringing about change. Using a set of quality "tools," teams define a system, assess a situation, analyze causes, try out improvement theories, study results, standardize improvement, and plan continuous improvement.

Environment That Celebrates Successes Even though many schools are now using team-based management or employing total quality, the fourth distinguishing feature of Koalaty Kid schools is the excitement that permeates the school environment. This excitement is focused on celebrating student successes, large and small. Displays of papers that meet or exceed requirements, photos of students recognized for exemplary behavior, and rosters of student achievements adorn classroom bulletin boards and school hallways. At assemblies and pep rallies, students cheer for one another's accomplishments as they are recognized. In hundreds of ways, the teachers, staff, volunteers, and parents communicate their delight when students reach goals.

Among the success stories that have resulted from Koalaty Kid are Mark Twain Elementary in Richardson, Texas. Historically the lowest-performing school in its district, after one year of implementing Koalaty Kid, schoolwide pass rates jumped from 72 percent to 93 percent in the writing/comprehension portion of the Texas Assessment of Academic Skills; the mathematics pass rate increased from 65 to 81 percent; and the overall pass rate rose from 35 to 71 percent.[25] To learn more, visit the Web link at http://evans.swlearning.com.

Quality in Higher Education

Many colleges and universities have also made substantial commitments to quality efforts. However, the percentages of higher educational institutions engaged in long-term efforts to measure and improve quality have been relatively small. Although the Baldrige Award established an Education category in 1999, it was not until 2002 that a university, the University of Wisconsin—Stout, won the award.

One of the early success stories at the university level is Oregon State University (OSU).[26] Following close study of the quality literature, a visit from Dr. W. Edwards Deming, company visits to Ford, Hewlett-Packard, and Dow, and attendance by the president and several top administrators at a seminar on problem-solving tools, administrators at OSU began the planning phase. The first pilot study at OSU was conducted in the physical plant area for a number of reasons: (1) quality was considered a high-priority issue; (2) it had a high probability of success; (3) management agreed that it was important; (4) no one else was working on it; and (5) it was also important to the customers of the organization. A multilevel team of 12 people chose to study the specific issue of ways to "decrease turnaround time in the remodeling process." The team made and implemented a number of recommendations. Among them were the development of a project manager position; installation of a customer

Quality Spotlight
Oregon State
University

service center to enhance work scheduling, control, and follow-up; implementation of customer surveys to assess communications; more consultation at the beginning of the process with customers; identification of equipment and materials that could be purchased during the design phase; and shop participation to identify potential problems during the design phase. The first pilot project reduced the remodeling project time by 10 percent. Using customer surveys, the team studied many other processes, such as those in recruitment and admissions. However, note that such early efforts focused on administrative systems—the manufacturing analogy of quality—and not in the core processes of teaching or research.

> *Business plays an important role in fostering quality improvement efforts in higher education by transferring knowledge and expertise on quality processes and implementation practices.*

In 1989 Xerox Corporation hosted the first Quality Forum, a gathering of academic and business leaders. Business leaders urged academia to teach quality principles and to use them in managing their organizations. Many companies established partnerships with colleges and universities. For example, Motorola's partnership with Purdue University led to the formation of the university's continuous quality improvement approach called *Excellence21*, a systemwide effort by the university to explore the principles of continuous improvement and total quality management. Projects were developed in the areas of

1. Faculty and Staff Development and Worklife Enrichment
2. Assessment of Student Learning Outcomes
3. Undergraduate Education
4. Graduate Education
5. Student Related (Student services)
6. Administrative Processes
7. Technology

Other universities established similar partnerships with industry leaders. However, these efforts revolved around project approaches. Two examples of schools that have addressed quality within their overall management systems are Penn State University and the University of Wisconsin–Stout.

 Quality Spotlight
Penn State University

Penn State University is a multi-campus "mega" university that serves more than 81,000 students each year, on 24 campuses, with a 2002–2003 year budget exceeding $1.8 billion, exclusive of their medical center's funds.[27] Since the early 1990s the university has shown a consistent commitment to continuous quality improvement (CQI) efforts. Since 1991, more than 450 CQI teams registered with the Center for Quality and Planning. The projects of 50–60 certified CQI teams each year are coordinated by the university council on continuous quality improvement (UCCQI) consisting of 10 members who meet three times per year.

Each year, Penn State hosts a Quality Expo to "share, learn, and celebrate" quality improvements and quality champions.[28] Some examples of noteworthy projects that have been completed there over the past 10 years include the following:[29]

- At the University Libraries, eliminating unnecessary steps in the wage payroll process yielded annual savings of $30,221, and changing the process for ordering library materials resulted in annual time savings valued at $60,748. Self-directed work teams in the Libraries' Acquisitions department have improved work processes, such as reducing the check-in process for periodicals, from two weeks to 48 hours and the time required to process labels for 6,000 serials from 27 to 15 days.

- By eliminating several steps in the processing of new faculty appointments, a CQI team in the dean's office of the College of Health and Human Development saved 500 to 750 hours per year.
- In the Outreach and Cooperative Extension division, quality improvement teams in their Conferences and Institutes department used existing technology to find a way to more easily track financial records across multiple years and more accurately monitor accounts to determine final costs and income. After training personnel in the new process, a savings of 4,300 staff hours per year was realized.
- By using the financial data warehouse, WPSX-TV, the university-sponsored TV station, reduced the time it takes to run reports and move data into Excel from six hours to under 15 minutes. Previously, a financial assistant could only run reports once a month because it was so labor intensive; now the report can be run every week due to the time savings.

Quality Spotlight
University of
Wisconsin-Stout

One of 13 publicly supported universities in the University of Wisconsin System, the University of Wisconsin–Stout, located in Menomonie, has about 1,200 faculty and staff and about 8,000 students.[30] Operating on a $95 million annual budget, UW–Stout offers 27 undergraduate and 16 graduate degrees through three academic colleges: the College of Technology, Engineering and Management; the College of Human Development; and the College of Arts and Sciences.

Nearly half of UW–Stout's programs are unique within the University of Wisconsin system, and several are not offered anywhere else in the United States. This distinctive array of degree offerings stems from UW–Stout's "Mission Driven–Market Smart" focus aimed at developing students for careers in industry and education. This special mission guides all key processes, including strategic planning, program development, partnership building, and teaching and learning. In addition to its success in placing graduates in jobs and earning high satisfaction scores from students and alumni, UW–Stout has been described as a "hidden treasure" in a popular national catalog for high school guidance counselors. UW–Stout uses a comprehensive set of methods for listening to and learning from students throughout their academic careers and beyond. Student needs, expectations, attitudes, and performance are tracked through surveys, course and program evaluations, and a variety of "success measures" that link student performance to educational effectiveness.

The university began conducting student satisfaction surveys in the mid-1970s. Since then, it has supplemented its efforts through participation in state and national student surveys. Survey results and other student-related information are evaluated from numerous perspectives. The university's integrated relational database system permits almost unlimited segmentation of data. For example, student performance and satisfaction can be evaluated for standard categories, such as academic programs, diversity group, gender, or for unique segments of students. This ability supports efforts to determine the root causes of problems and to pin down the relationship between processes and outcomes.

The results of these and other analyses are helping UW–Stout to sharpen its "Mission Driven–Market Smart" focus to the benefit of students and employers alike. UW-Stout seniors exceeded the national peer averages of "active" learning—traditional instruction reinforced with real-life experience—by 13 percent in 2000. Since 1996, the job placement rate for graduates has been at or above 98 percent. Moreover, alumni earn salaries that exceed the national average from other institutions and the average for graduates from UW system schools.

Such results also lead to satisfaction. For example, more than 90 percent of graduate program alumni and almost 90 percent of undergraduate alumni say that, if they could do it all over again, they would choose to attend UW–Stout. Among employers, UW–Stout also earns consistently high marks. In the university's five most recent follow-up surveys to learn how employers view its graduates, 99 percent to 100 percent of respondents rated UW–Stout graduates as well prepared for their positions.

One of the particular efforts to encourage colleges and universities to engage in quality practices is the **Academic Quality Improvement Project (AQIP)**. The goals of AQIP are to help member organizations improve their performance and maximize their effectiveness; reshape the relationship with members of The Higher Learning Commission (an accreditation agency) into a partnership; and provide the public with credible quality assurance concerning higher education providers. Participation in AQIP is a voluntary alternative to traditional academic accreditation. It focuses on application of TQ principles to educational institutions to better understand their key processes, track performance, and understand students and other stakeholders; involves faculty more directly in the improvement process; and provides concrete feedback to enable institutions to raise performance levels. The criteria used for AQIP assessment are closely aligned with the Malcolm Baldrige Criteria for Performance Excellence that we will discuss in the next chapter. Further information may be found at the AQIP Web link at http://evans. swlearning.com.

> *AQIP criteria focuses on institutional practices for helping students learn, accomplishing other distinct objectives, understanding student and stakeholder needs, valuing people, leading and communicating, supporting institutional operations, measuring effectiveness, planning continuous improvement, and building collaborative relationships—all of which are key elements of TQ.*

QUALITY IN SMALL BUSINESSES AND NOT-FOR-PROFITS

Small businesses and not-for-profits have generally been slow to adopt quality initiatives. In most cases, this lag is a result of a lack of understanding and knowledge of what needs to be done and how to do it, because managers are wrapped up in entrepreneurial activities that typically focus on sales strategies and market growth, day-to-day cash flow problems, and routine fire fighting. In addition, small firms and not-for-profits often lack the resources needed to establish and maintain more formal quality systems. However, in viewing the three principles of TQ, a focus on customers is clearly vital to small enterprises; the company president or founder is often the principal contact with key customers and knows them intimately. Most small businesses live or die from their customer relationship practices, but the other two TQ principles—teamwork and participation, and a process focus and continuous improvement—are generally not well addressed. Small business executives, especially in family-owned enterprises, often have a "command-and-control" attitude that dominates decision making, leaving little discretion and empowerment to employees. In addition, processes tend to be highly unstructured and not based on adequate data and information. Simply getting by each day often takes precedence over long-term planning and improvement activities.

Many other characteristics of small firms adversely affect the implementation of TQ principles. These characteristics include the following:[31]

- The lack of market clout, which may impact a small firm's ability to get suppliers involved in quality efforts
- Not recognizing the importance of human resource management strategies in quality, and therefore experiencing lower levels of employee empowerment, involvement, and quality-related training

- Lack of professional management expertise and the short-term focus, which often results in inadequate allocation of resources to TQ efforts
- Lower technical knowledge and expertise, making it difficult for smaller firms to effectively use quality tools and improvement techniques
- The informal nature of communication and lack of structured information systems, which inhibit implementation

Perhaps the most important factor in successful quality initiatives in small businesses is the recognition by the CEO or president that a quality focus can be beneficial and lead to achieving organizational goals.

Nevertheless, many successful small businesses have shown that quality initiatives can be successfully accomplished.

Small businesses often come to this conclusion as they grow or face critical market challenges; they simply cannot afford to be managed as they were in the past, and require a more systematic process-oriented infrastruc-

Quality Spotlight
Texas Nameplate Company

ture. One example is Texas Nameplate Company, Inc. (TNC), which manufactures and sells identification and information labels that are affixed to refrigerators, oilfield equipment, high-pressure valves, trucks, computer equipment, and other products made by more than 1000 customers throughout the United States and in nine foreign countries. With only 66 employees, it was the smallest company to receive a Baldrige Award when it did so in 1998. Their quality journey began when a large customer threatened to cut them off if they did not begin applying quality control tools. However, it was the persistence of TNC's president, Dale Crownover, who made the difference and kept faith in his people. Not only did Crownover begin training his people, but he instituted profit-sharing and gainsharing incentives, along with higher-than-industry-average pay scales, to reinforce the workforce's commitment to quality and foster company loyalty. Customer contact employees are empowered to resolve customer complaints without consulting management, and production workers are responsible for tailoring processes to optimize contributions to company goals and to meet team-set standards.

To help workers identify opportunities for improvement, each process at TNC is mapped using a flow chart. The average employee receives 75 hours of training in the first two years, much of it delivered on a just-in-time basis. About one in 10 workers is a multipurpose employee, trained in three or more jobs, allowing them to be moved to any area of the company that needs assistance to meet fluctuating customer and market demands. As a result of these efforts, the company disbanded its quality control department, replaced it with a cross-functional team, and made quality the responsibility of all employees. Defects fell from 2.4 percent to less than 1 percent, employee turnover improved, and market share increased by 45 percent in just three years. Was it hard? In one interview, Crownover stated, "Yeah, it was hard. The last five years of my life doing this was very hard. But let me tell you about the first five years I was president of this company. We had legal issues, EEOC, customer complaints, people quitting . . . that was hard!" We will discuss the importance of leadership for implementing quality further in later chapters.

Similar comments hold true for not-for-profits, who, unlike their business counterparts, are not driven by the bottom line (although tight budgets can certainly be a driving factor in pursuing quality) and whose managers often lack the business acumen and technical expertise needed to make an organizational transformation. Little literature exists on how to apply quality principles to not-for-profits, and employees use a "language" different from business, making it challenging for them to translate business concepts into meaningful applications. Among the key challenges that not-for-profits face are overcoming the fear of change, changing the mindset that not-for-profits are different and cannot effectively apply quality principles, identifying a vision and customers, understanding work processes, dealing with limited resources, and understanding relationships with government and large corporations.[32]

However, numerous not-for-profit organizations are adopting TQ principles because of their impact on the public and society—their major customers and stakeholders. The United Way of America, for example, began recognizing United Way organizations for quality achievements in 1994. The American Red Cross launched a multiyear, multimillion-dollar quality effort to enhance organizational effectiveness and improve its process of collecting, testing, and distributing blood. Their focus is to drive any variability, deviation, or error down to zero using initiatives such as the following:

- New technologies to reduce the potential for human error
- Restructuring and increasing the level of quality assurance staff
- Creating a more streamlined and comprehensive training system
- Reengineering the core manufacturing processes to make them more efficient and simplified so as to reduce and prevent errors
- Investing in facilities to enable more efficient and effective adoption of new technology[33]

QUALITY IN THE PUBLIC SECTOR

Quality in the public sector—federal, state, and municipal governments—has not achieved growth and momentum as rapidly as in the private sector. Nevertheless, many public sector entities have made remarkable strides to incorporate the principles of quality into their operations.

Quality in the Federal Government

The federal government has a surprisingly long history of quality improvement activities. Quality circle programs—a form of team participation—were developed in the late 1970s at several Department of Defense installations, such as the Norfolk Naval Shipyard and the Cherry Point Naval Air Station. NASA began its quality improvement efforts in the early 1980s, both internally and with its suppliers.[34] Quality caught the attention of a number of agencies and managers when President Ronald Reagan signed Executive Order 12637, "Productivity Improvement for the Federal Government," in 1988.[35] The order required senior managers to monitor and improve both quality and productivity. It also encouraged them to use employee involvement, training, and participation in decision making, along with the more traditional methods of incentives, recognition, and rewards, to enhance the process.

One of the mechanisms set up to promote quality during the 1980s was the Federal Quality Institute (FQI). The FQI was established within the U.S. Office of Personnel Management in Washington, D.C., as the "primary source of leadership, information, and consulting services on quality management in the federal government." The institute provides such products and services as seminars, start-up assistance, national and regional conferences, support of quality awards, research, a listing of private sector consultants, an information network, and publications. In 1990 the FQI was given responsibility for administering the President's Quality Award and the Quality Improvement Prototype Award, which are the federal government's equivalent of the Malcolm Baldrige National Quality Award given to private sector organizations.

During the Clinton administration, efforts toward the advancement of quality in the federal government continued. Under the direction of Vice President Al Gore, a series of awards, with the innovative title of "The Golden Hammer" Awards focused attention on the need for continuous improvement efforts to reduce government waste at the grassroots individual and organizational levels. In addition, a report entitled "Creating a Government That Works Better and Costs Less: Report of the National Performance Review" was published in the fall of 1993. The report outlined 384 recommendations and indicated 1,214 specific actions that the federal government should take to improve government operations and reduce costs.

One of the more recognizable results in improvements to federal services is the Internal Revenue Service. In the mid-1990s, The National Commission on Restructuring the Internal Revenue Service focused on ways of creating a more efficient system and structure that eases the burden of compliance and protects basic rights for the taxpayer, while ensuring that the Internal Revenue Service collects the proper amount of taxes. The Commission's objectives were that the taxpayer shall receive superior service from the IRS and that the IRS shall be accountable to the taxpayer for appropriated and collected revenues; that the IRS shall use contemporary, effective technology for ease of service and compliance; and that the administration of the laws governing federal revenue collection shall be done at the lowest cost possible to the government and in the least burdensome manner to the taxpayer while ensuring the protection of civil liberties and privacy. As a result of the Commission's 1997 report, *A New Vision for the IRS*, the IRS made a concerted effort to improve the quality of its services and performance. Many improvements are evident, including faster telephone service, electronic filing, and a comprehensive Web site with downloadable forms, help files, and a host of other information.

After George W. Bush became president in 2000, the criteria for the President's Quality Award (PQA) were revised. The award's criteria now focuses on recognizing accomplishments that further the administration's objectives as noted in the President's Management Agenda (see the Web link at http://evans.swlearning.com). Specifically, beginning in 2002, the program was redesigned to recognize organizations for their performance and results in any or all of the five following categories:

1. Budget and Performance Integration
2. Strategic Management of Human Capital
3. Competitive Sourcing
4. Improved Financial Performance
5. Expanded Electronic Government

According to the Office of Personnel Management's Web site, the aims of the process and the President's Quality Award (paraphrased) are:

> Organizations selected for recognition serve as role models and benchmarks for other organizations to attain similar success. Applications are evaluated in part, by the results attained and the transferability and sustainability of the improvement, and sharing of these best practices to provide significant leverage in creating a government that is citizen-centered, results-oriented, and market-based.

The criteria and program guidelines can be found from the Web link at http://evans.swlearning.com. Some recent PQA winners and brief descriptions of their quality focus follow:

- *James A. Haley Veterans' Hospital, Tampa, Florida* Having embraced the concepts of continuous quality improvement (CQI) since the early 1990s, the James A. Haley Veterans Hospital is a two-time recipient of a President's Quality Award. Haley Veterans' Hospital is a tertiary teaching hospital and nursing home that provides patients with a full range of primary and specialized care, as well as rehabilitative services and extended care. Since CQI's beginnings at Haley, hospital managers have used dozens of interdisciplinary teams made up of employees whose main goals are to find ways to improve patient care levels and seek innovation in hospital administration. One such administrative innovation is the use of Gallup telephone surveys with patients. The telephone surveys allow Haley's employees and managers to "listen and learn" from patients' hospital experiences.

- *Defense Supply Center Philadelphia, Philadelphia, Pennsylvania* The Defense Supply Center Philadelphia annually provides about $5 billion worth of food, clothing, textiles, medicines, medical equipment, and general and industrial supplies and services to America's armed forces, their eligible dependents, and other non-Defense Department customers worldwide. Defense Supply Center Philadelphia's employees go above and beyond the call of duty to provide quality support anywhere in the world it is needed at competitive prices. DSCP is an Inventory Control Point within the U.S. Department of Defense's Defense Logistics Agency.

- *Army Armament Research, Development and Engineering Center, Picatinny Arsenal, New Jersey* Picatinny Arsenal, home to the U.S. Army Tank-Automotive and Armaments Command's Armament Research, Development, and Engineering Center (ARDEC), has a distinguished history in armaments and munitions development and production dating back to the Revolutionary War. Today, ARDEC is leading the way in the development of tomorrow's armament and munitions systems. The organization's entire fabric is committed to providing its ultimate customer—the soldier—the most effective products found anywhere in the world. ARDEC realizes that quality is a journey, not a destination. The soldiers ARDEC represents are the real winners.

More details on PQA winners may be found at the Office of Personnel Management's Web site, which can be linked from http://evans.swlearning.com.

State and Local Quality Efforts

State and local government agencies have gained momentum in developing their own quality programs and processes, albeit at a much slower rate than the private sector. Massachusetts, for example, formed a Quality Improvement Council to oversee and facilitate a broad quality program. In North Carolina, pilot projects for improvement in the quality of services are under way in the Department of Administration and the Division of Motor Vehicles. State quality award programs, discussed in the next chapter, provide a basis for many state and local agencies to learn about quality and pursue performance excellence in the same manner as private business.

Quality Spotlight
City of Madison
Wisconsin

One of the earliest examples of a successful public-sector quality initiative involved the city of Madison, Wisconsin. Joseph Sensenbrenner, mayor of Madison from 1983 to 1989, was one of the leaders in bringing quality principles to city government.[36] After a 1983 audit disclosed problems at the city garage, such as long delays in repair and equipment unavailability, Sensenbrenner attempted to apply quality improvement approaches, where the manager and mechanics were surprised to see "top management" personally visible and committed to their problems. Sensenbrenner obtained the cooperation of the union president and formed a team to gather data from individual mechanics and the repair process itself. The team found that many delays resulted from insufficient stocking of repair parts, which, in turn, was caused by having more than 440 different types, makes, models, and years of equipment—all obtained by purchasing from the lowest bidder. Solving the problem required teamwork and breaking down barriers between departments. The concept of an internal customer was virtually unknown. When the 24-step purchasing policy was changed to 3 steps, employees were stunned and delighted that someone was listening to them. They studied the potential of a preventive maintenance program and discovered, for example, that city departments did not use truck-bed linings when hauling corrosive materials such as salt. Mechanics rode along on police patrols and learned that squad cars spent most of their time idling; this information was used to tune engines properly. Other departments helped gather data. As a result, the average vehicle turnaround time was reduced from nine days to three with a net annual savings of about $700,000. The lessons learned in the city garage were expanded to other departments from painting to health. By the time Sensenbrenner left office in 1989, Madison's city departments each ran between 20 and 30 quality improvement projects at a time; five agencies focused on long-term commitment to new management practices, including continuous quality improvement skills and data-gathering techniques; the city provided training in quality to every employee; several state agencies eager to follow Madison's approach initiated joint efforts; and city workers continued to invent service improvements for internal and external customers.

A noteworthy effort over an extended period of time has resulted in TQ approaches being spread throughout the government of Jefferson County, which contains the city of Louisville, Kentucky.[37] Key to this effort was Rebecca Jackson, County Clerk, who introduced total quality and continuous improvement concepts to her office workforce of 320 employees, soon after she was elected in 1989. She set about challenging her employees to develop a customer focus in offices as varied as the motor-vehicle license tag department, local tax collections, voter registrations, county elections, public records office (deeds, mortgages, wills, etc.), and marriage and other professional licensing departments.

Quality Spotlight
Jefferson County, Kentucky

The voice of the customer was solicited and analyzed via customer comment cards that asked for feedback on staff work. More than 200 people responded every week. Each received a written reply, thanking them for their positive comments and outlining corrective action to be taken in problem areas. To build morale and serve as a catalyst for examining and improving procedures and processes, anyone who submitted a suggestion received a pen. Anyone whose suggestion was adopted was "mugged": he or she received a black mug imprinted with the office seal, which was presented with a certificate of appreciation at weekly meetings for top management.

Jackson helped the staff to develop a set of common values, language, and tools. Formal training sessions were held for management and staff. Employees studied how the office worked, from the budgeting process to personnel policies. As a result, significant service time improvements were made. For example, the time needed to renew an auto tag was reduced from two hours to 30 minutes. Employees learned to treat people as customers, with smiles, greetings, and a "thank you" as they left. Employees acted as professionals by owning problems and finding solutions. A recent innovation under Jackson's guidance has been to create a Web site where customers can find all of the popular forms and information, such as court docket files, budget info, application forms, studies, and reports available to download. This availability

Quality concepts and principles are universal and can be applied in all types of organizations. The difficulty, of course, is developing an infrastructure to make it happen and the discipline to sustain efforts over time.

often saves people a trip to the courthouse just to pick up forms that they need to fill out to obtain service.[38] Jackson was so successful in turning around the operations of the County Clerk's Office, that in 1998 she was named Public Official of the Year, an award presented by the National Association of County Recorders, Election Officials, and Clerks.

QUALITY IN PRACTICE
SERVICE QUALITY AT THE RITZ-CARLTON HOTEL COMPANY[39]

Caesar Ritz defined the concept of a luxury hotel in the 1890s. In 1992 The Ritz-Carlton Hotel Company became the first hospitality organization to receive the Malcolm Baldrige National Quality Award; in 1999 they became the second company to win the award a second time, a testament to their continuous journey of improvement. The hotel industry is a very competitive business, one in which consumers place great emphases on reliability, timely delivery, and value. The Ritz-Carlton focuses on the principal concerns of its main customers and strives to provide them with highly personalized, caring service. Attention to employee performance and information technology are two of the company's many strengths that helped it to achieve superior quality.

The Ritz-Carlton operates from an easy-to-understand definition of service quality that is aggressively communicated and internalized at all levels of the organization. Its Three Steps of Service, Motto, Employee Promise, Credo, and Basics—collectively known as the Gold Standards—are shown in Figure 2.2, and instilled in all employees through extensive training approaches. They allow employees to think and act independently with innovation for both the benefit of the customer and the company. The company's approaches for selecting and training employees were discussed earlier in this chapter.

The Ritz-Carlton uses many sources of information to understand its customers. These include alliances with travel partners such as airlines and credit card companies; focus groups and customer satisfaction results; complaints, claims, and feedback from the salesforce; customer interviews; travel industry publications and studies; and even special psychological studies to understand what customers mean, not what they say, and how to

---

Figure 2.2 The Ritz-Carlton Three Steps of Service, Motto, and Credo

THREE STEPS OF SERVICE

1
A warm and sincere greeting. Use the guest name, if and when possible.

2
Anticipation and compliance with guest needs.

3
Fond farewell. Give them a warm good-bye and use their names, if and when possible.

"We Are Ladies and Gentlemen Serving Ladies and Gentlemen"

THE RITZ-CARLTON®
CREDO

The Ritz-Carlton Hotel is a place where the genuine care and comfort of our guests is our highest mission.

We pledge to provide the finest personal service and facilities for our guests who will always enjoy a warm, relaxed yet refined ambience.

The Ritz-Carlton experience enlivens the senses, instills well-being, and fulfills even the unexpressed wishes and needs of our guests.

© 1992, 1998, The Ritz-Carlton Hotel Company. All rights reserved.

---

appeal to the customer in the language they most understand.

A formal strategic planning process sets business directions to achieve the company's long-term vision: "To Be the Premier Worldwide Provider of Luxury Travel and Hospitality Products and Services." Upper managers at the corporate and hotel level conduct monthly performance reviews of the strategic plan, focusing on key indicators that reflect employee pride and joy, customer loyalty, financial performance, and process performance. Quarterly reviews focus on opportunities for improvement and innovation. A variety of comparative data on competitors and other world-class organizations is used to evaluate and improve their practices. For example, data revealed that front desk turnover was higher than usual. The company found out that certain airlines were paying higher wages and attracting their employees. The Ritz-Carlton reevaluated its compensation policy to match the airlines and actually reduced its total costs by eliminating a supervisor who was required to constantly monitor new employees.

The Ritz-Carlton gathers and uses customer-satisfaction and quality-related data on a daily basis. Information systems involve every employee and provide critical, responsive data on guest preferences, quantity of error-free products and services, and opportunities for quality improvement. They track a set of service quality indicators (SQI), shown in Figure 2.3, which represent the 12 most serious defects that can occur during regular operations. Each day an index is computed and disseminated to the workforce and reviewed by hotel managers.

Each production and support process is assigned an "executive owner" at the corporate office and a "working owner" at the hotel level, who are responsible for the development and improvement of these processes. They have the authority to define the measurements and determine the resources needed to manage these processes. The "GreenBook," a handbook for employees, describes a nine-step quality improvement process to guide the design, control, and improvement of all processes, and is emphasized during new employee training and continual development. The Ritz-Carlton even has a process to overcome cultural resistance to change: stress the importance of the change, express confidence that the change can be made, provide a reason why

Figure 2.3 Ritz-Carlton Service Quality Indicators

SQI Defects	Points
1. Missing Guest Preferences	10
2. Unresolved Difficulties	50
3. Inadequate Guestroom Housekeeping	1
4. Abandoned Reservation Calls	5
5. Guestroom Changes	5
6. Inoperable Guestroom Equipment	5
7. Unready Guestroom	10
8. Inappropriate Hotel Appearance	5
9. Meeting Event Difficulties	5
10. Inadequate Food/Beverage	1
11. Missing/Damaged Guest Property/Accidents	50
12. Invoice Adjustment	3

people should make the change as a group, and allow time to find an accommodation to the change.

These examples show only a few of The Ritz-Carlton's quality practices and the results have been impressive. At the time of winning its second Baldrige Award, overall "top box" customer satisfaction (using a scale of 1 to 5, with the "top box" being a 5) was 70 percent against 52 percent for its foremost competitor. Employee satisfaction on issues of decision-making authority, teamwork, communication, and empowerment exceeded service company norms by a significant margin. The time to process a new hire from walk-in to job offer dropped from 21 days to 1 day in three years. Total revenue per hour worked showed a steady upward trend, and pretax return on investment improved from 5.3 percent in 1995 to 12.9 percent in 1999. One lesson the hotel learned is not to underestimate the value of even one idea or quality improvement effort.

Key Issues for Discussion

1. What value does a focus on the Gold Standards have for The Ritz-Carlton?
2. What must a company do to reduce job offer processing times so dramatically?
3. How does information play a central role in everything that The Ritz-Carlton does?

QUALITY IN PRACTICE
PEARL RIVER SCHOOL DISTRICT[40]

The Pearl River School District (PRSD) is a 100-year-old school district located in Rockland County, 20 miles north of New York City on the west side of the Hudson River. It is primarily located in the hamlet of Pearl River and is required by law to provide a free education for all children in the district. PRSD is one of eight public school districts in the county. It has strong support and involvement of parents, and students have expectations of participating in cocurricular activities and attending college. The district's mission is simple: *Every child can and will learn.*

PRSD's quality approach is based on its core values:

- Our students are our customers, and the product we deliver is to allow them to achieve to their highest ability.
- Educational opportunity is for all students.
- Learning is an active process where students discover and create knowledge.
- Tracking academic performance is a consistent and constant practice.
- Active involvement from all stakeholders is integral to district operations.
- District employees are highly valued resources.
- The district recognizes the value it has in the community and the people it serves.
- Our business operations are cost-effective while maintaining quality and protecting program.

Three district goals guide its focus and direction:

1. Improve academic performance.
2. Improve the perception of the district by incorporating quality principles and values in all areas of operations.
3. Maintain fiscal stability and improve cost-effectiveness.

The students are the primary customers of the school district's educational services. Students expect that the district will teach them how to discover and create knowledge and allow them the opportunity to attain the highest level of achievement. For most students, meeting this expectation means they will graduate from high school with a New York State Regents diploma, which represents the highest level of achievement. In a recent survey, 90 percent of the 8th graders entering high school report that they expect to earn a Regents diploma. Furthermore, 100 percent of these students expect that they will be prepared to enter and be successful in college. To accomplish these requirements, students avail themselves of a wide offering of academic, extra, and cocurricular activities with a continuous emphasis on achievement. Students' needs are represented through student government activities at all buildings, by student representatives reporting directly to the Board of Education twice a month in public meetings, and by surveys of present and past graduates. Every student has his/her progress reviewed quarterly by an administrator and teacher or teachers. Central office administrators monitor these reviews. Special education teachers, the coaches and director of the athletic teams, and guidance counselors support students.

Pearl River's primary stakeholder groups are parents, the business community, and district residents who have no children in the district. Parent and community needs are represented in such systems as PTA, memberships on all hiring interview committees, membership on district planning and evaluation committees, and through yearly surveys and focus groups. The district reaches out in a variety of ways to include its senior citizens in the school activities. Through Parent University, the district offers adult education courses to more than 1,000 adults. The district provides training for parents to teach courses to other parents. The involvement of the various stakeholder groups in planning and implementation of district goals and objectives is an integral part of the daily regimen. Stakeholders require that the district provide strong student achievement, be perceived as a quality educational provider, and be financially stable and fiscally prudent with the taxpayers' resources. An important involvement of stakeholders is in the election of the five-member Board of Education, whose terms expire every three years, and the voting on the district's annual operating budget every May for the following school year. The district employees use a number of strategies to educate and involve stakeholders in the planning and evaluation of the district budget.

The chief reason the district is successful is that everything it does is aligned with its three strategic goals: (1) improve student academic achievement, (2) improve public perception of the district, and (3) maintain fiscal stability and improve cost-effectiveness. Students and parents see the district as being ranked in the first percentile of all school districts in the state in student academic achievement. Success also requires that taxpayers perceive the district as having low per-pupil cost and high academic achievement.

PRSD uses a continuous improvement cycle to drive the performance improvement. A disciplined performance review process is used to collect and analyze data to evaluate whether the district goals, objectives, and projects are being accomplished. This performance review cycle is structured according to the school year, starting in July with validation of the district mission, values, and goals. Throughout the school year, the district uses a number of formal and informal checkpoints to monitor and evaluate performance. Data are collected from student performance, environmental scanning, demographic and enrollment trends, student and stakeholder surveys, national standardized tests, NYS tests, NYS learning standards, audits, and inspections. Knowledge of student needs and expectations is important to PRSD because the students are viewed as customers. PRSD uses formative and summative data of students based on qualitative and quantitative collection points. Student utilization of district services is also measured, and surveys of alumni, both qualitative and quantitative, are used to determine whether the district is meeting the expectations of the world outside.

Stakeholders' needs are determined through surveys, focus groups, voting on the district budget, local business surveys, and higher education surveys. The faculty stakeholder group conducts both formal and informal surveys, and organizations like the labor management committee provide information on needs and expectations. Student and stakeholder needs are analyzed through a formal process to determine whether the needs are central to the mission, consistent with mandates from the federal government and the state, and whether the resources are available. A modified balanced scorecard (see Chapter 8) is used to organize key performance measures and aid in a structured review process. This process allows PRSD to prioritize and

organize goals so that they support each other and to ensure that they are directed at meeting their three strategic goals.

The work system design is an important part of the performance improvement system. More than 14 variables are considered in designing how to deliver curriculum and instruction to students. This system is evaluated as part of the annual planning cycle and adjusted throughout the year to align with the successful completion of district goals. Faculty and staff development is integrated with the work system design so as to improve employee performance. Every one of the employees has annual goals and an evaluation, which supports district goals. All faculty members participate in a minimum of 42 hours of professional development each year. All staff participate in a minimum of 21 hours of training. The district's continuous improvement cycle has been modified and customized so that the classroom teachers can use it. The process allows for curriculum alignment to meet federal and state standards, as well as faculty instructional delivery improvement so that all students learn. Also, all of the key student service and support processes are measured to ensure that they contribute to the district goals. The district is proactive in meeting all federal, state, and local regulatory, legal, and ethical requirements.

Figure 2.4 shows data on three key satisfaction measures that Effective Schools research has

Figure 2.4 Student Satisfaction Survey Results

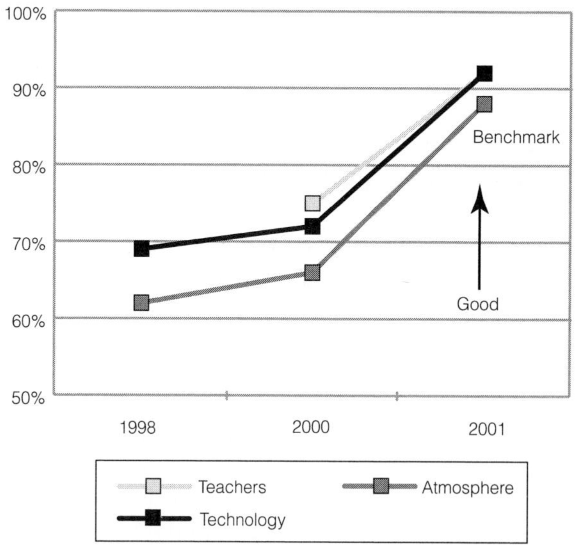

demonstrated are essential to positive student achievement results. Over the four years, student satisfaction with teachers, atmosphere, and technology steadily improved and surpassed the benchmark rate. Figure 2.5 summarizes milestones in the history of continuous improvement at PRSD, culminating in its receiving one of the first Baldrige Awards given for education in 2001.

Key Issues for Discussion

1. Discuss how the practices at PRSD reflect quality principles.
2. Thinking back on your own K–12 education, especially high school, what things stand out that PRSD probably does differently?

Figure 2.5 PRSD Continuous Improvement Timeline

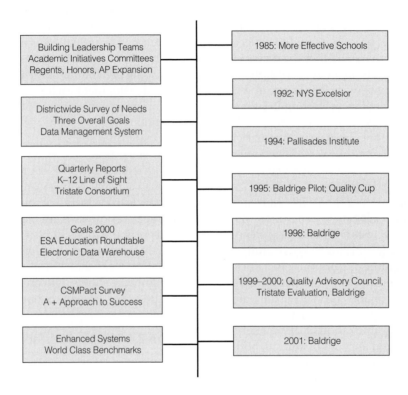

![Review Questions icon] **REVIEW QUESTIONS**

1. What is a system? Why is systems thinking important to quality management?
2. Explain how quality has moved beyond technical such issues as reliability, inspection, and process control in manufacturing.
3. Explain the quality concerns of each major function of a manufacturing system.
4. How can business support activities help to sustain quality in an organization? List the key business support activities and their role in quality.
5. What types of organizations fall under the definition of services? Why is service quality especially important in today's business environment?
6. How do service standards differ from manufacturing specifications? How are they similar?

7. Discuss the differences between manufacturing and service organizations. What are the implications of these differences for quality assurance?

8. Explain the roles of employees and information technology in providing quality service. How does The Ritz-Carlton Hotel Company use employees and information technology for quality service?

9. Summarize the status of quality in the health care industry. How are professional organizations promoting quality improvement in health care?

10. How do the recommendations of the President's Advisory Commission on Consumer Protection and Quality in the Health Care Industry address the basic principles of TQ described in Chapter 1?

11. Summarize the major quality initiatives used in education. How are the approaches at K–12 institutions similar to yet different from those used in the colleges and universities?

12. Why have small businesses and not-for-profits been slow to adopt quality initiatives?

13. What must small businesses and not-for-profits do to successfully establish a total quality focus?

14. Describe some of the key quality initiatives that have been taken in the government sector, both federal and state.

 ## DISCUSSION QUESTIONS

1. This chapter listed several dimensions of service quality (time, timeliness, and so on). List five service organizations and specify which dimension(s) each organization emphasizes. State whether you believe the emphasis gives the firm competitive advantage.

2. How might Deming's diagram of a production system in Chapter 1 (Figure 1.3) be applied to education? Specifically, sketch it out in detail for a college or university and explain its components.

3. Cite some examples from your own experience in which you felt service quality was truly top-notch and some in which it was not. What do you think might be some of the fundamental differences in the infrastructure and management practices of these organizations?

4. How is information technology used to improve service in your college or university?

5. What role has the Internet played in improving service quality? What barriers to service quality might it have?

6. Discuss the implications of the following statements with respect to introducing TQ principles in a college classroom.[41] Do you agree with them? How do they reflect TQ principles? What changes in traditional learning approaches would they require for both students and instructors?
   a. Embracing a customer focus doesn't mean giving students all As and abandoning standards.
   c. If students fail, the system has failed.
   d. Faculty members are customers of those who teach prerequisites.
   e. Treating students as customers means allowing students to choose not to come to class.
   f. Completing the syllabus is not a measure of success.
   g. New and tenured instructors should visit each other's classrooms.

      h. Eliminate performance appraisals based on classroom evaluations.

      i. No matter how good the test, luck will be involved.

7. Contrast the role of service quality at Amazon.com and Barnes and Noble (which operates traditional bookstores as well as an e-commerce site). What are the differences in their approaches? How might a company like Barnes and Noble exploit its dual marketing focus (stores and e-commerce) in a complementary fashion to provide services that Amazon.com would not be able to offer?

8. How have health care, not-for-profit, and government organizations benefited from quality improvement initiatives in manufacturing and service sectors? Can you find or think of specific examples where manufacturing and service businesses might be able to learn from quality practices developed by not-for-profit organizations?

9. Cite one or more examples of times when you received either high- or poor-quality service from a physician's office, dentist's office, or hospital. What do you think contributed most to your experience—well-designed procedures, technology, or the behavior of the professionals or staff?

10. Thinking of your experiences at a post office, driver's license bureau, or other government agency, describe your perception of the quality of the service, and suggest some TQ approaches that might help the agency improve.

 ## PROJECTS, ETC.

1. Interview some key managers at a nearby manufacturing company and construct a diagram similar to Figure 2.1 showing the company's key functions and their relationships. Summarize the major quality concerns of each function.

2. Interview some managers at a local service organization and summarize the role of employees and information technology in providing quality service. How are employees and information technology integrated into long-range improvement plans and strategies?

3. Develop a Deming-type diagram of a hospital as a production system. You might wish to talk with some health care professionals to better understand the terminology and key issues.

4. Arrange a tour of a local hospital or clinic. How is quality managed in the organization? What individuals or groups spearhead quality improvement efforts? Is the entire workforce involved to any degree? What quality-related improvements have they made in the past two years?

5. Interview administrative officials at your college or university to determine what quality efforts have been made to improve both administrative functions and educational effectiveness.

6. Arrange an interview with a local high school principal or school district superintendent. Determine whether any quality initiatives have been adopted during the past two years. Have teachers been trained in quality improvement approaches? How does the school or district gather information from its stakeholders? Are the interviewees aware of the Koalaty Kid program?

7. Visit the AQIP Web site (http://www.aqip.org) and report on how AQIP is promoting quality in colleges and universities.

8. School boards provide a critical link between schools, parents, and the community. According to the National School Board Association, school boards must help to create a vision and structure for the school system while focusing on accountability to ensure results and advocacy for improved performance. Interview members of a local school board or parents of children in a public school district that you know to determine how well the school board address the following tasks:[42]

a. Focuses on issues related to student achievement

b. Sets a common vision for student achievement and a clear definition of student success

c. Uses reliable data to make informed decisions about how to support student achievement goals and how to measure progress

d. Brings diverse opinions to bear and create community consensus on student achievement goals

e. Sets benchmarks and discusses progress toward student achievement goals

f. Plays a leadership role in defining standards of achievement for all students

g. Develops a process for maintaining accountability within the schools and the school board itself

h. Models teamwork and partnership

i. Incorporates mechanisms for feedback from parents, administrators, teachers, and the greater community

j. Creates policies that clearly support student achievement goals

9. Have quality initiatives been adopted by your local government? Interview some local politicians and managers to answer this question: Can you, as a customer, obtain easy access to these people?

10. Talk to a local not-for-profit organization manager or small business owner about quality. How aware are they of quality principles and tools? What challenges do they see in trying to build quality into their organizations?

CASES

Additional cases are available in the Bonus Materials Folder on the CD-ROM.

I. Toyota Motor Corporation, Ltd.[43]

The Toyota brand name has earned an international reputation for quality. The roots of Toyota Motor Corporation, founded in 1937, stem from the Toyoda Automatic Loom Works. Sakichi Toyoda invented a loom with an automatic stopping function; whenever a thread broke or the machine ran out of thread, it stopped automatically. This approach was built into automotive assembly lines to improve quality and productivity and led to the development of the "Toyota Production System," which has commonly become known as *lean production*. A significant feature of lean production is the practice of continuous improvement by every worker, demanding the questioning of every process and testing of all assumptions. Errors and defects are viewed as learning opportunities to remove waste and improve efficiency. In 1951, Eiji Toyoda instituted a system of creative suggestions based on the motto "Good Thinking, Good Products," which is prominently displayed in every production facility. One example is the Rakuraku seat, a comfortable work chair mounted on the tip of an arm that allows a line worker to easily get into and out of cramped car-body interiors. In 2000, more than 650,000 suggestions were submitted—almost 12 per employee—and 99 percent were adopted.

At Toyota, everybody helps whenever they can. Even top and middle managers are well-known for getting their "hands dirty" by helping workers on the production line when necessary. Toyota uses games, competitions, and cultural events to promote its 3 C's: creativity, challenge, and courage. It trains workers extensively, not only in job skills, but also in personal development that focuses on positive attitudes and a sense of responsibility. Toyota's education system includes formal education, on-the-job training, and informal education.

Toyota is implementing a direct monitoring system that supports quality. For example, its French plant is connected by a broadband system to the head office, enabling it to transmit video, audio, and facility performance data. Engineers in Japan can monitor the data of the plant's operation in real time, check machinery utilization rates, diagnose malfunctions, and provide ideas for improvement. Information technology and e-commerce are also used to expand relationships with suppliers and customers. For example, customers may request quotes and gather information that previously was only available to dealers.

Shotaro Kamiya, first president of Toyota Motor Sales, stated, "The priority in receiving benefits from automobile sales should be in the order of the customer, then the car dealer, and lastly the maker. This attitude is the best approach in winning the trust of customers and dealers and ultimately brings growth to the manufacturer." The guiding principles of Toyota are as follows:

1. Honor the language and spirit of the law of every nation and undertake open and fair corporate activities to be a good corporate citizen of the world.
2. Respect the culture and customs of every nation and contribute to economic and social development through corporate activities in the communities.
3. Dedicate ourselves to providing clean and safe products and to enhancing the quality of life everywhere through all our activities.
4. Create and develop advanced technologies and provide outstanding products and services that fulfill the needs of customers worldwide.
5. Foster a corporate culture that enhances individual creativity and teamwork value, while

honoring mutual trust and respect between labor and management.
6. Pursue growth in harmony with the global community through innovative management.
7. Work with business partners in research and creation to achieve stable, long-term growth and mutual benefits, while keeping ourselves open to new partnerships.

Toyota has approximately 40 production facilities in more than 20 countries and regions outside Japan. When Toyota began expanding outside of Japan, many believed that the culture could not be copied or applied to foreign cultures, especially in the United States. With a focus of incorporating the best elements of Japanese and local traditions, while avoiding the weaknesses of both, Toyota as proven that its approaches and culture can work everywhere.

One popular phrase at Toyota is "change or die." The company continually seeks to redefine itself to adapt to changes in society and the business environment. Toyota's recent vision is captured by the phrase *harmonious growth*—a harmony between man, society, and the environment.

> *We wish to make Toyota not only strong but a universally admired company, winning the trust and respect of the world. We must be a company that is accepted wholeheartedly by people around the world, who would think it natural if Toyota became No. 1 in size, since we provide attractive products that excel in environmental protection and in safety and thus contribute immensely to local communities. That is the goal of "Harmonious Growth" and what I regard as corporate virtue.*
> —Hiroshi Okuda, Chairman

Discussion Questions

1. What do Toyota's guiding principles mean for its management system? In particular, how do they reflect the principles of total quality?
2. We noted that SSM Health Care learned from manufacturing companies in their quality journey. What can nonmanufacturing companies learn and apply from Toyota's philosophy and practices? Suggest specific things that education and government might learn.

II. The Nightmare on Telecom Street[44]

H. James Harrington, a noted quality consultant, related the following story in *Quality Digest* magazine:

I called to make a flight reservation just an hour ago. The telephone rang five times before a recorded voice answered. "Thank you for calling ABC Travel Services," it said. "To ensure the highest level of customer service, this call may be recorded for future analysis." Next, I was asked to select from one of the following three choices: "If the trip is related to company business, press 1. Personal business, press 2. Group travel, press 3." I pressed 1.

I was then asked to select from the following four choices: "If this is a trip within the United States, press 1. International, press 2. Scheduled training, press 3. Related to a conference, press 4." Because I was going to Canada, I pressed 2.

Now two minutes into my telephone call, I was instructed to be sure that I had my customer identification card available. A few seconds passed and a very sweet voice came on, saying, "All international operators are busy, but please hold because you are a very important customer." The voice was then replaced by music. About two minutes later, another recorded message said, "Our operators are still busy, but please hold and the first available operator will take care of you." More music. Then yet another message: "Our operators are still busy, but please hold. Your business is important to us." More bad music. Finally the sweet voice returned, stating, "To speed up your service, enter your 19-digit customer service number." I frantically searched for their card, hoping that I could find it before I was cut off. I was lucky; I found it and entered the number in time. The same sweet voice came back to me, saying, "To confirm your cus-tomer service number, enter the last four digits of your social security number." I pushed the four numbers on the keypad. The voice said: "Thank you. An operator will be with you shortly. If your call is an emergency, you can call 1-800-CAL-HELP, or push all of the buttons on the telephone at the same time. Otherwise, please hold, as you are a very important customer." This time, in place of music, I heard a commercial about the service that the company provides.

At last, a real person answered the telephone and asked, "Can I help you?" I replied, "Yes, oh yes." He answered, "Please give me your 19-digit customer service number, followed by the last four digits of your social security number so I can verify who you are." (I thought I gave these numbers in the first place to speed up service. Why do I have to rattle them off again?)

I was now convinced that he would call me Mr. 5523-3675-0714-1313-040. But, to my surprise, he said: "Yes, Mr. Harrington. Where do you want to go and when?" I explained that I wanted to go to Montreal the following Monday morning. He replied: "I only handle domestic reservations. Our international desk has a new telephone number: 1-800-1WE-GOTU. I'll transfer you." A few clicks later a message came on, saying: "All of our international operators are busy. Please hold and your call will be answered in the order it was received. Do not hang up or redial, as it will only delay our response to your call. Please continue to hold, as your business is important to us."

Discussion Questions

1. Summarize the service failures associated with this experience.
2. What might the travel agency do to improve its customers' service experience?

III. Child Focus, Inc.[45]

Child Focus, Inc. (CFI), whose mission is to join with communities in strengthening families and improving the quality of life for children, offers a wide variety of programs in Clermont, Hamilton, and Brown counties in Ohio. With an agency budget in excess of $11 million dollars, the spectrum of services includes Head Start programs for children ages 0–5, parenting education, family literacy, GED test preparation, substance abuse prevention, partial hospitalization, mental health prevention and counseling services in schools, foster care, independent living, case management, outpatient individual, family, and group therapy, diagnostic testing, psychiatric services, and professional training. CFI's 240 employees have a broad range of professional education including high school, associate's, bachelor's, master's, Ph.D., R.N., and M.D. degrees. All staff share the authority, dedication, and commitment to promote the mission of serving children and families. Facilities include intranet, Internet, a Web site (http://www.child-focus.org), specifically designed management information systems with necessary office equipment, 22 vehicles to provide client transportation, and two commercial kitchens that serve more than 800 meals a day. Facilities and programs are supervised by a volunteer Board of Trustees and by the accreditation standards of the National Association for the Education of the Young Child, Day Care Licensing Regulations, Head Start Performance Standards, and Ohio Departments of Education, Mental Health, Alcohol and Drug Addiction Services, and Job and Family Services.

As CFI continues to expand its programs through new and larger contracts, the biggest challenge is to provide quality services. Personnel and human resources issues are another challenge. They continually strive to find qualified staff who are willing to work with some of the most challenging children and dysfunctional families. Although their turnover rate is approximately 15

percent, most of it is in less-skilled positions. Consequently, this loss of staff increases training costs. Training existing staff to meet higher educational standards and continuing to find office and service space to meet growing needs is also a challenge.

CFI's diversity of programming, reporting, and funding to multiple agencies and organizations requires continuous management at all levels within the agency. The governing Board of Trustees for Child Focus is a diverse group of volunteers that have experience as attorneys, teachers, homemakers, and CFI consumers. Federal, state, and county legislative and regulatory changes can affect programming or present financial challenges. These entities, in turn, may have competing philosophies, which complicate administration or delay program implementation.

CFI management has several procedures in place to identify and manage these organizational challenges. Customer, staff, and collaborators' recommendations and complaints are identified through evaluation and administrative programs in both the Early Childhood and Behavioral Health divisions and are continuously monitored by staff, management, and the Board of Trustees. Through a continuous strategic planning process, CFI identifies ways in which to improve and expand its services through program modification or development.

The CEO is committed to building a total quality organization. If you were asked to help in this quality journey, what questions would you want answered? What advice would you provide?

ENDNOTES

1. "Hyundai Gets Hot," *Business Week,* December 17, 2001, 84–85.
2. "Michigan Hospital Promises to Deliver," *Cincinnati Enquirer,* July 17, 1991, A2.
3. Marilyn Adams, "Air service faces continued heat from fliers," USAToday.com, accessed June 1, 2000.
4. Ackoff, Russell L., *Recreating the Corporation: A Design of Organizations for the 21st Century,* Oxford, 1999.
5. "A Profile of Hershey Foods Corporation," Hershey Foods Corporation, Hershey, PA 17033, 7.
6. Jeff Sabatini, "Flawless (Nearly)," *Automotive Manufacturing & Production,* November 1999, 60–62.
7. D. A. Collier, "The Customer Service and Quality

Challenge," *The Service Industries Journal* 7, no. 1 (January 1987), 79.
8. Frederick F. Reichheld and W. Earl Sasser, Jr., "Zero Defections: Quality Comes to Services," *Harvard Business Review* 68, no. 5 (September-October 1990), 105–112.
9. Dean S. Elmuti and Yunus Kathawala, "Small Service Firms Face Implementation Challenges," *Quality Progress,* April 1999, 67–75.
10. Claes Fornell, *Q4, 2002: Retail, Finance, and e-Commerce,* National Quality Research Center, University of Michigan Business School, CFI Group, available at http://www.theacsi.org/scores_commentaries/

commentaries/Q4_02_comm.htm, accessed February 18, 2003.

11. Ron Zemke, "Auditing Customer Service: Look Inside as Well as Out," *Employee Relations Today* 16 (Autumn 1989), 197–203.

12. Adapted from the 1992 and 1999 Ritz-Carlton's Malcolm Baldrige National Quality Award application summaries; Cheri Henderson, "Putting on the Ritz," *TQM Magazine* 2, no. 5 (November–December 1992), 292–296; and remarks by various Ritz-Carlton managers at the 2000 Quest for Excellence Conference, Washington D.C.

13. "Quality '93: Empowering People with Technology," advertisement in *Fortune*, September 20, 1993.

14. "New JCAHO Standards Emphasize Continuous Quality Improvement," *Hospitals*, August 5, 1991, 41–44.

15. This information is adapted from NCQA's Web site, http://www.ncqa.org.

16. http://www.hcqualitycommission.gov.

17. Maureen Bisognano, "New Skills Needed in Medical Leadership," *Quality Progress*, June 2000, 32–41.

18. Robert Burney, "TQM in a Surgery Center," *Quality Progress* 27, no. 1 (January 1994), 97–100.

19. Nada R. Sanders, "Health Care Organizations Can Learn From the Experiences of Others," *Quality Progress*, February 1997, 47–49.

20. See, for example, Christina Del Valle, "Readin', Writin', and Reform," *Business Week/Quality Special Issue*, October 25, 1991, 140–142; Myron Tribus, "Quality Management in Education," *Journal for Quality and Participation* (January–February 1993), 12–21. See also Christopher W. L. and Paula E. Morrison, "Students Aren't Learning Quality Principles in Business Schools," *Quality Progress* 25, no. 1 (January 1992), 25–27; John A. Byrne, "Is Research in the Ivory Tower 'Fuzzy, Irrelevant, and Pretentious'?" *Business Week*, October 29, 1990, 62–66.

21. This section is adapted from an extensive account in Lloyd Dobyns and Clare Crawford-Mason, *Quality or Else* (Boston: Houghton-Mifflin, 1991), 221–230.

22. Kathleen A. Sharples, Michael Slusher, and Mike Swaim, "How TQM Can Work in Education," *Quality Progress* 29, no. 5 (May 1996), 75–78.

23. ASQ Quality Advocate, ASC Quality Central e-zine, available at http://www.asq.org/news/news_releases/100102edsurvey.html, accessed October 11, 2002.

24. Adapted from the http://www.koalatykid.org Web site. Permission to reprint is granted by the ASQ Koalaty Kid Alliance.

25. Kennedy Smith, "Koalaty Kid: A student-focused initiative to improve the quality of education," *Quality Digest*, August 2002, 49–51.

26. L. Edwin Coate, "TQM at Oregon State University," reprinted with permission from *Journal for Quality and Participation* (December 1990), 56–65. See also L. Edward Coate, *Implementing Total Quality Management in a University Setting* (Corvallis, OR: Oregon State University, July 1990); Ralph G. Lewis and Douglas H. Smith, *Total Quality in Higher Education* (Delray Beach, FL: St. Lucie Press, 1994).

27. http://www.psu.edu.

28. Everett, Carol Lindborg, "Penn State's Commitment to Quality Improvement," *Quality Progress* 35, no. 1 (January 2002), 44–48.

29. "CQI: Making a Difference at Penn State, 1991–1999 Highlights," available at http://www.psu.edu/president/pia/cqi/highlights.pdf.

30. Adapted from Baldrige Award Recipient Profile, University of Wisconsin–Stout, National Institute of Standards and Technology, U.S. Department of Commerce. Courtesy of UW–Stout.

31. S. L. Ahire, D. Y. Golhar, "Quality Management in Large vs. Small Firms," *Journal of Small Business Management* 34, no. 2 (1996), 1–13.

32. Madhav N. Sinha "Helping Those Who Help Others," *Quality Progress*, July 1997; and Renee Oosterhoff Cox, "Quality in Nonprofits: No Longer Uncharted Territory," *Quality Progress*, October 1999, 57–61.

33. Kennedy Smith, "American Red Cross Undergoes Quality Transfusion," *Quality Digest*, March 2003, 6–7.

34. Ned Hamson, "The FQI Story: Today and Tomorrow," *Journal for Quality and Participation* (July–August 1990), 46–49.

35. Executive Order No. 12637, vol. 7. U.S. Code Congressional and Administrative News, 100th Congress—Second Session (St. Paul, MN: West Publishing Co.), B21–B23.

36. Joseph Sensenbrenner, "Quality Comes to City Hall," *Harvard Business Review* (March–April 1991), 64–75.

37. Adapted from *CQM Voice* 9, no. 1 (Spring 1998) available at: http://cqmextra.cqm.org/voice.nsf/.

38. See http://www.co.jefferson.ky.us/.

39. See note 12.

40. Adapted from 2001 Malcolm Baldrige National Quality Award Education Application, courtesy of Pearl River School District, 275 East Central Avenue, Pearl River, NY 10965; http://www.pearlriver.k12.ny.us.

41. Adapted from Ronald E. Turner, "TQM in the College Classroom," *Quality Progress* 28, no. 10 (October 1995), 105–108.

42. "The Key Work of School Boards," National School Board Association brochure. NSBA, 1680 Duke Street, Alexandria, VA 22314.

43. Our thanks go to a former student, Boris Méndez Rojas, for his research in developing the information in this case.

44. H. James Harrington, "Looking for a Little Service," *Quality Digest*, May 2000; http://www.qualitydigest.com.

45. Child Focus, Inc., 2003 Greater Cincinnati Chamber of Commerce Small Business Awards Applica-

tion. Our thanks go to Tara Dawson for providing this information.

BIBLIOGRAPHY

Berry, Leonard L., Valarie A. Zeithaml, and A. Parasuraman. "Five Imperatives for Improving Service Quality." *Sloan Management Review*, Summer 1990, 29–38.

Carr, Maureen P., Francis W. Jackson, and Diane Cesarone. *The Crosswalk: Joint Commission Standards and Baldrige Criteria.* Oakbrook Terrace, IL : Joint Commission on Accreditation of Healthcare Organizations, 1997.

Cullen, Thomas Patrick. *Managing Service Quality in the Hospitality Industry.* Ithaca, NY: Hotel School, Cornell University, 2000.

Fitzsimmons, James A., and Mona J. Fitzsimmons. *New Service Development: Creating Memorable Experiences.* Thousand Oaks, CA: Sage Publications, 2000.

Gantenbein, Douglas, and Marcia Stepanek. "Kaiser Takes the Cybercure," *Business Week,* February 7, 2000.

Garvin, David A. *Managing Quality.* New York: The Free Press, 1988.

Hallowell, Roger. *Virtuous Cycles: Improving Service and Lowering Costs in E-Commerce.* Boston: Division of Research, Harvard Business School, 2001.

King, Carol A. "Service Quality Assurance Is Different." *Quality Progress* 18, no. 6 (June 1985), 14–18.

Medina-Borja, Alexandra, and Konstantinos Triantis. "A Methodology to Evaluate Outcome Performance in Social Services and Government Agencies." *Annual Quality Congress Proceedings* 55th (May 2001), 707–719.

Rust, Roland T., Christine Moorman, and Peter R. Dickson. *Getting Returns from Service Quality: Is the Conventional Wisdom Wrong?* Cambridge, MA: Marketing Science Institute, 2000.

Watson, Gregory H. "Peter F. Drucker: Delivering Value to Customers." *Quality Progress* 35, no. 5, (May 2002).

Zemke, Ron. "The Emerging Art of Service Management." *Training* 29 (January 1992), 36–42.

CHAPTER 3

PHILOSOPHIES AND FRAMEWORKS

In the 1890s, Caesar Ritz defined the standards for a luxury hotel; these evolved into the quality responsibilities of the employees—the "Ladies and Gentlemen Serving Ladies and Gentlemen"—of today's Ritz-Carlton Hotel Company: anticipating the wishes and needs of the guests, resolving their problems, and exhibiting genuinely caring conduct toward guests and each other. The Ritz-Carlton management recognized that the key to ensuring that these responsibilities are realized was to create a "Skilled and Empowered Work Force Operating with Pride and Joy." This quality-focused philosophy led the company to be a two-time recipient of the Malcolm Baldrige National Quality Award.

The concept of "pride and joy" in work—and its impact on quality—is one of the foundations of the philosophy of the late W. Edwards Deming. Deming, along with Joseph M. Juran and Philip B. Crosby, are regarded as true "management gurus" in the quality revolution. Their insights on measuring, managing, and improving quality have had profound impacts on countless managers and entire corporations around the world. The *Quality Profiles* on the following page highlight two companies that reflect these philosophies.

This chapter presents the quality management philosophies of these three leaders, their similarities and differences, and also examines their individual contributions to modern practice. In addition, it discusses the contributions of other key individuals who have helped to shape current thinking in quality management. These philosophies became the cornerstone for quality management practice and frameworks, such as the Deming Prize, the Malcolm Baldrige National Quality Award, the ISO 9000 standards, and the Six Sigma philosophy, which we also introduce in this chapter, and which form the basis for much of the remainder of this book.

THE DEMING PHILOSOPHY

No individual has had more influence on quality management than Dr. W. Edwards Deming (1900–1993). Deming received a Ph.D. in physics and was trained as a statistician, so much of his philosophy can be traced to these roots. He worked for Western Electric during its pioneering era of statistical quality control in the 1920s and 1930s. Deming recognized the importance of viewing management processes statistically. During World War II he taught quality control courses as part of the U.S. national defense effort, but he realized that teaching statistics only to engineers and factory workers would never solve the fundamental quality problems that manufacturing needed to address. Despite numerous efforts, his attempts to convey the message of quality to upper-level managers in the United States were ignored.

Shortly after World War II Deming was invited to Japan to help the country take a census. The Japanese had heard about his theories and their usefulness to U.S. companies during the war. Consequently, he soon began to teach them statistical quality control. His thinking went beyond mere statistics, however. Deming preached the importance of top management leadership, customer/supplier partnerships, and continuous improvement in product development and manufacturing processes. Japanese managers embraced these ideas, and the rest, as they say, is history. Deming's influence on Japanese industry was so great that the Union of Japanese Scientists and Engineers established the Deming Application Prize in 1951 to recognize companies that show a high level of achievement in quality practices. Deming also received Japan's highest honor, the Royal Order of the Sacred Treasure, from the emperor. The former chairman of NEC Electronics once said, "There is not a day I don't think about what Dr. Deming meant to us."

Although Deming lived in Washington, D.C., he remained virtually unknown in the United States until 1980, when NBC telecast a program entitled "If Japan Can . . . Why Can't We?" The documentary highlighted Deming's contributions in Japan and his later work with Nashua Corporation. Shortly afterward, his name was frequently on the lips of U.S. corporate executives. Companies such as Ford, GM, and Procter &

QUALITY PROFILES

TEXAS NAMEPLATE COMPANY, INC., AND SUNDARAM-CLAYTON

TEXAS NAMEPLATE COMPANY, INC.

Founded in 1946, Texas Nameplate Company, Inc. (TNC), with only 66 employees, manufactures and sells identification and information labels that are affixed to refrigerators, oil-field equipment, high-pressure valves, trucks, computer equipment, and other products made by more than 1,000 customers throughout the United States and in nine foreign countries. TNC has honed the raw attributes inherent to its small size—from streamlined communications and rapid decision-making to shared goals and accessible leaders—into competitive advantages. The result is a closely knit organization that is finely tuned to the requirements of its customers. TNC aims to create a continuous learning environment that enables empowered teams of workers to take charge of processes and to deliver products and services with a "star quality." Through its "Customer Site Visit" program, a team of TNC employees visits customer facilities to identify opportunities for improving products and services. The results of these visits are shared with everyone at TNC. Customer contact employees are empowered to resolve customer complaints without consulting management, and production workers are responsible for tailoring processes to optimize contributions to company goals and to meet team-set standards. TNC reduced its defects from 3.65 percent to about 1 percent in four years. Customers consistently give the company an "excellent" rating (5 to 6 on a scale of 6) in 12 key business areas, including product quality, reliable performance, on-time delivery, and overall satisfaction, and in its employee survey, satisfaction rates in five areas employees say are the most important: fair pay, job content satisfaction, recognition, fairness/respect, and career development, exceed national norms by a significant margin.

Sundaram-Clayton (S-C) is a manufacturer of air-brake systems and castings, headquartered in Chennai, India, and is part of an Indian industrial group called TVS–Suzuki. S-C became India's first-ever winner of the Deming Prize for Overseas Companies. In discussing how and why S-C adopted a Japanese type of quality system, CEO Venu Srinivasan pointed to a long history of conformance to procedures that was part of the culture of the firm. However, he also said that they developed their own unique approach, based on encouragement from their Japanese quality advisors. Srinivasan took over as CEO in 1977, and conducted an analysis of the company's strengths, weaknesses, opportunities, and threats, which revealed—to the company's horror—that a 90 percent market share was no insulation against top-class competition. Concluding that short-term tactics or defensive strategies could not deliver what a long-term transition to excellence could, Srinivasan set the company on the route to total quality with a focus on its people.

Workers spend a minimum of 45 hours a year in classroom training, well above the industry average of four hours, starting with how and why to keep machines and the shop floor clean using the Japanese "5 Ss": seiri (clearing up), seiton (organizing), seiso (cleaning), seiketsu (standardizing), and shitsuke (training). They also learn to use quality problem-solving tools and implement them in small, self-managed teams. When S-C won the Deming Prize, sales per employee had increased three times over the prior year, and frame assembly line rejections had dropped from 12 percent to 0.5 percent over 10 years.

Source: Baldrige Award Recipient Profiles, National Institute of Standards and Technology, U.S. Department of Commerce.

Gamble invited him to work with them to improve their quality. To their surprise, Deming did not lay out "a quality improvement program" for them. His goal was to change entire perspectives in management, and often radically. Deming worked with passion until his death in December 1993 at the age of 93, knowing he had little time left to make a difference in his home country. When asked how he would like to be remembered, Deming replied, "I probably won't even be remembered." Then after a long pause, he added, "Well, maybe . . . as someone who spent his life trying to keep America from committing suicide."[1]

Foundations of the Deming Philosophy

Unlike other management gurus and consultants, Deming never defined or described quality precisely. In his last book, he stated, "A product or a service possesses quality if it helps somebody and enjoys a good and sustainable market."[2] In Deming's view, variation is the chief culprit of poor quality. In mechanical assemblies, for example, variations from specifications for part dimensions lead to inconsistent performance and premature wear and failure. Likewise, inconsistencies in human behavior in service frustrate customers and hurt companies' reputations. To accomplish reductions in variation, Deming advocated a never-ending cycle of product/service design, manufacture/service delivery, test, and sales, followed by market surveys and then redesign and improvement. He claimed that higher quality leads to higher productivity, which in turn leads to long-term competitive strength. The Deming "chain reaction" theory (see Figure 3.1) summarizes this view. The theory is that improvements in quality lead to lower costs because they result in less rework, fewer mistakes, fewer delays and snags, and better use of time and materials. Lower costs, in turn, lead

> *The Deming philosophy focuses on continual improvements in product and service quality by reducing uncertainty and variability in design, manufacturing, and service processes, driven by the leadership of top management.*

to productivity improvements. With better quality and lower prices, a firm can achieve a higher market share and thus stay in business, providing more and more jobs. Deming stressed that top management must assume the overriding responsibility for quality improvement.

Figure 3.1 The Deming Chain Reaction

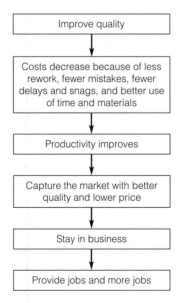

Deming's philosophy underwent many changes as he himself continued to learn. In his early work in the United States, he preached his "14 Points" (see Table 3.1), which are discussed later in the chapter. The 14 Points caused some confusion and misunderstanding among businesspeople, because Deming did not provide a clear rationale for them. Near the end of his life, however, he synthesized the underlying foundations of the 14 Points in what he called "A System of Profound Knowledge." Understanding the elements of this "system" provides critical insights needed for designing effective management practices and making decisions in today's complex business environment.

Deming's Profound Knowledge system consists of four interrelated parts:

1. Appreciation for a system
2. Understanding of variation
3. Theory of knowledge
4. Psychology

Each of these parts is explained here.

Systems We noted the importance of systems in Chapter 2. The components of any system must work together if the system is to be effective. Traditional organizations typically manage according to the functions in vertical organization charts. However, when interactions occur among the parts of a system (for instance, among functions and departments in an organization), managers cannot manage the system well by simply managing the parts in isolation; they must understand the processes that cross functional boundaries, align these processes toward a common vision or goal, and optimize their interactions. Suboptimization (doing the best for individual com-

---

Table 3.1 Deming's 14 Points

1. Create and publish to all employees a statement of the aims and purposes of the company or other organization. The management must demonstrate constantly their commitment to this statement.
2. Learn the new philosophy, top management and everybody.
3. Understand the purpose of inspection, for improvement of processes and reduction of cost.
4. End the practice of awarding business on the basis of price tag alone.
5. Improve constantly and forever the system of production and service.
6. Institute training.
7. Teach and institute leadership.
8. Drive out fear. Create trust. Create a climate for innovation.
9. Optimize toward the aims and purposes of the company the efforts of teams, groups, staff areas.
10. Eliminate exhortations for the workforce.
11. (a) Eliminate numerical quotas for production. Instead, learn and institute methods for improvement.
    (b) Eliminate MBO [management by objective]. Instead, learn the capabilities of processes and how to improve them.
12. Remove barriers that rob people of pride of workmanship.
13. Encourage education and self-improvement for everyone.
14. Take action to accomplish the transformation.

Source: Originally published in *Out of the Crisis* by W. Edwards Deming. © 1986 by The W. Edwards Deming Institute. Revised by W. Edwards Deming in January 1990. Reprinted by permission of MIT Press, pp. 23–24.

ponents) results in losses to everybody in the system. According to Deming, it is poor management, for example, to purchase materials or service at the lowest price or to minimize the cost of manufacture if it is at the expense of the system. For instance, inexpensive materials may be of such inferior quality that they will cause excessive costs in scrap and repair during manufacture and assembly. Minimizing the cost of manufacturing alone might result in products that do not meet designers' specifications and customer needs. Such situations lead to a win-lose effect. Purchasing wins, manufacturing loses; manufacturing wins, customers lose; and so on. To manage any system, managers must understand the interrelationships among the systems' components and among the people who work in it.

> *The aim of any system should be for all stakeholders—stockholders, employees, customers, community, and the environment—to benefit over the long term.*

Deming stressed that systems must be focused toward a purpose. Stockholders can realize financial benefits, employees can receive opportunities for training and education that will enhance their joy in work, customers can receive products and services that meet their needs and create satisfaction, the community can benefit from business leadership, and the environment can benefit from responsible management.

Systems thinking applies to managing people also. Pitting individuals or departments against each other for resources is self-destructive to an organization. The individuals or departments will perform to maximize their own expected gain, not that of the entire firm. Therefore, optimizing the system requires internal cooperation. Similarly, using sales quotas or arbitrary cost-reduction goals will not motivate people to improve the system and customer satisfaction; the people will perform only to meet the quotas or goals and optimize their individual rewards. Traditional performance appraisals do not consider interactions within the system. Many factors affect an individual employee's performance, including the following:

- The training received
- The information and resources provided
- The leadership of supervisors and managers
- Disruptions on the job
- Management policies and practices

Few performance appraisals recognize such factors and often place blame on individuals who have little ability to control their environment. We will discuss this situation further in Chapter 6.

Variation The second part of Profound Knowledge is a basic understanding of statistical theory and variation. We see variation everywhere, from hitting golf balls to the meals and service in a restaurant. A device called a quincunx illustrates a natural process of variation. A computer-simulated quincunx is shown in Figure 3.2.[3] In a quincunx, small balls are dropped from a hole in the top and hit a series of pins as they fall toward collection boxes. The pins cause each ball to move randomly to the left or the right as it strikes each pin on its way down. Note that most balls end up toward the middle of the box. Figure 3.3 shows the frequency distribution of where the balls landed in one simulation. Note the roughly symmetrical bell shape of the distribution. A normal distribution is bell-shaped. Even though all balls are dropped from the same position, the end result shows variation.

The same kind of variation exists in any production and service process, generally due to factors inherent in the design of the system, which cannot easily be controlled. Today, modern technology has improved our ability to produce many physical parts with very little variation; however, the variation that stems from

Figure 3.2 A Quincunx in Action

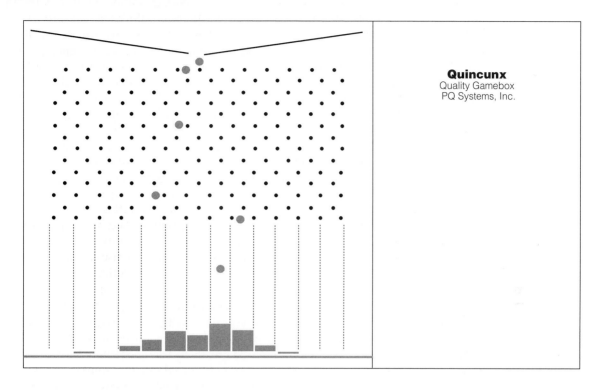

Figure 3.3 Results from a Quincunx Experiment

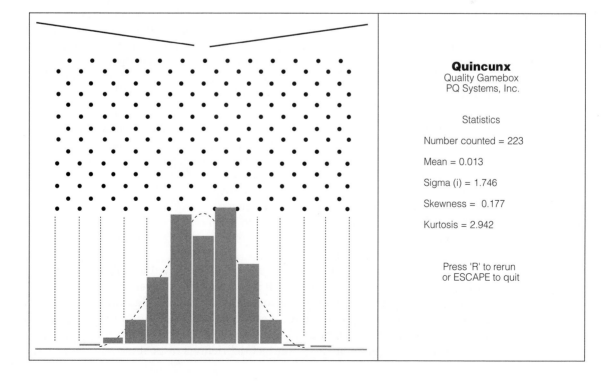

human behavior and performance continues to hamper quality efforts. Deming suggested that management first understand, and then work to reduce variation through improvements in technology, process design, and training. With less variation, both the producer and consumer benefit. The producer benefits by needing less inspection, experiencing less scrap and rework, and having more consistent human performance, resulting in higher productivity and customer satisfaction. The consumer has the advantage of knowing that all products and services have similar quality characteristics and will perform or be delivered consistently. This advantage can be especially critical when the consumer is another firm using large quantities of the product in its own manufacturing or service operations.

Statistical methods are the primary tools used to identify and quantify variation. Deming proposed that every employee in the firm be familiar with statistical techniques and other problem-solving tools. Statistics can then become the common language that every employee—from top executives to line workers—uses to communicate with one another. Its value lies in its objectivity; statistics leaves little room for ambiguity or misunderstanding. We will explore issues of variation and statistics further in Chapter 11.

> *Excessive variation results in products that fail or perform erratically and inconsistent service that does not meet customers' expectations.*

Theory of Knowledge The third part of Profound Knowledge is the "theory of knowledge," the branch of philosophy concerned with the nature and scope of knowledge, its presuppositions and basis, and the general reliability of claims to knowledge. Deming's system was influenced greatly by Clarence Irving Lewis, author of *Mind and the World,* who stated, "There is no knowledge without interpretation. If interpretation, which represents an activity of the mind, is always subject to the check of further experience, how is knowledge possible at all? . . . An argument from past to future at best is probable only, and even this probability must rest upon principles which are themselves more than probable."[4] Basically, managers need to understand how things work and why decisions that affect the future should be effective. Any rational plan, however simple, requires prediction concerning conditions, behavior, and comparison of performance, and such predictions should be grounded in theory.

For example, it is easy to learn a "cookbook" approach to statistics—being able to run a computer program or a Microsoft Excel procedure. Doing so, however, runs the risk of using the tools inappropriately. Understanding the assumptions and theory behind statistical tools and techniques is vital to applying them correctly. Countless managers use a similar cookbook approach to managing by reading the latest self-help book and blindly following the author's recommendations. Many companies jump on the latest popular approach advocated by business consultants, only to see

> *Experience only describes—it cannot be tested or validated—and alone is no help in management. Theory, on the other hand, helps one to understand cause-and-effect relationships that can be used for prediction and rational management decisions.*

the approach fail. Copying an example of success, without understanding it with theory, may lead to disaster.

Deming emphasized that knowledge is not possible without theory, and experience alone does not establish a theory. It is one reason why Deming never gave managers any "solutions" or prescriptions for achieving quality. He wanted them to learn and discover what works and what is appropriate for their individual organizations. The modern concept of organizational learning reflects the theory of knowledge. For example, many project managers conduct debriefings or postmortem reviews upon completion of projects. These reviews allow them to understand what went wrong and what went right, helping to develop a knowledge base and provide concrete information to improve in the future. Objective data and a systematic problem-solving process provide a rational basis for making decisions.

Psychology Psychology helps us understand people, interactions between people and circumstances, interactions between leaders and employees, and any system of management. It is critical to designing a work environment that promotes employee satisfaction and well-being. Much of Deming's philosophy is based on understanding human behavior and treating people fairly. People differ from one another. A true leader must be aware of these differences and work toward optimizing everybody's abilities and preferences. Most managers operate under the assumption that all people are alike. However, a true leader understands that people learn in different ways and at different speeds, and manages the system accordingly.

People are born with a need for love and esteem in their relationships with other people. Some circumstances provide people with dignity and self-esteem. Conversely, circumstances that deny people these advantages will smother intrinsic motivation. Fear does not motivate people; instead, it prevents the system from reaching its full potential. If people cannot enjoy their work, they will not be productive and focused on quality principles. Psychology helps us to nurture and preserve these positive innate attributes of people; otherwise, we resort to carrots and sticks that offer no long-term values.

People can be motivated intrinsically and extrinsically; however, the most powerful motivators are intrinsic.

One of Deming's more controversial beliefs is that pay is not a motivator, which industrial psychologists have been saying for decades. The chairman of General Motors once stated if GM doubled the salary of every employee, nothing would change. Monetary rewards are a way out for managers who do not understand how to manage intrinsic motivation. When joy in work becomes secondary to getting good ratings, employees are ruled by external forces and must act to protect what they have and avoid punishment.

Impacts of Profound Knowledge Peter Scholtes, a noted consultant, makes some salient observations about the failure to understand the components of Profound Knowledge:[5]

When people don't understand systems:

- They see events as individual incidents rather than the net result of many interactions and interdependent forces.
- They see the symptoms but not the deep causes of problems.
- They don't understand how an intervention in one part of [an organization] can cause havoc in another place or at another time.
- They blame individuals for problems even when those individuals have little or no ability to control the events around them.
- They don't understand the ancient African saying, "It takes a whole village to raise a child."

When people don't understand variation:

- They don't see trends that are occurring.
- They see trends where there are none.

- They don't know when expectations are realistic.
- They don't understand past performance so they can't predict future performance.
- They don't know the difference between prediction, forecasting, and guesswork.
- They give others credit or blame when those people are simply either lucky or unlucky, which usually occurs because people tend to attribute everything to human effort, heroics, frailty, error, or deliberate sabotage, no matter what the systemic cause.
- They are less likely to distinguish between fact and opinion.

When people don't understand psychology:

- They don't understand motivation or why people do what they do.
- They resort to carrots and sticks and other forms of induced motivation that offer no positive effect and impair the relationship between the motivator and the one being motivated.
- They don't understand the process of change and the resistance to it.
- They revert to coercive and paternalistic approaches when dealing with people.
- They create cynicism, demoralization, demotivation, guilt, resentment, burnout, craziness, and turnover.

When people don't understand the theory of knowledge:

- They don't know how to plan and accomplish learning and improvement.
- They don't understand the difference between improvement and change.
- Problems will remain unsolved, despite their best efforts.

Little of Deming's system of Profound Knowledge is original. Walter Shewhart developed the distinction between common and special causes of variation in the 1920s; business schools began to teach many of the behavioral theories to which Deming subscribed in the 1960s; management scientists refined systems theory in the 1950s through the 1970s; and scientists in all fields have long understood the relationships among prediction, observation, and theory. Deming's major contribution was to tie these concepts together in the context of business. He recognized their synergy and developed them into a unified universal theory of management.

Deming's 14 Points

Deming's 14 Points listed in Table 3.1 date back several decades to when many organizations were ruled by autocratic managers who were driven by short-term profits and who had little regard for engaging the workforce or interest in quality improvement. Deming was emphatic in his belief that these managerial practices needed a radical overhaul and proposed the 14 Points for achieving quality excellence. Although management practices today are vastly different from when Deming first began to preach his philosophy, the 14 Points still convey important insights for managers. We will briefly consider the key lessons of each.

Point 1: *Create a Vision and Demonstrate Commitment* An organization must define its values, mission, and vision of the future to provide long-term direction for its management and employees. Deming believed that businesses should not exist simply for profit; they are social entities whose basic purpose is to serve their customers and employees. To fulfill this purpose, they must take a long-term view, invest in innovation, training, and research, and take responsibility for providing jobs and improving a firm's competitive position. This responsibility lies with top management, who must show commitment.

Making a commitment to drive improvement within an organization, perhaps through a Baldrige-based or Six Sigma approach that we will discuss later in this chapter, is still difficult for managers. Even when managers have conducted a thorough assessment of their organization and know what they *need* to change, many do not effectively follow up on opportunities.[6] Reasons range from denial ("We can't be that bad!") to excuses ("We have a lot of irons on the fire right now."). Effective leadership begins with commitment, and we will revisit this issue in Chapter 5.

Point 2: *Learn the New Philosophy* Historical methods of management built on early twentieth century principles of Frederick Taylor, such as quota-driven production, work measurement, and adversarial work relationships, will not work in today's global business environment. Deming recognized this problem a long time ago and sought to change the prevailing attitudes that ignored the importance of quality improvement. Specifically, companies cannot survive if products of poor conformance quality or poor fitness for use leave their customers dissatisfied. Instead, companies must take a customer-driven approach based on mutual cooperation between labor and management and a never-ending cycle of improvement. To effectively focus on the customers' needs, everyone, from the boardroom to the stockroom, must learn the principles of quality and performance excellence.

Today, many of these principles are indeed ingrained in managers and front-line employees through training and reinforcement of organizational values. However, people change jobs and organizations generally have a short memory—both need to continually renew themselves to learn new approaches and relearn many older ones. This concept of "organizational learning" will be addressed in Chapter 9.

Point 3: *Understand Inspection* Deming knew that inspection had been the principal means for quality control; companies employed dozens or even hundreds of people who inspected for quality on a full-time basis. Routine inspection acknowledges that defects are present, but does not add value to the product. Rather, it is rarely accurate, and encourages the production of defective products by letting someone else catch and fix the problem. The rework and disposition of defective material decreases productivity and increases costs. In service industries, rework cannot be performed; external failures are the most damaging to business.

Deming encouraged workers to take responsibility for their work, rather than leave the problems for someone else down the production line. Simple statistical tools can be used to help control processes and eliminate mass inspection as the principal activity in quality control. Inspection should be used as an information-gathering tool for improvement, not as a means of "assuring" quality or blaming workers.

Today, this new role of inspection has been integrated into the quality management practices of most companies. However, few managers truly understand the concept of variation and how it affects their processes and inspection practices. By understanding and seeking to reduce variation, managers can eliminate many sources of unnecessary inspection, thus reducing non-value-added costs associated with operations.

Point 4: *Stop Making Decisions Purely on the Basis of Cost* Purchasing departments have long been driven by cost minimization and competition among suppliers without regard for quality. In 1931 Walter Shewhart noted that price has no meaning without quality.[7] Yet, by tradition, the purchasing manager's performance has been evaluated by cost. Deming recognized that the direct costs associated with poor quality materials that arise during production or during warranty periods, as well as the loss of customer goodwill, can far exceed the cost "savings" perceived by purchasing. Thus, purchasing must understand its role as a supplier to production. This relationship causes individuals to rethink the meaning of an "organizational boundary." It is not simply the four walls around the production floor. The supplier and manufacturer must be considered as a "macro organization."

Deming also urged businesses to establish long-term relationships with fewer suppliers, leading to loyalty and opportunities for mutual improvement. Management previously justified multiple suppliers for reasons such as providing protection against strikes or natural disasters, while ignoring "hidden" costs such as increased travel to visit suppliers, loss of volume discounts, increased setup charges resulting in higher unit costs, and increased inventory and administrative expense. Most importantly, constantly changing suppliers solely on the basis of price increases the variation in the material supplied to production, because each supplier's process is different. In contrast, a reduced supply base decreases the variation coming into the process, thus reducing scrap, rework, and the need for adjustment to accommodate this variation. A long-term relationship strengthens the supplier-customer bond, allows the supplier to produce in greater quantity, improves communication with the customer, and therefore enhances opportunities for process improvement. Suppliers know that only quality goods are acceptable if they want to maintain a long-term relationship.

Today's emphasis on supply chain management (SCM) reflects the achievement of Point 4. SCM focuses heavily on a system's view of the supply chain with the objective of minimizing total supply chain costs and developing stronger partnerships with suppliers.

Point 5: *Improve Constantly and Forever* Improvements are necessary in both design and operations. Improved design of goods and services comes from understanding customer needs and continual market surveys and other sources of feedback, and from understanding the manufacturing and service delivery process. Improvements in operations are achieved by reducing the causes and impacts of variation, and engaging all employees to innovate and seek ways of doing their jobs more efficiently and effectively. When quality improves, productivity improves and costs decrease, as the Deming chain reaction (Figure 3.1) suggests.

Traditionally, continuous improvement was not a common business practice; today it is recognized as a necessary means for survival in a highly competitive and global business environment. Quality improvement will be discussed extensively in Part III of this book. The tools for improvement are constantly evolving, and organizations need to ensure that their employees understand and apply them effectively, which requires training, the focus of the next Point.

Point 6: *Institute Training* People are an organization's most valuable resource; they want to do a good job, but they often do not know how. Management must take responsibility for helping them. Not only does training result in improvements in quality and productivity, but it adds to worker morale, and demonstrates to workers that the company is dedicated to helping them and investing in their future. In addition, training reduces barriers between workers and supervisors, giving both more incentive to improve further. For example, at Honda of America in Marysville, Ohio, all employees start out on the production floor, regardless of their job classification.

Training must transcend such basic job skills as running a machine or following the script when talking to customers. Training should include tools for diagnosing, analyzing, and solving quality problems and identifying improvement opportunities. Today, many companies have excellent training programs for technology related to direct production, but still fail to enrich the ancillary skills of their workforce. Here is where some of the most lucrative opportunities exist to make an impact on key business results.

Point 7: *Institute Leadership* Deming recognized that one of biggest impediments to improvement was a lack of leadership. The job of management is leadership, not supervision. Supervision is simply overseeing and directing work; leadership means providing guidance to help employees do their jobs better with less effort. In many companies, supervisors know little about the job itself because the position is often used as an entry-level job for college graduates. The supervisors have never worked in the department and cannot train the workers, so their principal responsibility is to get the product out the door. Supervision should provide the link between management and the workforce. Good supervisors are not police or paperpushers, but rather coaches, helping workers to do a better job and develop their skills. Leadership can help to eliminate the element of fear from the job and encourage teamwork.

Leadership was, is, and will continue to be a challenging issue in every organization, particularly as new generations of managers replace those who have learned to lead. Thus, this Point of Deming's will always be relevant to organizations.

Point 8: *Drive Out Fear* Driving out fear underlies many of Deming's 14 Points. Fear is manifested in many ways: fear of reprisal, fear of failure, fear of the unknown, fear of relinquishing control, and fear of change. No system can work without the mutual respect of managers and workers. Workers are often afraid to report quality problems because they might not meet their quotas, their incentive pay might be reduced, or they might be blamed for problems in the system. One of Deming's classic stories involved a foreman who would not stop production to repair a worn-out piece of machinery. Stopping production would mean missing his daily quota. He said nothing, and the machine failed, causing the line to shut down for four days. Managers are also afraid to cooperate with other departments, because the other managers might receive higher performance ratings and bonuses, or because they fear takeovers or reorganizations. Fear encourages short-term thinking.

Managers fear losing power. One example is presented by Bushe.[8] After a statistical quality control program was implemented in an automotive plant, worker groups were sometimes able to offer better advice about system improvements than the corporate engineering staff, which ran counter to the plant's well-established culture. Middle managers were no longer the "experts." Their fear diminished their support for the program, which was eventually eliminated.

Fear is a cultural issue for all organizations. Creating a culture without fear, as we will discuss in Chapter 9, is a slow process but can be destroyed in an instant with a transition of leadership and a change in corporate policies. Therefore, today's managers need to continue to be sensitive to the impact that fear can have on their organizations.

Point 9: *Optimize the Efforts of Teams* Teamwork helps to break down barriers between departments and individuals. Barriers between functional areas occur when managers fear they might lose power. Internal competition for raises and performance ratings contributes to building barriers. The lack of cooperation leads to poor quality because other departments cannot understand what their internal customers want and do not get what they need from their internal suppliers.

Perhaps the biggest barrier to team efforts in the United States results from issues between union and management. With some notable exceptions, the history of labor/management relations in U.S. firms has been largely adversarial. Lack of sensitivity to worker needs, exploitation of workers, and poor management practices and policies frequently resulted in strained relations between managers and their subordinates. Labor leaders also must bear their share of the blame. They resisted many management efforts to reduce rigid, rule-based tasks, preferring to adhere to the structured approaches rooted in Frederick W. Taylor's historical principles of scientific management.[9]

Despite occasional efforts to promote labor/management cooperation and attempts to find common ground for employee involvement and participation initiatives, managers remain skeptical that unions and union members will contribute their best efforts. Unions still seem to hold a core belief that management is trying to undercut their power and is working to eliminate the union via direct work initiatives that appeal to workers. Downturns in the economy, which put pressure on management to reduce costs by downsizing or seeking union "give-backs," also undercut gains in cooperation and labor/management trust levels that may have been realized in more prosperous periods.

A recent example involved four unions at a Canadian hospital. A two-stage quality improvement (QI) initiative was introduced that involved a TQ effort and a reengineering campaign. Union leaders' responses to QI were found to be closely related to the extent to which the leaders perceived QI as a threat to their vested interests in union survival and protecting members' well-being. The researchers found that the development of more positive shared relationships between the QI implementation team and the union was affected by the extent to which the unions and management accommodated each other's vested interests and by the parties' balance of power. This illustration shows that training and employee involvement are important means of removing such barriers.[10] We will discuss these issues in greater detail in Chapter 6.

Point 10: *Eliminate Exhortations* Many early attempts to improve quality focused solely on behavioral change. However, posters, slogans, and motivational programs calling for Zero Defects, Do It Right the First Time, Improve Productivity and Quality, and so on, are directed at the wrong people. They assume that all quality problems are due to human behavior and that workers can improve simply through motivational methods. Workers become frustrated when they cannot improve or are penalized for defects.

Motivational approaches overlook the major source of many problems—the system. Causes of variation stemming from the design of the system are management's problem, not the workers'. If anything, workers' attempts to fix problems only increase the variation. Improvement occurs by understanding the nature of special and common causes. Thus, statistical thinking and training, not slogans, are the best routes to improving quality. Motivation can be better achieved from trust and leadership than from slogans and goals.

Point 11: *Eliminate Numerical Quotas and Management by Objective (MBO)* Many organizations manage by the numbers. Measurement has been, and often still is, used punitively. Standards and quotas are born of short-term perspectives and create fear. They do not encourage improvement, particularly if rewards or performance appraisals are tied to meeting quotas. Workers may short-cut quality to reach the goal. Once a standard is reached, little incentive remains for workers to continue production or to improve quality; they will do no more than they are asked to do.

Arbitrary management goals, such as increasing sales by 5 percent next year or decreasing costs next quarter by 10 percent, have no meaning without a method to achieve them. Deming acknowledged that goals are useful, but numerical goals set for others without incorporating a method to reach the goal generate frustration and resentment. Further, variation in the system year-to-year or quarter-to-quarter—a 5 percent increase or a 6 percent decrease, for example—makes comparisons meaningless. Management must understand the system and continually try to improve it, rather than focus on short-term goals.

Point 12: *Remove Barriers to Pride in Workmanship* People on the factory floor and even in management were often treated as, in Deming's words, "a commodity." Factory workers are given monotonous tasks, provided with inferior machines, tools, or materials, told to run defective items to meet sales pressures, and report to supervisors who know nothing about the job. Salaried employees are expected to work evenings and weekends to make up for cost-cutting measures that resulted in layoffs of their colleagues. Many are given the title of "management" so that overtime need not be paid. Even employees in the quality profession are not immune.[11] An inspection technician stated, "This profession always seems to end up being called the troublemakers." A quality engineer stated, "The managers over me now give little direction, are very resistant to change, and do little to advance their people." A quality supervisor said, "Someone less qualified could perform my job . . . for less money." How can these individuals take pride in their work? Many cannot be certain they will have a job next year.

Deming believed that one of the biggest barriers to pride in workmanship is performance appraisal. Performance appraisal destroys teamwork by promoting competition for limited resources, fosters mediocrity because objectives typically are driven by numbers and what the boss wants rather than by quality, focuses on the short term and discourages risk taking, and confounds the "people resources" with other resources. If all individuals are working within the system, then they should not be singled out of the system to be ranked. Some people have to be "below average," which can only result in frustration if those individuals are working within the confines of the system. Deming sorted performance into three categories: the majority of performances that are within the system, performances outside the system on the superior side, and performances outside the system on the inferior side. Statistical methods provide the basis for these classifications. Superior performers should be compensated specially; inferior performers need extra training or replacement.

Although many companies will not eliminate performance appraisals completely, some have made substantial changes. Many now separate performance appraisal from annual salary reviews, using appraisal to recognize accomplishment of results and the use of quality processes. We will have more to say about this issue in Chapter 6.

Point 13: *Encourage Education and Self-Improvement* The difference between this Point and Point 6 is subtle. Point 6 refers to training in specific job skills; Point 13 refers to continuing, broad education for self-development. Organizations must invest in their people at all levels to ensure success in the long term. A fundamental mission of business is to provide jobs as stated in Point 1, but business and society also have the responsibility to improve the value of the individual. Developing the worth of the individual is a powerful motivation method.

Today, many companies understand that elevating the general knowledge base of their workforce—outside of specific job skills—returns many benefits. However, others still view this task as a cost that can be easily cut when financial trade-offs must be made.

Point 14: *Take Action* Any cultural change begins with top management and includes everyone. Changing an organizational culture generally meets with skepticism and resistance that many firms find difficult to deal with, particularly when many of the traditional management practices Deming felt must be eliminated are deeply ingrained in the organization's culture. We will discuss this challenge more in Chapter 9.

Many people have criticized Deming because his philosophy is just that: a philosophy. It lacks specific direction and prescriptive approaches and does not fit into the traditional American business culture. As we noted earlier, Deming did not propose specific methods for implementation because he wanted people to study his ideas and derive their own approaches. As he often stated, "There is no instant pudding." Despite the controversy, many firms organized their quality approaches around Deming's philosophy. Some companies, such as 1991 Baldrige Award winner Zytec Corporation, now a part of Artesyn Technologies, met with great success. Another example is Hillerich & Bradsby.[12]

Quality Spotlight
Hillerich &
Bradsby

Hillerich & Bradsby Co. (H&B) has been making the Louisville Slugger brand of baseball bat for more than 115 years. In the mid-1980s, the company faced significant challenges from market changes and competition. CEO Jack Hillerich attended a four-day Deming seminar, which provided the basis for the company's current quality efforts. Returning from the seminar, Hillerich decided to see what changes that Deming advocated were possible in an old company with an old union and a history of labor/management problems. Hillerich persuaded union officials to attend another Deming seminar with five senior managers. Following the seminar, a core group of union and management people developed a strategy to change the company. They talked about building trust and changing to system "to make it something you want to work in." Employees were interested, but skeptical. To demonstrate their commitment, managers examined Deming's 14 Points, and picked several they believed they could make progress on through actions that would demonstrate a serious intention to change. One of the first changes was the elimination of work quotas that were tied to hourly salaries and a schedule of warnings and penalties for failures to meet quotas. Instead, a team-based approach was initiated. Although only a few workers took advantage of the change, overall productivity actually improved as rework decreased because workers were taking pride in their work to produce things the right way first. H&B also eliminated performance appraisals and commission-based pay in sales. The company also focused its efforts on training and education, resulting in an openness for change and capacity for teamwork. Today, the Deming philosophy is still the core of H&B's guiding principles.

Deming's legacy lives on through the W. Edwards Deming Institute (http://deming.org).

THE JURAN PHILOSOPHY

Joseph Juran (1904–) was born in Romania and came to the United States in 1912. He joined Western Electric in the 1920s as it pioneered in the development of statistical methods for quality. He spent much of his time as a corporate industrial engineer and, in 1951, did most of the writing, editing, and publishing of the *Quality Control Handbook*. This book, one of the most comprehensive quality manuals ever written, has been revised several times and continues to be a popular reference.

Like Deming, Juran taught quality principles to the Japanese in the 1950s and was a principal force in their quality reorganization. Juran also echoed Deming's conclusion that U.S. businesses face a major crisis in quality due to the huge costs of poor quality and the loss of sales to foreign competition. Both men felt that the solution to this crisis depends on new thinking about quality that includes all levels of the managerial hierarchy. Upper management in particular requires training and experience in managing for quality.

Unlike Deming, however, Juran did not propose a major cultural change in the organization, but rather sought to improve quality by working within the system familiar to managers. Thus, his programs were designed to fit into a company's current strategic business planning with minimal risk of rejection. He argued that employees at different levels of an organization speak in their own "languages." (Deming, on the other hand, believed statistics should be the common language.) Juran stated that top management speaks in the language of dollars; workers speak in the language of things; and middle management must be able to speak both languages and translate between dollars and things. Thus, to get top management's attention, quality issues must be cast in the language they understand—dollars. Hence, Juran advocated the use of quality cost accounting and analysis to focus attention on quality problems. At the operational level, Juran focused on increasing conformance to specifications through elimination of defects, supported extensively by statistical tools for analysis. Thus, his philosophy fit well into existing management systems.

Juran proposed a simple definition of quality: "fitness for use."

Juran's definition of quality suggests that it should be viewed from both external and internal perspectives; that is, quality is related to "(1) product performance that results in customer satisfaction; (2) freedom from product deficiencies, which avoids customer dissatisfaction." How products and services are designed, manufactured and delivered, and serviced in the field all contribute to fitness for use. Thus, the pursuit of quality is viewed on two levels: (1) the mission of the firm as a whole is to achieve high design quality; and (2) the mission of each department in the firm is to achieve high-conformance quality. Like Deming, Juran advocated a never-ending spiral of activities that includes market research, product development, design, planning for manufacture, purchasing, production process control, inspection and testing, and sales, followed by customer feedback. The interdependency of these functions emphasizes the need for competent companywide quality management. Senior management must play an active and enthusiastic leadership role in the quality management process.

Juran's prescriptions focus on three major quality processes, called the **Quality Trilogy:** (1) *quality planning*—the process of preparing to meet quality goals; (2) *quality control*—the process of meeting quality goals during operations; and (3) *quality improvement*—the process of breaking through to unprecedented levels of performance. At the time he proposed this structure, few companies were engaging in any significant planning or improvement activities. Thus, Juran was promoting a major cultural shift in management thinking.

Quality planning begins with identifying customers, both external and internal, determining their needs, translating customer needs into specifications, developing product features that respond to those needs, and developing the processes capable of producing the product or delivering the service. Thus, like Deming, Juran wanted employees to know who uses their products, whether in the next department or in another organization. Quality goals based on meeting the needs of customers and suppliers alike at a minimum combined cost are then established. Next, the process that can produce the product to satisfy customers' needs and meet quality goals under operating conditions must be designed. Strategic planning for quality— similar to the firm's financial planning process—determines short-term and long-term goals, sets priorities, compares results with previous plans, and meshes the plans with other corporate strategic objectives.

As a parallel to Deming's emphasis on identifying and reducing sources of variation, Juran stated that quality control involves determining what to control, establishing units of measurement to evaluate data objectively, establishing standards of performance, measuring actual performance, interpreting the difference between actual performance and the standard, and taking action on the difference.

Unlike Deming, however, Juran specified a detailed program for quality improvement. Such a program involves proving the need for improvement, identifying specific projects for improvement, organizing support for the projects, diagnosing the causes, providing remedies for the causes, proving that the remedies are effective under operating conditions, and providing control to maintain improvements. Juran's approach is reflected in the practices of a wide variety of organizations today.

Many aspects of the Juran and Deming philosophies are similar. The focus on top management commitment, the need for improvement, the use of quality control techniques, and the importance of training are fundamental to both philosophies. However, they did not agree on all points. For instance, Juran believed that Deming was wrong to tell management to drive out fear. According to Juran, "Fear can bring out the best in people."[13] The Juran Institute, founded by Dr. Juran, provides substantial training in the form of seminars, videotapes, and other materials (http://www.juran.com).

THE CROSBY PHILOSOPHY

Philip B. Crosby (1926–2001) was corporate vice president for quality at International Telephone and Telegraph (ITT) for 14 years after working his way up from line inspector. After leaving ITT, he established Philip Crosby Associates in 1979 to develop and offer training programs. He also authored several popular books. His first book, *Quality Is Free*, sold about 1 million copies and was largely responsible for bringing quality to the attention of top corporate managers in the United States. The essence of Crosby's quality philosophy is embodied in what he calls the "Absolutes of Quality Management" and the "Basic Elements of Improvement." Crosby's Absolutes of Quality Management include the following points:

- *Quality means conformance to requirements, not elegance.* Crosby quickly dispels the myth that quality follows the transcendent definition discussed in Chapter 1. Requirements must be clearly stated so that they cannot be misunderstood. Requirements act as communication devices and are ironclad. Once requirements are established, then one can take measurements to determine conformance to those requirements. The nonconformance detected is the absence of quality. Quality problems become nonconformance problems, that is, variation in output. Setting requirements is the responsibility of management. Crosby maintained that once the requirements are specified, quality is judged solely on whether they have been met. Therefore these requirements must be clearly defined by management and not left by default to front-line personnel.
- *There is no such thing as a quality problem.* Problems must be identified by those individuals or departments that cause them. Thus, a firm may experience accounting problems, manufacturing problems, design problems, front-desk problems, and so on. In other words, quality originates in functional departments, not in the quality department, and therefore the burden of responsibility for such problems falls on these functional departments. The quality department should measure conformance, report results, and lead the drive to develop a positive attitude toward quality improvement. This Absolute is similar to Deming's third Point.

- *There is no such thing as the economics of quality; doing the job right the first time is always cheaper.* Crosby supports the premise that "economics of quality" has no meaning. Quality is free. What costs money are all actions that involve not doing jobs right the first time. The Deming chain reaction sends a similar message.
- *The only performance measurement is the cost of quality, which is the expense of nonconformance.* Crosby noted that most companies spend 15 to 20 percent of their sales dollars on quality costs. A company with a well-run quality management program can achieve a cost of quality that is less than 2.5 percent of sales, primarily in the prevention and appraisal categories. Crosby's program calls for measuring and publicizing the cost of poor quality. Quality cost data are useful to call problems to management's attention, to select opportunities for corrective action, and to track quality improvement over time. Such data provide visible proof of improvement and recognition of achievement. Juran supported this approach.
- *The only performance standard is "Zero Defects (ZD)."* Crosby felt that the Zero Defects concept is widely misunderstood and resisted. Many thought it to be a motivational program. It is described as follows:

> *Zero Defects is a performance standard. It is the standard of the craftsperson regardless of his or her assignment. . . . The theme of ZD is do it right the first time. That means concentrating on preventing defects rather than just finding and fixing them.*
>
> *People are conditioned to believe that error is inevitable; thus they not only accept error, they anticipate it. It does not bother us to make a few errors in our work . . . to err is human. We all have our own standards in business or academic life—our own points at which errors begin to bother us. It is good to get an A in school, but it may be OK to pass with a C.*
>
> *We do not maintain these standards, however, when it comes to our personal life. If we did, we should expect to be shortchanged every now and then when we cash our paycheck; we should expect hospital nurses to drop a constant percentage of newborn babies. . . . We as individuals do not tolerate these things. We have a dual standard: one for ourselves and one for our work.*
>
> *Most human error is caused by lack of attention rather than lack of knowledge. Lack of attention is created when we assume that error is inevitable. If we consider this condition carefully, and pledge ourselves to make a constant conscious effort to do our jobs right the first time, we will take a giant step toward eliminating the waste of rework, scrap, and repair that increases cost and reduces individual opportunity.*[14]

Juran and Deming, on the other hand, would point out the uselessness, or even hypocrisy of exhorting a line worker to produce perfection because the overwhelming majority of imperfections stems from poorly designed manufacturing systems beyond the workers' control.

Crosby's Basic Elements of Improvement were *determination, education,* and *implementation.* Determination means that top management must take quality improvement seriously. Everyone should understand the Absolutes, which can be accomplished only through education. Finally, every member of the management team must understand the implementation process.

Unlike Juran and Deming, Crosby's approach was primarily behavioral. He emphasized using management and organizational processes rather than statistical techniques to change corporate culture and attitudes. Like Juran and unlike Deming however, his approach fit well within existing organizational structures.

COMPARISONS OF QUALITY PHILOSOPHIES

Despite their significant differences to implementing organizational change, the philosophies of Deming, Juran, and Crosby are more alike than different. Each views quality as imperative in the future competitiveness in global markets; makes top management commitment an absolute necessity; demonstrates that quality management practices will save, not cost money; places responsibility for quality on management, not the workers; stresses the need for continuous, never-ending improvement; acknowledges the importance of the customer and strong management/worker partnerships; and recognizes the need for and difficulties associated with changing the organizational culture.

The individual nature of business firms complicates the strict application of any one specific philosophy. Although each of these philosophies can be highly effective, a firm must first understand the nature and differences of the philosophies and then develop a quality management approach tailored to its individual organization. Any approach should include goals and objectives, allocation of responsibilities, a measurement system and description of tools to be employed, an outline of the management style that will be used, and a strategy for implementation. After taking these steps, the management team is responsible for leading the organization through successful execution. We address these issues further in Chapter 9.

OTHER QUALITY PHILOSOPHERS

Other notable figures in the quality arena include A. V. Feigenbaum and Kaoru Ishikawa. Feigenbaum and Ishikawa were both awarded the title of Honorary Members of the American Society for Quality in 1986.[15] At that time the society had only four living honorary members, two of whom were W. Edwards Deming and Joseph M. Juran. Obviously, the title of "Honorary Member" is not given lightly by the ASQ. In this section we briefly review the accomplishments that made them part of this elite group, and also introduce another influential thinker in the quality movement, Genichi Taguchi.

A. V. Feigenbaum

A. V. Feigenbaum's career in quality began more than 40 years ago. For 10 years, he was the manager of worldwide manufacturing and quality control at General Electric. In 1968 he founded General Systems Company of Pittsfield, Massachusetts, and serves as its president. Feigenbaum has traveled and spoken to various audiences and groups around the world over the years. He was elected as the founding chairman of the board of the International Academy of Quality, which has attracted active participation from the European Organization for Quality Control, the Union of Japanese Scientists and Engineers (JUSE), as well as the American Society for Quality.

Feigenbaum is best known for coining the phrase **total quality control**, which he defined as ". . . an effective system for integrating the quality development, quality maintenance, and quality improvement efforts of the various groups in an organization so as to enable production and service at the most economical levels which allow full customer satisfaction." His book *Total Quality Control* was first published in 1951 under the title *Quality Control: Principles, Practice, and Administration*. He viewed quality as a strategic business tool that requires involvement from everyone in the organization, and promoted the use of quality costs as a measurement and evaluation tool.

Feigenbaum's philosophy is summarized in his Three Steps to Quality:

1. *Quality Leadership:* A continuous management emphasis is grounded on sound planning rather than reaction to failures. Management must maintain a constant focus and lead the quality effort.
2. *Modern Quality Technology:* The traditional quality department cannot resolve 80 to 90 percent of quality problems. This task requires the integration of office staff as well as engineers and shop-floor workers in the process who continually evaluate and implement new techniques to satisfy customers in the future.
3. *Organizational Commitment:* Continuous training and motivation of the entire workforce as well as an integration of quality in business planning indicate the importance of quality and provide the means for including it in all aspects of the firm's activities.

The Japanese latched on to this concept of total quality control as the foundation for their practice called companywide quality control (CWQC), which began in the 1960s. Feigenbaum also popularized the term *hidden factory,* which described the portion of plant capacity wasted due to poor quality. Many of his ideas remain embedded in contemporary thinking, and have become important elements of the Malcolm Baldrige National Quality Award criteria. These aspects include the principles that the customer is the judge of quality; quality and innovation are interrelated and mutually beneficial; managing quality is the same as managing the business; quality is a continuous process of improvement; and customers and suppliers should be involved the process.

Kaoru Ishikawa

An early pioneer in the quality revolution in Japan, Kaoru Ishikawa was the foremost figure in Japanese quality until his death in 1989. He was instrumental in the development of the broad outlines of Japanese quality strategy, and without his leadership, the Japanese quality movement would not enjoy the worldwide acclaim and success that it has today. Dr. Ishikawa was a professor of engineering at Tokyo University for many years. As a member of the editorial review board for the Japanese journal *Quality Control for Foremen,* founded in 1962, and later as the chief executive director of the QC Circle Headquarters at the Union of Japanese Scientists and Engineers (JUSE), Dr. Ishikawa influenced the development of a participative, bottom-up view of quality, which became the trademark of the Japanese approach to quality management. However, Ishikawa was also able to get the attention of top management and persuade them that a companywide approach to quality control was necessary for total success.

Ishikawa built on Feigenbaum's concept of total quality and promoted greater involvement by all employees, from the top management to the front-line staff, by reducing reliance on quality professionals and quality departments. He advocated collecting and analyzing factual data using simple visual tools, statistical techniques, and teamwork as the foundations for implementing total quality. Like others, Ishikawa believed that quality begins with the customer and therefore, understanding customers' needs is the basis for improvement, and that complaints should be actively sought. Some key elements of his philosophy are summarized here.

1. Quality begins with education and ends with education.
2. The first step in quality is to know the requirements of customers.
3. The ideal state of quality control occurs when inspection is no longer necessary.
4. Remove the root cause, not the symptoms.

5. Quality control is the responsibility of all workers and all divisions.
6. Do not confuse the means with the objectives.
7. Put quality first and set your sights on long-term profits.
8. Marketing is the entrance and exit of quality.
9. Top management must not show anger when facts are presented by subordinates.
10. Ninety-five percent of problems in a company can be solved with simple tools for analysis and problem solving.
11. Data without dispersion information (i.e., variability) are false data.

Genichi Taguchi

A Japanese engineer, Genichi Taguchi—whose philosophy was strongly advocated by Deming—explained the economic value of reducing variation. Taguchi maintained that the manufacturing-based definition of quality as conformance to specification limits is inherently flawed. For example, suppose that a specification for some quality characteristic is 0.500 ± 0.020. Using this definition, the actual value of the quality characteristic can fall anywhere in a range from 0.480 to 0.520. This approach assumes that the customer, either the consumer or the next department in the production process, would accept any value within the 0.480 to 0.520 range, but not be satisfied with a value outside this tolerance range. Also, this approach assumes that costs do not depend on the actual value of the quality characteristic as long as it falls within the tolerance specified (see Figure 3.4).

But what is the real difference between 0.479 and 0.481? The former would be considered as "out of specification" and either reworked or scrapped while the latter would be acceptable. Actually, the impact of either value on the performance characteristic of the product would be about the same. Neither value is close to the nominal specification 0.500. The nominal specification is the ideal target value for the critical quality characteristic. Taguchi's approach assumes that the smaller the variation about the nominal specification, the better is the quality. In turn, products are more consistent, and total costs are less. The following example supports this notion.

The Japanese newspaper *Ashai* published an example comparing the cost and quality of Sony televisions at two plants in Japan and San Diego.[16] The color density of all the units produced at the San Diego plant were within specifications, while some of those shipped from the Japanese plant were not (see Figure 3.5). However, the average loss per unit of the San Diego plant was $0.89 greater than that of the Japanese plant. This increased cost occurred because workers adjusted units that were out of specification at the San Diego plant, adding cost to the process. Furthermore, a unit adjusted to minimally meet specifications was more likely to generate customer complaints than a unit close to the original target value, therefore incurring

---

Figure 3.4 Traditional Economic View of Conformance to Specifications

Figure 3.5 Variation in U.S.-Made Versus Japanese-Made Television Components

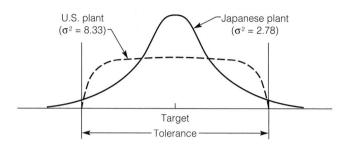

higher field service costs. Figure 3.5 shows that fewer U.S.-produced sets met the target value for color density. The distribution of quality in the Japanese plant was more uniform around the target value, and though some units were out of specification, the total cost was less. Taguchi measured quality as the variation from the target value of a design specification, and then translated that variation into an economic "loss function" that expresses the cost of variation in monetary terms. We will discuss the mathematics of this approach in Chapter 12.

Taguchi also contributed to improving engineering approaches to product design. By designing a product that is insensitive to variation in manufacture, specification limits become meaningless. He advocated certain techniques of experimental design to identify the most important design variables in order to minimize the effects of uncontrollable factors on product variation. Thus, his approaches attacked quality problems early in the design stage rather than reacting to problems that might arise later in production.

QUALITY MANAGEMENT AWARDS AND FRAMEWORKS

The philosophies of Deming, Juran, Crosby, and others provide much guidance and wisdom in the form of "best practices" to managers around the world, leading to the development of numerous awards and certifications for recognizing effective application of TQ principles. Although awards justifiably recognize only a select few, the award or certification criteria provide frameworks for managing from which every organization can benefit. The two frameworks that have had the most impact on quality management practices worldwide are the U.S. Malcolm Baldrige National Quality Award and international ISO 9000 certification process. Recently, the concept of Six Sigma has evolved into a unique framework for managing quality.

THE MALCOLM BALDRIGE NATIONAL QUALITY AWARD

In Chapter 1 we noted that the Malcolm Baldrige National Quality Award (MBNQA) has been one of the most powerful catalysts of total quality in the United States, and indeed, throughout the world. More importantly, the award's *Criteria for Performance Excellence* establish a framework for integrating total quality principles and practices in any organization. This framework provides the foundation for much of the next six chapters. In this section we present an overview of the MBNQA, its criteria, and the award process.

History and Purpose

Recognizing that U.S. productivity was declining, President Reagan signed legislation mandating a national study/conference on productivity in October 1982. The American Productivity and Quality Center (formerly the American Productivity Center) sponsored seven computer networking conferences in 1983 to prepare for an upcoming White House Conference on Productivity. The final report on these conferences recommended that "a National Quality Award, similar to the Deming Prize (discussed later in this chapter) in Japan, be awarded annually to those firms that successfully challenge and meet the award requirements. These requirements and the accompanying examination process should be very similar to the Deming Prize system to be effective." The Malcolm Baldrige National Quality Improvement Act was signed into law (Public Law 100-107) on August 20, 1987. The focus of the program was defined as follows:

- Helping to stimulate American companies to improve quality and productivity for the pride of recognition while obtaining a competitive edge through increased profits;
- Recognizing the achievements of those companies that improve the quality of their goods and services and providing an example to others;
- Establishing guidelines and criteria that can be used by business, industrial, governmental, and other enterprises in evaluating their own quality improvement efforts; and
- Providing specific guidance for other American enterprises that wish to learn how to manage for high quality by making available detailed information on how winning enterprises were able to change their cultures and achieve eminence.

The award is named after President Reagan's Secretary of Commerce, who was killed in an accident shortly before the Senate acted on the legislation. Malcolm Baldrige was highly regarded by world leaders, having played a major role in carrying out the administration's trade policy, resolving technology transfer differences with China and India, and holding the first Cabinet-level talks with the Soviet Union in seven years, which paved the way for increased access for U.S. firms in the Soviet market. Up to three companies can now receive an award in each of the original categories of manufacturing, small business, and service (prior to 1999, only two). Congress approved award categories in nonprofit education and health care in 1999. Table 3.2 shows the recipients through 2003.

The award has evolved into a comprehensive National Quality Program, administered through the National Institute of Standards and Technology in Gaithersburg, Maryland, of which the Baldrige Award is only one part. The National Quality Program is a public–private partnership, funded primarily through a private foundation. The program's Web site at www.baldrige.org provides current information about the award, the performance criteria, award winners, and a variety of other information.

The Criteria for Performance Excellence

The award examination is based upon a rigorous set of criteria, called the *Criteria for Performance Excellence*, designed to encourage companies to enhance their competitiveness through an aligned approach to organizational performance management that results in:

1. Delivery of ever-improving value to customers, resulting in improved marketplace success
2. Improvement of overall company performance and capabilities
3. Organizational and personal learning

Table 3.2 Malcolm Baldrige Award Recipients

Year	Manufacturing	Small Business	Service
1988	Motorola, Inc. Westinghouse Commercial Nuclear Fuel Division	Globe Metallurgical, Inc.	
1989	Xerox Corp. Business Products and Systems Milliken & Co.		
1990	Cadillac Motor Car Division IBM Rochester	Wallace Co., Inc.	Federal Express (FedEx)
1991	Solectron Corp. Zytec Corp. (now part of Artesyn Technologies)	Marlow Industries	
1992	AT&T Network Systems (now Lucent Technologies, Inc., Optical Networking Group) Texas Instruments Defense Systems & Electronics Group (now part of Raytheon Systems Co.)	Granite Rock Co.	AT&T Universal Card Services (now part of Citigroup) The Ritz-Carlton Hotel Co. (now part of Marriott International)
1993	Eastman Chemical Co.	Ames Rubber Corp.	
1994		Wainwright Industries, Inc.	AT&T Consumer Communication Services (now the Consumer Markets Division of AT&T) Verizon Information Services (formerly GTE Directories, Inc.)
1995	Armstrong World Industries Building Products Operations Corning Telecommunications Products Division		
1996	ADAC Laboratories	Custom Research Inc. Trident Precision Manufacturing, Inc.	Dana Commercial Credit Corp.
1997	3M Dental Products Division Solectron Corp.		Merrill Lynch Credit Corp. Xerox Business Services
1998	Boeing Airlift and Tanker Programs Solar Turbines, Inc.	Texas Nameplate Company, Inc.	
1999	STMicroelectronics, Inc.–Region Americas	Sunny Fresh Foods	BI The Ritz-Carlton Hotel Company, L.L.C.

Continued

Table 3.2 Malcolm Baldrige Award Recipients *(continued)*

Year	Manufacturing	Small Business	Service
2000	Dana Corporation–Spicer Driveshaft Division (now Torque Traction Technologies, Inc.) KARLEE Company	Los Alamos National Bank	Operations Management International, Inc.
2001	Clarke American Checks, Inc.		Pal's Sudden Service
2002	Motorola, Inc. Commercial, Government and Industrial Solutions Sector		Branch-Smith Printing Division
2003	Medrad, Inc.	Stoner, Inc.	Boeing Aerospace Support Caterpillar Financial Services Corp. (U.S.)

Year	Healthcare	Education
2001		Chugach School District Pearl River School District University of Wisconsin–Stout
2002	SSM Health Care	
2003	Baptist Hospital, Inc. Pensacola, FL Saint Luke's Hospital of Kansas City	Community Consolidated School District #15, Palatine, IL

The criteria consist of a hierarchical set of categories, items, and areas to address. The seven categories are as follows:

1. *Leadership:* This category examines how an organization's senior leaders address values, directions, and performance expectations, as well as a focus on customers and other stakeholders, empowerment, innovation, and learning. Also examined are an organization's governance and how the organization addresses its public and community responsibilities.
2. *Strategic Planning:* This category examines how an organization develops strategic objectives and action plans. Also examined is how the chosen objectives and plans are deployed and how progress is measured.
3. *Customer and Market Focus:* This category examines how an organization determines requirements, expectations, and preferences of customers and markets. Also examined is how the organization builds relationships with customers and

determines the key factors that lead to customer acquisition, satisfaction, loyalty and retention, and to business expansion.

4. *Measurement, Analysis, and Knowledge Management:* This category examines how an organization selects, gathers, analyzes, manages, and improves its data, information, and knowledge assets.

5. *Human Resource Focus:* This category examines how an organization's work systems and employee learning and motivation enable employees to develop and utilize their full potential in alignment with the organization's overall objectives and action plans. Also examined are the organization's efforts to build and maintain a work environment and employee support climate conducive to performance excellence and to personal and organizational growth.

6. *Process Management:* This category examines the key aspects of an organization's process management, including key product, service, and business processes for creating customer and organizational value, and key support processes involving all work units.

7. *Business Results:* This category examines an organization's performance and improvement in key business areas—customer satisfaction, product and service performance, financial and marketplace performance, human resource results, operational performance, and governance and social responsibility. Also examined are performance levels relative to competitors.

The 2003 criteria can be found on the CD-ROM accompanying this book, and it will be used in various cases and exercises. We encourage you to read the entire document for clarifying notes and explanations. Also, slightly different versions of the criteria are written for education and health care, primarily to conform to unique language and practices in these sectors. *Because the criteria are updated each year, we suggest that you obtain the current version.* A single free copy of the criteria can be obtained from the National Institute of Standards and Technology. Write to the Baldrige National Quality Program, National Institute of Standards and Technology (NIST), Administration Building, Room A600, 100 Bureau Drive, Stop 1020, Gaithersburg, MD 20899-1020; call 301-975-2036; send a fax to 301-948-3716; e-mail nqp@nist.gov; or download the criteria from the Web site http://www.baldrige.org.

The seven categories form an integrated management system as illustrated in Figure 3.6. The umbrella over the seven categories reflect the fact that organizations must focus on customers through their strategy and action plans as a basis for all key decisions. Leadership, Strategic Planning, and Customer and Market Focus represent the "leadership triad," and suggest the importance of integrating these three functions. Human Resource Focus and Process Management represent how the work in an organization is accomplished and leads to Business Results. These functions are linked to the leadership triad. Finally, Measurement, Analysis, and Knowledge Management support the entire framework by providing the foundation for a fact-based system for improvement.

Each category consists of several *items* (numbered 1.1, 1.2, 2.1, etc.) that focus on major requirements on which businesses should focus. Each item, in turn, consists of a small number of *areas to address* (e.g., 6.1a, 6.1b) that seek specific information on approaches used to ensure and improve competitive performance, the deployment of these approaches, or results obtained from such deployment.

For example, the Leadership category consists of two examination items, each having three areas to address (items with only one area to address have the same title):

1.1   Organizational Leadership
       a. Senior Leadership Direction

Figure 3.6 Baldrige Criteria Framework

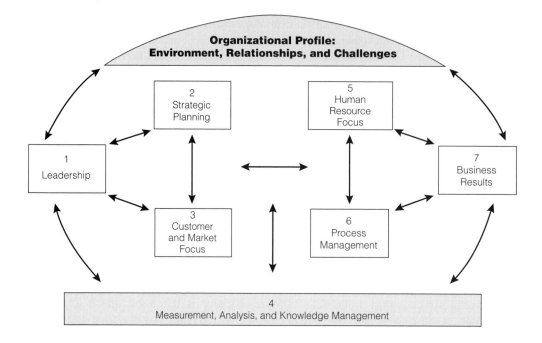

b. Organizational Governance
c. Organizational Performance Review
1.2   Social Responsibility
a. Responsibilities to the Public
b. Ethical Behavior
c. Support of Key Communities

The Senior Leadership Direction area asks organizations to answer the following questions:

- How do senior leaders set and deploy organizational values, short- and longer-term directions, and performance expectations? How do senior leaders include a focus on creating and balancing value for customers and other stakeholders in their performance expectations? How do senior leaders communicate organizational values, directions, and expectations through your leadership system, to all employees, and to key suppliers and partners? How do senior leaders ensure two-way communication on these topics?
- How do senior leaders create an environment for empowerment, innovation, and organizational agility? How do they create an environment for organizational and employee learning? How do they create an environment that fosters and requires legal and ethical behavior?

To illustrate how companies address these items in their applications, consider some of the information for the Leadership category provided by The Ritz-Carlton Hotel Company (see the *Quality in Practice* in Chapter 2 for basic information about the company) in its 1992 and 1999 applications (with a caveat that the scope of the Leadership criteria changed substantially over the years). When Horst Schulze became president in 1983, he and his leadership team personally took charge of managing for quality because they realized that managing for quality could not be delegated. They personally established the Gold Standards, which are the foundation of The Ritz-Carlton quality philosophy. The Gold Standards, in their simplicity, represent an easy-to-understand definition of service quality, and are aggressively communicated and internalized at all levels of the organization.

The constant and continuous reinforcement techniques of the Gold Standards, led by senior leaders, include lectures at new employee orientation, developmental training, daily line-up meetings, administration of both positive and negative reinforcement, mission statements displayed, distribution of Credo cards, the Credo as first topic of internal meetings, and peer pressure. As a result, employees have an exceptional understanding and devotion to the company's vision, values, quality goals, and methods.

Since 1984, all members of senior leadership have personally ensured that each new hotel's goods and services are characteristic of The Ritz-Carlton on opening day. An important aspect of this quality practice takes place during the concentrated and intense "seven-day countdown" when senior leaders work side-by-side with new employees using a combination of hands-on behavior modeling and reinforcement. During these formative sessions, which all new employees must attend, the president and COO personally interacts with every new employee, both individually and in a group setting. He personally creates the employee-guest interface image and facilitates each department's first vision statement. Throughout the entire process, the senior leaders monitor work areas for "start-up," instill Gold Standards, model the company's relationship management, insist upon 100 percent compliance to customers' requirements, and recognize outstanding achievement.

Senior leaders set direction through seven specific decisions:

10-Year Vision: To be the premier Worldwide Provider of Luxury Travel and Hospitality Products and Services
5-Year Mission: Product and Profit Dominance
3-Year Objectives: The Vital Few Objectives
1-Year Tactics: Key Production and Business Processes
Strategy: Customer and Market Focus Strategy with Action Plans
Methods: TQM—Application of Quality Sciences; Malcolm Baldrige National Quality Award Criteria; The GreenBook, 2nd Edition (the company's handbook of quality processes and tools)
Foundation: Values and Philosophy, The Gold Standards, Credo; Motto, Three Steps of Service, Basics, Employee Promise

Leadership effectiveness is evaluated on key questions of a semiannual employee satisfaction survey and through audits on public responsibility. Gaps in leadership effectiveness are addressed with development/training plans and extensive use of developmental job assignments.

In the Baldrige criteria, areas to address that request information on approach or deployment begin with the word *how*. This wording means that the organization should be able to describe methods, measures, and evaluation, learning, and improvement factors in explaining their approach for meeting the criteria requirements. It also implies that these approaches are performed on a regular basis

> *The Baldrige criteria define both an integrated infrastructure and a set of fundamental practices for a high-performance management system.*

and embedded in the practices of the organization, and are not simply ad hoc ways of doing business.

One thing they do not do is prescribe specific quality tools, techniques, technologies, systems, or starting points, and are not associated with any one quality philosophy. Companies are encouraged to develop and demonstrate creative, adaptive, and flexible approaches to meeting basic requirements. Many innovative approaches have been developed by Baldrige winners and are now commonly used by many other companies. We will see many examples in the "Leading Practices" sections of subsequent chapters. The Bonus Materials provide a detailed description of the Baldrige Award evaluation process.

Criteria Evolution

As the important management practices of any organization should be, the specific award criteria are evaluated and improved each year. Over the years, the criteria have been streamlined and simplified to make them more relevant and useful to organizations of all types and sizes. For example, the initial set of criteria in 1988 had 62 items with 278 areas to address. By 1991 the criteria had only 32 items and 99 areas to address. The 1995 criteria were reduced to 24 items and 54 areas to address. In 1997 further refinements to develop the shortest list of key requirements necessary to compete in today's marketplace, improve the linkage between process and results, and make the criteria more generic and user-friendly resulted in 20 items and 30 areas to address. In 1999, the criteria were reworded in a question format that managers can easily understand.

Most significantly, the word *quality* was judiciously dropped in the mid-1990s. For example, prior to 1994, the Strategic Planning category was titled "Strategic Quality Planning." The change to "Strategic Planning" signifies that quality should be a part of business planning, not a separate issue. Throughout the document, the term *performance* has been substituted for quality as a conscious attempt to recognize that the principles of total quality are the foundation for a company's entire management system, not just the quality system. As Dr. Curt Reimann, former director and architect of the Baldrige Award Program noted, "The things you do to win a Baldrige Award are exactly the things you'd do to win in the marketplace. Our strategy is to have the Baldrige Award criteria be a useful daily tool that simulates real competition."

To this end, the most significant changes in the criteria reflect the maturity of business practices and total quality approaches. The criteria evolved from a primary emphasis on product and service quality assurance in the late 1980s, to a broad focus on performance excellence in a global marketplace by the late 1990s. The improvements include the following shifts in emphasis:

- From quality assurance and strategic quality planning to a focus on process management and overall strategic planning
- From a focus on current customers to a focus on current and future customers and markets
- From human resource utilization to human resource development and management
- From supplier quality to supplier partnerships
- From individual quality improvement activities to cycles of evaluation and improvement in all key areas
- From data analysis of quality efforts to an aggregate, integrated organizational level review of key company data
- From results that focus on limited financial performance to a focus on a composite of business results, including customer satisfaction and financial, product, service, and strategic performance

In addition, criteria updates are designed to address emerging and relevant issues facing business. In 2003, for example, the criteria strengthened its emphasis on organizational governance and ethics in the wake of the Enron, WorldCom, and Arthur Andersen fiascos that occurred the year before.

Using the Baldrige Criteria

The Baldrige Award criteria form a model for business excellence in any organization—manufacturing or service, large or small. The former Texas Instruments Defense Systems and Electronics Group (now part of Raytheon), for example, used the criteria to provide focus and coherence to the activities across the corporation.[17] They were able to tackle a part of total quality that previously had been unreachable: implementing quality efforts in staff, support, and nonmanufacturing areas. TI asked every business unit to prepare a mock award application as a way of measuring its progress. This task represented a radical change for some operations because, until that time, most staff functions were not required to measure their processes or their results. The Defense Systems & Electronics Group's self-assessment revealed that they were a long way from applying for and winning the Baldrige Award. But the group aggressively adopted the criteria as a blueprint for improving its business. Many executives did not believe that the criteria could be applied to defense contractors, but TI's experience clearly showed that it could.

Many other types of organizations have used the criteria. For example, although the legal profession in general has not adopted quality management practices, the Trial Division of Nationwide Insurance, which operates 56 law offices in 20 states, uses the Baldrige model as a key component of its business plan. Senior leaders introduced it to all of the company's managing trial attorneys and encouraged individual offices to apply for local or state Baldrige-based awards.[18] The incorporation of Education and Health Care in the award program in 1999 reflected of the growing interest in these sectors. Many school districts now use the criteria, particularly after the publicity that resulted from the 2001 winners. Some states even mandate Baldrige assessment, and traditional accreditation bodies now allow Baldrige as an alternative means of preparing for accreditation. One large Chicago-area hospital applied for the Baldrige-based Lincoln Award for Excellence and prepared for its accreditation visit by JCAHO at the same time, recognizing the synergy and overlap of Baldrige principles and JCAHO standards. In 2002, the first health care organization received a Baldrige award, which will undoubtedly boost interest in the health care sector.

Many small businesses (defined as those with 500 or fewer employees) believe that the Baldrige criteria are too difficult to apply to their organizations because they cannot afford to implement the same types of practices as large companies. This assumption is simply not true, as the *Quality Profile* on Texas Nameplate at the beginning of this chapter illustrates. For example, the ability to obtain customer and market knowledge through independent third party surveys, extensive interviews, and focus groups, which are common practices among large companies, may be limited by the resources of a small business. What is important, however, is whether the company is using appropriate mechanisms to gather information and use it to improve customer focus and satisfaction. Similarly, large corporations frequently have sophisticated computer/ information

> *Approaches that organizations use to address the Baldrige criteria requirements need not be formal or complex, and can easily be implemented by small businesses.*

systems for data management, while small businesses may perform data and information management with a combination of manual methods and personal computers. Also, systems for employee involvement and process management may rely heavily on informal verbal communication and less on formal written documentation. Thus, the size or nature of a business does not affect the appropriateness of the criteria, but rather the context in which the criteria are applied.

Companies use the Baldrige Criteria in different ways—for self-assessment or internal recognition programs, even if they do not intend to apply for the award. The benefits of using the criteria for self-assessment include accelerating improvement efforts, energizing employees, and learning from feedback—particularly if external examiners are involved. For instance, Honeywell, Inc., uses it as a companywide framework for understanding, evaluating, and improving their business. Honeywell's mandate is to use the model for managing the business and engaging senior management in an annual assessment process. This framework is used by general managers to exchange information, ask for help, and learn from each other.[19] Even the U.S. Postal Service has decided to use the Baldrige Criteria as a basis to reestablish a quality system by identifying the areas that need the most improvement and providing a baseline to track progress. Using the award criteria as a self-assessment tool provides an objective framework, sets a high standard, and compares units that have different systems or organizations.

The approaches used for self-assessment vary. They may include simple questionnaires developed from the criteria, for which answers are compiled and used as a basis for an improvement plan; facilitated assessments in which key business leaders gather together to examine their organization against the criteria; and full written "applications" that are evaluated by trained internal or external examiners.[20] Assessments are often linked to the organization's strategic planning process, which serves as a means of implementing the opportunities for improvement that are identified through the process. The Bonus Materials folder on the CD-ROM contains a brochure entitled "Why Baldrige?" that provides a simple overview of why the Baldrige approach is valuable to any organization.

Impacts of the Baldrige Program

An economic evaluation study of the Baldrige program by the U.S. Department of Commerce concluded that a conservative estimate of the present value of the net social benefits associated with the program was $24.65 billion in constant 2000 dollars. This return was achieved by a $119 million investment in total social costs associated with the program, a 207:1 ratio. More importantly, the program changed the way in which many organizations around the world manage their operations, and helped significantly to bring the principles of TQ into the daily culture of these organizations. The true benefactors are the customers and other stakeholders who received better products and services.

Most states in the United States have developed award programs similar to the Baldrige Award. State award programs generally are designed to promote an awareness of productivity and quality, foster an information exchange, encourage firms to adopt quality and productivity improvement strategies, recognize firms that have instituted successful strategies, provide role models for other businesses in the state, encourage new industry to locate in the state, and establish a quality-of-life culture that will benefit all residents of the state.[21] Each state is unique, however, and thus the specific objectives will vary. For instance, the primary objectives of Minnesota's quality award are to encourage all Minnesota organizations to examine their current state of quality and to become more involved in the movement toward continuous quality improvement, as well as to recognize outstanding quality achievements in the state. Missouri, on the other hand, has as its objectives to educate all Missourians in quality improvement, to foster the pursuit of quality in all aspects of Missouri life, and to recognize quality leadership. Other states, such as Tennessee and Ohio, use their award programs to provide developmental advice to organizations just starting on their quality journey. Information and links to state award programs can be found at the Baldrige Award Web site, http://www.baldrige.org.

Baldrige and Deming

It is no secret that W. Edwards Deming was not an advocate of the Baldrige Award.[22] (Joseph Juran, however, was highly influential in its development.) The competitive nature of the award is fundamentally at odds with Deming's teachings. However, many of Deming's principles are reflected directly or in spirit within the criteria. In fact, Zytec, which implemented its total quality system around Deming's 14 Points, received a Baldrige Award. We provide a discussion of how the Baldrige Criteria support each of Deming's 14 Points in the Bonus Materials folder.

INTERNATIONAL QUALITY AWARD PROGRAMS

As we noted earlier, the Baldrige Award was inspired by Japan's Deming Prize, although the two are quite different. Subsequently, Baldrige inspired many other nations to establish their own quality awards, as shown in Figure 3.7. We briefly discuss the Deming Prize and other award programs here.

The Deming Prize

The Deming Application Prize was instituted in 1951 by the Union of Japanese Scientists and Engineers (JUSE) in recognition and appreciation of W. Edwards Deming's achievements in statistical quality control and his friendship with the Japanese people. The Deming Prize has several categories, including prizes for individuals, factories, and small companies, and the Deming application prize, which is an annual award presented to a company or a division of a company that has achieved distinctive performance improvements through the application of companywide quality control. As defined by JUSE, companywide quality control (CWQC) is a system of activities to assure that quality products and services required by customers are economically designed, produced, and supplied while respecting the principle of customer orientation and the overall public well-being. These quality assurance activities involve market research, research and development, design, purchasing, production, inspection, and sales, as well as all other related activities inside and outside the company. Through everyone in the company understanding both statistical concepts and methods, through their application to all the aspects of quality assurance and through repeating the cycle of rational planning, implementation, evaluation, and action, CWQC aims to accomplish business objectives.

The Deming Prize is awarded to all companies that meet a prescribed standard. However, the small number of awards given each year is an indication of the difficulty of achieving the standard. The objectives are to ensure that a company has so thoroughly deployed a quality process that it will continue to improve long after a prize is awarded. The application process has no "losers." For companies that do not qualify, the examination process is automatically extended up to two times over three years. Deming Prize winners are also eligible for the Japan Quality Medal, which was

Figure 3.7 Countries with Quality Awards Around the World

established to encourage winners to continue practicing and enhancing their quality efforts. Since its inception in 1969, fewer than 20 companies have received it, because it demands sustained performance to rigorous standards over a five-year period. In 1998, Phillips Semiconductors in Taiwan was the first non-Japanese company to win the Japan Quality Medal.

The judging criteria for the Deming Prize establishes a framework for a CWQC system. The criteria consist of a checklist of 10 major categories, with each major category divided into subcategories, or "checking points." For example, the policy category includes policies pursued for management, quality, and quality control; methods for establishing policies; appropriateness and consistency of policies; utilization of statistical methods; communication and dissemination of policies; checks of policies and the status of their achievement; and the relationship between policies and long- and short-term plans. Details and additional information about the Deming Prize are provided in the Bonus Materials folder on the CD-ROM with this book.

European Quality Award

In October 1991 the European Foundation for Quality Management (EFQM) in partnership with the European Commission and the European Organization for Quality announced the creation of the European Quality Award. EFQM was, and remains, a nonprofit organization. The award was designed to increase awareness throughout the European Community, and businesses in particular, of the growing importance of quality to their competitiveness in the increasingly global market and to their standards of life. The European Quality Award consists of two parts: the European Quality Prize, given to companies that demonstrate excellence in quality management practice by meeting the award criteria, and the European Quality Award, awarded to the most successful applicant. In 1992 four prizes and one award were granted for the first time.

Applicants must demonstrate that their TQ approach has contributed significantly to satisfying the expectations of customers, employees, and other constituencies. The award process is similar to the Deming Prize and Baldrige Award. The assessment is based on customer satisfaction, business results, processes, leadership, people satisfaction, resources, people management, policy and strategy, and impact on society. Figure 3.8 shows the integrated management framework for the European Quality Award, now known as the Business Excellence Model.[23] Like Baldrige, results—including customer, people (employee), and society results—constitute a high percentage of the total score. These results are driven by "Enablers" the means by which an organization approaches its business responsibilities, and a foundation of innovation and learning. The categories are roughly equivalent to those in Baldrige. However, the results criteria of people satisfaction, customer satisfaction, impact on society, and business results are somewhat different.[24] The impact on society results category focuses on the perceptions of the company by the community at large and the company's approach to the quality of life, the environment, and the preservation of global resources. The European Quality Award criteria place greater emphasis on this category than is placed on the public responsibility item in the Baldrige Award criteria.

Sixteen countries participate in the award program. Recent winners include:

- **Large Organizations and Business Units:** Dexia—Sofaxis, France; *Operational Units (subcategory):* Bosch Sanayi ve Ticaret AS, Turkey; *Public Sector (subcategory):* Customs and Tax Region Aarhus, Denmark

Figure 3.8 European Quality Award Framework

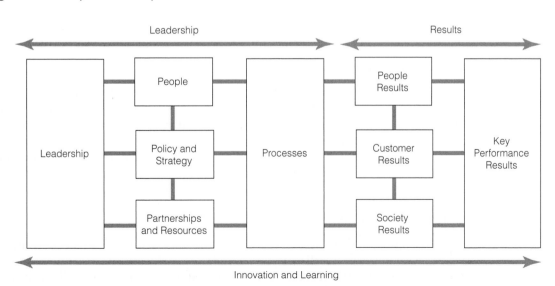

Source: Used with permission of EFQM. © EFQM, 1999. The EFQM Excellence Model is a registered trademark.

- **Small and Medium-sized Organizations (SMEs):** *Subsidiary SMEs (subcategory)*: Banc International d'Andorra—Banca Mora, Principality of Andorra; *Independent SMEs (subcategory)*; ASLE, Workers Incorporated Companies Association, Spain; Maxi SA Coco-Mat, Greece; Springfarm Architectural Mouldings Ltd., Northern Ireland (Award Winner)

Canadian Awards for Business Excellence

Canada's National Quality Institute (NQI) (http://www.nqi.ca) recognizes Canada's foremost achievers of excellence through the prestigious Canada Awards for Excellence. NQI is a nonprofit organization designed to stimulate and support quality-driven innovation within all Canadian enterprises and institutions, including business, government, education, and health care. The Canadian Awards for Business Excellence quality criteria are similar in structure to the Baldrige Award criteria, with some key differences. Separate, but similar, criteria are used for business organizations, public sector organizations, and "healthy workplace" organizations. The major categories and items within each category are:

1. *Leadership:* Strategic direction, leadership involvement, and outcomes
2. *Customer Focus:* Voice of the customer, management of customer relationships, measurement, and outcomes
3. *Planning for Improvement:* Development and content of improvement plan, assessment, and outcomes
4. *People Focus:* Human resource planning, participatory environment, continuous learning environment, employee satisfaction, and outcomes
5. *Process Optimization:* Process definition, process control, process improvement, and outcomes
6. *Supplier Focus:* Partnering and outcomes

These categories seek similar information as the Baldrige Award criteria. For example, the People Focus category examines the development of human resource planning and implementation and operation of a strategy for achieving excellence through people. It also examines the organization's efforts to foster and support an environment that encourages and enables people to reach their full potential. Recipients of Canada's top quality award in 2002 include Dana Canada Inc., Spicer Driveshaft Group, Canada Post, Saskatoon Operations, Homewood Health Centre, and Mullen Trucking.

Australian Business Excellence Award

The Australian Quality Awards (now called Business Excellence Award) were developed independently from the MBNQA in 1988. The Awards were previously administered by the Australian Quality Awards Foundation, a subsidiary of the Australian Quality Council, a private, for-profit organization. In 2002, Standards Australia International [SAI] formally acquired a range of products and services previously owned by the Australian Quality Council [AQC]. SAI's Professional Services Division became the new home of the AQC and in recognition of the importance of business excellence to SAI, the division has been renamed Business Excellence Australia.

Four levels of awards are given:

1. *The Business Improvement Level*—encouragement recognition for "Progress toward Business Excellence" or "Foundation in Business Excellence"
2. *The Award Level*—representing Australian best practices; recognition as a Winner or Finalist

3. *The Award Gold Level*—open only to former Award winners; represents a revalidation and ongoing improvement
4. *The Australian Business Excellence Prize*—open only to former Award winners; represents international best practices evident throughout the organization

The assessment criteria address leadership, strategy and planning, information and analysis, people, customer focus, processes, products and services, and organizational performance within the framework shown in Figure 3.9. In this model, leadership and customer focus are the drivers of the management system and enablers of performance. Strategy, policy and planning, information and analysis, and people are the key internal components of the management system. Quality of process, product and service are focused on how work is done to achieve the required results and obtain improvement. Organizational performance is the outcome of the management system—a results category. As with Baldrige, the framework emphasizes the holistic and interconnected nature of the management process. The criteria are benchmarked with the Baldrige criteria and the European Business Excellence Model. One of the distinctive aspects of Australia's program is solid union support.

The 2003 winners were *Gold Award:* Boeing Australia Limited; *Silver Award:* Boeing Australia Limited, CORE—the Public Correctional Enterprise; *Bronze Award:* Fremantle Ports, Tasmanian Alkaloids; *Business Excellence Award:* Corporate Capability Development, QLD Department of Employment and Training, Counter Disaster and Rescue Services, QLD Department of Emergency Services, Open Learning Institute of TAFE QLD, Safety and Health Division, Department of Natural Resources and Mines. In addition some special "category awards" were Australia Post Shared Services Division (*Strategy and Planning Award*), City of Perth (*Information and Knowledge Award*), and Riteway Express (*People Award*).

Some previous recipients include Abbot International division of Abbot Australasia Pty Ltd., Avis Australia; BHP Research, Ericcson Australia Pty Ltd., ICI Pharmaceuticals, Integral Energy, Ford Motor Company of Australia, Limited, Ford Motor Company Plastics Plant, Noyce Lawyers (a legal firm), Toyota Motor Corporation Australia Limited, the TVS Partnership Pty, Ltd. (see case study in Chapter 6), and the Wesley Hospital.

Figure 3.9 Australia Business Excellence Award Framework

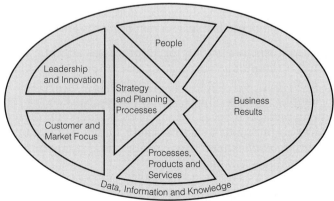

Source: http://www.businessexcellenceaustralia.com.au/.

ISO 9000:2000

As quality became a major focus of businesses throughout the world, various organizations developed standards and guidelines. Terms such as *quality management, quality control, quality system,* and *quality assurance* acquired different, sometimes conflicting meanings from country to country, within a country, and even within an industry.[25] When the European Community moved toward the European free trade agreement, which went into effect at the end of 1992, quality management became a key strategic objective. To standardize quality requirements for European countries within the Common Market and those wishing to do business with those countries, a specialized agency for standardization, the International Organization for Standardization (IOS), founded in 1946 and composed of representatives from the national standards bodies of 91 nations, adopted a series of written quality standards in 1987. They were revised in 1994, and again (significantly) in 2000. The most recent version is called the **ISO 9000:2000** family of standards.

The IOS took a unique approach in adopting the "ISO" prefix in naming the standards. *Iso* is a scientific term for equal (as in isotherm lines on a weather map, which show equal temperatures). Thus, organizations certified under the ISO 9000 standard are assured to have quality equal to their peers. The standards have been adopted in the United States by the American National Standards Institute (ANSI) with the endorsement and cooperation of the American Society for Quality (ASQ). The standards are recognized by about 100 countries, including Japan.

> *ISO 9000 defines **quality system standards**, based on the premise that certain generic characteristics of management practices can be standardized, and that a well-designed, well-implemented, and carefully managed quality system provides confidence that the outputs will meet customer expectations and requirements.*

The standards were created to meet five objectives:

1. Achieve, maintain, and seek to continuously improve product quality (including services) in relationship to requirements.
2. Improve the quality of operations to continually meet customers' and stakeholders' stated and implied needs.
3. Provide confidence to internal management and other employees that quality requirements are being fulfilled and that improvement is taking place.
4. Provide confidence to customers and other stakeholders that quality requirements are being achieved in the delivered product.
5. Provide confidence that quality system requirements are fulfilled.

The standards prescribe documentation for all processes affecting quality and suggest that compliance through auditing leads to continuous improvement. In some foreign markets, companies will not buy from suppliers who are not certified to the standards. For example, many products sold in Europe, such as telecommunication terminal equipment, medical devices, gas appliances, toys, and construction products require product certifications to assure safety. Often, ISO certification is necessary to obtain product certification. Thus, meeting these standards is becoming a requirement for international competitiveness.

Structure of the ISO 9000:2000 Standards

The ISO 9000:2000 standards focus on developing, documenting, and implementing procedures to ensure consistency of operations and performance in production and service delivery processes, with the aim of continual improvement, and supported by fundamental principles of total quality. The standards consist of three documents:

1. *ISO 9000—Fundamentals and vocabulary.* This document provides fundamental background information and establishes definitions of key terms used in the standards.
2. *ISO 9001—Requirements.* This document provides the specific requirements for a quality management system, to which users must conform in order to obtain third-party certification. An example of one of the requirements is "The supplier's management with executive responsibility shall define and document its policy for quality, including objectives for quality and commitment to quality. The quality policy shall be relevant to the supplier's organizational goals and the expectations and needs of its customers. The supplier shall ensure that this policy is understood, implemented, and maintained at all levels of the organization." Thus, the requirements state precisely what the organization needs to do. The requirements are organized into four major sections: Management Responsibility; Resource Management; Product Realization; and Measurement, Analysis, and Improvement.[26]
3. *ISO 9004—Guidelines for Performance Improvements.* This document provides guidelines to assist organizations in improving their quality management systems beyond the minimum requirements in ISO 9001, but does not prescribe any requirements that must be followed.

The requirements provide a structure for a basic quality assurance system. Management Responsibility addresses what top management must do to ensure an effective quality system, such as promoting the importance of quality throughout the organization, developing and implementing the quality management system, identifying and meeting customer requirements, defining an organizational quality policy and quality objectives, clearly defining responsibilities for quality, and controlling documents and records. Resource Management ensures that an organization provides sufficient people, facilities, and training resources. Product Realization refers to controlling the production/service process from receipt of an order or quote through design, materials procurement, manufacturing or service delivery, distribution, and subsequent field service. Measurement, Analysis, and Improvement focuses on control procedures for assuring quality in products and processes, analysis of quality-related data, and correction, prevention, and improvement planning activities. A list of the requirements and some discussion of the registration process are provided in the Bonus Materials folder on the CD-ROM.

The standards are intended to apply to all types of businesses, including electronics and chemicals, and to services such as health care, banking, and transportation. For example, in July 2000, the B2B (business-to-business) firm, bestroute.com, became the first e-commerce distributorship to achieve ISO registration. Interpreting the standards to e-business required some unique strategies to ensure compliance. The company focused on the key concept of the standard that is common to any industry: customer service. The company developed and documented processes for all aspects of bestroute.com's customer service—from call routing to return processing to phone etiquette. As the customer service manager observed, "In the end, the processes we established, implemented and are keeping on top of in order to comply with the standard are the very same things we needed to do to keep customers happy."[27]

Factors Leading to ISO 9000:2000

The original ISO 9000:1994 series standards consisted of 20 fundamental elements of a basic quality system that included such things as management responsibility, design control, purchasing, product identification and traceability, process control, inspection and testing, corrective and preventive action, internal quality audits, training, and statistical techniques.

The original standards and the 1994 revision met with considerable controversy.[28] The standards only required that the organization have a documented, verifiable process in place to ensure that it consistently produces what it says it will produce. A company could comply with the standards and still produce a poor-quality product—as long as it did so consistently! Many never used the standards to drive improvement. Dissatisfaction with ISO 9000 resulted in the European Union calling for deemphasizing ISO 9000 registration, citing the fact that companies were more concerned with "passing a test" than on focusing their energies on quality processes. The Australian government stopped requiring ISO 9000 registration for government contracts. The Australian *Business Review Weekly* noted that "its reputation among small and medium businesses continues to deteriorate. Some small businesses have almost been destroyed by the endeavor to implement costly and officious quality assurance ISO 9000 systems that hold little relevance to their businesses."

The deficiencies in the old ISO 9000 standards led to a joint effort 1994 by the Big Three automobile manufacturers—Ford, Chrysler, and General Motors—as well as several truck manufacturers, to develop QS-9000, an interpretation and extension of ISO 9000 for automotive suppliers. The goal was to develop fundamental quality systems that provide for continuous improvement, emphasizing defect prevention and the reduction of variation and waste in the supply chain. QS-9000 is based on ISO 9000 and includes all ISO requirements. However, QS-9000 went well beyond ISO 9000 standards by including additional requirements such as continuous improvement, manufacturing capability, and production part approval processes. Now, even QS-9000 is considered inadequate and is being phased out.

ISO 9000:2000 is a response to the widespread dissatisfaction that resulted from the old standards. The new standards have a completely new structure, based on eight principles—"comprehensive and fundamental rules or beliefs for leading and operating an organization" that reflect the basic principles of total quality that we introduced in Chapter 1, and many of the core values and concepts of the Baldrige and European Quality Award criteria. These eight principles were voted on, and overwhelmingly approved, at a conference in 1997 attended by 36 representatives of countries that have delegates in the TC 176 technical committee, charged with the responsibility of revising the ISO 9000 standards.[29] The principles and their explanation as defined by the IOS are shown in Table 3.3.

With this underlying philosophy, the ISO 9000:2000 revision aligns much closer to the performance excellence concept of Baldrige. For example,

- Organizations now need a process to determine customer needs and expectations, translate them into internal requirements, and measure customer satisfaction and dissatisfaction.
- Managers must communicate the importance of meeting customer and regulatory requirements, integrate ISO 9000 into business plans, set measurable objectives, and conduct management reviews. No longer can top management delegate the program to people lower in the organization. Organizations now must view work as a process and manage a system of interrelated processes. This approach is significantly different from the "document what you do" requirements of earlier versions.

Table 3.3 ISO 9000:2000 Quality Management Principles

Principle 1: Customer Focus
Organizations depend on their customers and therefore should understand current and future customer needs, should meet customer requirements, and strive to exceed customer expectations.

Principle 2: Leadership
Leaders establish unity of purpose and direction of the organization. They should create and maintain the internal environment in which people can become fully involved in achieving the organization's objectives.

Principle 3: Involvement of People
People at all levels are the essence of an organization and their full involvement enables their abilities to be used for the organization's benefit.

Principle 4: Process Approach
A desired result is achieved more efficiently when activities and related resources are managed as a process.

Principle 5: System Approach to Management
Identifying, understanding, and managing interrelated processes as a system contributes to the organization's effectiveness and efficiency in achieving its objectives.

Principle 6: Continual Improvement
Continual improvement of the organization's overall performance should be a permanent objective of the organization.

Principle 7: Factual Approach to Decision Making
Effective decisions are based on the analysis of data and information.

Principle 8: Mutually Beneficial Supplier Relationships
An organization and its suppliers are interdependent and a mutually beneficial relationship enhances the ability of both to create value.

Source: http://www.iso.ch/9000e/QMP.html. Used with permission.

- Analysis now needs to be done to provide information about customer satisfaction and dissatisfaction, products, and processes with the focus on improvement.
- Evaluation of training effectiveness and making personnel aware of the importance of their activities in meeting quality objectives are stressed.
- In the previous standards, organizations were required to perform corrective and preventive action, but now must have a planned process for improvement.

Implementation and Registration

Implementing ISO 9000 is not an easy task.[30] The ISO 9000 standards originally were intended to be advisory in nature and to be used for two-party contractual situations (between a customer and supplier) and for internal auditing. However, they quickly evolved into criteria for companies who wished to "certify" their quality management or achieve "registration" through a third-party auditor, usually a laboratory or some other accreditation agency (called a registrar). This process began in the United Kingdom. Rather than a supplier being audited for compliance to the standards by each customer, the registrar certifies the company, and this certification is accepted by all of the supplier's customers.

Recertification is required every three years. Individual sites—not entire companies—must achieve registration individually. All costs are borne by the applicant, so the process can be quite expensive. A registration audit may cost anywhere from $10,000 to more than $40,000, while the internal cost for documentation and training may exceed $100,000.

Benefits of ISO 9000

Many diverse organizations have realized significant benefits from ISO 9000 that range from higher customer satisfaction and retention, better quality products, and improved productivity. At DuPont, for example, ISO 9000 has been credited with increasing on-time delivery from 70 to 90 percent, decreasing cycle time from 15 days to 1.5 days, increasing first-pass yields from 72 to 92 percent, and reducing the number of test procedures by one-third. Sun Microsystems' Milpitas plant was certified in 1992, and managers believe that it helped deliver improved quality and service to customers.[31] In Canada, Toronto Plastics, Ltd. reduced defects from 150,000 per million to 15,000 per million after one year of ISO implementation.[32] The first home builder to achieve registration, Michigan-based Delcor Homes, reduced its rate for correctable defects from 27.4 to 1.7 in two years and improved its building experience approval rating from the mid 60s to the mid 90s on a 100-point scale.[33] Thus, using ISO 9000 as a basis for a quality system can improve productivity, decrease costs, and increase customer satisfaction. In addition, organizations have found that using ISO 9000 resulted in increased use of data as a business management tool, increased management commitment, more efficient management reviews, and improved customer communication.[34]

Current information can be obtained from the ISO Web site (http://www.iso.ch).

SIX SIGMA

Six Sigma, which has garnered a significant amount of credibility over the last decade because of its acceptance at such major firms as Allied Signal (now part of Honeywell) and General Electric, is not as new a concept as it seems. This concept is facilitated through use of basic and advanced quality improvement and control tools by teams whose members are trained to provide fact-based decision-making information. The term *Six Sigma* is based on a statistical measure that equates to 3.4 or fewer errors or defects per million opportunities. An ultimate "stretch" goal of all organizations that adopt a Six Sigma philosophy is to have all critical processes, regardless of functional area, at a Six Sigma level of capability.

Six Sigma can be described as a business improvement approach that seeks to find and eliminate causes of defects and errors in manufacturing and service processes by focusing on outputs that are critical to customers and a clear financial return for the organization.

Evolution of Six Sigma

Motorola pioneered the concept of Six Sigma as an approach to measuring product and service quality. The late Bill Smith, a reliability engineer at Motorola, is credited with originating the concept during the mid-1980s and selling it to Motorola's CEO, Robert Galvin. Smith noted that system failure rates were substantially higher than predicted by final product test, and suggested several causes, including higher system complexity that resulted in more opportunities for failure, and a fundamental flaw in traditional quality thinking. He concluded that a much higher level of internal quality was required and convinced Galvin of its importance.[35] As a result, Motorola set the following goal in 1987:

> *Improve product and services quality ten times by 1989, and at least one hundred fold by 1991. Achieve six-sigma capability by 1992. With a deep sense of urgency, spread dedication to quality to every facet of the corporation, and achieve a culture of continual improvement to assure total customer satisfaction. There is only one ultimate goal: zero defects—in everything we do.*

The core philosophy of Six Sigma is based on some key concepts:[36]

1. Think in terms of key business processes and customer requirements with a clear focus on overall strategic objectives.
2. Focus on corporate sponsors responsible for championing projects, support team activities, help to overcome resistance to change, and obtain resources.
3. Emphasize such quantifiable measures as **defects per million opportunities (dpmo)** that can be applied to all parts of an organization: manufacturing, engineering, administrative, software, and so on.
4. Ensure that appropriate metrics are identified early in the process and that they focus on business results, thereby providing incentives and accountability.
5. Provide extensive training followed by project team deployment to improve profitability, reduce non-value-added activities, and achieve cycle time reduction.
6. Create highly qualified process improvement experts ("green belts," "black belts," and "master black belts") who can apply improvement tools and lead teams.
7. Set stretch objectives for improvement.

Quality Spotlight
General Electric

The recognized benchmark for Six Sigma implementation is General Electric. The efforts by General Electric in particular, driven by former CEO Jack Welch, brought significant media attention to the concept and made Six Sigma a popular approach to quality improvement. In the mid-1990s, quality emerged as a concern of many employees at GE. Jack Welch invited Larry Bossidy, then CEO of Allied Signal, who had phenomenal success with Six Sigma, to talk about it at a Corporate Executive Council meeting. The meeting caught the attention of GE managers and as Welch stated, "I went nuts about Six Sigma and launched it," calling it the most ambitious task the company had ever taken on.[37] To ensure success, GE changed its incentive compensation plan so that 60 percent of the bonus was based on financials and 40 percent on Six Sigma, and provided stock option grants to employees in Six Sigma training. In their first year, they trained 30,000 employees at a cost of $200 million and got back about $150 million in savings. From 1996 to 1997, GE increased the number of Six Sigma projects from 3,000 to 6,000 and achieved $320 million in productivity gains and profits. By 1998, the company had generated $750 million in Six Sigma savings over and above their investment, and would receive $1.5 billion in savings the next year.

GE had many early success stories. GE Capital, for example, fielded about 300,000 calls each year from mortgage customers who had to use voice mail or call back 24 percent of the time because employees were busy or unavailable. A Six Sigma team analyzed one branch that had a near perfect percentage of answered calls and applied their learning of their best practices to the other 41 branches, resulting in a 99.9 percent chance of customers' getting a representative on the first try. A team at GE Plastics improved the quality of a product used in CD-ROMs and audio CDs from a 3.8 sigma level to 5.7 level and captured a significant amount of new business from

Sony.[38] GE credits Six Sigma with a 10-fold increase in the life of CT scanner X-ray tubes, a 400 percent improvement in return on investment in its industrial diamond business, a 62 percent reduction in turnaround time at railcar repair shops, and $400 million in savings in its plastics business.[39]

One of the key learnings GE discovered was that Six Sigma is not only for engineers. Welch observed the following:[40]

- Plant managers can use Six Sigma to reduce waste, improve product consistency, solve equipment problems, or create capacity.
- Human resource managers need it to reduce the cycle time for hiring employees.
- Regional sales managers can use it to improve forecast reliability, pricing strategies, or pricing variation.
- For that matter, plumbers, car mechanics, and gardeners can use it to better understand their customers' needs and tailor their service offerings to meet customers' wants.

After many years of implementation, Six Sigma has become a vital part of GE's company culture. In fact, as GE continues to acquire new companies, integrating Six Sigma into different business cultures is a significant challenge. Six Sigma is a priority in acquisitions and addressed early in the acquisition process.

Many other organizations such as Texas Instruments, Allied Signal (which merged with Honeywell), Boeing, 3M, Home Depot, Caterpillar, IBM, Xerox, Citibank, Raytheon, and the U.S. Air Force Air Combat Command have developed quality improvement approaches designed around the Six Sigma concept and also report significant results. Between 1995 and the first quarter of 1997, Allied Signal reported cost savings exceeding $800 million from its Six Sigma initiative. Citibank groups reduced internal callbacks by 80 percent, credit processing time by 50 percent, and cycle times of processing statements from 28 days to 15 days.[41]

Six Sigma as a Quality Framework

Six Sigma provides a blueprint for implementation of a total quality system. In many ways, Six Sigma is the realization of many fundamental concepts of "total quality management," notably, the integration of human and process elements of improvement.[42] Human issues include management leadership, a sense of urgency, focus on results and customers, team processes, and culture change; process issues include the use of process management techniques, analysis of variation and statistical methods, a disciplined problem solving approach, and management by fact. However, it is more than simply a repackaging of older quality approaches, such as the traditional notion of total quality management. Some of the contrasting features include:

- TQM is based largely on worker empowerment and teams; Six Sigma is owned by business leader champions.
- TQM activities generally occur within a function, process, or individual workplace; Six Sigma projects are truly cross-functional.
- TQM training is generally limited to simple improvement tools and concepts; Six Sigma focuses on a more rigorous and advanced set of statistical methods and a structured problem-solving methodology DMAIC—define, measure, analyze, improve, and control—which will be discussed in detail in Chapter 10.
- TQM is focused on improvement with little financial accountability; Six Sigma requires a verifiable return on investment and focus on the bottom line.

In addition, Six Sigma has elevated the importance of statistics and statistical thinking in quality improvement. Six Sigma's focus on measurable bottom-line results, a disciplined statistical approach to problem solving, rapid project completion, and organizational infrastructure make it a powerful methodology for improvement.

BALDRIGE, ISO 9000, AND SIX SIGMA

We examined three major frameworks for quality management systems: the Baldrige Criteria for Performance Excellence, ISO 9000, and Six Sigma. Although each of these frameworks are process-focused, data-based, and management-led, each offers a different emphasis in helping organizations improve performance and increase customer satisfaction. For example, Baldrige focuses on performance excellence for the entire organization in an overall management framework, identifying and tracking important organizational results; ISO focuses on product and service conformity for guaranteeing equity in the marketplace and concentrates on fixing quality system problems and product and service nonconformities; and Six Sigma concentrates on measuring product quality and driving process improvement and cost savings throughout the organization.

Although the 2000 revision of ISO 9000 incorporated many of the Baldrige criteria's original principles, it still is not a comprehensive business performance framework.

ISO 9000 provides a set of good basic practices for initiating a quality system, and is an excellent starting point for companies with no formal quality assurance program.

Nevertheless, it is an excellent way to begin a quality journey. In fact, it provides more detailed guidance on process and product control than Baldrige, and provides systematic approaches to many of the Baldrige criteria requirements in the Process Management category. Thus, for companies in the early stages of developing a quality program, the standards enforce the discipline of control that is necessary before they can seriously pursue continuous improvement. The requirements of periodic audits reinforce the stated quality system until it becomes ingrained in the company.

Implementing Six Sigma fulfills in part many of the elements of ISO 9000:2000, including the Quality Management System, Resource Management, Product Realization, and Measurement, Analysis, and Improvement sections of the standards.[43] For instance, Six Sigma helps to demonstrate management commitment through periodic review of Six Sigma plans and projects, providing champions to sponsor projects, providing training resources, and communicating progress and achievements.

Because Baldrige and Six Sigma provide much more comprehensive views of quality management, we will focus on them throughout the remainder of this book. A critical question is whether an organization using Baldrige will be more successful if it also uses Six Sigma, and vice versa. If one views Six Sigma as only a small part of the Process Management category, one might believe that the impact would be marginal. However, let us examine the role of Six Sigma in each of the seven Baldrige categories. Six Sigma enhances the ability of leadership to focus on the critical factors that make a business successful and select appropriate strategies and action plans. Therefore, Six Sigma can strengthen management practices in Leadership and Strategic Planning. Understanding customer requirements and linking them to processes and delivery systems is a principal focus of Baldrige. By focusing on critical to quality (CTQ) customer requirements—one of the important concepts in Six Sigma, organizations gain better knowledge about customer requirements, a key component of the Customer Focus category. Six Sigma methodology is driven by a management-by-fact methodology. This basis can improve an organization's ability to meet the requirements in the Measurement, Analysis, and Knowledge Management category. The role of people in championing projects and providing the technical and application-specific knowledge is vital. Six Sigma can improve work systems, training, and the work environment—all critical components of the Human Resource Focus Baldrige category. With Six Sigma, process management is not a by-product, but it is one of the primary organizational goals. The DMAIC methodology provides a structured approach to category 6, Process Management. Finally, Six Sigma's focus on business results leads organizations to track and monitor appropriate metrics.

Taking a broad view, Six Sigma contributes to nearly 80 percent of the points available in a Baldrige assessment. Although no formal studies have investigated these synergies, many organizations have successfully married the two, including Texas Instruments, Motorola, Compaq, Solectron, Boeing, and others. In fact, Jack Swaim of Compaq Computer (now Hewlett-Packard) and a former Baldrige examiner, observed that Six Sigma can provide the impetus for change, while the Baldrige Core Values provide the keys to sustainability. He also suggests that pursuing Baldrige first can make it easier to implement Six Sigma. We also believe that Six Sigma can lay the foundation for a broader Baldrige perspective, and is reflected by a comment from another colleague, Cynthia Scribner at Raytheon, who noted that Six Sigma makes a great unifying story for a Baldrige application. Unfortunately, consultants and advocates appear to support their own perspectives, and such synergies are seldom exploited. The Bonus Materials folder on the CD-ROM contains additional discussion of the synergies between Baldrige and Six Sigma.

So how should an organization choose? The correct answer is that it should not be either/or, but rather, any combination of these systems.

Although different, Baldrige and Six Sigma are highly compatible and can each have a place in the management system of a successful organization.

One example of merging Baldrige with Six Sigma is Baxter Healthcare International.[44] The Business Excellence organization is a small group of people focused on helping internal clients improve their operations. Specific areas of responsibility in Business Excellence include:

- The Baxter Award for Operational Excellence (an internal Baldrige Award)
- Deployment of the Baxter Integrated Management System (the Baldrige model)
- The Corporate Quality Manual
- The Baxter Quality Institute (an internal quality training group)
- The Quality Leadership Process (a method of deploying performance excellence in manufacturing)
- Lean Manufacturing Initiative
- Six Sigma Initiatives

They rolled all of these areas together into a unified service offering. For example, consider the following fictitious scenario. The supply chain organization determined that their operating cost and cash flow contributions are not meeting the targets. Business Excellence would set out to help them in the following way. First, they work with members of the leadership team to develop an organizational profile of the supply chain organization. This initial assessment helps the team focus on who they are and what their specific challenges are. Next, they perform a simple Baldrige assessment online and then use the output to generate a feedback report of strengths and opportunities for improvement with strong emphasis on the integration of the model. Then they distill the feedback report down to 10–12 cross-cutting themes for the leadership team to focus on. These themes are built into an Excel spreadsheet for a "prioritization matrix" exercise, designed to identify the top two or three critical opportunities or issues that the group will focus on. Next, they bring in the Six Sigma approach and drill down into these opportunities to determine potential projects. When these projects have been identified and scoped sufficiently to make a decision to move forward, project charters are developed and assigned to Six Sigma specialists to implement them.

QUALITY IN PRACTICE
BUILDING BUSINESS EXCELLENCE IN HUNGARY[45]

One of Europe's major success stories since the fall of the Iron Curtain is Hungary, whose economy grew even during the recent worldwide recession. Quality improvement is credited by many as the reason for the country's success. Some of the firms that achieved recognition include Burton-Apta, a manufacturer of ceramic products and systems used in kilns; Westel Mobile Telecommunications Co. and Herend Porcelain Manufacturing.

Burton-Apta engaged in quality initiatives beginning in the 1970s. A breakthrough occurred in 1986 when Shoji Shiba, a Japanese professor, brought the concept of TQ to Hungary. Burton-Apta learned about quality concepts and established a quality council. The company received ISO 9000 certification in 1993, the first Hungarian National Quality Award in the mid-sized business category in 1997, the European Quality Prize in 1999, and finally the European Quality Award (EQA) in 2000. Because it was no longer eligible for the EQA, the company decided to conduct self-assessments to maintain its focus on continuous improvement. These self-assessments resulted in improvements in many areas, including management commitment, strategy and planning, human resources, customer satisfaction, employee satisfaction, social impact, and business results. Some of the specific opportunities for improvement that were identified and acted upon included the following:

- Managers taking more responsibility as role models and systematically disseminating best practices from all over Hungary and abroad
- Incorporating the opinions of all stakeholders in strategic planning activities

- Developing a career and recruitment plan that includes evaluation of managers by themselves, employees, and outside experts; increased employee empowerment; and a more efficient suggestion system
- Improvements in safety, increased compensation and other employee benefits, and better recognition of employees
- Special emphasis on the environment that exceeds that of other midsized companies in the region

Westel Mobile Telecommunications Co. Ltd. is the leading provider of Hungarian wireless telecommunications service. Westel uses self-assessment to appraise the performance of the organization and its overall leadership. It began using the Baldrige criteria in 1994, and in 1995 became Hungary's first telecom provider to achieve ISO 9000 certification. In 1996, 25 managers participated in Westel's first EFQM self-assessment. Criterion owners were appointed, each responsible for ensuring areas for improvement were prioritized and improvement plans developed, built into the business plan, and implemented. In 2001, Westel received the European Quality Award.

Westel's assessment and review system is shown in Figure 3.10. This system is focused on ensuring delivery of the company's vision and mission via policies, strategies, and processes that deliver stakeholder satisfaction. The company's recent mission and vision aim are for Westel to be trusted and relied on by all stakeholders. Society, which includes the general population, peer and key people, the press, authorities and regulatory

Figure 3.10 Westel's Assessment and Review System

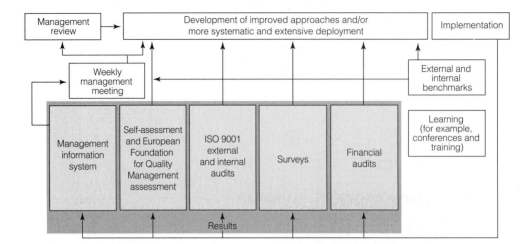

bodies, is included in the list of stakeholders. Westel meets its societal obligations through direct employment, job creation, and sponsorship of and donations to various programs, such as the Hungarian Olympic committee and the Budapest Festival Orchestra. It also focuses heavily on environmental responsibility; as one example, it encourages clients to dispose of batteries in special bio waste bins.

Herend Porcelain Manufacturing, in business since 1826, achieved ISO 9000 certification in 1995, but decided to strengthen its TQ system by being driven by employee and customer satisfaction. This decision led to implementation of the ISO 14001 environmental management system and the British Standards Institute health and safety management system as part of their quality management system. Employees became more involved and empowered to improve such areas as professional skills, quality attitudes, environmental protection and safety, communication and problem solving, and compliance with customer needs and expectations, making continuous improvement a daily routine.

Herend takes a data-driven approach to managing, using 132 different indicators to follow up on goals stated in their mission and strategic

plan. Reviews and assessments of approaches and processes are performed by internal audits. These assessments go far beyond simple certification of conformance and focus on overall performance, as well as determining areas for improvement, increasing customer satisfaction, and improving organizational effectiveness. Herend won the first Hungarian National Quality Award in 1996.

Key Issues for Discussion

1. Westel operates in an industry sector with both expressed and latent (those that customers do not express) customer and market needs and expectations. Why are latent needs important in the telecommunications industry? What does their importance mean for managing such a company?

2. Each of these firms uses some sort of self-assessment process to understand their management practices. Could the results they realized have been achieved without these self-assessments? Why or why not?

3. How important do you think a national quality award is to a nation's economic growth?

QUALITY IN PRACTICE
SIX SIGMA INTEGRATION AT SAMSUNG[46]

Samsung Electronics Co. (SEC) of Seoul, Korea, was founded in 1969 and sold its first product, a television receiver, in 1971. Today Samsung is well-known in the home, mobile, office networks, and core components businesses. Since its inception, SEC has used a variety of quality tools and approaches, but Six Sigma was added to upgrade its approaches and improve SEC's competitive position in world markets.

Strategically, SEC wants to be a borderless, global brand that is a household word wherever its products and services are available. Its strategic objective is to create both qualitative and quantitative growth and deliver competitive value to all stakeholders—customers, partners, and shareholders—while maintaining profitability. To accomplish this objective, their emphasis is on optimizing the supply chain to make operations as efficient and timely as possible. SEC integrated Six Sigma into its entire business process as a way to perfect its fundamental approach to product, process, and personnel development (see Figure 3.11).

As a foundation for its Six Sigma thrust, SEC began by pursuing a pervasive goal of developing its internal resources, especially people, to put innovation first in the development and design of products, in manufacturing and marketing, and in the growth of employees. The Six Sigma process began in late 1999 and early 2000 with training for SEC's management, champions, and other employees responsible for planning and deployment. Within three years, about one-third of its 49,000 employees received formal training. In 2000, manufacturing began to use Six Sigma improvement processes, and then expanded its scope to include "Design for Six Sigma" (see Chapter 13) in designing new products. Next, Six Sigma was applied to business and internal support processes where customer needs and interactions have become increasingly critical. These processes include transactional activities such as completing an invoice, designing procedures to improve cycle time, and improving processes in human resources, accounting, business planning, sales, call centers, and customer service. All business processes are candidates for Six Sigma improvement, and SEC's finance and marketing people have begun to embrace it.

Through Sigma Park, an intranet site available to all SEC facilities worldwide, SEC provides reference materials, benchmarking opportunities, reports to senior management, and enhancement for Six Sigma projects whose team members span several continents. Cross-border organizational learning is advanced as the Six Sigma methodologies are applied consistently from location to location.

In 2000 and 2001, SEC completed 3,290 Six Sigma projects, which contributed to a 50 percent (an average) reduction in defects. No thought is given to improvement in quality and productivity without Six Sigma. These initiatives contributed to

Figure 3.11 Samsung's Integration of Six Sigma

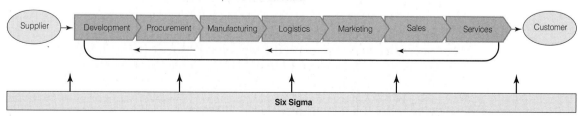

the company's recent growth. For example, SEC became one of the top 10 electronic and electrical equipment manufacturing companies in the world, with the best operating profit ratios and superior fiscal soundness. Its debt to equity ratio also is lower than that of any top ranking company; and it reached the number one position in *BusinessWeek*'s 2002 information technology guide. Employees believe that quality is the single most important reason for the company's higher sales, lower costs, satisfied customers, and profitable growth.

The four factors that made Six Sigma successful at SEC are the following:

1. Strong proactive support with required resources provided by top management
2. Acceptance and implementation of Six Sigma's basic disciplines by employees
3. Linkage with all innovative and infrastructure activities
4. Accurate and fair evaluation of all successful Six Sigma projects, with meaningful recognition and rewards for employees

A flattening of the organizational structure, making it easier for key decisions to be made at lower levels, was another factor contributing to SEC's success. SEC intends to use Six Sigma and innovation to remain a leader in the digital economy.

Key Issues for Discussion

1. Although this case application suggests that Six Sigma was deployed quite easily at Samsung, what specific challenges do you think the company faced after it decided to begin its Six Sigma thrust? How might its prior focus on quality have made Six Sigma easier to implement?
2. Suggest some specific types of Six Sigma projects within the supply chain in Figure 3.11 that Samsung might have undertaken.

 # REVIEW QUESTIONS

1. Explain the Deming chain reaction.
2. How does Deming's definition of quality compare with the definitions discussed in Chapter 1?
3. Summarize the four components of Profound Knowledge. How do they mutually support each other?
4. Explain the implications of not understanding the components of Profound Knowledge as suggested by Peter Scholtes.
5. Summarize Deming's 14 Points. How does each point relate to the four components of Profound Knowledge?
6. Explain Juran's Quality Trilogy.
7. How is Juran's philosophy similar to or different from Deming's?
8. What are Crosby's Absolutes of Quality Management and Basic Elements of Improvement? How are they similar to or different from Deming's 14 Points?
9. Summarize the key contributions of Feigenbaum, Ishikawa, and Taguchi to modern quality thinking.
10. How does Taguchi's approach to measuring variation support the Deming philosophy?
11. What does JUSE mean by *company-wide quality control*? How do the Deming Prize criteria relate to this concept?
12. Summarize the purposes of the Malcolm Baldrige National Quality Award.
13. Explain the Baldrige Award framework and why each element is important in any quality system.
14. Describe the key issues addressed in each of the seven categories of the Criteria for Performance Excellence.

15. How do companies that do not apply for the award commonly use the Baldrige Award criteria?
16. How do the Baldrige criteria support Deming's 14 Points? (See the Bonus Materials.)
17. Explain the differences among the Baldrige, European, Canadian, and Australian Quality Awards.
18. Briefly summarize the key elements of ISO 9000. Are these activities something that every company should be doing? Why or why not?
19. List the reasons companies pursue ISO 9000 registration. What benefits can registration provide?
20. Why has ISO 9000 been controversial? How has the 2000 revision addressed some of the controversial issues?
21. Describe the evolution of Six Sigma. What impact has it had on General Electric?
22. What are the similarities and differences among Six Sigma, ISO 9000, and the Baldrige approaches? (See also the Bonus Materials for this chapter.)

 DISCUSSION QUESTIONS

1. Mary Matthews works for an airline as a reservation clerk. Her duties include answering the telephone, making reservations, and providing information to customers. Her supervisor told her to be courteous and not to rush callers. However, the supervisor also told her that she must answer 25 calls per hour so that the department's account manager can prepare an adequate budget. Mary comes home each day frustrated because the computer is slow in delivering information that she needs, and sometimes reports no information. Without information from the computer, she is forced to use printed directories and guides. What is Mary's job? What might Deming say about this situation? Drawing upon Deming's principles, outline a plan to improve this situation.
2. What implications might the Theory of Knowledge have for Wall Street analysts who react to quarterly earnings reports?
3. Discuss the interrelationships among Deming's 14 Points. How do they support each other? Why must they be viewed as a whole rather than separately?
4. The following themes form the basis for Deming's philosophy. Classify the 14 Points into these categories and discuss the commonalties within each category.
   a. Organizational purpose and mission
   b. Quantitative goals
   c. Revolution of management philosophy
   d. Elimination of seat-of-the-pants decisions
   e. Cooperation building
   f. Improvement of manager/worker relations
5. Think of a system with which you are familiar, such as your college, fraternity, or a student organization. What is the purpose of that system? What would it mean to optimize that system?
6. List some examples of variation that you observe in your daily life. How might they be reduced?
7. Suggest ways that management can recognize the existence of fear in an organization. What strategies might managers use to deal with and eliminate fear?
8. Discuss how Deming's 14 Points can apply to an academic environment. How can learning and classroom performance be improved by applying Deming's philosophy?

9. In a videotape made in 1993, Deming related a story of a woman executive who spent an entire day flying from city to city, changing planes several times, because her company's travel department received a cheaper fare than if she had taken a direct flight. How does this example violate the concepts of Profound Knowledge and the 14 Points, and what should the company do about it?

10. The original version of Deming's 14 Points (developed in the early 1980s) is given in Table 3.4. Contrast each of these with the revised version in Table 3.1 early in the chapter. Explain the implications of the changes. Why might Deming have made these changes?

11. Create a matrix diagram in which each row is a category of the Baldrige Award criteria and four columns correspond to a level of organizational maturity with respect to quality:
    • Traditional management practices
    • Growing awareness of the importance of quality
    • Development of a solid quality management system
    • Outstanding, world-class management practice

    In each cell of the matrix, list two to five characteristics that you would expect to see for a company in each of the four situations for that criteria category. How might this matrix be used as a self-assessment tool to provide directions for improvement?

12. Contrast the categories of the Baldrige Award with the Deming Prize (see the Bonus Materials). How are they similar? Different?

13. Discuss the implications of the Baldrige criteria for e-commerce. What are the specific challenges that e-commerce companies face within each category of the criteria?

14. What philosophical changes might be required to implement a Six Sigma process in a hospital, government agency, or not-for-profit organization? Are they likely to be easy or difficult?

15. How might the principles of Six Sigma be used to improve a quality process in a school or university? What elements of the Six Sigma philosophy might be difficult to obtain support for in the educational environment? Why?

PROJECTS, ETC.

1. Study the annual reports of some major companies issued over a period of several years. Do you see evidence of implementation of the quality philosophies discussed in this chapter?

2. Design a questionnaire or survey instrument to determine the degree to which an organization is "Demingized." Explain how you developed the questions.

3. Visit the National Quality Program Web site (http://www.baldrige.org) and write a report on the information that can be found there.

4. Select a category from the Baldrige Education criteria on the CD-ROM and interview your school administrators using the criteria questions as a basis for the interview. Write a report assessing your school against the criteria.

5. Carefully compare the Baldrige business, education, and health care criteria available on the CD-ROM. Evaluate the differences in the criteria categories among the sectors. If you were to write criteria for a not-for-profit organization such as a United Way agency, or a government entity, such as a state department of taxation or a municipal government, what specific changes would you suggest in the criteria to meet their unique culture and requirements?

Table 3.4 Original Version of Deming's 14 Points

1. Create constancy of purpose toward improvement of product and service, with the aim of becoming competitive and to stay in business and to provide jobs.
2. Adopt the new philosophy. We are in a new economic age. Western management must awaken to the challenge, must learn their responsibilities, and take on leadership for change.
3. Cease dependence on inspection to achieve quality. Eliminate the need for inspection on a mass basis by building quality into the product in the first place.
4. End the practice of awarding business on the basis of price tag alone. Instead, minimize total cost. Move toward a single supplier for any one item, on a long-term relationship of loyalty and trust.
5. Improve constantly and forever the system of production and service to improve quality and productivity, and thus constantly decrease costs.
6. Institute training on the job.
7. Institute leadership. The aim of supervision should be to help people and machines and gadgets do a better job. Supervision of management is in need of overhaul, as well as the supervision of production workers.
8. Drive out fear so everyone can work effectively for the company.
9. Break down barriers between departments. People in research, design, sales, and production must work as a team, to foresee problems of production and those that may be encountered with the product or service.
10. Eliminate slogans, exhortations, and targets for the work force that ask for zero defects or new levels of productivity. Such exhortations only create adversarial relationships, as the bulk of the causes of low quality and low productivity belong to the system and thus lie beyond the power of the work force.
11a. Eliminate work standards (quotas) on the factory floor. Substitute leadership.
11b. Eliminate management by objective. Eliminate management by numbers, numerical goals. Substitute leadership.
12a. Remove barriers that rob hourly workers of their right to pride of workmanship. The responsibility of supervisors must be changed from sheer numbers to quality.
12b. Remove barriers that rob people in management and engineering of their right to pride in workmanship. This means, *inter alia*, abolishment of the annual or merit rating and of management by objective.
13. Institute a vigorous program of education and self-improvement.
14. Put everybody in the company to work to accomplish the transformation. The transformation is everybody's job.

Source: Reprinted from *Out of the Crisis* by W. Edwards Deming by permission of MIT Press and the W. Edwards Deming Institute. © 1986 by The W. Edwards Deming Institute, pp. 23–24.

6. Does your state have a quality award program? If so, obtain some current information about the program and report on it. If not, contact your state representative to see why not.
7. Interview some managers at a local company that is pursuing or has pursued ISO 9000 registration. Report on the reasons for achieving registration, the perceived benefits, and the problems the company encountered during the process. If they had previously been registered to the older ISO 9000:1994 standards, how has the recent ISO 9000:2000 revision affected their plans and progress?
8. Visit *Quality Digest's* ISO 9000 Registered Company Database at http://www.qualitydigest.com and report on the number of registered companies. How widespread is ISO 9000 in the United States?

9. Find a company that has implemented a Six Sigma process. What changes have they made in the organization in order to develop their Six Sigma approach?

CASES

Additional cases are available in the Bonus Materials Folder on the CD-ROM.

I. TECSMART ELECTRONICS[47]

TecSmart Electronics designs, manufactures, and repairs electronic power supplies for a variety of original equipment manufacturers in the computer, medical, and office products field. The company's focus is summed up by three simple words: quality, service, and value. The top management team started its quality journey in the mid-1980s, basing it on Deming's 14 Points. They established a Deming Steering Committee to guide the process and champion each of the 14 Points, and trained most of the employees by sending them to Deming seminars. Although the Deming philosophy provided the foundation to carry the company into the twenty-first century, the current CEO decided to pursue a Baldrige focus and began a process of self-assessment against the criteria to identify opportunities for improvement.

As a first preparatory step, the executive team spent a day off site to think about its management practices and create an initial list of its strengths, which are summarized here.

- Senior leaders set company objectives and guide cross-functional teams to review and develop individual plans for presentation to employees. Each department manager develops a supporting objective for each company objective, and nearly every employee works on a team to support these objectives.
- Senior leaders participate in quarterly communication meetings with all employees to discuss company issues and answer questions. All employees receive full financial information from their managers each month.
- Senior leaders teach courses in TecSmart University on change management, customer service, quality, and leadership; meet with

customers, suppliers, and benchmarking partners; and are actively engaged in professional and community organizations.
- The company collects operational data in every department and evaluates its information requirements in monthly senior staff meetings and cross-functional task team meetings.
- TecSmart sets Six Sigma goals for most of its processes and converted process measurements to parts per million on all product lines.
- All employees are trained in a five-step problem-solving process based on defining problems, collecting data, analyzing the cause of the problem, developing a solution, and implementing change.
- Inputs to the strategic planning process include customer feedback, market research, and benchmarking information from customers, suppliers, competitors, and industry leaders. Team analyses are evaluated at an off-site planning meeting by all managers, resulting in long-range strategic planning documents, which are discussed with the rest of the workforce as well as major suppliers for feasibility. Once agreed upon, department teams develop detailed action plans with measurable goals. The CEO reviews progress every month.
- TecSmart uses more than a dozen different processes to gather customer information, and validates the information by consolidation and cross-referencing.
- All employees receive customer relationship training. Customer service employees help define service standards, which are tracked on a routine basis.
- All complaints are handled by the vice president of sales and resolved within two days.

The vice president is responsible for ensuring that any process that generated a complaint is improved.

- Customer satisfaction data is acquired from sales representatives, executive phone calls and visits, and satisfaction surveys. These data are reviewed and compared by the executive team during the strategic planning process.
- TecSmart uses self-managed work groups in which employees make most day-to-day decisions while managers focus on coaching and process improvement. Hourly workers can make process changes with the agreement of only one other person, and salespeople are authorized to travel whenever they feel it necessary for customer service.
- The average employee receives 72 hours of internal quality/service-related training, and quality training is mandatory for all salespeople, engineers, office staff, and managers.
- Employees are surveyed each year to gauge how effectively the company implemented Deming's 14 Points, rating each on a scale of 1–10.
- Cross-functional teams guide product development, which includes four interim reviews by executive management. Meetings are held with customers to identify needs and requirements and to review progress at the end of each phase of the development process.

- New product introduction teams work with design engineers and customers to ensure that design requirements are met during manufacturing and testing. All processes are formally documented, using statistical process control to monitor variation and provide a basis for corrective action. Statistical methods are used to optimize processes.
- Quality is assessed through internal audits, employee opinion surveys, and customer feedback.
- Suppliers are involved in early stages of a product development program. Quality requirements for suppliers have been identified, and certified suppliers' materials are exempt from incoming inspection.

Discussion Questions

1. Discuss how the practices that TecSmart identified support Deming's 14 Points.
2. How do these practices support the Baldrige criteria? Specifically, identify which of the questions in the criteria each of these practices address.
3. What are some of the obvious opportunities for improvement relative to the Baldrige criteria? What actions would you recommend that TecSmart do to improve its pursuit of performance excellence using the Baldrige criteria?

II. Can Six Sigma Work in Health Care?

Colin David is the CEO of a Southwest Louisiana Regional Medical Center (SLRMC), a small non-profit hospital with 150 beds and 825 employees, offering a wide range of outpatient and inpatient services. Colin had just returned from a health care conference during which one of the keynote speakers—from the financial services industry—discussed the philosophy and benefits of Six Sigma and urged health care organizations to consider moving toward a Six Sigma framework. Colin was quite excited. However, he knew that changing the culture in a hospital was indeed difficult. However, he felt that if he could accomplish that, SLRMC could truly become a nationally recognized leader in the industry. In discussing the

concept, the executive management team was also excited at the possibilities. They identified four key areas where they thought that Six Sigma could lead to significant benefits: patient services, quality assessment, financial management, and human resources. As time was running short for the meeting, the team concluded with one major action item: the directors in charge of each of these four areas were to develop a set of strategic Six Sigma projects that would form the basis for the initiative. However, after the meeting broke up, Colin realized that in their initial euphoria over the potential of Six Sigma, they had not thought of how to introduce it to the hospital staff and physicians, or how to manage the initiative. Colin decided that it would be best to call in a consultant to help. Because *you* were highly recommended, you have a meeting scheduled with Colin in one week. What would be your agenda for this meeting? What questions would you need answered before proposing a Six Sigma implementation plan? How would you design an infrastructure to support Six Sigma at SLRMC?

III. CapStar Health System, Inc.: Understanding the Organizational Environment

The complete CapStar case study, a fictitious example of a Baldrige application, can be found on the CD-ROM accompanying this book. (The case is based on the 2002 Baldrige criteria, which has some key differences in the criteria questions as compared to later criteria, however these differences are not relevant for this case.) Read the Organizational Profile, which is a description of the organizational environment, relationships, and challenges that impact CapStar's performance excellence approaches. In examining the scope of the first six categories (excluding results) in the 2003 Baldrige Health Care criteria (also available on the CD-ROM), list the *most relevant factors* from the Organizational Profile that would affect your assessment of the management practices for this organization. For example, in considering the Human Resource Focus category, you might note that one of CapStar's strategic challenges is that its chief competitor has been aggressively pursuing CapStar's key physi-

cians. Therefore, you might expect to see that their human resource practices would focus closely on physician satisfaction and well-being. You might also note that CapStar's nonmanagement workforce is 41 percent professional, 22 percent technical, 14 percent clerical, and 13 percent service. These percentages would suggest that work systems and reward/recognition approaches need to be tailored to meet the unique needs of these employee segments. Thus, in your listing of the most relevant factors for the Human Resource Focus category, the first two factors might be the following:

- A key competitor is aggressively pursuing CapStar's key physicians.
- The nonmanagement workforce is 41 percent professional, 22 percent technical, 14 percent clerical, and 13 percent service.

Complete this list for each category and briefly justify why these factors would be important.

IV. GeoOrb Polymers, North America: Understanding the Organizational Environment

The complete GeoOrb Polymers, North America case study, a fictitious example of a Baldrige application based on the 2003 business criteria, can be found on the CD-ROM accompanying this book.

Read the Organizational Profile and perform the same type of analysis as requested in Case III for CapStar Health Systems.

ENDNOTES

1. John Hillkirk, "World-Famous Quality Expert Dead at 93," *USA Today,* December 21, 1993.

2. W. Edwards Deming, *The New Economics for Industry, Government, Education* (Cambridge, MA: MIT Center for Advanced Engineering Study, 1993).

3. The quincunx simulator is contained in the Quality Gamebox, a registered trademark of Productivity-Quality Systems, Inc., 10468 Miamisburg-Springboro Road, Miamisburg, OH 45342; 937-885-2255; 800-777-3020. The Quality Gamebox software is distributed with this book with permission of PQ Systems, Inc.

4. Clarence Irving Lewis, *Mind and the World* (Mineola, NY: Dover, 1929).

5. Peter R. Scholtes, "Communities as Systems," *Quality Progress,* July 1997, 49–53.

6. Matthew W. Ford and James R. Evans, "Managing Organizational Self-Assessment: Follow-Up and Its Influence Factors," working paper, Department of Management & Marketing, Northern Kentucky University, 2003.

7. Walter A. Shewhart, *Economic Control of Quality of a Manufactured Product* (New York: Van Nostrand, 1931).

8. Gervase R. Bushe, "Cultural Contradictions of Statistical Process Control in American Manufacturing Organizations," *Journal of Management* 14 (May 1988), 19–31.

9. "Detroit vs. the UAW: At Odds over Teamwork," *Business Week,* August 24, 1987, 54–55.

10. Yonatan Reshef and Helen Lam, "Union Responses to Quality Improvement Initiatives: Factors Shaping Support and Resistance," *Journal of Labor Research,* Winter 1999, 11–131.

11. Brad Stratton, "The Price Is Right: ASQC Annual Salary Survey," *Quality Progress* 21, no. 9 (September 1988), 24–29.

12. Adapted from March Laree Jacques, "Big League Quality," *Quality Progress,* August 2001, 27–34.

13. Jeremy Main, "Under the Spell of the Quality Gurus," *Fortune,* August 18, 1986, 30–34.

14. Philip B. Crosby, *Quality Is Free* (New York: McGraw-Hill, 1979), 200–201.

15. Facts in this section were obtained from "Profile: the ASQC Honorary Members A. V. Feigenbaum and Kaoru Ishikawa," *Quality Progress* 19, no. 8 (August 1986), 43–45; and Bruce Brocka and M. Suzanne Brocka, *Quality Management: Implementing the Best Ideas of the Masters* (Homewood, IL: Business One Irwin, 1992).

16. April 17, 1979; cited in L. P. Sullivan, "Reducing Variability: A New Approach to Quality," *Quality Progress* 17, no. 7 (July 1984), 15–21.

17. Adapted from Jerry R. Junkins, "Insights of a Baldrige Award Winner," *Quality Progress* 27, no. 3 (March 1994), 57–58. Used with permission of Texas Instruments.

18. Nancy Blodgett, "Service Organizations Increasingly Adopt Baldrige Model," *Quality Progress,* December 1999, 74–78.

19. Paul W. DeBaylo, "Ten Reasons Why the Baldrige Model Works," *The Journal for Quality and Participation,* January/February 1999, 1–5.

20. DeBaylo, *ibid.*

21. Paul M. Bobrowski, and John H. Bantham, "State Quality Initiatives: Mini-Baldrige to Baldrige Plus," *National Productivity Review* 13, no. 3 (Summer 1994), 423–438.

22. Letter from W. Edwards Deming, *Harvard Business Review,* January–February 1992, 134.

23. Kevin Shergold and Deborah M. Reed, "Striving for Excellence: How Self-Assessment Using the Business Excellence Model Can Result in Step Improvements in All Areas of Business Activities," *TQM Magazine* 8, no. 6 (1996), 48–52.

24. B. Nakhai, and J. Neves, "The Deming, Baldrige, and European Quality Awards," *Quality Progress,* April 1994, 33–37.

25. Michael J. Timbers, "ISO 9000 and Europe's Attempts to Mandate Quality," *Journal of European Business,* March–April 1992, 14–25.

26. http://www.bsi.org.uk/iso-tc176-sc2/. "Transition Planning Guidance for *ISO/DIS 9001:2000*," ISO/TC 176/SC 2/N 474, December, 1999.

27. Richard C. Randall, "Quality in the Dot.Com World," *Quality Progress,* February 2001, 86–87.

28. Amy Zuckerman, "ISO/QS-9000 Registration Issues Heating Up Worldwide," *The Quality Observer,* June 1997, 21–23.

29. Amy Zuckerman and Rosalind McClymont, "Tracking the Ongoing ISO 9000 Revisions," *Business Standards,* 2, no. 2 (March–April 2000), 13–15; Jack West, with Charles A. Cianfrani and Joseph J. Tsiakals, "A Breeze or a Breakthough? Conforming to ISO 9000:2000," *Quality Progress,* March 2000, 41–44. See also by West et al., "Quality Management Principles: Foundation of ISO 9000:2000 Family, Part 5," *Quality Progress,* February 2000, 113–116; and "Quality Management Principles: Foundation of ISO 9000:2000 Family, Part 6," *Quality Progress,* March 2000, 79–81.

30. Implementation guidelines are suggested by the case study by Steven E. Webster, "ISO 9000 Certification, A Success Story at Nu Visions Manufacturing," *IIE Solutions,* April 1997, 18–21.

31. ISO 9000 Update, *Fortune,* September 30, 1996, 134[J].

32. Astrid L. H. Eckstein, and Jaydeep Balakrishnan, "The ISO 9000 Series: Quality Management Systems for the Global Economy," *Production and Inventory Management Journal* 34, no. 4 (Fourth Quarter 1993), 66–71.

33. "Home Builder Constructs Quality with ISO 9000," *Quality Digest,* February 2000, 13.

34. Sandford Liebesman and James Mroz, "ISO 9000:2000 Experiences: First Results Are In," *Quality Progress,* April 2002, 52–59.

35. "Origin of Six Sigma: Designing for Performance Excellence," *Quality Digest,* (May 2000), 30; and Harry, Mikel and Richard Schroeder. *Six Sigma* (New York: Currency, 2000), 9–11.

36. A composite of ideas suggested by Stanley A Marash, "Six Sigma: Business Results Through Innovation," *ASQ's 54th Annual Quality Congress Proceedings,* 2000, 627–630; and Dick Smith and Jerry Blakeslee, *Strategic Six Sigma: Best Practices from the Executive Suite* (New York: Wiley, 2002).

37. Jack Welch, *Jack: Straight from the Gut* (New York: Warner Books, 2001), 329–330.

38. Jack Welch, *ibid,* 333–334.

39. "GE Reports Record Earnings with Six Sigma," *Quality Digest,* December 1999, 14.

40. See note 37.

41. Rochelle Rucker, "Six Sigma at Citibank," *Quality Digest,* December 1999, 28–32.

42. Ronald D. Snee, "Guest Editorial: Impact of Six Sigma on Quality Engineering," *Quality Engineering* 12, no. 3 2000, ix–xiv.

43. Ronald D. Snee and Roger W. Hoerl, *Leading Six Sigma* (Upper Saddle River, NJ: Prentice-Hall, 2002).

44. The authors are grateful to Joe Sener, VP Busi-

ness Excellence for Baxter International, for providing this information.

45. Pál Molnár, "Hungary's Journey to Business Excellence," *Quality Progress,* February 2003, 55–64. © 2003 American Society for Quality. Reprinted with permission.

46. Adapted from Jong-Yong Yun and Richard C.H. Chua, "Samsung Uses Six Sigma to Change its Image,"

Six Sigma Forum Magazine 2, no. 1 (November 2002), 13–16. © 2002 American Society for Quality. Reprinted with permission.

47. This case was inspired by the Zytec Application Summary, 1991 Winner of the Malcolm Baldrige National Quality Award.

BIBLIOGRAPHY

Breyfogle, Forrest W., III, James M. Cupello, and Becki Meadows. *Managing Six Sigma.* New York: Wiley-Interscience, 2001.

Brocka, Bruce, and M. Suzanne Brocka. *Quality Management: Implementing the Best Ideas of the Masters.* Homewood, IL: Business One Irwin, 1992.

Bush, David, and Kevin Dooley."The Deming Prize and the Baldrige Award: How They Compare." *Quality Progress* 22, no. 1 (January 1989), 28–30.

DeCarly, Neil J., and W. Kent Sterett. "History of the Malcolm Baldrige Award." *Quality Progress* 23, no. 3 (March 1990), 21–27.

Deming, W. Edwards. *The New Economics for Industry, Government, Education.* Cambridge, MA: MIT Center for Advanced Engineering Study, 1993.

———. *Out of the Crisis.* Cambridge, MA: MIT Center for Advanced Engineering Study, 1986.

Duncan, W. Jack, and Joseph G. Van Matre. "The Gospel According to Deming: Is It Really New?" *Business Horizons,* July–August 1990, 3–9.

Eckes, George. *The Six Sigma Revolution,* New York: John Wiley & Sons, 2001.

Harry, Mikel J. "Framework for Business Leadership." *Quality Progress,* April 2000.

Harry, Mikel J. *The Vision of Six Sigma: A Roadmap for Breakthrough.* Phoenix, AZ: Tri Star Publishing, 1997.

Hoerl, Roger W. "Six Sigma and the Future of the Quality Profession." *Quality Progress,* June 1998.

Hunt, V. Daniel. *Managing for Quality.* Homewood, IL: Business One Irwin, 1993.

Juran, J. M. *Juran on Quality by Design.* New York: The Free Press, 1992.

———. "Product Quality—A Prescription for the West." *Management Review,* June–July 1981.

———. "The Quality Trilogy." *Quality Progress* 19 (August 1986), 19–24.

Kivenko, Ken. "Improve Performance by Driving Out Fear." Quality Progress 27, no. 10 (October 1994), 77–79.

Lowe, J. *Jack Welch Speaks.* New York: John Wiley & Sons, 1998.

Ohio Quality and Productivity Forum Roundtable. "Deming's Point Four: A Study." *Quality Progress* 21, no. 12 (December 1988), 31–35.

Raturi, A., and D. McCutcheon. "An Epistemological Framework for Quality Management," working paper. Cincinnati, OH: University of Cincinnati, Department of Quantitative Analysis and Information Systems, March 1990.

Reimann, Curt W. "The Baldrige Award: Leading the Way in Quality Initiatives." *Quality Progress* 22, no. 7 (July 1989), 35–39.

Scherkenbach, William W. *Deming's Road to Continual Improvement.* Knoxville, TN: SPC Press, 1991.

P A R T 2

THE MANAGEMENT SYSTEM

For quality to succeed in an organization, it must become a part of everyone's daily activities. A total quality system must be built on effective managerial practices that focus on customers; provide leadership to all employees; integrate quality into strategic business planning; involve and motivate everyone; build quality into all products and processes; and provide useful information to maintain high performance, continuously improve, and lead to sustainable competitive advantage. The Baldrige framework, introduced in Chapter 3, provides a structure for designing an organization around high-performance management practices. Part 2 of this book addresses the seven key elements of the Baldrige criteria on which a total quality foundation should be built.

Chapter 4 examines the role and importance of customers and customer satisfaction in achieving strategic business objectives, and describes various approaches for acquiring customer knowledge and measuring satisfaction. Chapter 5 focuses on leadership and strategic planning activities, emphasizing the importance of leadership in driving quality throughout an organization, and the natural role that leaders play in strategic planning, as well as introducing useful tools that support strategic planning efforts. Chapter 6 examines the role of human resources in achieving total quality, including the design of high-performance work systems and effective management of human resources. Chapter 7 discusses process management, including approaches for controlling and improving design, production, delivery, and support processes by which work gets accomplished. Chapter 8 deals with measurement and strategic information management, focusing on the importance of using a balanced set of performance measures and business results to guide organizational decisions and direction. In each of these chapters, we describe "leading practices" that high-performance organizations, primarily Baldrige winners, use in deploying the principles of total quality and examine how each topic is also addressed in ISO 9000 and Six Sigma initiatives.

Finally, Chapter 9 addresses the all-important topic of how to build a true quality organization by developing a culture that provides the motivation and direction for everyone to work toward the organization's vision. It also emphasizes that quality is a journey and must be sustained. As both managers and workers enter and leave the organization, TQ requires constant renewal. This chapter looks toward the future; as you read it, we hope that you will also look toward your future and what these principles will mean to the rest of your life.

CHAPTER 4

FOCUSING ON CUSTOMERS

Feargal Quinn is the executive chairman of Superquinn, a 5,600-employee, 19-store chain of supermarkets in Ireland. In every deed, the focus is on persuading the customer to return.[1] Quinn calls it the "boomerang principle." His tireless and inventive exploration of this principle earned him the reputation as Ireland's "pope of customer service." Superquinn inspires such intense devotion that many customers say that they drive out of their way—and past several of its biggest competitors—to shop there. At Superquinn, you don't have to pay for broccoli stalks and carrot tops you never use; the store provides scissors to cut off what you don't want. The checkout technology provides a running tab on a screen that faces the customer, and then organizes the final receipt by product category, rather than the order in which products were scanned. Every store features a professionally staffed playhouse where mothers can leave young children while they shop. The program costs the company a bundle, but it has earned even more in loyal customers and reputation. Kindergarten teachers around the country (Ireland doesn't have preschool) recognize "Superquinn kids" as the most socialized and school-ready of each new class. Each month, Superquinn managers are required to spend time in customers' shoes, shopping, asking questions, lodging complaints, waiting in line. Superquinn's fresh produce, butchers, and fishmongers are mixed in with futuristic flat screen displays, digital shelf labels, and kiosks that link customers to their bank, their SuperClub account, as well as to wine recommendations and interactive recipe planners. Quinn notes that "What seems reasonable or even valuable from the perspective of the company is often glaringly wrong from the point of view of the customer."

In Japanese, a single word, *okyakusama*, means both "customer" and "honorable guest." World-class organizations are obsessed with meeting and exceeding customer expectations. Many companies such as The Ritz-Carlton Hotel Company, Disney, and Nissan Motor Co.'s Infiniti division were built on the notion of satisfying the customer. Home Depot, cited by Wal-Mart's CEO as the best retail organization in the United States, has as its service philosophy: "Every customer has to be treated like your mother, your father, your sister, or your brother."[2]

Other firms have to *learn* to be customer-focused. Many entrepreneurial start-up companies, for example, create new markets with innovative products; however, this process essentially tells customers what they want. As customers became more sophisticated and competition increases, these firms often face a competitive crisis and must begin to listen

> *To create satisfied customers, the organization needs to identify customers' needs, design the production and service systems to meet those needs, and measure the results as the basis for improvement.*

more closely to customers. Many organizations simply have not developed adequate management practices in this area. A Deloitte and Touche research study noted that 83 percent of executives surveyed said that the quality of their customer relationships will be a critical factor to compete in the twenty-first century, yet only 56 percent of them felt they had strong capabilities in this area.[3]

The organization must also use customer focus as a key driver for its strategic planning activities. This chapter focuses on this concept of customer-driven quality. The *Quality Profiles* on the following page provide two examples of organizations that focus considerable attention on their customers.

THE IMPORTANCE OF CUSTOMER SATISFACTION AND LOYALTY

Avis recognizes two ways to increase market share in the rental car business: (1) by buying large volumes of corporate business with extremely low rates, and (2) by improving customer satisfaction levels, thereby increasing repurchase intent and repeat business. Avis stated that it will not buy business at low rates for the sole purpose of increasing market share. Avis's marketing department uses a full range of research and analysis to keep pace with changing market

> *Customer wants and needs drive competitive advantage, and statistics show that growth in market share is strongly correlated with customer satisfaction.*

QUALITY PROFILES

CUSTOM RESEARCH INCORPORATED AND BI

Custom Research Inc. (CRI), is a national marketing research firm based in Minneapolis with about 100 employees. CRI adopted a highly focused customer-as-partner approach in 1988, and leverages an intensive focus on customer satisfaction, a team-oriented workforce, and information technology to pursue individualized service and satisfied customers. Senior management aimed for high levels of consistency and competence in delivering its services by organizing, systematizing, and measuring quality. Each research project is monitored on four essentials: accuracy, on time, on budget, and meeting or exceeding client expectations. CRI's business system is focused on a "Surprise and Delight" strategy, supported by five key business drivers: people, processes, requirements, relationships, and results.

Customer surveys have shown that CRI meets or exceeds its clients' expectations on 97 percent of its projects. More impressive is the fact that 70 percent of its clients said that the company *exceeded* expectations. CRI was rated by 92 percent of clients as "better than competition" on the key dimension "overall level of service." CRI received a Baldrige award in 1996.

BI develops business improvement and incentive programs to help other companies to achieve their own goals by enhancing the performance of the people who hold the keys to success—customers' employees, distributors, or consumers. As one of the three major players offering such programs across the country, BI employs more than 1,400 associates. Most are located at its headquarters in Minneapolis. Others are in Eden Valley, Minnesota; Sioux Falls, South Dakota; and in 21 U.S. sales offices. BI works behind the scenes to help their customers succeed by integrating communications, training, measurement, and rewards to improve performance. Almost every BI account requires a customized product or service. Improvement efforts are driven by the goal of customer delight and grouped under a process management system known as the "BI Way," which includes training, problem-solving techniques, process improvement, incentives, and a focus on results. BI has identified five corporate objectives that are front and center in every decision made by the company: revenue, productivity, customer satisfaction, associate satisfaction, and added value. Every action at BI must support at least one of these objectives, and all plans, improvement teams, and measures that track progress and quantify the company's success are tied to these objectives. BI first began using the Baldrige approach to quality and performance improvement in 1990, and applied for 10 consecutive years before winning in 1999, clearly demonstrating a commitment to continuous improvement and the persistence needed to reach a high level of performance.

Company revenue grew by a cumulative 47 percent over the second half of the 1990s. BI consistently outperformed its two key competitors on customer-focused results. In 1998, for instance, a key measure of overall customer satisfaction scored 8.5 on a 10-point scale compared with competitor ratings of 7.9 and 7.6; on-time performance scored 8.1 compared to 7.9 and 7.7 for competitors; and a measure of accurate performance was 8.1 versus 7.8 and 7.7 for competitors. Associate retention was 83 percent, which was particularly strong in a tight Twin Cities labor market.

Source: Malcolm Baldrige National Quality Award, Profiles of Winners, National Institute of Standards and Technology, Department of Commerce.

trends and develops programs that respond to customers' needs. Through information technology, Avis queries all customers at car return to monitor trends and levels of customer satisfaction. It also calls 1,500 customers each month to assess in detail satisfaction levels in each of nine service delivery areas.[4]

Customer satisfaction is also an important factor for the bottom line. One study found that companies with a 98 percent customer retention rate are twice as profitable as those at 94 percent. Studies have also shown that dissatisfied customers tell at least twice as many friends about bad experiences than they tell about good ones. Johnson Controls, Inc. (JCI), discovered that 91 percent of contract renewals came from customers who were either satisfied or very satisfied. A percentage point increase in the overall satisfaction score was worth $13 million in service contract renewals annually. JCI also learned that those customers who gave a not satisfied rating had a much higher defection rate. After seeing the financial impact of customer satisfaction, JCI made improving customer satisfaction a key initiative.[5]

Even though satisfaction is important, modern firms need to look further. Achieving strong profitability and market share requires *loyal* customers—those who stay with a company and make positive referrals. Satisfaction and loyalty are very different concepts. To quote Patrick Mehne, the chief quality officer at The Ritz-Carlton Hotel Company: "Satisfaction is an attitude; loyalty is a behavior." Customers who are merely satisfied may often purchase from competitors because of convenience, promotions, or other factors. For example, Cadillac generally receives high ratings in the American Customer Satisfaction Index (discussed later in this chapter); however, its market share has declined. This lack of correlation suggests that satisfaction of Cadillac owners does not necessarily influence their next purchase. Loyal customers place a priority on doing business with a particular organization, and will often go out of their way or pay a premium to stay with the company. Loyal customers spend more, are willing to pay higher prices, refer new clients, and are less costly to do business with. As an example, although Home Depot customers spend only about $38 each visit, they shop 30 times annually and spend more than $25,000 throughout a lifetime.[6] Carl Sewell, owner of Sewell Cadillac in Dallas, calculated that the average lifetime value of a loyal customer for his dealership was $332,000.[7]

> *A firm cannot create loyal customers without first creating satisfied customers.*

Statistics also show that the typical company gets 65 percent of its business from existing customers, and it costs five times more to find a new customer than to keep an existing one happy.[8]

One study of a Tennessee commercial bank found that a 0.1 percentage point improvement in overall customer satisfaction translated into a 0.6 percentage point increase in customer retention. Customer satisfaction occurs when products and services meet or exceed customer expectations—our principal definition of quality. To exceed expectations, an organization must deliver ever-improving value to its customers. Value, as defined in Chapter 1, is quality related to price. Consumers no longer buy solely on the basis of price. They compare the total package of products and services that a business offers (sometimes called the **consumer benefit package**) with the price and with competitive offerings. The consumer benefit package influences the perception of quality and includes the physical product and its quality dimensions; presale support, such as ease of ordering; rapid, on-time, and accurate delivery; and postsale support, such as field service, warranties, and technical support. If competitors offer better choices for a similar price, consumers will rationally select the package with the highest perceived quality. One example is Midwest Express Airlines, a Milwaukee-based operation that caters to business travelers.

Midwest Express earned its reputation for providing the "best care in the air" by offering passengers luxury service at competitive coach or discounted fares. The airline offers free coffee and newspapers each morning at its gates, fresh-baked chocolate-chip cookies on afternoon flights, and steak and shrimp at dinner—in planes with wide leather seats, no more than two across. Such practices have produced a host of awards from travel magazines and consumer groups. It outperforms its competitors financially and in terms of the percentage of seats filled.[9]

If a competitor offers the same quality package of goods and services at a lower price, customers would generally choose the one having the lower price. However, lower prices require lower costs if the firm is to continue to be profitable. Quality improvements in operations reduce costs. Thus, understanding exactly what customers want and their perception of value is absolutely crucial to competitive success. Businesses must focus on both continually improving both the consumer benefit package and improving the quality of their internal operations.

In addition to value, satisfaction and loyalty are influenced greatly by service quality, integrity, and the relationships that organizations build with customers.[10] One study found that customers are five times more likely to switch because of perceived service problems than for price concerns or product quality issues.[11] As one small business owner stated, "We build customer loyalty by telling our customers the truth, whether it is good or bad news."[12]

The American Customer Satisfaction Index[13]

In 1994 the University of Michigan Business School and the American Society for Quality (ASQ) released the first American Customer Satisfaction Index (ACSI), an economic indicator that measures customer satisfaction at the national level. It was the first cross-industry benchmark in the United States to measure customer satisfaction. Similar indexes previously existed in Sweden and Germany. One of the goals is to raise the public's perception and understanding of quality, as do the consumer price index and other economic indicators. This increased awareness will help to interpret price and productivity measures and promote customer-driven quality.

The ACSI is based on customer evaluations of the quality of goods and services purchased in the United States and produced by both domestic firms and foreign firms with a substantial U.S. market share. The 1994 ACSI provides a baseline against which customer satisfaction levels can be tracked over time. It is designed to answer the questions: Are customer satisfaction and evaluations improving or declining for the nation's output of goods and services? Are they improving or declining for particular sectors of industry or specific industries? The index quantifies the value that customers place on products, and thus drives quality improvement. Companies can use the data to assess customer loyalty, identify potential barriers to entry within markets, predict return on investments, and pinpoint areas in which customer expectations are not being satisfied.

The econometric model used to produce ACSI links customer satisfaction to its determinants: customer expectations, perceived quality, and perceived value. Customer satisfaction, in turn, is linked to customer loyalty, which has an impact on profitability.

The index uses a tested, multi-equation econometric model to produce four levels of indexes: a national customer satisfaction index and indexes for seven industrial sectors, 40 specific industries, and 203 companies and agencies within those industries. ACSI is based on results of telephone interviews conducted in a national sample of 46,000 consumers who recently bought or used a company's product or service. This model is summarized in Figure 4.1.

Figure 4.1 ACSI Model

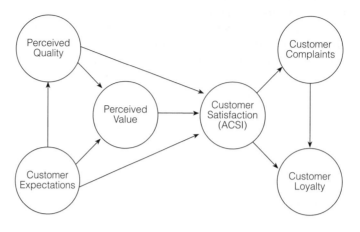

Source: Courtesy of National Quality Research Center (see endnote 13).

The initial 1994 results showed that nondurable manufacturing scored relatively high in customer satisfaction while public administration and government services scored relatively low. However, the overall national index declined continually until 1997, from 74.5 to 71.7, but gradually improved since then, and stood at 73.8 in the first quarter of 2003. Some of the largest improvements occurred in the retail, finance, and e-commerce sectors. In fact, Amazon.com achieved the highest score in the index, closely followed by eBay.

The ACSI is updated on a rolling basis with one to three sectors of the economy measured each quarter. Magazines such as *Fortune* and *Business Week* generally report current ACSI results; a question later in this chapter will ask you to research recent trends. Company scores and other information are available from http://acsi.asq.org/ and the Web links at evans.swlearning.com, http://www.bus.umich.edu/, and http://www.cfigroup.com/.

In April 2000, a similar European Customer Satisfaction Model was announced. It is administered by the European Organization for Quality (EOQ) and is based on customer evaluations of the quality of goods and services that are purchased in Europe and produced by both European Community and Non-European Community companies that have substantial European market share. It provides both national and European indexes (ECSI). ECSI has been built to be compatible with ACSI to allow comparison of results outside Europe. More about the index may be found http://www.eoq.org.

CREATING SATISFIED CUSTOMERS

Figure 4.2 provides a view of the process in which customer needs and expectations are translated into perceptions during the design, production, and delivery processes. True customer needs and expectations might be called **expected quality**. Expected quality is what the customer assumes will be received from the product. The producer identifies these needs and expectations and translates them into specifications for products and services. **Actual quality** is the outcome of the production process and what is delivered to the customer. However, actual quality may differ considerably from expected quality if information gets lost or is misinterpreted from one step to the next in Figure 4.2. For instance, ineffective market research efforts may incorrectly assess the true customer needs and expectations. Designers of products and services may develop specifications that inadequately reflect these needs. Manufacturing operations or customer-contact personnel may not deliver according to the specifications.

Customers will assess quality and develop perceptions (**perceived quality**) by comparing their expectations (expected quality) with what they receive (actual quality). If expected quality is higher than actual quality, then the customer will probably be dissatisfied. On the other hand, if actual quality exceeds expectations, then the customer will be satisfied or even surprisingly delighted. Because perceived quality drives consumer behavior, producers should make every effort to ensure that actual quality conforms to expected quality. One complication comes from the customer who sees and believes that the quality of the product is considerably different from what he or she actually receives (actual quality), which might be shaped by advertising or prior negative experiences. Thus, perceptions are not always accurate, and may even change over time, for example, when a customer finds that the initial quality of an automobile is high, but begins to experience problems in the long run.

Understanding these relationships requires a system of customer satisfaction measurement and the ability to use customer feedback for improvement. This model suggests that producers must take great care to ensure that customer needs are met or exceeded both by the design and production process (discussed further in Chapter 7). This effort requires that producers look at processes through the customers' eyes, not the organization's. An organization's focus is often reflected by the

Figure 4.2 Customer-Driven Quality Cycle

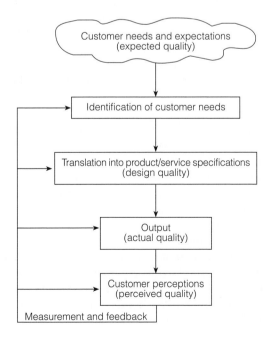

measures that it uses to evaluate its performance. When an organization's principal focus is on such things as production schedules and cost, productivity, or output quantity rather than ease of product use, availability, or cost of ownership, it is difficult to create a customer-focused culture.

Many organizations still focus more on processes and products from an internal perspective, rather than taking the perspective of the external customer.

Many causes of dissatisfaction are not attributable to production or service defects or employee mistakes.[14] Customers may not use the product correctly or may have unreasonable expectations about what it can do, marketing sometimes makes promises it cannot keep, or advertising is misleading. These issues suggest that companies need to pay greater attention to overall customer experiences that impact perceptions. Such attention might include better user manuals or information on product packaging as well as unambiguous advertising.

Leading Practices

Successful companies in every industry engage in a variety of customer-oriented practices that lead to profitability and market share. These generic practices, and some specific examples, are described in the following list.

1. *They clearly define key customer groups and markets, considering competitors and other potential customers, and segment their customers accordingly.* For example, Motorola's Commercial, Government, and Industrial Solutions Sector segments its customers in two ways, first by world region, and second by sales distribution channel (direct and indirect). The Ritz-Carlton Hotel Company ranks potential and current customers by volume, geography, and profit. GTE Directories (now Verizon Information Services) segments its customers into three distinct groups: advertisers, consumers, and companies that contract for Yellow Pages services. Such segmentation recognizes differences among customer groups and allows organizations to tailor their approaches to the unique needs of the groups.

2. *They understand both near-term and longer-term customer needs and expectations (the "voice of the customer") and employ systematic processes for listening and learning from customers.* At Whirlpool, when customers rate a competitor's product higher in satisfaction surveys, engineers take it apart to find out why. They also have hundreds of consumers fiddle with computer-simulated products while engineers record the users' reactions on videotape.[15] GTE Directories uses four basic approaches for identifying customer needs and monitoring satisfaction: (1) primary research, which includes focus groups, surveys, and interviews; (2) secondary research from monitoring competitors; (3) customer performance tracking that studies consumer behavior; and (4) customer feedback from sales representatives. Pearl River School District uses formative and summative assessment data on individual students and groups; student surveys; student utilization of offerings, facilities, and services; alumni surveys; educational research, active student participation in committees; and business focus groups.

3. *They understand the linkages between the voice of the customer and design, production, and delivery processes.* This practice ensures that no critical requirements fall through the cracks, and minimizes the potential gaps between expected quality and actual quality. Recognizing that many of its customers must drive hundreds of miles to one of less than 200 Lexus dealerships in the United States, the corporation designed a new service—they converted a truck into a mobile service station that can go to the customer's home. Ames Rubber Corporation uses a closed-loop communication system, called Continuous Supplier and Customer

Involvement. New products begin with a series of customer meetings to create a product brief, which outlines technical, material, and operational requirements. The product brief is then forwarded to internal departments to select materials, processes, and procedures as approved by the customer. The customer evaluates prototypes until completely satisfied. Finally, a trial production run is made. Not until the customer approves the results does full-scale production commence. Pal's Sudden Service derives service standards from its customer data and information, and incorporates them into staff training, reviewing them daily by store owners, operators, and assistant managers to build customer service skills. The *Quality in Practice* case, Software Support Center, in the Bonus Materials folder on the CD-ROM is an example of building operational improvements to increase customer satisfaction.

4. *They build relationships with customers through commitments that promote trust and confidence, provide easy accessibility to people and information; set effective service standards; train customer contact employees; and effectively follow-up on products, services, and transactions.* Eastman Chemical Company has a no-fault return policy on its plastics products believed to be the only one of its kind in the chemical industry. A customer may return any plastics product for any reason for a full refund. This policy was a direct result of Eastman's customer surveys. Eastman Chemical also provides a toll-free number through which customers can contact virtually anyone in the company—including the president—24 hours a day, seven days a week. Senior managers at Branch-Smith Printing visit key customers at least annually, and send a customer newsletter to former, current, and potential customers four times a year, containing information useful to graphic designers or production operations and offers a Help Desk e-mail address. Customer relationship management includes attention to training and developing customer-contact employees, and empowering them to do whatever is necessary to satisfy the customer.

5. *They have effective complaint management processes by which customers can easily comment, complain, and receive prompt resolution of their concerns.* Every customer relations representative at GTE Directories tries to handle customer complaints on the first call. They are authorized to propose immediate solutions, including credit adjustments, free advertising, or even advertising in other media to offset omissions or misprints. If immediate resolution is not possible, they must resolve the complaint within 10 days. The Ritz-Carlton uses Guest Incident Action forms, which are aggregated on a monthly basis at each hotel, to ensure that complaints were handled effectively and steps taken to eliminate the cause of the problem. Customer service or sales reps who receive a complaint at Branch-Smith Printing are responsible for providing resolution options within 48 hours, recording the complaint, and delivering it to the quality manager who must determine the cause and modify work instructions or conduct retraining as necessary.

6. *They measure customer satisfaction, compare the results relative to competitors, and use the information to evaluate and improve internal processes.* BI uses three approaches to track customer satisfaction: a Transactional Customer Satisfaction Index for immediate feedback, an annual Relationship Customer Satisfaction Index to learn about specific attributes of satisfaction and intent for repeat business, and a competitive study to see how it performs relative to competitors. SSM Health Care uses standardized patient satisfaction surveys that are customized to its five major patient segments, informal discussions with patients and families, and focus groups to understand satisfaction and dissatisfaction. They use online analytical processing software to drill down to a particular nursing unit, for

example, to examine inpatient loyalty and compare those to other units within a hospital or across the corporation. Then they distribute results electronically that identify specific improvements that will give the greatest gains in patient satisfaction to executives and patient satisfaction coordinators.

The remainder of this chapter expands upon these important themes.

IDENTIFYING CUSTOMERS

To understand customer needs, a company must know who its customers are. Most employees think that "customers" are those people who ultimately purchase and use a company's products. These end users, or **consumers**, certainly are an important group. Identifying consumers is a top management task related to the company's mission and vision. However, consumers are not the only customer group of concern to a business. The easiest way to identify customers is to think in terms of customer-supplier relationships.

AT&T uses a customer-supplier model as shown in Figure 4.3. Every process receives inputs from suppliers and creates outputs for customers. The feedback loops suggest that suppliers must also be considered as customers. They need appropriate information about the requirements they must meet. This model can be applied at the organization level, the process level, and the performer level (see the discussion of the "Three Levels of Quality" in Chapter 1.)

At the organization level, a business has various **external customers** that may fall between the organization and the consumer, and who have distinct needs and expectations. For example, manufacturers of consumer products distribute to retail stores such as Wal-Mart and grocery stores. The retail stores are external customers of the manufacturers. They have specific needs for timely delivery, appropriate product displays, accurate invoicing, and so forth. Because these stores allocate shelf space for the manufacturers' products, they represent important customers. The manufacturers are customers of the chemical companies, printing companies, and other suppliers of such things as materials and packaging materials.

At the process level, departments, and key cross-functional processes within a company have **internal customers** who contribute to the company's mission and depend on the department's or function's products or services to ultimately serve consumers and external customers. For instance, manufacturing is a customer of purchasing, a nursing unit is a customer of the hospital laundry, and reservations is a customer of the information systems department for an airline or hotel. Figure 2.1 in Chapter 2 is a good example of the internal customer-supplier relationships within a typical manufacturing firm.

Figure 4.3 AT&T's Customer-Supplier Model

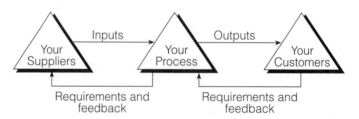

At the performer level, each employee receives inputs from others and produces some output for their internal customers. Such internal customers may be the assembly line worker at the next station, an executive's secretary, the order taker who passes along orders to the food preparer at McDonald's, or an X-ray technician who must meet a physician's request.

Identifying customers begins with asking some fundamental questions:

1. What products or services are produced?
2. Who uses these products and services?
3. Who do employees call, write to, or answer questions for?
4. Who supplies the inputs to the process?

Eventually, everyone can better understand their role in satisfying not only their internal customers, but also the external customers.

The natural customer-supplier linkages among individuals, departments, and functions build up the "chain of customers" throughout an organization that connect every individual and function to the external customers and consumers, thus characterizing the organization's value chain.

If an organization remembers that its customers include its employees and the public, then it consciously maintains a work environment conducive to the well-being and growth of all employees. Efforts in this area should go beyond the expected training and job-related education. Health, safety, and ergonomics (the study of physical capabilities of people in the design of workplaces, tools, instruments, and so on) should be included in quality improvement activities. Many companies offer special services such as counseling, recreational and cultural activities, non-work-related education, day care, flexible work hours, and outplacement to their employees. Texas Instruments, for instance, provides preventive health screenings at little or no cost to encourage personal involvement in health management. The company-sponsored employee association, called "Texins," uses fitness activities, recreational clubs, and family events to promote employee well-being.

The public is also an important customer of business. A company must look ahead to anticipate public concerns and assess the possible impacts on society of its products, services, and operations. Business ethics, environmental concerns, and safety are important societal issues. Companies can have a powerful influence on communities as corporate citizens through their contributions to charitable activities and the personal involvement of their employees. Based on a company's actions in promoting education, health care, and ethical conduct, the public judges a company's community behavior, which, in turn, can impact sales and profitability.

Finally, everyone is his or her own customer. As we discussed in Chapter 1, quality must be personalized or it will have little meaning at any other level. Robert Galvin, former CEO of Motorola, once told the Economic Club of Chicago, "Quality is a very personal obligation. If you can't talk about quality in the first person . . . then you have not moved to the level of involvement of quality that is absolutely essential."

Customer Segmentation

Customers generally have different requirements and expectations. A company usually cannot satisfy all customers with the same products or services. This issue is particularly important for companies that do business globally (just think of the differences in regulations for automobiles in various countries or the differences in electrical power systems in the United States versus Europe). Therefore, companies that segment customers into natural groups and customize the products or services are better able to respond to customers' needs. Juran suggests classifying customers into two main groups: the *vital few* and the *useful many*.[16] For example, organizers of conventions and meetings book large blocks of hotel rooms and have large catering needs. They represent the vital few and deserve special attention on an individual basis. Individual travelers and families are the useful many and typically need only standardized attention as a group. As another example, telecommunications services might be segmented as follows:

1. Residential customers, grouped according to dollar amount billed.
2. Business customers, grouped according to size of business, number of different services used, and volume of usage.
3. Third-party resellers, who purchase telecommunications capacity in bulk and manage their own customer groups.[17]

Another way of segmenting customers with an eye toward business results is by profitability. Many companies often spend a lot of money trying to acquire customers who are not profitable and probably will never be. Profit potential can be measured by the **net present value of the customer** (**NPVC**).[18] NPVC is the total profits (revenues associated with a customer minus expenses needed to serve a customer) discounted over time. For instance, the profit associated with customers at an automobile dealer consist of the profit from the sale of a car plus the profit from service visits. The number of transactions associated with repeat customers can easily be estimated. As another example, frequent fliers represent high NPVC customers to an airline. By segmenting them according to their frequency, an airline can determine the net value of offering increasing levels of benefits to fliers at higher frequency levels as a means of retaining current customers or enticing potential customers. Firms can also use NPVC to eliminate customers with low or negative values that represent a financial liability. For example, the Fleet Financial Group dropped its basic savings account interest rate, hoping to lose customers who had only savings accounts.[19]

> *Customer segmentation might be based on geography, demographic factors, ways in which products are used, volumes, or expected levels of service.*

> *Segmentation allows a company to prioritize customer groups, for instance by considering for each group the benefits of satisfying their requirements and the consequences of failing to satisfy their requirements.*

Determination of benefits and consequences allows the company to align its internal processes

Quality Spotlight
Fidelity
Investments

according to the most important customer expectations or their impact on shareholder value. For instance, Fidelity Investments realized that some customers that do limited business with Fidelity were using costly resources of service representatives too frequently. They began teaching them how to use the company's lowest cost channels: its automated phone lines and its Web site, which was made friendlier and easier to use. They could still talk to service reps, but the phone system identified their calls and routed them into longer queues as a disincentive to call, so the most profitable customers could be served more quickly. Fidelity was willing to lose some of these customers, because their profitability would increase; however, 96 percent of them stayed and most switched to lower-cost channels.[20]

UNDERSTANDING CUSTOMER NEEDS

David A. Garvin suggests that products and services have many dimensions of quality:[21]

1. *Performance:* A product's primary operating characteristics. Using an automobile as an example, characteristics would include such things as acceleration, braking distance, steering, and handling.

2. *Features:* The "bells and whistles" of a product. A car may have power options, a tape or CD deck, antilock brakes, and power seats.
3. *Reliability:* The probability of a product's surviving over a specified period of time under stated conditions of use. A car's ability to start on cold days and frequency of failures are reliability factors.
4. *Conformance:* The degree to which physical and performance characteristics of a product match preestablished standards. A car's fit and finish and freedom from noises and squeaks can reflect this dimension.
5. *Durability:* The amount of use one gets from a product before it physically deteriorates or until replacement is preferable. For a car it might include corrosion resistance and the long wear of upholstery fabric.
6. *Serviceability:* The speed, courtesy, and competence of repair work. An automobile owner might be concerned with access to spare parts, the number of miles between major maintenance services, and the expense of service.
7. *Aesthetics:* How a product looks, feels, sounds, tastes, or smells. A car's color, instrument panel design, control placement, and "feel of the road," for example, may make it aesthetically pleasing.

Table 4.1 gives some examples of these dimensions for both a manufactured product and a service product. They form the basis for what customers want. A driver seeking performance, for example, might look to BMW, while one who values reliability might prefer a Toyota. Others who want different features might choose Chrysler or Lincoln. Therefore, companies need to focus on the key drivers of customer satisfaction that lead to business success. Considerable marketing efforts go into correctly identifying customer needs. Ford, for example, identified about 90 features that customers want in sales and service, including a ride to their next stop when they drop off a car for service and appointments within one day of a desired date. Ford then trimmed the list to seven service standards and six sales standards against which dealers have begun to measure themselves.[22]

For services, research shows that five key dimensions of service quality contribute to customer perceptions:

1. *Reliability:* The ability to provide what was promised, dependably and accurately. Examples include customer service representatives responding in the promised

Table 4.1 Quality Dimensions of a Manufactured Product and Service

Quality Dimension	Manufactured Product (Stereo Amplifier)	Service Product (Checking Account)
Performance	Signal-to-noise ratio; power	Time to process customer requests
Features	Remote control	Automatic bill paying
Conformance	Workmanship	Accuracy
Reliability	Mean time to failure	Variability of time to process requests
Durability	Useful life	Keeping pace with industry trends
Serviceability	Ease of repair	Resolution of errors
Aesthetics	Oak cabinet	Appearance of bank lobby

Source: Adapted from Paul E. Pisek, "Defining Quality at the Marketing/Development Interface," *Quality Progress* 20, no. 6 (June 1987), 28–36.

time, following customer instructions, providing error-free invoices and statements, and making repairs correctly the first time.

2. *Assurance:* The knowledge and courtesy of employees, and their ability to convey trust and confidence. Examples include the ability to answer questions, having the capabilities to do the necessary work, monitoring credit card transactions to avoid possible fraud, and being polite and pleasant during customer transactions.

3. *Tangibles:* The physical facilities and equipment, and the appearance of personnel. Tangibles include attractive facilities, appropriately dressed employees, and well-designed forms that are easy to read and interpret.

4. *Empathy:* The degree of caring and individual attention provided to customers. Some examples might be the willingness to schedule deliveries at the customer's convenience, explaining technical jargon in a layperson's language, and recognizing regular customers by name.

5. *Responsiveness:* The willingness to help customers and provide prompt service. Examples include acting quickly to resolve problems, promptly crediting returned merchandise, and rapidly replacing defective products.

As one example, credit card users might have the following expectations for four key business activities associated with the card:

1. *Applying for an account:* Accessible, responsive, accurate, and professional
2. *Using the card:* Easy to use and hassle free, features, credit limit
3. *Billing:* Accurate, timely, easy to understand
4. *Customer service:* Accessible, responsive, and professional

A Japanese professor, Noriaki Kano, suggested three classes of customer requirements:

1. *Dissatisfiers:* Requirements that are expected in a product or service. In an automobile, a radio, heater, and required safety features are examples, which are generally not stated by customers but assumed as given. If these features are not present, the customer is dissatisfied.

2. *Satisfiers:* Requirements that customers say they want. Many car buyers want a sunroof, power windows, or antilock brakes. Although these requirements are generally not expected, fulfilling them creates satisfaction.

3. *Exciters/delighters:* New or innovative features that customers do not expect. The presence of unexpected features, such as a weather channel button on the radio or separate rear-seat audio controls that allow children to listen to different music than their parents, leads to high perceptions of quality.

Meeting customer expectations (that is, providing satisfiers) is often considered the minimum required to stay in business. To be truly competitive, companies must surprise and delight customers by going beyond the expected. Teams at Custom Research Inc., all have the same goal of "surprising and delighting" their clients. Client requirements are determined during client interviews, and drive account plans to ensure that each project meets or exceeds client requirements through clearly agreed-upon service standards, as well as longer-term process plans to improve the company's key processes. Feedback at the end of each project and annual interviews of major clients measure satisfaction and drive improvements. Thus, successful companies continually innovate and study customer perceptions to ensure that needs are being met.

> *As customers become familiar with them, exciters/delighters become satisfiers over time. Eventually, satisfiers become dissatisfiers.*

For instance, antilock brakes and air bags certainly were exciters/delighters when they were first introduced. Now, most car buyers expect them. Satellite navigational systems for automobiles are a more-recent example of exciters/delighters that are becoming more commonplace and may soon be viewed as satisfiers. As technology evolves, consumer expectations continually increase.

In the Kano classification system, dissatisfiers and satisfiers are relatively easy to determine through routine marketing research. For example, the hot-selling Ford F-150 pickup truck relied on extensive consumer research at the beginning of the redesign process. Perhaps one of the best examples of understanding customer needs and using this information to improve competitiveness is Frank Perdue's chicken business.[23] Perdue learned what customers' key purchase criteria were; these criteria included a yellow bird, high meat-to-bone ratio, no pinfeathers, freshness, availability, and brand image. He also determined the relative importance of each criterion, and how well the company and its competitors were meeting each one. By systematically improving his ability to exceed customers' expectations relative to the competition, Perdue gained market share even though his chickens were premium-priced. Among Perdue's innovations was using a jet engine that dried the chickens after plucking, allowing the pinfeathers to be singed off.

However, traditional market research efforts may not be effective in understanding exciters/delighters, and may even backfire. For example, Ford listened to a sample of customers and asked whether they wanted a fourth door on the Windstar minivan. Only about one-third thought it was a great idea, so Ford scrapped the idea. Chrysler, on the other hand, spent a lot more time living with owners of vans and observing their behavior, watching them wrestle to get things in and out, noting all the occasions where a fourth door would really be convenient, and was very successful after introducing a fourth door.[24] Thus, a company must make special effort to identify exciters/delighters. Sony and Seiko, for instance, go beyond traditional market research and produce dozens, even hundreds, of Walkman audio products and wristwatches with a variety of features to help them understand what excites and delights the customer. Those models that do not sell are simply dropped from the product lines. To practice this strategy effectively, marketing efforts must be supported by highly flexible manufacturing systems that permit rapid setup and quick response. Producing breakthrough products or services often requires that companies ignore consumer feedback and take risks. As Steve Jobs of Apple Computer noted about the iMac, "That doesn't mean we don't listen to customers, but it's hard for them to tell you what they want when they've never seen anything remotely like it. Take desktop video editing. I never got one request from someone who wanted to edit movies on his computer. Yet now that people see it, they say, 'Oh my God, that's great!'"[25]

Besides consumers, companies must also pay attention to the needs of external customers. In designing its Icy Rider sled, Rubbermaid used a combination of field research, competitive product analysis, and consumer focus groups. It also listened to major retailers, such as Wal-Mart, who wanted such products to be stackable and save space.[26]

Understanding the needs of internal customers is as important as understanding those of external customers. This point is reflected in the AT&T customer-supplier model in Figure 4.3, which the company uses to help employees comprehend internal customer-supplier issues. For example, in many service industries, customer-contact employees depend on a variety of information and support from internal suppliers, such as the information systems department, warehousing and production scheduling, and engineering and design functions. Failure to meet the needs of customer-contact employees will have a detrimental effect on external customers. One company,

GTE Supply, negotiates contracts, purchases products, and distributes goods for internal telephone operations customer groups at each GTE local telephone company. In response to complaints from its internal customers, GTE Supply began to survey its internal customers to identify needs and information for improvement. This approach dramatically improved satisfaction levels, reduced costs, and decreased cycle times.[27]

GATHERING AND ANALYZING CUSTOMER INFORMATION

Customer requirements, as expressed in the customer's own terms, are called the **voice of the customer**. However, the customer's meaning is the crucial part of the message. As the vice president of marketing at Whirlpool stated, "The consumer speaks in code."[28] Whirlpool's research showed that customers wanted clean refrigerators, which could be interpreted to mean that they wanted easy-to-clean refrigerators. After analyzing the data and asking more questions, Whirlpool found out what most consumers actually wanted was refrigerators that looked clean with minimum fuss. As a result, Whirlpool designed new models to have stucco-like fronts and sides that hide fingerprints.

When former Disney executive Paul Pressler assumed the CEO position at Gap, he met with each of Gap's top 50 executives, asking them such standard questions as "What about Gap do you want to preserve and why?" "What about Gap do you want to change and why?" and so on. But he also added one of his own: "What is your most important tool for figuring out what the consumer wants?"[29] Some of the key approaches to gathering customer information include the following:

> *Companies use a variety of methods, or "listening posts," to collect information about customer needs and expectations, their importance, and customer satisfaction with the company's performance on these measures.*

- Comment cards and formal surveys
- Focus groups
- Direct customer contact
- Field intelligence
- Complaint analysis
- Internet monitoring

The Bonus Materials folder on the CD-ROM contains more information and examples about these approaches.

Some companies use unconventional and innovative approaches to understand customers. Texas Instruments created a simulated classroom to understand how mathematics teachers use calculators; and a manager at Levi Strauss used to talk with teens who were lined up to buy rock concert tickets. Other approaches for obtaining useful customer and market information might be rapid innovation and field trials of products and services to better link research and development with design; close tracking of technological, competitive, societal, environmental, economic, and demographic factors that may affect customer requirements and expectations; and interviewing lost customers to determine the factors they use in their purchase decisions.

Voice of the customer data typically consist of a large number of verbal comments or other textual information. Such information needs to be sorted and consolidated into logical groups so that managers can understand the key issues. One useful tool for organizing large volumes of information efficiently and identifying natural patterns or groupings in the information is the **affinity diagram**. An affinity diagram is a main ingredient of the KJ method, developed in the 1960s by Kawakita Jiro, a Japanese anthropologist, which is a technique for gathering and organizing a large number of ideas or facts.[30] For example, suppose that a banking team determined that the most important requirement for mortgage customers is timely closings.[31] Through focus groups and other customer interviews, customers listed the following as key elements of timely closings:

1. Expeditious processes
2. Reliability
3. Consistent and accurate information
4. Competitive rates
5. Notification of industry changes
6. Prior approvals
7. Innovation
8. Modem link between computers
9. Buyer orientation
10. Diversity of programs
11. Mutual job understanding
12. Flexibility
13. Professionalism
14. Timely and accurate status reports

The company's team would group these items into logical categories (Post-It® notes are often used because they can be easily moved around on a wall) and provide a descriptive title for each category. The result is an affinity diagram, shown in Figure 4.4, which indicates that the key customer requirements for timely closings are communication, effective service, and loan products. Through organization of an affinity diagram, information can be used to better design a company's products and processes to meet customer requirements.

Affinity diagrams can be used for many other applications. For example, they can be used to organize any large group of complex ideas or issues, such as potential reasons for quality problems, or things a company must do to successfully market a product.

Figure 4.4 Affinity Diagram

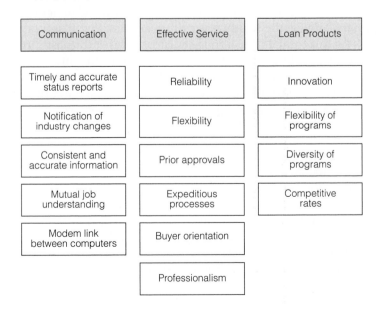

CUSTOMER RELATIONSHIP MANAGEMENT

Truly excellent companies foster close relationships with customers that lead to loyalty. For example, Lexus owners who become accustomed to the at-home pickup of their vehicles for service, free loaners, and other special dealer touches may find it difficult to give up these services when it is time to purchase a new car. In Bank of Montreal's Private Client Services group, bankers provide services according to the preferences of their clients who value convenience and time, not the traditions of the bank. These preferences might mean meeting in the client's home or office instead of the bank.[32] Dell, Inc. offers a variety of customer-friendly services that includes loading all the customer's software, even proprietary applications, at the factory and configuring it the way it is going to be used, saving hours of work by highly paid computer technicians.[33]

> *An organization builds customer loyalty by developing trust, communicating with customers, and effectively managing the interactions and relationships with customers through approaches and its people.*

Moments of truth may be direct contacts with customer representatives or service personnel, or when customers read letters, invoices, or other company correspondence. Problems result from unkept promises, failure to provide full service, service not provided when needed, incorrectly or incompletely performed service, or failure to convey the correct information. At moments of truth, customers form perceptions about the quality of the service by comparing their expectations with the actual outcomes.

> *In services, customer satisfaction or dissatisfaction takes place during **moments of truth**—every instance in which a customer comes in contact with an employee of the company.*

Consider an airline, for example. (The phrase "moment of truth" was popularized by the CEO of Scandinavian Airlines System, Jan Carlzon.) Moments of truth occur when a customer makes a reservation, buys tickets, checks baggage, boards a flight, orders a beverage, requests a magazine, deplanes, and picks up baggage. Multiply these instances by the number of passengers and the number of daily flights, and it is easy to see that hundreds of thousands of moments of truth occur each day. Each occurrence influences a positive or negative image about the company. Southwest Airlines recognizes the power of customer focus.[34] Known for its legendary service, the Southwest culture ensures that it serves the needs of its Customers (with a capital C) in a friendly, caring, and enthusiastic manner. Every one of the approximately 1,000 customers who write to the airline get a personal response (not a form letter) within four weeks, and frequent fliers get birthday cards. The airline even moved a flight up a quarter-hour when five medical students who commuted weekly to an out-of-state medical school complained that the flight got them to class 15 minutes late. To quote the CEO, "We dignify the Customer." This statement applies to internal customers also; it is not unusual to find pilots helping ground crews unload baggage. As one executive stated, "We are not an airline with great customer service. We are a great customer service organization that happens to be in the airline business." Southwest's customer commitment was apparent in the hours after the September 11 terrorist attacks. The top executives swiftly agreed to grant refunds to all customers who asked for them, regardless of ticket restrictions, despite the fact that it might have cost them several hundred million dollars. Refund claims never came; in fact, one loyal customer sent in $1,000 to support Southwest after the attacks. Southwest has consistently been the most profitable U.S. airline.

Quality Spotlight
Southwest
Airlines

Excellent customer relationship management depends on five aspects:

1. Accessibility and commitments
2. Selecting and developing customer contact employees
3. Relevant customer contact requirements
4. Effective complaint management
5. Strategic partnerships and alliances

Each aspect is addressed in the next sections.

Accessibility and Commitments

Customer-focused organizations provide customers easy access to their employees. Procter & Gamble was the first company to install a toll-free number for its products in 1974. Customers of Ames Rubber Corporation have immediate access to top division management, manufacturing personnel, quality engineers, sales and service representatives, and technical support staff. Today, e-mail and Web site access are becoming the media of choice for many consumers.

Companies that truly believe in the quality of their products make strong commitments to their customers. Effective commitments address the principal concerns of customers, are free from conditions that might weaken customers' trust and confidence, and are communicated clearly and simply to customers. A customer commitment might be as simple as guaranteeing that your call or e-mail inquiry will be returned promptly. (Have you ever encountered a Web site with a disclaimer "We cannot always answer every question that we receive"?) Many commitments take the form of explicit guarantees and warranties. FedEx is highly recognized for its guarantee, which refunds full charges if a shipment is even a minute late. Xerox replaces any product that a customer does not find satisfactory, for any reason, within three years of purchase.

Extraordinary guarantees that promise exceptional, uncompromising quality and customer satisfaction, and back that promise with a payout intended to fully recapture the customer's goodwill with few if any strings attached are one of the strongest actions a company can take to improve itself.[35] L.L. Bean's guarantee is a good example: "Everything we sell is backed by a 100 percent unconditional guarantee. We do not want you to have anything from L.L. Bean that is not completely satisfactory. Return anything you buy from us at any time for any reason it proves otherwise." By translating every element of customer dissatisfaction into financial costs, such guarantees quickly alert the company to problems and direct priorities. Workers gain better knowledge of the business and quality improves, which, in turn, results in increased sales and higher profits.

Selecting and Developing Customer Contact Employees

Customer-contact employees are particularly important. They are the people whose main responsibilities bring them into regular contact with customers—in person, by telephone, or through other means. Procter & Gamble calls its consumer relations department the "voice of the company." A staff of more than 250 employees handles in excess of 3 million contacts each year. Their mission is stated as "We are a world-class consumer response center. We provide superior service to consumers who contact Procter & Gamble, encourage product repurchase, and help build brand loyalty. We protect the Company's image and the reputation of our brands by resolving complaints before they are escalated to government agencies or the media. We capture

Quality Spotlight
Procter & Gamble

and report consumer data to key Company functions, identify and share consumer insights, counsel product categories on consumer issues and trends, and manage consumer handling and interaction during crises." Today, companies rely on call centers—more than 60,000 in the United States and growing at 20 percent per year—as their primary means of customer contact. Call centers can be a means of competitive advantage by serving customers more efficiently and personalizing transactions to build relationships. However, they must be supported by appropriate technology, such as automating routine

> *Companies must carefully select customer contact employees, train them well, and empower them to meet and exceed customer expectations.*

calls to minimize the necessity of answering the same questions over and over, and routing calls to people with appropriate skills. Inefficient processes can only lead to frustrated customers.

Many companies begin with the recruiting process, selecting those employees who show the ability and desire to develop good customer relationships. Major companies such as Procter & Gamble seek people with excellent interpersonal and communication skills, strong problem-solving and analytical skills, assertiveness, stress tolerance, patience and empathy, accuracy and attention to detail, and computer literacy. Job applicants often go through rigorous screening processes that might include aptitude testing, customer-service role-playing exercises, background checks, credit checks, and medical evaluations.

Quality Spotlight
The Ritz-Carlton Hotel Company

Companies committed to customer relationship management ensure that customer-contact employees understand the products and services well enough to answer any question, develop good listening and problem recovery skills, and feel able to handle problems. Effective training not only increases employees' knowledge, but improves their self-esteem and loyalty to the organization. The Ritz-Carlton Hotel Company follows orientation training with on-the-job training and, subsequently, job certification. The company reinforces its values daily, recognizes extraordinary achievement, and appraises performance based on expectations explained during the orientation, training, and certification processes. For many organizations, customer relationship training involves every person who comes in contact with customers, including receptionists.

Customers dislike being transferred to a seemingly endless number of employees to obtain information or resolve a problem. TQ-focused companies empower their front-line people to do whatever is necessary to satisfy the customer. At The Ritz-Carlton, all employees are empowered to do whatever it takes to provide "instant pacification." No matter what their normal duties are, other employees must assist if aid is requested by a fellow worker who is responding to a guest's complaint or wish. Ritz-Carlton employees can spend up to $2,000 to resolve complaints with no questions asked. However, the actions of empowered employees should be guided by a common vision; that is, employees require a consistent understanding of what actions they may or should take.

Customer-contact employees also need access to the right technology and company information to do their jobs. FedEx, for example, furnishes employees with the information and technology they need to continually improve their performance. The Digitally Assisted Dispatch System (DADS) communicates to all couriers through screens in their vans, enabling quick response to pickup and delivery dispatches; it allows couriers to manage their time and routes with high efficiency. Information technology improves productivity, increases communication, and allows customer contact employees to handle almost any customer issue.

Customer Contact Requirements

Front-line personnel who come in daily contact with customers have a significant amount of responsibility for customer satisfaction. **Customer contact requirements** are measurable performance levels or expectations that define the quality of customer contact with representatives of an organization. These expectations might include technical requirements such as response time (answering the telephone within two rings), or behavioral requirements (using a customer's name whenever possible). Walt Disney Company, widely recognized for extraordinary customer service, clearly defines contact requirements in their guidelines for Guest Service, which include making eye contact and smiling, greeting and welcoming every guest, seeking out guests who may need assistance, providing immediate service recovery, displaying approachable body language, focusing on the positive rather than rules and regulations, and thanking each and every guest.[36] The Florida Power and Light *Quality in Practice* case in the Bonus Materials folder on the CD-ROM provides a good example of how customer expectations determine contact requirements.

Companies need to communicate these requirements to all customer-contact employees. This communication often initially takes place during new employee orientations. However, to maintain the consistency and effectiveness of these standards, companies must continually reinforce their standards. Additionally, many customer-contact employees depend on internal customers for support, who also must understand the role they play in meeting the requirements. The key to satisfying external customers is to satisfy internal customers first. At Southwest Airlines, for example, the philosophy is that if employees can provide the same service to one another as they do to passengers, the airline will benefit.[37] Each operating division identifies an internal customer. Mechanics who service planes target the pilots who fly them, and marketers treat reservation agents as customers. Departments even provide free ice cream or pizza as tokens of customer appreciation or for a job well done. Use of the customer-supplier model approach effectively communicates the importance of these relationships.

Finally, a company should implement a process for tracking adherence to the requirements and providing feedback to the employees to improve their performance. Information technology supplies the data for effectively tracking conformance to customer contact requirements.

Effective Complaint Management

Despite all efforts to satisfy customers, every business experiences unhappy customers. Complaints can adversely affect business if not dealt with effectively. A company called TARP, formerly known as Technical Assistance Research Programs, Inc., conducted studies that revealed the following information:

1. The average company never hears from 96 percent of its unhappy customers. For every complaint received, the company has 26 more customers with problems, six of whom have problems that are serious.
2. Of the customers who make a complaint, more than half will again do business with that organization if their complaint is resolved. If the customer feels that the complaint was resolved quickly, the figure jumps to 95 percent.
3. The average customer who has had a problem will tell nine or ten others about it. Customers who have had complaints resolved satisfactorily will only tell about five others of the problem resolution.[38]

4. With the advent of the Internet, TARP also found that 4 percent of satisfied customers post their feelings on the Web, while 15 percent of unsatisfied customers do the same.[39]

Leading organizations consider complaints as opportunities for improvement. Encouraging customers to complain, making it easy for them to do so, and effectively resolving complaints increases customer loyalty and retention. A compelling story was related by a Wal-Mart customer in a letter to *Fortune* magazine. He had telephoned Wal-Mart's headquarters to complain about its store in La Plata, Argentina. The switchboard immediately rang the vice president of international operations, who thanked him for calling, asked detailed questions, and inquired whether he was willing to repeat his story to the Latin American VP, to whom he was transferred immediately. He was then asked if he would be willing to talk to the Argentinian store manager; 10 minutes later he received the call from La Plata. The customer observed, "On my next trip to Argentina, a year later, the store had been transformed. No wonder Wal-Mart is the world's largest retailer."

Many customers do not complain because they feel it wouldn't do any good or they are uncomfortable with the process. Leading firms actively solicit complaints. Nissan, for instance, telephones each person who buys a new car or brings one in for significant warranty work. Its objective is to resolve all dissatisfaction within 24 hours.[40]

Companies involved in customer relationship management train customer-contact personnel to deal with angry customers. Customer service personnel need to listen carefully to determine the customer's feelings and then respond sympathetically, ensuring that the complaint is understood. They should make every effort to resolve the problem quickly. Many companies have well-defined processes for dealing with complaints. For example, at BI, all complaints, regardless of where they come from, are forwarded directly to the business unit manager related to the complaint.[41] The manager follows the Service Recovery Process (see Figure 4.5), and contacts the customer directly for clarification of the issue and additional information. Findings are then communicated to the account executive, sales manager, account manager, and all involved business unit associates via e-mail. This process enables the BI team to work in conjunction with the customer to address the failure and provide a solution that meets the customer's needs. A written follow-up of the resolution is shared with all BI team members working with the customer.

Complaints provide a source of product and process improvement ideas. Leading-edge companies encourage employees to bring complaints to the surface in a variety of formal and informal ways, such as a response center to encourage employees to call with ideas and process improvements as well as complaints, and rewards and recognition for employees involved in the processes. Costs associated with complaints can be significant, and include lost business, complaint handling costs, and claims and compensation. Typically, cross-functional teams study the information, determine the real source of the complaints, and make recommendations. Technology is often used to capture, analyze, and report complaint data. Eastman Chemical, for example, discovered that most complaint investigations stopped after learning who caused the problem, and corrective actions did not address the true causes. After developing a process to drill down to the actual sources of complaints and prevent their occurrence, Eastman nearly halved the level of cus-

To improve products and processes effectively, companies must do more than simply fix the immediate problem. They need a systematic process for collecting and analyzing complaint data and then using that information for improvements.

Figure 4.5 BI Service Recovery Process

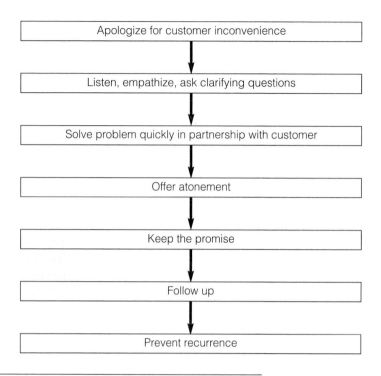

Source: Courtesy of Guy Schoenecker, president and chief quality officer.

tomer complaints in three years, resulting in improved customer satisfaction, increased sales, reduced waste, and lower costs.[42] Finally, the complaint process itself needs to be monitored, evaluated, and improved. Companies typically track the percentage of customers who are satisfied with complaint resolution, the cost of resolving complaints, and the time required to resolve them.

Strategic Partnerships and Alliances

Today's suppliers are being asked to take on greater responsibilities to help their customers. As companies focus more on their core competencies—the things they do best—they are looking outside their organizations for assistance with noncritical support processes. **Customer-supplier partnerships**—long-term relationships characterized by teamwork and mutual confidence—represent an important strategic alliance in achieving excellence and business success. Benefits of such partnerships include access to technology or distribution channels not available internally, shared risks in new investments and product development, improved products through early design recommendations based on supplier capabilities, and reduced operations costs through better communications. For example, FedEx and Jostens formed a strategic partnership that enabled both to benefit from new sales of scholastic jewelry and yearbooks.[43] They took advantage of each other's strengths: Jostens provided a high-quality product with superior service, and FedEx provided reliable high-volume, short-interval delivery for these time-critical products.

Many companies work closely with suppliers that share common values. This close relationship improves supplier capabilities by teaching them quality-related tools and approaches. Although many companies have formal supplier certification programs (discussed in Chapter 7) in which they rate their suppliers, some companies ask suppliers to rate *them* as customers. Motorola uses a 15-member council of suppliers that rates Motorola's practices and offers suggestions for improving, for example, the accuracy of production schedules or design layouts that Motorola provides.[44] Some typical questions that companies might ask of their suppliers might be[45] What expectations do you have that are not being met? What type of technical assistance would you like from us? What type of feedback would you like from us? What benefits are you looking for in a partnership? Better two-way communication can improve both products and relationships.

Exploiting CRM Technology

Customer relationship management (CRM) software is designed to help companies increase customer loyalty, target their most profitable customers, and streamline customer communication processes. More than $11 billion was spent on CRM-related U.S. sales at the turn of the century and is growing significantly.[46] A typical CRM system includes market segmentation and analysis, customer service and relationship building, effective complaint resolution, cross-selling goods and services, order processing, and field service.

CRM helps firms gain and maintain competitive advantage by:

- Segmenting markets based on demographic and behavioral characteristics
- Tracking sales trends and advertising effectiveness by customer and market segment
- Identifying which customers should be the focus of targeted marketing initiatives with predicted high customer response rates
- Forecasting customer retention (and defection) rates and providing feedback as to why customers leave a company
- Studying which goods and services are purchased together, leading to good ways to bundle them
- Studying and predicting which Web characteristics are most attractive to customers and how the Web site might be improved

Technology is a key enabler of CRM. CRM systems provide a variety of useful operational data to managers, including the average time spent responding to customer questions, comments, and concerns, average order tracking (flow) time, total revenue generated by each customer (and sometimes their family or business) from all goods and services bought by the customer—the total picture of economic value of the customer to the firm, cost per marketing campaign, and price discrepancies.

Quality Spotlight
Tsutaya

One company that exploits technology in developing customer relationships is Tsutaya, Japan's largest video, book, and CD chain.[47] Using a point-of-sale system that facilitates real-time inventory tracking between headquarters and franchises and a Web and wireless site called Tsutaya Online (TOL), Tsutaya tracks purchases, demographic data, spending behavior, and by implication, lifestyles and interests. This system enables them to offer personalized product recommendations. For example, if you bought a CD by a certain artist, TOL will e-mail a digital music clip when the next album debuts. Tsutaya also developed a sophisticated recommendation engine to match a customer's video rental history and mood to the ideal movie selection. Many other companies, such as Amazon.com and BMG Music Service, use technology in similar ways.

MEASURING CUSTOMER SATISFACTION

Customer feedback is vital to a business. Through feedback, a company learns how satisfied its customers are with its products and services and sometimes about competitors' products and services. Measurement of customer satisfaction completes the loop shown in Figure 4.2. Measures of customer satisfaction allow a business to do the following:

1. Discover customer perceptions of how well the business is doing in meeting customer needs, and identify causes of dissatisfaction and failed expectations as well as drivers of delight.
2. Compare the company's performance relative to competitors to support planning and better strategic initiatives.
3. Discover areas for improvement in the design and delivery of products and services, as well as for training and coaching of employees.
4. Track trends to determine whether changes actually result in improvements.

For example, the city of Portland, Oregon, mails a survey annually to about 10,000 of its citizens, asking them to rate the performance of the police department, water bureau, environmental services, and public transportation. The city also asks them if they feel safe walking at night in their neighborhoods, parks, and downtown;

An effective customer satisfaction measurement system results in reliable information about customer ratings of specific product and service features and about the relationship between these ratings and the customer's likely future market behavior.

whether the streets are clean enough, how they feel about recreation services offered, and how they rate the livability of the city. The results are benchmarked against six other cities, and if Portland is not doing as well, the mayor tries to find out why.[48] However, it is important to understand that customer satisfaction is a psychological attitude. It is not easy to measure, and can only be observed indirectly. The ACSI model in Figure 4.1 shows that customer satisfaction is influenced by customer expectations and perceptions of quality and value. Thus, it is difficult to reduce these complex relationships into a single measure.

Customer satisfaction measures may include product attributes such as product quality, product performance, usability, and maintainability; service attributes such as attitude, service time, on-time delivery, exception handling, accountability, and technical support; image attributes such as reliability and price; and overall satisfaction measures. At FedEx, customers are asked to rate everything from billing to the performance of couriers, package condition, tracking and tracing capabilities, complaint handling, and helpfulness of employees. Measurements are based on a bona fide customer requirement or need.

The most helpful customer data include comparisons with key competitors. Companies often rely on third parties to conduct blind surveys to determine who key competitors are and how their products and services compare. Competitive comparisons often clarify how improvements in quality can translate into better customer satisfaction or whether key quality characteristics are being overlooked.

Designing Satisfaction Surveys

The first step in developing a customer satisfaction survey is to determine its purpose. Surveys should be designed to clearly provide the users of the survey results with the information they need to make decisions. A critical question to consider is Who is the customer? Managers, purchasing agents, end users, and others all may be affected by a company's products and services. Xerox, for instance, sends specific surveys to buyers, managers, and users. Buyers provide feedback on their perceptions of the sales processes, managers provide input on billing and other administrative processes, and users provide feedback on product performance and technical support. And customer satisfaction measurement should not be confined to external customers. Information from internal customers also contributes to the assessment of the organization's strengths and weaknesses. Often the problems that cause employee dissatisfaction are the same issues that cause dissatisfaction in external customers. Many companies use employee opinion surveys or similar vehicles to seek employee feedback on the work environment, benefits, compensation, management, team activities, rewards and recognition, and company plans and values. However, other indicators of employee satisfaction are absenteeism, turnover, grievances, and strikes, which can often supply better information than surveys that many employees may not take seriously.

The next question to address is who should conduct the survey. Independent third-party organizations often have more credibility to respondents and can ensure objectivity in the results. After these preliminary steps are completed, it is necessary to define the sample frame; that is, the target group from which a sample is chosen. Depending on the purpose of the survey, it might be the entire customer base or a specific segment. For example, a manufacturer of commercial lawn tractors might design different surveys for golf course superintendents who purchase the tractors and another for end users who ride them daily.

The next step is to select the appropriate survey instrument. Formal written surveys are the most common means of measuring customer satisfaction, although other techniques, such as face-to-face interviews, telephone interviews, and focus groups are used. Written surveys have the advantage of low data collection costs, self-administration, and ease of analysis; when used, they should be kept short and simple. In addition, they can probe deeply into the issues. However, they suffer from high nonresponse bias, require large sample sizes, and measure predetermined perceptions of what is important to customers, thus reducing the scope of qualitative information that can be obtained. Face-to-face interviews and focus groups, on the other hand, require much smaller sample sizes and can generate a significant amount of qualitative information, but incur high costs and participant time commitments. Telephone interviews fall somewhere in between these extremes. Telephone interviews appear to be the preferred approach for companies with a limited number of business customers; mail-based surveys are used to track routine transactions, where key attributes are stable over time. For example, Toyota uses mail surveys to identify unhappy customers and then telephones them for more details. This approach is cost-effective when the majority of customers are satisfied.[49]

One should avoid leading questions, compound questions that address more than one issue or idea, ambiguous questions, acronyms and jargon that the respondent may not understand, and double negatives. For example, the question "How would you rate our service?" is too ambiguous and provides little actionable information. A better question would be "How would you rate the response time of our technical support desk?" Another poor example is "Should Burger Mart increase its food portions at a higher price?" This question addresses two different issues. Open-ended

*The types of questions to ask in a survey must be properly worded to achieve **actionable** results. By actionable, we mean that responses are tied directly to key business processes, so that what needs to be improved is clear; and information can be translated into cost/revenue implications to support the setting of improvement priorities.*

questions such as "If this were your business, what would you do differently?" often lead to honest opinions. Most surveys also ask for basic demographic information to stratify the data.

A "Likert" scale is commonly used to measure the response (see Table 4.2). Likert scales allow customers to express their degree of opinion. Five-point scales have been shown to have good reliability and are often used. Responses in the "5" range tell a company what it is doing very well. Responses in the "4" range suggest that customer expectations are being met, but that the company may be vulnerable to competitors. Responses in the "3" range mean that the product or service barely meets customer expectations and that much room for improvement exists. Responses in the "1" or "2" range indicate serious problems. However, most scales like these exhibit response bias; that is, people tend to give either high or low values. If responses are clustered on the high side, it is difficult to discriminate among responses, and the resulting skewness in the distribution causes the mean value to be misleading.

Many customer satisfaction measures evaluate service characteristics. Developing measurable service quality characteristics can be difficult. For instance, a quality characteristic such as "availability" is ambiguous and not as easy to measure as the accuracy of order filling. Typically, such quality characteristics are translated into specific statements that clearly describe the concept. For example, any of the following statements could be used to describe "availability."

1. The doctor was available to schedule me at a good time.
2. I could get an appointment with the doctor at a time I desired.
3. My appointment was at a convenient time.

One example of a simple satisfaction survey for Hilton Hotels is shown in Figure 4.6. The survey asks direct and detailed questions about the guest bathroom, including such potential dissatisfiers as shower water pressure and temperature and bathtub/sink drainage, likelihood of future recommendation, and space for open-ended comments. A seven-point Likert scale is used in this example.

The final task is to design the reporting format and the data entry methods. Modern technology, such as computer databases in conjunction with a variety of statistical analysis tools, assists in tracking customer satisfaction and provides information for continuous improvement. As a final note, surveys should always be pretested to determine whether instructions are understood, identify questions that may be misunderstood or poorly worded, determine how long it takes to complete the survey, and determine the level of customer interest.

Table 4.2 Examples of Likert Scales Used for Customer Satisfaction Measurement

Very Poor	Poor	Neither Poor nor Good	Good	Very Good
1	2	3	4	5
Strongly Disagree	Disagree	Neither Agree nor Disagree	Agree	Strongly Agree
1	2	3	4	5
Very Dissatisfied	Dissatisfied	Neither Satisfied nor Dissatisfied	Satisfied	Very Satisfied
1	2	3	4	5

Figure 4.6 Hilton Hotel Guest Survey

| | | Completely fill in your response | ● Correct | | **GUEST**Scope | | | | | |

Please rate your satisfaction with the comfort level of your accommodations.

	Level of Satisfaction							N/A
	Low		Avg.			High		
	1	2	3	4	5	6	7	
Accommodations look and smell clean and fresh:	☐	☐	☐	☐	☐	☐	☐	☐
Clean and comfortable linens:	☐	☐	☐	☐	☐	☐	☐	☐
Comfort level of pillow:	☐	☐	☐	☐	☐	☐	☐	☐
Comfort level of mattress:	☐	☐	☐	☐	☐	☐	☐	☐
Easily regulated room temperature:	☐	☐	☐	☐	☐	☐	☐	☐
Housekeeping during stay:	☐	☐	☐	☐	☐	☐	☐	☐
Overall satisfaction with this Hilton:	☐	☐	☐	☐	☐	☐	☐	
Likelihood you would recommend Hilton:	☐	☐	☐	☐	☐	☐	☐	
Likelihood, **if returning to the area**, you would return to this Hilton:	☐	☐	☐	☐	☐	☐	☐	
Value of accommodations for price paid:	☐	☐	☐	☐	☐	☐	☐	

Primary purpose of visit?   ☐ Individual business   ☐ Convention/Meeting   ☐ Pleasure
How many times have you been a guest at this Hilton?   ☐ 1   ☐ 2   ☐ 3   ☐ 4   ☐ 5+
Did you have a hotel product or service problem during your stay?   ☐ Yes   ☐ No
If yes—did you report it to the staff?   ☐ Yes   ☐ No
If yes—was it resolved to your satisfaction?   ☐ Yes   ☐ No
If yes—what was the nature of the problem? _____
_____

Please share any thoughts on any other aspects of your visit; including the names of any
staff members who made your stay more enjoyable: _____
_____
_____
_____
_____

Name:	Daytime Phone:
Date of Stay:	Room:
PLEASE DO NOT WRITE BELOW THIS LINE FD2	

Source: Reprinted with permission of UniFocus, LP. © 2000 UniFocus.

Quality Spotlight
Granite Rock

Granite Rock Company is a California manufacturer of high-quality construction materials for road and highway construction and maintenance, and for residential and commercial building construction. Its major product lines include rock, sand and gravel aggregates, ready-mix concrete, blacktop, and other products. Surveying its principal customer groups is one of the key approaches Granite Rock uses to improve customer satisfaction. The surveys ask respondents to rate factors in buying concrete, not only from Granite Rock, but from competitors as well. (Figure 4.7 shows such a survey.) Through information obtained from the surveys, Granite Rock determined that the most important factors to customers in order of importance are on-time delivery, product quality, scheduling (ability to deliver products on short notice), problem resolution, price, credit terms, and salespeople's skills. Annually, the company surveys customers and noncustomers to obtain a "report card" on their service

Figure 4.7 Granite Rock Customer Importance Survey

```
┌─────────────────────────────────────────────────────────────┐
│             What is important to YOU ?                        │
│                                                               │
│ Please rate each of the following on a scale from 1 to 5 with 5│
│ being most important in your decision to purchase from a supplier.│
│                                                               │
│                                              Building         │
│                               Concrete       Materials        │
│ Importance          Least . . . Most      Least . . . Most    │
│                                                               │
│ Responsive to special needs  1  2  3  4  5   1  2  3  4  5    │
│ Easy to place orders         1  2  3  4  5   1  2  3  4  5    │
│ Consistent product quality   1  2  3  4  5   1  2  3  4  5    │
│ On-time delivery             1  2  3  4  5   1  2  3  4  5    │
│ Accurate invoices            1  2  3  4  5   1  2  3  4  5    │
│ Lowest prices                1  2  3  4  5   1  2  3  4  5    │
│ Attractive credit terms      1  2  3  4  5   1  2  3  4  5    │
│ Salespeople's skills         1  2  3  4  5   1  2  3  4  5    │
│ Helpful dispatchers          1  2  3  4  5   1  2  3  4  5    │
│ Courteous drivers            1  2  3  4  5   1  2  3  4  5    │
│ Supplier resolves problems                                    │
│    fairly and quickly        1  2  3  4  5   1  2  3  4  5    │
│                                                               │
│ Please write in any other items not listed above which are very│
│ important to you in making your purchase decision:            │
│ _____  │
│ _____  │
└─────────────────────────────────────────────────────────────┘
```

(see Figure 4.8). Granite Rock repeats the survey every three or four years as priorities change, particularly if the economy changes. The surveys also ask open-ended questions about what customers like and dislike.[50]

Analyzing and Using Customer Feedback

Deming stressed the importance of using customer feedback to improve a company's products and processes (refer to Figure 1.3 in Chapter 1). By examining trends in customer satisfaction measures and linking satisfaction data to its internal processes, a business can see its progress and areas for improvement. As the next step, the company assigns to an employee or group of employees the responsibility and accountability for developing improvement plans based on customer satisfaction results. Many companies, for example, tie managers' annual bonuses to customer satisfaction results. This practice acts as an incentive for managers and a direction for their efforts.

Appropriate customer satisfaction measurement identifies processes that have high impact on satisfaction and distinguishes between low performing processes low performance and those that are performing well.

One way to ensure that measurement is appropriate is to collect information on both the importance and the performance of key quality characteristics. For example, a hotel might ask how important check-in speed, check-out speed, staff attitude, and so on, are, as well as how the customer rates the hotel on these attributes. Evaluation of such data can be accomplished using a grid similar to the one shown in Figure 4.9, on which mean performance and importance scores for individual attributes are plotted.[51] Results in the diagonal quadrants (the shaded areas) are good. A firm ideally wants high performance on important characteristics and not to waste resources on characteristics of low importance. Results off the diagonal indicate that the firm either is wasting resources to achieve high perfor-

Figure 4.8 Granite Rock Customer Report Card

Please write in the names of the suppliers you use most often for concrete. Then grade each company using this scale:

A= The *Best*
B= Above Average
C= *Same* As Competition
D= Needs Improvement
F= *Terrible*

1
Please write in the Concrete Supplier you use MOST OFTEN

2
Please write in your #2 Concrete Supplier

3
Please write in your #3 Concrete Supplier

1.   Reliable Delivery

	1	2	3
A. Do your orders arrive on time?			

2.   Consistent Quality

A. How is their concrete's workability?			
B. How does it pump?			
C. Is the slump right?			
D. How about set time?			
E. How about psi strength?			

3.   Dependable Service

A. Are they responsive to special needs?			
B. Is it easy to place orders or requests with them?			
C. Are their invoices accurate?			

4.   Competitive Pricing

A. Are their prices competitive?			
B. Are their credit terms competitive?			

5.   People Who Care

A. Do their salespeople understand your needs?			
B. Are their dispatchers helpful?			
C. Are their drivers courteous?			
D. Do they address problems fairly and quickly?			

6. Overall Rating			

mance on unimportant customer attributes (overkill), or is not performing acceptably on important customer attributes, leaving the firm vulnerable to competition. The results of such an analysis can help target areas for improvement and cost savings, as well as provide useful input for strategic planning. Often, competitor data are also plotted, providing a comparison against the competition. Granite Rock Company, featured in the last section, uses this approach. The results of their importance survey and competitive performance survey are summarized and plotted on an importance/performance graph to assess the strengths and vulnerabilities of the company and its competitors. The scales are chosen so that each axis represents the industry average. Granite Rock looks at the distance between its ratings and those of the competitors. If the ratings are close, customers cannot differentiate Granite Rock from its competitors on that particular measure. By posting these graphs on bulletin boards at each plant, the company ensures that all employees, particularly salespeople, are fully informed of the survey results.

Many companies have integrated customer feedback into their continuous improvement activities and in redesigning products and services. For example,

Quality Spotlight
Skilled Care
Pharmacy

Skilled Care Pharmacy (see Case Study in Chapter 1), located in Mason, Ohio, is a $25 million dollar privately held regional provider of pharmaceutical products delivered within the long-term care, assisted living, hospice, and group home environments. Skilled Care developed a Customer Grade Card, benchmarked from Baldrige winner Wainwright Industries, to measure customer satisfaction. The Grade Card uses a school-like A-B-C-D scoring system shown in Figure 4.10. The scores from the four questions covering Quality, Responsiveness, Delivery, and Communication are converted from letters to numbers and averaged. Any questions that were graded C or below generate an immediate phone call or personal visit to the customer by the Customer Care Team to investigate and resolve the issue. An example of how the feedback was used for improvement involved some low scores received for "Delivery." Management determined there was potential risk of losing valuable customers. Upon investigation, it became evident that the issue was not timely delivery, but their system of cut-off times for ordering medications for same-day delivery. If the customer missed the cut-off time, then they did not receive their order until the next day, and, Skilled Care was considered to be "late." Their response to this customer need was to extend pharmacy ordering hours and to aggressively modify staff schedules for the order processing and pharmacy departments. In turn, they were able to offer an additional five hours for customers to phone or fax medication orders for receipt the same day. As a result, satisfaction scores for "Delivery" rose dramatically.

Why Many Customer Satisfaction Efforts Fail[52]

Determining and using customer satisfaction information should be viewed as a key business process. Just going through the motions can often lead to failure. A. Blanton Godfrey suggests several reasons why customer satisfaction efforts fail to produce useful results.

1. *Poor measurement schemes.* Just tracking the percentage of "satisfied and very satisfied" customers on a 5-point Likert scale provides little actionable information. Many surveys provide biased results because few dissatisfied customers respond, or the surveys lack adequate sample sizes or randomization. Survey designers need appropriate understanding of statistical concepts.
2. *Failure to identify appropriate quality dimensions.* Many surveys address issues the company thinks are important, not what customers think. This error results from a lack of capturing reliable information about customer needs and expectations.
3. *Failure to weight dimensions appropriately.* Even if organizations measure the right things, they may not understand which dimensions are important. As a result, they spend too much effort on dimensions with the lowest scores that may not be important to the customers. Use of techniques such as importance-performance analysis can help focus attention to the key dimensions.

Figure 4.9 Performance-Importance Comparison

Importance	Performance	
	Low	High
Low	Who cares?	Overkill
High	Vulnerable	Strengths

Figure 4.10 Skilled Care's Customer Grade Card Scoring System

A = Customer Totally Satisfied		100 points
B = Customer Generally Satisfied		90 points
C = Customer Generally Dissatisfied		50 points
D = Customer Totally Dissatisfied		0 points

4. *Lack of comparison with leading competitors.* Quality and perception of quality is relative. Without appropriate comparative data, competitors may be improving much faster than an organization realizes.

5. *Failure to measure potential and former customers.* Without an understanding of why non-customers do not do business with a company, or more importantly, why customers leave, an organization risks losing market share to competitors and may be headed for demise.

6. *Confusing loyalty with satisfaction.* As we noted at the beginning of this chapter, these two concepts are different. Customer retention and loyalty provide an indication of the organization's future.

Customer Perceived Value [53]

Measuring **customer perceived value (CPV)** is an alternative to traditional customer satisfaction measurement that focuses more on customer loyalty than on satisfaction.

> *CPV measures how customers assess benefits—such as product performance, ease of use, or time savings—against costs, such as purchase price, installation cost or time, and so on, in making purchase decisions.*

Sellers that provide the greatest CPV at the time of the purchasing decision always win the sale. CPV measurement includes potential buyers rather than just existing customers, is forward-looking rather than retrospective, and examines choices relative to alternatives rather than relative to expectations. Typical questions that are asked include "What benefits are important to you?" and "How well do you believe that each product or supplier will deliver those benefits?" and focus on perceptions of future value rather than past experiences.

CPV methodology identifies the most important product attributes that prospective customers use to compare one offering against another, and their relative importance and performance. One approach for assessing importance is to ask the customer to place a percentage value of importance on each attribute so the total sums to 100 percent, thus eliminating the common problem of giving high ratings to each factor. Asking customers to rate the performance of different offerings on each attribute on a 10-point scale can assess relative performance; the difference in ratings is the relative performance. For example, in comparing two casual dining restaurants, A and B, we might find the following:

Attribute	Relative Importance	Relative Performance (A—B rating)
Menu variety	30	-2
Food quality	20	+3
Atmosphere	10	0
Value	40	+1

By multiplying the relative importance values by relative performance and summing, we see that overall, restaurant A has a higher perceived value but could improve its perceived value by improving its menu variety. Such information becomes the basis for strategic decisions.

CUSTOMER FOCUS IN THE BALDRIGE CRITERIA, ISO 9000, AND SIX SIGMA

Category 3 of the 2003 Malcolm Baldrige National Quality Award Criteria for Performance Excellence (available on the CD-ROM) is titled *Customer and Market Focus.* Item 3.1, *Customer and Market Knowledge,* examines an organization's processes for gaining knowledge about requirements, expectations, and preferences of customers and markets, with the aim of keeping products and services relevant, and for developing new opportunities. The criteria ask how an organization determines its target customers, customer groups, and market segments, considering potential customers and competitors' customers; and how an organization listens and learns to determine customer requirements and expectations and their relative importance. The item also asks how an organization uses customer and marketing information, loyalty and retention data, win/loss analysis, and complaints to plan products and services and to make improvements. Finally, the item asks how an organization improves its customer listening and learning approaches so that it can keep current with changing business needs and directions. Continuous improvement of business processes is a core concept of the Baldrige criteria.

Item 3.2, *Customer Relationships and Satisfaction,* examines an organization's processes for building customer relationships and determining customer satisfaction, with the aim of acquiring new customers, retaining existing customers, and developing new opportunities. The item asks how an organization builds relationships to meet and exceed expectations and to increase loyalty, provides easy access for customers to seek information or assistance or to comment and complain, how customer contact requirements are determined and deployed, how complaints are resolved effectively and promptly, how the organization aggregates, analyzes, and learns from complaint information, and how approaches to all aspects of customer relationships are kept current with changing business needs and directions. This item also addresses an organization's satisfaction and dissatisfaction determination processes, how they may differ among customer groups or segments, how measurement captures actionable information for business development and improvement, how the organization follows up with customers on products, services, and transaction quality, how it determines customers' satisfaction relative to competitors so that it may improve future performance, and finally, how satisfaction determination approaches are kept current.

Customer focus is a key requirement of ISO 9000:2000. For example, in the Management Responsibility section, one requirement is "Top management shall ensure that customer requirements are determined and are met with the aim of enhancing customer satisfaction." This puts the responsibility for customer focus on senior leadership. In the Product Realization section, the standards require that the organization determine customer requirements, including delivery and post-delivery activities, and any requirements not stated by the customer but necessary for specified or intended use. In addition, the organization must establish procedures for communicating with customers about product information and other inquiries, and for obtaining feedback, including complaints. In the Measurement, Analysis, and Improvement sections, the standards require that the organization monitor customer perceptions as to whether the organization has met customer requirements; that is, customer satisfaction. Note that even though some basic customer-focused processes are required, the scope is not as broad as in Baldrige.

Customers are sometimes a "hidden" part of Six Sigma efforts, because the focus tends to be on the improvement projects and measurement issues. However, a focus on the customer is vital at every stage of Six Sigma projects. For instance, product design (and design of associated manufacturing or service delivery processes) will be far more successful if the "voice of the customer," is included. A fundamental aspect of Six Sigma methodology is identification of critical to quality (CTQ) characteristics that are vital to customer satisfaction.

During the process of producing a product or service, it is important to gather information needed by internal customers for process control activities to ensure that the product is meeting the CTQs. If the CTQs are not being met, then the organization needs to develop a better measurement and control system.[54] Often, internal data that can improve control processes—such as whether materials arrived on time, how often an accounting report had incorrect data, or how many employees were absent from work—are kept in departmental records, where they are difficult to access. The solution may require a Six Sigma study to determine the types of data and information that are needed to provide necessary monitoring and control, and how the information gap (if one exists) can be closed.

Finally, at the delivery stage, customer satisfaction measures can provide clear information about the success of Six Sigma efforts. An interesting result of the impact of service recovery on customer satisfaction was reported in a *Fortune* magazine article:

> *A global hotel chain was stunned to discover a perverse consequence of its customer-centric Six Sigma quality initiative. Apparently guests were mildly pleased by the chain's sincere efforts to provide a hassle-free stay. But what really moved the customer-satisfaction needle was how well the hotel responded when something went wrong. Guests who had experienced a problem that was quickly and politely resolved rated the hotel service higher than guests who had had no problems at all. What's more, more guests with happy resolution of their hassle said they were likely to recommend the hotel than did the trouble-free guests.[55]*

In fact, many common Six Sigma projects revolve around developing appropriate customer satisfaction measurement processes, as well as trying to improve the design and delivery of CTQs identified through voice of the customer processes.

QUALITY IN PRACTICE

UNDERSTANDING THE VOICE OF THE CUSTOMER AT LaROSA'S PIZZERIAS[56]

"All business is the same, it just looks different" is a favorite quote of T. D. Hughes, CEO of LaRosa's, Inc. LaRosa's is a privately held chain of neighborhood pizzerias with 54 locations in Cincinnati, Ohio, northern Kentucky, and Southeast Indiana, that offers full-service dine-in, carryout, and home delivery. LaRosa's competes against such national chains as Pizza Hut, Papa John's, Uno's and other local restaurants, yet holds a 45 to 50 percent share in its market area. LaRosa's has been a leader among local businesses in adopting and promoting total quality principles. T. D.'s quote provides a foundation for learning from other organizations and adopting high-performance

practices that have proven successful, no matter what business they come from. One of these is the Voice of the Customer process.

In 1997, as part of a new strategic planning process, LaRosa's identified growth as a key strategic goal. Because the local market was essentially saturated, however, the Executive Management Team worked on strategies for growing the company for three years and produced no tangible results. One of the reasons for the impasse was the lack of sound, factual data. The Executive Management Team had developed three growth strategies, but could not agree on which one to follow because of a lack of a fact-based foundation for the decision.

In 2000, a project team was formed to tackle this issue, and was given complete latitude to make any recommendation for an Italian/pizzeria concept based on customer needs and expectations. The team consisted of the marketing director (team leader), two executive vice presidents, the director of operations, two franchise owners, an external strategic business partner, and the CEO, who was the team sponsor. The key tool that successfully led to an understanding of their customers and to a new and innovative restaurant design was Voice of the Customer (VOC). VOC is a structured methodology for listening to customers that is promoted by the Center for Quality of Management (CQM), an industrial consortium based in Boston (http://www.cqm.org). The basis for VOC is asking customers to express their needs and expectations through their experiences. LaRosa's completed 16 in-depth one-on-one interviews with current and potential customers both inside and outside of their current market area to provide examples of dining incidents these individuals had experienced, seeking "the good, the bad, and the ugly." Here are some responses from customers of current competitors and potential competitors in other markets.

1. "So there I was, like herded cattle, standing on the hard concrete floor, cold wind blasting my ankles every time the door opened, waiting and waiting for our name to be called."
2. "And then I saw a dirty rag being slopped around a dirty table!"
3. "The manager said, 'That's not a gnat, that's black pepper,' so I said I know the difference between black pepper and a gnat, black pepper doesn't have little wings on it!"
4. "When they're that age, going to the bathroom is a full-contact sport—they're reaching and grabbing at everything, and you're trying to keep them from touching anything because the bathroom is so dirty."

What were the customers actually saying? One of the challenges that LaRosa's faced was to translate the "customer voices" into actionable terms. In these examples, LaRosa's understood the customers as saying that restaurant design should consider the diverse comfort needs of all guests, that it provide a facility that customers implicitly trust, that customers feel cared for by service staff,

and that restroom cleanliness affirms guests' trust in restaurant cleanliness. In analyzing all the responses gathered, LaRosa's was able to prioritize the most important customer requirements: (1) assurance that the kitchen is clean (which is reflected by the cleanliness of the restrooms), (2) prompt service, (3) food and drinks at their proper temperature, (4) fresh food, (5) meeting the unique needs of adult guests as well as families, (6) exceeding service expectations, (7) an easy to read and understand menu, and (8) caring staff.

The experience of using VOC changed the company focus from a "product-out" to a "market in" mentality. It gave them a decision-making tool based on factual data and broke down communication silos within the company, and eliminated the age-old sales and marketing versus operations conflict. The Executive Management Team and directors were able to agree on a growth strategy that had eluded them for three years. The result was a new restaurant design concept that explicitly addressed the voice of the customer. To meet the diverse needs of customers, for example, LaRosa's developed a larger waiting area, a casual bar area with more of an adult atmosphere in addition to the family dining areas, both table and booth seating, and a private dining area for parties. LaRosa's also initiated an improved kids' program highlighted by Luigi's Closet, a small area in which children can select a toy or activity to keep them busy and crackers to eat while waiting for dinner. The Bonus Materials folder on the CD-ROM provides some photographs of the result.

The new restaurant jumped to second in sales behind LaRosa's flagship location. The dining room check average is 25 percent higher than the market average, profitability as a percent of gross sales is well above the chain average, and secret shopper satisfaction results show that it is performing at the top of the chain.

Key Issues for Discussion

1. How does VOC differ from other forms of market research into customer needs and expectations? What advantages and possible disadvantages does it have?
2. What impact did the VOC process have for LaRosa's?
3. Conduct a mock VOC for your school or college. What did you learn?

QUALITY IN PRACTICE
CUSTOMER FOCUS AT AMAZON.COM

Warren Buffett, the well-known financier and CEO of Berkshire Hathaway, has never been a big backer of technology businesses.[57] However, he owns $459 million worth of Amazon.com's bonds, making him one of Amazon's biggest debt holders. Buffet observes, "I've been using a computer for eight or ten years now and I still really pay for only three things on the Internet: *The Wall Street Journal,* online bridge, and books from Amazon.com. That they are one of only three companies online that have gotten money out of my pocket tells me they are doing something right."

The concept of Amazon began in 1994 when Jeff Bezos, its founder and CEO, read a study that predicted the Internet would explode in popularity. He settled on selling books online because almost every book was already catalogued electronically, yet no physical bookstore could carry them all. Bezos has a rare talent for a relentless focus on the customer, and a studied disregard for short-term pressures to show results on the "bottom line." The original Amazon model envisioned giving customers access to a gigantic selection without the time, expense, and hassle of opening stores and warehouses and dealing with inventory. However, Bezos quickly discovered that the only way to make sure customers get a good experience and that Amazon gets inventory at good prices was to operate his own warehouses so he could control the transaction from start to finish. In its 2002 Annual Report a letter from the 1997 Annual Report was reproduced, explaining Amazon's customer-focused philosophy in these words:

> From the beginning, our focus has been on offering our customers compelling value. We realized that the Web was, and still is, the World Wide Wait. Therefore, we set out to offer customers something they simply could not get any other way, and began serving them with books. We brought them much more selection than was possible in a physical store (our store would now occupy 6 football fields), and presented it in a useful, easy-to-search, and easy-to-browse format in a store open 365 days a year, 24 hours a day. We maintained a dogged focus on improving the shopping experience, and in 1997 substantially enhanced our store. We now offer customers gift certificates, 1-Click℠ shopping, and vastly more reviews, content, browsing options, and recommendation features. We dramatically lowered prices, further increasing customer value. Word of mouth remains the most powerful customer acquisition tool we have, and we are grateful for the trust our customers have placed in us. Repeat purchases and word of mouth have combined to make Amazon.com the market leader in online bookselling.[58]

In its 2002 Annual Report, Bezos's letter made numerous points to explain how that vision of customer service had developed and expanded, including:

- We have deep selection that is unconstrained by shelf space.
- We turn our inventory 19 times in a year.
- We personalize the store for each and every customer.
- We trade real estate for technology (which gets cheaper and more capable every year).
- We display customer reviews critical of our products.
- You can make a purchase with a few seconds and one click.
- We put used products next to new ones so you can choose.
- We share our prime real estate, our product detail pages, with third parties, and, if they can offer better value, we let them.
- Customer experience costs that remain variable, such as the variable portion of fulfillment costs, improve in our model as we reduce defects. Eliminating defects improves costs and leads to better customer experience.[59]

Many of the customer-pleasing features of Amazon's operations are not noticed, or even known, by Amazon's customers. These fall into the categories of technology, order fulfillment, and retailing strategies. In technology, the company's Web site has been, and remains, leading edge. In an effort to serve customer needs, Amazon was one of the early pioneers to develop software for collaborative filtering of customer data. Basically, the filter is used to suggest similar or related products to a customer after he or she has focused on a product or product category. For example, if a customer browses or purchases *The Management and Control of Quality*, other books in quality management would then be suggested on the viewer's Web browser. These suggestions are based on what other readers of the text had purchased, in addition to the target text. Web features and capabilities have expanded over the years, to include features such as "look inside the book" for a chapter preview, in-store pickup of orders, shipping choices (priority vs. regular), and affinity group selections (Wedding Registry, Baby Registry, personal Wish List, etc.).

In order fulfillment, the capabilities of its high-tech warehouses continue to drive costs down, as mentioned earlier. For example, Amazon has a nearly perfect process for sorting multiple item orders. As it expands its offerings and adds more retail partners, Amazon's fulfillment capabilities pay dividends to its partners, as well as adding revenues to Amazon. By reducing the time it takes to get all the items in an order into the sorting system, Amazon shipped 35 percent more units with the same number of people than it had in earlier years.[60]

Its retailing strategy is based more and more on partnerships with those who, in most businesses, would be considered competitors. Amazon proclaims that it seeks "to offer Earth's Biggest Selection and to be Earth's most customer-centric company, where customers can find and discover anything they might want to buy online." However, at any time, its competitor-partners may be offering the same item through their linked Web sites at a different price. For example, when a book is being viewed, the web page will also permit the viewer to go to a linking web page of a partner's book company, where the same title used (or even new) book is being sold for a lower price. Its partners include well-known retailers such as Borders Books, Waldenbooks, Waterstone, Target Stores, Lands' End, and thousands of other lesser-known companies, large and small. In fact, through what

is called their Associates Program, Amazon.com provides a link to 900,000 Web sites carrying specialty items and where online auctions are taking place every day.

With millions of customers and potential customers accessing its global sites in the United States, the United Kingdom, Germany, Japan, and Canada daily, Amazon.com's sophisticated technology allows it to build an in-depth and potentially valuable database of many of its customers. In 1999, Amazon.com experimented with a highly controversial feature on its Web site. It started featuring thousands of individual bestseller lists categorized by Zip codes, workplaces, and colleges—wherever its customers were ordering from. With a mouse click on its World Wide Web site, browsers could peek behind the scenes at the books that specific groups were reading, the compact discs they were listening to, and the videos they were watching. Amazon described it as "fun," happily announcing the feature, Purchase Circles, in a press release. Soon, however, citing customer complaints, the company began backtracking. Customers were allowed to opt out of having their data collected, as long as they were savvy enough to read the fine print and send an e-mail to the company. Companies could choose not to be included by sending a fax.[61] Despite the controversy, Amazon .com still has Purchase Circles on its Web site.

Key Issues for Discussion

1. How does Amazon.com's CRM software help it to gain market share and maintain its competitive advantage?
2. How are operating efficiencies realized in order fulfillment activities of Amazon.com? Will costs continue to fall, given that their warehouses are currently operating at less than 50% of capacity? (*Note:* This measure is expected to change over time, depending on the state of the economy.)
3. What are the customer privacy risks, besides the ones mentioned in the case, that Amazon.com must guard against in order to continue to grow its business?

Additional *Quality in Practice* case studies may be found in the Bonus Materials folder on the CD-ROM.

REVIEW QUESTIONS

1. Explain the difference between satisfaction and loyalty. Why is loyalty more important?
2. What is a *consumer benefit package*? Why is it important in understanding satisfaction and loyalty?
3. Describe the model used in computing the American Customer Satisfaction Index. How might a business use the information from the ACSI database?
4. Explain the *customer-driven quality cycle*. What do expected quality, actual quality, and perceived quality mean, and how do they relate with one another?
5. List and provide an example of the six leading practices of customer-focused quality.
6. Define the principal types of customers that an organization encounters.
7. Explain the AT&T customer-supplier model.
8. Why is it important to segment customers? Describe some ways of defining customer segments.
9. Explain the different dimensions of quality defined by David Garvin and the key dimension of service quality. How are these dimensions similar and different?
10. What is the *voice of the customer*?
11. What is the Kano model, and what are its implications for quality management?
12. List the major approaches to gathering customer information. What are the advantages and disadvantages of each?
13. Describe how affinity diagrams and tree diagrams are used to organize and work with customer-related information.
14. Explain the concept of *moments of truth*.
15. Explain the importance of accessibility and commitments such as guarantees to building customer relationships.
16. Who are customer contact employees? Why are they critical to an organization?
17. Define the term *customer contact requirements*. Why are they important?
18. Explain the role of training and empowerment of customer-contact employees in achieving customer satisfaction.
19. Why should a company make it easy for customers to complain? How should complaint information be used?
20. Outline a generic complaint management process.
21. Why are strategic partnerships and alliances useful to an organization?
22. How can customer relationship management (CRM) software help companies develop and improve a focus on customers?
23. Why does an organization measure customer satisfaction?
24. Describe the key steps that must be addressed in designing customer satisfaction surveys.
25. Explain the concept of importance-performance analysis and its benefit to an organization.
26. Why do many customer satisfaction efforts fail?
27. What specific issues of customer focus are addressed in the Baldrige Award criteria?

DISCUSSION QUESTIONS

1. Can you describe a customer-focused organization similar to Superquinn with which you have had personal experience? What aspects of the organization impressed you the most?

2. A service representative of a major U.S. airline told a customer about an internal memo that had been circulated called "No Waivers, No Favors," which promises significant and negative consequences to any employee giving a customer special treatment outside of the airline's strict policies. As the employee noted, "Now, nobody is doing anything until we find out what happens to us if we are a little lenient about enforcing a rule. People are scared." Why do you think that management adopted this policy? What implications will it probably have for customers?

3. Why do you think that many firms fail to recognize the importance of customers until they are faced with a crisis?

4. Construct a list of at least 20 different names for a "customer," for example, buyer, client, and so on.

5. Think about a prescription that a doctor may write. Describe the different types of customers involved in the process of filling the prescription.

6. How might a bank quantify the value of a loyal customer? Try to develop a quantitative model.

7. How might your school use the customer-driven quality cycle in Figure 4.2?

8. Consider a fraternity or other student organization and make a list of all of its customers.

9. How might a college or university segment its customers? What specific needs might each of these customer groups have?

10. Recall the AT&T customer-supplier model in Figure 4.3. For each of the following departments in a typical company, discuss who are their internal or external customers and suppliers.
    a. Operations
    b. Information Systems
    c. Human Resources
    d. Mailroom
    e. Payroll

11. For services, how do the quality dimensions defined by David Garvin relate to the five dimensions of reliability, assurance, tangibles, empathy, and responsiveness identified by other researchers? Do they all fit into one of these categories?

12. Which of the five key dimensions of service quality—reliability, assurance, tangibles, empathy, or responsiveness—would the following items from a retail banking customer survey address?
    a. Following through on promises
    b. Offering convenient banking hours
    c. Providing prompt customer service
    d. Properly handling any problems that arise
    e. Maintaining clean and pleasant branch office facilities
    f. Demonstrating knowledge of bank products and services
    g. Giving undivided attention to the customer
    h. Never being too busy to respond to customer requests
    i. Charging reasonable service fees

     j. Maintaining a professional appearance

     k. Providing error-free bank statements

     l. Keeping customer transactions confidential

13. Deer Valley Resort in Park City, Utah, is viewed by many as the Ritz-Carlton of ski resorts, providing exceptional services and a superior ski vacation experience.[62] The resort offers curbside ski valet service to take equipment from vehicles, parking lot attendants to ensure efficient parking, and a shuttle to transport guests from the lot to Snow Park Lodge. Guests walk to the slopes on heated pavers to prevent the pavement from freezing and assist in snow removal. The central gathering area by the base lifts is wide and level, allowing plenty of room to put on equipment and easy access to the lifts. At the end of the day, guests can store their skis without charge at each lodge. The resort limits the number of skiers on the mountain to reduce lines and congestion, and offers complimentary mountain tours for both expert and intermediate skiers. Everyone is committed to ensuring that each guest has a wonderful experience, from "mountain hosts" stationed at the top of the lifts to answer questions and provide directions, to the friendly workers at the cafeterias and restaurants, whose food is consistently rated number one by ski enthusiast magazines. "Our goal is to make each guest feel like a winner," says Bob Wheaton, vice president and general manager. "We go the extra mile on the mountain, in our ski school, and throughout our food-service operation because we want our guests to know they come first." What dimensions of quality—as described by David Garvin and specific to services that are described in this chapter—are evident at Deer Valley?

14. Give several examples of dissatisfiers, satisfiers, and exciters/delighters in products or services that you recently purchased. Why did you classify them into these categories?

15. Consider the following customer expectations for a fast-food (quick-service) restaurant. Would you classify them as dissatisfiers, satisfiers, and exciters/delighters?

     a. Special prices on certain days

     b. Food is safe to eat

     c. Hot food is served hot

     d. Service is friendly

     e. Background music

     f. Playland for children

     g. Restaurant is clean inside

     h. Food is fresh

     i. A "one-bite" money-back guarantee

     j. Orders can be phoned in for pickup at a separate window

16. In the context of a fast-food restaurant, make a list of different characteristics that might describe "freshness." Classify them by means of an affinity diagram or tree diagram. What does your response mean for measuring satisfaction of this attribute?

17. Prepare a list of moments of truth that you encounter during a typical quarter or semester at your college or university.

18. Write a generic customer satisfaction policy that a firm might use to convey trust to its customers and as a means of determining employee values, policies, and training initiatives.

19. Customer satisfaction is generally discussed from the consumer viewpoint. However, it is equally important from a business-to-business transaction perspective. Discuss what suppliers to other businesses can do to improve satisfaction.

20. If you were the manager of a small pizza restaurant (dine-in and limited delivery), what customer contact requirements might you specify for your employees who take phone orders, work the cash register, and serve as waiters? How would you train them?

21. Comment on the following questions that you might see on customer satisfaction surveys. Discuss some of the problems with these questions and how they might be improved.
    a. The staff is professional.
    b. ETAs are adequate.
    c. Waiting time was reasonable.
    d. Food safety is important to my purchase decision.
    e. The service representative was friendly and helpful.

22. A local franchise of a national car rental firm conducted a survey of customers to determine their perceptions of the importance of key product and service attributes as well as their perceptions of the company's performance.[63] The results are given in Tables 4.3 and 4.4. In Table 4.3, importance was measured on a four-point scale ranging from "not at all important" to "very important." Note that Table 4.4 is segmented by personal and business use, and that two different scales were used (the percentage values are based on the percentage of "yes" responses; all others are on a 5-point scale from "poor" to "excellent"). What conclusions might you make from these data? What possible improvements can you suggest?

Table 4.3 Importance Ratings of Product/Service Attributes

Mechanical condition of car	4.00
Cleanliness of vehicle	3.93
Friendliness of staff	3.86
Check-out speed/efficiency	3.80
Getting reserved car or better	3.80
Check-in speed/efficiency	3.79
Cleanliness of facility	3.66
Employee appearance	3.45
Getting nonsmoking car	3.45
Speed of coach service	3.24

Table 4.4 Customer Ratings of Performance

	Personal use	Business use
Mechanical condition of car	4.815	4.750
Cleanliness of vehicle	4.893	4.563
Friendliness of staff	4.929	4.688
Check-out speed/efficiency	4.759	4.688
Getting reserved car or better	96%	100%
Check-in speed/efficiency	4.821	4.750
Cleanliness of facility	4.893	4.500
Employee appearance	100%	100%
Getting nonsmoking car	86%	100%
Speed of coach service	100%	100%

23. One of our former students discovered a way to receive great service: ask for a satisfaction survey before the end of the transaction. In one experience, the student observed an instant change in how she was treated. What does such an experience tell you about the company?

24. Analyze the following customer satisfaction results (on a 5-point scale) for a fast-food restaurant. What recommendations would you make to the managers?

Attribute	Importance	Performance
Fresh buns	4.83	4.80
Cheese is melted	4.26	4.82
Drink is not watery	4.88	4.64
Fries are crisp	4.85	4.80
Fries are salty	4.12	4.48
Service is fast	4.93	4.61
Open 24 hours	3.91	4.81
Good variety of food	4.46	3.87
Nutritional data displayed	3.76	4.65
Children's menu available	4.80	3.97
Tables kept clean	4.91	4.89
Low-fat items available	3.62	4.55

25. How does the Baldrige criteria address the issues raised in the discussion of the reasons why many customer satisfaction efforts fail? Can addressing the criteria help to mitigate these reasons?

PROJECTS, ETC.

1. Perform some research to examine trends in the American Customer Satisfaction Index over the last three years. What economic sectors show improvement? Which don't? How has the overall index changed?

2. Determine whether your school implements any of the leading practices of customer focus in a systematic manner and write a report describing their approaches.

3. Based on the information in this chapter, propose new approaches for measuring customer satisfaction for your faculty and instructors that go beyond the traditional course evaluation processes that your school may use.

4. You may have visited or purchased items from large computer and software retail stores. In a group brainstorming session, identify those characteristics of such a store that would be most important to you, and design a customer survey to evaluate customers' importance and the store's performance.

5. Table 4.5 lists customer requirements as determined through a focus group conducted by Western America Airlines. Develop an affinity diagram, classify these requirements into appropriate categories, and design a questionnaire to survey customers. Be sure to address any other pertinent issues/questions as well as customer information that would be appropriate to include in the questionnaire.

6. Interview some managers of small businesses to determine how they respond to complaints and use complaint information in their organizations.

7. Describe some ways that companies can improve Web sites and make them

Table 4.5 Airline Customer Requirements

- Quality food
- Ability to solve problems and answer questions during flight
- Efficient boarding procedures
- Appealing interior appearance
- Well-maintained seats
- Reservation calls answered promptly
- Timely and accurate communication of information prior to boarding
- Good selection of magazines and newspapers
- Efficient and attentive flight attendants
- Good beverage selection
- Clean lavatories
- Efficient ticket line and waiting procedures
- Convenient ground transportation
- Courteous reservations personnel
- Good quality audio/visual system
- Sufficient quantity of food
- Interesting in-flight magazine

- Courteous and efficient gate personnel
- In-flight telephone access
- Good variety of audio/visual programming
- Flight attendants knowledgeable of airline programs and policies
- Correct explanation of fares and schedules
- Efficient seat selection process
- Courteous and efficient sky cap
- Timely and accurate communication of flight information (in-flight)
- Convenient baggage check-in
- Timely baggage check-in
- Comfortable seating and leg room
- Assistance for passengers with special needs
- Courteous ticket counter personnel
- Convenient parking close to terminal
- Ability to solve baggage claim problems
- Ability of reservation agents to answer questions

more customer-focused. You might consider examining a variety of Web sites and identifying "best practices."

8. Gather several customer satisfaction surveys or comment cards from local establishments. Analyze them as to their ability to lead to actionable information that will help the organization, and propose any improvements or redesign you deem appropriate.

9. This exercise provides an experience with developing an affinity diagram for analyzing complaints and would best be performed by the class as a whole.[64] Each student writes one or more descriptions of personal experiences of frustration and dissatisfaction with products and services. Two examples might be: "Every time I purchase a CD, the seal is difficult and time-consuming to remove. I have even cracked the case a few times while trying to remove it." "I purchased a new pair of running shoes, and the laces were too long." These experiences should be written on large sticky notes and posted on the classroom wall. Students then group the responses in to logical categories and develop descriptive headers for each group that explain the causes of dissatisfaction and then create the affinity diagram. For instance, the shoe example might fall into a group titled "Product components are incompatible." An alternative project is to use positive comments about products and services.

10. A number of pizza chains or restaurants are undoubtedly located around your college campus. Using a focus group of students, conduct an interview to determine what factors are important in selecting a restaurant or pizza delivery. Once you have identified these factors, design a satisfaction survey to compare perceptions among the most popular restaurants in your area. Ask a sample of students who visited at least to two of them to complete the survey. Analyze the results and draw conclusions in a written report.

11. Many companies host visitors for plant tours, benchmarking information, and so on. Design a customer satisfaction questionnaire for a medium-sized manufacturing plant that might do so. Why would such a survey be useful?

CASES

Additional cases are available in the Bonus Materials Folder on the CD-ROM.

I. The Case of the Missing Reservation

Mark, Donna, and their children, along with another family, traditionally attended Easter brunch at a large downtown hotel. This year, as in the past, Donna called and made a reservation about three weeks prior to Easter. Because half the party consisted of small children, they arrived 20 minutes prior to the 11:30 reservation to ensure being seated early. When they arrived, however, the hostess said that they did not have a reservation. She explained that guests sometimes failed to show and that she would probably have a table available for them before long. Mark and Donna were quite upset and insisted that they had made a reservation and expected to be seated promptly. The hostess told them, "I believe that you made a reservation, but I can't seat you until all the people on the reservation list are seated. You are welcome to go to the lounge for complimentary coffee and punch while you wait." When Mark asked to see the manager, the hostess replied, "I am the manager," and turned to other duties. The party was eventually seated at 11:45, but was not at all happy with the experience.

The next day, Mark wrote a letter to the hotel manager explaining the entire incident. Mark was in the MBA program at the local university and taking a course on quality management. In the class, they had just studied issues of customer focus and some of the approaches used at The Ritz-Carlton Hotel, a 1992 and 1999 Baldrige Award winner. Mark concluded his letter with the statement, "I doubt that we would have experienced this situation at a hotel that truly believes in quality." About a week later, he received the following letter:

We enjoy hearing from our valued guests, but wish you had experienced the level of service and accommodations that we strive to achieve here at our hotel. Our restaurant manager received your letter and asked me to respond as Total Quality Lead.

Looking back at our records, we did not show a reservation on the books for your family. I have addressed your comments with the appropriate department head so that others will not have to experience the same inconveniences that you did.

Thank you once again for sharing your thoughts with us. We believe in a philosophy of "continuous improvement," and it is through feedback such as yours that we can continue to improve the service to our guests.

Discussion Questions

1. Were the hostess's actions consistent with a customer-focused quality philosophy? What might she have done differently?
2. How would you have reacted to the letter that Mark received? Could the Total Quality Lead have responded differently? What does the fact that the hotel manager did not personally respond to the customer tell you?

II. American Parkinson's Disease Association Center[65]

Parkinson's disease (PD) is a complex neurological disorder whose major characteristics are tremor, slowness of movement, and muscle rigidity. With advancing disease, patients may have trouble with balance and gait, as well as cognitive problems. Awareness of PD increased in recent years when celebrities Muhammad Ali and Michael J. Fox developed the disease.

Patients with PD are commonly referred to

neurologists. However, due to the complex nature of the disease and its management, it is common for neurologists themselves to refer patients to PD sub-specialists. The American Parkinson's Disease Association (APDA) is a nonprofit voluntary health agency committed to serving the Parkinson community through a comprehensive program of research, patient education, and support. The goals of APDA are

- To sponsor pioneering research into the cause, diagnosis, treatment, and cure for PD.
- To develop a grassroots network of information and referral centers and support groups nationwide.
- To establish fundraising chapters in strategic areas throughout the country.
- To publish and distribute a quarterly newsletter, educational booklets, audio-visual and other educational and supportive materials about PD.
- To sponsor educational conferences for professionals, patients, caregivers, and families throughout the country.
- To raise public awareness and understanding of PD.

The Cincinnati office of APDA is a nonprofit information and referral center for PD. The primary purpose of the center is to support and educate by counseling and providing literature to patients and individuals who are associated with the disease. The center implements positive coping skills and goals for patients, caregivers, and other health care personnel; and informs patients and caregivers of the reason and rationale for their therapies. Services are delivered to customers by telephone, mail, Internet, person-to-person contact, support group, and chapter work. The center also conducts an annual symposium, sponsored by area neurologists, hospitals, as well as pharmaceutical companies, to address hot topics such as new drugs and surgical treatments.

The center employs a medical director, who is a neurologist specializing in PD, a registered nurse as project coordinator, and an assistant. The assistant herself has PD and her real-life experience enables her to empathize with customers. The center is affiliated with a local university, which provides an accountant to help the center with financial matters. The Center is regulated by the APDA and OSHA regulations. Because it is not a medical establishment, it is not subject to health department regulations. Operating funds come from grant money given by APDA and other grant money from pharmaceutical companies.

The key customers are the Parkinson's patients, their caregivers, family members, support groups, and the professionals (neurologists, geriatricians and nursing homes) who work with these patients. Customers use the center for information and referrals to improve their response to the disease and overall well-being. The center responds to every client on an individual basis. APDA is the main supplier of all media materials. Pharmaceutical companies provide their drug and general information. Surgical companies and hospital supply companies also provide information on their devices.

An important strategic challenge the center faces is involving community neurologists and primary care physicians outside the university system as allies in their efforts. Community neurologists often refer their complicated patients to the university hospital and its affiliated neurology clinic. However, they do so with reservations. These reasons include losing their patients to university neurologists, conflicts of interest related to pharmaceutical-sponsored clinical trials, and a general feeling that academic neurologists do not treat them with respect.

Discussion Questions

1. Describe the supply chain structure for this center.
2. On what issues should the center focus in order to build relationships with its customers and suppliers?
3. Can you suggest specific activities and practices that they might engage in to develop into a total quality organization?

III. GOLD STAR CHILI: CUSTOMER AND MARKET KNOWLEDGE[66]

Gold Star Chili has hired you as a consultant to help them improve their approaches to focusing on customers. Management prepared a Baldrige-like application as a basis for beginning a self-assessment (portions of which relating to customer focus are included next). Examine their response in the context of the leading practices described in this chapter. What are Gold Star's strengths? What are its weaknesses and opportunities for improvement? What specific advice, including useful tools and techniques that might help Gold Star, would you suggest?

Company Background

Gold Star Chili, Inc., based in Cincinnati, Ohio, was founded in 1965 as a family-owned system of franchised and company-owned restaurants. Gold Star currently operates 118 regional locations (99 of which are franchised; the remaining are company restaurants or are co-owned). The Gold Star menu is based on a unique, "Cincinnati-style" chili recipe, flavored with a proprietary blend of spices from around the world. The chili is prepared in a central commissary, designed to reduce equipment needs at individual restaurants, promote consistency, and reduce labor costs.

Gold Star operates in a highly competitive market against other multilocation chili firms and traditional fast-food competitors such as McDonald's, Taco Bell, and Kentucky Fried Chicken. It trails its major competitor, Skyline, which has a larger advertising campaign, in market share. In the late 1980s, Gold Star recruited a non-family member to serve as CEO in order to expand the number of restaurants and geographic coverage. In early 1997 Gold Star launched a Total Quality initiative, "The Gold Star Way."

Customer Focus Practices

Gold Star is committed to achieving exceptional customer satisfaction through the creation of lasting relationships and by offering a consistently high-caliber set of products and services that customers perceive as an excellent value. Through the effective application of its "one customer at a time" philosophy, each associate strives to provide the level of customer service that permits the company to create and keep customers for life. Through attention to each customer's needs at each "moment of truth," its focus is on not only satisfying, but delighting each customer. Through careful implementation and adherence to the "Gold Star Way," the company seeks to develop an enhanced understanding of customers and markets.

Gold Star Chili defines two key customer groups: direct customers who use Gold Star products and services, and indirect customers with whom Gold Star has other relationships. Direct customers are divided into six customer segments, determined by product use: restaurant customers, franchisees, franchise applicants, retail customers, retail wholesalers, and mail-order customers. Indirect customers include product suppliers, service suppliers, co-packers, brokers/consultants, shareholders, and regulatory agencies.

To learn from customers, Gold Star uses multiple listening posts, including market research, focus groups, customer comment cards, satisfaction surveys, and roundtable meetings, advisory council group meetings, and one-on-one meetings. In determining restaurant consumer requirements, market research is conducted every two to three years. Gold Star benchmarks consumer preferences in eating habits, consumer loyalty, product awareness, and attribute ratings for quality, service, and value of Gold Star restaurants and competitors. Focus groups determine consumer preferences against the competition. Customers expect product consistency, a clean and pleasant atmosphere, and consistent service. Recently, Gold Star implemented a Voice of the Customer process with consumers, as well as with franchisees and associates.

Each restaurant has postage-paid comment cards (see Figure 4.11) available at counters and tables. Monthly, the Gold Star office receives on average 200–300 comment cards. A customer service representative enters each comment into a database and produces monthly reports on consumer satisfaction of each restaurant. From time to time, consumers will call directly to the corporate offices to make a formal complaint; these calls are also tabulated into the monthly customer comment report. The primary communication with restaurant customers occurs at the customer-server interface. In addition, store managers are encouraged to talk with guests regularly. An 800 number is also provided for consumers of retail products.

Franchisees are attracted by the relatively low investment required to join the Gold Star family of restaurants, the opportunity to operate a profitable business, and to benefit from the strong brand equity built into the Gold Star name. They expect consistency in chili product, effective corporate direction in the form of advice, market feedback, and promotional activities. Prior to the addition of a new restaurant, a geodemographic analysis of potential locations is performed to ensure that any new facility will not take more than 10 percent of its business from another Gold Star location. Gold Star's Franchisee Service Representatives (FSRs) take product orders from individual franchisees by telephone on a daily/weekly basis. These frequent interactions create a continuous dialogue

Figure 4.11 Customer Comment Card

We would like to have your comments.
NO POSTAGE NECESSARY! Please Mail:
DATE: _____ TIME: ____ $_{PM}^{AM}$ LOCATION:
_____

Servers Name: _____
What Did You Order: _____

QUALITY

	👍 👎			👍 👎
Good value	☐ ☐	Taste		☐ ☐
Quality of food	☐ ☐	Portion		☐ ☐
Temperature of food	☐ ☐	Appearance of food		☐ ☐

SERVICE

Speed	☐ ☐	Hospitality		☐ ☐
Accuracy	☐ ☐	Appearance of server		☐ ☐

CLEANLINESS

Inside store	☐ ☐
Outside store	☐ ☐
Rest rooms	☐ ☐

What radio station(s) do you listen to most often?
_____

How would you rate your overall dining experience?

1	2	3	4	5	6	7	8	9	10
POOR				GOOD					EXCELLENT

COMMENTS: _____
_____
_____

OPTIONAL: Name: _____
Address: _____
Phone: _____

between the franchisee and the FSR as well as the delivery person who delivers product.

Numerous opportunities are created to listen and learn from franchisees, including a Franchise Advisors Council consisting of elected owners who meet monthly to review and determine business decisions that affect the chain. The council members are also assigned to committee groups that meet with department heads to review business practices in areas of marketing, purchasing, menu pricing, operational costs, and gross profit analysis. Gold Star also conducts quarterly business meetings with restaurant owners and key managers. These meetings cover operations issues affecting the chain; outside suppliers are welcome to attend the meetings also. In 1996, a comprehensive survey of franchisees was initiated. Many complained that the survey was too long and not anonymous. Consequently, the survey was redesigned in 1997 into a short, five-question "Franchise Satisfaction Survey" that is sent to all locations on a quarterly basis (see Figure 4.12).

Through the data received from market research and focus group studies, Gold Star can determine consumer awareness, preferences, and dislikes. Feedback from advisory council meetings and quarterly business meetings help guide the company in determining training needs for management development of franchisees and their staff. Satisfaction survey results help target areas of opportunity and create action plans. The relative importance of product and service features to franchisees is tracked through the quarterly meetings, as well as through learning from daily and weekly phone calls to FSRs and face-to-face discussions with delivery personnel.

More than 70 percent of customers eat in a Gold Star restaurant at least once a month, and 20 to 30 percent eat at least once per week. The loyalty of the customer base permits servers and store managers to get to know customers personally and learn much about consumer needs. Marketing consultants perform an annual telephone survey of 300 "heavy chili users" to learn more about what consumers seek in chili products.

Gold Star Chili is an active participant in roundtable events sponsored by the Greater Cincinnati Chamber of Commerce. It participates with the Cincinnati Restaurant Association and the National Restaurant Association. These connections help maintain awareness of business trends, and advances in new technology. Changing business needs are assessed by reviewing the annual reports of competing restaurants, and an annual market research study that permits benchmarking against the restaurant/convenience food industry in general. Gold Star also reviews market research questions and redesigns questions to gain better feedback. Service industry trade literature is read regularly. In some instances, store operators have developed their own set of customer satisfaction tracking tools, for example, tracking tip amounts.

Gold Star uses several interlinked approaches to determine customer satisfaction and to strengthen relationships. The comment card program and toll-free number make it easy for the consumer to provide feedback. The operations department has four directors of operations,

Figure 4.12 Franchisee Satisfaction Survey

Franchisee Satisfaction Survey

Gold Star Chili

Franchisee: _____

Please complete this survey and mail by return date.
Rating and comments should pertain to all departments.

RATING SCALE	
A	TOTALLY SATISFIED
B	GENERALLY SATISFIED
C	GENERALLY DISSATISFIED
D	TOTALLY DISSATISFIED

	Rating
Communication Staff effectively communicates to you and listens to your needs and makes you feel important; Is easy to contact.	
Quality Quality food and products. Consistent and accurate services provided.	
Timeliness On-time deliveries; Handles emergencies; Speedy solutions.	
Dependability Promises kept; Trust in overall direction of the company.	
Cooperativeness Responds to needs; Flexible; Courteous; Sensitive to franchisee's needs.	

Please help us continuously improve by providing comments when a grade of "B" or less is given.

How does Gold Star Chili rate against other companies that you work with:
Please circle one: A   B   C   D

Comments:

_____

_____

_____

_____

Suggestions:

_____

_____

_____

_____

each overseeing half of the franchise community. Restaurant owners are given the director's phone number, pagers, cell phone numbers, e-mail addresses, and home phone numbers. All potential franchise owners meet with the executive staff prior to purchasing a franchise to establish a relationship.

Every worker is trained to ask the customer about his or her experience and see whether anything can be done to make it better. Comment cards are responded to within 24 hours of receipt, with a letter apologizing for an error or thanking them for a compliment. All department heads treat franchisees as internal customers, and have signed a pledge guaranteeing to return calls within 24 hours. If a franchisee reports a problem with product quality, Gold Star often hand-delivers replacement product the same day.

Restaurant customers with complaints most often present them directly to the server or manager. Usually the manager will attempt to recover from the service incident by offering partial or total credit, or a coupon redeemable for free food. Gold Star Chili uses a formal customer response system. All complaints are channeled to a customer service representative (CSR). All complaints, verbal or written, are logged onto a Comment Action form. If the comment is determined to be critical, then a call is made to the customer. The CSR must make two attempts to contact the customer within 24 hours. If the CSR cannot make contact, then a letter is sent to the customer along with free coupons. Afterwards, the CSR will report the outcome directly to the franchisee. Occasionally, a three-way conference is conducted between the CSR, the franchisee, and the customer. The Comment Action form is logged into the database and forwarded to the appropriate department for review and signature. The CSR prepares a monthly complaint log highlighting all comments, which are reviewed by senior management. A summary of comments is sent to all franchisees to provide a picture of how customers view the entire corporation and the impacts that each store may have on the reputation of the others. This practice has been highly effective in informing franchisees of key issues that might need attention.

Gold Star's mission is to create lasting relationships based upon respect, trust, and support given to customers. Many franchisees build relationships through local store marketing. Many owner/managers are active in the community with sponsorships of teams or school programs. Gold Star provides owners with school achievement awards they can distribute to local schools.

Gold Star keeps its approaches to customer access and relationships current through benchmarking Baldrige Award winners and attending regional and national conference to learn best practices.

Gold Star measures customer satisfaction for each of the major customer groups, consumers, franchise operators, associates, and suppliers, using comment cards and satisfaction surveys. Consumer comment cards rate key attributes as "thumbs up" or "thumbs down," and the overall dining experience on a scale from 1 to 10. The other satisfaction surveys use a score of A, B, C, or D for five attrib-

utes, and have a section for open comments. Action plans are set for any scores that fall below A. The franchise operator and supplier surveys also seek ratings against other companies they deal with. The associate survey asks for specific likes and dislikes about working for Gold Star Chili.

The majority of follow-up with dine-in customers is done face-to-face. At each restaurant, the server visits the table two to three times to ensure that everything is acceptable and to see if customer needs are being met.

Through various meetings between corporate and franchisees, Gold Star obtains information about satisfaction relative to competitors. The franchise satisfaction survey gives specific and reliable information from stores. For consumers, satisfaction relative to competitors is obtained from focus groups. The customer satisfaction report is sent out monthly to make all franchisees more aware of actions taking place in stores, and for sharing both positive and negative comments.

As with other approaches to customer relationships, Gold Star keeps its approaches to satisfaction determination current through benchmarking Baldrige Award winners and best practice research. For example, Gold Star was able to implement changes to the satisfaction survey process by following the method used by a past winner.

IV. CapStar Health Systems: Customer Focus

The complete CapStar case study, a fictitious example of a Baldrige application, can be found on the CD-ROM accompanying this book. If you have not read the Organizational Profile yet (see Case III in Chapter 3), please do so first. Examine their response to Category 3 in the context of the leading

practices described in this chapter (you need not consider the actual Baldrige criteria for this activity). What are their strengths? What are their weaknesses and opportunities for improvement? What specific advice, including useful tools and techniques that might help them, would you suggest?

ENDNOTES

1. Adapted from the article on Feargal Quinn by Polly Labarre in "Who's Fast in 2002," *Fast Company*, November 2001, 88–94.

2. Patricia Sellers, "Companies That Serve You Best," *Fortune*, May 31, 1993, 6.

3. "Making Customer Loyalty Real: Lessons from Leading Manufacturers," Special Advertising Section, *Fortune*, June 21, 1999.

4. AVIS 1992 Annual Report and Quality Review.

5. Steve Hoisington and Earl Naumann, "The Loyalty Elephant," *Quality Progress*, February 2003, 33–41.

6. "Companies That Serve You Best" (see note 2).

7. Carl Sewell and Paul B. Brown, *Customers for Life* (New York: Doubleday-Currency, 1990).

8. Jane Norman, "Royal Treatment Keeps Customers Loyal," *Cincinnati Enquirer*, May 31, 1998, E3, E5.

9. David Leonhardt, "Big Airlines Should Follow Midwest's Recipe," *Business Week,* June 28, 1999.

10. J. M. Juran, *Juran on Quality by Design* (New York: The Free Press, 1992), 7.

11. The Forum Corporation, "Customer Focus Research," executive briefing, Boston, 1988.

12. "Companies That Serve You Best" (see note 2).

13. Model developed by National Quality Research Center, University of Michigan Business School for the American Customer Satisfaction Index, (ACSI). Cosponsored with American Society for Quality Control, 1994.

14. John A. Goodman, Dianne Ward, and Scott Broetzmann, "It Might Not Be Your Product," *Quality Progress,* April 2002, 73–78.

15. "How to Listen to Consumers," *Fortune,* January 11, 1993, 77.

16. J. M. Juran, *Juran on Quality by Design* (New York: The Free Press, 1992), chapter 3.

17. AT&T Quality Steering Committee, *Achieving Customer Satisfaction,* AT&T Bell Laboratories, 1990.

18. Michael J. Stahl, William K. Barnes, Sarah F. Gardial, William C. Parr, and Robert B. Woodruff, "Customer-Value Analysis Helps Hone Strategy," *Quality Progress,* April 1999, 53–58.

19. "Time to Put Away the Checkbook: Now Fleet Needs to Bring Order to Its Furious Expansion," *Business Week,* June 10, 1996, 100.

20. Larry Selden and Geoffrey Colvin, "Will This Customer Sink Your Stock?" *Fortune,* September 30, 2002, 127–132.

21. David A. Garvin, "What Does Product Quality Really Mean?" *Sloan Management Review* 26, no. 1 (1984), 25–43.

22. Rahul Jacob, "Why Some Customers Are More Equal Than Others," *Fortune,* September 19, 1994, 215–224.

23. Robert D. Buzzell and Bradley T. Gale, The PIMS Principles: Linking Strategy to Performance (New York: The Free Press, 1987).

24. "Getting an Edge," *Across the Board,* February 2000, 43–48.

25. "Apple's One-Dollar-a-Year Man," *Fortune,* January 24, 2000, 71–76.

26. Bruce Nussbaum, "Designs for Living," *Business Week,* June 2, 1997, 99.

27. James H. Drew and Tye R. Fussell, "Becoming Partners with Internal Customers," *Quality Progress* 29, no. 10 (October 1996), 51–54.

28. "How to Listen to Consumers," *Fortune,* 11 January, 1993, 77.

29. Patricia Sellers, "Gap's New Guy Upstairs," *Fortune,* April 14, 2003, 110–116.

30. "KJ" is a registered trademark of the Kawayoshida Research Center.

31. This example is adapted from Donald L. McLaurin and Shareen Bell, "Making Customer Service

More Than Just a Slogan," *Quality Progress* 26, no. 11 (November 1993), 35–39.

32. Jane Carroll, "Mickey's Not for Everybody," *Across the Board,* February 2000, 11.

33. See note 3, "Making Customer Loyalty Real . . .".

34. Richard S. Teitelbaum, "Where Service Flies Right," *Fortune,* August 24, 1992, 117–118; Southwest Airlines, available at http://iflyswa.com; Kevin Freiberg and Jackie Freiberg, "NUTS! Southwest Airlines' Crazy Recipe for Business and Personal Success (Austin, TX: Bard Press, 1996); "Holding Steady," *Business Week,* February 3, 2003, 86.

35. Christopher Hart, "What Is an Extraordinary Guarantee?" *The Quality Observer* 3, no. 5 (March 1994), 15.

36. The Disney Institute, *Be Our Guest,* Disney Enterprises, Inc., 2001, 86.

37. Teitelbaum (see note 34).

38. Karl Albrecht and Ronald E. Zemke, *Service America* (Homewood, IL: Dow Jones-Irwin, 1985).

39. John Goodman, Pat O'Brien, and Eden Segal, "Turning CFOs Into Quality Champions—Show Link to Enhanced Revenue and Higher Margins," *Quality Progress* 33, no. 3 (March 2000), 47–56.

40. "Focusing on the Customer," *Fortune,* June 5, 1989, 226.

41. BI 1999 Malcolm Baldrige National Quality Award Application Summary.

42. Gary Hallin and Robert J. Latino, "Eastman Chemical's Success Story," *Quality Progress,* June 2003, 50–54.

43. AT&T Corporate Quality Office, *Supplier Quality Management: Foundations* (1994), 52.

44. Myron Magnet, "The New Golden Rule of Business," *Fortune,* February 21, 1994, 60–64.

45. Patricia C. La Londe, "Surveys As Supplier Relationship Tool" ASQ's 54th Annual Quality Congress proceedings, Indianapolis, IN, 2000, 684–686.

46. "Behind the Numbers," *CIO Magazine,* November 2, 2000, available at http://www2.cio.com/.

47. Eric Almquist and Carla Heaton, "Customers Are Disappearing," *Across the Board,* July–August, 2002, 61–63.

48. Lucy McCauley, "How May I Help You?" *Fast Company,* March 2000, 93.

49. John Goodman, David DePalma, and Scott Breetzmann, "Maximizing the Value of Customer Feedback," *Quality Progress* 29, no. 12 (December 1996), 35–39.

50. Malcolm Baldrige National Quality Award Profiles of Winners, 1988–1993; and materials provided by Granite Rock, including the 1992 Malcolm Baldrige Application Summary; Edward O. Welles, "How're We Doing?" *Inc.,* May 1991; Martha Heine, "Using Customer Report Cards Ups Service," undated reprint from *Concrete Trader;* and "Customer Report Cards at Granite Rock," available at http://www.baldrigeplus.com.

51. Importance-performance analysis was first introduced by J.A. Martilla and J.C. James, "Importance-Performance Analysis," *Journal of Marketing,* 41,1977, 77–79.

52. A. Blanton Godfrey, "Beyond Satisfaction," *Quality Digest,* January 1996, 15.

53. David C. Swaddling and Charles Miller, "Don't Measure Customer Satisfaction," *Quality Progress,* May 2002, 62–67.

54. Mike Carnell, "Gathering Customer Feedback," *Quality Progress,* 36, no. 1 (January 2003), 60.

55. Michael Schrage "Make No Mistake?" *Fortune,* December 11, 2001.

56. Our thanks go to Brian Cundiff of LaRosa's Inc. for providing this case.

57. Fred Vogelstein. "Mighty Amazon," *Fortune,* May 26, 2003, 64.

58. 1997 Amazon.com, Inc. Annual Report, as quoted in the 2002 Amazon.com, Inc. Annual Report, 4.

59. 2002 Amazon.com, Inc. Annual Report, 1–2.

60. Robert D. Hof and Heather Green, "How Amazon Cleared the Profitability Hurdle," *Information Technology*, February 4, 2002, available at http://www. businessweek .com/magazine/content/02_05/b3768079.htm.

61. David Streitfeld, "Amazon.com's Data-Mining Technology Stirs Internet Privacy Controversy," *Washington Post,* as quoted by http://www.onlineathens. com/stories/082899/new_0828990006.shtml.

62. Courtesy of Deer Valley Resort.

63. Adapted from Ralph F. Altman and Marilyn M. Helms, "Quantifying Service Quality: A Case Study of a Rental Car Agency," *Production and Inventory Management* 36, no. 2 (Second Quarter 1995), 45–50. Reprinted with permission of APICS—The Educational Society for Resource Management, Falls Church, VA.

64. Edna White, Ravi Behara, and Sunil Babbar, "Mine Customer Experiences," *Quality Progress,* July 2002, 63–67.

65. Our thanks go to two former students, Arif Dalvi, M.D., and Peggy Vogt, for their work on which this case is based.

66. We thank our student team, Sudipta Bhattacharya, Terry Fitzpatrick, Gordon Jamieson, and Jeremy Smith, for their work on the initial version of this case for the fourth edition of this book; Kim Olden of Gold Star Chili for providing current information; and Gold Star Chili, Inc., for granting permission to use this material.

BIBLIOGRAPHY

AT&T Quality Steering Committee. *Achieving Customer Satisfaction.* Quality Technology Center, AT&T Bell Laboratories, 1990.

Hayes, Bob E. *Measuring Customer Satisfaction: Development and Use of Questionnaires,* 2nd ed. Milwaukee, WI: ASQC Quality Press, 1997.

Hoffman, K. Douglas, and John E.G. Bateson. *Essentials of Services Marketing.* Fort Worth: Harcourt College Publishers, 2002.

Janda, Swinder, Phillip J. Trocchia, and Kevin P. Gwinner. "Consumer Perceptions of Internet Retail Service Quality," *International Journal of Service Industry Management* 13, no. 5 (2002), 412–431.

Johnston, Robert. "The Determinants of Service Quality: Satisfiers and Dissatisfiers," *International Journal of Service Industry Management* 6, no. 5 (1995), 53.

Kyrillidou, Martha, and Fred M. Heath. *Measuring Service Quality.* Champaign, IL : University of Illinois Graduate School of Library and Information Science, 2001.

Malcolm Baldrige National Quality Award. 2003 Criteria for Performance Excellence.

Mittal, Banwari, and Jagdish N. Sheth. *Value Space: Winning the Battle for Market Leadership: Lessons from the World's Most Admired Companies.* New York: McGraw-Hill, 2001.

Nogami, Glenda Y. "Eight Points for More Useful Surveys." *Quality Progress* 29, no. 10 (October 1996), 93–96.

Raju, P. S., and Subhash C. Lonial. "The Impact of Quality Context and Market Orientation on Organizational Performance in a Service Environment." *Journal of Service Research* 4, no. 2 (2001), 140–154.

Rosenberg, Jarrett. "Five Myths about Customer Satisfaction," *Quality Progress* 29, no. 12 (December 1996), 57–60.

Sanes, Christina. "Customer Complaints = Golden Opportunities." 1993 ASQC Quality Congress Transactions, Boston, 45–51.

Schlesinger, Leonard A. "'Hardwiring' an Organization's Service Performance," *Managing Service Quality* 13, no. 1 (2003), 6–9.

Whitely, Richard C. *The Customer-Driven Company.* Reading, MA: Addison-Wesley, 1991.

Wong, Amy, and Amrik Sohal. "Customers' Perspectives on Service Quality and Relationship Quality in Retail Encounters," *Managing Service Quality* 12, no. 6 (2002), 424–433.

Zeithaml, A. Parasuraman, and Leonard L. Berry. *Delivering Quality Service.* New York: The Free Press, 1990.

Zimmerman, Richard E., Linda Steinmann, and Vince Schueler. "Designing Customer Surveys That Work." *Quality Digest* (October 1996), 22–28.

CHAPTER 5

LEADERSHIP AND STRATEGIC PLANNING

Jack Welch, retired CEO of General Electric, is probably regarded as the most-admired CEO of his generation. The following dialogue about General Electric's Six Sigma quality initiative took place between a *Fortune* magazine reporter and Welch:[1]

> Fortune: *Jack, you're doing a total-quality thing ten or 15 years after the rest of corporate America did it. Why are you doing it, and why now?*
>
>   Welch: *There was only one guy in the whole country who hated quality more than me. I always believed quality would come from just operating well and fast, and all these slogans were nonsense.*
>
>   *The guy who hated quality more was Larry Bossidy. He hated quality totally. Then he left GE and went to Allied Signal. In order to resurrect Allied*

Signal, Larry went out, saw Motorola, and did some stuff on Six Sigma. And he called me one day and he said, "Jack, this ain't b.s.—this is real stuff, this is really great stuff."

We poll 10,000 employees every year. In '95 they came back and said, we desperately need a quality issue. So Six Sigma was something we adopted then. The results are fantastic. We're going to get $1.2 billion of gain this year. For years our operating margin was never over ten. It's been improving, and it's going to be 16.7 this year. Our working-capital turns were four for 35 years. It will be nine this year.

The one thing that all quality experts agree on is that strong leadership, especially from senior managers, is absolutely necessary to develop and sustain a TQ culture. A co-director of the Juran Center for Leadership in Quality at the University of Minnesota observed:

- Despite substantial efforts, only a few U.S. organizations have reached world-class excellence.
- Even fewer companies have sustained such excellence during changes in leadership.
- Most corporate quality failures rest with leadership.[2]

Leaders may seek to motivate employees and develop enthusiasm for quality with rhetoric, but actions often speak louder than words, as seen in Welch's behavior. The former CEO of Motorola, Robert Galvin, made a habit of making quality the first item on the agenda of executive staff meetings—and then leaving the meeting before the discussion of financial issues. His leadership guided Motorola to become one of the first winners of the Malcolm Baldrige National Quality Award. As one professional observed, managers manage for the present; leaders lead for the future.

> *Leadership is the ability to positively influence people and systems under one's authority to have a meaningful impact and achieve important results.*

Leaders create clear and visible quality values, and integrate these values into the organization's strategy. **Strategy** is the pattern of decisions that determines and reveals a company's goals, policies, and plans to meet the needs of its stakeholders. Through an effective strategy, a business creates a sustainable competitive advantage.

The principal role of strategic planning is to align work processes with strategic directions, thereby ensuring that improvement and learning reinforce organizational priorities. In today's business environment, quality is a key element of strategic planning. This chapter describes the role of leadership and strategic planning for quality and performance excellence, with an emphasis on the application of leadership concepts in a TQ environment and the process of formulating and implementing TQ-based strategies.

> *Strategic planning is the process of envisioning the organization's future and developing the necessary goals, objectives, and action plans to achieve that future.*

LEADERSHIP FOR QUALITY

Despite the countless articles and books written about it, leadership is one of the least-understood concepts in business. Even though many theories of leadership have been developed, no single approach adequately captures the essence of the concept. Most definitions of leadership reflect an assortment of behaviors, for example:

QUALITY PROFILES

SOLAR TURBINES, INC., AND CORNING TELECOMMUNICATIONS

PRODUCTS DIVISION

San Diego-based Solar Turbines, Inc., a wholly owned subsidiary of Caterpillar Inc. since 1981, is the world's largest supplier of mid-range industrial gas turbine systems, with more than 10,000 systems installed throughout the world. Following its six "strategies to win," the company increased its share of the worldwide market for new turbine equipment to a position of strong market leadership since 1992. Five of Solar's strategies focus on meeting customer requirements, building the performance capabilities necessary to quickly deliver superior products, and engaging the full potential of its workforce. Sustained progress in these areas enabled the company to realize its sixth strategy, delivering investor-grade returns in a low-margin industry. Teams at every level, from executive leadership to shop floor work teams, are effectively linked to others, ensuring that decisions and actions do not occur in isolation or without understanding of businesswide impacts.

Solar's strategic focus paid off. From 1994 to 1998, the year Solar received a Baldrige Award, new product development cycle time was reduced from 39 to 22 months; warranty claims decreased significantly, and nonrecoverable commissioning costs declined. Because of its quality gains, maintenance costs for customers are 42 percent lower than the average for all suppliers. Revenues generated per employee increased 61 percent between 1993 and 1997.

The Telecommunications Products Division (TPD) of Corning, Inc., produces hair-thin optical fiber used to transmit large amounts of data over long distances for three distinct customer groups (cable manufacturers, end users, and joint-venture fiber-making companies) in more than 30 countries. In a highly competitive industry, the division's Executive Leadership Team integrated the principles of total quality into its "Plan to Win," which embodies six fundamental components: strategic direction; customer focus; formalized systems of process management; a culture of continuous improvement; measurement of progress using the Baldrige criteria; and foundation values of people, processes, and technology. The approach develops strategic direction by carefully linking vision, mission, strategy, plans, goals, and individual employee objectives. Customer focus is ensured through their Customer Response System, used to gather customer inputs, establish priorities, and initiate action plans to increase customer satisfaction. Processes are designed to be formalized, closed-loop systems, ensuring that short-term plans, goals, and individual employee contributions contribute to meeting long-term strategic aims. TPD uses surveys and other feedback mechanisms to ensure that individual employees understand how their personal work objectives contribute to meeting the division's key strategic objectives.

In 1994, 98 percent of customers rated the quality of TPD products as "very good" or "excellent" and 99 percent of end-user customers viewed TPD as the industry and technological leader. These ratings stem from many internal improvements. For example, returns of unsatisfactory products were reduced by a factor of more than 24 over a 10-year period, while performance in meeting customer shipping requirements improved tenfold. TPD also reduced hazardous waste levels by six times in the seven years preceding its winning the Baldrige Award in 1995. TPD achieved these results even as the price of optical fiber dropped by almost 50 percent.

Source: Malcolm Baldrige National Quality Award Profiles of Winners, National Institute of Standards and Technology, Department of Commerce.

- Vision that stimulates hope and mission that transforms hope into reality
- Radical servanthood that saturates the organization
- Stewardship that shepherds its resources
- Integration that drives its economy
- The courage to sacrifice personal or team goals for the greater community good
- Communication that coordinates its efforts
- Consensus that drives unity of purpose
- Empowerment that grants permission to make mistakes, encourages the honesty to admit them, and gives the opportunity to learn from them
- Conviction that provides the stamina to continually strive toward business excellence[3]

In practice, the notion of leadership can be as elusive as the notion of quality itself. This section briefly summarizes the principal concepts of leadership and prominent leadership practices in quality management.

When we think of leadership, we generally think of *executive leadership*, which focuses on the roles of senior managers in guiding an organization to fulfill its mission and meet its goals. The critical importance of senior managers' roles in business excellence is affirmed by numerous research studies and from practitioners' perspectives. In the Baldrige criteria, as well as other frameworks such as the ISO 9000 and Japan's Deming Prize, leadership is the first category. The many activities that senior executives perform include the following:

- Defining and communicating business directions
- Ensuring that goals and expectations are met
- Reviewing business performance and taking appropriate action
- Creating an enjoyable work environment that promotes creativity, innovation, and continual improvement
- Soliciting input and feedback from customers
- Ensuring that employees are effective contributors to the business
- Motivating, inspiring, and energizing employees
- Recognizing employee contributions
- Providing honest feedback

As we move further into the new economy, some of the cherished views about leadership being centered at the top of the organization are being seriously challenged. Today's fluid, "de-jobbed" organizations—in which parts of the work are being done by traditional departments, parts are being done by temporary project teams, parts are being done by business partners in another organization, and parts are being done by external contract employees who are indistinguishable from the company's own workers—require a broader view of leadership:

- The formal, organizational, leadership that is responsible for integrating, resourcing, and orchestrating the activities of the various project teams
- The ad hoc leadership required within project teams
- Leadership in every member of every project team that incorporates the initiative, the self-management capacity, the readiness to make hard decisions, the embodiment of organizational values, and the sense of business responsibility that in the traditional organization were limited to the top people in the organization[4]

For example, formal organizational leadership is manifested in developing clear values, creating a competitive advantage, defining customer and market focus, and encouraging continual learning. Ad hoc leadership within project teams is seen by observing the leader working to make those around her or him successful, by removing barriers to team performance, establishing good lines of communication, and resolving problems. Individual leadership is revealed through people maintaining the focus and discipline to consistently complete jobs, being proactive in identifying and solving problems, working for win-win agreements, and making continuous learning a personal habit. These core skills—vision, empowerment, intuition, self-understanding, and value congruence—are reflected in the practices of quality leaders in organizations throughout the world.

> *Effective leadership requires five core leadership skills: vision, empowerment, intuition, self-understanding, and value congruence.[5]*

Leaders are visionaries; they manage for the future, not the past (think back to the first of Deming's 14 Points). Vision is crucial at every level during times of change. Leaders recognize the radical organizational changes taking place today as opportunities to move closer to total quality. Jack Welch, for example, pushed GE to become a leader among traditional Old Economy companies in embracing the Internet after noticing his wife Christmas shopping on the Web. "I realized that if I didn't watch it, I would retire as a Neanderthal," he was reported as saying, "So I just started reading everything I could about it." He began by pairing 1,000 Web-savvy mentors with senior people to get his top teams up to Internet speed quickly.[6] Visionary leaders create mental and verbal pictures of desirable future states and share these visions with their organizational partners, including customers, suppliers, and employees.

Leaders empower employees to assume ownership of problems or opportunities, and to be proactive in implementing improvements and making decisions in the best interests of the organization. At Motorola, for example, every department has Participative Management Process teams consisting of 8–12 members who set objectives to support corporate goals. Individual employees develop goals and plans, track progress, and receive bonuses based on successful and timely achievement of goals. The philosophy at GTE Directories Corporation summarizes this facet of leadership nicely: *Put a stake in the ground, get out of the way, and stay the course.* Empowerment threatens many managers who are accustomed to wielding their power, often coercively through fear of punishment or sanctions.[7] True power is not based upon formal position and authority, but rather aids in spreading power downward and outward and developing leadership at lower levels of the organization. It is this notion that Deming was trying to convey in one of his 14 Points: Institute Leadership.

Leaders are not afraid to follow their intuition. Even in the face of uncertainty and change, they must anticipate the future and must be prepared to make difficult decisions that will help the organization to be successful. When he was appointed CEO of Xerox in 1982, David Kearns had already witnessed firsthand the implementation of TQM at Fuji Xerox. On his return from Japan, he had begun listing the factors that made the Japanese better than their American counterparts. After eliminating those factors he felt were insignificant, three elements remained: cost, quality, and expectations.[8] His intuition in this case led him to develop the Leadership Through Quality initiative at Xerox.

Self-understanding requires the ability to look at one's self and then identify relationships with employees and within the organization. It requires an examination of oneself's weaknesses as well as strengths. One manager told Roger Milliken, chairman and CEO of Milliken & Co., "There are only five managers [out of 400] in this room who know how to listen." Milliken recognized the need to do something. At the end of the meeting, Milliken stood up on a banquet chair, and raising his right arm, asked all of the assembled executives to repeat after him: "I will listen. I will not shoot the messenger. I recognize that management is the problem."[9] Many leaders have an insatiable appetite for knowledge and self-learning as well as a drive to develop their skills and use them effectively.

Finally, value congruence occurs when leaders integrate their values into the company's management system. Values are basic assumptions and beliefs about the nature of the business, mission, people, and relationships of an organization. Specifically, values include trust and respect for individuals, openness, teamwork, integrity, and commitment to quality. They become standards by which choices are made and create an organizational structure in which quality is a routine part of activities and decisions throughout the organization. For example, the founder and first CEO of Solectron Corporation, Winston Chen, developed the Solectron Beliefs, a set of basic values to use as the model for behavior of all employees: Customer First, Respect for the Individual, Quality, Supplier Partnership, Business Ethics, Shareholder Value, and Social Responsibility. His successor, Ko Nishimura, continues to reaffirm the Solectron Beliefs year after year, and personally coaches the leadership team to live them. He has stated that if the company's behavior does not reflect the Beliefs, then the behavior—not the Beliefs—must change. His leadership led Solectron to become the first two-time Baldrige award winner. Employees quickly recognize leaders who do not apply the values they espouse or who do so inconsistently. This incongruence causes employees to constantly doubt management's message.

Good leaders should "lead for quality," that is, they should ensure that the principles of TQ are adopted and used throughout their organizations. Some actions might include the following:

- Gathering data before expressing an opinion and backing up actions with facts
- Being aware that quality is defined by customers and acting on that awareness
- Using quality tools when appropriate and making their benefits visible to all
- Expecting and driving commitment and accountability throughout the organization

As A. V. Feigenbaum noted, "The passion is in living and working in the spirit of a quality ethic—which means having a deep belief that what you do to make quality better makes everything in the organization better."[10]

Leading Practices for Leadership

In firms committed to total quality, various leadership practices share common elements. True leaders promote quality and business performance excellence in several ways.

1. *They focus on creating and balancing value for customers and other stakeholders that serves as a basis for setting business directions and performance expectations at all levels of the organization.* An organization's vision and values emanates from senior leaders, as seen from the previous discussion of Solectron, and should revolve around customers, both external and internal. For example, FedEx's concise motto of *People, Service, Profits* conveys that commitment to the people—the employees of FedEx—come first. If employees are treated with respect and have empathetic leaders, they will provide exceptional service to customers, and profits will follow. BI developed a three-pronged approach to business excellence: a pervasive customer focus, strong associate focus, and its internal quality management philosophy called the "BI Way." This philosophy, which includes training, problem-solving techniques, process improvement, incentives, and a focus on results, brings TQ principles into the fabric of the company. Rhetoric cannot stand alone; leaders must demonstrate commitment

to the vision and values. At FedEx, every business decision is evaluated against the People-Service-Profits hierarchy, in that order. At BI, every associate takes part in the improvement process, but the company's leaders drive the process and give it priority and energy.

2. *They create and sustain a leadership system and environment for empowerment, innovation, agility, and organizational learning.* Leaders provide an environment with few bureaucratic rules and procedures. Such an environment encourages managers to experiment and take risks, permits employees to talk openly about problems, supports teamwork, and promotes employees' understanding of their responsibilities for quality. Solectron managers, for example, foster teamwork and give workers responsibility for meeting quality goals. They encourage a strong family atmosphere, promote clear and effective communications, and recognize and reward groups for exceptional performance. Besides monetary awards, Solectron often buys lunch for an entire division or brings in ice cream for the whole corporation. At Custom Research, Inc., the top four senior leaders ensure that employees have the responsibility, training, and information they need to do their jobs through empowering everyone to do whatever it takes to serve clients, working with nine other senior people to set strategy, and making middle managers the real leaders.

3. *They set high expectations and demonstrate substantial personal commitment and involvement in quality, often with a missionary-like enthusiasm.* A leader can inspire people to do things they do not believe they can do. Frances Hesselbein, president of the Peter F. Drucker Foundation for Non-Profit Management, and former CEO of the Girl Scouts of the USA, says, "The leader for today and the future will be focused on how to be [rather than how to do]—how to develop quality, character, mind-set, values, principles and courage."[11] Motorola set aggressive goals of reducing defects per unit of output in every operation by 100-fold in four years and reducing cycle time by 50 percent each year. The 3M Company seeks to generate 25 percent of sales from products less than two years old. To promote such "stretch goals," leaders provide the resources and support necessary to meet them, especially training.

Leaders, such as Jack Welch in this chapter's opening quotation, display a passion about quality and actively live their values. By "walking the talk," leaders serve as role models for the whole organization. Many CEOs lead quality training sessions, serve on quality improvement teams, work on projects that do not usually require top-level input, and personally visit customers. Senior managers at the former Texas Instruments Defense Systems & Electronics Group, for example, led 150 of 1,900 cross-functional teams. In small businesses, such as Marlow Industries, CEO and president Raymond Marlow chairs the TQM Council and has daily responsibility for quality-related matters.

4. *They integrate quality values into daily leadership and management and communicate extensively through the leadership structure and to all employees.* General Electric redefined its promotion standards around quality. Managers will not be considered for promotions, but will face dismissal, unless they visibly demonstrate support for the company's Six Sigma quality strategy.[12] Successful leaders continually promote their vision throughout the organization using many forms of communication: personal interaction, talks, newsletters, seminars, e-mail, and video. For example, senior managers at Eastman Chemical use every opportunity, including personal visits to teams, in-plant television broadcasts, and bimonthly quality management forums, to communicate the company's vision, values, and goals. Flattening the organizational structure often enhances

communication. Texas Instruments Defense Systems and Electronics Group reduced the number of organizational layers from eight to five and increased the number of employees per supervisor as a way of speeding up communication.

5. *They review organizational performance—including their own performance as leaders— to assess organizational success and progress, and translate review findings into priorities for improvement and opportunities for innovation for the organization as a whole as well as their own leadership effectiveness.* To maintain a commitment to improvement, leaders must maintain a sense of the organization's energy level. This awareness requires a process for reviewing performance measures and using the results to drive improvements. Reviews help to build consistency behind goals and allocation of resources. For example, Motorola's Commercial, Government, and Industrial Solutions Sector (CGISS) process includes semiannual organizational performance review meetings, quarterly operations reviews, monthly customer and business performance meetings, and quarterly Performance Excellence Steering Committee meetings, among others. One illustration of the outcomes was the formation of a cross-functional team to address short-term and long-term global safety and security opportunities. Annually, senior leaders are calibrated against their peers on results and behaviors and work on identifying development plans on both dimensions.

6. *They create an environment that fosters legal and ethical behavior, and a governance system that addresses management and fiscal accountability and protection of stockholder and stakeholder interests.* SSM Health Care, for example, implemented a systemwide organizational ethics effort called the Corporate Responsibility Process (CRP). The CRP aligns with the elements of the national Office of Inspector General's model compliance plan, but goes beyond compliance to ensure that corporate values are reflected in all work processes. Employees, physicians, volunteers, and suppliers can use a confidential help line to raise questions, and any reported issues are investigated and acted upon. KPMG identified the CRP as a best practice nationwide. Likewise, Motorola CGISS has a Board of Directors Ethics Committee, a Corporate Compliance Officer, Ethics Hotline, and Leadership Standards Model to support its business practices.

7. *They integrate public responsibilities and community support into their business practices.* Leadership responsibilities include the protection of public health, safety, and the environment that may be affected by a company's products and services. For instance, Eastman Chemical Company helped to develop the Chemical Manufacturers Association's Responsible Care principles, which require member companies to assume responsibility for public health, safety, and environmental protection in everything they do. Solectron France was the first French company to have its Environmental Management and Audit System certified by the European Economic Community, and sites in Malaysia and China helped to train local governments in best practices for recycling, hazardous material handling, and auditing.

   Support of key communities, such as education, health care, professional organizations, and community services, are important roles for companies and a leadership responsibility. BI, for instance, emphasizes education and direct volunteer efforts. Its associates designed and teach a "School to Work" curriculum in the local school district. BI donates a consistent percentage of its profits to the community each year, and matches funds raised by its associates for charitable causes. GTE Directories' community activities include corporate philanthropy, and a Volunteer Initiatives Program that provides funding to nonprofit organizations based on employee volunteer time.

From all these examples, we see that leadership is the "driver" of the entire quality system. Without leadership, a total quality initiative simply becomes the "flavor of the month," which is the major reason that total quality efforts fail in many organizations. Effective leadership practice, however, is built upon a sound foundation of organizational structure and theory.

LEADERSHIP THEORY AND PRACTICE

Leadership involves both people and measurement and control systems, thus it has both a "soft" side and a "hard" side. To understand how leadership is developed and practiced, it is important to understand its foundations in management theory. Dozens of leadership theories have been derived from literally thousands of leadership studies. Unlike some areas of quality management that are only a few decades old, leadership theories can often be traced back 50–75 years or more. A comprehensive review of these theories is well beyond the scope of this text. However, the theories are quite important within the context of TQ; therefore, we provide a brief summary of the most popular leadership approaches and discuss their implications in a TQ environment. The well-informed manager, engineer, or technician should be aware of such approaches and use them to broaden his or her understanding of how leadership can affect behavior in the workplace and lead to the successful adoption of TQ. Table 5.1 summarizes some of the key theories that have influenced today's leadership styles.

The purpose of leadership theories is to explain differences in leadership styles and contexts.

Table 5.1 Classification of Leadership Theories

Leadership Theory	Pioneer/Developer	Type of Theory
"Great man" model[13]	Ralph Stogdill	Trait
Ohio State Studies[14]	E. A. Fleishman, E. F. Harris, et al.	Leader behavior
Michigan Studies[15]	Rensis Likert	
Theory X–Theory Y model[16]	Douglas MacGregor	
Managerial Grid model[17]	Robert Blake; Jane S. Mouton	
Leadership effectiveness model[18]	Fred E. Fiedler	Contingency (Situational)
Supervisory contingency decision model[19]	V. H. Vroom and P. W. Yetton V. H. Vroom and A. G. Jago	
Managerial roles[20]	Henry Mintzberg	Role approach
Charismatic theory[21]	R. J. House; J. A. Conger	Emerging theories
Transformational theory[22]	James M. Burns; N. M. Tichy and D. O. Ulrich; B. M. Bass	
Substitutes for leadership[23]	Jon P. Howell, et al.	
Emotional intelligence[24]	Daniel Goleman	

Because many of the traditional and contingency leadership theories are developed more fully in principles of management and organizational behavior courses, their characteristics will not be explored in detail here. Instead, a summary of the concepts of these theories is included on the CD-ROM in the Bonus Materials folder for review purposes. In the next section we will briefly describe characteristics of the "emerging" leadership theories that are generating active discussion in academic settings and being applied to management situations today.

Contemporary and Emerging Leadership Theories

Traditional leadership theories were largely based on an assumption of rational thinking. Emerging leadership theories build on or enlarge traditional theory by attempting to answer questions raised, but not answered, by earlier approaches. According to the various contemporary leadership theories developed over the last 20 or 30 years, leadership effectiveness can be improved with the correct mix of the leader's style of management, the characteristics of those who are led, and the situation.

> *Some of the newer theories include attributional, transactional, and emotional intelligence theories, which enter the realm of human emotions to explain how good leaders seem to succeed, and where mediocre ones show mixed results or fail to accomplish their goals.*

Attributional theory states that leaders' judgment on how to deal with subordinates in a specific situation is based on their attributions of the internal or external causes of the behaviors of their followers. For example, if a leader observes an employee producing poor-quality material, the leader may attribute the problem to internal factors within the person's control, such as poor effort, commitment, or lack of ability. Alternately, the leader could attribute the problem to external factors, such as bad material or defective equipment. Depending on these attributions (and how/whether they are justified), the leader will decide whether to use punishment (reprimand, demotion, firing) or corrective solutions (problem finding, job redesign, training) to resolve the problem. Readers who are interested in learning more about this approach are referred to Hellriegel and colleagues.[25]

Transactional (charismatic) theory assumes that certain leaders may develop the ability to inspire their subordinates to exert extraordinary efforts to achieve organizational goals, owing to the leader's vision and understanding of how to tap into the developmental needs of the subordinates. An emerging leadership theory that falls within the transactional category shows potential for dealing with the leadership needs of organizations that want to develop a total quality management process. This approach, called **Transformational Leadership theory**, can help to explain the impact of leadership in a TQ environment.[26] According to this model, leaders adopt many of the behaviors discussed earlier in this chapter. They take a long-term perspective, focus on customers, promote a shared vision and values, work to stimulate their organizations intellectually, invest in training, take some risks, and treat employees as individuals. The CEOs and executive team members of nearly every Malcolm Baldrige Award recipient have modeled this leadership behavior. Some empirical evidence found in research suggests that transformational leadership is strongly correlated with lower turnover, higher productivity and quality, and higher employee satisfaction than other approaches.

Not all managers in TQ organizations ought to be transformational leaders, however. The charismatic transformational leader, such as a Jack Welch, is rare, and most effective at the top. An organization pursuing TQ needs both those who establish visions and those who are effective at the day-to-day tasks needed to achieve them.[27]

Another emerging concept of leadership is called the **Substitutes for Leadership theory**.[28] This research takes the intriguing view that in many organizations, if characteristics of subordinates (team members), the nature of the tasks that they perform, and the guidance and incentives provided by the organization are aligned, then formal leadership tends to be unproductive or counterproductive. It is suggested that this leadership approach may be useful in cases of low leadership effectiveness where the leader cannot be removed for various political or other reasons (the owner's incompetent son or daughter is the "leader"), or where team member training or competence is especially high (a surgical team), or where the situation is particularly dynamic (battling oil well fires in the desert). In such situations, self-management, professional education, or even computer technology can be developed or built in to substitute for leadership. The implication for a TQ-focused organization is that each situation calls for just the right amount of leadership (not too much and not too little) in order to attain high-quality results.

One of the newest of the emerging leadership theories is called the **Emotional Intelligence theory**.[29] Goleman defines five components of emotionally intelligent leaders: (1) self-awareness, (2) self-regulation, (3) motivation, (4) empathy, and (5) social skill. His premise is that too much reliance was placed on the rational side of leadership in leadership research studies and training done over the years. He argues that expectations for emotional intelligence are generally not captured in performance evaluation systems, but that the self-management (components 1 through 3) and interpersonal skills (components 4 and 5) represented by the five components are as essential for executive-level leaders as "traditional" intelligence (measured by IQ tests) and technical competence. The significance of emotional intelligence for effective total quality lies in translating the "vision" of an integrated leadership system and long-range planning process into action. Without credible self-management, represented by the first three components, it will be difficult for subordinates within the organization to "buy into" the vision of the leader. Without mature empathy and social skills, represented by the last two components, it will be difficult for the leader to work effectively with customers, suppliers, and others outside the organization in order to build rapport needed for long-term enterprise effectiveness, which is critical for a TQ-focused organization.

Applying Leadership Theory in a TQ Environment

Quality Spotlight
The Ritz-Carlton

Chapter 3 describes how senior leadership at The Ritz-Carlton Hotel Co. modeled many of the behaviors of effective leaders as developed within existing leadership theories. (You might wish to review this material before continuing.) By examining characteristics of several of the emerging leadership theories, we can see how they are applied in practice at The Ritz-Carlton.

Horst Schulze, the retired CEO of The Ritz-Carlton, and his senior leadership team take care that leaders' judgments on how to deal with subordinates in a specific situation are based on positive attributions (attribution theory). The assumption of worker competency is a given at Ritz-Carlton, even extending to the company motto of "We are ladies and gentlemen serving ladies and gentlemen."

Aspects of Transformational Leadership theory are evident during the new hotel start-up process, when senior leaders are visible, doing what transformational leaders do. These activities include taking a long-term perspective, focusing on customers, promoting a shared vision and values, working to stimulate their organizations intellectually, investing in training, taking some risks, and treating employees as individuals.

Can it be that The Ritz-Carlton's staff is expected to be like a team of oil-well fire-fighters? The Substitutes for Leadership theory provides some support for this notion. As outlined earlier, if characteristics of subordinates (team members), the nature of the tasks that they perform, and the guidance and incentives provided by the organization are aligned, then formal leadership tends to be unproductive or counterproductive. The Ritz-Carlton's leadership model incorporates a high level of team member training (focusing on the Gold Standards) and competence (often seen in highly professional jobs, such as surgical teams), and the situation is often very dynamic. Thus, workers must often be self-led. They "substitute for leadership" and are empowered to take action without waiting for supervisory approval.

By empowering employees as leaders at every level, The Ritz-Carlton provides an environment that will lead to the development and use of greater emotional intelligence, as outlined in Emotional Intelligence theory. Thus, the employee-guest interface and relationship management approaches that The Ritz-Carlton teaches every employee, provide interpersonal skills and supplement self-management. The components of emotionally intelligent leaders—self-awareness, self-regulation, motivation, empathy, and social skill—are regularly seen in employees' ability to be self-managed (components 1 through 3) and in their use of interpersonal skills (components 4 and 5).

CREATING THE LEADERSHIP SYSTEM

The **leadership system** refers to how leadership is exercised, formally and informally, throughout an organization. These elements include how key decisions are made, communicated, and carried out at all levels. They include structures and mechanisms for decision making, selection and development of leaders and managers, and reinforcement of values, directions, and performance expectations. It builds loyalties and teamwork based upon shared values, encourages initiative and risk taking, and subordinates organization to purpose and function. An effective leadership system also includes mechanisms for leaders' self-examination and improvement.

> *An effective leadership system respects the capabilities and requirements of employees and other stakeholders, and sets high expectations for performance and performance improvements.*

To illustrate these themes, the leadership system at Solar Turbines, Inc., shown in Figure 5.1, operates in three distinct, yet highly integrated modes. First, through a functional organizational structure led by the president's staff ("1" in Figure 5.1), Solar maintains a focus on functional excellence through the recruitment, hiring, development of critical skills, and the application of tools and common processes to continuously improve functional effectiveness. Second, three cross-functional leadership structures ("2" in the figure), comprised of managers and technical experts selected from multiple levels of the organization, facilitate companywide teamwork and decision making. This Expanded Leadership Team, consisting of the Operations Council (74 leaders from across the business) and the Expanded Leadership Group (more than 400 managers and supervisors), enables Solar to develop the next generation of business leaders. It also promotes rapid, effective communication among employees with cross-functional teaming occurring at all levels of the organization. The third leadership structure is the set of 10 interlocking committees ("3" in the figure) that coordinate and integrate all business areas. These committees, listed in Table 5.2, provide a mechanism to strengthen organizational learning through cross-functional sharing, companywide communication, and strategic direction setting. Members of the president's staff chair key committees and, along with other senior

Figure 5.1 Solar Turbines, Inc. Leadership System

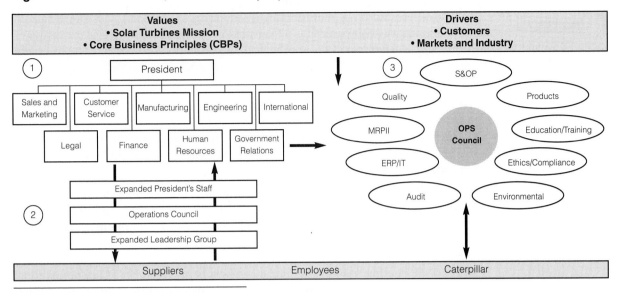

Source: Authorization by Solar Turbines, Incorporated.

Table 5.2 Solar Turbines, Inc., Committee Structure

Committee	Purpose	Conducted
Operations Council	Communicate business status, develop strategies and business plans	Biannually
Quality Council	Customer satisfaction, operational quality	Monthly
Sales and Operations Planning	Current and future performance to plan, supplier performance	Monthly
MRP II Steering Committee	Process improvement, benchmarking, teams, employee satisfaction, internal Baldrige assessments	Monthly
Products Committee	New product development, product strategy	Monthly
Education Steering Committee	Training and education, human resource development	Quarterly
Environmental Council	Environmental health, safety, products and processes	Quarterly
ERP/IT Council	Information technology planning and deployment, enterprise resource planning	Monthly
Audit Committee	Internal/external policy, regulatory compliance, and business controls	Quarterly
Ethics and Compliance Committee	Contract review, ethics, legal compliance, and oversight	Quarterly

Source: Authorization by Solar Turbines, Incorporated.

business leaders, actively participate to provide guidance, learn, share, and support each other's decisions as a leadership team.[30]

In contrast to the large manufacturing environment at Solar, Custom Research Inc. (a small services company) has a four-person steering committee as the center of the leadership system (see Figure 5.2). The senior leaders developed the company vision, exemplified by the CRI Star shown in Figure 5.3. The Star defines the five driving forces of the business:

1. Developing competent and empowered people
2. Managing work through technology-driven processes
3. Meeting or exceeding unique client requirements and expectations
4. Building partnering relationships with major clients and suppliers
5. Producing growth and profit results

The steering committee sets the company directions, integrates performance excellence goals, and promotes the development of all employees. Committee members interact frequently with associates and review overall company performance daily. They meet formally each month to evaluate performance and identify areas for improvement.

The use of steering teams of senior managers is prevalent in TQ organizations. Such teams assume many responsibilities such as incorporating total quality principles into the company's strategic planning process and coordinating the overall effort. At AT&T, the steering team is characterized by several essential elements.[31]

- *Leadership*: Promoting and articulating the quality vision, communicating responsibilities and expectations for management action, aligning the business management process with the quality approach, maintaining high visibility for commitment and involvement, and ensuring that business-wide support is available in the form of education, consulting, methods, and tools

Figure 5.2 Custom Research Inc. Leadership System

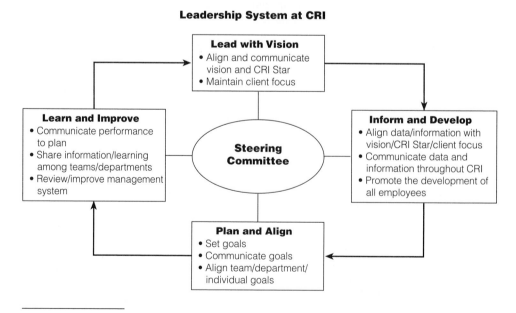

Source: Courtesy of CRI.

Figure 5.3 CRI Star

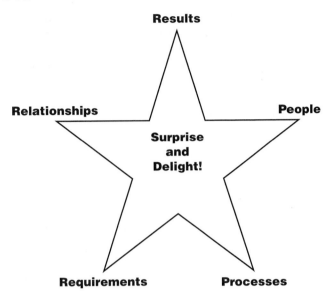

Source: Courtesy of CRI.

- *Planning*: Planning strategic quality goals, understanding basic customer needs and business capabilities, developing long-term goals and near-term priorities, formulating human resource goals and policies, understanding employees' perceptions about quality and work, ensuring that all employees have the opportunity and skills to participate, and aligning reward and recognition systems to support the quality approach
- *Implementation*: Forming key business process teams, chartering teams to manage and improve these processes, reviewing improvement plans, providing resources for improvement, enlisting all managers in the process, reviewing quality plans of major organizational units, and working with suppliers and business partners in joint quality planning
- *Review*: Tracking progress through customer satisfaction and internal measures of quality, monitoring progress in attaining improvement objectives, celebrating successes, improving the quality system through auditing and identifying improvement opportunities, planning improvements, and validating the impact of improvements

Corporate charters, bylaws, and policies document the rights and responsibilities of owners/shareholders, board of directors, and the CEO, and describe how the organization is managed to ensure accountability, transparency of operations, and fair treatment of all stakeholders. Governance processes may include approving strategic direction, monitoring and evaluating CEO performance, succession planning, financial auditing, executive compensation, disclosure, and shareholder reporting. Effective

*An important aspect of the leadership system is **governance**, which refers to the system of management and controls exercised in the stewardship of an organization.*

governance processes can mitigate the types of problems manifested by stock manipulations, financial misreporting, and corporate and personal greed that occurred with Enron, WorldCom, Arthur Andersen and others, and which seriously damaged business credibility. In fact, evidence indicates that good governance and integrity are important ingredients for success. Johnson Controls, Inc., for instance, is ranked among the top five companies with the best corporate governance practices, and these five companies' stocks have outperformed the S&P 500 for the three years through 2003.

Leadership and Social Responsibilities

An important aspect of an organization's leadership is its responsibility to the public and practice of good citizenship. This responsibility includes ethics and protection of public health, safety, and the environment. Several factors are forcing organizations to think seriously about this issue.[32]

- *Regulatory pressures.* France, for instance, requires all companies listed on the Paris Stock exchange to include information about their social and environmental performance within their financial statements, and the United Kingdom (the first nation with a minister for corporate social responsibility) requires pension-fund managers to disclose the degree to which social and environmental criteria are part of their investment decisions.
- *Changing demographics.* Better-educated individuals demand that companies with which they do business conform to higher standards. Investors can choose among many socially responsible portfolios.
- *Pressure from nongovernmental organizations.* Europeans, in particular, trust organizations such as Amnesty International and Greenpeace more than corporations such as Bayer, Shell, and Microsoft.
- *Greater transparency.* The Internet allows news, especially bad news, to travel faster, and allows people to voice their opinions more openly.

Planning activities, such as product design (see Chapter 7) should anticipate adverse impacts from production, distribution, transportation, use, and disposal of a company's products. For example, State Farm Insurance put in place physical, electronic, and organizational safeguards to protect customer information. They continually review their policies and practices, monitor computer networks, and test the strength of security in order to help ensure the safety of customer information. It is the responsibility of senior leaders to ensure that problems are prevented, forthright responses are made should problems occur, and that information is made available to maintain public awareness, safety, and confidence. Organizations should not only meet all local, state, and federal laws and regulatory requirements, but should treat these as

> *Practicing good citizenship refers to leadership and support—within the limits of an organization's resources—of publicly important purposes, including improving education, community health, environmental excellence, resource conservation, community service, and professional practices.*

opportunities for continuous improvement beyond mere compliance. Good citizenship might entail leading efforts to help define the obligations of the industry to its communities.

At Solar Turbines, for example, its Social Responsibility Core Business Principle and Environmental, Health, and Safety Policy guide the company's responsibility and citizenship actions. Solar's environmental health and safety strategy for its internal operation is to surpass compliance and strive for industry leadership. Prod-

Quality Spotlight
Solar Turbines

ucts and services must comply with local, state, and federal standards in each locale as well as country-specific and governing body standards for emissions and effluent discharge. Solar's strategy has yielded significant reduction in the use of hazardous raw materials and production of hazardous waste, increased recycling and reuse, improved energy efficiency, and reduced water consumption. Solar and one of its key suppliers partnered with Cal-Poly State University to establish a Vibration and Rotor Dynamics Laboratory. The Solar Volunteers Club, founded in 1988, provides opportunities to employees, families and friends to play an active role in local communities. Another group provides assistance to Solar retirees and/or spouses, and meaningful ways to interact with their communities, with each other, and with the company. Frances Hesselbein, quoted earlier in this chapter, says that leaders must determine how to answer the question that young people so frequently raise: "Why should I not be cynical [about what corporate leaders say and do]?"[33]

STRATEGIC PLANNING

One of the critical aspects of any organization that requires the attention of senior leadership is strategic planning. As an old saying goes, "If you don't know where you are going, any road will take you there." Through strategic planning, leaders mold an organization's future and manage change by focusing on an ideal vision of what the organization should and could be three, five, or more years in the future. The objective of strategic planning is to build a posture that is so strong in selective ways that the organization can achieve its goals despite unforeseeable external forces.

The concept of strategy holds different meanings for different people. One characterization of strategy is:

> *A strategy is a pattern or plan that integrates an organization's major goals, policies, and action sequences into a cohesive whole. A well-formulated strategy helps to marshal and allocate an organization's resources into a unique and viable posture based on its relative internal competencies and shortcomings, anticipated changes in the environment, and contingent moves by intelligent opponents.[34]*

A focus on both customer-driven quality and operational performance excellence, as opposed to traditional financial and marketing goals, is essential to an effective strategy. To be competitive and profitable, an organization must focus on the drivers of customer satisfaction, customer retention, and market share; and build operational capability, including speed, responsiveness, and flexibility, to contribute to short- and longer-term productivity growth and cost/price competitiveness. For many firms, quality is an essential element of business strategy.

Leading Practices for Strategic Planning

Effective organizations share several common approaches in their strategic planning efforts.

1. *Top management, employees, and even customers or suppliers actively participate in the planning process.* Strong leadership is necessary to establish the credibility of a total quality focus and integrate quality principles into the business planning process. At The Ritz-Carlton Hotel Company, for example, senior leadership also serves as the senior quality group. Similarly, senior executives at AT&T Transmission Systems comprise the company's quality council. This council prioritizes quality objectives and reviews the progress of quality improvement

efforts. Each member of the council chairs a separate steering committee responsible for the deployment of quality objectives.

Employees represent an important resource in strategic planning. Not only can the company capitalize on employee knowledge of customers and processes, but also employee involvement greatly enhances the effectiveness of strategy implementation. Such "bottom-up" planning facilitates better understanding and assessment of customer needs. At The Ritz-Carlton, teams at all levels—corporate, management, and employee—set objectives and devise action plans. Each hotel designates a quality leader who serves as a resource and advisor to teams for developing and implementing plans. At Solar Turbines, Inc., the strategy development process involves people from all parts of its worldwide organization, customers, and suppliers. Sales, marketing, service, engineering, and manufacturing people in functional and cross-functional teams perform information gathering, analysis, and conclusions. This information is carried forward to the leadership system committees and the Operations Council where it is integrated and synthesized into strategies and critical success factor goals.

It is not unusual for customers and suppliers to be involved in strategic planning efforts because of their importance in the supply chain. Customers and suppliers may offer vital advice to an organization as it plans for the future.

2. *They have systematic planning systems for strategy development and deployment.* Using a systematic process helps to optimize the use of resources, ensure the availability of trained employees, and ensure bridging between short-term and longer-term requirements that may entail capital expenditures or supplier development, for example. For example, Figure 5.4 shows the strategic planning process for Eastman Chemical Company. Eastman drives its approach by using its mission, vision, major improvement opportunities (MIOs), and other critical planning as inputs. These factors lead to the development of an overall strategy, and MIOs and key initiatives for each organizational unit. Deployment is achieved by a project management focus and cycles of review and improvement.

3. *They gather and analyze a variety of data about external and internal factors as inputs to the strategic planning process.* Effective strategic planning depends upon a clear understanding of customer and market needs and expectations, competitive environment and capabilities, financial and societal risks, human resource and other operational capabilities and needs, and supplier/partner capabilities and needs. The Ritz-Carlton, for instance, evaluates all action plans on how effectively they address customer requirements. A key goal is to become the first hospitality company with 100 percent customer retention; all plans must address this goal. The approaches for gathering customer information described in Chapter 4 are used in the annual planning processes. Similarly, AT&T Consumer Communications Services identified five key determinants of customer satisfaction: call quality, customer service, billing, price, and company reputation. Company goals are directly aligned with these requirements and used to set targets for process improvements and new services. Solar Turbines, Inc., looks at six external factors that affect its business: customer needs and wants, market trends and opportunities, industry trends, competitive dynamics, governmental and regulatory issues, and technological innovations that can change the nature of products and services.

4. *They align short-term action plans with long-term strategic objectives and organizational challenges, and communicate them throughout the organization, using measurements to track progress.* SSM Health Care, for instance, identified three specific

Figure 5.4 Strategic Planning Process at Eastman Chemical Company

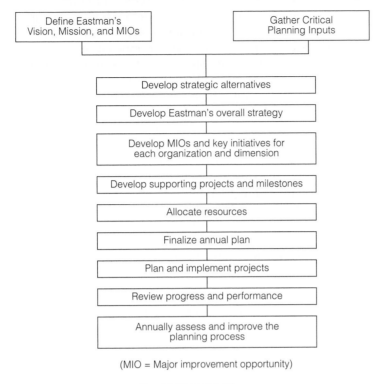

(MIO = Major improvement opportunity)

action plans during one year to help meet its strategic objective of "Exceptional patient, employee, and physician satisfaction": improve patient satisfaction with pain management, implement Nursing Shared Accountability model, and increase diversity representation within leadership. Key indicators to track the success of these actions plans, such as nurse turnover rate and the number of minorities in managerial professional ranks, were developed and monitored. Communication ensures that strategies will be deployed effectively at the "three levels of quality"—the organization level, process level, and individual job level. At BI, for example, the Strategic Business and Quality Plan (SBQP) is communicated to all BI leaders and then all vice presidents facilitate division planning with their teams. The result is a divisional SBQP with measurable objectives and action plans, which is communicated to all associates within the division. Each director, regional sales manager, and team leader then facilitates a planning session with his or her individual team, which results in a department, region, or team plan with objectives and action plans of its own. The Strategic Planning Team meets quarterly to report progress of each action plan against its timeline and reviews results measurements against corporate objectives.

5. *They derive human resource plans from strategic objectives and action plans.* Whenever an organization seeks to do something different, people are invariably impacted. Thus, it is important to consider organizational change and plan for necessary human resource changes that may be needed. These changes might include new

training initiatives, work reorganization, or compensation and incentive approaches. AT&T, for instance, links its training and education to strategic plans to establish current and future competencies for both the organization and the individual. The Consumer Communications Services division develops long-term and short-term plans in four areas: competencies, organization effectiveness, performance, and people. Short-term plans in the first area include strengthening the linkage among identification, assessment, employee development, and business needs, and refining roles and responsibilities to increase employee empowerment. Long-term plans center around the continuous learning environment and formulating new systems for empowering and developing employees.[35] Motorola's Commercial, Government, and Industrial Solutions Sector ties the following human resource plans into its strategic planning process: breakthrough changes in work design, team member development, education, and training; compensation, recognition, and benefits; and human resources needs identification and recruitment. When GE decided to adopt a Six Sigma framework for the organization, it was necessary to train 12,000 black-belt leaders to implement the plan. Incentives for project champions in upper management were restructured to account for 40 percent of their bonuses.[36]

Strategy Development

Henry Mintzberg, an unconventional thinker when it comes to management and organizational structures, argued that competitive success requires strategic thinking by senior leaders in the organization.[37] He describes strategy development as

> . . . capturing what the manager learns from all sources (both soft insights from his or her personal experiences and the experiences of others throughout the organization and the hard data from market research and the like) and then synthesizing that learning into a vision of the direction that the business should pursue.

In many organizations, strategy development is nothing more a group of managers sitting around in a room and generating ideas. Effective strategy development requires a systematic process. Although specific approaches vary from one company to another, all generally follow the basic model shown in Figure 5.5. The organization's leaders first explore and agree upon (or reaffirm) the mission, vision, and guiding principles of the organization, which form the foundation for the strategic plan.

A mission statement might include a definition of products and services the organization provides, technologies used to provide these products and services, types of markets, important customer needs, and distinctive competencies or the expertise that sets the firm apart from others. The mission of Solectron is ". . . to provide worldwide respon-

*The **mission** of a firm defines its reason for existence; it answers the question "Why are we in business?"*

siveness to our customers by offering the highest quality, lowest total cost, customized, integrated, design, supply chain and manufacturing solutions through long-term partnerships based on integrity and ethical business practices." The mission of the Cadillac Motor Car Company is stated in a similar fashion: "To engineer, produce, and market the world's finest automobiles, known for uncompromised levels of distinctiveness, comfort, convenience, and refined performance."

A firm's mission guides the development of strategies by different groups within the firm. It establishes the context within which daily operating decisions are made and sets limits on available strategic options. In addition, it governs the trade-offs

Figure 5.5 Strategic Planning Process

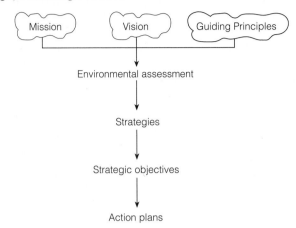

The **vision** describes where the organization is headed and what it intends to be; it is a statement of the
future that would not happen by
itself.

Values, or **guiding principles**,
guide the journey to a vision by
defining attitudes and policies for
all employees, which are reinforced
through conscious and subcon-
scious behavior at all levels of the
organization.

among the various performance measures and
between short- and long-term goals. Finally, it
can inspire employees to focus their efforts
toward the overall purpose of the organization.

The vision articulates the basic characteristics that shape the organization's strategy. A
vision should be brief, focused, clear, and inspi-
rational to an organization's employees. It
should be linked to customers' needs and
convey a general strategy for achieving the mission. For example, PepsiCo states, "We will be
an outstanding company by exceeding customer expectations through empowered
people, guided by shared values." Texas Instru-
ment's vision is stated as: ". . . to become a premier electronics company providing
world leadership in digital solutions for the networked society—a society transformed by personalized electronics, all speaking the same digital language, all able to
communicate anytime, anywhere." Solectron's is simple: "Be the best and continuously improve."

A vision must be consistent with the culture and values of the organization.
PepsiCo's shared values are diversity (respecting individual differences), integrity
(doing what we say), honesty (speaking openly and working hard to understand and
resolve issues), teamwork (working on real customer needs), accountability (committing fully to meeting expectations), and balance (respecting individual decisions
to achieve professional and personal balance in life).

The mission, vision, and guiding principles serve as the foundation for strategic
planning. Top management and others who lead, especially the CEO, must articulate
them. They also have to be transmitted, practiced, and reinforced through symbolic
and real action before they become "real" to the employees and the people, groups,
and organizations in the external environment that do business with the firm.

Although an organization's mission, vision, and values rarely change, the environment in which the organization exists usually does. Thus, strategy development
requires an **environmental assessment** of key factors noted in the Leading Practices

section: customer and market requirements, expectations, and opportunities; technological and other innovations that might affect products or operations; organizational strengths and weaknesses, including human and other resources; financial, societal and ethical, regulatory, and other potential risks; changes in the global or national economy; and factors unique to the organization, such as partner and supply chain needs, strengths, and weaknesses. This information is usually gathered and maintained as inputs to the planning process. Such environmental assessments are often accompanied by SWOT (strengths, weaknesses, opportunities, threats) analyses, and help identify critical success factors on which a strategy must focus. From these environmental assessments, organizations develop strategies, objectives, and action plans.

> **Strategies** *are broad statements that set the direction for the organization to take in realizing its mission and vision.*
>
> **Strategic objectives** *are what an organization must change or improve to remain or become competitive.*
>
> **Action plans** *are things that an organization must do to achieve its strategic objectives.*

A strategy might be directed toward becoming a preferred supplier, a low-cost producer, a market innovator, or a high-end or customized service provider. Strategic objectives set an organization's longer-term directions and guide resource allocation decisions. They are typically focused externally and relate to customer, market, product, service, or technological opportunities and challenges. Strategic objectives set an organization's long-term direction and guide resource allocation decisions. For example, a strategic objective for a supplier in a highly competitive industry might be to develop and maintain a price leadership position.

Action plans include details of resource commitments and time horizons for accomplishment. For the supplier seeking to develop a price leadership position, action plans might include the design of efficient processes and creation of an accounting system that tracks activity-level costs. Action plans form the basis for effective implementation, or what is called *deployment*, of a strategy.

Strategy Deployment

Deployment of strategy includes defining the business in terms of its key processes that deliver value to customers, identify what portions of these processes contribute the most to strategic objectives, and encouraging employees to complete process changes and improvements that will achieve the objectives. Essentially, deployment links the planners (who focus on "doing the right thing") with the doers (whose focus is on "doing things right").

> **Strategy deployment** *refers to developing detailed action plans, defining resource requirements and performance measures, and aligning work unit, supplier, or partner plans with overall strategic objectives.*

Many organizations simply do a poor job of deployment, despite having elegant and comprehensive strategy development approaches. Consider the following three indicators of poor deployment:[38]

1. *Lack of alignment across the organization.* Organizational goals should be linked, or aligned, with division, department, team, and individual goals. Everyone should be able to answer the question: What does strategy mean in terms that I can act on?
2. *Misallocation of resources.* Good strategic planning dedicates resources to making improvements or changes in those areas that are critical to a company's

strategic advantage. Spreading resources too thin to make a real difference in key areas of the business or allocating them to projects that have no real impact on strategy is ineffective.

3. *Insufficient operational measures.* Companies need appropriate measurement systems at the operational level to successfully implement a strategy. These systems help guide employees and determine how well their work supports the strategy.

The traditional approach to deploying strategy is top-down. From a TQ perspective, subordinates are both customers and suppliers, and therefore their input is necessary. An iterative process in which senior management asks what lower levels of the organization can do, what they need, and what conflicts may arise can avoid many of the implementation problems that managers typically face.

Japanese firms introduced a deployment process known as **hoshin kanri**, or *hoshin planning*. In the United States, this process is often referred to as **policy deployment**, or *management by planning*. Many companies, notably Florida Power and Light, Hewlett-Packard, and AT&T among many others, have adopted this process. The literal Japanese translation of hoshin kanri is "pointing direction."[39] The idea is to point, or align, the entire organization in a common direction. Florida Power and Light defines policy deployment as "the executive deployment of selected policy-driven priorities and the necessary resources to achieve performance breakthroughs." Hewlett-Packard calls it "a process for annual planning and implementation which focuses on areas needing significant improvement." AT&T's definition is "an organization-wide and customer-focused management approach aimed at planning and executing breakthrough improvements in business performance." Regardless of the particular definition, policy deployment emphasizes organization-wide planning and setting of priorities, provides resources to meet objectives, and measures performance as a basis for improving performance. Policy deployment is essentially a TQ-based approach to executing a strategy by ensuring that all employees understand the business direction and are working according to a plan to make the vision a reality.

M. Imai provides an example of policy deployment:

> To illustrate the need for policy deployment, let us consider the following case: The president of an airline company proclaims that he believes in safety and that his corporate goal is to make sure that safety is maintained throughout the company. This proclamation is prominently featured in the company's quarterly report and its advertising. Let us further suppose that the department managers also swear a firm belief in safety. The catering manager says he believes in safety. The pilots say they believe in safety. The flight crews say they believe in safety. Everyone in the company practices safety. True? Or might everyone simply be paying lip service to the idea of safety?
>
> On the other hand, if the president states that safety is company policy and works with his division managers to develop a plan for safety that defines their responsibilities, everyone will have a very specific subject to discuss. Safety will become a real concern. For the manager in charge of catering services, safety might mean maintaining the quality of food to avoid customer dissatisfaction or illness.
>
> In that case, how does he ensure that the food is of top quality? What sorts of control points and checkpoints does he establish? How does he ensure that there is no deterioration of food quality in flight? Who checks the temperature of the refrigerators or the condition of the oven while the plane is in the air?
>
> Only when safety is translated into specific actions with specific control and checkpoints established for each employee's job might safety be said to

have been truly deployed as a policy. Policy deployment calls for everyone to interpret policy in light of his own responsibilities and for everyone to work out criteria to check his success in carrying out the policy.[40]

Figure 5.6 provides a simplified description of the policy deployment process.[41] With policy deployment, top management is responsible for developing and communicating a vision, then building organization-wide commitment to its achievement.[42] The long-term strategic plan forms the basis for shorter-term planning. This vision is deployed through the development and execution of annual objectives and plans. All levels of employees actively participate in generating strategy and action plans to attain the vision. At each level, progressively more detailed and concrete means to accomplish the objectives are determined. Objectives should be challenging, but people should feel that they are attainable. To this end, middle management negotiates with senior management regarding the objectives that will achieve the strategies, and what process changes and resources might be required to achieve those objectives. Middle management then negotiates with the implementation teams the final short-term objectives and the performance measures that are used to indicate progress toward accomplishing the objectives.

Figure 5.6 The Policy Deployment Process

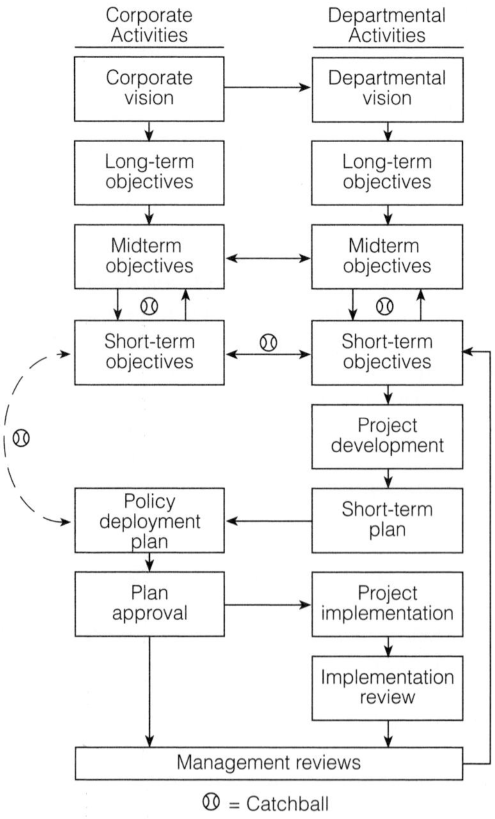

Source: Kersi F. Munshi, "Policy Deployment: A Key to Long-Term Success," *ASOC Quality Congress Transactions* (Boston, 1993), 236–244.

Management reviews at specific checkpoints ensure the effectiveness of individual elements of the strategy. The implementation teams are empowered to manage actions and schedule their activities. Periodic reviews (monthly or quarterly) track progress and diagnose problems. Management may modify objectives on the basis of these reviews, as evidenced by the feedback loop in the figure. Top management evaluates results as well as the deployment process itself through annual reviews, which serve as a basis for the next planning cycle.

Note, however, that top management does not develop action plans; it sets overall guidelines and strategies. Departments and functional units develop specific implementation plans. Hence, the process in Figure 5.6 includes both corporate and departmental activities. In practice, policy deployment entails a high degree of detail, including the anticipation of possible problems during implementation. The emphasis is on the improvement of the process, as opposed to a results-only orientation.

The negotiation process is called *catchball* (represented by the baseball symbol in Figure 5.6). Leaders communicate midterm objectives and measures to middle managers who develop short-term objectives and recommend necessary resources, targets, and roles/responsibilities. These issues are discussed and debated until agreement is reached. The objectives then cascade to lower levels of the organization where short-term plans are developed. Catchball is an up, down, and sideways communication process as opposed to an autocratic, top-down management style. It marshals the collective expertise of the whole organization and results in realistic and achievable objectives that do not conflict. In the spirit of Deming, the process focuses on optimizing the system rather than on individual goals and objectives. Clearly, this process can only occur in a TQ culture that nourishes open communication.

Strategic objectives and action plans often require significant changes in human resource requirements, such as redesigning the work organization or jobs to increase employee empowerment and decision making, promoting greater labor/management cooperation, modifying compensation and recognition systems, or developing new education and training initiatives.

Effective deployment aligns resources and policies. For example, a strategic objective of increasing the number of patents generated might require hiring more engineers, developing a creativity training program, and changing its financial incentive approaches. Finally, organizations need performance measures or indicators for tracking progress relative to action plans.

An increasingly important part of strategic planning is projecting the competitive environment. This activity helps to detect and reduce competitive threats, to shorten reaction time, and to identify opportunities. Organizations might use a variety of modeling, scenario, or other techniques and judgments to project the competitive environment. Projections of key performance measures and comparisons with competitors, benchmarks, and past performance help an organization evaluate its performance in achieving its objectives, strategies, and ultimately, its vision.

LINKING HUMAN RESOURCE PLANS AND BUSINESS STRATEGY

Prior to developing a TQ focus, most organizations neglected the strategic importance of human resource management. Now TQ-focused firms, such as Armstrong Building Products Operations (BPO), recognize that human resource management plays a key role in overall strategic planning. BPO's overall HR strategy is as follows:

- To provide the opportunity for employees to reach their full potential by developing a high performance organization which supports the operation's Vision,

Mission, and Goal. The behavior in deploying the strategy will be consistent with our corporate Operating Principles

- To attract, develop, challenge and retain a diverse workforce to assure we have the skills and organization to build our business
- To involve and empower employees to improve processes and participate in decisions that affect the business
- To recognize and reward performance that contributes to the business strategy and goals
- To continuously improve those elements of the work environment that enhance employees' well-being, satisfaction, and productivity[43]

At Armstrong BPO, the translation of business needs to HR plans is performed by the same team that is accountable for business results, thus helping to ensure focus, alignment, and proper allocation of resources.

Strategic human resource plans often include one or more of the following:

- Redesign of the work organization to increase empowerment and decision making or team-based participation
- Initiatives for promoting greater labor/management cooperation, such as union partnerships
- Initiatives to foster knowledge sharing and organizational learning
- Partnerships with educational institutions to help ensure the future supply of well-prepared employees

Whatever the choices, it is vital that they support the organization's overall strategy. Without proper alignment, the work that people do can be focused in an entirely different direction than the organization intends to go. For example, Dell Computer discovered that its sales grew well beyond their technical support service capabilities. Faced with rapid turnover (many male reps view it as their first job on the way to some other technical career), Dell opened a call center in Bangalore, India, to field calls, even from North America, drawing upon the strong level of technical expertise available there.[44]

THE SEVEN MANAGEMENT AND PLANNING TOOLS

Managers may use a variety of tools and techniques, known as the **seven management and planning tools**, to implement policy deployment.

1. *Affinity diagram*: A tool for organizing a large number of ideas, opinions, and facts relating to a broad problem or subject area
2. *Interrelationship diagraph*: A tool for identifying and exploring causal relationships among related concepts or ideas
3. *Tree diagram*: A tool to map out the paths and tasks necessary to complete a specific project or reach a specified goal
4. *Matrix diagram*: "Spreadsheets" that graphically display relationships between ideas, activities, or other dimensions in such a way as to provide logical connecting points between each item
5. *Matrix data analysis*: A tool to take data and arrange them to display quantitative relationships among variables to make them more easily understood and analyzed
6. *Process decision program chart*: A method for mapping out every conceivable event and contingency that can occur when moving from a problem statement to possible solutions

7. *Arrow diagrams*: A tool for sequencing and scheduling project tasks

These tools are particularly useful in structuring unstructured ideas, making strategic plans, and organizing and controlling large, complex projects. Thus, they can benefit all employees involved in quality planning and implementation. These tools had their roots in post–World War II operations research developments in the United States, but were combined and refined by several Japanese companies over the past several decades as part of their planning processes. They were popularized in the United States by the consulting firm GOAL/QPC, and have been used by a number of firms since 1984 to improve their quality planning and improvement efforts. Many companies formally integrated these tools into policy deployment activities. The Bonus Materials folder describes these management and planning tools in detail, and illustrates how they can be used in policy deployment. These seven tools provide managers with improved capability to make better decisions and facilitate the implementation process. With proper planning, managers can use their time more effectively to continuously improve and innovate.

LEADERSHIP, STRATEGY, AND ORGANIZATIONAL STRUCTURE

The effectiveness of the both the leadership system and the strategic planning system depends in part on **organizational structure**—the clarification of authority, responsibility, reporting lines, and performance standards among individuals at each level of the organization. It is also true that effective strategy deployment is dependent upon, and tends to shape, organizational structure.

Traditional organizations tend to develop structures that help them to maintain stability. They tend to be highly structured, both in terms of rules and regulations, as well as the height of the "corporate ladder," sometimes with seven or more layers of managers between the CEO and the first-line worker. In contrast, organizations in the rapidly changing environments characteristic of modern organizations have to build flexibility into their organization structures. Hence, they tend to have fewer written rules and regulations and flatter organizational structures.

Several factors having to do with the context of the organization affect how work is organized. They include the following:[45]

1. *Company operational and organizational guidelines.* Standard practices that have developed over the firm's history often dictate how a company organizes and operates.
2. *Management style.* The management team operates in a manner unique to a given company. For example, management style might be formal or informal, or democratic or autocratic. If the organization operates in a highly structured, formal atmosphere, organizing a quality effort around informal meetings would probably meet with little success.
3. *Customer influences.* Customers, particularly governmental agencies, may require formal specifications or administrative controls. Thus, the organization needs to understand and respond to these requirements.
4. *Company size.* Large companies have the ability to maintain formal systems and records, whereas smaller companies may not.
5. *Diversity and complexity of product line.* An organization suitable for the manufacture of a small number of highly sophisticated products may differ dramatically from an organization that produces a high volume of standard goods.
6. *Stability of the product line.* Stable product lines generate economies of scale that influence supervision, corrective action, and other quality-related issues. Frequent changes in products necessitate more control and commensurate changes to the quality system.

7. *Financial stability.* Quality managers need to recognize that their efforts must fit within the overall budget of the firm.
8. *Availability of personnel.* The lack of certain skills may require other personnel, such as supervisors, to assume duties they ordinarily would not be assigned.

An organization chart shows the *apparent structure* of the formal organization. However, some organizations refuse to be tied down by a conventional organization chart, even to the extent that employees make a running joke of titles. For example, Semco S/A, a radically unconventional manufacturer of industrial equipment (mixers, washers, air conditioners, bakery plant units) located in São Paulo, Brazil, has what is called a "circular" organization chart with four concentric circles. They avoid the use of the term *levels*. The titles that go with these are Counselors (CEO and the equivalent of vice presidents), Partners (business unit heads), Coordinators (supervisory specialists and functional leaders), and Associates (everyone else). If anyone desires, he or she can think up a title for external use that describes his or her area or job responsibility. As owner and CEO Ricardo Semler explains:

> Consistent with this philosophy, when a promotion takes place now at Semco we simply supply blank business cards and tell the newly elevated individual: "Think of a title that signals externally your area of operation and responsibility and have it printed." If the person likes "Procurement Manager," fine. If he wants something more elegant, he can print up cards saying, "First Pharaoh in Charge of Royal Supplies." Whatever he wants. But inside the company, there are only four options. (Anyway, almost all choose to print only their name.)[46]

Although many different organizational structures exist, most are variations or combinations of three basic types: (1) the line organization, (2) the line and staff organization, and (3) the matrix organization.

The line organization is a functional form, with departments that are responsible for marketing, finance, and operations. In the traditional organization, the quality department ("Quality Control," "Quality Assurance," or some similar name) is generally distinct from other departments. In a TQ organization, the role of quality should be invisible in the organization chart, because quality planning and assurance are part of the responsibility of each operating manager and employee at every level. In theory, this organizational form could exist in a fairly large organization if all employees were thoroughly indoctrinated in the philosophy of quality and could be counted on to place quality as the top priority in all aspects of their daily work. In practice, this particular structure is not generally successful except when used in small firms.

The line and staff organization is the most prevalent type of structure for medium-sized to large firms. In such organizations, line departments carry out the functions of marketing, finance, and production for the organization. Staff personnel, including quality managers and technical specialists, assist the line managers in carrying out their jobs by providing technical assistance and advice. Variations on the basic line and staff organization can include geographic or customer organizations. In this traditional form of organization structure, instead of technical experts who assist line managers and workers in attaining quality, quality managers and inspectors may take on the role of guardians of quality. This guardian-type role also happens when the quality assurance function is placed too low in the organization or when pressure from higher levels of the organization forces quality inspectors to ease up on quality so that more products can be shipped. The major cause of this problem is too much responsibility with insufficient authority.

The matrix-type organization was developed for use in situations where large, complex projects are designed and carried out, such as defense weapons systems or large construction projects. Firms that do such work have a basic need to develop an organizational structure that will permit the efficient use of human resources while maintaining control over the many facets of the project being developed. In a matrix-type organization, each project has a project manager and each department that is providing personnel to work on the various projects has a technical or administrative manager. Thus, a quality assurance technician might be assigned to the quality assurance department for technical and administrative activities but would be

As more and more companies accept the process view of organizations, they are structuring the quality organization around functional or cross-functional teams.

attached to Project A for day-to-day job assignments. The technician would report to the project manager of Project A and to his or her "technical boss" in the quality assurance department. When Project A is completed, the technician might be reassigned to Project B under a new project manager. He or she would still be reporting to the "technical boss" in quality assurance, however.

The matrix type of organization for project work has a number of advantages. It generally improves the coordination of complex project work as well as improving the efficiency of personnel use. Its major drawback is that it requires split loyalty for people who report to two supervisors. This division of loyalty can be especially troublesome or even dangerous in a quality assurance area. For example, in a nuclear power plant project, a project manager who is under pressure to complete a project by a certain deadline might try to influence quality assurance personnel to take shortcuts in completing the inspection phase of the project. The quality manager, who might be hundreds of miles away from the site, would often not have the influence over the inspectors that the project manager would have. A generic example is shown in Figure 5.7, and a specific example (GTE Directories) is shown in Figure 5.8. In this organizational structure, the management board leads the quality effort, meeting

Figure 5.7 Team-Based Organizational Chart

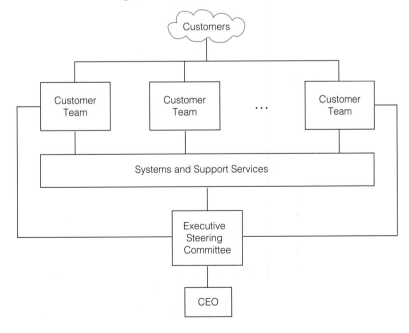

Figure 5.8 Team-Based Organizational Chart

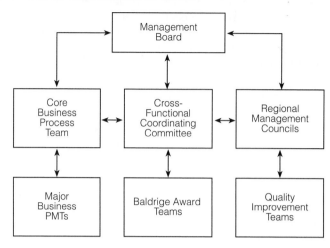

Source: Courtesy of GTE Directories Corporation.

twice each month to discuss and review management and quality issues. Quality is implemented through various teams: core business process team, cross-functional coordinating committee, regional management councils, major business process management teams (PMTs), Malcolm Baldrige National Quality Award (MBNQA) teams, and quality improvement teams. The regional management councils identify and address key regional issues; the cross-functional coordinating committee reviews major proposals for consistency with the strategic plan and business priorities. Such team-based organization structures spread the ownership and the accountability for quality throughout the organization. The "quality department" serves as an internal consulting group, providing advice, training, and organizational development to the teams.

We see that a "one-size fits all" quality organization is inappropriate. The organization must be tailored to reflect individual company differences and provide the flexibility and the ability to change. What is important, however, is that senior leaders drive quality and performance excellence concepts throughout the organization through effective communication and as role models, and ensure that strategic planning focuses all key stakeholders in achieving the organization's mission and vision.

LEADERSHIP AND STRATEGIC PLANNING IN THE BALDRIGE CRITERIA, ISO 9000, AND SIX SIGMA

Category 1 of the 2003 Malcolm Baldrige National Quality Award Criteria for Performance Excellence is *Leadership*. As the first of the seven categories, it signifies the critical importance of leadership to business success. Item 1.1, *Organizational Leadership*, examines how senior leaders guide an organization by setting directions; communicating and deploying values and performance expectations; creating and balancing value for customers and other stakeholders, and creating an environment for empowerment, innovation, organizational agility, organizational and employee learning, and legal and ethical behavior. The criteria also ask how the organization's governance system addresses management and fiscal accountability and protection of stakeholder interests. In addition, the criteria ask how senior leaders review organizational performance and capabilities through its performance measurement system and use review findings to drive improvement and change. Finally, the criteria ask how the performance of senior leaders is evaluated and how they use the results to improve leadership effectiveness and the leadership system.

Item 1.2, *Social Responsibility*, addresses how an organization fulfills its public responsibilities, ensures ethical behavior, and practices good citizenship. These responsibilities include how the organization addresses impacts and risks of products, services, and operations on society in a proactive manner; how it ensures ethical business practices in all stakeholder interactions; and how the organization, its senior leaders, and employees identify, support, and strengthen key communities as part of good citizenship practices.

Category 2, *Strategic Planning*, examines how an organization develops strategic objectives and action plans, how they are deployed, and how progress is measured. Item 2.1, *Strategy Development*, examines an organization's strategic planning process and how it uses key data and information in developing strategies and objectives, with the aim of guiding and strengthening overall performance, competitiveness, and future success.

Item 2.2, *Strategy Deployment*, looks at how an organization translates strategic objectives into action plans to accomplish the objectives and assesses progress relative to the action plans. Particular attention is given to changes in product/services, customers/markets, and operations. The criteria seek information on key measures and indicators for tracking progress and how the measures help to align all important work units and stakeholders in meeting objectives. It also seeks projections of key performance measures as a basis for comparing past performance and performance relative to competitors and benchmarks.

Leadership underlies many of the requirements of ISO 9000:2000. The entire section on Management Responsibility is concerned with the role of leadership in driving a quality system. For example, the standards require that "Top management shall provide evidence of its commitment to the development and implementation of the quality management system and continually improving its effectiveness by a) communicating to the organization the importance of meeting customer as well as statutory and regulatory requirements, b) establishing the quality policy, c) ensuring that quality objectives are established, d) conducting management reviews, and e) ensuring the availability of resources." More specific responsibilities are spelled out in detail in other clauses of the standards. Although strategic planning is not addressed as broadly as it is in the Baldrige criteria, the ISO 9000 standards do require that top management ensure that quality objectives are established at relevant functions and levels within the organization, that they be measurable and consistent with the quality policy, that planning be carried out in order to meet quality system requirements and the quality objectives, and that the integrity of the quality management system is maintained when changes are planned and implemented.

Leadership is a fundamental value of Six Sigma. Driving organizational change to create and sustain a Six Sigma culture simply cannot be done without strong leadership. In other words, Six Sigma cannot be an add-on or a "flavor of the month." It must become the way business is done in organizations that adopt it. Leaders in twenty-first-century organizations are finding that not only must they move from hierarchically structured organizations to learning organizations, but also they must then take the next step of moving from learning organizations to teaching organizations. For example, Noel Tichy, former director of GE's John F. Welch Leadership

Center at Crotonville (their GE "university") helped to revitalize GE under the guidance of Jack Welch. He and Jack developed the concept of the virtuous teaching cycle (VTC) that guides their entire leadership development process, of which the Six Sigma approach is a vital part. The VTC includes some of the following concepts and assumptions, as well as others:[47]

- Leadership at all levels [as opposed to leadership at the top]
- Teamwork [as opposed to passive-aggressive behavior]
- Teachable point of view (TPOV) throughout [as opposed to a rigid, top-down process]
- Organizational knowledge grows [as opposed to organizational knowledge being depleted]
- Boundrylessness [as opposed to a boundary-laden, turf-oriented organization]

In this fashion, leadership development for Six Sigma needs to be both top-down and bottom-up. In Chapter 6, we will deal with training and development of Six Sigma leaders, from the team level up to project champions.

A Six Sigma framework is a way to turn performance improvement concepts into concrete actions. Thus, it must be integrated into strategic planning processes. Specific Six Sigma improvement projects provide a means of ensuring that strategies and action plans are implemented and lead to results to close the gaps identified in the strategic planning process.

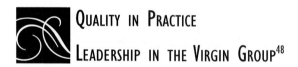

QUALITY IN PRACTICE
LEADERSHIP IN THE VIRGIN GROUP[48]

One must look hard for the application of systematic quality principles in an organization such as Virgin Enterprises, whose major product lines include music, video, clothing, financial services, national and international air travel, Internet car sales in Britain, and national train travel services. Here is an organization—actually, a loose conglomeration of separate, stand-alone companies—that "grew like Topsy" with only the vision of its charismatic founder and guru, Sir Richard Branson (knighted in March 2000), to guide it. Yet, specific principles and practices behind the apparent organizational chaos helped to make this British, global firm a competitor.

Sir Richard, CEO of the Virgin Group, is one example of the new breed of global leaders identified by business researchers Manfred Kets de Vries and Elizabeth Florent-Treacy.[49] The group is headquartered in a suburb of London in the United Kingdom, but has an increasing presence in the United States and Asia, as well as Europe. Something of the philosophy and structure of the firms can be seen in the following excerpt from the group's Web site.

Having successfully run a student magazine in London in the late 1960s, Richard Branson and his colleagues decided to set up a record company. After days of argument and discussion they settled on the name Virgin. It sounded trendy and, as Richard said at the time, "We thought it was good because we could apply it to other businesses, not just music."

Today, 96 percent of British consumers have heard of Virgin and it is one of the world's top 50 brands. Sometimes it appears in the list of well-known brands in countries where it doesn't even trade.

Virgin achieved all this notoriety in a unique way. The group's origins date back to the mail-order record company, record shops, and recording studio, which were all founded in the early 1970s. As Richard Branson grew the businesses during that decade, he followed British economist E. F. Schumacher's "small is beautiful" philosophy and always set up new businesses, rather than managing Virgin as one big conglomerate. When he set up Virgin Atlantic Airways in 1984, this philosophy continued, as it did with all the new businesses since. So today Virgin is not really a group at all. Financial results are not aggregated centrally and each business runs its own affairs, but each is a part of a collection of shared ownership, shared leadership and shared values. In many respects Virgin resembles a mixture of a branded venture capital organization and a Japanese keiretsu (or society of business). The Japanese seem to think so anyway!

What ties all the businesses together are the values of the brand and the philosophy of management. In the eyes of consumers, Virgin stands for value, quality, innovation, fun, and a sense of competitive challenge. Not all of its new businesses can achieve these values, especially when they grow out of old companies in need of rejuvenation (or Virginisation!). It is then that the organization brings its management skills to bear.

Management believes passionately in Virgin values and in what they are doing, and are convinced that together they can create the first British global brand name of the twenty-first century. Realizing this ambition is a highly motivating challenge and has already seen the creation of 200 companies worldwide, which currently employ more than 25,000 people.

Richard was born in 1950 of middle-class professional parents (his father was a lawyer, his mother, an actress and flight attendant), and was a teenage entrepreneur and "ordinary" student in the elite Stowe school. He quit without taking his final senior examinations in order to start a magazine called *Student*. There he was editor, publisher, and advertising manager. The venture was not an outstanding financial success, so in 1970, Branson advertised recordings of alternative music at a 15 percent discount over record stores in his magazine, thus beginning what was soon to be called Virgin Records. In 1984, after several ups and downs, Virgin Records was solidly successful. Branson then took another risk and started a unique, low-fare trans-Atlantic airline called Virgin Atlantic. In 1986, the company went public, but after a financial market downturn in 1987, Branson again took the company private in 1988. Other ventures followed throughout the 1990s to bring the company to its present level of prominence.

Branson attributed his early success in the record company to the fact that they created independent, stand-alone companies. The difference was that other record companies at this time were selling rights to recordings to other companies. As Branson pointed out in an interview,

Actually, a lot of companies evolved out of the record company. If you needed a record company, you needed shops to sell your products; you needed an export company to export your records; you needed foreign companies to distribute your records abroad and market them as well; you needed editing suites to edit your videos, and so on.[50]

The independent Virgin firms were developing, growing, and signing local groups to make recordings in Germany, France, Japan, and the United States.

In starting and growing Virgin Atlantic, Branson's friends and advisors thought that he had lost his way. In 1984, it was not economically feasible to make a profit in an airline. However, Branson felt that part of the problem was that airlines were managed abysmally at that time. He said:

Their way of doing business was really terrible. As far as service quality was concerned, the airline business was perhaps the worst run of almost any business I can think of. The big airlines tried to get away with as much as they could. They were either national airlines or just ex-national airlines. They charged as much as they could. Their costs had gone through the roof. They offered the customers the minimum because they could afford to do so, being monopolies or duopolies. We decided to get in there and compete and offer good-quality service. Looking back on that decision, the past ten years have been exhilarating, great fun.

The very fact that Virgin Atlantic has remained in business for 20 years is a tribute to the tenacity of Branson and the firm's management. Table 5.3 summarizes the essence of Virgin's competitive advantage.

Key Issues for Discussion

1. Given the freewheeling style of Branson and his managers, do you think that the Virgin

enterprises can be classified as a "TQ" organization? Why or why not?

2. How well do you think that Branson and his managers perform the strategic planning process? What are some indications that they do, or do not do, strategic planning?

3. How well do you think that Branson and his managers perform managerial and leadership tasks? How might these tasks be better balanced?

4. What leadership theory do you think best fits the senior leadership of The Virgin Group? What theory would best fit Branson, as leader? Why might there be a difference?

Table 5.3 Key Points of Virgin's Unique Competitive Advantage

The key to Virgin's competitive advantage is the creative talents of individual employees, which is made apparent in the following areas:

Corporate Culture

- Putting the world "right"
- The notion of "family"; "People are our greatest asset."
- Cultural glue based on sense of community, bonds of group, not codified
- Friendly, egalitarian, nonhierarchical atmosphere
- Anybody with a crazy idea gets a hearing
- Empowerment: "We're in the business of making millionaires."
- Motivating people is key to organization's success: "If your staff is enjoying their work, they will perform well. Consequently, customers will enjoy their experience with your company."
- Staff should have happy memories of their time in the organization

Leadership Style

- Reassuring contact with followers
- Social worker, both with followers and in vision for new products (e.g., Mates condoms)
- Pragmatic idealist
- Extremely competitive
- Counterbalanced by strong executive role constellation
- Top person should enjoy himself so that others will feel free to have fun
- "Renaissance entrepreneur": 100 percent involvement in startup of new ventures, then delegate

Organizational Design

- Truly entrepreneurial and intrapreneurial organization; organic growth rather than acquisition
- "Small is beautiful"; small, autonomous units, small head office
- Work as an exciting adventure, challenging the status quo
- "If you do something for fun and create the best possible product, then the profit will come."
- No formal board meetings; employees encouraged to contact Branson directly with ideas, problems
- "Communication from bottom to top"; lateral communication
- Speed: employees get a quick response directly from Branson, or just "go ahead and do it"

Continuous Transformation and Change

- Share the wealth with people who have new ideas; create a sense of ownership
- Attract and develop mavericks
- Environment offers high degree of freedom and encourages original ideas; "Drive for change."
- "Creative adaptation"; avoiding the not-invented-here syndrome

Building a Global Organization

- *Keiretsu-like* system: more than 500 small companies around the world operating quasi-independently

Source: "An Interview with Richard Branson," in *The New Global Leaders* (San Francisco: Jossey-Bass, 1999), 56–57.

Quality in Practice
Strategic Planning at Branch-Smith Printing Division[51]

Branch-Smith, Inc., is a fourth-generation, family business founded by Aaron Smith in 1910. The Branch-Smith Printing Division in Ft. Worth, Texas, has only 70 full-time employees and specializes in creating multipage, bound materials with services ranging from design to mailing for specialty customers. The company produces publications, magazines, catalogs, directories, and books, as well as some general commercial printing, typically in quantities generally less than 20,000. It offers a complete array of turnkey services to customers, including design, image scanning, electronic and conventional prepress work, printing, binding, and mailing/delivery.

Within the Printing Division, the context of the business is set through their Vision Statement: *"Market Leading Business Results through an Expert Team providing Turnkey Solutions to Customer Partners."* This vision expresses the desire to produce strong and sustainable results through balanced performance improvement. It creates success for long-term customers and rewards for their employees who bring solutions to bear on our opportunities. The mission is stated as: *"The mission of the Branch-Smith Printing Division is to provide expert solutions for publishers."* This purpose guides Branch-Smith Printing in meeting customers' needs on its own terms. Publishers work with them because Branch-Smith focuses on serving publishers' niche requirements for printing as well as offering the vertically integrated value-added services that result in lower costs, reduced cycle times, and on-time delivery. An important component of the solution is easy accessibility for the customer, and timely and appropriate information. It is also expressed in its Quality Policy, which states: *"Branch-Smith Printing will seek to continuously improve results for all stakeholders through the application of its Innovating Excellence Process."*

The printing industry is very competitive with numerous companies seeking market share. Branch-Smith Printing stands out among competitors based on its approach for identifying and serving a specific niche, focusing on development of long-term relationships, partnering with sup-

pliers, and involvement in standard defining industry associations. To ensure a competitive position, it focuses on serving a select market niche that most other printers have difficulty serving well. Many competitors focus on attracting jobs with greater quantity outputs because of the limitations of their equipment. They charge much higher prices for the shorter runs, thus giving Branch-Smith an advantage in this market. Its equipment and technologies are directed to cost-effectively serve this niche through sheet-fed press versus the popular web printing. This technology allows for faster changeovers from one type of print to another and process automation offers cost savings.

Although Branch-Smith is a small family business, they engage in a formal planning process annually with monthly updates during management reviews. The process is built around a continuous learning cycle that begins with lessons learned from previous years to determine and implement improvements. The strategic planning process (SPP) is a key tool the company uses to visualize the ideal future and create strategies and plans to achieve it, and to incorporate improvement opportunities into prioritized action plans. Strategic planning occurs formally each year with updates and tracking conducted monthly during management reviews. Ongoing updates throughout the year allow the company to correct direction or to proactively respond to risks and opportunities.

Figure 5.9 represents the full strategic planning, deployment, and review process. A month prior to strategic planning, assignments are made to PLT members to research information needed for strategic decision making. The assignment list includes 28 specific areas for understanding organizational and supplier/partner capabilities, market conditions, stakeholder input and requirements, competitive information, industry issues, and risks. Branch-Smith gathers information through a customer survey, lost revenues, and complaints to identify customer needs and their importance, trends and directions of the printing industry, and market requirements from industry association networking. Involvement in professional associations provides industry knowledge and benchmarks concerning customer needs and competitor actions, including emerging tools and competitors. Trade magazines and discussions with key suppliers provide additional input about customer needs, competitor directions, and supplier capabilities. Trends and directions in technology and other environmental changes are also identified through involvement with trade associations and external benchmarking groups, and through general understanding of the business climate gained through newspapers, journals, and periodicals.

One important source of information for strategic planning regarding human resource needs and capability is an annual employee survey. Human resource and operational capabilities are identified through review of aggregate measures of performance and productivity, which are enhanced with feedback from scheduled ISO audits that identify processes in need of improvement. Primary inputs on process efficiency and capability come from in-process productivity measures, revenue lost due to complaints, and other measures, which include spoilage cost, frequency, and reason. These measures are recorded daily through electronic, shop-floor data collection. Strategic partnerships with key suppliers help to gather information about availability of materials and supplier growth plans to help determine their capability to meet Branch-Smith's changing needs. Finally, part of the annual operational review involves understanding suppliers' current financial position and trends in profitability and utiliza-

tion, which is compared to external economic conditions to identify areas of potential risk and opportunity over the short- and longer-term.

The formal planning activity is conducted during the fall of each year by the Print Leadership Team (PLT) through a series of meetings on and off site. Step 1 of Figure 5.9 ensures that lessons learned and improvement cycles are built into the SPP. The PLT analyzes the effectiveness of the overall planning and deployment process to determine and implement improvements. The effectiveness of the leadership system is also evaluated and areas for improvement for the coming year are determined. These improvements are documented as potential actions for the strategic plan. In Step 2, the company reviews its vision, mission, and values to ensure they still reflect the current environment. Next, management reviews and revises objectives, which are intended to communicate to employees and all stakeholders what the company expects to accomplish in the next three to five years.

In Step 3, the company conducts an operational review to analyze the results of the organization's key performance measures for the prior year. They then review and incorporate information into the plan from annual Baldrige-based self-evaluation or from external review feedback. This analysis provides an understanding of key strengths and weaknesses for the SWOT (strengths, weaknesses, opportunities, and threats) analysis in Step 5. Step 4 involves a business analysis to evaluate the external environment to forecast changing trends and gain

Figure 5.9 Branch-Smith Strategic Planning Process

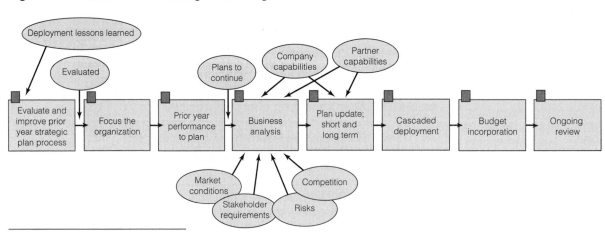

Source: Used with permission of AIM, Inc.

market requirements. PLT members bring forward
defined inputs, including literature and studies for
scanning the environment and identifying new
opportunities for products, services, competitive
advantage, marketing, and technology approaches.
From the review of this information, the PLT
develops a list of potential opportunities and
threats for each environmental element. In Step 5, a
SWOT analysis is conducted based upon the issues
identified in Steps 1, 3, and 4. SWOT elements are
used to identify and prioritize key areas to address.

Based upon the SWOT review, the PLT
develops short- and longer-term strategies and
actions to move the company toward its vision and
objectives. They add in action plans that are still in
process from the prior year to allow them to also be
prioritized, set appropriate measures and goals for
objectives and strategies, and sort and prioritize
the action plans. Action plans are assigned to PLT
members to develop (or update) steps, timelines,
resources, costs, and measures of success. These
plans are then entered into the Quality Improvement Database (QID) for review and tracking. A
final balancing meeting is held to review the plan
as a whole and make needed adjustments to timing
of plans and financial and human resource requirements to balance the plan to resource constraints.
In Step 6, the company creates documents and
methods to support deployment of the plan.

Results of strategic planning are first communicated to employees through a deployment meeting.
Leaders, with their departmental teams or other
appropriate members, then discuss the plans during
follow-up sessions. Teams and individuals update
goals and mission statements for their departments
that support the division plans, thus aligning
actions, measures, and goals throughout the organization. Other stakeholders receive a variety of communications to detail our plans and strategies for
informational and planning purposes. For example,

a supplier appreciation luncheon is held to provide
a more direct opportunity to present plans to key
supplier partners and receive feedback on plans and
needs. In Step 7, financial resource requirements to
accomplish the action plans are rationalized into
short- and longer-term budget projections. Then, in
Step 8, ongoing tracking of action plans is conducted through monthly management review of
overall progress to plans and key measures.
Throughout the year as needed, the strategic plan is
updated with new or modified action plans to
reflect the changes to the environment.

Key Issues for Discussion

1. Compare Branch-Smith's approach to the
generic strategic planning process described
in this chapter. What are some of its unique
features?
2. Branch-Smith's current objectives are "1) To
continuously improve business results through
a process improvement focus, partnership with
our suppliers, and strong financial performance. 2) To become the partner of choice for
our customers through: a targeted marketing
plan, excellent execution to customer requirements, and relationship development. To
become the partner of choice, our value
package must be continually improved. 3) To
become the employer of choice through: a
caring, involved culture; continually improving
training systems; providing growth opportunities; and industry leading compensation, benefits, and reward and recognition systems. We
extend the same quality environment to
coworkers as we extend to customers."

How do these objectives address the
strategic challenges cited in the case? What
types of activities might the company deploy
to achieve these objectives?

REVIEW QUESTIONS

1. Define leadership. Why is it necessary for successful total quality management?
2. How does leadership relate to strategic planning?
3. List the key roles that senior executives play as leaders of their organizations.
4. List the five core leadership skills. Of what value are these skills in TQ?
5. What are the leading leadership practices of top managers in TQ-based organizations? Provide some examples of each.
6. Explain the traditional theories of leadership and their implications for total quality.
7. How do emerging theories differ from traditional theories? What implications do they have for TQ?
8. Define the term *leadership system*. What elements should an effective leadership system have?
9. What is the role of steering teams in many leadership systems?
10. Why are public responsibility and community support important elements of leadership?
11. What characteristics and focus does the leader of the future need, according to Frances Hasselbein, chair and president of the Peter F. Drucker Foundation?
12. What is a strategy? What elements do most strategies contain?
13. What are the leading practices for effective strategic planning?
14. Explain the basic strategic planning process.
15. Define mission, vision, and guiding principles. What is the purpose of each?
16. What is hoshin kanri? Provide a simplified description of this process.
17. How does catchball play an important role in policy deployment?
18. List and explain the major uses for the seven management and planning tools.
19. Describe the key contextual factors that affect organizational structure. What implications do they have for quality?
20. Describe the types of organizational structure commonly used. What are the advantages or disadvantages of each?
21. What types of organizational structures are common in TQ-based organizations today?
22. Explain how leadership and strategic planning are addressed in the Baldrige, ISO 9000:2000, and Six Sigma frameworks.

 ## DISCUSSION QUESTIONS

1. We emphasized that leadership is the "driver" of a total quality system. What does this statement imply and what implications does it have for future CEOs? Middle managers? Supervisors?
2. Provide examples from your own experiences in which leaders (not necessarily company managers—consider academic unit heads, presidents of student organizations, and even family members) exhibited one or more of the five core leadership skills described in this chapter. What impacts did these skills have on the organization?
3. State some examples in which leaders you have worked for exhibited some of the leading practices described in this chapter. Can you provide examples for which they have not?

4. Review Deming's 14 Points in Chapter 3. What aspects of leadership theories are evident in them, either individually or as a holistic philosophy?

5. Referring to the Traditional Leadership Theories document in the Bonus Materials folder on the CD-ROM, give examples of different "situational conditions" that would affect leadership styles according to Fiedler's model. As a company moves from a little to a high degree of TQ adoption, how do the situational conditions change? What do these changes mean for leadership?

6. How might concepts of the theory of emotional maturity be used to explain the failures of leadership in organizations such as Enron and Worldcom? How does it explain leadership success in a TQ environment?

7. How does the Xerox Leadership Through Quality strategy support TQ?

8. How can TQ principles improve the process of strategic planning?

9. The Johnson & Johnson credo was written in 1943 by its chairman Robert Wood Johnson: "We believe our first responsibility is to the doctors, nurses and patients, to mothers and fathers and all others who use our products and services. In meeting their needs, everything we do must be of high quality." What would you expect to see in Johnson & Johnson's leadership and strategic planning approaches that reflect this philosophy?

10. Examine the following mission statements. Do you think they have a true purpose or are they merely cosmetic devices because someone felt that no major company can be seen without one?[52]
    a. Our single focus will continue to be helping customers all over the world succeed in their businesses. When we do that—when we make them winners—then employees, dealers, and stockholders win as well.
    b. XYZ strives to understand and fulfill the needs of all our customers by providing the highest level of reliability and service at all times.
    c. XYZ creates value by providing transportation-related products and services with superior quality, safety, and environmental care to demanding customers in selected segments.
    d. We are dedicated to being the world's best at bringing people together—giving them easy access to each other and to the information and services they want and need—anytime, anywhere.
    e. To serve the most vulnerable.

11. Try to match the following companies with their actual mission statement in question 10. Could you think of more appropriate mission statements for any of these organizations?
    a. Volvo
    b. AT&T
    c. The International Red Cross
    d. Caterpillar
    e. DHL Worldwide Express

12. Contrast the following vision statements in terms of their usefulness to an organization.
    a. To become the industry leader and achieve superior growth and market share.
    b. To become the best-managed electric utility in the United States and an excellent company overall and be recognized as such.
    c. Being the best at everything we do, exceeding customer expectations; growing our business to increase its value to customers, employees, shareowners, and communities in which we work.

13. Propose three applications for each of the seven management and planning tools discussed in the chapter (see the Bonus Materials for detailed informa-

tion). You might consider some applications around school, such as in the classroom, studying for exams, and so on.

14. Discuss how each of the following quality values (which are the core values and concepts underlying the Baldrige criteria) are reflected in each item of the Baldrige criteria for Strategic Planning (i.e., Item 2.1 Strategy Development, and Item 2.2 Strategy Deployment): customer-driven, visionary leadership, organizational and personal learning, valuing employees and partners, agility, managing for innovation, focus on the future, management by fact, social responsibility, focus on results and creating value, and systems perspective.

See the description of the seven management and planning tools in the Bonus Materials on the CD-ROM.

PROBLEMS

1. "Let's plan a graduation party for our seniors," suggested Jim Teacher, president of the Delta Mu Zeta fraternity at State U. Everyone on the fraternity council thought that it was a good idea, so they agreed to brainstorm ideas for the party.

    "First, we have to pick a date," suggested Joe. "It'll have to be after final exams are over, but before graduation."

    "That narrows it down pretty quickly to June 8, 9, or 10. The 11th is a Sunday and the 12th is graduation day," said Jim. "I propose that we try for Thursday the 8th, with the alternate date of Friday, the 9th. We'll have to take a vote at the fraternity meeting tomorrow."

    "Now, let's list things that have to be done in order to get ready for the party," suggested Amber.

    They quickly produced the following list (not in any order): Pick date. Plan menu. Get food delivered. Estimate costs. Locate and book a hall. Determine budget. Select music. Hire a DJ. Plan decorations. Set up, decorate hall. Determine how much can be paid from treasury and what the cost of the special assessment will be for each member. Design and print invitations. Set up mailing list. Dress rehearsal (day before party) "dummy activity." Mail invitations. Plan ceremony for seniors. Rehearse ceremony. Plan after-party cleanup and bill paying. Have the party. Cleanup and pay bills.

    Next, they selected Joe as the "project manager" based on his prior fraternity party planning experience and because he was taking a quality management course and was studying the seven management and planning tools.

    a. Put yourself in Joe's position. Develop an interrelationship digraph for the party planners. Draw arrows from one activity to the next one that must occur. Note that the activities that have the most arrows going into them will tend to be the long-range results. Activities having the most arrows originating from them will tend to be the initial activities.

    b. What can you conclude from the graph? How would this digraph help make the job of organizing the party easier for the project team?

2. Creative Design Group (CDG) designs brochures for companies, trade groups, and associations. Their emphasis on customer service is based on speed, quality, creativity, and value. They want each brochure to "wow" the customer in its design, meet or exceed the preparation deadline, and be of superior quality at a

reasonable price. Value is emphasized over price, because the president, Trendy Art, believes that CDG's experienced staff should emphasize high quality and creativity instead of price. They accomplish their primary objectives 97 percent of the time.

To carry out their objectives, the small company has four designers, a customer service/estimator (CSE), and Trendy, who is the creative director and strategic visionary. The work environment, in a converted garage behind Trendy's house, features modern (though not always state-of-the-art) computer hardware and software, excellent lighting, and modern communications for sending design documents to clients and printers. Designers generally work independently of each other, consulting with the CSE about requests for status updates or client-initiated changes. They also consult with Trendy, who signs off on the creative design, after consultation with each client. A casual dress code and work policies, and a number of perks for workers, such as health insurance, flextime, generous vacation and sick leave benefits, a 401(k) retirement plan, and competitive wages have, in the past, made it easy to attract and retain talented people. However, with fewer talented people graduating from design schools in the area, and more competitive firms bidding up salaries, turnover has become an issue.

The CSE, Green Ishied, is the contact point for all projects, which may number 10–20 active at any one time. He must ensure that projects are carefully estimated and prepare proposals, track progress of each project, and communicate with clients on status and change requests. He is also responsible for advertising and promotion of the firm.

Trendy's husband, Hy, is a CPA and part-time accountant for the company. He noticed recently that costs are increasing, the percentage of their bids accepted is decreasing, and the ROI is slipping.

Develop an affinity diagram that captures the major organizational features and issues. How could this diagram help Trendy develop a three- to five-year strategic plan for CDG?

3. Given the situation in problem 2, Trendy determined several long-range objectives, among which are outdistancing the competition so as to grow the business by 10 percent per year for each of the next five years (a 61 percent compound growth rate), and adding a new designer every two years. These factors should be the key ingredients for her goal of increasing her profitability by 10 percent per year. To accomplish her objectives, she must deal with the two major issues of the increasing competition and employee recruitment and retention in order to develop effective action plans to support her long-range plan. Develop a tree diagram, starting with "Develop action plans" as the main theme. At the next level, include the two main issues. One, for example is, "Develop a plan to meet competition." Then break out each of the issues into two or three feasible proposals, such as "Make advertising more effective," under the previous item of "Develop a plan to meet competition." Finally, add another level of specificity with two to four items, such as: "Place ads in business newspaper," "Redesign Web page," and so on, under the "Make advertising more effective" item.

4. Jim Teacher (see problem 1) was able to get some estimating information from the president of another fraternity that had planned and carried out a similar party for graduating seniors last year. They had not kept financial information, but they did have the actual hours that it took to complete each activity. From these data, Jim obtained the following time estimates for Delta Mu Zeta.

Pick date	1 day	Design and print invitations	3 days
Plan menu	2 days	Set up mailing list	5 days
Get food delivered	1 day	Dress rehearsal (day before	
Estimate costs	3 days	party) "dummy activity"	0 days
Locate and book a hall	5 days	Mail invitations	1 day
Determine budget	3 days	Plan ceremony for seniors	2 days
Select music	2 days	Rehearse ceremony	1 day
Hire a DJ	3 days	Plan after-party cleanup and	
Plan decorations	2 days	bill paying	2 days
Set up, decorate hall	1 day	Have the party	1 day
Determine how much can be		Cleanup and pay bills	1 day
paid from treasury and what			
the cost of the special assess-			
ment will be for each member	1 day		

    a. You are Joe, the project manager. Use the interrelationship digraph developed in problem 1 to draw an arrow diagram, making sure that activities are sequenced in the correct order.

    b. If you are familiar with PERT/CPM through other courses, use the preceding data to calculate the minimum time that the project will take; that is, compute the critical path.

5. Using the result of problems 2 and 3, Trendy Art decided that, along with improving her recruiting processes for new and replacement hiring, it was time to replace the computer system with state-of-the-art hardware and software. Knowing that no one at CDG had the expertise to design the type of system that they needed, Trendy looked around, analyzed three competing firms' proposals, and finally settled on Creative Computer Group (CCG) to act as consultants and system integrators. Before signing the contract, Trendy decided to ask Hy and Green Ishied (the CSE) to meet with her and the CEO of CCG to clarify the system design requirements and the wording of the contract.

    Trendy, Hy, and Green all agreed that the system needed to be completely integrated, with the capability to gather cost and scheduling data directly from the designers, and to produce all necessary business reports, as well as having graphics capability. Both cost and design information would have to be available to everyone in the firm. Therefore, the network should be capable of interfacing both Macintosh and PC desktops via USB connections, with common printers. It should also provide for high bandwidth Internet access and capability to send and receive graphic and text data files. Charlie Nerd, the president of CCG, said that all of those requirements could be met by the system that he would design. Because it was such an important project for his company, he would personally be the project manager for the installation and testing of the new system. After outlining the plans for the system, Charlie asked if they had any questions. Trendy, Hy, and Green had no immediate questions, but promised to get back to Charlie with a few within three days.

    a. Given the following information, perform a matrix data analysis to determine why (or if) CCG should get the contract to install the computer system. Justify your analysis.

    b. What questions would you suggest that Trendy, Hy, and Green get back to Charlie on?

Supplier Characteristics	Weights	Rating for CCG	Rating for COG	Rating for COW	Weighted Value CCG	Weighted Value COG	Weighted Value COW
System design reliability	0.3	8	6	5			
Delivery timeliness	0.2	7	4	9			
Cost	0.2	5	7	6			
System service	0.2	9	6	4			
Experience	0.1	4	9	6			
Totals	1.0						

Note: Independent ratings on a scale of 1–10 (where 10 is best) were performed by the Small Business Council of Qualdale, where CDG is located.

Suppliers: CCG = Creative Computer Group
　　　　　　 COG = Computer Organizational Group
　　　　　　 COW = Computer Operations Workgroup

　　c. Construct a process decision program chart, but closely reflecting CCG's training needs. What special considerations would need to be included in training graphic designers with little business knowledge and business-oriented people (such as Hy and Green) with little artistic design knowledge, about each other's areas of work in order to use an integrated system?

Projects, Etc.

1. Using the information in this chapter, design a questionnaire that might be used to understand leadership effectiveness in an organization.
2. Interview someone you know about the leadership characteristics of their supervisor. What leadership style does he or she appear to reflect?
3. Interview managers at some local organizations to determine whether they have well-defined missions, visions, and guiding principles. If they do, how are these translated into strategy? If not, what steps should they take?
4. Joseph Conklin proposes 10 questions for self-examination to help you understand your capacity for leadership.[53] Answer the following questions, and discuss why they are important for leadership.
　　a. How much do I like my job?
　　b. How often do I have to repeat myself?
　　c. How do I respond to failure?
　　d. How well do I put up with second guessing?
　　e. How early do I ask questions when making a decision?
　　f. How often do I say "thank you"?
　　g. Do I tend to favor a loose or strict interpretation of the rules?
　　h. Can I tell an obstacle from an excuse?
　　i. Is respect enough?
　　j. Have I dispensed with feeling indispensable?

5. Find several examples of mission and vision statements for *Fortune* 500 companies. Critique these statements with respect to their usefulness, relevance to the organization, and ability to inspire and motivate employees.

6. Does your university or college have a mission and strategy? How might policy deployment be used in a university setting? Discuss with a senior executive administrator at your college or university (such as the VP of administration or the VP of academic affairs/provost) how policy deployment is, or might be, done.

7. Liz Keim, then president of the American Society for Quality (ASQ), wrote an opinion piece in September 2002, entitled "Corporate Wrongdoing: A Betrayal of Quality Principles: *Malfeasance and accounting cover-ups are the worst forms of waste*" (available at: http://www.asq.org/news/interest/090902ethics.html). Read her discussion, summarize it, and discuss her main points with a CEO or chief financial officer in a large service organization, such as a bank, a telecommunications firm, or a manufacturing organization. Determine if and how corporate ethical documents, policies, and practices have changed since these corporate scandals became public in 2001, 2002, and later.

8. Research the leadership and strategic planning practices of recent Baldrige Award winners. Discuss different approaches that these firms use and why they seem appropriate for their organizations. How do they reflect the leading practices described in this chapter?

9. In your role as a student, develop your own statements of mission, vision, and guiding principles. How would you create a strategy to achieve your mission and vision?

10. Compare the organizational structures of several companies. What differences are reflected in their quality approaches and results?

 # CASES

Additional cases, including Baldrige assessment cases, are available in the Bonus Materials Folder on the CD-ROM.

I. JOHNSONVILLE FOODS[54]

Ralph C. Stayer, owner and CEO of Johnsonville Foods Co. in Sheboygan Falls, Wisconsin, has been profiled by Tom Peters in his book *Thriving on Chaos* and the PBS video program, *The Leadership Alliance*.[55] Stayer revealed his leadership secrets in the book that he co-authored with James A. Belasco under the intriguing title of *Flight of the Buffalo*.[56] Stayer was responsible for initiating the process that transformed a sleepy, family-owned sausage-making company into a nationally recognized firm that is using an innovative self-management process to remain healthy in an increasingly competitive industry. In the first chapter of his book, Stayer compares his company to a herd of buffalo that follows a single leader wherever the leader wants them to go. In the old West when buffalo hunters wanted to kill a lot of buffalo, they just killed the lead buffalo. The

rest of the herd was easily cut down, because they would stop and mill around the fallen leader, waiting for him to lead them to safety.

Stayer wanted to change the leadership paradigm to encourage his employees to become responsible, interdependent workers, more like a flock of wild geese. Geese fly in their typical "V" formation, with different birds taking the lead at different points in time. Essentially, they share the leadership load. He stated that the leadership principles for the new paradigm include the following points:

1. Leaders transfer ownership of the work to those who execute the work.
2. Leaders create the environment for ownership where each person wants to be responsible.

3. Leaders coach the development of personal capabilities.
4. Leaders learn fast themselves and encourage others also to learn quickly.[57]

Ralph Stayer began to transform Johnsonville in the early 1980s before the firm reached a point of crisis. It was a small regional meat packer that was strong in Wisconsin and beginning to make some inroads into surrounding states. Over the next 10 years, through his efforts and those of the company's "associates," their return on assets doubled, sales increased nine times, and product and quality levels improved significantly, even though the company was in a mature and declining industry.

Stayer tried the "prescriptions" of job descriptions, MBO, communication improvement methods, and even an early version of quality circles to transform the company's culture. None stood the test of time nor his gut feel for what changes were needed in the company. He felt that his small entrepreneurial firm had the potential to be great, but was only performing up to the average measures in the industry.

The Palmer Sausage decision, detailed in a 1985 Harvard Business School case, was the turning point for employee learning and empowerment.[58] Palmer Sausage Co., a larger regional competitor, had a product that it wanted to distribute, but the firm was consolidating plants and contacted Johnsonville about the possibility of providing some extra capacity. Although this "golden opportunity" would help the company grow, Johnsonville would have to build a new plant, hire additional workers, and make other improvements. Meanwhile, if Palmer didn't like Johnsonville's product it could cancel the contract with a 30-day notice, leaving Johnsonville in a vulnerable position with unused plant capacity and too many workers on the payroll. Instead of making an executive decision, Ralph Stayer empowered his workers and managers to study the problem and decide whether to accept Palmer's offer. Many small groups met and discussed the decision and decided to accept the offer.

The employees rose to the challenge. Initially, they worked six or seven days per week while the new plant was being built. The new employees were brought on board and trained, and the old employees rapidly learned new skills. The quality levels for both Johnsonville and Palmer products rose, despite the strain of high production. The new plant was successfully brought on line in 1987.

A result that is perhaps even more significant is the degree to which employees have taken over both strategic and operating management responsibilities at Johnsonville Foods. In Stayer's words:

Profoundly, Johnsonville people learned what they needed to do. They learned to be responsible for more of the strategic decisions at Johnsonville. They changed the career tracking system and set new team performance standards. Then they went on transforming themselves from buffalo into geese.

Teams of line employees at Johnsonville now make capital budgeting, new product development, scheduling, hiring and firing, quality and productivity measurement, and a number of other strategic and operating decisions.

In summary, Stayer sees the key to leadership success as doing the job of changing the leadership paradigm, owning up to being part of the problem as a traditional manager, empowering employees to do the jobs that they care capable of doing and growing into, coaching and rewarding performance in multiple ways, and learning, learning, learning.

Discussion Questions

1. From a strategic management standpoint, does Ralph Stayer provide sufficient planning and control to keep the company on track?
2. What type of management style does he seem to follow? Does it fit any of the leadership theories that were developed in the chapter?
3. How easy or difficult would it be for other companies to duplicate the leadership style of Stayer and the organizational systems practiced at Johnsonville Foods?

II. A STRATEGIC BOTTLENECK[59]

An international bottle manufacturer produces glass containers for customers that include condiment producers, breweries, and wineries. The growing demand for plastic containers, and a history of higher production costs due to high scrap and return rates drove the business to focus its improvement efforts on cost and customer performance. However, the unique characteristics of the bottle manufacturing process and the way in which the company measured and motivated its workforce's performance made these improvements difficult to accomplish.

Bottle plants are traditionally organized around two primary functions: forming and selecting. Forming is where raw materials are melted in furnaces and molten glass is cut and formed by fast-moving, noisy, and dangerous machines that turn out thousands of bottles each minute. The workforce is primarily older males. In the selecting department, the work is relatively quiet and clean. The majority of workers are female, and the work is focused on spotting and removing bottles that fail to meet height, weight, dimension, centricity, and thickness specifications.

The principal performance measure in the forming department is the pack-to-melt ratio, calculated by dividing the total weight of bottles shipped by the total weight of the raw materials used. Individual and team performance goals are typically tied to this measure. The focus is on throughput and getting the highest percentage of produced bottles packed and shipped to customers. In the selecting department, customer satisfaction is the key measure of work performance, and compensation is based on how much product is accepted by the customer. As you can imagine, relations between the two departments were quite strained.

To achieve its strategic goals of lower cost and improved customer performance, what could this company do to align the goals of the forming and selecting departments?

III. CORRYVILLE FOUNDRY COMPANY[60]

Corryville Foundry Company (CFC) was founded in the mid-1940s in a 3,000-square-foot building with nine people as a small family business to produce castings. In the 1960s, as business grew, the company expanded its facilities and its capability to develop its own tooling patterns, eventually moving into a 40,000-square-foot building. Over this time period, the foundry industry declined from more than 12,000 companies to about 4,000.

With such a shrinking market, CFC began to listen more to its customers. They discovered that customers were not happy with the quality of the products they had been receiving. In 1989 CFC made a commitment to quality by hiring a quality assurance manager, Ronald Chalmer. Chalmer felt that upper management was committed to quality and saw an opportunity to change the company's culture. He also firmly believed in Deming's philosophy. One of the first things he did was to work with upper management in developing a mission statement:

> Our mission at CFC is to improve the return on investment. We can accomplish this by changing attitudes and incorporating a quality/team environment. This will improve the quality of our products, enhance our productivity (which in turn will allow us to quote competitive prices), and elevate our service and response

> level to our customers. There are several factors which make positive change imperative.
>
> The standards for competitive levels of quality and service are becoming more demanding. The emergence of the "World Market" has brought on new challenges. We are in a low-growth, mature market. In order for CFC to improve return on investment, we must develop a strategy to improve quality and responsiveness in all areas of the company. We need to have all employees recognize the importance of product quality and service and move toward more favorable pricing. We need to change thinking throughout the organization to get employees involved, to encourage teamwork, to develop a more flexible workforce and adaptable organization. We need to instill pride in the workplace and the product.
>
> We believe that we can best achieve the desired future state by study of and adherence to the teachings of W. Edwards Deming.

Under Chalmer's direction, CFC made some substantial improvements in the quality of castings, particularly reducing scrap and reject rates. He worked closely with the factory workers directly responsible for the products, asking them what they needed to get the job done and ensuring management commitment to provide the necessary resources. For example, CFC invested in a new controller for the furnaces that provided a digital readout of temperature. With this technology, workers were able to categorize the metal temperatures needed for each casting type and were able to adjust the process as needed. The success of this project led the company to empower employees to control many other aspects of the system.

Three years later, the president and CEO retired. The new CEO, who had been a vice president of a major manufacturing company, did not feel that the mission statement provided a clear and vivid direction. Consequently, he set up a planning retreat for senior management (including Chalmer) to develop a new strategic vision.

Discussion Questions

1. Comment on the current mission statement. Does it provide the strategic direction necessary for success for this company?
2. How can the mission statement be improved? Suggest a better statement of mission, vision, and guiding principles.

IV. CapStar Health Systems: Leadership and Strategic Planning

The complete CapStar case study, a fictitious example of a Baldrige application, can be found on the CD-ROM accompanying this book. If you have not read the Organizational Profile yet (see Case III in Chapter 3), please do so first. Examine their response to Categories 1 and 2 in the context of the leading practices described in this chapter (you need not consider the actual Baldrige criteria for this activity). What are their strengths? What are their weaknesses and opportunities for improvement? What specific advice, including useful tools and techniques that might help them, would you suggest?

ENDNOTES

1. Jack Welch, Herb Kelleher, Geoffrey Colvin, and John Huey "How to Create Great Companies and Keep Them That Way," *Fortune*, no. 1 (January 11, 1999), 163.
2. Debbie Phillips-Donaldson, "On Leadership," *Quality Progress*, August 2002.
3. Rick Edgeman, Su Mi Park Dahigaard, Jens J. Dalhgaard, and Franz Scherer, "On Leaders and Leadership," *Quality Progress*, October 1999, 49–54.
4. William Bridges "Leading the De-Jobbed Organization," in Frances Hesselbein, Marshall Goldsmith, and Richard Beckhard (eds.), *The Leader of the Future* (San Francisco: Jossey-Bass, 1996), 16–17.
5. R. E. Byrd, "Corporate Leadership Skills: A New Synthesis," *Organizational Dynamics*, Summer 1987, 34–43.
6. Award, the Newsletter of Baldrigeplus, May 7, 2000. Available at http://www.baldrigeplus.com.
7. J. R. P. French, Jr., and B. H. Raven, "The Bases of Social Power," in D. Cartwright and A. Zanders (eds.), *Group Dynamics: Research and Theory*, 2d ed. (New York: Harper & Row, 1960), 607–623.
8. Xerox Quality Solutions, *A World of Quality: The Timeless Passport* (Milwaukee, WI: ASQC Quality Press, 1993), 5.
9. Robert Haavind et al., *The Road to the Baldrige Award* (Boston: Butterworth-Heinemann, 1992), 50–51.
10. Debbie Phillips-Donaldson, "Champions of Quality: The New Breed," *Quality Progress*, November 2001, 35–39.
11. Frances Hesselbein, *Hesselbein on Leadership* (San Francisco: Jossey-Bass, 2002), 8.
12. Robert Slater, *Jack Welch and the GE Way* (New York: McGraw-Hill, 1999), 219.
13. R. M. Stogdill, *Handbook of Leadership* (New York: The Free Press, 1974).
14. E. A. Fleishman and E. F. Harris "Patterns of Leadership Behavior Related to Employee Greivances and Turnover." *Personnel Psychology* (1962), 15, 43-56.
15. Rensis Likert, *The Human Organization: Its Management and Value* (New York: McGraw-Hill, 1967).
16. Douglas McGregor, The Human Side of Enterprise (New York: McGraw-Hill, 1960).
17. R. R. Blake and J. S. Mouton, *The Managerial Grid* (Houston: Gulf Publishing, 1965).
18. Frederick E. Fiedler, *A Theory of Leadership Effectiveness* (New York: McGraw-Hill, 1967).
19. V. H. Vroom and A. G. Jago, *The New Leadership* (Englewood Cliffs, NJ: Prentice Hall, 1988).
20. Henry Mintzberg, *Mintzberg on Management: Inside Our Strange World of Organizations* (New York: The Free Press, 1989). Also, *The Nature of Managerial Work* (New York: Harper & Row, 1973); "The Manager's Job: Folklore

and Fact," *Harvard Business Review* (July/August 1975).

21. R. J. House "A 1976 Theory of Charismatic Leadership" in J.G. Hunt and L.L. Larson (Eds.) *Leadership: The Cutting Edge* (Carbondale, IL: Southern Illinois University Press, 1977), 189-207. Also, J.A. Conger, *The Charismatic Leader: Behind the Mystique of Exceptional Leadership* (SanFrancisco: Jossey-Bass, 1989).

22. James M. Burns; N. M. Tichy and D. O. Ulrich, etc. (see note 26).

23. Jon P. Howell, et al. (see note 28).

24. Daniel Golema.(see note 29).

25. Reprinted by permission from Don Hellriegel, John W. Slocum, Jr., and Richard W. Woodman, *Organizational Behavior*, 6th ed. (St. Paul, MN: West, 1992), 413–414. All rights reserved.

26. The term *transformational leadership* has been attributed to James M. Burns. See his book, *Leadership* (New York: Harper & Row, 1978). Other sources are N. M. Tichy and D. O. Ulrich, "The Leadership Challenge: A Call For the Transformational Leader," *Sloan Management Review* 26 (1984), 59–68; N. M. Tichy and M. A. Devanna, *The Transformational Leader* (New York: John Wiley & Sons, 1986); B. M. Bass, *Leadership and Performance Beyond Expectations* (New York: The Free Press, 1985).

27. Philip Atkinson, "Leadership, Total Quality and Cultural Change," *Management Services,* June 1991, 16–19.

28. Jon P. Howell, David E. Bowen, Peter W. Dorfman, Steven Kerr, and Phillip M. Podsakoff "Substitutes for Leadership: Effective Alternatives for Ineffective Leadership" *Organizational Dynamics,* Summer 1990. Also see Steve Kerr and John Jermier, "Substitutes for Leadership: Their Meaning and Measurement" *Organizational Behavior and Human Performance,* December, 1978; and Jon P. Howell, Peter W. Dorfman, and Steven Kerr, "Moderator Variables in Leadership Research," *Academy of Management Review,* January, 1986.

29. Daniel Goleman, "What Makes a Leader?" *Harvard Business Review,* November–December, 1998, 93–102; and Daniel Goleman, *Working with Emotional Intelligence* (New York: Bantam Books, 1998).

30. Solar Turbines, Inc., Malcolm Baldrige National Quality Award Application Summary, 1999, 4.

31. AT&T Quality Steering Committee, *Leading the Quality Initiative,* AT&T Bell Laboratories, 1990, 13–14.

32. A. J. Vogl, "Does It Pay to Be Good?" *Across the Board,* January/February 2003, 16–23.

33. Frances Hasselbein. *Hasselbein on Leadership.* (San Francisco: Jossey-Bass, a Wiley imprint) 2002, 13.

34. James Brian Quinn, *Strategies for Change: Logical Incrementalism* (Homewood, IL: Richard D. Irwin, 1980).

35. AT&T Consumer Communication Services, Summary of 1994 Application for the Malcolm Baldrige National Quality Award.

36. Noel Tichy and Nancy Cardwell, *The Cycle of Leadership* (New York: HarperCollins, 2002), 185; and

James M. Lucas. "The Essential Six Sigma," *Quality Progress,* January, 2002, 28.

37. Henry Mintzberg, "The Fall and Rise of Strategic Planning," *Harvard Business Review,* January–February 1994, 107–114.

38. Victor Cvascella, "Effective Strategic Planning," *Quality Progress,* November 2002, 62–67.

39. Bob King, *Hoshin Planning: The Developmental Approach* (Methuen, MA: GOAL/QPC, 1989).

40. M. Imai, *Kaizen: The Key to Japan's Competitive Success* (New York: McGraw-Hill, 1986), 144–145.

41. Adapted from Kersi F. Munshi, "Policy Deployment: A Key to Long-Term TQM Success," *ASQC Quality Congress Transactions* (Boston, 1993), 236–244.

42. The Ernst & Young Quality Improvement Consulting Group, *Total Quality: An Executive's Guide for the 1990s* (Homewood, IL: Dow Jones-Irwin, 1990).

43. Armstrong Building Products Operations Malcolm Baldrige National Quality Award Application Summary, 1995.

44. Brad Grimes, "You Call This Service?" *PCWorld,* December 2002, 143–152.

45. Kermit F. Wasmuth, "Organization and Planning," in Loren Walsh, Ralph Wurster, and Raymond J. Kimber (eds.), *Quality Management Handbook* (Wheaton, IL: Hitchcock Publishing Company, 1986), 9–34.

46. Ricardo Simler, *Maverick* (New York: Warner Books, 1993), 196.

47. Noel M. Tichy and Nancy Cardwell, *The Cycle of Leadership: How Great Leaders Teach Their Organizations to Win* (New York: HarperCollins, 2002), 57.

48. Adapted from Manfred F. R. Kets de Vries, "Charisma in Action: The Transformational Abilities of Virgin's Richard Branson and ABB's Percy Barnevik," *Organizational Dynamics,* no. 3, (January 1, 1998), 6.

49. Manfred F. R. Kets de Vries and Elizabeth Florent-Treacy, *The New Global Leaders: Richard Branson, Percy Barnevik, and David Simon* (San Francisco: Jossey-Bass Publishers, 1999), xiii–xiv. © 1999. This material used by permission of John Wiley & Sons, Inc.

50. Manfred F. R. Kets de Vries and Elizabeth Florent-Treacy, "An Interview with Richard Branscom," *The New Global Leaders* (San Francisco: Jossey-Bass, 1999), 40.

51. Branch-Smith Printing, Application Summary, 2002. Courtesy of David Branch, President.

52. "Missions for All Seasons," *Across the Board,* April, 2000, 12.

53. Joe Conklin, "What It Takes to Be a Leader," *Quality Progress,* November 2001, 83.

54. Information for this case study was adapted from several sources, including Ralph Stayer, "How I Learned to Let My Workers Lead," *Harvard Business Review,* November/December 1990, 66–83; James A. Belasco and Ralph C. Stayer, *Flight of the Buffalo: Soaring to Excellence, Learning to Let Employees Lead* (New York: Warner Books, Inc., 1993); Tom Peters, *Thriving on Chaos: Handbook for a Management Revolution* (New York: Alfred

A. Knopf, 1987). Additional information is also available in the Harvard cases by M. J. Roberts, Johnsonville Sausage Co. (A), [#9-387-103]; Johnsonville Sausage Co. (B), [#9-393-063]; HBR Videotape [9-888-517].

55. Tom Peters, *Thriving on Chaos: Handbook for a Management Revolution* (New York: Alfred A. Knopf, 1987); Tom Peters, "The Leadership Alliance," videotape, Video Publishing House, Inc., 1988.

56. James A. Belasco and Ralph C. Stayer, *Flight of the Buffalo: Soaring to Excellence, Learning to Let Employees Lead* (New York: Warner Books, 1993).

57. *Ibid.*, 19.

58. Johnsonville Sausage, Harvard Business School (1985), Cases #9-387-103 and #9-393-063.

59. Adapted from Victor Cvascella, "Effective Strategic Planning," *Quality Progress*, November 2002, pp. 62–67. Copyright © 2002, American Society for Quality. Reprinted with permission.

60. This fictitious case stems from a real company. We thank our students John P. Rosiello and David Seilkop for contributing the research.

BIBLIOGRAPHY

AT&T Quality Steering Committee. *Batting 1000: Using Baldrige Feedback to Improve Your Business.* AT&T Bell Laboratories, 1992.

AT&T Quality Steering Committee. *Policy Deployment.* AT&T Bell Laboratories, 1992.

Bennis, Warren, Grechen M. Spreitzer, and Thomas G. Cummings (eds.). *The Future of Leadership: Today's Top Leadership Thinkers Speak to Tomorrow's Leaders.* San Francisco: Jossey-Bass, 2001.

Bennis, Warren G., and Robert J. Thomas. *Geeks and Geezers.* Boston: Harvard Business School Press, 2002.

Blanchard, Ken. *The Heart of a Leader: Insights on the Art of Influence.* Tulsa, OK: Honor Books, 1999.

Bossidy, Larry, Ram Charan, and Charles Burch. *Execution: The Discipline of Getting Things Done.* New York: Crown Books—Random House, 2002.

Brager, Joan. "The Customer-Focused Quality Leader." *Quality Progress* 25, no. 5 (May 1992), 51–53.

Camison, Cesar. "Total Quality Management and Cultural Change: A Model of Organizational Development," *International Journal of Technology Management* 16, nos. 4–6 (1998), 479.

Cole, Robert E. "Corporate Strategy—Learning from the Quality Movement: What Did and Didn't Happen, and Why?" *Californina Management Review* 41,no. 1 (1998), 43.

Collins, James. *Good to Great: Why Some Companies Make the Leap . . . And Others Don't.* New York: Harper-Collins, 2001.

Conger, J., and R. Kanugo. "Toward a Behavioral Theory of Charismatic Leadership in Organizational Settings." *Academy of Management Review,* October 1987, 637–647.

Easton, George S., and Sherry L. Jarrell. "The Effects of Total Quality Management on Organizational Performance: An Empirical Investigation," *The Journal of Business* 71, no. 2 (1998), 253.

Evans, James R., and James W. Dean, Jr. *Total Quality: Management, Organization, and Strategy,* 3rd ed. Cincinnati: South-Western Publishing, 2003.

Emery, F. E., E. L. Trist, and J. Woodward. *Management and Technology.* London: Her Majesty's Stationery Office, 1958.

Franz, Douglas. "To Put G.E. Online Meant Putting a Dozen Industries Online," *New York Times*, March 29, 2000.

Hart, Christopher W. L., and Christopher E. Bogan. *The Baldrige.* New York: McGraw-Hill, 1992.

Hesselbein, Frances, Marshall Goldsmith, and Richard Beckhard (eds.) *The Leader of the Future: New Visions, Strategies, and Practices for the next Era.* San Francisco: Jossey-Bass, Publishers, 1996.

Juran, J. M. *Juran on Quality by Design.* New York: The Free Press, 1992.

Kenyon, David A., "Strategic Planning with the Hoshin Process," *Quality Digest*, May 1997, 55–63.

Kouzes, James M., and Barry Z. Posner. *The Leadership Challenge,* 3rd ed. San Francisco: Jossey-Bass, 2002.

Lawrence, P. R., and J. W. Lorsch. *Organization and Environment.* Boston: Harvard University, Division of Research, Graduate School of Business Administration, 1967.

"Learning to Compete Through Quality," *The Quality Observer,* January 1997, 10-24.

Profiles of Malcolm Baldrige Award Winners. Boston: Allyn & Bacon, 1992.

Rue, L. W., and L. Byars. *Management Theory and Application,* 9th ed. New York: McGraw-Hill/Irwin, 1999.

Sample, Steven B. *The Contrarian's Guide to Leadership.* San Francisco: Jossey-Bass, 2001.

Smergut, Peter. "Total Quality Management and the Not-for-Profit," *Administration in Social Work*, 22, no. 3 (1998), 75.

St. Lawrence, Dennis, and Bob Stinnett. "Powerful Planning with Simple Techniques." *Quality Progress* 27, no. 7 (July 1994), 57–64.

Taylor, Glenn L., and Martha N. Morgan, "The Reverse Appraisal: A Tool for Leadership Development," *Quality Progress* 28, 12, (December 1995), 81–87.

Tedesco, Frank M. "Building Quality Goals into the Business Plan." *The Total Quality Review* 4, no. 1 (March/April 1994), 31–34.

Tichy, Noel M., Andrew McGill, Andrew R. McGill (eds.). *The Ethical Challenge: How to Build Honest Business Leaders.* New York: John Wiley and Sons, 2003.

U.S. Department of Commerce and Booz-Allen & Hamilton, Inc. "Total Quality Management (TQM): Implementer's Workshop." May 1990.

Waldman, David A. "A Theoretical Consideration of Leadership and Total Quality Management." *Leadership Quarterly* 4 (1993), 65–79.

Welch, Jack, and John Byrne. *Jack: Straight from the Gut.* New York: Warner Books, 2001.

Welch, Jack, Rik Kirkland, and Geoffrey Colvin. "Jack: The Exit Interview," *Fortune,* September 17, 2001.

Whiteley, Richard C. *The Customer-Driven Company.* Reading, MA: Addison-Wesley, 1991.

CHAPTER 6

HUMAN RESOURCE PRACTICES

Toyota's Georgetown, Kentucky, plant has been a three-time winner of the J. D. Power Gold Plant Quality Award. When asked about the "secret" behind the superior Toyota paint finishes, one manager replied, "We've got nothing, technology-wise, that anyone else can't have. There's no secret Toyota Quality Machine out there. The quality machine is the workforce—the team members on the paint line, the suppliers, the engineers—everybody who has a hand in production here takes the attitude that we're making world-class vehicles."[1] The human resource is the *only* one that competitors cannot copy, and the *only* one that can synergize, that is, produce output whose value is greater than the sum of its parts. Deming emphasized that no organization can survive without good people, people who are improving. After leadership, people are the most important component of total quality. FedEx, for instance, has found direct statistical correlation between customer and employee satisfaction; a drop in employee satisfaction scores precedes a drop in customer satisfaction by about two months. Heskett, Sasser, and Schlesinger of the Harvard Business School have conducted research in a number of service operations in industries ranging from communications to banking to fast food, and observed similar relationships.[2] They found that as employee satisfaction increased, so did customer satisfaction and loyalty to the organization. If employees were satisfied with their working conditions and jobs, they stayed with the company, became familiar with customers and their needs, had the opportunity to correct errors because the customers knew and trusted them, and had outcomes of higher productivity and high service quality. Customers of these firms became more loyal, thus providing more repeat business, were willing to complain about service problems so that employees could fix them, and benefited from the relationship by seeing lower costs and better service, thus leading to a new cycle of increased customer satisfaction.

> *Businesses are learning that to satisfy customers, they must first satisfy employees.*

Satisfying employees, however, can go well beyond simple job security. As *Fortune* magazine noted,

> . . . *the real test comes in tough times. Priorities may change, layoffs may be unavoidable. FORTUNE's [2003 list of the] 100 Best Companies, however, are still trying hard to do right by their staff. For example, at No. 21-ranked Pfizer, rather than cut benefits, the company actually expanded them. Employees now receive three weeks' vacation after one year of service; previously, they had to wait five years. The company also increased its adoption aid benefit from $5,000 to $10,000. And it began offering a vision plan as part of its health-insurance coverage. J.M. Family Enterprises, a Deerfield Beach, Fla., Toyota distributor ranked 14 on our list, also put more perks on its already lavish list of benefits—which include on-site hair salons, a medical clinic staffed with two physicians, a lap pool, and recognition cruises on a company yacht. In the past year, it opened an on-site child-care center and began offering retirees with 10 years' service a health-insurance plan in which the premium is split 50-50.*[3]

The role of people at work certainly changed as business and technology evolved over the years. Prior to the Industrial Revolution, skilled craftspeople had a major stake in the quality of their products because their families' livelihoods depended on the sale of those products. They were motivated by pride in their work as well as the need for survival. Frederick W. Taylor promulgated the departure from the craftsmanship concept. Taylor concluded that a factory should be managed on a scientific basis. So he focused on work methods design, the establishment of standards for daily work, selection and training of workers, and piecework incentives. Taylor separated planning from execution, concluding that foremen and workers of those days lacked the education necessary to plan their work. The foreman's role was to ensure that the workforce met productivity standards. Other pioneers of scientific management, such as Frank and Lillian Gilbreth and Henry Gantt, further refined the Taylor system through motion study, methods improvement, ergonomics, scheduling, and wage incentive systems.

The Taylor system dramatically improved productivity. However, it also changed many manufacturing jobs into a series of mundane and mindless tasks. Without a systems perspective and a focus on the customer, the responsibility for quality shifted from workers to inspectors, and as a result, quality eroded. The Taylor philosophy also contributed to the development of labor unions and established an adversarial relationship between labor and management that has yet to be completely overcome.

QUALITY PROFILES

SUNNY FRESH FOODS AND MERRILL LYNCH CREDIT CORPORATION

Sunny Fresh Foods (SFF) manufactures and distributes more than 160 different types of egg-based food products to more than 12,000 U.S. food service operations, such as quick service restaurants, schools, hospitals, convenience stores, and food processors. A subsidiary of Cargill, Inc., SFF operates three manufacturing facilities with a total of 380 employees. At SFF, a satisfied, motivated workforce is a vital ingredient of the company's successful operational and business performance. As measured in annual surveys, employees' rising level of satisfaction and their nearly complete awareness of how their jobs affect customers correlate directly with increasing customer satisfaction. SFF refers to its workers as "stakeholders" and ensures that they share in the benefits of continuous improvement. For example, although the base pay is set slightly below the industry midpoint for salaried workers, incentives can increase earnings above the 75th percentile. In addition, extensive reward and recognition systems, including monetary rewards for exemplary safety performance to extra vacation days for quality achievements, also help to motivate employees to contribute to the company's progress toward its improvement goals.

Innovations and a near perfect record for on-time delivery helped SFF earn sole-supplier status from several major national restaurant chains. In its 1999 customer survey, SFF earned scores of 100 percent on three of its five key indicators of satisfaction: on-time delivery, technical support, and customer service access. Scores on the other two—product performance and product freshness—topped 90 percent. SFF ranks second in its industry market share, up from 14th in 1988. SFF was a 1999 Baldrige Award recipient.

Merrill Lynch Credit Corporation (MLCC) provides a wide variety of liability management services including home financing, personal credit, and investment and business financing. MLCC's 830 employees, known as partners, market and sell all its products through a nationwide network of more than 14,000 financial consultants at Merrill Lynch Private Client sales offices. MLCC considers partner empowerment critical to its success. Partners are encouraged to take initiative and responsibility, especially in areas such as flexibility, cooperation, rapid response, and learning. Cross- and just-in-time training, cross-functional teams, and flow re-engineering teams help partners achieve success. MLCC strives to be the employer of choice and offers multiple methods of improving partner satisfaction, including alternative work arrangements.

MLCC also emphasizes process management and measurement systems to link every partner to company objectives, and makes heavy use of technology to enable partners to meet the ever-increasing expectations of clients and the company's financial consultants. Using process improvement techniques, the percentage of legal submissions returned late was reduced from 20 percent in the first half of 1995 to zero percent in the second half of 1996. Net income rose 100 percent from 1994 to 1996 and exceeded the industry group average. Return on equity increased approximately 74 percent and return on assets increased by about 36 percent during the same period. Partner satisfaction with the company's recognition programs improved from 42 percent in 1994 to 70 percent in 1996, when the company was named a Baldrige recipient.

Source: Malcolm Baldrige National Quality Award, Profiles of Winners, National Institute of Standards and Technology, Department of Commerce.

Nevertheless, the Taylor system was the key force behind the explosive economic development of the twentieth century.

On the other hand, the Taylor system failed to exploit an organization's most important asset—the knowledge and creativity of the workforce. As executives at The Ritz-Carlton Hotel Company have stated, human beings don't serve a function, they have a purpose, and the role of the human resources function is to unleash the power of the workforce to achieve the goals of the organization.[4] Rather than directing and supervising workers, managers today must empower and challenge them. Studies show that this new philosophy results in higher quality, lower costs, less waste, better utilization, increased capacity, reduced turnover and absenteeism, faster implementation of change, greater human skill development, and better individual self-esteem.[5] It also requires more attention to the psychological aspects of work—one of the key principles of the Deming philosophy.

The focus on customer satisfaction and flexibility to meet ever-changing customer demands brings new approaches to work design and employee development. In this chapter, we address human resource management within a total quality environment, focusing on the design and management of high-performance work systems.

THE SCOPE OF HUMAN RESOURCE MANAGEMENT

Human resource management (HRM) consists of those activities designed to provide for and coordinate the people of an organization.[6] These activities include determining the organization's human resource needs; assisting in the design of work systems; recruiting, selecting, training and developing, counseling, motivating, and rewarding employees; acting as a liaison with unions and government organizations; and handling other matters of employee well-being. HRM evolved from research at the Hawthorne Works of the Western Electric Company in the late 1920s. Interestingly, both Deming and Juran were working for Western Electric at the time, which may have influenced their views on quality and the workforce. Many other individuals contributed to understanding motivation, employee development, and effective job design.

HRM is a modern term for what has been traditionally referred to as *personnel administration* or *personnel management*. In their traditional role, personnel managers in a business organization interviewed job applicants, negotiated contracts with the union, kept time cards on hourly workers, and occasionally taught a training course.

> *The objectives of an effective HRM system are to build a high-performance workplace and maintain an environment for quality excellence to enable employees and the organization to achieve strategic objectives and adapt to change.*

Today their role has changed dramatically. Human resource managers may still perform the traditional tasks of personnel managers, but the scope and importance of their area of responsibility expanded significantly. Instead of being corporate watchdogs, human resource managers now take on a strategic leadership role in their organizations. They must view human resource requirements in an integrated way, that is, aligned with the organization's strategic directions, and at the same time, oversee day-to-day operations and maintenance of the HRM system. For example, the importance of human resources at a company such as BI is reflected in the fact that a senior vice president within the Office of the President leads HR.

Just as all managers are responsible for quality even though their organizations may have quality professionals, all managers have a responsibility for human resources, even if the formal organizational structure has HRM professionals. Developing skills through training and coaching, promoting teamwork and participation, motivating and recognizing employees, and providing meaningful communication are important human resource skills that all managers must do for total quality to succeed. At Xerox, for instance, managers are directly accountable for the development and implementation of human resource plans that support the quality goals of the company. Thus, understanding HRM practices is necessary for a total quality environment and a critical task for all managers.

Leading companies have revolutionized all (or nearly all) of their major human resource policies and procedures.[7] Table 6.1 contrasts traditional HRM policies with those supporting a total quality perspective. In traditional organizations, HRM units identify, prepare, direct, and reward employees for following rather narrow objectives. In TQ organizations, HRM units develop policies and procedures to ensure that employees can perform multiple roles, improvise when necessary, and direct themselves toward continuous improvement of both product quality and customer service. Many companies use the new HRM paradigm to develop a more cooperative, productive, flexible, and innovative work environment that recognizes the value of the human resource in meeting customer needs and achieving strategic business objectives.

Leading Practices

TQ-based HRM practices work to accomplish the following tasks:

1. Communicate the importance of each employee's contribution to total quality.
2. Stress quality-related synergies available through teamwork.
3. Empower employees to "make a difference."
4. Reinforce individual and team commitment to quality with a wide range of rewards and reinforcements.[8]

These goals are realized by leading companies through the following practices:

- *They promote teamwork and skill sharing across work units and locations.* Teams encourage free-flowing participation and interaction among its members. FedEx has more than 4,000 Quality Action teams; Boeing Airlift and Tanker Division has more than 100 integrated product teams (IPTs) that are typically made up of engineering, work-team, customer, and supplier representatives. Granite Rock, with fewer than 400 employees, has about 100 functioning teams, ranging from 10 corporate quality teams to project teams, purchasing teams, task forces, and function teams composed of people who do the same job at different locations. Special efforts keep the teams relevant and make sure that no teams exist just for the sake of having them. Texas Nameplate Company builds its leadership system upon a team framework that includes a senior leadership team (Business Excellence Leadership Team), a Daily Operations & Innovation Team, teams within each production and support service department for daily work activities, corrective action teams, and various other teams such as the Recognition Committee. SSM Health Care runs an annual Showcase for Sharing and a Sharing Conference, a Nursing Summit and Clinical Summit, and Clinical Collaborative Learning Sessions to share skills and best practices for its employees, physicians, and nurses.
- *They organize and manage work and jobs to promote cooperation, initiative, empowerment, innovation, and the culture of the organization, capitalizing on the diverse ideas and thinking of employees.* Sunny Fresh Foods, highlighted in this chapter's *Quality Profiles*, designs its work systems to emphasize safety, quality, compensation and recognition, and employee development in support of individual

Table 6.1 Traditional versus Total Quality Human Resource Paradigms

Corporate Context Dimension	Traditional Paradigm	Total Quality Paradigm
Corporate Culture	Individualism Differentiation Autocratic leadership Profits Productivity	Collective efforts Cross-functional work Coaching/enabling Customer satisfaction Quality

Human Resource Characteristics	Traditional Paradigm	Total Quality Paradigm
Communications	Top-down	Top-down Horizontal, lateral Multidirectional
Voice and involvement	Employment-at-will Suggestion systems	Due process Quality circles Attitude surveys
Job design	Efficiency Productivity Standard procedures Narrow span of control Specific job descriptions	Quality Customization Innovation Wide span of control Autonomous work teams Empowerment
Training	Job-related skills Functional, technical Productivity	Broad range of skills Cross-functional Diagnostic, problem solving Productive and quality
Performance measurement and evaluation	Individual goals Supervisory review Emphasize financial performance	Team goals Customer, peer, and supervisory review Emphasize quality and service
Rewards	Competition for individual merit increases and benefits	Team/group-based rewards Financial rewards, financial and nonfinancial recognition
Health and safety	Treat problems	Prevent problems Safety programs Wellness programs Employee assistance
Selection/promotion career development	Selected by manager Narrow job skills Promotion based on individual accomplishment Linear career path	Selected by peers Problem-solving skills Promotion based on group facilitation Horizontal career path

Source: Blackburn and Rosen, "Total Quality and Human Resources Management: Lessons Learned from Baldrige Award-Winning Companies," *The Academy of Management Executive* 7, no. 3 (1993), 49–66.

development and SFF's long-term goals. Many of its work systems are unique to the industry. Examples are a "ramp-in" schedule in which new employees are allowed to work for only a specified number of hours to learn their jobs and minimize the potential for repetitive stress injuries; and a rotation system by which employees rotate to another workstation every 20 minutes. This format ensures that workers can understand and respond to product quality issues at any stage of the process and understand their internal customers; it also fights boredom, reduces repetitive stress injuries, and promotes learning. In addition, SFF uses a "buddy" system in which new employees are matched with high-performing experienced employees who serve as role models for operational excellence and behavioral competencies. Merrill Lynch Credit Corporation uses a wide variety of approaches to promote learning and flexibility. Partners are cross-trained and may "float" to other jobs to address areas of increased volume; MLCC's approach to data analysis and problem solving requires lessons learned and countermeasures to be shared with all other areas; and best practices workshops are used to share approaches and techniques used by the best performers for critical process steps.

Innovation is frequently promoted through suggestion systems. Cadillac commits to answering all suggestions within 24 hours; 70 percent of the suggestions received involve quality issues. (Cadillac jumped to second place behind Lexus in the 2003 J.D. Power and Associates Initial Quality Survey.) Milliken either implements or rejects every suggestion within three days. Although no specific rewards are offered, employees still submit suggestions, and the company implements a high percentage of the suggestions that are submitted.

- *They empower individuals and teams to make decisions that affect quality and customer satisfaction.* Many companies talk about empowerment, but few truly practice it. At AT&T, design engineers have the authority to stop a design, and line operators can stop the production line if they detect a quality problem. At The Ritz-Carlton Hotels, each employee can "move heaven and earth" and spend up to $2,000 to satisfy a customer. To foster innovation at Trident Precision Manufacturing, employees "own" specific processes and are given the responsibility for identifying problems and opportunities for improvement. In addition, they have the authority to modify their processes using the company's documented process improvement procedure. Because of the high level of empowerment given to individuals and teams at Texas Nameplate, the company disbanded its quality control department, assigning its activities to various people who do the work.

- *They develop effective performance management systems, compensation, and reward and recognition approaches to support high performance work and a customer focus, and to motivate employees.* At Sunny Fresh Foods, the performance management process (PMP) is an ongoing process of setting expectations, coaching, and reviewing performance. Inputs include key results areas, behavioral competencies, and skill development. BI's process involves associates setting annual goals and objectives that link to division and department objectives, developing action plans, and measuring their performance. The process includes internal customer feedback from peers, a self-evaluation, and director feedback. At FedEx, performance management involves upward, downward, and peer feedback and focuses on goals rather than numbers. At STMicroelectronics, peer evaluations account for 40 percent of team members' performance; the remainder is based on attendance and team leader review. Annual development plans are included in each employee's performance review and their teams review progress and performance quarterly. STMicrolectronic's compensation system supports its job design by rewarding employees through pay increases and promotions as skills are developed and demonstrated. A variable pay program encourages individual, team, unit, and company goal achievement for all employees.

Leading companies also recognize and reward employee contributions beyond monetary compensation. Solectron has employee and team recognition processes at each site, including family-oriented Employee Appreciation Days. In one year, Trident Precision Manufacturing recognized or rewarded employees more than 1,200 times. Figure 6.1 shows the wide scope of recognition approaches used by Merrill Lynch Credit Corporation.

- *They have effective processes for hiring and career progression.* Paying attention to hiring profiles and succession planning is necessitated by the challenges of today's labor markets and the requirements of high-performance work. For example, Branch-Smith Printing specifies the set of skills required to perform a job. Candidates are screened with a set of questions designed to assess their skills to perform the job functions as defined in the job descriptions. They use behavior-based questions to assess whether candidates have the characteristics to excel in their team-based, quality-focused environment. Two additional assessments are given to candidates who meet the first criteria. One is a preemployment screening tool for assessing the attitudes of job candidates regarding integrity, responsibility, and work ethic. The second uses advanced technology

Figure 6.1 Recognition Approaches at Merrill Lynch Credit Corporation

Types of Recognition	Partner Category			
President's Award			3	4
Special Recognition Award			3	4
Partner Suggestion Program	1	2	3	4
Partner-of-the-Month Program			3	4
Honor Roll Program		2		
Partner-to-Partner Notes	1	2	3	4
Service Recognition Award	1	2	3	4
VICP/EIP Bonus Pool	1	2	3	4
ML&Co/MLCC Gifts	1	2	3	4
Perfect Attendance			3	4
Partner Appreciation Week	1	2	3	4
Partner Birthday Gifts	1	2	3	4
Summer/Holiday Parties	1	2	3	4

Legend: 1 = Senior management   2 = Management
3 = Supervisor   4 = All other partners

to predict job suitability and matches people with the job for which they are applying. At Pal's Sudden Service, employees advance on a planned basis to fill process team roles as they learn more job skills and operational positions. The most capable team members are selected to back up assistant managers and are put on a path for advancement to assistant manager, and possibly to owner/operator succession.

- *They make extensive investments in training and education.* These investments include ensuring that training addresses key organizational needs and contributes to the organizational mission and vision, is delivered effectively, evaluated, and reinforced on the job. At Wainwright Industries, associates are fully engaged in quality training efforts beginning with their first day on the job. During new associate orientation, senior managers explain the importance of quality and customer satisfaction and outline the company's approaches to continuous improvement. Follow-up sessions are held 24 and 72 days after the start of employment. The company invests up to 7 percent of its payroll in training and education. All associates take courses on quality values, communication techniques, problem solving, statistical process control, and synchronous manufacturing. With almost 13 percent of its workforce being minorities, Sunny Fresh Foods has translated training materials into Spanish and uses interpreters to facilitate understanding, and offers English as a Second Language classes during work hours. At Dana Commercial Credit, training and education needs and effectiveness are reviewed monthly, focusing on skill enhancement of those people, including senior managers, who have direct contact with customers. AT&T uses a systematic methodology called the Instructional Technology Approach to assess, analyze, and develop curricula to identify and address skill and development gaps.

- *They motivate employees to develop and use their full potential.* Organizations use a variety of means to motivate employees. For example, managers and supervisors at Motorola's Commercial, Government, and Industrial Solutions Sector engage employees in quarterly personal commitment dialogue sessions. To help achieve both personal and professional goals, Motorola offers tuition reimbursement, continuing education, promotion-from-within, and the Motorola incentive plan. Cross-functional "Communities of Practice" focus on critical business issues fostering individual learning and development. Competency assessments and career development dialogues enable managers and their employees to create ongoing developmental plans. Managers and supervisors use formal and informal coaching sessions to instill individual responsibility and ownership for personal development. BRAVO! (Motorola's spot recognition program) concentrates on rewarding behaviors and subsequent business results. Patent Awards recognize technical innovation, and annual merit increases, promotions, and stock options are also awarded.

- *They maintain a work environment conducive to the well-being and growth of all employees.* Satisfied employees are productive employees. Leading-edge firms include well-being factors such as health, safety, and ergonomics in their improvement activities. Ames Rubber Corporation, for example, has nine major long-range plans in effect, covering such areas as affirmative action, health benefits and safety, and accident reduction. FedEx teaches employees how to handle dangerous goods, lift heavy packages correctly, and drive safely. Leading companies also perform audits to identify risks and prevent accidents, focusing on root cause analysis. Texas Instruments, for example, uses safety, environmental, and ergonomic experts to institute preventive actions, investigate accidents, and provide training. At The Ritz-Carlton, project teams configure the best combination of technology and procedures to eliminate causes of safety and security problems.

Employee satisfaction is enhanced by such special services as counseling, recreational or cultural activities, non-work-related education, daycare, flexible working hours, and outplacement activities. Texas Instruments, for example, has a company-sponsored employee association called "Texins" that provides fitness activities, recreational clubs, and family events; the company also offers free counseling for personal and relationship problems. Granite Rock sponsors company picnics and parties at regular intervals. Solectron provides American culture and citizenship classes, wellness committees to communicate health information programs, employee assistance programs, sports and recreation programs, and tuition reimbursement.

- *They monitor the extent and effectiveness of human resource practices and measure employee satisfaction as a means of continuous improvement.* Employee surveys and measurement of key HRM indicators monitor employee satisfaction and identify problem areas. These surveys frequently ask employees to rate their supervisors on leadership, communication, and support. For instance, Merrill Lynch Credit Corporation surveys a subset of employees quarterly on 15 drivers of partner satisfaction. AT&T conducts an opinion survey every two years to measure employee attitudes and the effect of improvement efforts. Management compares the results within AT&T and with benchmarks of other high-performance companies. GTE Directories chartered a team to determine how the company should measure quality improvement team effectiveness. The team discovered that inconsistent evaluation guidelines made it difficult to manage the process, so they developed specific and measurable guidelines emphasizing customer satisfaction, measurable results, cross-functional involvement, and initiative. Sunny Fresh Foods identifies its key factors for employee well-being from performance reviews, exit interviews, and individual discussions. Results are segmented and analyzed by plant and employee group, which allows management at each plant to tailor initiatives for their employees.

Indicators such as the number of teams, rate of growth, percentage of employees involved, number of suggestions implemented, time taken to respond to suggestions, team activities, absenteeism, turnover rates, and grievances provide a basis for evaluation and improvement. Texas Instruments has a training council that uses a computerized system to monitor individualized training plans. This process, along with employee surveys, customer surveys, suggestions, and so on, helps to identify needs.

TEAMS IN ORGANIZATIONAL DESIGN AND QUALITY IMPROVEMENT

Traditionally, HRM has focused on individuals. This mind-set is built into the management system by such practices as management by objectives, individual performance evaluation, professional status and privileges, and individual promotion. Focusing on individuals contributes to rivalries, competition, favoritism, and self-centeredness, which collectively work against accomplishing the true mission of an organization: serving customers. Alfie Kohn, who studied issues of cooperation and competition among employees over five years, concluded that the ideal amount of competition in any company is *none at all.* Any informal competition that may develop is best discouraged; management should go out of the way to design cooperative work groups and incentive systems.[9] Research shows that the effectiveness of supervisors and subordinates alike is positively related to cooperation and negatively related to competitiveness. Even at the organizational level, cooperation between such departments as design and manufacturing, doctors and hospital administrators, and business managers and orchestra conductors is not the norm. A single person rarely has enough knowledge or experience to understand all aspects of the most important work processes; thus, team approaches are essential for process improvement.

*A **team** is a small number of people with complementary skills who are committed to a common purpose, set of performance goals, and an approach for which they hold themselves mutually accountable.*[10]

Teams, and the need for such team skills as cooperation, communication, skill diversity, and group decision making, represents a fundamental shift in how the work is performed in the United States and most countries in the Western world. Although organizations traditionally were formed around task or work goups, the focus of teams and teamwork has taken on a new meaning in a TQ environment. Teamwork breaks down barriers among individuals, departments, and line and staff functions, an action prescribed by one of Deming's 14 Points. Teams provide opportunities to individuals to solve problems that they may not be able to solve on their own. Employees who participate in team activities feel more empowered, are more satisfied with the rate of improvement in quality in their companies, and receive better training in both job-related and problem-solving skills.

Teams may perform a variety of problem-solving activities, such as determining customer needs, developing a flowchart to study a process, brainstorming to discover opportunities for improvement, selecting projects, recommending corrective actions, and tracking the effectiveness of solutions. Teams may also assume many traditional managerial functions. For example, an assembly team at GM's Saturn plant interviews and hires its own workers, approves parts from suppliers, chooses its equipment, and handles its own budget.

Many types of teams exist in different companies and industries. Among the most common are the following:

- *Management teams:* Teams consisting mainly of managers from various functions, such as sales and production that coordinate work among teams
- *Natural work teams:* Teams organized to perform entire jobs, rather than specialized, assembly line-type work
- *Self-managed teams (SMTs)*: Specially empowered work teams defined as "a highly trained group of employees, from 6 to 18, on average, fully responsible for turning out a well-defined segment of finished work—also known as **self-directed work teams**. The segment could be a final product, like a refrigerator or ball bearing; or a service, like a fully processed insurance claim. It could also be a complete but intermediate product or service, like a finished refrigerator motor, an aircraft fuselage, or the circuit plans for a television set."[11] More information on the evolution and activities of SMTs can be found in the Bonus Materials folder on the CD-ROM for this chapter.
- *Virtual teams:* A relatively new format in which team members communicate by computer, take turns as leaders, and jump in and out as necessary[12]
- *Quality circles:* Teams of workers and supervisors that meet regularly to address work-related problems involving quality and productivity[13]
- *Problem-solving teams:* Teams whose members gather to solve a specific problem and then disband (The difference between quality circles is that quality circles usually remain in existence for a much longer period of time.)

Bonus Materials

- *Project teams:* Teams with a specific mission to develop something new or to accomplish a complex task (Project teams have been in use since World War II, and probably before that. However, project teams recently gained a new measure of importance and respect in the context of Six Sigma.)

Management teams, natural work teams, self-managed teams, and virtual teams typically work on routine business activities—managing an organization, building a product, or designing an electronic system—and are an integral part of how work is organized and designed. Quality circles, problem-solving teams, and project teams, on the other hand, work more on an ad-hoc basis to address specific tasks or issues, often relating to quality improvement. Also, natural work teams, self-managed teams, and quality circles typically are *intraorganizational*; that is, members usually come from the same department or function. Management teams, problem-solving teams, virtual teams, and project teams, are usually *cross-functional*; they work on specific tasks or processes that cut across boundaries of several different departments regardless of their organizational home.

An example of the cross-functional nature of teams is the platform team approach to automotive vehicle development introduced by Chrysler.[14] This cross-functional team approach brings together professionals from engineering, design, quality, manufacturing, business planning, program management, purchasing, sales, marketing, and finance to work together to get a new vehicle to market. This idea, brought to Chrysler by its merger with smaller, more innovative AMC/Jeep was not accepted at Chrysler without significant upheaval and struggles. "You talk about internal strife," recalls one Chrysler loyalist, "This was war!"[15] Nevertheless, the concept was just what was needed to pull the company from bankruptcy and near collapse. The Dodge Viper, introduced in 1992, and the 1993 Jeep Grand Cherokee tested this approach, which led to the development of the Chrysler Concorde, Dodge Intrepid, and Eagle Vision in just 39 months, not only on time and under budget, but exceeding 230 product excellence targets. Today, all automobile manufacturers develop products using similar cross-functional team approaches.

Quality circles were one of the first types of teams to focus specifically on quality. The concept was developed by Kaoru Ishikawa of the University of Tokyo, and quality circles exploded in Japan. The Union of Japanese Scientists and Engineers (JUSE) estimated that registration in quality circles grew from 400 members in 1962 to 200,000 members in 1968 to more than 700,000 members in 1978. Today, millions of workers are involved. Toyota, for example, uses the problem-solving skills of circles and engineers to their advantage. When the firm found that 50 percent of its warranty losses were caused by 120 large problems and 4,000 small problems, the set of large problems were assigned to their engineers. The set of small problems were given to their quality circles.[16]

Quality circle concepts were not only known but also used by some U.S. firms in the late 1960s, according to existing evidence.[17] However, the concept received widespread publicity when a team of managers for Lockheed Missiles and Space Division in California made a trip to Japan in 1973 to view quality circles in action, and subsequently established them at Lockheed. After the success of the Lockheed program became known, many other manufacturing firms—including Westinghouse, General Electric, Cincinnati Milacron, Ford Motor Company, Dover Corporation, and Coors Brewing Company—established quality circle programs or began using similar team problem-solving approaches. Later, service organizations such as hospitals, school systems, and state and federal governmental units started quality circle programs.[18] After about five or six years of use in the United States, however, quality circles were labeled a "fad." Much of the feeling of disappointment in their promise resulted from management's failure to understand how to implement and manage them successfully. Still, they represented a starting point for many U.S. companies to develop and

The three basic functions of quality circles and problem-solving teams are to identify, analyze, and solve quality and productivity problems.

test out ideas on teamwork and participative management, and many are still active today. More importantly, they paved the way for more progressive kinds of teams.

Figure 6.2 illustrates the process by which these types of teams commonly operate. The methodology is a process of creative problem

solving as discussed in Chapter 13. Problem-solving tools are taught to members by team leaders with the assistance of a facilitator, who is a full-time or part-time resource person. To illustrate how this process works, consider an information systems (IS) team for a manufacturing company that faced a serious problem with internal customer satisfaction about its response to requests for application changes and help with using new software.[19] The team asked several internal customers to attend a meeting where the group brainstormed about what the problem was. They agreed on the statement "Our response time to fix people's PCs is 24 hours, and the customer needs a response of 8 hours or less." The team decided to collect data on cycle time and responsiveness to understand why delays were occurring. As they shared this information, they realized they had not known many of the facts. After analyzing the data, they decided to try a solution that assigned each person on the IS

Figure 6.2 Problem-Solving Functions of Teams

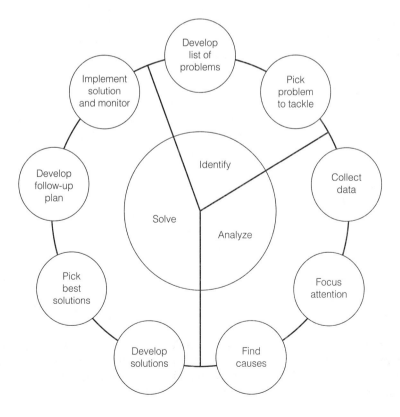

team as an account manager for each department. Their responsibility was to coordinate and communicate with accounts to monitor response time and customer satisfaction. If response time was not within the goal, the account manager was responsible for working with the IS team and department to handle the situation. As a means of control, they prompted the organization every two months for feedback about the solution and the process.

Building Effective Teams

Jumping into team approaches without adequate planning is an invitation to disaster. Robbins and Finley list 14 reasons why teams fail, although they are quick to point out that no one reason, and often multiple reasons, explain why it happens.[20] Their list includes organizational problems (bad policies, stupid procedures, bleary vision, ill-conceived reward system, confused goals, unresolved roles, antiteam culture), leadership problems (bad leadership, insufficient feedback and information, the wrong tools), and individual/team barriers (mismatched needs, hidden agendas, personality conflicts, lack of team trust, unwillingness to change). Thus, managers need to carefully evaluate how teams are introduced in their organizations and address team building as a critical work process.

Team implementation should always begin with a period of investigation, reflection, and soul searching. Many companies rush out and form the wrong kind of teams for a specific job. For example, quality circle-type teams cannot achieve the same type of results as a cross-functional problem-solving team or a self-managed team. Managers should examine their organization's goals, objectives, and culture to evaluate its readiness to develop and support team-based initiatives. This step may be the most difficult portion of the process, because it demands a hard self-appraisal of the organization as a whole. One enthusiastic manager can often get teams going, but solid support at a number of managerial levels is necessary to keep them going. Managers should then analyze the work required. Teams take a lot of maintenance, and if the work can be done faster and better by a single person, a team should not be used.

Self-managed teams (SMTs) represent the greatest challenge. Organizations that use SMTs typically arrive at them through one of two routes: organizational start-up with SMTs in place, or transformations from more limited team structures. The second is often a next logical step after other types of employee involvement programs reach maturity. Figure 6.3 shows the approach used by Boeing Airlift and Tanker Programs to develop self-managed teams, a result of a historic agreement between the company and union to support employee participation and empowerment.

Any organizational change, especially one as significant as initiating teams, is often met with resistance. Keys to overcoming resistance are early involvement by all parties, open and honest dialogue, and good planning. Management holds the key, however. As the organizational leaders, they must believe in workers and their ability to contribute. As leaders, managers must also show commitment and support by providing the right training, rewards, and recognition.

Teams go through a fairly predictable cycle of formation and growth, regardless of their charge and goals. Teams are generally formed in organizational settings by direction from a manager, leader, or governing body. They are typically given a broad objective (operate this process according to certain guidelines, put a man on the moon in this decade, design a process to make cookies using elves as workers, etc.). The team may also be given a time frame and resource limits, if it is a project team.

The key stages of a team's life cycle are called forming, storming, norming, performing, and adjourning.[21]

Figure 6.3 Boeing A&T Team Development Process

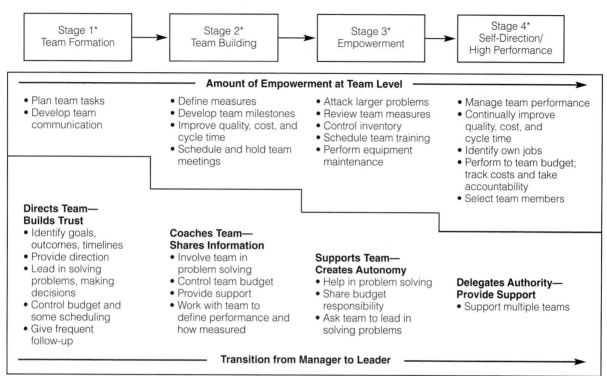

* Stages may overlap under certain conditions. Team maturity and level of process improvement already in place may impact stage application.

Source: Courtesy of Boeing Airlift and Tanker Programs.

Forming takes place when the team is introduced, meets together, and explores issues of their new assignment. *Storming* occurs when team members disagree on team roles and challenge the way that the team will function. The third stage, *norming*, takes place when the issues of the previous stage have been worked out, and team members agree on roles, ground rules, and acceptable behavior when doing the work of the team. Stage four, *performing*, characterizes the productive phase of the life cycle when team members cooperate to solve problems and complete the goals of their assigned work. In the *adjourning* phase, the team wraps up the project, satisfactorily completes its goals, and prepares to disband or move on to another project.

Peter Scholtes, a leading authority on teams for quality improvement, suggested 10 ingredients for a successful team. These items provide some guidance during the forming stage and can mitigate issues that might lead to "storming":

1. *Clarity in team goals.* As a sound basis, a team agrees on a mission, purpose, and goals.
2. *An improvement plan.* A plan guides the team in determining schedules and mileposts by helping the team decide what advice, assistance, training, materials, and other resources it may need.

3. *Clearly defined roles.* All members must understand their duties and know who is responsible for what issues and tasks.
4. *Clear communication.* Team members should speak with clarity, listen actively, and share information.
5. *Beneficial team behaviors.* Teams should encourage members to use effective skills and practices to facilitate discussions and meetings.
6. *Well-defined decision procedures.* Teams should use data as the basis for decisions and learn to reach consensus on important issues.
7. *Balanced participation.* Everyone should participate, contribute their talents, and share commitment to the team's success.
8. *Established ground rules.* The group outlines acceptable and unacceptable behaviors.
9. *Awareness of group process.* Team members exhibit sensitivity to nonverbal communication, understand group dynamics, and work on group process issues.
10. *Use of the scientific approach.* With structured problem-solving processes, teams can more easily find root causes of problems.[22]

Teams require various leadership and maintenance activities, especially if the team is large and the project or work assignment is complex. Typical roles that members must assume are the champion, sponsor, team leader, facilitator, timekeeper, scribe, and team member, as shown in Table 6.2 on page 268.

Six Sigma Project Teams

Project teams are fundamental to Six Sigma. Six Sigma projects require a diversity of skills that range from technical analysis, creative solution development, and implementation. Thus, Six Sigma teams not only address immediate problems, but also provide an environment for individual learning, management development, and career advancement. Six Sigma teams are comprised of several types of individuals:

- *Champions:* Senior-level managers who promote and lead the deployment of Six Sigma in a significant area of the business. Champions understand the philosophy and tools of Six Sigma, select projects, set objectives, allocate resources, and mentor teams. Champions own Six Sigma projects and are responsible for their completion and results; typically they also own the process that the project is focused on improving. They select teams, set strategic direction, create measurable objectives, provide resources, monitor performance, make key implementation decisions, and report results to top management. More importantly, champions work toward removing barriers—organizational, financial, personal—that might inhibit the successful implementation of a Six Sigma project.
- *Master Black Belts:* Full-time Six Sigma experts who are responsible for Six Sigma strategy, training, mentoring, deployment, and results. Master Black Belts are highly trained in how to use Six Sigma tools and methods and provide advanced technical expertise. They work across the organization to develop and coach teams, conduct training, and lead change, but are typically not members of Six Sigma project teams.
- *Black Belts:* Fully-trained Six Sigma experts with up to 160 hours of training who perform much of the technical analyses required of Six Sigma projects, usually on a full-time basis. They have advanced knowledge of tools and DMAIC methods, and can apply them either individually or as team leaders. They also mentor and develop Green Belts. Black Belts need good leadership and communication skills in addition to technical skills and process knowledge. They

should be highly motivated, eager to gain new knowledge, and well-respected among their peers. As such, Black Belts are often targeted by the organization as future business leaders.

- *Green Belts:* Functional employees who are trained in introductory Six Sigma tools and methodology and work on projects on a part-time basis, assisting Black Belts while developing their own knowledge and expertise. Typically, one of the requirements for receiving a Green Belt designation is to successfully complete a Six Sigma project. Successful Green Belts are often promoted to Black Belts.
- *Team Members:* Individuals from various functional areas who support specific projects.

The roles of the Six Sigma champion and the Master Black Belt leader are similar to those of the champion and sponsor described in Table 6.2. The role of a Black Belt is similar to a staff quality expert, while Green Belts are typically given the team leadership role.

Cooper and Noonan have begun compiling a national database on Six Sigma and teams.[23] Preliminary information from this database indicated that the most important lesson learned by the teams that were surveyed was "determine who the stakeholders are for the project and ask them for their input on how to improve the process." Other aspects considered important for team success included management support and participation, communication during projects about Six Sigma as well as project progress, alignment of team members with organizational vision, mission and values, and definition and use of sound metrics.

DESIGNING HIGH-PERFORMANCE WORK SYSTEMS

Performance simply means the extent to which an individual contributes to achieving the goals and objectives of an organization. *High-performance work* is characterized by flexibility, innovation, knowledge and skill sharing, alignment with organizational directions, customer focus, and rapid response to changing business needs and marketplace requirements. Teams often provide the infrastructure for high-performance work systems. As we noted in Chapter 1, organizations may be viewed at three levels: the individual level, the process level, and the organizational level. The design of high-performance work systems can be addressed using this framework. At the individual level, work systems should enable effective accomplishment of work activities and promote flexibility and individual initiative in managing and improving work processes. Natural work teams, quality circles, and self-managed teams can provide an ideal approach for achieving these objectives by involving, empowering, and training employees. At the process level, cooperation, cross-functional teamwork, and communication are key ingredients. Project teams and problem-solving teams can support these efforts. At the organizational level, compensation and recognition, and attention to employee well-being through health, safety, and support services are major factors for outstanding performance. Management teams can provide the necessary direction and support.

High-performance work *refers to work approaches used to systematically pursue ever-higher levels of overall organizational and human performance.*

In designing work systems, managers must make choices in five traditional areas of human resources: planning, staffing, appraising, compensating, and training and development. The dimensions of each of these five areas can be viewed on a continuum from a structured environment with rigid practices to an unstructured envi-

Table 6.2 Team Member Roles, Responsibilities, and Performance Attributes

Role Name	Responsibility	Definition	Attributes of Good Role Performance
Champion	Advocate	The person initiating a concept or idea for change/improvement	• Is dedicated to seeing it implemented • Holds absolute belief it is the right thing to do • Has perseverance and stamina
Sponsor	Backer; risk taker	The person who supports a team's plans, activities, and outcomes	• Believes in the concept/idea • Has sound business acumen • Is willing to take risk and responsibility for outcomes • Has authority to approve needed resources • Will be listened to by upper management
Team leader	Change agent; chair; head	A person who: • Staffs the team or provides input for staffing requirements • Strives to bring about change/improvement through the team's outcomes • Is trusted by followers to lead them • Has the authority for, and directs the efforts of, the team • Participates as a team member • Coaches team members in developing or enhancing necessary competencies • Communicates with management about the team's progress and needs • Handles the logistics of team meetings • Takes responsibility for team records	• Is committed to the team's mission and objectives • Has experience in planning, organizing, staffing, controlling, and directing • Is capable of making and maintaining channels that enable members to do their work • Is capable of gaining the respect of team members; serves as a role model • Is firm, fair, and factual in dealing with a team of diverse individuals • Facilitates discussion without dominating • Actively listens • Empowers team members to the extent possible within the organization's culture • Supports all team members equally • Respects each team member's individuality
Facilitator	Helper; trainer; adviser; coach	A person who: • Observes the team's processes and team members' interactions and suggests process changes to facilitate positive movement toward the team's goals and objectives • Intervenes if discussion develops into multiple conversations • Intervenes to skillfully prevent an individual from dominating the discussion or to engage an overlooked individual in the discussion the team as a whole	• Is trained in facilitating skills • Is respected by team members • Is tactful • Knows when and when not to intervene • Deals with the team's process, not content • Respects the team leader and does not override his or her responsibility • Respects confidential information shared by individuals or within the team • Will not accept facilitator role if expected to report to management information that is proprietary to the team

Table 6.2 *(continued)*

Role Name	Responsibility	Definition	Attributes of Good Role Performance
Facilitator		• Assists the team leader in bringing discussions to a close • May provide training in team building, conflict management, and so forth	• Will abide by the ASQ Code of Ethics
Timekeeper	Gatekeeper; monitor	A person designated by the team to watch the use of allocated time and remind the team members when their time objective may be in jeopardy	• Is capable of assisting the team leader in keeping the team meeting within the predetermined time limitations • Is sufficiently assertive to intervene in discussions when the time allocation is in jeopardy • Is capable of participating as a member while still serving as a timekeeper
Scribe	Recorder; note taker	A person designated by the team to record critical data from team meetings (Formal "minutes" of the meetings may be published and distributed to interested parties.)	• Is capable of capturing on paper, or electronically, the main points and decisions made in a team meeting and providing a complete, accurate, and legible document (or formal minutes) for the team's records • Is sufficiently assertive to intervene in discussions to clarify a point or decision in order to record it accurately • Is capable of participating as a member while still serving as a scribe
Team members	Participants: subject matter experts	The persons selected to work together to bring about a change/improvement, achieving this goal in a seated environment of mutual respect, sharing of expertise, cooperation, and support	• Are willing to commit to the purpose of the team • Are able to express ideas, opinions, and suggestions in a nonthreatening manner • Are capable of listening attentively to other team members • Are receptive to new ideas and suggestions • Are even-tempered and able to handle stress and cope with problems openly • Are competent in one or more fields of expertise needed by the team • Have favorable performance records • Are willing to function as team members and forfeit "star" status

Source: Bauer, John E. Grace L. Duffy, and Russell T. Westcott (eds.), *The Quality Improvement Handbook* (Milwaukee, WI: ASQ Quality Press, 2002), 43–44. © 2002 American Society for Quality. Reprinted with permission.

ronment with flexible practices, as shown in Table 6.3. Conventional HRM practices generally fall on the left side of each continuum. HRM choices that support a TQ environment are listed on the right-hand side of the table. Day-to-day management activities, which include how employees are selected and developed, how they are

---

Table 6.3 Choices in Designing Work Systems

Planning Choices

Informal	. . . .	Formal
Short term	. . . .	Long term
Explicit job analysis	. . . .	Implicit job analysis
Job simplification	. . . .	Job enrichment
Low employee involvement	. . . .	High employee involvement

Staffing Choices

Internal sources	. . . .	External sources
Narrow paths	. . . .	Broad paths
Single ladder	. . . .	Multiple ladders
Explicit criteria	. . . .	Implicit criteria
Limited socialization	. . . .	Extensive socialization
Closed procedures	. . . .	Open procedures

Appraising Choices

Behavioral criteria	. . . .	Results criteria
Purposes: Development, Remedial, Maintenance		
Low employee participation	. . . .	High employee participation
Short-term criteria	. . . .	Long-term criteria
Individual criteria	. . . .	Group criteria

Compensating Choices

Low base salaries	. . . .	High base salaries
Internal equity	. . . .	External equity
Few perks	. . . .	Many perks
Standard, fixed package	. . . .	Flexible package
Low participation	. . . .	High participation
No incentives	. . . .	Many incentives
Short-term incentives	. . . .	Long-term incentives
No employment security	. . . .	High employment security
Hierarchical	. . . .	High participation

Training and Development Choices

Short term	. . . .	Long term
Narrow application	. . . .	Broad application
Productivity emphasis	. . . .	Quality-of-work-life emphasis
Spontaneous, unplanned	. . . .	Planned, systematic
Individual orientation	. . . .	Group orientation
Low participation	. . . .	High participation

Source: Adapted from R. S. Schuler, "Human Resource Management Practice Choices," in *Readings in Personnel and Human Resource Management*, 3d ed., R. S. Schuler, S. A. Youngblood, and V. L. Huber, eds. (St. Paul, MN: West Publishing Company, 1988).

motivated at work, and how their performance is evaluated, can have a major impact on the success or failure of total quality efforts in an organization. In this section we address the most important elements in designing high-performance work systems that support a total quality focus.

Work and Job Design

Work design refers to how employees are organized in formal and informal units, such as departments and teams. **Job design** refers to responsibilities and tasks assigned to individuals. Both work and job design are vital to organizational effectiveness and personal job satisfaction. Unfortunately, managers often do not understand workers' needs. One research study found that the top five employee needs in the workplace are (1) interesting work, (2) recognition, (3) feeling "in" on things, (4) security, and (5) pay. Managers, however, believed pay to be number one. Many companies understand that the best way to influence job satisfaction and motivate

The design of work should provide individuals with both the intrinsic and extrinsic motivation to achieve quality and operational performance objectives.

workers is to make jobs more rewarding, which can entail introducing variety into work (consider the job rotation program at Sunny Fresh Foods in the *Quality Profiles*), emphasizing the importance and significance of the job, providing more autonomy and empowerment, and giving meaningful feedback.

An integrating theory that helps us understand how job design impacts motivation, satisfaction, and organizational effectiveness was proposed by Hackman and Oldham.[24] Their model, which has been validated in numerous organizational settings, is shown in Figure 6.4. The model contains four major segments:

1. Critical psychological states
2. Core job characteristics
3. Moderating variables
4. Outcomes

Three critical psychological states drive the model. *Experienced meaningfulness* is the psychological need of workers to have the feeling that their work is a significant contribution to the organization and society. *Experienced responsibility* indicates the need of workers to be accountable for the quality and quantity of work produced. *Knowledge of results* implies that all workers feel the need to know how their work is evaluated and the results of their evaluation.

Five core job characteristics have been identified as having an impact on the critical psychological states:

1. *Task significance:* The degree to which the job gives the participants the feeling that they have a substantial impact on the organization or the world, for example, solving a customer's problem rather than simply filing papers
2. *Task identity:* The degree to which the worker can perceive the task as a whole, identifiable piece of work from start to finish, for example, building an entire component rather than performing a small repetitive task
3. *Skill variety:* The degree to which the job requires the worker to use a variety of skills and talents, for example, physical skills in machining a part and mental skills in using a computer to track quality measurements
4. *Autonomy:* The degree to which the task permits freedom, independence, and personal control to be exercised over the work, for example, being able to stop a production line to solve a problem

Figure 6.4 Hackman and Oldham Work Design Model

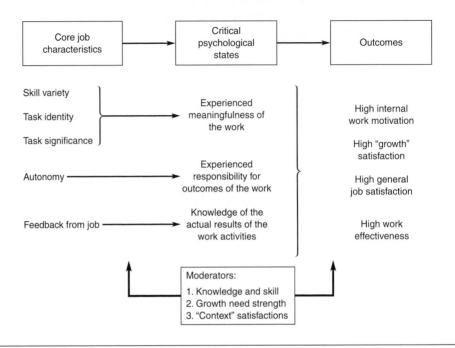

Source: J. Richard Hackman and Greg R. Oldham, *Work Redesign* (figure 4.6 from p. 90). © 1980 by Addison-Wesley Publishing Co., Inc. Reprinted by permission of Addison Wesley Longman.

5. *Feedback from the job:* the degree to which clear, timely information about the effectiveness of performance of the individual is available, not only from supervisors, but also from measurements that the worker might take directly.

Quality is related in a primary or secondary sense to all five of these core job characteristics. Quality of a product or service is undoubtedly increased by a worker's dedicated application of skills, which is enhanced by task identity and a feeling of task significance. More directly, quality of work is enhanced by a job design that incorporates autonomy and feedback relating to quality characteristics. The key outcomes of high general job satisfaction and high work effectiveness can then be seen as results that define and reinforce excellent quality.

As an example illustrating characteristics of the Hackman and Oldham model, consider the case of workers in a small Delaware firm that produces space suits for astronauts. The work requires a great deal of handcrafting, using conventional sewing machinery as well as high technology in testing the suits for proper functioning. Task significance and task identity are evident in the workers' ability to see the job's extreme importance and its fit into the complete unit (a space suit for an individual astronaut). Skill variety and autonomy are somewhat limited because conventional sewing techniques must be used and rigid specifications must be precisely followed. However, other motivating aspects of the job may compensate for the lack of these characteristics. Feedback on results is timely and individualized. Comprehensive testing and inspection of the space suits is performed to assure that no defective units are produced.

Several common approaches to work design—job enlargement, job rotation, and job enrichment—are supported by this model. IBM was apparently the first user of **job enlargement**, in which workers' jobs were expanded to include several tasks rather than one single, low-level task. This approach reduced fragmentation of jobs and generally resulted in lower production costs, greater worker satisfaction, and higher quality, but it required higher wage rates and the purchase of more inspection equipment. **Job rotation** is a technique by which individual workers learn several tasks by rotating from one to another. The purpose of job rotation is to renew interest or motivation of the individual and to increase his or her complement of skills. However, several studies showed that the main benefit was to increase workers' skills but that little, if any, motivational benefit could be expected.[25] Finally, **job enrichment** entails "vertical job loading" in which workers are given more authority, responsibility, and autonomy rather than simply more or different work to do. Garvin presents an interesting example of how Japanese managers in the air-conditioning industry view job enrichment as important to quality.[26] In Japan, newly hired workers are trained so that they can do every job on the line before eventually being assigned to only one job. Training frequently requires 6–12 months, in contrast to the standard training time of one to two days for newly hired production workers in U.S. air-conditioning companies. The advantage of this "enriched" training is that workers are better able to track a defect to its source and can frequently suggest remedies to problems because they understand the entire process from start to finish. Job enrichment has been used successfully in a number of firms, notably AT&T, which experienced better employee attitudes and performance, as well as Texas Instruments, IBM, and General Foods.

Employee Involvement

Tom Peters suggested involving everyone in everything, in such activities as quality and productivity improvement, measuring and monitoring results, budget development, new technology assessment, recruiting and hiring, making customer calls, and participating in customer visits.[27] **Employee involvement (EI)** refers to any activity by which employees participate in work-related decisions and improvement activities, with the objectives of tapping the creative energies of all employees and improving their motivation. Pete Coors, CEO of Coors Brewing, explained it simply, "We're moving from an environment where the supervisor says, 'This is the way it is going to be done and if you don't like it, go someplace else,' to an environment where the supervisor can grow with the changes, get his troops together and say, 'Look, you guys are operating the equipment, what do you think we ought to do?'"[28]

EI approaches can range from simple sharing of information or providing input on work-related issues and making suggestions to self-directed responsibilities such as setting goals, making business decisions, and solving problems, often in cross-functional teams.

The continuum of EI approaches is summarized in Table 6.4. As total quality matures in an organization, higher levels of employee involvement are evident. One of the most prominent employee involvement processes has been GE's "Work-Out" program.[29] Employees are encouraged to get together in a series of meetings to discuss reports, meetings, measurements, and approvals in their work area or department. The meetings are facilitated by an outside leader, but supervisors are forbidden to attend, except for a brief opening appearance, until the last day of a three-day session. At the final Work-Out session, the supervisor, and often, his or her boss, are at the front of the room, with no

Quality Spotlight
General Electric

Table 6.4 Levels of Employee Involvement

Level	Action	Primary Outcome
1. Information sharing	Managers decide, then inform employees	Conformance
2. Dialogue	Managers get employee input, then decide	Acceptance
3. Special problem solving	Managers assign a one-time problem to selected employees	Contribution
4. Intragroup problem solving	Intact groups meet weekly to solve local problems	Commitment
5. Intergroup problem solving	Cross-functional groups meet to solve mutual problems	Cooperation
6. Focused problem solving	Intact groups deepen daily involvement in a specific issue	Concentration
7. Limited self-direction	Teams at selected sites function full time with minimum supervision	Accountability
8. Total self-direction	Executives facilitate self-management in an all-team company	Ownership

Source: Copyright © Jack D. Orsburn, Linda Moran, Ed Musselwhite, and John H. Zenger, *Self-Directed Work Teams* (Burr Ridge, IL: Business One Irwin, 1990), 34. Reproduced with permission of The McGraw-Hill Companies.

idea of what has been discussed during the previous two days. The supervisor can only respond to items that the employees recommend in one of three ways:

1. Agree on the spot to implement the proposal.
2. Say no to the proposal.
3. Ask for more information.

Typically, more than 80 percent of the Work-Out recommendations received an immediate answer. For example, Armand Lauzon, head of plant services at GE Aircraft Engines factory in Lynn, Massachusetts, was confronted with 108 proposals at the end of a Work-Out session by his employees. He said yes to 100 recommendations on the spot, including one in which an employee had sketched a design for protective shields for machines on a brown paper bag. The employee asked whether his group could bid on the work. They got the bid when they quoted a cost of $16,000 versus an outside vendor's proposed cost of $96,000!

EI initiatives are by no means new.[30] Many programs and experiments have been implemented over more than 100 years by industrial engineers, statisticians, and behavioral scientists. Early attempts influenced modern practices considerably. Unfortunately, these approaches lacked the complementary elements of TQ, such as a customer orientation, top management leadership and support, and a common set of tools for problem solving and continuous improvement.

EI is rooted in the psychology of human needs and supported by the motivation models of Maslow, Herzberg, and McGregor. Employees are motivated through exciting work, responsibility, and recognition. EI provides a powerful means of achieving the highest order individual needs of self-realization and fulfillment. Thus, employee involvement should begin with a personal commitment to quality, as we discussed in Chapter 1.

EI offers many advantages over traditional management practices:

- Replaces the adversarial mentality with trust and cooperation
- Develops the skills and leadership capability of individuals, creating a sense of mission and fostering trust
- Increases employee morale and commitment to the organization
- Fosters creativity and innovation, the source of competitive advantage
- Helps people understand quality principles and instills these principles into the corporate culture
- Allows employees to solve problems at the source immediately
- Improves quality and productivity[31]

One of the easiest ways to involve employees on an individual basis is the **suggestion system**. An employee suggestion system is a management tool for the submission, evaluation, and implementation of an employee's idea to save cost, increase quality, or improve other elements of work such as safety. Companies typically reward employees for implemented suggestions. At Toyota, for instance, employees generate nearly 3 million ideas each year—an average of 60 per employee—of which 85 percent are implemented by management. Suggestion systems are often tied to incentives. Wainwright Industries developed a unique and effective approach that has been benchmarked extensively.[32] Suggestion programs were viewed as neither systematic nor continuous, and not woven into the fabric of daily operations. Their approach was designed to overcome these shortcomings in the following ways:

- Focusing employees on small, incremental improvements within their own areas of responsibility and control
- Recognizing all employees for their level of participation regardless of the value of the improvement
- Scaling team-based improvement efforts in a way that minimizes downtime and provides people with the tools and techniques to produce successful outcomes
- Positioning supervisors as the catalyst for cultural change through a coaching and support role in the employee involvement and improvement process

The process contains two main components: individual implemented improvements and team-based system improvements. Rather than submitting suggestions for someone else to approve and implement, employees are provided with training and given the responsibility to take the initiative to make improvements on their own without prior approval within the scope of their main job responsibilities. Upon making improvements, they complete a form to document what they have done and present it to the supervisors, whose role is not to approve or disapprove, but to acknowledge the improvement and to point out any issues that the employee needs to understand. All forms submitted during the week are placed into a random drawing for some type of award determined by the individual unit. At the end of each quarter, every individual who met his or her goal of implemented improvements receives some type of valued recognition. The team-based approach breaks large initiatives into smaller manageable projects. Breaking down large tasks allows employees to understand how their individual jobs fit into the big picture and maximizes participation reduces time requirements for any particular employee. Wainwright was able to cite more than 50 implemented improvements per employee per year, far exceeding those of most American and Japanese companies.

Fostering employee creativity has many benefits. Thinking about solutions to problems at work makes even routine work enjoyable; writing down the suggestions improves workers' reasoning ability and writing skills. Satisfaction is the by-product of an implemented idea and a job made easier, safer, or better. Recognition for suggestions leads to higher levels of motivation, peer recognition, and possible monetary rewards. Workers gain an increased understanding of their work, which may lead to promotions and better interpersonal relationships in the workplace. Table 6.5 summarizes strategies that can foster the success of suggestion systems.

Empowerment

Empowerment requires, as the management philosophy of Wainwright Industries states, *a sincere belief and trust in people.* A survey by Annandale, Virginia-based MasteryWorks Inc. concluded that employees leave their organizations because of trust, observing that "Lack of trust was an issue with almost every person who had left an organization."[33]

Examples of empowerment abound. Workers in the Coors Brewery container operation give each other performance evaluations, and even screen, interview, and hire new people for the line. At Motorola, sales representatives have the

> *Empowerment* simply means giving people authority—to make decisions based on what they feel is right, have control over their work, take risks and learn from mistakes, and promote change.

Table 6.5 Success Factors for Suggestion Systems

1. Ensure that management, first and foremost, is involved in the program. Involvement should begin at the top and filter down through all levels until all employees participate.
2. Push decision making regarding suggestion evaluation to lower levels.
3. Gain union support by pledging no layoffs due to productivity gains from adopted suggestions.
4. Train everyone in all facets of the suggestion system. Improve problem-solving capability by promoting creative problem solving through the use of the seven basic statistical tools.
5. Resolve all suggestions within one month.
6. Encourage all suggestors to personally describe their idea to a supervisor, engineer, or manager.
7. Promote pride in work, and quality and productivity gains from suggestions, rather than the big cash awards if possible.
8. Remove ceilings on intangible suggestion awards. Revise evaluations of intangible suggestions to value them more on par with tangible suggestions.
9. Eliminate restrictions prohibiting suggestions regarding a worker's immediate work area.
10. Continuously promote the suggestion program, especially through supervisor support.
11. Trust employees enough to make allowances for generation, discussion, and submittal of suggestions during work hours.
12. Keep the program simple.

Source: Muse and Finster, "A Comparison of Employee Suggestion Systems in Japan and the USA," University of Wisconsin Working Paper (1989).

authority to replace defective products up to six years after purchase, a decision that used to require top management approval. A Corning Glass plant replaced 21 different jobs with one "specialist" job and gave employee teams broad authority over production scheduling and division of labor.

The need to empower the entire workforce in order for quality to succeed has long been recognized. Juran wrote that "ideally, quality control should be delegated to the workforce to the maximum extent possible."[34] Five of Deming's 14 Points relate directly to the notion of empowerment:

Point 6: Institute training.
Point 7: Teach and institute leadership.
Point 8: Drive out fear. Create trust. Create a climate for innovation.
Point 10: Eliminate exhortations for the workforce.
Point 13: Encourage education and self-improvement for everyone.[35]

These points suggest involving employees more directly in decision-making processes, giving them the security and confidence to make decisions, and providing them with the necessary tools and training.

Empowered employees must have the wisdom to know what to do and when to do it, the motivation to do it, and the right tools to accomplish the task.[36] These requirements may mean significant changes in work systems, specifically, the following:

- Employees be provided education, resources, and encouragement.
- Policies and procedures be examined for needless restrictions on the ability of employees to serve customers.
- An atmosphere of trust be fostered rather than resentment and punishment for failure.
- Information be shared freely rather than closely guarded as a source of control and power.
- Workers feel their efforts are desired and needed for the success of the organization.
- Managers be given the required support and training to adopt a" hands-off" leadership style.
- Employees be trained in the amount of latitude they are allowed to take. Formulating decision rules and providing role-playing scenarios are excellent ways of teaching employees.[37]

Empowerment also means that leaders and managers must relinquish some of the power that they previously held. This power shift often creates management fears that workers will abuse this privilege. However, experience shows that front-line workers generally are more conservative than managers. For example, companies that have empowered employee groups to evaluate performance and grant pay raises to their peers have found that they are much tougher than managers were.

Empowerment gives managers new responsibilities. They must hire and develop people capable of handling empowerment, encourage risk taking, and recognize achievements. Giving employees information about company finances and the financial implications of empowered decisions is also important. At DuPont's Delaware River plant, management shares cost figures with all workers.[38] By sharing this information, management believes that workers will think more for themselves and identify with company goals. To help employees make decisions on issues affecting production, a department manager at the Eastman Chemical plant in Texas supplied operators with a daily financial report that showed how their decisions affected the bottom line. As a result, department profits doubled in four months and quality improved by 50 percent as employees began suggesting cost-saving improvements.[39]

Empowerment can be viewed as vertical teamwork between management and labor. It builds confidence in workers by showing them that the company has confidence in their ability to make decisions on their own. It generates commitment and pride. It also gives employees better experience and an opportunity to advance their careers. It benefits customers who buy the organization's products and services. For instance, empowered employees can often reduce bureaucratic red tape that customers encounter—such as seeking a supervisor's signature—which makes customer transactions speedier and more pleasant. John Akers, former chairman of IBM, said, "Empowering our employees and inculcating a sense that everyone owns his or her piece of the business not only unleashes the talent and energy of our people, but also flattens the organization and reduces stifling bureaucracy."[40]

Even though many workers prefer an empowered workplace to the old style of narrowly defined tasks, empowerment is not for everyone.[41] One worker at Eaton Corporation hated the idea of being her own boss and its associated responsibilities such as fixing broken machines and having to learn a wide variety of jobs, and left after nine months. This example suggests that selecting the right people for a particular work environment is an important task.

Recruitment and Career Development

Motorola ties recruitment and selection activities to results in order to gauge the quality of its recruiting efforts as it strives for TQ at every level.[42] The recruiting department is measured by a new quality-oriented criterion: success of recruits on the job. Instead of using the old measure of how much it costs to hire each recruit, recruiters are now measured on whether new hires were well trained coming into the company, brought in at the right salary level, or left the company after the first six months for a better job. Based on these and other data, the department decided it had to increase, rather than decrease, the amount spent on each recruit. Thus, in recruiting activities, Motorola plans and sets objectives for recruiting, charts progress over time in order to reduce "defects" in the hiring process, and determines whether the "output" of the process (excellent employees) is under control, rather than simply measuring inputs (dollars per recruit). Other major companies like Procter & Gamble seek entry-level college graduates who understand total quality principles. They specifically want their new employees to think in terms of creating quality and value for consumers, to understand their customers and needs, and to work toward results despite obstacles.

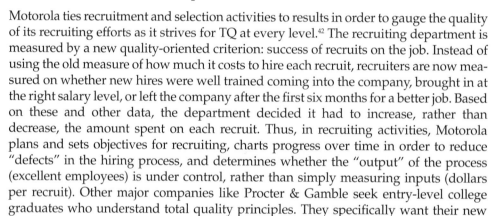

Meeting and exceeding customer expectations begins with hiring the right people whose skills and attitudes will support and enhance the organization's objectives.

Customer-contact employees make up one of the fastest-growing segments of the workforce. Limited availability of people with the skills to perform complex, rapidly changing jobs is forcing HRM managers to rethink their selection strategies. Traditional hiring practices have been based on cognitive or technical rather than interpersonal skills. The criterion is now shifting to attributes such as enthusiasm, resourcefulness, creativity, and the flexibility to learn new skills rapidly. The internal customer concept suggests that every employee needs good interpersonal skills. Even technical skill requirements are changing; to apply quality principles on the job, all workers must have basic mathematics and logical-thinking abilities. To ensure that job candidates have the requisite skills, new approaches, such as psychological testing and situational role playing, are now being used in the hiring process.

Career development is also changing because of TQ. As managerial roles shift from directing and controlling to coaching and facilitating, managers, who must deal with cross-functional problems, benefit more from horizontal movement than from upward movement in narrow functional areas. Flatter organizations limit promotion opportunities. Thus, career development expands learning opportunities and creates more challenging assignments rather than increasing spans of managerial control.

Training and Education

Companies committed to TQ invest heavily in training and education, recognizing that such investments add value to organizational capabilities. The leaders in quality—Deming, Juran, and Crosby—actively promoted quality training and education. Two of Deming's 14 Points, for example, are devoted to these issues. Xerox Business Products and Systems, for instance, invested more than $125 million in quality training. Customer service representatives at FedEx receive five weeks of training before they ever speak unsupervised with a customer. Even an 18-employee digital printing company in Reykjavik, Iceland—Umslag, ehf—spends 4 percent of total wages on training, which includes training in equipment repair to reduce the need to bring in expertise from Holland, languages to support growth in international business, and personal interests, such as computer programming, that can benefit the business.[43]

Training is one of the largest initial costs in a total quality initiative. Not surprisingly, it is one in which many companies are reluctant to invest. However, research indicates that companies that spend heavily on training their workers outperform companies that spend considerably less, as measured on the basis of overall stock market returns. Even if companies make the investment, they often take great pains to measure the benefits against the costs. Motorola used to calculate returns, but no longer. Its management *knows* that the benefits of quality-based training outweigh the costs by at least 30 to 1. Training and education have become an essential responsibility of HRM departments in TQ organizations, particularly as empowered employees require new knowledge and skills, which should not have to be cost-justified.

Training generally includes quality awareness, leadership, project management, communications, teamwork, problem solving, interpreting and using data, meeting customer requirements, process analysis, process simplification, waste reduction, cycle time reduction, error-proofing, and other issues that affect employee effectiveness, efficiency, and safety. Education needs might also include basic skills, such as reading writing, language, mathematics, or computer skills. Employees at Xerox learn a range of techniques, from the basic quality improvement tools through benchmarking. Motorola employees learn statistical methods and defect reduction approaches. Solectron Corporation, with a large multicultural workforce in its U.S. facilities, offers English as a second language courses, and training in communications, interpersonal skills, and technical manufacturing skills, all with bilingual trainers.

In a total quality environment, employees need to understand the goal of customer satisfaction, to be given the training and responsibilities to achieve this goal, and to feel that they do indeed make a difference. For example, at the Coors Brewing Company in Golden, Colorado, the customer satisfaction improvement program is focused on giving employees the appropriate skills, and on creating the environment in which employees have one responsibility and one hoped-for result: to satisfy and delight their customers, especially internal customers. Coors engaged in a massive training program to learn TQ principles, and then restructured its organization systems (compensation, evaluation, and so on) to support the new effort. The company

Quality Spotlight
Coors Brewing
Co.

succeeded in developing in its employees a passion for their jobs and pride in their work, which translated into measurable improvements in productivity, a remarkably low turnover rate, and the delivery of quality product and service throughout the system.[44]

Some employees, such as customer-contact personnel typically need a higher level of training in behavioral topics than manufacturing engineers, who may need advanced statistical skills.

Customer needs and strategic directions should drive training strategies.

FedEx, with its focus on efficiency and customer service, trains workers in team development and people issues. At IBM Rochester, managers tell the education department what they need, and programs are designed to meet those needs. By treating the training function as an internal supplier, the time taken to deliver training programs has been reduced from five days to two.

Many large companies have formal training departments, whose systems and approaches evolved along with their overall quality systems. Education and training can be delivered in a variety of ways, including on-the-job or traditional classroom environments. Today, computer-based and distance learning education are becoming increasingly popular. Training can also be accomplished through developmental assignments within or outside the organization. Specific approaches vary by company.

In some, managers train their workers directly in a top-down fashion; this approach was pioneered by Xerox, beginning with the CEO, David Kearns himself, during their transition to total quality. Others use self-paced methods employing advanced technology. The FedEx Quality Academy, established in 1991, uses a television network that broadcasts courses in a just-in-time fashion at the employees' work site. It also has a network of interactive video instruction, consisting of 1,200 workstations at 700 locations. More than 2,000 course titles are available for self-paced instruction. The Quality Academy tracks test scores, pass rates, and time spent online.[45] Honda of America uses interactive computer-based training modules on dedicated workstations in the plant.[46] Smaller companies often use outside consultants. The content should be customized to the company's needs; "packaged" seminars are often a waste of time.

Continual reinforcement of lessons learned in training programs is essential. Many companies send employees to courses, but then allow the knowledge to slip away. New knowledge can be reinforced in several ways. Motorola uses on-the-job coaching to reinforce training; The Ritz-Carlton has follow-up sessions to monitor instructional effectiveness. The Ritz-Carlton holds a "quality lineup" briefing session each day in every work area. During these sessions, employees receive instructions on achieving quality certification within the company. Work area teams set the quality certification performance standards of each position. Finally, companies need an approach for evaluating training effectiveness. The Ritz-Carlton requires employees to pass written and skill demonstration tests. Other companies use on-the-job evaluation or tests in simulated work environments. Many measure behavior and attitude changes. However, the true test of training effectiveness is results. By establishing a linkage between training and results (see the discussion of interlinking in Chapter 8), companies can show the impact on customer satisfaction and also identify gaps in training.

Compensation and Recognition

Without willing, sustained, individual effort and coordinated teamwork focused on meeting organizational goals, TQ is an impossible dream. However, when organizations ask employees to assume new challenges and responsibilities, the question

Compensation and recognition refer to all aspects of pay and reward, including promotions, bonuses, and recognition, either monetary and nonmonetary or individual and group.

"What's in it for me?" ultimately gets asked. Extrinsic and intrinsic rewards are the key to sustained individual efforts.

Compensation Compensation is always a sticky issue, closely tied to the subject of motivation and employee satisfaction. Although money can be a motivator, it often causes employees to believe they are being treated unfairly, and forces managers to deliver negative messages. Eventually, it diminishes intrinsic motivation and creates win-lose situations. The objectives of a good compensation system should be to attract, retain, and not demotivate employees. Other objectives include reducing unexplainable variation in pay (think about Deming's principles) and encouraging internal cooperation rather than competition. Most companies still use traditional financial measures, such as revenue growth, profitability, and cost management, as a basis for compensation; more progressive organizations use quality measures such as customer satisfaction, defect prevention, and cycle time reduction to make compensation decisions.

Many TQ-focused companies now base compensation on the market rate for an individual with proven capabilities, and then make adjustments as capabilities are increased, along with enhanced responsibilities, seniority, and business results. For example, General Motors' Powertrain Division, influenced strongly by Deming, decoupled compensation from performance appraisals. Compensation is determined from a "maturity curve" that considers an individual's seniority, level of expertise, and market for his or her services. Peers and subordinates have input as to an individual's rating on this curve. Distinctions based on contributions are limited to truly exceptional individuals. This example is an exception; few companies have eliminated merit ratings from their salary systems.

Many companies link compensation to company track records, unit performance, team success, or individual achievement.[47] At Kaiser Aluminum, such performance-based compensation incentives led to an 80 percent improvement in productivity and 70 percent decrease in poor quality costs over five years.[48] Team-based pay and **gainsharing**, an approach in which all employees share savings equally, are gaining in popularity and importance. Compensation for individuals is sometimes tied to the acquisition of new skills, often within the context of a continuous improvement program in which all employees are given opportunities to broaden their work-related competencies. However, legal restrictions in federal wage and hour laws make it difficult to implement some of these approaches. At a 1999 hearing of a subcommittee of the House Committee on Education and the Workforce, Pam Farr, a management consultant with the Cabot Advisory Group who had previously worked for Marriott Corporation as a human resources executive, testified:

> *A recent survey by William M. Mercer indicated that just 24 percent of large and midsize companies use team-based incentive pay. For companies that have chosen to implement team incentive pay programs, however, the results are overwhelmingly positive. A recent study by the Hay Group indicated that team-based and gainsharing plans are the most effective programs to help improve employee performance and satisfaction. A General Accounting Office study indicated that such programs significantly improve employer-employee relations, and reduce grievances, absenteeism and turnover. By removing the impediments to team-based pay systems, Congress will facilitate employee pay increases, employee work satisfaction and encourage productivity increases.[49]*

Nucor Corporation, one of the nation's largest steel producers, is well-known for having succeeded in attacking quality, productivity, participation, and compensation issues.[50] Nucor has more than 6,000 employees in plants in the United States and had annualized sales in excess of $4 billion in mid-1997. All employees, from the president on down, have the same benefits; the only differences in individual pay are related to responsibilities. Workers at Nucor's five nonunion steel mills earn base hourly rates that are less than half of the going rate for unionized steelworkers. Nucor uses pay incentives designed around groups of 40 to 50 workers, including secretaries and senior managers. They offer four basic compensation plans:

1. *Production Incentive Plan.* Employees involved directly in manufacturing are paid weekly bonuses on the basis of production of their work groups, which range from 20 to 40 workers each. These productivity and quality bonuses are based on the number of tons of steel of acceptable quality produced by a given production team. The formulas are nondiscretionary, based upon established production goals, and can average 80–150 percent of the base wage. This plan creates pressure for each individual to perform well, and in some facilities, is tied to attendance and tardiness standards. No bonus is paid if equipment is not operating, thus creating a strong emphasis on maintaining equipment in top operational condition at all times. The bonuses are paid every week to reinforce motivation. The average worker at Nucor earns several thousand dollars per year more than the average worker in the industry, while the company is able to sell its steel at competitive worldwide market prices.

2. *Department Manager Incentive Plan.* Department managers earn incentive bonuses paid annually based primarily on the return on assets of their facility.

3. *Nonproduction and Nondepartment Manager Incentive Plan.* Participants include accountants, engineers, secretaries, and other employees. The bonus is based on the facility's return on assets. Each month every operation receives a report showing progress, which is posted in the employee cafeteria or break area to keep employees appraised of their expected bonus levels throughout the year.

4. *Senior Officers Incentive Plan.* Senior officers do not receive profit sharing, pension, discretionary bonuses, or retirement plans. A significant part of their compensation is based upon Nucor's return on stockholder's equity above a certain minimum earnings. If Nucor does well, compensation is well above average, as much as several times base salary. If the company does poorly, compensation is limited to base salary, which is below the average pay at comparable companies.

The company was producing a ton of steel for less than half the average costs of a U.S. steel company.[51] For example, in September 1997, when other steel companies were attempting to raise prices for steel, Nucor announced that it was cutting the price of cold-rolled steel, one of the most widely used product lines, by 7 percent.[52] Nucor required fewer than four hours of labor per ton, Japanese companies required about five hours per ton, and other U.S. mills averaged more than six hours per ton. This comparison illustrates the use and benefits of team-based pay policies.

During downturns, managers at Nucor frequently find that their bonuses are cut, even while hourly workers continue to receive theirs, based on production rates. One difficult year, Nucor cut salaries for its 12 top executives by 5 percent and froze wages for its 3,500 employees. However, despite the tough times, it maintained their policy of no layoffs as it had throughout the history of the current company. The next year, when the United Steelworkers Union signed a contract to reduce wages and benefits in order to improve the competitiveness of the basic steel industry, Nucor announced a 5 percent wage increase. More about the Nucor story can be found on its Web site at http://www.nucor.com.

Special Recognition and Rewards Special recognition and rewards can be monetary or nonmonetary, formal or informal, individual or group. These rewards might include trips, promotional gifts, clothing, time off, or special company-sponsored awards and events. Most importantly, rewards should lead to behaviors that increase customer satisfaction. A Conference Board study found that a combination of cash and noncash recognition works better for clerical and hourly workers than for managers and professional/technical employees; for these groups, compensation-based incentives such as stock options are more successful.[53] As an example, in October 1994, Continental Airlines, new CEO Gordon Bethune calculated that late and canceled flights were costing the company $6 million per month to put passengers on rival airlines or send them to hotels. He declared that if Continental ranked among the top three airlines for on-time performance in any month, he would split half the savings (about $65 per person) with all nonexecutive employees. Within two months, Continental was first. To ensure that the bonuses made a vivid impression, Bethune issued the checks separately and traveled around the country to distribute thousands of them personally. The behavioral changes are best illustrated by a story executives like to retell. A catering truck pulls up to a plane but is 10 meals short. In the old days, the flight attendant would have told the driver to get the extra meals while the plane

Quality Spotlight
Continental
Airlines

Recognition provides a visible means of promoting quality efforts and telling employees that the organization values their efforts, which stimulates their motivation to improve.

sat at the gate for 40 minutes. The newly gung ho flight attendant, however, crisply tells the catering guy not to screw up again and shuts the cabin door. The plane pushes back on schedule, and she finds a bunch of investment bankers and offers them free liquor in place of the meal.[54]

Employees should contribute to the company's performance and recognition approaches. L.L. Bean, for example, gives dinners or certificates exchangeable for merchandise. Winners of "Bean's Best Awards" are selected by cross-functional teams based on innovative ideas, exceptional customer service, role modeling, expertise at their jobs, and exceptional management ability.[55]

Certain key practices lead to effective employee recognition and rewards:

- *Giving both individual and team awards.* At The Ritz-Carlton, individual awards include verbal and written praise and the most desirable job assignments. Team awards include bonus pools and sharing in the gratuity system. Many companies have formal corporate recognition programs, such as IBM's Market Driven Quality Award for outstanding individual and team achievements in quality improvement, or the Xerox President's Award and Team Excellence Award.

- *Involving everyone.* Recognition programs involve both front-line employees and senior management. Westinghouse had a Wall of Fame to recognize quality achievers at each site. Solectron rewards groups by buying lunch for entire divisions and bringing in ice cream for everyone in the plant. A Monsanto Company chemical plant ties worker bonuses to results at individual units and rewards workers for helping to prevent accidents.[56] What is particularly interesting is that different programs exist in different Monsanto plants—all developed with the participation of workers. Bonus plans that failed had been ones decreed by corporate headquarters, rather than those formulated in cooperation with employees.

- *Tying rewards to quality based on measurable objectives*. Leading companies recognize and reward behavior, not just results. Zytec rewarded employees for participating in the suggestion program by providing cash awards for each implemented suggestion. A group of peers selected the best improvement ideas each month, which were also rewarded with cash. Many rewards were linked to customer satisfaction measures. Awards that conflicted with quality values were modified or eliminated. Continuous feedback reinforced good performance and identified areas for improvement. When Custom Research, Inc. attains a specific corporate goal, the entire company is taken on a trip to destinations such as San Francisco and Disney World!
- *Allowing peers and customers to nominate and recognize superior performance*. Texas Instruments, for example, has a Site Quality Award to recognize the top 2 percent on the basis of peer nomination. Employees at FedEx who receive favorable comments from a customer are automatically nominated for the Golden Falcon Award. Recipients chosen by a review committee receive a gold pin, a congratulatory call from the CEO, recognition in the company newsletter, and 10 shares of company stock. AT&T Universal Card Services' World of Thanks award consisted of a globe-shaped pad of colored paper with "Thank You" written in different languages. Anyone in the company could write a message of thanks to someone else. In four years, employees used more than 130,000 of them![57]
- *Publicizing extensively*. Many companies recognize employees through newsletters, certificates and pins, special breakfasts or luncheons, and annual events such as competitions. Motorola, for example, developed a worldwide Total Customer Satisfaction (TCS) team competition. Approximately half of Motorola's 142,000 employees are on teams that compete locally, regionally, and internationally to attend the final one-day, corporate-wide competition held at a resort each year. The 1996 competition included 24 teams from eight countries. Teams were scored on such criteria as project selection, teamwork, analysis techniques, remedies, results, institutionalization (permanence, deployment, and team growth from the project), and presentation. Corporatewide results over eight years have been impressive, with an estimated savings of $2.4 billion per year.[58]
- *Making recognition fun*. Domino's Pizza stages a national Olympics, in which teams from the company's three regions compete in 15 events based on 15 job categories, such as doughmaking, driving, answering the telephone, and delivery. Winners, standing on platforms while the Olympic theme is played, receive medals, checks, and other forms of recognition. The finals are broadcast live to commissaries around the country. Domino's Olympics provides an excellent way to benchmark efforts throughout the corporation; winners attend three days of discussion with upper management to talk about what's good about the company, what needs improvement, and how those improvements can be made.[59]

Health, Safety, and Employee Well-Being

Because employees are key stakeholders of any organization, their health, safety, and overall well-being are important factors in the work environment. Health and safety have always been priorities in most companies, but working conditions now extend beyond basic issues of keeping the work area safe and clean. For example, as we learn more about ergonomic-related disorders such as carpal tunnel syndrome, employers have an even greater responsibility to incorporate health and safety factors into human resource plans. Other responsibilities include providing reasonable accommodations to workers with disabilities or ensuring that male and female employees are protected from sexual harassment from fellow workers and others.

Most companies provide many opportunities to contribute to the quality of working life. They can provide personal and career counseling, career development and employability services, recreational or cultural activities, daycare, special leave for family responsibilities or for community services, flexible work hours, outplacement services, and extended health care for retirees. Johnson & Johnson's Ethicon Endosurgery Division, in Blue Ash, Ohio, has a Wellness Center with exercise rooms and equipment to support employees in their manufacturing and R&D facility. Employees can use the center before or after working hours or during their breaks. In addition, those workers who are assembling products get regular, programmed "ergonomic" breaks every few hours, where they are required to do exercises designed to prevent repetitive motion injuries. All of these opportunities contribute to creating a more productive, safer, and more enjoyable in work environment.

Quality Spotlight
SAS Institute,
Inc.

SAS Institute, Inc., consistently one of *Fortune*'s "100 Best Companies to Work For," is a high-tech software development company based in Cary, North Carolina. SAS has a people-focused founder and CEO in the person of James Goodnight. Perhaps the most eye-opening policy of the firm is its mandated seven-hour workday. No "all-nighters" are expected of SAS employees. The multibillionaire Goodnight sets the example by leaving the office at 5 P.M., sharp. Many of the lavish employee perks at the sprawling corporate campus are family and lifestyle-oriented, from daycare centers, lactation rooms, a Montessori school, and a college prep private high school, to a 55,000-square-foot athletic facility, free massages, free car washes, and end-of-year bonuses. The payoff? SAS has about 4 percent turnover in an industry where 20 percent is the norm.[60]

Motivating Employees

Understanding human behavior and motivation are major elements of Deming's Profound Knowledge discussed in Chapter 3. Deming spoke of motivation as being primarily intrinsic (internal), and was suspicious of external forms of motivation, such as incentives and bonuses. Although thousands of studies have been performed over the years on human and animal subjects in attempts to define and refine the concept of motivation, it remains an extremely complex phenomenon that still is not fully understood. As managers in a TQ environment take on the roles of coaches and facilitators, their skills in motivating employees become even more crucial.

There is no such thing as an unmotivated employee, but the system within which people work can either seriously impede motivation or enhance it.

Saul W. Gellerman defined **motivation** as "the art of creating conditions that allow every one of us, warts and all, to get his work done at his own peak level of efficiency."[61] A more formal definition of motivation is *an individual's response to a felt need*. Thus, some stimulus, or activating event, must spur the need to respond to that stimulus, generating the response itself. For example, an individual worker given the goal or quality task of achieving zero defects on the parts that he or she produces may feel a need to keep his or her job. Consequently, the worker is motivated by the stimulus of fear and responds by carefully producing parts to achieve the goal. Another less insecure worker may feel the need for approval of his or her work by peers or superiors and be motivated by the stimulus of pride. The worker then responds to that need and that stimulus by producing high-quality parts.

Researchers have proposed many theories and models to describe how and why people are motivated. A theory is a way to describe, predict, and control what is observed in the world. Models graphically or symbolically show what a theory is saying in words. Often a model is so closely associated with a theory that the terms are used interchangeably. For example, Herzberg's Two-Factor theory describes two categories of factors, called "maintenance" and "motivational" factors. Maintenance factors are conditions that employees have come to expect, such as a safe working environment, a reasonable level of job security, supervision, and even adequate pay. Workers in a situation with these conditions will not be dissatisfied, but maintenance factors generally do not provide any motivation to work harder. Motivational factors, such as recognition, advancement, achievement, and the nature of the work itself are less tangible, but do motivate people to be more committed to and satisfied with their work. From Herzberg's theory arose the concept of job enrichment, described earlier in this chapter. With job enrichment, employees gain a sense of fulfillment (satisfaction) from completion of every cycle of a task. Acquiring cross-functional skills, working in teams, and increased empowerment are forms of job enrichment.

Theories and models are often classified according to common themes. James L. Bowditch and Anthony F. Buono categorize motivation theories as *content*, *process*, and *environmentally based* theories.[62] These theories are often studied in traditional management courses and are summarized in Table 6.6. In the behavioral sciences, as well as in the pure sciences, the originator of a theory is becoming more and more difficult to determine because many researchers' ideas often overlap. Thus, the information in Table 6.6 is merely suggestive of one or more names that have been associated with the development of the theory. The Bonus Materials folder for this chapter on the CD-ROM contains detailed descriptions of some of these key theories, and we suggest that you review them.

Motivation theories can be applied to support TQ in any organization. For example, Herzberg's theory suggests that ignoring maintenance factors such as supervision,

Table 6.6 A Classification of Motivation Theories

Motivation Theory	Pioneer/Developer	Type of Theory
Content Theories		
Hierarchy of Needs	Abraham Maslow	Need
Motivation and Maintenance	Frederick Herzberg	Need/satisfaction
Theory X-Y	Douglas McGregor	Managerial expectations
n-Ach, n-Aff, n-Pow	David McClelland	Acquired need
Process Theories		
Preference–Expectancy	Victor H. Vroom	Expectancy
Contingency	Porter and Lawler	Expectancy/reward
Goal Setting	Edward Locke	Goal
Path–Goal Theory of Leadership	Robert J. House	Goal
Environmentally Based Theories		
Operant Conditioning	B. F. Skinner	Reinforcement
Equity	J. Stacy Adams	Equity
Social Learning/Self-Efficacy	A. Bandura	Social Learning/Self-Efficacy
	Snyder and Williams	

working conditions, salary, peer relations, status, and security will produce dissatisfaction and negatively impact the work environment, while enhancing the motivating factors will produce a positive effect. Thus, understanding and applying the theories should result in more effective designs of work systems and the work environment.

Performance Appraisal

Considerable truth can be found in the statement, "How one is evaluated determines how one performs." This reality can be dangerous. Analog Devices, a successful Massachusetts analog and digital equipment manufacturer, embraced TQ but found its stock price steadily declining. One of its key measures (on which managers were rewarded) was new product introduction time, with an objective of reducing it from 36 to 6 months. The product development team focused on this objective; as a result, engineers turned away from riskier new products and designed mundane derivatives of old products that no longer met customers' needs. The company subsequently scrapped that goal.[63]

Performance appraisal is a process for evaluating and generating information about employees' effectiveness and efficiency at work.[64] However, performance appraisal is an exceedingly difficult HRM activity. Organizations typically use performance appraisals for a number of reasons: to provide feedback to employees who can then recognize and build on their strengths and work on their weaknesses, to determine salary increases, to determine training needs, to identify people for promotion, and to deal with human resource legalities. As such, they can provide a paper trail to fight wrongful-discharge suits and act as a formal warning system to marginal employees.[65] Many leading organizations use performance appraisal for changing corporate culture.

Conventional appraisal processes typically involve setting objectives for a certain period of time (typically for the year ahead), either unilaterally or jointly by the manager with his or her subordinate. Objectives might focus on development of knowledge or skills, results such as output and productivity, or behavior. Objective setting is followed by a supervisory review of accomplishments, strengths and weaknesses, or personal characteristics of the subordinate related to the job at the end of the review period. Often, the form used for performance rating has 10 to 15 tangible and intangible categories, such as quantity of work, quality of work, works well with others, takes initiative, and so on, to be rated on a five- or seven-point scale from "excellent" to "unsatisfactory" or "poor." The performance appraisal interview may be accompanied by announcements of raises, bonuses, or promotions. In some cases, company policy dictates a certain distribution of results, such as "no more than 10 percent of any department's employees may be rated as excellent" or "merit raises or bonuses will only be paid to employees who are rated as excellent or very good."

Dissatisfaction with conventional performance appraisal systems is common among both managers, who are the appraisers, and workers, who are appraised. General Motors, for example, discovered that 90 percent of its people believed they were in the top 10 percent. How discouraging is it to be rated lower? Many managers are inclined to give higher ratings because of potential negative impacts. Numerous research studies over the past several decades have pointed out the problems and pitfalls of performance appraisals.[66] Many legitimate objections can be made:[67]

- They tend to foster mediocrity and discourage risk taking.
- They focus on short-term and measurable results, thereby discouraging long-term planning or thinking and ignoring important behaviors that are more difficult to measure.

- They focus on the individual and therefore tend to discourage or destroy team-work within and between departments.
- The process is detection-oriented rather than prevention-oriented.
- They are often unfair, since managers frequently do not possess observational accuracy.
- They fail to distinguish between factors that are within the employees' control and system-determined factors that are beyond their control.

Many companies use peer review, customer evaluations, and self-assessments as a part of the appraisal process. One approach that has been gaining increasing acceptance and overcomes many of the objections cited earlier is called **360-degree feedback**.[68] In an ideal 360-degree approach, a group of individuals who interact with the employee (or team) on a frequent basis participate in both the goal-setting process and the performance appraisal process. This group might include suppliers, clients, peers, internal customers, managers, and subordinates. The process involves two-way communication in which both parties discuss such needs as service levels, response times, accuracy of work and so on, which are often expressed as written service contracts. At the end of the performance period, selected representatives who participated in the goal setting evaluate how well the goals of the service contracts have been met, and provide feedback. The final performance appraisal consists of discussing an aggregation of the comments and ratings with the employee, and serves as a process for setting goals for the next period and for employee development. Because the approach is new, little systematic research has been performed on its effectiveness; however, user feedback has been positive.

> *Performance appraisals are most effective when they are based on the objectives that support the strategic directions of the organization, best practices, and continuous improvement.*

In the spirit of Deming, many companies are replacing performance evaluation altogether with personal planning and development systems. Cadillac, for instance, replaced its traditional performance review with a personnel development planning process in which managers meet with employees to set future expectations, identify training needs, provide coaching, and reward continuous improvement. Eastman Chemical Company eliminated employee labeling, improved the focus on individual development planning, and encouraged employee involvement and ownership. Granite Rock does not emphasize past performance, but sets professional development goals in conjunction with the company's needs. No stigma is attached to failure; the thrust of the process is to develop each individual to the fullest.

Today, many leading organizations are focusing on identifying a small number of core competencies that are critical to the organization's success.[69] These core competencies are the behaviors, skills, and attributes every member is expected to have. They also use **mastery descriptions**, narratives of behavior that one who has mastered it would likely engage in. For example, a mastery description of *Customer Focus* might be:

> *Dedicated to meeting the expectations and requirements of internal and external customers. Knows who every one of his/her customers is and can state what that individual's expectations are. Gets firsthand customer information and uses it for improvements in products and services. Speaks and acts with customers in mind. Takes the client's side in well-founded complaints. Is skilled at managing customer expectations. Establishes and maintains effective relationships with customers and gains their trust and*

respect. Actively seeks customers' feedback on the quality of service he/she provides.

A behavioral frequency scale, in which appraisers indicate how frequently the appraisee does the things listed in the mastery descriptions (rarely, occasionally, frequently, or regularly, for example) is often used. This avoids numerical judgments of performance, defensive reactions, and provides a guide of what to do to improve.

Measuring Employee Satisfaction and HRM Effectiveness

Measurement of employee satisfaction and HRM effectiveness is useful to assess the linkages with company strategy and to provide a foundation for improvement. In fact, research has suggested that organizations that use people measures as part of a balanced set of measures to manage the business see significantly higher return on investment and return on assets than those that don't. The same holds true for organizations that say their employee surveys provide valuable information to guide decision making. Nevertheless, few organizations have well-defined people measures or use them to predict key business outcomes.[70]

> *HR measures allow companies to predict customer satisfaction, identify those issues that have the greatest impact on business performance, and allocate appropriate resources.*

Both outcome and process measures provide data by which to assess HRM effectiveness. Outcome measures might include "hard" measures of cost savings, productivity improvements, defect rate reduction, customer satisfaction improvements, cycle time reductions, and employee turnover, as well as "soft" measures of teamwork and management effectiveness, employee commitment, employee satisfaction, and empowerment. Typical process measures of success include the number of suggestions that employees make, the numbers of participants in project teams, and participation in educational programs. Team process effectiveness can be assessed by tracking the average time it takes to complete a process improvement project, and determining whether teams are getting better, smarter, and faster at performing improvements. Facilitators and program coordinators should also look for other indicators of success, such as improvements in team selection and planning processes, frequency of use of quality improvement tools by employees, employee understanding of problem-solving approaches, and senior management involvement. Employee surveys can also help in providing this information.

Questions in a typical survey might be grouped into such basic categories as quality of worklife, teamwork, communications, opportunities and training, facilities, leadership, compensation, benefits, and the company. Surveys might also address important team and individual behaviors, such as unity for a common purpose, listening effectively and acknowledging others' contributions, obtaining the participation of all members of the team, gathering and analyzing relevant data and information, sharing responsibility, using problem-solving processes and tools, and meeting company objectives for quality improvement. Many research-based and commercial survey instruments are available.[71] Like the customer satisfaction surveys we discussed in Chapter 4, many employee surveys also seek feedback on the importance of key issues.

Employee surveys also help organizations better understand the "voice of the employee," particularly with regard to employee satisfaction, management policies, and their internal customers and suppliers. Such feedback helps organizations improve their human resource management practices. For example, Marlow Industries uses a survey that addresses a broad variety of issues, including management support, the company's total quality system, organizational effectiveness, training, and continuous improvement. Table 6.7 shows most of the questions included in their survey. All responses are made on a five-item scale ranging from *totally disagree* to *very much agree*. Xerox produces its survey in 25 languages. Fifty-four questions are grouped into eight categories: Directions/communications, Valuing people, Trust, Learning, Feedback, Recognition, Participation/involvement, and Teamwork. Xerox compares results against similar companies such as Allied Signal, Honeywell, Sun Microsystems, Texas Instruments, and others.

In evaluating results, trends and long-term results should be emphasized, and they should be communicated to employees. A good system should report results on a regular basis, perhaps monthly or quarterly, with a summary year-end report, using graphical aids wherever possible. Detailed reports should go to lower-level managers, showing results at their level. Summary reports should go to higher management levels. Specific action, such as training, changes in reward or recognition, or improvements to support employee well-being should be taken based on results.

HRM in the Internet Age

Has the Internet Age changed what organizations need to know about HRM? The answer is surprisingly, no. Workers want to be treated with respect, have their basic needs addressed, understand the goals of their work, and have managers recognize their unique individual differences. They want to be given challenging, meaningful work in which they can experience pride of ownership, personal learning and growth, and be rewarded fairly and equitably when they perform.

However, things have certainly changed in the fast-paced Internet Age. Managers who don't recognize these changes and keep up with trends in job design, motivation, and leadership do so at their own peril. Take virtual teams, for example.[72] These types of teams use a combination of Internet, e-mail, phone, fax, video conferencing, PC-to-PC connections, and shared computer screen technologies to get their jobs done. Virtual teams are often given a distinct Web site for posting charts, meeting minutes, statistics, and other shared documents. Virtual teaming requires special attention to communication, technology, sponsorship, and leadership issues. For example, the team leader needs to be able to tackle issues that he or she might not have encountered with traditional teams. One of the biggest disadvantages is the lack of experience members have working with one another. They are not aware of each other's work standards and cannot scrutinize these ethics as consistently as traditional teams. This issue can be overcome by developing operating agreements by all team members, spelling out what they commit to do or not to do. Another factor is that communication is more complex because body language, voice inflection, and other communication cues are eliminated. Thus, virtual team members must be able to excel in relating their own ideas, and also understand the information others are trying to convey.

Today's organizations are characterized by much less employee loyalty, much more organizational uncertainty (and paradoxically, much more individual opportunity), and much more dependence of the organization on its human capital than ever before. As one writer put it: "We are all temps (temporary workers)!" HRM practices in the Internet Age will increasingly require employers to take nontraditional approaches to attract and retain highly-skilled employees, including special perks, increased levels of responsibility early in the employees' careers, and understanding of the effects of changes brought about by new technologies and new realities of employee lifestyles in the twenty-first century.

Table 6.7 Employee Quality Survey—Marlow Industries

Management Support

1. The president is an active supporter of quality at Marlow Industries.
2. Senior management (VPs) are active supporters of quality at Marlow Industries.
3. My supervisor is an active supporter of quality at Marlow Industries.
4. My supervisor is concerned more about the quality of my work than the quantity of my work.
5. My supervisor can help me to do my job better.
6. My supervisor encourages good housekeeping efforts.
7. I receive recognition for a top quality job done.

Total Quality System

1. Marlow Industries' Total Quality System is not a fad. It will be active long into the future.
2. The Total Quality system has made an improvement in the performance of my work.
3. The Total Quality system has made an improvement in my ability to do my job right the first time.
4. I understand the meaning of the Quality Policy.
5. I believe in the meaning of the Quality Policy.
6. I understand the meaning of the Quality Pledge.
7. I believe in the meaning of the Quality Pledge.
8. All departments within Marlow Industries support the Total Quality system.
9. My co-workers support quality first.
10. My co-workers believe in the Quality Pledge.
11. My "supplier" co-worker treats me as his/her "customer" and meets my needs.
12. I know who my internal "customer" is.
13. I am able to meet the requirements of my internal customer.
14. I believe that improving quality is the key to maintaining Marlow Industries' success.

Organizational Effectiveness

1. I receive feedback that helps me perform my job better.
2. I am encouraged to stop and ask questions if something does not seem right.
3. There is a high level of quality in the products we ship to our external customers.
4. Marlow Industries provides reliable processes and equipment so that I can do my job right the first time.
5. I do not use defective materials.
6. I am provided proper procedures to do my job right.
7. My fellow workers have a high level of enthusiasm about Marlow Industries' quality.
8. I believe control charts will help us improve quality.
9. I believe Marlow Industries offers a high quality working environment.
10. I enjoy my job.

Training

1. I have received training to be able to do my job right the first time.
2. I have received training on how to determine if the work I do conforms to Marlow Industries' workmanship standards, and other requirements of the customer.
3. I receive adequate safety training so that I am aware of the safety and health requirements of my job.
4. My supervisor has received adequate training to be able to do his/her job right the first time.
5. My co-worker has received adequate training to be able to do his/her job right the first time.
6. I have received ongoing training.
7. The training I have received has been very helpful to me in my job.

Job Satisfaction and Morale

1. I have a high level of personal job satisfaction.
2. My morale is high.
3. The morale of my work group is high.

Involvement

1. I feel involved at Marlow Industries.
2. I would like to be more involved at Marlow Industries.

Source: Courtesy Marlow Industries.

HUMAN RESOURCE FOCUS IN THE BALDRIGE CRITERIA, ISO 9000, AND SIX SIGMA

Category 5 of the 2003 Malcolm Baldrige National Quality Award Criteria for Performance Excellence is *Human Resource Focus*. This category examines how an organization's work systems and human resource practices lead to performance excellence and align with strategic objectives and action plans. Item 5.1, *Work Systems*, focuses on how work and jobs are organized to promote cooperation, initiative, empowerment, innovation, and organizational culture, how they capitalize on diversity within the organization, and how communication and skill sharing are accomplished across work units, jobs, and locations. It also examines the performance management system, and how compensation and recognition reinforce high-performance work. Finally, it addresses hiring and career progression approaches, including effective succession planning for senior leadership.

Item 5.2, *Employee Learning and Motivation*, focuses on how employee education, training, and career development support the achievement of objectives and build employee knowledge, skills, and capabilities. It examines how key organizational needs, such as performance measurement and improvement, technological change, ethical business practices, leadership development, and safety are addressed through education and training, how needs are determined, how education and training are delivered and reinforced on the job, and how the effectiveness of education and training are evaluated. This item also addresses how an organization motivates employees to develop and utilize their full potential, and attain job- and career-related development and learning objectives.

Item 5.3, *Employee Well-Being and Satisfaction*, examines how an organization ensures a safe and healthful work environment and support climate that contribute to the well-being, satisfaction, and motivation of all employees. It includes identifying appropriate measures and targets for key workplace factors so that status and progress can be tracked, and how preparation for emergencies or disasters is addressed. The criteria also asks how the organization determines the key factors that affect employee well-being, satisfaction, and motivation; how services, benefits, and policies support employees; how well-being, satisfaction, and motivation are assessed and measured; and how assessment findings are used to identify priorities for improving the work environment and employee support climate.

The focus of human resources in ISO 9000:2000 revolves primarily around training and the work environment, but does not address the subject as comprehensively as Baldrige does. The standards require that "Personnel performing work affecting product quality shall be competent on the basis of appropriate education, training, skills, and experience." The standards further require that organizations determine the level of competence that employees need, provide training or other means to ensure competency, evaluate the effectiveness of training or other actions taken, ensure that employees are aware of how their work contributes to quality objectives, and maintain appropriate records of education, training, and experience. The standards also address the work environment from the standpoint of providing buildings, workspace, utilities, equipment, and supporting services needed to achieve conformity to product requirements, as well as determining and managing the work environment, including safety, ergonomics, and environmental factors.

Human resource focus is essential to Six Sigma. We discussed the role of project teams in Six Sigma earlier in this chapter. One quality professional noted that "Six Sigma actually owes its success to all the quality efforts that have come before it, and teams are an integral part of Six Sigma implementation."[73] In addition to teams, selecting the right people to serve on teams, training and skill development, and reward and recognition approaches to drive behavior are vital to Six Sigma efforts. Six Sigma efforts often result in significant change recommendations to the organization; work processes change and employees need to do things differently. Understanding how changes affect people is a necessary issue that organizations must address after Six Sigma projects are completed; project champions, in particular, need to apply the principles discussed in this chapter to their organizations.

QUALITY IN PRACTICE
TD INDUSTRIES[74]

TD Industries is an employee-owned firm that provides mechanical, refrigeration, electrical, plumbing, building controls, and energy services to customers in Texas and the Southwest. Headquartered in Dallas, the company expanded rapidly in the 1990s, due to the tremendous growth rate of the area. In the early 1990s the company employed about 600 people and had revenues of approximately $75 million per year. By the end of 1998, employment had grown to 1,050 employees, with revenues of $182 million. It is interesting to note that the company added 98 jobs over the 1997–98 timeframe, but had 2,200 applications for those jobs! What made these jobs so attractive in an industry where the norm is hard physical work, highly cyclical demand, and typically a high employee turnover rate? To help answer this question, consider the company's vision:

> We are committed to providing outstanding career opportunities by exceeding our customers' expectations through continuous aggressive improvement.

Note the focus on its people as reflected in the goal of providing outstanding career opportunities. A list of some of the awards it has won attests to its ability to achieve this vision:

- 1998, Texas Quality Award (based on the Malcolm Baldrige criteria)
- 1997, No. 5 on *Fortune* Magazine's list of *"The 100 Best Companies to Work for in America"* [No. 2 in 1998 and No. 4 in 1999]
- 1996, National Member of the Year Associated Builders and Contractors
- 1996, Jack Lowe, CEO—Crystal Achievement Award National Association of Women in Construction
- 1996, National Carrier Distinguished Dealer Award
- 1995, Commercial Contractor of the Year, *Contracting Business*
- 1995, 1996, 1997, United Way Pacesetter/Elite Company

In testifying to the members of the U.S. House of Representatives Committee on Education and the Workforce (http://edworkforce.house.gov/) on May 20, 1998, regarding "The American Worker at a Crossroads Project," Ben Houston, President of TD Industries shared the company philosophy:

> We have humbly accepted the above awards on behalf of all Partners of TD Industries because we believe our culture is founded upon having fun while we accomplish the following: Trust, Servant Leadership, Quality, Sharing. To have fun, every meeting agenda item begins with Item #1—HUMOR. Our entire culture is based on a trusting relationship between all of our stakeholders—our clients, our communities, our partners, and our suppliers. We believe in the value of the individual, and attempt, in our culture, to recognize this value.
>
> TD Industries believes in Robert Greenleaf's philosophy as indicated in his book entitled, The Servant Leader. We believe that all individuals within TD Industries, regardless of their jobs, are leaders and managers of their own jobs. We also believe that in order to lead, one must first serve those that are to be led.
>
> We believe everything we do must strive towards meeting our stakeholders needs—our clients, our communities, our partners, and our suppliers. In order to ensure quality, teamwork among all TD

Partners, our clients, and suppliers is essential. Most opportunities for improvement are accomplished through quality work teams. We avoid the term "buy in" because it implies someone has the correct answer and must sell it to others. We prefer to have the best solution created by equal input from all participants.

In order to ensure improvement, TD Industries measures many items on an ongoing basis and the information is available to all TD Partners, but especially the work group that can affect the improvement. Items measured include the following:

1. *Partner Satisfaction:* An annual confidential questionnaire is compared with national groups, benchmarked against TD's own performance year by year to ensure that improvement is being made in all areas.
2. *Supervisors Survey:* Supervisors are confidentially rated annually by the partners who work with them, and the reports are given to the supervisors to be reviewed with their supervisor within three weeks.
3. *Customer Surveys:* Every area of customer contact is surveyed on a regular basis depending on the type of business. A goal of 9 out of 10 has been set, and all scores below 7 are reviewed with the client and the responsible manager and reviewed for lessons learned.
4. *One With Ones:* One with One reviews are required yearly with each partner and his or her supervisor and not at the same time as pay evaluations.
5. *Pay Evaluations:* Pay evaluations are done twice annually with training records and career paths being a portion of the review.
6. *Productivity Reports:* Sent to the partners doing the work.
7. *Safety Reports:* Sent to the partners doing the work.
8. *Continuous Improvement:* All partners, regardless of their position in the company, are asked to obtain a minimum of 32 hours of training in order to sharpen the skills of the individual, and assist in ensuring the contin-

uous improvement of the company's greatest resource—its employees.

In addition, formal training for leaders includes safety orientation; mentors; 90-day orientation; sixth-month benefit orientation; one-year TD Opportunities; second year Quality and years 3 through 6 Leadership Training on Diversity, Team Work, Leadership, and 7 Habits. Associated Builders and Contractors Wheels of Learning craft courses are offered as well as technical and management courses.

TD Industries provides many benefits to its employees: medical, dental, group term life, and long-term disability insurance; employee stock ownership plan (ESOP)/401(k)—30 percent of the profits go to partners in the ESOP and 401(k) plans; and other benefits such as paid personal time, holidays, sick pay, job injury pay, jury duty, wellness program, funeral pay, continuing education program (fully paid for by TD Industries through which many have obtained degrees at night), prescription safety glasses, and partner grant requests with up to $100 for a community service in which the partner works. Partners are encouraged to participate in many associations such as Associated Builders and Contractors and United Way in order to give back to the industry and community. Financial incentives are paid to virtually every partner based on improvements in the partner's own operation if partner satisfaction, supervisor scores and customer satisfaction are acceptable. Thirty percent of all pretax profits are distributed to the partners in the ESOP and 401(k). As Houston noted, "These items of SHARING close the loop of TRUST due to the sharing that TD Industries practices with all Partners."

Key Issues for Discussion

1. Explain how human resource activities at TD Industries work toward achieving the company's vision statement.
2. How do HRM processes at TD Industries support the fundamental principles of TQ: customer focus, participation and teamwork, and continuous improvement?

QUALITY IN PRACTICE
L.L. BEAN[75]

L.L. Bean Co., a sporting goods and apparel mail-order distributor and retailer headquartered in Freeport, Maine, has been known for quality and a focus on the customer since it was founded in 1912 by Leon Leonwood Bean, a Maine outdoorsman. "L.L.," as he was called, grew tired of coming home with wet, sore feet from the heavy leather woodsman's boots of his day. He invented a new kind of boot that combined lightweight leather tops with waterproof rubber bottoms, incorporating the best features of both materials. The practical advantages of his new L.L. Bean boots were readily apparent, and he soon sold 100 pairs to fellow sportsmen through the mail. Unfortunately, 90 pairs were sent back when the stitching gave way. But L.L. was true to his word, refunded his customers' money and started over with an improved boot.

L.L. Bean operated his business based on the following belief: "Sell good merchandise at a reasonable profit, treat your customers like human beings, and they will always come back for more." The company now sells more than 16,000 outdoor products, and even has eight stores in Japan. The Freeport flagship store is one of the most popular tourist destinations in Maine, receiving more than 3.5 million visitors a year. The company also has 12 factory outlet stores: six in New England, five in the mid-Atlantic states, and one in Oregon. L.L.'s products were originally sold only through the mail, but so many people dropped by his Freeport workshop to purchase items that he opened a showroom in 1917. Over the years, the company kept growing as L.L. added casual and sports apparel, gear and other footwear to his line. By 1951, people were dropping by day and night on their way to hunt and fish in Maine, and L.L. announced he had "thrown away the keys," deciding to keep the retail store open continuously. It has been open to the public 24 hours a day, 365 days a year, ever since.

Legendary stories are told of commitment to quality and service in its catalogs and inside and around the company. One such story was told of customer service representative who was informed of a late shipment, loaded a canoe on his car, and drove from Freeport to New York City (a distance of almost 300 miles, or 475 km) so that the customer could go hunting the next morning. Bean backs up its reputation for quality and customer focus with a "Guarantee of 100% Satisfaction" on all products.

For 20 years, Bean had enjoyed 20 percent annual growth in sales. In the 1990s, the firm was caught in a major industry downturn, with rising costs and shrinking demand. Bean launched a TQ and HR effort in the mid-1990s. The focus on quality was led by an 85-person total quality and human resources (TQHR) unit, composed of HR generalists, some HR specialists, and process improvement consultants.

Bean is a people-focused organization, so massive layoffs were not seen as a viable cost-cutting option. Bob Peixotto, vice president (total quality and human resources) stated, "People are the solution, not the problem." Traditionally, the company had paid an average of 15 percent of salary as a profit-sharing bonus, each year. During the 1990s, bonuses were unpredictable and sporadic. Limited voluntary retirements and staff reductions were carried out, but TQHR saw that the solution was to "work smarter, not harder."

As a direct marketing and retail business, large-scale complexity and dependence on world-class business logistics put people, total quality, and customer service at the heart of the company. To save time and meet customer needs, continual process review and improvement were essential. L.L. Bean began to rethink each of these elements.

L.L. Bean already had an intense customer focus, so the two key drivers of the total quality effort were people (their involvement in the business) and processes (business process management and improvement). A new people-process model helped to integrate TQ into the HR department. Total quality was defined by Bean employees as "managing an enterprise to maximize customer satisfaction in the most efficient and effective way by totally involving people in improving the way work is done." TQHR's mission was to support the company TQ mission by acting as a catalyst for total quality and superior performance.

For a retail organization like L.L. Bean, quality is not a production line issue. As Peixotto said, "It happens every time a customer representative receives a call in the telephone center. That interaction is where quality really happens, so a third goal was to change the infrastructure to support such customer interaction. This eventually meant a redesigned TQHR department."

To accomplish their TQ goals, departmental leadership decided to focus its own efforts on five operational themes:

1. Servicing line managers to meet employee needs, role revision for managers and management learning.
2. Practicing what it preached—with its own performance improvement and management being one example.
3. Acting as one unified department with a portfolio of products and services.
4. Regarding itself as a business, with regular feedback from internal customers being critical evidence of performance.
5. Continually reviewing and rethinking the TQHR process.

When TQHR reviewed its work to identify the types of business in which it should be involved, almost 50 different kinds emerged, including business process improvement, publishing, facilitation, management consulting, report management, legal care management, physical therapy, learning center operations, and career counseling.

Next, the department devised a portfolio of TQHR products or services for internal customers for which resources were needed. The final list of 109 included career assessment, ergonomic workstation design, quality assessments, and change management counseling. Six core processes were identified for delivering these products and services to other parts of the business, including recruiting and orienting people, developing people, separating people, organizational development planning, product and service development, and delivering products and services.

Peixotto explains, "These changes helped us to create a new TQHR paradigm, where departmental staff worked directly in customer areas and therefore at the front end of the business and total quality. Our role here was to act as consultants, not order takers for HR products or services." As a result of the rethinking, the new TQHR organiza-tion was divided into two sections—the resource center and service teams that work in internal-customer areas across all L.L. Bean's operations.

The resource center acts as a strategic HR think-tank, deciding what TQHR should be offering and examining the strategic needs of internal customers in relation to employee performance, productivity, and continuous improvement. The service teams are business partners, delivering products and services directly for internal customers, working away from their own operational area.

To accomplish work across departmental units, TQHR teams called "pods," were also introduced. These short-life teams are rapidly and flexibly deployed process-improvement consultants—"the catalysts for change who go after costs," in Peixotto's words. These pods are expert teams that address needs such as training and development, recruitment and compensation, and can assume both strategic and operational roles for their work. For example, the compensation pod is investigating new, major TQHR approaches such as team-based rewards and recognition.

Broadly skilled business people are assigned to work in TQHR. Their skills include both traditional HR competencies, such as training and recruitment, and specific process improvement skills such as systems, information technology, and industrial engineering. Thus, they can be deployed across the resource center, pods, or service teams.

Peixotto's unit also does not hesitate to use talent from elsewhere within the organization. For example, any L.L. Bean employee with appropriate skills is invited to attend the annual training courses in facilitation and process improvement. In return, these "outside" individuals guarantee TQHR 52 days of personal input a year to support its activities. He says, "They act as skilled personnel and change or process improvement missionaries. Broad and interrelated consultancy skills will always be TQHR's critical capability. But, as internal consultants, we never tell any part of the organization what it should be doing: our job is to listen first and then recommend action or tools for getting things done effectively."

Peixotto uses the TQHR unit as a test laboratory for the organization's HR tools or techniques to support its work in the continuous improvement process. It requires that TQHR anticipate internal-customer requirements or how their needs might change with new business priorities.

Then, they test out the tools and techniques that range from the basics—pay, incentives, training, competencies, performance measures, employee relations and so on—to more complex approaches, including job redesign and process improvement. They may be applied in one of two scenarios: (1) as tested templates for managers to use to save on their own time and resources and avoid reinventing the wheel; or (2) for service teams, where they have been invited to help in a function or business area. "The invitation is important," explains Peixotto, "because our role is to act as facilitators and enablers." TQHR also benchmarks itself with any organization that has proven best practices. Recently, performance management, leadership development, idea generation systems, compensation issues and workplace safety have been benchmarked.

TQHR departmental productivity savings have reduced operating expenses by $500,000. Additional direct savings from TQHR-driven initiatives in one year were $5.6 million from business process improvement projects, $2.75 million saved in health costs because of better working practices, and $2.1 million through workforce planning.

With a renewed focus on high customer service and quality standards, Peixotto's reengineered process is receiving high marks for internal customer satisfaction. The highest rated attributes of the TQHR unit are customer responsiveness, "easy to do business with," accessibility and flexibility. Previously, these qualities were among those the original HR department performed less well, which contributed to a loss of organizational credibility. Peixotto now feels that the redesigned and repositioned TQHR unit is well placed (and expert enough) to work in partnership with other support areas in the company. They are now begin-

ning to have a substantial impact on quality problems through the use of process improvement projects and, where appropriate, by reengineering processes or by specific departmental activities.

TQHR is now a kind of "amoebic unit," which Peixotto describes as teams separating and forming as required, continuously learning and operating as if every day is a new pilot project. He comments, "Change is the organization's constant. TQHR's job is to increase its own effectiveness first, to help people to understand their processes and to cope with the level of change we're creating. The big name of the game for the late 1990s will be managing change."

Bob Peixotto says that L.L. Bean's traditional HR department, the forerunner of the total quality and human resources unit, was viewed as "the necessary organizational stepchild and extra business cost." The reengineered, customer-focused department, in contrast, is described as "easy to do business with," accessible and flexible. If the name of the game for the turn of the century is to be managing change, the TQHR unit at L.L. Bean will surely be at the forefront.

Key Issues for Discussion

1. Discuss L.L. Bean's approach to blending human resource management with total quality. What lessons can be applied to other organizations?
2. How has the TQHR Department modeled the characteristics of teams given in Scholtes' list of successful team characteristics?
3. Because L.L. Bean is primarily a service firm, what special challenges does it face as it attempts to emphasize quality to its employees?

 ## REVIEW QUESTIONS

1. Discuss the impact of the Taylor system on quality, productivity, and human resource management. How has TQ changed business thinking about Taylor?
2. Define *human resource management*. Contrast it with the traditional role of personnel management.
3. Contrast traditional HRM approaches with those required in a TQ environment.
4. Summarize the leading HRM practices encountered in TQ organizations.
5. What is a *team*? Define the major types of teams found in organizations today.

6. Contrast the differences between quality circles and self-managed teams. What are the key characteristics of self-managed teams not found in quality circles?

7. What roles must be fulfilled within the structure of teams? What steps can team leaders take to coach less experienced team members to enhance team performance?

8. Discuss the four phases that teams typically go through during their life cycle.

9. Explain the important issues an organization must consider in developing successful teams.

10. How are the roles in Six Sigma teams similar to and different from traditional project teams?

11. What is *high-performance work*? What types of HR practices contribute to a high-performance work environment?

12. Explain the difference between *work design* and *job design*. How does the Hackman and Oldham model enhance understanding of how job design affects motivation, satisfaction, and organizational effectiveness?

13. What is *employee involvement*? Discuss some of the early developments of EI approaches. What are the advantages of EI over traditional management practices?

14. How can managers overcome resistance to EI initiatives?

15. What is *empowerment*? Discuss the changes that empowerment brings to organizations.

16. Discuss the role of training and education in supporting total quality.

17. What types of compensation practices support total quality?

18. What are the key practices that lead to effective recognition and reward approaches?

19. What issues must organizations consider with respect to health, safety, and employee well-being in the work environment?

20. In a TQ-based organization, what is the role of recruitment and career development? What challenges does TQ pose in these areas?

21. Define the term *motivation*. Why is motivation critical in a TQ environment?

22. Briefly summarize traditional performance appraisal processes. Within a TQ perspective, what objections have been raised concerning these processes? What steps can be taken to make performance appraisal more consistent with TQ principles?

23. What is *360-degree feedback*? How does it differ from traditional performance appraisal approaches? How does it address the major criticisms of traditional performance appraisal processes and support TQ efforts?

24. Why is it important to measure employee satisfaction and HRM effectiveness? Describe some common approaches.

25. Summarize the HRM issues addressed in the Malcolm Baldrige National Quality Award criteria, ISO 9000:2000, and the Six Sigma philosophy.

 ## Discussion Questions

1. What is your reaction to the quote about Toyota in the opening paragraph of the chapter? Would such an observation be true of most other organizations? Is it really true that competitors cannot copy the human resources of an organization? Why or why not?

2. Peter Drucker, arguably the most respected and influential writer on management, observed:

   Whatever his limitations and shortcomings—and he had many—no other American, not even Henry Ford (1863–1947), had anything like Taylor's impact. "Scientific Management: (and its successor, "Inudstrial Engineering") is the one American philosophy that has swept the world—more so even than the Constitution and the Federalist Papers. In the last century there has been only one worldwide philosophy that could compete with Taylor's: Marxism. And in the end Taylor has triumphed over Marx.[76]

   Comment on Drucker's observations about the Taylor system. Do you agree with his statement about Taylor versus Marx? Why or why not?

3. What can an organization do about individuals who "aren't good with numbers" if they have a policy that they become Green Belts, and later, Black Belts, as a prerequisite for promotion to higher levels of management?

4. How can a fraternity or student organization use leading HRM practices of companies to develop its own strategic HRM plans? If you are involved in such an organization, develop a strategic HRM plan that supports total quality.

5. Think of a job you have had. Apply the Hackman and Oldham model to evaluate how the job design impacted your motivation and satisfaction, as well as organizational effectiveness.

6. Recently, new "employee performance software" has been developed to track individual output. For example, British Airways uses it to ensure that customer service reps' time in the break room or on personal calls doesn't count on the clock. The technology can keep track so that extra incentive dollars are eventually directed in to the paychecks of those whose digital records merit them. It can also help managers understand how to assemble the most effective teams or who to lay off.[77] Discuss the implications of such technology from a TQ perspective.

7. Cite some examples of empowerment or lack of empowerment from your own experiences.

8. How might the concept of empowerment be employed in a classroom?

9. Undoubtedly you have received a recorded message prior to a call to company that says something like "For quality purposes, this call may be recorded." What do you think the real purpose of such an approach is? Is it to improve quality or to monitor poorly trained employees or catch them deviating from company scripts? Would an empowered organization need to use this method?

10. Many companies today seek the best available applicants and train them in TQ principles. What implications does this practice have for designing college curricula and choosing elective courses in a given program?

11. How might a jazz quartet be viewed as a metaphor for a team in a business situation?

12. Students in early grades often receive many kinds of recognition: stickers, candy, and so on, for good work. As we discussed, similar forms of recognition are common in the workplace. Yet little daily recognition is given at the high school and college level. Discuss possible reasons for this difference and design a recognition program that might be appropriate in your class.

13. Consider the statement, "How one is evaluated determines how one performs." What does this notion mean for your classes? Would your performance change if grades were abolished (as Deming strongly advocated)?

14. Discuss the controversy over performance appraisal. Do you agree with Deming's approach, or do you take the more traditional viewpoint toward performance review? Why?

15. Most colleges and universities use a course/instructor evaluation system. If your school has one, how is it used? Does it support continuous improvement or is it used strictly for performance appraisal? How might the evaluation instrument or process be modified to better reflect TQ principles?

16. Jack Welch, former CEO of General Electric, stated his passion for making people GE's core competency. He used a system in which executives in the bottom 10 percent of a forced performance ranking were eliminated. What do you think of this approach? How does it fit with a TQ philosophy? How would you respond to someone who says, "I think all my people are pretty good. If I fire the bottom 10 percent, that would just give me a new bottom 10 percent. Where does it end?" Read the paper at http://www.worklab-consulting.com (click on IQ) for some perspectives.

17. The training strategy that Xerox used is summarized as follows:
    a. The training is uniform—common tools and processes are taught across all of Xerox, to all employees, creating a "common language within Xerox" that fosters cohesive team functioning.
    b. Training is conducted in family groups, with all members starting and finishing training at the same time to facilitate the change process.
    c. Training starts at the top of the organization with the CEO and cascades downward to all employees.[78]

    What advantages does such strategy have? Do you see any possible disadvantages? Would this approach work in any business?

18. Discuss the conditions under which team incentives, gainsharing, and "pay for increased skills" reward systems may work. When is it a poor idea to install such systems?

19. A restaurant owner noted that "waitstaff skills are very trainable; human-being skills are not. I can train anyone to be knowledgeable about our wine list or how to clear a table properly. But I cannot teach people to care about how their actions affect others." Do you agree with the statement?

20. What motivates *you* to study and perform in the classroom? How do motivation theories apply to you personally? Discuss how these theories might lead to new ways of teaching and learning.

21. When simple theories such as those of Maslow, Herzberg, and McGregor explain motivation, why does the search continue for more complex ones or for ones that integrate several different theories, such as Porter and Lawler's theory? What implications do they have for quality? (Read the Bonus Materials on Theories of Motivation first.)

22. Suppose that someone told you that she was just promoted to manager of a department with several "star" employees who are constantly getting new job offers. Aside from compensation issues (assume they are well-paid), what might you suggest as means of ensuring that these employees remain loyal to the company? Labor relations between unions and management can make it difficult to establish TQ-oriented HRM practices within organizations.

23. The National Labor Relations Board (NLRB) ruled on two cases in 1993 and 1994 that complicate a company's determination of how far it can go legally to set up and use employee participation programs (EPPs) to make improvements in the workplace. The two cases involved a small, nonunion company, Electromation, and a large company, DuPont. These case decisions by a five-person board were based on interpretations of the 58-year-old National Labor Relations Act (NLRA, or Wagner Act) that prohibits unfair labor practices. The rulings are found in the

NLRB proceedings as *Electromation vs. International Brotherhood of Teamsters* (309 NLRB-No. 163), and *E. I. duPont de Nemours and Company vs. Chemical Workers Association, Inc.* (311 NLRB-No. 88). In the *Electromation* case, the nonunion company's management set up five employee action committees to deal with policies concerning absenteeism, smoking, communications, pay for premium positions, and attendance bonuses. In DuPont's case, management unilaterally (without bargaining with the union) changed the composition of safety and fitness committees to include nonmanagerial employees (where the committees had previously been composed only of management) at a unionized New Jersey plant. Stated briefly, the cases specified that "employer-dominated labor organizations" are prohibited. In both cases, the employee teams/committees were ruled to be "labor organizations" and to be "management dominated." Discuss the implications of these cases, particularly in the context of TQ. You might wish to conduct further research on these cases.

 ## PROJECTS, ETC.

1. Briefly review the history of HRM. Conduct a thorough literature search of one of the "branches" of HRM and relate it to current quality management issues. Search some current business periodicals (e.g., *Fortune, Business Week*) for articles dealing with HRM issues. Explain how they relate to the material in this chapter. Are any new approaches emerging?
2. Interview managers at a local organization about their HRM practices, focusing on work and job design issues. Report on your perceptions of how well their practices support a high-performance workplace.
3. Survey local companies to determine if and how they use suggestion systems. What levels of participation do they have? Are suggestions tied to rewards and recognitions?
4. Investigate the extent of team participation at some local companies. What kinds of teams do you find? Do managers believe these teams are effective?
5. Find a small to medium-sized company that is using Six Sigma teams. Have they changed the GE/Motorola model in the way that they train and use team leaders and resource people (Green, Black, and Master Black Belts)? Are they using those roles for management development purposes?
6. Survey several managers in one or two companies on the topic of motivation for quality. Try to find managers at each of the following levels to interview:
   a. Quality control/assurance
   b. Manufacturing or industrial engineering
   c. Upper-level management
   d. First-line supervision
   e. Line employees (perhaps a union steward or officer)
7. Research the impacts of the Internet Age on human resource practices in an actual firm. One possible approach would be to interview an HR manager at a company that is changing from a bricks-and-mortar to an Internet-based organization (such as a telephone company that is shifting to a broad-based communications firm). Another approach might be to visit the Web sites of several firms, examine HR practices that may be described , and compare and contrast your findings.

CASES

I. THE HOPEFUL TELECOMMUTER

Jennifer Smith was pregnant, and she was happy about it. She and her husband, Jim, had been planning to start a family for some time. However, she was concerned about her job as a Northeast Zone supply chain manager for health and beauty products for Big Bear Stores. Big Bear was a large, multibillion dollar foodstore chain that had stores in 47 states. It was a conventionally organized retailer divided into three geographic regions (Atlantic, Mid-American, and Western) with 12 zones (4 per region).

Zone supply chain managers, such as Jennifer, were the link between the store managers and their product-line suppliers. Jennifer had been ranked number one in customer and in supplier satisfaction surveys for health and beauty product lines for the last two years. She knew that she was eligible for six months of maternity leave under the federal Family Leave Act, and that the company would have to provide a job for her upon her return. What she didn't like was the thought that they did not have to, and probably would not, give her the same job that she was now holding so well.

Jennifer had talked with Jim, at length, about what to do. They agreed that she should approach her regional manager, Sarah Strong, the Zone VP, about the possibility of "telecommuting" to her job after the baby came. Jennifer thought that she could do 85–90 percent of the job at home on her own schedule. A large part of her job consisted of verbal and fax contacts with store managers and suppliers, as well as extensive use of a computer for manipulating databases, preparing spreadsheet reports, and sending and responding to e-mail. The other 10–15 percent of the time, when she had to be in the office for face-to-face meetings or had to take brief trips, her parents and Jim could keep the baby and cover for her at home.

When Jennifer approached Sarah Strong, she was interested, but would not commit herself to supporting Jennifer's request to telecommute. She said that the company had never done that before, and it might pose a number of difficulties. She did say that she would take her request forward to the two V.P.'s who could approve or disapprove it. Both senior managers would have to approve Jennifer's request, however. Sarah asked Jennifer to prepare some "talking points" concerning the benefits versus the limitations of the arrangement that she could present to the vice president of human resources, and the senior vice president of operations, Sarah's manager. She also asked her to prepare a cost estimate, in consultation with the Zone information systems manager.

The following was what Jennifer prepared for the estimated costs:

Laptop computer and docking station	$3,500.00
Setup DSL dedicated phone line	250.00
Fax machine	250.00
Computer desk and chair	375.00
Telephone line charges (6 months)	240.00
Total	$4,615.00

Discussion Questions

1. You are Jennifer. What "talking points" would you prepare to support your case? Include both the strengths and limitations of telecommuting. Keep in mind the needs of your "customers," the human resources VP, as well as Sarah, and the VP of operations.
2. What issues do you think that the VP of human resources might raise? What issues do you think the senior VP of operations might raise?
3. How does your answer demonstrate the principles of empowerment? How might it fit the components of the Hackman-Oldham Job Characteristics model?

II. CRYSTAL SILICON, INC.

Crystal Silicon, Inc. (CSI), manufactures ultra-pure silicon wafers for the semiconductor industry located in the midwestern United States.[79] The plant employs approximately 600 people. The hourly workforce is nonunion, and most are hired without much experience in the industry and are trained locally, because it is difficult to entice experienced and highly paid employees from the West Coast to move to the Midwest location.

Electronics engineer Vernon L. Essai (pronounced *S-eye*) founded CSI in the early 1980s. Essai had worked for Texas Instruments and Intel for 10 years. He learned the value of innovation and was able to stay ahead of the technology curve while running a small company by being agile and stressing high quality of products. He was finding it increasingly hard to attract innovative product designers in what had become a worldwide marketplace for people with talent.

CSI's management structure is pretty traditional, with a highly educated, technically trained design department, and the functional departments of marketing, production, administration, and finance, each presided over by one of the five vice presidents.

Direct supervisors conduct performance appraisals of all employees, and identify key objectives for personal development that are reviewed by the department managers. A principal focus of this process is to identify the things that employees will need to do for promotions and career development. Supervisors are trained to look for high potential in workers and continually try to motivate them to seek career development opportunities. These appraisals are supplemented by formal yearly performance evaluations. Hourly employees are rated on safety, quality, production output, dependability, initiative, judgment, teamwork, and attendance. Salaried employees are rated on safety, knowledge, planning and organization, execution and results, initiative, creativity, teamwork, and communication. These ratings directly affect their yearly merit increase. The HR department trains all new managers and supervisors on how to conduct performance appraisals.

During the yearly planning process, department managers work with senior managers to determine training needs. Senior management then meets with the HR director to determine what the budget can support.

Rewards are given for perfect attendance, and all employees participate in a financial incentive program, which is paid out quarterly. Financial bonuses are based upon results of on-time delivery, customer complaints, process yield, and lost work-day accidents. Bucking an industry trend, stock options have not been used to reward either senior managers for exceptional results, or design team members, who have "scored home runs" in designing innovative and profitable products. Essai was asked about it by one of the vice presidents, and he replied, "Why should I give away the company to people who are just doing their jobs? If we see that they are well paid for their work, why would they want to work harder for some gamble that our stock will go up in the future?"

CSI uses an employee survey to determine sources of dissatisfaction and opportunities for improvement. Survey questions measure behavioral impacts on productivity, profitability, customer satisfaction, and turnover. The data are segmented by type of employee (i.e., salaried vs. hourly) as well as by job type and department.

Despite CSI's careful attention to systematic employee appraisal, fair compensation, and financial rewards for accomplishment of goals, and in the face of a technology downturn, turnover recently increased substantially. The employee survey showed pockets of dissatisfaction among both hourly and salaried workers related to opportunities for challenge on the job and growth in knowledge of how to perform jobs better.

Discussion Questions

1. How does CSI's approach to performance appraisal support high performance work? Discuss the differences in evaluating hourly and salaried employees. Do these distinctions make sense?
2. Why are financial bonuses based only on the factors cited, despite the comprehensive categories on which employees are rated during performance appraisals?
3. How might a team approach be introduced

and developed to increase employee involvement, empowerment, and commitment?
What changes might be required in the roles
of managers and line workers if the plant
was reorganized into teams?

4. What advice might you give the company to

better leverage its performance appraisal
approach?

5. Can you advance some reasons why
turnover is increasing and employee dissatisfaction growing, based on HR processes and
leadership factors?

III. TVS PARTNERSHIP PROPRIETARY, LTD., BRISBANE, AUSTRALIA[80,81]

The environment of property development and
the need for architectural services has been very
volatile in Australia. In the mid-1990s the development of commercial properties, such as resorts,
office buildings, hotels, and apartment complexes,
went through a rapid boom and bust cycle. Many
developers eventually declared bankruptcy, and as
a result, numerous architectural and property
development firms either shrank in size or went
bankrupt also.

TVS Partnership Proprietary, Ltd.,[82] is a small,
closely held professional partnership that in 1990
had a staff of 12, and grew to about 22 people in the
parent organization, plus approximately 55 others
in subsidiary firms. From 1990 until 1997, TVS won
numerous design profession awards, as well as the
Australian Quality Award in 1993, which it was the
first small business in Australia to win.

To smooth out business cycles, TVS has diver-
sified into other services, such as interior design,
environmental design, landscape architecture, and
hotel property management. It invested in
research, developing the first solar house (Solar I)
in Australia, and pioneered in efforts to use "environmentally friendly" building design and management processes. During the period between
1990 and 1997, the firm grew by more than 50 percent in number of employees. Annual turnover
(revenue) increased by approximately 50 percent
per year for the last several years.

TVS was first introduced to formal concepts of
TQ in 1989. The organization is led by five directors. All five are involved in, and responsible for,
promoting quality, motivation, improvement, plan
review, competitive performance, goals and objectives, education and training, and customer and
supplier relations. Individual directors are responsible for overview and improvement of specific
areas of activity, such as finance and administration, office facilities, operations, research and
development, human resources, public relations,

and quality processes. They are very proud of
their leadership style.

The vision of TVS focuses on three areas—self,
customers, and community. "Success through service" was developed as a company slogan in 1990.
The firm broadened its perspective to a customer
focus about 1992. In 1993 it added a community
focus. The I-CARE philosophy, an acronym for
"Improvement that is continuous and relentless,"
extends across the TVS organization. It expresses
values, goals, and aspirations and provides a practical and tangible guide to work by individuals
within the firm. It is also, of course, a marketing
tool that is used to ensure that customers are
aware of the philosophy and implied quality that
they can expect to receive from the firm. The TVS
philosophy can be summarized by:

- Improvement that is continuous and relentless
- The power of teams
- The importance of its individual members
- The long-term focus
- Understanding and satisfying client needs
- Creative, cost-effective, and efficient solu-
tions that give more with less
- The integration of the specialist design disci-
plines—architecture (the built environment),
interior design (the human interface), and
landscape design (the natural environment)
- The value of efficient and appropriate
supporting processes and technology
- Management by measurement, data, and
analysis
- A long-term commitment to the local and
global environment
- The encouragement of honesty, trust,
integrity, and responsibility
- Innovation

Recruiting is based primarily on referral with
little advertising. In addition, TVS extends offers
to students who have worked at the firm through

a cooperative student program at Queensland University of Technology, and selects the best interns who graduate from various university hospitality programs (for its hotel division). During a probation period of four months the company tries to assess and retain new employees who are high achievers and people with good values.

Clarity of induction, through use of an induction manual, helps to ensure that all divisions and new employees are aligned with company goals. The I-CARE philosophy and principles are stressed for new hires. TVS enjoys very low turnover; average retention is about seven years. TVS's induction process allows the managing director to walk into any division and immediately feel comfortable. The values emphasized are honesty and integrity, customer focus, the concept of customer service, service to the community, fire and enthusiasm, commitment to grow, commitment to change, support of a dynamic theory of the firm, and understanding of the need for continuously changing processes.

Some weaknesses are apparent in the induction process, however, especially as it relates to transmission of the TQ philosophy. Those who were at TVS at the time of receiving the AQA are probably the most enthusiastic about TQ. Even the veteran draftsmen could explain the quality process and its components. However, this familiarity seems to be lacking in newer employees.

The induction manual was written just prior to receipt of the AQA Award and has not been revised since that date. In it, the current corporate philosophy, culture, teamwork, and the reward and recognition process are mentioned only in passing. The nature of the employee mix is now quite varied, compared to 1992. The firm now has technical staff, administrative staff, service staff, and professionals (architects, designers, managers, etc.). They need general knowledge about the firm and its everyday procedures, but also specialized knowledge pertaining to their division.

TVS experienced a serious drop in morale in 1994 due to three factors: (1) an external environmental slump, with many property developers going bankrupt, (2) a shift of the firm's offices to temporary quarters for six months while a new office was being built, and (3) new offshore expansion projects. At that point TVS developed a new strategic planning approach. The Leadership team (five directors, two associates, and the quality

manager), reorganized the management of the firm into teams, and dropped centralized job controls. Job costing was shifted to the teams, and an administrative team became facilitators. Quality control was also made a team responsibility.

Prior to setting up the teams, weekly alignment meetings for the whole office had been held to coordinate employee and company efforts. Everyone had to speak or pass at the meetings run without meeting facilitators. As the firm grew, even less input took place, because the less articulate staff became reluctant to speak in a large-group setting. Eventually, these weekly meetings were discontinued because they were becoming too unproductive.

Weekly meetings of smaller teams were used as a substitute for the alignment meetings. However, weekly meetings were sometimes problematic because of travel schedules and urgent tasks of directors and team leaders. Of 12 planned monthly meetings, the directors were able to attend only 8 to 10. Teams sometimes became jealous of each other's territories. Although these team meetings produced cohesion among group members, the level of interteam coordination suffered. When more people were needed on a team, some were moved to the team needing resources (not always happily).

TVS is currently finalizing another team reorganization to improve interteam coordination. Two people from each team will now meet weekly. Full office meetings will be held monthly. The cost coordination will fall on the shoulders of the project leader.

Compensation is an area where the directors of TVS have struggled. Before 1993 they set aside 10 percent of profit for salary increases and bonuses. They would meet and debate how much each person should get at each level. They came up with several elaborate schemes for allocating the amounts to each person systematically. In the end, this arrangement did not work well. After winning the AQA, they went back to the old allocation method.

TVS tried to diversify the types of reward and recognition systems. One such program, The Eagle Card, was a motivational system developed by an American management consultant. For outstanding performance, employees received Eagle Cards and various rewards associated with them. However, TVS determined that such approaches have a short life cycle, after which they must be replaced by a new scheme.

TVS's directors are flexible about the type of rewards and recognition used. They like to reward employees for outstanding performance as close to the event as possible. For example, they have done such things as paid for an employee's wedding, paid the deposit for a person's house, given an employee time off and paid for a trip to Bangladesh for humanitarian purposes, and bought a set of tires for an employee who needed them. They will give time off for a sabbatical, time to sort out family life, and so on. The downside is that employees occasionally feel that they did not receive a reward when they deserved one. Although the directors complied with the AQA criteria, which suggest that they should have a consistent, repeatable process for rewarding people, they struggled with the notion, feeling it was not right for their organization. The final success of many projects cannot be measured for a year or more after commencement.

TVS tried an employee shareholding plan in 1990. Many employees were not interested and did not appreciate the value of shares. The plan

was reviewed and the company directors eventually bought back the employees' shares. Problems arose with the valuation and transfer of shares between employees. Recently they began to issue shares to senior managers. It is now being proposed that the company will issue and sell shares to senior managers and associates on an invitation basis.

Discussion Questions

1. How may changes in the organizational structure affected human resource policies? What were the strengths and weaknesses in the human resources management approaches that TVS adopted?
2. Why has the HR function undergone so many changes in a short period of time? What might you recommend?
3. Creative and operations-oriented parts of an organization often view quality from different points of view. How could managers from the different divisions be encouraged to share their perspectives and knowledge to benefit the whole organization?

IV. CAPSTAR HEALTH SYSTEMS: HUMAN RESOURCE FOCUS

The complete CapStar case study, a fictitious example of a Baldrige application, can be found on the CD-ROM that accompanies this book. If you have not read CapStar's Organizational Profile yet (see Case III in Chapter 3), please do so first. Examine their response to Category 5 in the context of the leading practices described in this

chapter (you need not consider the actual Baldrige criteria for this activity). What are their strengths? What are their weaknesses and opportunities for improvement? What specific advice, including useful tools and techniques that might help them, would you suggest?

ENDNOTES

1. Robin Yale Bergstrom, "People, Process, Paint," *Production*, April 1995, 48–51.

2. James L. Heskett, W. Earl Sasser, Jr., and Leonard A. Schlesinger, *The Service Profit Chain* (New York: The Free Press, 1997), 101.

3. "How Companies Satisfy Employees," available at http://www.Fortune.com, January 7, 2003. See also "100 Best Companies to Work For," *Fortune,* January 20, 2003.

4. Town Hall discussion at the Quest for Excellence Conference, Washington D.C., March 2000.

5. Richard E. Walton, "From Control to Commitment in the Workplace," *Harvard Business Review* 63, no.

2 (March/April 1985), 77–84. © by the President and Fellows of Harvard College; all rights reserved.

6. Lloyd L. Byars and Leslie W. Rue, *Human Resource Management*, 6th ed. (New York: Irwin/McGraw-Hill, 2000), 6.

7. Richard Blackburn and Benson Rosen, "Total Quality and Human Resources Management: Lessons Learned from Baldrige Award-Winning Companies," *Academy of Management Executive* 7, no. 3 (1993), 49–66.

8. Blackburn and Rosen (see note 7).

9. Alfie Kohn, *No Contest: The Case Against Competition* (Boston: Houghton Mifflin, 1986).

10. Jon R. Katzenback and Douglas K. Smith, "The Discipline of Teams," *Harvard Business Review* (March/April 1993), 111–120.

11. Jack D. Orsburn, Linda Moran, Ed Musselwhite, and John H. Zenger, *Self-Directed Work Teams* (Homewood, IL: Business One-Irwin, 1990), 8.

12. Brian Dumaine, "The Trouble with Teams," *Fortune*, 5 September, 1994, 86–92.

13. Much of the brief history in this section has been adapted from J. M. Juran, "The QC Circle Phenomenon," *Industrial Quality Control,* January 1967, 329–336.

14. "Platform Approach at Chrysler," *Quality '93: Empowering People with Technology, Fortune* Advertisement, September 20, 1993.

15. Brock Yates, *The Critical Path* (Boston: Little, Brown and Co., 1996), 76.

16. Jeremy Main. *Quality Wars* (New York: The Free Press, 1994), 62.

17. Sidney P. Rubinstein, "QC Circles and U.S. Participative Movements," *1972 ASQC Technical Conference Transactions*, Washington, D.C., 391–396.

18. For more about the history and impact of quality circles in the early 1980s in the United States, see William M. Lindsay, *Measurement of Quality Circle Effectiveness: A Survey and Critique*, unpublished M.S. thesis, University of Cincinnati, College of Engineering (May 1986), 72, 117–120.

19. Helene F. Uhlfelder, "It's All About Improving Performance," *Quality Progress*, February 2000, 47–52.

20. Harvey A. Robbins and Michael Finley, *Why Teams Don't Work: What Went Wrong and How to Make it Right* (Princeton, NJ: Peterson's/Pacesetter Books, 1995), 14–15.

21. Samuel C. Certo, *Modern Management,* 9th ed. (Upper Saddle River, NJ:Prentice Hall, 2003), 389.

22. Peter R. Scholtes et al., *The Team Handbook: How to Use Teams to Improve Quality* (Madison, WI: Joiner Associates, Inc., 1988) 6-10–6-22.

23. Nancy Page Cooper and Pat Noonan. "Do Teams and Six Sigma Go Together?" *Quality Progress* 36, no. 6 (June 2003), 26–27.

24. Portions adapted from Chapter 4, "Motivation Through the Design of Work," in J. R. Hackman and G. R. Oldham, *Work Redesign* (Reading, MA: Addison-Wesley, 1980).

25. Hackman and Oldham, 25 (see note 24).

26. David A Garvin, *Managing Quality* (New York: The Free Press, 1988), 202–203.

27. Tom J. Peters, *Thriving on Chaos: Handbook for a Management Revolution* (New York: Alfred A. Knopf, 1988).

28. Alan Wolf, "Golden Opportunities," *Beverage World,* February 1991.

29. Robert Slater, *Jack Welch and the GE Way* (New York: McGraw-Hill, 1999), 153–155, 158–159.

30. A more comprehensive review of history and the forerunners of quality circles from the early 1900s can be found in William M. Lindsay, "Quality Circles and Participative Work Improvement: A Cross-Disciplinary History," in Dennis F. Ray (ed.), *Southern Management Association Proceedings* (Mississippi State, MS: Mississippi State University, 1987), 220–222.

31. Joseph J. Gufreda, Larry A. Maynard, and Lucy N. Lytle, "Employee Involvement in the Quality Process," in The Ernst & Young Quality Improvement Consulting Group, *Total Quality!: An Executive's Guide for the 1990s* (Homewood, IL: Richard D. Irwin, 1990).

32. From materials provided by Mike Simms, former plant manager.

33. "It's My Manager, Stupid," *Across the Board*, January 2000, 9.

34. J. M. Juran, *Juran on Leadership for Quality: An Executive Handbook* (New York: The Free Press, 1989), 264.

35. Phillip A. Smith, William D. Anderson, and Stanley A. Brooking, "Employee Empowerment: A Case Study," *Production and Inventory Management* 34, no. 3 (1993), 45–50.

36. John Troyer, "Empowerment," Guest Editorial, *Quality Digest*, October 1996, 64.

37. AT&T Quality Steering Committee, *Great Performances* (AT&T Bell Laboratories, 1991), 39; and William Smitley and David Scott, "Empowerment: Unlocking the Potential of Your Work Force," *Quality Digest* 14, no. 8 (August 1994), 40–46.

38. "Changing a Culture: DuPont Tries to Make Sure That Its Research Wizardry Serves the Bottom Line," *The Wall Street Journal*, March 27, 1992, A5.

39. Robert S. Kaplan, "Texas Eastman Company," Harvard Business School Case, No. 9-190-039.

40. John F. Akers, "World-Class Quality: Nothing Else Will Do," *Quality Progress* 24, no. 10 (October 1991), 26–27.

41. Timothy Aeppel, "Not All Workers Find Idea of Empowerment As Neat As It Sounds," The Wall Street Journal, September 8, 1997, A1.

42. Ronald Henkoff, "Make Your Office More Productive," *Fortune*, February 25, 1991, 76.

43. "Small Company's Training Policy Yields Big Results," *The Human Element* (a publication of the Human Development and Leadership Division of the American Society for Quality), 20, no. 1 (Spring 2003).

44. Alan Wolf, "Coors' Customer Focus," *Beverage World,* March 1991.

45. Bill Wilson, "Quality Training at FedEx," *Quality Digest* 15, no. 1 (January 1995), 40–43.

46. "Honda of America Launches Computerized Quality Assurance Training," *Quality Progress* 30, no. 10 (October 1997), 19–20.

47. "Bonus Pay: Buzzword or Bonanza?" *Business Week*, November 14, 1994, 62–64.

48. Woodrumm Imberman, "Pay for Performance Boosts Quality Output," *IIE Solutions*, October 1996, 34–36.

49. Quoted from "Statement of Pam Farr, President & COO, The Cabot Advisory Group on behalf of Cabot Advisory Group, Llc on The Rewarding Performance in Compensation Act before the House Committee on Education and the Workforce Subcommittee on Workforce Protections—April 13, 1999."

50. Nancy J. Perry, "Here Come Richer, Riskier Pay Plans," *Fortune*, December 19, 1988, 50–58; "The Nucor Story," available at http://www.nucor.com.

51. Frank C. Barnes, "Nucor (A)," in Robert R. Bell and John M. Burnham, *Managing Productivity and Change* (Cincinnati, OH: South-Western Publishing Company, 1991), 507.

52. Chris Adams, "Nucor Slashes Its Hot-Rolled Steel Prices by 7%," *The Wall Street Journal*, September 30, 1997, A3.

53. Bruce N. Pfau and Steven E. Gross, *Innovative Reward and Recognition Strategies in TQM*, The Conference Board, Report Number 1051, 1993.

54. Brian O'Reilly, "The Mechanic Who Fixed Continental," *Fortune*, December 20, 1999, 176–186.

55. Dawn Anfuso, "L.L. Bean's TQM Efforts Put People Before Processes," *Personnel Journal*, July 1994, 73–83.

56. "Bonus Pay: Buzzword or Bonanza?" *Business Week*, November 14, 1994, 62–64.

57. Bob Nelson, "Secrets of Successful Employee Recognition," *Quality Digest*, August 1996, 26–30.

58. Leigh Ann Klaus, "Motorola Brings Fairy Tales to Life," *Quality Progress*, June 1997, 25–28.

59. "Domino's Pizza, Inc., *"Profiles in Quality* (Boston: Allyn and Bacon, 1991), 90–93.

60. Michelle Conlin and Kathy Moore, "Photo Essay—SAS," *Business Week*, June 19, 2000, 192–202.

61. Saul W. Gellerman, *Motivation in the Real World* (New York: Dutton, 1992).

62. James L. Bowditch and Anthony F. Buono, *A Primer on Organizational Behavior*, 2d ed. (New York: John Wiley & Sons, 1990), 52.

63. Jeremy Main, *Quality Wars* (New York: The Free Press, 1994), 130.

64. Khalid A. Aldakhilallah and Diane H. Parente, "Redesigning a Square Peg: Total Quality Management Performance Appraisals," *Total Quality Management* 13, no. 1 (2002), 39–51.

65. George Eckes, "Practical Alternatives to Performance Appraisals," *Quality Progress* 27, no. 11 (November 1994), 57–60.

66. Douglas McGregor, "An Uneasy Look at Performance Appraisal," *Harvard Business Review*, September–October 1972; Herbert H. Meyer, Emanuel Kay, and John R. P. French, Jr., "Split Roles in Performance Appraisal," *Harvard Business Review*, January–February 1965; Harry Levinson, "Appraisal of What Performance?" *Harvard*

Business Review, January–February 1965; A. M. Mohrman, *Deming Versus Performance Appraisal: Is There a Resolution?* (Los Angeles: Center for Effective Organizations, University of Southern California, 1989).

67. John F. Milliman and Fred R. McFadden, "Toward Changing Performance Appraisal to Address TQM Concerns: The 360-Degree Feedback Process," *Quality Management Journal* 4, no. 3 (1997), 44–64.

68. Milliman and McFadden (see note 67).

69. Dick Grote, "The Secrets of Performance Appraisal: Best Practices from the Masters," *Across the Board*, May 2000, 14–20.

70. Brian S. Morgan and William A. Schiemann, "Measuring People and Performance: Closing the Gaps," *Quality Progress*, January 1999, 47–53.

71. See John D. Cook, Susan J. Hepworth, Toby D. Wall, and Peter B. Warr, *The Experience of Work* (London, Academic Press, 1981); and Dale Henderson and Fess Green, "Measuring Self-Managed Workteams," *Journal for Quality and Participation*, January–February 1997, 52–56.

72. Mark R. Hagen, "Teams Expand into Cyberspace," *Quality Progress*, June 1999, 90–93.

73. Nancy Page Cooper and Pat Noonan, "Do Teams and Six Sigma Go Together?" *Quality Progress*, June 2003, 25–28.

74. Courtesy of TD Industries. Ben Houston, president.

75. Adapted from the L.L. Bean Web site, http://www.llbean.com and from Chris Ashton, "HR at the Forefront of Change Management at L.L. Bean," *International Journal of Retail Distribution Management* 26, no. 4–5, April 14, 1998, 192. Copyright 1998, MCB University Press, Ltd (UK). Used with permission of L.L. Bean, Inc. and Chris Ashton.

76. Peter F. Drucker. Management Challenges for the 21st Century. (New York: HarperBusiness, 1999), 139.

77. Michelle Conlin, "The Software Says You're Just Average," *Business Week*, February 25, 2002, 126.

78. Xerox Business Products and Systems, Malcolm Baldrige National Quality Award application, 1989.

79. This case was inspired by a Baldrige assessment project by our former students, Leo Chan, Cara Hastings, and Eric Vaughn.

80. By William M. Lindsay and Arthur Preston, Senior Research Fellow, Queensland University of Technology. See William M. Lindsay and Arthur Preston. "Maintaining Quality Through Evolving Strategy: The TVS Partnership" *Industrial Management and Data Systems*, 100, no. 4, (2000), 164–171, for further details.

81. Appreciation is expressed to the TVS Partnership Proprietary, Ltd., and especially to directors Laurie Truce and Mark Thomson, as well as Penny Pinkham, Quality Manager and Administrative Team Leader, for their hospitality and cooperation in preparation of this case.

82. Application of The TVS Partnership—Architects to the Australian Quality Award Foundation, Australian Quality Award, Small Enterprise, 1993.

BIBLIOGRAPHY

Andersen, Bjorn, and Tom Fagerhaug. *Performance Management Explained: Designing and Implementing Your State-of-the-Art System.* Milwuakee, WI: American Society for Quality, 2002.

AT&T Quality Steering Committee. *Batting 1000: Using Baldrige Feedback to Improve Your Business.* AT&T Bell Laboratories (1992).

Great Performances! AT&T Bell Laboratories, 1991.

Badracco, Joseph L. *Leading Quietly.* Boston: Harvard Business School Press, 2002.

Bens, Ingrid. *Facilitation at a Glance!* Cincinnati: AQP, 1999.

Blackburn, Richard, and Benjamin Rosen. "Total Quality and Human Resources Management: Lessons Learned from Baldrige Award-Winning Companies." *Academy of Management Executive* 7, no. 3 (1993), 49–66.

Buckingham, Marcus, and Curt Coffman. *First, Break All the Rules: What the World's Greatest Managers Do Differently.* New York: Simon and Schuster, 1999.

Byrne, John. *Chainsaw: The Notorious Career of Al Dunlop in the Age of Profit-at-Any-Price.* New York: HarperBusiness, 2002.

Christison, William L. "Financial Information Is Key to Empowerment." *Quality Progress* 27, no. 7 (July 1994), 47–48.

Eure, Rob. "E-Commerce (A Special Report): The Classroom—On the Job; Corporate E-Learning Makes Training Available Anytime, Anywhere," *The Wall Street Journal,* March 12, 2001, R33.

Galford, Robert, Laurie Broedling, Edward G. Lawler, III, Tim Riley, et al. "Why Doesn't This HR Department Get Any Respect?" *Harvard Business Review,* 76, no. 2, March/April 1998, 24–40.

Hackman, J. Richard. *Leading Teams: Setting the Stage for Great Performance.* Boston: Harvard Business School Press, 2002.

Herzberg, Frederick. *Work and the Nature of Man.* Cleveland, OH: World, 1966.

_____."One More Time: How Do You Motivate Employees?" *Harvard Business Review* 46, (January/ February 1968), 53–62.

Kanfer, Ruth. "Motivation Theory in Industrial and Organizational Psychology." In Marvin D. Dunnette and Leaeta M. Hough (eds.). *Handbook of Industrial and Organizational Psychology,* 2nd ed., vol. 1. Palo Alto, CA: Consulting Psychologists Press, Inc., 1990, 75–170.

Katzenbach, Jon R. and Douglas K. Smith. *The Wisdom of Teams.* New York: HarperBusiness, 2003.

Kern, Jill P., John J. Riley, and Louis N. Jones (eds.). *Human Resources Management.* Quality and Reliability Series, sponsored by the ASQC Human Resources Division. New York: Marcel Dekker, Inc., and Milwaukee: ASQC Quality Press, 1987.

Lewin, Kurt. *A Dynamic Theory of Personality.* New York: McGraw-Hill, 1935.

Lindsay, William M., and Joseph A. Petrick. *Total Quality and Organization Development.* Boca Raton, FL: CRC/St. Lucie Press, 1997.

Locke, E. A., and G. P. Latham. *Goal Setting: A Motivational Technique that Works!* Englewood Cliffs, NJ: Prentice Hall, 1984.

Mayo, Elton. *The Human Problems of Industrial Civilization.* Cambridge, MA: Harvard Graduate School of Business, 1946.

Messmer, Max. "Rightsizing, Not Downsizing: How to Maintain Quality Through Strategic Staffing." *Industry Week,* August 3, 1993, 23–26.

Miner, John B. *Theories of Organizational Behavior.* Hinsdale, IL: Dryden Press, 1980.

Morgan, Ronald B., and Jacke E. Smith. *Staffing the New Workplace: Selecting and Promoting for Quality Improvement.* Milwaukee, WI: ASQ Press, 1996.

Mohrman, Susan Albers, Ramkrishnan V. Tenkasi, Edward E. Lawler, III, and Gerald E. Ledford, Jr. "Total Quality Management: Practice and Outcomes in the Largest U.S. Firms, " *Employee Relations* 17, no. 3 (1995), 26–41.

Moorhead, Gregory, and Ricky W. Griffin. *Organizational Behavior: Managing People and Organizations,* 6th ed. New York: Houghton-Mifflin Co., 2001.

Olian, Judy D., and Sara L. Rynes. "Making Total Quality Work: Aligning Organizational Processes, Performance Measures, and Stakeholders." *Human Resource Management,* Fall 1991, 303–333.

Palmer, Brian, and Mike Ziemlanski "Tapping Into People," Quality Progress, April 2000, 74–79.

Petrick, Joseph A., and Diana Furr. *Total Quality in Managing Human Resources.* Boca Raton, FL: CRC/St. Lucie Press, 1995.

Powell, Cash, Jr. "Empowerment, the Stake in the Ground for ABS." *Target,* January/February 1992.

Rubinstein, Sidney P. "Quality and Democracy in the Workplace." Quality *Progress* 21, no. 4 (April 1988), 25–28.

Semerad, James M. "Create a New Learning Environment." *APICS—The Performance Advantage,* April 1993, 34–37.

Scholtes, P. R. The Team Handbook, 2nd ed. Madison, WI: Joiner Associates, 1996.

Simmons, David E., Mark A. Shadur, and Arthur P. Preston. "Integrating TQM and HRM, " *Employee Relations* 17, no. 3 (1995), 75–86.

Snape, Ed, Adrian Wilkinson, Mick Marchington, and Ted Redman. "Managing Human Resources for TQM: Possibilites and Pitfalls, " *Employee Relations* 17, no. 3 (1995), 42–51.

Snell, Scott A., and James W. Dean. "Integrated

Manufacturing and Human Resource Management: A Human Capital Perspective." *Academy of Management Journal* 35, no. 3 (1992), 467–504.

Taylor, Frederick W. *The Principles of Scientific Management*. New York: Harper & Row, 1911.

Steers, Richard M. Lyman W. Porter, and Gregory A. Bigley. *Motivation and Leadership at Work*, 6th ed. New York: McGraw-Hill, 1996.

Tichy, Noel, and Eli Cohen. "The Teaching Organization," *Training and Development*, July, 1998.

Walton, Richard E. "From Control to Commitment in the Workplace." *Harvard Business Review* 63, no. 2 (March/April 1985), 77–85.

Yee, William, and Ed Musselwhite. "Living TQM With Workforce 2000." *1993 ASQC Quality Congress Transactions*. Boston, 141–146.

CHAPTER 7

PROCESS MANAGEMENT

The "New Economy," as many call it, is revolutionizing business. Despite the dot-com crash at the turn of the century, online shopping has matured, and Amazon.com has garnered high marks in the American Customer Satisfaction Index (see Chapter 4). However, the debut of online retailing was fraught with problems. For example, between Thanksgiving and Christmas, 1999, some 22 million shoppers spent more than $5 billion shopping online.[1] Traffic on sites such as Yahoo and Kbkids.com grew by 500 percent. Outpost.com, a computer and electronics retailer, sold $2 million of merchandise in one day. However, it wasn't long before Internet message boards were filled with comments like "I doubt I will ever shop again online for Christmas" and other comments unfit to print here.

As *Fortune* magazine noted, "It takes much more than a logo and a Website to run an e-tailing operation. Online retailers aren't so different from brick and mortar stores. They run out of stock, sell damaged merchandise, and hire rude sales help . . . hordes of companies flooded the market. Trouble is, many of them spent heavily to market and promote their brands but scrimped on infrastructure—the unglamorous side of the business, which focuses on delivering products to customers. The results were often disastrous." Amazon.com, for example, initially tried to have suppliers maintain inventory, but it found that it needed to build traditional distribution centers around the country to improve customer service and control over the product.[2] A. Blanton Godfrey notes that many organizations are "wired for failure"; that is, their processes are not designed effectively or aligned with each other.[3] He cites other examples in addition to the problems that confronted e-retailers. One example is overscheduling at airports. During the 4:15 to 4:30 P.M. time slot, 35 arrivals are scheduled in Atlanta, even though in optimal weather conditions the airport can handle only 25 in 15 minutes; with bad weather, this number drops to 17. Another company celebrated its largest sales contract in history only to discover that all qualified suppliers for critical materials were at capacity. A third example is the unwillingness of departments to work together. For example, when products fail in the plant or in service, it isn't because designers choose components they know will fail; they often have insufficient information about the problems that result from their choices.

These observations point to the importance of designing and managing effective processes—such as product design, order entry, manufacturing, distribution, and customer service—throughout the value chain. Deming and Juran observed that the overwhelming majority of quality problems are associated with processes; few are caused by the workers themselves. Rather, management is responsible to design and continuously improve the processes with which individuals work. Actually, it shares this responsibility with the workforce. The former president of Texas Instruments Defense Systems & Electronics Group (now part of Raytheon) had a sign in his office that sums up these issues nicely: "Unless you change the process, why would you expect the results to change?"

> *Process management* involves planning and administering the activities necessary to achieve a high level of performance in key business processes, and identifying opportunities for improving quality and operational performance, and ultimately, customer satisfaction.

Process management activities help to prevent defects and errors, eliminate waste and redundancy, and thereby lead to better quality and improved company performance through shorter cycle times, improved flexibility, and faster customer response.

Nearly every leading company views process management as a fundamental business activity (see the *Quality Profiles* on page 312). AT&T, for example, bases its methodology on the following principles:

- Process quality improvement focuses on the end-to-end process.
- The mind-set of quality is one of prevention and continuous improvement.
- Everyone manages a process at some level and is simultaneously a customer and a supplier.
- Customer needs drive process quality improvement.
- Corrective action focuses on removing the root cause of the problem rather than on treating its symptoms.
- Process simplification reduces opportunities for errors and rework.
- Process quality improvement results from a disciplined and structured application of the quality management principles.[4]

QUALITY PROFILES

STMICROELECTRONICS, INC.—REGION AMERICAS, AND BOEING AIRCRAFT AND

TANKER PROGRAMS

Headquartered in Carrollton, Texas, STMicroelectronics, Inc.—Region Americas (ST), a wholly owned subsidiary of a French firm, ranks among the world's top manufacturers of semiconductor integrated circuits, supplying consumer electronics, automotive, medical, telecommunications, and computer equipment markets. ST competes against about 20 semiconductor manufacturers with broad product lines as well as hundreds of smaller rivals that serve niche markets. In this industry, missteps in planning and execution quickly translate into competitive disadvantages. ST aims to distinguish itself through advances in technological innovation, increases in the breadth of its product and service offerings, and continuous improvement in just-in-time delivery, fast prototyping, rapid problem resolution, and other areas responsive to customers' high-priority requirements. In 1998, ST initiated a "gung ho" program to promote teaming and employee empowerment, resulting in the redesign of manufacturing work systems and jobs, all with the aim of encouraging and enabling employees to take control of their work.

ST is tightly aligned with its parent corporation's quest to become the world leader in environmental compliance. In 1997 and 1998, energy used to manufacture silicon wafers declined by 20 percent. Employee satisfaction levels in 1999 exceed the industry composite in 8 of 10 categories, and its supplier management program earned "best in class" rating in an independent evaluation of performance in 19 benchmark areas. ST was a 1999 Baldrige Award winner.

Boeing Airlift and Tanker (A&T) Programs designs, develops, and produces the C-17 Globemaster 111 airlifter, which is capable of carrying 170,000 pounds and is used by the U.S. Air Force to transport large, heavy cargo to sites around the world. In 1996, A&T signed a $14.2 billion agreement to deliver 80 C-17s to the Air Force. A few years later, the Defense Department threatened to cancel the C-17 program because of technical problems, cost overruns, and late deliveries. A&T overhauled its operations to become "process-focused and customer-driven," initiating partnerships with customers, unions, and suppliers, and replacing manager-controlled teams with empowered teams of workers. To help it perform to plan, A&T developed a seven-step approach to defining, managing, stabilizing, and improving processes and established performance measures that are indicators of efficiency and the chief drivers of customer satisfaction: quality, timeliness, and cycle time. Using this process, one team developed a dry sealant to precoat the 1.4 million fasteners used to assemble a C-17 to replace a wet sealant that was difficult to apply and cost more to dispose of than to buy. The innovation reduced rework, improved airframe quality, reduced structural fatigue, and enabled mechanics to work "faster, cleaner, and better."

Between 1995 and its winning a Baldrige Award in 1998, A&T maintained an on-time delivery record of 100 percent. Productivity increased from $200,000 per employee in 1994 to more than $300,000 in 1998. Performance on key quality measures has improved by 50 percent during 1994–1998, cycle time was cut by more than 80 percent, and supplier on-time delivery increased from 75.9 percent to 99.8 percent. The C-17's 1997 level of performance was nearly four times better than that of the next best competitor's aircraft, and return on net assets was nearly seven times better than the next best competitor.

Source: Malcolm Baldrige National Quality Award, Profiles of Winners, National Institute of Standards and Technology, Department of Commerce.

This chapter discusses philosophies and approaches for designing and managing important processes in an organization. In Chapter 13, we will discuss specific tools and techniques for process improvement in the context of Six Sigma.

THE SCOPE OF PROCESS MANAGEMENT

As we noted in Chapter 1, essentially all work in an organization is performed by some process. Common business processes include acquiring customer and market knowledge, strategic planning, research and development, purchasing, developing new products or services, fulfilling customer orders, managing information, measuring and analyzing performance, and training employees, to name just a few.

Value-creation processes (sometimes called *core processes*) are those most important to "running the business" and maintaining or achieving a sustainable competitive advantage. They drive the creation of products and services, are critical to customer satisfaction, and have a major impact on the strategic goals of an organization.

> *Leading companies identify important business processes throughout the value chain that affect customer satisfaction. These processes typically fall into two categories: value-creation processes and support processes.*

Value-creation processes typically include design, production/delivery, and other critical business processes. **Design processes** involve all activities that are performed to incorporate customer requirements, new technology, and past learning into the functional specifications of a product (i.e., a manufactured good or service), and thus define its fitness for use. **Production/delivery processes** create or deliver the actual product; examples are manufacturing, assembly, dispensing medications, teaching a class, and so on. These processes must be designed to ensure that the product will conform to specifications (the manufacturing definition of quality) and also be produced economically and efficiently. Product design greatly influences the efficiency of manufacture as well as the flexibility of service strategies, and therefore must be coordinated with production/delivery processes. The ultimate value of the product, and hence, the perceived quality to the consumer, depend on both these types of processes.

Support processes are those that are most important to an organization's value-creation processes, employees, and daily operations. They provide infrastructure for value-creation processes but generally do not add value directly to the product or service. A process such as order entry that might be thought of as a value creation process for one company (e.g., a direct mail distributor) might be considered as a support process for another (e.g., a custom manufacturer). In general, value creation processes are driven by external customer needs while support processes are driven by internal customer needs. Because value creation processes do add value to products and services, they require a higher level of attention than do support processes. Table 7.1 shows the value creation processes and their requirements defined by Pal's Sudden Service. Their support processes include accounting/finance, human resources, maintenance, management information systems, ordering, and stocking. Other critical support processes that lead to business success and growth might be research and development, technology acquisition, supply chain management and supplier partnering, mergers and acquisitions, project management, or sales and marketing. These processes will differ greatly among organizations, depending on the nature of products and services, customer and market requirements, global focus, and other factors.

> *Process management consists of three key activities: design, control, and improvement.*

Table 7.1 Value Creation Processes for Pal's Sudden Service

Process	Principal Requirements
Order Taking	Accurate, fast, friendly
Cooking	Proper temperature
Product Assembly	Proper sequence, sanitary, correct ingredients and amounts, speed, proper temperature, neat
Cash Collection	Accurate, fast, friendly
Slicing	Cut/size, freshness/color
Chili preparation	Proper temperature, quantity, freshness
Ham/chicken preparation	Proper temperature, quantity, freshness
Supply chain management	Price/cost, order accuracy
Property acquisition	Sales potential, adherence to budget
Construction	On time, within budget
Marketing & advertising	Clear message, brand recognition

Source: Courtesy of Pal's Sudden Service.

Designing a process begins with identifying and documenting the process. As we stated in Chapter 1, processes generally cut across traditional organizational functions, and accurately defining a process may take some investigation and thought. Documenting a process involves describing how it is performed. It will likely include developing a process flowchart and writing standard operating procedures and work instructions. A good process design focuses on the prevention of poor quality by ensuring that goods and services meet both external and internal customer requirements, and that the process is capable of achieving the requisite level of performance.

The distinction between control and improvement is illustrated in Figure 7.1. Any process performance measure naturally fluctuates around some average level. Abnormal conditions cause an unusual deviation from this pattern. Removing the causes of such abnormal conditions and maintaining level performance is the essence of control. Improvement, on the other hand, means changing the performance to a new level.

To apply the techniques of process management, processes must be (1) repeatable, and (2) measurable. *Repeatability* means that the process must recur over time. The cycle may be long, as with product development processes or patent applications; or it may be short, as with a manufacturing operation or an order entry process. *Measurement* provides the ability to capture important quality and performance indicators to reveal patterns about process performance. Each measurement should aim for a standard or target that is driven by customer requirements. Meeting these two conditions ensures that sufficient data can be collected to reveal useful information for evaluation and control, as well as learning that leads to improvement and maturity.

We may view process management according to the three levels of quality discussed in Chapter 1. Major value creation and support processes are generally defined at the organizational level; these activities require attention by senior managers. Each major process consists of many subprocesses that are managed by functional managers

Figure 7.1 Control versus Improvement

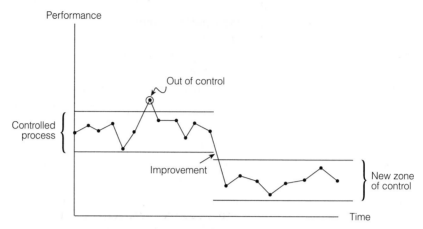

or cross-functional teams. Finally, each subprocess consists of many specific work steps performed by individuals at the performer level. Boeing Airlift and Tanker (A&T) Programs has developed an "enterprise process model" that views the entire business as eight interconnected process families. These major groupings range from enterprise leadership and new business development to production and post-delivery product support. Each family encompasses up to 10 major processes, which, in turn, are made up of several tiers of supporting subprocesses. A&T manages cross-cutting relationships as "mega-processes" that extend to suppliers and customers.

Individuals or groups, known as **process owners**, are accountable for process performance and have the authority to manage and improve their process. Process owners may range from high-level executives who manage cross-functional processes to workers who run a manufacturing cell or an assembly operation on the shop floor. Assigning process owners ensures that someone is responsible to manage the process and optimize its effectiveness.

Leading Practices

Process management requires a disciplined effort involving all managers and workers in an organization. Companies that are recognized world leaders in quality and customer satisfaction share some common practices.

- *They define and document important value creation and support processes, and manage them carefully.* Many companies use ISO 9000 as a basis for defining and documenting key processes. Branch-Smith Printing, for example, created more than 40 process maps as part of the process of converting to ISO 9000. Corning Telecommunications Products Division (TPD) has identified and documented more than 800 processes in all areas of its business, of which 50 are designated as "core business processes" that merit special emphasis in continuous improvement efforts. Each core process is owned and managed by a key business leader. Many organizations also recognize that managing supplier relationships (i.e., how performance requirements are communicated and ensured, mutual assistance and training, etc.) represents an important support process.

At DaimlerChrysler, for example, suppliers are involved early in the design process.[5] As a result, DaimlerChrysler often finds out about new materials, parts, and technologies before other automakers.

- *They translate customer requirements into product and service design requirements early in the design process, taking into account linkages between product design requirements and manufacturing or service process requirements, supplier capabilities, and legal and environmental issues.* One of the fundamental questions asked by SSM Health Care during their process design activities is "What are the customer's expected outcomes from the process?" Reviewing patient/customer feedback data, conducting specialized surveys or focus groups, and including customers on design teams help them answer this question. Leading companies coordinate design and production/delivery processes. AT&T Transmission Systems has a new product introduction center that evaluates designs based on manufacturing capabilities, recognizing that good designs both reduce the risk of manufacturing defects and improve productivity. The Bell Laboratories engineering research center supports the introduction of new processes by simulating the manufacturing environment needed to evaluate new technologies. An operational policy developed at Eastman Chemical encourages employees to maximize product value by operating the process at target levels, not just within some specification limits, thus better meeting design performance requirements. Eastman Chemical also reviews designs for safety, reliability, waste minimization, patent position, toxicity information, environmental risks, product disposal, and other customer needs. It also conducts a market analysis of key suppliers' abilities to manage costs, obtain materials, maintain production, and ship reliably.

- *They ensure that quality is built into products and services and use appropriate engineering and quantitative tools and approaches during the development process.* Eastman Chemical, for instance, uses laboratory modeling of processes, computer simulation, designed statistical experiments, and evaluation in customers' plants to assess the quality of its products prior to production. Texas Instruments locates its design centers strategically throughout its facilities. These centers offer expertise and systems with extensive capability for electrical and mechanical computer-aided design, system engineering, and manufacturing, and allow the evaluation of parts that have the best quality history, producibility, reliability, and other special engineering requirements. AT&T Universal Card Services used qualitative and quantitative research and testing to verify how accurately it understood customer needs. Before it introduced new products or services, market trials were conducted to determine whether they met customer and business requirements. The company's program management process had guidelines for deliverables, which addressed all quality requirements. Each phase of the process fulfilled specific requirements, which had to be completed, reviewed, and approved before the next phase of development began. IBM Rochester uses statistical techniques to study customers' priorities and trade-offs; validates this information with customer councils, satisfaction surveys, and other forms of feedback; and maintains a Software Partner Laboratory in which customers can certify that requirements are being met and that programs will operate correctly on their systems.

- *They manage the product development process to enhance cross-functional communication, reduce product development time, and ensure trouble-free introduction of products and services.* Leading companies use cross-functional teams to coordinate all phases of product development and reduce development times. Boeing A&T

has more than 100 integrated product teams (IPTs) that oversee the design, production, and delivery of the C-17 aircraft's more than 125,000 parts and supporting services. AT&T established nine expert breakthrough teams—called Achieving Process Excellence Teams—that identify process improvements for developing and deploying products faster in the market. They establish standards, procedures, and training for cross-functional communication that prevents problems from occurring. At The Ritz-Carlton Hotel Company, for instance, the interface of all design, marketing, operations, and legal functions throughout each project allows the company to anticipate requirements and evaluate progress. Customized hotel products and services, such as meetings and banquet events, receive the full attention of local hotel cross-functional teams. These teams involve all internal and external suppliers, verify production and delivery capabilities before each event, critique samples, and assess results. At Globe Metallurgical, a team consisting of employees from customer service, engineering, and quality assurance works together before product development even begins. Afterward, a team of customers and employees from purchasing, engineering, and quality assurance works with the first team to manage the development process. To ensure a trouble-free launch of its products, Solar Turbines uses advanced computerized design and analytical tools that ensure collaboration and sharing of data between manufacturing and key suppliers. Other tools, such as predictive modeling and rapid prototyping are used to validate function, performance, and manufacturability.

- *They define performance requirements for suppliers, ensure that requirements are met, and develop partnering relationships with key suppliers and other organizations.* At Dana Commercial Credit, strategic suppliers include financial institutions and law firms. Legal requirements are communicated at the early stages of a relationship; feedback from customers determines whether requirements are being met. Corning TPD classifies its suppliers in a hierarchy: Level 1 suppliers have a direct impact on customer satisfaction; Level 2 suppliers are important, but do not have direct linkage to customer satisfaction; Level 3 suppliers provide commodity-like products. Level 1 suppliers are supported by cross-functional teams and integrated into development activities. Armstrong conducts site visits and has a 5-level scale to help suppliers understand where they stand in meeting the company's expectations. STMicroelectronics developed an annual Supplier Quality & Service Plan, which sets goals for suppliers and specifies how ST will review performance, share data, and carry out other responsibilities in the relationship. Long-term partnerships with quality-minded suppliers enabled Texas Nameplate Company to nearly eliminate inspections of incoming materials. These "ship-direct-to-stock" suppliers are required to be defect-free for at least two years and meet all requirements specified on purchase orders.

- *They control the quality and operational performance of key processes and use systematic methods to identify significant variations in operational performance and output quality, determine root causes, make corrections, and verify results.* Leading companies establish measures and indicators to track quality and operational performance, and use them as a basis for controlling the processes and consistently meeting specifications and standards. The key measures used by SSM Health Care to monitor their processes are shown in Table 7.2. Daily, weekly, monthly, and quarterly performance assessments provide the opportunity to review and manage these measures and identify ways of preventing potential errors before they affect the patient. The Ritz-Carlton Hotel Company has a policy by which the first person who detects a problem is empowered to break away from

Table 7.2 SSM Health Care Process Requirements and Measures

Process	Key Requirements	Key Measures
Admit		
Admitting/ Registration	Timeliness	• Time to admit patients to the setting of care • Timeliness in admitting/registration rate on patient satisfaction survey questions
Assess		
Patient Assessment	Timeliness	• % of histories and physicals charted within 24 hrs or prior to surgery • Pain assessed at appropriate intervals, per hospital policy
Clinical laboratory and radiology services	Accuracy & Timeliness	• Quality control results/Repeat rates • Turnaround time • Response rate on medical staff satisfaction survey
Care Delivery/Treatment		
Provision of clinical care	Nurse responsiveness Pain management Successful clinical outcomes	• Response rate on patient satisfaction and medical staff survey questions • Wait time for pain medications • % CHF patients received med instructions/weighing • % Ischemic heart patients discharged on proven therapies • Unplanned readmits/Returns to ER or Operating Room • Mortality
Pharmacy/ Medication use	Accuracy	• Use of dangerous abbreviations in medication orders • Med error rate or adverse drug events resulting from med errors
Surgical services/ Anesthesia	Professional skill, competence/ communication	• Clear documentation of informed surgical and anesthesia consent • Perioperative mortality • Surgical site infection rates
Discharge		
Case management	Appropriate utilization	• Average length of stay (ALOS) • Payment denials • Unplanned readmits
Discharge from setting of care	Assistance and clear directions	• Discharge instructions documented and provided to patient • Response rate on patient satisfaction survey

Source: Courtesy of SSM Health Care.

routine duties, investigate and correct the problem immediately, document the incident, and then return to their routine. Many companies use statistical process control (see Chapter 14) and formal problem-solving processes to identify, analyze, and solve quality problems. Granite Rock, for instance, was the first in the construction materials industry to apply statistical process control in the management of production of aggregates, concrete, and asphalt products.

• *They continuously improve processes to achieve better quality, cycle time, and overall operational performance.* Leading companies employ systematic approaches for analyzing data and identifying improvements. Branch-Smith Printing, for example, uses a simple quality improvement process (QIP) shown in Figure 7.2 to evaluate and improve all production and delivery processes, using performance data and complaints to prioritize opportunities for process improvement. Leading companies use proven techniques such as process analysis and simplification and advanced technologies. Motorola's Commercial, Government, and Industrial Solutions Sector uses continuous improvement teams that meet regularly to proactively evaluate and improve processes. At IBM Rochester, cross-functional teams examine all elements of production and support processes, from order entry to delivery and installation. The teams evaluate and remove, change, and improve steps in these processes. The Ritz-Carlton has eight mechanisms devoted solely to the improvement of process, product, and service quality:

1. New hotel start-up improvement process: a cross-sectional team from the entire company that works together to identify and correct problem areas.
2. Comprehensive performance evaluation process: the work area team mechanism that empowers people who perform a job to develop the job procedures and performance standards.
3. Quality network: a mechanism of peer approval through which an individual employee can advance a good idea.
4. Standing problem-solving team: a standing work area team that addresses any problem it chooses.
5. Quality improvement team: special teams assembled to solve an assigned problem identified by an individual employee or leaders.
6. Strategic quality planning: annual work area teams that identify their missions, primary supplier objectives and action plans, internal objectives and action plans, and progress reviews.

Figure 7.2 QIP Process at Branch-Smith Printing

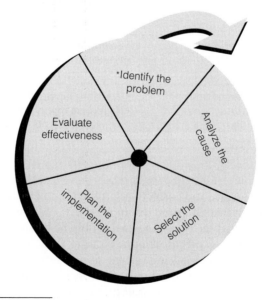

Used with permission of AIM, Inc.

7. Streamlining process: the annual hotel evaluation of processes, products, or services that are no longer valuable to the customer.

8. Process improvement: the team mechanism for corporate leaders, managers, and employees to improve the most critical processes.

- *They innovate to achieve breakthrough performance using such approaches as benchmarking and reengineering.* Briefly, benchmarking is the search for best practices in any company, in any industry, anywhere in the world, and reengineering is the radical redesign of business processes to achieve significant improvements in performance. As an example of benchmarking, when Granite Rock could not find any company that was measuring on-time delivery of concrete, it talked with Domino's Pizza, a worldwide leader in on-time delivery of a rapidly perishable product (a characteristic shared with freshly mixed concrete) to acquire new ideas for measuring and improving its processes. AT&T has a corporate database to share benchmarking information among its business units. The database contains data from more than 100 companies and 250 benchmarking activities for key processes such as hardware and software development, manufacturing, financial planning and budgeting, international billing, and service delivery. AT&T obtains this information from customers, visits to other companies, trade shows and journals, professional societies, product brochures, and outside consultants. Pal's Sudden Service uses benchmarking extensively. Managers are continually on the lookout for benchmarking candidates, and each one compiles a running list of potential subjects. Pal's uses benchmarking to obtain meaningful competitive comparisons, new best practices for achieving higher performance goals, or new organizational directions, as well as to constantly remind the entire organization that performance can always be improved.

To illustrate the concept of reengineering, Intel Corporation previously used a 91-step process costing thousands of dollars to purchase ballpoint pens—the same process used to purchase forklift trucks! The improved process was reduced to eight steps. In rethinking its purpose as a customer-driven, retail service company rather than a manufacturing company, Taco Bell eliminated the kitchen from its restaurants. Meat and beans are cooked outside the restaurant at central commissaries and reheated. Other food items such as diced tomatoes, onions, and olives are prepared off-site. This innovation saved about 11 million hours of work and $7 million per year over the entire chain.[6]

PRODUCT DESIGN PROCESSES

Companies today face incredible pressures to continually improve the quality of their products while simultaneously reducing costs, to meet ever-increasing legal and environmental requirements, and to shorten product life cycles to meet changing consumer needs and remain competitive. The ability to achieve these goals depends on a large extent on product design (by which we also imply *redesign*). The complexity of today's products makes design a difficult activity; a single state-of-the-art integrated circuit may contain millions of transistors and involve hundreds of manufacturing steps. Nevertheless, improved designs not only reduce costs, but increase quality. For example, a network interface card from around 1990 contained about 40 chips; five years later, the entire system board of a Macintosh Performa 5200 had just 19. Fewer components mean fewer points of failure and less chance of assembly error.[7]

Most companies have some type of structured product development process. Although we tend to equate product development with manufactured goods, it is important to realize that design processes apply to services as well. For example, in the late 1980s, Citibank designed a new mortgage approval procedure that reduced turnaround times from 45 to less than 15 days; FedEx has consistently developed new variations of its package delivery services.[8]

The typical product development process, shown in Figure 7.3, consists of six phases:

1. *Idea Generation.* As emphasized in Chapter 4, new or redesigned product ideas should incorporate customer needs and expectations. However, true innovations often transcend customers' expressed desires, simply because customers may not know what they like until they have it. A good example is Chrysler's decision to develop the minivan, despite research that showed that people balked at such an odd-looking vehicle.[9]

2. *Preliminary Concept Development.* In this phase, new ideas are studied for feasibility, addressing such questions as: Will the product meet customers' requirements? Can it be manufactured economically with high quality? Objective criteria are required for measuring and testing the attributes associated with these questions. One tool for assisting in this and subsequent steps is quality function deployment, which will be described in Chapter 12.

3. *Product/Process Development.* If an idea survives the concept stage—and many do not—the actual design process begins by evaluating design alternatives and determining engineering specifications for all materials, components, and parts. This phase usually includes prototype testing, in which a model (real or simulated) is constructed to test the product's physical properties or use under actual operating conditions, as well as consumer reactions to the prototypes. For example, in developing the user interface for an automobile navigation system, BMW conducted extensive consumer tests with a keyboard, a rotating push button, and a joystick (the push button was ultimately selected).[10] Boeing's 777 jet was built using digital prototypes. Design reviews are frequently conducted to identify and eliminate possible causes for manufacturing and marketing problems. In addition to the actual product design, companies develop, test, and standardize the processes used in manufacturing, which include selecting the appropriate technology, tooling, and suppliers, and performing pilot runs to verify results.

Figure 7.3 Structured Product Development Process

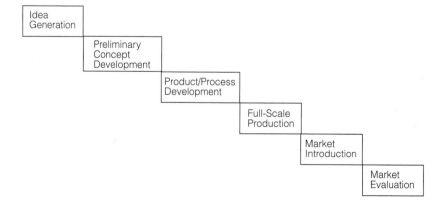

4. *Full-Scale Production*. If no serious problems are found, the company releases the product to manufacturing or service delivery teams.
5. *Market Introduction*. The product is distributed to customers.
6. *Market Evaluation*. Deming and Juran both advocated an ongoing product development process that relies on market evaluation and customer feedback to initiate continuous improvements. In fact, Deming's introductory lecture to Japanese managers in 1950 contrasted the "old way" of product design—design it, make it, and try to sell it—with a "new way":

- Design the product (with appropriate tests).
- Make it and test it in the production line and in the laboratory.
- Put it on the market.
- Test it in service through market research; find out what the user thinks of it, and why the nonuser has not bought it.
- Redesign the product, in light of consumer reactions to quality and price.[11]

This philosophy is one of the key ingredients in a successful TQ culture.

Many companies view customers as significant partners in product development, thus integrating market evaluation throughout the process. Ames Rubber Company, for example, uses a four-step approach to product development that maintains close communication with the customer.[12] Typically, Ames initiates a new product through a series of meetings with the customer and sales/marketing or the technical services group. From these meetings, management prepares a product brief listing all technical, material, and operational requirements. The brief is forwarded to internal departments, such as engineering, quality, and manufacturing. The technical staff then selects materials, processes, and procedures, and submits its selections to the customer. Upon the customer's approval, a prototype is made. Ames delivers the prototype to the customer, who evaluates and tests it and reports results to the company. Ames makes the requested modifications and returns the prototype for further testing. This process continues until the customer is completely satisfied. Next, Ames makes a limited preproduction run. Data collected during the run are analyzed and shared with the customer. Upon approval, full-scale production commences.

Quality Spotlight
Ames Rubber Company

Design approaches often differ depending on the nature of products or services. For example, approaches to designing entirely new products will be unlike those that address minor changes and improvements. Design approaches might consider factors such as functional performance, cost, manufacturability, safety, and environmental impacts. We address some of these issues next.

Cost, Manufacturability, and Quality

General Electric found that 75 percent of its manufacturing costs are determined by design. With products in which parts alone represent 65 to 80 percent of the manufacturing cost, design may account for 90 percent or more of the total manufacturing cost. Other companies exhibit similar figures. For Rolls Royce, design determines 80 percent of the final production costs.

Product design can significantly affect the cost of manufacturing (direct and indirect labor, materials, and overhead), redesign, warranty, and field repair; the efficiency by which the product can be manufactured, and the quality of the output.

Simplifying the design can often improve cost as well as quality. By cutting the number of parts, material costs generally go down, inventory levels fall, the number of suppliers shrinks, and production time can be shortened. Back in the days of dot matrix printers (ask your instructor!), IBM, for example, realized many benefits of design simplification. IBM had been buying its dot matrix printers from Seiko Epson Corporation, then the world's low-cost producer. When IBM developed a printer with 65 percent fewer parts that was designed to snap together during final assembly without the use of fasteners, the result was a 90 percent reduction in assembly time and major cost reductions.

Many aspects of product design can adversely affect manufacturability and, hence, quality.[13] Some parts may be designed with features difficult to fabricate repeatedly or with unnecessarily tight tolerances. Some parts may lack details for self-alignment or features for correct insertion. In other cases, parts so fragile or so susceptible to corrosion or contamination may be damaged in shipping or by internal handling. Sometimes a design simply has more parts than are needed to perform the desired functions, which increases the chance of assembly error. Thus, problems of poor design may show up as errors, poor yield, damage, or functional failure in fabrication, assembly, test, transport, and end use.

Designs with numerous parts increase the incidence of part mix-ups, missing parts, and test failures. Parts that are similar but not identical create the possibility that an assembler will use the wrong part. Parts without details to prevent insertion in the wrong orientation lead to more frequent improper assembly. Complicated assembly steps or tricky joining processes can cause incorrect, incomplete, unreliable, or otherwise faulty assemblies. Finally, the designer's failure to consider conditions to which parts will be exposed during assembly such as temperature, humidity, vibration, static electricity, and dust, may result in failures during testing or use.

Design for manufacturability (DFM) is the process of designing a product for efficient production at the highest level of quality.

Table 7.3 summarizes important design guidelines for improving manufacturability and thus improving quality and reducing costs. Many industries have developed more specific guidelines. For example, guidelines for designing printed circuit boards include:

> *DFM is intended to prevent product designs that simplify assembly operations but require more complex and expensive components, designs that simplify component manufacture while complicating the assembly process, and designs that are simple and inexpensive to produce but difficult or expensive to service or support.*

- Placing all components on the topside of the board
- Grouping similar components whenever possible
- Maintaining a 0.60-inch clearance for insertable components

Design Quality and Social Responsibility

Safety in consumer products represents a major issue in design, and certainly an important part of a company's public responsibilities. Liability concerns cause many companies to forgo certain product development activities. For example, Unison Industries, Inc., of Rockford, Illinois, developed a new solid-state electronic ignition system for piston-engine aircraft. The company dropped the product after prototype testing. Unison says it was sued over crashes involving aircraft on which its products were not even installed. Getting removed from the lawsuits proved costly in itself.[14] In a survey of more than 500 chief executives, more than one-third worked for firms that canceled the introduction of products because of liability concerns. Many companies closed plants and laid off workers, and more than 20 percent of the executives said they believed their companies lost market share to foreign competitors because of product liability costs.

> *All parties responsible for design, manufacture, sales, and service of a defective product are now liable for damages.*

Table 7.3 Design Guidelines for Quality Assurance

Minimize Number of Parts
- Fewer parts and assembly drawings → Lower volume of drawings and instructions to control

- Less complicated assemblies → Lower assembly error rate
- Fewer parts to hold to required quality characteristics → Higher consistency of part quality
- Fewer parts to fail → Higher reliability

Minimize Number of Part Numbers
- Fewer variations of like parts → Lower assembly error rate

Design for Robustness (Taguchi method)
- Low sensitivity to component variability → Higher first-pass yield; less degradation of performance with time

Eliminate Adjustments
- No assembly adjustment errors → Higher first-pass yield
- Eliminates adjustable components with high failure rates → Lower failure rate

Make Assembly Easy and Foolproof
- Parts cannot be assembled wrong → Lower assembly error rate
- Obvious when parts are missing → Lower assembly error rate
- Assembly tooling designed into part → Lower assembly error rate
- Parts are self-securing → Lower assembly error rate
- No "force fitting" of parts → Less damage to parts; better serviceability

Use Repeatable, Well-Understood Processes
- Part quality easy to control → Higher part yield
- Assembly quality easy to control → Higher assembly yield

Choose Parts That Can Survive Process Operations
- Less damage to parts → Higher yield
- Less degradation of parts → Higher reliability

Design for Efficient and Adequate Testing
- Less mistaking "good" for "bad" product and vice versa → Truer assessment of quality; less unnecessary rework

Lay Out Parts for Reliable Process Completion
- Less damage to parts during handling and assembly → Higher yield; higher reliability

Eliminate Engineering Changes on Released Products
- Fewer errors due to changeovers and multiple revisions/versions → Lower assembly error rate

Source: D. Daetz, "The Effect of Product Design on Product Quality and Product Cost," *Quality Progress* 20, no. 6 (June 1987), pp. 63–67.

According to the theory of strict liability, anyone who sells a product that is defective or unreasonably dangerous is subject to liability for any physical harm caused to the user, the consumer, or the property of either.[15] This law applies when the seller is in the business of selling the product, and the product reaches the consumer without a substantial change in condition even if the seller exercised all possible care in the preparation and sale of the product. The principal issue is whether a defect, direct or indirect, exists. If the existence of a defect can be established, the manufacturer usually will be held liable. A plaintiff need prove only that (1) the product was defective, (2) the defect was present when the product changed ownership, and (3) the defect resulted in injury. In 1997 Chrysler was ordered to pay $262.5 million in a case involving defective latches on minivans; thus, the economic consequences can be significant.

Attention to design quality can greatly reduce the possibility of product liability claims as well as provide supporting evidence in defense arguments. Liability makes documentation of quality assurance procedures a necessity. A firm should record all evidence that shows the designer established test and monitoring procedures of critical product characteristics. Feedback on test and inspection results along with corrective actions taken must also be documented. Even adequate packaging and handling procedures are not immune to examination in liability suits, because packaging is still within the manufacturer's span of control. Managers should address the following questions:[16]

- Is the product reasonably safe for the end user?
- What could possibly go wrong with it?
- Are any needed safety devices absent?
- What kind of warning labels or instructions should be included?
- What would attorneys call "reasonable foreseeable use"?
- What are some extreme climatic or environmental conditions for which the product should be tested?
- What similarities does the product have with others that may have encountered previous problems?

In addition to legal issues, environmental concerns have an unprecedented impact on product and process designs. Hundreds of millions of home and office appliances are disposed of each year. The problem of what to do with obsolete computers is a growing design and technological waste problem today.[17] A monitor contains eight pounds of lead; a CPU has another three to five pounds, as well as other hazardous metals, such as mercury. According to a 1997 Carnegie Mellon University study, 150 million dead but not decaying PCs will be buried in U.S. landfills by 2005. In Europe, the European Commission proposed a ban on materials such as lead-based solder in PCs and the imposition of recycling responsibilities on manufacturers beginning in January 2004. Pressures from environmental groups clamoring for "socially responsive" designs, states and municipalities that are running out of space for landfills, and consumers who want the most for their money all cause designers and managers to look carefully at the concept of **design-for-environment**, or **DfE**.[18]

DfE is the explicit consideration of environmental concerns during the design of products and processes, and includes such practices as designing for recyclability and disassembly.

DfE offers the potential to create more desirable products at lower costs by reducing disposal and regulatory costs, increasing the end-of-life value of products, reducing material use, and minimizing liabilities. Recyclable products are designed to be taken apart and their components repaired, refurbished, melted down, or otherwise salvaged for reuse. Recyclability appeals to environmentalists as well as city and state officials, each of whom are fighting the effects of waste disposal. At the same time, however, it creates new issues for designers and consumers. For example, designers must strive to use fewer types of materials, such as plastics, with properties that allow for reuse. *Business Week* cites several U.S. firms already working on or marketing such products, including Whirlpool, 3M, and General Electric.[19] The latter's plastics division, which serves the durable goods market, uses only thermoplastics in its products. Unlike many other varieties of plastics, thermoplastics can be melted down and recast into other shapes and products, thus making them recyclable. Designers must also refrain from using certain methods of fastening, such as glues and screws, in favor of quick connect-disconnect bolts or other such fasteners. These changes in design will have an impact on tolerances, durability, and quality of products. Such design changes affect consumers who will be asked to recycle products (perhaps to recover a deposit), in spite of inconveniences such as transporting them to a recycling center.

Repairable products are not a new idea, but the concept lost favor when, in the 1960s and 1970s, the United States became known as the "throwaway society." Many products are discarded simply because the cost of maintenance or repair is too high when compared with the cost of a new item. Now **design for disassembly** promises to bring back easy, affordable product repair. For example, Whirlpool Corporation is developing a new appliance designed for repairability, with its parts sorted for easy coding. Thus, repairability has the potential of pleasing customers, who would prefer to repair a product rather than discard it. At the same time, companies are challenged to consider fresh approaches to design that build both cost-effectiveness and quality into the product. For instance, even though it is more efficient to assemble an item using rivets instead of screws, this approach is contrary to a design-for-disassembly philosophy. An alternative might be an entirely new design that eliminates the need for fasteners in the first place.

Streamlining the Product Development Process

The importance of speed in product development cannot be overemphasized. To succeed in highly competitive markets, companies must churn out new products quickly. In 1990, the former Digital Equipment Corp., for example, was about to launch a new generation of computer disk drives. However, because of product design problems, the product was very late and competitors had already released enhanced technology drives at much lower prices. What could have been a huge win became a great failure.[20]

Nearly every industry is focused on reducing product development cycles. Whereas automakers once took four to six years to develop new models, most are striving to do it within 24 months. In fact, Toyota's goal is just 18 months! Boeing took 54 months to design its 777 airplane; yet the company would like to reduce it to 10 because the market changes so quickly. The product development process can be improved with various advanced technologies, such as computer-aided design (CAD), computer-aided manufacturing (CAM), flexible manufacturing systems (FMS), and computer-integrated manufacturing (CIM). These technologies automate and link design and manufacturing processes, reducing cycle times as well as removing opportunities for human error, thus improving quality. Such automation is a significant factor at Toyota.[21]

Successful product development demands the involvement and cooperation of many different functional groups within an organization to identify and solve design problems and try to reduce product development and introduction times. All departments play crucial roles in the design process. The designer's objective is to design a product that achieves the desired functional requirements. The manufacturing engineer's objective is to produce it efficiently. The salesperson's goal is to sell the product, and the finance person's goal is to make a profit. Purchasing seeks parts that meet quality requirements. Packaging and distribution deliver the product to the customer in good operating condition. Clearly, all business functions have a stake in the product; therefore, all should work together.

One of the most significant barriers to efficient product development is poor intraorganizational cooperation.

Unfortunately, the product development process often is performed without such cooperation. In many large firms product development is accomplished in a serial fashion, as suggested in Figure 7.3. In the early stages of development, design engineers dominate the process. Later, the prototype is transferred to manufacturing for production. Finally, marketing and sales personnel are brought into the process. This approach has several disadvantages. First, product development time is long. Second, up to 90 percent of manufacturing costs may be committed before manufacturing engineers have any input to the design. Third, the final product may not be the best one for market conditions at the time of introduction.

An approach that alleviates these problems is called **concurrent engineering**, or **simultaneous engineering**. Typical benefits include 30 to 70 percent less development time, 65 to 90 percent fewer engineering changes, 20 to 90 percent less time to market, 200 to 600 percent improvement in quality, 20 to 110 percent improvement in white collar productivity, and 20 to 120 percent higher return on assets.[22]

Concurrent engineering is a process in which all major functions involved with bringing a product to market are continuously involved with product development from conception through sales. Such an approach not only helps achieve trouble-free introduction of products and services, but also results in improved quality, lower costs, and shorter product development cycles.

Concurrent engineering involves multifunctional teams, usually consisting of 4 to 20 members and including every specialty in the company. The functions of such teams are to determine the character of the product and decide what design methods and production methods are appropriate; analyze product functions so that all design decisions can be made with full knowledge of how the item is supposed to work; perform a design for manufacturability study to determine whether the design can be improved without affecting performance; formulate an assembly sequence; and design a factory system that fully involves workers.

Concurrent engineering has been a major force behind the resurgence of U.S. automobile companies by enabling them to dramatically reduce product development time. In the past, automobile development followed a sequential process in which styling engineers dreamed up a concept and sent the concept to product engineers to design components. They in turn would send the designs to manufacturing and suppliers. This process was costly and inefficient; each handoff lost something in time and money. What appeared feasible for one group often proved impossible for another to accomplish. By the time the vehicle was finally produced, marketing was faced with selling a product for which they had no input. Often the vehicle was priced incorrectly for the target market.

In 1980 Ford launched Team Taurus, modeled after program management concepts in the aerospace industry. Program managers headed product teams that included representatives from design, engineering, purchasing, marketing, quality assurance, sales, and service. Cadillac adopted simultaneous engineering in 1985. Vehicle teams, composed of disciplines from every area of the organization, were responsible for managing all steps of product development. They defined the target market and the overall vehicle goals, and managed the timing, profitability, and continuous improvement of the vehicle's quality, reliability, durability, and performance. Chrysler's adaptation of simultaneous engineering enabled it to develop and introduce the celebrated Viper sports car in just two years. Among U.S. automakers Chrysler was an innovator in fast product development.[23]

One approach often used to facilitate product development is the **design review**. The purpose of a design review is to stimulate discussion, raise questions, and generate new ideas and solutions to help designers anticipate problems before they occur. Generally, a design review is conducted in three major stages: preliminary, intermediate, and final. The preliminary design review establishes early communication between marketing, engineering, manufacturing, and purchasing personnel and provides better coordination of their activities. It usually involves higher levels of management and concentrates on strategic issues in design that relate to customer requirements and thus the ultimate quality of the product. A preliminary design review evaluates such issues as the function of the product, conformance to customer's needs, completeness of specifications, manufacturing costs, and liability issues.

After the design is well established, an intermediate review takes place to study the design in greater detail to identify potential problems and suggest corrective action. Personnel at lower levels of the organization are more heavily involved at this stage. Finally, just before release to production, a final review is held. Materials lists, drawings, and other detailed design information are studied with the purpose of preventing costly changes after production setup.

In summary, a total approach to product development and process design involves the following activities:[24]

1. Constantly thinking in terms of how one can design or manufacture products better, not just solving or preventing problems
2. Focusing on "things done right" rather than "things gone wrong"
3. Defining customer expectations and going beyond them, not just barely meeting them or just matching the competition
4. Optimizing desirable features or results, not just incorporating them
5. Minimizing the overall cost without compromising quality of function

Various tools that fall under the rubric of "Design for Six Sigma" will be discussed in Chapter 12 and contribute to achieving these objectives.

DESIGNING PROCESSES FOR QUALITY

The design of the processes that produce and deliver goods and services can have a significant impact on cost (and hence profitability), flexibility (the ability to produce the right types and amounts of products as customer demand or preferences change), and the quality of the output. Standardized processes establish consistency of output. For example, in producing a new, very small CD player, Sony had to develop entirely new manufacturing processes, because no process in existence was able to make this product as small and as accurate as the design required. FedEx developed a wireless data collection system that employs laser scanners to manage millions of packages daily through its six main hubs, improving not only customer service, but saving labor costs as well.[25]

However, standardized processes may not be able to meet the needs of different customer segments as we discussed in Chapter 4. Today, many companies use a strategy of *mass customization*—providing personalized, custom-designed products to meet individual customer preferences at prices comparable to mass-produced items. Motorola, for instance, produces one-of-a-kind pagers from more than 29 million combinations of options in a mass assembly process at a low cost. Dell Computer configures each computer system to customer specifications. At Levi Strauss, customers are measured for custom-fit jeans at local stores; the jeans are produced at a central factory and delivered to the customer's store. Mass customization requires significant changes to traditional manufacturing processes that focus on either customized, crafted products or mass-produced, standardized products.[26] These products include flexible manufacturing technologies, just-in-time systems, information technology, and an emphasis on cycle time reduction.

> *The goal of process design is to develop an efficient procedure to satisfy both internal and external customer requirements.*

The design of a process begins with the process owner. A process owner might be an individual, a team, a department, or some cross-functional group. A basic approach to process design is suggested by Motorola:

1. *Identify the product or service:* What work do I do?
2. *Identify the customer:* Who is the work for?
3. *Identify the supplier:* What do I need and from whom do I get it?
4. *Identify the process:* What steps or tasks are performed? What are the inputs and outputs for each step?
5. *Mistake-proof the process:* How can I eliminate or simplify tasks? What "poka-yoke" (i.e., mistake-proofing) devices (see Chapter 13) can I use?
6. *Develop measurements and controls, and improvement goals:* How do I evaluate the process? How can I improve further?

Steps 1 through 3 address such questions as "What is the purpose of the process?" "How does the process create customer satisfaction?" and "What are the essential inputs and outputs of the process?" Step 4 focuses on the actual process design by defining the specific tasks performed in transforming the inputs to outputs. Step 5 focuses on making the process efficient and capable of delivering high quality. Step 6 ensures that the process will be monitored and controlled to the level of required performance. This monitoring involves gathering in-process measurements and/or customer feedback on a regular basis and using this information to control and improve the process.

The actual process design is the specification of how the process works. The first phase is to list in detail the sequence of steps—value-adding activities and specific tasks—involved in producing a product or delivering a service, usually depicted as a flowchart (see Chapter 13 for further discussion). Such a graphical representation provides an excellent communication device for visualizing and understanding the process. Flowcharts can become the basis for job descriptions, employee-training programs, and performance measurement. They help managers to estimate human resources, information systems, equipment, and facilities requirements. As design tools, they enable management to study and analyze processes prior to implementation in order to improve quality and operational performance. Figure 7.4 shows The Ritz-Carlton's Three Steps of Service process. The process is highly structured and defines the procedures for anticipating and complying with customer needs. All employees who come in contact with customers are trained to follow this process.

Special Considerations in Service Process Design

The fundamental differences between manufacturing and service processes deserve special attention in process design. This aspect is especially important because support processes are basically services. Some common examples of service processes are preparing an invoice, taking a telephone order, processing a credit card, and checking out of a hotel. First, the outputs of service processes are not as well defined, as are manufactured products. For example, even though all banks offer similar tangible goods such as checking, loans, automatic tellers, and so forth, the real

> *Service process designers must concentrate on doing things right the first time, minimizing process complexities, and making the process immune to inadvertent human errors, particularly during customer interactions.*

Figure 7.4 The Ritz-Carlton Hotel Company: Three Steps of Service Process

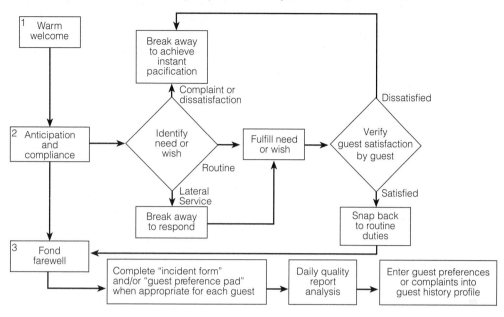

differentiating factor among banks is the service they provide. Second, most service processes involve a greater interaction with the customer, often making it easier to identify needs and expectations. On the other hand, customers often cannot define their needs for service until after they have some point of reference or comparison.

Fast-food restaurants, for example, have carefully designed their processes for high degree of accuracy and fast response time.[27] New hands-free intercom systems, better microphones that reduce ambient kitchen noise, and screens that display a customer's order are all focused on these requirements. Timers at Wendy's count every segment of the order completion process to help managers identify problem areas. Kitchen workers wear headsets to hear orders as they are placed. Even the use of photos on drive-through order boards make it more likely for customers to select these items; less variety means faster order fulfillment.

Service processes often involve both internal and external activities, a factor that complicates quality design. In a bank, for example, poor service can result from the way that tellers treat customers and also from poor quality of computers and communications equipment beyond the control of the tellers. Internal activities are primarily concerned with efficiency (quality of conformance), while external activities—with direct customer interaction—require attention to effectiveness (quality of design). All too often, workers involved in internal operations do not understand how their performance affects the customers they do not see. The success of the process depends on everyone—workers involved in internal as well as external activities—understanding that they add value to the customer.

Designing a service essentially involves determining an effective balance of these components. The goal is to provide a service whose

Services have three basic components: physical facilities, processes, and procedures; employees' behavior; and employees' professional judgment.[28]

elements are internally consistent and directed at meeting the needs of a specific target market segment. Too much or too little emphasis on one component will lead to problems and poor customer perceptions. For example, too much emphasis on procedures might result in timely and efficient service, but might also suggest insensitivity and apathy toward the customer. Too much emphasis on behavior might provide a friendly and personable environment at the expense of slow, inconsistent, or chaotic service. Too much emphasis on professional judgment might lead to good solutions to customer problems but also to slow, inconsistent, or insensitive service.

A useful approach to designing effective services is first to recognize that services differ in the degree of customer contact and interaction, the degree of labor intensity, and the degree of customization. For example, a railroad is low in all three dimensions. On the other hand, an interior design service would be high in all three dimensions. A fast-food restaurant would be high in customer contact and labor intensity, but low in customization.

Services low in all three dimensions of this classification are more similar to manufacturing organizations. The emphasis on quality should be focused on the physical facilities and procedures; behavior and professional judgment are relatively unimportant. As contact and interaction between the customer and the service system increases, two factors must be taken into account. In services low in labor intensity, the customer's impression of physical facilities, processes, and procedures is important. Service organizations must exercise special care in choosing and maintaining reliable and easy-to-use equipment. With higher levels of contact and interaction, appropriate staff behavior becomes increasingly important.

As labor intensity increases, variations between individuals become more important; however, the elements of personal behavior and professional judgment will remain relatively unimportant as long as the degrees of customization and contact and interaction remain low. As customization increases, professional judgment becomes a bigger factor in the customer's perception of service quality. In services that are high in all three dimensions, facilities, behavior, and professional judgment must be equally balanced.

In services, quality standards take the place of the dimensions and tolerances applicable in manufacturing. Examples of standards set by one of the airline industry leaders, Swissair, include:

- Ninety percent of calls are answered within 30 seconds.
- Ninety percent of passengers are checked in within three minutes of arrival.
- Baggage claim time is only 10 minutes between the first and last customer.

However, service standards are inherently more difficult to define and measure than manufacturing specifications. They require extensive research into customer needs and attitudes regarding timeliness, consistency, accuracy, and other service requirements, as discussed in previous chapters. Even though many product specifications developed for manufactured products are focused on meeting a target, such as a product dimension, service targets typically are "smaller is better." Thus, the true service standard is zero defects, and any other standards (such as those of Swissair) should be construed as interim standards and targets only.

In designing high-quality service processes, consider the following questions:[29]

- What service standards are already in place?
- Which of these standards have been clearly communicated to all service personnel?
- Have these standards been communicated to the public?

- Which standards require refinement?
- What is the final result of the service provided? What should it ideally be?
- What is the maximum access time that a patron will tolerate without feeling inconvenienced?
- How long should it take to perform the service itself?
- What is the maximum time for completion of service before the customer's view of the service is negatively affected?
- At what point does service begin, and what indicator signals the completion of the service?
- How many different people must the consumer deal with in completing the service?
- What components of the service are essential? Desirable? Superfluous?
- What components or aspects of service must be controlled in order to deliver a service encounter of equal quality each time one occurs?
- Which components can differ from encounter to encounter while still leading to a total service encounter that meets standards?
- What products that affect its service performance does a service organization obtain from other sources?

As you can see, service process design is not a trivial exercise!

PROJECTS AS VALUE-CREATION PROCESSES

Some organizations are project-focused because of the nature of their work. They tend to deliver unique, one-of-a-kind products or services tailored to the specific needs of an individual customer. Examples include performing clinical trials for pharmaceutical companies, market research studies, consulting, and systems installation. **Project management** involves all activities associated with planning, scheduling, and controlling projects. Good project management ensures that an organization's resources are used efficiently and effectively. Such management is particularly important for Six Sigma, because projects generally cut across organizational boundaries and require the coordination of many different departments and functions.

*In many companies, value creation processes take the form of **projects**—temporary work structures that start up, produce products or services, and then shut down.*[30]

Traditional project management methodologies were developed before the advent of total quality; hence, TQ approaches were not often incorporated. Such approaches as identifying customer requirements, using a customer-supplier model, teamwork principles, cycle time reduction, and in-process measurements can improve the quality of the result. For example, although each project is unique, many projects have similar underlying processes, and attention to these processes can improve the overall quality of the project effort.

To illustrate, consider Custom Research Incorporated (CRI), which conducts unique market research studies for many different organizations. A Cycle Time Task Force identified nine common processes for all marketing research studies: identification of client requirements/expectations, questionnaire design, questionnaire programming, sampling, data collection, data tabulation, report and analysis, internal communication, and client communication. A Process Task Force was formed to map and improve each process. For example, CRI developed a "one-entry system" that eliminates the need to enter data into its computer system more than once, and

Quality Spotlight
Custom Research, Inc.

allows questionnaires to be tested for validity and reliability, eliminating several programming steps and helping to reduce cycle time. An account team is in charge of every research project. Project-related problems anywhere in the process are recognized and reported by the team. Team members use their problem-solving skills to determine whether the variation is due to common or special causes, analyze the reasons for the occurrence, and implement changes that will prevent it from occurring. When each project is completed, the account team completes a Project Quality Recap documenting problems and solutions and rating the performance of internal departments. Teams refer to the Recaps on file when they have similar projects or subsequent projects from the same client.[31]

Organizations such as Custom Research use a pure project organizational structure whereby team members are assigned exclusively to projects and report only to a project manager. This approach makes it easier to manage projects, because project teams can be designed for efficiency by including the right mix of skills; however, it can result in inefficiencies because of duplication of resources across the organization, for example, having a different information technology support person on each project. However, in a typical manufacturing or service firm, projects are not the major value creation process, but they often charter projects to meet infrequent needs, such as a new facility layout or technology rollout. Such projects cut across organizational boundaries, making communication across the organization difficult, and require more careful management approaches. Functional managers may be reluctant to provide the resources, and employees assigned to projects might relegate a project to a lower priority than their daily, functional job, making it difficult for the project manager to control the project.

A practical solution to this dilemma is a matrix organizational structure, which "loans" people and other resources to projects while still maintaining functional control over them. Project managers coordinate the work across the functions to minimize duplication of resources and facilitate communication across the organization, but coordination requires that resources be negotiated (see Chapter 5). Such organizational structures are often used in Six Sigma organizations.

A typical Six Sigma project team consists of a project manager, technical consultant, project champion, external customer or process owner, and the core project team. We discussed Six Sigma project teams in Chapter 6. The key leadership role belongs to the project manager, who is generally trained as a Six Sigma green belt (SSGB) or black belt (SSBB). Project managers are often generalists who have diverse backgrounds and experience and lead the project activities, plan and track progress of the work, and provide direction to the project team. In addition, they must manage the relationships and communication among the members of the project team. Thus, the project manager's ability to facilitate is usually more important than his or her ability to supervise. The project manager must also have sufficient technical expertise to resolve disputes among functional specialists.

> *Successful project managers have four key skills: a bias toward task completion, technical and administrative credibility, interpersonal and political sensitivity, and leadership ability.*

Project Life Cycle Management

A project typically unfolds in stages, which can be called a **life cycle**. Taking a quality perspective, Kloppenborg and Petrick[32] defined the stages of the typical quality-focused project management process as the following:

1. *Project Quality Initiation:* Define directions, priorities, limitations, and constraints.
2. *Project Quality Planning:* Create a blueprint for the scope of the project and resources needed to accomplish it.

3. *Project Quality Assurance:* Use appropriate, qualified processes to meet technical project design specifications.
4. *Project Quality Control:* Use appropriate communication and management tools to ensure that managerial performance, process improvements, and customer satisfaction is tracked.
5. *Project Quality Closure:* Evaluate customer satisfaction with project deliverables and assess success and failures that provide learning for future projects and referrals from satisfied customers.

These phases of the project life cycle will be discussed in more detail later in the chapter.

These basic components are applicable to any project management endeavor, but are directly relatable to Six Sigma design and improvement projects. The roles and accountability of each member of the project team in each stage of the project life cycle are summarized in Table 7.4.

Project Quality Initiation Projects are implemented to satisfy some need of a customer or process owner; thus, the first step in managing a project is to clearly define the goals of the project, and when and how they must be accomplished. Initiation also includes identifying a project champion, project manager, and other team members. The customer must be a vital participant in all stages of the process, not just at the beginning and the end.

Project Quality Planning All project-management decisions involve four factors: *time, resources, costs,* and *performance*. Project managers need to know how much time a project should take and when specific activities should be started and completed so that deadlines can be established and progress of the project monitored. They must also determine the resources, such as people and equipment available for the project, and how they should be allocated among the various activities. Projects usually have limited budgets and costs generally depend on the resources expended; thus, they must be monitored and controlled. Project managers seek ways to minimize costs without jeopardizing deadlines. Finally, performance, which can be defined as how well the results of the project meet customer requirements, should be a measurable entity. Software packages, such as Microsoft Project®, incorporate various quantitative analysis tools for scheduling, budgetary analysis, and tracking factors of time, resources, and costs, and should be selected at this stage.

The project-planning process involves determining the set of activities that must be performed, who will do them, how long each is estimated to take, and when they should be completed to meet the organization's goals. The project-planning process consists of the following steps:

1. *Project definition.* Define the project, its objectives, and deliverables. Determine the activities that must be completed and the sequence required to perform them.
2. *Resource planning.* For each activity, determine the resource needs: personnel, time, money, equipment, materials, and so on.
3. *Project scheduling.* Specify a time schedule for each activity.
4. *Project tracking and control.* Establish the proper control methods to be used for tracking progress. Develop alternative plans in anticipation of problems in meeting the planned schedule.

When projects are late, it is often because of failure to perform these four tasks adequately.

Table 7.4 Project Life Cycle Accountability Matrix

Role/Stage	Project Quality Initiation	Project Quality Planning	Project Quality Assurance	Project Quality Control	Project Quality Closure
Champion	Select project manager; promote Six Sigma use; align and select project; commit to charter	Determine decision-making authority; commit to plan; allocate resources needed for project success	Conduct external customer communications; mentor project manager; clear obstacles as needed	Conduct external customer communications; mentor project manager; approve or reject process improvements; clear obstacles as needed	Sign off on completed project; recognize and reward participants; assess project to improve system
External Customer (or Process Owner)	Identify and prioritize expectations; commit to charter	Contribute process knowledge; identify customer satisfaction standards and trade-off values; commit to plan	Participate in ongoing communications; assist in obtaining approvals for changes in processes	Confirm ongoing satisfaction level; accept deliverables	Verify when usage training and support are completed; assess project to improve system; ensure that new processes are implemented; sign off
Master Black Belt (Technical Consultant)	Assist in strategic project selection; promote Six Sigma vision, tools, and process	Assist in identifying data collection and analysis needs; provide training resources; ensure that processes are statistically sound	Participate in ongoing communications; mentor project manager; facilitate cross-project sharing and learning	Provide expertise in design of process improvements; support project manager (SSBB and/or SSGB)	Assist in development of management presentations; do project sign-offs; ensure that project results are publicized; disseminate best practices and lessons learned
Project Manager (SSBB and/ or SSGB)	Select core team; identify risks; empower performance; commit to charter	Identify customer satisfaction standards and trade-off values; plan for short-term training if needed; develop quality and communications plans; commit to plan	Conduct customer/ management communications; select tools; confirm qualified processes used; oversee data gathering and analysis; manage quality audits and planning	Track progress, critical success factors, and costs versus plan; implement mid-course corrections; measure customer satisfaction; manage process improvements	Notify champion of project completion; recognize and reward participants; assess project to improve system
Core Team	Determine team operating principles; flowchart project; identify lessons learned; commit to charter	Plan project; contribute special expertise; identify suppliers; qualify the process; identify data to collect; commit to plan	Use qualified processes; gather data, find root causes; conduct quality audits; plan future work	Measure customer satisfaction; test deliverables; correct defects; endorse deliverables	Provide customer support and training; assess project to improve system

Source: Adapted from Timothy J. Kloppenborg and Joseph A. Petrick, *Managing Project Quality* (Vienna, VA: Management Concepts, 2003), 11.

Project Quality Assurance Project quality assurance can be thought of as "customer relationship management" while the project is in process. It requires communication, interpersonal, and diplomacy skills on the part of the project manager. He or she must manage upward to the project champion and out to the client, while keeping a firm, but participative, hand on the pulse of team members and those who are actually doing the "hands-on" project work. Project quality assurance allows the project manager to estimate how successfully the final "deliverable" will perform, not just whether it will be on time and below budgeted cost. Software packages such as Microsoft Project are not designed to track "deliverable" performance measures, although some of the project tracking data for estimated final costs and estimated completion dates may be of interest to customers. As suggested in Table 7.4, performance tracking is often subjective, but can be quantified using communication processes and customer surveys, tracking and controlling changes in the project plan, and performing regular project reviews or audits.

Project Quality Control Project quality control involves systematically reviewing the time, resources, cost, and performance measures as the project is being carried out. Because of the uncertainty of task times, unavoidable delays, or other problems, projects rarely, if ever, progress on schedule. Managers must therefore monitor performance of the project and take corrective action when needed. A typical project control system includes the following:

- A project plan covering expected scope, schedule, cost, and performance goals or requirements
- A continuous monitoring system that measures the current results or status against the project plan through the use of monitoring tools
- A reporting system that identifies deviations from the project plan by means of trends and forecasts
- Timely actions to take advantage of beneficial trends or to correct deviations

Project Quality Closure Project closeout is one of those mundane but vitally important processes that facilitate future improvement in project management performance. It consists of such steps as the following:

- Ensuring that the project has been signed off by those who must do so
- Ensuring that all bills have been paid and all financial records have been completed
- Ensuring that team members have not only been thanked, but provided for, which may involve following up with recommendations for reassignment to new projects or departments
- Ensuring that "lessons learned" are examined and documented, often by performing a final project audit
- Ensuring that project successes and best practices are communicated and disseminated to other parts of the organization

PROCESS CONTROL

An international study by Landor & Associates, an independent design and image firm, showed conclusively that Coca-Cola is the number one brand in the minds of soft-drink consumers around the world, and affirmed that the company is totally committed to quality. Coca Cola has stated, "Our commitment to quality is something for which we will never lose our taste."[33] However, in early June, 1999, quite a few people in Europe did when almost 100 Belgian children fell ill after drinking Coca-Cola. This incident caused the Belgian Health Ministry to require Coca-Cola to recall millions of cans of product in Belgium and to cease product distribution. Later, France and the Netherlands also halted distribution of Coke products as the contamination scare spread. It was quickly determined that contaminated carbon dioxide had been used during the carbonation process at the Antwerp bottling facility. According to the official statement from Coca-Cola, "Independent laboratory testing showed that the cause of the of the off-taste in the bottled products was carbon dioxide. That carbon dioxide was replaced and all bottles with off-taste have been removed from the market. The issue affects the taste of the soft drinks only. . . . The second issue involves an external odor on some canned products. In the case of the Belgian distribution system, a substance used in wood treatment has caused an offensive odor on the outside bottom of the can. Independent analysis determined that the product is safe. The Company, in conjunction with its bottling partner in Belgium, is taking all necessary steps to eliminate this offensive odor."[34] After two weeks, the company was allowed to begin producing and distributing products in the three countries. Then, at the end of June, Coca-Cola Beverages Poland found that 1,500 bottles of its Bonaqua water product contained mold. This discovery resulted in 246,000 glass bottles being withdrawn from the market in Poland, and replaced with plastic containers.

Although the Coca-Cola Company acted swiftly to resolve the problems and recover its image and reputation, this case demonstrates the importance of *process control*. **Control** is the activity of ensuring conformance to the requirements and taking corrective action when necessary to correct problems and maintain stable performance. Not recognizing when contamination occurs in a bottling process for instance, signifies a lack of control. Control charts, which will be discussed thoroughly in Chapter 14, are an important tool for controlling processes.

Process control is important for two reasons. First, process control methods are the basis for effective daily management of processes. Second, long-term improvements cannot be made to a process unless the process is first brought under control.

Any control system has three components: (1) *a standard or goal*, (2) *a means of measuring accomplishment*, and (3) *comparison of actual results with the standard, along with feedback to form the basis for corrective action*. Goals and standards are defined during planning and design processes. They establish what is supposed to be accomplished. These goals and standards are reflected by measurable quality characteristics, such as dimensions of machined parts, numbers of defectives, customer complaints, or waiting times. For example, golf balls must meet five standards to be considered as conforming to the Rules of Golf: minimum size, maximum weight, spherical symmetry, maximum initial velocity, and overall distance.[35] Methods for measuring these quality characteristics may be automated or performed manually by the workforce. Golf balls are measured for size by trying to drop them through a metal ring—a conforming ball sticks to the ring while a nonconforming ball falls through; digital scales measure weight to one-thousandth of a gram; and initial velocity is measured in a special machine by finding the time it takes a ball struck at 98 mph to break a ballistic screen at the end of a tube exactly 6.28 feet away.

Measurements supply the information concerning what has actually been accomplished. Workers, supervisors, or managers then assess whether the actual results meet the goals and standards. If not, then remedial action must be taken. For example, workers might check the first few parts after a new production setup (called setup verification) to determine whether they conform to specifications. If not, the worker adjusts the setup. Sometimes this process occurs automatically. For instance, in the production of plastic sheet stock, thickness depends on temperature. Sensors monitor the sheet thickness; if it begins to go out of tolerance, the system can adjust the temperature in order to change the thickness.

However, in many industries, data are collected through some type of manual inspection process. Such processes that rely on visual interpretation of product characteristics or manual reading of gauges and instruments may encounter error rates of from 10 to 50 percent. This high rate occurs for several reasons:

- *Complexity*: The number of defects caught by an inspector decreases with more parts and less orderly arrangement.
- *Defect rate*: When the product defect rate is low, inspectors tend to miss more defects than when the defect rate is higher.
- *Inspection rate*: The inspector's performance degrades rapidly as the inspection rate increases.[36]

These factors can be mitigated by using automated technology, or at the very least, minimizing the number of quality characteristics that must be inspected, reducing time pressures, using repeated inspections (if the same item is inspected by several people, a higher percentage of total defects will be caught), and improving the design of the workspace to facilitate the inspection task.

Short-term corrective action generally should be taken by those who own the process and are responsible for doing the work, such as machine operators, order-fulfillment workers, and so on. Long-term remedial action is the responsibility of management. The responsibility for control can be determined by checking the three components of control systems. A process owner must have the means of knowing what is expected (the standard or goal) through clear instructions and specifications; they must have the means of determining their actual performance, typically through inspection and measurement; and they must have a means of making corrections if they discover a variance between what is expected of them and their actual performance. If any of these criteria is not met, then the process is the responsibility of management, not the process owner.

Both Juran and Deming made this important distinction. If process owners are held accountable for or expected to act on problems beyond their control, they become frustrated and end up playing games with management. Juran and Deming stated that the majority of quality problems are management-controllable—the result of common cause variation. For the smaller proportion of problems resulting from special causes, process owners must be given the tools to identify them and the authority to take action. This philosophy shifts the burden of assuring quality from inspection departments and "quality control" personnel to workers on the shop floor and in customer-contact positions. For example, DaimlerChrysler manufactures the PT Cruiser at the company's Toluca Assembly Plant in Mexico. To ensure quality, the Toluca plant verifies parts, processes, fit, and finish every step of the way, from stamping and body to paint and final assembly. The control practices include visual management through quality alert systems, which are designed to call immediate attention to abnormal conditions. The system provides visual and audible signals for each station for tooling, production, maintenance, and material flow.[37]

In manufacturing, control is usually applied to incoming materials, key processes, and final products and services.

Clearly, if incoming materials are of poor quality, then the final product will certainly be no better. In a TQ environment, customers should not have to rely on heavy inspection of purchased items. The burden of supplying high-quality product should rest with the suppliers themselves. Occasional inspection might be used to audit compliance, but suppliers should be expected to provide documentation and statistical evidence that they are meeting required specifications. The Bonus Materials folder on the CD-ROM contains supplementary material on supplier and partnering process management.

Because unwanted variation can arise during production, in-process control is needed throughout the production process. When the process owner assumes the role of inspector, the occurrence of special causes of variation can quickly be recognized and immediate adjustments to stabilize the process can be made. Done properly, this activity can eliminate the need for independent inspection.

Final inspection represents the last point in the manufacturing process at which the producer can verify that the product meets customer requirements, and avoid external failure costs. For many consumer products, final inspection consists of functional testing. For instance, a manufacturer of televisions might do a simple test on every unit to make sure it operates properly. However, the company might not test every aspect of the television, such as picture sharpness or other characteristics. These aspects might already have been evaluated through in-process controls. Computerized test equipment is quite widespread, allowing for 100 percent inspection to be conducted rapidly and cost-effectively.

> *Effective quality control systems include documented procedures for all key processes; a clear understanding of the appropriate equipment and working environment; methods for monitoring and controlling critical quality characteristics; approval processes for equipment; criteria for workmanship, such as written standards, samples, or illustrations; and maintenance activities.*

Cincinnati Fiberglass, a small manufacturer of fiberglass parts for trucks, uses a control plan for each production process that includes the process name, tool used, standard operating procedure, tolerance, inspection frequency, sample size, person responsible, reporting document, and reaction plan. Of particular importance is the ability to trace all components of a product back to key process equipment and operators and to the original material from which it was made. Process control also includes monitoring the accuracy and variability of equipment, operator knowledge and skills, the accuracy of measurement results and data used, and environmental factors such as time and temperature. An example of process control in the food industry—the HACCP approach—is discussed in the Bonus Materials folder on the CD-ROM.

Control should be the foundation for organizational learning. Many companies are adopting an approach that has been used in the U.S. military, called **after-action review**, or **debrief**. This review consists of asking four basic questions:

1. What was supposed to happen?
2. What actually happened?
3. Why was there a difference?
4. What can we learn?

Thus, rather than simply correcting unacceptable events, the focus is on preventing them from occurring again in the future.

Process Control in Services

Many people think that process control applies only to manufacturing. This assumption could not be further from the truth. The approach used by The Ritz-Carlton Hotel Company to control quality is proactive because of their intensive personalized service environment.[38] Systems for collecting and using quality-related measures are widely deployed and used extensively throughout the organization. Each hotel tracks service quality indicators on a daily basis. The Ritz-Carlton recognizes that many customer requirements are sensory, and thus, difficult to measure. However, by selecting, training, and certifying employees in their knowledge of The Ritz-Carlton Gold Standards of service, they are able to assess their work through appropriate sensory measurements—taste, sight, smell, sound, and touch—and take appropriate actions.

The company uses three types of control processes to deliver quality:

1. Self-control of the individual employee based on their spontaneous and learned behavior.
2. Basic control mechanism, which is carried out by every member of the workforce. The first person who detects a problem is empowered to break away from routine duties, investigate and correct the problem immediately, document the incident, and then return to their routine.
3. Critical success factor control for critical processes. Process teams use customer and organizational requirement measurements to determine quality, speed, and cost performance. These measurements are compared against benchmarks and customer satisfaction data to determine corrective action and resource allocation.

In addition, The Ritz-Carlton conducts both self-audits and outside audits. Self audits are carried out internally at all levels, from one individual or function to an entire hotel. Process walk-throughs occur daily in hotels while senior leaders assess field operations during formal reviews at various intervals. Outside audits are performed by independent travel and hospitality rating organizations. All audits must be documented, and any findings must be submitted to the senior leader of the unit being audited. They are responsible for action and for assessing the implementation and effectiveness of recommended corrective actions.

An example of a structured quality control process in the service industry is the "10-Step Monitoring and Evaluation Process" set forth by the Joint Commission on Accrediting Health Care Organizations. This process, shown in Table 7.5, provides a detailed sequence of activities for monitoring and evaluating the quality of health care in an effort to identify problems and improve care. Standards and goals are defined in steps 2 through 5; measurement is accomplished in step 6; and comparison and feedback is performed in the remaining steps.

The most common quality characteristics in services, time (waiting time, service time, delivery time) and number of nonconformances, can be measured rather easily. Insurance companies, for example, measure the time to complete different transactions such as new issues, claim payments, and cash surrenders. Hospitals measure the percentage of nosocomial infections and the percentage of unplanned re-admissions to the emergency room, intensive care, or operating room within, say, 48 hours. Other quality characteristics are observable. They include the types of errors (wrong kind, wrong quantity, wrong delivery date, etc.) and behavior (courtesy, promptness, competency, and so on). Hospitals might monitor the completeness of medical charts and the quality of radiology readings, measured by a double-reading process.

Simple data collection procedures capture the measurements for service quality control. Time is easily measured by taking two observations: starting time and finishing time. Many observed data assume only "yes" or "no" values. For example, a survey of pharmaceutical operations in a hospital might include the following questions:

- Are drug storage and preparation areas within the pharmacy under the supervision of a pharmacist?
- Are drugs requiring special storage conditions properly stored?
- Are drug emergency boxes inspected on a monthly basis?
- Is the drug emergency box record book filled out completely?

Table 7.5 10-Step Monitoring and Evaluation Process for Health Care Organizations

- *Step 1: Assign Responsibility.* The emergency department director is responsible for, and actively participates in, monitoring and evaluation. The director assigns responsibility for the specific duties related to monitoring and evaluation.
- *Step 2: Delineate Scope of Care.* The department considers the scope of care provided within emergency services to establish a basis for identifying important aspects of care to monitor and evaluate. The scope of care is a complete inventory of what the emergency department does.
- *Step 3: Identify Important Aspects of Care.* Important aspects of care are those that are high-risk, high-volume, and/or problem-prone. Staff identify important aspects of care so that monitoring and evaluation focuses on emergency department activities with the greatest impact on patient care.
- *Step 4: Identify Indicators.* Indicators of quality are identified for each important aspect of care. An indicator is a measurable variable related to a structure, process, or outcome of care. Examples of possible indicators (all of which would need to be further defined) include insufficient staffing for sudden surges in patient volume (structure), delays in physicians reporting to the emergency room (process), and transfusion errors (outcome).
- *Step 5: Establish Thresholds for Evaluation.* A threshold for evaluation is the level or point at which intensive evaluation of care is triggered. A threshold may be 0% or 100% or any other appropriate level. Emergency department staff should establish a threshold for each indicator.
- *Step 6: Collect and Organize Data.* Appropriate emergency department staff should collect data pertaining to the indicators. Data are organized to facilitate comparison with the thresholds for evaluation.
- *Step 7: Evaluate Care.* When the cumulative data related to an indicator reach the threshold for evaluation, appropriate emergency department staff evaluate the care provided to determine whether a problem exists. This evaluation, which in many cases will take the form of peer review, should focus on possible trends and performance patterns. The evaluation is designed to identify causes of any problems or methods by which care or performance may be improved.
- *Step 8: Take Actions to Solve Problems.* When problems are identified, action plans are developed, approved at appropriate levels, and enacted to solve the problem or take the opportunity to improve care.
- *Step 9: Assess Actions and Document Improvement.* The effectiveness of any actions taken is assessed and documented. Further actions necessary to solve a problem are taken and their effectiveness is assessed.
- *Step 10: Communicate Relevant Information to the Organization-wide Quality Assurance Program.* Findings from and conclusions of monitoring and evaluation, including actions taken to solve problems and improve care, are documented and reported monthly through the hospital's established channels of communication.

Source: "Medical Staff Monitoring and Evaluation—Departmental Review," Chicago. Copyright by the Joint Commission on Accreditation of Health Care Organizations, Oakbrook Terrace, IL. Reprinted with permission (undated).

Even though human behavior is easily observable, the task of describing and classifying the observations is far more difficult. The major obstacle is developing operational definitions of behavioral characteristics. For example, how does one define courteous versus discourteous, or understanding versus indifference? Defining such distinctions is best done by comparing behavior against understandable standards. For instance, a standard for "courtesy" might be to address the customer as "Mr." or

"Ms." Failure to do so is an instance of an error. "Promptness" might be defined as greeting a customer within five seconds of entering the store, or answering letters within two days of receipt. These behaviors can easily be recorded and counted. Figure 7.5 shows some behavioral questions used in a patient survey by a group of Southern California hospitals.[39]

PROCESS IMPROVEMENT

Process improvement is an important business strategy in competitive markets because

- Customer loyalty is driven by delivered value.
- Delivered value is created by business processes.

Figure 7.5 Sample Hospital Staff Behavior Questions

Admissions
11. Altogether, how long did you have to wait to be admitted?
        More than 1 hour: _____ (1)   1 hour: _____ (2)   30 min.: _____ (3)   15 min.: _____ (4)
12. If you had to wait 30 minutes or longer before someone met with you, were you told why?
        YES: _____ (1)   NO: _____ (2)   Did not wait 30 minutes: _____ (3)

Nursing Staff
21. Did a nurse talk to you about the procedures for the day?
        Never: _____ (1)   Sometimes: _____ (2)   Often: _____ (3)   Always: _____ (4)
22. Were you on IV fluids?
        YES: _____ (1)   NO: _____ (2)
        A. If YES, did the IV fluids ever run out?
                YES: _____ (1)   NO: _____ (2)

Medical Staff
28. Did the doctor do what he/she told you he was going to do?
        Never: _____ (1)   Sometimes: _____ (2)   Often: _____ (3)   Always: _____ (4)

Housekeeping
36. Did the housekeeper come into your room at least once a day?
        YES: _____ (1)   NO: _____ (2)
39. Was the bathroom adequately supplied?
        Always: _____ (1)   Often: _____ (2)   Sometimes: _____ (3)   Never: _____ (4)

X-Ray
When you received services from the X-ray technician, were the procedures explained to you?
        Always: _____ (1)   Often: _____ (2)   Sometimes: _____ (3)   Never: _____ (4)

Food
34. Generally, were your meals served at the same time each day?
        Always: _____ (1)   Often: _____ (2)   Sometimes: _____ (3)   Never: _____ (4)

Source: Adapted from K. M. Casarreal, J. L. Mill, and M. A. Plant, "Improving Service Through Patient Surveys in a Multihospital Organization," Hospital & Health Services Administration, Health Administration Press, Ann Arbor, MI, March/April 1986, 41–52. © 1986, Foundation of the American College of Health Care Executives.

- Sustained success in competitive markets requires a business to continuously improve delivered value.
- To continuously improve value creation ability, a business must continuously improve its value creation processes.[40]

Quality Spotlight
Dell and
Microsoft

A good illustration is Dell. Although it has had some of the highest quality ratings in the PC industry, CEO Michael Dell became obsessed with finding ways to reduce machine failure rates. He concluded that failures were related to the number of times a hard drive was handled

Improvement should be a proactive task of management and be viewed as an opportunity, not simply as a reaction to problems and competitive threats.

during assembly, and insisted that the number of "touches" be reduced from an existing level of more than 30 per drive. Production lines were revamped and the number was reduced to fewer than 15. Soon after, the reject rate of hard drives fell by 40 percent and the overall failure rated dropped by 20 percent.[41] Another example is Microsoft. In 1996, CEO Bill Gates noticed that Microsoft was printing 350,000 sales reports per year, and that 114 different forms were used in procurement alone.[42] After many discussions with other top managers and employees, a directive was issued that basically stated that all paper forms and reports must be eliminated unless a compelling need could be found for them. The results included:

- The total number of paper forms at Microsoft was reduced from 1,000 to 60; of these, 10 are required by law, 40 are required by outside parties, and 10 are seldom used.
- Only one procurement form now exists.
- Savings for the first year (1997–98) were estimated at $40 million.
- Studies by accounting firms suggest that the average form costs $145 to process, and that the average cost of a similar average electronic transaction, as verified by Microsoft, is $5.

Microsoft accomplished this process improvement by using the company intranet, "Frequently Asked Questions" (FAQ), search capabilities, and links to related pages for each electronic form; scanning outside documents and putting them into the internal system; and developing a self-service approach so that individuals could handle 90 percent of their administrative information processing needs on their own desktop PCs.

Many opportunities for improvement exist, including the obvious reductions in manufacturing defects and cycle times. Organizations should also consider improving employee morale, satisfaction, and cooperation; improving managerial practices; improving the design of products with features that better meet customers' needs, and that can achieve higher performance, higher reliability, and other market-driven dimensions of quality; and improving the efficiency of manufacturing systems by reducing workers' idle time and unnecessary motions, and by eliminating unnecessary inventory, unnecessary transportation and material handling, and scrap and rework.

The concept of continuous improvement dates back many years. One of the earliest examples in the United States was at National Cash Register Company (NCR). After a shipment of defective cash registers was returned in 1894, the company's founder discovered unpleasant and unsafe working conditions. He made many changes, including better lighting, new safety devices, ventilation, lounges, and lockers. The company offered extensive evening classes to improve employees' education and skills, and instituted a program for soliciting suggestions from factory workers. Workers received cash prizes and other recognitions for their best ideas; by the 1940s the company was receiving an average of 3,000 suggestions each year.

Over the years, many other companies such as Lincoln Electric and Procter & Gamble developed innovative and effective improvement approaches. However, many of these focused almost exclusively on productivity and cost. A focus on quality improvement, on the other hand, is relatively recent, stimulated by the success of the Japanese. Toshiba in 1946, Matsushita Electric in 1950, and Toyota in 1951 initiated some of the earliest formal continuous improvement programs. Toyota, in particular, pioneered just-in-time (JIT), which showed that companies could make products efficiently with virtually zero defects. JIT established a philosophy of improvement, which the Japanese call **kaizen** (pronounced kī-zen).

Kaizen[43]

Kaizen, which is a Japanese word that means gradual and orderly continuous improvement, is a philosophy that encompasses all business activities and everyone in an organization. In the kaizen philosophy, improvement in all areas of business—cost, meeting delivery schedules, employee safety and skill development, supplier relations, new product development, or productivity—serve to enhance the quality of the firm. Thus, any activity directed toward improvement falls under the kaizen umbrella. Activities to establish traditional quality control systems, install robotics and advanced technology, institute employee suggestion systems, maintain equipment, and implement just-in-time production systems all lead to improvement.

Kaizen focuses on small, gradual, and frequent improvements over the long term with minimum financial investment, and participation by everyone in the organization.

At Nissan Motor Co., Ltd., for instance, management seriously considers any suggestion that saves at least 0.6 seconds in a production process. The concept of kaizen is so deeply ingrained in the minds of both managers and workers that they often do not even realize they are thinking in terms of improvement. The Kaizen Institute (http://www.kaizen-institute.com) suggests some basic tips for implementing kaizen. These suggestions include discarding conventional fixed ideas; thinking of how to do something, not why it cannot be done; not seeking perfection; not making excuses, but questioning current practices; and seeking the "wisdom of ten people rather than the knowledge of one." By instilling kaizen into people and training them in basic quality improvement tools, workers can build this philosophy into their work and continually seek improvement in their jobs. This process-oriented approach to improvement encourages constant communication among workers and managers.

Three things are required for a successful kaizen program: operating practices, total involvement, and training.[44] First, operating practices expose new improvement opportunities. Practices such as just-in-time reveal waste and inefficiency as well as poor quality. Second, in kaizen, every employee strives for improvement. Top management, for example, views improvement as an inherent component of corporate strategy and provides support to improvement activities by allocating resources effectively and providing reward structures that are conducive to improvement. Middle management can implement top management's improvement goals by establishing, upgrading, and maintaining operating standards that reflect those goals; by improving cooperation between departments; and by making employees conscious of their responsibility for improvement and developing their problem-solving skills through training. Supervisors can direct more of their attention to improvement rather than "supervision," which, in turn, facilitates communication and offers better guidance to workers. Finally, workers can engage in improvement through suggestion systems and small group activities, self-development programs that teach practical problem-solving techniques, and enhanced job performance skills. All these improvements require significant training, both in the philosophy and in tools and techniques.

The kaizen philosophy has been widely adopted and is used by many firms in the United States and around the world. For example, at ENBI Corporation, a New York manufacturer of precision metal shafts and roller assemblies for the printer, copier, and fax machine markets, kaizen projects have resulted in a 48 percent increase in productivity, a 30 percent reduction in cycle time, and a 73 percent reduction in inventory.[45] Kaizen has been successfully applied in the Mercedes-Benz truck factory in Brazil, resulting in reductions of 30 percent in manufacturing space, 45 percent in inventory, 70 percent in lead time, and 70 percent in setup time over a three-year period. Sixteen employees have full-time responsibility for kaizen activities.[46]

Flexibility and Cycle Time Reduction

Success in globally competitive markets requires a capacity for rapid change and flexibility. Electronic commerce, for instance, requires more rapid, flexible, and customized responses than traditional market outlets. Flexibility might demand special strategies such as modular designs, sharing components, sharing manufacturing lines, and specialized training for employees. It also involves outsourcing decisions, agreements with key suppliers, and innovative partnering arrangements.

> *Flexibility refers to the ability to adapt quickly and effectively to changing requirements. It might mean rapid changeover from one product to another, rapid response to changing demands, or the ability to produce a wide range of customized services.*

One important business metric that complements flexibility is cycle time. **Cycle time** refers to the time it takes to accomplish one cycle of a process (e.g., the time from when a customer orders a product to the time that it is delivered, or the time to introduce a new product). Reductions in cycle time serve two purposes. First, they speed up work processes so that customer response is improved. Second, reductions in cycle time can only be accomplished by streamlining and simplifying processes to eliminate non-value-added steps such as rework. This approach forces improvements in quality by reducing the potential for mistakes and errors. By reducing non-value-added steps, costs are reduced as well. Thus, cycle time reductions often drive simultaneous improvements in organization, quality, cost, and productivity. Significant reductions in cycle time cannot be achieved simply by focusing on individual subprocesses; cross-functional processes must be examined all across the organization. Through these activities, the company comes to understand work at the organizational level and to engage in cooperative behaviors.

Quality Spotlight
Proctor & Gamble

One example of cycle time reduction is Procter & Gamble's over-the-counter (OTC) clinical division, which conducts clinical studies that involve testing drugs, health care products, or treatments in humans.[47] Such testing follows rigorous design, conduct, analysis, and summary of the data collected. P&G had at least four different ways to perform a clinical study and needed to find the best way to meet its research and development needs. They chose to focus on cycle time reduction. Their approach built on fundamental TQ principles: focusing on the customer, fact-based decisions, continual improvement, empowerment, the right leadership structure, and an understanding of work processes. An example is shown in Figure 7.6. The team found that final reports took months to prepare. Only by mapping the existing process did they

Figure 7.6 Final Report "Is" and "Should" Process Map Example

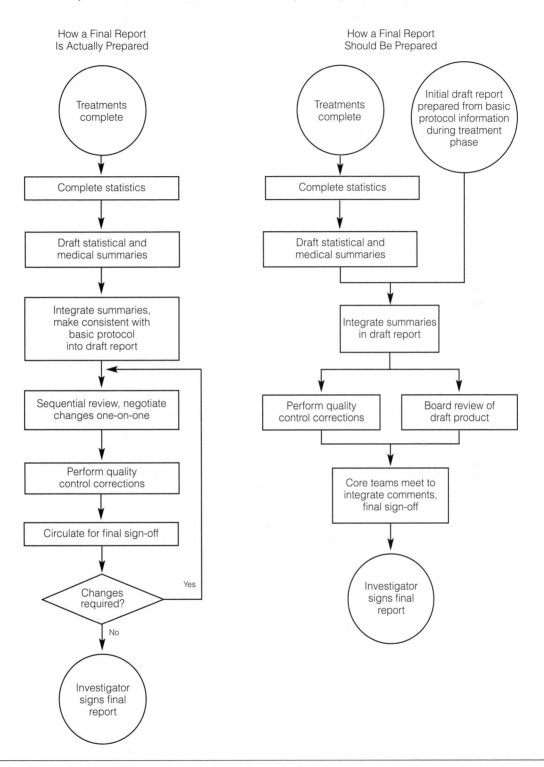

Source: David A. McCamey, Robert W. Bogs, and Linda M. Bayuk, "More, Better, Faster From Total Quality Effort," *Quality Progress,* August 1999, 43–50. © 1999. American Society for Quality. Reprinted with permission.

fully understand the causes of long production times and the amount of rework and recycling during review and sign-off. By restructuring the activities from sequential to parallel work and identifying critical measurements to monitor the process, they were able to reduce the time to less than four weeks.

Agility is a term that is commonly used to characterize flexibility and short cycle times. Agility is crucial to such customer-focused strategies as mass customization, which requires rapid response and flexibility to changing consumer demand. Enablers of agility include close relationships with customers to understand their emerging needs and requirements, empowering employees as decision makers, effective manufacturing and information technology, close supplier and partner relationships, and breakthrough improvement (discussed next).

Breakthrough Improvement

Breakthrough improvement refers to discontinuous change, as opposed to the gradual, continuous improvement philosophy of kaizen. Breakthrough improvements result from innovative and creative thinking; often these are motivated by **stretch goals**, or **breakthrough objectives**.

When a goal of 10 percent improvement is set, managers or engineers can usually meet it with some minor improvements. However, when the goal is 1,000 percent improvement, employees must be creative and think "outside of the box." The seemingly impossible is often achieved, yielding dramatic improvements and boosting morale. Motorola's Six Sigma thrust was driven by a goal of improving product and services quality ten times within two years, and at least 100-fold within four years.

Stretch goals force an organization to think in a radically different way, and to encourage major improvements as well as incremental ones.

For stretch goals to be successful, they must derive unambiguously from corporate strategy. Organizations must not set goals that result in unreasonable stress to employees or punish failure. In addition, they must provide appropriate help and tools to accomplish the task. Two approaches for breakthrough improvement that help companies achieve stretch goals are *benchmarking* and *reengineering*.

Benchmarking The development and realization of improvement objectives, particularly stretch objectives, is often aided through the process of benchmarking. **Benchmarking** is defined as "measuring your performance against that of best-in-class companies, determining how the best-in-class achieve those performance levels, and using the information as a basis for your own company's targets, strategies, and implementation,"[48] or more simply, "the search of industry best practices that lead to superior performance."[49] The term **best practices** refers to approaches that produce exceptional results, are usually innovative in terms of the use of technology or human resources, and are recognized by customers or industry experts.

Through benchmarking, a company discovers its strengths and weaknesses and those of other industry leaders and learns how to incorporate the best practices into its own operations. Benchmarking can provide motivation to achieve stretch goals by helping employees to see what others can accomplish. For example, to meet a stretch target of reducing the time to build new 747 and 767 airplanes at Boeing from 18 months (in 1992) to 8 months, teams studied the world's best producers of everything from computers to ships. By 1996 the time had been reduced to 10 months.[50]

The concept of benchmarking is not new.[51] In the early 1800s Francis Lowell, a New England industrialist, traveled to England to study manufacturing techniques at the best British mill factories. Henry Ford created the assembly line after taking a tour of a Chicago slaughterhouse and watching carcasses, hung on hooks mounted on a monorail, move from one workstation to another. Toyota's just-in-time production system was influenced by the replenishment practices of U.S. supermarkets. Modern benchmarking was initiated by Xerox and has since become a common practice among leading firms.

An organization may decide to engage in benchmarking for several reasons. It eliminates "reinventing the wheel" along with associated wasted time and resources. It helps identify performance gaps between an organization and competitors, leading to realistic goals. It encourages employees to continuously innovate. Finally, because it is a process of continuous learning, benchmarking emphasizes sensitivity to the changing needs of customers.[52]

Three major types of benchmarking have emerged in business. **Competitive benchmarking** involves studying products, processes, or business performance of competitors in the same industry to compare pricing, technical quality, features, and other quality or performance characteristics of products and services. For example, a television cable company might compare its customer satisfaction rating or service response time to other cable companies; a manufacturer of TVs might compare its unit production costs or field failure rates against competitors. Significant gaps suggest key opportunities for improvement. Competitive benchmarking was refined into a science by Xerox during the 1970s and 1980s.

Process benchmarking emerged soon after. It centers on key work processes such as distribution, order entry, or employee training. This type of benchmarking identifies the most effective practices in companies that perform similar functions, no matter in what industry. For example, Xerox adapted the warehousing and distribution practices of L.L. Bean for its spare parts distribution system. Texas Instruments studied the kitting (order preparation) practices of six companies, including Mary Kay Cosmetics, and designed a process that captured the best practices of each of them, cutting kitting cycle time in half. A General Mills plant in Lodi, California, had an average machine changeover time of three hours. Then somebody said, "From three hours to 10 minutes!" Employees went to a NASCAR track and videotaped the pit crews, and studied the process to identify how the principles could be applied to the production changeover processes. Several months later, the average time fell to 17 minutes.[53] The U.S. Marine Corps studied companies such as Wal-Mart and United Parcel Service to improve its supply chain processes, changing its inventory policies and learning to employ modern technology like handheld computers. Thus, companies should not aim benchmarking solely at direct competitors or similar organizations; in fact, they would be mistaken to do so. If a company simply benchmarks within its own industry, it may merely be competitive and have a slight edge in those areas in which it is the industry leader. However, if benchmarks are adopted from outside the industry, a company may learn ideas and processes as well as new applications that allow it to surpass the best within its own industry and to achieve distinctive superiority.

Finally, **strategic benchmarking** examines how companies compete and seeks the winning strategies that have led to competitive advantage and market success. The typical benchmarking process can be described by the process used at AT&T.

1. *Project conception:* Identify the need and decide to benchmark.
2. *Planning:* Determine the scope and objectives, and develop a benchmarking plan.
3. *Preliminary data collection:* Collect data on industry companies and similar processes as well as detailed data on your own processes.

4. *Best-in-class selection:* Select companies with best-in-class processes.
5. *Best-in-class collection:* Collect detailed data from companies with best-in-class processes.
6. *Assessment:* Compare your own and best-in-class processes and develop recommendations.
7. *Implementation planning:* Develop operational improvement plans to attain superior performance.
8. *Implementation:* Enact operational plans and monitor process improvements.
9. *Recalibration:* Update benchmark findings and assess improvements in processes.[54]

Reengineering   The process of **reengineering** has been defined as "the fundamental rethinking and radical redesign of business processes to achieve dramatic improvements in critical, contemporary measures of performance, such as cost, quality, service, and speed."[55] Such questioning often uncovers obsolete, erroneous, or inappropriate assumptions. Radical redesign involves tossing out existing procedures and reinventing the process, not just incrementally improving it. The goal is to achieve quantum leaps in performance. For example, IBM Credit Corporation

> *Reengineering involves asking basic questions about business processes: Why do we do it? and Why is it done this way?*

cut the process of financing IBM computers, software, and services from seven days to four hours by rethinking the process. Originally, the process was designed to handle difficult applications and required four highly trained specialists and a series of handoffs. The actual work took only about 1.5 hours; the rest of the time was spent in transit or delay. By questioning the assumption that every application was unique and difficult to process, IBM Credit Corporation was able to replace the specialists by a single individual supported by a user-friendly computer system that provided access to all the data and tools that the specialists would use.

Successful reengineering requires fundamental understanding of processes, creative thinking to break away from old traditions and assumptions, and effective use of information technology. PepsiCo has embarked on a program to reengineer all of its key business processes, such as selling and delivery, equipment service and repair, procurement, and financial reporting. In the selling and delivery of its products, for example, customer reps typically experience stockouts of as much as 25 percent of product by the end of the day, resulting in late-day stops not getting full deliveries and the need to return to those accounts. Many other routes return with overstock of other products, increasing handling costs. By redesigning the system to include handheld computers, customer reps can confirm and deliver that day's order and also take a future order for the next delivery to that customer.[56]

Benchmarking can greatly assist reengineering efforts. Reengineering without benchmarking probably will produce 5 to 10 percent improvements; benchmarking can increase this percentage to 50 or 75 percent. When GTE reengineered eight core processes of its telephone operations, it examined the best practices of some 84 companies from diverse industries. By studying outside best practices, a company can identify and import new technology, skills, structures, training, and capabilities.[57]

PROCESS MANAGEMENT IN THE BALDRIGE CRITERIA, ISO 9000, AND SIX SIGMA

Category 6 of the 2003 Malcolm Baldrige National Quality Award Criteria for Performance Excellence is *Process Management*. Item 6.1, *Value Creation Processes*, examines how an organization identifies and manages its key processes for creating customer value and achieving business success and growth. This process includes how an organization incorporates customer and supplier input into determining its key process requirements; how processes are designed to meet these requirements; and how new technology, organizational learning, cycle time, productivity, cost control, and other efficiency and effectiveness factors are designed into processes. This criteria item also seeks to understand how key performance measures and indicators are used for controlling and improving processes, how costs associated with inspections, tests, and audits are minimized, and how defects and rework are prevented. Finally, it calls for information on how value creation processes are improved to achieve better performance, reduce variability, improve products and services, keep processes current with business needs and directions, and how improvements are shared with other organizational units. It might include Six Sigma approaches, use of ISO 9000:2000, or other process improvement tools. Item 6.2, *Support Processes*, calls for similar information about key support processes, particularly on how they are designed to meet appropriate internal and external customer requirements, and how they are controlled and improved.

Many aspects of ISO 9000:2000 deal with process management activities (in fact, the entire standards are focused on an organization's ability to understand, define, and document its processes). For example, one of the requirements is that organizations plan and control the design and development of products and manage the interfaces between different groups involved in design and development to ensure effective communication and clear assignment of responsibility. The standards also address the management of inputs and outputs for design and development activities, and use of systematic reviews to evaluate the ability to meet requirements, identify any problems, and propose necessary actions; purchasing processes; control of production and service, including measurement and process validation; control of monitoring and measuring devices used to evaluate conformity; analysis and improvement; monitoring and measurement of quality management processes; and continual improvement, including preventive and corrective action. The standard requires that an organization use its quality policy, objectives, audit results, data analysis, corrective and preventive actions, and management reviews to continually improve its quality management system's effectiveness.

Six Sigma is based on understanding and improving processes on a project-by-project basis. Two of the advantages of Six Sigma are that projects are clearly linked to strategic needs and organizational objectives, and that projects are managed under a common framework. This linkage enables projects to be timely and relevant, and ensures that controls are put in place to leverage the improvements that are identified.

The Six Sigma team-project approach provides a natural fit with the requirements of product and process design, control, and improvement. A good system for process management is a prerequisite to Six Sigma. Obviously, to effectively design or improve a process you first need to understand it. If an organization does not have an ongoing system of process management, it will be quite difficult to implement Six Sigma. Some key processes that are necessary to implement Six Sigma include the following:

- Project selection and definition
- Financial review
- Training
- Leadership for project leaders
- Project leader mentoring
- Certification for Six Sigma specialists

- Project tracking and reporting
- Information management and dissemination

It is important to note that Six Sigma is not a substitute for continuous improvement. Because of its reliance on specialists—the "black belts" who lead the high-profile projects—it becomes quite easy to ignore simple improvements that can be achieved at the process owner level. In fact, it can easily alienate process owners who, instead of seeking continuous improvements, leave them to the specialists. Thus, the objectives are somewhat different, yet both approaches can easily support one another. Process owners should be trained in Six Sigma methods and be involved in formal Six Sigma projects, but still have responsibility for continuous improvement on a daily basis.

QUALITY IN PRACTICE
GOLD STAR CHILI: PROCESS MANAGEMENT[58]

(We encourage you to read the Gold Star Chili case in Chapter 4 first for background information about the company.) Gold Star Chili, a chain of chili restaurants in the greater Cincinnati area, views process management activities as critical to its business success. Quality improvement teams, technology, and strong relationships with suppliers ensure that their chili is produced in a consistent fashion with respect to taste, viscosity, and general quality.

Figure 7.7 shows a process-based organization of the company. Three major value-creation processes link the operation of the company to its customers and other stakeholders:

1. Franchising
2. Restaurant operations
3. Manufacturing/distribution

Sustaining these processes are various support processes, such as research and development, human resources, accounting, purchasing, operations, training, marketing, and customer satisfaction, as well as design processes for new products, menus, and facilities. Production/delivery processes are coordinated at the corporate office and documented in manuals provided to each store. Internal customer needs are addressed in quality improvement team meetings.

The franchising process, outlined in Figure 7.8, is designed to ensure a smooth and successful start-up that meets company objectives. The process has been refined over time and includes extensive interaction with prospective and approved franchisees. New technology has been

introduced to facilitate the process. For example, a site-selection software package is used to evaluate market potential using a variety of demographic data. Computer-aided design is also used for site development. Because franchise process delays are costly, the process helps to eliminate variability, reduce cycle time, and cut down on problems that might occur during development and introduction. Procedure manuals have been developed to provide each store with the necessary information and training to ensure that they operate efficiently.

Restaurant processes include Cash Register, Steam Table, Drive-Thru, Tables, Bussers, and Management. These processes are designed to ensure that the principal requirements of all customers, such as being served in a timely manner and receiving their order accurately, are met. Prior to the opening of each restaurant, training sessions ensure that these processes are performed correctly and according to company standards. Each employee is cross-trained to perform each function.

Chili production is performed at the Gold Star Commissary. A nine-member team, cross-trained to perform each process, is responsible for adding beef, spices, tomatoes, and water during production. The chili must pass a series of strict tests before being shipped to restaurants. Control of chili production is assisted by various pieces of equipment for precise measurement. For example, a Bostwick Viscosity Meter determines the consistency of the chili, determining whether it is too thick or thin, and a flow meter adds the proper amount of water. Other equipment analyzes the fat content of the ground beef used in the chili.

Figure 7.7 Gold Star Chili, Inc. Organization

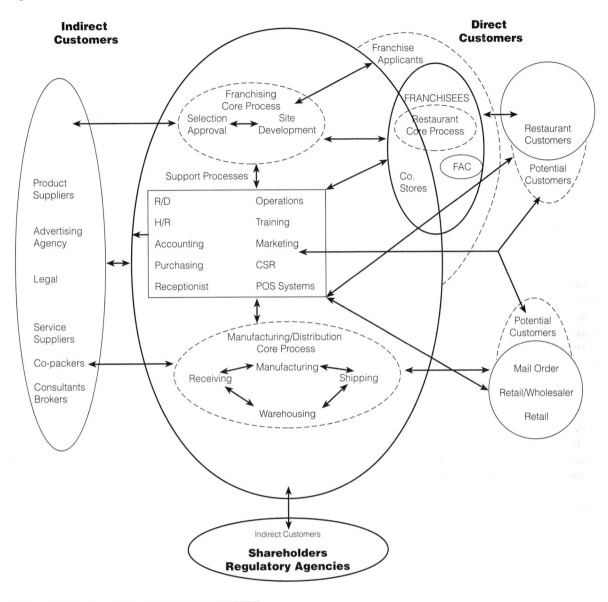

Source: Courtesy of Gold Star Chili. Used with permission.

The final taste test is performed by members of the commissary to ensure that each batch meets established standards.

The commissary team also serves as a quality improvement team. Since July 1996, they have met informally on a daily basis to discuss processes and feedback from internal and external customers; they use a formal improvement process in reporting their activities. They use information from customer comment cards, measurements of waiting time for drive-through service, and feedback from restaurant managers to analyze and adjust processes as necessary. Store performance and quality are measured quarterly through visits by corporate employees. Monthly meetings of key process leaders and daily team meetings analyze

Figure 7.8 Gold Star Chili Franchising Process

GOLD STAR CHILI, INC.

650 Lunken Park Drive
Cincinnati, Ohio 45226
(513) 231-4541

Steps to a Gold Star Chili Franchise

1. Submit a fully completed franchise application. We will respond to you within 15 business days on your applications.

2. You will receive for your review our Uniform Franchise Offering Circular and Exhibits. At this time you will sign and date the Receipt of Offering Circular.

3. Ten days after we receive your Receipt of Offering Circular, you will be sent a Confidentiality Agreement which you must hold for 5 days, then sign, date, and return to us.

4. Schedule and complete a meeting with support staff of Gold Star Chili in our Cincinnati location.

5. Attend a two-day orientation in Cincinnati. You will work with our Operations and Training personnel who will review your qualifications and objectives.

6. You will then be notified of your approval or disapproval of your request to become a Gold Star Chili Franchisee.

7. Gold Star personnel will begin the process of identifying and approving a restaurant location. A scope of work per Gold Star standards will be completed.

8. Sign Gold Star Chili Franchise Agreement and pay initial fee.

9. Begin construction.

10. Complete the training program.

11. Develop an opening plan.

12. Open your Gold Star Chili Restaurant.

Source: Courtesy of Gold Star Chili. Used with permission.

processes for improvement opportunities, such as changes in procedures or the introduction of new technology. For example, several restaurants discovered large clumps of beef in the chili. The team determined that a new beef pump was not grinding the meat correctly.

The selection of suppliers is driven by two criteria: quality and price. Gold Star partners with key product suppliers for restaurant equipment and food products. They seek out local companies and educate them in their business needs and practices. For example, they have invited suppliers to attend a seminar on the Gold Star Chili total quality philosophy and suppliers' role in the process. To ensure that raw materials meet Gold Star specifications, potential and current suppliers visit the commissary to be informed about what Gold Star requires and what technologies the company expects them to have. Suppliers are required to meet or exceed quality standards and provide products at reasonable prices. Gold Star recently embarked on establishing a supplier scorecard to measure and monitor supplier performance. The scorecard includes ratings on on-time delivery or service, accuracy of invoicing and shipping documents, customer service, cost and value, technical expertise, and supplier quality initiatives, and seeks to identify strengths and targeted areas for improvement in each key area.

Gold Star attempts to establish long-term relationships with its suppliers. Company managers visit suppliers' facilities on a regular basis to solicit comments and complaints, and to discuss areas for improvement. During these discussions, suppliers often provide Gold Star with information about new technologies, suggestions for process improvements, and other helpful knowledge. For example, by sharing information with one key paper supplier, the supplier was able to redesign Gold Star's purchasing process, enabling the supplier to increase minimum order levels for deliveries, which reduced Gold Star's overall costs. The company conducts annual cost audits to determine whether costs might be lowered without sacrificing quality. If an alternative supplier is found with similar quality, service, and lower costs, Gold Star will approach its current supplier with the opportunity to lower costs.

Key Issues for Discussion

1. How does the organization structure in Figure 7.7 reflect Deming's view of a production system as discussed in Chapter 1?
2. As a small, privately held company, Gold Star is relatively new at applying total quality management approaches to its process management. Based on the information provided here, what suggestions might you provide in the process management area as the company matures in its journey to total quality?

QUALITY IN PRACTICE
BRINGING PROCESS MANAGEMENT TO EDUCATION[59]

In 1991, 200 angry parents, mostly Hispanic, confronted Gerald Anderson in his first week as superintendent of the Brazosport Independent School District (BISD), then considered among the worst districts in Texas. They demanded to know why their children had the worst test scores and what he was going to do about it. He seized the challenge, developing process-based techniques that raised achievement levels of all students. Today, this 13,500-student school district 50 miles south of Houston is the largest Exemplary school district in the state of Texas, a designation earned by only 121 districts based on tough accountability ratings. Brazosport was one of only two educational institutions to receive site visits for the Malcolm Baldrige National Quality Award in the first year of education sector eligibility (1999). Schools across the country have begun to benchmark their processes.

Brazosport is particularly noteworthy because of the socioeconomic diversity of its students. The success of BISD has been a never-ending journey of dedication and hard work, based on a philosophy of no excuses, and the belief that all children can learn regardless of family background, sex, or socioeconomic status. The strategy that Brazosport employed was an eight-step process to improve the learning process. The process, based on TQ principles and Effective Schools research that identifies characteristics of schools where all students succeed, is summarized here.

1. Educators examine results of state proficiency tests, identifying areas where students need to improve.
2. Teachers develop a time line, determining what they will teach and how much time they'll spend on each objective based on the needs of the students.

3. Teachers devise daily 10-minute segments to work on concepts where students need help. Each teacher gets an instructional focus sheet stating the objectives to be taught, dates for teaching each objective, and dates when students will be assessed on them.
4. Students are constantly assessed to determine whether they have mastered the concepts, giving teachers new data.
5. Students receive tutorial time so that teachers can reteach areas that students have not mastered.
6. Students who master the concepts take part in enrichment activities.
7. Teachers receive maintenance booklets to help them reteach key concepts and keep students on track. They meet frequently in teams to review progress.
8. Principals monitor the instructional process by visiting classrooms and meeting with teachers to discuss students' progress.

"The process is nothing but effective teaching practices," states Patricia Davenport, former director of curriculum and instruction at Brazosport. However, its uniqueness lies in its implementation as a disciplined process. Brazosport piloted the program for two years in Velasco Elementary, its school with the highest percentage of economically disadvantaged students—82 percent—and the lowest test scores on the state assessment. In two years' time, students went from less than 30 percent mastering the state assessment to 70 percent.

Figure 7.9 shows the results of standardized mathematics tests over an eight-year period. Similar results were achieved in writing and reading as well. The American Productivity and Quality Center, a Houston-based consulting firm, trains school districts across the nation in this process.

Figure 7.9 Mathematics Standardized Test Results for Brazosport Independent School District

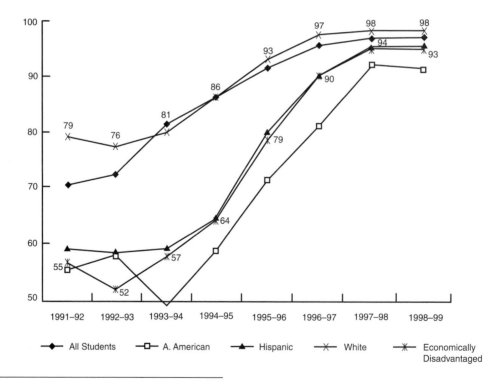

Source: Brazosport Independent School District, Freeport, Texas.

Key Issues for Discussion

1. How does the eight-step process exemplify principles of total quality and process management?

2. What infrastructure would a school district need to make this process effective? Comment specifically on leadership and human resource issues that would need to be addressed.

REVIEW QUESTIONS

1. Define process management and its key components. Why is it important to any business?
2. Summarize the principles on which AT&T bases its process management methodology.
3. Define and illustrate the principal categories of processes.
4. Why must processes be repeatable and measurable?
5. Summarize the leading practices in process management.
6. Describe the product design and development process.
7. How can product design affect manufacturability? Explain the concept and importance of design for manufacturability.
8. Summarize the key design practices for high quality in manufacturing and assembly.
9. Discuss social responsibility issues relating to product design facing businesses today.
10. Discuss the importance of and impediments to reducing the time for product development.
11. Describe the basic approach used for designing value-creation and support processes.
12. Explain the differences between designing manufactured products and services. How should the design of services be approached?
13. Describe the three components of any control system.
14. How can one check whether process owners have true responsibility for controlling a process?
15. Explain the concept of after-action review.
16. Why is it important to establish strong relationships with suppliers? What are some good supplier management practices? (See Bonus Materials.)
17. What is the purpose of supplier certification? Explain some of the common practices for supplier certification. (See Bonus Materials.)
18. Explain the Japanese concept of kaizen. How does it differ from traditional Western approaches to improvement?
19. How are projects considered as vital value-creation processes?
20. Explain the life cycle of a project from a TQ perspective.
21. What aspects of Six Sigma projects are process-related? Briefly define them.
22. What is flexibility and why is it important to a modern organization?
23. What are the key impacts of cycle time reduction?
24. What is a stretch goal? How can stretch goals help an organization?
25. Define benchmarking and list its benefits.
26. What is reengineering? How does it relate to TQ practices?
27. Discuss how process management is addressed in the Baldrige criteria, ISO 9000:2000, and Six Sigma.

DISCUSSION QUESTIONS

1. Identify some of the key processes associated with the following business activities for a typical company: sales and marketing, supply chain management, managing information technology, and managing human resources.

2. Provide some examples of processes that are repeatable and measurable and some that are not.

3. List some of the common processes that a student performs. How can these processes be improved?

4. Are classroom examinations a means of control or improvement? What should they be?

5. Why are modern products more difficult to manufacture than traditional products such as bicycles or hand tools?

6. How can kaizen be applied in a classroom?

7. The kaizen philosophy seeks to encourage suggestions, not to find excuses for failing to improve. Typical excuses are "If it's not broken, don't fix it," "I'm too busy to work on it," and "It's not in the budget." Think of at least five other excuses why people don't try to improve.

8. How might Six Sigma projects be applied to course design?

9. What is the "product development process" a school might use for designing and introducing a new course? How might it be improved to reduce "time-to-market"?

10. How can a manager effectively balance the three key components of a service system design?

11. In a true story related by our colleague Professor James W. Dean, Jr., the general manager of an elevator company was frustrated with the lack of cooperation between the mechanical engineers who designed new elevators and the manufacturing engineers who determined how to produce them.[60] The mechanical engineers would often completely design a new elevator without consulting with the manufacturing engineers, and then expect the factory to somehow figure out how to build it. Often the new products were difficult or nearly impossible to build, and their quality and cost suffered as a result. The designs were sent back to the mechanical engineers (often more than once) for engineering changes to improve their manufacturability, and customers sometimes waited for months for deliveries. The general manager believed that if the two groups of engineers would communicate early in the design process, many of the problems would be solved. At his wits' end, he found a large empty room in the plant and had both groups moved into it. The manager relaxed a bit, but a few weeks later he returned to a surprise. The two groups of engineers had finally learned to cooperate—by building a wall of bookcases and file cabinets right down the middle of the room, separating them from each other! What would you do in this situation?

12. Legal Sea Foods operates several restaurants and fish markets in the Boston area and other East Coast locations. The company's standards of excellence mandate that it serves only the freshest, highest-quality seafood. It guarantees the quality by buying only the "top of the catch" fish daily. Although Legal Sea Foods tries to make available the widest variety every day, certain species of fish are subject to migratory patterns and are not always present in New England waters. Weather conditions may also prevent local fishermen from fishing in certain areas.

    Freshly caught fish are rushed to the company's quality control center where they are cut and filleted in an environmentally controlled state-of-the-art facility. All shellfish come from government-certified beds and are tested in an in-house microbiology laboratory for wholesomeness and purity. There are even special lobster storage tanks so that all lobsters are held under optimum conditions, in clean, pollution-free water. Every seafood item is inspected for quality eight separate times before it reaches the table.

At Legal Sea Foods' restaurants, each meal is cooked to order. Even though servers make every effort to deliver all meals within minutes of each other, they will not jeopardize the quality of an item by holding it beneath a heat lamp until the entire order is ready. The service staff is trained to work as a team for better service. More than one service person frequently delivers food to a table. When any item is ready, the closest available person serves it. Customer questions can be directed to any employee, not just the person who took the initial order.

   a. What are the major processes performed by Legal Sea Foods? How does the process design support its goal of serving only the freshest, highest-quality seafood?

   b. Where would Legal Sea Foods fall on the three-dimensional classification of service organizations? Is its process design consistent with this classification?

13. The president of Circle H assigned you to perform a complete investigation to determine the causes of certain quality problems and to recommend appropriate corrective action. You have authority to talk to any other person within the company.

The early stages of your investigation establish that the three reasons most often cited by customers are symptomatic of some major quality problems in the company's operations. In proceeding with the audit, you decide to review all available data, which may yield indications of the root causes of these problems.

Further investigation reveals that, over a recent four-month period, a procedural change was made in the order approval process. You wish to find out whether this change caused a significant difference in the amount of time required to process an order from field sales through shipping. You therefore decide to investigate this particular situation.

On completion of your investigation into the problems with order processing, you determine that the change in procedures for order approval led to an increase in the amount of time required to restock goods in the customers' stores. You want to recommend corrective action for this problem, but you first do additional investigation as to why the change was made. You learn that, because of large losses on delinquent accounts receivable, the change was made to require that the credit manager approve all restock orders. This approval requirement added an average of three hours to the amount of internal processing time needed for a restock order.

On review of your report, the president of Circle H takes note of administrative problems whose existence he had never suspected. To assure that corrective action will be effective and sustained, the president assigns you to take charge of the corrective action program.[61]

   a. What types of data would be most useful to review for clues as to why the three major customer complaints occurred?

   b. How would you investigate whether the change in the order approval process had a significant effect on order processing time?

   c. Given your knowledge of problems in both order processing and accounts receivable, what should you do?

14. McDonald's used to make food to stock, storing sandwiches in a large tray used to fulfill customer orders. When sales went flat in the mid 1990s and independent

market testing showed a widening gap with competition in food quality, McDonald's recognized that the make-to-stock process was not meeting customer demands. After five years of lab and market testing, McDonald's rolled out the new "Just for You" system, which began in March 1998, to create a make-to-order environment. This shift required a massive change in technology with computers to coordinate orders; food production equipment using "rapid toasters" and temperature-controlled "launching zones" to replace the old heat lamps and holding bins; new food preparation tables, and retraining efforts for the entire domestic food production organization of more than 600,000 crew members. However, this system has apparently backfired. Sales did not improve as expected and customers complained about slow service. The new system increased the average service time 2 to 3 minutes per order, and 15-minute waits were not uncommon. McDonald's stock price decreased, and rivals such as Wendy's captured additional market share.[62] What lessons does this experience suggest for process management? What might McDonald's have done differently?

15. The Cincinnati Water Works (CWW) serves approximately 1 million customers.[63] Its billing system allows customer service representatives (CSRs) to retrieve information from customer accounts quickly using almost any piece of data such as customer name, address, phone number, social security number, and so on. Besides a customer's account history, the system contains everything that was said in a call, including documentation of past problems and their resolution. An integrated voice response system provides automated phone support for bill paying and account balances, tells customers of the approximate wait time to speak to a CSR, and allows the customers to leave a message for a CSR to return a call. An information board in the department shows the number of customers waiting, average length of time waiting, and the number of CSRs that are busy and doing post-call work. A pop-up screen provides CSRs with customer data before the phone rings so that he or she will have the customer's information before they even say hello. Work orders taken by CSRs, such as a broken water main or leaking meter, are routed automatically to a field service supervisor for immediate attention. This system is also used internally to allocate maintenance workers when a problem arises at a pumping station or treatment facility. A geographic information system is used for mapping the locations of water mains and fire hydrants, and provides field service employees, meter readers, and contractors exact information to accomplish their work. Handheld meter readers are used to locate meters and download data into computers. Touch pad devices provide exterior connections to inside meters, eliminating the necessity to enter a house or building. CWW is also investigating automated meter readers and radio frequency devices that simply require a company van to drive by the building to automatically obtain readings. Discuss how technology has affected the processes of CWW. What specific types of improvements (quality, cycle time, etc.) were these applications designed to address? Can you think of similar uses of these technologies in other service applications?

 PROJECTS, ETC.

1. Identify some of the major processes a student encounters in a college or university. What types of noneducational institutions perform similar processes and might be candidates for benchmarking?

2. Write down *your* process for preparing for an exam. How could this process be improved to make it shorter and/or more effective? Compare your process to those of your classmates. How might you collectively develop an improved process?

3. Interview a plant manager at a local factory to determine his or her philosophy on process management. What techniques does the company use?

4. Investigate design-for-environment practices in some of your local industries. Describe company policies and the methods and techniques that they use to address environmental concerns in product design.

5. Christina Clark works at a food service operation for a large amusement park. She has been charged with developing a process control plan based on HACCP principles for meeting food safety requirements (see the Bonus Materials). For example, the requirements for hot dogs include:

   - *Receiving*: Refrigerated hot dogs should be between –40 and 34 degrees Fahrenheit when received.
   - *Storage*: Storage temperature should be between –40 and 34 degrees Fahrenheit.
   - *Cooking*: Hot dogs should be heated to a temperature of 145 ± 5°F within 30 minutes of placing on the grill.
   - *Cooked Storage*: Leftover hot dogs must be covered and placed in refrigeration immediately and reach a temperature of 40°F or lower within 4 hours.
   - *Reheating*: Hot dogs must be reheated to an internal temperature of 165 ± 5°F within 20 minutes, one time only.

   Develop a process control plan for ensuring that these requirements are met. Design any forms or "standard operating procedures" that you think would be helpful in implementing your plan.

6. Design a process for the following activities:
   a. Preparing for an exam
   b. Writing a term paper
   c. Planning a vacation
   d. Making breakfast for your family
   e. Washing your car

   Draw a flowchart for each process and discuss how ways in which both quality and cycle time might be improved.

7. Design an instrument for evaluating the "process orientation" of an organization. For example, what characteristics would you look for in firms that have a strong process orientation?

CASES

Additional cases, including Baldrige assessment cases, are available in the Bonus Materials Folder on the CD-ROM.

I. THE STATE UNIVERSITY EXPERIENCE

Wow! That State University video was really cool. It has lots of majors; it's close to home so I can keep my job; and Mom and Dad loved it when they visited. I wish I could know what it's really like to be a student at State. Hmmm, I think I'll ask Mom and Dad to take a campus tour with me. . . .

I'm sure that we took our tour on the hottest day of the summer. The campus is huge—it took us about two hours to complete the tour and we didn't even see everything! I wasn't sure that the tour guide knew what he was doing. We went into a gigantic lecture hall and the lights weren't even on. Our tour guide couldn't find them so we had to hold the doors open so the sunlight could come in. About three-fourths of the way through the tour, our guide said, "State University isn't really a bad place to go to school; you just have to learn the system." I wonder what he meant by that? . . .

This application is really confusing. How do I let the admissions office know that I am interested in physics, mechanical engineering, and industrial design? Even my parents can't figure it out. I guess I'll call the admissions office for some help. . . .

I'm so excited! Mom just handed me a letter from State! Maybe they've already accepted me. What? What's this? They say I need to send my transcript. I did that when I mailed in my application two weeks ago. What's going on? I hope it won't affect my application. I'd better check with Admissions. . . .

You can't find my file? I thought you were only missing my transcript. I asked my counselor if she had sent it in yet. She told me that she sent it last week. Oh, you'll call me back when you locate my file? O.K. . . .

Finally, I've been accepted! Wait a minute. I didn't apply to University College; that's a two-year program. I wanted physics, M.E., or industrial design. Well, since my only choice is U. College and I really want to go to State, I guess I'll

send in the confirmation form. It really looks a lot like the application. In fact, I know I gave them a lot of the same information. I wonder why they need it again? Seems like a waste of time. . . .

Orientation was a lot of fun. I'm glad they straightened out my acceptance at U. College. I think I will enjoy State after all. I met lots of other students. I saw my advisor and I signed up for classes. All I have left to do is pay my tuition bill. Whoops. None of my financial aid is on this bill. I know I filled out all of the forms because I got an award letter from State. There is no way my parents and I can pay for this without financial aid. It says at the bottom, I'll lose all of my classes if I don't pay the bill on time. . . .

I'm not confirmed on the computer? I sent in my form and the fee a long time ago. What am I going to do? I don't want to lose all of my classes. I have to go to the admissions office or my college office and get a letter that says I am a confirmed student. O.K. If I do that tomorrow, will I still have all of my classes? . . .

I can't sleep; I'm so nervous about my first day. . . .

Discussion Questions

1. What breakdowns in service processes has this student experienced?
2. What types of process management activities should State University administrators undertake?

II. The PIVOT Initiative at Midwest Bank, Part I[64]

Midwest, a bank holding company, is located in Ohio. Its main subsidiary provides a diverse line of banking and financial products and services regionally; and selected business activities are conducted nationally. Consumer, small business, and investment products and services are offered through a network of retail banking centers located primarily within Ohio and Kentucky. Midwest Bank also has a growing presence in Florida with 13 retail banking centers. Commercial banking products and services are offered through nine regional offices. Customers can also access this Midwest's financial and banking products and

services 24-hours per day via its network of ATMs, a 24-hour telephone customer service center, or online. This bank has served the financial needs of its customers for 100 years, and currently 3,200 associates serve approximately 600,000 customers.

The PIVOT Initiative

The PIVOT initiative, the name that Midwest gave its Six Sigma process improvement approach, started with the selection of three pilot projects, one of which was in the Commercial Processing Department (CPD) that works as Midwest Bank's cash vault. CPD already operated at a high level of sigma (4.26) as found early in Yellow Belt Six Sigma training. CPD processes a high dollar volume of transactions. One costly error in the previous year resulted in a loss of over a quarter million dollars and brought the department to the forefront of change initiatives. Once the project was chosen, the bank selected six associates to run the first PIVOT project.

A project coordinator working from the project office was selected as project manager for the Six Sigma functions of the project. An operations financial manager was in charge of financial impact analysis and equipment purchasing. The assistant vice president and team supervisor, were subject matter experts from within CPD. Another project coordinator was brought on board for her bank wide knowledge and overall project support. The project analyst for CPD and five other areas was in charge of the departmental project management and was the Six Sigma analyst for the team. The Six Sigma analyst was responsible for data integrity, graphical analysis, and data stratification. After their weeklong Six Sigma course, the six team members ran the project from project definition to the control stage. The team followed the Six Sigma DMAIC process steps (Define, Measure, Analyze, Improve, Control) during the CPD PIVOT project to define the project and get it underway.

DMAIC Define Stage

The senior vice president and vice president over CPD were the champions for this project and initially worked to establish the problem definition statement. These champions were responsible for the process every day and also held accountable for the errors in the department.

Because the two largest potential sources of errors (strapping and deposit processing) did not influence each other in the process and had separate causes for creating errors, the champions separated them. The problem statement defined the number of errors the department was accountable for during the previous year and the dollar losses of these errors. In this case study, the number of errors and the actual dollar losses are only approximate. The (disguised) problem statement was:

In (the previous year) the number of internal and external defects for the CPD

was 150, resulting in Bank losses of $400,000 as well as significant potential risk exposure. Included in the losses is an anomaly of $280,000. The remainder represents a gap of $120,000 versus the goal of $0 of total losses due to Commercial Processing Department operations. Our objective is to reduce the internal error ratio by December of the current year and the total amount of losses by over 50% in the following 12 months. Projects from this business case will reduce loss expense and risk exposure, while increasing customer satisfaction.

Much debate centered on whether to include the anomaly loss since it skewed the numbers considerably. However, the decision was finally made to include it. Support for the CPD PIVOT project centered on risk mitigation, which is difficult to quantify, and on dollar losses required to carry the project. Based on the potential reduction of approximately $400,000 in losses and the future risk mitigation, the steering committee approved the project launch, and the CPD PIVOT team moved onto the Measure stage.

(See "The PIVOT Initiative at Midwest Bank, Part II" in Chapter 10 for a continuation of this case.)

Discussion Questions

1. What conclusions can you reach on the importance of team preparation and member selection to the "Define" stage, and eventual success of Six Sigma projects, such as the PIVOT project?
2. How do the roles of the PIVOT team members, described in the case, match or not match the roles in Table 7.4 in the chapter? Why do you think that they differ?
3. What factors do you think weighed in the decision to include the $280,000 "anomaly" in the project justification? If you were the project champion, how would you assess this justification in deciding on whether the project was significant enough to move forward?

III. Stuart Injection Molding Company[65]

Stuart Injection Molding Company (SIMC) is a small business that specializes in custom plastic molding for many different industries, including appliances and various consumer products such as toys. Adele Stuart, daughter of the company's founder and current CEO wishes to expand into the automotive sector. However, she realizes that to do so will require more formalized systems and eventually ISO 9000 registration. Although many basic procedures for assuring quality are in place, most have been conducted informally, and the company never compiled a formal quality manual that documents the system and outlines specific responsibilities for managers and workers. Recognizing the lack of a manual as a major deficiency, they called you in as a consultant to help. After spending some time in the plant talking with many employees, you jotted down several notes and observations:

- The plant manager (PM) is responsible for ensuring the success of the quality management system by providing the necessary resources and reviewing system performance. However, SIMC has a quality assurance (QA) department that is responsible for the majority of implementation issues, such as maintaining measuring and test equipment, verifying process capability, performing inspection, selecting methods for monitoring process performance, and auditing the system.
- All functional departments recognize their responsibility for quality planning and producing high-quality products. For example, the marketing and sales department conducts market research to understand customer needs and handles customer complaints; the project engineering department performs design reviews; the manufacturing department conducts in-process inspection for the purpose of maintaining control and coordinates continuous improvement processes. Maintenance, supplier relations, receiving, and human resources departments support these functions.
- Most products are custom-designed with the customer. When a new job is contracted, a

cross-functional team is selected that includes members from project engineering, quality assurance, manufacturing, and sales. This team develops all the specifications to ensure that design meets customer requirements and can be made according to these requirements, selects materials and process tolerances, determines production routings and inspection plans, develops a production control plan and measurement system, and monitors a trial production run. The customer must approve all design changes.
- The company uses a variety of contemporary tools to simplify and optimize the product while also focusing on reducing production cost and waste. These tools include quality function deployment, geometric dimensioning and tolerancing, design for manufacturing and assembly, value engineering, design of experiments, failure mode and effects analysis, and cost/performance/risk analysis.
- Inspection is routine during the production process. QA lab personnel perform all phases of inspection and testing. Production operators use a "first-piece" inspection process to validate the start-up for a new product. Receiving inspection is performed on material, purchased parts, and subassemblies used in processing, manufacturing, and assembly. Operators also perform in-process inspections during production and final inspection on finished products. When contractually required, statistical process control techniques are used to ensure control of key process characteristics. Gauging instruction sheets are maintained by QA for at least one year.
- Nonconforming products are labeled with a "Do Not Use" tag and kept from being shipped. This tag describes the nonconformance, documents the disposition decision, and records the reinspection results. If they are repaired or reworked, they are reinspected. Products that do not fully comply with specific requirements are not shipped without customer authorization. When nonconformities are detected, a cross-functional team investigates them and corrective actions are initiated to prevent their recurrence.

- SIMC has a continuous improvement philosophy that pervades the entire organization. Processes are improved beyond minimum requirements when further improvements benefit customers. Quality performance and productivity are continuously monitored to identify opportunities for improvement. Everyone in the organization is encouraged to come forward with ideas for improving products, processes, systems, and productivity within the working environ-

ment. Some examples of opportunities for quality and productivity improvement are the reduction of cycle times, less scrap, rework and repair rates, less unscheduled machine downtime, and process performance variation.

Based on this information, what would you recommend to the company? Specifically on their process management activities, note any additional information that you might need.

IV. CapStar Health Systems: Process Management

The complete CapStar case study, a fictitious example of a Baldrige application, can be found on the CD-ROM that accompanies this book. If you have not read the organizational profile yet (see Case III in Chapter 3), please do so first. Examine their response to Category 6 in the context of the leading practices described in this chapter. (You

need not consider the actual Baldrige criteria for this activity.) What are their strengths? What are their weaknesses and opportunities for improvement? What specific advice, including useful tools and techniques that might help them, would you suggest?

ENDNOTES

1. Adapted from Katrina Brooker, "The Nightmare Before Christmas," *Fortune,* January 24, 2000, 24–25.

2. Robert Hof, Debra Sparks, Ellen Neuborne, and Wendy Zellner, "Can Amazon Make It?" *Business Week,* July 10, 2000, 38–43.

3. A. Blanton Godfrey, "Planned Failures," *Quality Digest,* March 2000, 16.

4. AT&T Quality Steering Committee, *Process Quality Management & Improvement Guidelines,* AT&T Publication Center, AT&T Bell Laboratories (1987).

5. Justin Martin, "Are You As Good As You Think You Are?" *Fortune,* September 30, 1996, 142–152.

6. Michael Hammer and James Champy, *Reengineering the Corporation* (New York: HarperBusiness, 1993), 177–178.

7. Steven H. Wildstrom, "Price Wars Power Up Quality," *Business Week,* September 18, 1995, 26.

8. Philip A. Himmelfarb, "Fast New-Product Development at Service Sector Companies," *Quality Digest,* April 1996, 41–44.

9. Justin Martin, "Ignore Your Customer," *Fortune,* May 1, 1995, 121–126.

10. Wolfgang Schneider, "Test Drive Into the Future," BMW Magazine 2, 1997, 74-77.

11. Peter J. Kolesar, "What Deming Told the Japanese in 1950," *Quality Management Journal* 2, no. 1 (Fall 1994), 9–24.

12. Ames Rubber Corporation, Application Summary for the 1993 Malcolm Baldrige National Quality Award.

13. Adapted from Douglas Daetz, "The Effect of Product Design on Product Quality and Product Cost," *Quality Progress,* June 1987, 63–67. © 1987, Hewlett-Packard Co. All rights reserved. Reprinted with permission.

14. Carolyn Lochhead, "Liability's Creative Clamp Holds Firms to the Status Quo," *Insight,* August 29, 1988, 38–40.

15. John H. Farrow, "Product Liability Requirements," *Quality Progress,* May 1980, 34–36; Mick Birmingham, "Product Liability: An Issue for Quality," *Quality,* February 1983, 41–42.

16. Randall Goodden, "Quality and Product Liability," *Quality Digest,* October 1995, 35–41.

17. David Pescovitz, "Dumping Old Computers—Please Dispose of Properly," *Scientific American* 282, no. 2 (February 2000), 29; http://www.sciam.com/2000/0200issue/0200techbus2.html.

18. Early discussions of this topic can be found in Bruce Nussbaum and John Templeton, "Built to Last—Until It's Time to Take It Apart," *Business Week,* September 17, 1990, 102–106. A more recent reference is Michael Lenox, Andrew King, and John Ehrenfeld, "An Assessment of Design-for-Environment Practices in

Leading U.S. Electronics Firms," *Interfaces* 30, no. 3 (May/June 2000), 83–94.

19. Nussbaum and Templeton (see note 18).

20. Charles Huber and Robert Launsby, "Straight Talk on DFSS," *Six Sigma Forum Magazine*, August 2002, 21.

21. Valerie Reitman and Robert L. Simison, "Japanese Car Makers Speed Up Car Making," *The Wall Street Journal* (December 29, 1995), 17.

22. Don Clausing and Bruce H. Simpson, "Quality by Design," *Quality Progress*, January 1990, 41–44.

23. For the fascinating story of how Chrysler redesigned itself, along with their design process, see Brock Yates, *The Critical Path* (Boston: Little, Brown and Co., 1996).

24. "A Smarter Way to Manufacture," *Business Week*, April 30, 1990.

25. Kelly Scott, "How Federal Express Delivers Customer Service," *APICS—The Performance Advantage*, November 1999, 44–46.

26. Rebecca Duray and Glenn W. Milligan, "Improving Customers Satisfaction Through Mass Customization," *Quality Progress*, August 1999, 60–66.

27. Sarah Anne Wright, "Putting Fast-Food to the Test," *The Cincinnati Enquirer*, July 9, 2000, F1, 2.

28. John Haywood-Farmer, "A Conceptual Model of Service Quality," *International Journal of Operations and Production Management* 8, no. 6 (1988), 19–29.

29. Charles D. Zimmerman, III, and John W. Enell, "Service Industries," Sec. 33 in J. M. Juran (ed.), *Juran's Quality Control Handbook*, 4th ed. (New York: McGraw-Hill, 1988).

30. Paula K. Martin and Karen Tate, "Projects That Get Quality Treatment," *The Journal for Quality and Participation*, November/December 1998, 58–61.

31. Custom Research Incorporated, "Highlights of CRI's Best Practices," 1996 Baldrige Application Abstract, 13–14.

32. Timothy J. Kloppenborg and Joseph A. Petrick, *Managing Project Quality* (Vienna, VA: Management Concepts, 2003), 9, 11.

33. "Coca-Cola: A Taste for Quality," The Coca-Cola Company, Atlanta, Georgia.

34. http://www.thecoca-colacompany.com/news/NewsDetail.asp?NewsDate=6/15/99.

35. "Testing for Conformity: An Inside Job," *Golf Journal*, May 1998, 20–25.

36. Douglas H. Harris and Frederick B. Chaney, *Human Factors in Quality Assurance* (New York: John Wiley & Sons, Inc., 1969).

37. "DaimlerChrysler's Quality Practices Pay Off for PT Cruiser," News and Analysis, *Metrologyworld.com*, (accessed March 23, 2000).

38. Adapted from The Ritz-Carlton Hotel Company, Application Summaries for the Malcolm Baldrige National Quality Award, 1992 and 1999.

39. Adapted from K. M. Casarreal, J. I. Mills, and M. A. Plant, "Improving Service Through Patient Surveys in a Multihospital Organization," *Hospital & Health Services Administration*, Health Administration Press, Ann Arbor, MI (March/April 1986), 41–52. © 1986, Foundation of the American College of Health Care Executives.

40. Robert A. Gardner, "Resolving the Process Paradox," *Quality Progress*, March 2001, 51–59.

41. Andrew E. Serwer, "Michael Dell Turns the PC World Inside Out," *Fortune*, September 8, 1997, 76–86.

42. Bill Gates with Collins Hemingway, *Business @ the Speed of Thought* (New York: Warner Books, 1999).

43. Masaaki Imai, *KAIZEN—The Key to Japan's Competitive Success* (New York: McGraw-Hill, 1986).

44. Alan Robinson (ed.), *Continuous Improvement in Operations* (Cambridge, MA: Productivity Press, 1991).

45. Lea A. P. Tonkin, "Kaizen Blitz℠ 5: Bottleneck-Bashing comes to Rochester, NY," *Target* 12, no. 4 (September–October 1996), 41–43.

46. Mark Oakeson, "Makes Dollars & Sense for Mercedes-Benz in Brazil," IIE Solutions (April 1997), 32–35.

47. David A. McCamey, Robert W. Bogs, and Linda M. Bayuk, "More, Better, Faster From Total Quality Effort," Quality Progress, August 1999, 43–50.

48. Lawrence S. Pryor, "Benchmarking: A Self-Improvement Strategy," *Journal of Business Strategy*, November/December 1989, 28–32.

49. Robert C. Camp, *Benchmarking: The Search for Industry Best Practices That Lead to Superior Performance* (Milwaukee. WI: ASQC Quality Press and UNIPUB/Quality Resources, 1989).

50. Shawn Tully, "Why to Go for Stretch Targets," *Fortune*, November 14, 1994, 45–58.

51. Christopher E. Bogan and Michael J. English, "Benchmarking for Best Practices: Winning Through Innovative Adaptation," *Quality Digest*, August 1994, 52–62.

52. Cathy Hill, "Benchmarking and Best Practices," The 54th Annual Quality Congress Proceedings of the American Society for Quality, 2000.

53. John Hackl, "New Beginnings: Change is Here to Stay," *Quality Progress*, February 1998, 5.

54. AT&T Consumer Communication Services Summary of 1994 Application for the Malcolm Baldrige National Quality Award.

55. Hammer and Champy (see note 6).

56. P. Kay Coleman, "Reengineering Pepsi's Road to the 'Right Side Up' Company," *Insights Quarterly* 5, no. 3 (Winter 1993), 18-35.

57. Bogan and English (see note 51).

58. We wish to thank Andy Assaley, Scott Atkinson, Frank Cornell, and Eugene Wulsin for their work on which this case is based. Courtesy Gold Star Chili, Inc.

59. Adapted from Cindy Kranz, "Schools Intend to Improve," *Cincinnati Enquirer*, October 15, 2001, pp. B1, B5.

60. James R. Evans and James W. Dean, Jr. *Total Quality: Management, Organization, and Strategy*, 3rd ed., Cincinnati, OH: South-Western College Publishing, 2003.

61. Adapted from ASQ Quality Auditor Certification Brochure, July 1989.

62. John E. Ettlie, "What the Auto Industry Can Learn from McDonald's," *Automotive Manufacturing & Production*, October 1999, 42; David Stires, "Fallen Arches," *Fortune*, April 29, 2002, 74–76.

63. Adapted from a student project by one of the author's students, Tim Planitz, December 2001.

64. Appreciation is expressed to one of the author's students, Michael Wolf, who wrote the paper on which this case is based, as part of the requirements for MGT 699, Total Quality Management, 2002, at Northern Kentucky University, and Cathy Ernst, senior vice president at the bank.

65. We thank our former students Nick Dattilo, Brian Kessler at Woodcraft Pattern Works, Inc., and Tameka Flowers, on whose research this case is based.

BIBLIOGRAPHY

Ahmed, Pervaiz K. and Mohammed Rafiq. "Integrated Benchmarking: A Holistic Examination of Select Techniques for Benchmarking Analysis," *Benchmarking for Quality Management & Technology* 5, no. 3 (1998), 225–242.

Andersen, Bjorn. *Business Process Improvement Toolbox*. Milwaukee, WI: ASQ Quality Press, 1999.

AT&T Quality Steering Committee. *Batting 1000*. AT&T Bell Laboratories, 1992.

———. *Process Quality Management & Improvement Guidelines*. AT&T Bell Laboratories, 1987.

Boser, Robert B., and Cheryl L. Christ. "Whys, Whens, and Hows of Conducting a Process Capability Study." Presentation at the ASQC/ASA 35th Annual Fall Technical Conference, Lexington, Kentucky, 1991.

Brassard, Michael and Diane Ritter. *The Memory Jogger II*. Methuen, MA: GOAL/QPC, 1994.

Burke, Charles J. "10 Steps to Best-Practices Benchmarking," *Quality Digest* (February 1996), 23–28.

Camp, Robert C. *Business Process Benchmarking: Finding and Implementing Best Practices*. Milwaukee, WI: ASQC Quality Press, 1995.

DeToro, Irving, and Thomas McCabe. "How to Stay Flexible and Elude Fads," *Quality Progress*, March 1997, 55–60.

Duncan, Acheson J. *Quality Control and Industrial Statistics*, 5th ed. Homewood, IL: Richard D. Irwin, 1986.

Gitlow, H., S. Gitlow, A. Oppenheim, and R. Oppenheim. *Tools and Methods for the Improvement of Quality*. Homewood, IL: Irwin, 1989.

Goetsch, David L. and Stanley B. Davis. *Understanding and Implementing ISO 9000:2000*. Upper Saddle River, NJ: Prentice Hall, 2002.

Godfrey, Blan. "Future Trends: Expansion of Quality Management Concepts, Methods and Tools to All Industries," *Quality Observer* 6, no. 9 (September 1997), 40–43, 46.

Hurley, Heather. "Cycle-Time Reduction: Your Key to a Better Bottom Line," *Quality Digest* (April 1996), 28–32.

Lapin, Lawrence L. *Statistics for Modern Business Decisions*, 4th ed. San Diego: Harcourt Brace Jovanovich, Inc., 1987.

Lloyd's Register Quality Assurance, Ltd., "Getting the Most from ISO 9000." 1999.

Lowenthal, Jeffrey N. *Six Sigma Project Management: A Pocket Guide*. Milwaukee, WI: ASQ Quality Press, 2001.

Melan, Eugene H. *Process Management: A Systems Approach to Total Quality*. Portland, OR: Productivity Press, 1995.

O'Dell, Karla, and C. Jackson Grayson, Jr. *If Only We Knew What We Know*. New York: Free Press, 1999.

Ouelette, Steven M., and Michael V. Petrovich. "Daily Management and Six Sigma: Maximizing Your Returns." Proceedings of ASQ's 56th Annual Quality Congress, 2002.

Pande, Peter S., Robert P. Neuman, and Roland R. Cavanagh. *The Six Sigma Way Team Fieldbook: An Implementation Guide for Process Improvement Teams*. New York: McGraw-Hill Trade, 2001.

Pyzdek, Thomas. "Six Sigma Is Primarily a Management Program." *Quality Digest*, June 1999, 26.

Reilly, Norman B. *The Team Based Product Development Guidebook*. Milwaukee, WI: ASQ Quality Press, 1999.

Robbins, C. L., and W. A. Robbins. "What Nurse Managers Should Know about Sampling Techniques." *Nursing Management* 20, no. 6 (June 1989), 46–48.

Rosenfeld, Manny. "Only the Questions That Are Asked Can Be Answered," *Quality Progress*, April 1994, 71–73.

Sherman, Strat. "Stretch Goals: The Dark Side of Asking for Miracles," *Fortune*, November 13, 1995, 231–232.

CHAPTER 8

PERFORMANCE MEASUREMENT AND STRATEGIC INFORMATION MANAGEMENT

In the early 1990s, Boeing's assembly lines were morasses of inefficiency. A manual numbering system dating back to World War II bomber days was used to keep track of an airplane's four million parts and 170 miles of wiring; changing a part on a 737's landing gear meant renumbering 464 pages of drawings. Factory floors were covered with huge tubs of spare parts worth millions of dollars. In an attempt to grab market share from rival Airbus, the company discounted planes deeply and was buried by an onslaught of orders. The attempt to double production rates, coupled with implementation of a new production control system, resulted in Boeing being forced to shut down its 737 and 747 lines for 27 days in October 1997, leading to a $178 million loss and a shakeup of top management. Much of the blame was focused on Boeing's financial practices and lack of real-time data. With a new CFO and finance team, the company created a "control panel" of vital measures such as material costs, inventory turns, overtime, and defects using a color-coded spreadsheet. For the first time, Boeing was able to generate a series of bar charts showing which of its programs were creating value and which were destroying it. The results were eye-opening; not only did they help improve operations, but they also helped formulate a growth plan. As one manager noted, "The data will set you free."[1]

A supply of consistent, accurate, and timely data across all functional areas of business provides real-time information for the evaluation, control, and improvement of processes, products, and services to meet both business objectives and rapidly changing customer needs.

Data are simply representations of facts that come from some type of measurement process. **Measurement** is the act of quantifying the performance dimensions of products, services, processes, and other business activities. **Measures and indicators** refer to the numerical information that results from measurement. For example, the presence or absence of surface defects for a brass sink fixture might be assessed by visual inspection. A useful measure of quality might be the percentage of fixtures that have surface defects. As another example, the diameters of machined ball bearings might be measured with a micrometer. Statistics such as the mean diameter and standard deviation provide information to evaluate the ability of the production process to meet specifications. For services, examples of measurements would be the percentage of orders filled accurately and the time taken to fill a customer's order. The term *indicator* is often used for measurements that are not a direct or exclusive measure of performance. For instance, you cannot directly measure dissatisfaction, but you can use the number of complaints or lost customers as indicators of dissatisfaction. Measurements and indicators provide a scorecard of business performance that can be used at all levels of the organization. The aim of measurement and analysis is to guide an organization toward the achievement of key business results and strategic objectives, and to anticipate and respond to rapid or unexpected internal or external changes.

Although Deming believed in using data as a basis for problem solving, he was highly critical of overemphasizing measurement. He often stated that the most important figures, such as the value of a loyal customer, are unknown and unknowable. Although this generalization certainly has merit, considerable value lies in using objective data for planning and decision making. Osborne and Gaebler make three insightful observations:

1. If you don't measure results, you can't tell success from failure.
2. If you can't see success, you can't reward it—and if you can't reward success, you are probably rewarding failure.
3. If you can't recognize failure, you can't correct it.[2]

Information is data in context of a business or organization. Information is derived from the analysis of data. Good information allows managers to make decisions on the basis of facts, not opinions. When Dr. Noriaki Kano consulted with Florida Power and Light (FPL), the company told him that lightning was the principal cause of service interruptions. Kano asked why groundings or arresters had not prevented the interruptions; FPL replied that these would not work with Florida's severe lightning. Kano asked for the data to back up this conclusion, but FPL could not produce any. About 18 months later, when Kano next visited the company, they had

Quality Profiles

Wainwright Industries, Inc. and ADAC Laboratories

ADAC Laboratories

Wainwright Industries, Inc., headquartered in St. Peters, Missouri, is a family-owned business that manufactures stamped and machined parts for U.S. and foreign customers in the automotive, aerospace, home security, and information processing industries. Annual sales total $30 million, and the company employs 275 associates. Craftsmanship, teamwork, and innovation have been commitments at Wainwright since its inception in 1947. Delivering products and services of unequaled quality that generate total customer satisfaction is Wainwright's principal objective. This commitment led the company to a Malcolm Baldrige National Quality Award in the small business category in 1994.

Wainwright Industries aligns the company's business objectives with customers' critical success factors: price, line defects, delivery, and partnership. This alignment process prompted the development of five key strategic indicator categories: safety, internal customer satisfaction, external customer satisfaction, defect rate, and business performance. Within each category, Wainwright developed specific indicators and goals. For instance, for external customer satisfaction, they measure a satisfaction index and compile complaints each month; for business performance, they track sales, capital expenditure, and market share for drawn housings.

Wainwright constantly looks for ways to improve, searching inside and outside the organization for ideas and examples on how to streamline processes, cut delivery times, make training programs more effective, or enhance any other facet of its customer-focused operations. Its empowered workforce provides a rich source of ideas; each associate averages more than one implemented improvement per week. Ninety-five percent of all purchase orders are processed within 24 hours. The lead time for making one of Wainwright's principal products—drawn housings for electric motors—was reduced to 15 minutes from its former level of 8.75 days.

ADAC Laboratories is a 710-person Silicon Valley-based maker of high-technology health care products such as diagnostic imaging and healthcare information systems. ADAC used quality management principles to change the company culture after successfully coming out of a turnaround in the mid-1980s. ADAC replaced its executive-driven Quality Council with two weekly meetings open to all employees as well as customers and suppliers. During these meetings, numerous employees present data on key measures of customer satisfaction, quality, productivity, and operational and financial performance. The company made significant investments in data collection systems targeted to key needs and activities, such as tracking design defects and customer calls for support.

The company's corporate planning process, known as DASH, yields a strategic plan for the next three to five years and an annual business plan. Consistent with ADAC's primary core value, "Customers come first," the DASH process begins with a thorough, fact-based analysis of customer requirements today's and tomorrow's. This analysis mines data gathered from a variety of sources, including surveys, lost-order information, interviews conducted by customer-contact employees, logs of service calls, and focus groups. Results are integrated with those from analyses of competitive forces, risks, company capabilities, and supplier capabilities.

ADAC consistently brings products to market faster than its larger competitors. Through its performance excellence processes; defect rates measured at final inspection fell about 40 percent, and if a system breaks down, ADAC technicians will have it back in operation within an average of 17 hours after receiving the call, less than a third of the time it used to take. On eight measures of service satisfaction, ADAC was the sole leader in five categories and tied for the top spot in the remaining ones.

Source: Malcolm Baldrige National Quality Award, Profiles of Winners, National Institute of Standards and Technology, Department of Commerce.

collected data and found that interruptions occurred even when strong lightning was not present. In addition, they discovered that many utility poles did not have sufficient groundings, a situation they had not recognized until they collected the data.[3]

Having too much data, however, can be as bad as not having any. It is important to gather the right information. When Ford studied Mazda's management approaches, former CEO Donald Peterson observed, "Perhaps, most important, Mazda had been able to identify the types of information and records that were truly useful. It didn't bother with any other data. [At Ford] we were burdened with mountains of useless data and stifled by far too many levels of control over them."[4]

Despite the fact that more than half of the workforce in the United States is engaged in the generation, processing, or dissemination of data and/or information, many companies do a poor job of systematically collecting appropriate data, getting it to the right people, and analyzing it properly. Bill Gates notes that middle mangers need as much business data as top managers, but often have no way to get it. He also says that that face-to-face meetings devoted to status updates are a symptom of poor information flow, because that type of information could be handled much more effectively using electronic transfer of data and e-mail.[5] Organizations ignore measurement for a variety of reasons: they don't know what to measure; they don't want to spend the time or effort to do it; they don't see the value of measurement; or they are afraid to uncover problems. Dealing with data and information should be addressed from a process perspective, and TQ concepts can be applied to the generation, analysis, and use of data and information. This chapter introduces basic concepts of performance measurement and analysis and strategic information management.

THE STRATEGIC VALUE OF INFORMATION

Organizations need information and performance measures for three reasons:[6]

1. To lead the entire organization in a particular direction; that is, to drive strategies and organizational change.
2. To manage the resources needed to travel in this direction by evaluating the effectiveness of action plans.
3. To operate the processes that make the organization work and continuously improve.

Many managers and quality professionals view measurement activities only in terms of outputs from the production system. This limited approach is a mistake because a broad base of measurements, tied together by strong information systems, can help to align a company's operations with its strategic directions. A good analogy for information systems within an organization might be the central nervous system in the body. (Bill Gates, in fact, refers to information as the "digital nervous system" of an organization.) The central nervous system sends messages to and from the brain to various points in the body where the work gets done, such as lifting, walking, thinking, or digesting food. Effective information systems provide the right information to the right people at the right time. By having a central source of information accessible to everyone, individuals in manufacturing can have input on product design and sales; designers can obtain immediate feedback about manufacturing and financial implications of decisions; and everyone can share information for solving problems. Empowered individuals with the right information can make more timely decisions and can take action to better serve customers.

Data and information support analysis at the "three levels of quality"—individual, process, and organization—as discussed in Chapter 1. At each of these levels the primary focus of data and information is control, diagnosis, and planning, respectively. The types of information and how it is disseminated and aligned with organizational levels are equally vital to success. At the individual level, such data as quality performance, adherence to schedules, and costs of operations provide real-time information to identify assignable reasons for variation, determine their causes, and take corrective action as needed. This assessment might require lean communication channels consisting of bulletins, computerized quality reports, and digital readouts of part dimensions to provide immediate information on what is happening and how things are progressing. At the process level, operational performance data such as yields, cycle times, and productivity measures help managers determine whether their processes are accomplishing their objectives, whether they are using resources effectively, and whether they are improving. Information at this level generally is aggregated; for example, daily or weekly scrap reports, customer complaint data obtained from customer service representatives, or monthly sales and cost figures faxed in from field offices. At the organization level, product and service quality and operational performance data from all areas of the firm, along with relevant customer, financial, human resource, and other organizational effectiveness data, form the basis for measuring shareholder value and for strategic planning and decision making by senior leadership. Such information is highly aggregated and obtained from many different sources throughout the organization.

Measurement-managed companies are more likely to be in the top third of their industry financially, complete organizational changes more successfully, reach clear agreement on strategy among senior managers, enjoy favorable levels of cooperation and teamwork among management, undertake greater self-monitoring of performance by employees, and have a greater willingness by employees to take risks.[7]

Good data and information management provide many benefits:

- They help the company know that customers are receiving appropriate levels of service because indicators are used to measure service attributes.
- They provide concrete feedback to workers to verify their progress.
- They establish a basis for reward and recognition.
- They provide a means of assessing progress and signaling the need for corrective action.
- They reduce the costs of operations through better planning and improvement actions.

Leading Practices

Successful companies recognize the importance of reliable and appropriate data and information in strategic planning and daily customer-focused decision making. Data and information are the forces that drive quality excellence and improve operational and competitive performance. Some of the key practices are summarized here.

1. *They develop a comprehensive set of performance indicators that reflect internal and external customer requirements and the key factors that drive the organization.* Performance indicators span the entire business operation, from suppliers to customers, and from front-line workers to top levels of management. Boeing Airlift and Tanker Programs, for example, defines performance measurements in five key categories that support company goals: customer satisfaction, program performance, workforce effectiveness, operational and process performance, and financial results. Collecting data that no one uses or wants, however, wastes

valuable time and resources. Leading companies select appropriate measures and indicators using well-defined criteria. Boeing A&T uses five criteria to select data: important to customers, effective in measuring performance, effective in forecasting results, actionable, and easily collected with integrity. As another example, Clarke American structures its performance measurements along two dimensions: how they are used—to either *change the business* or *run the business*—and whether they are predictive (*leading*) or diagnostic (*lagging*). "Change the business" measures are those most critical to the achievement of strategic objectives and evaluate organizational performance, such as total order cycle time and implemented ideas. "Run the business" measures are those used for daily operations and include measures of accuracy, responsiveness, and timeliness for deliveries.

2. *They use comparative information and data to improve overall performance and competitive position.* Comparative information includes comparisons relative to direct competitors as well as best-practices benchmarking, either inside or outside one's industry. Such information allows organizations to know where they stand in relation to competitors and other leading companies, provides the impetus for breakthrough improvement, and helps them understand their own processes before they compare performance levels. For example, Corning Telecommunications Products Division (TPD) uses a Competitive Analysis Process to gather publicly available data to analyze competitors' intentions and capabilities, including manufacturing capacity, cost, and cost of incremental capacity, and determines product capability and quality through direct evaluation of competitors' products. At Custom Research Inc. (CRI), the Steering Committee uses a benchmarking matrix to identify areas where benchmarking could benefit the company most; it is targeted on five key processes. All employees are encouraged to informally benchmark through industry and other organizations, conferences, and seminars, and bring back what they learn to CRI. Employees at SSM Health Care attended Disney Institute training and visited two other hospitals that have used the Disney approach to develop its K.I.D.S. RULE customer service program at Cardinal Glennon Children's Hospital in St. Louis.

3. *They continually refine information sources and their uses within the organization.* Antiquated measurement approaches lead to poor decisions. Leading companies continually improve their performance measurement systems, staying abreast of new techniques. They conduct ongoing review and update their sources and uses of data, shorten the cycle time from data gathering to access, and broaden access to everyone who requires data for management and improvement. During quarterly "measurement summits" at ADAC Laboratories, representatives from all departments review the types of data collected according to three criteria: whether the data support key business drivers; address one of the "five evils"—waste, defects, delays, accidents, or mistakes; or support objective analysis for improvement. Teams at Corning TPD brainstorm and research new measurements, consult with experts, and test the measurements for three to six months before full implementation.

4. *They use sound analytical methods to conduct analyses, use the results to support strategic planning and daily decision making.* Strong analytical capability is the necessary precursor of good analysis. Leading companies employ a variety of statistical tools and structured approaches for analyzing data and turning them into useful information. Fuji-Xerox, a Japanese subsidiary of Xerox, uses a variety of statistical techniques such as regression and analysis of variance to develop mathematical models relating such factors as copy quality, machine

malfunctions, and maintenance time to customer satisfaction results. SSM Health Care uses regression/impact analysis to identify opportunities for improvement from the patient satisfaction surveys. Through this statistical tool, the areas with the lowest satisfaction and highest importance to the customer can be determined. At Pal's Sudden Service, an automated data collection, integration, and analysis system, SysDine, generates store-level and companywide reports on sales, customer count, product mix, ideal food and material cost, and turnover rates and also has an automated correlation routine available for analyzing key data to support organizational performance reviews and strategic planning. As a result, they are able to identify how changes in one performance area affect all other areas, make accurate performance projections, and understand how to optimize their management system.

5. *They involve everyone in measurement activities and ensure that performance information is widely visible throughout the organization.* No longer do "quality control" departments perform inspection and measurement activities. Instead, organizations expect all process owners to collect and analyze data from their individual processes as a basis for problem solving and improvement activities. Motorola, for instance, strives to measure every task performed by every one of its employees. At GTE Directories, functional and cross-functional teams throughout the company work to maintain up-to-date scope, management, and quality of key operational measurement data. The owner of data at Texas Nameplate Company is the person who has access to the data and responsibility to use them.

   Performance information can quickly pinpoint areas that need improvement; but just knowing that one is doing a good job can also be a powerful motivator. Thus, organizations need to share performance information with all employees. For example, The Ritz-Carlton disseminates its Service Quality Indicator statistics to the workforce on a daily basis. Solar Turbines shares comparative data in its leadership and all-employee meetings showing projected comparisons with each of its "top tier measures." Branch-Smith Printing puts its performance analysis into charts for review in preparation for their strategic planning process. Results from each management review are posted for all employees, who use this for information, evaluation, and improvement processes. Department-specific analyses are communicated by posting "Resource Performance Charts" in all functional areas. The charts include the department or group goals, performance levels, and the relationship of goals to division strategies.

6. *They ensure that data and information are accurate, reliable, timely, secure and confidential as appropriate.* At Branch-Smith Printing, for example, to ensure production data and information integrity and reliability, shop floor data collection information goes through a four-step manual process. Daily production information is (1) input, inspected, and approved by the employee, (2) reviewed and edited by the employee's supervisor, (3) verified by accounting personnel, and (4) inspected by the quality manager before the PSI end of month closing. Feedback on its accuracy flows from the supervisor to the employee, the accounting personnel to the supervisor, and the quality manager to the accounting assistant. STMicroelectronics designs its systems to bypass human data entry whenever possible and performs validity checks at the database level.

   To ensure data and information security and confidentiality, the SSM Health Care established a department for Compliance Administration and Security, which is responsible for ensuring appropriate authorized access to its computer systems. A formal computer authorization process for granting access to systems and a process of routinely requiring passwords to be changed have been implemented. The department leader also is working with the project manager for HIPAA compliance and heads up the HIPAA Technical Security team to ensure that the confidentiality of electronic patient records is in compliance with federal standards.

7. *They ensure that hardware and software systems are reliable and user-friendly, and that data and information are accessible to all who need it them.* The reliability of hardware and software is crucial to ensure the integrity of performance measurement systems. At Branch-Smith Printing, server uptime is protected with redundant power supplies and hard drives. Two servers have two identical mirrored drives so that if a device on the primary fails, we can remove one of the drives and install it in the sister machine, and have the server operating again in just minutes. At Motorola, special interest groups or technical advisory boards and working groups have been formed across the corporation to involve users in establishing and updating desktop hardware and software standards to reduce costs, ensure reliability, and improve ease of use.

Leading companies provide rapid access to data and information to all employees who need the information. Xerox, for example, maintains one of the most extensive computer networks in the world, linking hundreds of sites on four continents to provide information 24 hours a day, seven days a week. At Milliken and STMicroelectronics, databases and online reports are available to every associate to support daily operations and empower employees to take appropriate action.

8. *They systematically manage organizational knowledge and identify and share best practices.* Managing information and knowledge can require a significant commitment of resources as the sources of information grow dramatically each year. Information from internal operations, from the Internet, and from business-to-business (B2B) and business-to-consumer (B2C) communications challenges organizational abilities to provide the information that people need to do their work, keep current, and improve. Clarke American, for example, has an automated information collection and distribution system that provides a central repository for information for partners, customers, and associates. To help manage knowledge, SSM Health Care determines the need for and priority of comparative data and best practices by answering these questions: Does the benchmarking effort relate to strategies and action plans? Is the data available and reliable? Does the benchmarking effort relate to the department level indicators? They also foster best practice sharing throughout the organization via an annual Sharing Conference that highlights 40 or more best practices from around the system; having quality improvement teams notify the Quality Resource Center of new projects and send their storybooks to be shared with other entities; having teams participating in share lessons learned through teleconferences and face-to-face meetings; and using the system's intranet site and e-mail newsletters.

All of these practices encourage "management by fact," one of the key elements of total quality.

THE SCOPE OF PERFORMANCE MEASUREMENT

Traditionally, most businesses relied on organizational performance data based almost solely on financial or accounting-based factory productivity considerations, such as return on investment, earnings per share, direct labor efficiency, and machine utilization.[8] Unfortunately, many of these indicators are inaccurate and stress quantity over quality.[9] They reward the wrong behavior; lack predictive power; do not capture key business changes until it is too late; reflect functions, not cross-functional processes; and give inadequate consideration to difficult-to-quantify resources such as intellectual capital.[10] For example, financial measures reflect past decisions; they do not focus on factors that create value and predict financial success. Measurements such as direct labor efficiency promote building unnecessary inventory and lead to overcontrol of direct labor, thus preventing workers from assuming their own responsibility for control and from focusing on process improvement. An emphasis on machine utilization encourages having fewer, but larger, general-purpose machines, which results in more complex material flows and increased inventory and throughput time. In traditional manufacturing and service operations, cost was the key measure of performance, particularly in highly competitive markets. Today, however, quality drives key decisions, which requires a much broader set of performance measures that are aligned to an organization's strategy.

The Balanced Scorecard

Robert Kaplan and David Norton pose the following scenario:[11]

> *Imagine entering the cockpit of a modern jet airplane and seeing only a single instrument there. How would you feel about boarding the plane after the following conversation with the pilot?*
>
> *Q: I'm surprised to see you operating the plane with only a single instrument. What does it measure?*
>
> *A: Airspeed. I'm really working on airspeed this flight.*
>
> *Q: That's good. Airspeed certainly seems important. But what about altitude? Wouldn't an altimeter be helpful?*
>
> *A: I worked on altitude for the last few flights and I've gotten pretty good on it. Now I have to concentrate on proper airspeed.*
>
> *Q: But I notice you don't even have a fuel gauge. Wouldn't that be useful?*
>
> *A: You're right; fuel is significant, but I can't concentrate on doing too many things well at the same time. So on this flight I'm focusing on airspeed. Once I get to be excellent at airspeed, as well as altitude, I intend to concentrate on fuel consumption on the next set of flights.*

Clearly, you would be a bit uneasy about taking this flight. However, the analogy with business is not that far-fetched. Many companies still manage their organizations by concentrating primarily on financial measures.

To make decisions that further the overall organizational goals of meeting, or exceeding, customer expectations and making productive use of limited resources, companies need good data and information about customers and markets, human resource effectiveness, supplier performance, product and service quality, and other key factors, in addition to traditional financial performance and accounting measures.

Art Schneiderman at Analog Devices first developed the concept of a balanced scorecard in 1987.[12] Analog Devices established and openly published a set of nonfinancial performance goals as part of its five-year strategic plan. A one-page summary that combined these performance goals with the key financial goals was originally referred to as the "Quarterly Performance Audit," but quickly became known as the "Scorecard." Robert Kaplan and David Norton of the Harvard Business School studied Analog Devices and promoted the concept in

Harvard Business Review articles and a book. The purpose of the balanced scorecard is "to translate strategy into measures that uniquely communicate your vision to the organization." Their version of the balanced scorecard consists of four perspectives:

- *Financial Perspective:* Measures the ultimate results that the business provides to its shareholders. They include profitability, revenue growth, return on investment, economic value added (EVA), and shareholder value.
- *Internal Perspective:* Focuses attention on the performance of the key internal processes that drive the business. They include such measures as quality levels, productivity, cycle time, and cost.
- *Customer Perspective:* Focuses on customer needs and satisfaction as well as market share. This includes service levels, satisfaction ratings, and repeat business.
- *Innovation and Learning Perspective:* Directs attention to the basis of a future success—the organization's people and infrastructure. Key measures might include intellectual assets, employee satisfaction, market innovation, and skills development.

Quality Spotlight
Pearl River
School District

Organizations need to know what is happening now and what might happen in the future. For example, customer survey results about recent transactions might be a leading indicator for customer retention (a lagging indicator); employee satisfaction might be a leading indicator for turnover, and so on.

> *A good balanced scorecard contains both leading and lagging measures and indicators.* ***Lagging measures*** *(outcomes) tell what has happened;* ***leading measures*** *(performance drivers) predict what will happen.*

Pearl River School District uses a modified balanced scorecard that includes leading and lagging indicators relative to strategic objectives under each of its three district goals (Figure 8.1). Lagging indicators represent long-term results and lead indicators are either short-term or line-of-sight predictors for lagging indicators. For example, stakeholder satisfaction rates are key factors in the level of support the district can expect in their annual budget vote. The fourth and eighth grade New York State exams are designed to be predictors of student success on the Regents examinations.

Leading and lagging measures and indicators can help to establish cause-and-effect relationships across perspectives. Figure 8.2 shows the causal relationships among the key measures in IBM Rochester's balanced scorecard. This model suggests that improving internal capabilities such as people skills, product/service quality, and products and channels, will lead to improved customer satisfaction and loyalty, which in turn, lead to improved financial and market share performance. Understanding such relationships is important in using data and information for strategic and operational decisions.

Kaplan and Norton's balanced scorecard is only one version of performance measurement systems that have emerged as companies recognized the need for a broad set of performance measures that provide a comprehensive view of business performance. For instance, Raytheon's version defines customer, shareholder, process, and people perspectives. The Malcolm Baldrige Criteria for Performance Excellence Results category groups performance measures into six sets:

- Customer
- Product and service
- Financial and market
- Human resource
- Organizational effectiveness
- Governance and social responsibility

Figure 8.1 Pearl River School District Balanced Scorecard

Strategic Objectives	Lag Indicators (long-term)	Lead Indicators (predictive)
Academic Performance		
Academic Achievement	Regents Diploma Rate	Achievement on 4th and 8th grade NYS exams
		CTPIII Reading and Math Achievement
		Special Education Opportunity
College Admissions	AP Participation Rate	Passing rate on Regents exams
	AP Performance Rate	SAT I & II Participation Rate
		Scholar Athlete Teams
Perception		
Parent/Community Satisfaction	Maintain 2:1 Plurality on Budget Votes	Stakeholder Satisfaction Surveys
		Adult Education Enrollment
	Market Share	Student Satisfaction Surveys
		Prospective Homeowner Requests
		New Resident Survey
Fiscal Stability		
Cost-Effective Fiscal Management	Contain Per-Pupil Expenditure	Reduce Costs in Non-Instructional Areas

Source: Courtesy of Pearl River School District.

Figure 8.2 Causal Relationships Among Categories of IBM Rochester's Balanced Scorecard

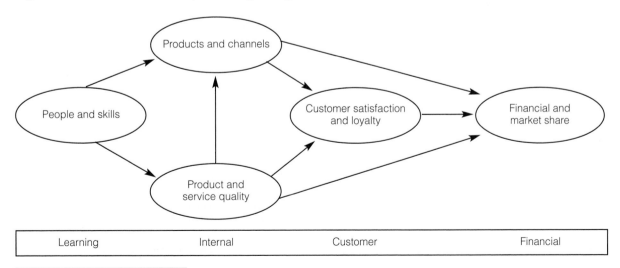

Source: Courtesy of IBM Rochester, MN.

These categories are summarized in Figure 8.3, along with examples of measures in each category. This set is quite similar to the balanced scorecard, and in fact, any measure in the balanced scorecard can easily be assigned to one of these categories. We will briefly discuss each of these categories. As we describe specific examples, note that the specific measures an organization chooses are tied to the key factors that make it competitive in its industry.

Figure 8.3 Business Performance Measures and Indicators

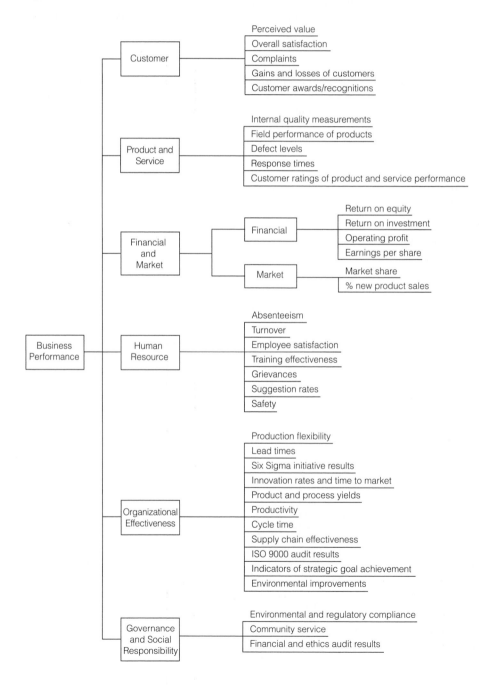

Customer-Focused Measures

We discussed the importance of measuring customer satisfaction in Chapter 4. Relevant measures and indicators of an organization's performance as viewed by customers include direct measures of customer satisfaction and dissatisfaction, customer retention, gains and losses of customers and customer accounts, customer complaints, and warranty claims. Other indicators of customer satisfaction include measures of perceived value, loyalty, positive referral, and customer relationship building. Customer satisfaction should be measured over three areas at a minimum: product quality, service quality, and cycle times. For example, 3M's automotive trades business has as its direct customers automotive distributors, while end users are the secondary group. Service quality and cycle times are key satisfaction measures for distributors, while product quality is the principal satisfaction indicator for end users. 3M's measurements include the following:

- In-stock service levels
- On-time delivery
- Order completeness
- Emergency response time
- Ease of dealing with supplier
- Ease of contact with customer service department
- Complaint handling
- Accuracy of shipment
- Order cycle time
- Product quality and performance[13]

Product and Service Measures

Measures and indicators of product and service performance that have strong correlation with customer satisfaction and decisions relative to future purchases and relationships are important for organizations to track. They might include internal quality measurements, field performance of products, defect levels, response times, data collected from customers or third parties on ease of use or other attributes, and customer surveys on product and service performance. STMicroelectronics, for example, tracks the number of nonconforming production lots, which play a significant role in complaints received by their customers. They also track different measures for different customer segments. For instance, the telecommunications industry has a very short cycle-to-market requirement; key measures that address this factor are delivery time, flexibility, response delay, early warning, quality/reliability, and response quality.

Financial and Market Measures

Financial measures are generally tracked by senior leadership to gauge overall company performance and are often used to determine incentive compensation for senior executives. Measures of financial performance might include revenue, return on equity, return on investment, operating profit, pretax profit margin, asset utilization, earnings per share, and other liquidity measures. In a capital-intensive industry such as airplane production, key financial measures at Boeing Airlift and Tanker Programs are return on sales, return on net assets, and net asset turnover. The Ritz-Carlton Hotel Company, on the other hand, monitors earnings before taxes, depreciation, and amortization, administrative costs, and gross profit among its key financial indicators. A useful financial performance indicator is the *cost of quality*, which managers use to prioritize improvement projects and gauge the effectiveness of total quality efforts and which we will discuss this later in this chapter. It is one of Solar Turbine's key measures.

Marketplace performance indicators could include market share, measures of business growth, new product and geographic markets entered, and percentage of new product sales as appropriate. In a commodity market in which Sunny Fresh Foods competes, its performance drivers include their share of the U.S. market and total pounds of egg products sold. In the highly competitive semiconductor industry, STMicroelectronics looks not only at sales growth, but at differentiated product sales.

Human Resource Measures

Many companies do not measure human resource results, despite the critical importance of human resources in achieving quality and performance objectives. We addressed this issue in Chapter 6. HR measures can relate to employee well-being, satisfaction, training and development, work system performance, and effectiveness. Examples include safety, absenteeism, turnover, and employee satisfaction. Other measures might include the extent of training, training effectiveness, and measures of improvement in job effectiveness. Texas Nameplate Company measures the percent of net earnings for its risk-based compensation (gain sharing) program, because it significantly impacts employee productivity, motivation, and satisfaction. Because of the important relationship that Boeing Airlift and Tanker Programs has with its unions, A&T tracks grievance backlog reduction as a way of quantifying improving relationships. The Ritz-Carlton tracks percent turnover closely, because this measure is a key indicator of employee satisfaction and the effectiveness of their selection and training processes.

Organizational Effectiveness Measures

This category includes measures and indicators that relate to attaining key organizational goals, and includes unique and innovative measures to track business development and operational improvement. They might include measures related to design, production, delivery, and support process performance. Examples of common measures are cycle times, production flexibility, lead times, setup times, time to market, product/process yields, and delivery performance. Boeing A&T, for instance, tracks the mean time between corrective maintenance of its aircraft; increasing this time indicates improved quality of the aircraft systems. Other examples are reduced emission levels and waste stream reductions, Six Sigma initiative results, and ISO 9000 assessment audits. STMicroelectronics tracks key indicators of strategic goal achievement, such as R&D investment and number of patents granted. Texas Nameplate uses toxic chemicals in its etching process; thus, it monitors the pH level and amount of suspended metals in water discharge to meet local regulations. With the increased focus on supply chain management, many companies are now reviewing cost savings; total supply chain management costs; reductions in inventory and cycle time; and indicators of better communication, such as those achieved via electronic commerce. Solar Turbines, for example, monitors supplier lead times for two critical components—forgings and castings.

Many organizational effectiveness measures focus on process (both value-creation and support) performance. Process data can reflect defect and error rates of intermediate operations, and also efficiency measures such as cost, cycle time, productivity, schedule performance, machine downtime, preventive maintenance activity, rates of problem resolution, energy efficiency, and raw material usage. For example, Motorola measures nearly every process in the company in terms of defects, errors and time. All processes within the company, including design, order entry, manufacturing, and marketing, are measured for improvements in error rates and cycle times. American Express analysts monitor telephone conversations for politeness, tone of voice, accuracy of the transaction, and other customer service aspects. Comparisons between judgments of the analysts and judgments of customers in post-transaction interviews determine the relevance of specific internal measurements. Because of the importance of hiring skilled people, The Ritz-Carlton embarked on a major project to improve the cycle time from when a potential new-hire walks in the door until a job offer is tendered; it became one of their key measures in this category.

Governance and Social Responsibility Measures

Monitoring measures and indicators in this category helps maintain an ethical organization that is a good citizen in its communities. Measures and indicators relate to organizational accountability, stakeholder trust, and ethical behavior. They might include measures of regulatory/legal compliance, financial and ethics review results, and measures of community service, such as volunteer hours and presentations to educational or civic groups. Key financial measures that are tied strongly to corporate governance include those found in income statements, balance sheets, as well as distributions of stock and stock options, and management stock purchase and sales activity.

The Role of Comparative Data

Looking at data without a basis for comparison can easily lead to a false sense of achievement. For example, a performance measure may be improving, but at a rate slower than its competition. Without that information, it would be difficult for an organization to recognize the need for further improvements or an accelerated pace of change to close the gap. Comparative and benchmark information also provide the motivation to seek breakthrough improvements.

Organizations need comparative data, such as industry averages, best competitor performance, and world-class benchmarks to gain an accurate assessment of performance and know where they stand relative to competitors and best practices.

Comparative data should be driven by an organization's needs and priorities, and focus on areas most critical to competitive strategy. Comparative data may be obtained in many ways and include third-party surveys and benchmarking approaches. The Ritz-Carlton Hotel Company, for instance, uses ratings and awards from travel industry publications and salesforce reports to assess its competitive status. Boeing A&T seeks information from three sources:

1. *Best-in-Boeing:* high-performing processes identified through various company-level councils
2. *Best-in-Industry:* companies identified through various benchmarking centers, the International Benchmarking Clearinghouse, and their internal Business Environmental Assessment group
3. *World Class:* leading-edge companies, winners of national awards, or those cited by customers, suppliers, and industry experts

Figure 8.4 shows the performance of lead time from order placement until delivery for Texas Nameplate Co. TNC's results are compared against two major competitors and industry averages from a third party survey. The results show that TNC has consistently maintained a position of leadership in this measure. A good source of comparative benchmarks is the performance of Baldrige-winning organizations.

Figure 8.4 Texas Nameplate Performance Results for Delivery Lead TIme

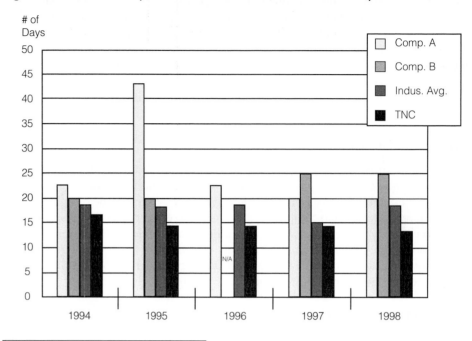

Source: Courtesy of Texas Nameplate Company.

DESIGNING EFFECTIVE PERFORMANCE MEASUREMENT SYSTEMS

The purposes of a performance measurement system include the following:

- Providing direction and support for continuous improvement
- Identifying trends and progress
- Facilitating understanding of cause-and-effect relationships
- Allowing performance comparison to benchmarks
- Providing a perspective of the past, present, and future

In addition, they should be intelligible to a majority of employees, provide real-time information for decisions, and support personal and organizational learning.[14] Balanced scorecards often fail for a variety of reasons, including incorrectly identifying the real drivers of customer satisfaction; not defining measures appropriately to focus attention on the places within a process where they will have the greatest impact; negotiating goals rather than basing them on customer requirements, process limitations, and improvement capabilities; or not linking nonfinancial and expected financial results in a quantitative fashion.[15] Thus, organizations must carefully design their performance measurement systems.

Addressing these issues requires an organization to align its measurement system to its

In designing a performance measurement system, organizations must consider how the measures will support senior executive performance review and organizational planning to address the overall health of the organization, and how the measures will support daily operations and decision making.

vision and strategy and select meaningful process-level measurements. Many organizations make two fundamental mistakes: (1) not measuring key characteristics critical to company performance or customer satisfaction, and (2) taking irrelevant or inappropriate measurements. In the first case, the organization often fails to meet customer expectations or performance goals. In the second, the measurement system directs attention to areas that are not important to customers, thus wasting time and resources. The number of performance indicators seems to grow with the size and complexity of the organization. In many organizations, performance indicators have been around for a long time, and few managers can probably say where, when, and why they developed. In most cases, somebody just decided they were good to have. For example, IDS Financial Services, a subsidiary of American Express, used to measure more than 4,000 individual tasks: functions like phone calls, mail coding, and application acceptance. Many of these tasks were subject to 100 percent inspection. Now, after redesigning its information management system, IDS measures 80 service processes and uses statistical sampling.

Mark Graham Brown suggests some practical guidelines for designing a performance measurement system:[16]

- Fewer is better. Concentrate on measuring the vital few key variables rather than the trivial many.
- Measures should be linked to the factors needed for success, namely, the key business drivers.
- Measures should include a mix of past, present, and future to ensure that the organization is concerned with all three perspectives.
- Measures should be based around the needs of customers, shareholders, and other key stakeholders.
- Measures should start at the top and flow down to all levels of employees in the organization.
- Multiple indexes can be combined into a single index to give a better overall assessment of performance.
- Measures should be changed or at least adjusted as the environment and strategy changes.
- Measures need to have targets or goals that are based on research rather than arbitrary numbers.

Linking Measures to Strategy

A balanced scorecard approach helps in identifying the right measures by aligning them with the organization's vision and strategy. It provides a means of setting targets and allocating resources for short-term planning, communicating strategies, aligning departmental and personal goals to strategies, linking rewards to performance, and supplying feedback for organizational learning. IBM Rochester's quality scorecard groups 19 key performance measures into seven areas: customer satisfaction, software performance, hardware performance, service, delivery, administration, and image. Each is reported quarterly as a single index, with color-coded "quality" and "status" columns. In the quality column, red indicates an adverse trend, yellow a flat trend, and green an improving trend; in the status column, red means "not on track to attain plan," yellow means "plan attainment at risk," and green means "tracking to plan." This system provides a concise, visual summary of overall organizational performance.

Effective performance measures that are aligned with business strategy are driven by factors that determine what is important to the success of the business. These factors include the following:

- The nature of a company's products and services
- Principal customers and their key performance requirements and expectations
- Organizational culture; its purpose, mission, and vision
- Capabilities and core competencies, such as human resources, facilities, and technologies
- Supplier, supply chain requirements, and partnering relationships
- Regulatory environment
- Position in the market and competitive environment
- Principal factors that determine competitive success, such as product innovation, price leadership, or e-services
- Strategic challenges the organization faces

For example, the First National Bank of Chicago asked its customers what they considered as good-quality features of a product and the delivery of those features.[17] Responses included timeliness, accuracy, operations efficiency, economics, and customer responsiveness. These responses initiated the development of performance indicators such as lockbox processing time, bill keying accuracy, customer service inquiry resolution time, and money transfer timeliness. A computer software company might not need to collect extensive data on environmental quality issues whereas a chemical company certainly would. A pizza franchise that delivers bulk orders to fraternities and parties around a college campus would have a different set of performance measures and indicators than one in a quiet suburban residential neighborhood. Thus, an organization first needs to fully understand its internal capabilities and external environment.

Measures should logically be tied to key business drivers. MBNA, the Wilmington, Delaware, credit card company that markets custom cards to "affinity groups" such as professional associations, universities, and sports team fans, views speed of service as one of its key business drivers. Thus, it measures the time to process customer address changes, the percentage of times phones are picked up within two rings, and the times

> *The things an organization needs to do well to accomplish its vision are often called **key business drivers** or **key success factors**. They represent things that separate an organization from its competition and define strengths to exploit or weaknesses to correct.*

Quality Spotlight
Armstrong Building Products Operations

taken to transfer calls from the switchboard.[18] Armstrong Building Products Operations identified five components of value that drive its business strategy: customer satisfaction, sales growth, operating profit, asset management, and high-performance organization. Each of these components is supported by key measurements and analysis approaches. For example, product quality, a key driver of customer satisfaction, is measured by dimensions and squareness, fire performance, acoustics and color, dimensional stability, competitor product quality analysis, and claims. Likewise, service quality is measured by on-time delivery and missed-item promises, pricing and billing, and information support for customers. Another key business driver, operating profit, is measured by process effectiveness, units per employee, scrap and downtime, and cost of quality. Organizational performance measures include recordable injury rate, number of improvements/work orders, percentage of employees recognized, gain-sharing savings, and employee satisfaction trends and turnover rate.

Key performance measures should be aligned with strategies and action plans. Setting targets for each measure provides the basis for strategy deployment as discussed in Chapter 5. Figure 8.5 shows an example from Merrill Lynch Credit Corporation (MLCC), a 1997 Baldrige Award recipient. MLCC defines its Critical Few Objectives from its long-term focused strategies, Client Satisfaction, Partner Satisfaction, Business

Figure 8.5 Merrill Lynch Credit Corporation's Alignment of Measures with Strategies and Processes

* Proprietary Information Deleted

Long-Term Focus	MLCC Critical Few Objective Requirements (Form 1)	Resources ($)	Key Performance Measures	Targets		Core Process No.							
				*	*	1.0	2.0	3.0	4.0	5.0	6.0	7.0	8.0
1.0 Client Satisfaction	1.1 Increase end-user satisfaction		% Good to excellent/Excellent	*	*	●	●	●	●	○	●		
	1.2 Increase field/FC satisfaction	*	% Good to excellent/Excellent	*	*	○	○		●		●		
	1.3 Increase internal client satisfaction		% Good to excellent/Excellent	*	*	○	○	●	●	●	●	●	
2.0 Partner Satisfaction	2.1 Increase partner satisfaction		% Overall partner satisfaction	*	*	●	●	●	●	●	●	●	
	2.2 Reduce partner turnover		% Turnover	*	*	○	○			●	●	○	
	2.3 Develop managerial skills/capability model	*	Determine leadership req'mnts	*	*	●	●		○		●	●	
	2.4 Deploy partner productivity measurement standards		% Partners reviewed	*	*	○	○				●	●	
	2.5 Ensure proper staffing levels		% Budget vs. actual	*	*	○	○	●			●		
3.0 Business Growth	3.1 Increase origination volume		Overall units/$ Volume (billions)	*	*	●	●	●			●		
	3.2 Increase FC effectiveness	*	% Approval ratio	*	*	●	●	●			●		
	3.3 Institutionalize liability management		# of client impressions # of FC impressions	*	*	●	●	●			●		
4.0 Shareholder Value	4.1 Reduce operating expenses		% Revenue/Expense ratio	*	*	●	●	●	○		●	●	
	4.2 Increase process productivity	*	Application approval cycle time	*	*	●	●		○	○	●	●	
	4.3 Develop MLCC-wide compliance program		% Approved compliance procedures in place	*	*					●	●	●	

Legend: ● = High Impact   ○ = Medium Impact   Blank = Low or No Impact

Business Priority Matrix

Support Process Alignment

Growth, and Shareholder Value. For each of these, they define key performance measures and targets by which to evaluate progress toward meeting these objectives. They also align each of the objectives with their eight primary value-creation processes: Design, Market, Pre-Origination, Order, Underwrite, Approve, Audit/Fund, and Setup Service. Such an approach ensures that process owners focus on the right measurements that support the company's strategy.

Process-Level Measurements

What makes a good performance measurement system? Many organizations define specific criteria for selecting measures and indicators. IBM Rochester, for example, asks the following questions:

- Does the measurement support our mission?
- Will the measurement be used to manage change?
- Is it important to our customers?
- Is it effective in measuring performance?
- Is it effective in forecasting results?
- Is it easy to understand/simple?
- Are the data easy/cost-efficient to collect?
- Does the measurement have validity, integrity, and timeliness?
- Does the measure have an owner?

Many organizations use the acronym *SMART* to characterize good measures and indicators: *simple, measurable, actionable, related* (to customer requirements and to each other), and *timely*. Process measures should also clearly align with customer requirements. For example, product reliability might be measured by the number of repair calls, billing accuracy by the percentage of billing inquiries or complaints, knowledgeable customer representatives by supervisor observations or analysis of recorded calls, ease of use by number of calls to a help desk, and so on.

> *Good measures and indicators are* ***actionable***; *that is, they provide the basis for decisions at the level at which they are applied.*

At the process level, product and service quality indicators focus on the outcomes of manufacturing and service processes. A common indicator of manufacturing quality is the number of **nonconformities per unit**, or **defects per unit**. Because of the negative connotation of "defect" and its potential implications in liability suits, many organizations use the term *nonconformance*; however, quite a few still use the term *defect*. In this book, both terms are used interchangeably to be consistent with current literature and practice. In services, a measure of quality analogous to defects per unit is **errors per opportunity**. Each customer transaction provides an opportunity for many different types of errors.

Nonconformities per unit or errors per opportunity are often reported as rates per thousand or million. A common measure is **dpmo—defects per million opportunities**. Thus, a defect rate of 2 per 1,000 is equivalent to 2,000 dpmo. At some Motorola factories, quality is so good that they measure defects per billion!

Many companies classify defects into three categories:

1. *Critical defect*: A critical defect is one that judgment and experience indicate will surely result in hazardous or unsafe conditions for individuals using, maintaining, or depending on the product and will prevent proper performance of the product.
2. *Major defect*: A major defect is one not critical but likely to result in failure or to materially reduce the usability of the unit for its intended purpose.

3. *Minor defect*: A minor defect is one not likely to materially reduce the usability of the item for its intended purpose, nor to have any bearing on the effective use or operation of the unit.[19]

Critical defects may lead to serious consequences or product liability suits; thus, they should be monitored and controlled for carefully. On the other hand, minor defects might not be monitored as closely, because they do not affect fitness for use. For many products, however, even minor defects can lead to customer dissatisfaction. To account for each category, many companies create a composite index in which major and critical defects are weighted more heavily than minor defects. For example, FedEx has an extensive quality measurement system that includes a composite measure, called the service quality indicator (SQI), which is a weighted sum of 10 factors that reflect customers' expectations of company performance. FedEx's SQI is shown in Table 8.1. Different weights reflect the importance of each failure; losing a package, for instance, is more serious than delivering it a few minutes late. The index is reported weekly and summarized on a monthly basis.

Identifying and Selecting Process Measures

To generate useful process performance measures a systematic process is required.[20]

1. *Identify all customers of the system and determine their requirements and expectations.* Organizations need answers to key questions: Who are my customers? and What do they expect? Many of the "customer listening" approaches introduced in Chapter 4 can be used in this step. Customer expectations change over time; thus, regular feedback must be obtained.
2. *Define the work process that provides the product or service.* Key questions include: What do I do that affects customer needs? and What is my process? The use of

---

Table 8.1 FedEx Service Quality Indicator and Factors

Error Type / Description	Weight
1. *Complaints reopened*—customer complaints (on traces, invoices, missed pickups, etc.) reopened after an unsatisfactory resolution	3
2. *Damaged packages*—packages with visible or concealed damage or spoilage due to weather or water damage, missed pickup, or late delivery	10
3. *International*—a composite score of performance measures of international operations	
4. *Invoice adjustments*—customer requests for credit or refunds for real or perceived failures	1
5. *Late pickup stops*—packages that were picked up later than the stated pickup time	3
6. *Lost packages*—claims for missing packages or with contents missing	10
7. *Missed proof of delivery*—invoices that lack written proof of delivery information	1
8. *Right date late*—delivery past promised time on the right day	1
9. *Traces*—package status and proof of delivery requests not in the COSMOS IIB computer system (the FedEx "real time" tracking system)	3
10. *Wrong day late*—delivery on the wrong day	5

Source: Service Quality Indicators at FedEx (internal company document).

flowcharts for process mapping can stimulate the definition of work processes and internal customer-supplier relationships.

3. *Define the value-adding activities and outputs that compose the process.* This step—identifying each part in the system in which value is added and an intermediate output is produced—weeds out activities that do not add value to the process and contribute to waste and inefficiency. Analysis performed in this step identifies the internal customers within the process along with their needs and expectations.

4. *Develop specific performance measures or indicators.* Each key activity identified in step 3 represents a critical point where value is added to the output for the next (internal) customer until the final output is produced. At these checkpoints, performance can be measured. Key questions include: What factors determine how well the process is producing according to customer requirements? What deviations can occur? What sources of variability can occur?

5. *Evaluate the performance measures to ensure their usefulness.* Questions to consider include: Are measurements taken at critical points where value-adding activities occur? Are measurements controllable? Is it feasible to obtain the data needed for each measure? Have operational definitions for each measurement been established? Operational definitions are precise definitions of measurements that have no ambiguities. For example, when measuring "invoice errors," a precise definition of what is an error and what is not is needed. Does an error include an omission of information, wrong information, or misspelling? Operational definitions provide a common understanding and enhance communication throughout the organization.

To illustrate this approach, consider the process of placing and filling a pizza order. Customer expectations include a quick response and a fair price. The process that provides this service is shown in Figure 8.6. To begin, the order taker is an (internal) customer of the caller (who provides the pizza order). Later, the caller is a customer of the deliverer (either at the pickup window or the caller's home). Also, the cook is a customer of the order taker (who prepares the documentation for the ordered pizza).

Some possible performance measures include:

- Number of pizzas, by type per hour. If this number is high relative to the kitchen's capacity, then perhaps cooking time and/or preparation is being short-cut or delivery times are stretched out.
- Order accuracy (as transmitted to the kitchen). This measure can indicate a lack of attention or knowledge on the part of the order taker.
- Number of pizzas rejected per number prepared. A high number for this measure can indicate a lack of proper training of cooks, resulting in poor products and customer complaints.
- Time to delivery. This measure might indicate a problem within the restaurant or inadequate training of the driver. (Of course, as happened with Domino's, measuring delivery time could encourage drivers to drive too fast and lead to safety problems.)
- Number of errors in collections. Errors here can result in lost profits and higher prices.
- Raw materials (dough, etc.) or finished pizzas inventory. A high number might result in spoilage and excess costs. Low inventory might result in lost orders or excessive customer waiting time.

Notice that these measures—only a few among many possible measures—are related to customer expectations and business performance.

Figure 8.6 Example of a Pizza Ordering and Filling Process for Home Delivery

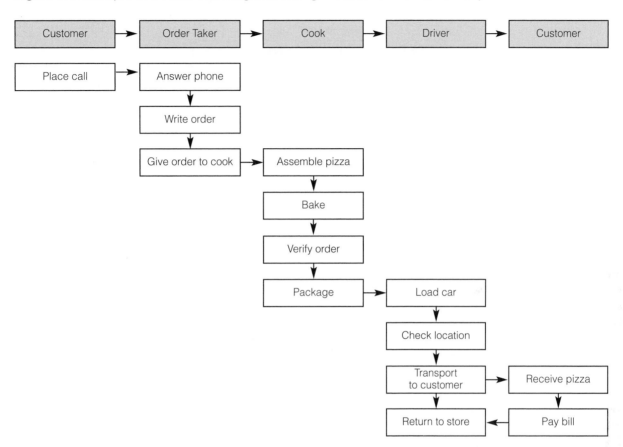

Many organizations use **dashboards**, which typically consist of a small set of measures (five or six) that provide a quick summary of process performance (this term is sometimes also used to describe a balanced scorecard at the organizational level). This preference stems from the analogy to an automobile's dashboard—a collection of indicators (speed, RPM, oil pressure, temperature, etc.) that summarize performance. Dashboards often use graphs, charts, and other visual aids to communicate key measures and alert managers when performance is not where it should be.

Aligning Strategic and Process-Level Measurements[21]

It is possible that all work processes could be meeting their requirements while the organization is not achieving its longer-term goals. Thus, aligning strategic and process-level measurements is vital to a high-performing organization, and can be viewed as an approach for strategy deployment (see Chapter 5). Figure 8.7 illustrates how goals and measures might be aligned for a hypothetical retail manufacturer. Alignment might even go further, down to the team and individual levels. Note that alignment is tied fundamentally to the performance goals; the measures support goal attainment. The organization does not have to have one set of performance measures that everyone produces and reports, but rather, measures are used where they are

Figure 8.7 An Example of Aligning Strategic and Process-Level Performance Measures

Corporate Level

Goals	Measures
Profitability	% earnings growth
Market share	Market share product index
Store presence	Linear shelf space per store
Inventory control	Inventory turns
Self-managed teams	% teams operational

Factory Level

Goals	Measures
Revenue growth	% sales growth
Scrap rate	% over expected
New customer orders	% increase
Inventory control	Inventory turns
On-time shipping	% on-time shipments
Self-managed teams	% employees certified
Safety	OSHA reportables

Production Line Level

Goals	Measures
Scrap rate	% over expected
Schedule fulfillment	% on-target
Productivity	Tons per operating hour
Changeover time	% reduction per machine
Self-managed teams	% employees certified

Source: R. I. Wise, "A Method for Aligning Process-Level and Strategy-Level Performance Metrics," *The Quality Management Forum*, 25, no. 1 (Spring 1999), 4–6. American Society for Quality, 11th Annual Quality Management Conference.

most appropriate. Production line data, for example, might be reviewed only at the line level for daily operations control, while some data might be integrated at the next level for process improvement. Information that supports review of organizational-level performance is passed on to the corporate level.

Enterprise Resource Planning (ERP)—systems are software packages that integrate organizational information systems and provide an infrastructure for managing information across the enterprise.[22] They integrate all aspects of a business—accounting, customer relationship management, supply chain management, manufacturing, sales, human resources, and so on—into a unified information system, and provide more timely analysis and reporting of sales, customer, inventory, manufacturing, human resource, and accounting data. The three most prominent vendors for ERP software are SAP, Oracle, and PeopleSoft. For example, when a salesperson fills an order, the system can check the customer's credit and their own manufacturing capacity, record the order, schedule the shipment, log the order on the production schedule, order parts from suppliers, and update financial and accounting records. ERP systems allow companies to share different databases in a networking environment and store and process all company data in a unique database, and distribute it to a large group of users. Typical ERP applications span financial, human resource, operations and supply chain, and sales and marketing data. Many ERP systems now offer performance measurement system modules that are focused on helping manage the wide scope of data that are collected in the system.

ANALYZING AND USING PERFORMANCE DATA

All the different types of data that we discussed support operational-level decisions, senior leadership performance reviews, priority setting, and strategic planning. However, simply reporting numbers or showing them on graphs and charts are not enough. Data require sound analysis to turn them into information. **Analysis** refers to an examination of facts and data to provide a basis for effective decisions. Examples of possible analyses include the following:

- Examining trends and changes in key performance indicators
- Making comparisons relative to other business units, competitor performance, or best-in-class benchmarks
- Calculating means, standard deviations, and other statistical measures
- Seeking to understand relationships among different performance indicators using sophisticated statistical tools such as correlation and regression analysis

The capabilities of today's spreadsheet and database software, such as Microsoft Excel and Access, make analysis simple to do by nearly any employee. Also, some evidence suggests that organizations that use more sophisticated statistical tools for analysis tend to have better business results. The fact that effective analysis requires more advanced statistical thinking might explain the lack of good approaches in most organizations. Thus, organizations are advised to develop improved statistical expertise among their employees which is one of the key benefits of Six Sigma.

Volumes of data acquired at the process level, while useful for daily operations decisions and process control, generally are not appropriate for senior executive review or strategic planning. For instance, some companies develop an aggregate customer satisfaction index (CSI) by weighting satisfaction results, market share, and gains or losses of customers. Previously we discussed how FedEx aggregates different quality components into a single index. Corning Telecommunications Products Division aggregates data and information into key financial and business-level analyses that quantify the impact of decisions on financial and market performance. Its data researchers examine relationships among quality, price, and image as they relate to the attraction and retention of customers. They also quantify the relationships between process capability, people and process productivity, and unit costs.

Organizations need a process for transforming data, usually in some integrated fashion, into information that top management can understand and work with.

As we noted in our discussion of the balanced scorecard, managers must also understand the linkages between key measures of business performance. Examples of such analyses are:

- How product and service quality improvement correlates with key customer indicators such as customer satisfaction, customer retention, and market share
- Financial benefits derived from improvements in employee safety, absenteeism, and turnover
- Benefits and costs associated with education and training
- Relationships between product and service quality, operational performance indicators, and overall financial performance

- Profit impacts of customer satisfaction and retention
- Market share changes as a result of changes in customer satisfaction
- Impacts of employee satisfaction on customer satisfaction

Establishing causal relationships between external lagging results and internal leading measures provides a visible and obvious direction for improvement. For instance, FedEx correlates the 10 quality components with customer satisfaction through extensive market research. Additionally, it conducts focus groups and other surveys to validate these relationships. Trident Precision Manufacturing correlates quality, cost, delivery, and service data with customer satisfaction data to verify their understanding of their customers. GTE Directories uses a proprietary third-party model and software to perform similar analyses.

Interlinking is the term that describes the quantitative modeling of cause-and-effect relationships between external and internal performance measures, such as the relationship of customer satisfaction measures to internal process measures (e.g., product quality or employee performance).[23] A simple interlinking model was developed by Florida Power and Light.[24] In studying the telephone operation of its customer service centers, FPL sampled customers to determine their level of satisfaction with waiting times on the telephone. Satisfaction began to fall significantly at about two minutes (see Figure 8.8). FPL also found that customer satisfaction is directly related to how callers perceive the competence of the phone representatives. Research showed that excessive waiting times caused a bias in the ratings. Eliminating this bias made a substantial contribution toward accurately measuring customer satisfaction with the phone contact experience. To improve customer satisfaction, FPL developed a system to notify customers of the anticipated wait and give them a choice of holding

Figure 8.8 Interlinking Model of Customer Satisfaction and Time on Hold

Customer Satisfaction Rating	Time on Hold
1.32	<30 sec.
1.57	30–60 sec.
1.67	1–2 min.
2.14	2–3 min.

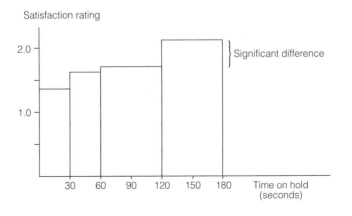

or deferring the call to a later time. Customers were actually willing to wait longer on hold without being dissatisfied if they knew the length of the wait, which improved customer satisfaction even when call traffic was heavy.

Another example is the controls group of Johnson Controls Inc., which examined the relationship between satisfaction levels and contract renewal rates. They found that 91 percent of contract renewals came from customers who were either satisfied or very satisfied, and customers who gave a "not satisfied" rating had a much higher defection rate. By examining the data, they found that a one percentage point increase in the overall satisfaction score was worth $13 million in service contract

Quality Spotlight
Johnson
Controls Inc.

renewals annually. As a result, Johnson Controls made improving customer satisfaction a key strategic initiative.[25]

Not all interlinking models need to be based on sophisticated statistical and computer models.

Ames Rubber Corporation found that simple graphs establish important correlations among measures that impact business decisions and strategy. For example, it discovered that internal yields increase as employee turnover decreases, and that lost time accidents decrease with increasing training hours, leading to new initiatives for training and HR policies.

By using such interlinking models, managers can determine objectively the effects of additional resources or changes in the system to reduce waiting time. Improving the process is only appropriate once a linkage to customer satisfaction is established. This practice is "management by fact"; without it, it is only "management by guess." The objectives and benefits of interlinking include:

- Screening out weak or misleading performance measures
- Focusing management attention on key performance measures that do make a difference
- Predicting performance such as customer satisfaction levels
- Setting target standards for performance
- Requiring areas such as marketing and operations to coordinate their data analysis efforts
- Making wise decisions faster than competitors do
- Seeing relationships among performance variables that competitors miss
- Enhancing communication within the organization based on good data analysis and management by fact.[26]

Interlinking is becoming more widespread based on support by new software technology for analyzing data, particularly data mining. **Data mining** is the process of searching large databases to find hidden patterns in data, using analytical approaches and technologies such as cluster analysis, neural networks, and fuzzy logic. Data mining computer programs can sort through millions of pieces of information and identify subtle correlations between many variables, which is far more than the human mind is capable of doing. For example, data mining might discover that a particular supplier has a higher defect rate on parts costing less than $5, or that consumers who purchase a backup disk drive also tend to purchase a software utility package. Using data mining, MCI developed a set of 22 detailed and highly secret statistical profiles to identify potential customers who might leave for a rival company.[27] Data mining is relatively inexpensive and can provide new competitive knowledge. However, it requires clean data, even though it establishes correlations among variables, it cannot necessarily establish cause and effect. Also, it can easily lead to useless insights or overlook insights that are important. Nevertheless, the technology holds considerable promise.

THE COST OF QUALITY

In most firms, cost accounting is an important function. All organizations measure and report costs as a basis for control and improvement. The concept of the **cost of quality (COQ)** emerged in the 1950s. Traditionally, the reporting of quality-related costs had been limited to inspection and testing; other costs were accumulated in overhead accounts. As managers began to define and isolate the full range of quality-related costs, a number of surprising facts emerged.[28] First, quality-related costs were much larger than previously reported, generally in the range of 20 to 40 percent of sales. Second, quality-related costs were not only related to manufacturing operations, but to ancillary services such as purchasing and customer service departments as well. Third, most of the costs resulted from poor quality and were avoidable. Finally, while the costs of poor quality were avoidable, no clear responsibility for action to reduce them was assigned, nor was any structured approach formulated to do so. As a result, many companies began to develop cost of quality programs. The "costs of quality"—or more specifically, the costs of *poor* quality—are those costs associated with avoiding poor quality or those incurred as a result of poor quality.

Juran noted that workers and supervisors speak in the "language of things"—units, defects, and so on. Unfortunately, quality problems expressed as the number of defects typically have little impact on top managers who are generally

> *COQ approaches have numerous objectives, but perhaps the most important one is to translate quality problems into the "language" of upper management—the language of money.*

more concerned with financial performance. But if the magnitude of quality problems can be translated into monetary terms, such as "How much would it cost us to run this business if there were no quality problems?" the eyes of upper managers are opened. Dollar figures can be added meaningfully across departments or products, and compared to other dollar measures. Middle managers, who must deal with both workers and supervisors as well as top management, must have the ability to speak in both languages. Quality cost information serves a variety of other purposes, too. It helps management evaluate the relative importance of quality problems and thus identify major opportunities for cost reduction. It can aid in budgeting and cost control activities. Finally, it can serve as a scoreboard to evaluate the organization's success in achieving quality objectives.

To establish a cost of quality approach, one must identify the activities that generate cost, measure them, report them in a way that is meaningful to managers, and analyze them to identify areas for improvement. The following sections discuss these activities in greater detail.

Quality Cost Classification

Quality costs can be organized into four major categories: prevention costs, appraisal costs, internal failure costs, and external failure costs. **Prevention costs** are investments made to keep nonconforming products from occurring and reaching the customer, including the following specific costs:

- *Quality planning costs*, such as salaries of individuals associated with quality planning and problem-solving teams, the development of new procedures, new equipment design, and reliability studies
- *Process control costs*, which include costs spent on analyzing production processes and implementing process control plans
- *Information systems costs* expended to develop data requirements and measurements

- *Training and general management costs*, including internal and external training programs, clerical staff expenses, and miscellaneous supplies

Appraisal costs are those associated with efforts to ensure conformance to requirements, generally through measurement and analysis of data to detect nonconformances. Categories of appraisal costs include the following:

- *Test and inspection costs* associated with incoming materials, work-in-process, and finished goods, including equipment costs and salaries
- *Instrument maintenance costs* due to calibration and repair of measuring instruments
- *Process measurement and control costs*, which involve the time spent by workers to gather and analyze quality measurements

Internal failure costs are incurred as a result of unsatisfactory quality found before the delivery of a product to the customer; some examples include the following:

- *Scrap and rework costs*, including material, labor, and overhead
- *Costs of corrective action*, arising from time spent determining the causes of failure and correcting production problems
- *Downgrading costs*, such as revenue lost when selling a product at a lower price because it does not meet specifications
- *Process failures*, such as unplanned machine downtime or unplanned equipment repair

External failure costs occur after poor-quality products reach the customer, specifically:

- *Costs due to customer complaints and returns*, including rework on returned items, cancelled orders, and freight premiums
- *Product recall costs* and *warranty claims*, including the cost of repair or replacement as well as associated administrative costs
- *Product liability costs*, resulting from legal actions and settlements

Experts estimate that 60 to 90 percent of total quality costs are the result of internal and external failure and are the responsibility of, but not easily controllable by management. In the past, managers reacted to high failure costs by increasing inspection. Such actions, however, only increase appraisal costs. The overall result is little, if any, improvement in quality or profitability. In practice, an increase in prevention usually generates larger savings in all other cost categories. In a typical scenario, the cost of replacing a poor-quality component in the field might be $500; the cost of replacement after assembly might be $50; the cost of testing and replacement during assembly might be $5; and the cost of changing the design to avoid the problem might be only 50 cents.

Better prevention of poor quality clearly reduces internal failure costs, as fewer defective items are made. External failure costs also decrease. In addition, less appraisal is required, because the products are made correctly the first time. However, because production is usually viewed in the short term, many managers fail to understand or implement these ideas.

A convenient way of reporting quality costs is through a breakdown by organizational function as shown in Figure 8.9. This matrix serves several purposes. First, it allows all departments to recognize their contributions to the cost of quality and participate in a cost of quality program. Second, it pinpoints areas of high quality cost and turns attention toward improvement efforts. Such a report can be implemented easily on a spreadsheet. Quality costs are often reported as an *index*, that is, the ratio of the

Figure 8.9 Cost of Quality Matrix

	Design Engineering	Purchasing	Production	...	Finance	...	Accounting	Totals

Prevention costs
  Quality planning
  Training
  . . .								

Appraisal costs
  Test and inspection
  Instruments
  . . .								

Internal failure costs
  Scrap
  Rework
  . . .								

External failure costs
  Returns
  Recall costs
  . . .								

Totals								

current value to a base period. The Bonus Materials folder for this chapter on the CD-ROM contains further information about computing and using quality cost indexes.

Quality costs in different categories are rarely distributed evenly.

If we rank internal failure costs from largest to smallest, for example, chances are that 70 or 80 percent of all internal failure costs are due to only one or two manufacturing problems. Identifying these "vital few," as they are called, leads to corrective action that has a high return for a low dollar input. This technique, which we will study formally in a later chapter, is called *Pareto analysis*. In this fashion, quality costs can be used to identify trends or areas that require significant attention. For example, a steady rise in internal failure costs and decline in appraisal costs might indicate a problem in assembly, testing equipment maintenance, or a lack of proper control of purchased parts. Of course, such information can only signal areas for improvement; it cannot tell managers what the specific problems are.

For most companies embarking on a quality cost program, management typically finds that the highest costs occur in the external failure category, followed by internal failure, appraisal, and prevention, in that order. Clearly, the order should be reversed; that is, the bulk of quality costs should be found in prevention, some in appraisal, perhaps a small amount in internal failure, and virtually none in external failure. Thus, companies should first attempt to reduce external failure costs to zero by investing in appraisal activities to discover the sources of failure and take corrective action. As quality improves, failure costs will decrease, and the amount of appraisal can be reduced with the shift of emphasis to prevention activities.

Quality Costs in Service Organizations

The nature of quality costs differs between service and manufacturing organizations. Traditional external failure costs such as warranty and field support are less relevant to services than to manufacturing. Process-related costs, such as customer-service and complaint-handling staff and lost customers are more critical.

In manufacturing, quality costs are primarily product-oriented; for services, however, they are generally labor-dependent, with labor often accounting for up to 75 percent of total costs.

Internal failure costs might not be as evident in services as in manufacturing. For example, a small distributor focused a great deal of attention on minimizing inventories while trying to improve service. The company knew that backorders existed, but believed that they were simply the nature of the business. Further analysis revealed nearly one backorder for every five orders. After examining the process, the cost of backorders was determined to be $30 per transaction, for an annual cost of $200,000. The reasons included suppliers not meeting delivery dates, errors in sales orders, and other non-value-added operations.[29] Internal failure costs tend to be much lower for service organizations with high customer contact, which have little opportunity to correct an error before it reaches the customer. By that time, the error becomes an external failure.

Work measurement and sampling techniques are often used extensively to gather quality costs in service organizations. For example, work measurement can be used to determine how much time an employee spends on various quality-related activities. The proportion of time spent multiplied by the individual's salary represents an estimate of the quality cost for that activity. Consumer surveys and other means of customer feedback are also used to determine quality costs for services. In general, however, the intangible nature of the output makes quality cost accounting for services difficult.

Capturing Quality Costs Through Activity-Based Costing[30]

The importance of quality has had a major impact on the role of accounting systems in business. Standard accounting systems are generally able to provide quality cost data for direct labor, overhead, scrap, warranty expenses, product liability costs, and maintenance, repair, and calibration of test equipment. However, most accounting systems are not structured to capture important cost-of-quality information. Costs such as service effort, product design, remedial engineering effort, rework, in-process inspection, and engineering change losses must usually be estimated or collected through special efforts. Some costs due to external failure, such as customer dissatisfaction and future lost revenues, are impossible to estimate accurately. Although prevention costs are the most important, appraisal costs, internal failure, external failure, and prevention costs (in that order) are usually easier to collect.

Traditional accounting systems focused on promoting the efficiency of mass production, particularly production with few standard products and high direct labor. Traditional systems accurately measure the resources that are consumed in proportion to the number of units produced of individual products. Today's products are characterized by much lower direct labor, and many activities that consume resources are unrelated to the volume of units produced. As a result of automation, direct labor typically is only 15 percent of manufacturing cost and can be as low as 5 percent in high-tech industries. Meanwhile, overhead costs have grown to 55 percent or more, and are spread across all products using the same formula. Because of these changes, traditional accounting systems present an inadequate picture of manufacturing efficiency and effectiveness and do a poor job of allocating the expenses of these support resources to individual products. Moreover, they attach no value to such elements as rework or bottlenecks that impede processing. Because these costs are hidden, managers typically have little incentive to cut them.

Activity-based costing organizes information about the work (or activity) that consumes resources and delivers value in a business. People consuming resources in work ultimately achieve the value that customers pay for. Examples of activities might be moving, inspecting, receiving, shipping, and order processing. To get a handle on these activities, cross-functional teams of workers, managers, and clerical employees map each step of every business process using flowcharts. These flowcharts pinpoint the operations that add value and reveal the ones that do not.

Activity-based costing allocates overhead costs to the products and services that use them. Knowing the costs of activities supports efforts to improve processes. Once activities can be traced to individual products or services, then additional strategic information is made available. The effects of delays and inefficiencies become readily apparent. The company can then focus on reducing these hidden costs.

With the new information provided by activity-based costing, managers can make better decisions about product designs, process improvements, pricing, and product mix. Other benefits include the facilitation of continuous improvement activities to reduce overhead costs, and the ease with which relevant costs can be determined. For instance, Caterpillar Inc. used activity-based costing to determine the value of intangibles such as better quality and faster time-to-market to persuade the board to approve a $2 billion modernization effort. LTV incorporated activity-based costing into its Integrated Process Management Methodology.[31] The accounting department supports the manufacturing and other departments by providing information on product costing and operating activities to evaluate performance, identify deficiencies, and assess quality costs arising from internal and external failure of products and customer product requirements. The system helps managers to integrate customer requirements with product improvement strategies.

MEASURING THE RETURN ON QUALITY

Total Quality efforts should lead to the achievement of outstanding business results. However, a successful quality initiative does not guarantee financial success. (Many argue that without it, however, a company will eventually be doomed to failure.) Many companies fail to pay enough attention to the financial returns on quality-related investments. Financial returns not only demonstrate when the efforts are going in the right direction, but can help identify changes and improvements that need to be made before staying on the wrong path too long. For example, AT&T's chairman receives a quarterly report from each business unit that describes quality improvements and their financial impacts.

Traditionally, measuring reductions in quality-related costs through COQ was the principal method of documenting the benefits of quality. However, this approach only focuses on the internal view of quality. More attention is being paid to the external view and accounting for increases in revenues associated with improved quality and customer satisfaction. Balancing quality costs against expected revenue gains has become known as **return on quality (ROQ)**. ROQ is based on four main principles:[32]

- *Quality is an investment*. Thus, it is not fundamentally different from investing in equipment or buildings.

- *Quality efforts must be made financially accountable.* Because businesses evaluate other investments in this way, and quality efforts should be subject to the same types of financial justification.
- *It is possible to spend too much on quality.* Customers might not be willing to pay the premiums associated with higher levels of quality, or the process improvement benefits might not justify the expense.
- *Not all quality expenditures are equally valid.* An improvement in product design or customer response might be much more important from a strategic point of view than improving the capability of a minor process in the manufacturing plant.

The foundation for the approach stems from the model in Chapter 1 (Figure 1.4) relating quality and profitability shown, which proposes that quality improvement leads to financial returns through improvements in customer satisfaction and loyalty. Sophisticated statistical methods are often used to estimate these effects and the financial implications. Thinking of quality as a financially justifiable investment in this fashion is fundamental to project selection in Six Sigma.

ROQ was applied to evaluating a training program to improve customer service skills of branch staff at Chase Manhattan Bank.[33] The intended outcomes of the program included the ability of the branch staff to identify behavior that creates a positive memorable customer experience, analyze interactions with customers, identify what customers want, and understand the nature of caring customer service. By using a test and control group, estimating the net present value of the loss avoided from customers not becoming dissatisfied as a result of the training program, $471,000, and comparing this figure to the net present value of training costs, $326,000, the return on investment was computed to be 44.4 percent. This analysis showed that a systemwide training program would likely be profitable. Results were circulated among Chase managers and the company moved forward with expansion of the training program.

MANAGING INFORMATION AND KNOWLEDGE ASSETS

Simply collecting data is not enough. Companies must ensure that data are valid and accurate, that the hardware and software systems that process the data are reliable, and that data and information are available to all who need them in a timely fashion, and secure from those that should not have access to them.

Data Validity

The familiar computer cliché, "Garbage in, garbage out," applies equally well to organizational performance data. Any measurement is subject to error, and hence the credibility of data can be suspect. *Reliability* of a measurement refers to how well the measuring instrument—manual instruments, automated equipment, or surveys and questionnaires—consistently measures the "true value" of the characteristic. Measurement reliability in manufacturing demands careful attention to *metrology*, the science of measurement. This topic is discussed in Chapter 12 in the context of Six Sigma. A useful approach to ensuring data reliability is for internal cross-functional teams or external auditors to conduct periodic audits of the processes used to collect the data. Standardized forms, clear instructions, and adequate training lead to more consistent performance in data collection. The former AT&T Universal Card Services, for example, used

*Data used for planning and decision making need to be valid and accurate. A measure is **valid** if it measures what it says it measures accurately.*

standard data entry templates and procedures to facilitate the consistency and uniform editing of manually input data. Data collected automatically from interfaces with other systems use standard record formats and edits, and are reconciled at each handoff. Also, a central data dictionary defined critical data elements according to source, meaning, format, and valid content of each. AT&T followed stringent guidelines and standards for developing, maintaining, documenting, and managing data systems.

Like any business process, information creation should be managed with total quality principles.[34] The quality of information can be improved by capturing data only once, and as close to the origin of the data as possible; eliminating human error by capturing data electronically where possible; using a single database whenever feasible; eliminating all unnecessary handling of data by intermediaries, such as data entry clerks; placing accountability on the creators of data and information; ensuring proper training; and defining targets and measures of data quality. Maintaining computer systems, backing up databases, and building error-checking capabilities into software provides added measures for ensuring data and information validity and availability. Frequent computer crashes or network problems can wreak havoc on operations and customer responsiveness.

Data Accessibility and Security

A company's efforts are wasted if collected data are not available to the right employees when needed. A customer service representative who tells a customer that he or she needs to find some information and will call back the next day cannot satisfy that customer in a timely fashion. At Milliken, all databases, including product specifications, process data, supplier data, customer requirements, and environmental data are available to every associate throughout the computer network. Electronic charts displayed throughout the plant and in business support departments show key quality measures and trends. Data accessibility empowers employees and encourages their participation in quality improvement efforts. Figure 8.10 shows how a wide variety of data is made accessible to all stakeholders at Pearl River School District. Sharing data is becoming increasingly important in business networks and supply chains.

Modern information technology plays a critical role in data accessibility. Many companies have state-of-the-art online computer networks supplemented by local processing capabilities. Prudential Insurance Company agents take portable computers to customer's homes or places of business.[35] This practice reduces the time needed to answer a client's questions and increases the accuracy and reliability of the answers. Sales and service offices are connected electronically. Each can obtain information about the current status of contracts being serviced by another office, and thus can be of assistance to customers who contact them directly. They can also electronically forward requests for action to the appropriate office.

In many companies, business information is only accessible to top managers and others on a need-to-know basis. In TQ-focused companies, business information is accessible to everyone.

Wainwright Industries posts all business information—quality, customer satisfaction, and financial performance—in a room accessible to all employees, customers, suppliers, and visitors. Organizations that share results often exhibit better performance because information provides the basis for better decisions, and employees understand why certain decisions are made.

Confidentiality and security are critical in managing data, particularly with the increasing use of electronic data transfer. Using firewalls to prevent external systems attacks and passwords to ensure that only authorized users have access to sensitive

Figure 8.10 Data Accessibility at Pearl River School District

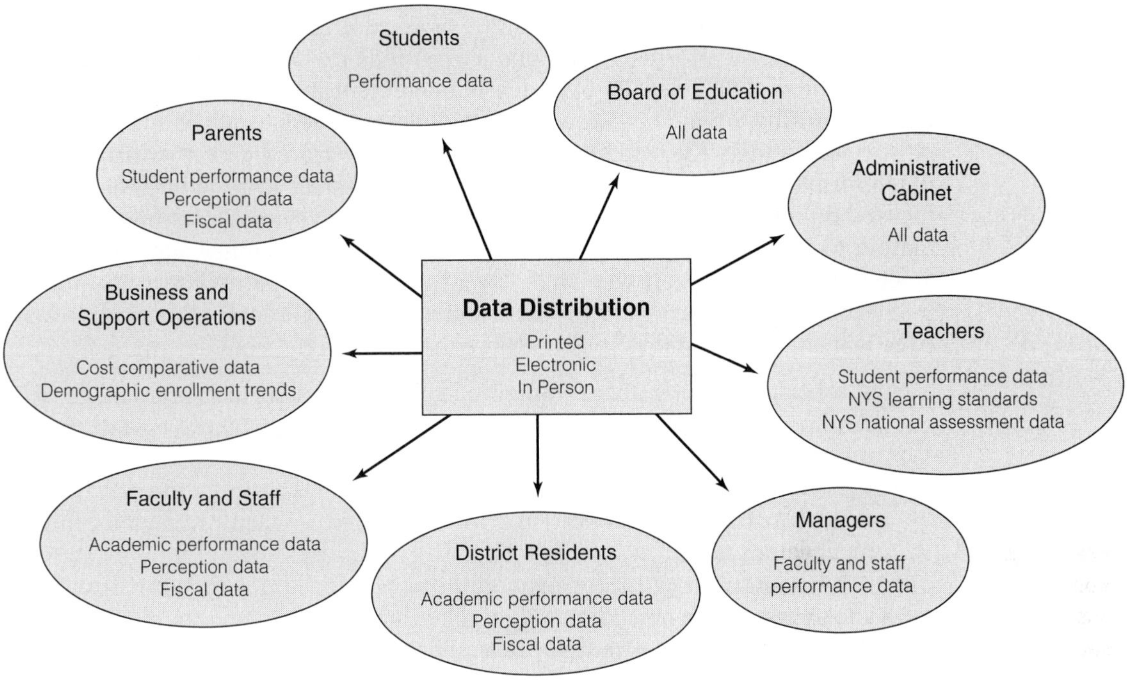

data such as customer records and financial information are vital in an information management system. At Clarke American, for instance, when an associate leaves the company, the Termination Identification Process System (TIPS) automatically notifies Systems Assurance to remove access to all facilities and systems.

Knowledge Management

One Hewlett-Packard manager noted, "The fundamental building material of a modern corporation is knowledge." H. James Harrington observed, "All organizations have it, but most don't know what they know, don't use what they do know and don't reuse the knowledge they have."[36] Knowledge is perishable and if it is not renewed and replenished, it becomes worthless. **Explicit knowledge** includes information stored in documents or other forms of media. **Tacit knowledge** is information that is formed around intangible factors resulting from an individual's experience, and is personal and content-specific. These two aspects represent the "know-how" that an organization has available to use, invest, and grow. Employees, software, patents, databases, documents, guides, policies and procedures, and technical drawings are repositories of an organization's knowledge assets. Customers, suppliers, and partners may also hold key knowledge assets. Knowledge assets have become more important than financial and physical assets in many organizations.

Knowledge assets refer to the accumulated intellectual resources that an organization possesses, including information, ideas, learning, understanding, memory, insights, cognitive and technical skills, and capabilities.

Process improvement requires new knowledge to result in better processes and procedures. Increasing the knowledge of the organization, both in an individual sense as well as for the organization as a whole, is the essence of learning and ties closely to Deming's concept of the theory of knowledge (see Chapter 3). Knowledge can easily be lost if information is not documented or when individuals are promoted or leave the organization. **Knowledge management** involves the process of identifying, capturing, organizing, and using knowledge assets to create and sustain competitive advantage. Knowledge management differs from *information management* in that information management is focused on data whereas knowledge management is focused on information. A knowledge management system allows intangible information to be managed as an organizational asset in a manner similar to tangible assets. Skandia, a large Swedish financial services company, internally audits its intellectual capital every year for inclusion in its annual report. An effective knowledge management system should include the following:

- A way of capturing and organizing explicit as well as tacit knowledge of how the business operates, including an understanding of how current business processes function
- A systems-approach to management that facilitates assimilation of new knowledge into the business system and is oriented toward continuous improvement/innovation
- A common framework for managing knowledge and some way of validating and synthesizing new knowledge as it is acquired
- A culture and values that support collaborative sharing of knowledge across functions and encourages full participation of all employees in the process[37]

A benchmarking study co-sponsored by the American Productivity and Quality Center reported that 79 percent of managers from the 70 responding companies felt that managing organizational knowledge is central to the organization's strategy, but 59 percent stated that their firm was performing this management function poorly or not at all.[38] Also, 88 percent believed that a climate of openness and trust is important for knowledge sharing, but 32 percent of the respondents believed that their organization did not have such a climate. In many companies, the gap was attributed to a lack of commitment to knowledge management on the part of top managers.

The transfer of knowledge within organizations and the identification and sharing of best practices often set high-performing organizations apart from the rest. Many organizations perform similar activities at different locations or by different people. For example, consider a sales organization with district managers spread out over the country, or a clinical research organization that performs research studies for drug companies in a project environment, or a school district with teachers teaching the same subjects at different locations throughout the district. What happens when one individual develops an innovative practice? How is this knowledge shared among others performing similar jobs? In most organizations, the answer is that knowledge is probably never shared.

The ability to identify and transfer best practices within the organization is sometimes called **internal benchmarking**. In this particular area, the most mature organizations may falter, even those that are adept at benchmarking other organizations. The American Productivity and Quality Center (APQC) noted that executives have long felt frustrated by their inability to identify or transfer outstanding practices from one location or function to another. They know that some facilities have superior practices and processes, yet operating units continue to reinvent or ignore solutions and repeat mistakes.[39] Research identified three categories of barriers:

1. Lack of motivation to adopt the practice
2. Inadequate information about how to adapt the practice and make it work
3. Lack of "absorptive capacity," the resources and skill to make and manage the change

APQC suggests that although most people have a natural desire to learn and share their knowledge, organizations have a variety of logistical, structural, and cultural hurdles to overcome, including the following:

- Organizational structures that promote "silo" thinking in which locations, divisions, and functions focus on maximizing their own accomplishments and rewards, or, as Deming called it, "suboptimization"
- A culture that values personal technical expertise and knowledge creation over knowledge sharing
- The lack of contact, relationships, and common perspectives among people who don't work side-by-side
- An overreliance on transmitting "explicit" rather than "tacit" information—the information that people need to implement a practice that cannot be codified or written down
- Not allowing or rewarding people for taking the time to learn and share and help each other outside of their own small corporate village.

Internal benchmarking requires a process: first, identifying and collecting internal knowledge and best practices; second, sharing and understanding those practices; and third, adapting and applying them to new situations and bringing them up to best-practice performance levels.

Technology, culture, leadership, and measurement are enablers that can help or hinder the process. Many organizations create internal databases by which employees can share their practices and knowledge. For example, Texas Instruments has a Best Practices Knowledge Base delivered via Lotus Notes, Intranet, and TI's network systems. Information is often organized around business core and support processes. Cultural issues include how to motivate and reward people for sharing best practices and establishing a supportive culture. As with any TQ effort, senior leadership must take an active role by tying initiatives to the company's vision and strategy, communicating success stories at executive meetings, removing implementation barriers, reinforcing and rewarding positive behaviors, leading by example, and communicating the importance of best practice sharing with all employees. Finally, measuring the frequency of use and satisfaction with best-practice databases, linking practices to financial and customer satisfaction, focusing on cycle time to implement best practices, and measuring the growth of virtual teams that share information are ways in which the organization can monitor the effectiveness of their approaches.

One example of an internal best practice learning process is Royal Mail, the largest business unit within the Post Office Group in the United Kingdom (UK), which handles an average of 64 million letters per day using approximately 160,000 people at 1,900 operational sites throughout the UK.[40] Each potential good practice (a term used to recognize that a practice may not be the best, but is good enough to provide significant performance gains) requires formalized documentation that includes a description of the practice; names and telephone numbers of the contacts; date; process diagram; description of the major steps, who performs them, and what is needed to do the work; implementation resources; and risks and barriers. These good practice descriptions are scrutinized by a panel for evaluation of their potential for transferability to other parts of the business. The panel characterizes the good practice as either mandatory, where all units and staff are required to adopt it, or recommended, where application is optional, depending on local conditions. Royal Mail uses six measurements for evaluating its approach:

1. The number of potential national good practices reaching national process groups
2. The proportion of national good practices becoming confirmed good practices
3. The extent of implementation
4. The cycle time from first submission to entry in the national database
5. The benefit gained compared to the anticipated benefit
6. Satisfaction from members of the national and business unit process groups

MEASUREMENT AND INFORMATION MANAGEMENT IN THE BALDRIGE CRITERIA, ISO 9000, AND SIX SIGMA

Category 4 of the 2003 Malcolm Baldrige National Quality Award Criteria for Performance Excellence is titled *Measurement, Analysis, and Knowledge Management.* This category is positioned as the foundation for all other categories in the systems framework that underlies the Baldrige philosophy and provides a key feedback structure linking business results. This category examines how an organization selects, gathers, analyzes, manages, and improves its data, information, and knowledge assets. Item 4.1, *Measurement and Analysis of Organizational Performance,* focuses on the major components of an effective performance measurement system. It addresses an organization's selection, management, and use of data and information for performance measurement and analysis in support of organizational planning and performance improvement. The criteria ask how an organization gathers and integrates data and information for monitoring daily operations and supporting organizational decision making, and how measures are selected and used. The criteria also ask how an organization selects and uses comparative data and information to support operational and strategic decision making and innovation. In addition, the criteria asks what analyses are used to support senior leaders' assessment of overall organizational performance and strategic planning, how results are communicated throughout the organization, and how the performance measurement system is kept current with changing business needs and directions.

Item 4.2, *Information and Knowledge Management,* looks at how an organization ensures the availability of high-quality, timely data and information for all key users—employees, suppliers and partners, and customers. This process includes ensuring that data, information, and organizational knowledge possess all the characteristics that users expect: integrity, reliability, accuracy, timeliness, and appropriate levels of security and confidentiality. In addition, the criteria ask how an organization ensures that hardware systems and software are reliable, secure, and user-friendly so that access is facilitated and encouraged. It also addresses how an organization builds and manages its knowledge assets to improve organizational efficiency, effectiveness, and innovation by capturing, protecting, and disseminating organizational knowledge.

ISO 9000:2000 provides a basic framework for managing data and information. The document and data control requirements of ISO 9000 require companies to define a process for ensuring that any critical information that is required for the performance of a business process is accurate, up-to-date, and effective for its intended purpose. Because ISO 9000 places an emphasis on processes that, in many cases are cross-functional, it forces companies to break down some of the organizational and functional silos that inhibit effective sharing of information.[41]

The measurement, analysis, and improvement requirements of ISO 9000:2000 deal with the measurement of product and process characteristics, performance of the quality system, and search for continuous improvement, requiring that management make decisions based on analysis and trends of product and process performance indicators, internal auditing, and customer feedback. Specific requirements include the following:

- Establishing, planning, and implementing measurement, monitoring, and improvement activities
- Monitoring information about customer satisfaction as a performance metric
- Establishing measurement and monitoring methods to assure that product and process requirements are attained
- Acquiring and analyzing data to determine improvement effectiveness
- Promoting continuous improvement using auditing reports, data analysis, and management reviews

Using a balanced scorecard approach or the Baldrige measurement framework can clearly provide the foundation for meeting these requirements for firms that pursue ISO 9000.

Six Sigma emphasizes fact-based decisions and provides organizations with tools to generate measurable results from Six Sigma projects. Six Sigma methodology requires measuring and reporting performance goals, and using performance indicators to control and sustain improvements. Project selection is based on understanding the financial as well as the nonfinancial benefits to the organization, such as cost savings, increased sales, reduced cycle times, or improved customer satisfaction. Thus, measurements are vital in "selling" Six Sigma projects to top management.

Six Sigma can have a significant impact on the cost of quality because of its focus on financial return; in fact, one survey observed that the top three measures used to quantify Six Sigma success are cost takeout, productivity, and revenue generation.[42] Many Six Sigma projects focus on reducing the costs of poor quality that result from low sigma levels of performance, and improved designs that will increase customer satisfaction and hence, revenue. The different categories of the cost of quality described earlier in this chapter provide many opportunities for Six Sigma projects. For example, a company might identify all costs that would vanish if sigma performance levels were increased. The list might include costs associated with credits given to customers because of late delivery, billing errors, scrap and rework, unplanned downtime, extra inventory to buffer against defects, errors in specifications and drawings, and accounts payable mistakes. Quantifying these costs establishes the justification for Six Sigma projects. Six Sigma projects can also be categorized in different levels, based upon their impact on results:[43]

1. Level 1 projects directly affect an organization's profit margin (projects have a clear, hard dollar impact on profitability).
2. Level 2 projects result in redeployment of resources inside an organization to increase operating efficiency or productivity.
3. Level 3 projects directly affect operations by avoiding expenditures or increasing the chances of obtaining higher future revenues.

QUALITY IN PRACTICE

KNOWLEDGE MANAGEMENT FOR CONTINUOUS IMPROVEMENT AT CONVERGYS[44]

Convergys Corporation (NYSE: CVG), a member of the S&P 500 and the *Forbes* Platinum 400, is the global leader in integrated billing, employee care, and customer care services provided through outsourcing or licensing. Convergys serves top companies in telecommunications, Internet, cable and broadband services, technology, financial services, and other industries in more than 40 countries, and also provides integrated, outsourced, human resource services to leading companies across a broad range of industries. Convergys software processes more than 1.5 million individual bills each day to support more than 120 million subscribers, and manages more than 1.7 million separate customer and employee contacts, both live and via electronic interaction. Convergys employs more than 48,000 people in 48 customer contact centers, data centers, and other offices in the United States, Canada, Latin America, Europe, the Middle East, and Asia. Convergys is on the Internet at http://www.convergys.com, and has world headquarters in Cincinnati.

The outsourced customer service industry is maturing rapidly, is extremely dynamic, and the environment continues to become more and more complex. Some factors contributing to this situation include consolidation of providers, stiff price competition, and new competition from both the expansion to offshore markets such as India and the Philippines as well as traditional systems integrators who are further penetrating the business process outsourcing (BPO) market. In addition, Convergys is a fairly young organization, having grown through a series of acquisitions that number more than 20 in the last 20 years. This high number of mergers created a unique challenge as cultures collided and as employees were challenged to integrate the myriad of processes, procedures, and systems. With this environment and the expectations of clients, shareholders and employees to constantly improve, Convergys developed a vision: "To establish a high performance culture focused on continuously improving the value we provide to our clients, shareholders and employees."

To deploy continuous improvement (CI) as a

key part of the company's culture and achieve this vision, Convergys followed a two-step approach:

1. Establish leadership support and financial relevance.
2. Support and encourage total participation—establish CI as part of everyone's job.

First, they built leadership support by linking CI to important business initiatives in a highly visible way. With this strong foundation, they turned more attention to getting all employees involved in improving the business. To accomplish this goal, Convergys needed a tool to help facilitate sharing and accelerating improvement efforts. The tool they chose was a Web-based employee intranet that called the CI Portal (see Figure 8.11).

The CI Portal provides an infrastructure for companywide knowledge management activities. One of the primary ways employees use it is to submit, track, and manage improvement efforts (see Figure 8.12). Additionally all improvement efforts and success stories from throughout the organization can be assessed through the CI Portal. Since its inception in the fourth quarter of 2000, more than 24,00 improvement efforts have been submitted in the pipeline, 300 of which were completed, successful improvements by mid-2003.

Convergys also introduced a Best Practices Knowledgebase to the CI Portal (see Figure 8.13). The purpose of the knowledge base is to encourage and facilitate the sharing of best practices that improve the value of services provided to their clients. Furthermore, through this knowledge base, best practices can be adopted and leveraged across the organization. To facilitate the sharing of knowledge across the organization, the knowledge base was designed to make it easy to record a best practice in a consistent format that makes it understood by others with little difficulty. Additionally, best practices are categorized in a way that makes it easy to find those that are relevant to a diverse set of needs. To ensure the ongoing credibility of the Best Practices Knowledgebase, a potential best practice is reviewed and endorsed before it can be designated as a best practice. Once the proper documentation is in

Figure 8.11 Convergys CI Portal

place, the potential best practice is forwarded to a vice president deemed to be a subject matter expert in the area of the idea. The VP is asked to review the practice and decide whether its use should be encouraged across the organization. The VP then designates the practice as a Best Practice.

Another reason employees go to the CI Portal is to access resources to help them facilitate or accelerate improvement efforts. More than 40 specific improvement tools that are accessible through the CI Portal support their standard improvement

methodology, which is referred to as The Improvement Process or TIP. Figure 8.14 shows TIP as accessed in the CI Portal. For each step of TIP, CI Tools are identified that support that step.

CI Tools are approaches, tips, and techniques that facilitate problem solving and making improvements. CI Tools are basically proven methods that assist in making fact-based decisions. CI Tools can be used in a variety of ways. Independently, each tool can help to solve a common business issue. CI Tools also support a

Figure 8.12 Process for Submitting and Managing Improvement Efforts

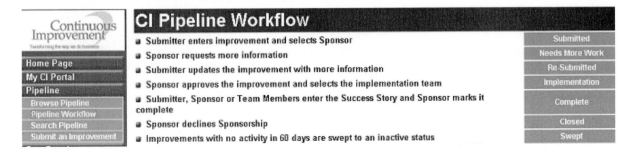

Figure 8.13 Example of Best Practice Knowledgebase

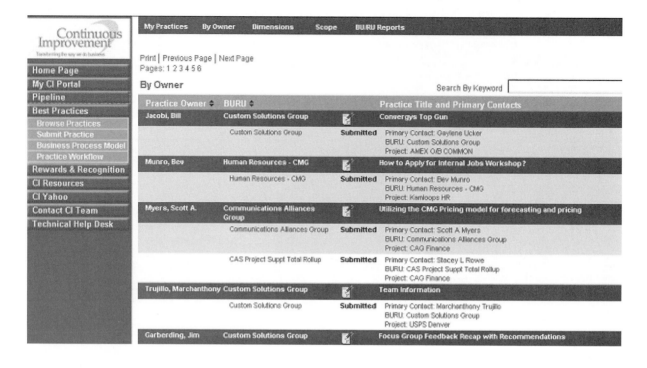

Figure 8.14 The Improvement Process (TIP)

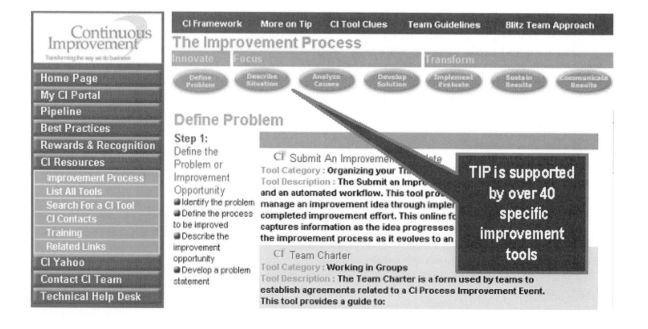

structured improvement effort. CI Tools are documented in the CI Portal in a simple, consistent, easy-to-use format. Figure 8.15 shows a short list of the types of tools included in the CI Portal as well as the consistent format.

Access to TIP and CI tools through the CI Portal provides an ongoing source of continual training for employees on an as-needed basis and a way to refresh and reinforce continuous improvement approaches. Additionally, self-paced training modules have been developed specifically for CI and the CI Portal and are available to all employees to augment learning and personal development. Examples of the self-paced courses including the following:

- Driving Improvements with the CI Portal
- Accelerating Improvements with TIP and CI Tools
- Improving Business Processes

Continuous improvement (CI) is an integral part of Convergys's culture and its value proposition. Through CI, Convergys has been able to generate significant financial benefits, such as maintaining higher profit margins than its competition. In 2002 alone, more than 2,000 management employees (or 45 percent of management) were directly involved in CI activities. In a 24-month period, more than 2,400 improvement ideas were submitted. Furthermore, thousands more embraced the CI culture. Several clients also acknowledged their approach to continuous improvement as a point of differentiation.

CI and the uses of the CI Portal keep expanding. The focus will continue to be on how employees can be better equipped to facilitate making their own improvements. Additionally, Convergys continues to learn how to most effectively leverage the knowledge and experience of its employees through the sharing of success stories and best practices, and, in the process, strengthen CI as a competitive advantage.

Key Issues for Discussion

1. How does Convergys's CI Portal help to align improvement ideas and projects with the firm's strategic goals?
2. What is the specific process used to take employees' ideas from the concept stage to the "best practice" stage?
3. How are the best practices and tools used to promote learning and develop a knowledge-based organization via the CI Portal?

Figure 8.15 CI Tools

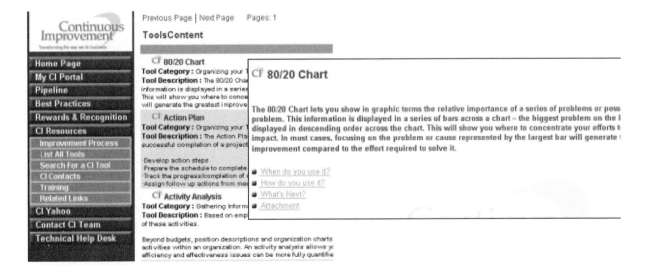

QUALITY IN PRACTICE

MODELING CAUSE-AND-EFFECT RELATIONSHIPS AT IBM ROCHESTER[45]

IBM's AS/400 Division in Rochester, Minnesota, winner of the 1990 Malcolm Baldrige National Quality Award, struggled with the dilemma of having a wealth of information and a plethora of measurements without understanding which factors have the greatest impact on overall business performance. To better ascertain which factors were most critical, IBM initiated a study to determine whether any relationships existed among the numerous measurements. Interviews with division managers identified measurements they felt were most important. A list of more than 50 key measurements was considered. This list included traditional measurements such as market share, overall customer satisfaction, employee morale, job satisfaction, warranty costs, inventory costs, product scrap, and productivity.

The key measurements were defined in three general areas: business-related, such as revenue and productivity; quality-related, such as customer satisfaction and warranty costs; and people-related, such as employee satisfaction and morale. Customer satisfaction data were derived from customer satisfaction surveys of AS/4000 customers and measured the percentage of customers responding

satisfied or very satisfied on five-point-scale surveys. Employee satisfaction data were derived from an annual survey of AS/400 division employees. An unweighted index represented the percentage of employees responding favorably to a set of survey questions. These survey questions, among other things, addressed employees' satisfaction with their job, their immediate manager, and their level of skills. Productivity was computed as the measurement of revenue produced per number of employees, calculated on an annual basis. Quality is reflected by the cost of quality. Although numerous measurements of the cost of quality included scrap and rework expenses, warranty costs (expenses) had the highest correlation to the other measurements used in this study. Warranty costs include labor, parts, and service expended during the warranty period of an AS/400. An aggregate of both hardware and software maintenance and service was used in this calculation to represent the total required costs associated with servicing an AS/400 at a customer's location, including replacement costs. Warranty cost per employee is calculated on an annual basis.

Table 8.2 IBM AS/400 Division Data 1984–1994

	Market Share	Customer Satisfaction	Productivity	Cost of Quality	Employee Satisfaction	Job Satisfaction	Manager	Satisfaction with Right Skills
Market Share	1.00	0.71	0.97	−0.86	0.84	0.84	—	0.97
Customer Satisfaction	0.71	1.00	—	−0.79	0.70	—	—	0.72
Productivity	0.97	—	1.00	—	0.93	0.92	0.86	0.98
Cost of Quality	−0.86	−0.79	—	1.00	—	—	—	—
Employee Satisfaction	0.84	0.70	0.93	—	1.00	0.92	0.92	0.86
Job Satisfaction	0.84	—	0.92	—	0.92	1.00	0.70	0.84
Satisfaction with Manager	—	—	0.86	—	0.92	0.70	1.00	0.92
Right Skills	0.97	0.72	0.98	—	0.86	0.84	0.92	1.00

Using 10 years of data, the researchers identified a strong correlation among market share, customer satisfaction, productivity, warranty cost, and employee satisfaction. Table 8.2 shows those measurements that have a correlation equal to or greater than 0.7. Figure 8.16 shows a model that describes the cause-and-effect relationship among the factors (only those measurements with a correlation factor equal to or greater than 0.7 are shown). This model suggests that to improve employee satisfaction, a manager must focus on improving job satisfaction, satisfaction with management, and satisfaction with having the right skills for the job. To improve job satisfaction, a manager must focus on improving satisfaction with management and satisfaction with having the right skills for the job. Improving satisfaction with having the right skills for the job will improve employee satisfaction and job satisfaction and will positively impact productivity, market share, and customer satisfaction. Improving employee satisfaction will directly impact productivity and customer satisfaction and will decrease warranty costs. Decreasing warranty costs will directly impact customer satisfaction and market share. Improving customer satisfaction will directly impact market share.

The study was not meant to explore every possible impact or relationship between operational measurements. However, it does suggest the need to take an enterprise view of measurements and understand the impact of one measurement on another. Most organizations are hierarchical and functionally oriented. Typically, customer satisfaction, employee satisfaction, quality, and productivity are each managed by a different group. Therefore, analyses and decisions are generally performed by each separate group without consideration for overall integration among these measurements. Additionally, reviews of these measurements are typically done through separate meetings or reports. A company needs to understand these relationships and review the measurements in aggregate. Otherwise, actions may be taken that have the opposite desired outcome on upstream results. For instance, if an action is taken that impacts employee satisfaction such as a layoff, the company must consider counteractions to prevent a decline in productivity, customer satisfaction, and market share.

Key Issues for Discussion

1. Explain why the relationships shown in Figure 8.16 make sense in theory.
2. Can these results apply to other businesses? Why or why not?

Figure 8.16 The Relationship Between Market Share, Customer Satisfaction, Productivity, Cost of Quality, and Employee Satisfaction

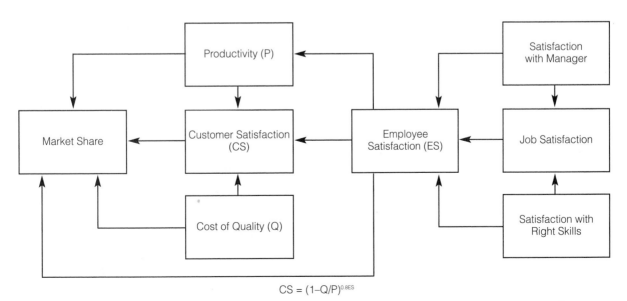

$$CS = (1-Q/P)^{0.8ES}$$

REVIEW QUESTIONS

1. Define measurement.
2. Explain the difference between measures and indicators.
3. Why do organizations need performance measures?
4. Explain the use of data and information at the "three levels of quality" in an organization.
5. What are the benefits of good data and information systems?
6. Summarize the leading practices related to data and information management.
7. What is the balanced scorecard? Describe its four components.
8. Explain the difference between leading and lagging measures. How are they used within a balanced scorecard?
9. What are the six key categories of results measures in the Malcolm Baldrige Criteria? Provide examples of measurements and indicators in each category.
10. Explain the types of measures commonly used for product and service quality.
11. What is the role of comparative data in a performance measurement system?
12. What two fundamental mistakes do organizations frequently make about measurement?
13. Explain the importance and utility of linking performance measures to strategy.
14. What do we mean by the term *actionable* in reference to measures and indicators?
15. Describe the process of defining process-level measurements.
16. Why are cost of quality programs valuable to managers?
17. List and explain the four major categories of quality costs. Give examples of each.
18. Discuss how index numbers are often used to analyze quality cost data.
19. How do quality costs differ between service and manufacturing organizations?
20. How does activity-based costing facilitate the acquisition of quality cost data?
21. What do we mean by validity and reliability of data? Why are these concepts important?
22. What is return on quality (ROQ)? Why is it a useful approach for organizations?
23. Why is accessibility of data important? How does information technology improve accessibility?
24. Describe ways by which data can be analyzed to generate useful managerial information?
25. What is interlinking? Provide an example.
26. How is information and analysis addressed in the Baldrige criteria, ISO 9000:2000, and Six Sigma?

DISCUSSION QUESTIONS

1. Classify the measurements described in Figure 8.3 into one of the "three levels of quality": organization, process, and individual performer.
2. Under which perspective of the balanced scorecard would you classify each of the following measurements?
   a. On-time delivery to customers
   b. Time to develop the next generation of products
   c. Manufacturing yield
   d. Engineering efficiency
   e. Quarterly sales growth

   f. Percent of products that equal 70 percent of sales

   g. Cash flow

   h. Number of customer partnerships

   i. Increase in market share

   j. Unit cost of products

3. Many "course and instructor evaluation" systems consist of inappropriate or ineffective measurements. Discuss how the principles in this chapter can be used to develop an effective measurement system for instructor performance.

4. How can measurement be used to control and improve the daily operations of your college or university?

5. What types of performance measurements might be used by a fraternity or student organization?

6. In making cheese, companies test milk for somatic cell count to prevent diseases. They also test for bacteria to determine how clean the milk is, and perform a freezing-point test to see whether the milk was diluted with water (milk with water in it freezes at a lower temperature, which increases production costs because all the excess water must be extracted). Final cheese products are subjected to tests for weight, presence of foreign elements or chemicals, and for taste and smell. What customer-related measures might interlink with these internal measures?

7. What information would you need to fully answer the questions that IBM Rochester uses for selecting measures and indicators? Where would you get this information?

8. Discuss what the different categories of quality costs might mean to your college and university. How can they be measured?

9. Many quality experts such as Joseph Juran and Philip Crosby advocate cost-of-quality evaluations. Deming, however, states that "the most important figures are unknown and unknowable." How can these conflicting opinions be resolved?

10. Should a quality department have to cost-justify an expensive piece of measuring equipment based on a return on quality argument, or should the department manager simply point to "increased competition" as justification?

11. Using information you learned in prior courses in statistics or quantitative methods, discuss some analytical approaches that organizations can use for analyzing performance data.

12. How does the adoption of a Six Sigma approach within an organization change the amount and types of data that may be gathered routinely, as well as for specific projects?

 ## PROBLEMS

(See the Bonus Materials folder for this chapter for information about analyzing quality costs.)

1. Derecho Inventions, which designs prototype components for the telecom industry has begun a quality program. About a year ago, for the first time, they began to measure quality costs. They were so shocked by their initial figure of 60 percent internal and external failure costs that they immediately launched a Six Sigma quality improvement effort. The percentage of total quality costs recently, after six months of improvements for the firm, are distributed as follows:

Prevention	20%
Appraisal	33%
Internal failure	32%
External failure	15%

What conclusions can you reach from these data?

2. Analyze the following cost data. What percent of sales are each category of cost? What are the implications of these data for management?

	Product		
	A	**B**	**C**
Total sales	$1,537,280	$ 933,600	$1,397,120
Total quality costs as % of sales	21%	18%	12%
External failure	**35%**	**25%**	**13%**
Internal failure	**52%**	**30%**	**37%**
Appraisal	**12%**	**42%**	**35%**
Prevention	**1%**	**3%**	**15%**

Note: Bold figures represent percentages of quality costs by product.

3. Analyze the following cost data. What are the implications of these data for management? Chart these data. Calculate the quality indexes as a relationship to the cost of sales. How do these data differ from those given in problem 2?

	Product B		
	1 Qtr	2 Qtr	3 Qtr
Total sales	$1,000,000	$900,000	$1,200,000
Quality Categories as a Percent of Quality Cost			
External failure	**25%**	**15%**	**10%**
Internal failure	**30%**	**30%**	**25%**
Appraisal	**42%**	**45%**	**40%**
Prevention	**3%**	**10%**	**25%**
Total quality costs	$210,000	$162,000	$144,000

Note: Bold figures represent percentages of quality costs by product.

4. Compute a sales dollar base index for Midwest Sales, Inc., to analyze the following quality cost information, and prepare a memo to management.

	Quarterly Costs (in thousands of dollars)			
	1	2	3	4
Total sales	4,120.0	4,206.0	4,454.0	4,106.0
External failure	280.8	208.2	142.8	128.6
Internal failure	468.2	372.4	284.4	166.4
Appraisal	194.2	227.7	274.4	266.2
Prevention	28.4	29.2	50.2	80.2
Total quality costs	971.6	837.5	751.8	641.4

5. D.B. Smith Company recycles computers. It buys and salvages parts and materials from obsolete systems. It considers that it has done a "quality" job if it can salvage 60 percent of the "book value" of equipment that it buys. The book value of a particular lot that it bought was $1,700,000. What conclusions can be drawn from the following cost data incurred in processing the lot? Customer returns are simply scrapped and replaced. Be sure and specify your assumptions about categories of quality costs.

Cost Category	Amount
Quality equipment design	$ 25,000
Scrap	330,000
Inspection and retest	340,000
Customer returns	90,000
Supplier quality surveys	8,000
Repair	80,000

6. Analyze the following cost data. What are the implications of these data for management?

How do these data differ from those in problem 3?

	Product		
	A	B	C
Total sales	$2,500,000	$1,800,000	$2,600,000
Quality cost as a % of sales	30	20	25
External failure	**42%**	**20%**	**15%**
Internal failure	**45%**	**25%**	**30%**
Appraisal	**12%**	**52%**	**40%**
Prevention	**1%**	**3%**	**15%**

Note: Bold figures represent percentages of quality costs by product.

7. Compute a labor cost base index for Miami Valley Steel Co. to analyze the following quality cost information and prepare a memo to management.

	Quarterly Costs (in thousands of dollars)			
	1	2	3	4
External failure	1000	900	950	725
Internal failure	3500	3250	3000	2200
Appraisal	900	1200	1150	860
Prevention	400	500	550	800
Total Quality Cost	5800	5850	5650	4585
Total Labor Cost	19500	19000	21000	19000

8. Prepare a graph or chart showing the different quality cost categories and percentages for the Great Plates Printing Company.

Cost Element	Amount
Customer complaint remakes	$ 28,000
Printing plate revisions	28,000
Quality improvement projects	14,000
Gauging	100,000
Other waste	39,000
Correction of typographical errors	210,000
Proofreading	450,000
Quality planning	57,000
Press downtime	285,000
Bindery waste	53,000
Checking and inspection	42,000

9. Jeans Are Us, Inc., operates a distribution center in Cincinnati where it receives and breaks down bulk orders from suppliers' factories, and ships out products to retail customers. Prepare a graph or chart showing the different quality cost categories and percentages for the company's quality costs that were incurred over the past year.

Cost Element	Amount
Checking outbound boxes for errors	$710,000
Quality planning	10,000
Downtime due to conveyor/computer problems	405,000
Packaging waste	75,000
Incoming product inspection	60,000
Customer complaint rework	40,000
Correcting erroneous orders before shipping	40,000
Quality training of associates	30,000
Quality improvement projects	20,000
Other waste	55,000
Correction of typographical errors—pick tickets	10,000

10. The following cost of quality data were collected at the installment loan department of the Edison Bank. Classify these data into the appropriate cost of quality categories and analyze the results. What suggestions would you make to management?

Loan Processing

1. Run credit checks:	$ 2675.01
2. Review documents:	3,000.63
3. Make document corrections; gather additional information:	1,032.65
4. Prepare tickler file; review and follow up on titles, insurance, second meetings:	155.75
5. Review all output:	2,243.62
6. Correct rejects and incorrect output:	425.00
7. Reconcile incomplete collateral report:	78.34
8. Handle dealer problem calls; address associate problems; research and communicate information:	2,500.00
9. Compensate for system downtime:	519.01
10. Conduct training:	1,500.00

Loan Payment

1. Receive, inspect, and process payments:	800.00
2. Respond to inquiries when no coupon is presented with payments:	829.65

Loan Payoff

1. Receive, inspect, and process payoff and release documents:	224.99
2. Research payoff problems:	15.35

11. Given the following cost elements, determine the total percentage in each of the four major quality cost categories for the HiTeck Tool Company.

Cost Element	Amount
Incoming test and inspection	$ 7,500
Scrap	35,000
Quality training	0
Inspection	25,000
Test	5,000
Adjustment cost of complaints	21,250
Quality audits	2,500
Maintenance of tools and dies	9,200
Quality control administration	5,000
Laboratory testing	1,250
Design of quality assurance equipment	1,250

Cost Element (continued)	Amount
Material testing and inspection	$ 1,250
Rework	70,000
Quality problem-solving by product engineers	11,250
Inspection equipment calibration	2,500
Writing procedures and instructions	2,500
Laboratory services	2,500
Rework due to vendor faults	17,500
Correcting imperfections	6,250
Setup for test and inspection	10,750
Formal complaints to vendors	10,000

12. Use Pareto analysis to investigate the following quality losses at Oakton Paper Mill. What conclusions do you reach?

Category	Annual Loss
Downtime	$ 28,000
Testing costs	14,000
Rejected paper	375,000
Odd lot	70,000
Excess inspection	21,000
Customer complaints	105,000
High material costs	39,000
Quality improvement training	8,000

13. Use Pareto analysis to investigate the following quality losses at Beecom Software Corp. What conclusions do you reach?

Category	Annual Loss
Rework costs	$ 30,000
Rejected disks (loaded)	360,000
Rejected disks (blank)	89,000
Inspection costs (extra)—incoming	18,000
Inspection costs (extra)—outgoing	28,000
Customer returns	185,000
Training and system improvement costs	67,000
System downtime	138,000

14. National Computer Repairs, Inc., has a thriving business repairing and upgrading computers. The following are costs of quality that they collected over the past year. Use Pareto analysis to investigate their quality losses and to suggest which areas they should address first in an effort to improve their quality.

Category	Annual Loss
Customer returns	$120,000
Inspection costs—outgoing	35,000
Inspection costs—incoming	15,000
Workstation downtime	50,000
Training/system improvement	30,000
Rework costs	50,000

15. Excelsior Inn, a medium-sized hotel (approximately 450 rooms) gathered a considerable amount of data with which to estimate its return on quality. The site manager wants to determine what the return would be if she invested in additional service. Her evidence indicates that additional effort in making sure that

rooms (in particular, the bathrooms) are clean will result in increases in market share, which can easily be translated into dollars of profit. In the following table are data taken from a pilot study where various amounts of additional labor, above the present standard, were applied to room cleaning. These data are expressed in annual dollar amounts, based on wages and fringe benefits of current employees servicing the rooms. Customers who stayed in those rooms were then surveyed to determine their levels of satisfaction/dissatisfaction. Analysts then matched percentages of dissatisfied customers with the annual dollars of improvement efforts from the study.

a. Using linear regression (for example, the Data Analysis tool or Add Trendline option in Excel), determine the equation that can be used to estimate the reduction in customer dissatisfaction, based on additional cleaning effort. What would be the appropriate level of effort to apply, based on your calculations?

b. If each point of market share increase brings in approximately $600,000 of profit per year, and the cost per year is your suggested investment in improvement from part (a). What would be the return on quality (improvement), based on a three year discounted cash flow at 10 percent of the investment costs, if the site manager estimated that she could realize a 2.5 percent increase in market share?

| Excelsior Inn | Return on Quality |
Service Improvement Investment (in thousands of dollars)	Percent of Customers Dissatisfied
0	0.200
50	0.150
150	0.100
260	0.076
290	0.067
300	0.059
450	0.052
600	0.045
750	0.040
900	0.035
1050	0.031
1200	0.027
1350	0.024
1500	0.021
1650	0.017
1800	0.014
1950	0.010
2100	0.007

16. The Herzberg company has collected information about customer behavior and lost sales as a result of service problems. They estimate that, given the current level of service and historical data on complaints, the company will lose a total of 900,000 sales from customers who experience problems over a five-year period.

a. At an average of $20 profit per sale, what is the average lost profit per year?

b. Suppose the company can reduce its annual number of lost sales by 10 percent by investing $300,000 to enhance its service through training and better technology. How much profit can be earned as a result? What is the return on this quality investment?

PROJECTS, ETC.

1. Interview managers at a local airline, hospital, governmental agency, or police department to determine what types of performance measures or indicators they use. Can you construct a balanced scorecard for them?
2. Many restaurants and hotels use "tabletop" customer satisfaction surveys. Find several of these from local businesses. What internal performance indicators might be good leading indicators for the customer satisfaction items in the surveys?
3. Interview managers at a local company to identify the key factors that drive their business. What performance measures or indicators does the company use? Are these indicators consistent with their business factors?
4. Interview managers at a local company to determine which, if any, of the leading practices described in this chapter they follow. What advice would you give them?
5. Using as many measures in Figure 8.3 as you can, draw a diagram similar (but with more detail) to the IBM Rochester model in Figure 8.2 showing leading/lagging and cause-and-effect relationships among these measures.
6. Interview some local quality or production managers to determine whether their companies conduct cost-of-quality evaluations. If they do, how do they use the information? What types of quality costs do they measure?
7. Design a spreadsheet template for conducting quality cost analyses and apply it to problems in this chapter.
8. Interview Black Belts or Project Champions in an organization that has adopted a Six Sigma approach. Discuss their requirements for data and find out how easy or difficult it is to gather the data needed to support their teams and recommendations to management.

CASES

Additional cases, including Baldrige assessment cases, are available in the Bonus Materials Folder on the CD-ROM.

I. COYOTE COMMUNITY COLLEGE

Coyote Community College is a comprehensive, two-year public college that serves and strengthens the greater Albuquerque, New Mexico, community by providing postsecondary education and learning opportunities to all who want to identify and develop their abilities and interests. Since 1968, Coyote's programs and services have been providing accessible, affordable, high-quality higher education opportunities in a learning environment that encourages challenging, innovative teaching methods and delivery systems that enhance student learning.

Coyote is a commuter college with a main campus in downtown Albuquerque and two branch campuses: one located in Bernalillo, 20 miles north of Albuquerque, and the other in Armijo, southeast of downtown Albuquerque. The campus in Albuquerque accounts for 44 percent of Coyote's enrollment, the Bernalillo campus accounts for 25 percent, and the Armijo campus accounts for 31 percent.

Coyote's innovative, community-centered educational programs are designed to meet a variety of academic, career, and personal educational goals.

Program offerings fall into one of three general areas: (1) General Education, University Transfer Education, and Developmental Education; (2) Workforce Development, Certificate Programs, and Continuing Education; and (3) Community Education and Outreach. The majority of these programs lead to the award of diplomas, degrees, or certificates. Coyote also provides high-quality student support services and resources in collaboration with community agencies to enable students to formulate their goals and pursue them realistically. These services include academic and occupational counseling, job and educational placement services, assistance in obtaining financial aid, and special needs programs.

Programs and offerings in the area of General Education, University Transfer Education, and Developmental Education enable students to achieve academic and personal goals, enter the job market, or, in some cases, to successfully transfer to four-year colleges and universities. Coyote offers Associate of Arts (AA) degrees in liberal arts, business administration, education, hotel and restaurant management, computer science, pre-engineering, and biological sciences. AA degrees are intended for students transferring to four-year colleges and universities such that no remedial coursework is required upon transfer. Occupational programs in technical, vocational, and paraprofessional fields lead to an Associate of Science (AS) degree or a certificate. Occupational programs also provide retraining and upgrading of skills in these fields so that students are qualified to meet current needs of the labor market. AS degrees are generally not intended for transfer to four-year institutions. Students who do transfer with AS degrees are required to take additional remedial courses as required by each specific degree program. Students may select from 30 occupational programs, including computer technology, computer applications, day care management, nursing, retailing, computer-aided design/computer-aided manufacturing (CAD/CAM), graphic design technology, biotechnology, heating-ventilating-air conditioning (HVAC), hydrological technology, and contract administration.

In the area of Developmental Education, Coyote offers General Education Development (GED) preparation courses, courses in English as a Second Language (ESL), and strong remedial courses in math, reading, and writing. Sixty per-

cent of all Coyote students enrolled in traditional college courses enroll in at least one remedial course, and 15 percent enroll in an ESL course.

In the area of Workforce Development, Certificate Programs, and Continuing Education, Coyote provides custom-designed, on-site training courses and services that meet the needs of local businesses. In partnership with several local employers, Coyote offers contract training for computer networking technicians, water management specialists, office managers, contract administrators, and prison guards. Coyote also offers intensive ESL and remedial English and math courses under contract. In addition, Coyote offers a wide variety of short-term certification courses, such as Network Administrator, Network Engineer, Advanced Office Automation, Systems Engineer, Quality Auditor, Purchasing Manager, and Certified Nursing Assistant, to the general public and by contract. Continuing Education programs address those students who wish to improve professional skills, acquire new skills, or expand their fields of knowledge and general interest.

In the area of Community Education and Outreach, Coyote provides programs and community services that offer multicultural, recreational, and community development activities to meet the needs of lifelong learners. These activities, which include a Women in Transition program, the Coyote Cultural Center, an Elder Learning Center, and a day care center, also encourage the use of community college facilities and services by all citizens of the community for educational and cultural purposes.

Students at Coyote are divided among (1) those enrolled in traditional college credit degree curricula, (2) those enrolled in noncredit contract training and in short-term certificate courses, and (3) those involved in the community outreach programs. Because of demands placed on their resources and time by employers, family, and others, students tend to pursue the education intermittently, and approximately 75 percent of students attend part-time.

Coyote employs 280 full-time faculty, 830 adjunct (part-time) faculty, 40 administrators, and 150 support staff. The faculty are members of the National Education Association union. Fifty percent of full-time faculty holds a master's degree, 40 percent hold doctoral degrees, and 10 percent hold bachelor's degrees. Adjunct faculty, many of whom are working in the field in which they teach, hold at least a bachelor's degree. Seventy-five percent of the administrators hold a master's degree or higher.

Although Coyote's primary stakeholders are its students, key stakeholders also include college faculty and staff, four-year colleges and universities to which Coyote's students transfer, local employers, the New Mexico State Board of Community Colleges, Coyote's Board of Governors (BOG), and the surrounding community at large, including local taxpayers. The requirements of the primary stakeholders are shown in Figure 8.17.

Coyote's oversight body is the BOG. The members of Coyote's BOG are elected by voters in seven geographical districts within the two-county region the college serves. Funding for programs and for most construction and equipment comes from a property tax levy in the two-county region and annual appropriations by the New Mexico legislature. Coyote's BOG approves spending over $50,000, intergovernmental agreements, bond spending, building improvements, and construction. The BOG also provides continuous evaluation and assessment of Coyote's policies, procedures, and practices to ensure that the college is fulfilling its mission and achieving its purposes. In addition, Coyote has a private nonprofit foundation for private contributions, which are increasing every year.

Coyote is accredited by the North Central Association of Colleges and Schools (NCACS), and 12 individual programs are certified or accredited by other appropriate organizations. Coyote was reviewed by the NCACS in 1998 and is scheduled for another review in 2008. Coyote is also responsive to a variety of federal, state, and local regulations, including the Occupational Safety and Health Administration (OSHA) requirements, Environmental Protection Agency (EPA) regulations, federal and state financial aid regulations, and affirmative action guidelines. Coyote complies with the Americans with Disabilities Act (ADA). Coyote is also proud of its partnerships with the colleges and universities to which the majority of its credit students transfer. Faculty members from these universities serve on Coyote's Curriculum Advisory Teams. In addition, articulation agreements with all four-year institutions in the region are in place for all of Coyote's university transfer programs (AA degrees), as well as for more than 50 percent of the occupational degree programs.

A key differentiator of online programs offered by out-of-state colleges is convenience. Students can attend online courses any time of the day or night to accommodate their busy and sometimes changing schedules. Coyote is responding to this need by developing both online and video-based programs. In addition, Coyote's key differentiator is that it focuses on preparing graduates to be successful in the local community. Input of local employers in the planning process, new program design, and student internships enables Coyote's graduates to find desirable jobs in the local community more easily and to succeed at those jobs. Coyote's growing, individualized, technology-based delivery of educational programs with related support services (individualized program design and certification), which is targeted to employed adult students with needs for specific skill development, is another important competitive advantage. Planning is focused on providing learning excellence through use of state-of-the-art learning technologies to expand the off-campus student population while retaining the current levels of on-campus students.

The principal factors that determine competitive success include accessibility, flexibility in scheduling, affordability, ability to offer high value at a low cost, the effectiveness of the curriculum, the time to complete programs, and the range of programs offered. Dr. Gayle Brooks, who previously served as Deputy Provost at McMoto Industrial University, was selected as Coyote's president in 1992, with a mandate to reverse a six-year-long trend of declining enrollment and diminishing student success. In the last eight years, Coyote has shown steady increases in enrollment and in student success as judged by student employment rates and acceptance rates by four-year colleges and universities. The foundation of this turnaround was the establishment of a common mission, vision, and values. These provide continuing direction for the college and drive specific goals to stretch Coyote's capabilities. In 1994, under the direction of Dr. Brooks, Coyote developed and adopted LEARN, a three-point philosophy of education. These points are:

- *Learning Excellence:* All aspects of the education process are learner-centered, and the needs of the learner are paramount. Recognition of the diversity of learning styles and rates of learning is fundamental. Technology is used as a tool to facilitate learning.

- *Assessment:* Assessment of learning is ongoing for both learners and learning facilitators. Technology is a tool to facilitate the assessment of processes associated with learning.
- *Recognizing Needs:* It is imperative to identify and respond to the needs of all of Coyote's stakeholders. Needs vary by stakeholder, as shown in Figure 8.17.

As a result of implementing LEARN, Coyote recently identified the following three key technology-based strategies designed to improve student learning and meet learner requirements. Each of these strategies is currently at different levels of implementation within the college:

1. *Incorporation of technologies into the traditional classroom:* In order to enhance student learning, instructors are being encouraged to incorporate multimedia into traditional delivery techniques.
2. *Technology mediation allowing individually paced learning:* Computer-based instruction allows learners to begin precisely at their current level of knowledge and progress through structured materials at their own pace. Monthly start dates of sequenced courses allow students to proceed to the next course when ready, with no delays or potential loss of learning due to waiting.

3. *Distance learning delivery methods:* A variety of technologies allow Coyote to meet learner needs. An interactive video system (teleclasses) ties the three campuses together to decrease the need for students to drive from one campus to another. This system also allows Coyote to offer some traditionally low enrollment courses that meet specific student needs, including upper-level foreign language and math classes. Online courses offered via the Internet and video-based courses (telecourses) offered via cable television and video cassette checkout meet the needs of students with difficult schedules and geographic constraints.

The leadership at Coyote wants to develop a balanced scorecard. To customize it for the educational environment, they renamed the categories as

1. Funder/Financial Perspective
2. Student/Participant Perspective
3. Internal Process Perspective
4. Innovation and Resource Perspective

Based on the description of this college and its environment, what specific types of measures should they include in each of these perspectives of the balanced scorecard? How would they be measured?

Figure 8.17 Stakeholders and Requirements

Stakeholder	Requirements
Students	Acquisition of needed skills and knowledge, learning skill development, accessibility, flexibility in scheduling, affordability, increased capacity for self-directed learning, responsive services, effective curriculum
Faculty/Staff	Receive professional development, feedback, support, recognition
Four-year colleges and universities	Strong student academic foundations compatible with higher learning
Employers	Current/future employees' acquisition of needed skills/knowledge/attitude, cost-efficient learning, innovative problem-solving and team skills, leadership skills, computer proficiency, professional proficiency
SBCC and BOG	Return for dollar
Taxpayers and community	Fulfillment of education needs that are not met by other institutions, support to region/state, efficient expenditure of funding

II. Ultra-Productivity Fasteners, Part I

The Ultra-Productivity Fasteners Company was founded in 1959 to supply a variety of fasteners—rivets, clips, and screws—to appliance manufacturers. These fasteners are used in the assembly of major appliances, including dishwashers, washing machines, clothes dryers, and ranges. In 1981 Ultra-Productivity successfully penetrated the automotive market. Currently, the appliance market with three major OEM customers represents 60 percent of the annual sales. Two automotive customers account for approximately 30 percent of the sales; the remaining 10 percent of sales are made to a variety of smaller customers.

In the design phase, appliance manufacturers expect rapid response in the design and manufacture of special fasteners, and technical assistance in properly applying existing fastener designs. In the production and warranty phases, appliance manufacturers expect just-in-time delivery; fasteners that consistently meet specifications; fasteners that can be used on the product line without difficulty, and frequently with automated equipment; and fasteners that will not break during handling, shipping, or repair.

Requirements of the automotive customers are similar, but the need for fasteners that will not break is more critical because of the additional vibration and safety considerations. Just-in-time delivery is a primary requirement for automotive customers because a lack of fastener may hold up assembly of an automobile.

Ultra-Productivity is one of three major manufacturers in the fastener market, in addition to a large number of small regional manufacturers. The market for fasteners is extremely competitive; price is a key consideration in the purchase decision. Ultra-Productivity is headquartered in Louisville, Kentucky, with a major manufacturing plant at that location. Two other manufacturing plants are located at Lansing, Michigan, and Atlanta, Georgia. The Louisville and Lansing plants are of comparable size, with approximately 300 production workers each. The Atlanta plant is only one-third the size of other plants with approximately 100 production employees. Although quality has always been an important consideration, a formal, companywide quality improvement program was initiated in 1989 after a major automotive contract was lost.

Assignment

Summarize the key factors that drive this company's business and define a set of product and service performance indicators that would be consistent with these factors and provide both operational-level managers and senior leadership with the information needed to make key decisions. The Bonus Materials folder on the CD-ROM contains a follow-up to this case called *Ultra-Productivity Fasteners, Part 2.*

III. CapStar Health Systems: Information and Analysis

The complete CapStar case study, a fictitious example of a Baldrige application, can be found on the CD-ROM accompanying this book. If you have not read the Organizational Profile yet (see Case III in Chapter 3), please do so first. Examine their response to Category 4 in the context of the leading practices described in this chapter (you need not consider the actual Baldrige criteria for this activity). What are their strengths? What are their weaknesses and opportunities for improvement? What specific advice, including useful tools and techniques that might help them, would you suggest?

ENDNOTES

1. Jerry Useem, "Boeing Versus Boeing," *Fortune,* October 2, 2000, 148–160.

2. D. Osborne and T. Gaebler, *Reinventing Government: How the Entrepreneurial Spirit Is Transforming the Public Sector* (Reading, MA: Addison-Wesley Publishing Co., 1992).

3. Noriaki Kano, "A Perspective on Quality Activities in American Firms," *California Management Review,* Spring 1993, 12–31.

4. Blan Godfrey, "Future Trends: Expansion of Quality Management Concepts, Methods, and Tools to All Industries," *Quality Observer* 6, no. 9 (September 1997), 40–43, 46.

5. Bill Gates with Collins Hemingway, *Business @ the Speed of Thought* (New York: Warner Books, 1999).

6. Kicab Casteñeda-Méndez, "Performance Measurement in Health Care," *Quality Digest,* May 199, 33–36.

7. Laura Struebing, "Measuring for Excellence," *Quality Progress,* December 1996, 25–28.

8. Robert S. Kaplan and David P. Norton, "The Balanced Scorecard—Measures That Drive Performance," *Harvard Business Review,* January/February 1992, 71–79. © 1992 by the President and Fellows of Harvard College; all rights reserved.

9. Ernest C. Huge, "Measuring and Rewarding Performance," in Ernst & Young Quality Consulting Group, *Total Quality: An Executive's Guide for the 1990s* (Homewood IL: Irwin, 1990).

10. New Corporate Performance Measures, A Research Report, Report Number 1118-95-RR, New York: The Conference Board, 1995.

11. Robert S. Kaplan and David P. Norton, *The Balanced Scorecard* (Boston, MA: Harvard Business School Press, 1996), 1.

12. Consult Schneiderman's Web site, http://www.schneiderman.com for many interesting papers about the history, design, and use of balanced scorecards and other aspects of measurement.

13. John Geanuracos and Ian Meiklejohn, *Performance Measurement: The New Agenda; Using Non-Financial Indicators to Improve Profitability* (London: Business Intelligence, 1993).

14. Roberto Antonio Martins, "Use of Performance Measurement Systems: Some Thoughts Toward a Comprehensive Approach," Second International Conference on Performance Measurement, University of Cambridge, July 2000.

15. Arthur M. Schneiderman, "Why Balanced Scorecards Fail," *Journal of Strategic Performance Measurement* 3, no. 1 (January 1999), 6–11.

16. Mark Graham Brown, *Keeping Score: Using the Right Metrics to Drive World-Class Performance* (New York: Quality Resources, 1996).

17. "First National Bank of Chicago," *Profiles in Quality* (Boston, MA: Allyn and Bacon, 1991).

18. Justin Martin, "Are You as Good as You Think You Are?" *Fortune,* September 30, 1996, 142–152.

19. Glenn E. Hayes and Harry G. Romig, *Modern Quality Control* (Encino, CA: Benziger, Bruce & Glencoe, Inc., 1977).

20. U.S. Office of Management and Budget, "How to Develop Quality Measures That Are Useful in Day-to-Day Measurement," U.S. Department of Commerce, National Technical Information Service (January 1989).

21. Robert I. Wise, "A Method for Aligning Process Level and Strategy Level Performance Metrics," American Society for Quality, 11th Annual Quality Management Conference.

22. Marcelo Telles de Menezes and Roberto Antonio Martins, "Performance Measurement After ERP Implementation: Some Empirical Evidences," Proceedings, Third World Congress on Intelligent Manufacturing Processes & Systems, Cambridge, MA, June 2000, 146–151.

23. David A. Collier, *The Service/Quality Solution* (Milwaukee, WI: ASQC Quality Press, and Burr Ridge, IL: Richard D. Irwin, 1994).

24. Bob Graessel and Pete Zeidler, "Using Quality Function Deployment to Improve Customer Service," *Quality Progress* 26, no. 11 (November 1993), 59–63.

25. Steve Hoisington and Earl Naumann, "The Loyalty Elephant," *Quality Progress,* February 2003, pp. 33–41.

26. Collier (see note 23), 235–236.

27. "Coaxing Meaning Out of Raw Data," *Business Week,* February 3, 1997, 134–138.

28. Frank M. Gryna, "Quality Costs," in *Juran's Quality Control Handbook,* 4th ed. (New York: McGraw-Hill, 1988).

29. ASQ Quality Costs Committee, "Profiting from Quality in the Service Arena," *Quality Progress,* May 1999, 81–84.

30. The reader is referred to the text by Cooper and Kaplan (1991) cited in the bibliography for a thorough treatment of this topic.

31. L. Reid, "Continuous Improvement Through Process Management," *Management Accounting* (September 1992), 37–44.

32. R. T. Rust, A. J. Zahorik, and T. L. Keiningham, "Return on Quality (ROQ): Making Service Quality Financially Accountable," *Journal of Marketing* 59, no. 2 (April 1995), 58–70.

33. Roland T. Rust, Timothy Keiningham, Stephen Clemens, and Anthony Zahorik, "Return on Quality at Chase Manhattan Bank," *Interfaces* 29, no. 2 (March/April 1999), 62–72.

34. Larry English, "Data Quality: Meeting Customer Needs," *Data Management Review,* November 1996, 44–51, 86.

35. Ethan I. Davis, "Quality Service at The Prudential," in Jay W. Spechler, *When America Does It Right* (Norcross, GA: Industrial Engineering and Management Press, 1988), 224–232.

36. H. James Harrington, "Creating Organizational Excellence—Part Four," *Quality Digest,* April 2003, 14.

37. Chuck Cobb, "Knowledge Management and Quality Systems," The 54th Annual Quality Congress Proceedings, 2000, American Society for Quality, 276–287.

38. Robert J. Heibeler, "Benchmarking Knowledge Management," *Strategy and Leadership* 24, no. 2 (March/April, 1996), as cited in Verna Allee, *The Knowledge Evolution: Expanding Organizational Intelligence* (Boston: Butterworth-Heinemann, 1997), 8.

39. Carla O'Dell and C. Jackson Grayson, "Identifying and Transferring Internal Best Practices," APQC White Paper, 2000; http://www.apqc.org/free/whitepapers/cmifwp/index.htm.

40. Mohamed Zairi and John Whymark, "The transfer of best practices: How to build a culture of benchmarking and continuous learning—Part 1," *Benchmarking: An International Journal* 7, no. 1 (2000), 62–78.

41. Cobb (see note 37).

42. Brian Swayne and Brent Harder, "Where Has All the Magic Gone?" *Six Sigma Forum Magazine* 2, no. 3 (May 2003), 22–32.

43. George Byrne and Bob Norris, "Drive Baldrige Level Performance," *Six Sigma Forum Magazine* 2, no. 3 (May 2003), 13–21.

44. We wish to gratefully acknowledge Ms. Julie Coughlin of Convergys for providing this case.

45. Adapted from Steven H. Hoisington and Tse-Hsi Huang, "Customer Satisfaction and Market Share: An Empirical Case Study of IBM's AS/400 Division," in Earl Naumann and Steven H. Hoisington (eds.) *Customer-Centered Six Sigma* (Milwaukee, WI: ASQ Quality Press, 2001). Reprinted with permission of ASQ Quality Press.

BIBLIOGRAPHY

Allen, Derek R. and Morris Wolburn. *Linking Customer and Employee Satisfaction to the Bottom Line.* Milwaukee, WI: ASQ Quality Press, 2002.

American National Standard: Guide to Inspection Planning, ANSI/ASQC E-2-1984. Milwaukee, WI: American Society for Quality Control, 1984.

AT&T Quality Steering Committee. Process Quality Management & Improvement Guidelines. AT&T Bell Laboratories, 1987.

Brown, Mark Graham. *Keeping Score: Using the Right Metrics to Drive World-Class Performance.* New York: Quality Resources, 1996.

Brown, Mark Graham. *Winning Score : How to Design and Implement Organizational Scorecards.* New York: Productivity Press, 2000.

Case, Kenneth E., and Lynn L. Jones. *Profit Through Quality: Quality Assurance Programs for Manufacturers.* Norcross, GA: American Institute of Industrial Engineers, 1978.

Cooper, Robin, and Robert S. Kaplan. *The Design of Cost Management Systems: Text, Cases, and Readings.* New York: Prentice Hall, 1991.

Cupello, James M. "A New Paradigm for Measuring TQM Progress." *Quality Progress* 27, no. 5 (May 1994), 79–82.

Donnell, Augustus, and Margaret Dellinger. *Analyzing Business Process Data: The Looking Glass.* AT&T Bell Laboratories, 1990.

Haavind, Robert. *The Road to the Baldrige Award.* Boston: Butterworth-Heinemann, 1992.

Hart, Christopher W. L., and Christopher E. Bogan. *The Baldrige.* New York: McGraw-Hill, 1992.

Henriques, Diana B., and Jacques Steinberg. "Right Answer, Wrong Score: Test Flaws Take Toll." *New York Times,* May 20, 2001; and Diana B. Henriques and Jacques Steinberg. "When a Test Fails the Schools, Careers and Reputations Suffer." *New York Times,* May 21, 2001. Source: http://deming.eng.clemson.edu/pub/psci/psn/inthenewsarchive.htm.

Juran, Joseph M. *Juran on Quality By Design.* New York: The Free Press, 1992.

Kaplan, Robert S., and David P. Norton. *The Balanced Scorecard.* Boston: Harvard Business School Press, 1996.

Kaplan, Robert S., and David P. Norton. *The Strategy-Focused Organization: How Balanced Scorecard Companies Thrive in the New Business Environment.* Boston: Harvard Business School Press, 2000.

Neely, Andrew, Chris Adams, and Mike Kennerley. *The Performance Prism: The Scorecard for Measuring and Managing Business Success.* New York: Financial Times-Prentice Hall, 2002. Performance Measurement Association. http://www.performanceportal.org.

Rice, George O. "Metrology." In Loren Walsh, Ralph Wurster, and Raymond J. Kimber (eds.), *Quality Management Handbook.* New York: Marcel Dekker, 1986, 517–530.

Rosander, A. C. *The Quest for Quality in Services.* Milwaukee, WI: ASQC Quality Press, 1989.

Schneiderman, Arthur M."Measurement, the Bridge between the Hard and Soft Sides." *Journal of Strategic Performance Measurement* 2, no 2 (April/May 1998), 14.

Schneiderman, Arthur M. "Are There Limits to TQM?" *Strategy & Business* 11 (Second Quarter 1998), 35.

Schneiderman, Arthur M. "Why Balanced Scorecards Fail!" *Journal of Strategic Performance Measurement,* January 1999, 6.

Stewart, Thomas. *The Wealth of Knowledge.* New York: Currency, 2001

Whitley, Richard C. *The Customer-Driven Company.* Reading, MA: Addison-Wesley, 1991.

Wilkerson, David, and Clifton Cooksey. *Customer Service Measurement.* Arlington, VA: Coopers & Lybrand, 1994.

Yakhou, Mehenna, and Boubekeur Rahali. "Integration of Business Functions: Roles of Cross-Functional Information Systems." *APICS—The Performance Advantage* 2, no. 12 (December 1992), 35–37.

CHAPTER 9

BUILDING AND SUSTAINING TOTAL QUALITY ORGANIZATIONS

At the Seventh Annual National Conference on Federal Quality in July 1994, 12-year-old Kelly Potter addressed the luncheon crowd of 2,000 participants.[1] Kelly's elementary school in Nazareth, Pennsylvania, participates in Koalaty Kid, a program sponsored by the American Society for Quality, which promotes teaching of quality principles in elementary schools (see Chapter 2). Her message was not earthshaking. She thanked her family and school system members for their support and discussed how quality improvement techniques were used in her school for such things as cafeteria operations and homework assignments. She even applied these techniques to prepare her speech. The audience exploded with a standing ovation. Brad Stratton, then editor of *Quality Progress*, observed, "I don't think they were applauding her verbal message, as much as her nonverbal message which was this: Hey people! This stuff is so simple that kids can do it! Kids!"

The principles of total quality—focus on the customer, involve everyone, and continuously improve—are simple to understand and represent common sense. Yet many companies have experienced great difficulty in implementing total quality and even deciding whether to do it. This difficulty often results from some common misconceptions, such as that TQ means doing lots of "things" like collecting data and

431

organizing teams, or that it only applies to large companies. A total quality strategy does, however, require significant changes in organization design, processes, and culture. Such broad change has been a stumbling block for many companies, and researchers have noted that upwards of 70 percent of all change initiatives fail.

Success takes top management involvement and cooperation from the workforce and workers' organizations, as well as support from middle managers. Without all of these factors, a traditional culture cannot change to a TQ culture in a sustainable fashion. We emphasize that the journey is not easy, yet many organizations—large and small, for-profit and not-for-profit—embark on it successfully (see the *Quality Profiles* on the facing page). In this chapter we reflect on many of the concepts discussed throughout the previous eight chapters, and discuss some of the barriers and pitfalls to developing a sustainable quality-based organization.

Building and sustaining a TQ organization requires a readiness for change, the adoption of sound practices and implementation strategies, and an effective organizational infrastructure.

MAKING THE COMMITMENT TO TQ

A survey of manufacturing firms cited the top three obstacles to TQ implementation among companies that do not have a formal TQ effort as:

1. Lack of a strong motivation
2. Lack of time to devote to quality initiatives
3. Lack of a formalized strategic plan for change[2]

Most firms—even Baldrige Award winners—have moved toward total quality because of threats to its survival. Xerox, for example, watched its market share fall from 80 percent to 13 percent in a little more than a decade (see the *Quality in Practice* case in Chapter 1); and Boeing Airlift and Tanker Programs was on the verge of having its contract with the U.S. government canceled. Although not facing dire crises, perceived future threats were the impetus for FedEx, Solectron, and Wainwright. When faced with a threat to survival, an organization effects change more easily; under these circumstances, they generally implement TQ quickly and smoothly. However, an organization will generally have more difficulty in gaining support for TQ, or any significant change for that matter, when not facing a crisis. This reluctance is a reflection of the attitude "If it ain't broke, don't fix it." Unfortunately, complacency today often leads to crises tomorrow. Leaders with foresight view TQ as an opportunity to get better, and to maintain or enhance existing market leadership positions. In such cases, one might even attempt to manufacture a crisis mentality to effect change.[3]

The motivation to adopt a TQ philosophy usually stems from one of two basic reasons—either a firm reacts to competition that poses a threat to its survival, or TQ represents an opportunity to improve and grow the business.

When organizations cite a lack of time as the reason for not pursuing TQ, one often finds that the organization has plenty of time to correct errors, rework defective products, and waste time in complex processes that have resulted from years of inefficiency. They do not recognize the Crosby philosophy that "Quality is Free." In most cases, lack of time is simply an excuse for not wanting to devote the effort necessary to pursue TQ or failure to understand the benefits that can result. The

QUALITY PROFILES

AMERICAN ELECTRIC POWER AND PAL'S SUDDEN SERVICE

The Conesville, Ohio, plant of American Electric Power (AEP) was a recipient of Ohio's Governor's Award for Excellence, the state equivalent of the Baldrige Award, in 2001. The plant is one of the largest in Ohio and one of the most complex in the United States. The plant's difficult journey to performance excellence began with a major reorganization when the plant was forced to cut 25 percent of its workforce. In a two-day meeting in 1995, amidst a tense and emotional atmosphere, new leaders outlined a mission, vision, and goals for the first time, making trust and caring the principal core values. The old culture that was characterized by a conservative, top-down leadership style, functional silos, an adversarial unionized workforce, and a highly political atmosphere, had to be dismantled.

A leadership team, which included union representatives, was established, new employee development programs were created in an atmosphere of empowerment and learning, all with a new focus on external and internal customers. The cultural changes included an employee-developed behavior-based safety program, weekly newsletters, systems thinking, opening the books to all, improved manager communications, and solving problems internally rather than escalating grievances. In a few short years, the plant received the AFL-CIO National Labor-Management Award, grievances fell from 37 to zero, and it received national recognition for its school-to-work program. Coupled with a new performance management program, a balanced scorecard, and a process-focused management approach, the plant achieved record high productions, a more than 100 percent increase in employee productivity, a 45 percent reduction in operation and maintenance costs, and greater than $5 million in process improvement savings.

A privately owned, quick-service restaurant chain, Pal's Sudden Service, serves hamburgers, hot dogs, chipped ham, chicken, French fries, and beverages as well as breakfast biscuits with country ham, sausage, and gravy to primarily drive-through customers at 17 locations, all within 60 miles of Kingsport, Tennessee. The company aims to distinguish itself from fast-food competitors by offering competitively priced food of consistently high quality, delivered rapidly, cheerfully, and without error. The company's Business Excellence Process is the key integrating element, a management approach to ensuring that customer requirements are met in every transaction, today and in the future. Carried out under the leadership of Pal's two top executives and its 17 store owner/operators, the Business Excellence Process spans all facets of the operation from strategic planning (done annually with two-year horizons) to online quality control. Every component process, including those for continual improvement and product introduction, is interactively linked, producing data that directly or indirectly inform the others. In customer satisfaction, including food quality, service, and order accuracy, Pal's is outperforming its primary competitor. Pal's order handout speed improved more than 30 percent since 1995, decreasing from 31 seconds to 20 seconds, almost four times faster than its top competitor. Errors in orders are rare, averaging less than one for every 2,000 transactions. In addition, Pal's consistently receives the highest health inspection scores in its market and in the entire state of Tennessee.

Sources: Ohio Award for Excellence Governor's Award Winner presentation, and the Malcolm Baldrige National Quality Award, Profiles of Winners, National Institute of Standards and Technology, Department of Commerce.

third reason—lack of a change process—also is typically the result of a lack of discipline and a fire-fighting mentality. We will address organizational change extensively in this chapter.

As we noted in Chapter 5, leadership is the essential ingredient for success.[4] Gaining commitment from top executives is not easy, however. As one quality director noted, "It's a hard sell if management is not predisposed." Dale Crownover, CEO of Texas Nameplate Company, believes the best way to sell quality to top executives is to show them where money is being lost due to absenteeism, downtime, not having procedures in place, lack of job descriptions, and poor training. Other quality managers note the importance of viewing quality as an integrated part of the business, and showing that quality projects are good for business, for example, demonstrating the return on quality that we discussed in Chapter 8. Interviews with Baldrige winners suggest ten ways that middle managers or quality professionals can sell the TQ concept to senior leaders:

1. Learn to think like top executives who are paid, after all, to satisfy the concerns of three key groups of stakeholders: customers, investors, and employees.
2. Position quality as a way to address the priority goals of these three groups of stakeholders.
3. Align your objectives with those of senior management. If the organization's goal is to reduce cycle time, show how your program will reduce cycle time. If the goal is to increase market share, show how your plan will do that.
4. Make your arguments as quantitative as possible.
5. When approaching top management, make your first pitch to someone who is likely to be sympathetic to your proposal.
6. Focus on getting an early win, even if it's a small one.
7. Be sure your efforts won't be undercut by corporate accounting policies that may exaggerate the costs of quality or fail to recognize its full financial benefits.
8. Develop allies—both those who are internal and can lend credibility to your position and those who are external and can tell how quality improved the bottom line at their organizations.
9. Develop metrics for return on quality, so you can show that your efforts are paying off.
10. Never stop selling quality.

ORGANIZATIONAL CULTURE AND TOTAL QUALITY

Any organizational activity can be viewed in one of three ways, depending on the intensity of commitment to the activity:

1. *Function*: A task or group of tasks to be performed that contribute to the mission or purpose of an organization
2. *Process*: A set of steps, procedures, or policies that define how a function is to be performed and what results are expected
3. *Ideology*: A set of values or beliefs that guide an organization in the establishment of its mission, processes, and functions

Many managers view quality as a set of tasks to be performed by specialists in quality control or individuals in their particular jobs. Other managers have a broader perspective and see quality as a process in which many people at the operating level from a number of functional areas of the organization are involved in cross-functional activities. Still other managers take the broadest viewpoint in which quality is an ideology

For total quality to truly succeed, it must define and drive the culture of the organization.

or philosophy that pervades and defines the culture of the entire organization.

Culture (often called *corporate culture*) is an organization's value system and its collection of guiding principles. A survey conducted by the Wyatt Company, a Washington, D.C., consulting firm, found that the barriers to change cited most often were employee resistance and "dysfunctional corporate culture"—one whose shared values and behavior are at odds with its long-term health.[5] An example of a dysfunctional culture is a high-tech company that stresses individual rewards while innovation depends on teamwork. To change their management practices, organizations must first address their fundamental values.

Cultural values are often seen in the mission and vision statements of organizations (see Chapter 5). For example, it is not unusual to see statements like "We will

Culture is reflected by the management policies and actions that a company practices.[6] Therefore, organizations that believe in the principles of total quality are more likely to implement the practices successfully. Conversely, actions set culture in motion. As total quality practices are used routinely within an organization, its people learn to believe in the principles, and cultural changes can occur.

continuously strive to improve the level of quality in all our products" or "Teamwork is essential to our mutual success" in corporate mission and vision statements. Culture is a powerful influence on behavior because it is shared widely and because it operates without being talked about, and indeed, often without being thought of.

A concise summary of the principles on which modern, high-performing TQ organizations are built and managed is given in the set of *Core Values and Concepts* that form the basis for the Baldrige criteria. They include the following:

- Visionary Leadership
- Customer Driven
- Organizational and Personal Learning
- Valuing Employees and Partners
- Agility
- Focus on the Future
- Managing for Innovation
- Management by Fact
- Social Responsibility
- Focus on Results and Creating Value
- Systems Perspective

These values are embedded throughout the Criteria for Performance Excellence. For example, if you review the criteria for Item 1.1, Organizational Leadership, you can easily find direct or implied references to almost all of these values. They must become a living, breathing part of an organization's culture if it is to be successful in achieving its mission and vision and a leader in its industry and markets.

Likewise, Six Sigma has evolved into a unique continuous improvement and business development culture within organizations that adopt it. Six Sigma shares many synergies with the Baldrige framework, and can provide a complementary foundation for pursuing higher levels of performance excellence using the Baldrige framework. In observing the evolution of Six Sigma from purely a technical focus to a much broader management paradigm, we can make some interesting parallels with Baldrige.[7] In fact, when we review the Baldrige Core Values and Concepts, we see many synergies with Six Sigma:

- **Visionary Leadership** Leadership is one of the major contributing factors ensuring Six Sigma's success across the organization. Most testimonials on why Six Sigma works focus on "continued top management support and enthusiasm."[8] A general manager of a $1.2 billion electronics business in Atlanta states that "Six Sigma has to be part of every discussion on the performance of the business—Six Sigma results are discussed daily with the boss."[9]

- **Customer-Driven Excellence** One of the key reasons to pursue Six Sigma is to be ahead of, responsive to, and focused on customers. Customer requirements, both external and internal, are paramount in choosing which Six Sigma projects to undertake. For example, a sales and marketing VP at GE Aircraft Engines directly attributes the success of the division to the Six Sigma initiative: "It has helped our salespeople focus on building relationships with our customers [whose demands] for increased value have forced us to place a greater emphasis on speed, quality, and productivity."[10] Critical to quality issues are one of the mainstays of Six Sigma at the design, processing, delivery, and recovery (if needed) stages of the relationship with customers.

- **Organizational and Personal Learning** A key aspect of Six Sigma is to create a learning environment where both the individuals and the organization learn and act based on that learning, improving all the time both from internal and external perspectives. Six Sigma provides a structured environment for taking the best ideas from every source, internally and externally, and rethinking the who-what-when-where-why-how of all the processes both within the organization and as they interface with the outside world.

- **Valuing Employees and Partners** Besides hardware and software, people are needed to make Six Sigma work. Six Sigma supports a culture where every individual has the opportunity to contribute not only by doing their work, but also by improving their work. Most successful companies believe that training in Six Sigma is worth the investment.

- **Agility** Organizations must have the ability to respond quickly and flexibly to changing customer needs, wants and desires, and in response to other internal factors and changes in the business environment. Six Sigma supports both process management and directed positive change on a timely basis while taking into consideration all the appropriate relationships.

- **Focus on the Future** A company that focuses on the future needs a goal, a plan for achieving that goal, and a working methodology to fulfill that plan. Six Sigma offers a methodology for improving the overall performance of an organization, giving it access to the resources that will allow it to continue to grow, develop, and succeed.

- **Managing for Innovation** Within Six Sigma, both incremental change and breakthrough change are supported and expected, and this change is directed not only at what the company produces but also how the company itself works internally and interfaces with the rest of the world. Although Six Sigma was originally applied to manufacturing processes, companies such as GE have shown that the theory applies everywhere.[11]

- **Management by Fact** Six Sigma demands the effective use of data to analyze business issues. Six Sigma uses measurement to discover opportunities, to drive business results, and to drive improvement.

- **Social Responsibility** Although not specifically addressed in Six Sigma, it would be almost impossible for an organization to use all the other principles and concepts of Six Sigma, deliver better products and services, and grow in revenue and profitability without being a good citizen in its community.

- **Focus on Results and Creating Value** Six Sigma breaks the barrier between quality and business results, focusing directly on value-added processes and achieving improved business results for the organization. No project is considered complete until the benefit has been shown and a team of financial auditors signs off.
- **Systems Perspective** One of the characteristics stated and implicit in both Baldrige and Six Sigma is that efforts are expected to encompass the whole organization. Although the pieces are important, taken in total, integrated, and in relationship to one another, the system makes up the real value of the organization. Processes differ significantly, but all must be viewed from a system's perspective and their impact on and benefit to the ultimate customer, which is certainly consistent with Baldrige.

These core values often are embodied in the strategies and leadership philosophies of major organizations. For example, the total quality philosophy at Procter & Gamble focuses on delivering superior consumer satisfaction and boils down to four principles:[12]

Quality Spotlight
Procter & Gamble

- *Really know our customers and consumers.* Know those who resell our products and those who finally use them—and then meet and exceed their expectations.
- *Do the right things right.* This task requires hard data and sound statistical analysis to select the "right things" and to direct continual improvement in how well we do those things.
- *Concentrate on improving systems.* In order to achieve superior consumer satisfaction and leadership financial goals, we must continually analyze and improve the capability of our basic business systems and subsystems.
- *Empower people.* This principle means removing barriers and providing a climate in which everyone in the enterprise is encouraged and trained to make his or her maximum contribution to business objectives.

The P&G Statement of Purpose captures the "what," "how," and expected "results" of their quality efforts.

> We will provide products of superior quality and value that best fill the needs of the world's consumers. We will achieve that purpose through an organization and a working environment which attracts the finest people; fully develops and challenges our individual talents; encourages our free and spirited collaboration to drive the business ahead; and maintains the Company's historic principles of integrity, and doing the right thing.
>
> Through the successful pursuit of our commitment, we expect our brands to achieve leadership share and profit positions so that, as a result, our business, our people, our shareholders, and the communities in which we live and work, will prosper.

A similar philosophy is described by the American Express Quality Leadership approach. The fundamental beliefs about quality that provide the philosophical underpinnings and guide decision making at American Express are as follows:

- Quality is the foundation of continued success.
- Quality is a journey of continuous improvement and innovation.
- Quality provides a high return, but requires the investment of time and resources.
- Quality requires committed leadership.
- Quality begins by meeting or exceeding the expectations of customers and employees.

- Quality requires teamwork and learning at all levels.
- Quality comes from the energy of a diverse community of motivated and skilled people who are given and take responsibility.

Of course, it is easy to make bold statements; making them "real" requires a significant cultural change in many organizations.

Cultural Change

To understand some of the issues associated with changing an organization's culture to a TQ philosophy, it is useful to reflect on the principal differences that distinguish TQ from traditional management practices, many of which we addressed in earlier chapters. Many traditional practices stem from the fundamental structure of U.S. business, which derives from the Adam Smith principles of division of labor in the eighteenth century and their reinforcement during Frederick Taylor's scientific management era.[13] Although they were quite appropriate in their time and contributed to past economic success, the principles no longer suffice. Japan, by contrast, built its management system on the teachings of Deming, Juran, Drucker, and other modern business philosophers, whose focus relied on fundamental TQ principles. A clear understanding of these differences can help to avoid many of the problems that firms face when trying to implement TQ, as well as defining the changes necessary to establish a TQ culture. The Bonus Materials folder on the CD-ROM for this chapter provides some of the key differences that distinguish TQ organizations from older, traditional organizations.

Quality Spotlight
Wainwright
Industries

One powerful example of cultural change is the case of Wainwright Industries, which has been cited several times in previous chapters.[14] During the 1970s and 1980s, Wainwright lost millions in sales; operations slowed to three days a week; and tensions grew between employees and management. Recognizing that the problem lay with management, the CEO made some radical changes. Workers were called "associates," and everyone was put on salary. Associates are paid even if they miss work and still receive time-and-a-half for overtime. The company has maintained better than 99 percent attendance since this change. Managers shed their white shirts and ties, and everyone from the CEO down wears a common uniform, embroidered with the label Team Wainwright. A team of associates developed a profit-sharing plan, whereby everyone receives the same bonus every six months. Everyone has access to the privately held company's financial records. In addition, all reserved parking spaces were removed; walls—including those for the CEO's office—were replaced with glass. Customers, both external and internal, are treated as partners, with extensive communication. The most striking example occurred when one worker admitted having accidentally damaged some equipment, even though most workers were afraid to report such incidents. The CEO called a plantwide meeting and explained what had happened. Then he called the man up, shook his hand, and thanked him for reporting the accident. Reporting of accidents increased from zero to 90 percent, along with suggestions on how to prevent them. As we noted in Chapter 6, Wainwright's culture can be summed up as a *sincere belief and trust in people.*

Joshua Hammond of the American Quality Foundation urges business leaders in the United States to develop approaches that maximize their own cultural strengths. A successful quality strategy needs to fit within the existing organization culture, which is the reason the Baldrige

Impatient managers often seek immediate cultural change by adopting off-the-shelf quality programs and practices, or by imitating other successful organizations. In most cases, this approach is setting themselves up for failure.

Award criteria are nonprescriptive. No magic formula works for everyone. One study of Baldrige Award winners concluded that each has a unique "quality engine" that drives the quality activities of the organization.[15] Some examples are summarized in Table 9.1. This table does not suggest that all other aspects of TQ are ignored; they are not. The quality engine customizes the quality effort to the organizational culture and provides focus.

Building on Best Practices

The organizational infrastructure, as evidenced by an organization's management systems and practices, is vital to successful TQ implementation. **Best practices** are simply those that are recognized by the business community (and often verified through some type of research) to lead to successful performance. Such companies as Disney, Microsoft, and many Baldrige winners have recognized best practices and are routinely contacted by other companies to learn about their approaches.

Research performed by H. James Harrington with Ernst & Young and the American Quality Foundation, called the International Quality Study (IQS), suggested that trying to implement all the best practices of world-class organizations may not be a good strategy.[16] In fact, implementing the wrong practices can actually hurt the organization. The study indicated that only five best practices are "universal," and the chances are only 5 percent that they may not improve performance. They are:

1. Cycle-time analysis
2. Process value analysis
3. Process simplification
4. Strategic planning
5. Formal supplier certification programs

Table 9.1 Some Examples of Quality Engines

Company	Quality Engine	Focus
IBM Rochester	Market-driven quality	Customer needs determined early in the planning and design process
Motorola	Process control	Defect prevention; Six-Sigma quality
Pal's Sudden Service	Process focus	Everything—from new product introduction to hiring to work systems—viewed as a process that impacts customer satisfaction
Xerox	Benchmarking	Competitive and best-in-class benchmarks
FedEx	Technology	Using technology to speed processes and improve customer service
Texas Nameplate	Employee empowerment and involvement	Teams and active participation of employees in all aspects of the business
Clarke American Checks	Strategic planning	Involving all stakeholders in a "First in Service" strategy focused on running and changing the business
Dana Spicer Driveshaft	Measurement	Use of measurements to track and improve quality and to align business strategies

Au: ok to add "determined"?

Beyond these five, best practices depend on a company's current level of perfor-mance. Three measures of performance are ROA (return on assets: after-tax income divided by total assets), which is a measure of profitability; VAE (value added per employee: sales less the costs of materials, supplies, and work done by outside con-tractors), a measure of productivity; and quality, as measured by an external cus-tomer satisfaction index.

Low performers—those with less than 2 percent ROA and $53,000 VAE (in 1996 dollars), and low quality—can reap the highest benefits by concentrating on funda-mentals. These fundamentals include departmental and cross-functional teamwork, training in customer relationships, problem solving and suggestion systems, using internal customer complaint systems for new product and service ideas, empha-sizing cost reduction when acquiring new technology, using customer satisfaction measures in strategic planning, increased training for all levels of employees, and focusing quality strategy on "building it in" and "inspecting it in." Among those things that low performers should *not* do is use quality as a basis for senior manage-ment assessment, use world-class benchmarking or benchmarking marketing and sales processes, rely on surveys to obtain feedback from customers, emphasize empowerment, and remove quality control inspection.

Medium performers—those with ROA from 2 to 6.9 percent, VAE between $53,000 and $84,000, and medium quality levels—achieve the most benefits from promoting department-level improvement teams, training employees in problem solving and other specialized topics, listening to supplier suggestions about new products, emphasizing the role of enforcement for quality assurance, making regular and con-sistent measurements of progress and sharing quality performance information with middle management, and emphasizing quality as a key to the company's reputation. Medium performers should not emphasize quality and team performance in assessing senior management, increase training in general knowledge subjects, use cross-functional teams or teams with customers on them to create design specifica-tions, shift primary responsibilities for compliance with quality standards away from the quality assurance function, or select suppliers based on their general reputation.

High performers—with ROA exceeding 6.9 percent, VAE over $84,000, and high quality levels respectively—gain the most from providing customer-relationship training for new employees, emphasizing quality and teamwork for senior manage-ment assessment, encouraging widespread participation in quality meetings among nonmanagement employees, using world-class benchmarking, communicating strategic plans to customers and suppliers, conducting after-sales service to build customer loyalty, and emphasizing competitor-comparison measures and customer satisfaction measures when developing plans. Practices that could get these firms into trouble include increasing participation in department-level improvement teams, focusing technology on production processes, relying on customer surveys as a primary input for improvement, and using cross-functional teams with customers on them to create design specifications.

Strangely, the IQS Best Practices Report was interpreted by some news media as a criticism of TQ.[17] They translate the report as simply saying that many quality prac-tices are a waste of time and ineffective. On the contrary, the results are the first sig-nificant effort to develop a prescriptive theory (back to Deming again) of TQ implementation, rather than relying on intuition and anecdotal evidence. This view-point is similar to the contingency approaches in motivation and leadership theory and contradicts the notion of one magic quick fix for quality. Rather, companies advance in stages along a learning curve in their application of TQ and must carefully design their programs to optimize its effect.

The Role of Employees in Cultural Change

Juran and others suggest that a company must foster five key behaviors to develop a positive quality culture:[18]

1. It must create and maintain an awareness of quality by disseminating results throughout the organization.
2. It must provide evidence of management leadership, such as serving on a quality council, providing resources, or championing quality projects (Six Sigma, for example).
3. The company must encourage self-development and empowerment through the design of jobs, use of empowered teams, and personal commitment to quality.
4. The company must provide opportunities for employee participation to inspire action, such as improvement teams, product design reviews, or Six Sigma training.
5. The company must provide recognition and rewards, including public acknowledgment for good performance as well as tangible benefits.

It is interesting to note that these suggestions generally revolve around people, and we emphasize that people are the most important element in a successful quality organization. Each category of employees plays a critical role. Senior managers must ensure that their plans and strategies are successfully executed within the organization. Middle managers provide the leadership by which the vision of senior management is translated into the operations of the organization. In the end, the workforce delivers quality and, for TQ to succeed, must feel not only empowerment, but ownership. Most process problems—upwards of 80 percent—are owned by managers, as one AT&T manager observed; in his organization 60 percent of these issues could be addressed by first- and second-level managers while the remaining were the responsibility of middle and top managers.

Three key players for successful TQ implementation are senior management, middle management, and the workforce.

Senior Management Many organizations today find themselves in a leadership vacuum because the environment has changed more rapidly than they ever imagined. Their leadership styles have not kept pace, and they find themselves falling back on approaches that were "good enough" for their predecessors, but frequently inadequate today.

In an extensive research project, Henry Mintzberg studied managers who had formal authority and defined 10 managerial roles that leaders must play.[19] These roles were (1) figurehead, (2) leader, (3) liaison, (4) monitor, (5) disseminator, (6) spokesperson, (7) entrepreneur, (8) disturbance handler, (9) resource allocator, and (10) negotiator. Mintzberg pointed out that the importance of each role is contingent on the environmental and organizational factors that face managers who must lead. These contingencies include the industry or environmental surroundings of the organization, its age and size, the organizational level at which the leader operates, and the part of the organization (e.g., operating core, technostructure, or support structure) in which the leader resides. For example, in a pharmaceutical firm, where government regulation and the need for constant protection of the "ethical" quality image abound, the top management leader must spend a tremendous amount of time as figurehead, liaison, and spokesperson. In a small, family-owned foundry with a history of labor unrest, the CEO would tend to spend much more time as entrepreneur, disturbance handler, and negotiator in order to develop a quality product and image.

Senior managers' responsibilities include the following tasks:

1. Ensure that the organization focuses on the needs of the customer.
2. Cascade the mission, vision, and values of the organization throughout the organization.
3. Identify the critical processes that need attention and improvement.
4. Identify the resources and trade-offs that must be made to fund the TQ activity.
5. Review progress and remove any identified barriers.
6. Improve the macroprocesses in which they are involved, both to improve the performance of the process and to demonstrate their ability to use quality tools for problem solving.[20]

These responsibilities require a commitment of time that is often perceived to take away from other duties. However, if senior managers recognize that quality management is simply good business management, then they are less likely to encounter conflict. Senior leaders must be willing to deal openly with resistance in an honest environment. Perhaps their three most compelling challenges are to embrace the TQ philosophy, communicate it effectively throughout the organization, and create a fact-based organization in which, as one executive told one of the authors, they can "ask what customers think and have the guts to face the results."

Middle Management   Leonard Sayles, a veteran leadership consultant and researcher, observed that middle managers have traditionally not been expected to be leaders, but to be guardians of "generally approved management principles" (GAMP).[21] GAMP rests on time-honored assumptions and practices:

- Clear and fixed work goals and technology
- Relying on centralized specialist groups
- Focusing on numbers, such as meeting budgeted targets
- Being as autonomous as possible and ignoring the work system
- Delegating as much as possible and managing solely by results
- Compartmentalizing people issues and technology issues

Sayles suggests that GAMP no longer works. The principles were probably effective in simple, stable organizations and the business environment of 40 or 50 years ago. Critical leadership roles in today's rapidly changing business environment involve coordination, technology development, system and process integration, and continuous improvement. Coordination involves ensuring that strategies and plans are actually carried out at the operating levels of the firm. In the past, employees required direction in the form of precise instructions on what to do and how to do it. Today, managers find themselves monitoring progress, disseminating information and suggestions between local and distant line staff and outside experts, and acting as a spokesperson inside and outside the firm. Technology development requires that managers constantly scan the environment to be aware of technological developments that may threaten or enhance the operations of the company. System and process integration means optimizing the system to meet strategic goals such as customer service, and using tools of quality measurement and continuous improvement.

Middle management has been tagged by many as a direct obstacle to creating a supportive environment for TQ.[22] Because of their position in the company, middle managers have been accused of feeding territorial competition and stifling information flow. They have also been blamed for not developing or preparing employees for change. Unwilling to take initiatives that contribute to continuous improvement, middle managers appear to be threatened by continuous improvement efforts. Often, they are left out of the equation, with attention being paid to top management and the front-line workforce. However, middle management's role in creating and sustaining a TQ culture is critical. Middle managers improve the operational processes that are the foundation of customer satisfaction. They can make or break cooperation and teamwork; and they are the principal means by which the remaining workforce prepares for change.

Middle managers must exhibit behaviors that are supportive of total quality, as they act as role models for first-level managers and employees. Such behaviors include listening to employees as customers, creating a positive work environment, being role models for first-level managers and supervisors, implementing quality improvements enthusiastically, challenging people to develop new ideas and reach their potential, encouraging supervisors to empower their people, setting challenging goals and providing positive feedback, and following through on promises. These changes are often difficult for middle managers to accept. The perceived threats from an empowered workforce, which often lead to flatter organizations, are indeed serious issues that organizations must tackle.

Transforming middle managers into change agents requires a systematic process that dissolves traditional management boundaries and replaces them with an empowered and team-oriented state of accountability for organizational performance. This process involves the following:

1. *Empowerment*: Middle managers must be accountable for the performance of the organization in meeting objectives.
2. *Creating a common vision of excellence*: This vision is then transformed into critical success factors that describe key areas of performance that relate to internal and external customer satisfaction.
3. *New rules for playing the organizational game*: Territorial walls must be broken, yielding a spirit of teamwork. Today's managers must assume the role of coach. One new approach is "interlocking accountability," in which managers are accountable to one another for their performance. The second is "team representation," in which each manager is responsible for accurately representing the ideas and decisions of the team to others outside the team.
4. *Implementing a continuous improvement process*: These projects should improve their operational systems and processes.
5. *Developing and retaining peak performers*: Middle managers must identify and develop future leaders of the organization.

The Workforce If total quality does not occur at the workforce level, it will not occur at all. The workforce implements quality policies. This task requires ownership. Ownership goes beyond empowerment; it gives the employee the right to have a voice in deciding what needs to be done and how to do it.[23] It is based on a belief that what is good for the organization is also good for the individual, and vice versa. At Westinghouse, workers defined ownership as "taking personal responsibility for our jobs . . . for assuring that we meet or exceed our customers' standards and our own. We believe that ownership is a state of mind and heart that is characterized by a personal and emotional commitment to approach every decision and task with the confidence and leadership of an owner." Self-managed teams, discussed in Chapter 6, represent one form of ownership.

Increased ownership requires increased sharing of information with the workforce and a commitment to the workforce in good times and in bad. As we discussed earlier in this chapter, Wainwright Industries develops trust and belief in each associate. Its continuous improvement process involves everyone and is associate-driven. Although Wainwright cannot guarantee a job for life, its commitment to job security is based on the philosophy that the training and development Wainwright gives to its employees makes them highly employable and marketable, even if the company should suffer financial hardship. With such commitments, the company can more easily develop the loyalty and commitment needed within the workforce as they jointly strive to apply the principles of total quality.

CHANGE MANAGEMENT

Change makes people uncomfortable, thus, managing change is seldom pleasant. Managing change usually requires a well-defined process, just like any other business process. Thinking of change management as a process helps to define the steps necessary to achieve the desired outcomes. It also forces the organization to think of its employees as customers who will be affected by the change. Most change processes include three basic stages. The first stage involves questioning the organization's current state and dislodging accepted patterns of behavior. The second stage is a state of flux, where new approaches are developed to

Organizations contemplating change must answer some tough questions, such as, Why is the change necessary? What will it do to my organization (department, job)? What problems will I encounter in making the change? and perhaps the most important one—What's in it for me?

replace suspended old activities. The final period consists of institutionalizing the new behaviors and attitudes. American Express, for example, views its change process as consisting of five steps:[24]

Quality Spotlight
American Express

1. *Scope the change:* Why are we doing this?
2. *Create a vision:* What will the change look like?
3. *Drive commitment:* What needs to happen to make the change work?
4. *Accelerate the transition:* How are we going to manage the effort on an ongoing basis?
5. *Sustain momentum:* What have we learned and how can we leverage it?

Often reward systems get in the way of cultural change and must be adjusted for the new culture to take hold. In many companies, telephone operators are rewarded for the speed with which they process calls, rather than for how completely they satisfy the customers who call. Unless this type of reward system is changed, management's pleas to increase customer satisfaction will fall upon deaf ears. Willingness to make such changes indicates management's commitment to the new culture.

It is important to differentiate between organizational changes resulting from strategy development and implementation (i.e., "strategic change"), and organizational changes resulting from operational assessment activities (i.e., "process change").[25] *Strategic change* stems from strategic objectives, which are generally externally focused and relate to significant customer, market, product/service, or technological opportunities and challenges. An organization must change these aspects to remain or become competitive. Strategic change is broad in scope, is driven by environmental forces, and is tied closely to the organization's ability to achieve its goals. Some examples are General Electric's implementation of Six Sigma throughout the corporation, and Hewlett-Packard's decision to merge with Compaq. In contrast, *process change* deals with the operations of an organization. Some examples of process change are a health care organization that discovered weaknesses in the organization's ability to collect and analyze information, followed by a $50 million information system upgrade; or an AT&T division that found that many employees did not recall the division's strategic vision, which prompted managers to increase meetings and interactions with employees to improve communication.

Although change to a business process tends to have lasting effects, the change tends to be narrow in scope. Unlike strategic change, which motivates organization-wide changes in behavior, process change is often confined to a particular unit, division, or function of the organization. For example, changing an organization's process for measuring customer satisfaction usually requires substantive adjustment to a limited number of functional areas, such as marketing or information systems. In Table 9.2, we describe the characteristics of strategic change in contrast with process change. Strategic changes are the ones that impact culture the most rapidly. However, an accumulation of continuously improving process changes can also lead to a positive and sustainable culture change.

Implementation Barriers to Creating a TQ Culture

One reason for TQ failure is a lack of what Deming called "constancy of purpose" in his original version of the 14 Points. The people who implement quality initiatives often have conflicting goals and priorities. For example, the general manager of a large defense electronics contractor unveiled a big quality program, then plunged into dealing with the unit's plummeting revenues and layoffs. Quality went nowhere. Changes in leadership can be devastating. At Florida Power and Light, John J. Hudiburg drove hard to win the Deming Prize, but his successor reduced the scope of the quality effort.[26] Other organizations continually try to implement the latest fads, only to disband them after a short time in favor of something else. This inconsistency causes an incredible amount of cynicism on the part of the workforce. An organization must have a clear understanding of why it is embarking on a TQ effort and must stay focused for the long haul.

> *Numerous barriers exist to successfully transform organizations to a sustained culture of total quality. Understanding these barriers can help significantly in managing change processes.*

Table 9.2 Strategic versus Process Change

	Strategic Change	**Process Change**
Theme of change	Shift in organizational direction	Adjustment of organizational processes
Driving force	Usually environmental forces—market, rival, technological change	Usually internal— "How can we better align our processes?"
Typical antecedent	Strategic planning process	Self-assessment of management system
How much of the oranization changes?	Typically widespread	Often narrow—divisional or functional
Examples	Entering new markets Seeking low-cost position Mergers and acquisitions	Improving information systems Establishing hiring guidelines Developing improved customer satisfaction measures

Another reason for failure is the lack of a holistic view of quality (which is why we use the term *total* in TQ!). Many approaches to "implementing quality" are one-dimensional and are consequently prone to failure. For example, some firms emphasize the use of quality tools such as statistical process control, but may only deploy them in a narrow part of the organization, such as manufacturing. These firms will see some improvement, but because the entire organization is not involved success will be limited. Others take a problem-solving approach in which defects in both production and customer service are identified and corrected through quality circles or other team approaches. However, they may ignore customer relationship management processes or strategic planning issues. Again, improvements will be achieved, but they will be sporadic and limited. By essentially delegating quality to front-line employees, management demonstrates a lack of leadership, which will not create the sustained culture required for longevity. A third approach might emphasize design, but ignore many potential means for continuous process improvement. Total quality requires a comprehensive effort that encompasses all of the elements discussed in this book thus far. What is really required is a total change in thinking, not a new collection of tools. A focus on tools and techniques is easy; what is hard is understanding and achieving the changes in human attitudes and behavior that are necessary. We see this holistic theme throughout the book as we discuss the "three levels of quality"—individual, process, and organization—all of which are necessary to define a true TQ organization. The level to which an organization evolves reflects its maturity in developing a TQ culture. Even though it is easy to train individuals to perform quality tasks, it is certainly more difficult to establish cross-functional cooperation and to build the entire organization around a TQ framework.

Another danger lies in the lack of understanding cultural issues and the tendency to imitate others—the easy way out. Many of the experts and consultants have rewritten total quality management around their own discipline, such as accounting, engineering, human resources, or statistics. Their "one best model" of TQ may not mesh with an organization's culture; most successful companies develop their own unique approaches to fit their own requirements. Research has shown that imitation of TQ efforts made by one successful organization may not lead to good results in another. To go back to Deming, no knowledge is possible without theory, or to use one of his more descriptive phrases, "There is no instant pudding."

> *Perhaps the most significant failure encountered in most organizations is a lack of alignment between components of the organizational system.*

The importance of systems as one of Deming's components of Profound Knowledge cannot be overemphasized. In the Baldrige criteria, **alignment** is defined as consistency of plans, processes, actions, information, decisions, results, analysis, and learning to support key organization-wide goals. Effective alignment requires common understanding of purposes and goals and use of complementary measures and information for planning, tracking, analysis, and improvement at each of the three levels of quality. A well-aligned organization has its processes focused on achieving a shared vision and strategy. Aligning the organization is a challenging task that is accomplished through a sound strategy and effective deployment. The most damaging alignment problem to which many TQ failures have been attributed is the lack of alignment between expectations that arise from TQ change processes and reward systems. In one survey, an overwhelming percentage (65.8 percent) of managers surveyed ranked the number one barrier to TQ as "Management's compensation is not linked to achieving quality goals."[27] Although we addressed this issue in Chapter 6, ignoring the "What's in it for me?" question can destroy—and it has in numerous cases—any TQ effort.

Certain mistakes are made repeatedly.[28] Some of the more common mistakes include the following:

1. TQ is regarded as a "program," despite the rhetoric that may state the contrary.
2. Short-term results are not obtained, causing management to lose interest—often either no attempt is made to get short-term results, or management believes that measurable benefits lie only in the distant future.
3. The process is not driven by a focus on the customer, a connection to strategic business issues, and support from senior management.
4. Structural elements in the organization block change, such as compensation systems, promotion systems, accounting systems, rigid policies and procedures, specialization and functionalization, and status symbols such as offices and perks.
5. Goals are set too low. Management does not shoot for stretch goals or use outside benchmarks as targets.
6. The organizational culture remains one of "command and control" and is driven by fear or game-playing, budgets, schedules, or bureaucracy.
7. Training is not properly addressed. Too little training is offered to the workforce or it may be of the wrong kind, such as classroom training only or a focus on tools and not problems. Training must be matched to strategy and business needs so as not to be viewed as frivolous.
8. The focus is mainly on products, not processes.
9. Little real empowerment is given and is not supported in actions.
10. The organization is too successful and complacent. It is not receptive to change and learning, and clings to the "not invented here" syndrome.
11. The organization fails to address three fundamental questions: Is this another program? What's in it for me? How can I do this on top of everything else?
12. Senior management is not personally and visibly committed and actively participating.
13. The organization overemphasizes teams for cross-functional problems, which leads to the neglect of individual efforts for local improvements.
14. Employees operate under the belief that more data are always desirable, regardless of relevance—"paralysis by analysis."
15. Management fails to recognize that quality improvement is a personal responsibility at all levels of the organization.
16. The organization does not see itself as a collection of interrelated processes making up an overall system. Both the individual processes and the overall system need to be identified and understood.

Although this list is extensive, it is by no means exhaustive. It reflects the immaturity that many companies exhibit when trying to implement TQ. TQ requires a new set of skills and learning, including interpersonal awareness and competence, team building, encouraging openness and trust, listening, giving and getting feedback, group participation, problem solving, clarifying goals, resolving conflicts, delegating and coaching, empowerment, and continuous improvement as a way of life.[29]

The process must begin by creating a set of feelings and attitudes that lead to lasting values and organizational commitment. It must develop by planning a long-term TQ strategy. Finally, it must be realized through training, continuous feedback and open communications, and empowerment.

SUSTAINING THE QUALITY ORGANIZATION

Getting started often seems easy by comparison with sustaining a quality focus. Numerous organizational barriers and challenges get in the way. New efforts usually begin with much enthusiasm, in part because of the sheer novelty of the effort. After awhile, reality sets in and doubts surface. Real problems develop as early supporters begin to question the process. At this point, the organization can resign itself to inevitable failure or persist and seek to overcome the obstacles.

> *Sustaining total quality requires viewing quality efforts as a journey, not an end, as well as the ability to develop into a "learning organization."*

Quality as a Journey

Successful TQ organizations realize that quality is a never-ending journey. As an old Chinese proverb says, a journey begins with a single step. Perhaps the best way to understand this concept is through an example.[30] In the 1980s, Techneglas, a Columbus, Ohio, producer of glass for television picture tubes, realized that the quality of its products had to be improved to meet the ever-increasing demands of its customers. Although the company trained its employees in SPC during the mid-1980s, the program was short-lived. In 1992, management realized the need for an organized approach for developing SPC, hired an outside consulting firm, and formed a management steering committee. After their first meeting, they realized that the program they were creating had to be much more than SPC, and had to incorporate a broader notion of TQM. Their initial efforts focused around Deming's principles, for example, using SPC to eliminate mass inspection; improving supervision to provide workers with the proper tools, equipment, and processes and drive out fear, establishing new education and training programs; and working with suppliers to ensure statistical evidence of product quality. They also established problem-solving teams, and improved communication between top management and the workforce. By 1993, most operating departments were actively involved, a quality mission statement had been issued, pilot SPC projects were in progress, and teams had been created. A quality council consisting of engineers and assistant supervisors from each department was created to move the implementation process a step down from the management steering committee. Each person on the council was responsible for TQM implementation for his or her respective area. The council focused on SPC applications, teams, and standard operating procedures.

In 1996, a TQM facilitator was added to the organization, which eventually expanded to a facilitator for each department. Figure 9.1 shows the key steps in their implementation process. By May of 1997, the quality policy had been drafted and more than 300 employees received SPC training. Fourteen pilot programs were completed or were in progress. By the end of December, more than 100 standard operating procedures had been written. The plant's workforce continues to believe that TQM implementation is the key to continued improvement for the future.

Even though it is clear that Techneglas has not reached the level of maturity in their management systems as reflected in the Baldrige criteria, they made a serious commitment to the TQ concept and carefully orchestrated a process to make it happen. Surprisingly, or perhaps not, many companies still have not yet made this type of commitment. As the Techneglas example shows, TQ requires discipline, time, and planning just to establish the basics, fundamentals in which many companies are unwilling to invest.

Many Baldrige-winning companies started from similar humble beginnings. As their systems matured, they discovered the benefits of the Baldrige framework and

Figure 9.1 Techneglas TQM Implementation Model

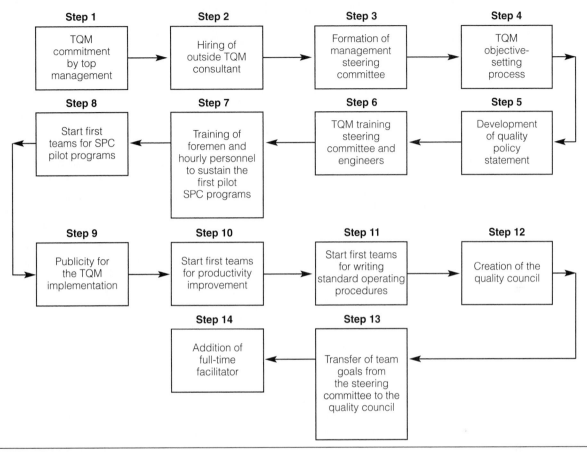

Source: William A. Hines, "The Stops and Starts of Total Quality Management," *Quality Progress,* February 1998, 61–64. ©1998. American Society for Quality. Reprinted with permission.

assessment process as a means for continual improvement. For example, at Armstrong Building Products Operations, the evolution of quality occurred in several phases beginning in 1983:[31]

Phase I (1983–1985)
    Commitment to try
    Philip Crosby system
    Quality improvement teams
Phase II (1985–1990)
    Process improvement
    Quality plans added to business plans
    Supplier quality management
Phase III (1989–1992)
    Vision clearly defined
    Empowered employees; flatter organization
    Use of Baldrige criteria for self-assessment

Phase IV (1991–1994)
   Product and service leadership
   Baldrige Award applications (1995 winner)
   Business results
Phase V (post–1994)
   High performance change process
   "Nonnegotiable" business strategies
   Achieving value for employees, customers, shareholders

Similarly, ADAC Laboratories began its TQ approach in 1991 by benchmarking other leading organizations, forming a monthly Quality Committee, developing a commitment to customer satisfaction, investing in field service, and designing a new strategic planning process.[32] In 1992 ADAC developed its vision, began weekly quality meetings, adopted the Baldrige criteria and conducted a self-assessment, and strengthened quality incentives and rewards. During 1993 the Baldrige criteria were widely deployed, benchmarking was performed in all areas, systematic and comprehensive training programs were started, and quality performance was monitored on a twice-weekly basis. In the next two years, policy deployment (see Chapter 5) was introduced, the ADAC business approach was refined based on TQ and mutual learning principles, the company focused on people-value-added, breakthrough improvement became a priority, and ADAC pursued ISO 9000 registration.

Although the Baldrige Award is not the principal motivator, engaging in the Award process can make a difference. Custom Research Incorporated, for example, stated

> The pursuit [of the Baldrige Award] forced us to improve faster than we would have on our own. As soon as we received the previous year's feedback, we needed to start the current year's application. We were forced to show improvement every year in all aspects of our company. The site visits also motivated our staff. The extensive preparation required for the site visits created tremendous work and tension. But it also created enthusiasm and energy like nothing our company had ever done. . . . We learned from this journey that stubborn persistence does pay off. It paid off for us in both winning the award and in showing us how to improve in order to achieve results. . . . This tremendous opportunity to be reviewed and to receive feedback is one reason we encourage other companies to apply for the Baldrige. Even when we didn't win, it was well worth it. In fact, it was the smartest thing our company ever did. The process of "living under the microscope" proved valuable to our self-awareness. . . . We don't just talk about the Baldrige concept, we implement the principles every day throughout the company. . . . We've actually built an entire company culture around the Baldrige version of performance excellence.[33]

The Learning Organization

Psychologists suggest that individuals go through four stages of learning:

1. Unconscious incompetence: You don't know that you don't know.
2. Conscious incompetence: You realize that you don't know.
3. Conscious competence: You learn to do, but with conscious effort.
4. Unconscious competence: Performance comes effortlessly.

As discussed in Chapter 1, many companies in the United States languished in stage 1 until receiving a wake-up call in the 1980s with regard to quality. Unfortunately, as many organizations move into stage 2, they tend to shoot the messenger and refuse to accept the state of incompetence. This attitude can be explained by recognizing that organizations have both static and dynamic components. If organizations exist to structure the work of groups of people, then they must be expected to produce some tangible product or provide some service. The static part of the organization is intended to document, regularize, and maintain the rational requirements for work through relatively stable processes, policies, procedures, rules, and communications on which everyone, at least tacitly, agrees and depends. The static part of an organization thus inherently resists change. The degree of dynamism in organizations is moderated by factors such as culture, leadership, learning, and linkages between people and structures.

> *Organizations are dynamic entities. Managers must consider the dynamic component in order to deal with instability in the environment, imperfect plans, the need for innovation, and the common human desire for variety and change.*

Therefore, both the culture and the organizational structure should be designed to support the established direction in which the organization is moving, and modified whenever that direction changes significantly. Managers, especially those who do not understand the nature of leadership, are often hesitant to make needed organizational changes as the organization grows, even when the need for change becomes obvious. This need to change, to move through the four stages of learning repeatedly, is embodied in a concept called the *learning organization.*

The concept of organizational learning is not new. It has its roots in general systems theory[34] and systems dynamics[35] developed in the 1950s and 1960s, as well as theories of learning from organizational psychology. Peter Senge, a professor at the Massachusetts Institute of Technology (MIT), has become the major advocate of the learning organization movement. He defines the **learning organization** as:

> . . . an organization that is continually expanding its capacity to create its future. For such an organization, it is not enough merely to survive. "Survival learning" or what is more often termed "adaptive learning" is important—indeed it is necessary. But for a learning organization, "adaptive learning" must be joined by "generative learning," learning that enhances our capacity to create.[36]

The conceptual framework behind this definition requires an understanding and integration of many of the concepts and principles that are part of the TQ philosophy. Senge repeatedly points out, "Over the long run, superior performance depends on superior learning." What he means is that organizations cannot count on being successful in the long run if they merely have committed leaders who use TQ principles for strategic planning and policy deployment, practice TQ in daily operations, and use it for continuous improvement of the current process.

Learning organizations have become skilled in creating, acquiring, and transferring knowledge and in modifying the behavior of their employees and other contributors to their enterprises. A good example of a learning organization (and a learning individual!) is General Electric and Jack Welch. In his first letter to GE shareholders in 1981, he noted, "This commitment to the utmost in quality and personal excellence is our surest path to continued business success. Quality is our best assurance of customer allegiance. It is our strongest defense against foreign competition and the only path to sustained growth and earnings." Welch's approach to business improvement has gone through three cycles of learning:

Quality Spotlight
General Electric

1. In the first cycle (early 1980s to late 1980s), he focused GE on the elimination of variety in its portfolio of businesses by reducing the nonperforming business

units as judged by market performance. The elimination of unprofitable businesses permitted a better use of working capital. However, only so much gain can result from trimming the organization or eliminating bureaucracy, which led to the next phase of learning.

2. During the late 1980s to mid-1990s, he focused the company on simplifying and eliminating non-value-added activities through creative efforts of teams using Work-Outs and the Change Action Process (later renamed the Change Acceleration Process). Work-Out is a tool for involving all people from all ranks, levels, and functions of the organization in problem solving and improvement. Work-Out demolished the artificial barriers and walls within the organization and fostered the idea of "boundaryless learning."

3. Throughout his learning journey, Welch challenged his people to keep looking for creative ways to apply new learning from any source to improve the business. In 1995, Welch discovered Six Sigma and studied its implementation at both Motorola and Allied Signal. This phase of discovery focused on the elimination of variation from already lean business operations to drive gains in productivity and financial performance with a better focus on the customer.

Welch's process for continuous learning led to the discovery that business must simplify first, then automate best practices that have been designed for robust performance in the face of variation in business conditions. As Welch noted, "It is this passion for learning and sharing that forms the basis for the unrelenting optimism with which we view the future, and for the conviction that our greatest days lie ahead."

Quality Spotlight
Motorola

Another example is Motorola. Although Motorola introduced the concept of Six Sigma back in 1986, it is significantly different today. Motorola's "second generation" Six Sigma is an overall high-performance system that executes business strategy.[37] Its results are evident in Motorola's Commercial, Government, and Industrial Solutions Sector division receiving a Baldrige Award in 2002. Their new approach to Six Sigma is based on the following four steps.

1. *Align executives to the right objectives and targets.* This step means creating a balanced scorecard of strategic goals, metrics, and initiatives to identify the improvements that will have the most impact on the bottom line. Projects are not limited to traditional product and service domains but extend to market share improvements, better cash flow, and improved human resource processes.

2. *Mobilize improvement teams around appropriate metrics.* Teams use a structured problem-solving process to drive fact-based decisions; however, the focus on defects and defects per million opportunities (dpmo) sigma levels is less important, particularly in human intensive processes such as marketing and human resources. For example, the definition of a defect as "employee performance that falls below a certain level" can be controversial and be easily manipulated. Continuous measures such as invoice delivery time or credit approval response time are replacing count-based measures such as the number of overdue invoices or the percentage of dissatisfied customers.

3. *Accelerate results.* Motorola uses an action learning framework methodology that combines formal education with real-time project work and coaching to quickly take employees from learning to doing. Project teams receive support from coaches on a just-in-time basis. Projects are driven to be accomplished quickly, rather than over a long period of time. Finally, a campaign management approach helps integrate various project teams so that the cumulative impact on the organization is, in fact, accelerated.

4. *Govern sustained improvement.* Leaders actively and visibly sponsor the key improvement projects required to execute business strategy and review them in the context of outcome goals. An important step is for leaders to actively share best practices and knowledge about improvements with other parts of the organization that can benefit.

Six Sigma continues to be Motorola's method of choice for driving bottom line improvements. More efforts will be focused on product design that enhances the overall customer experience across the value chain. As such, Six Sigma projects increasingly involve key customers, suppliers, and other business partners.

The key to developing learning organizations, according to Senge, is a new approach to leadership. Leaders must develop the capability to integrate creative thinking and problem solving throughout the organization. In the words of Walter Wriston, former CEO of Citibank, "The person who figures out how to harness the collective genius of the people in his or her organization is going to blow the competition away." Finally, leaders in learning organizations must help people to restructure their views of reality. Instead of the traditional focus on reacting to events and responding to historical trends, leaders must encourage and model decision making based on understanding the causes of events and the behavior behind the trends in order to make positive changes to the system. Thus, real improvements (second generation TQ) can only be made by understanding the root causes, instead of treating the symptoms.

David Garvin, who defines the learning organization as " . . . an organization that is skilled at creating, acquiring, and transferring knowledge, and at modifying its behavior to reflect new knowledge and insights,"[38] criticized Senge and others for not providing an operational framework for implementing a learning organization[39] (something that Senge attempts to correct in another book[40]). Interestingly, Garvin observes that simply trying to change and make improvements is not enough. Thus, companies that are trying but failing to make significant changes have not yet become skilled learning organizations. Also, colleges and universities who know and teach about TQ but don't put the concepts into practice to improve their own teaching, research, and administrative processes, are not exhibiting the characteristics of learning organizations.

Learning organizations have to become good at performing five main activities, including systematic problem solving, experimentation with new approaches, learning from their own experiences and history, learning from the experiences and best practices of others, and transferring knowledge quickly and efficiently throughout the organization.[41]

Virtually all of these skills have been defined as TQ terms with the same basic meanings as Garvin suggests:

- Kaizen—continuous quality improvement
- Experimental design
- Santayana review[42]
- Benchmarking
- Dissemination and "holding the gains"

Garvin later raised the important issue of what happens to knowledge when key people leave (retire, die, or move on to other organizations). If knowledge is not widely shared via reports, company intranets, policies and procedures, and face-to-face discussions, it can be easily lost. He states that it must become a part of the organization's norms and values to do such sharing, because it probably is not part of the old style of thinking in most organizations, where it is believed that "knowledge is power."

Sitkin and others proposed that a sharp distinction lies between the concepts of what they called "Total Quality Control" (TQC) and "Total Quality Learning" (TQL) approaches (see Table 9.3).[43] They argued that TQC practices applied to the quality precepts of customer satisfaction, continuous improvement, and treating the organization as a system result in a traditional closed cybernetic control system. A closed-loop control system has a standard, a way of measuring actual performance versus the standard, feedback on variances between actual versus standard, and a way to modify the system. The TQL approach, in contrast, applies practices to the precepts in an open-system way that is experimentally oriented, rather than control-oriented. The authors argued that the control aspects of TQC are appropriate to stable, routine environments where repetitive operations (such as high-volume manufacturing or service delivery) take place. The environment that contains innovative, highly uncertain operations (such as production of newly designed semiconductors or research and engineering departments) would require a TQL focus that was experimentally oriented and tolerant of mistakes in order to successfully invent new products and approaches. Their theory suggests that TQ implementation practices need to be modified in order to fit various environmental and contextual factors such as stage of the life cycle of the product, industry in which the company operates, and level of education and training of the workforce. Indeed, the Ernst & Young Best Practices report discussed earlier in this chapter confirmed the importance of exploring contingent factors in the implementation of TQ practices.

SELF-ASSESSMENT PROCESSES

One way for organizations to build and subsequently sustain a TQ organization is to conduct self-assessments of where it stands relative to best practices and key

Table 9.3 Linking the Distinctive Principles Associated with TQC and TQL to Common Underlying TQM Precepts

	Principles Derived from Common Precepts	
Shared TQM Precepts	**Control-Oriented Principles (TQC)**	**Learning-Oriented Principles (TQL)**
Customer Satisfaction	Monitor and assess known customer needs	Scan for new customers, needs, or issues
	Benchmark to better understand existing customer needs	Test customer need definitions
	Respond to customer needs	Stimulate new customer need definitions and levels
Continuous Improvement	Exploit existing skills and resources	Explore new skills and resources
	Increase control and reliability	Increase learning and resilience
Treating the Organization as a Total System	First-order learning (cybernetic feedback)	Second-order learning
	Participation enhancement focus	Diversity enhancement focus

Source: Sim B. Sitkin, Kathleen M. Sutcliffe, and Roger G. Schroeder, "Distinguishing Control from Learning in Total Quality Management: A Contingency Perspective," *Academy of Management Review* 19, no 3 (1994), 537–564.

Self-assessment should identify both strengths and opportunities for improvement, creating a basis for evolving toward higher levels of performance. Thus, a major objective of most self-assessment projects is the improvement of organizational processes based on opportunities identified by the evaluation.

requirements. **Self-assessment** is the holistic evaluation of processes and performance. The *self* part of the term means that it should be conducted internally rather than simply relying on an external consultant, which promotes greater involvement of the organization's people, yielding a higher level of understanding and buy-in.

At a minimum, a self-assessment should address the following:

- *Management involvement and leadership.* To what extent are all levels of management involved?
- *Product and process design.* Do products meet customer needs? Are products designed for easy manufacturability?
- *Product control.* Is a strong product control system in place that concentrates on defect prevention before the fact, rather than defect removal after the product is made?
- *Customer and supplier communications.* Does everyone understand who the customer is? To what extent do customers and suppliers communicate with each other?
- *Quality improvement.* Is a quality improvement plan in place? What results have been achieved?
- *Employee participation.* Are all employees actively involved in quality improvement?
- *Education and training.* What is done to ensure that everyone understands his or her job and has the necessary skills? Are employees trained in quality improvement techniques?
- *Quality information.* How is feedback on quality results collected and used?

Many self-assessment instruments that provide a picture of the state of quality in the organization are available.[44] The Baldrige National Quality Program provides one simple instrument called *Are We Making Progress?* It provides a way of capturing the voice of the employee and developing baseline measurements of an organization's progress using the Baldrige criteria. The *Are We Making Progress?* Survey is available in the Bonus Materials folder on the CD-ROM. Most self-administered surveys, however, can only provide a rudimentary assessment of an organization's strengths and weaknesses. The most complete way to assess the level of TQ maturity in an organization is to evaluate its practices and results against the Malcolm Baldrige National Quality Award criteria by using trained internal or external examiners, or by actually applying for the Baldrige or a similar state award and receiving comprehensive examiner feedback. Of course, many companies, especially smaller firms, that are just starting on a quality journey should begin with the basics, for example, a well-documented and consistent quality assurance system such as ISO 9000 that was discussed in Chapter 3.

Because the Baldrige process is based on self-assessment against the criteria, it is not surprising that some of the best examples of learning organizations are Baldrige winners. In pursuing their TQ efforts that eventually led to the award, they have continually and systematically translated the examiner feedback into improvements in their management practices. A vice president at Texas Instruments Defense Systems & Electronics (DS&E) Group noted that "participating in the Baldrige Award process energized improvement efforts."[45] By 1997, just before its purchase by Raytheon,

Quality Spotlight
Texas Instruments

DS&E had reduced the number of in-process defects to one-tenth of what they were at the time it won the Baldrige. Production processes that took four weeks several years before were reduced to one week, with 20 to 30 percent less cost.

In 1994 the Texas Instruments Corporation launched the TI Business Excellence Standard (TI-BEST), an assessment and improvement process that grew out of DS&E's Baldrige Award experience.[46] The process is applied to TI businesses around the world. The four steps of TI-BEST are as follows:

1. Define business excellence for your business.
2. Assess your progress.
3. Identify improvement opportunities.
4. Establish and deploy an action plan.

This process provides a systematic approach to learning and improvement and benefits the organization by

- Providing a framework that ties efforts together.
- Providing a vehicle for identifying best practices.
- Providing a structure for sharing knowledge and learning methods and techniques others have used to make improvements.
- Allowing employees to speak the same language of quality, thereby increasing communication and organizational alignment toward common goals.
- Fostering teamwork across the company.
- Improving the ability to measure improvements by documenting processes and results.
- Providing a process to accelerate improvement across the organization.
- Involving every employee in continuous improvement toward world-class benchmarks.

The complete TI approach to business excellence, displayed on meeting room walls throughout the organization, is summed up in Figure 9.2. In this model, business excellence is achieved through the three core principles of total quality. This core is supported by a focus on operational excellence through achieving customer satisfaction with processes and teamwork and empowerment (think back to the role of Process Management and Human Resource Focus in the Baldrige framework in Chapter 3). The approach is implemented by an annual improvement process (Strategic Planning) and measured by a balanced scorecard involving customer, process, HR, and financial measurements and indicators. TI is one of only two semiconductor companies in the world to have gained market share in each of the four consecutive years prior to 1997, and during that time has jumped from last place to first in return on net assets, compared to Intel, Motorola, and National Semiconductor.

Quality Spotlight
Sun
Microsystems

Many other companies learn from Baldrige winners and benchmark them routinely. Scott McNealy, CEO of Sun Microsystems, for example, invited three CEOs of Baldrige winners (FedEx, Motorola, and Xerox) to visit his company to discuss their quality processes. From those meetings came the core principles and strategies that Sun uses today. The key lessons that Sun learned were:

- Quality must be elevated to the level of a "core management process."
- Quality must be the first agenda item of every executive management and board meeting.
- Quality can be managed only if it is measured.
- Quality starts with the employee.
- Achievement in quality must be a factor in compensation.

Figure 9.2 Texas Instruments' Approach to Quality

Office of Best Practices

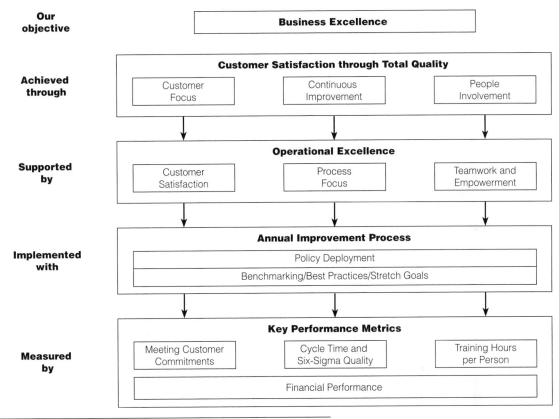

Source: © 1997 American Society for Quality (ASQ). Reprinted with permission.

In explaining this approach, McNealy noted that "Sun was launched as a company in 1982, just about the time that Xerox was starting its Leadership Through Quality process. We wanted to learn as much as we could about what worked and what didn't work before we started solving problems that had already been solved."[47] Assessment findings often identify specific processes and activities that require extensive modification.[48] A Baldrige assessment, for example, might find that the organization lacks a systematic approach for determining customer satisfaction relative to its competitors. A number of actions might be taken to address this opportunity. The organization might consider instituting a competitive analysis program, sponsoring an industry-wide customer satisfaction research program, benchmarking best-in-class organizations, or undertaking some other initiatives to improve its intelligence gathering practices. Although interventions of such scope commonly involve many employees, involvement of senior management in direction setting, resource provision, and subsequent monitoring is usually necessary for effective implementation.

Leveraging Self-Assessment: The Importance of Follow-Up

This lack of follow-through might seem a bit surprising. Why would organizations take the time to conduct a self-assessment and then not follow up on the results? After all, improvement opportunities usually offer significant gains in organizational effectiveness and competitive performance. Some managers may not follow up because they truly do not sense a problem—despite information suggesting otherwise. Often, however, managers get the message but choose not to respond. Many managers react negatively or by denial: "These are wrong," "This is not how it is here," and "These [examiners] missed the boat" are often heard. Such remarks are particularly likely when the report suggested that the organization was a less-than-stellar performer in areas perceived as strengths by senior managers.

Although some research suggests a positive relationship between the conduct of self-assessment and performance outcomes, other evidence suggests that many organizations derive little benefit from conducting self-assessment and achieve few of the process improvements suggested by self-study.

Other mangers may not know what to do with the information. Managers possessing little understanding of how the organization operates may not know which levers to pull in order to effect change or simply do it to appease their superiors. Typical comments include, "There's some good stuff here, but I have no idea where to go from here," and "It's hard for me to understand how to turn this [assessment report] into action." After reading his copy of the feedback report, the head of one manufacturing company muttered, "Well, we've satisfied [the boss's demand for conducting the self-assessment] for another year. Now we can put this all away and get back to business."

Managers must take a positive approach to self-assessment findings, no matter how unpleasant they might appear—"OK, what should we do to improve these areas?" Positive reactions often reinforce long-held but suppressed views about how the organization func-

Following up requires senior leaders to engage in two types of activities: action planning and subsequently tracking implementation progress.

tioned. For example, at a meeting where results were being presented to the top management team, the chief engineering manager, upon hearing of low evaluations related to the organization's communications processes, exclaimed, "I've been telling you guys this for years! Maybe now you'll believe me that we need to do something."

The action plan identifies particular activities necessary to address the improvement opportunities. Effective action plans share some common characteristics. First, key actions to address the opportunities must be identified. A meeting to discuss the findings with key employees is often an excellent way to begin. Once identified, action plans should be documented and the who, what, when, where, and how of each action item specified. A draft version of the action plan should be communicated to inform those directly affected and gain their cooperation. Finally, the action plan should be reviewed to ensure that it effectively addresses the key opportunities identified by the self-assessment findings.

Many managers consider their job finished when action plans are set in motion. However, planned changes are rarely implemented as initially intended. Moreover, people responsible for implementing the plans may need to use encouragement or involvement in order to effectively execute their portions of the intended change. Change implementation demands a second component of effective follow-up—tracking the progress of action plan execution—to provide managers with crucial feedback on whether the intervention is effective.

To leverage self-assessment findings, managers must do four things:

1. *Prepare to be humbled.* "Humbling" is a word we often hear from managers who have recently digested assessment findings. Many of them have trouble believing that the performance levels of the organization are as low as they appear. Managers can temper their expectations by learning about the self-assessment activities and experiences of other organizations. Hearing it from peers, through phone calls to colleagues, and attending conferences, permit managers to learn firsthand about the self-assessment experiences of others.

2. *Talk though the findings.* Follow-up can be enhanced when the top management team discusses the self-assessment findings. Discussing the issues, concerns, and ideas can generate greater shared perspective among executives and improve consensus.

3. *Recognize institutional influences.* Managers should be sensitive to the institutional forces working on their self-assessment activities, such as pressures from customers. Institutional influence can be covertly transmitted through the literature, presentations, and conversation that managers encounter. During the planning phase of the assessment, frank discussion about the environmental motivators of the project can sensitize managers to these outside influences.

4. *Grind out the follow-up.* Even though follow-up activities may not be as exciting as plotting competitive strategy or entertaining customers, they provide infrastructure for realizing the process improvements possible from self-assessment.

IMPLEMENTING ISO 9000, BALDRIGE, AND SIX SIGMA

Organizations can take many routes to building a quality culture, but none of them represents the "one best way." Organizations might pursue Baldrige, ISO 9000, Six Sigma, or some combination of all three. Recently, some organizations are integrating principles of lean production into Six Sigma (which we will discuss further in the next chapter).

Whatever approach or combination of approaches an organization uses should make the most sense—and work—in the organization.

Many organizations start with ISO 9000 because of its prescriptive nature and process orientation. One of the first things to do is to establish a **quality policy** that identifies key objectives of products and services such as fitness for use, performance, safety, and dependability; and basic procedures for such key activities as process control, inspection, testing, control of nonconforming product, corrective action, control of measuring and test equipment, and maintenance of essential records and documentation.

Management must also identify and provide appropriate resources to achieve the objectives set forth in their quality policy. These resources might include people with special skills, manufacturing equipment, inspection technology, and computer software. Individuals must be given the responsibility to initiate actions to prevent the occurrence of defects and errors, to identify and solve quality-related problems, and to verify the implementation of solutions. The system should also include an audit program to determine if the activities and results of the quality system comply with plans.

ISO 9000 requires that all the elements required for a quality system, such as control processes, measuring and test equipment, and other resources needed to achieve the required quality of conformance, be documented in a **quality manual**, which serves as a permanent reference for implementing and maintaining the system. A quality manual need not be complex; a small company might need only a dozen pages while a large organization might need manuals for all key functions. Sufficient records should be maintained to demonstrate conformance to requirements and verify that the quality system is operating effectively. Typical records that might be maintained are inspection reports, test data, audit reports, and calibration data. They should be readily retrievable for analysis to identify trends and monitor the effectiveness of corrective actions. Other documents, such as drawings, specifications, inspection procedures and instructions, work instructions, and operation sheets are vital to achieving quality and should likewise be controlled.

Finally, the system needs to be maintained and kept up to date. This maintenance can be facilitated through **internal audits**, which focus on identifying whether documented procedures are being followed and are effective, and reporting the issues to management for corrective action. Internal audits generally include a review of process records, training records, complaints, corrective actions, and previous audit reports. A typical internal audit begins by asking those who perform a process regularly to explain how it works.[49] Their statements are compared to written procedures, and compliance and deviations are noted. Next, the trail of paperwork or other data are examined to determine whether the process is consistent with the intent of the written procedure and the worker's explanation. Internal auditors also need to analyze whether the process is meeting its intent and objectives, thus focusing on continuous improvement.

ISO 9000 can be implemented in an organization that has not fully embraced TQ and result in significant benefits. In fact, it may even be redundant in a mature organization that has used Baldrige or Six Sigma as a framework for some time. These organizations most likely do all the things required by the standards, and perhaps the only thing missing is the formal documentation. However, as we noted in Chapter 3, although ISO 9000:2000 is compatible with a total quality philosophy, it represents only a subset of it, and is not as complete a management framework as Baldrige.

Implementation of ISO 9000 requires the resources and support of top management, but the details fall mainly within the province of operating managers, supervisors, and employees to identify, develop, and document critical work processes. Meeting the registration standards can be a painstaking and costly undertaking, often requiring organizations to develop and institute many new procedures and train many people. One consultant notes four major barriers to successfully implementing ISO 9000:[50]

1. *Misinterpretation of the requirements.* Significant assistance can be found through public seminars, consultants, books, and registrars.
2. *Overcontrol of the quality system.* Processes and procedures can easily fall into the trap of "paralysis by analysis" where so much control is involved that the actual work does not get done properly and resources are wasted. The purpose of control is to ensure that customer requirements and internal needs are met; thus, defining these aspects clearly can help set the proper direction.
3. *Excessive documentation.* Although ISO 9000 requires appropriate documentation, some organizations go overboard and document everything in the smallest detail. Documentation should reflect the requirements of the standards but need not include unnecessary details, which can become a burden for those using the documentation as well as for those responsible for keeping it up to date.
4. *Failing to identify current gaps in requirements.* ISO does not require that all procedures be designed from scratch. Organizations typically have many existing procedures in place that may only need minor updating to meet the standards. Thus, efforts to assess current practices against the standards to determine what needs to be done and avoid "reinventing the wheel" should be done at the early stages of implementation efforts.

Perhaps the best way to understand the process of building the Baldrige framework into an organization is to review the "Top 10" list of lessons learned by SSM Health Care in their quality journey:

1. Don't wait until you're "ready."
2. It takes longer than you think.
3. Everyone must be involved and understand what's important.
4. It's important not just to understand the Baldrige criteria, but also to understand the connections among the criteria.
5. In well-run organizations, everything is intentional.
6. Never confuse activity with accomplishment.
7. You don't know what you don't know until someone tells you.
8. So, you say you want to be exceptional . . . prove it.
9. If you're in this to win, don't bother.
10. Leadership is not seeing which way the parade is moving and running to the front.

These observations clearly indicate the challenge that TQ and Baldrige present. Implementing Baldrige requires repetitive cycles of self-assessment, priority-setting, action planning to address gaps and opportunities for improvement, and reflection of results, all driven by an organization's vision, strategic challenges, and capabilities.

A major benefit of Baldrige is that it naturally provides a framework for organizational learning, and therefore helps to enhance and sustain an organization, no matter what its current level of maturity. For example, in the Leadership category, the requirement of Organizational Performance Review focuses organizations to provide a picture of their "state of health" and examine how well they are currently performing and also how well they are moving toward the future. This review capitalizes on the information generated from the measurement and analysis of business results and is intended to provide a reliable means to guide both improvement and change at the strategic planning level. It also provides a natural linkage among categories 2, 4, and 7 in the criteria as illustrated in Figure 9.3.

As we indicated throughout the preceding chapters, a fully implemented Six Sigma process is a strategic approach that is driven and supported by top management, but is deployed throughout the organization at every level. Several key principles are necessary for effective implementation of Six Sigma:[51]

- *Committed leadership from top management.* In most companies, Six Sigma represents a major cultural shift, and changing an organization's culture requires intimate involvement by top leadership. Motorola's former CEO Bob Galvin passionately led the Six Sigma effort with aggressive goals: 10-fold reduction in defects in the first three years, and 100-fold improvement in the next three years. Managers at GE participate in hands-on approaches such as personally spending time in every Six Sigma training wave, speaking and answering questions for students, dropping in (usually unannounced) on weekly and monthly Six Sigma reviews, and making site visits at the manufacturing and call-taking operations to observe firsthand the degree to which Six Sigma in ingrained in the culture.
- *Integration with existing initiatives, business strategy, and performance measurement.* Six Sigma should not be pursued just because other companies are doing it. It should have a clear justification in terms of a company's mission and strategic direction. However, with its focus on customers and the bottom line, this integration usually is not too difficult. At companies like GE and Allied Signal, Six Sigma has been extended to all areas of the company, such as product development and financial services. For example, GE first identifies all critical customer performance features and subjects them to a rigorous statistical design process, thus designing products for Six Sigma levels.

Figure 9.3 Organizational Learning in the Baldrige Criteria

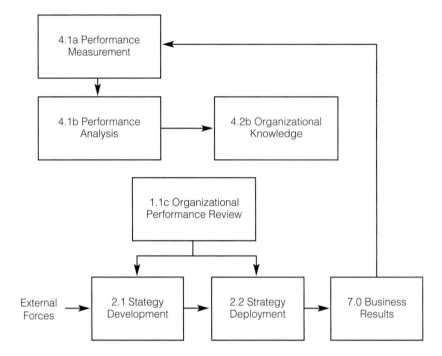

- *Process thinking.* As one of the foundation principles of total quality, a process focus is, not surprisingly, a necessary prerequisite. Mapping business processes is one of the key activities in Six Sigma efforts, as is a disciplined approach to the information gathering, analysis, and problem solving.
- *Disciplined customer and market intelligence gathering.* The ultimate goal is to improve those characteristics that are most important to customers; thus knowledge of customer needs is vital. Approaches that we discussed in Chapter 4 are essential to help focus Six Sigma projects on customers.
- *A bottom-line orientation.* Six Sigma projects must produce real savings or revenues in both the short term and long term. Most Six Sigma projects are designed to be completed within three to six months. GE has a financial analyst certify the results of every project.
- *Leadership in the trenches.* Within GE, Six Sigma includes a diverse population of technical and nontechnical people, managers, and others from key business areas who work together as a team to attack a problem using the DMAIC approach. All employees participate, not just those that hold the "belts."
- *Training.* Although many companies that embraced total quality provide employees with only basic awareness training, Six Sigma companies train nearly everyone in rigorous statistical and problem-solving tools. GE's Green Belt training is delivered to all GE employees and is available in strategic locations across the world. It is typically rolled out over a four-month period and is scheduled to help facilitate the trainee in leading a "green belt project" to not only yield savings but also practice in a real-life situation what is being learned in the training.

- *Continuous reinforcement and rewards.* Six Sigma companies have significantly changed performance measurement and reward systems. At GE, 40 percent of executive incentives are tied to Six Sigma goals and progress. Before any savings are credited to an individual, the Black Belt overseeing the project must show that the problems are fixed permanently. All employees, even executives, who want to be considered for promotion must be trained in Six Sigma and complete a project. Some companies also pool the savings at the business unit level and share the savings with the Six Sigma team members.

A succinct way of describing a successful game plan for implementing Six Sigma is to consider Iomega, the global producer of PC storage devices: *invest in people, make data-based decisions, and achieve and measure results.* The company credits Six Sigma for taking responsibility for quality out of the hands of a few specialists and spreading it throughout the company. Inventory and incoming bad material were both decreased by 80 percent, technical support call wait time was reduced from 80 minutes to 2 minutes on average, and direct labor productivity increased by 65 percent since the Six Sigma program started in 1998, producing more than $120 million in savings through 2001.[52]

A VIEW TOWARD THE FUTURE

It is always a fascinating exercise to try to look into the future and think about how things will be five or ten years from today. For decades, Peter Drucker has been particularly successful in discerning future business, economic, and societal trends long before they were fulfilled. For example, he predicted the rise of Medicare some 20 years before Congress passed its legislation. Drucker advises a pragmatic approach to assessing the future. He noted: "Traditional planning asks, 'What is most likely to happen?' Planning for uncertainty asks, instead, 'What has already happened that will create the future?'"[53]

In reflecting on quality in the past century, A.V. Feigenbaum and Donald S. Feigenbaum observed:

> [Quality] has become one of the 20th century's most important management ideas. It has exorcised the traditional business and graduate management school notion that a company's success means making products and offering services quicker and cheaper, selling them hard and providing a product service net to try to catch those that don't work well. It has replaced this notion with the business principle that making products better is the best way to make them quicker and cheaper and that what is done to make quality better anywhere in an organization makes it better everywhere in the organization.[54]

What the future will hold is never predictable. We face a serious challenge in sustaining the principles of quality amidst the continuing emergence of short-lived management fads, changing leadership driven by pressures of the stock market, e-commerce, and a myriad of other factors. In the January 2000 issue of *Quality Progress,* the American Society for Quality invited 21 individuals to provide comments on quality in the new century.[55] We conclude this chapter with a sample of those comments, and invite you to reflect on what they mean for you as you continue your education and embark on your future careers.

> "Those who understand that quality is derived from effectively managing systems will provide leadership in the new millennium. How many CEOs do you know who arise from the ranks of quality? Few, if any. Yet, I believe tomorrow's business leaders will have deep roots in quality and advanced understanding of how it nourishes their organizations' broader management systems." —Alexander Chong

"The new millennium presents us with some fundamental challenges:

- *Altered labor markets with higher skill levels, a greater gender balance and increasing diversity.*

- *Competitive demands for continuous improvement, customer responsiveness and levels of business excellence that are not price prohibitive.*

These can only be met through an emphasis on quality with equality."
—*Eileen Drew*

"The 21st century will see leading edge companies apply to information the quality principles successfully applied to manufacturing. This will usher in the next economic revolution—the 'realized' Information Age, created by applying information quality management to information and knowledge processes." —Larry P. English

"Quality is necessary for public education to thrive in the future. We have a moral imperative to use quality to make a difference in the lives of our children." —Diane Rivers

"The quality perspective will shape the redefinition of the role of government. This new role will mean serving as a facilitator of relationships and innovative partnerships across all sectors, with less focus on direct delivery of service. Those who understand this context will thrive." —Tina Sung

Finally, Miles Maguire, Editor of *Quality Progress* noted:

In the first 10 seconds of the new century . . . the world will witness the birth of 44 infants . . . by the time a year has passed almost 140 million children will have been born. . . . Consider all the new technologies and products and concepts and ideologies that have taken hold in the last decade: flip phones, fax machines, hiphop, SUVs, global markets, cyberschooling, eco-tourism, eco-terrorism, extreme sports, e-commerce, gene therapy, streaming media and digital encryption—to name just a few. And now consider how the next decade, the first 1 percent of the new millennium, will bring at least as great a proliferation of ideas, innovations, and improvements. These developments will set a higher standard of expectations, creating a marketplace with a dizzying diversity of demands that can scarcely be imagined. What will the voice of the 21st century customer be telling us? We'll have to listen carefully to find out.[56]

QUALITY IN PRACTICE
THE EASTMAN WAY[57]

Eastman Chemical Company recognizes that people create quality; this recognition is embodied in a philosophy known as the Eastman Way (see Figure 9.4). The Eastman Way describes a culture based on key beliefs and principles of respect, cooperation, fairness, trust, and teamwork. Developing such a culture depends not only on learning how to recognize and reward behavior, but also understanding the processes and procedures that work against achieving corporate goals.

The wake-up call came in the late 1970s when a key customer told the company that its product was not as good as its competitors' and indicated that if things did not change, Eastman would lose business. Eastman's first realization was that customer feedback was essential to survival. In 1983 the company developed a quality policy; soon after, it began training employees in statistical process control, flowcharting, and other basic tools. Production employees were encouraged to post their quality results, which became known as "rat sheets." As one employee stated, "You are asking all of us to post all of our mistakes. How will these things be used?" This clash between the traditional, hierarchical, disciplinary organizational culture and the open, honest environment demanded by TQ led to the Eastman Way.

Another key effort started in 1985 was a quality management process that focused on internal and external customers and suppliers and the application of the Deming (PDSA) Cycle. In 1986 senior managers implemented their own quality management process, focusing on understanding customer needs and satisfaction measurements. Later that year the quality focus expanded from individuals to the concept of interlocking teams. (By 1995, 99 percent of employees actively participated in teams.) In 1987 Eastman focused on employee empowerment, and discovered that a company cannot successfully empower employees who don't care, don't have authority, and don't have appropriate skills. Efforts to overcome these obstacles were addressed.

In 1988 Eastman applied for the Baldrige Award, learning a great deal from the site visit and examiners' feedback, and from a Deming seminar attended by 400 managers. In the next year, quality systems were registered to ISO 9000, and Eastman implemented a process, evaluation, control, and improvement system. In 1990 Eastman assessed all of its divisions using the Baldrige criteria. One key improvement made, based on this assessment, was a change in the employee appraisal system, moving from ranking to development. In 1991 Eastman developed its vision: to be the world's preferred chemical supplier. Accomplishing this goal required measuring performance in many different areas, including customer satisfaction, employee morale, supplier cooperation, and local community support. The company was reorganized from a typical hierarchical structure to a set of strategic business units linked in a hub-and-spoke fashion to the CEO. In 1992 Eastman implemented a supplier recognition program and began helping suppliers in their own quality efforts. In 1993 the company received the Baldrige Award.

Figure 9.4 The Eastman Way

Eastman people are the key to success. We have recognized throughout our history the importance of treating each other fairly and with respect. We will enhance these beliefs by building upon the following values and principles:

Honesty and integrity. We are honest with ourselves and others. Our integrity is exhibited through relationships with co-workers, customers, suppliers, and neighbors. Our goal is truth in all relationships.

Fairness. We treat each other as we expect to be treated.

Trust. We respect and rely on each other. Fair treatment, honesty in our relationships, and confidence in each other create trust.

Teamwork. We are empowered to manage our areas of responsibility. We work together to achieve common goals for business success. Full participation, cooperation, and open communication lead to superior results.

Diversity. We value different points of view. Men and women from different races, cultures, and backgrounds enrich the generation and usefulness of these different points of view. We create an environment that enables all employees to reach their full potential in pursuit of company objectives.

Employee well-being. We have a safe, healthy, and desirable workplace. Stability of employment is given high priority. Growth in employee skills is essential. Recognition for contributions and full utilization of employees' capabilities promote job satisfaction.

Citizenship. We are valued by our community for our contributions as individuals and as a company. We protect public health and safety and the environment by being good stewards of our products and our processes.

Winning attitude. Our can-do attitude and desire for excellence drive continual improvement, making us winners in everything we do.

Source: "To Be the Best," Eastman Chemical Company publication ECC-67, January 1994. © 1996 American Society for Quality. Reprinted with permission.

During its quality journey, Eastman identified and removed several roadblocks that impeded motivation:

- *Fear of losing one's job.* The company promised never to lay off anyone because of quality improvement.
- *The performance appraisal system.* Although those rated near the top complained, it was a clear disincentive to the majority of the workforce.
- *The employee suggestion system.* The original system rewarded individuals with money, which interfered with suggestions for improvements by teams.

To sustain its efforts, Eastman uses seven steps for accelerated continuous improvement.

1. *Focus and pinpoint.* "Focus" is about getting everyone on the same page with regard to goals; "pinpoint" is about specifying in measurable terms what is expected.
2. *Communicate.* Communication is done companywide by publicizing key result areas, the vision, and the mission statement so that employees can answer the questions: What is being improved? Why is it important to the customer, to the company, and to me? What has the management team committed to do to help? And what, specifically, is the company asking me to do?
3. *Translate and link.* Teams translate the companywide objectives into their own language and environment.
4. *Create a management action plan.* Management creates a plan with specific actions to reach a goal, including metrics to measure success. Each team member is asked to know what tasks need to be done, why they are important, and what the team's role is in getting them done.
5. *Improve processes.* Teams use a six-step process similar to those described in Chapter 13.
6. *Measure progress and provide feedback.* Eastman is adamant about the importance of unambiguous, visual feedback to employees and appropriate measures of performance. Eastman's rules include:
   - Feedback should be visual, frequent, simple, and specific.
   - The baseline performance should be shown for comparison.
   - The past, current period, and future goals should be posted.
   - The best-ever score should be posted.
   - A chart should be immediately understandable.
   - A good scorecard allows comments and annotations.
7. *Reinforce behaviors and celebrate results.* Eastman reinforces the learning that leads to positive results by encouraging teams at celebrations to answer the questions: What did you do? Why did it work? Why is it important for the customer, the company, and the team? How did the team accomplish its achievement?

Eastman points out that its formula cannot be blindly followed by others, but must be adapted to the specific corporate culture. Nevertheless, the human principles are universal.

Key Issues for Discussion

1. Trace the development of total quality at Eastman. What lessons can you derive that would be useful to other organizations?
2. How does Eastman exhibit principles of a learning organization?

QUALITY IN PRACTICE

MERGING DIVERGENT QUALITY SYSTEMS AT HONEYWELL[58]

AlliedSignal and Honeywell each had years invested in their quality management systems (QMSs) when they merged in 1999 into Honeywell International. AlliedSignal was a leading supporter of, and participant in, the Six Sigma movement. By the time of the merger, AlliedSignal was five years into its Six Sigma program, which was key to the company's effort to capture growth and productivity opportunities more rapidly and efficiently. Meanwhile, Honeywell had developed its own Baldrige-based QMS—the Honeywell Quality Value (HQV) program. The merger between

AlliedSignal and Honeywell required merging and reshaping these two diverse approaches, which was renamed Six Sigma Plus. Six Sigma Plus combines the characteristics of the former AlliedSignal's Six Sigma program and the former Honeywell's HQV method, including lean enterprise, a lean manufacturing component; and activity-based management (ABM), which aids in analyzing customer profitability and targeting future costs for new product development.

Key to making Six Sigma Plus universal in each of Honeywell International's businesses was committing to a strategy of approaching every improvement project with the same logical method, the DMAIC process. Their leadership criteria were also logical and rigorous. Candidates for Six Sigma Plus leadership positions were expected to possess an aptitude for learning, the ability to lead, the ability to mentor others, and the desire to continue to progress through the organization.

Honeywell International's CEO Michael R. Bonsignore made clear the future of Six Sigma at the new company: "As a new organization, our challenge is to continue the performance improvements of our predecessors, delight customers, and achieve aggressive growth. Six Sigma Plus will drive growth and productivity by energizing all of Honeywell International's 120,000 employees worldwide—providing the skills and tools to create more value for our customers, improve our processes and capitalize on the power of the Internet through e-business. I am determined to make it a way of life at Honeywell International."

Edward M. Romanoff, Honeywell International's communications director for Six Sigma Plus and productivity, stated: "Lean helps us to reengineer a process to focus only on customer value-added elements. ABM helps us to understand the profitability of our products and services and to tailor our business models appropriately. The HQV process is being streamlined, timed to affect our annual operating plans, and geared to help our businesses prioritize remedial process improvements that affect customers and the financial well-being of the business. These two pieces—Six Sigma and HQV—come together nicely in that the latter provides the framework for how one should run a business in total, and Six Sigma gives you the quantitative specifics of what and how to improve."

"The Baldrige criteria might mandate that a company measure a given product's performance from a customer's perspective," explains Ray Stark, VP of Six Sigma and Productivity. "And if no such reporting mechanism existed, the Baldrige examiner would suggest that best-performing companies have this kind of system and that your company should put one in place. With a Six Sigma QMS, we would not only say you should put something in place, but we would give you the specific measurements that would help you understand the capability of the product. And it would be done in a way that would allow you to index its quality against a yardstick that we call Six Sigma."

Being able to effectively use Stark's yardstick meant training. Employees of the former AlliedSignal needed to learn about the HQV elements added to their Six Sigma program to create Six Sigma Plus, but the bigger challenge was training employees of the former Honeywell in Six Sigma methodology, a program that had not been developed or implemented there.

But "training" didn't accurately characterize Honeywell International's project based educational system. "Our program is not about training, it's about learning," explains Romonoff. "You can put people in a classroom and give them statistical training. You can give them hypothetical examples to make your point and people do learn, some faster than others. But the part that's unique here is that people come into this mentored environment with a project beforehand. It's something that they or their business particularly needs done. And they're given that project and asked to go and learn about these tools and how they can apply them to get a desired result or 'outcome.' It's very much results-orientated." Management expects this newly gained knowledge to trickle down the corporate structure as soon as the training is completed. Employees who complete the program are expected to go back to their business and complete two to three Six Sigma projects per year. Additionally, they are to mentor as many as 10 groups of employees a year in their Six Sigma Plus learning curve.

"So if that's 10 teams at 10 people each, you've got 100 employees that can be potentially impacted by this one individual," explains Stark. "So it's very important that these people have the team-dynamic skills to deal with different types of people, behaviors and situations. At the end of the day, what we want is at least a simple understanding of the applications of these tools by every employee."

Honeywell International employees who become skilled in Six Sigma Plus tools can earn certification in the following core areas of proficiency:

- Green Belt—A person with working knowledge of Six Sigma Plus methodology and tools, who has completed training and a project to drive high-impact business results.
- Black Belt—A highly skilled Six Sigma Plus expert who has completed four weeks of classroom learning and, over the course of four to six months, demonstrated mastery of the tools through the completion of a major process improvement project.
- Master Black Belt—The Six Sigma Plus expert most highly skilled in the methodologies of variation reduction. After a year-long project-based certification program, Master Black Belts train and mentor Black Belts, help select and lead high-value projects, maintain the integrity of the sigma measurements, and develop and revise Six Sigma Plus learning materials.
- Lean Expert—A person who has completed four weeks of lean training and one or more projects that have demonstrated significant, auditable business results and the appropriate application of Six Sigma Plus lean tools.
- Lean Master—A person highly skilled in implementing lean principles and lean tool utilization in diverse business environments. Certification involves one year of intense study and practice in advanced lean tools, teaching, and mentoring.
- ABM Expert—A person who has demonstrated proficiency in activity-based management (ABM) through a business application involving product costing, process costing, or customer profitability analysis. Certification involves attending an ABM training course, defining a meaningful project, displaying knowledge of the ABM tools and using the data for key decision making. ABM experts frequently link Six Sigma Plus tools to projected and actual financial results.
- ABM Master—A person who has the skills of an expert plus the ability to develop and deliver ABM learning courses. Certification typically takes one year and involves demonstrating the use of ABM data for multiple purposes with repeatable and sustainable

results. ABM Masters are proficient in the use of advanced cost management tools and have the ability to tailor cost data and analysis to a business's vision and strategy.
- TPM Expert—A person who applies total productive maintenance (TPM) and reliability methodologies and tools to assist or lead teams in optimizing asset capacity-productivity at minimum life cycle cost. A TPM Expert is responsible for determining critical equipment and measuring its overall effectiveness, thus enabling growth and productivity through optimum asset utilization.
- TPM Master—A highly skilled individual experienced in the use of TPM and reliability tools and methodologies. TPM Masters' responsibilities include assisting leadership in identifying high-leverage asset improvement opportunities; leading critical, high-leverage improvement projects in a business; and leading cultural paradigm shifts from reactive to proactive asset management.

This commitment to training and expansion of Six Sigma Plus around the world has paid significant dividends. One of Honeywell's European divisions, Aerospace Services, merged activity-based management and lean manufacturing techniques at its Raunheim, Germany, facility. The site repairs auxiliary power units, propulsion engines, and components that provide air conditioning and other power-related features aboard aircraft. The site impressed customers over a recent two-year period with a 43 percent reduction in component repair time. It helped Honeywell achieve a $47 million increase in revenue and was a major factor in $900,000 worth of productivity improvements. An Industrial Control team developed a reliable, cost-effective family of chips and assembled components for the burgeoning data communications market. As a result, Industrial Control achieved a 500 percent increase in revenue growth, resulting in a year-over-year increase in operating profits of several million dollars. Cycle time was reduced 35 percent, and yields increased from 75 percent to 93 percent.

Key Issues for Discussion

1. Trace the development of Six Sigma, the Honeywell Quality Value (HQV) program, and Six Sigma Plus, before and after the

AlliedSignal and Honeywell merger. What role did the corporate culture of each organization play in the results from the Six Sigma Plus initiative?

2. How does top management show its support of Six Sigma Plus? Do you believe that an adequate structure exists to continue building and sustaining the quality effort at Honeywell for the foreseeable future?

3. What are the unique features of Six Sigma Plus that are not part of the standard Six Sigma process discussed in earlier chapters?

 ## REVIEW QUESTIONS

1. Why do companies decide to adopt TQ? What approach to TQ is more prevalent? Why?

2. Summarize ways by which senior leaders can be sold on the TQ concept.

3. Explain the difference between *function, process,* and *ideology* in viewing such organizational activities as TQ.

4. What is *culture*? How are cultural values reflected in organizations?

5. How can an organization develop a TQ-supportive corporate culture?

6. Summarize the differences between a traditional organization and a TQ-focused organization (see Bonus Materials).

7. What lessons can be learned from Wainwright Industries about changing a company's culture?

8. What are best practices? What are the major conclusions and implications of the Best Practices report of Ernst & Young and the American Quality Foundation? How do they relate to Deming's philosophy?

9. Describe the role of senior management, middle management, the workforce, and unions in TQ implementation. Describe the responsibilities of each group and how they can support one another.

10. What must organizations do to successfully prepare for change?

11. Explain the differences between "strategic change" and "process change."

12. Discuss the barriers to successful TQ implementation. What are some of the common mistakes that organizations make when attempting to implement TQ?

13. Define the term *alignment*. Of what importance is alignment in successfully implementing TQ?

14. Explain the importance of viewing quality as a journey.

15. Describe the four stages of learning. How is this model of organizational learning reflected in the Baldrige criteria?

16. What is a learning organization? Why is this concept important to total quality?

17. Explain how General Electric and Motorola exemplify organizational learning.

18. What is self-assessment? Explain the importance of self-assessment in building a TQ organization. What issues should self-assessment address?

19. Why is follow-up important as a part of self-assessment processes? What two key activities should comprise follow-up? What advice should managers heed to leverage self-assessment?

20. What basic things must organizations do to begin implementing ISO 9000, Baldrige, and Six Sigma?

DISCUSSION QUESTIONS

1. What might the term *dysfunctional corporate culture* mean? What implications does it have regarding quality? Discuss how each of the Baldrige Core Values and Concepts are explicitly or implicitly reflected in each of the first six categories of the Baldrige criteria.

2. For each of the Baldrige Core Values and Concepts, discuss things that you might observe in a site visit to TQ and non-TQ organizations.

3. Consider each of the management practices discussed in the Bonus Materials in the context of TQ versus traditional management. Propose some approaches for how an organization might move form the traditional practice to a TQ orientation. What specific organizational changes would be necessary?

4. Create a matrix diagram in which each row is a category of the Baldrige criteria and four columns correspond to the following:
   • Traditional management practices
   • Growing awareness of the importance of quality
   • Development of solid quality management system
   • Outstanding, world-class management practice
   In each cell of the matrix, list two to five characteristics that you would expect to see for a company in each of the preceding four situations for that category. How might this matrix be used as a self-assessment tool to provide directions for improvement?

5. Develop a hierarchy of the Baldrige Award criteria's Areas to Address that would guide an organization just starting to pursue TQ toward world-class performance. In other words, what Areas to Address would be more appropriate for new organizations to concentrate on, and in what sequence should they progress toward fully meeting the Baldrige criteria?

6. What steps might an organization take to overcome the implementation barriers and common mistakes cited in this chapter?

7. Discuss typical reasons for each of the following barriers to TQ implementation:
   a. Poor planning
   b. Lack of top management commitment
   c. Workforce resistance
   d. Lack of proper training
   e. Teamwork complacency
   f. Failure to change the organization properly
   g. Ineffective measurement of quality improvement

8. Describe some personal experiences in which you traveled through the four stages of learning described in this chapter.

9. What might the learning organization concept mean to a college or university?

10. In one company, the overriding focus of implementing TQ was ability to reduce costs. How does this narrow view of TQ inhibit the effectiveness of the organization?

11. You have undoubtedly seen a flock of geese flying overhead. How do the following behaviors of this species provide some insight for organizations wishing to implement TQ?
    a. As each bird flaps its wings, it creates an uplift for the bird behind. By using a "V" formation, the whole flock adds 71 percent more flying range than if each bird flew alone.

    b. Whenever one falls out of formation, it suddenly feels the resistance of trying to fly alone, and quickly gets back into formation to take advantage of the lifting power of the birds immediately in front.

    c. When the lead bird gets tired, it rotates back into formation and another flies at the point position.

    d. The birds in formation honk from behind to encourage those up front to maintain their speed.

    e. When one gets sick or wounded or shot down, two birds drop out of formation and follow their fellow member down to help or provide protection. They stay with this member of the flock until it can fly again or dies. Then they launch out on their own, with another formation or to catch up with their own flock.

12. What is your opinion on the future of quality? Do you agree with the comments made in the concluding section of this chapter? Why or why not?

 # Projects, Etc.

1. Examine some corporate Web sites and comment on the cultural values that are reflected by the information you find. How important do these organizations view quality to their success?

2. For each item in the Baldrige criteria, determine whether each of the core values and concepts are reflected (a) strongly, (b) moderately, or (c) little to not at all. Summarize your results in a matrix (rows represent core values and columns represent the items).

3. Talk to individuals that you know from some local organizations (companies, schools, government agencies) about the organization's commitment to quality principles. What factors do they attribute to either the success or failure of their organization's approaches?

4. Interview a manager at a local organization to classify the organization on the scale from "traditional to TQ" based on the list of factors described in the Bonus Materials.

5. List some key factors that differentiate quality implementation among small and large companies. What things would smaller companies be better at than large companies? If possible, study some companies to verify your hypotheses.

6. Interview your fellow students to identify a set of "best learning practices." Develop a plan for sharing these throughout your school.

7. Find an organization that has implemented ISO 9000, Baldrige, or Six Sigma. Prepare a report on the implementation issues and challenges that the organization faced. How did they address them, and what was the result of their efforts?

Cases

Additional cases are available in the Bonus Materials Folder on the CD-ROM.

I. The Parable of the Green Lawn[59]

A new housing development has lots of packed earth and weeds, but no grass. Two neighbors make a wager on who will be the first to have a lush lawn. Mr. Fast N. Furious knows that a lawn will not grow without grass seed, so he immediately buys the most expensive seed he can find because everyone knows that quality improves with price. Besides, he'll recover the cost of the seed through his wager. Next, he stands knee-deep in his weeds and tosses the seed around his yard. Confident that he has a head start on his neighbor, who is not making much visible progress, he begins his next project.

Ms. Slo N. Steady, having grown up in the country, proceeds to clear the lot, till the soil, and even alter the slope of the terrain to provide better drainage. She checks the soil's pH, applies weed killer and fertilizer, and then distributes the grass seed evenly with a spreader. She applies a mulch cover and waters the lawn appropriately. She finishes several days after her neighbor, who asks if she would like to concede defeat. After all, he does have some blades of grass poking up already.

Mr. Furious is encouraged by the few clumps of grass that sprout. While these small, green islands are better developed than Ms. Steady's fledgling lawn, bare spots and weeds surround them. If he maintains these footholds, he reasons, they should spread to the rest of the yard. He notices that his neighbor's lawn is more uniform and is really starting to grow. He attributes this progress to the Steady children, who water the lawn each evening. Not wanting to appear to be imitating his neighbor, Mr. Furious instructs his children to water his lawn at noon.

The noon watering proves to be detrimental, so he decides to fertilize the remaining patches of grass. Since he wants to make up for the losses the noon watering caused, he applies the fertilizer at twice the recommended application rate. Most of the patches of grass that escape being burned by the fertilizer, however, are eventually choked out by the weeds.

After winning the wager with Mr. Furious, Ms. Steady lounges on the deck enjoying her new grill, which she paid for with the money from the wager. Her lawn requires minimal maintenance, so she is free to attend to the landscaping. The combination of the lawn and landscaping also results in an award from a neighborhood committee that determines that her lawn is a true showplace. Mr. Furious still labors on his lawn. He blames the poor performance on his children's inability to properly water the lawn, nonconforming grass seed, insufficient sunlight, and poor soil. He claims that his neighbor has an unfair advantage and her success is based on conditions unique to her plot of land. He views the loss as grossly unfair; after all, he spends more time and money on his lawn than Ms. Steady does.

He continues to complain about how expensive the seed is and how much time he spends moving the sprinkler around to the few remaining clumps of grass that continue to grow. But Mr. Furious thinks that things will be better for him next year, because he plans to install an automatic sprinkler system and make a double-or-nothing wager with Ms. Steady.

Discussion Questions

1. Within the context of the continual struggles to create a "world-class" lawn and "world-class" business, draw analogies between the events when total quality is implemented.
2. Specifically, translate the problems described here into business language. What are the implementation barriers to achieving total quality?

II. The Yellow Brick Road to Quality[60]

In the film *The Wizard of Oz*, Dorothy learned many lessons. Surprisingly, managers can learn a lot also. For each of the following summaries of scenes in the film, discuss the lessons that organizations can learn in pursuing change and a TQ culture.

1. Dorothy was not happy with the world as she knew it. A tornado came along and transported her to the Land of Oz. Dorothy's house was dropped by the tornado on the Wicked Witch of the East, killing the witch. "Ding, dong, the witch is dead!" rang throughout Munchkinland, but Dorothy had enraged the dead witch's sister. Dorothy only temporarily lost her home support provided by family back in Kansas. All is not good, however, in the Land of Oz. Dorothy's problem is to find her way home to Kansas. Her call to action was precipitated by a crisis—the tornado that transported her to an alien land.

2. In the throes of a Kansas tornado, Dorothy is transported to an unfamiliar land. Immediately, she realizes her world is different and the processes and people she encounters are different, yet bear some similarity to her Kansas existence. She is lost and confused and uncertain about the next steps to take. She realizes she is in a changed state—the Land of Oz—and must devise a plan to get home.

3. Dorothy is a hero for killing the Wicked Witch of the East. Glinda the Good Witch sends Dorothy on her way to meet the Wizard of Oz who will help her get back to Kansas. The Wicked Witch of the West tries to get Dorothy's newly acquired ruby slippers, but to no avail. Dorothy and Toto leave for Oz via the Yellow Brick Road. Along the way, they are joined by Scarecrow, Tin Man, and Lion. Through their teamwork, they provide mutual support to endure the vexing journey. They overcome many risks and barriers, including the sleeping poppy field, flying monkeys, and a haunted forest on the way to Oz.

4. Dorothy and her entourage finally reach Oz and meet the Wizard. Rather than instantly granting their wishes, the Wizard gives them an assignment—to obtain the Wicked Witch's broom. They depart for the West.

5. Charged with the task of obtaining the broom, Dorothy and company experience several encounters with near disaster, including Dorothy's incarceration in the witch's castle while an hourglass counts the time to her death. In a struggle to extinguish the Scarecrow's fire (incited by the Wicked Witch), Dorothy tosses a bucket of water, some of which hits the Witch and melts her. Dorothy is rewarded with the broomstick and returns to Oz.

6. Returning to Oz, the group talks with the Wizard, expecting him to help Dorothy return to Kansas. After defrocking the Wizard, they find out he does not know how. The Wizard tries to use a hot air balloon to return and accidentally leaves Dorothy and Toto behind upon takeoff. Glinda arrives and helps Dorothy realize she can return to Kansas on her own with the help of the ruby slippers.

7. Dorothy awakens from her dream and experiences a new understanding and appreciation for her home and family in Kansas. "Oh, Auntie Em, there's no place like home."

III. Westerfield Construction[61]

Westerfield Construction hired a new quality manager, Kelly Deters, to help integrate its quality system into everyday business operations. One of her initial projects was to lead the development and implementation of a customer service life cycle (CSLC), which is the identification, analysis, involvement, management, data sharing, and evaluation of all the contact points between the company and its customers, along with strong feedback mechanisms. Deters began by assessing the readiness of the organization for change. She determined that the executive team was able to inspire others and act as role models, and were strong and effective leaders. The company had a functioning quality council of executive and middle managers, whose purpose was to review and become personally involved in selected change initiatives. Communications among the team, middle managers, and employees had improved significantly, largely because of frequent open forums that were initiated by the CEO. Deters concluded that the firm's strategy supported its mission and vision, and that organizational culture supported change in the company. These factors all pointed to a favorable environment for change, leading her to believe that she would be able to successfully implement the CSLC.

Because the CSLC was cross-functional, it touched almost every part of the organization, including some that did not recognize their relationship with other parts of the company. Deters built a cross-functional team of employees to review the business plan and customer strategies to provide context and alignment with the vision and company strategy. She also had a consultant train the team in the use of the seven management and planning tools (see Chapter 5). Resources were available to the team for benchmarking outstanding organizations with established CSLCs. Sufficient budget, time, and other resources were also provided to her by the executive team. The CSLC team used the tools prior to developing an action plan for implementation. They developed measures to monitor the effectiveness of the CSLC and drive continuous improvements. She decided to phase in the implementation in two functional areas that had strong existing customer relationships: estimating and project management.

Within six months the CSLC was operational and the team was rewarded for its efforts; each team member was given a day off with pay, and the company newsletter ran articles about customer service, satisfaction, and the progress of the CSLC team. An executive manager was given the responsibilities for managing the new process, and before the team disbanded, lessons learned were identified and shared for future projects.

Discussion Questions

1. In examining the process that Deters used to manage the development and implementation of this project, what factors contributed to her success?
2. Try to develop a model in the form of a flowchart that characterizes an effective change process based on this case.

ENDNOTES

1. Brad Stratton, "Cynicism vs. Kelly Potter," *Quality Progress* 27, no. 9 (September 1994), 5.

2. Gary Salengna and Farzaneh Fazel, "Obstacles to Implementing Quality," *Quality Progress,* July 2000, 53–57.

3. Brian Dumaine, "Times Are Good? Create a Crisis," *Fortune,* June 28, 1993, 123–130.

4. Susan E. Daniels and Mark R. Hagen, "Making the Pitch in the Executive Suite," *Quality Progress,* April 1999, 25–33.

5. Thomas A. Stewart, "Rate Your Readiness to Change," *Fortune,* February 7, 1994, 106–110.

6. James R. Evans and Matthew W. Ford, "Value-Driven Quality," *Quality Management Journal* 4, no. 4 (1997), 19–31.

7. For a more complete treatise of the relationship between Six Sigma and Baldrige, see James R. Evans and Kenneth Pipke, "Six Sigma & Baldrige—A Synergistic Team," *Quality Management Forum,* Fall 2002.

8. "What have been the results of Six Sigma?" *Quality Progress* 31, no. 6 (June, 1998), 39.

9. Paul, L. "Practice Makes Perfect," *CIO Enterprise* 12, no. 7 (January 15, 1999), Section 2.

10. Cohen, A. "General Electric," *Sales and Marketing Management,* October 1997.

11. C. Hendricks, and R. Kelbaugh. "Implementing Six Sigma at GE," *The Journal for Quality and Participation,* July/August 1998.

12. "Total Quality at Procter & Gamble," The Total Quality Forum, Cincinnati, Ohio (August, 1991), 6–8.

13. Paul R. Keck, "Why Quality Fails," *Quality Digest,* November 1995, 53–55.

14. Gregory P. Smith, "A Change in Culture Brings Dramatic Quality Improvements," *The Quality Observer,* January 1997, 14–15, 37.

15. James H. Davis, *Who Owns Your Quality Program? Lessons from Baldrige Award Winners* (New York: Coopers & Lybrand, undated).

16. "Special Report: Quality," *Business Week,* November 30, 1992, 66–75; and H. James Harrington, "The Fallacy of Universal Best Practices," Report TR 97-003, Ernst & Young, 1997.

17. Cyndee Miller, "TQM's Value Criticized in New Report," *Marketing News,* 1992; Gilbert Fuchsberg, " 'Total Quality' Is Termed Only Partial Success," *The Wall Street Journal,* October 1, 1992, B1, B7.

18. Joseph M. Juran and A. Blanton Godfrey (eds.), *Juran's Quality Handbook* 5th ed. (New York: McGraw-Hill, 1999); and Frank M. Gryna, *Quality Planning and Analysis,* Fourth ed. (New York: McGraw-Hill, 2001). This concept is summarized in Mary Anne Watson and Frank M. Gryna "Quality Culture in Small Business: Four Case Studies," *Quality Progress,* January 2001, 41–48.

19. Henry Mintzberg, *Mintzberg on Management* (New York: The Free Press, 1989), 15–21.

20. Arthur R. Tenner, and Irving J. DeToro, *Total Quality Management: Three Steps to Continuous Improvement* (Reading, MA: Addison-Wesley, 1992).

21. Leonard Sayles, *The Working Manager* (New York: The Free Press, 1993), 25–32.

22. Mark Samuel, "Catalysts for Change," *The TQM Magazine* 2, no. 4 (1992), 198–202.

23. Davis (see note 15).

24. Janet Young, "Driving Performance Results at American Express," *Six Sigma Forum Magazine* 1, no. 1 (November 2001), 19–27.

25. Matthew W. Ford and James R. Evans, "Baldrige Assessment and Organizational Learning: The Need for Change Management," *Quality Management Journal* 8, no. 3 (2001), 9–25.

26. "Where Did They Go Wrong?" *Business Week/Quality 1991,* October 25, 1991, 34–38.

27. Nabil Tamimi and Rose Sebastianelli, "The Barriers to Total Quality Management," *Quality Progress,* June 1998, 57–60.

28. Core body of knowledge working council findings, "Issues in Implementation of TQ," a report of the Total Quality Leadership Steering Committee and Working Councils, Total Quality Forum, Cincinnati, Ohio (November 1992), 255–257.

29. Thomas H. Patten, Jr., "Beyond Systems—The Politics of Managing in a TQM Environment," *National Productivity Review,* 1991/1992.

30. William A. Hines, "The Stops and Starts of Total Quality Management," *Quality Progress,* February 1998, 61–64. © 1998. American Society for Quality. Reprinted with permission.

31. Henry A. Bradshaw, "From Leadership to Customer Satisfaction: The Total Quality Management System," Presentation Material from the 1996 Regional Malcolm Baldrige Award Conference, Boston, June 6, 1996.

32. Doug Keare, "Lessons Learned and Quality Journey," presentation notes, 1997 Quest for Excellence Conference, Washington, DC.

33. Custom Research Incorporated, "Six Lessons Learned From Our Baldrige Journey," available at http://www.cresearch.com/mb/mb02/mb02_con.htm.

34. L. von Bertalanffy, "The Theory of Open Systems in Physics and Biology," *Science* 111 (1950), 23–29.

35. J. W. Forrester, *Industrial Dynamics* (New York: John Wiley & Sons, 1961).

36. Peter M. Senge, *The Fifth Discipline: The Art and Practice of the Learning Organization* (New York: Doubleday Currency, 1990), 14.

37. Matt Barney, "Motorola's Second Generation," *Six Sigma Forum Magazine* 1, no. 3 (May 2002), 13–22.

38. David A. Garvin, *Learning in Action: A Guide to Putting the Learning Organization to Work* (Boston: Harvard Business School Press, 2000), 11.

39. David A. Garvin. "Building a Learning Organization," *Harvard Business Review,* July/August 1993, 80.

40. Peter M. Senge, Charlotte Roberts, Richard B. Ross, Brian J. Smith, and Art Kleiner, *The Fifth Discipline Field Book: Strategies and Tools for Building a Learning Organization* (New York: Currency-Doubleday, 1994).

41. Garvin (see note 38).

42. This intriguing label deserves a special explanation. It was coined by Joseph Juran in *Juran on Quality by Design* (New York: The Free Press, 1992), 409–413. It refers to the remark once made by philosopher George Santayana, who said, "Those who cannot remember the past are condemned to repeat it."

43. Sim B. Sitkin, Kathleen M. Sutcliffe, and Roger G. Schroeder. "Distinguishing Control from Learning in Total Quality Management: A Contingency Perspective," *Academy of Management Review* 19, no. 3 (1994), 537–564.

44. See, for example, Mark Graham Brown, "Measuring Up Against the 1997 Baldrige Criteria," *Journal for Quality and Participation* 20, no. 4 (September 1997), 22–28.

45. Ann B. Rich, "Continuous Improvement: The Key to Success," *Quality Progress* 30, no. 6 (June 1997).

46. Brad Stratton, "TI Has Eye on Alignment," *Quality Progress* 30, no. 10 (October 1997), 28–34.

47. Larry Hambly, "Sun Microsystems Embeds Quality into Its DNA," *The Quality Observer,* July 1997, 16–20, 45.

48. Many examples of these interventions and of management's involvement in them have been documented in the popular literature. See, for example, D. H. Myers, and J. Heller, "The Dual Role of AT&T's Self-Assessment Process," *Quality Progress,* January 1995, 79–83; D. Zaremba, and T. Crew, "Increasing Involvement in Self-Assessment: The Royal Mail Approach," *TQM Magazine,* February 1995, 29–32; and M. Blazey, "Insights into Organizational Self-Assessments," *Quality Progress,* October 1998, 47–52.

49. Tom Taormina, "Conducting Successful Internal Audits," *Quality Digest,* June 1998, 44–47.

50. Kim, Young, "ISO 9000—Making Companies Competitive," *Quality in Manufacturing,* November/December 1994, 26.

51. Jerome A. Blakeslee, Jr., "Implementing the Six Sigma Solution," *Quality Progress,* July 1999, 77–85;

© 1999. American Society for Quality. Reprinted with permission; and Kim M. Henderson and James R. Evans, "Successful Implementation of Six Sigma: Benchmarking General Electric Company," *Benchmarking: An International Journal* 7, no. 4 (2000), 260–281.

52. Robert A. Green, "Seeking Six Sigma Standardization," *Quality Digest,* August 2001, 49–52.

53. Peter F. Drucker. "Planning for Uncertainty," in *Managing in a Time of Great Change* (New York: Truman Talley Books/Dutton, 1995) , 39–40.

54. A.V. Feigenbaum and Donald S. Feigenbaum, "New Quality for the 21st Century," *Quality Progress,* December 1999, 27–31.

55. "21 Voices for the 21st Century," *Quality Progress,* January 2000, 31–39.

56. Miles Maguire, "The Voice of the 21st Century Customer," *Quality Progress,* January 2000, 41.

57. Adapted from Weston F. Milliken, "The Eastman Way," *Quality Progress* 29, no. 10 (October 1996), 57–62.

58. Robert Green, "Dedicated Teams Successfully Merge Two Divergent Quality Systems," *Quality Digest,* December 2000, 24–28. Adapted from Quality Digest, http://www.qualitydigest.com with permission.

59. Adapted from James A. Alloway, Jr., "Laying Groundwork for Total Quality," *Quality Progress* 27, no. 1 (January 1994), 65–67. © 1994 American Society for Quality. Reprinted with permission.

60. David M. Lyth and Larry A Mallak, "'We're Not in Kansas Anymore, Toto' or Quality Lessons from the Land of Oz," *Quality Engineering* 10, no. 30 (1998), 579–588.

61. Based on Gregory S. Shinn, "Intentional Change by Design," *Quality Progress,* May 2001, 46–51.

BIBLIOGRAPHY

Brown, Mark Graham. *Baldrige Award-Winning Quality. How to Interpret the Baldrige Criteria for Performance Excellence,* 12th ed. Milwaukee: ASQ Quality Press, 2003.

Burns, T., and G. M. Stalker. *The Management of Innovation.* London: Tavistock, 1961.

Conti, Tito. "Stakeholder-Based Strategies to Enhance Corporate Performance." Denver, CO: Annual Quality Congress Proceedings, May 2002, 373–381.

Emery, F. E., E. L. Trist, and J. Woodward. *Management and Technology.* London: Her Majesty's Stationery Office, 1958.

Ford, Matthew W. and James R. Evans. "Baldrige Assessment and Organizational Learning: The Need for Change Management." *Quality Management Journal* 8, no. 3 (July 2001), 9–25.

Hutton, David W. *From Baldrige to the Bottom Line: A Road Map for Organizational Change and Improvement.* Milwaukee: ASQ Quality Press, 2000.

Lawrence, P. R., and J. W. Lorsch. *Organization and Environment.* Boston: Harvard University, Division of Research, Graduate School of Business Administration, 1967.

Miller, Ken. *The Change Agent's Guide to Radical Improvement.* Milwaukee: ASQ Quality Press, 2002.

Rue, Leslie W., and Lloyd L. Byars. *Management: Skills and Applications, with Powerweb,* 10th ed. New York: McGraw-Hill/Irwin, 2002.

Schmidt, Warren H., and Jerome P. Finnigan. *A Race Without a Finish Line.* San Francisco: Jossey-Bass Publishers, 1992.

Silverman, Lori with Annabeth L. Propst. *Critical SHIFT: The Future of Quality in Organizational Performance.* Milwaukee: ASQ Quality Press, 1999.

Van der Wiele, Ton, Alan Brown, Robert Millen, and Daniel Whelan. "Improvement in Organizational Performance and Self-Assessment Practices by Selected American Firms." *Quality Management Journal* 7, no. 4, (October 2000), 8–22.

Six Sigma and the Technical System

Even though a strong foundation of managerial practices is absolutely essential for success, quality is made on the factory floor and on the front lines of service systems. Assuring quality of products and services is assisted by the appropriate use of effective analytical tools and techniques for analyzing data, solving problems, improving and controlling processes, and reducing the potential for failure. In this part of the book, we focus on these issues, using the philosophy and structure of Six Sigma to guide the organization of these chapters.

Chapter 10 expands upon the concepts of Six Sigma that were introduced in Chapter 3, focusing on project selection and teamwork, tools and methodology, and the relationship with concepts of lean production. Chapter 11 builds upon the Deming philosophy introduced in Chapter 3, particularly the role of statistics and statistical thinking in evaluating process effectiveness and making informed decisions. In Chapter 12 we focus on design for Six Sigma, an emerging philosophy supported by a collection of tools and methodologies for building quality and reliability into products and services. In Chapter 13, we present a variety of approaches and tools for quality improvement, that are key components of process management. In Chapter 14, we address statistical process control, focusing on the construction and use of the most common types of control charts. Each chapter in this section of the book provides numerous problems for practice in developing these technical skills.

CHAPTER

10

PRINCIPLES OF SIX SIGMA

Six Sigma has evolved from a simple quality metric to an overall strategy to accelerate improvements and achieve unprecedented performance levels by focusing on characteristics that are critical to customers and identifying and eliminating causes of errors or defects in processes.[1] The Six Sigma approach aims to reduce defect levels to only a few parts per million for an organization's key products and processes. Accomplishing such a daunting task requires the effective implementation of statistical principles and various tools for diagnosing quality problems and facilitating improvement.

In Chapters 3 through 9 we introduced Six Sigma as a quality management framework, discussed some of the basic principles of Six Sigma as they relate to customers, leadership and strategic planning, human resources, process management, and measurement, and addressed some key issues for successful implementation. Beginning with this chapter, we focus on the technical, rather than the managerial, issues associated with Six Sigma, and present a wide variety of tools and techniques for improving products and processes. In this chapter we integrate the philosophy of Six Sigma introduced in earlier chapters by discussing the underpinnings of Six Sigma and its methodology. In the remaining chapters of the book, we describe in detail the key tools for quality improvement that support Six Sigma efforts.

THE STATISTICAL BASIS OF SIX SIGMA

In Chapter 8 we introduced the metrics used for measuring quality performance. Six Sigma began by stressing a common measure for quality. In Six Sigma terminology, a **defect**, or **nonconformance**, is any mistake or error that is passed on to the customer. A **unit of work** is the output of a process or an individual process step. A measure of output quality is **defects per unit (DPU)**:

Although we view quality improvement tools and techniques from the perspective of Six Sigma, it is important to understand that they are simply a collection of methods that have been used successfully in all types of quality management and improvement initiatives, from generic TQM efforts, to ISO 9000, and in Baldrige processes.

$$\text{Defects per unit} = \text{Number of defects discovered}/\text{Number of units produced}$$

However, this type of output measure tends to focus on the final product, not the process that produces the product. In addition, it is difficult to use for processes of varying complexity, particularly service activities. Two different processes might have significantly different numbers of opportunities for error, making appropriate comparisons difficult. The Six Sigma concept redefines quality performance as **defects per million opportunities (dpmo)**:

$$\text{dpmo} = \text{DPU} \times 1,000,000/\text{opportunities for error}$$

For example, suppose that an airline wishes to measure the effectiveness of its baggage handling system. A DPU measure might be lost bags per customer. However, customers may have different numbers of bags; thus the number of opportunities for error is the average number of bags per customer. If the average number of bags per customer is 1.6, and the airline recorded 3 lost bags for 8000 passengers in one month, then

$$\text{dpmo} = \frac{3}{(8,000)(1.6)} \times 1,000,000 = 234.375$$

The use of dpmo allows us to define quality broadly. In the airline case, a broad definition might mean every opportunity for a failure to meet customer expectations from initial ticketing until bags are retrieved.

Six Sigma represents a quality level of at most *3.4 defects per million opportunities*. Figure 10.1 explains the theoretical basis for Six Sigma in the context of manufacturing specifications. Motorola chose this figure because field failure data suggested that Motorola's processes drifted

A six sigma quality level corresponds to a process variation equal to half of the design tolerance while allowing the mean to shift as much as 1.5 standard deviations from the target.

by this amount on average. The allowance of a shift in the distribution is important, because no process can be maintained in perfect control. As will be discussed in Chapter 14, many common statistical process control (SPC) plans are based on sample sizes that only allow detection of shifts of about two standard deviations. Thus, it would not be unusual for a process to drift this much and not be noticed. The area under the shifted curves *beyond* the Six Sigma ranges (the tolerance limits) is only 0.0000034, or 3.4 parts per million. Thus, if the process mean can be controlled to within 1.5 standard deviations of the target, a maximum of 3.4 defects per million can be expected. If it is held exactly on target (the shaded distribution in Figure 10.1), only 2.0 defects per billion would be expected.

In a similar fashion we could define three-sigma quality, five-sigma quality, and so on. The easiest way to understand it is to think of the distance from the target to

QUALITY PROFILES

KARLEE COMPANY AND LOS ALAMOS NATIONAL BANK

KARLEE COMPANY
LOS ALAMOS NATIONAL BANK

KARLEE Company is a contract manufacturer of precision sheet metal and machined components for the telecommunications, semiconductor, and medical equipment industries. It provides a full range of manufacturing services from initial component design to assembled, integrated products. Located in Garland, Texas, KARLEE's 550 team members have met or exceeded sales growth goals every year since 1994, while continuing to improve customer satisfaction and operational performance. Serving four major customers, KARLEE's customer focus is exemplified by constant, scheduled communications. Each primary customer is assigned a three-person customer service team to provide ongoing and proactive support. KARLEE leadership and team members actively support the community. Activities include tutoring at a local elementary school, coaching a high school team for a national robotics competition, and adopting needy families in the Garland community. To improve the work environment and production processes, KARLEE uses manufacturing cells, consisting of state-of-the-art computer numerical control equipment, machining centers, and robotic loading systems as well as concepts, such as lean manufacturing principles and statistical process control, which often are not used by smaller companies. Continued mastery of these techniques has helped the company to improve efficiency and productivity and, as a result, benefit customers by reducing delivery times and controlling costs. In 2000, KARLEE went from lead-time assemblies of two to three weeks to quick turn assemblies of one to two days. These increased turns remained consistent in the presence of sales growth of 49 percent for these products.

Los Alamos National Bank (LANB) is an independent community bank that provides a full range of financial services to the consumer, commercial, and government markets in northern and central New Mexico. LANB has 167 employees and locations in Los Alamos, White Rock, and Santa Fe, and is the primary financial institution for 66 percent of Los Alamos County residents. It is the largest Guaranteed Rural Housing lending institution in New Mexico and the leading originator of Fannie Mae loans in northern New Mexico. Because of streamlined procedures, LANB approves home equity loans in two days or fewer while its competitors take from one to six weeks. The Cerro Grande fires of May 2000 truly tested the culture that LANB had built. It was a catastrophe that forced the evacuation of Los Alamos, burned nearly 50,000 acres and destroyed more than 280 homes. Overnight, bank employees moved their entire operation to the Santa Fe branch and provided uninterrupted service to their customers. Not surprisingly, LANB has a high level of customer loyalty. One-third of bank customers have five or more banking relationships with the bank, an industry benchmark at more than five times the national average. In one recent survey, 80 percent of the bank's customers said they were "very satisfied" with the service they received. Returns on key financial indicators exceed local competitors and the national average. Employee satisfaction results have been well above those of banks its size in five of eight key indicators, and have exceeded the norm for banks of its size in six of 12 dimensions important to its mission and culture.

Source: Malcolm Baldrige National Quality Award Winners' Profiles, U.S. Department of Commerce, National Institute of Standards and Technology.

Figure 10.1 Theoretical Basis for Six Sigma

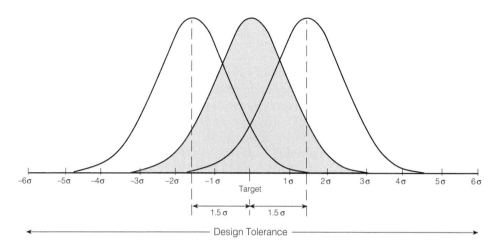

the upper or lower specification (half the tolerance), measured in terms of standard deviations of the inherent variation, at the sigma level. A k-sigma quality level satisfies the equation:

k * process standard deviation = tolerance / 2

Note that in Figure 10.1, if the design specification limits were only 4 standard deviations away from the target, the tails of the shifted distributions begin to exceed the specification limits by a significant amount.

Table 10.1 shows the number of defects per million for different sigma quality levels and different amounts of off-centering. Note that a quality level of 3.4 defects per million can be achieved in several ways, for instance;

- with 0.5-sigma off-centering and 5-sigma quality
- with 1.0-sigma off-centering and 5.5-sigma quality
- with 1.5-sigma off-centering and 6-sigma quality[2]

In many cases, controlling the process to the target is less expensive than reducing the process variability. This table can help assess these trade-offs.

The sigma level can easily be calculated on an Excel spreadsheet using the formula

=NORMSINV(1 − Number of Defects/Number of Opportunities) + SHIFT

or equivalently,

=NORMSINV(1 − dpmo/1,000,000) + SHIFT

SHIFT refers to the off-centering as used in Table 10.1. Using the airline example discussed earlier, if we had 3 lost bags for 8000(1.6) = 12,800 opportunities, we would find =NORMSINV(1 − 3/12800) + 1.5 = 4.99828 or about a 5-sigma level. The truth is less impressive. It was reported that 3.67 mishandled baggage reports per 1,000 passengers were filed in May 2003, which was up from 3.31 per 1,000 a year earlier.[3] This result yields a sigma level of only 4.33, assuming 1.6 bags per passenger.

Table 10.1 Number of Defectives (Parts per Million) for Specified Off-Centering of the Process and Quality Levels

Off-Centering	Quality Level						
	3-sigma	3.5-sigma	4-sigma	4.5-sigma	5-sigma	5.5-sigma	6-sigma
0	2,700	465	63	6.8	0.57	0.034	0.002
0.25-sigma	3,577	666	99	12.8	1.02	0.1056	0.0063
0.5-sigma	6,440	1,382	236	32	**3.4**	0.71	0.019
0.75-sigma	12,288	3,011	665	88.5	11	1.02	0.1
1-sigma	22,832	6,433	1,350	233	32	**3.4**	0.39
1.25-sigma	40,111	12,201	3,000	577	88.5	10.7	1
1.5-sigma	66,803	22,800	6,200	1,350	233	32	**3.4**
1.75-sigma	105,601	40,100	12,200	3,000	577	88.4	11
2-sigma	158,700	66,800	22,800	6,200	1,300	233	32

Source: Pandu R. Tadikamalla, "The Confusion over Six-Sigma Quality," *Quality Progress* 27, no. 11 (November 1994). Reprinted with permission of Pandu R. Tadikamalla and *Quality Progress.*

Although originally developed for manufacturing in the context of tolerance-based specifications, the Six Sigma concept has been operationalized to any process and has come to signify a generic quality level of at most 3.4 defects per million opportunities.

Six Sigma has been applied in product development, new business acquisition, customer service, accounting, and many other business functions. For example, suppose that a bank tracks the number of errors reported in customers' checking account statements. If they find 12 errors in 1,000 statements, it is equivalent to an error rate of 12,000 per million, somewhere between 3.5 and 4 sigma levels. The difference between a 4- and 6-sigma quality level can be surprising. Put in practical terms, if your cellular phone system operated at a 4-sigma level, you would be without service for more than four hours each month, whereas at 6-sigma, it would only be about 9 seconds a month; a 4-sigma process would result in 1 nonconforming package for every three truckloads while a 6-sigma process would have only one nonconforming package in more than 5,000 truckloads. And, if you play 100 rounds of golf each year, you would only miss one putt every 163 years at a 6-sigma level! What may be more surprising to realize is that a change from 3 to 4 sigma represents a 10-fold improvement; from 4 to 5 sigma, a 30-fold improvement; and from 5 to 6 sigma, a 70-fold improvement—difficult challenges for any organization.

However, not all processes should operate at a Six-Sigma level.[4] The appropriate level should depend on the strategic importance of the process and the cost of improvement relative to the benefit. It is generally easy to move from a 2 or 3-sigma level to a 4-sigma level, but moving beyond that requires much more effort and sophisticated statistical tools.

At Motorola, Six Sigma became part of the common language of all employees. To them, it means near perfection, even if they do not understand the statistical details. (Some tell their coworkers, "Have a 6-sigma weekend!") Since stating its goal, Motorola has made great strides in meeting this goal, achieving 6-sigma capability in many processes and 4- or 5-sigma levels in most others. Even in those departments that have reached the goal, Motorola employees continue their improvement efforts in order to reach the ultimate goal of zero defects.

In addition to a focus on defects, Six Sigma seeks to improve all aspects of operations. Thus, other key metrics include cycle time, process variation, yield, and throughput. Selecting the appropriate metric depends on the scope and objectives of the project, making Six Sigma a universal approach for improvement in all aspects of a business.

PROJECT SELECTION FOR SIX SIGMA

One of the requirements for achieving Green Belt status (see Chapter 6) is to successfully complete a basic Six Sigma project by solving a meaningful business problem that positively impacts customers or business performance. Often Green Belt projects address small problems within a department or work function. As employees develop their skills, become Black Belts, and start applying Six Sigma on a routine basis, they begin to address larger and more complex issues, such as problems associated with key value-creation or cross-functional processes, such as supply chains.

According to Kepner and Tregoe, a **problem** is a deviation between what should be happening and what actually is happening that is important enough to make someone think the deviation ought to be corrected.[5] Research using more than 1,000 published cases describing quality problem solving activities suggests that virtually every instance of quality problem-solving falls into one of five categories:

> *A useful way of classifying quality- and performance-related problems that can help identify potential Six Sigma projects is by problem type.[6]*

1. *Conformance problems* are defined by unsatisfactory performance by a well-specified system. Users are not happy with system outputs, such as quality or customer service levels. The system has worked before, but for some reason it is not performing acceptably. The causes of deviations must be identified, and the system restored to its intended mode of functioning.

2. *Unstructured performance problems* result from unsatisfactory performance by a poorly specified system. That is, the task is nonstandardized and not fully specified by procedures and requirements. An example would be poor sales. No one right way of selling a product means the problem cannot be cured by enforcing standards that do not exist. Unstructured problems require more creative approaches to solving them.

3. *Efficiency problems* result from unsatisfactory performance from the standpoint of stakeholders other than customers. Typical examples are cost and productivity issues. Even though the quality of the outputs may be acceptable, the system's performance does not achieve internal organizational goals. Identification of solutions often involves streamlining processes.

4. *Product design problems* involve designing new products that better satisfy user needs—the expectations of customers that matter most to them. In Six Sigma, those vital characteristics are called "critical to quality" (CTQ) issues as we discussed in Chapter 4.

5. *Process design problems* involve designing new processes or substantially revising existing processes. The challenge here is determining process requirements, generating new process alternatives, and linking these processes to customer needs. Techniques discussed in Chapter 7, such as benchmarking and reengineering, are useful tools for process design.

One of the more difficult challenges in Six Sigma is the selection of the most appropriate problems to attack. In the words of Russell Ackoff, managers must learn "mess management." Ackoff, a noted authority on problem solving, defines a **mess** as a "system of external conditions that produces dissatisfaction."[7] High costs, excessive defects, a rash of customer complaints, or low customer satisfaction often characterize quality- and performance-related messes. Such messes often trigger opportunities for Six Sigma projects.

Lynch and colleagues point out two ways to generate projects: top-down and bottom-up.[8] Top-down projects generally are tied to business strategy and are aligned with customer needs. Their major weakness is that they are often too broad in scope to be completed in a timely manner. In addition, top managers may underestimate the cost and overestimate the capabilities of the team or teams to which the project is assigned. In a bottom-up approach, Black Belts (or MBBs) choose the projects that are well-suited to the capabilities of teams. However, a major drawback of this approach is that the projects may not be tied closely to strategic concerns of top management, thus receiving little support and low recognition from the top. Perhaps the best way to ensure success is for executive champions, who understand the impact of projects from a strategic perspective, to work closely with the technical experts in choosing the most relevant projects that fit within the capabilities of Six Sigma teams.

A Six Sigma project might span an entire division or be as narrow as a single production operation. Factors that should be considered when selecting Six Sigma projects include the following:

- Financial return, as measured by costs associated with quality and process performance, and impacts on revenues and market share
- Impacts on customers and organizational effectiveness
- Probability of success
- Impact on employees
- Fit to strategy and competitive advantage

As we noted several times in earlier chapters, Six Sigma projects are driven by expected financial returns. Reducing costs associated with poor quality, such as scrap, rework, excessive cycle times, delays, and lost customers often provide an obvious justification for pursuing a project. A Cost of Quality process (discussed in Chapter 8) often facilitates identifying opportunities and measuring results.

One of the pitfalls experienced in organizations new to Six Sigma is a lack of ability of senior managers to estimate what the resources they allocate (or fail to allocate) to Six Sigma projects will "buy" in the way of bottom-line returns. Thus, it becomes important to be able to differentiate between, and to estimate fairly accurately, the differences in resources required to bring a $250,000 project versus a $50,000 project to a successful conclusion. Six Sigma projects should lead to improved customer satisfaction and organizational performance. Such improvements can lead directly to higher sales or market share, thus providing financial justification for selecting a project.

Projects chosen should have a high likelihood of success. Considerable risk comes in choosing problems that can best be compared with "solving world hunger." At the outset of a Six Sigma initiative, it is beneficial to pick the "low-hanging fruit"—projects that are easy to accomplish, or even can be completed by a single individual in order to show early successes. This visible success helps to build momentum and support for future projects. Studies show that many projects are significantly over-budget, behind schedule, or do not result in desired outcomes.[9] Thus, good project management, as we discussed in Chapter 7, is essential.

Six Sigma projects should fit within the capabilities of the people and teams that work on them. Many indirect benefits accrue. The training received as Green or Black Belts improves employee and organizational knowledge, and participating in Six Sigma projects improves team and leadership skills, as pointed out in Chapter 6. Six Sigma can motivate employees to innovate and improve their work environment, and ultimately their satisfaction on the job and personal self-esteem. Many projects offer opportunities to reduce frustration with inadequate work processes or to provide increased value to customers; these types of projects are certainly important candidates for selection.

Finally, Six Sigma projects should support the organization's vision and competitive strategy. In Chapter 5 we stressed the importance of creating action plans that help an organization achieve its chosen strategies. At GE, for example, business goals work their way down the organization, helping employees to distinguish between projects that will not have a significant effect on business performance and those that do.[10]

Of course, most organizations probably have more opportunities for Six Sigma projects than available resources to do them. In many cases, project selection is often political in nature. Senior executives who champion Six Sigma projects might exercise political influence to get their pet projects recognized and accepted. However, taking a more objective viewpoint is more effective. Prioritizing and selecting projects using some rational criteria can contribute to greater effectiveness. Project steering committees that include at least a portion of the organization's senior leadership often guide these decisions. This group can act as a filter for the voices of both the external and internal customers in evaluating and prioritizing projects.

Simple scoring models may be used to evaluate and prioritize potential projects. An example of a project selection matrix is shown in Figure 10.2. The top box shows the customer importance ratings on a set of key CTQs using the scale at the bottom left. The numbers in the main table are based on the scale on the bottom right, and are determined by the steering committee. By multiplying these rankings by the customer importance ratings, we can arrive at a total score in the right-hand column (Project ranking metric). The higher the number, the more the project affects customer issues. This process takes the guesswork and opinions out of the project selection process and focuses on the important issues to the customer and the organization.

SIX SIGMA PROBLEM SOLVING

Problem solving is the activity associated with changing the state of what is actually happening to what should be happening. Many years ago, Juran defined **breakthrough** as the accomplishment of any improvement that takes an organization to unprecedented levels of performance. Breakthrough attacks chronic losses or, in Deming's terminology, common causes of variation. The objectives of Six Sigma projects often focus on breakthrough improvements that add value to the organization and its customers through systematic approaches to problem solving.

Successful quality and business performance improvement depends on the ability to identify and solve problems; this ability is fundamental to the Six Sigma philosophy. Many nonquantitatively inclined managers (which may include 75 or 80

Figure 10.2 Example of a Project Selection Matrix

Customer Issues	Missing parts ordered	Late delivery	Damaged orders	Wrong orders	More parts than ordered	On hold too long
Customer importance	8	5	7	10	3	3

Project	Project ranking based on correlation to customer issues						Project ranking metric
Order fill process flow optimization	5	8	3	3	5	0	146
Replenishment cycle time reduction project	5	8	5	0	0	0	115
Customer service feedback reporting	5	3	3	8	0	5	171
Delivery vendor certification	0	10	8	0	0	0	106
IT upgrade process integration	7	5	0	8	8	3	194

Customer importance	Relationship to customer importance
0	Not important
3	Slightly important
5	Important
8	Very important
10	Critical

Project rank	Relationship to customer issue
0	No correlation
3	Very little correlation
5	Some correlation
8	High correlation
10	Complete correlation

Source: William Michael Kelly, "Three Steps to Project Selection," *Six Sigma Forum Magazine* 2, no. 1 (November 2002), 29–32. © 2002, American Society for Quality. Reprinted with permission.

percent of the population) have difficulty in grasping the concept of a systematic fact-based, often statistical, problem-solving approach. Yet, using such an approach is vital to effectively identifying sources of problems, understanding their causes, and developing improvement solutions.

"Speaking the same language" builds confidence and assures that solutions are developed objectively, rather than by intuition. Leaders in the quality revolution—

Deming, Juran, and Crosby (see Chapter 3)—proposed specific methodologies for improvement in the early days of the quality revolution. Although each methodology is distinctive in its own right, they share many common themes:[11]

> *A structured problem-solving process provides all employees with a common language and a set of tools to communicate with each other, particularly as members of cross-functional teams.*

1. *Redefining and analyzing the problem:* Collect and organize information, analyze the data and underlying assumptions, and reexamine the problem for new perspectives, with the goal of achieving a workable problem definition.
2. *Generating ideas:* "Brainstorm" to develop potential solutions.
3. *Evaluating and selecting ideas:* Determine whether the ideas have merit and will achieve the problem solver's goal.
4. *Implementing ideas:* Sell the solution and gain acceptance by those who must use them.

These themes are reflected in the principal problem solving methodology used by Six Sigma, DMAIC—define, measure, analyze, improve, and control—which we discuss next. (We will discuss several other types of quality problem solving methodologies in Chapter 13.)

The DMAIC Methodology

One of the first things that a Green Belt in training learns are the five steps in the DMAIC methodology.

1. Define After a Six Sigma project is selected, the first step is to clearly define the problem. This activity is significantly different from project selection. Project selection generally responds to symptoms of a problem and usually results in a rather vague problem statement. One must describe the problem in operational terms that facilitate further analysis. For example, a firm might have a history of poor reliability of electric motors it manufactures, resulting in a Six Sigma project to improve motor reliability. A preliminary investigation of warranty and field service repair data might suggest that the source of most problems was brush wear, and more specifically, suggest a problem with brush hardness variability. Thus, the problem might be defined as "reduce the variability of brush hardness." This process of drilling down to a more specific problem statement is sometimes called **project scoping**.

A good problem statement should also identify customers and the CTQs that have the most impact on product or service performance, describe the current level of performance or the nature of errors or customer complaints, identify the relevant performance metrics, benchmark best performance standards, calculate the cost/revenue implications of the project, and quantify the expected level of performance from a successful Six Sigma effort. The Define phase should also address such project management issues as what will need to be done, by whom, and when.

2. Measure This phase of the DMAIC process focuses on how to measure the internal processes that impact CTQs. It requires an understanding of the causal relationships between process performance and customer value. These concepts were discussed in Chapter 8. However, once they are understood, procedures for gathering facts—collecting good data, observation, and careful listening—must be defined and implemented. Data from existing production processes and practices often provide important information, as does feedback from supervisors, workers, customers, and field service employees. Many of the technical issues of measurement that must be considered in a Six Sigma project are discussed in Chapter 11.

Data collection should not be performed blindly. One must first ask some basic questions:

- What questions are we trying to answer?
- What type of data will we need to answer the question?
- Where can we find the data?
- Who can provide the data?
- How can we collect the data with minimum effort and with minimum chance of error?

The first step in any data collection effort is to develop **operational definitions** for all performance measures that will be used. For example, what does it mean to have "on-time delivery"? Does it mean within one day of the promised time? One week? One hour? What is an error? Is it wrong information on an invoice, a typographical mistake, or either? Clearly, any data are meaningless unless they are well defined and understood without ambiguity.

The Juran Institute suggests 10 important considerations for data collection:

1. Formulate good questions that relate to the specific information needs of the project.
2. Use appropriate data analysis tools and be certain the necessary data are being collected.
3. Define comprehensive data collection points so that job flows suffer minimum interruption.
4. Select an unbiased collector who has the easiest and most immediate access to the relevant facts.
5. Understand the environment and make sure that data collectors have the proper experience.
6. Design simple data collection forms.
7. Prepare instructions for collecting the data.
8. Test the data collection forms and the instructions and make sure they are filled out properly.
9. Train the data collectors as to the purpose of the study, what the data will be used for, how to fill out the forms, and the importance of remaining unbiased.
10. Audit the data collection process and validate the results.[12]

These guidelines can greatly improve the process of uncovering relevant facts necessary to identify and solve problems.

3. Analyze A major flaw in many problem-solving approaches is a lack of emphasis on rigorous analysis. Too often, we want to jump to a solution without fully understanding the nature of the problem and identifying the source of the problem. The Analyze phase of DMAIC focuses on *why* defects, errors, or excessive variation occur, which often result from one or more of the following:

- A lack of knowledge about how a process works, which is particularly critical if different people perform the process. Such lack of knowledge results in inconsistency and increased variation in outputs.
- A lack of knowledge about how a process *should* work, including understanding customer expectations and the goal of the process.
- A lack of control of materials and equipment used in a process.

- Inadvertent errors in performing work.
- Waste and complexity, which manifest themselves in many ways, such as unnecessary steps in a process and excess inventories.
- Hasty design and production of parts and assemblies; poor design specifications; inadequate testing of incoming materials and prototypes.
- Failure to understand the capability of a process to meet specifications.
- Lack of training.
- Poor instrument calibration and testing.
- Inadequate environmental characteristics such as light, temperature, and noise.

Finding the answers requires identifying the key variables that are most likely to create errors and excessive variation—the root causes. NCR Corporation defines **root cause** as "that condition (or interrelated set of conditions) having allowed or caused a defect to occur, which once corrected properly, permanently prevents recurrence of the defect in the same, or subsequent, product or service generated by the process."[13] As with a medical analogy, eliminating symptoms of problems usually provides only temporary relief; eliminating root causes provides long-term relief.

One useful approach for identifying the root cause is the "5 Why" technique.[14] This approach forces one to redefine a problem statement as a chain of causes and effects to identify the source of the symptoms by asking why, ideally five times. In a classic example at Toyota, a machine failed because a fuse blew. Replacing the fuse would have been the obvious solution; however, this action would have only addressed the symptom of the real problem. Why did the fuse blow? Because the bearing did not have adequate lubrication. Why? Because the lubrication pump was not working properly. Why? Because the pump axle was worn. Why? Because sludge seeped into the pump axle, which was the root cause. Toyota attached a strainer to the lubricating pump to eliminate the sludge, thus correcting the problem of the machine failure.

After potential variables are identified, experiments are conducted to verify them. These experiments generally consist of formulating some hypothesis to investigate, collecting data, analyzing the data, and reaching a reasonable and statistically supportable conclusion. Statistical thinking and analysis (Chapter 11) plays a critical role in this phase. It is one of the reasons why statistics is an important part of Six Sigma training (and one that engineering and many business curricula often ignore). Other experiments might employ computer simulation techniques.

4. Improve Once the root cause of a problem is understood, the analyst or team needs to generate ideas for removing or resolving the problem and improve the performance measures and CTQs. This idea-gathering phase is a highly creative activity, because many solutions are not obvious. One of the difficulties in this task is the natural instinct to prejudge ideas before thoroughly evaluating them. Most people have a natural fear of proposing a "silly" idea or looking foolish. However, such ideas may actually form the basis for a creative and useful solution. Effective problem solvers must learn to defer judgment and develop the ability to generate a large number of ideas at this stage of the process, whether practical or not.

A number of processes and tools to facilitate idea generation can be used. One of the most popular is brainstorming. Brainstorming, a useful group problem-solving procedure for generating ideas, was proposed by Alex Osborn "for the sole purpose of producing checklists of ideas" that can be used in developing a solution to a problem.[15] With brainstorming, no criticism is permitted, and people are encouraged to generate a large number of ideas through combination and enhancement of existing ideas. Wild ideas are encouraged and frequently trigger other good ideas from somewhere else.

Checklists are often used as a guide for generating ideas. Osborn proposed about 75 fundamental questions based on the following principles:

- Put to other uses?
- Adapt?
- Modify?
- Magnify?
- Minify?
- Substitute?
- Rearrange?
- Reverse?
- Combine?

By consciously seeking ideas based on this list, one can generate many unusual and often useful ideas.

After a set of ideas have been proposed, it is necessary to evaluate them and select the most promising. This process includes confirming that the proposed solution will positively impact the key process variables and the CTQs, and identifying the maximum acceptable ranges of these variables.

Problem solutions often entail technical or organizational changes. Often some sort of decision or scoring model is used to assess possible solutions against important criteria such as cost, time, quality improvement potential, resources required, effects on supervisors and workers, and barriers to implementation such as resistance to change or organizational culture. To implement a solution effectively, responsibility must be assigned to a person or a group who will follow through on what must be done, where it will be done, when it will be done, and how it will be done. Project management techniques are helpful in implementation planning.

5. Control The Control phase focuses on how to maintain the improvements, which includes putting tools in place to ensure that the key variables remain within the maximum acceptable ranges under the modified process. These improvements might include establishing the new standards and procedures, training the workforce, and instituting controls to make sure that improvements do not die over time. Controls might be as simple as using checklists or periodic status reviews to ensure that proper procedures are followed, or employing statistical process control charts (see Chapter 14) to monitor the performance of key measures.

The following example shows how DMAIC was used at American Express to improve the number of customers who received renewal cards.[16] (In this example, data have been masked to protect confidentiality.)

Define and Measure: On average in 1999, American Express received 1,000 returned renewal cards each month. Of these renewals, 65 percent are due to the fact that the card members changed their addresses and did not tell the company. The U.S. Post Office calls these forwardable addresses. Amex does not currently notify a card member when they receive a returned plastic card.

Analyze: Analysis of the data noted significant differences in the causes of returned plastics between product types. Optima, the revolving card product, had the highest incidence of defects, but was not significantly different from other card types in the percentage of defects. Renewals had by far the highest defect rate among the three areas of replacement, renewal, and new accounts. After additional testing, returns with forwardable addresses were overwhelmingly the largest percentage and quantity of returns.

Improve: An experimental pilot study was run on all renewal files issued, comparing records against the National Change of Address database. As a result, they were able to reduce the dpmo rate by 44.5 percent, from 13,500 to 6,036 defects per million opportunities. This action enabled over 1,200 card members who would not have automatically received their credit cards to receive them, increasing revenue and customer satisfaction.

Control: Amex began tracking the proportion of returns over time as a means of monitoring the new process to ensure that it remains in control.

Tools and Techniques

Two of the unique features of DMAIC are its emphasis on customer requirements and the use of statistical tools and methodologies. This approach requires an understanding and commitment to statistical thinking and the use of problem-solving approaches at a level that may be foreign to managers and other employees in many organizations.

The tools used in DMAIC have been around for a long time. For example, Deming long advocated using statistics to understand and reduce variation, and Juran promoted the use of many simple tools for quality problem solving and improvement. Thomas Pyzdek, a noted quality consultant, states that more than 400 tools are now available in the "TQM Toolbox."[17] However, most organizations rarely go beyond the basic improvement tools and fail to recognize the benefits from more sophisticated statistical tools such as design of experiments. Six Sigma recognized the power of advanced statistical methods and took them beyond the realm of engineering. In addition, a unique feature about Six Sigma is the integration of these tools and the DMAIC methodology into management systems across the organization.[18]

These tools are integrated into standard Six Sigma curricula, which typically involve a blend of technical topics and project management and leadership topics. Figure 10.3 shows a typical Six Sigma Black Belt training curriculum at General Electric. The topics covered may be categorized into seven general groups:[19]

- *Elementary statistical tools* (basic statistics, statistical thinking, hypothesis testing, correlation, simple regression)
- *Advanced statistical tools* (design of experiments, analysis of variance, multiple regression)
- *Product design and reliability* (quality function deployment, failure mode, and effects analysis)
- *Measurement* (process capability, measurement systems analysis)
- *Process control* (control plans, statistical process control)
- *Process improvement* (process improvement planning, process mapping, mistake proofing)
- *Implementation and teamwork* (organizational effectiveness, team assessment, facilitation tools, team development)

Most of these topics are addressed in other chapters of this book. It can be seen that Six Sigma has greatly expanded the requisite knowledge for true performance breakthroughs.

Design for Six Sigma

We introduced issues associated with product design in Chapter 7 and emphasized the importance of integrating design with sourcing and production. **Design for Six**

Figure 10.3 Six-Sigma Black Belt Training

Week 1	Week 2	Week 3	Week 4
• Overview	• Statistical thinking	• Design of experiments	• Control plans
• Process improvement planning	• Hypothesis testing	• Analysis of variance	• Statistical process control
• Process mapping	• Correlation	• Multiple regression	• Mistake-proofing
• Quality function deployment	• Simple regression	• Facilitation tools	• Team development
• Failure mode and effects analysis	• Team assessment		
• Organizational effectiveness concepts			
• Basic statistics			
• Process capability			
• Measurement systems analysis			

Source: Roger W. Hoerl, "Six Sigma and the Future of the Quality Profession," *Quality Progress*, June 1998, 35–48. © 1998. American Society for Quality. Reprinted with permission.

Sigma (DFSS) is a relatively recent approach to product development that focuses on delivering the right product at the right time and at the right cost. DFSS is a complex systems engineering analysis methodology that is enhanced with statistical methods to enhance traditional design processes. Its focus is to optimize CTQs for Six Sigma product and system performance by balancing cost, schedule, and quality; recognizing that Six Sigma margins are not always the optimal design margins.[20] Some features of DFSS include the following:

- A high-level architectural view of the design
- Use of CTQs with well-defined technical requirements
- Application of statistical modeling and simulation approaches
- Predicting defects, avoiding defects, and performance prediction using analysis methods
- Examining the full range of product performance using variation analysis of subsystems and components

DFSS uses many tools including multivariable optimization, design of experiments, statistical analysis techniques, probabilistic simulation techniques, and failure mode and effects analysis, many of which are discussed in subsequent chapters.

One of the early applications of DFSS was at GE's Medical Systems Division. The Lightspeed Computed Tomography (CT) System was the first GE product to be completely designed and developed using DFSS. Lightspeed allows doctors to capture multiple images of a patient's anatomy simultaneously at a speed six times faster than traditional scanners. As a result, productivity doubled while the images had much higher quality. Jack Welch announced that all GE products designed after that time would be designed using the DFSS approach.[21] We will develop the concept of Design for Six Sigma in more detail in Chapter 12.

Team Processes and Project Management

We introduced teams in Chapter 6. Teams are vital to Six Sigma projects because of the interdisciplinary nature of such projects. Six Sigma teams rely on several different types of professionals (roles), including Champions, Master Black Belts, Black Belts, and Green Belts that we described in Chapter 6. An effective Six Sigma process deploys this leadership structure throughout the organization. As noted earlier, team-related topics, including organizational effectiveness, team assessment, facilitation tools, and team development, are part of standard Six Sigma training. Team leaders and team members must understand their roles as project managers and organizational leaders (refer back to Table 6.2).

More than any other type of organizational structure, the team structure depends on cooperation, communication, and clarity. Eckes estimates that 60 percent of failures of Six Sigma teams are due to failures in the "mechanics" of team operations, as opposed to poor project selection or improper use of tools.[22] He cites contributing factors such as lack of application of meeting skills, improper use of agendas, failure to determine meeting roles and responsibilities, lack of setting and keeping ground rules, and lack of appropriate facilitative behaviors. Electronic communications, virtual teams, and motivation were discussed earlier, but they must also be used effectively if teams are to be successful.

Projects are the vehicles that are used to organize team efforts and to implement the DMAIC process. Although projects are set up as temporary organization structures, their flexibility allows cross-functional teams to complete significant work in minimum time, if well managed. One of the challenges of implementing Six Sigma projects is to coordinate them with normal work activities. Some slack time, as well as physical and financial resources, must be allocated to project teams in order for them to achieve their objectives. Team members and project leaders cannot be expected to carry a full load of routine work and still participate fully and effectively on Six Sigma project teams.

Projects fail for a variety of reasons, including not adhering to schedules, poor planning, and "scope creep" when the nature of the project gradually loses its focus and becomes unwieldy, mismatching of skills, and insufficient knowledge transfer.[23] Being able to manage a large portfolio of projects, as would be found in Six Sigma environments, is vital to organizational success. The project management body of knowledge defines 69 tools that a project manager must master, but few have done so. Achieving professional certification in project management can significantly assist Six Sigma efforts.

SIX SIGMA IN SERVICES AND SMALL ORGANIZATIONS

Because Six Sigma was developed in the manufacturing sector, and most publicity has revolved around such companies as Motorola and GE, many people in the service sector think that Six Sigma does not apply to their organizations. Nothing can be further from the truth.[24] These characteristics are present in all business processes; thus, Six Sigma can easily be applied to a wide variety of transactional, administrative, and service areas. In fact, it is generally agreed that 50 percent or more of the total savings opportunity in an organization lies outside of manufacturing. Within the service sector, Six Sigma is beginning to be called *transactional Six Sigma*.

All Six Sigma projects have three key characteristics: a problem to be solved, a process in which the problem exists, and one or more measures that quantify the gap to be closed and can be used to monitor progress.

However, while Six Sigma applies equally well in service areas, it is true that services have some unique characteristics relative to manufacturing processes. We discussed these briefly in Chapter 1. First, the culture is usually less scientific and service employees typically do not think in terms of processes, measurements, and data. The processes are often invisible, complex, and not well defined or well documented. Also, the work typically requires considerable human intervention, such as customer interaction, underwriting or approval decisions, or manual report generation. These differences make opportunities difficult to identify, and projects difficult to define. Finally, similar service activities are often done in different ways. If you have three people doing the same job, perhaps in three different locations, it is unlikely that they will do the job in the same way.

Because service processes are largely people-driven, measurements are often nonexistent or ill-defined, because many believe that defects cannot be measured. Therefore, one must create measurement systems before collecting any data. Applying Six Sigma to services requires examination of four key measures of the performance:

- *Accuracy*, as measured by correct financial figures, completeness of information, or freedom from data errors
- *Cycle time*, which is a measure of how long it takes to do something, such as pay an invoice
- *Cost*, that is, the internal cost of process activities (in many cases, cost is largely determined by the accuracy and/or cycle time of the process; the longer it takes, and the more mistakes that have to be fixed, the higher the cost)
- *Customer satisfaction*, which is typically the primary measure of success

Fortunately, important similarities can be shown between manufacturing and nonmanufacturing processes. First, both types of processes have "hidden factories," those places where the defective "product" is sent to be reworked or scrapped (revised, corrected, or discarded in nonmanufacturing terms). Find the hidden factory and you also find opportunities to improve the process. Performing manual account reconciliation in accounting, revising budgets repeatedly until management will accept them, and making repeat sales calls to customers because all the information requested by the customer was not available are all examples of the hidden factory.

Consider how a janitorial service company might use DMAIC. In the Define stage, a key question would be to define what a defect represents. One might first create a flowchart of the cleaning process, specifying what activities are performed. One example of a defect might be leaving streaks on windows because it is a source of customer dissatisfaction, a CTQ. In the Measure stage, not only would the firm want to collect data on the frequency of defects, but also information about what products and tools employees use. The Analyze stage might include evaluating differences among employees to determine why some appear better at cleaning than others. Developing a standard operating procedure might be the focus of the Improve stage. Finally, Control might entail teaching employees the correct technique and measuring improvement over time.

In one application at CNH Capital, Six Sigma tools were applied to decrease asset management cycle time in posting repossessions to a bid list and remarketing Web site.[25] Cycle time was reduced 75 percent, from 40 days to 10 days, resulting in significant ongoing dollar savings. A facility management company had a high level of "days sales outstanding." Initially, they tried to fix this issue by reducing the term of days in its billing cycle, which, however, upset customers. Using Six Sigma, they found that a large percentage of accounts with high days sales outstanding received invoices having numerous errors. After understanding the source of the errors and making process changes, the invoice process improved and days sales outstanding was reduced. At DuPont, a Six Sigma project was applied to improve cycle time for an employee's application for long-term disability benefits.[26] Some examples of financial applications of Six Sigma include the following:[27]

- Reduce the average and variation of days outstanding of accounts receivable.
- Close the books faster.
- Improve the accuracy and speed of the audit process.
- Reduce variation in cash flow.
- Improve the accuracy of journal entries (most businesses have a 3–4 percent error rate).
- Improve accuracy and cycle time of standard financial reports.

These are but a few of the many potential applications of Six Sigma in service organizations.

Small organizations are often confused and intimidated by the size, costs, and extensive technical training they see in large organizations that implement "formal" Six Sigma processes. For this reason, they often don't even try to adopt these approaches. Small organizations are usually lean by necessity, but not always effectively so. Their processes often operate at quality levels of two to three sigma, and they are not even aware of it. Spanyi and Wurtzel provide some sage advice to small organizations thinking about adopting Six Sigma or lean production:[28]

- Obtain management commitment.
- Identify key processes and goals.
- Prioritize the improvement projects.
- Be systematic.
- Don't worry about training Black and Green Belts.
- Use just-in-time practices to learn the Six Sigma tools necessary to successfully carry out specific projects.
- Communicate successes and reward and recognize performers.

Small companies often need to bring in consultants for training or improvement initiatives in the early stages of learning. These types of initiatives can help to develop in-house expertise and put them on the right track.

SIX SIGMA AND LEAN PRODUCTION

Lean production refers to approaches initially developed by the Toyota Motor Corporation that focus on the elimination of waste in all forms, including defects requiring rework, unnecessary processing steps, unnecessary movement of materials or people, waiting time, excess inventory, and overproduction. A simple way of defining it is "getting more done with less."[29] It involves identifying and eliminating non-value-added activities throughout the entire value chain to achieve faster customer response, reduced inventories, higher quality,

A Toyota assembly plant fairly hums: Every movement has a purpose, and there is no slack. Tour a typical auto plant, and you see stacks of half-finished parts, assembly lines halted for adjustment, workers standing idle. At Toyota the workers look like dancers in a choreographed production: retrieving parts, installing them, checking the quality, and doing it all in immaculate surroundings.[30]

and better human resources. As one article about Toyota observed, to see the Toyota production system in action is to "behold a thing of beauty."

Lean production is facilitated by a focus on measurement and continuous improvement, cross-trained workers, flexible and increasingly automated equipment, efficient machine layout, rapid setup and changeover, just-in-time delivery and scheduling, realistic work standards, worker empowerment to perform inspections and take corrective action, supplier partnerships, and preventive maintenance. Some of the benefits claimed by proponents of lean production include the following:

- At least 60 percent reduction in cycle times
- 40 percent improvement in space utilization
- 25 percent greater throughput
- 50 percent reduction in work-in-process and finished goods inventories
- 50 percent improvement in quality
- 20 percent improvements in working capital and worker productivity

However, as one industry expert observed, it takes "an incredible amount of detailed planning, discipline, hard work, and painstaking attention to detail." Surveys have noted that midsized and large companies are likely to be familiar with lean principles and have systems in place; however, few small manufacturing shops have much familiarity with the principles. Thus, considerable opportunity exists for this important economic sector.

Some of the key tools used in lean production include:

- *The 5S's*. The 5S's are derived from Japanese terms: *seiri* (sort), *seiton* (set in order), *seiso* (shine), *seiketsu* (standardize), and *shitsuke* (sustain). They define a system for workplace organization and standardization. Sort refers to ensuring that each item in a workplace is in its proper place or identified as unnecessary and removed. Set in order means to arrange materials and equipment so that they are easy to find and use. Shine refers to a clean work area. Not only is this important for safety, but as a work area is cleaned, maintenance problems such as oil leaks can be identified before they cause problems. Standardize means to formalize procedures and practices to create consistency and ensure that all steps are performed correctly. Finally, sustain means to keep the process going through training, communication, and organizational structures.
- *Visual controls*. Visual controls are indicators for tools, parts, and production activities that are placed in plain sight of all workers so that everyone can understand the status of the system at a glance. Thus, if a machine goes down, or a part is defective or delayed, immediate action can be taken.
- *Efficient layout and standardized work*. The layout of equipment and processes is designed according to the best operational sequence, by physically linking and arranging machines and process steps most efficiently, often in a cellular arrangement. Standardizing the individual tasks by clearly specifying the proper method reduces wasted human movement and energy.
- *Pull production*. In this system (also described as *kanban* or *just-in-time*), upstream suppliers do not produce until the downstream customer signals a need for parts.
- *Single minute exchange of dies (SMED)*. SMED refers to rapid changeover of tooling and fixtures in machine shops so that multiple products in smaller batches can be run on the same equipment. Reducing setup time adds value to the operation and facilitates smoother production flow.
- *Total productive maintenance*. Total productive maintenance is designed to ensure that equipment is operational and available when needed.

- *Source inspection.* Inspection and control by process operators guarantees that product passed on to the next production stage conforms to specifications.
- *Continuous improvement.* Continuous improvement provides the link to Six Sigma. In order to make lean production work, one must get to the root causes of problems and permanently remove them. Teamwork is an integral part of continuous improvement in lean environments. Many techniques that we discuss in subsequent chapters are used.

Quality Spotlight
Sunset
Manufacturing

One example of the application of lean concepts is found at Sunset Manufacturing, Inc., of Tualatin, Oregon, a 35-person, family-owned machine shop.[31] Because of competitive pressures and a business downturn, Sunset began to look for ways to simplify operations and cut costs. They established a lean steering committee to coordinate and drive the process. The committee chartered a kaizen team to reduce setup time on vertical milling machines by 50 percent. The team used SMED and the 5S's approach as their basic tools. Several actions were taken, including (1) standardizing parts across milling machines, (2) reorganizing the tool room, (3) incorporating the SMED approach in machine setups, and (4) and implementing what was termed "dance cards," which gave operators the specific steps required for the SMED of various machines and products. The results were impressive. Tool preparation time dropped from an average of 30 minutes to less than 10 minutes, isolation and identification of worn tools was improved, improved safety and appearance in the tool room due to 5S's application was apparent, machine setup time was reduced from an average of 216 minutes to 36 minutes (an 86 percent improvement). Estimated savings were $33,000 per year, with an implementation cost of less than half of that amount. The net impact was to allow smaller lots to be run, a 75 percent reduction in setup scrap, emergence of a more competitive organization, and a morale boost for team members.

Six Sigma is a useful and complementary approach to lean production. For example, a cycle time reduction project might involve aspects of both. Lean tools might be applied to streamline an order entry process. This application leads to the discovery that significant rework occurs because of incorrect addresses, customer numbers, or shipping charges and results in high variation of processing time. Six Sigma tools might then be used to drill down to the root cause of the problems and identify a solution. Because of these similarities, many industry training programs and consultants have begun to focus on "Lean Six Sigma," drawing upon the best practices of both approaches. Both are driven by customer requirements, focus on real dollar savings, have the ability to make significant financial impacts on the organization, and can be used in nonmanufacturing environments.

However, some differences clearly exist between lean production and Six Sigma. First, they attack different types of problems. Lean production addresses visible problems in processes, for example, inventory, material flow, and safety. Six Sigma is more concerned with less visible problems, for example, variation in performance. Another difference is that lean tools are more intuitive and easier to apply by anybody in the workplace, while many Six Sigma tools require advanced training and expertise of Black Belt or Master Black Belt specialists, or consultant equivalents. For example, the concept of the 5S's is easier to grasp than statistical methods. Thus, organizations might be well advised to start with basic lean principles and evolve toward more sophisticated Six Sigma approaches.

LEAN SIX SIGMA AND SERVICES[32]

Lean production can easily be applied to nonmanufacturing environments. Pure service firms such as banks, hospitals, and restaurants have benefited from lean principles. In these contexts, lean production is often called **lean enterprise**. For example, banks require quick response and efficiency to operate on low margins, making many of their processes, such as check sorting and mortgage approval, natural candidates for lean enterprise solutions.[33] Handling of paper checks and credit card slips, for instance, involves a physical process not unlike an assembly line. The faster a bank moves checks through its system, the sooner it can collect its funds and the better its returns on invested capital.

One North American financial institution applied lean enterprise principles to check processing operations. They followed one check as it made its way through the bank's systems, documenting the time spent in actual processing and in waiting, rework, and handling. They found that almost half of the bank's processing capacity was consumed by nonprocessing activities such as fixing jams and setting up machines. Further investigation revealed wide variations in productivity between individual operators on a single shift. When the work practices of the least and most productive operators were compared, it became evident that although all were engaged in the same task, differences in the way they performed it were creating huge swings in productivity.

To adopt a lean manufacturing approach, the bank first matched the flow of incoming checks to processing capacity. At the end of each business day, the check processing operation was swamped with more checks than it could handle; this bottleneck created the false impression that capacity was constrained. The bank applied just-in-time principles to the processing of incoming checks and spread the check flow evenly through the day. A second bottleneck occurred at the beginning of the day; standard practice dictated that all checks presented for morning processing were sorted three times. This process prevented the processing operation from handling the morning check volume in time to meet the account posting deadline. However, many of the checks did not need to be completed by the morning deadline, and once the sorting of these low-priority items was shifted to later in the day when volumes were lower, capacity increased by 122 percent.

By uncovering and freeing up "phantom" capacity that had previously been taken up by waiting time, maintenance, and rework, they could increase actual capacity by more than 25 percent without investing in additional equipment. The bank was able to both sell its services to other banks at an attractive price and to expand capacity during the most time-sensitive period of the day, when its services could be priced at a premium. In all, these one-off improvements resulted in a more than doubling of the margin contributed by the operation.

A medical laboratory had been improving cycle time from test sample receipt to shipment for several years and had achieved a 30 percent reduction, primarily by using new technology. However, doctors were still asking for faster responses. Using performance benchmarking, the lab quality coordinator found some examples of manufacturing plants that had reduced cycle time by as much as 90 percent with little capital investment. The coordinator discovered that these improvements were not achieved simply by making each step work faster, but also by identifying and reducing waste that existed between the process steps, such as movement, waiting, and inventory. By learning about lean production techniques and changing the flow of test samples in the lab, the organization was able to reduce cycle time by another 20 percent within seven months.[34]

Six Sigma is even being successfully implemented in local government settings. Consider the case of the city of Ft. Wayne, Indiana. Before he was elected mayor of the city, Graham Richard had founded a quality learning network in 1991. Thanks to the TQM Network, more than 40 small and medium-sized companies, nonprofit organizations, and local government now provide Six Sigma training to their employees.

When he took office in January 2000, Mayor Richard quickly enrolled the city of Fort Wayne into membership in the Northeast Indiana TQM Network. Michele Hill, was appointed to the city's newly created position of quality enhancement manager, and was assisted by Roger Hirt, a Six Sigma Master Black belt formerly with General Electric. Ten city employees from a variety of departments initially received Six Sigma Black Belt training and each completed a city approved project. As a result of some of these projects, the city reduced larcenies by 19 percent in a targeted area, increased fire code re-inspections by 23 percent, reduced the time to re-inspect by 17 days, and increased the amount of transportation engineering change orders within an accepted tolerance by 21 percent.

Perhaps the most shining example of Six Sigma's potential in a municipal setting comes from a most unglamorous process: waste activated sludge. Cheryl Cronin, of the Fort Wayne's Water Pollution Control Plant, set her sights on increasing the amount of waste activated sludge processed through the plant's centrifuge. It might not sound exciting but the results were impressive. As a direct result of Cronin's project, the city avoided $1.7 million in improvements to the WPC Plant's digester, the digester's use of alternative fuels dropped 98 percent, and the operating time on the process decreased by four hours per day. "With tools like Six Sigma in the hands of City workers, we can not only provide quality training for our employees, but now we can also measure and improve customer satisfaction," Cronin said. "This is a win-win situation for everyone living in Fort Wayne or using services offered by the city."

QUALITY IN PRACTICE

AN APPLICATION OF SIX SIGMA TO REDUCE MEDICAL ERRORS[35]

Medication administration and laboratory processing/results reporting are examples of complex systems in health care that are known to be error prone. As described in the report of the National Academy of Sciences/Institute of Medicine, medication errors are a substantial source of preventable errors in hospitals, but result in part from poorly designed complex systems. At Froedtert Hospital in Milwaukee, Wisconsin, errors with IV medication drips and laboratory processing and results reporting were well documented. Additionally, errors in ordering, transporting, analyzing, and reporting clinical laboratory tests were known to be a significant source of error at the hospital. It is for these reasons that these two areas were targeted for initial study.

A consortium was created by four Milwaukee-based organizations committed to the development of an approach to reduce errors and improve patient safety. The consortium members include the Medical College of Wisconsin, Froedtert Memorial Lutheran Hospital, the American Society for Quality, and SecurTrac, a company formed specifi-

cally to develop technologies to improve patient safety. The consortium is currently addressing three major efforts: (1) improved identification and reporting of health care errors, (2) deployment of the Six Sigma methodology to reduce errors, and (3) testing and implementation of technical solutions to improve patient safety. At the center of this approach is the effort to determine whether the Six Sigma error reduction methodology can be successfully applied in health care.

Using Six Sigma methods and selected statistical tools, Froedtert Hospital's processes for medication delivery were evaluated with the goal of designing an approach that would decrease the likelihood of errors. The design employed the classic Six Sigma process steps. A multidisciplinary group of physicians, nurses, pharmacists, and administrators identified medication delivery by continuous IV infusions as a process subject to substantial error. Continuous IV infusions are used in many clinical settings and errors can severely impact patient well-being. Initially, the focus was on five specific IV medications. Soon it was realized that the number was too small to permit quantification of error rates. The scope of the project was expanded to 22 medications delivered by continuous IV infusion. Team members developed a process map (flowchart) to delineate each step in the procedure for continuous IV medication infusion. The process map revealed nine steps: (1) physician order, (2) order review, (3) pharmacist order entry, (4) dose preparation, (5) dose dispensing, (6) infusion rate calculation, (7) IV pump setup, (8) pump programming, and (9) pump monitoring.

Each of the steps was subjected to a failure modes and effect analysis (FMEA—see Chapter 12) and scored on a scale of 1 to 10 for three categories: frequency of occurrence, detectability, and severity. The scores were multiplied together to yield a risk priority number (RPN) for each step. Eighteen months of retrospective medication error reports were reviewed to provide additional data for the RPN calculation. This review confirmed the FMEA results that IV rate calculations and IV pump setup were the two most error-prone steps in the IV infusion process. Initial efforts to delineate and reduce errors focused on these two steps.

Because it was not known how often errors went unrecognized or unreported, an audit was conducted to determine whether the prescribed dose rate matched the actual infusion rate. Two weeks of audit data were collected and the resulting 124 data points were rated on a discrepancy scale of 1 to 3 (1 for a ≤ 1 ml/hr discrepancy, 2 for a 1–5 ml/hr discrepancy, 3 for a ≥ 5ml/hr discrepancy). Ten of the audits were rated at level 2 and four were rated at level 3. Root cause analysis was employed to determine the cause of the discrepancies. Work was then begun to affect the accuracy of infusion rates.

Using Six Sigma methods and statistical tools, the team also examined the hospital's clinical laboratory process. Key elements in the acquisition, laboratory analysis, and reporting of patient specimens were identified. The steps included (1) physician order, (2) order entry, (3) matching the order to the patient, (4) collecting the specimen, (5) labeling the specimen, (6) transporting the specimen, (7) analyzing the specimen, (8) reporting the results, and (9) entering the results into the patient's chart. Each of these steps is subject to error. Applying Six Sigma analysis, the steps subject to the most errors were identified. These steps

were: order entry by the unit clerical staff, transportation of the specimens to the lab, and analysis of specimens in the lab. To identify, define, and reduce these errors, a laboratory error reduction task force was established. It included members from administration, lab, nursing, clerical staff, information systems, and quality management. The task force first developed a process map so that all members could appreciate the complexity and vulnerability of the entire process. The process map provided the task force with the tools to analyze the clinical laboratory problem in depth. The FMEA technique was employed to arrive at a risk priority number (RPN) so that steps in the laboratory analysis process could be prioritized in terms of their vulnerability to error. Again, order entry, transportation, and analysis of specimens were identified. Statistical tools, including correlation and regression, analysis of variance, confidence intervals, and hypothesis testing, were employed to evaluate the laboratory process further.

The analysis of medication delivery by IV infusions served as a good example of deployment of Six Sigma methodology to reduce error and improve patient safety in a health care setting. Significant variability in the ordering and processing of IV drips was identified. Lack of standardization in many steps of the process posed the greatest risk for system failure. Those steps with the highest degree of variability and the greatest chance for error were

1. MD ordering practices (i.e., lack of standardization in medication description, dosage, concentration, etc.)
2. IV drip preparation (lack of standardization by pharmacy and nursing of IV bag concentrations)
3. RN labeling and documentation of IV concentrations

In these three areas, a multidisciplinary task force created standards to reduce variation. Specific interventions included implementation of standardized physician order sheets, a policy requiring preparation of all IV medications in a standard concentration, and use of color-coded labels when nonstandard concentrations were in use. Thirty days after implementation, measurable improvement was evident. Level 1 discrepancies fell from 47.4 percent to 14 percent. Level 2 discrepancies fell from 21.1 percent to 11.8 percent and level 3 discrepancies fell from 15.8 percent to 2.9 percent. Though far from achieving a six-sigma level of performance, substantial efforts continue to move toward that goal.

The laboratory project proved to be more complex. It was evident early on that the scope of this complex system was too broad for an initial effort. The project was broken down into smaller individual steps of the larger process. Once refocused, the appointed task force identified opportunities to reduce variation in select steps of the laboratory process. Alternate means of identifying specimens, changes in the approach to "point of care" laboratory analysis, decentralization of some laboratory tests, and a revised system to order and process

stat lab tests was put into place. Effectiveness monitoring continues as does measurement of sustainable error reductions. These efforts marked the beginning of a long laboratory redesign process aimed at driving out error, reducing turnaround time, and improving patient safety.

Key Issues for Discussion

1. How did the team use process mapping as a key part of the Six Sigma process? What value did process mapping have?
2. Why were the teams and task forces multidisciplinary in nature? What benefits does this approach have?

QUALITY IN PRACTICE
FORD'S DRIVE TO SIX SIGMA QUALITY[36]

Ford Motor Company began developing its Six Sigma quality approach, called Consumer Driven Six Sigma, in 1999. However, the company didn't really get serious about reclaiming their motto of the 1980s, "Quality is Job 1," until 2001—when JD Power and Associates' Initial Quality Study ranked Ford last among the big seven automakers. By 2003, the same survey ranked Ford number four and found that they were the most improved auto maker of the group.

The company now has more than 200 Master Black Belts, 2200 Black Belts, nearly 40,000 Green Belts, and 3000 Project Champions. Ford's training of Green, Black, Master Black Belts, and Project Champions generally follows the conventional Six Sigma training process. Black Belt training is "hands-on" and "just in time." Each trainee gets one week of full-time training per month for four months. The other three weeks of the month require that the trainees apply their training to a live project. Their Six Sigma teams typically have a member of management, a Master Black Belt (MBB), a Black Belt (BB), and several Green Belts (GB) assigned to take on various roles in a project.

BBs are expected to handle two to three projects at a time. They can choose their own projects, but are asked to choose them carefully to ensure that they contribute to waste elimination or customer satisfaction improvement. The goal is that at least

half of the reduction of "Things Gone Wrong" (in "Ford-speak") will be improved through successful Six Sigma projects. Ford has implemented a unique project tracking system that has helped to promote organizational learning. The system allows members of project teams to observe what other teams are working on via an internal database.

Leaders are also expected to have hands-on involvement as project champions. Senior leaders are required to partner with MBBs to run performance cells. These cells are managed similar to a manufacturing operation and benefit from the technical expertise of the MBB and the administrative experience of the manager. The process keeps new projects coming in and ensures that projects that are underway stay on track.

An example of a typical project was the one led by Master Black Belt Pauline Burke. The problem was recognized after customers complained that body side moldings on the Ford Focus were lifting at the edges. It became evident to Burke that this issue was a "mega project" when the number of CTQ (critical to quality) issues began to multiply. In total, the project required nine months to complete, compared to the average of four months for a typical Six Sigma project at Ford.

Burke and her team followed the DMAIC problem-solving process rigorously. The Define stage uncovered four critical issues:

1. The tape that was designed to secure the molding was not contacting the car body enough.
2. Holes located on the body and used to line up the molding were too high, hitting an indent on the body sides.
3. Pressure used to apply the tape was too low.
4. The body was not clean enough, so the tape was not sticking well.

In the Measure stage, measurements were taken on the location of the holes, flatness of the molding, pressure being applied, and percent of area being cleaned. Analysis required that team experts, stakeholders such as maintenance personnel and tier 1 and tier 2 suppliers, as well as management, use the data. They were all seeking to understand the process and to discover ways in which it could be improved. In Stage 4 of DMAIC, improvements were proposed, including moving holes on the body side down by 2 millimeters; changing molds for the body side molding to ensure flatness and 100 percent contact between the molding, tape, and body side; using optimum pressure to apply the molding (as determined by a design of experiment process); and replacing the head on the cleaning fixture to ensure optimum cleaning of the body side.

One element of the Control stage was to monitor the hole locations using routine quality checks. It was also necessary to ensure that the supplier implemented a new procedure for checking the moldings for flatness. Other quality checks were performed to meet specifications for optimum pressure used to apply the moldings to the body, and to maintain cleaning equipment. The project resulted in savings of $100,000 and no customer complaints since the improvements were implemented.

Overall, Ford's Six Sigma approach contributed impressively to the bottom line. More than 6,000 projects have been completed in just three years, and Six Sigma has saved more than $1 billion since its inception. Louise Goeser, Ford's vice president of quality, cited a number of benefits of the company's Six Sigma effort, including improved quality of products, better measurement of results and success, and improved decision making. However, she also noted some challenges, such as selecting projects that are linked to strategic objectives and the company's Revitalization plan. Ford's goal is corporatewide adoption of Six Sigma tools and methodology, so that everyone from the CEO down will possess data-driven decision-making skills.

The slogan, "Quality is Job 1," has been given a new emphasis with the development of three components: operating systems to define standards and processes, quality leadership to engage all employees, and Consumer Driven Six Sigma to be the primary data-driven decision process. These elements have helped to integrate Six Sigma into the overall quality program. Finally, the company plans to continue its emphasis on value creation and waste prevention, while widening and deepening deployment. This focus will involve increasing use of Design for Six Sigma, strengthening ties with suppliers, and continued integration of Six Sigma tools, methods and mindset as a mechanism for delivering results based on corporate objectives.

Key Issues for Discussion

1. Why do you think that the 2001 J.D. Power and Associates results were so poor even though the company had started its Six Sigma process in 1999?
2. Why did it take almost twice the average project time in order to complete the Ford Focus body-molding project? What were some possible technical difficulties encountered in analyzing and correcting the CTQ issues that were uncovered in the design stage of that project?
3. A major roadblock in Ford's Six Sigma effort was employee skepticism. How do you think they overcame it?

REVIEW QUESTIONS

1. What is a defect? Explain how to compute defects per million opportunities (dpmo).
2. Explain the theoretical basis for Six Sigma quality. How does it relate to the process capability index Cp?

3. Describe the Six Sigma problem-solving approach (DMAIC). How is it similar to or different from the other problem-solving approaches discussed in this chapter?

4. What are the key principles for effective implementation of Six Sigma?

5. What are the major types of tools used in Six Sigma projects?

6. What is Kepner and Tregoe's definition of a problem? How does this definition apply to quality issues? Provide some examples.

7. Explain the difference between structured, semistructured, and ill-structured problems. What implications do these classifications have for solving problems?

8. What are the four major components of problem solving? Why is it important to have some type of systematic problem-solving methodology in an organization?

9. List and explain the five categories into which all quality problem-solving can be classified.

10. Why do messes arise in organizations?

11. What is a root cause? How does the "5 Why" technique help uncover the root cause?

12. Describe some techniques used to generate ideas.

13. List and explain some of the tools and approaches used in "lean" organizations. How does the lean operating concept relate to Six Sigma?

14. What are some reasons why the lean approach appeals to small organizations?

15. In manufacturing, the concept of a "hidden factory" describes the necessity of repair and rework of defective products. List some places where the "hidden factory" can exist in service businesses.

 ## DISCUSSION QUESTIONS

1. The January 22, 2001, issue of *Fortune* contained an article "Why You Can Safely Ignore Six Sigma," that was highly critical of Six Sigma. Here are some of the criticisms levied against Six Sigma:
   a. The results often don't have any noticeable impact on company financial statements. Thus, Six Sigma success doesn't correlate to higher stock value. This criticism applies to 90 percent of the companies that implement Six Sigma.
   b. Only early adopters can benefit.
   c. Six Sigma focuses on defects, which are hard to objectively determine for service businesses.
   d. Six Sigma can't guarantee that your product will have a market.
   How would you respond to these statements?

2. Some of the key processes associated with business activities for a typical company include sales and marketing, supply chain management, managing information technology, and managing human resources. What types of Six Sigma projects might be considered in order to improve each of these activities?

3. "Resistance to change" is a common theme in the behavioral sciences. What part do you believe that resistance to change plays in management's fostering of successful versus unsuccessful adoptions of Six Sigma approaches? What impact does workers' resistance or lack of resistance have?

4. List some of the common processes that a student performs. How can these processes be improved using a Six Sigma approach?

5. Why are modern products that often require high tolerances, short production runs, and heavy customer input difficult to manufacture in order to meet Six Sigma specifications?

6. How can lean concepts be applied in a classroom?

7. The Six Sigma philosophy seeks to develop technical leadership through "Belt" training, then use it in team-based projects designed to improve processes. To what extent are these two concepts (technical experts versus team experts) at odds? What must be done to prevent them from blocking success in improvement projects?

8. How might a Six Sigma project be done to improve a registration process in a university? An admission process?

9. How can a manager effectively balance the key components of a Six Sigma implementation design related to who, what, where, when, why, and how it could be done?

10. In 1995 Jack Welch sent a memo to his senior managers telling them that they would have to require every employee to have started Six Sigma training to be promoted. Furthermore, 40 percent of the managers' bonuses were to be tied to the successful introduction of Six Sigma. Do you believe that this directive was a motivational action, or did it violate W. Edwards Deming's maxim that managers and leaders must "cast out fear"? Why or why not?

11. A consultant told the story of two Six Sigma teams that made separate presentations on how they would improve processes in their own areas. At the end of the second presentation, the consultant asked a basic question that stopped both Black Belt team leaders in their tracks: "Haven't you both just proposed making improvements based on eliminating parts of processes in the other group's areas? It seems that the implementation costs in one area will cancel out the savings in the other area!" What had the Black Belts failed to recognize? What would you recommend to prevent this situation from happening in other organizations?

 ## PROBLEMS

1. An insurance firm set a standard that policy applications be processed within three days of receipt. If, out of a sample of 1,000 applications, 50 fail to meet this requirement, at what sigma level is this process operating?

2. During one month, 35 preflight inspections were performed on a military aircraft. Eighteen nonconformances were noted. Each inspection checks 60 items. What sigma level does this incidence of nonconformance correspond to?

3. Over the last year 1,054 injections were administered at a clinic. Quality is measured by the proper amount of dosage as well as the correct drug. In two instances, the incorrect amount was given, and in one case, the wrong drug was given. At what sigma level is this process?

4. *The Wall Street Journal* reported on February 15, 2000, that about 750,000 airplane components are manufactured, machined, or assembled for Boeing Co. by workers from the Seattle Lighthouse for the Blind. A Boeing spokeswoman noted that the parts have an "exceptionally low" rejection rate of one per thousand. At what sigma level is this process operating?

5. An electronics firm manufactures 500,000 circuit boards per month. A random sample of 5,000 boards is inspected every week for five characteristics. During a recent week, two defects were found for one characteristic, and one defect each was found for the other four characteristics. If these inspections produced defect counts that were representative of the population, what is the overall sigma level for the process? What is the sigma level for the characteristic that showed two defects?

PROJECTS, ETC.

1. Three popular Web sites for Six Sigma are http://www.ge.com/sixsigma, http://www.isixsigma.com, and http://www.sixsigmaformum.com. Explore these sites and consider the following questions.
   a. How does GE use Six Sigma to enhance customer perception of its products and services?
   b. What is the apparent purpose of the isixsigma Web site?
   c. Who are the customers of the sixsigmaforum Web site?
   d. Is there basic agreement about what the Six Sigma concept includes, based on what the three Web sites present? Why or why not?
   e. How do these Web sites differ in their concept of what Six Sigma includes?
2. Identify an important problem around your school or in some related function, such as a student organization, and apply the DMAIC process to develop an improved solution. You might wish to consult Chapter 13 during this effort to learn some useful tools.
3. Find a local company that is using Six Sigma or lean principles. Write a case study of their experiences, focusing on the challenges they faced during their implementation efforts.

CASES

I. IMPLEMENTING SIX SIGMA AT GE FANUC[37]

GE Fanuc Automation in Charlottesville, Virginia, is a joint venture between General Electric and Fanuc Ltd. of Japan, a company that specializes in computer numerical control (CNC) and robotic technology. The division has annual sales of about $700 million from the manufacture and sale of factory automation products, which serve the automotive, food-processing and packaging, paper, pharmaceutical, robotics, chemical, and energy markets. The headquarters and main manufacturing plant is at its Charlottesville facility, and includes more than 500,000 square feet of floor space divided among seven buildings on 50 acres of land. GE Fanuc implemented their Six Sigma program in 1996, shortly after Jack Welch announced the quality ini-

tiative for the entire company. The program required a major cultural and attitude change at GE-Fanuc and around the world at GE sites, but it has resulted in a stronger, quality-driven company.

The Six Sigma way of thinking is ingrained in everything the company and its employees do. "From our corporate decisions all the way out to the factory floor, Six Sigma has raised our employees' mindset to look at data instead of emotion," says Sheila O'Donnell-Good, GE Fanuc's Six Sigma business leader. "If you go out on the floor and visit each line, you're going to see a lot of good data driving decision making. . . . We have ingrained our tool sets within our people, so Six Sigma is a philosophy and an outlook that allows us to examine a broken process, get to a solution, and put controls on in the end. We also see it as a business strategy that helps us gain a competitive edge because it's a differentiator between us and our competitors."

"At one time, GE was a Three-Sigma company and the cost of failure was estimated at 15 percent of sales. But achieving Six Sigma represents a $4 billion cost reduction opportunity through reduced cost of failure," says O'Donnell-Good. She adds that the savings are "really greater if you think about it because there have been significant improvements through this program other than the cost-of-failure reduction."

Six Sigma teams are established to improve or correct processes. Don Splaun, manager of advanced manufacturing technology, headed a Six Sigma team that wanted to eliminate the Environmental Stress Screen (ESS) test on circuit boards. Splaun felt the test was costly and unnecessary because the ESS was followed by a second and final test. The test was designed to eliminate premature failure in the boards, but required running the boards through a high-temperature oven for seven hours.

Initially, Splaun estimated that GE Fanuc was paying about $12,000 to $18,000 in electricity plus $2,000 to $70,000 a year in maintenance costs per oven and labor costs for loading and unloading the oven. Concentrating on the field-control product line, team members collected and analyzed data to determine whether the final test was as effective as the ESS. Operators filled out data sheets with information such as board name, date, and whether the board passed or failed the ESS test and subsequent tests. These data helped team members determine whether boards that failed were false failures or dead on arrivals (DOAs), which aren't related to the ESS. Of 7,703 boards that were tested, 311 failed in the first pass. Of these, 284 (91.3 percent) were false failures and 26 (8.4 percent) were dead on arrival (DOA). Only 1 board (0.3 percent) actually failed during the ESS. DOAs were also found bad at the final test, indicating that the final test is an effective screen. Thus, Splaun and his team found only 1 failure out of 7,703 units, which was equivalent to 130 defects per million observations (dpmo), a yield of 99.99 percent, and a sigma level of 5.15.

This analysis indicated that the final test captured the same failures as the ESS in a more time- and cost-effective manner, so the ESS and the ovens used for the test could be eliminated. To con-

trol the improvement, the company began to track the number of failures and defective boards on the line to ensure that product quality remains high after elimination of ESS. The actual benefits that resulted from the project are summarized here.[38]

Direct Labor & Materials Savings		$84,742
Inventory Reduction	$48,400	
Energy/Maintenance	$16,000	
Total Hard Savings		$149,142
Labor Cost Avoidance	$18,000	
Total Savings		$167,142

Removing the test from the manufacturing process also reduced the cycle time by a day.

GE Fanuc is only one example of the application of Six Sigma within General Electric. The impact of Six Sigma across the GE corporation is clearly described in the company's 1999 Annual Report:

> In 1999, the Six Sigma initiative was in its fifth year—its fifth trip through the operating system. From a standing start in 1996, with no financial benefit to the Company, it flourished to the point where it produced more than $2 billion in benefits in 1999.[39]

Jack Welch, then CEO of GE stated: "We want being a product/services customer of GE to be analogous to bringing your car in for a 50,000-mile check and driving out with 100 more horsepower, better gas mileage and lower emissions."

In the initial stages of Six Sigma, the company's effort consisted of training more than 100,000 people in its science and methodology and focusing thousands of "projects" on improving efficiency and reducing variance in internal operations—from industrial factories to financial services back rooms. From there, the firm's operating system steered the initiative into design engineering to prepare future generations of "Design for Six Sigma" products—and drove it rapidly across the customer-interactive processes of the financial services businesses. Medical Systems used it to open up a commanding technology lead in several diagnostic platforms and achieve dramatic sales increases and customer satisfaction improvements. Every GE product business and financial service activity [now] uses Six Sigma in its product design and fulfillment processes.

Welch concluded: "Today, Six Sigma is focused squarely where it must be—on helping our customers win. A growing proportion of Six Sigma projects now under way are done on customer processes, many on customer premises. The objective is not to deliver flawless products and services that we think the customer wants when we promise them—but rather what customers really want when they want them."

Discussion Questions

1. How was GE's corporate-level vision of Six Sigma put into practice at the GE Fanuc manufacturing site?

2. What is the difference between direct labor savings and labor cost avoidance savings from a managerial perspective?
3. Verify that the number of defective boards found in the test (one) gives a dpmo of 130.
4. If you were Splaun and were asked to make a presentation to other team leaders and managers (which, in fact, happened), what conclusions would you draw that may be useful to future teams about the way that the project was conducted?

II. THE PIVOT INITIATIVE AT MIDWEST BANK,[40] PART 2

This case is a continuation of PIVOT Initiative at Midwest Bank in Chapter 7. You should review that case for background on the project and a description of the Define stage of the DMAIC approach. In this case, the focus is on the remaining steps—Measure, Analyze, Improve, and Control.

The Measure stage demanded an intense data collection effort by the PIVOT team. They used a tool called an *XY matrix* (see example in Table 10.2), designed to rank factors for potential error causes (Xs) and for customer outputs (Ys). The team gathered data and studied departmental process flows, seeking to find root causes of the problem, and to identify and agree on key CTQs that impact the customer. During the process, it was difficult for everyone, especially the subject matter experts (SMEs), to ignore their perceptions in speculating about possible causes of errors, which became known as "tribal knowledge." Six Sigma theory strongly discourages any attempt to let unproven assumptions creep into recommendations. All factors must be statistically proven through in-depth analysis to justify recommendations.

For CPD, the principal customer outputs selected were risk mitigation, error reduction, and reducing dollar loss, which were then stratified against potential error causes. The matrix was then used to calculate an overall ranking to guide the team toward the most probable causes of errors. After deciding to focus on the top seven potential causes, the CPD department's staff began the task of gathering data for each of them to verify their impact on errors in the process.

The Six Sigma analyst stratified the data collected across the potential error categories. During the Analysis stage, analysis of an extensive array of

graphs developed from the data permitted the team to see trends in the process and to begin seeking strategic solutions. Construction of the graphs required more than 48 hours of team effort. Trends pointed to problems with the manual strapping process. However, the tribal knowledge suggested that errors were due to insufficient staffing, but the initial analysis of the data did not match this hypothesis. As a result, the team began to search for a way to prove or disprove the tribal knowledge.

It was suggested that the data were not properly stratified with regard to staffing and that analysis should be applied across a longer timeframe. CPD set out to collect more data from past months, and the Six Sigma analyst began developing the graphs needed to examine the new data. Over the next week, some 100 different graphs were created, depicting data in single strands and also paired with variables that interacted with one another. The team's Six Sigma training had emphasized the importance of *fully* exploring all data interactions, using graphs to illustrate relationships between variables. Despite the team's best efforts to find a relationship, staffing and volume did not appear to affect strapping errors. This finding disproved the tribal knowledge, while providing a multitude of additional graphs for analysis.

Strong correlations were seen in the graphs involving human factors and manual processes. CPD's processes called for numerous manual steps when handling cash. The graphs' trends suggested that whenever a manual process occurred, the number of errors increased, especially in the cash strapping area where, despite many years of experience, associates were making more than 100 errors

Table 10.2 Examples of an XY Matrix

XY Matrix

Project: CDP Pivot

Output Variables (Ys)	Reduce Loss Potential	Mitigate Risk	Reduce Defects	Rank	% Rank
Output Rating	9	10	10		
Input Variables (Xs)	**Association Table**				
Customer Compliance	9	10	10	281	15.11%
Experience	10	10	9	280	15.05%
Manual Processes	10	9	10	280	15.05%
Human Factor	10	8	10	280	15.05%
Training	8	10	10	272	14.62%
Volume	9	9	10	271	14.57°h
Interdepartmental Processing Flow	10	10	5	240	12.90%
Timeliness of Courier	3	5	8	157	8.44%
Timeliness Standards	3	3	9	147	7.90%
Staffing	5	3	6	135	7.26%
Theft	2	4	2	78	4.19%

each year. These errors caused the bank to lose thousands of dollars through miss-strapped cash. On the deposit side, manual errors created a much larger dollar loss per error. The one anomaly loss accounted for almost $280,000 dollars without any repercussions for the associate making the error. A manual process caused the error, but several team members felt that the overall attitude toward dollar errors was insufficient. Associates on the deposit side were far more concerned about quantity of deposit errors, than they were about the dollar losses from each error. These human factor elements began to cause the team great concern, because it was likely to be difficult to come to agreement on immediate solutions for such a complicated issue.

To further evaluate the process, the team decided to utilize an advanced Six Sigma tool called the Failure Modes and Effects Analysis

(FMEA, discussed further in Chapter 12). The FMEA paralleled the process map constructed in the Measure stage, but concentrated more on the inputs to the processes. Once the steps were laid out, the team brainstormed potential fallouts or errors from the process. Each of these errors was then charted until the potential effect of the individual problem was found. After the causes and effects were mapped out, each process step was then ranked on three categories: severity, occurrence, and detection, to create an overall ranking of potential failures (RPN) in the process and spearhead the team's efforts (see the example in Table 10.3). The highest-ranking index of the team was strapping cash, with an RPN of 360. Of the top 10 potential errors, 77 percent involved human factors as the root cause of the problem. These issues focused the team on the need to alleviate

Table 10.3 Typical Pivot FMEA Showing Key Process Steps

#	Process Function (step)	Potential Failure Modes (process) (defects)	Potential Failure Effects (Ys)	SEV	Potential Causes of Failures (Xs)	OCC	Current Process Controls	DET	RPN	Recom-mended Actions	Responsible Person and Target Date	Taken Actions
2	Customer Makes Deposit	No deposit ticket	Deposited in wrong account	10	Human factor	3	Magnet verifies A/C# and name	8	180	Extensive customer ed. possible fee assessments	SMEs Sept.	
14	Check Deposits to Processing	Customer fraud	Bank takes loss	9	Bank takes loss	2	Currently verify payee/ systemic controls	10	180	Data collection concerning all deposited checks	SMEs	Verifying deposit ownership and check verify <15
24	Processor Verifies Deposit	Lost check	Bank takes loss	9	Human factor	2	Research and correct if possible	10	180	Dollar standard and dual control	Team 7/31/02	
31	Cash In Ticket/Ship Processing	Lost deposit	Bank takes loss	9	Human factor	1	Research and correct if possible	1	9	Explore possible upload w/FTP	Team 7/31/02	
33	Strap Cash	Lost cash	Bank takes loss	9	Human factor	4	Manual process	10	360	Automate process with a strapper	SME	Approval CBA submitted
51	Processing Completes Deposit	Miss post	Deposit delayed or bank loss	8	Human factor	4	Manual process	8	256	Explore possible upload w/FTP	Team 7/31/02	

the human interaction with the process, and especially on fixing strapping errors.

With statistically proven error causes available, the PIVOT team turned its attention to the Improve stage to develop corrective actions. One of the most beneficial tools used to find solutions to error causes was the *Countermeasures Matrix*. A portion of this matrix is shown in the form of the Countermeasures Tree Diagram in Figure 10.4. This diagram helped the team organize potential solutions to the most risky issues and to ensure that root causes were effectively addressed. The diagram categorized the proposed solutions by effectiveness and feasibility on a scale of 1 to 5, based on team opinion, statistical information, and cost estimates. Some of the solutions emerged in earlier stages of the process, while others came after intense scrutiny.

After two or three potential solutions were identified for each root cause, the team disbanded to conduct individual research on the feasibility and effectiveness of each solution. These activities included bringing in vendors, visiting other cash vaults around the city, and researching literature and online sources. Five major countermeasures were recommended as part of the total package of seven recommendations to eliminate strapping errors, and 14 recommendations concerning deposit errors. The five were:

1. Purchase a cash strapping machine.
2. Assess a $5 charge to the clients for incorrect deposits.
3. Eliminate double keying of deposits in both CPD and Processing departments.

Figure 10.4 Countermeasures Tree

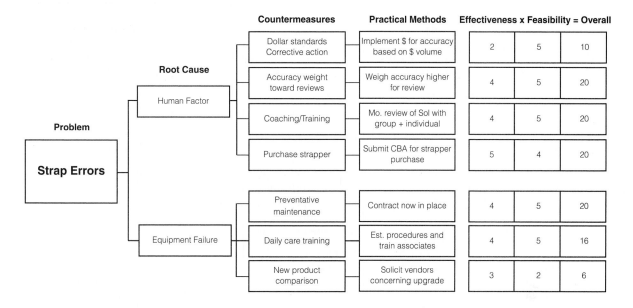

4. Implement a new vacation scheduling system for deposit processing associates to reduce the number of errors attributable to inexperienced personnel on the job.
5. Implement a dollar loss corrective action program to discourage associates from making large dollar errors in CPD's deposit section.

The potential advantages and barriers for each countermeasure are shown in Table 10.4. None of them were likely to provide a perfect solution to the problem, but each could contribute substantially to meeting the goals of the project.

The CPD PIVOT team started out slowly in the Control stage as many solutions were left to the subject matter experts to implement while some of the minor solutions were immediately implemented into daily CPD processes. Some of the recommended improvements were easy to sell and showed immediate results, while others were extremely difficult. A pilot study of the $5 charge for incorrect deposits showed promise for substantially reducing the 44 percent of deposit errors attributable to improper deposit preparation by large corporate clients. The large anomaly deposit loss had been due to an improperly completed deposit ticket.

The most difficult recommendation to handle was number 5. After the team began falling behind on execution of solutions, it took some negotiation

between the champions and the department head to regain momentum in implementing countermeasures for the project. The corrective action plan for dollar losses mirrored the branch plan, as it was introduced to CPD associates. Its success had not been accurately measured.

The project has had a significant impact on errors within the department. Some of the solutions have proved to be effective. Overall errors are down by 30 percent. Although this percentage does not perfectly match the goal, several solutions are still in their infancy, with a strong potential for that number to be further reduced. The second metric involved dollar losses that the bank incurred. Dollar losses plummeted 57 percent from the same period last year. In a dollar-focused environment, these solutions proved to be essential to the survival of the business and a drive toward increased competitiveness within the banking market.

Discussion Questions

1. How difficult did it appear to be to find the "root cause" of the errors? What do you think contributed to the difficulty?
2. What types of quantitative analysis would need to be done in order to justify the implementation of the five major recommendations?
3. For which of the adopted changes would it be most difficult to "hold the gains"? Why?

Table 10.4 Countermeasures Selection and Control

Countermeasure	Potential Advantage	Potential Barrier	Cost	Result
Purchase strapping machine	Eliminate 98.2% of strapping errors with 99.95% accuracy	Cost	Very high purchase cost	• Delayed in finding vendor • Currently only handles $20 bills
Assess $5 customer charge for incorrect deposits	Reduce 44% of deposit errors	Loss of customers	• Low out of pocket • Hard to quantify customer impact	After quantified risky study, has been implemented, with some concerns
Eliminate double keying of deposits	Reduce deposit data entry errors by 24%	IT must confirm current system can handle increased volumes	Moderate, $5,000	Await testing
New vacation schedule policy	Reduce the 79% of deposit errors when experienced associates on vacation	Employee dissatisfaction	No out of pocket cost	Implemented policy for one associate per group to be on vacation at a time
Dollar loss corrective action for associates	Reduce the magnitude of dollar losses, not just volume, in deposit sections	Supervisor and employee dissatisfaction	No out of pocket cost	Implemented policy based on similar branch bank policy

ENDNOTES

1. Ronald D. Snee, "Why Should Statisticians Pay Attention to Six Sigma?" *Quality Progress*, September 1999, 100–103.

2. Pandu R. Tadikamalla, "The Confusion over Six-Sigma Quality," *Quality Progress* 27, no. 11, November 1994, 83–85. Reprinted with permission of Pandu R. Tadikamalla and *Quality Progress*.

3. "Up, Up, and Away?" *Fortune*, July 21, 2003, 149.

4. Kervin Linderman, Roger G. Schroeder, Srilata Zaheer, and Adrian S. Choo, "Six Sigma: A Goal-Theoretic Perspective," *Journal of Operations Management* 21, (2003), 193–203.

5. Charles H. Kepner and Benjamin B. Tregoe, *The Rational Manager* (New York: McGraw-Hill, 1965).

6. Gerald F. Smith, "Too Many Types of Quality Problems," *Quality Progress*, April 2000, 43–49.

7. Russell Ackoff, "Beyond Problem Solving," presented at the Fifth Annual Meeting of the American Institute for Decision Sciences (now the Decision Sciences Institute), Boston (November 16, 1973).

8. Donald P. Lynch, Suzanne Bertolino, and Elaine Cloutier, "How to Scope DMAIC Projects," *Quality Progress* 36, no. 1 (January, 2003), 37–44.

9. Jeffrey K. Pinto, "The Power of Project Management," *Industry Week*, August 18, 1997, 138–140.

10. " Six Sigma at GE-Lunar, Manufacturing and Technology Matters," Erdman Center for Manufacturing and Technology Management, University of Wisconsin-Madison School of Business, Fall/Winter 2002, 1–3.

11. A. VanGundy, "Comparing 'Little Known' Creative Problem-Solving Techniques," in *Creativity Week III, 1980 Proceedings* (Greensboro, NC: Center for Creative Leadership, 1981). The reader is also referred to James R. Evans, *Creative Thinking in the Decision and Management Sciences* (Cincinnati, OH: South-Western Publishing Co., 1991), for a thorough treatment of creative problem solving.

12. "The Tools of Quality Part V: Check Sheets," *Quality Progress* 23, no. 10 (October 1990), 53.

13. "NCR Corporation," in *Profiles in Quality* (Needham Heights, MA: Allyn and Bacon, 1991).

14. Howard H. Bailie, "Organize Your Thinking with a Why-Why Diagram," *Quality Progress* 18, no. 12 (December 1985), 22–24.

15. A. F. Osborn, *Applied Imagination*, 3d ed. (New York: Scribners, 1963); S. J. Parnes, R. B. Noller, and A. M. Biondi (eds.), *Guide to Creative Action* (New York: Scribners, 1977).

16. Chris Bott, Elizabeth Keim, Sai Kim, and Lisa Palser, "Service Quality Six Sigma Case Studies," *ASQ's 54th Annual Congress Proceedings*, 2000, 225–231.

17. Thomas Pyzdek, *The Six Sigma Handbook* (Tuscon, AZ: McGraw-Hill/Quality Publishing, 2001), 301.

18. A. Blanton Godfrey, "Six Sigma Quality," *Quality Digest*, May 1999, 22.

19. Roger W. Hoerl, "Six Sigma and the Future of the Quality Profession," *Quality Progress*, June 1998, 35–42. ©1998, American Society for Quality. Reprinted with permission.

20. This definition is adapted from Maurice L. Berryman, "DFSS and Big Payoffs," *Six Sigma Forum Magazine* 2, no. 1 (November 2002), 23–28.

21. Charles Humber and Robert Launsby, "Straight Talk on DFSS," *Six Sigma Forum Magazine* 1, no. 4 (August 2002).

22. George Eckes, *The Six Sigma Revolution* (New York: John Wiley & Sons, 2001), 251–254.

23. H. James Harrington, "Creating Organizational Excellence—Part Two," *Quality Digest*, February 2003, 14.

24. This discussion of the applicability of Six Sigma to services is adapted from Soren Bisgaard, Roger W. Hoerl, and Ronald D. Snee, "Improving Business Processes With Six Sigma," *Proceedings of ASQ's 56th Annual Quality Congress*, 2002 (CD-ROM), and Kennedy Smith, "Six Sigma for the Service Sector," *Quality Digest*, May 2003, 23–28.

25. Adapted from Elizabeth Keim, LouAnn Fox, and Julie S. Mazza, "Service Quality Six Sigma Case Studies," *Proceedings of the 54th Annual Quality Congress of the American Society for Quality*, 2000 (CD-ROM).

26. Lisa Palser, "Cycle Time Improvement for a Human Resources Process," *ASQ's 54th Annual Quality Congress Proceedings*, 2000 (CD-ROM).

27. Roger Hoerl, "An Inside Look at Six Sigma at GE," *Six Sigma Forum Magazine* 1, no. 3 (May 2002), 35–44.

28. Andrew Spanyi and Marvin Wurtzel. "Six Sigma for the Rest of Us," *Quality Digest* 23, no. 7 (July, 2003), 26.

29. Gary Conner, "Benefiting from Six Sigma," *Manufacturing Engineering* 130, no. 2 (February, 2003).

30. Alex Taylor III, "How Toyota Defies Gravity," *Fortune*, December 8, 1997, 100–108.

31. Gary Conner, "Benefitting from Six Sigma," *Manufacturing Engineering*, February, 2003, 53–59.

32. Anthony R. Goland, John Hall, and Devereaux A. Clifford, "First National Toyota," *The McKinsey Quarterly* no. 4, (1998), 58–66.

33. Goland et al. (see note 32).

34. Duke Okes, "Organize Your Quality Toolbelt," *Quality Progress*, July 2002, 25–29.

35. Adapted from Cathy Buck, "Application of Six Sigma to Reduce Medical Errors," *Proceedings of the 55th Annual Quality Congress of the American Society for Quality*, 2001 (CD-ROM). © 2001, American Society for Quality. Reprinted with permission.

36. Kennedy Smith. "Six Sigma at Ford Revisited," *Quality Digest* 23, no. 6 (June 2003), 28–32. Adapted from Quality Digest, www.qualitydigest.com, with permission.

37. Adapted from an article in *Industrial Maintenance and Plant Operations*, Copyright © 2000 Cahners Business Information, A Division of Reed Elsevier, Inc., as available at http://www.impomag.com; and materials supplied by Don Splaun, manager of advanced manufacturing technology at GE-Fanuc, Charlottesville, VA.

38. Final figures provided at the end of the project by Don Splaun.

39. Adapted from the GE 1999 Annual Report.

40. Appreciation is expressed to one of the author's students, Michael Wolf, who wrote the paper on which this case is based, as part of the requirements for MGT 699, Total Quality Management, 2002, at Northern Kentucky University, and Cathy Ernst, senior vice president at the bank.

BIBLIOGRAPHY

Alukal, George, and Anthony Manos. "Lean Manufacturing," *The Quality Management Forum* 28, no. 3 (Summer 2002), 4–7.

Breyfogle, Forrest W., III, James M. Cupello, and Becki Meadows. *Managing Six Sigma*. New York: John Wiley & Sons, 2001.

Brue, Greg. *Six Sigma for Managers*. New York, McGraw-Hill, 2002

Eckes, George. *The Six Sigma Revolution*. New York: John Wiley & Sons, 2001.

George, Michael L. *Lean Six Sigma: Combining Six Sigma Quality with Lean Speed*. New York: McGraw-Hill, 2002.

Stamatis, D. H. *Six Sigma and Beyond: Foundations of Excellent Performance*. Boca Raton, FL: St. Lucie/CRC Press, 2002.

Tomas, Sam. "Six Sigma: Motorola's Quest for Zero Defects." *APICS, The Performance Advantage*, July 1991, 36–41.

"What Is Motorola's Six Sigma Product Quality?" *American Production and Inventory Control Society 1990 Conference Proceedings*. Falls Church, VA: *APICS*, 27–31.

CHAPTER 11

STATISTICAL THINKING AND APPLICATIONS

Brian Joiner, a noted quality management consultant, relates the following case:

> *Ed was a regional VP for a service company that had facilities around the world. He was determined that the facilities in his region would get the highest customer satisfaction ratings in the company. If he noticed that a facility had a major drop in satisfaction ratings in one month or had "below average" ratings for three months in a row, he would call the manager and ask what had happened—and make it clear that next month's rating had better improve. And most of the time, it did!*[1]

As the average satisfaction score dropped from 65 to 60 between February and March, Ed's memo to his managers read:

> *Bad news! We dropped five points! We should all focus on improving these scores right away! I realize that our usage rates have increased faster than anticipated, so you've really got to hustle to give our customers great service. I know you can do it!*

As Joiner observed, "Do you look at data this way? This month versus last month? This month versus the same month last year? Do you sometimes look at the latest data point? The last two data points? I couldn't understand why people would only want to look at two data points. Finally, it became clear to me. With any two data points, it's easy to compute a trend: 'Things are down 2 percent this month from last month. This month is 30 percent above the same month last year.' Unfortunately, we learn nothing of importance by comparing two results when they both come from a stable process . . . and most data of importance to management are from stable processes."

Many managers who do not understand how to use statistics effectively make similar mistakes. Statistical concepts are crucial to good quality management and are the key in dealing with processes and their inherent variation. They are fundamental to Six Sigma practice and studies; in fact, Six Sigma has elevated the importance of statistics in business analysis. Statistical methods have applications in many other areas of quality management, including product and market analysis, product and process design, process control, testing and inspection, identification and verification of process improvements, and reliability analysis. All managers, supervisors, and production and clerical workers should have some knowledge of the technical aspects of statistical methods. Companies large and small need to understand statistical aspects of data analysis to make good decisions (see the *Quality Profiles* for Granite Rock and Branch-Smith).

Readers of this text are assumed to have prior knowledge of elementary statistics. This chapter provides a brief review of some important statistical concepts and applications in Six Sigma and other quality control and improvement activities, but the chapter is not intended to replace a rigorous treatment of statistical methods. However, we have found that statistics is a subject for which you learn something new every time you review the concepts, so we encourage you to do so. A complete treatment of statistical methods for Six Sigma can be found in Breyfogle's book in the Bibliography at the end of this chapter.

STATISTICAL THINKING

Statistics is a science concerned with "the collection, organization, analysis, interpretation, and presentation of data."[2] Measurement processes provide data. The data may be dimensions of bolts being produced on a production line, order entry errors per day in an order entry department, or numbers of flight delays per week at an airport.

The importance of statistical concepts in quality management cannot be overemphasized. Indeed, statistics is essential in implementing a continuous improvement philosophy. The use of statistical methods in quality dates back to 1903, when the Bell System faced a problem designing its central offices.[3] A telephone subscriber takes the phone off the hook and gets a dial tone, meaning that he is connected to a trunk line that goes to the central office. The question was, "How many of those lines do you need?" Theoretically, every subscriber could use the phone at the same time, but in reality only a few percent actually do. Analysts collected and analyzed statistical information on the demand day-by-day, hour-by-hour, and identified the peak periods to determine how many lines were required to meet a service standard (the probability of not getting a dial

> *Raw data collected from the field do not provide the information necessary for quality control or improvement. Data must be organized, analyzed, and interpreted. Statistics provide an efficient and effective way of obtaining meaningful information from data, allowing managers and workers to control and improve processes.*

Quality Profiles

Granite Rock Company and Branch-Smith Printing Division

Founded in 1900, Granite Rock produces rock, sand, and gravel aggregates; ready-mix concrete; asphalt; road treatments; and recycled road-base material. It also retails building materials made by other manufacturers and runs a highway-paving operation. It competes in a six-county area extending from San Francisco southward to Monterey. Most of its major competitors are firms owned by multinational construction-material companies.

Charts for each product line help executives assess Granite Rock's performance relative to competitors on key product and service attributes, ranked according to customer priorities. After annual improvement targets are set, the executive committee expects branches and divisions to develop their own implementation plans. Coordination across divisions is fostered by 10 Corporate Quality Teams that oversee and help align improvement efforts across the entire organization.

As part of Granite Rock's effort to reduce process variability and increase product reliability, many employees are trained in statistical process control, root-cause analysis, and other quality-assurance and problem-solving methods. This workforce capability helps the company exploit the advantages afforded by investments in computer-controlled processing equipment. Its newest batch plant features a computer-controlled process for mixing batches of concrete, enabling real-time monitoring of key process indicators. With the electronically controlled system, which Granite Rock helped a supplier design, the reliability of several key processes has reached the six-sigma level.

Applying statistical process control to all product lines has helped the company reduce variable costs and produce materials that exceed customer specifications and industry-and government-set standards. For example, Granite Rock's concrete products consistently exceed the industry performance specifications by 100 times.

Branch-Smith, Inc., is a fourth-generation family business. The Branch-Smith Printing Division (BSPD) specializes in creating multipage, bound materials with services ranging from design to mailing for specialty customers. The company takes the time to find out precisely which niche it could most successfully fill in the ultra-competitive printing arena. Aware that more than 1000 printing firms crowd the Dallas/Fort Worth market, Branch-Smith used a study of the industry to determine a primary customer base. This careful, data-driven approach—typical of how the company operates—pointed toward clients with printing needs too small for larger shops, but which fit well with what BSPD did best, providing expert solutions and leveraging cost advantages normally associated with web press operations while capitalizing on its specialized sheet-fed printing capabilities. Every Branch-Smith function is geared toward providing the best possible customer service at the lowest possible cost. To that end, databases and software tools are used extensively to gather information about, and to improve, processes involving customer service, all phases of production, continuous improvement, and decision making. An important tool called the Quality Information Database, or QID, places key data dealing with suppliers, opportunities for improvement, customer complaints, and internal nonconformance in a central location. The company's Management Review Team—responsible, among other things, for establishing and monitoring the organization's direction—uses this data to document and track progress. BSPD experienced a 72 percent growth over four years and held that gain in 2002, when the industry declined 6.6 percent. Even though BSPD is a small business in a highly fragmented industry, its market share in the Dallas/Fort Worth area has almost tripled, increasing from 0.50 percent in 1997 to 1.46 percent in 2002.

Sources: Malcolm Baldrige National Quality Award, Profiles of Winners, and 2002 Quest for Excellence video script, National Institute of Standards and Technology, Department of Commerce.

tone). In the 1920s, Bell Labs thought that statistical tools would have applications in the factory, and began to experiment with statistical sampling, eventually leading to the development of control charts. Joseph Juran was involved in trying to sell this new technology in the factories, but had little success until World War II, when the push to improve quality in the military began with the implementation of statistical methods in factories in earnest. The rest, as they say, is history.

Simply knowing statistical tools and methods is not enough; one must understand the role that the science of statistics plays in managerial decisions. Managers need to *think* statistically. **Statistical thinking** is a philosophy of learning and action based on these principles:

1. All work occurs in a system of interconnected processes.
2. Variation exists in all processes.
3. Understanding and reducing variation are keys to success.[4]

Understanding processes provides the context for determining the effects of variation and the proper type of managerial action to be taken. By viewing work as a process, we can apply statistical tools to establish consistent, predictable processes, study them, and improve them. While variation exists everywhere, many business decisions do not often account for it, and managers frequently confuse common and special causes of variation. We must understand the nature of variation before we can focus on reducing it.

Any production process contains many sources of variation, as illustrated in Figure 11.1. Different lots of material vary in strength, thickness, or moisture content, for example. Cutting tools have inherent variation in their strength and composition. During manufacturing, tools experience wear, vibrations cause changes in machine settings, and electrical fluctuations cause variations in power. Operators do not position parts on fixtures consistently, and physical and emotional stress affect operators' consistency. In addition, measurement gauges and human inspection capabilities are not uniform. Even when measurements of several items by the same instrument are the same, it is due to a lack of precision in the measurement instrument; extremely precise instruments always reveal slight differences.

The complex interactions of these variations in materials, tools, machines, operators, and the environment are not easily understood. Variation due to any of these individual sources appears at random; individual sources cannot be identified or explained. However their combined effect is stable and can usually be predicted statistically. These factors are present as a natural part of a process and are referred to as **common causes** of variation. Common causes are a result of the design of the product and production system and generally account for about 80 to 95 percent of the

---

Figure 11.1 Sources of Variation in a Production Process

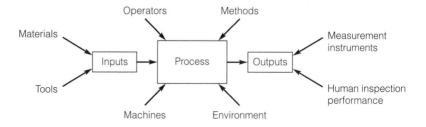

observed variation in the output of a production process. Therefore, common cause variation can only be reduced if the product is redesigned, or if better technology or training is provided for the production process. For example, Wilson Sporting goods acknowledged that small irregularities in golf balls can cause the heavier core of golf balls to be off center, resulting in balls that don't roll straight, with up to 1 in 12 high-end balls having this problem. To solve the problem, Wilson introduced a new ball design, the True ball, with a lighter core and heavier cover.[5] As an example of common cause variation in a process, suppose that boards are to be cut to the precise length of 55 inches. If the worker is provided with only a handsaw, a table, and a 12-inch ruler, it will be virtually impossible for him or her to cut lengths of this precision consistently, and a significant amount of measurable variation will exist. However, suppose that a 60-inch metal tape measure, a fixture for holding the boards, and an electric saw are available, and workers are trained in how to use them properly. Clearly, the output from this system will have less variability and more consistent quality.

The remaining variation in a production process is the result of **special causes**, often called **assignable causes** of variation. Special causes arise from external sources that are not inherent in the process. They appear sporadically and disrupt the random pattern of common causes. Hence, they tend to be easily detectable using statistical methods, and usually economical to correct. For instance, the worker cutting boards may be distracted by a supervisor and mark the boards incorrectly before cutting, resulting in several pieces that may be an inch too short. Common factors that lead to special causes are a bad batch of material from a supplier, a poorly trained substitute machine operator, a broken or worn tool, or miscalibration of measuring instruments. Unusual variation that results from such isolated incidents can be explained or corrected.

*A system governed only by common causes is called a **stable system**. Understanding a stable system and the differences between special and common causes of variation is essential for managing any system.*

Some of the operational problems created by variation include the following:[6]

- *Variation increases unpredictability.* If we don't understand the variation in a system, we cannot predict its future performance.
- *Variation reduces capacity utilization.* If a process has little variability, then managers can increase the load on the process because they do not have to incorporate slack into their production plans.
- *Variation contributes to a "bullwhip" effect.* This well-known phenomenon occurs in supply chains; when small changes in demand occur, the variation in production and inventory levels becomes increasingly amplified upstream at distribution centers, factories, and suppliers, resulting in unnecessary costs and difficulties in managing material flow.
- *Variation makes it difficult to find root causes.* Process variation makes it difficult to determine whether problems are due to external factors such as raw materials or reside within the processes themselves.
- *Variation makes it difficult to detect potential problems early.* Unusual variation is a signal that problems exist; if a process has little inherent variation, then it is easier to detect when a problem actually does occur.

Management can make two fundamental mistakes in attempting to improve a process:

1. To treat as a special cause any fault, complaint, mistake, breakdown, accident, or shortage when it actually is due to common causes.

2. To attribute to common causes any fault, complaint, mistake, breakdown, accident, or shortage when it actually is due to a special cause.

In the first case, tampering with a stable system can increase the variation in the system. In the second case, the opportunity to reduce variation is missed because the amount of variation is mistakenly assumed to be uncontrollable.

How often do managers make decisions based on a single data point or two, seeing trends when they don't exist, or manipulating financial figures they cannot truly control? The lack of broad and sustained use of statistical thinking in many organizations is due to two reasons.[7] First, statisticians historically functioned as problem solvers in manufacturing, research, and development, and thereby focused on individual clients rather than on organizations. Second, statisticians focused primarily on technical aspects of statistics rather than emphasizing process definition, measurement, control, and improvement—the key activities that lead to bottom-line results.

Senior management needs to champion the use of statistical thinking by defining the strategy and goals of the approach, clearly and consistently communicating the benefits and results, providing the necessary resources, coaching others, and recognizing and rewarding the desired behavior. To help managers work in this fashion, many organizations are creating core groups of highly trained professionals who are skilled in statistical thinking tools and can help others to use them effectively. This task requires an environment conducive to learning new behaviors and concepts.

Statistical thinking can be applied at all levels of an organization.[8] At the organizational level, it helps executives to understand the business system and its core processes, use data from the entire organization to assess performance, develop useful measurement systems, and encourage employees to experiment to improve their work. At the process level, it can motivate managers to develop and assess standardized project management systems, set realistic goals, keep employees better informed, and focus on the process without blaming employees for variation. Finally, at the individual or personal level, statistical thinking can help employees to be knowledgeable about variation, to analyze work data better, and to identify important measures and improvement opportunities. Thus, every manager and employee can benefit from statistical thinking and using total quality tools. Technology, such as today's powerful PCs and user-friendly software for data analysis and visualization such as Microsoft Excel and other spreadsheet packages, has greatly facilitated the ability to use statistics and quality tools in daily work.

Deming's Red Bead and Funnel Experiments[9]

Statistical thinking is at the heart of the Deming philosophy and his principles of Profound Knowledge (see Chapter 3). Frank H. Squires, a well-known expert on quality, credited W. Edwards Deming with keeping statistics in the forefront of the worldwide quality improvement movement. Squires stated:

> *The triumph of statistics is the triumph of Dr. Deming. When others have wavered or been lukewarm in their support for statistics, Dr. Deming has stood firm in his conviction that statistics is the heart of quality control. Indeed, he goes further and makes statistical principles central to the whole production process.*[10]

In his four-day management seminars, Deming used two simple, yet powerful experiments to educate his audience about statistical thinking. The first is the "Red Bead" experiment, which proceeds as follows. A Foreman (usually Deming) selects several volunteers from the audience: Six Willing Workers, a Recorder, two Inspectors, and a Chief Inspector. The materials for the experiment include 4,000 wooden beads—800 red and 3,200 white—and two Tupperware boxes, one slightly smaller than the other. Also, a paddle with 50 holes or depressions is used to scoop up 50 beads, which is the prescribed workload. In this experiment, the company is "producing" beads for a new customer who needs only white beads and will not take red beads. The Foreman explains that everyone will be an apprentice for three days to learn the job. During apprenticeship, the workers may ask questions. Once production starts, however, no questions are allowed. The procedures are rigid; no departures from procedures are permitted so that no variation in performance will occur. The Foreman explains to the Willing Workers that their jobs depend on their performance and if they are dismissed, many others are willing to replace them. Furthermore, no resignations are allowed.

The company's work standard, the Foreman explains, is 50 beads per day. The production process is simple: Mix the raw material and pour it into the smaller box. Repeat this procedure, returning the beads from the smaller box to the larger one. Grasp the paddle and insert it into the bead mixture. Raise the paddle at a 44-degree angle so that every depression will hold a bead. The two Inspectors count the beads independently and record the counts. The Chief Inspector checks the counts and announces the results, which are written down by the Recorder. The Chief Inspector then dismisses the worker. When all six Willing Workers have produced the day's quota, the Foreman evaluates the results.

Figure 11.2 shows the results of the first day's production generated with the Quality Gamebox computer simulation software. The Foreman is disappointed. He reminds the Willing Workers that their job is to make white beads, not red ones. The company is on a merit system, and it rewards only good performance. Marty only made 7 red beads and deserves a pay increase. The data do not lie; he is the best worker. Dennis made 14 red beads. Everyone likes him, but he must be placed on probation. The Foreman announces that management has set a goal of no more than 7 red beads per day per worker, and sees no reason why everyone cannot be as good as Marty.

Figure 11.2 First Day's Production (The paddle shows the result of the last Willing Worker, Ann)

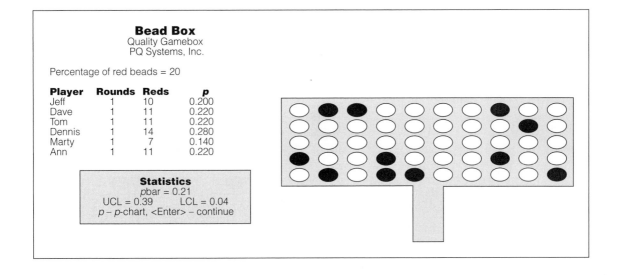

Figure 11.3 shows the cumulative results for the second day. We see that after two days, Jeff had produced 23 red beads, Dave 24, Tom 20, Dennis 21, Marty 17, and Ann 23. (The second day's results can be found by subtraction: Jeff produces 13 beads, Dave 13, Tom 9, Dennis 7, Marty 10, and Ann 12.) The overall performance was not good. Management is watching carefully. The Foreman reminds them again that their jobs depend on performance. Marty is a big disappointment. The merit increase obviously went to his head. The Foreman chastises him in front of the other workers. Dennis, on the other hand, showed remarkable improvement; probation and the threat of losing his job made him a better worker—only 7 red beads—a 50 percent reduction in defects! He met the goal; if he can do it, anyone can. Dennis gets a special commendation from the plant manager.

At the beginning of the third day, management announces a Zero Defects Day. Everyone will do their best on this last day of the apprenticeship program. The Foreman is desperate and he tells the Willing Workers again that their jobs are their own responsibility. From Figure 11.4, production figures can be determined (by computing the difference between the cumulative output of day 3 and day 2), and show that Jeff produces 12 red beads, Dave 18, Tom 17, Dennis 9, Marty 6, and Ann 11. Clearly, Marty learned a lesson the day before, but the group's overall performance is not good. Management is bitterly disappointed at the results. The Zero Defect Day program did not improve quality substantially; in fact, more red beads were produced today than ever before. Costs are getting out of control, and there is talk of shutting down the entire plant. Dave and Tom receive pink slips informing them that tomorrow will be their last day; their work is clearly much worse than the others. But the Foreman is optimistic. He puts up a poster saying "Be a Quality Worker!" to encourage the others to reach the goal.

On the fourth day (see Figure 11.5), we find that the number of red beads produced by the six Willing Workers is 8, 11, 8, 9, 8, and 9. The production is still not good enough. The Foreman announces that management has decided to close the plant after all.

Figure 11.3 Second Day's Cumulative Results

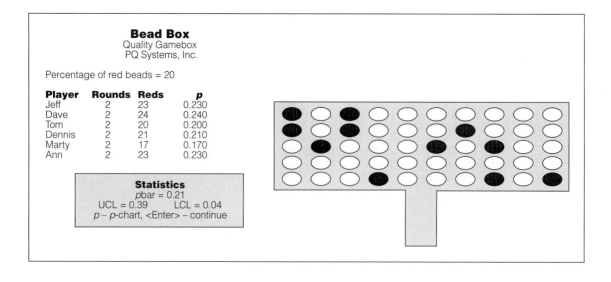

Figure 11.4 Third Day's Cumulative Results

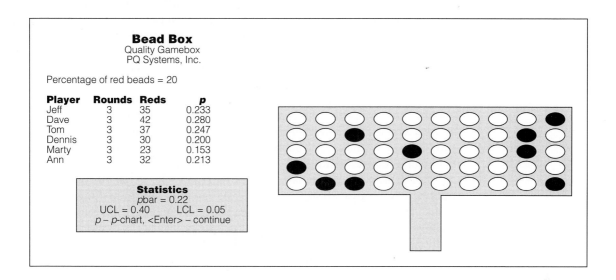

The Red Bead experiment offers several important lessons for managers:

- *Variation exists in systems and, if stable, can be predicted*. If we plot the fraction of red beads produced by each worker each day, we can observe this variation easily. Figure 11.6 is a plot of the fraction of red beads produced over time. All points fluctuate about the overall average, which is 0.21, falling roughly between 0.10 and 0.40. In Chapter 14 we will learn to calculate *statistical limits of variation* (0.04 and 0.38)—limits between which we would expect results from a

Figure 11.5 Fourth Day's Cumulative Results

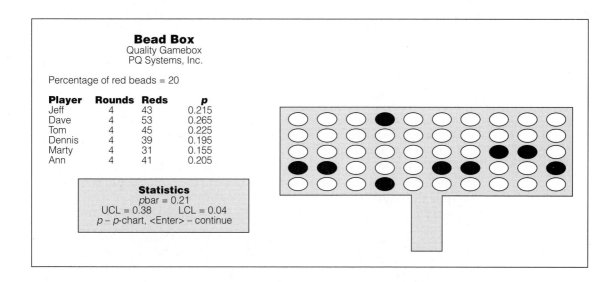

stable system to fall. This variation shows that that the system of production is indeed stable; that is, the variation arises from common causes. Although the exact number of red beads in any particular paddle is not predictable, we can describe statistically what we expect from the system.

- *All the variation in the production of red beads, and the variation from day to day of any Willing Worker, came entirely from the process itself.* In this experiment, Deming deliberately eliminated the source of variability that managers usually believe is the most significant: people. Each worker was basically identical, and no evidence showed that any one of them was better than another. They could not control the number of red beads produced, and could do no better than the system would allow. Neither motivation nor threats had any influence. Unfortunately, many managers believe that all variation is controllable and place blame on those who cannot do anything about it.

- *Numerical goals are often meaningless.* A Foreman who gives out merit pay and puts people on probation, supposedly as rewards and punishment of performance, actually rewards and punishes the performance of the process, not the Willing Workers. To rank or appraise people arbitrarily is demoralizing, especially when workers cannot influence the outcomes. No matter what the goal is, it has no effect on the actual number of red beads produced. Exhorting workers to "Do their best" only leads to frustration. Management has no basis to assume that the best Willing Workers of the past will be the best in the future.

- *Management is responsible for the system.* The experiment shows bad management. Procedures are rigid. The Willing Workers have no say in improving the process. Management is responsible for the incoming material, but does not work with the supplier to improve the inputs to the system. Management designed the production system and decided to rely on inspection to control the process. These decisions have far more influence on the outcomes than the efforts of the workers. Three inspectors are probably as costly as the six workers and add practically no value to the output.

Deming's second experiment is the Funnel Experiment. Its purpose is to show that people can and do affect the outcomes of many processes and create unwanted variation by "tampering" with the process, or indiscriminately trying to remove common causes of variation. In this experiment, a funnel is suspended above a table with a target drawn on a tablecloth. The goal is to hit the target. Participants drop a marble through the funnel and mark the place where the marble eventually lands. Rarely will the marble rest on the target. This variation is due to common causes in the process. One strategy is to simply leave the funnel alone, which creates some variation of points around the target. This may be called *Rule 1*. However, many people believe they can improve the results by adjusting the location of the funnel. Three possible rules for adjusting the funnel are:

Rule 2. Measure the deviation from the point at which the marble comes to rest and the target. Move the funnel an equal distance in the opposite direction from its current position [Figure 11.7(a)].

Rule 3. Measure the deviation from the point at which the marble comes to rest and the target. Set the funnel an equal distance in the opposite direction of the error from the target [Figure 11.7(b)].

Rule 4. Place the funnel over the spot where the marble last came to rest.

Figure 11.8 shows a computer simulation of these strategies using the Quality Gamebox. Clearly the first rule—leave the funnel alone—results in the least variation.

Figure 11.6 Run Chart of Fraction of Red Beads Produced

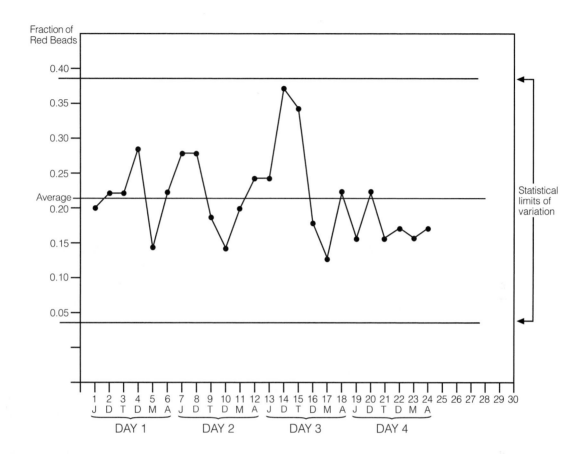

Figure 11.7 Two Rules for Adjusting the Funnel

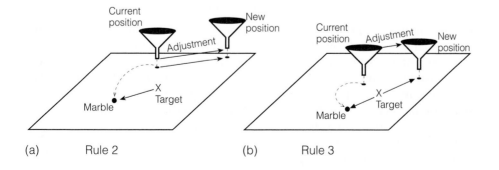

Figure 11.8 Results of the Funnel Experiment

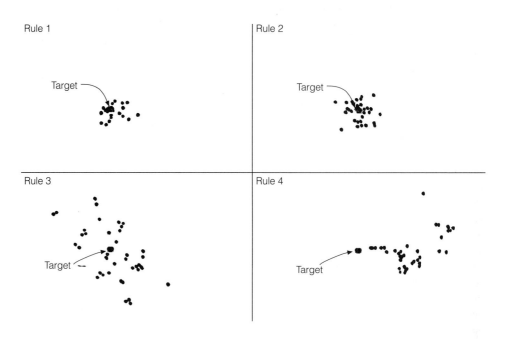

People use these rules inappropriately all the time, causing more variation than would normally occur. An amateur golfer who hits a bad shot tends to make an immediate adjustment. If the last manufactured part is off-specification, adjust the machine. If a schedule was not met last month, change the process. If the last quarter's earnings report was less than expected, dump the stock. If an employee's performance last week was subpar (or exceptional), punish (or reward) the employee. In all these cases, the error is usually compounded by an inappropriate reaction. All of these policies stem from a lack of understanding of variation, which originates from not understanding the process.

STATISTICAL FOUNDATIONS

To apply statistics properly, you need to have a basic understanding of probability distributions and sampling. These concepts are the focus of this section.

Random Variables and Probability Distributions

Random variables and probability distributions are the foundation for understanding statistical methods. The collectively exhaustive set of outcomes from an experiment makes up a *sample space*. A mathematical function that assigns numerical values to every possible outcome in a sample space is called a *random variable*. A random variable can be either discrete or continuous, depending on the specific numerical values it may assume. A *discrete random variable* can take on only finite values. An example would be the number of defects observed in a sample. A *continuous random variable* can take on any real value over a specified interval of real numbers. An example would be the diameters of bearings being manufactured in a factory. Of course, the actual observed values for the variable are limited by the precision of the measuring device. Hence, only a finite number of actual observations would occur. In theory, this result would still be a continuous random variable. Random variables are the key component used in the development of probability distributions.

A *probability distribution* represents a theoretical model of the relative frequency of a random variable. Relating probability distributions to the random variables that they represent allows a classification of the distributions as either discrete or continuous. The Bonus Materials folder for this chapter on the CD-ROM contains a review of the more useful probability distributions in quality applications. You are undoubtedly quite familiar with the normal distribution and its use as a common assumption in statistical models. Unfortunately, most business processes do not produce normal distributions.[11] Lack of a normal distribution often results from the tendency to control processes tightly, which eliminates many sources of natural variation, as well as from human behavior, physical laws, and inspection practices. For example, data on the number of days customers take to pay bills typically show that many customers like to prepay; others send payments that arrive just after the due date. This behavior causes spikes in the distribution that do not conform to normality. In a hot-dip galvanizing process, a zinc layer forms when the base material reaches the temperature of molten zinc. However, if the part is removed before the critical temperature is reached, no zinc will adhere at all. Thus, all parts will have some minimum zinc thickness and the left side of the distribution will not tail off gradually as does a normal distribution. Measuring perpendicularity as the absolute deviation from 90 degrees instead of the actual angle can easily lead to nonnormality. Therefore, it is important to fully understand the nature of your data before applying statistical theory that depends on normality assumptions.

Sampling

Sampling forms the basis for applications of statistics. Suppose that you worked in a 1,000-bed hospital and wanted to determine the attitudes of a certain group of patients about the quality of care they received while in the hospital. Several factors should be considered before making this study:

1. What is the objective of the study?
2. What type of sample should be used?
3. What possible error might result from sampling?
4. What will the study cost?

One approach to tackling this problem would be to take a complete census—a survey of every person in the entire population. However, the objective of the study will dictate which method should be used to perform the study in the most effective and efficient manner. This decision requires sensitivity to the needs of the user and an understanding of the strengths and weaknesses of the specific techniques being used. Would sampling work just as well? If the user needs the results next week to make a decision involving the expenditure of $1,000, the study will require a different design from one in which the results influence a decision that will be made in six months and has a $1 million expenditure. Sampling provides a distinct advantage over a complete census in that much less time and cost are required to gather the data. In many cases, such as inspection, sampling may be more accurate than 100 percent inspection because of reduction of inspection errors. However, sampling is frequently subject to a higher degree of error.

The second issue relates to different methods of sampling. The following are some of the most common:

1. *Simple random sampling*: Every item in the population has an equal probability of being selected.
2. *Stratified sampling*: The population is partitioned into groups, or strata, and a sample is selected from each stratum.
3. *Systematic sampling*: Every nth (4th, 5th, etc.) item is selected.
4. *Cluster sampling*: A typical group (division of the company, for example) is selected, and a random sample is taken from within the group.
5. *Judgment sampling*: Expert opinion is used to determine the location and characteristics of a definable sample group.

In choosing the appropriate type of sampling method, an analyst must consider what the sample is designed to do.

> *A good sampling plan should select a sample at the lowest cost that will provide the best possible representation of the population, consistent with the objectives of precision and reliability that have been determined for the study.*

Suppose that your objective is to provide a report to top management of the hospital to help them decide whether to expand the use of quality control measures within the hospital. Some issues that would have to be considered before choosing a sample would be the time frame for completing the study, the size and cost limitations of the sample, the accessibility of the population of patients, and the desired accuracy. Assume that you have six weeks to complete the study, a limited operating budget of $1,500, and a population of 800 maternity patients (the category in which you are interested) who could be involved in the quality study. Further assume that the accuracy of your study requires a sample of at least 400 patients and that the cost of each response would vary from $2 to $4, depending on how the survey is administered. Obviously, you would have to select a sample, because a complete census of all patients would not be feasible because of the budget limitation. Time limitations would make travel to conduct face-to-face interviews virtually impossible. Thus, the only feasible alternatives would be mailed questionnaires, telephone interviews, or a combination of the two.

Given this information, what type of sample should be chosen? Each type has advantages and disadvantages. A simple random sample would be easy to select but might not include sufficient representation by floor or ward. If a list of the patients, perhaps in alphabetical order, was available, a systematic sample of every fourth name could easily be selected. It would have the same disadvantages as the random sample, however. On the other hand, a cluster sample or judgment sample could be selected to include more representatives from floors or wards. However, cluster and judgment samples frequently take more time to identify and select appropriate sampling units. Also, because more subjective judgment is involved, a biased, nonrepresentative sampling plan is more likely to be developed.

> *Errors in sampling generally stem from two causes: **sampling error** and **systematic error** (often called nonsampling error).*

The third issue in sampling relates to error. Sampling error occurs naturally and results from the fact that a sample may not always be representative of the population, no matter how carefully it is selected. The only way to reduce sampling error is to take a larger sample from the population. Systematic errors, however, can be reduced or eliminated by design.

Sources of systematic error include the following:

1. *Bias*: The tendency to systematically over- or under-estimate true values
2. *Noncomparable data*: Data that come from two populations but are erroneously considered to have come from one

3. *Uncritical projection of trends*: The assumption that what has happened in the past will continue into the future
4. *Causation*: The assumption that because two variables are related, one must be the cause of changes in the other
5. *Improper sampling*: The use of an erroneous method for gathering data, thus biasing results (for example, using electronic mail surveys to get opinions from a population having few individuals with electronic mail services)

These sources of error can be overcome through careful planning of the sampling study. Bias can be reduced by frequent interaction with end users of the study as well as cross-checking of research designs with knowledgeable analysts. Noncomparable data can be avoided by a sensitivity to conditions that could contribute to development of dissimilar population segments. In the hospital example, data gathered from different floors, wards, or shifts could prove to be noncomparable. In production firms, different shifts, machines, or products may define different populations, even though the characteristics being measured are the same for each. Uncritical projection of trends can be avoided by analysis of the underlying causes of trends and a constant questioning of the assumption that tomorrow's population will be the same as yesterday's. Reasons for causation must be investigated. Relationships between variables alone are not sufficient to conclude that causality exists. Causation can often be tested by holding one variable constant while changing the other to determine effects of the change. Finally, improper sampling can be avoided by a thorough understanding of sampling techniques and a determination of whether the method being used is capable of reaching any unit in the population in an unbiased fashion. This section concludes with some examples of sampling applications in quality.

Simple Random Sampling A simple random sample is a small sample of size n drawn from a large population of size N in such a way that every possible sample of size n has an equal chance of being selected. For example, if a box of 1,000 plastic components for electrical connectors is thoroughly mixed and 25 parts are selected randomly without replacement, the random aspect of this definition has been satisfied. Simple random sampling forms the basis for most scientific statistical surveys, such as auditing, and is a useful tool for quality assurance studies. Many statistical procedures depend on taking random samples. If random samples are not used, bias may be introduced. For instance, if the items are rolled in coils, sampling only from the exposed end of the coil (a convenience sample) can easily result in bias if the production process that produced the coils varies over time.

Simple random samples can be selected by using a table of random numbers (see Appendix C). A unique number is assigned to each element of the population by using serial numbers, by placing the items in racks or trays with unique row and column numbering, or by associating with each item a physical distance (such as depth in a card file). Numbers are then chosen from the table in a systematic fashion. A sample is formed by selecting the items that correspond to the chosen random numbers. The selection may begin at any point in the table and move in any direction, using any set of digits that serves the sampler's purpose. An illustration of the use of the random number table for simple random sampling follows.

A particular nursing unit has 30 patients. Five patient records are to be sampled to verify the correctness of a medical procedure. To determine which patients to select, assign numbers 1 through 30 to the 30 patients. Select, for example, the first row in Appendix C and examine consecutive two-digit integers until five different numbers between 01 and 30 are found. (Any two-digit number greater than 30 is rejected because it does not correspond to an item in the given population.) Thus, the following sequence of random numbers and decisions occurs.

Number	Decision
63	reject
27	select
15	select
99	reject
86	reject
71	reject
74	reject
45	reject
11	select
02	select
15	duplicate
14	select

Based on the preceding sequence, 2, 11, 14, 15, and 27 are selected.

Simple random sampling is generally used to estimate population parameters such as means, proportions, and variances. To use simple random sampling effectively, you must also determine the appropriate sample size. The Bonus Materials folder for this chapter on the CD-ROM addresses issues of sample size determination.

Other Types of Sampling Procedures Alternatives to simple random sampling are available and are discussed briefly here. These methods have distinct advantages over simple random sampling in many situations.

1. **Stratified Random Sampling** A stratified random sample is one obtained by separating the population into nonoverlapping groups, and then selecting a simple random sample from each group. The groups might be different machines, wards in a hospital, departments, and so on. For example, suppose a population of 28,000 items is produced on three different machines:

Machine	Group Size
1	20,000
2	5,000
3	3,000

Assume that a specific confidence level requires a sample of 525 units in this case. One could draw these units randomly from the entire population. Under stratified random sampling, a simple random sample of 250 units from machine 1, 150 units from machine 2, and 125 units from machine 3 might be taken. Formulas are available for combining the results of individual samples into an overall estimate of the population parameter of interest. This technique will demonstrate quality differences that may exist among machines.

Stratified random sampling will provide results similar to simple random sampling but with a smaller total sample size. It produces a smaller bound on the error of the estimation than would be produced by a simple random sample of the same size. These statements are particularly true if measurements within each group are homogeneous, that is, if the units within strata are alike.

2. **Systematic Sampling** In some situations, particularly with large populations, selecting a simple random sample using random number tables and searching through the population for the corresponding element is impractical. With

systematic sampling, the population size is divided by the sample size required, yielding a value for n. The first item is chosen at random from among the first n items. Thereafter, every nth item is selected. For example, suppose that a population has 4,000 units and a sample of size 50 is required. Select the first unit randomly from among the first 80 units. Every 80th (4,000/50) item after that would be selected.

Systematic sampling is based on the assumption that if the first element is chosen at random, the entire sample will have the properties of a simple random sample. This method should be used with caution because quality characteristics may vary in some periodic fashion with the length of the sampling interval and thus bias the results.

3. **Cluster Sampling** In cluster sampling, the population is first partitioned into groups of elements called clusters. A simple random sample of the clusters is selected. The elements within the clusters selected constitute the sample. For example, suppose that products are boxed in groups of 50. Each box can be regarded as a cluster. We would draw a sample of boxes and inspect all units in the boxes selected.

Cluster sampling tends to provide good results when the elements within the clusters are not alike (heterogeneous). In this case, each cluster would be representative of the entire population.

4. **Judgment Sampling** With judgment sampling, an arbitrary sample of pertinent data is examined and the percentage of nonconformances is calculated. Because judgment sampling is not random, the risks associated with making an incorrect conclusion cannot be quantified. Thus, it is not a preferred method of sampling.

STATISTICAL METHODOLOGY

Figure 11.9 summarizes the basic statistical methodology used in quality applications. The first major component of statistical methodology is the efficient collection, organization, and description of data, commonly referred to as **descriptive statistics**. Frequency distributions and histograms are used to organize and present data. Measures of central tendency (means, medians, proportions) and measures of dispersion (range, standard deviation, variance) provide important quantitative information about the nature of the data. For example, an airline might investigate the problem of lost baggage and determine that the major causes of the problem are lost or damaged identification tags, incorrect tags on the bags, and misrouting to baggage claim areas. An examination of frequencies for each of these categories might show that lost or damaged bags accounted for 50 percent of the problems, incorrect tags for 30 percent, and misrouting for only 20 percent. The airline might also compute the average number of baggage errors per 1,000 passengers each month. Such information is useful in identifying quality problems and as a means of measuring improvement.

The second component of statistical problem solving is **statistical inference**. Statistical inference is the process of drawing conclusions about unknown characteristics of a population from which data were taken. Techniques used in this phase include confidence intervals, hypothesis testing, and experimental design. For example, a chemical manufacturer might be interested in determining the effect of temperature on the yield of a new manufacturing process. Because of variation in yields, a confidence interval might be constructed to quantify the uncertainty of sample data. In a controlled experiment, the manufacturer might test the hypothesis that the temperature has an effect on the yield against the alternative hypothesis that temperature has no effect. If the temperature is, in fact, a critical variable, steps will

Figure 11.9 Basic Statistical Methodology for Quality

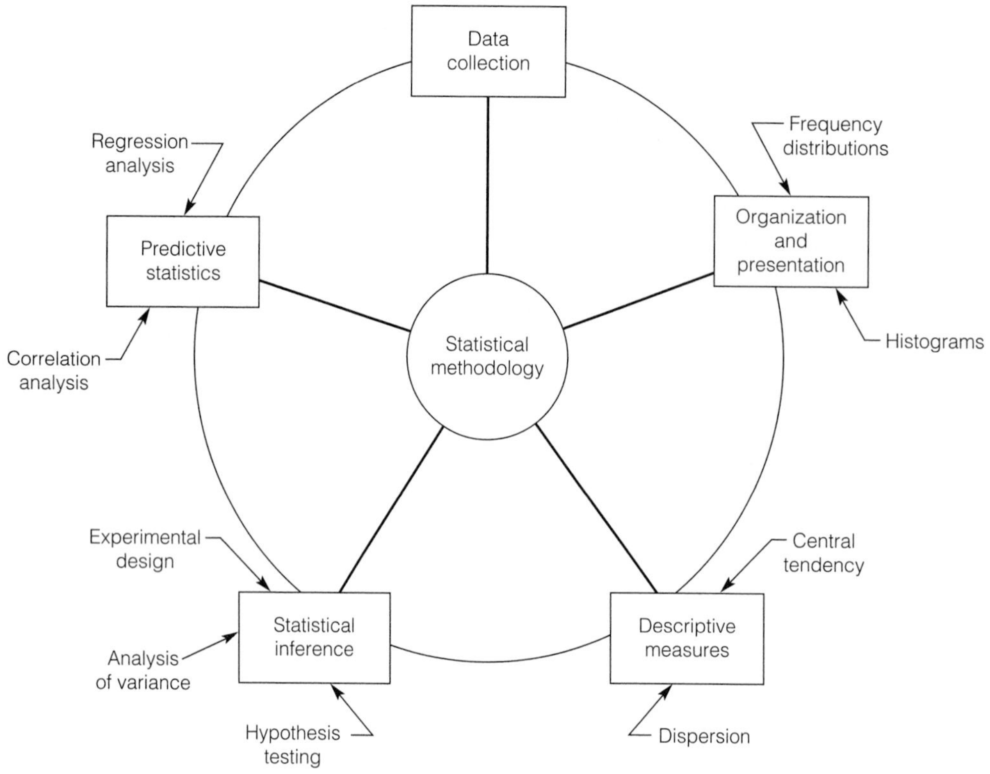

be required to maintain the temperature at the proper level and to draw inferences as to whether the process remains under control, based on samples taken from it. Experimental design is important for helping to understand the effects of process factors on output quality and for optimizing systems.

The third component in statistical methodology is **predictive statistics**, the purpose of which is to develop predictions of future values based on historical data. Correlation analysis and regression analysis are two useful techniques. Frequently, these techniques can clarify the characteristics of a process as well as predict future results. For example, in quality assurance, correlation is frequently used in test instrument calibration studies. In such studies, an instrument is used to measure a standard test sample that has known characteristics. The actual results are compared to standard results, and adjustments are made to compensate for errors.

Descriptive Statistics

A *population* is a complete set or collection of objects of interest; a *sample* is a subset of objects taken from the population. Characteristics of a population, such as the mean μ, standard deviation σ, or proportion π, are generally known as *parameters* of the population. In statistical notation, they are written as follows:

$$\text{Population mean: } \mu = \frac{1}{N} \sum_{i=1}^{N} x_i$$

$$\text{Population standard deviation: } \sigma = \sqrt{\frac{\sum_{i=1}^{N} (x_i - \mu)^2}{N}}$$

$$\text{Population proportion: } \pi = \frac{Q}{N}$$

where x_i is the value of the ith observation, N is the number of items in a population, and Q is the number of items exhibiting a criterion of interest, such as manufacturing defects or on-time departures of aircraft.

The sample mean, sample standard deviation, and sample proportion are computed as follows:

$$\text{Sample mean: } \bar{x} = \frac{1}{n} \sum_{i=1}^{n} x_i$$

$$\text{Sample standard deviation: } s = \sqrt{\frac{\sum_{i=1}^{n} (x_i - \bar{x})^2}{n-1}}$$

$$\text{Sample proportion: } p = \frac{q}{n}$$

where n is the number of items in a sample, and q is the number of items in a sample exhibiting a criterion of interest.

The purpose of sampling is to gain knowledge about the characteristics of the population from the information contained in a sample. For instance, the sample statistic $\bar{x}$ is generally used as a point estimator for the population parameter μ, s as a point estimator for σ, and p as a point estimator for π. The actual numerical values of $\bar{x}$, s, and p, which represent the single "best guess" for each unknown population parameter, are called *point estimates*. Other useful statistics to describe a set of data include the median, range, and coefficient of skewness.

Statistical Analysis with Microsoft Excel

Spreadsheets are the most useful tools for managers and analysts. In this part of the book, we will use Microsoft Excel whenever appropriate to perform statistical calculations and display graphs or charts. The disk accompanying this book contains all of the major spreadsheets used in examples in this book that will help you in working many end-of-chapter problems. The files available on the disk are identified by their name (NAME.XLS) in the text.

Microsoft Excel provides a set of data analysis tools, called the *Analysis ToolPak*, that are useful in complex statistical analyses. You provide the data and parameters for each analysis; the tool uses the appropriate statistical functions and then displays the results in an output table. Some tools generate charts in addition to output tables. To view a list of available analysis tools, click *Data Analysis* on the *Tools* menu. If the *Data Analysis* command is not on the *Tools* menu, run the Setup program to install the

Analysis ToolPak. After you install the Analysis ToolPak, you must select it in the Add-In Manager. Excel also provides many other statistical worksheet functions. To see a list of available functions, click *Edit Formula* on the formula bar, and then click the down-arrow in *Insert Function*. We strongly encourage you to learn how to use the capabilities of Excel for quality assurance applications. Much more information can be found in the Help files available with Excel.

We will assume that the sample of U-bolt measurements in Table 11.1 is representative of the population from which they were drawn. These data were entered into an Excel spreadsheet in the range A2:A121. Figure 11.10 shows the Descriptive Statistics dialog box that is displayed after choosing "Descriptive Statistics" from the *Tools/Data Analysis* options. An explanation of the items in this dialog box follows. (This information can also be obtained from the Help files in Excel.)

Input Range Enter the cell reference for the range of data you want to analyze. The reference must consist of two or more adjacent ranges of data arranged in columns or rows. Excel will compute individual statistics for each row or column; thus, all data in Table 11.1 are entered in a single column.

Grouped By To indicate whether the data in the input range are arranged in rows or in columns, click *Rows* or *Columns*.

Labels in First Row/Labels in First Column If the first row of the input range contains labels, select the Labels in First Row check box. If the labels are in the first column of the input range, select the Labels in First Column check box. This check box is clear

---

Table 11.1 Measurements of U-Bolts (U-bolt Data.XLS)

10.65	10.70	10.65	10.65	10.85
10.75	10.85	10.75	10.85	10.65
10.75	10.80	10.80	10.70	10.75
10.60	10.70	10.70	10.75	10.65
10.70	10.75	10.65	10.85	10.80
10.60	10.75	10.75	10.85	10.70
10.60	10.80	10.70	10.75	10.75
10.75	10.80	10.65	10.75	10.70
10.65	10.80	10.85	10.85	10.75
10.60	10.70	10.60	10.80	10.65
10.80	10.75	10.90	10.50	10.85
10.85	10.75	10.85	10.65	10.70
10.70	10.70	10.75	10.75	10.70
10.65	10.70	10.85	10.75	10.60
10.75	10.80	10.75	10.80	10.65
10.90	10.80	10.80	10.75	10.85
10.75	10.70	10.85	10.70	10.80
10.75	10.70	10.60	10.70	10.60
10.65	10.65	10.85	10.65	10.70
10.60	10.60	10.65	10.55	10.65
10.50	10.55	10.65	10.80	10.80
10.80	10.65	10.75	10.65	10.65
10.65	10.60	10.65	10.60	10.70
10.65	10.70	10.70	10.60	10.65

Figure 11.10 Microsoft Excel Descriptive Statistics Dialog Box

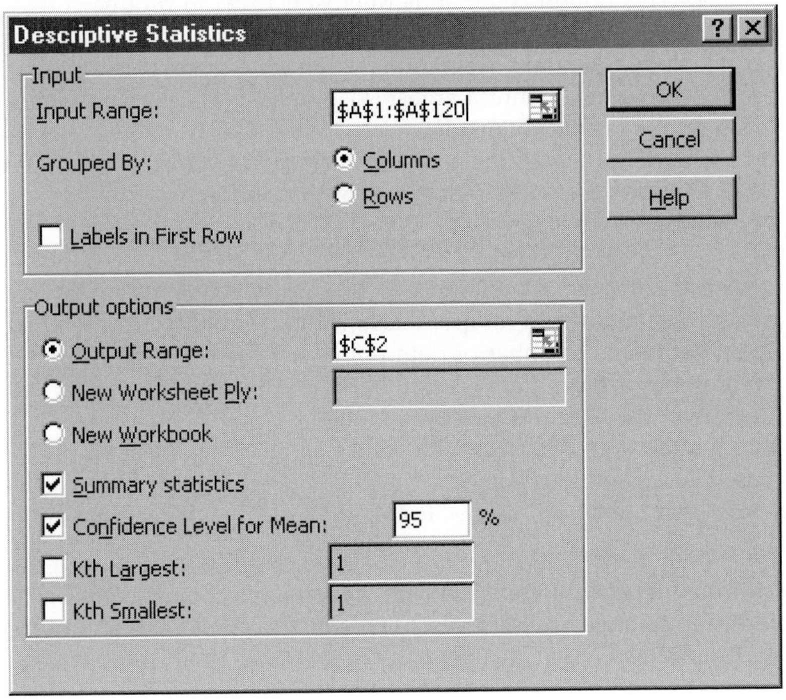

if the input range has no labels; Microsoft Excel generates appropriate data labels for the output table.

Confidence Level for Mean Select this option to include a row in the output table for the confidence level of the mean. In the box, enter the desired confidence level. For example, a value of 95 percent calculates the confidence level of the mean at a significance of 5 percent.

Kth Largest Select this option to include a row in the output table for the kth largest value for each range of data. In the box, enter the number to use for k. If you enter 1, this row contains the maximum of the data set.

Kth Smallest Select this option to include a row in the output table for the kth smallest value for each range of data. In the box, enter the number to use for k. Enter 1 and this row will contain the minimum of the data set.

Output Range Enter the reference for the upper-left cell of the output table. This tool produces two columns of information for each data set. The left column contains statistics labels and the right column contains the statistics. Microsoft Excel writes a two-column table of statistics for each column or row in the input range, depending on the Grouped By option selected.

New Worksheet Ply Click to insert a new worksheet in the current workbook and paste the results starting at cell A1 of the new worksheet. To name the new worksheet, type a name in the box.

New Workbook Click to create a new workbook and paste the results on a new worksheet in the new workbook.

Summary Statistics This option commands Microsoft Excel to produce one field for each of the following statistics in the output table: Mean, Standard Error (of the mean), Median, Mode, Standard Deviation, Variance, Kurtosis, Skewness, Range, Minimum, Maximum, Sum, Count, Largest (#), Smallest (#), and Confidence Level. Figure 11.11 shows the results obtained.

A second useful data analysis tool is the *Histogram* tool, which is described as follows. Figure 11.12 shows the Excel dialog box for this option.

Input Range Enter the reference for the range of data to be analyzed.

Bin Range (optional) Enter the cell reference to a range that contains an optional set of boundary values that define bin ranges. These values should be in ascending order. Microsoft Excel counts the number of data points between the current bin number and the adjoining higher bin, if any. A number is counted in a particular bin if it is equal to or less than the bin number down to the last bin. All values below the first bin value are counted together, as are the values above the last bin value. If the bin range is omitted, Microsoft Excel creates a set of evenly distributed bins between the data's minimum and maximum values. In this example, we defined the bin range in cells F3:F11.

Labels Select if the first row or column of the input range contains labels. Clear this check box if the input range has no labels; Microsoft Excel generates appropriate data labels for the output table.

Figure 11.11 Microsoft Excel Descriptive Statistics Results

	A	B	C	D
1	10.65			
2	10.75		*Column1*	
3	10.75			
4	10.60		Mean	10.71708333
5	10.70		Standard Error	0.007927716
6	10.60		Median	10.7
7	10.60		Mode	10.65
8	10.75		Standard Deviation	0.086843778
9	10.65		Sample Variance	0.007541842
10	10.60		Kurtosis	-0.53752485
11	10.80		Skewness	-0.0420018
12	10.85		Range	0.4
13	10.70		Minimum	10.5
14	10.65		Maximum	10.9
15	10.75		Sum	1286.05
16	10.90		Count	120
17	10.75		Confidence Level(95.0%)	0.015697649

Figure 11.12 Microsoft Excel Histogram Dialog Box

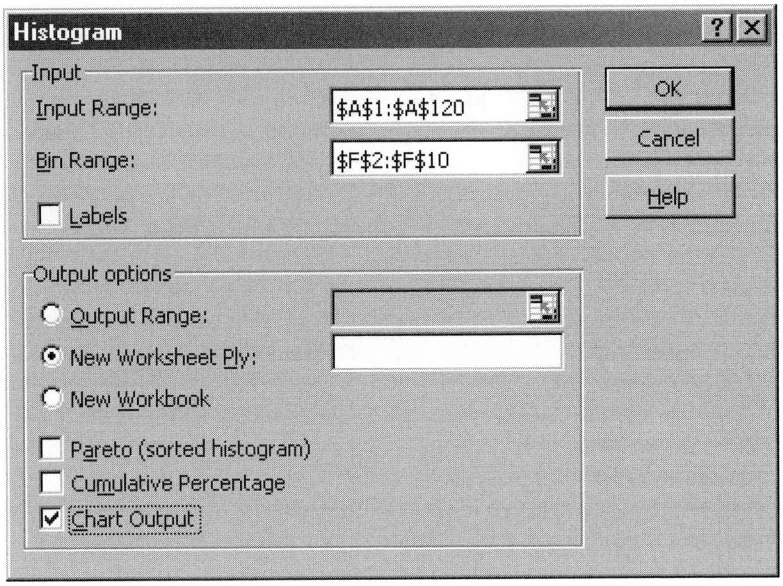

Output Range Enter the reference for the upper-left cell of the output table. Microsoft Excel automatically determines the size of the output area and displays a message if the output table will replace existing data.

Pareto (sorted histogram) Select to present data in the output table in descending order of frequency. If this check box is cleared, Microsoft Excel presents the data in ascending order and omits the three rightmost columns that contain the sorted data.

Cumulative Percentage Select to generate an output table column for cumulative percentages and to include a cumulative percentage line in the histogram chart. Clear to omit the cumulative percentages.

Chart Output Select to generate an embedded histogram chart with the output table.

Figure 11.13 shows the frequency distribution and histogram generated. We will use these results in another example later in this chapter.

Statistical Inference

Statistical inference is concerned with drawing conclusions about populations based on sample data. To be able to make probability statements about the relationship between sample statistics and population parameters and draw inferences, we first need to understand sampling distributions.

Sampling Distributions Different samples will produce different estimates of the population parameters. Therefore, sample statistics such as $\bar{x}$, s, and p are random variables that have their own probability distribution, mean, and variance. These probability distributions are called sampling distributions. In quality, the sampling distributions of $\bar{x}$ and p are of the most interest.

Figure 11.13 Histogram and Frequency Distribution

	A	B
1	Bin	Frequency
2	10.50	2
3	10.55	2
4	10.60	13
5	10.65	25
6	10.70	22
7	10.75	24
8	10.80	16
9	10.85	14
10	10.90	2
11	More	0

When using simple random sampling, the expected value of $\bar{x}$ is the population mean μ, or

$$E(\bar{x}) = \mu$$

The standard deviation of $\bar{x}$ (often called the **standard error of the mean**) is given by the formula

$$\sigma_{\bar{x}} = \frac{\sigma}{\sqrt{n}}$$ for infinite populations or sampling with replacement from an infinite population

$$\sigma_{\bar{x}} = \sqrt{\frac{N-n}{N-1}}\frac{\sigma}{\sqrt{n}}$$ for finite populations

When $n/N \leq 0.05$, $\sigma_{\bar{x}} = \sigma/\sqrt{n}$ provides a good approximation for finite populations.

The last step is to characterize the form of the probability distribution of $\bar{x}$. If the true population distribution is unknown, the Central Limit Theorem (CLT) can provide some useful insights:

If simple random samples of size n are taken from any population having a mean μ and a standard deviation of σ, the probability distribution of the sample mean approaches a normal distribution with mean μ and standard deviation (standard error) $\sigma_{\bar{x}} = \sigma/\sqrt{n}$ as n becomes very large. In more precise mathematical terms: As n $\to \infty$ the distribution of the random variable z = $(\bar{x} - \mu)/(\sigma/\sqrt{n})$ approaches that of a standard normal distribution.

The power of the central limit theorem can be seen through computer simulation using the *Quality Gamebox* software that is included on the CD-ROM accompanying

this text. Figure 11.14 shows the results of sampling from a triangular distribution for sample sizes of 1, 2, 5, and 10. For samples as small as five, the sampling distribution begins to develop into the symmetric bell-shaped form of a normal distribution. Also observe that the variance decreases as the sample size increases. The approximation to a normal distribution can be assumed for sample sizes of 30 or more. If the population is *known* to be normal, the sampling distribution of $\bar{x}$ is normal for any sample size.

Next, consider the sampling distribution of p, in which the expected value of p, $E(p) = \pi$. Here π is used as the population parameter and is not related to the *number* $\pi \approx 3.14159$. The standard deviation of p is

$$s_p = \sqrt{\frac{\pi(1 - \pi)}{n}}$$

for infinite populations.

For finite populations, or when $n/N > 0.05$, modify s_p by

$$s_p = \sqrt{\frac{N - n}{N - 1}} \sqrt{\frac{\pi(1 - \pi)}{n}}$$

In applying the central limit theorem (CLT) to p, the sampling distribution of p can be approximated by a normal distribution for large sample sizes.

This and subsequent chapters explore various applications of the CLT to statistical quality control in the areas of process capability determination and control charting. Consider the following example as we illustrate an application of sampling distributions.

The mean length of shafts produced on a lathe has historically been 50 inches, with a standard deviation of 0.12 inch. If a sample of 36 shafts is taken, what is the probability that the sample mean would be greater than 50.04 inches?

Figure 11.14 Illustration of the Central Limit Theorem

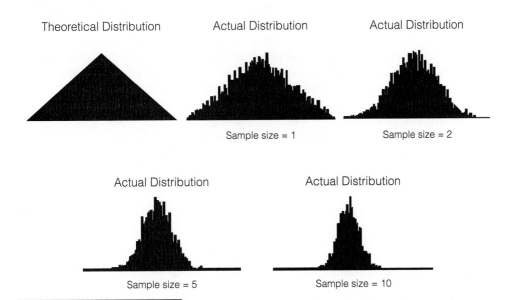

Source: Courtesy of P–Q Systems, Inc.

The sampling distribution of the mean is approximately normal with mean 50 and standard deviation of $0.12/\sqrt{36}$. Thus,

$$z = \frac{\bar{x} - \mu}{\sigma/\sqrt{n}} = \frac{50.04 - 50}{0.12/\sqrt{36}} = 2.0$$

In the standard normal table, the value of 2.0 yields the probability of 0.4772 between the mean and this value. The area for $z \geq 2.0$ then is found by

$$P(z \geq 2.0) = 0.5000 - 0.4772 = 0.0228$$

Thus, the probability of a value equal to or greater than 50.04 inches as the mean of a sample of 36 items is only 0.0228 if the population mean is 50 inches. The applicability of sampling distributions to statistical quality is that "shifts" in the population mean can quickly be detected using small representative samples to monitor the process.

Similarly, if a sample size of 64 is used, $\sigma/\sqrt{n} = 0.12/8 = 0.015$ and

$$z = \frac{\bar{x} - \mu}{\sigma/\sqrt{n}} = \frac{50.04 - 50}{0.015} = 2.67$$

and $P(z \geq 2.67) = 0.5000 - 0.4962 = 0.0038$. As the sample size increases, it is less likely that a mean value of at least 50.04 will be observed purely by chance. If it did, some special cause would likely be present.

Confidence Intervals A confidence interval (CI) is an interval estimate of a population parameter that also specifies the likelihood that the interval contains the true population parameter. This probability is called the level of confidence, denoted by $1 - \alpha$, and is usually expressed as a percentage. For example, we might state that "a 90 percent CI for the mean is 10 ± 2." The value 10 is the point estimate calculated from the sample data, and 2 can be thought of as a margin for error. Thus, the interval estimate is [8, 12]. However, this interval may or may not include the true population mean. If we take a different sample, we will most likely have a different point estimate, say 11.4, which determines the interval estimate [8.4, 12.4]. Again, this interval may or may not include the true population mean. If we chose 100 samples, leading to 100 different interval estimates, we would expect that 90 percent of them—the level of confidence—would contain the true population mean. We would say we are 90 percent confident that the interval we obtain from sample data contains the true population mean. Commonly used confidence levels are 90, 95, and 99 percent; the higher the confidence level, the more assurance we have that the interval contains the true population parameter. As the confidence level increases, the confidence interval becomes larger to provide higher levels of assurance.

Some common confidence intervals are

- Confidence interval for the mean, standard deviation known, sample size = n:

$$\bar{x} \pm z_{\alpha/2}\sigma/\sqrt{n}$$

- Confidence interval for the mean, standard deviation unknown, sample size = n:

$$\bar{x} \pm t_{\alpha/2, n-1}(s/\sqrt{n})$$

- Confidence interval for a proportion, sample size = n:

$$p \pm z_{\alpha/2}\sqrt{\frac{p(1-p)}{n}}$$

- Confidence interval for difference between two means, independent samples, equal variance, sample sizes $= n_1$ and n_2:

$$\bar{x}_1 - \bar{x}_2 \pm (t_{\alpha/2,\, n_1 + n_2 - 2})\, s_p \sqrt{\frac{1}{n_1} + \frac{1}{n_2}}$$

- Confidence interval for differences between two proportions, sample sizes $= n_1$ and n_2:

$$p_1 - p_2 \pm z_{\alpha/2} \sqrt{\frac{p_1(1 - p_1)}{n_1} + \frac{p_2(1 - p_2)}{n_2}}$$

Hypothesis Testing Hypothesis testing involves drawing inferences about two contrasting propositions (hypotheses) relating to the value of a population parameter, one of which is assumed to be true in the absence of contradictory data. For instance, suppose that a company is testing out a prototype process that is designed to reduce manufacturing cycle time. They can evaluate the proposed process by testing a hypothesis that the mean cycle time is the same as the current process.

A hypothesis test involves the following steps:

1. Formulate the hypotheses to test.
2. Select a level of significance that defines the risk of drawing an incorrect conclusion about the assumed hypothesis that is actually true.
3. Determine a decision rule on which to base a conclusion.
4. Collect data and calculate a test statistic.
5. Apply the decision rule to the test statistic and draw a conclusion.

To illustrate hypothesis testing, let us examine a producer of computer-aided design software for the aerospace industry that receives numerous calls for technical support. Tracking software is used to monitor response and resolution times. The company has a service standard of four days for the mean resolution time. However, the manager of the technical support group has been receiving some complaints of long resolution times. During one week, a sample of 44 customer calls resulted in a sample mean of 5.23 and standard deviation of 13.5. Even though the sample mean exceeds the four-day standard, does the manager have sufficient evidence to conclude that the mean service time exceeds four days, or is this particular sample mean simply a result of sampling error?

The hypothesis tested is

H_0: Mean response time ≤ 4

H_1: Mean response time > 4

The appropriate test statistic is

$$t = \frac{\bar{x} - 4}{s/\sqrt{n}}$$

The decision rule is to reject H_0 if $t > t_{n-1,\,\alpha}$. We compute the value of the test statistic as

$$t = \frac{\bar{x} - 4}{s/\sqrt{n}} = \frac{5.23 - 4}{13.5/\sqrt{44}} = \frac{1.24}{2.035} = 0.609.$$

Because $t_{43,\,.05} = 1.6811$, we cannot reject the null hypothesis. Therefore, the manager finds no sufficient statistical evidence that the mean response time exceeds 4.

Enumerative and Analytic Studies

A static population, such as employees in a company or its customer base, can be analyzed to estimate population parameters such as the mean, variance, or proportion. Confidence intervals and hypothesis tests can be applied. However, the purpose of sampling from a process is generally to predict the future. The characteristics of the population may change over time as a plot of sample means or variances might show. In such cases, confidence intervals and hypothesis tests are not appropriate *unless the time series can be shown to be stationary,* that is, have a constant mean and variance over time. Examining a trend chart of the data over time can usually provide more stationary parameters. Deming called the analysis of a static population an **enumerative study**, and the analysis of a dynamic time series an **analytic study**. Applying classical statistical inferences to an analytic study is not appropriate because they provide no basis for prediction. Thus, it is important to understand how to apply statistical tools properly.

One of the biggest mistakes that people make in using statistical methods is confusing data that are sampled from a static population (cross-sectional data) with data sampled from a dynamic process (time series data).

In the hypothesis testing example, for instance, we need to assume that the data are stationary during the week over which they were collected to apply this tool correctly. If we sampled the data over a long period of time and the characteristics of the population (mean or variance) changed over that time, then conducting a hypothesis test would not be appropriate.

Design of Experiments

Design of experiments (DOE), developed by R. A. Fisher in England, dates back to the 1920s. A designed experiment is a test or series of tests that enables the experimenter to compare two or more methods to determine which is better, or determine levels of controllable factors to optimize the yield of a process or minimize the variability of a response variable.[12] For example, a paint company might be interested in determining whether different additives have an effect on the drying time of paint in order to select the additive that results in the shortest drying time. As another example, suppose that two machines produce the same part. The material used in processing can be loaded onto the machines either manually or with an automatic device. The experimenter might wish to determine whether the type of machine and the type of loading process affect the number of defectives and then to select the machine type and loading process combination that minimizes the number of defectives.

As a practical tool for quality improvement, experimental design methods have achieved considerable success in many industries. In a celebrated case, Ina Tile Company, a Japanese ceramic tile manufacturer, had purchased a $2 million kiln from West Germany in 1953.[13] Tiles were stacked inside the kiln and baked. Tiles toward the outside of the stack tended to have a different average size and more variation in dimensions than those further inside the stack. The obvious cause was the uneven temperatures inside the kiln. Temperature was an uncontrollable factor, a noise factor. To try to eliminate the effects of temperature would require redesign of the kiln itself, a very costly alternative. A group of engineers, chemists, and others who were familiar with the manufacturing process brainstormed and identified seven major controllable variables that could affect the tile dimensions:

1. Limestone content
2. Fineness of additive

3. Content of agalmatolite
4. Type of agalmatolite
5. Raw material quantity
6. Content of waste return
7. Content of feldspar

The group designed and conducted an experiment using these factors. The experiment showed that the first factor, the limestone content, was the most significant factor; the other factors had smaller effects. By increasing the limestone content from 1 percent to 5 percent and choosing better levels for other factors, the percentage of size defects was reduced from 30 percent to less than 1 percent. Limestone was the cheapest material in the tile. In addition, the experiment revealed that a smaller amount of agalmatolite, the most expensive material in the tile, could be used without adversely affecting the tile dimension. Both the effect of the noise factor and the cost of the product were reduced at the same time! This discovery was a breakthrough in the ceramic tile industry.

As another example, ITT Avionics Division, a leading producer of electronic warfare systems, experienced a high defect rate when using a wave solder machine to solder assemblies on printed circuit boards.[14] The wave solder machine, developed to eliminate hand soldering, transports printed circuit boards through a wave of solder under computer control. A brainstorming session identified 14 process variables. From three sets of designed experiments, the subsequent data resulted in decisions that lowered the defect rate from seven or eight to 1.5 per board. With 2,500 solder connections per board, this translated to a a defect rate of 600 defects per million connections. Another division, ITT's Suprenant Company, an electrical wire and cable manufacturer and a supplier to Ford, saved an estimated $100,000 per year in scrap, reduced product variability by a factor of 10, and improved the run rate of an extruding operation by 30 percent.

Historically, experimental design was not widely used in industrial quality improvement studies because engineers had trouble working with the large number of variables and their interactions on many different levels in industrial problems. However, improved computer software and more sophisticated training have recently experimental design an important tool for quality improvement.

Factorial Experiments One of the most common types of experimental designs is called a **factorial experiment**. In a factorial experiment, all combinations of levels of each factor are considered. For example, suppose that temperature and reaction time are identified as important factors in the yield of a chemical process. If the experiment is designed to analyze the effect of two levels of each factor (for instance, temperature at 100 and 120 degrees, and time at 60 and 75 minutes), then there would be $2^2 = 4$ possible combinations to test:

Temperature	Time
100 degrees	60 minutes
100 degrees	75 minutes
120 degrees	60 minutes
120 degrees	75 minutes

In general, an experiment with m factors at k levels would have k^m combinations. Each combination should be performed in a random fashion to eliminate any potential systematic bias.

The purpose of a factorial experiment is to estimate the effects of each factor. For instance, what is the effect of a 20-degree change in temperature? Of a 15-minute change in reaction time? These questions are answered easily by finding the differences of the averages at each level. For instance, suppose we obtained the following results:

Temperature	Time	Yield (%)
100 degrees	60 minutes	85
100 degrees	75 minutes	88
120 degrees	60 minutes	90
120 degrees	75 minutes	80

The average yield for a temperature of 100 degrees is $(85 + 88)/2 = 86.5$. The average yield for a temperature of 120 degrees is $(80 + 90)/2 = 85$. Thus, the average difference in yield from increasing the temperature from 100 to 120 degrees is $85 - 86.5 = -1.5$ percent. Similarly, the average difference in increasing the time from 60 to 75 minutes is $(88 + 80)/2 - (85 + 90)/2 = 84 - 87.5 = -3.5$ percent. These differences—how the changes in the level of one factor affect the response—are called *main effects*. Thus, we might conclude that increasing temperature or time decreases the yield of the process.

However, in many situations, the effect of changing one factor depends on the level of other factors. For example, the effect of temperature may depend on the reaction time. In this example, we see that if the temperature is held constant at 100 degrees, an increase in reaction time results in a higher yield. However, when the temperature is 120 degrees, an increase in reaction time decreases the yield. This *interaction* is easy to determine by graphing the results as shown in Figure 11.15. If the lines are nearly parallel, then no interaction exists. In this case, we see an interaction. We may quantify the interaction by taking the average of difference of the yield when the temperature is increased from 100 to 120 degrees at a constant reaction time of 60, and subtracting the average of difference of the yield when the temperature is increased from 100 to 120 degrees at a constant reaction time of 75:

Temperature $\times$ Time Interaction $= (90 - 85)/2 - (80 - 88)/2 = 6.5$ percent

Figure 11.15 Interaction Effects

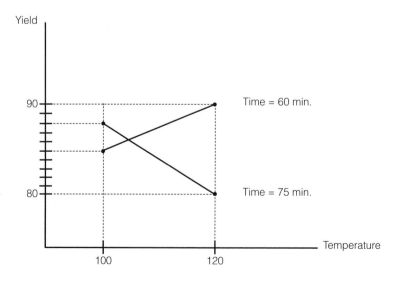

The closer this quantity is to zero, the smaller the interaction effect. In this case, a significant interaction is apparent. When interactions are present, main effects have little meaning; individual factors must be interpreted relative to levels of the other factors. We see that higher temperature and lower time appear to optimize the yield. The following example shows a simple application of a three-factor experiment not unlike those used in industrial and business settings.

Many one-tenth scale remote control (RC) model car racing enthusiasts believe that spending more money on high-quality batteries, using expensive gold-plated connectors, and storing batteries at low temperatures will improve battery life performance in a race.[15] To test this hypothesis, an electrical test circuit was constructed to measure battery discharge under different configurations. Each factor (battery type, connector type, and temperature) was evaluated at two levels, resulting in $2^3 = 8$ experimental conditions shown in Table 11.2.

Calculations of the main effects are as follows:

Battery cost
   Low = (72 + 93 + 75 + 94)/4 = 83.5 minutes
   High = (612 + 490 + 493 + 489)/4 = 521 minutes
   Main effect = High − Low = 437.5 minutes
Connector type
   Gold-plated = (94 + 75 + 490 + 493)/4 = 288 minutes
   Standard = (72 + 93 + 612 + 489)/4 = 316.5 minutes
   Main effect = Standard − Gold-plated = 28.5 minutes
Temperature
   Cold = (72 + 75 + 490 + 612)/4 = 312.25 minutes
   Ambient = (93 + 489 + 493 + 94)/4 = 292.25 minutes
   Main effect = Ambient − Cold = 20 minutes

These results suggest that high cost batteries do have a longer life, but that the impacts of gold plating or battery temperature do not appear to be significant. Because only one factor appears to be significant, calculation of interaction effects are not required. These conclusions can be tested more rigorously using analysis of variance, which will be discussed briefly next. Indeed, an analysis of variance confirms

Table 11.2 Experimental Design for Testing Battery Performance

Experimental Run	Battery Type	Connector Type	Battery Temperature	Discharge Time (minutes)
1	High cost	Gold-plated	Ambient	493
2	High cost	Gold-plated	Cold	490
3	High cost	Standard	Ambient	489
4	High cost	Standard	Cold	612
5	Low cost	Gold-plated	Ambient	94
6	Low cost	Gold-plated	Cold	75
7	Low cost	Standard	Ambient	93
8	Low cost	Standard	Cold	72

that the battery cost factor is statistically significant while the other factors are indistinguishable from experimental error.

Classical design of experiments can require many, often costly, experimental runs to estimate all main effects and interactions. A Japanese engineer, Dr. Genichi Taguchi, proposed another approach to DOE. He developed an approach to designing experiments that focused on the critical factors while deemphasizing their interactions, which greatly reduced the number of required experiments. However, Taguchi's approach violates some traditional statistical principles and has been criticized by the statistical community.[16] To add to the shortcomings of his approach, Taguchi introduced some statistically invalid and misleading analyses, ignored modern graphical approaches to data analysis, and failed to advocate randomization in performing the experiments. Even though many of these issues are subject to debate, numerous companies have used Taguchi's approaches effectively.

Analysis of Variance (ANOVA)

Because of Six Sigma, practitioners have "rediscovered" such techniques as analysis of variance, or ANOVA, which has long been an important tool in statistical analysis. ANOVA is a methodology for drawing conclusions about equality of means of multiple populations. In its simplest form—one-way ANOVA—we are interested in comparing means of observed responses of several different levels of a single factor. ANOVA tests the hypothesis that the means of all populations are equal against the alternative hypothesis that at least one mean differs from the others. To conduct an ANOVA, we need to

1. Carefully define the purpose and assumptions of the experiment.
2. Gather data related to the factor levels of interest.
3. Compute ANOVA statistics.
4. Interpret the meaning of the data.
5. Take action.

Let us suppose that the model race car enthusiasts in the previous example were interested in determining whether any significant differences exist between various brands of batteries (the factor levels). Understanding possible differences in battery performance could be a first step in examining whether connection or temperature has an effect on performance. Table 11.3 shows discharge times for three different brands of batteries, gathered through a measurement process.

Microsoft Excel provides a simple procedure to conduct a one-way ANOVA. Select *ANOVA: Single Factor* from the *Tools/Data Analysis* options. In the dialog box

Table 11.3 Battery Discharge Time Data by Brand

	Brand		
Observation	**A**	**B**	**C**
1	493	108	94
2	490	95	75
3	489	115	93
4	612	82	72

that pops up, enter the input range of the data in your spreadsheet and check whether it is stored in rows or columns. Table 11.4 shows the results of applying this tool. What does it tell us?

The objective of ANOVA is to statistically test the differences between the means of the groups (the time to discharge for the various brands of batteries) to determine whether they are the same or at least one mean is different. To make this determination, ANOVA partitions the total variability of the data into two parts, the variation between groups and the variation within groups. If the total variation between groups is relatively small compared to the variation within groups, it suggests that the populations are essentially the same. A relatively large variation between groups, however, suggests that differences exist in the unknown population means. The variation in the data is computed as a sum of squared (SS) deviations from the appropriate sample mean, and scaled as a variance measure, or "mean square" (MS). By dividing the mean square between groups by the mean square within groups, an F statistic is computed. If this value is larger than a critical value, F_{crit}, then the data suggest that a difference in means exist.

An examination of the SUMMARY section in Table 11.4 shows that Group A's mean value and variance are considerably larger than the others. In the ANOVA part of the table, the mean square between groups is significantly larger than the mean square within groups, resulting in an F statistic of 183.0412. When this value is compared to the critical F value (4.256), for 2 and 9 degrees of freedom at a 0.05 level of significance (from an F-table, available in any statistics text), we can reject the hypothesis that the means for the three battery types are the same. In fact, $F = 183$ is so much larger than 4.256, that we only have a 5.13×10^{-8} probability (the p-value in the output) that we could be wrong and should have failed to reject the hypothesis!

The model race car enthusiasts could conclude that a significant difference exists between the battery types. Other statistical tests are available to demonstrate what

Table 11.4 Results of Microsoft Excel ANOVA Procedure

Summary

Groups	Count	Sum	Average	Variance
A	4	2084	521	3683.333
B	4	400	100	212.6667
C	4	334	83.5	135

ANOVA

Source of Variation	SS	df	MS	F	P-value	F crit
Between Groups	491892.67	2	245946.33	183.0412	5.13E-08	4.256492
Within Groups	12093	9	1343.6667			
Total	503985.67	11				

factor levels differ from the others (although in this case, it is fairly obvious). The next step might be to explore other variables (connector type, battery temperature) to see how they might affect battery discharge time. It would require more sophisticated ANOVA methods. We encourage you to consult more complete statistics books, such as Montgomery or Lipson and Sheth.[17]

You can probably identify many applications of ANOVA in Six Sigma projects, when differences among critical quality characteristics must be explored. However, ANOVA requires that some statistical assumptions be satisfied for proper interpretation of the results, namely that the populations from which the samples are drawn are normally distributed and have equal variances, and that the data are randomly and independently obtained. These assumptions should be validated if possible.

Regression and Correlation

Regression analysis is a tool for building statistical models that characterize relationships between a dependent variable and one or more independent variables, all of which are numerical. The relationship may be linear, one of many types of nonlinear forms, or there may be no relationship at all. A regression model that involves a single independent variable is called *simple regression*. A regression model that involves several independent variables is called *multiple regression*. To develop a regression model, you first must specify the type of function that best describes the data. This step is important, because using a linear model for data that are clearly nonlinear, for instance, would probably lead to poor business decisions and results. The type of relationship can usually be seen in a scatter diagram, and we always recommend that you create one first to gain some understanding of the nature of any potential relationship.

Correlation is a measure of a linear relationship between two variables, X and Y, and is measured by the (population) correlation coefficient. Correlation coefficients will range from –1 to +1. A correlation of 0 indicates that the two variables have no linear relationship to each other. Thus, if one changes, we cannot reasonably predict what the other variable might do using a linear equation (we might, however, have a well-defined nonlinear relationship). A correlation coefficient of +1 indicates a perfect positive linear relationship; as one variable increases, the other will also increase. A correlation coefficient of –1 also shows a perfect linear relationship, except that as one variable increases, the other decreases.

To illustrate regression, we will use a common issue in quality that we will discuss again in a later chapter—ensuring that instruments are properly calibrated. In principle, it is a simple matter to check calibration. One connects the instrument to a known source, such as an extremely accurate voltage generator to check a voltmeter or a precision gauge block to check a micrometer. A reading is then obtained to determine whether the instrument is capable of accurately measuring the known variable. In practice, numerous sources of variation in the process may make calibration difficult.

The data in Figure 11.16 represent actual readings obtained from the calibration of a voltmeter versus the standard source readings from an accurate voltage generator. The source readings were purposely not set in even integer increments so as to minimize possible bias of the inspector taking the actual readings. To determine whether the instrument is accurate, we can develop a regression equation for the data. Using the Regression tool in Microsoft Excel, we obtain the results shown in Figure 11.16. The estimated regression equation is

$$Y = 0.0265 + .9914X$$

Figure 11.16 Microsoft Excel Regression Results

	A	B	C	D	E	F	G	H	I	J
1	Voltmeter Calibration									
2				SUMMARY OUTPUT						
3	Actual (Y)	Source (X)								
4	1.09	1.05		*Regression Statistics*						
5	2.12	2.15		Multiple R	0.999967043					
6	3.08	3.12		R Square	0.999934087					
7	4.09	4.08		Adjusted R Square	0.999925848					
8	5.11	5.11		Standard Error	0.027282724					
9	6.08	6.07		Observations	10					
10	7.2	7.23								
11	8.3	8.34		ANOVA						
12	9.59	9.66			*df*	*SS*	*MS*	*F*	*Significance F*	
13	10.41	10.49		Regression	1	90.33725522	90.33726	121364.4	5.16118E-18	
14				Residual	8	0.005954776	0.000744			
15				Total	9	90.34321				
16										
17					*Coefficients*	*Standard Error*	*t Stat*	*P-value*	*Lower 95%*	*Upper 95%*
18				Intercept	0.02648404	0.018447595	1.435636	0.189028	-0.016056219	0.069024299
19				Source (X)	0.991364042	0.002845689	348.374	5.16E-18	0.984801867	0.997926217

The value of R^2 is .9999, indicating an excellent fit. Note also that the value of the intercept is close to 0 and the slope is close to 1, which is where they should be. We would conclude that the instrument is in near perfect calibration, as the scatter chart in Figure 11.17 also indicates.

Figure 11.17 Scatter Chart of Voltmeter Calibration Readings

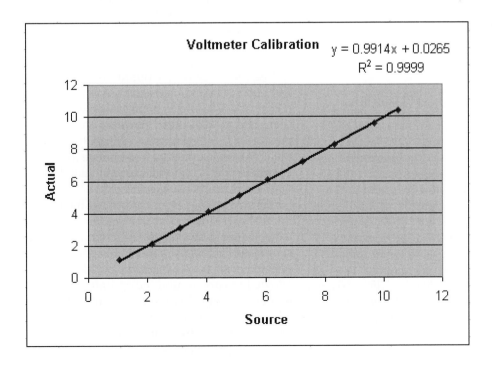

Quality in Practice

Improving Quality of a Wave Soldering Process Through Design of Experiments[18]

A Printed Circuit Assembly–Encoder (PCA-Encoder) is a critical component for the base carriage assembly for a printer. The PCA-Encoder is produced by putting the electronic components on printed circuit boards (panels) that contain eight small boards, and then soldering the components using a wave soldering process. Any defect in any of the solder joints will lead to the failure of the circuit. Thus, it is important to ensure that soldering is defect-free. Typical soldering defects are blowholes (insufficient solder) and bridges (solder between two joints). At a Hewlett-Packard India Ltd. plant in Bangalore, India, a high level of soldering defects was observed, necessitating 100 percent inspection for all circuit boards. Any defects identified required manual rework, which consumed much time.

A study was undertaken to optimize the wave soldering process for reducing defects, thereby eliminating the inspection stage after the process. The quality engineers conducted a detailed study on the solder defects to understand what aspects of the wave soldering process might affect the resulting quality. These were identified as

1. Conveyor speed
2. Conveyor angle
3. Solder bath temperature
4. Solder wave height
5. Vibration of wave
6. Preheater temperature
7. Air knife
8. Acid number (solid content in the flux), which is difficult to control because of environmental conditions

The engineers decided to use experimental design because of the long time frame required to adjust process parameters by trial and error, and the lack of insight into the possible joint effects of different parameters. Based on discussions with technical personnel, seven factors at three levels were selected for the experiment, as shown in Table 11.5. Conveyor speed and conveyor angle were fixed. A full factorial experiment would take 1,458 trials to conduct, which was not deemed to be practical. From statistical theory in the design of experiments, the seven main effects could be estimated by conducting only 18 trials as shown in Table 11.6.

Table 11.5 Factors and Levels for Experimentation

Factor	Code	Level 1	Level 2	Level 3
Bath temperature (°C)	A	248[a]	252	
Wave height[b]	B	4.38	4.40[a]	4.42
Overheated preheater (OH-PH) (PH-1)	C	340	360[a]	380
Preheater-1 (PH-1) (°C)	D	340	360[a]	380
Preheater (PH-2) (°C)	E	340	360[a]	380
Air Knife	F	0	3[a]	6
Omega[c]	G	0	2[a]	4

[a]Existing level

[b]The wave height is measured as the rpm of the motor pumping the solder.

[c]Omega refers to the vibration of the solder wave.

The experimental outcomes (response) were the number of defective solder joints in a frame (352 joints). Each experiment was repeated three times.

Using analysis of variance, it was observed that bath temperature, wave height, and omega had a significant effect on the soldering defects. By setting the factors at the optimum levels identified through the experiments, the predicted defect level was 1670 ppm as opposed to the current rate of more than 6000 ppm. However, the predicted average and the result of a confirmatory experiment were not sufficient to eliminate inspection completely, so additional experimental designs were conducted to reduce defects.

The next experiment considered the results of the first experiment and some of the uncontrollable factors. However, the different levels of the significant factors from the first experiment were selected in such a way that the new levels were allowed to vary around the optimum level of the first experiment. Based on the results of these additional experiments, new optimum levels of factors were identified and implemented with significant improvements. Figure 11.18 shows the

Table 11.6 Data Corresponding to the First Experiment

Exp. No.	(1) Bath Temp. (°C)	(2) Wave Height	(3) OH-PH (°C)	(4) PH-2 (°C)	(5) PH-1 (°C)	(6) Air Knife	(7) Omega	Response 1	2	3
1	248	4.38	340	340	340	0	0	1	2	1
2	248	4.38	360	360	360	3	2	0	2	0
3	248	4.38	380	380	380	6	4	0	1	0
4	248	4.40	340	340	360	3	4	1	0	1
5	248	4.40	360	360	380	6	0	4	2	0
6	248	4.40	380	380	340	0	2	8	1	6
7	248	4.42	340	360	340	6	2	2	4	3
8	248	4.42	360	380	360	0	4	4	1	0
9	248	4.42	380	340	380	3	0	2	2	4
10	252	4.38	340	380	380	3	2	1	3	1
11	252	4.38	360	340	340	6	4	1	2	1
12	252	4.38	380	360	360	0	0	6	3	2
13	252	4.40	340	360	380	0	4	3	3	4
14	252	4.40	360	380	340	3	0	4	3	8
15	252	4.40	380	340	360	6	2	2	1	1
16	252	4.42	340	380	360	6	0	2	7	3
17	252	4.42	360	340	380	0	2	2	1	3
18	252	4.42	380	360	340	3	4	4	2	1

Figure 11.18 Solder Defects After Experimental Design Optimization

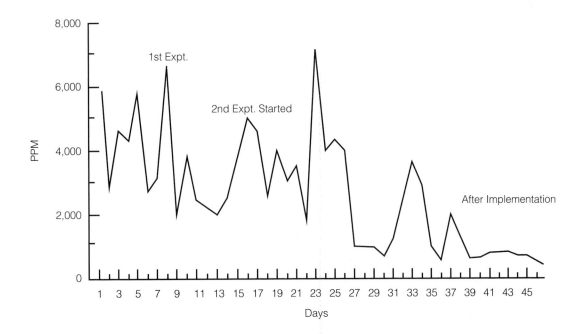

ppm level during the course of the experimentation, which took only 45 days.

Key Issues for Discussion

1. Why did the first experimental design not find the true optimum combination of factors

to achieve the maximum reduction of defects?

2. What were some of the advantages of using experimental design over a traditional trial-and-error approach?

QUALITY IN PRACTICE

APPLYING STATISTICAL ANALYSIS IN A SIX SIGMA PROJECT AT GE FANUC[19]

(This Quality in Practice features another project performed at the GE Fanuc plant. We encourage you to read the related case in Chapter 10 for some additional background.)

In mid-2002 a team at the GE Fanuc manufacturing plant in Charlottesville, Virginia, led by Six Sigma Black Belt Donald Splaun was given the go-ahead to investigate Black Belt Project #P52320. The objective of the project was to evaluate Printed Wire Board (PWB) Fabricated Board Finishes to determine if the high-priced nickel-gold (Ni-Au) finished boards that were being used were necessary as mounting platforms for fine pitch surface-mounted devices (SMDs) or for fine-pitched Ball Grid Array (BGA) electronic controller boards. SMDs are electronic components, such as microprocessors, that are placed on the top of electronic circuit boards (fabricated boards) and then have their electrical wire leads soldered into place. Fine pitch SMDs don't have much space between their electrical wire leads, making it difficult to put just the right amount of solder on them to make the proper electrical connect to the circuit boards on which they are mounted. The completed boards with all components properly mounted on them are then used in electrical assemblies to control the operations of industrial machinery.

Splaun had seven people on his analysis team, plus a financial representative to verify the dollar costs and savings; a Master Black Belt reviewer, who would evaluate the project to prevent obvious gaps in the analysis; and perhaps most importantly from a managerial standpoint, a Champion/Sponsor, who would ensure project visibility and that resources were allocated to complete the project. Team members and their job functions were:

Team Members Titles and Functions
Team Leader and Black Belt
Process engineer and fabricated board expert
Advanced manufacturing engineer responsible for SMD board assembly
Sourcing agent who purchases the boards
Test engineer who tests and evaluates boards
Producibility engineer who works with design teams
Production line operator who runs boards
Supplier quality analysis technician responsible for incoming board quality

Outside Resources
Financial representative to assist in cost calculations
Champion/Sponsor
Reviewer and Master Black Belt

After being formed, the team used a 12-step DMAIC process developed by GE Fanuc, to guide them through the project (see Table 11.7). The first three pre-project definition substeps (A, B, and C) required them to identify project CTQs, develop a team charter and have it approved, and define a process map.

Project team members identified the CTQs by using a standard cause-and-effect matrix, and weighted rankings of CTQ factors to prioritize them. The team determined there were three CTQs, two of which were business factors and the other a project factor:

- *Business CTQ factors*: Variable cost productivity (VCP) improvement, composed of the CTQs of internal cost reduction and contribution margin improvement
- *Project CTQ factor*: Benefits associated with

Table 11.7 GE Fanuc 12-Step DMAIC Process

Step	Description	Tools	Deliverables
Define			
A	Identify project CTQs		Project CTQs (1)
B	Develop team charter		Approved charter (2)
C	Define process map		High-level process map (3)
Measure			
1	Select CTQ characteristics	Customer, QFD, FMEA	Project Y (4)
2	Define performance standards	Customer, Blueprints	Performance standard for Project Y (5)
3	Measurement system analysis	Continuous Gage R&R, Test/Retest, Attribute R&R	Data collection plan and MSA (6), Data for Project Y (7)
Analyze			
4	Establish process capability	Capability indices	Process capability—Project Y (8)
5	Define performance objectives	Team, Benchmarking	Improvement goal for Project Y (9)
6	Identify variation sources	process and graphical Analysis, Hypothesis tests	Prioritized list of all Xs (10)
Improve			
7	Screen potential causes	DOE-screening	List of vital few Xs (11)
8	Discover variable relationships	Factorial designs	Proposed solution (12)
9	Establish operating tolerances	Simulation	Piloted solution (13)
Control			
10	Define and validate measurement system on Xs (independent variables) in actual application	Continuous Gage R&R, MSA Test/Retest, Attribute R&R	
11	Determine process capability	Capability indices	Process capability Y, X (14)
12	Implement process control	Control charts, Mistake proof, FMEA	Sustained solution (15), Documentation (16)

additional Ni-Au cost of $190,000 per year, suspected to be unnecessary

The team developed their charter to define the problem and working relationships. The problem clearly and succinctly stated as: *GE Fanuc currently specifies Ni-Au on fine-pitch SMD and BGA boards. The purpose of this project is to evaluate if this specification is necessary.*

The team also identified tools and databases that were to be used in the study, not only to ensure that everyone was working from a common source, but also to take advantage of the training that had been provided to team members. The tools included two statistical/spreadsheet software packages (Minitab and Excel) and a plantwide integrated database (SAP) that contained information on board characteristics, usage, specifications, costs, and so on.

Based on a 29-step process flowchart, it was decided that the analysis would require the use of a moderately complex experimental design. This design was required to determine the effects of supplier differences and finishes, because relatively few defects were being observed in manufacturing the boards. Data would have to be gathered from the experiment and from supplier surveys to help the team track potential causes that could have a bearing on the functionality and cost of each of the alternative boards or board materials being considered.

The experiment was designed to sample and test 288 CX3A1 boards:

- 96 hot air solder leveled (HASL) boards, 32 from each supplier
- 96 nickel-gold (Ni-Au) boards, 32 from each supplier
- 96 silver (Ag) boards, 32 from each supplier and to evaluate three suppliers.

The three suppliers were:
- Vendor G, Singapore/China (one or two GE Fanuc production suppliers)
- Vendor P, Taiwan/China (second major GE Fanuc supplier)
- Vendor D, USA (current prototype/fast turn supplier)

The cause-and-effect matrix identified 13 characteristics (Xs, or independent variables) that were considered important to measure during the experiment for each of the three finish types (Ys, or dependent variables). The primary hypothesis was that no significant differences in numbers of defects would be incurred, regardless of finish. In addition, a hypothesis that no significant interaction effects existed between suppliers, coatings, and any of the 13 characteristics considered essential for quality board functioning was investigated. The data collection and analysis process consisted of eight carefully defined steps conducted over a six-day period, involving almost $ 37,500 worth of boards and hard-to-measure production delays while the test boards were run on what is normally high speed, highly automated production machines.

After the data were collected, numerous ANOVA computer runs were made to pinpoint problem areas and test hypotheses. It was especially important to test the capabilities of each of the three types of board finishes to determine whether they were equivalent to the current, and very expensive, Ni-AU finished boards. It was also necessary to get some data to prove or disprove

hypotheses about supplier capabilities as well. Table 11.8 shows a typical computer printout and analysis of one of the 13 variables that was tested, called "Wave Solder Skips."

Of 15 ANOVA analysis runs performed on the 13 experimental variables that were measured, eight showed no significance, primarily because those variables had zero defects. Other findings included:

- Ni-Au boards are not significantly different from or better than horizontally processed HASL or Silver Boards for fine pitch SMD processing, therefore the firm can save money by switching from Ni-Au to HASL or Silver.
- The company should not use Vendor D for production. Results and suggestions for improvement of their prototype quality should be discussed with them.
- Ni-Au is worse for wave soldering, based on a defect measure of "insufficient solder fill."
- Vendor G was found to have an issue with a defect measure of "GR False Failures" (to be reviewed with the supplier).
- The GE Fanuc PWB Fab Specifications should be changed to reflect these conclusions.

From these analyses, the summary conclusion was that GE Fanuc did not need nickel-gold boards for fine pitch SMD.

The estimated savings from this project ranged from 7.1 percent on two-layer boards to 22.8 percent on four-layer boards, with an average of 14.3 percent savings on these 89 board types, and total estimated savings of $190,000 per year.

Key Issues for Discussion

1. Why did the experimental design have to be so complex? Why were so many individuals involved in this project?
2. What might have been some contributing factors that caused the company to select the Ni-Au over the cheaper boards in the past?
3. For Table 11.8, what can you conclude, given the F values and the p-values in the table? What steps should the team take, regarding use of vendors and further testing for this particular independent variable?

Table 11.8 Typical ANOVA Output for Vendor and Finish Analysis

Solder Skips, Analysis All
Two-Way Analysis of Variance
Analysis of Variance for Wave Solder Skips

Source	DF	SS	MS	F	P
Vendors	2	36.55	18.27	15.27	0.000
Finish	2	16.44	8.22	6.87	0.001
Interaction	4	23.39	5.85	4.89	0.001
Error	279	333.94	1.20		
Total	287	410.32			

Process Variable Averages

Manufacturers	Mean Number of Defects
Vendor C	0.03
Vendor D	0.80
Vendor G	0.06

Finish

HASL	0.271
Ni-Au	0.021
Silver	0.604

 REVIEW QUESTIONS

1. What is statistical thinking? Why is it important to managers and workers at all levels of an organization?
2. Explain the difference between common and special causes of variation.
3. Explain the two fundamental mistakes that managers make when attempting to improve a process. Can you cite any examples in your personal experience in which such mistakes were made?
4. What are the lessons of the Red Bead and Funnel Experiments? Can you cite any examples in your experience where someone acted counter to these lessons?
5. Discuss the differences among the three major components of statistical methodology (descriptive statistics, statistical inference, and predictive statistics). Why might this distinction be important to a manager?
6. Provide some examples of discrete and continuous random variables in a quality management context.
7. Define a population and a sample. What are their major characteristics?
8. Explain the difference between the standard deviation and the standard error of the mean. How are they related?

9. State the meaning of the central limit theorem in your own words. How important is it to the development and use of statistical quality control techniques?
10. What two factors influence sampling procedures?
11. Discuss the basic questions that must be addressed in a sampling study.
12. Describe the different methods of sample selection and provide an example in which each would be most appropriate.
13. What are the sources of systematic error in sampling? How can systematic error be overcome?
14. What is the purpose of design of experiments?
15. Describe a factorial experiment. Provide some examples of factorial experiments that you might use to solve some type of quality-related problem.
16. What limitations of simple factorial experiments can be overcome by using ANOVA?
17. What is the statistical basis for ANOVA; that is, what is it designed to test, statistically?

 ## PROBLEMS

Note: Data sets for several problems in this chapter are available in the Excel workbook *C11Data.xls* on the CD-ROM accompanying this text. Click on the appropriate worksheet tab as noted in the problem (e.g., Prob. 11-1) to access the data.

1. Use the data for Staunton Steam Laundry for the weights of loads of clothes processed through their washing department in a week. (See Prob. 11-1 in *C11Data.xls* for data). Apply the Descriptive Statistics and Histogram tools in Excel to compute the mean, standard deviation, and other relevant statistics, as well as a frequency distribution and histogram for the following data. From what type of distribution might you suspect the data are drawn?
2. Apply the Descriptive Statistics and Histogram analysis tools in Excel to compute the mean, standard deviation, and other relevant statistics, as well as a frequency distribution and histogram for the following data (Prob. 11-2 in *C11Data.xls*). From what type of distribution might you suspect the data are drawn?
3. The data (Prob. 11-3 in *C11Data.xls*) represent the weight of castings (in kilograms) being made in the Harrison Metalwork foundry. Based on this sample of 100 castings, compute the mean, standard deviation, and other relevant statistics, as well as a frequency distribution and histogram. What do you conclude from your analysis?
4. The data (Prob. 11-4 in *C11Data.xls*) show the weight of castings (in kilograms) being made in the Harrison Metalwork foundry after process changes took place. Compute the mean, standard deviation, and other relevant statistics, as well as a frequency distribution and histogram. Based on this sample of 100 castings, what do you conclude from your analysis?
5. Georgia Tea is sold in 2 liter (2000 milliliter) bottles. The mean volume of tea in the bottle is 2 liters and the standard deviation is 15 milliliters. If the process requires a 2 percent (total) or less probability of over- or underfilling, what should the upper and lower fill limits be?
6. New Orleans Punch is sold in 16-ounce cans. The mean number of ounces placed in a can is 15.8 with a standard deviation of 0.1 ounce. Assuming a normal distribution, what is the probability that the filling machine will cause

an overflow in a can, that is, the probability that more than 16 ounces will be placed in the can?

7. Kiwi Blend is sold in 950 milliliter (ml) cans. The mean volume of juice placed in a can is 945 ml with a standard deviation of 15 ml. Assuming a normal distribution, what is the probability that the filling machine will cause an overflow in a can, that is, the probability that more than 945 ml will be placed in the can?

8. Outback Beer bottles have been found to have a standard deviation of 5 ml. If 5 percent of the bottles contain less than 535 ml, what is the average filling volume of the bottles?

9. The standard deviation of the weight of filled salt containers is 0.4 ounce. If 2.5 percent of the containers contain less than 16 ounces, what is the mean filling weight of the containers?

10. In filling bottles of L & E Cola, the average amount of overfilling should be kept as low as possible. If the mean fill volume is 12.1 ounces and the standard deviation is 0.05 ounce, what percentage of bottles will have less than 12 ounces? More than 12.1 ounces (assuming no overflow)?

11. In a filling line at E & L Foods, Ltd., the mean fill volume for rice bubbles is 480 grams and the standard deviation is 3 grams. What percentage of containers will have less than 475 grams? More than 486 grams (assuming no overflow)?

12. The frequency table that follows represents the weight of castings (in kilograms) being made in the Harrison Metalwork foundry (see Problem 11-3 in *C11Data.xls* for "raw" data).
   a. Based on this sample of 100 castings, find the mean and standard deviation of the sample. (*Note:* If only the given data are used, it will be necessary to research formulae for calculating the mean and standard deviations using grouped data from a statistics text.)
   b. Use an Excel spreadsheet if not already done for Problem 3, to plot the histogram for the data.
   c. Plot the data on normal probability paper to determine whether the distribution of the data is approximately normal. (*Note:* The Regression tool in Excel has a normal probability plot that may be used here.)

Frequency Table

	Upper Cell Boundaries	Frequencies	Cumulative %
Cell 1	37.5	1	1.00%
Cell 2	37.8	3	4.00%
Cell 3	38.1	8	12.00%
Cell 4	38.4	26	38.00%
Cell 5	38.7	29	67.00%
Cell 6	39.0	15	82.00%
Cell 7	39.3	13	95.00%
Cell 8	39.6	4	99.00%
Cell 9	39.9	1	100.00%

13. The frequency table that follows shows the weight of castings (in kilograms) being made in the Harrison Metalwork foundry after process changes took place (see Problem 11-4, in *C11Data.xls*, for "raw" data).
   a. Based on this sample of 100 castings, find the mean and standard deviation of the sample. (*Note:* If only the given data are used, it will be necessary to research formulae for calculating the mean and standard deviations using grouped data from a statistics text.)

b. Use an Excel spreadsheet, if not already done for Problem 4, to plot the histogram for the data.

c. Plot the data on normal probability paper to determine whether the distribution of the data is approximately normal. (*Note:* The Regression tool in Excel has a normal probability plot that may be used here.)

Frequency Table

	Upper Cell Boundaries	Frequencies	Cumulative %
Cell 1	37.5	1	1.00%
Cell 2	37.8	3	4.00%
Cell 3	38.1	8	12.00%
Cell 4	38.4	23	35.00%
Cell 5	38.7	25	60.00%
Cell 6	39.0	23	83.00%
Cell 7	39.3	10	93.00%
Cell 8	39.6	6	99.00%
Cell 9	39.9	1	100.00%

14. A utility requires service operators to answer telephone calls from customers in an average time of 0.1 minute or less. A sample of 30 actual operator times was drawn, and the results are given in the following table. In addition, operators are expected to determine customer needs and either respond to them or refer the customer to the proper department within 0.5 minute. Another sample of 30 times was taken for this job component and is also given in the table. If these variables can be considered to be independent, is the average time taken to perform each component statistically different from the standard?

Component	Mean Time	Standard Deviation
Answer	0.1023	0.0183
Service	0.5290	0.0902

Note: Problems 15–19 address sample size determination and refer to theory covered in the Bonus Material for this chapter as contained on the student CD-ROM.

15. Determine the appropriate sample size to estimate the proportion of sorting errors at a post office at a 95 percent confidence level. Historically, the sorting error rate is 0.025, and you wish to have an allowable statistical error of 0.01.

16. You are asked by a motel owner to develop a customer satisfaction survey to determine the percentage of customers who are dissatisfied with service. In the past year, 20,000 customers were serviced. He desires a 95 percent level of confidence with an allowable statistical error of ±– 0.02. From past estimates, the manager believes that about 7 percent of customers have expressed dissatisfaction. What sample size should you use for this survey?

17. A local telephone company interviewed 150 customers to determine their satisfaction with service. Twenty-seven expressed dissatisfaction. Compute a 90 percent confidence interval for the proportion satisfied with an allowable error of 0.05.

18. A management engineer at Country Squire Hospital determined that she needs to take a work sampling study to see whether the proportion of idle time in the diagnostic imaging department had changed since being measured in a previous study several years ago. At that time, the percentage of idle time was 10 percent. If the engineer can only take a sample of 800 observations due to cost factors, and can tolerate an allowable error of 0.02, what percent confidence level can be obtained from the study?

19. Using the Discovery Sampling table in the bonus materials, suppose that a population consists of 2,000 units. The critical rate of occurrence is 1 percent, and you wish to be 99 percent confident of finding at least one nonconformity. What sample size should you select?

20. A process engineer at Sival Electronics is trying to determine whether a newer, more costly design involving a gold alloy in a computer chip is more effective than the present, less expensive silicon design. She wants to obtain an effective output voltage at both high and low temperatures, when tested with high and low signal strength. She hypothesizes that high signal strength will result in higher voltage output, low temperature will result in higher output, and the gold alloy will result in higher output than the silicon material. She hopes that the main and interaction effects with the expensive gold will be minimal. The following data were gathered in testing of all 2^n combinations. What recommendation would you make, based on these data?

Signal	Material	Temperature	Output Voltage
High	Gold	Low	18
High	Gold	High	12
High	Silicon	Low	16
High	Silicon	High	10
Low	Gold	Low	8
Low	Gold	High	11
Low	Silicon	Low	7
Low	Silicon	High	14

21. The process engineer at Sival Electronics was trying to determine whether three suppliers would be equally capable of supplying the mounting boards for the new "gold plated" components that she was testing. The following table shows the coded defect levels for the suppliers, according to the finishes that were tested. Lower defect levels are preferable to higher levels. Using one-way ANOVA, analyze these results. What conclusion can be reached, based on these data?

	Supplier 1	Supplier 2	Supplier 3
Finish 1	11.9	6.8	13.5
Finish 2	10.3	5.9	10.9
Finish 3	9.5	8.1	12.3
Finish 4	8.7	7.2	14.5
Finish 5	14.2	7.6	12.9

 PROJECTS, ETC.

1. A computer version of Deming's Funnel Exercise is available (free) at http://www.qualitystation.com/Funnel-Free.htm. Download and run the funnel simulation. Does it simulate the same rules as described in this chapter?

2. Devise an experiment similar to the battery performance test example to test different levels of some factor and conduct a statistical analysis of the results. Write up your experiment and results in a report along with the conclusions that you reach from the analysis. You might wish to consult the following paper: "101 Ways to Design an Experiment, or Some Ideas About Teaching Design of Experiments" by William G. Hunter, Technical Report No. 413 dated

June 1975 at http://www.stat.wisc.edu/department/handouts/technical413/technical413.html for some ideas.
3. Using one sheet of paper, design and build a helicopter. Some methods of making a paper helicopter can be found at: http://www.exploratorium.edu/science_explorer/roto-copter.html and http://www.faa.gov/education/resource/helicopt.htm.

Use design of experiments to develop a design that keeps the helicopter airborne for as long as possible.

Cases

I. The Disciplinary Citation[20]

A local delivery service has 40 drivers who deliver packages throughout the metropolitan area. Occasionally, drivers make mistakes, such as entering the wrong package number on a shipping document, failing to get a signature, and so on. A total of 240 mistakes were made in one year as shown in Table 11.9. The manager in charge of this operation has issued disciplinary citations to drivers for each mistake.

Discussion Questions

1. What is your opinion of the manager's approach? How does it compare with the Deming philosophy?
2. How might the analysis of these data help the manager to understand the variation in the system? (Plot the data to obtain some insight.) How can the data help the manager to improve the performance of this system?

Table 11.9 Delivery Driver Citations

Driver No.	1	2	3	4	5	6	7	8	9	10	11	12	13	14
Mistakes	6	1	0	14	0	2	18	2	5	13	1	4	6	5
Driver No.	15	16	17	18	19	20	21	22	23	24	25	26	27	28
Mistakes	0	0	1	3	15	24	3	4	1	2	3	22	4	8
Driver No.	29	30	31	32	33	34	35	36	37	38	39	40		
Mistakes	2	6	8	0	9	20	9	0	3	14	1	1		

II. The Quarterly Sales Report[21]

Suppose that Ron Hagler, the vice president of sales for Selit Corp., had just gotten a report on the past five years of quarterly sales data for the regions under his authority (see Table 11.10). Not happy with the results, he got on the phone to his secretary. "Marsha, tell the regional managers I need to speak with them this afternoon. Everyone must attend."

Marsha had been Hagler's secretary for almost a decade. She knew by the tone in his voice that he meant business, so she contacted the regional managers about the impromptu meeting at 2 P.M. At 1:55 P.M., the regional managers filed into the room. The only time they were called into a meeting together was when Hagler was unhappy.

Hagler wasted no time. "I just received the

Table 11.10 Five Years of Sales Data by Region (Data in thousands)

1999 Sales

Region	First Quarter	Second Quarter	Third Quarter	Fourth Quarter
Northeast	$ 924	$ 928	$ 956	$1,222
Southwest	1,056	1,048	1,129	1,073
Northwest	1,412	1,280	1,129	1,181
North Central	431	470	439	431
Mid-Atlantic	539	558	591	556
South Central	397	391	414	407

2000 Sales

Region	First Quarter	Second Quarter	Third Quarter	Fourth Quarter
Northeast	$ 748	$ 962	$ 983	$1,024
Southwest	1,157	1,146	1,064	1,213
Northwest	1,149	1,248	1,103	1,021
North Central	471	496	506	573
Mid-Atlantic	540	590	606	643
South Central	415	442	384	448

2001 Sales

Region	First Quarter	Second Quarter	Third Quarter	Fourth Quarter
Northeast	$ 991	978	1,040	$1,295
Southwest	1,088	4,322	1,256	1,132
Northwest	1,085	1,125	910	999
North Central	403	440	371	405
Mid-Atlantic	657	602	596	640
South Central	441	366	470	426

2002 Sales

Region	First Quarter	Second Quarter	Third Quarter	Fourth Quarter
Northeast	$ 756	$1,008	$1,038	$ 952
Southwest	4,352	1,353	1,466	1,196
Northwest	883	851	997	878
North Central	466	536	551	670
Mid-Atlantic	691	723	701	802
South Central	445	455	363	462

2003 Sales

Region	First Quarter	Second Quarter	Third Quarter	Fourth Quarter
Northeast	$1,041	$1,020	$ 976	$1,148
Southwest	1,330	1,003	1,197	1,337
Northwest	939	834	688	806
North Central	588	699	743	702
Mid-Atlantic	749	762	807	781
South Central	420	454	447	359

quarterly sales report. Northeast sales were fantastic. Steve, you not only improved 17.6 percent in the fourth quarter, but you also increased sales a whopping 20.6 percent over the previous year. I don't know how you do it!" Steve smiled. His philosophy to end the year with a bang by getting customers to stockpile units had paid off again. Hagler had failed to notice that Steve's first quarter sales were always sluggish.

Hagler continued: "Terry, Southwest sales were also superb. You showed an 11.7 percent increase in the fourth quarter and an 11.8 percent increase over the previous year." Terry also smiled. She wasn't sure how she did so well, but she sure wasn't going to change anything.

"Jan, Northwest sales were up 17.2 percent in the fourth quarter, but down 8.2 percent from the previous year," said Hagler. "You need to find out what you did previously to make your sales go through the roof. Even so, your performance in the fourth quarter was good." Jan tried to hide his puzzlement. Although he had received a big order in November, it was the first big order he had received in a long time. Overall, sales for the Northwest were declining.

Hagler was now ready to deal with the "problem" regions. "Leslie, North Central sales were down 5.5 percent in the fourth quarter, but up 4.7 percent from the previous year. I don't understand how your sales vary so much. Do you need more incentive?" Leslie looked down. She had been working very hard the past five years and had acquired numerous new accounts. In fact, she received a bonus for acquiring the most new business in 1998.

"Kim, Mid-Atlantic sales were down 3.2 percent in the fourth quarter and down 2.6 percent from the previous year. I'm very disappointed in your performance. You were once my best sales representative. I had high expectations for you. Now, I can only hope that your first quarter results show some sign of life." Kim felt her face get red. She knew she had sold more units in 2003 than in 2002. "What does Hagler know anyway," she thought to herself. "He's just an empty suit."

Hagler turned to Dave, who felt a surge of adrenaline. "Dave, South Central sales were the worst of all! Sales were down 19.7 percent in the fourth quarter and down 22.3 percent from the previous year. How can you explain this? Do you value your job? I want to see a dramatic improvement in this quarter's results or else!" Dave felt numb. It was a tough region, with a lot of competition. Sure, accounts were lost over the years, but those lost were always replaced with new ones. How could he be doing so badly?

How can Ron improve his approach by applying principles of statistical thinking? Use any analyses of the data that you feel are appropriate to fully explain your thinking and help him.

III. The HMO Pharmacy Crisis[22]

John Dover had just completed an intensive course, "Statistical Thinking for Continuous Improvement," that was offered to all employees of a large health maintenance organization (HMO). There was no time to celebrate, however. Dover worked as a pharmacy assistant in the HMO's pharmacy and he was under a lot of pressure, because his manager, Juan de Pacotilla, was about to be fired. Pacotilla's dismissal appeared imminent because of numerous complaints and even a few lawsuits over inaccurate prescriptions. Pacotilla now was asking Dover for his assistance in trying to resolve the problem.

"John, I really need your help," said Pacotilla. "If I can't show some major improvement or at least a solid plan by next month, I'm history."

"I'll be glad to help," replied Dover, "but what can I do? I'm just a pharmacy assistant."

"Your job title isn't important. I think you're just the person who can get this done," said Pacotilla. "I realize that I've been too far removed from day-to-day operations in the pharmacy, but you work there every day. You're in a much better position to find out how to fix the problem. Just tell me what to do, and I'll do it."

"But what about the statistical consultant you hired to analyze the data on inaccurate prescriptions?" asked Dover.

"To be honest, I'm really disappointed with that guy. He has spent two weeks trying to come up with a new modeling approach to predict weekly inaccurate prescriptions. I tried to explain to him that I don't want to predict the mistakes; I want to eliminate them. I don't think I got through, however, because he said we need a month of additional data to verify the model before he can apply a new method he just read about in a journal to identify 'change points in the time series,' whatever that means. But get this, he will only identify the change points and send me a list. He says it's my job to figure out what they mean and how to respond. I don't know much about statistics. The only thing I remember from my course in college is that it was the worst course I ever took. I'm becoming convinced that statistics really doesn't have much to offer in solving real problems. Since you've just gone through the statistical thinking course, maybe you can see something I can't. I realize it's a long shot, but I was hoping you could use this as the project you need to officially complete the course."

"I used to feel the same way about statistics, too," replied Dover. "But the statistical thinking course was interesting because it didn't focus on crunching numbers. I have some ideas about how we can approach making improvements in prescription accuracy. I think it would be a great project. But we might not be able to solve this problem ourselves. As you know, there is a lot of finger pointing going on. Pharmacists blame the doctors' sloppy handwriting and incomplete instructions for the problem. Doctors blame the pharmacy assistants, who do most of the computer entry of the prescriptions, claiming that they are incompetent. Pharmacy assistants blame the pharmacists for assuming too much about their knowledge of medical terminology, brand names, known drug interactions, and so on."

"It sounds like there's no hope," said Pacotilla.

"I wouldn't say that at all," replied Dover. "It's just that there might be no quick fix we can do by ourselves in the pharmacy. Let me explain what I'm thinking about doing and how I would propose attacking the problem using what I just learned in the statistical thinking course."

How do you think John should approach this problem, using what he has just learned? Assume that he really did pick up a solid understanding of the concepts and tools of statistical thinking in the course.

ENDNOTES

1. Adapted from Brian L. Joiner, *Fourth Generation Management* (New York: McGraw-Hill, 1994), 129.

2. J. M. Juran and Frank M. Gryna, Jr., *Quality Planning and Analysis,* 2d ed. (New York: McGraw-Hill, 1980), 35.

3. Scott M. Paton, "Juran: A Lifetime of Quality: An Exclusive Interview with a Quality Legend," *Quality Digest,* August 2002, 19–23.

4. Adapted from Galen Britz, Don Emerling, Lynne Hare, Roger Hoerl, and Janice Shade, "How to Teach Others to Apply Statistical Thinking," *Quality Progress,* June 1997, 67–79. © 1997, American Society for Quality. Reprinted with permission.

5. Kimberly Weisul, "So Your Lie May Always Be True," *Business Week,* February 25, 2002, 16.

6. Steven A. Melnyk and R. T. Christensen, "Variance is Evil," *APICS The Performance Advantage,* June 2002, 19.

7. Ronald D. Snee, "Getting Better Business Results: Using Statistical Thinking and Methods to Shape the Bottom Line," *Quality Progress,* June 1998, 102–106.

8. Britz, et al. (see note 4).

9. Based on descriptions given in W. Edwards Deming, *The New Economics For Industry, Government, Education* (Cambridge, MA: MIT Center for Advanced Engineering Study, 1993).

10. Frank H. Squires, "The Triumph of Statistics," *Quality,* February 1982, 75.

11. Thomas Pyzdek, "Non-Normal Distributions in the Real World," *Quality Digest,* December 1999, 36–41.

12. Johannes Ledolter, and Claude W. Burrill, *Statistical Quality Control* (New York: John Wiley & Sons, 1999).

13. N. Raghu Kackar, "Off-Line Quality Control, Parameter Design, and the Taguchi Method," *Journal of Quality Technology* 17, no. 4 (October 1985), 176–188.

14. Bruce D. Nordwall, "ITT Uses Process Control Methods to Increase Plant Productivity," *Aviation Week & Space Technology,* May 11, 1987, 69–74.

15. Eric Wasiloff and Curtis Hargitt, "Using DOE to Determine AA Battery Life," *Quality Progress,* March 1999, 67–71. © 1999, American Society for Quality. Reprinted with permission.

16. Joseph J. Pignatiello, Jr., and John S. Ramberg, "The Top 10 Triumphs and Tragedies of Genichi Taguchi," presented at the 35th ASQC/ASA Fall Technical Conference, Lexington, KY, 1991.

17. Douglas C. Montgomery, *Design and Analysis of Experiments* (New York: John Wiley & Sons, Inc., 1996); Charles Lipson and Narendra J. Sheth. *Statistical Design and Analysis of Engineering Experiments* (New York: McGraw-Hill Book Co., 1973).

18. Kalyan Kumar Chowdhury, E.V. Gigo, and R. Raghavan, "Quality Improvement Through Design of Experiments: A Case Study," *Quality Engineering,* 12, no. 3 (2000), 407–416. Copyright 2000 by Marcel Dekker, Inc.

19. Courtesy of Donald B. Splaun, Jr., Manager, Advanced Manufacturing Technology, GE-Fanuc, Inc.

20. Based on an anecdote in W. Edwards Deming, *Out of the Crisis* (Cambridge, MA: MIT Center for Advanced Engineering Study, 1986).

21. Adapted from Britz, et al. (see Note 4).

22. Adapted from Britz, et al. (see Note 4).

BIBLIOGRAPHY

Breyfogle, Forrest W. III. *Implementing Six Sigma*, 2nd ed., New York: John Wiley & Sons, 2003.

Chatfield, Christopher. *Statistics for Technology: A Course in Applied Statistics*, 3rd ed. New York: CRC Press, 1983.

Deming, W. Edwards. *The New Economics for Industry, Government, Education*, 2nd ed. Cambridge, MA: MIT Press, 2000.

———. *Out of the Crisis*. Cambridge, MA: MIT Press, 2000.

Duncan, Acheson J. *Quality Control and Industrial Statistics*, 5th ed. Homewood, IL: Richard D. Irwin, 1986.

Griffith, Gary. *Quality Technician's Handbook*, 5th ed. New York: Prentice Hall, 2002.

Gunter, Bert. "Process Capability Studies Part I: What Is a Process Capability Study?" *Quality Progress* 24, no. 2 (February 1991), 97–99.

Pyzdek, Thomas, *The Six Sigma Handbook*. New York: McGraw-Hill, 2003.

Robbins, C. L., and W. A. Robbins. "What Nurse Managers Should Know about Sampling Techniques." *Nursing Management* 20, no. 6 (June 1989), 46–48.

Scherkenbach, William W. *Deming's Road to Continual Improvement*. Knoxville, TN: SPC Press, 1991.

Scholtes, Peter R. "Communities as Systems," *ASQC 50th Annual Quality Congress Proceedings*, 1996, 258–265.

Tedaldi, Michael, Fred Seaglione, and Vincent Russotti. *A Beginner's Guide to Quality in Manufacturing*. Milwaukee, WI: ASQC Quality Press, 1992.

Chapter 12

Design for Six Sigma

During World War II, 60 percent of the aircraft destined for the Far East proved unserviceable; 50 percent of electronic devices failed while still in storage; the service life of electronic devices used in bombers was only 20 hours; and 70 percent of naval electronics devices failed.[1] Clearly, our ability to improve product performance has increased immensely over the last half-century. Nevertheless, businesses and consumers are still plagued with product failures or service upsets. Computers occasionally arrive DOA—dead on arrival—and most readers have undoubtedly encountered the "blue screen of death" that results from software crashes. Consumers don't receive the products they ordered, or are given inaccurate information. More serious problems have occurred, such as injuries or deaths resulting from automobile tire separation or defective infant cribs and toys. Most of these problems fundamentally result from poor design or inadequate design processes.

Design for Six Sigma (DFSS) represents a set of tools and methodologies used in the product development process for ensuring that goods and services will meet customer needs and achieve performance objectives, and that the processes used to make and deliver them achieve six sigma capability. DFSS consists of four principal activities:[2]

1. *Concept development*, in which product functionality is determined based upon customer requirements, technological capabilities, and economic realities
2. *Design development*, which focuses on product and process performance issues necessary to fulfill the product and service requirements in manufacturing or delivery
3. *Design optimization*, which seeks to minimize the impact of variation in production and use, creating a "robust" design
4. *Design verification*, which ensures that the capability of the production system meets the appropriate sigma level

DFSS can be viewed as a key approach within the overall product development process that we discussed in Chapter 7. DFSS is relatively new, but it is rapidly becoming recognized and incorporated into traditional product development processes, and is not only applied to engineered products, but also to business transactions and production processes.

General Electric is one company that embraced DFSS. For example, in its 1998 annual report, GE stated that "Every new product and service in the future will be DFSS. . . . They were, in essence, designed by the customer, using all of the critical-to-quality performance features (CTQs) the customer wanted in the product and then subjecting these CTQs to the rigorous statistical Design for Six Sigma Process." In its 2000 annual report, GE noted that more than half its sales would come from DFSS products in 2001.

> *Like Six Sigma itself, most tools for DFSS have been around for some time; its uniqueness lies in the manner in which they are integrated into a formal methodology, driven by the Six Sigma philosophy, with clear business objectives in mind.*

In this chapter, we focus on some of the more important tools and best practices that support DFSS efforts. However, we barely scratch the surface of the full scope of DFSS, and we encourage you to refer to some of the more complete references at the end of this chapter.

TOOLS FOR CONCEPT DEVELOPMENT

Concept development is the process of applying scientific, engineering, and business knowledge to produce a basic functional design that meets both customer needs and manufacturing or service delivery requirements. Concept development is a highly creative activity that can be enhanced by such techniques as brainstorming and brainwriting—a written form of brainstorming—and is focused first on identifying potential ideas. After potential ideas have been identified, they are evaluated using cost/benefit analysis, risk analysis, and other techniques. Finally, the best concept is selected, often using some type of scoring matrix to weight the selection criteria.

The first question one must ask during concept development is: What is the product (good or service) intended to do? In Chapter 4 we stressed the importance of understanding the voice of the customer; it is the starting point for concept development. How the voice of the customer is translated into physical or operational specifications and production processes for a product or service can mean the difference between a successful product and an outright failure.

For example, consumers expect a camera to take good pictures. In developing a new camera, Japanese engineers at one company studied pictures developed at

QUALITY PROFILES

DANA CORPORATION—SPICER DRIVESHAFT AND 3M DENTAL PRODUCTS DIVISION

DANA CORPORATION
3M DENTAL PRODUCTS

Dana Corporation–Spicer Driveshaft Division (now Torque Traction Technologies, Inc.) is North America's largest independent manufacturer of driveshafts and related components for light, medium, heavy duty, and off-highway vehicles. Spicer Driveshaft has 17 manufacturing, assembly, and administrative facilities around the United States, employing more than 3,400 people.

The company uses Customer Platform Teams as one of the focal points for identifying customer requirements and building and maintaining new business, product offerings, and customer relationships. These teams include sales, engineering, quality, and warranty personnel that use a variety of formal and informal methods to listen and learn from customers. All senior leaders are involved in a two-phase strategic planning process that addresses long-term direction and short-term objectives, which are linked and aligned from headquarters to the individual manufacturing plants. A comprehensive diversity plan is used to help develop candidates for promotion from within the organization, improve community involvement efforts, and establish a mentoring program.

From 1997 to 1999, sales increased by nearly 10 percent; economic value added increased from $15 million to $35 million; inventory as a percentage of sales decreased from 6.8 percent to 6.3 percent; and working capital decreased from 13 percent to 10.2 percent of sales. Internal defect rates decreased more than 75 percent from 1996 to 2000 and are approaching best-in-class levels. Employees are encouraged to develop and implement changes and innovative ideas and evaluate their results. Ideas submitted by employees average about three per month, which is approaching best-in-class. In 1999, almost 80 percent of ideas were implemented. The employee turnover rate is below 1 percent, which is better than the best competitor; and the attendance rate has remained above 98 percent for the last six years. The division received a Baldrige Award in 2000.

Launched in 1964, 3M Dental Products Division (DPD), a Baldrige winner in 1997, is a business unit of 3M Corporation, manufacturing and marketing more than 1,300 products used by dentists around the world, including restorative and crown and bridge materials and dental adhesive and infection control products. Innovation is a key success factor enabling the company to be a leader in the competitive dental products marketplace. Insights into changing customer requirements—combined with knowledge of technological, societal, and environmental trends—are the starting point for product and process innovations. Dentists, distributors, and major suppliers are involved in the division's systematic approach to translating key customer requirements into design requirements, prototypes, and, ultimately, reliable, quality products. Examples of customer involvement include simulated operations on "Fletchers," mannequins with human-like mouth features and conditions. Dentists use these mannequins to evaluate variations of prototype material or hardware products. Through this and other methods, customer feedback is received at least three times during the development cycle. The company's business performance management matrix provides a systematic and comprehensive tool for aligning key business drivers and goals down, through, and across all business and functional units. More than 40 cross-functional teams arrange new product introduction, solves problems, and manage and improve business processes.

In 1997 new product sales accounted for 45 percent of total sales, accelerating from 12 percent in 1992. Additionally, the number of patents per employee, an indicator of innovation, is better than twice the rate of its closest competitor. 3M DPD has been the industry leader in overall satisfaction of its U.S. distributors since 1989 and in overall satisfaction of dentists since 1987.

Source: Malcolm Baldrige National Quality Award, Profiles of Winners, National Institute of Standards and Technology, Department of Commerce.

photo labs and talked with customers to determine the major causes of poor pictures. The three biggest problems were underexposures, out-of-focus, and out-of-film (attempting to take pictures past the end of the roll). They developed the first camera that included a built-in flash to prevent underexposure, an autofocus lens, and an automatic rewind feature. Today, most popular models have these features to meet customer requirements. Other design considerations include the product's weight, size, appearance, safety, life, serviceability, and maintainability. When decisions about these factors are dominated by engineering considerations rather than by customer requirements, poor designs that fail in the market are often the result.

> *Developing a basic functional design involves translating customer requirements into measurable technical requirements and, subsequently, into detailed design specifications.*

Technical requirements, sometimes called design characteristics, translate the voice of the customer into technical language, specifically into measures of product performance. For example, consumers might want portable stereos with "good sound quality." Technical aspects of a stereo system that affect sound quality include the frequency response, flutter (the wavering in pitch), and the speed accuracy (inconsistency affects the pitch and tempo of the sound). Technical requirements are actionable; they lead to design specifications such as the electrical properties of stereo system components. Two of the most powerful tools for meeting technical requirements are *quality function deployment* and *concept engineering*.

Quality Function Deployment

A major problem with the traditional product development process is that customers and engineers speak different languages. A customer might express a desire to own a car that is easy to start. The translation of this requirement into technical language might be "car will start within 10 seconds of continuous cranking." Or, a requirement that "soap leaves my skin feeling soft" demands translation into pH or hardness specifications for the bar of soap. The actual intended message can be lost in the translation and subsequent interpretation by design or production personnel.

The Japanese developed an approach called **quality function deployment (QFD)** to meet customers' requirements throughout the design process and also in the design of production systems. The term, a translation of the Kanji characters used to describe the process, can sound confusing. QFD is a planning process to guide the design, manufacturing, and marketing of goods by integrating the voice of the customer throughout the organization. Through QFD, every design, manufacturing, and control decision is made to meet the expressed needs of customers. It uses a type of matrix diagram to present data and information.

QFD originated in 1972 at Mitsubishi's Kobe shipyard site. Toyota began to develop the concept shortly thereafter, and has used it since 1977 with impressive results. Between January 1977 and October 1979, Toyota realized a 20 percent reduction in start-up costs on the launch of a new van. By 1982, start-up costs had fallen 38 percent from the 1977 baseline, and by 1984, were reduced by 61 percent. In addition, development time fell by one-third at the same time quality improved. Xerox and Ford initiated the use of QFD in the United States in 1986 (at that time, more than 50 percent of major Japanese companies were already using the approach). Today, QFD is used successfully by manufacturers of electronics, appliances, clothing, and construction equipment, by firms such as General Motors, Ford, Mazda, Motorola, Xerox, Kodak, IBM, Procter & Gamble, Hewlett-Packard, and AT&T. The 1992 model

Cadillac was planned and designed entirely with QFD. Two organizations, the American Supplier Institute, Inc., a nonprofit organization, and GOAL/QPC, a Massachusetts consulting firm, have publicized and developed the concept in the United States.

At the strategic level, QFD presents a challenge and the opportunity for top management to break out of its traditional narrow focus on results, which can only be measured after the fact, and to view the broader process of how results are obtained. Under QFD, all operations of a company are driven by the voice of the customer, rather than by edicts of top management or the opinions or desires of design engineers. At the tactical and operational levels, QFD departs from the traditional product planning process in which product concepts are originated by design teams or research and development groups, tested and refined, produced, and marketed. Often, a considerable amount of wasted effort and time is spent redesigning products and production systems until customer needs are met. If customer needs can be identified properly in the first place, then such wasteful effort is eliminated, which is the principal focus of QFD.

QFD benefits companies through improved communication and teamwork between all constituencies in the value chain, such as between marketing and design, between design and manufacturing, and between purchasing and suppliers.

Product objectives are better understood and interpreted during the production process because all key design information is captured and synthesized. This approach helps to understand trade-offs in design, and promote consensus among managers. Use of QFD focuses on the drivers of customer satisfaction and dissatisfaction, making it a useful tool for competitive analysis of product quality by top management. Productivity as well as quality improvements generally follow QFD. Perhaps most significant, though, QFD reduces the time for new product development. QFD allows companies to simulate the effects of new design ideas and concepts. Through this benefit, companies can reduce product development time and bring new products into the market sooner, thus gaining competitive advantage. Details of the QFD process and its use are presented next.

The House of Quality A set of matrixes is used to relate the voice of the customer to a product's technical requirements, component requirements, process control plans, and manufacturing operations. The first matrix, the customer requirement planning matrix shown in Figure 12.1, provides the basis for the QFD concept. The figure demonstrates why this matrix is often called the **House of Quality**.

Building the House of Quality consists of six basic steps:

1. Identify customer requirements.
2. Identify technical requirements.
3. Relate the customer requirements to the technical requirements.
4. Conduct an evaluation of competing products or services.
5. Evaluate technical requirements and develop targets.
6. Determine which technical requirements to deploy in the remainder of the production/delivery process.

To illustrate the development of the House of Quality and the QFD process, the task of designing a new fitness center in a community with two other competing organizations is presented.

> *Step 1: Identify customer requirements.* The voice of the customer is the primary input to the QFD process. As discussed in Chapter 4, many methods can be used to gather valid customer information. The most critical and most difficult

Figure 12.1 The House of Quality

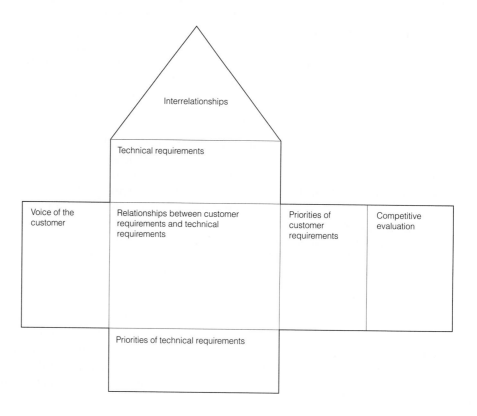

step of the process is to capture the essence of the customer's needs and expectations. The customer's own words are vitally important in preventing misinterpretation by designers and engineers. Figure 12.2 shows the voice of the customer in the House of Quality for the fitness center, perhaps based on a telephone survey or focus groups. They are grouped into five categories: programs and activities, facilities, atmosphere, staff, and other. These groupings can easily be done using affinity diagrams, for example.

Step 2: List the technical requirements that provide the foundation for the product or service design. Technical requirements are design characteristics that describe the customer requirements as expressed in the language of the designer or engineer. Essentially, they are the "hows" by which the company will respond to the "whats"—customer requirements. They must be measurable, because the output is controlled and compared to objective targets. For the fitness center, these requirements include the number and type of program offerings and equipment, times, staffing requirements, facility characteristics and maintenance, fee structure, and so on. Figure 12.3 adds this information to the House of Quality.

The roof of the House of Quality shows the interrelationships between any pair of technical requirements. Various symbols denote these relationships. A typical scheme uses the symbol • to denote a very strong relationship, ○ for a

Figure 12.2 Voice of the Customer in the House of Quality

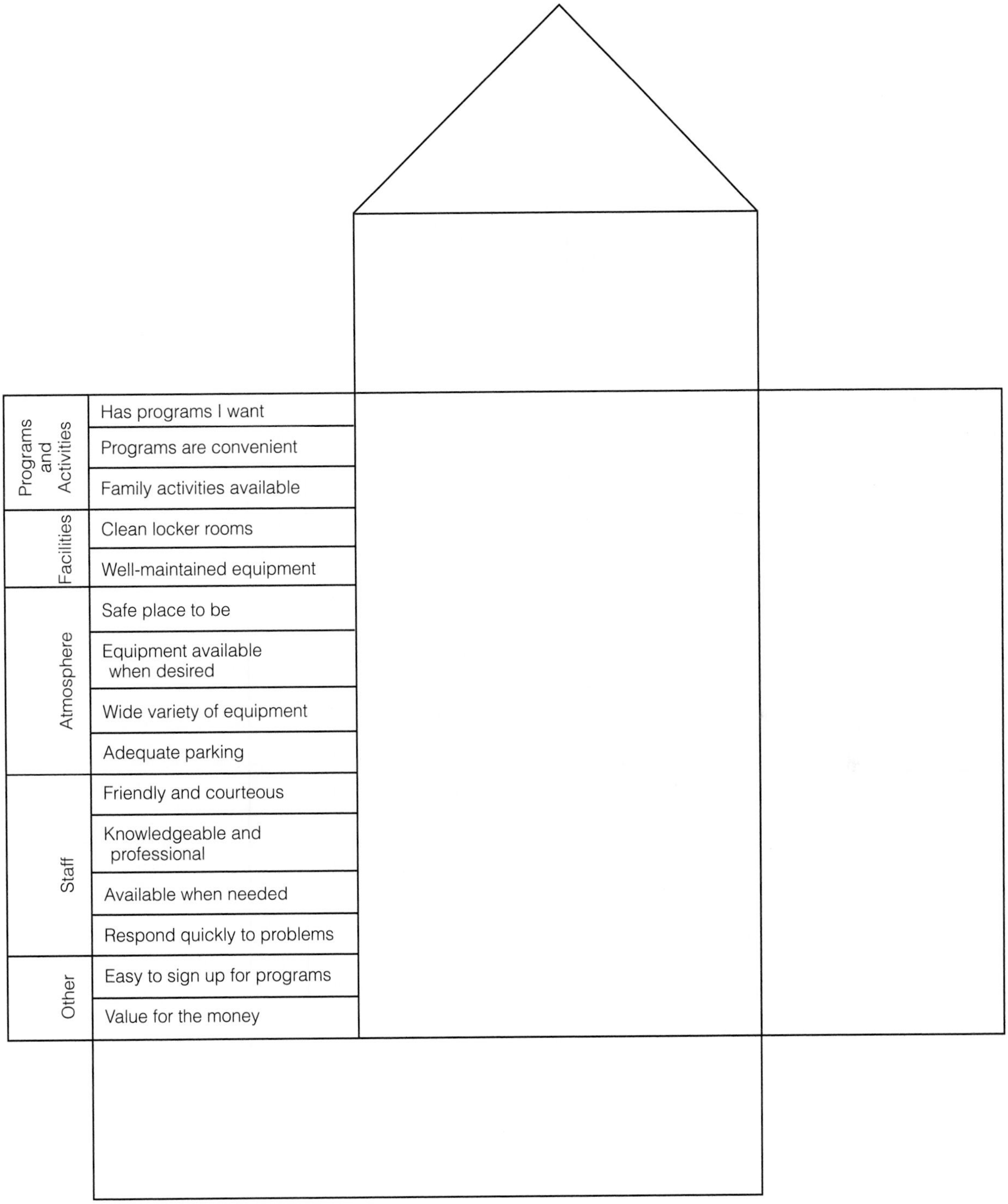

Programs and Activities	Has programs I want	
	Programs are convenient	
	Family activities available	
Facilities	Clean locker rooms	
	Well-maintained equipment	
Atmosphere	Safe place to be	
	Equipment available when desired	
	Wide variety of equipment	
	Adequate parking	
Staff	Friendly and courteous	
	Knowledgeable and professional	
	Available when needed	
	Respond quickly to problems	
Other	Easy to sign up for programs	
	Value for the money	

Figure 12.3 Technical Requirements in the House of Quality

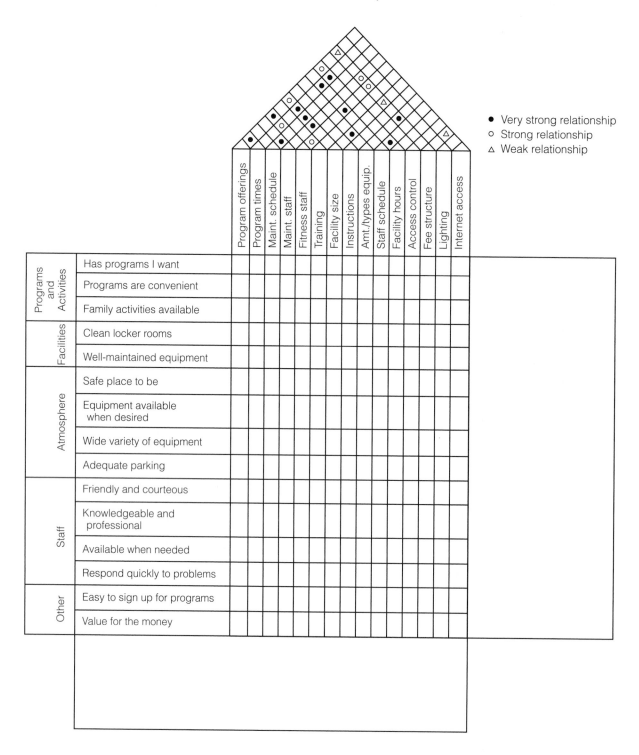

strong relationship, and Δ to denote a weak relationship. These relationships indicate answers to questions such as "How does a change in a technical characteristic affect others?" For example, increasing program offerings will probably require more staff, a larger facility, expanded hours, and higher costs; hiring more maintenance staff, building a larger facility, and buying more equipment will probably result in a higher membership fee. Thus, design decisions cannot be viewed in isolation. This relationship matrix helps to assess trade-offs.

Step 3: Develop a relationship matrix between the customer requirements and the technical requirements. Customer requirements are listed down the left column; technical requirements are written across the top. In the matrix itself, symbols indicate the degree of relationship in a manner similar to that used in the roof of the House of Quality. The purpose of the relationship matrix is to show whether the final technical requirements adequately address customer requirements. This assessment is usually based on expert experience, customer responses, or controlled experiments.

The lack of a strong relationship between a customer requirement and any technical requirement shows that the customer needs either are not addressed or that the final design will have difficulty in meeting them. Similarly, if a technical requirement does not affect any customer requirement, it may be redundant or the designers may have missed some important customer need. For example, the customer requirement "clean locker rooms" bears a very strong relationship to the maintenance schedule and only a strong relationship to the number of maintenance staff. "Easy to sign up for programs" would probably bear a very strong relationship to Internet access and only a weak relationship to the hours the facility is open. Figure 12.4 shows an example of these relationships.

Step 4: Add competitor evaluation and key selling points. This step identifies importance ratings for each customer requirement and evaluates competitors' existing products or services for each of them (see Figure 12.5). Customer importance ratings represent the areas of greatest interest and highest expectations as expressed by the customer. Competitive evaluation highlights the absolute strengths and weaknesses in competing products. By using this step, designers can discover opportunities for improvement. It also links QFD to a company's strategic vision and indicates priorities for the design process. For example, if an important customer requirement receives a low evaluation on all competitors' products (for instance, "family activities available"), then by focusing on this need a company might gain a competitive advantage. Such requirements become key selling points and the basis for formulating marketing strategies.

Step 5: Evaluate technical requirements of competitive products and services and develop targets. This step is usually accomplished through intelligence gathering or product testing and then translated into measurable terms. These evaluations are compared with the competitive evaluation of customer requirements to determine inconsistencies between customer requirements and technical requirements. If a competing product is found to best satisfy a customer requirement but the evaluation of the related technical requirements indicates otherwise, then either the measures used are faulty or else the product has an image difference (either positive toward the competitor or negative toward the company's product), which affects customer perceptions. On the basis of customer importance ratings and existing product strengths and weaknesses, targets for each technical requirement are set, as shown in Figure 12.6. For

Figure 12.4 Relationship Matrix

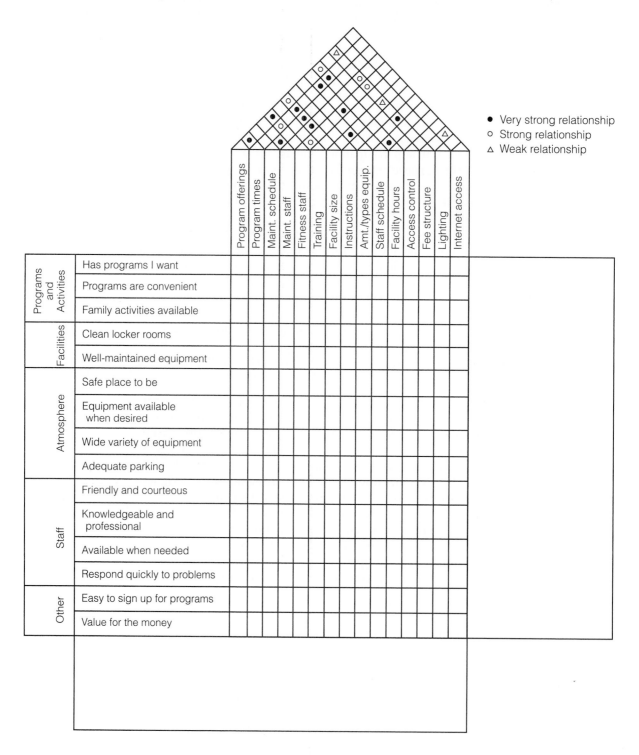

Figure 12.5 Competitive Evaluation

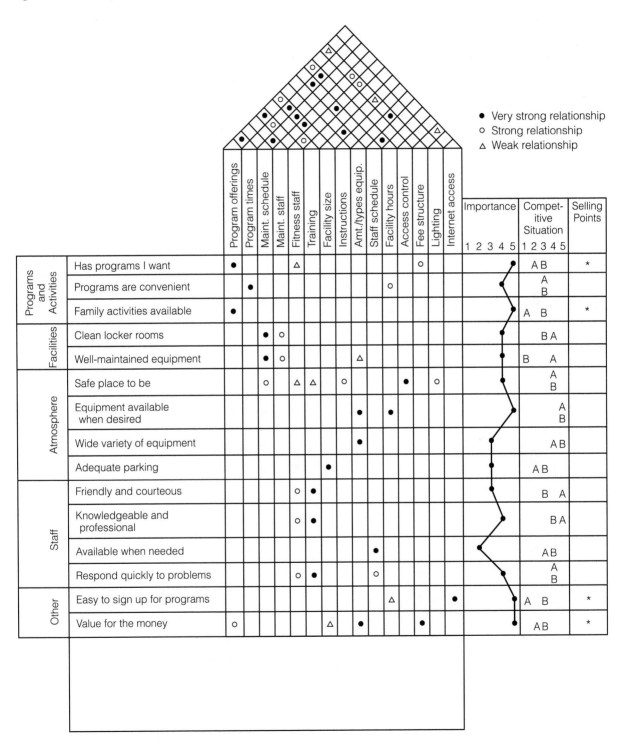

Figure 12.6 Completed House of Quality

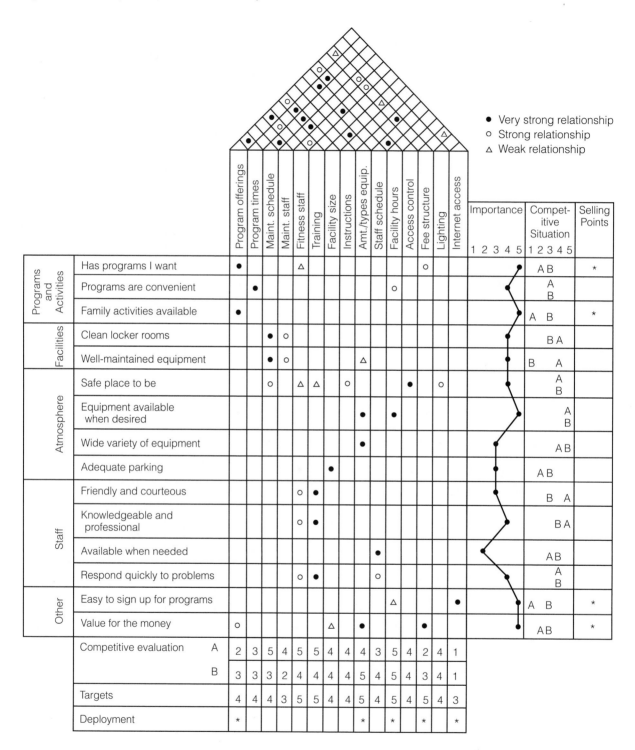

example, customers rated programs and family activities of high importance while competitive evaluation shows them to be quite low. Setting a higher target for these requirements will help to meet this critical need and be a source of competitive advantage.

Step 6: Select technical requirements to be deployed in the remainder of the process. The technical requirements that have a strong relationship to customer needs, have poor competitive performance, or are strong selling points are identified during this step. These characteristics have the highest priority and need to be "deployed" throughout the remainder of the design and production process to maintain a responsiveness to the voice of the customer. Those characteristics not identified as critical do not need such rigorous attention. For example, program offerings, amount and types of equipment, facility hours, fee structure, and Internet access have been identified in Figure 12.6 as the key issues to address in designing the fitness center.

The QFD Process The House of Quality provides the marketing function with an important tool to understand customer needs and gives top management strategic direction. However, it is only the first step in the QFD process. The voice of the customer must be carried throughout the production/delivery process. Three other "houses of quality" are used to deploy the voice of the customer to (in a manufacturing setting) component parts characteristics, process plans, and quality control.

The second house is similar to the first house but applies to subsystems and components. The technical requirements from the first house are related to detailed requirements of subsystems and components (see Figure 12.7). At this stage, target values representing the best values for fit, function, and appearance are determined. For example, program offerings might be broken down into fitness programs, children's programs, family programs, and so on, each with its own unique set of design requirements, and hence, its own House of Quality.

In manufacturing, most of the QFD activities represented by the first two houses of quality are performed by product development and engineering functions. At the next stage, the planning activities involve supervisors and production line operators. In the third house, the process plan relates the component characteristics to key process operations, the transition from planning to execution. (For the fitness center,

Figure 12.7 The Four Houses of Quality

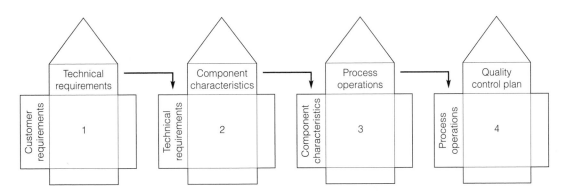

this step might involve creating a project plan for selecting, designing, and evaluating programs.) Key process operations are the basis for a *control point*. A control point forms the basis for a quality control plan delivering those critical characteristics that are crucial to achieving customer satisfaction, as specified in the last house of quality. At this point, for example, the fitness center might design membership surveys for evaluating programs, checklists for maintenance, performance appraisal approaches for the staff, and measures of equipment failures and problems. These activities are what must be measured and evaluated on a continuous basis to ensure that processes continue to meet the important customer requirements defined in the first House of Quality. Thus, the QFD process provides a thread from the voice of the customer, through design and production/delivery activities, to daily management and control. In that way, it provides the basis for more advanced methodologies such as design of experiments, and for effective implementation of statistical process control, which we discuss in a later chapter.

> *The vast majority of applications of QFD in the United States concentrate on the first and, to a lesser extent, the second houses of quality.*

Lawrence Sullivan, who brought QFD to the West, suggested that the third and fourth houses of quality offer far more significant benefits than the first two, especially in the United States.[3] In Japan, managers, engineers, and workers are more naturally cross-functional and tend to promote group effort and consensus thinking. In the United States, workers and managers are more vertically oriented and tend to suboptimize for individual and/or departmental achievements. Companies in the United States tend to promote breakthrough achievements, which often inhibits cross-functional interaction. If a U.S. company can maintain the breakthrough culture with emphasis on continuous improvement through more effective cross-functional interactions as supported by QFD, it can establish a competitive advantage over foreign competitors. The third and fourth houses of quality utilize the knowledge of about 80 percent of a company's employees—supervisors and operators. If their knowledge goes unused, this potential is wasted.

Concept Engineering

Concept engineering (CE) emerged from a consortium of companies that included Polaroid and Bose along with researchers at MIT, and is promoted and taught by the Center for Quality of Management (http://www.cqm.org). CE is a focused process for discovering customer requirements and using them to select superior product or service concepts that meet those requirements. Although similar to QFD in many respects, it puts the voice of the customer into a broader context and employees numerous other techniques to ensure effective processing of qualitative data. Five major steps comprise the process:

1. *Understanding the customer's environment.* This step involves first project planning activities such as team selection, identifying fit with business strategy, and gaining team consensus on the project focus. It also includes collecting the voice of the customer to understand the customer's environment—physical, psychological, competitive, and so on.
2. *Converting understanding into requirements.* In this step, teams analyze the customer transcripts to translate the voice of the customer into more specific requirements using the KJ method we introduced in Chapter 4. Essentially this step focuses on identifying the technical requirements we discussed in the context of QFD, selecting the most significant requirements, and "scrubbing" the requirements to refine them into clear and insightful statements.

3. *Operationalizing what has been learned.* This step involves determining how to measure how well a customer requirement is met. For example, a requirement developed for a project at Polaroid was "Document photographer delivers document photo quickly while the customer waits." The principal requirement is about throughput time, so the concept of "quickly" needs to be operationalized and measured.[4] Once potential metrics are defined, they are evaluated to reduce the number of metrics that need to be used while ensuring that they cover all key requirements. This evaluation usually requires some sort of customer questionnaire to identify the importance of the requirements and prioritize them.

4. *Concept generation.* This step focuses on generating ideas for solutions that will potentially meet customers' needs. One unique approach is to brainstorm ideas that might resolve each individual customer requirement, select the best ones, and then classify them under the more traditional functional product characteristics. This approach helps to develop a "market in" rather than a "product out" orientation. Creative thinking techniques are applied here to increase the number and diversity of potential ideas.

5. *Concept selection.* Finally, the potential ideas are evaluated with respect to meeting requirements, trade-offs are assessed, and prototyping may begin. The process ends with reflection on the final concept to test whether the decision "feels right" based on all the knowledge acquired.

As an example, Bose Corporation, a leader in high-end audio products, used concept engineering to improve its European delivery system while decreasing overhead cost to the company.[5] The delivery system included every activity from the time a dealer realizes that he or she needs a product from Bose until the product is delivered. In personal visits to dealers in France, Germany, Holland, Spain, Belgium, and the United Kingdom, Bose developed an interview guide that addressed the following:

1. How do you describe the perfect supplier?
2. Please describe your process of ordering.
3. Where does customer service fit into your business?
4. General questions about your impressions of Bose.

In processing the qualitative data obtained from the interviews, Bose focused on the question, "What scenes or images come to mind when you visualize a supplier's delivery system?" From an analysis of more than 100 customer requirements, 24 were selected as key requirements for a world-class delivery system. This analysis led the team to the conclusion that supplier reliability and system efficiency build confidence and create trusting relationships. Next, these requirements were stated in measurable terms and questionnaires were developed to ensure that the requirements truly reflected the opinions of the dealers. For example, a requirement might be "Have a simple and swift return policy for faulty or damaged products." This requirement might then be measured by the amount of information required to process a product return.

The team spent nearly three days generating potential solutions for each customer requirement. As they discussed the strengths of each idea, new ideas often emerged, even from seemingly bizarre ideas. The four strongest ideas were chosen, and the team wrote a story or scenario with specific changes that needed to be made to the delivery system as a way of presenting the solution; this form of presentation would enable those outside of the team to understand how the new systems would work in delighting the customer. Although the process was quite tedious, the team members agreed that it was an excellent approach for arriving at an effective solution and turned them "into believers."

Like QFD, concept engineering leaves a strong audit trail back to the voice of the customer. This evidence makes it difficult for skeptics to challenge the results and easier to convert them. The process helps to build consensus and gives the team confidence in selling the concept to management. It takes a lot of discipline and patience, but the end result is well worth the effort.

TOOLS FOR DESIGN DEVELOPMENT

After a concept is selected, the detailed design process begins, with a focus on establishing product specifications, which represent the transition from a designer's concept to a producible design, while also ensuring that it can be produced economically, efficiently, and with high quality. We will focus our attention on manufactured goods, although similar considerations apply to services. To illustrate these concepts, consider a microprocessor. The drawing in Figure 12.8 shows some of the critical dimensions and tolerances for the microprocessor. The "ratio" notation (0.514/0.588) denotes the permissible range of the dimension. Unless otherwise stated, the nominal dimension is the midpoint. Thus, the specification of 0.514/0.588 may be interpreted as a nominal dimension of 0.551 with a tolerance of plus or minus 0.037. Usually, this is written as 0.551 ± 0.037. The manufacturing-based definition of quality conformance to specifications is based on such tolerances.

Specifications apply to services as well. At Starbucks, the national chain of coffeehouses, milk must be steamed to at least 150 degrees Fahrenheit but never more than 170 degrees, and every espresso shot must be pulled within 23 seconds of service or tossed.[6] Government regulations often determine specifications for food and pharmaceutical products. For example, the U.S. Food and Drug Administration (FDA) sets quality standards regarding the number of unsavory items that find their way into food products.[7] Packaged mushrooms are allowed to contain up to 20 maggots of any size per 100 grams of drained mushrooms or 15 grams of dried mushrooms, while 100 grams of peanut butter may have an average of 30 insect fragments and one rodent hair. (Need we say more?)

Manufacturing specifications consist of nominal dimensions and tolerances. Nominal refers to the ideal dimension or the target value that manufacturing seeks to meet; tolerance is the permissible variation, recognizing the difficulty of meeting a target consistently.

Common cause variation cannot be reduced unless the production technology (at least one of the 5 Ms) is changed. If a process is incapable of producing within design specifications, management must weigh the cost of acquiring new technology against the consequences and related cost of allowing nonconformities in production. These costs may include, among others, 100 percent inspection, allowing nonconforming parts further in the production process, and possible loss of present and future customers.

Tolerance design involves determining the permissible variation in a dimension. To design tolerances effectively, engineers must understand the necessary trade-offs. Narrow tolerances tend to raise manufacturing costs but they also increase the interchangeability of parts within the plant and in the field, product performance, durability, and appearance. Also, a tolerance reserve or factor of safety is needed to account for engineering uncertainty regarding

Tolerances are necessary because not all parts can be produced exactly to nominal specifications because of natural variations (common causes) in production processes due to the "5 Ms": men and women, materials, machines, methods, and measurement.

Figure 12.8 Microprocessor Specifications

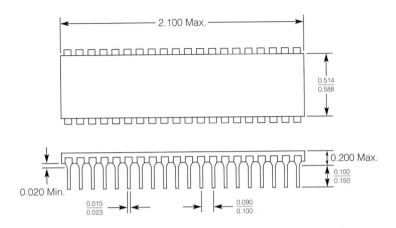

the maximum variation allowable and compatibility with satisfactory product performance. Wide tolerances, on the other hand, increase material utilization, machine throughput, and labor productivity, but have a negative impact on product characteristics, as previously mentioned. Thus, factors operating to enlarge tolerances include production planning requirements; tool design, fabrication, and setup; tool adjustment and replacement, process yield; inspection and gauge control and maintenance; and labor and supervision requirements.

Traditionally, tolerances are set by convention rather than scientifically. A designer might use the tolerances specified on previous designs or base a design decision on judgment from past experience. Setting inappropriate tolerances can be costly. For instance, in one company, a bearing seat had to be machined on a large part, costing more than $1,000. Because of the precision tolerance specified by design engineers, one or two parts per month had to be scrapped when the tolerance was exceeded. A study revealed that the bearings being used did not require such precise tolerances. When the tolerance was relaxed, the problem disappeared. This one design change resulted in approximately $20,000 in savings per year.

All too often, tolerance settings fail to account for the impact of variation on product functionality, manufacturability, or economic consequences. In a review of Audi's TT Coupe when it was first introduced, automobile columnist Alan Vonderhaar noted, "There was apparently some problem with the second-gear synchronizer, a device that is supposed to ease shifts. As a result, on full-power upshifts from first to second, I frequently got gear clashes." He observed others with the same problem from Internet newsgroups and concluded, "It appears to be an issue that surfaces just now and again, here and there throughout the production mix, suggesting it may be a tolerance issue— sometimes the associated parts are close enough to specifications to get along well, other times they're at the outer ranges of manufacturing tolerance and cause problems."[8]

Many statistical tools that we discussed in Chapter 10, including statistical inference, regression, and design of experiments, play an important role in design development. In this section we introduce two other general approaches: *design failure modes and effects analysis*, and *reliability prediction*.

Design Failure Mode and Effects Analysis

The purpose of **design failure mode and effects analysis (DFMEA)** is to identify all the ways in which a failure can occur, to estimate the effect and seriousness of the failure, and to recommend corrective design actions. A DFMEA usually consists of specifying the following information for each design element or function:

- *Failure modes*—ways in which each element or function can fail. This information generally takes some research and imagination. One way to start is with known failures that have occurred in the past. Documents such as quality and reliability reports, test results, and warranty reports provide useful information.
- *Effect of the failure on the customer*—such as dissatisfaction, potential injury or other safety issue, downtime, repair requirements, and so on. Maintenance records, customer complaints, and warranty reports provide good sources of information. Consideration should be given to failures on the function of the end product, manufacturability in the next process, what the customer sees or experiences, and product safety.
- *Severity, likelihood of occurrence, and detection rating.* Severity might be measured on a scale of 1 to 10, where a "1" indicates that the failure is so minor that the customer probably would not notice it, and a "10" might mean that the customer might be endangered. The frequency of occurrence based on service history or field performance provides an indication of the significance of the failure. Based on severity and likelihood, a risk priority can be assigned to identify critical failure modes that must be addressed.
- *Potential causes of failure.* Often failure is the result of poor design. Design deficiencies can cause errors either in the field or in manufacturing and assembly. Identification of causes might require experimentation and rigorous analysis.
- *Corrective actions or controls.* These controls might include design changes, "mistake proofing" (see Chapter 13), better user instructions, management responsibilities, and target completion dates.

Figure 12.9 gives an example of a simple DFMEA for an ordinary household light socket.

Using DFMEA will not only improve product functionality and safety, but also reduce external failure costs—particularly warranty costs, as well as decrease manufacturing and service delivery problems. It can also provide a defense against frivolous lawsuits. DFMEA should be conducted early in the design process to save costs and reduce cycle times, and provide a knowledge base to improve subsequent design efforts. This approach can also be used for processes to identify hazardous conditions that may endanger a worker or operational problems that can disrupt a production process and result in scrap, downtime, or other non-value-added costs.

Reliability Prediction

Reliability—the ability of a product to perform as expected over time—is one of the principal dimensions of quality. Reliability is an essential aspect of both product and process design. Sophisticated equipment used today in such areas as transportation (airplanes), communications (satellites), and medicine (pacemakers) requires high reliability. High reliability can also provide a competitive advantage for many consumer goods. Japanese automobiles gained large market shares in the 1970s primarily because of their high reliability. As the overall quality of products continues to improve, consumers expect higher reliability with each purchase; they simply are not satisfied with products that fail unexpectedly. However, the increased complexity of

Figure 12.9 DFMEA Example for a Common Household Lamp

Failure Mode and Effects Analysis
Analyst *J.A. White*

Product *2C Lamp*

Component Name	Failure Mode	Cause of Failure	Effect of Failure on System	Correction of Problem	Comments
Plug part no. P-3	Loose wiring	Use vibration, handling	Will not conduct current; may generate heat	Molded plug and wire	Uncorrected, could cause fire
	Not a failure of plug per se	User contacts prongs when plugging or unplugging	May cause severe shock or death	Enlarged safety tip on molded plug	Children
Metal base and stem	Bent or nicked	Dropping, bumping, shipping	Degrades looks	Distress finish, improved packaging	Cosmetic
Lamp socket	Cracked	Excessive heat, bumping, forcing	May cause shock if contacts metal base and stem; may cause shock upon bulb replacement	Improve material used for socket	Dangerous
Wiring	Broken, frayed, from lamp to plug	Fatigue, heat, carelessness, childbite	Will not conduct current; may generate heat, blow breakers, or cause shock	Use of wire suitable for long life in extreme environment anticipated	Dangerous; warning on instructions
	Internal short circuit	Heat, brittle insulation	May cause electrical shock or render lamp useless	Use of wire suitable for long life in extreme environment anticipated	
	Internal wire broken	Socket slipping and twisting wires	May cause electrical shock or render lamp useless	Use of indent or notch to prevent socket from turning	

Source: K. E. Case and L. L. Jones, *Profit Through Quality: Quality Assurance Programs for Manufacturers,* QC & RE Monograph Series No. 2 (New York: Institute of Industrial Engineers, 1978).

modern products makes high reliability more difficult to achieve. Likewise in manufacturing, the increased use of automation, complexity of machines, low profit margins, and time-based competitiveness make reliability in production processes a critical issue for survival of the business.

Basic Concepts and Definitions Like quality, reliability is often defined in a similar "transcendent" manner as a sense of trust in a product's ability to perform satisfactorily or resist failure. However, reliability is an issue that requires a more objective, quantitative treatment. Formally, reliability is defined as *the probability that a product, piece of equipment, or system performs its intended function for a stated period of time under specified operating conditions.* This definition has four important elements: probability, time, performance, and operating conditions.

First, reliability is defined as a *probability*, that is, a value between 0 and 1. Thus, it is a numerical measure with a precise meaning. Expressing reliability in this way provides a valid basis for comparison of different designs for products and systems. For example, a reliability of 0.97 indicates that, on average, 97 of 100 items will perform their function for a given period of time and under certain operating conditions. Often reliability is expressed as a percentage simply for descriptive purposes.

The second element of the definition is *time*. Clearly a device having a reliability of 0.97 for 1,000 hours of operation is inferior to one having the same reliability for 5,000 hours of operation, assuming that the mission of the device is long life.

Performance is the third element and refers to the objective for which the product or system was made. The term *failure* is used when expectations of performance of the intended function are not met. Two types of failures can occur: **functional failure** *at the start of product life due to manufacturing or material defects such as a missing connection or a faulty component,* and **reliability failure** *after some period of use.*

Examples of reliability failures include the following: a device does not work at all (car will not start); the operation of a device is unstable (car idles rough); or the performance of a device deteriorates (shifting becomes difficult). Because the nature of failure in each of these cases is different, the failure must be clearly defined.

The final component of the reliability definition is *operating conditions*, which involves the type and amount of usage and the environment in which the product is used. For example, typical operating conditions and environments for a wristwatch are summarized in Table 12.1. Notice that reliability must include extreme environments and conditions as well as the typical on-the-arm use.

By defining a product's intended environment, performance characteristics, and lifetime, a manufacturer can design and conduct tests to measure the probability of product survival (or failure). The analysis of such tests enable better prediction of reliability and improved product and process designs.

Reliability engineers distinguish between inherent reliability, which is the predicted reliability determined by the design of the product or process, and the achieved reliability, which is the actual reliability observed during use. Actual reliability can be less than the inherent reliability due to the effects of the manufacturing process and the conditions of use.

Table 12.1 Some Typical Watch Environments

Environment	Condition	Quantifiable Characteristics	Exposure Time
Typical use	On-the-arm	31°C (88°F)	16 hours/day
Transportation	In packing box	Vibration and shock (−20°C to +80°C)	Specifications for truck/rail/air shipping
Handling accident	Drop to hard floor	1,200 g, 2 milliseconds	1 drop/year
Extreme temperature	Hot, closed automobile	85°C (185°F)	4–6 hours, 5 times/year
Humidity and chemicals	Perspiration, salt, soaps	35°C (95°F) with 90% pH, rain	500 hours/year
Altitude	Pike's Peak	15,000 feet, −40°C	1 time

Source: Adapted from William R. Taylor, "Quality Assessed in New Products Via Comprehensive Systems Approach," *Industrial Engineering* 13, no. 3 (March 1981), 28–32.

Reliability Measurement In practice, reliability is determined by the number of failures per unit time during the duration under consideration (called the **failure rate**). The reciprocal of the failure rate is used as an alternative measure. Some products must be scrapped and replaced upon failure; others can be repaired. For items that must be replaced when a failure occurs, the reciprocal of the failure rate (having dimensions of time units per failure) is called the mean time to failure (MTTF). For repairable items, the mean time between failures (MTBF) is used.

In considering the failure rate of a product, suppose that a large group of items is tested or used until all fail, and that the time of failure is recorded for each item. Plotting the cumulative percentage of failures against time results in a curve such as the one shown in Figure 12.10. The slope of the curve at any point (that is, the slope of the straight line tangent to the curve) gives the instantaneous failure rate (failures per unit time) at any point in time. Figure 12.11 shows the failure rate curve, generally called a product life characteristics curve, corresponding to the cumulative failure curve in Figure 12.10. This curve was obtained by plotting the slope of the curve at every point. Notice that the slope of the curve and thus the failure rate may change over time. Thus, in Figure 12.11, the failure rate at 500 hours is 0.02 failures per hour while the failure rate at 4,500 hours is 0.04 failures per hour. The average failure rate over any interval of time is the slope of the line between the two endpoints of the interval on the curve. As shown in Figure 12.12, the average failure rate over the entire 5,000-hour time period is 0.02 failures per hour. Many research institutes and large manufacturers conduct extensive statistical studies to identify distinct patterns of failure over time.

Gathering enough data about failures to generate as smooth a curve as is shown in Figure 12.12 is not always possible. If limited data are available, the failure rate is computed using the following formula:

$$\text{Failure rate} = \lambda = \frac{\text{Number of failures}}{\text{Total unit operating hours}}$$

Figure 12.10 Cumulative Failure Curve Over Time

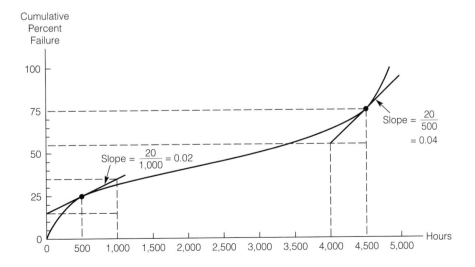

Figure 12.11 Failure Rate Curve

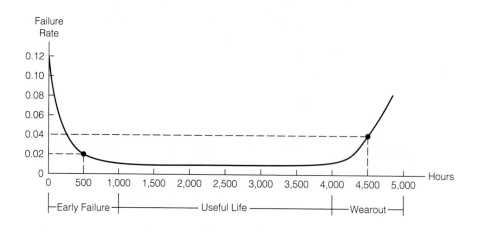

Figure 12.12 Average Failure Rate over a Time Interval

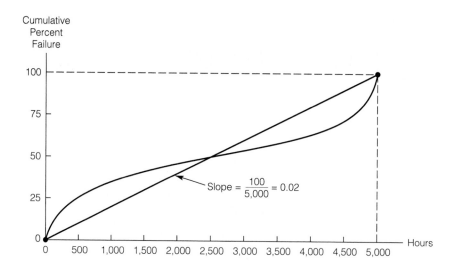

or alternatively,

$$\lambda = \frac{\text{Number of failures}}{(\text{Units tested}) \times (\text{Number of hours tested})}$$

A fundamental assumption in this definition allows for different interpretations. Because the total unit operating hours equal the number of units tested times the number of hours tested, no difference occurs in total unit operating hours between testing 10 units for 100 hours or one unit for 1,000 hours. However, the difference in Figure 12.11 is clear because the failure rate varies over time. For example, if useful life began at 10 hours and the wearout period began at 200 hours, a failure would almost certainly occur before 1,000 hours, whereas a failure would not be likely to occur in 100-hour tests. During a product's useful life, however, the failure rate is assumed to be constant, and different test lengths during this period of time should show little difference. This assumption is the reason that time is an important element of the definition of reliability.

To illustrate the computation of λ, suppose that 10 units are tested over a 100-hour period. Four units failed with one unit each failing after 6, 35, 65, and 70 hours; the remaining six units performed satisfactorily until the end of the test. The total unit operating hours are

$$
\begin{array}{rcl}
1 \times 6 &=& 6 \\
1 \times 35 &=& 35 \\
1 \times 65 &=& 65 \\
1 \times 70 &=& 70 \\
1 \times 100 &=& \underline{600} \\
&& 776
\end{array}
$$

Therefore, λ = (4 failures)/(776 unit operating hours) = 0.00515 failures per hour. In other words, in a one-hour period, about 0.5 percent of the units would be expected to fail. On the other hand, over a 100-hour period, about (0.00515)(100) = 0.515 or 51.5 percent of the units would be expected to fail. In the actual test, only 40 percent failed. The failure rate curve in Figure 12.11 is an example of a typical product life characteristics curve for such components, for example, as semiconductors.

Many electronic components commonly exhibit a high, but decreasing, failure rate early in their lives (as evidenced by the steep slope of the curve), followed by a period of a relatively constant failure rate, and ending with an increasing failure rate.

In Figure 12.11, three distinct time periods are evident: early failure (from 0 to about 1,000 hours), useful life (from 1,000 to 4,000 hours), and wearout period (after 4,000 hours). The first is the early failure period, sometimes called the **infant mortality period**. Weak components resulting from poor manufacturing or quality control procedures will often lead to a high rate of failure early in a product's life. This high rate usually cannot be detected through normal test procedures, particularly in electronic semiconductors. Such components or products should not be permitted to enter the marketplace. The second phase of the life characteristics curve describes the normal pattern of random failures during a product's useful life. This period usually has a low, relatively constant failure rate caused by uncontrollable factors, such as sudden and unexpected stresses due to complex interactions in materials or the environment. These factors are usually impossible to predict on an individual basis. However, the collective behavior of such failures can be modeled statistically. Finally, as age takes over, the wearout period begins, and the failure rate increases.

New car owners generally experience this phenomenon. During the first few months of ownership, owners may have to return their car to the dealer or remove the initial bugs caused by poor workmanship or manufacturing processes, such as wheel alignment or rattles. Such defects are monitored by J. D. Power's Initial Quality metrics of which you are probably aware. During its prime lifetime, the car may have few failures; however, as parts begin to wear out, the number and rate of failures begin to increase until replacement becomes desirable.

Knowing the product life characteristics curve for a particular product helps engineers predict behavior and make decisions accordingly. For instance, if a manufacturer knows that the early failure period for a microprocessor is 600 hours, it can test the chip for 600 hours (or more) under actual or simulated operating conditions before releasing the chip to the market.

Figure 12.13 Cumulative Probability for Tire Mileage

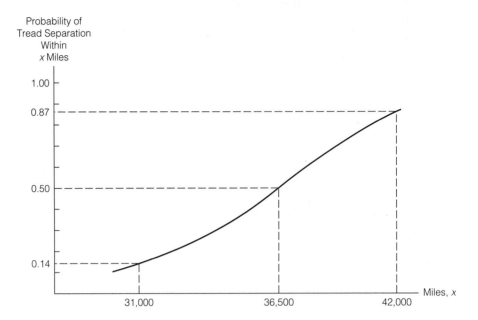

Knowledge of a product's reliability is also useful in developing warranties. As an illustration, consider a tire manufacturer who must determine a mileage warranty policy for a new line of tires. From engineering test data, the reliability curve shown in Figure 12.13 was constructed. This graph shows the probability of tread separation within a certain number of miles. Half the tires will fail by 36,500 miles, 87 percent will wear out by 42,000 miles, and only 14 percent will wear out by 31,000 miles. Thus, if a 31,000-mile warranty is established, management can compute the expected cost of replacing 14 percent of the tires. On the other hand, these data may indicate a poor design in relation to similar products of competitors. Design changes might be necessary to improve reliability. Note that in this example time is not measured chronologically, but in terms of product usage.

Mathematics of Reliability Reliability was defined earlier as the probability that an item will *not* fail over a given period of time. However, the probability distribution of failures is usually a more convenient figure to use in reliability computations. Recall that during the useful life of a product the failure rate is assumed to be constant. Thus, the fraction of good items that fail during any time period is constant. One can assume then that the probability of failure over time can be modeled mathematically by an exponential probability distribution. Not only is this model mathematically justified, but it has been empirically validated for many observable phenomena, such as failures of lightbulbs, electronic components, and repairable systems such as automobiles, computers, and industrial machinery.

If λ is the failure rate, the probability density function representing failures is given by the exponential density

$$f(t) = \lambda e^{-\lambda t} \quad t \geq 0$$

The probability of failing during a time interval (t_1, t_2) can be shown to be

$$e^{-\lambda(t_2 - t_1)}$$

Specifically, the probability of failure in the interval $(0, T)$ is given by the cumulative distribution function

$$F(T) = 1 - e^{-\lambda T}$$

Because reliability is the probability of *survival*, the **reliability function** is calculated as

$$R(T) = 1 - F(T) = e^{-\lambda T}$$

This function represents the probability that the item will not fail within T units of time.

Consider, for example, an item having a reliability of 0.97 for 100 hours of normal use. Determine the failure rate λ by solving the equation $R = e^{-\lambda T}$ for λ. Substituting $R = 0.97$ and $T = 100$ into this equation yields

$$0.97 = e^{-\lambda(100)}$$
$$\ln 0.97 = -100\lambda$$
$$\lambda = -(\ln 0.97)/100$$
$$= 0.0304/100$$
$$\approx 0.0003 \text{ failure per hour}$$

Thus, the reliability function is $R(T) = e^{-.0003T}$. The cumulative fraction of items that are expected to fail and survive after each 10-hour period may then be tabulated as given in Table 12.2. Note that the fraction failing in any 10-hour period is constant.

The reciprocal of the failure rate is often used in reliability computations. For non-repairable items, $\theta = 1/\lambda$ is defined as the *mean time to failure* (MTTF). Thus, in the preceding example for $\lambda = 0.0003$ failure per hour, $\theta = 1/.0003 = 3,333$ hours. That is,

Table 12.2 Cumulative Fraction Failing and Surviving

Time, T	Failures, F(T)	Survivors, R(T)
10	0.003	0.997
20	0.006	0.994
30	0.009	0.991
40	0.012	0.988
50	0.015	0.985
60	0.018	0.982
70	0.021	0.979
80	0.024	0.976
90	0.027	0.973
100	0.030	0.970

one failure can be expected every 3,333 hours on the average. The probability distribution function of failures and the reliability function can be equivalently expressed using the MTTF as

$$F(T) = 1 - e^{-T/\theta}$$

and

$$R(T) = e^{-T/\theta}$$

Suppose, for example, that an electronic component has a failure rate of $\lambda = 0.0001$ failure per hour. The MTTF is $\theta = 1/0.0001 = 10,000$ hours. The probability that the component will not fail in 15,000 hours is

$$R(15,000) = e^{-15,000/10,000}$$
$$= e^{-1.5}$$
$$= 0.223$$

For repairable items, θ is usually called the *mean time between failures* (MTBF). For example, suppose that a machine is operated for 10,000 hours and experiences four failures that are immediately repaired. The mean time between failures is

$$MTBF = 10,000/4 = 2,500 \text{ hours}$$

and the failure rate is

$$\lambda = 1/2,500 = 0.0004 \text{ failure per hour}$$

Predicting System Reliability Many systems are composed of individual components with known reliabilities. The reliability data of individual components can be used to predict the reliability of the system at the design stage. Systems of components may be configured in *series*, in *parallel*, or in some mixed combination. Block diagrams are useful ways to represent system configurations where blocks represent functional components or subsystems.

We first consider a **series system,** illustrated in Figure 12.14. In such a system, all components must function or the system will fail. If the reliability of component i is R_i, the reliability of the system is the product of the individual reliabilities, that is

$$R_S = R_1 R_2 \ldots R_n$$

This equation is based on the multiplicative law of probability. For example, suppose that a personal computer system is composed of the processing unit, modem, and printer with reliabilities of 0.997, 0.980, and 0.975, respectively. The reliability of the system is therefore given by

$$R_S = (0.997)(0.980)(0.975) = 0.953$$

Note that when reliabilities are less than one, system reliability decreases as additional components are added in series. Thus, the more complex a series system is, the greater the chance of failure.

Figure 12.14 Series System

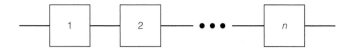

If the reliability function is exponential, for example, $R_i = e^{-\lambda_i T}$, then

$$
\begin{aligned}
R_S &= e^{-\lambda_1 T} e^{-\lambda_2 T} \cdots e^{-\lambda_n T} \\
&= e^{-\lambda_1 T - \lambda_2 T \ldots - \lambda_n T} \\
&= e^{-\left(\sum_{i=1}^{n} \lambda_i\right) T}
\end{aligned}
$$

Suppose that a two-component series system has failure rates of 0.004 and 0.001 per hour. Then

$$
\begin{aligned}
R_S(T) &= e^{-(0.004 + 0.001)T} \\
&= e^{-0.005T}
\end{aligned}
$$

The probability of survival for 100 hours would be

$$
\begin{aligned}
R_S(100) &= e^{-0.005(100)} \\
&= e^{-0.5} \\
&= 0.6065
\end{aligned}
$$

A parallel system is illustrated in Figure 12.15. In such a system, failure of an individual component is less critical than in series systems; the system will successfully operate as long as one component functions. Hence, the additional components are *redundant*. Redundancy is often built into systems to improve their reliability. However, as mentioned earlier, trade-offs in cost, size, weight, and so on must be taken into account.

The reliability of the parallel system in Figure 12.15 is derived as follows. If R_1, R_2, . . . , R_n are the reliabilities of the individual components, the probabilities of failure are $1 - R_1, 1 - R_2, \ldots, 1 - R_n$, respectively. Because the system fails only if each component fails, the probability of system failure is

$$(1 - R_1)(1 - R_2) \ldots (1 - R_n)$$

Hence, the system reliability is computed as

$$R_S = 1 - (1 - R_1)(1 - R_2) \ldots (1 - R_n)$$

If all components have identical reliabilities R, then

$$R_S = 1 - (1 - R)^n$$

Figure 12.15 Parallel System

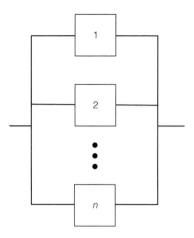

The computers on the space shuttle were designed with built-in redundancy in case of failure. Five computers were designed in parallel. Thus, for example, if the reliability of each is 0.99, the system reliability is

$$R_S = 1 - (1 - 0.99)^5 = 0.9999999999$$

Most systems are composed of combinations of series and parallel systems. Consider the system shown in Figure 12.16(a). To determine the reliability of such a system, first compute the reliability of the parallel subsystem B:

$$R_B = 1 - (1 - 0.9)^3 = 0.999$$

This level of reliability is equivalent to replacing the three parallel components B with a single component B having a reliability of 0.999 in series with A, C, and D, as shown in Figure 12.16(b). Next, compute the reliability of the equivalent series system:

$$R_S = (0.99)(0.999)(0.96)(0.98) = 0.93$$

A second type of series-parallel arrangement is shown in Figure 12.17(a). System reliability is determined by first computing the reliability of the series systems ABC and DE:

$$R_{ABC} = (0.95)(0.98)(0.99) = 0.92169$$

$$R_{DE} = (0.99)(0.97) = 0.9603$$

The result is an equivalent parallel system shown in Figure 12.17(b). The system reliability is then computed as

$$R_S = 1 - (1 - 0.92169)(1 - 0.9603) = 0.9969$$

Figure 12.16 Series-Parallel System and Equivalent Parallel System Example 1

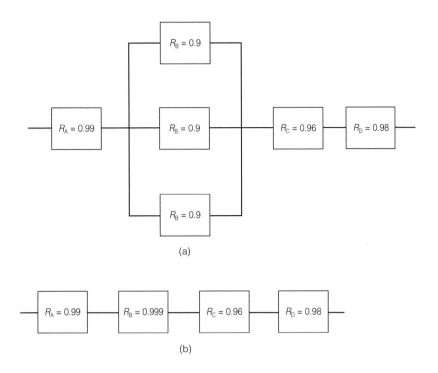

(a)

(b)

Figure 12.17 Series-Parallel System and Equivalent Parallel System Example 2

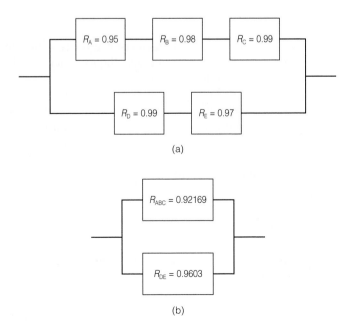

(a)

(b)

By appropriately decomposing complex systems into series and/or parallel components as shown in these examples, the system reliability can be easily computed. Reliability requirements are determined during the product design phase. The designer may use these techniques to determine the effects of adding redundancy, substituting different components, or reconfiguring the design.

TOOLS FOR DESIGN OPTIMIZATION

Designers of products and processes should make every effort to *optimize* their designs. A good analogy for understanding this concept is to consider the task of a major league baseball manager who must design the best player lineup. Although variation will be a factor among individuals as well as with the opposing team's defense, the manager would like to set the lineup that best plays to their strengths and overcomes their weaknesses. Some of the more useful approaches for accomplishing robust design are design of experiments, which we discussed in Chapter 11, and the Taguchi loss function, which we present next. We will also discuss some approaches for optimizing reliability.

> *Design optimization includes setting proper tolerances to ensure maximum product performance and making designs **robust**, that is, insensitive to variations in manufacturing or the use environment.*

The Taguchi Loss Function

A scientific approach to tolerance design uses the **Taguchi loss function**, the concept of which was introduced in Chapter 3. Recall that, as opposed to "goalpost" specifications, Taguchi suggests that no strict cut-off point divides good quality from poor quality. Rather, Taguchi assumes that losses can be approximated by a quadratic function so that larger deviations from target correspond to increasingly larger losses. For the case in which a specific target value, T, is determined to produce the optimum performance, and in which quality deteriorates as the actual value moves away from the target on either side (called "nominal is best"), the loss function is represented by

$$L(x) = k(x - T)^2$$

where x is any actual value of the quality characteristic and k is some constant. Thus, $(x - T)$ represents the deviation from the target, and the loss increases by the square of the deviation. Figure 12.18 illustrates this function.

The constant k is estimated by determining the cost associated with a certain deviation from the target, as the following example illustrates. Assume that a certain quality characteristic has a specification of 0.500 ± 0.020. An analysis of company records reveals that if the value of the quality characteristic exceeds the target of 0.500 by the tolerance of 0.020 on either side, the product is likely to require an adjustment during the warranty period and cost $50 for repair. Then,

$$50 = k(0.020)^2$$

$$k = 50/0.0004 = 125,000$$

Therefore, the loss function is

$$L(x) = 125,000(x - T)^2$$

Figure 12.18 Nominal-Is-Best Loss Function

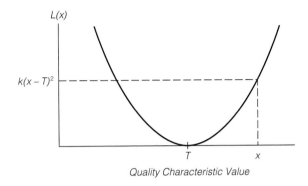

Thus, if the deviation is only 0.010, the estimated loss is

$L(0.010) = 125,000(0.010)^2 = \$12.50$

If the distribution of the variation about the target value is known, the average loss per unit can be computed by statistically averaging the loss associated with possible values of the quality characteristic. In statistical terminology, this average loss per unit is simply the expected value of the loss. To keep the mathematics simple, consider the following example.

Suppose that two processes, A and B, have the following distributions of a quality characteristic with specification 0.50 ± 0.02. In process A, the output of the process has values ranging from 0.48 to 0.52, all of which are equally likely. For process B, 60 percent of the output is expected to have a value of 0.50, 15 percent has a value of 0.49, and so

Value	Process A Probability	Process B Probability
0.47	0	0.02
0.48	0.20	0.03
0.49	0.20	0.15
0.50	0.20	0.60
0.51	0.20	0.15
0.52	0.20	0.03
0.53	0	0.02

Notice that the output from process A is spread equally over the range from 0.48 to 0.52 and lies entirely within specifications. In process B, output is concentrated near the target value, but does not entirely lie within specifications. Using the loss function

$L(x) = 125,000(x - 0.50)^2$

the expected loss for each process can be computed as follows:

Value, x	Loss	Process A Probability	Weighted Loss	Process B Probability	Weighted Loss
0.47	112.5	0.00	0	0.02	2.25
0.48	50.0	0.20	10	0.03	1.50
0.49	12.5	0.20	2.5	0.15	1.875
0.50	0.0	0.20	0	0.60	0
0.51	12.5	0.20	2.5	0.15	1.875
0.52	50.0	0.20	10	0.03	1.50
0.53	112.5	0.00	0	0.02	2.25
		Expected loss	25.0		11.25

Clearly process B incurs a smaller total expected loss even though some output falls outside specifications.

The expected loss is computed using a simple formula that involves the variance of the quality characteristic, σ^2, and the square of the deviation of the mean value from the target $D^2 = (\bar{x} - T)^2$. The expected loss is

$$EL(x) = k(\sigma^2 + D^2)$$

For instance, in process A, the variance of the quality characteristic is 0.0002 and $D^2 = 0$ because the mean value is equal to the target. Thus,

$$EL(x) = 125{,}000(0.0002 + 0) = 25$$

A similar computation can be used to determine the expected loss for process B.

To relate this calculation to the Sony television example cited in Chapter 3, k was determined to be 0.16. Because the mean of both distributions of color density fell on the target value, $D^2 = 0$ for both the U.S. and the Japanese plants. However, the variance of the distributions differed. For the San Diego plant, $\sigma^2 = 8.33$ and for the Japanese plant, $\sigma^2 = 2.78$. Thus the average loss per unit was computed to be

San Diego plant: 0.16(8.33) = $1.33

Japanese plant: 0.16(2.78) = $0.44

or a difference of $0.89 per unit.

The expected loss provides a measure of variation that is independent of specification limits. Such a measure stresses continuous improvement rather than acceptance of the status quo simply because a product "conforms to specifications."

Not all quality characteristics have nominal targets with tolerances on either side. In some cases, such as impurities in a chemical process or fuel consumption, "smaller is better." In other cases, "larger is better" as with breaking strength or product life. The loss function for the smaller-is-better case is

$$L(x) = kx^2$$

and for the larger-is-better case is

$$L(x) = k(1/x^2)$$

These formulas can be applied in a manner similar to the previous examples. The following example shows how the Taguchi loss function may be used to set tolerances. The desired speed of a cassette tape is 1.875 inches per second. Any deviation from this value causes a change in pitch and tempo and thus poor sound quality. Suppose that adjusting the tape speed under warranty when a customer complains and returns a cassette player costs a manufacturer $20. (This repair expense does not include other costs due to customer dissatisfaction and therefore is at best a lower bound on the actual loss.) Based on past information, the company knows the average customer will return a player if the tape speed is off the target by at least 0.15 inch per second. The loss function constant is computed as

$$20 = k(0.15)^2$$
$$k = 888.9$$

and thus the loss function is

$$L(x) = 888.9(x - 1.875)^2$$

At the factory, the adjustment can be made at a much lower cost of $3, which consists of the labor to make the adjustment and additional testing. What should the tolerance be before an adjustment is made at the factory?

To use the loss function, set $L(x) = \$3$ and solve for the tolerance:

$$3 = 888.9 \text{ (one-half tolerance)}^2$$

$$\text{tolerance} = \pm \sqrt{3/888.9} = \pm 0.058$$

Therefore, if the tape speed is off by more than 0.058 inches per second, adjusting it at the factory is more economical. Thus, the specifications should be 1.875 ± 0.058 or 1.817 to 1.933.

Optimizing Reliability

Many techniques are used to optimize the reliability of products. These include:

- *Standardization.* One method of ensuring high reliability is to use components with proven track records of reliability over years of actual use. If failure rates of components can be established, then standard components can be selected and used in the design process. The use of standardized components not only achieves higher reliability, but also reduces costs because standardized components are used in many different products.
- *Redundancy.* Redundancy provides backup components that can be used when the failure of any one component in a system can cause a failure of the entire system. The section on reliability prediction provided examples of how redundant components can increase reliability dramatically. Redundant components are designed either in a standby configuration or a parallel configuration. In a *standby system,* the standby unit is switched in when the operating unit fails; in the *parallel configuration,* both units operate normally but only one is required for proper functioning. Redundancy is crucial to systems in which failures can be extremely costly, such as aircraft or satellite communications systems. Redundancy, however, increases the cost, size, and weight of the system. Therefore, designers must trade off these attributes against increased reliability.

- *Physics of failure.* Many failures are due to deterioration because of chemical reactions over time, which may be aggravated by temperature or humidity effects. Understanding the physical properties of materials and their response to environmental effects helps to eliminate potential failures or to make the product robust with respect to environmental conditions that affect reliability. Reliability engineers must work closely with chemists, materials science engineers, and others who can contribute to a better understanding of failure mechanisms.

TOOLS FOR DESIGN VERIFICATION

The final phase of DFSS is verification of product and process designs. Sometimes verification is required by government regulation or for legal concerns. For products, reliability evaluation provides a means for obtaining data about product performance as both a verification approach and a means for design improvement. Verifying measurement systems and the capability of processes to meet specifications are also important in achieving Six Sigma performance. We introduce these approaches in this section.

> *Design verification is necessary to ensure that designs will meet customer requirements and can be produced to specifications.*

Reliability Testing

The reliability of a product is determined principally by the design and the reliability of the components of the product. However, reliability is such a complex issue that it cannot always be determined from theoretical analysis of the design alone. Hence, formal testing is necessary, which involves simulating environmental conditions to determine a product's performance, operating time, and mode of failure.

Testing is useful for a variety of other reasons. Test data are often necessary for liability protection, as means for evaluating designs or vendor reliability, and in process planning and selection. Often, reliability test data are required in military contracts. Testing is necessary to evaluate warranties and to avoid high costs related to early field failure. Good testing leads to good reliability and hence good quality.

Product testing is performed by various methods. The purpose of *life testing*, that is, running devices until they fail, is to measure the distribution of failures to better understand and eliminate their causes. However, such testing can be expensive and time-consuming. For devices that have long natural lives, life testing is not practical. **Accelerated life testing** involves overstressing components to reduce the time to failure and find weaknesses. This form of testing might involve running a motor faster than typically found in normal operating conditions. However, failure rates must correlate well to actual operating conditions if accelerated life testing is to be useful. Other testing studies the robustness of products. For example, one company performed a variety of tests on its computers. Products were disassembled and destructive testing was performed on the electromechanical, mechanical, and physical properties of components. *Environmental testing* consisted of varying the temperature from –40°F (the temperature inside trucks in the northern United States and Canada) to 165°F (the temperature inside trucks in the southwestern United States) to shock the product to see whether it could withstand extremes. Because old wiring exhibits a wide range of variation, AC power was varied from 105 to 135 volts. *Vibration and shock testing* were used to simulate trucks driving from the East to the West Coast to determine the product's ability to withstand rough handling and accidents.

Semiconductors are the basic building blocks of numerous modern products such as DVD players, automotive ignition systems, computers, and military weapons systems.

Semiconductors have a small proportion of defects, called *latent defects*, that can cause them to fail during the first 1,000 hours of normal operation. After that, the failure rate stabilizes, perhaps for as long as 25 years, before beginning to rise again as components wear out. These infant mortalities can be as high as 10 percent in a new technology or as low as 0.01 percent in proven technologies. The sooner a faulty component is detected, the cheaper is its replacement or repair. A correction on an integrated circuit fabrication line costs about 50 cents; at the board level it might cost $5; at the system level about $50; and in the field, $500. If a printed circuit board contains 100 semiconductors, a failure rate of 0.01 percent would cause a board failure rate of 1 percent.

Burn-in, or *component stress testing*, involves exposing integrated circuits to elevated temperatures in order to force latent defects to occur. For example, a device that might normally fail after 300 hours at 25°C might fail in less than 20 hours at 150°C. Survivors are likely to have long, trouble-free operating lives. Studies and experience have demonstrated the economic advantages of burn-in. For example, a large-scale study of the effect of burn-in on enhancing reliability of dynamic MOS memories was conducted in Europe. The failure rate without burn-in conditioning and testing to eliminate infant mortality was 0.24 percent per thousand hours, while burn-in and testing reduced the rate to 0.02 percent per thousand hours. When considering the cost of field service and warranty work, for instance, reduction of semiconductor failure rates in a large system by an order of magnitude translates roughly into an average of one repair call per year versus one repair call per month. Because burn-in requires considerable time—48 to 96 hours is common—designers attempt to produce equipment that can perform some functional tests during the burn-in cycle rather than after. Modern systems exist to test and burn-in integrated circuits. One system has the capacity of 18,000 DRAMs (dynamic random access memory) per load and is flexible in its burn-in and test procedures to accommodate future types without modification of the hardware. The system can accumulate and display information on the devices under test, both for real-time evaluation and for lot documentation.

Measurement System Evaluation

Accurately assessing Six Sigma performance depends on reliable measurement systems. Measuring quality characteristics generally requires the use of the human senses—seeing, hearing, feeling, tasting, and smelling—and the use of some type of instrument or gauge to measure the magnitude of the characteristic. Common types of measuring instruments used in manufacturing today fall into two categories: low-technology and high-technology. Low-technology instruments are primarily manual devices that have been available for many years; high-technology instruments describe those that depend on modern electronics, microprocessors, lasers, or advanced optics. The Bonus Materials folder for this chapter on the CD-ROM contains a discussion and some pictures of various types of measuring instruments.

Metrology Gauges and instruments used to measure quality characteristics must provide correct information, which is assured through **metrology**—the science of measurement. Originally, metrology only measured the physical attributes of an object. Today, metrology is defined broadly as the collection of people, equipment, facilities, methods, and procedures used to assure the correctness or adequacy of measurements, and is a vital part of global competitiveness. In testifying before the U.S. Congress, the director of the Office of Standards Services at the National Institute of Standards and Technology noted that efficient national and international trade requires weights and measures organizations that assure uniform and accurate measures used in trade, national or regional measurement standards laboratories, standards development organizations, and accredited and internationally recognized calibration and testing laboratories.[9]

The need for metrology stems from the fact that every measurement is subject to error. The evaluation of data obtained from inspection and measurement is not meaningful unless the measurement instruments are accurate, precise, and reproducible.

Whenever variation is observed in measurements, some portion is due to measurement system error. Some errors are systematic (called bias); others are random. The size of the errors relative to the measurement value can significantly affect the quality of the data and resulting decisions.

Accuracy is defined as the closeness of agreement between an observed value and an accepted reference value or standard. The lack of accuracy reflects a systematic bias in the measurement such as a gauge out of calibration, worn, or used improperly by the operator. Accuracy is measured as the amount of error in a measurement in proportion to the total size of the measurement. One measurement is more accurate than another if it has a smaller relative error.

Precision is defined as the closeness of agreement between randomly selected individual measurements or results. Precision, therefore, relates to the variance of repeated measurements. A measuring instrument with a low variance is more precise than another having a higher variance. Low precision is due to random variation that is built into the instrument, such as friction among its parts. This random variation may be the result of a poor design or lack of maintenance.

For example, suppose that two instruments measure a dimension whose true value is 0.250 inch. Instrument A may read 0.248 inch, while instrument B may read 0.259 inch. The relative error of instrument A is $(0.250 - 0.248)/0.250 = 0.8\%$; the relative error of instrument B is $(0.259 - 0.250)/0.250 = 3.6\%$. Thus, instrument A is said to be more accurate than instrument B. Now suppose that each instrument measures the dimension three times. Instrument A records values of 0.248, 0.246, and 0.251; instrument B records values of 0.259, 0.258, and 0.259. Instrument B is more precise than instrument A because its values are clustered closer together.

A measurement system may be precise but not necessarily accurate at the same time. The relationships between accuracy and precision are summarized in Figure 12.19. The figure illustrates four possible frequency distributions of 10 repeated measurements of some quality characteristic. In Figure 12.19 (a), the average measurement is not close to the true value. Moreover, a wide range of values fall around the average. In this case, the measurement is neither accurate nor precise. In Figure 12.19 (b), even though the average measurement is not close to the true value, the range of variation is small. Thus, the measurement is precise but not accurate. In Figures 12.19(c) and (d), the average value is close to the true value—that is, the measurement is accurate—but in 12.19 (c) the distribution is widely dispersed and therefore not precise, while the measurement in 12.19 (d) is both accurate and precise. Thus, Figure 12.19 demonstrates the vital nature of properly calibrating and maintaining all instruments used for quality measurements.

When a technician measures the same unit multiple times, the results will usually show some variability. **Repeatability**, or **equipment variation**, is the variation in multiple measurements by an individual using the same instrument. This measure indicates how precise and accurate the equipment is. **Reproducibility**, or **operator variation**, is the variation in the same measuring instrument when it is used by different individuals to measure the same parts, and indicates how robust the measuring process is to the operator and environmental conditions. Causes of poor

Figure 12.19 Accuracy versus Precision

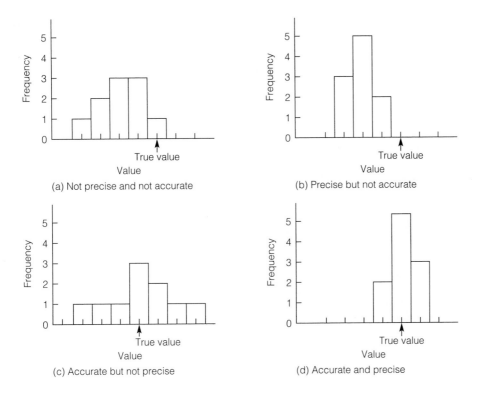

(a) Not precise and not accurate

(b) Precise but not accurate

(c) Accurate but not precise

(d) Accurate and precise

reproducibility might be poor training of the operators in the use of the instrument or unclear calibrations on the gauge dial. Statistical approaches can be used to quantify and evaluate equipment and operator variation.

The importance of measurement analysis is summed up by the following equation:

$$\sigma^2_{total} = \sigma^2_{process} + \sigma^2_{measurement}$$

which states that the total observed variation in production output is the sum of the true process variation (which is what we actually want to measure) plus variation due to measurement. If the measurement variation is high, the observed results will be biased, and process capability measurements, for example, may look worse than they actually are. Thus, an objective of quality control is to reduce measurement error as much as possible.

Measurement System Evaluation and Verification The accuracy, repeatability, and reproducibility of any measurement system must be quantified and evaluated. Accuracy can be measured by comparing the observed average of a set of measurements to the true value of a reference standard. Repeatability and reproducibility require a study of variation and can be addressed through statistical analysis. A repeatability and reproducibility study is conducted in the following manner.[10]

1. Select m operators and n parts. Typically at least 2 operators and 10 parts are chosen. Number the parts so that the numbers are not visible to the operators.
2. Calibrate the measuring instrument.
3. Let each operator measure each part in a random order and record the results. Repeat this procedure for a total of r trials. At least two trials must be used. Let M_{ijk} represent the kth measurement of operator i on part j.
4. Compute the average measurement for each operator:

$$\bar{x}_i = \left(\sum_j \sum_k M_{ijk} \right) / nr$$

The difference between the largest and smallest average is

$$\bar{x}_D = \max_i \{\bar{x}_i\} - \min_i \{\bar{x}_i\}$$

5. Compute the range for each part and each operator:

$$R_{ij} = \max_k \{M_{ijk}\} - \min_k \{M_{ijk}\}$$

These values show the variability of repeated measurements of the same part by the same operator. Next, compute the average range for each operator:

$$\bar{R}_i = \left(\sum_j R_{ij} \right) / n$$

The overall average range is then computed as

$$\bar{\bar{R}} = \left(\sum_i \bar{R}_i \right) / m$$

6. Calculate a "control limit" on the individual ranges R_{ij}:

$$\text{control limit} = D_4 \bar{\bar{R}}$$

where D_4 is a constant that depends on the sample size (number of trials, r) and can be found in Appendix B at the end of this book. Any range value beyond this limit might result from some assignable cause, not random error. Possible causes should be investigated and, if found, corrected. The operator should repeat these measurements using the same part. If no assignable cause is found, these values should be discarded and all statistics in step 5 as well as the control limit should be recalculated.

Once these basic calculations are made, an analysis of repeatability and reproducibility can be performed. The repeatability, or equipment variation (EV) is computed as

$$EV = K_1 \bar{\bar{R}}$$

Reproducibility, or operator (or appraisal) variation (AV) is computed as

$$AV = \sqrt{(K_2 \bar{x}_D)^2 - (EV^2/nr)}$$

The constants K_1 and K_2 depend on the number of trials and number of operators, respectively. Some values of these constants are given in Table 12.3. These constants provide a 99 percent confidence interval on these statistics.

An overall measure of repeatability and reproducibility (R&R) is given by

$$R\&R = \sqrt{(EV)^2 + (AV)^2}$$

Repeatability and reproducibility are often expressed as a percentage of the tolerance of the quality characteristic being measured. The American Society for Quality suggests the following guidelines for evaluating these measures of repeatability and reproducibility:

- Under 10% error: This rate is acceptable.
- 10 to 30% error: This rate may be acceptable based on the importance of the application, cost of the instrument, cost of repair, and so on.
- Over 30% error: Generally, this rate is not acceptable. Every effort should be made to identify the problem and correct it.

To illustrate a gauge repeatability and reproducibility study, suppose that a gauge used to measure the thickness of a gasket having a specification of 0.50 to 1.0 mm is to be evaluated. Ten parts have been selected for measurement by three operators. Each part is measured twice with the results as shown in the spreadsheet in Figure 12.20. (Slight rounding differences from manual calculations may be evident.)

The average measurement for each operator, $\bar{x}_i$, is

$$\bar{x}_1 = 0.830 \qquad \bar{x}_2 = 0.774 \qquad \bar{x}_3 = 0.829$$

Thus, $\bar{x}_D = 0.830 - 0.774 = 0.056$. The average range for each operator is

$$\bar{R}_1 = 0.037 \qquad \bar{R}_2 = 0.034 \qquad \bar{R}_3 = 0.017$$

The overall average range is $\bar{\bar{R}} = (0.037 + 0.034 + 0.017)/3 = 0.0293$. From Appendix B at the end of the book, $D_4 = 3.267$ because the two trials were conducted. Hence the control limit is $(3.267)(0.0293) = 0.096$. Because all range values fall below this limit, no assignable causes of variation are suspected. Compute the repeatability and reproducibility measures:

Table 12.3 Values of K_1 and K_2

Number of Trials	2	3	4	5
K_1	4.56	3.05	2.50	2.21
Number of Operators	2	3	4	5
K_2	3.65	2.70	2.30	2.08

$$\text{EV} \;=\; (4.56)(0.0293) = 0.134$$

$$\text{AV} \;=\; \sqrt{[(0.056)(2.70)]^2 - (0.134)^2/(10)(2)} = 0.147$$

$$\text{R\&R} \;=\; \sqrt{(0.134)^2 + (0.147)^2} = 0.199$$

If the tolerance of the gasket is $1.00 - 0.50 = 0.50$, these measures expressed as a percent of tolerance are:

Equipment variation $= 100(0.134)/0.50 = 26.8\%$

Operator variation $= 100(0.147)/0.50 = 29.4\%$

Total $R\&R$ variation $= 100(0.199)/0.50 = 39.8\%$

Even though individually the equipment and operator variation may be acceptable, their combined effect is not. Efforts should be made to reduce the variation to an acceptable level.

Figure 12.20 Spreadsheet for Repeatability and Reproducibility Analysis (R&R.XLS)

	A	B	C	D	E	F	G	H	I	J	K	L	M	N
1	**Gauge Repeatability and Reproducibility**													
2	This spreadsheet is designed for up to three operators, three trials, and ten samples. Enter data ONLY in yellow shaded cells.													
3														
4	**Number of operators**				3		**Upper specification limit**			1				
5	**Number of trials**				2		**Lower specification limit**			0.5				
6	**Number of samples**				10									
7														
8	Data		**Operator 1**				**Operator 2**				**Operator 3**			
9			**Trial**				**Trial**				**Trial**			
10	Sample #	**1**	**2**	**3**	Range	**1**	**2**	**3**	Range	**1**	**2**	**3**	Range	
11	1	0.630	0.590		0.040	0.560	0.560		0.000	0.510	0.540		0.030	
12	2	1.000	1.000		0.000	1.040	0.960		0.080	1.050	1.010		0.040	
13	3	0.830	0.770		0.060	0.800	0.760		0.040	0.810	0.810		0.000	
14	4	0.860	0.940		0.080	0.820	0.780		0.040	0.810	0.810		0.000	
15	5	0.590	0.510		0.080	0.430	0.430		0.000	0.460	0.490		0.030	
16	6	0.980	0.980		0.000	1.000	1.040		0.040	1.040	1.000		0.040	
17	7	0.960	0.960		0.000	0.940	0.900		0.040	0.950	0.950		0.000	
18	8	0.860	0.830		0.030	0.720	0.740		0.020	0.810	0.810		0.000	
19	9	0.970	0.970		0.000	0.980	0.940		0.040	1.030	1.030		0.000	
20	10	0.640	0.720		0.080	0.560	0.520		0.040	0.840	0.810		0.030	
21	Range average				0.037				0.034				0.017	
22	Sample average				0.830				0.774				0.829	
23														
24												Tolerance analysis		
25	Average range	0.029				Repeatability (EV)				0.134		26.75%		
26	X-bar range	0.056				Reproducibility (AV)				0.147		29.37%		
27					Repeatability and Reproducibility (R&R)					0.199		39.73%		
28					Control limit for individual ranges					0.096				
29					Note: any ranges beyond this limit may be the result									
30					of assignable causes. Identify and correct. Discard									
31					values and recompute statistics.									

*One of the most important functions of metrology is **calibration**—the comparison of a measurement device or system having a known relationship to national standards against another device or system whose relationship to national standards is unknown.*

Calibration Measurements made using uncalibrated or inadequately calibrated equipment can lead to erroneous and costly decisions. For example, suppose that an inspector has a micrometer that is reading 0.002 inch too low. When measurements are made close to the upper limit, parts that are as much as 0.002 inch over the maximum tolerance limit will be accepted as good, while those at the lower tolerance limit or that are as much as 0.002 inch above the limit will be rejected as nonconforming. A typical calibration system involves the following activities:

- Evaluation of equipment to determine its capability
- Identification of calibration requirements
- Selection of standards to perform the calibration
- Selection of methods and procedures to perform the calibration
- Establishment of calibration frequency and rules for adjusting this frequency
- Establishment of a system to ensure that instruments are calibrated according to schedule
- Implementation of a documentation and reporting system
- Evaluation of the calibration system through an established auditing process

The National Institute of Standards and Technology (NIST) maintains national measurement standards, and provides technical advice on making measurements consistent with national standards. NIST works with various metrology laboratories in industry and government to assure that measurements made by different people in different places yield the same results. Thus, the measurement of "voltage" or "resistance" in an electrical component has a precise and universal meaning. This process is accomplished in a hierarchical fashion. NIST calibrates the reference-level standards of those organizations requiring the highest level of accuracy. These organizations calibrate their own working-level standards and those of other metrology laboratories. These working-level standards are used to calibrate the measuring instruments used in the field. The usual recommendation is that equipment be calibrated against working-level standards that are 10 times as accurate as the equipment. When possible, at least a four-to-one accuracy ratio between the reference and working-level standards is desired; that is, the reference standards should be at least four times as accurate as the working-level standards.

Many government regulations and commercial contracts require regulated organizations or contractors to verify that the measurements they make are *traceable* to a reference standard. For example, world standards exist for length, mass, and time. For other types of measurement, such as chemical measurements, industry standards exist. Organizations must be able to support the claim of traceability by keeping records that their own measuring equipment has been calibrated by laboratories or testing facilities whose measurements can be related to appropriate standards, generally national or international standards, through an unbroken chain of comparison.[11] The purpose of requiring traceability is to ensure that measurements are accurate representations of the specific quantity subject to measurement, within the uncertainty of the measurement. Not only should there be an unbroken chain of comparisons, each measurement should be accompanied by a statement of uncertainty associated with the farthest link in the chain from NIST, that is, the last facility providing the measurement value. This accountability can be assured by purchasing an instrument that is certified against a higher level (traceable) standard, or contracting with a calibration agency that has such standards to certify the instrument.

Process Capability Evaluation

Process capability is important to both product designers and manufacturing engineers, and is critical to achieving Six Sigma performance. Knowing process capability allows one to predict, quantitatively, how well a process will meet specifications and to specify equipment require-

> *Process capability* is the range over which the natural variation of a process occurs as determined by the system of common causes, that is, what the process can achieve under stable conditions.

ments and the level of control necessary. For example, suppose that the inside diameter of a bushing that supports a steel shaft must be between 1.498 and 1.510 inches for an acceptable fit. If the diameter is too small, it can be enlarged through a rework process. However if it is too large, the part must be scrapped. If the variation in the machining process results in diameters that typically range from 1.495 and 1.515 inches, we would say that the process is not capable of meeting the specifications. Management then faces three possible decisions: (1) measure each piece and either rework or scrap nonconforming parts, (2) develop a better process by investing in new technology, or (3) change the design specifications.

Unfortunately, product design often takes place in isolation, with inexperienced designers applying tolerances to parts or products while having little awareness of the capabilities of the production process to meet these design requirements. Even experienced designers may be hard-pressed to remain up-to-date on the capabilities of processes that involve constant equipment changes, shifting technology, and difficult-to-measure variations in methods at scores of plants located hundreds or thousands of miles away from a centralized product design department. Process capability should be carefully considered in determining design specifications in a DFSS environment.

Process Capability Studies A **process capability study** is a carefully planned study designed to yield specific information about the performance of a process under specified operating conditions. Typical questions that are asked in a process capability study include the following:

- Where is the process centered?
- How much variability exists in the process?
- Is the performance relative to specifications acceptable?
- What proportion of output will be expected to meet specifications?
- What factors contribute to variability?

Many reasons exist for conducting a capability study. Manufacturing may wish to determine a performance baseline for a process, to prioritize projects for quality improvement, or to provide statistical evidence of quality for customers. Purchasing might conduct a study at a supplier plant to evaluate a new piece of equipment or to compare different suppliers. Engineering might conduct a study to determine the adequacy of R&D pilot facilities or to evaluate new processes.

Three types of studies are often conducted.

1. A *peak performance study* determines how a process performs under ideal conditions.
2. A *process characterization study* is designed to determine how a process performs under actual operating conditions.
3. A *component variability study* assesses the relative contribution of different sources of total variation.

The methods by which each study is conducted vary. A peak performance study is conducted under carefully controlled conditions over a short time interval to ensure that no special causes can affect variation. A process characterization study is performed over a longer time interval under actual operating conditions to capture the variations in materials and operators. A component variability study uses a designed experiment to control the sources of variability. Although this section considers a process characterization study, the general approach applies to a peak performance study with appropriate modifications.

The six steps in a process capability study are similar to those of any systematic study and include the following:

1. Choose a representative machine or segment of the process.
2. Define the process conditions.
3. Select a representative operator.
4. Provide materials that are of standard grade, with sufficient materials for uninterrupted study.
5. Specify the gauging or measurement method to be used.
6. Provide for a method of recording measurements and conditions, in order, on the units produced.

To obtain useful information, the sample size should be fairly large, generally at least 100. Process capability only makes sense if all special causes of variation have been eliminated and the process is in a state of statistical control (we will discuss this further in Chapter 14). For this discussion, we assume that the process is in control.

Two statistical techniques are commonly used to evaluate process capability. One is the frequency distribution and histogram, the other is the control chart. The use of frequency distributions and histograms is covered in this section, but the discussion of control charts is deferred to Chapter 14.

To illustrate the evaluation of process capability, let us consider the U-bolt data we used in Chapter 11 (Table 11.1). Using Microsoft Excel tools, we calculated the basic descriptive statistics for these data, and constructed a frequency distribution and histogram. These charts were shown in Figures 11.11 and 11.13. To recap, we saw that the mean dimension is $\bar{x} = 10.7171$, and the sample standard deviation $s = 0.0868$. The histogram suggests that the data are approximately normally distributed. Using this information, we can estimate the yield of conforming product for various manufacturing specifications analytically.

One of the properties of a normal distribution is that 99.73 percent of the observations will fall within three standard deviations from the mean. Thus, a process that is in control can be expected to produce a large percentage of output between $\mu - 3\sigma$ and $\mu + 3\sigma$, where μ is the process average. Therefore, the *natural tolerance limits* of the process are $\mu \pm 3\sigma$. A six standard deviation spread is commonly used as a measure of process capability. Thus, for the example, nearly all U-bolt dimensions are expected to fall between $10.7171 - 3(0.868) = 10.4566$ and $10.7171 + 3(0.0868) = 10.9766$. These calculations tell the production manager that if the design specifications are between 10.45 and 11.00, for instance, the process will be capable of producing nearly 100 percent conforming product.

Suppose, however, that design specifications are such that the dimension must lie between 10.55 and 10.90. Calculate the expected percentage of nonconforming U-bolts by computing the area under a normal distribution having a mean of 10.7171 and standard deviation 0.0868 to the left and right of these specifications, as illustrated in Figure 12.21. Converting 10.55 to a standard normal value yields $z = (10.55 - 10.7171)/0.0868 = -1.93$. Appendix A at the end of the book gives a value for the area to the *left* of $z = -1.93$ as $0.5000 - 0.4732 = 0.0268$. Similarly, the z value corresponding to 10.90 is $z = (10.90 - 10.7171)/0.0868 = 2.11$. The area to the *right* of $z = 2.11$ is $0.5000 - 0.4826 = 0.0174$. Therefore, the probability that a part will not meet specifications is

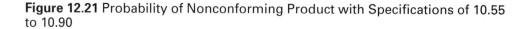

Figure 12.21 Probability of Nonconforming Product with Specifications of 10.55 to 10.90

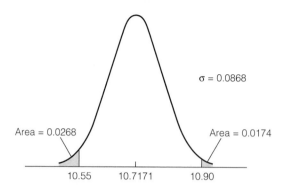

0.0268 + 0.0174 = 0.0442 or, expressed as a percentage, is 4.42 percent, which is only slightly better than a 2-sigma level. Similar computations can be used to estimate the percentage of nonconforming parts for other tolerances.

Not all process output will fit neatly into a normal curve; one can usually obtain important capability information directly from the histogram. Figure 12.22 shows some typical examples of process variation histograms that might result from a capability study. Figure 12.22(a) shows an ideal situation in which the natural variation is well within the specified tolerance limits. In Figure 12.22(b), the variation and tolerance limits are about equal; any shift of the distribution will result in nonconformances. The histogram in 12.22(c) shows a distribution with a natural variation greater than the specification limits; in this case, the process is not capable of meeting specifications. The histograms in Figures 12.22(d), (e), and (f) correspond to those in Figures 12.22(a), (b), and (c), except that the process is off-center from the specified tolerance limits. The capability of each is the same as in Figures 12.22(a), (b), and (c), but the shift in the mean of the distribution results in a higher level of nonconformance. Thus, in Figure 12.22(d), the process is capable; it is simply not adjusted correctly to the center of the specifications. In Figure 12.22(g), the bimodal shape suggests that perhaps the data were drawn from two different machines or that two different materials or products were involved. The small distribution to the right in Figure 12.22(h) may be the result of including pieces from a trial setup run while the machine was being adjusted. The strange distribution in Figure 12.22(i) might be the result of the measurement process, such as inadequate gauging or rounding of data, and not inherent in the process itself. Finally, the truncated distribution in Figure 12.22(j) is generally the result of sorting nonconforming parts; one would expect a smoother tail of the distribution on the left. Therefore, one must be careful to ensure that observed variation comes from the process itself, not from external influences. Thus, a good control system is a necessity, because a histogram alone will not provide complete information.

An important issue that is often ignored in process capability studies is the error resulting from using the sample standard deviation, s, rather than the true standard deviation, σ. A simple table can be constructed to find confidence intervals on the true value for σ for a given sample size. Such a table is shown in Table 12.4 and is easily explained by an example. For a given sample size, σ will be less than or equal to s

Figure 12.22 Examples of Process Variation Histograms and Specifications

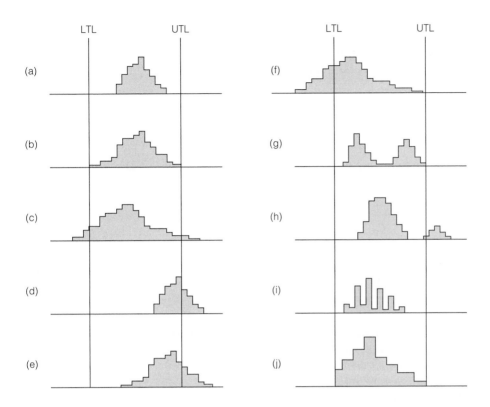

times the factor in that row with probability p, where p is the column heading. Thus, for a sample size of 30, $\sigma \leq 0.744s$ with probability 0.005; $\sigma \leq 1.280s$ occurs 95 percent of the time; and so on. A 90 percent confidence interval for σ can be found by using the factors in the columns corresponding to $p = 0.050$ and $p = 0.950$. Thus, for a sample size of 30, a 95 percent confidence interval would be (0.825s, 1.280s). The interpretation of process capability information should be tempered by such an analysis.

The process capability index, C_p (sometimes called the process potential index), is defined as the ratio of the specification width to the natural tolerance of the process. C_p relates the natural variation of the process with the design specifications in a single, quantitative measure.

Process Capability Indexes In Figure 12.22 we saw that the distribution of process output can differ in both location and spread relative to the specifications. The relationship between the natural variation and specifications is often quantified by a measure known as the **process capability index**.

In numerical terms, the formula is

$$C_p = \frac{UTL - LTL}{6\sigma}$$

where

UTL = upper tolerance limit

LTL = lower tolerance limit

σ = standard deviation of the process

The process capability index can be used for setting objectives and improving processes. Suppose that a quality manager in a firm has a process with a standard deviation of 1 and a tolerance spread of 8. The value of C_p for this situation is 1.33. The manager realizes that the natural spread is within specifications at this time, but new contracts call for increasing the value of the capability index. Targets are set for increasing the index to 1.66 within three months, to 2.00 within six months, and to 2.33 within a year. Given that the tolerance spread (UTL – LTL) is held at the previous level of 8, the following table shows the required process standard deviation for each phase of the project.

C_p	UTL – LTL	6σ	σ
1.33	8	6	1
1.66	8	4.8	0.8
2.00	8	4	0.67
2.33	8	3.43	0.57

Operationally, this task involves reducing the variability in the process from a standard deviation of 1.000 to 0.444, which results in the desired increase of C_p from the current level of 1.33 to the final level of 2.33, which might be accomplished using process improvement and technology upgrades.

Two important facts about the C_p index should be pointed out. One relates to process conditions and the other relates to interpretation of the values that have been calculated. First, the calculation of the C_p has no meaning if the process is not under statistical control. The natural spread (6σ) should be calculated using a sufficiently large sample to get a meaningful estimate of the population standard deviation (σ). Second, a C_p of 1.00 would require that the process be perfectly centered on the mean of the tolerance spread to prevent some units from being produced outside the limits. The goal of all units being produced within specifications with a C_p of 1.33 is much easier to achieve, and still easier with a C_p of 2.00. Based on the experience of a number of practitioners, they have suggested a "safe" lower limit C_p of 1.5. A value above this level will practically guarantee that all units produced by a controlled process will be within specifications. Many firms require C_p values of 1.66 or greater from their suppliers.

The previous discussion assumed that the process was centered; clearly the value of C_p does not depend on the mean of the process. To include information on process centering, one-sided indexes are often used. One-sided process capability indexes are as follows:

$$C_{pu} = \frac{\text{UTL} - \mu}{3\sigma} \quad \text{(upper one-sided index)}$$

$$C_{pl} = \frac{\mu - \text{LTL}}{3\sigma} \quad \text{(lower one-sided index)}$$

$$C_{pk} = \min(C_{pl}, C_{pu})$$

Table 12.4 Ratio of Population to Sample Standard Deviation

Number of Samples	Fraction of Population Less Than or Equal to Value in Table							
	0.005	0.010	0.025	0.050	0.100	0.950	0.975	0.995
2	0.356	0.388	0.446	0.510	0.608	15.952	31.911	159.516
3	0.434	0.466	0.521	0.578	0.659	4.407	6.287	14.142
4	0.483	0.514	0.567	0.620	0.693	2.919	3.727	6.468
5	0.519	0.549	0.599	0.649	0.717	2.372	2.875	4.396
6	0.546	0.576	0.624	0.672	0.736	2.090	2.453	3.484
7	0.569	0.597	0.644	0.690	0.751	1.918	2.202	2.979
8	0.588	0.616	0.661	0.705	0.763	1.797	2.035	2.660
9	0.604	0.631	0.675	0.718	0.774	1.711	1.916	2.440
10	0.618	0.645	0.688	0.729	0.783	1.645	1.826	2.278
11	0.630	0.656	0.699	0.739	0.791	1.593	1.755	2.154
12	0.641	0.667	0.708	0.748	0.798	1.551	1.698	2.056
13	0.651	0.677	0.717	0.755	0.804	1.515	1.651	1.976
14	0.660	0.685	0.725	0.762	0.810	1.485	1.611	1.910
15	0.669	0.693	0.732	0.769	0.815	1.460	1.577	1.854
16	0.676	0.700	0.739	0.775	0.820	1.437	1.548	1.806
17	0.683	0.707	0.745	0.780	0.824	1.418	1.522	1.764
18	0.690	0.713	0.750	0.785	0.828	1.400	1.499	1.727
19	0.696	0.719	0.756	0.790	0.832	1.385	1.479	1.695
20	0.702	0.725	0.760	0.794	0.836	1.370	1.461	1.666
21	0.707	0.730	0.765	0.798	0.839	1.358	1.444	1.640
22	0.712	0.734	0.769	0.802	0.842	1.346	1.429	1.617
23	0.717	0.739	0.773	0.805	0.845	1.335	1.415	1.595
24	0.722	0.743	0.777	0.809	0.848	1.325	1.403	1.576
25	0.726	0.747	0.781	0.812	0.850	1.316	1.391	1.558
26	0.730	0.751	0.784	0.815	0.853	1.308	1.380	1.542
27	0.734	0.755	0.788	0.818	0.855	1.300	1.370	1.526
28	0.737	0.758	0.791	0.820	0.857	1.293	1.361	1.512
29	0.741	0.762	0.794	0.823	0.859	1.286	1.352	1.499
30	0.744	0.765	0.796	0.825	0.861	1.280	1.344	1.487
31	0.748	0.768	0.799	0.828	0.863	1.274	1.337	1.475
36	0.762	0.781	0.811	0.838	0.872	1.248	1.304	1.427
41	0.774	0.792	0.821	0.847	0.879	1.228	1.280	1.390
46	0.784	0.802	0.829	0.854	0.885	1.212	1.260	1.361
51	0.793	0.810	0.837	0.861	0.890	1.199	1.243	1.337
61	0.808	0.824	0.849	0.871	0.898	1.179	1.217	1.299
71	0.820	0.835	0.858	0.879	0.905	1.163	1.198	1.272
81	0.829	0.844	0.866	0.886	0.910	1.151	1.183	1.250
91	0.838	0.852	0.873	0.892	0.915	1.141	1.171	1.233
101	0.845	0.858	0.879	0.897	0.919	1.133	1.161	1.219

Source: Thomas D. Hall, "How Close Is *s* to σ?" *Quality*, December 1991, 45. *Note:* The table published in this article was incorrect. An error notice was published in a subsequent issue and the correct table was made available by *Quality* magazine, and is shown here.

To illustrate these computations for the U-bolt example, we found a mean of 10.7171. Thus,

$$C_{pl} = \frac{10.7171 - 10.50}{3(.0868)} = .83$$

$$C_{pu} = \frac{11.0 - 10.7171}{3(.0868)} = 1.086$$

$$C_{pk} = \min\{.83, 1.086\} = .83$$

We see that the process is more capable of satisfying the upper specification limit than the lower specification limit. The low value of C_{pk} indicates that the worst case is unacceptable. This index is often used in specifying quality requirements in purchasing contracts. Figure 12.23 shows a spreadsheet, available on the CD-ROM accompanying this book, designed to compute these indexes.

We note that Six Sigma performance corresponds to process variation equal to half the design tolerance, or a C_p value of 2.0 (see Chapter 10, Figure 10.1). However, because Six Sigma allows a mean shift of up to 1.5 standard deviations from the target, C_{pk} must be held to 1.5.

Some controversy exists over C_p and C_{pk} as measures of process capability, particularly with respect to the economic loss function philosophy of Taguchi.[12] For example, a process may have a high C_{pk} even when its mean is off target and close to the specification limits, as long as the process spread is small.[13] Several alternative measures have been proposed and are discussed in one of the Bonus Materials documents for this chapter on the CD-ROM.

Figure 12.23 Spreadsheet for Process Capability Calculations (PROCESS_CAPABILITY.XLS)

	A	B	C	D	E	F	G	H	I	J	K	L	M	N	O	P
1	**Process Capability Analysis**															
2																
3	This spreadsheet is designed to handle up to 150 observations. Enter data ONLY in yellow-shaded cells.															
4																
5	Nominal specification				10.75		Average			10.7171			Cp	0.96		
6	Upper tolerance limit				11		Standard deviation			0.0868			Cpl	0.833		
7	Lower tolerance limit				10.5								Cpu	1.086		
8													Cpk	0.833		
9																
10	DATA	1	2	3	4	5	6	7	8	9	10	11	12	13	14	15
11	1	10.650	10.800	10.500	10.800	10.700	10.800	10.750	10.650	10.850	10.650	10.800	10.650			
12	2	10.750	10.850	10.800	10.800	10.700	10.700	10.850	10.700	10.800	10.550	10.700	10.850			
13	3	10.750	10.700	10.650	10.800	10.650	10.650	10.750	10.650	10.500	10.800	10.750	10.800			
14	4	10.600	10.650	10.650	10.700	10.600	10.750	10.800	10.850	10.650	10.650	10.700	10.600			
15	5	10.700	10.750	10.700	10.750	10.550	10.700	10.850	10.700	10.750	10.600	10.750	10.700			
16	6	10.600	10.900	10.850	10.750	10.650	10.650	10.600	10.750	10.750	10.600	10.650	10.650			
17	7	10.600	10.750	10.800	10.700	10.600	10.850	10.850	10.850	10.800	10.850	10.850	10.800			
18	8	10.750	10.750	10.700	10.700	10.700	10.600	10.650	10.850	10.750	10.650	10.700	10.650			
19	9	10.650	10.650	10.750	10.800	10.650	10.900	10.650	10.750	10.700	10.750	10.700	10.700			
20	10	10.600	10.600	10.750	10.800	10.750	10.850	10.750	10.750	10.700	10.650	10.600	10.650			

It is important to remember that C_p and C_{pk} are simply point estimates from some unknown distribution because they are based on samples. A confidence interval for C_{pk} can be expressed as[14]

$$C_{pk} \pm z_{\alpha/2} \sqrt{\frac{1}{9n} + \frac{C_{pk}^2}{2n-2}}$$

For example, suppose the point estimate is 1.15 and the sample size $n = 45$. Using this formula, a 95% confidence interval is (0.89, 1.41). Although 1.15 may seem good, it is quite possible that the true population parameter is less than one because of sampling error. If a sample size of 400 were used instead to obtain the same point estimate, the confidence interval would be (1.06, 1.24), providing a better indication that the capability is indeed good.

Process capability indexes depend on the assumption that the distribution of output is normal. When a normal distribution does not apply, such as in the chemical industry, when suppliers often pick and choose material that will meet the specifications of customers (which often results in a uniform distribution), or when output is affected by tool wear and exhibits a highly skewed distribution, process capability indexes can be below 1 even though all measurements are within specification limits. Finally, process capability may be affected by measurement error. If the measurement error is large, then process capability indexes must be viewed with caution.

Quality in Practice

Testing Audio Components at Shure, Inc.[15]

Shure Incorporated is a global, privately held company headquartered in Evanston, Illinois, with manufacturing facilities in Illinois, Texas, and Mexico, and sales offices in Germany and Hong Kong. Shure's mission is to

- Deliver high-performing, quality, rugged and reliable audio products.
- Provide superior customer service and support.

Shure's philosophy is to be market-driven and customer-focused in their chosen markets. Each market segment has its own quality and reliability needs.

- *Performance Audio:* Musical performers and those who record and monitor their work on stage or in the studio. Anyone who has attended a rock concert can attest to the rough treatment microphones receive from the entertainers, some actually throwing them across the stage.
- *Presentation and Installation Audio:* Anywhere a sound system is installed, such as houses of

worship, hotels, conference rooms, clubs, theaters, and auditoriums. Many users are unfamiliar with the acoustical characteristics of the equipment they are using and sound technicians are often not on site, so the equipment really needs to run by itself.

- *Radio and TV:* Broadcast industry both in studio and on location in the field. Technicians need to have total confidence in the equipment they are using on a live, remote broadcast, because they cannot go back and redo that on-the-spot interview.
- *Consumer Market:* Phonograph cartridges and low-cost microphones, including audiophiles, hip-hop DJs, and home recording. Scratch DJs literally take a record and pull it back and forth to the beat of a song, causing tremendous pressure on the phonograph stylus.
- *Mobile Communications:* Audio subsystems, such as hands-free cellular, within the automotive environment. Microphones need to perform in a variety of temperatures.

S. N. Shure began the company by launching a one-man operation in 1925 that sold radio parts kits. It was the microphone that marked the company's entry into manufacturing in 1932, and the microphone remains Shure's flagship product to this day. Because of its emphasis on engineering research, Shure products became known early on for their outstanding quality and durability. During World War II, Shure was awarded a U.S. government contract to provide microphones to the military, and needed to meet strict specifications for performance and ruggedness. Shure took the extra step to develop a rigorous in-house testing program that remains in place today.

In addition to microphones (both wired and wireless) and phonograph cartridges, Shure manufactures a number of other audio electronics products, including mixers, digital signal processors, personal monitoring systems, and digital feedback reducers. Shure's quality philosophy is reliability oriented. Products are tested for reliability well beyond the warranty period, with the goal of providing the customer long-term service and satisfaction. Testing is designed to simulate actual operating conditions. Shure has more than 80 test procedures in place. The following are a few examples:

- *Microphone Drop Test:* To determine whether a microphone is capable of dynamic shock stress. Initial performance data are taken on the mic. Then the mic is dropped numerous times onto a hardwood floor from a height of 6 feet at random angles. The mic is "talked out" after every two drops. After the drop tests, level and response are tested and compared to the initial data. Any unit not meeting original print specifications is considered a failure.
- *Perspiration Test:* To evaluate the corrosion resistance of painted/plated parts exposed to an acid solution simulating sweat. Parts are placed in a perspiration chamber that consists of a stand supporting the parts over a large glass jar containing acid solution. Parts are inspected daily for amounts of corrosion for a period of seven days. Parts are then compared to good control parts to determine amount of corrosion present.
- *Cable and Cable Assembly Flex:* To ensure that any cable that would normally be subjected

to random twisting motion under tension will meet field requirements. Cable flex test equipment provides for two independent motions: rocking motion and rotation, and twisting motion and rotation. Cables not meeting flex life specification are considered a failure.
- *Sequential Shipping:* To evaluate the packaging effectiveness and mechanical integrity of the product under simulated shipping conditions. This test is used for all Shure products. Products packaged for shipping are given the following tests, in order: drop test, vibration test, rough handling test. When the product is removed from its packaging, it must appear and operate as new. If appropriate, an electrical test is performed and compared to initial electrical test data.
- *Cartridge Drop and Scrape Test:* To determine ability of stylus to withstand accidental drops and side impacts. A cartridge mounted in a tonearm is dropped onto a moving record at least 100 times. The cartridge is scraped across a moving record 100 times. This test simulates and exceeds any abuse given to the cartridge and stylus in normal use.
- *Temperature Storage:* To determine ability to withstand extreme temperatures for extended periods of time. Initial performance data are taken. For high temperature, the product is placed in a preheated high temperature chamber for seven days. The product is allowed to stabilize at room temperature for 24 hours and then the same performance data are taken. For low temperature, the product is placed in a low temperature chamber for seven days, allowed to stabilize to room temperature for 24 hours, and tested.

By performing these and other rigorous tests, Shure consistently meets its goal of exceeding customers' product performance and reliability expectations.

Key Issues for Discussion

1. Describe how the definition of reliability presented in this chapter applies to the performance tests described here. Do these tests measure inherent reliability or achieved reliability?

2. For the examples of product testing provided in this case, discuss what quality/reliability measurements might be taken and how the data might be analyzed. For example, are the measurements attributes or variables? Would they be analyzed using descriptive statistics, Pareto charts, and so on?

QUALITY IN PRACTICE

APPLYING QUALITY FUNCTION DEPLOYMENT TO A UNIVERSITY SUPPORT SERVICE[16]

Most applications of QFD focus on manufacturing firms or the needs of the external customer. However, QFD can be applied effectively in service organizations, taking into account the needs of internal customers. Tennessee Technological University applied QFD to their Research Resources Center (RRC), an internal service system. Originally created as a support facility for faculty and student research, the RRC has grown to offer many more services, including test preparation, manuscript preparation, resumes, flyers, brochures, faxing, copying, typing, and computer applications. The RRC is staffed weekdays from 7:30 A.M. to 4:30 P.M. with highly experienced support personnel. Jody, the head coordinator of the RRC, is proficient in specialty computer applications. She has a workstation at her disposal loaded with word-processing, graphics, and desktop publishing software. Peripherals such as a laser printer, color printer, and a full-page scanner allow her to generate high-quality output. Candy specializes in word processing, and Marie specializes in copying, collating, and stapling or binding. All three are proficient in most of the RRC functions.

Jobs can be classified as student, teacher, or rush. Most jobs are single-task oriented and can be completed by one RRC professional. The professional may be dependent on student workers to process job orders accurately and place them in the appropriate incoming jobs bin. Some jobs, however, are dependent on the other employees' functions. For instance, Candy types the tests, and Marie makes the copies and packages the final product. In these instances, Marie functions as an internal customer. She becomes dependent on another professional employee to accomplish her job.

Students involved in scholarship and work study programs are also employed part time to support RRC personnel. The RRC, functioning as a unit of the College of Business, is bound by the same regulations as other university offices: It has little control over the student employment selection process.

The responsibilities of the students include taking work orders and assisting customers in low-tech functions, such as making copies and finding research materials. No formal training is provided. The student workers are briefly informed of the RRC's functions and told to be courteous to customers. When student workers have questions, they ask one of the professionals. The student workers are primarily used as an interface between RRC professionals and customers.

A security issue is associated with some of the documents that the RRC processes. Some faculty members choose to have the RRC type and print their tests. In these instances, student workers cannot be involved in any process related to the test. The order is taken by one of the professionals, the job is executed, and the final product is locked in a file cabinet in a room where student workers are not allowed. Additionally, some student documents may not be handled by student workers. Project papers submitted for typing should not be viewed by a student worker who, by chance, may be in the same class and have the same assignment.

Because of limited space in the RRC, little distinction can be made between back office and front office. A counter is set up to the right of the door as customers walk in. All workers are stationed behind this counter. As customers need assistance, they are met at the counter by student workers who assist them. If a customer requires a job, then the appropriate work-order forms are filled out. During this time, the customer is in full view of the operations. Some frequent customers prefer to relay their job orders directly to the professionals. Due to the customized nature of many of the jobs, this direct
contact is sometimes appropriate. Some customers, however, prefer to do business with certain RRC representatives, which means that RRC

professionals occasionally have to leave the work they are doing to serve the customer.

The area to the left of the counter is available for customer use (see Figure 12.24). Four large tables are centrally located for faculty members and students to use for study purposes. The waiting area is merely the area between the counter and these tables. Service lines are not structured, and service personnel attempt to serve customers on a first-come, first-served basis. When customers have work orders that can be completed quickly, they may choose to wait at the counter. Occasionally, a queue develops in front of the service counter.

QFD was used to analyze where a concerted effort might increase the RRC's quality level as perceived by the customer. Customer requirements were grouped along the five dimensions of service quality (in rank order of importance): reliability, responsiveness, assurance, empathy, and tangibles. These categories were further broken down into secondary requirements as shown in the House of Quality (Figure 12.25). Existing operations in the RRC were observed internally over a

three-month period and the following components were identified:

- *Planning:* Layout, resources equipment, resources personnel, and system capacity
- *Procedures:* Housekeeping, customer handling, documents handling, information handling, nonroutine situations, inventory, and job and personnel scheduling
- *Personnel:* Selection, skills training, and attitude and morale

The roof of the House of Quality illustrates the relationships between these service components. An expert from RRC was used to assess these relationships. The completed House of Quality reveals that three service components—resource personnel, documents handling, and information handling—are the most important design issues related to customer perceptions of service quality. In redesigning the current process, the primary focus was placed on these issues.

The study resulted in a number of recommendations to enable the RRC to deliver a higher level

Figure 12.24 RRC Old Layout

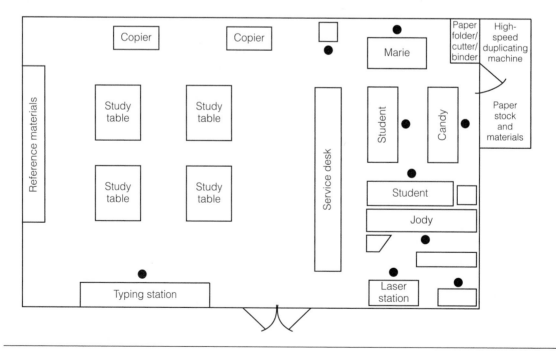

Source: R. Natarajan et al., "Applying QFD to Internal Service System Design," *Quality Progress*, February 1999, 65–70. © 1999, American Society for Quality. Reprinted with permission.

Figure 12.25 RRC House of Quality

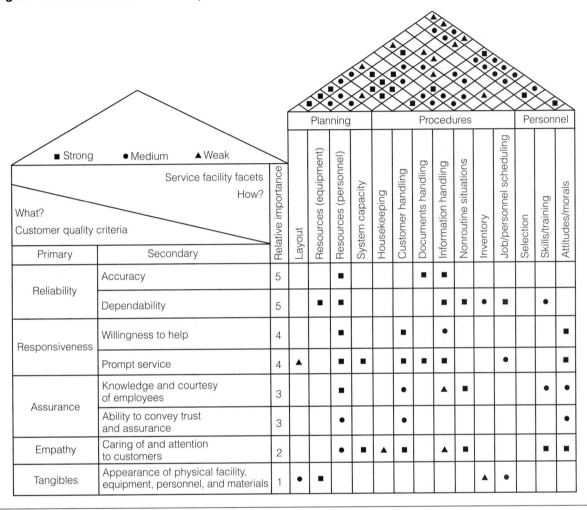

Primary	Secondary	Relative importance	Layout	Resources (equipment)	Resources (personnel)	System capacity	Housekeeping	Customer handling	Documents handling	Information handling	Nonroutine situations	Inventory	Job/personnel scheduling	Selection	Skills/training	Attitudes/morals
Reliability	Accuracy	5			■				■	■						
Reliability	Dependability	5		■	■					■	■	●	■		●	
Responsiveness	Willingness to help	4			■			■		●						■
Responsiveness	Prompt service	4	▲		■	■		■	■	■			●			■
Assurance	Knowledge and courtesy of employees	3			■				●	▲	■				●	●
Assurance	Ability to convey trust and assurance	3			●				●							●
Empathy	Caring of and attention to customers	2			●	■	▲	■		▲	■				■	■
Tangibles	Appearance of physical facility, equipment, personnel, and materials	1	●	■									▲	●		

■ Strong   ● Medium   ▲ Weak

Service facility facets — How?

What? Customer quality criteria

Source: R. Natarajan et al., "Applying QFD to Internal Service System Design," *Quality Progress*, February 1999, 65–70. © 1999, American Society for Quality. Reprinted with permission.

of service. One recommendation was to incorporate a better document-handling procedure. The RRC took the documents (resumes, tests, papers, and so on) and placed them in one incoming work bin. Staff members were good at sorting through the work orders and almost always identified the high-priority orders and completed them in plenty of time. But occasionally a work order was not noticed until it was almost too late. These orders were rushed and tended to be more prone to errors.

To prevent errors, procedures needed to be established that would separate the work orders into separate bins for high-priority jobs and normal jobs. Bins might also be placed at each person's workstation so employees did not have to sort through everyone else's work. Thus, employees would have a better idea of the work they had to do and might better allocate their time.

As mentioned earlier, the RRC had no formal training program. Although it might not be feasible for such a small organization to have a formal training program, some training procedures had to be considered. Employees needed to be thoroughly trained on documenting and routing work orders. An error in the work order inevitably resulted in an error in the final document. For instance, if a worker was not familiar with the work orders, he or she might document margin size in the wrong location. The professional, accustomed to seeing that information in a particular location, might not notice the correct margin settings, resulting in a flawed document.

Another suggested improvement was the facility layout. Many self-serve machines and resources were scattered around the room (see Figure 12.24). If they were centrally located, a customer could immediately target his or her needs upon entering the facility. Also, the service counter had no identifiable queuing system. If customers met the service counter head-on when entering the facility and key personnel were strategically positioned behind the counter, a quasi-service queue could be created as customers directed themselves to specific service personnel. A proposed new layout is suggested in Figure 12.26. This layout would also facilitate document flow with Jody's design, Candy's typing, and Marie's copying and folding, cutting, and binding in the same area.

These recommendations resulted in changes that were within the control of RRC personnel and therefore considered feasible. For instance, the

layout was changed to facilitate smoother traffic flow and improve customer contact with service providers. Self-serve equipment, such as copiers, computers, and printers were grouped in the new layout for easy access.

Key Issues for Discussion

1. Do you agree with the relative importance of measures of the voice of the customer in Figure 12.25? Explain why these rankings are reasonable, or provide counterarguments for a different ranking.
2. Using the relative importance ratings of the customer attributes and setting a scale of 1 = weak, 3 = medium, and 5 = strong for the relationship matrix, compute a weighted score for each of the technical requirements in Figure 12.25. Do your scores support the conclusions of the study in terms of the key service components to deploy in the QFD process?
3. What other recommendations might you suggest based on the information provided in this case?

Figure 12.26 RRC Proposed Layout

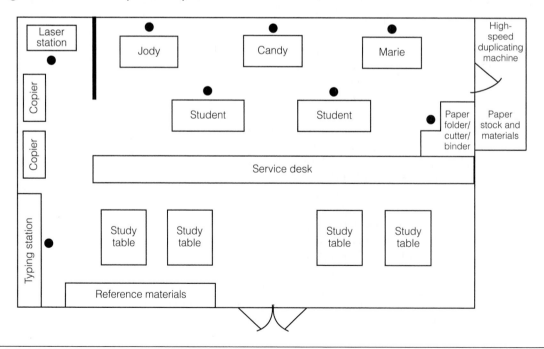

Source: R. Natarajan et al., "Applying QFD to Internal Service System Design," *Quality Progress*, February 1999, 65–70. © 1999, American Society for Quality. Reprinted with permission.

REVIEW QUESTIONS

1. What is Design for Six Sigma? Explain the four basic elements of DFSS and the various tools and methodologies that comprise this body of knowledge.
2. What are the principal benefits of QFD?
3. Outline the process of building the House of Quality. What departments and functions within the company should be involved in each step of the process?
4. Explain concept engineering. Why is it an important tool for assuring quality in product and process design activities?
5. Explain the difference between nominal dimensions and tolerances. How should tolerances be realistically set?
6. What is design failure mode and effects analysis (DFMEA)? Provide a simple example illustrating the concept.
7. What is the importance of reliability and why has it become such a prominent area within the quality disciplines?
8. Define reliability. Explain the definition thoroughly.
9. What is the difference between a functional failure and a reliability failure?
10. What is the definition of failure rate? How is it measured?
11. Explain the differences and relationships between the cumulative failure rate curve and the failure rate curve.
12. How is the average failure rate over a time interval computed?
13. Explain the product life characteristics curve and how it can be used.
14. What is a reliability function? Discuss different ways of expressing this function.
15. Explain how to compute the reliability of series, parallel, and series-parallel systems.
16. Describe different forms of product testing.
17. What does the term *latent defect* mean?
18. What is a "robust" design?
19. Explain the role of the Taguchi loss function in process and tolerance design.
20. Provide some examples of low-tech and high-tech measuring instruments (see Bonus Materials).
21. Describe the science of metrology.
22. What is the difference between accuracy, precision, and reproducibility?
23. What is calibration and why is it important to a good quality assurance system?
24. How is an R&R study performed? What is its purpose?
25. Explain the term *process capability*. How can process capability generally be improved?
26. What are the three major types of process capability studies? Describe the methodology of conducting a process capability study.
27. Define the process capability indexes, C_p, C_{pl}, and C_{pu}, and explain how they may be used to establish or improve quality policies in operating areas or with suppliers.
28. What are the advantages and disadvantages of the C_{pm} capability index (see Bonus Materials)?

PROBLEMS

Note: Data sets for several problems in this chapter are available in the Excel work-book *C12Data.xls* on the CD-ROM accompanying this text. Click on the appropriate worksheet tab as noted in the problem (e.g., Prob. 12-1) to access the data.

1. Bob's Big Burgers conducted consumer surveys and focus groups and identi-fied the most important customer expectations as
   - Healthy food
   - Speedy service
   - An easy-to-read menu board
   - Accurate order filling
   - Perceived value

   Develop a set of technical requirements to incorporate into the design of a new facility and a House of Quality relationship matrix to assess how well your requirements address these expectations. Refine your design as necessary, based upon the initial assessment.

2. Bob's Big Burgers (Problem 1) acquired some additional information. It found that consumers placed the highest importance on healthy food, followed by value, followed by order accuracy and service. The menu board was only casu-ally noted as an important attribute in the surveys. Bob faces three major com-petitors in this market: Grabby's, Queenburger, and Sandy's. Studies of their products yielded the information shown in Table 12.5. Results of the consumer panel ratings for each of these competitors are shown in Table 12.6 (a 1–5 scale, with 5 being the best). Using this information, modify and extend your House of Quality from Problem 1 and develop a deployment plan for a new burger. On what attributes should the company focus its marketing efforts?

3. Fingerspring, Inc., is working on a design for a new personal digital assistant (PDA). Marketing staff conducted extensive surveys and focus groups with

Table 12.5 Competitors' Product Information

Company	Price	Size (oz.)	Calories	Sodium (mg)	Fat (%)
Grabby's	1.55	5.5	440	75	13
Queenburger	2.25	7.5	640	95	23
Sandy's	1.75	6.0	540	80	16

Table 12.6 Consumer Panel Ratings

Attribute	Grabby's	Queenburger	Sandy's
Menu board	4	4	5
Order accuracy	4	5	3
Healthy food	4	2	3
Speedy service	3	5	4
Taste appeal	2	4	3
Visual appeal	3	4	3
Value	5	3	4

potential customers to determine the characteristics that the customers want and expect in a PDA. Fingerspring's studies have identified the most important customer expectations as

- Initial cost
- Reliability
- Ease of use
- Features
- Operating cost
- Compactness

Develop a set of technical requirements to incorporate into the design of a House of Quality relationship matrix to assess how well your requirements address these expectations. Refine your design as necessary, based upon the initial assessment.

4. Fingerspring, Inc. (Problem 3), faces three major competitors in this market: Harespring, Springbok, and Greenspring. It found that potential consumers placed the highest importance on reliability (measured by such things as freedom from operating system crashes and battery life), followed by compactness (weight/bulkiness), followed by flexibility (features, ease of use, and types of program modules available). The operating cost was only occasionally noted as an important attribute in the surveys. Studies of their products yielded the information shown in Table 12.7. Results of the consumer panel ratings for these competitors are shown in Table 12.8 (a 1–5 scale, with 5 being the best). Using this information, modify and extend your House of Quality from Problem 3 and develop a deployment plan for a new PDA. On what attributes should the company focus its marketing efforts?

Table 12.7 Competitors' Product Information

Company	Price	Wt. (oz.)	Size (In.)	Features	Operating Program	Battery life (hrs)	Opr. Cpsts (Batt./Prg/)
Harespring	575	4.0	4.8 x 3.2	15	PalmOS®	50	High
Springbok	195	7.5	5.1 x 3.3	9	Hardmark*	12	Low
Greenspring	450	8.8	5.3 x 3.3	12	Easyware**	25	Moderately high

Note: PalmOS® is one of the most recognized operating software programs for PDAs.
*New unproven software, unique to Springbok
**Well-received proprietary software, used on many PDAs for several years

Table 12.8 Consumer Panel Ratings

Attribute	Harespring	Springbok	Greenspring
Initial cost	3	5	4
Reliability	5	2	3
Ease of use	4	1	3
Features	4	2	3
Operating cost	5	3	4
Weight	5	3	3
Size	4	4	4

5. Given the cumulative failure curve in Figure 12.27, sketch the failure rate curve.
6. Compute the average failure rate during the intervals 0 to 30, 30 to 60, and 60 to 90, and 0 to 100, based on the information in Figure 12.27.
7. The life of a watch battery is normally distributed with a mean of 1,000 days and standard deviation of 60 days.
   a. What fraction of batteries is expected to survive beyond 1,100 days?
   b. What fraction will survive fewer than 880 days?
   c. Sketch the reliability function.
   d. What length of warranty is needed so that no more than 10 percent of the batteries will be expected to fail during the warranty period?
8. Lifetred, Inc., makes automobile tires that have a mean life of 50,000 miles with a standard deviation of 3,000 miles.
   a. What fraction of tires is expected to survive beyond 56,000 miles?
   b. What fraction will survive fewer than 47,000 miles?
   c. Sketch the reliability function.
   d. What length of warranty is needed so that no more than 10 percent of the tires will be expected to fail during the warranty period?
9. Compute the failure rate for six transformers that were tested for 600 hours each, three of which failed after 100, 175, and 350 hours.
10. Assuming an exponential distribution, a particular lightbulb has a failure rate of 0.002 units per hour. What is the probability of failure within 400 hours? What is the reliability function?
11. The MTBF of a circuit is 1,200 hours. Calculate the failure rate.
12. The MTBF for an Internet service provider's Web server unit is normally distributed with a mean of 180 days and a standard deviation of 10 days. Each failure costs the company $750,000 in lost computing time and repair costs. A shutdown for preventive maintenance can be scheduled during nonpeak times and will cost $500,000. As the manager in charge of computer operations, you are to determine whether a preventive maintenance program is worthwhile. What is your recommendation based on a 1% probability of failure? A 0.5% probability of failure? Assume 365 operating days per year.

Figure 12.27 Cumulative Failure Curve

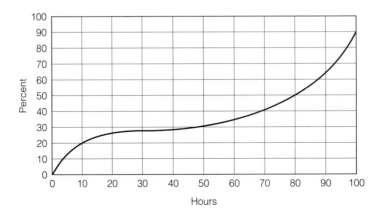

13. For a particular piece of equipment, the probability of failure during a given week is as follows:

Week of Operation	Probability of Failure
1	0.25
2	0.08
3	0.07
4	0.10
5	0.20
6	0.30

Management is considering a preventive maintenance program that would be implemented at the end of a given week of production. The production loss and downtime costs associated with an equipment failure are estimated to be $2,500 per failure. If it costs $500 to perform the preventive maintenance, when should the firm implement the preventive maintenance program? What is the total maintenance and failure cost associated with your recommendation, and how many failures can be expected each year? Assume 52 weeks of operation per year.

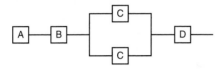

14. An electronic missile guidance system consists of the following components: Components A, B, C, and D have reliabilities of 0.96, 0.98, 0.90, and 0.99, respectively. What is the reliability of the entire system?

15. A manufacturer of portable radios purchases major electronic components as modules. The reliabilities of components differ by supplier. Suppose that the configuration of the major components is given by:

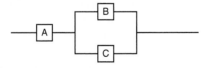

The components can be purchased from three different suppliers. The reliabilities of the components are as follows:

Component	Supplier 1	Supplier 2	Supplier 3
A	.95	.92	.94
B	.80	.86	.90
C	.90	.93	.85

Transportation and purchasing considerations require that only one supplier be chosen. Which one should be selected if the radio is to have the highest possible reliability?

16. In a complex manufacturing process, three operations are performed in series. Because of the nature of the process, machines frequently fall out of adjustment and must be repaired. To keep the system going, two identical machines are used at each stage; thus, if one fails, the other can be used while the first is repaired (see accompanying figure).

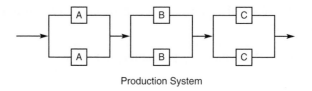

Production System

The reliabilities of the machines are as follows:

Machine	Reliability
A	.80
B	.90
C	.98

    a. Analyze the system reliability, assuming only one machine at each stage.
    b. How much is the reliability improved by having two machines at each stage?
17. An automated production system consists of three operations: turning, milling, and grinding. Individual parts are transferred from one operation to the next by a robot. Hence, if one machine or the robot fails, the process stops.
    a. If the reliabilities of the robot, turning center, milling machine, and grinder are 0.98, 0.94, 0.98, and 0.90, respectively, what is the reliability of the system?
    b. Suppose that two grinders are available and the system does not stop if one fails. What is the reliability of the system?
18. Two scales were used to weigh the same 25 samples of hamburger patties for a fast-food restaurant in Australia. Results are shown in *C12dataset* file for *Prob.12-18* on the student CD-ROM. The samples were weighed in grams, and the supplier has ensured that each patty weighs 114 grams. Which scale is more accurate? Which is more precise? Which is the better scale?
19. A gauge repeatability and reproducibility study at Frankford Brake Systems collected the data found in the *C12dataset* file for *Prob.12-19* on the student CD-ROM. Analyze these data. The part specification is 1.0 ± 0.06 mm.
20. A gauge repeatability and reproducibility study was made at Precision Parts, Inc., using three operators, taking three trials each on identical parts. The data that can be found in the *C12dataset* file for *Prob.12-20* on the student CD-ROM were collected. Do you see any problems after analyzing these data? What should be done? The part specification for a collar that was measured was 1.6 ± 0.2 inches.
21. A genetic researcher is trying to test two laboratory thermometers (that can be read to 1/100,000th of a degree Celsius) for accuracy and precision. She measured 25 samples with each and obtained the results found in the *C12dataset* file for *Prob.12-21* on the student CD-ROM. The true temperature being measured is 0 degrees C. Which instrument is more accurate? Which is more precise? Which is the better instrument?
22. A specification for the length of an auto part is 5.0 ± 0.05 centimeters (cm). It costs $25 to scrap a part that is outside the specifications. Determine the Taguchi loss function for this situation.
23. A blueprint specification for the thickness of a dishwasher part is 0.300 ± 0.024 centimeters (cm). It costs $9 to scrap a part that is outside the specifications. Determine the Taguchi loss function for this situation.

24. A team was formed to study the auto part described in Problem 22. While continuing to work to find the root cause of scrap, the team found a way to reduce the scrap cost to $17.50 per part.
    a. Determine the Taguchi loss function for this situation.
    b. If the process deviation from target can be held at 0.020 cm, what is the Taguchi loss?

25. A team was formed to study the dishwasher part described in Problem 23. While continuing to work to find the root cause of scrap, they found a way to reduce the scrap cost to $4 per part.
    a. Determine the Taguchi loss function for this situation.
    b. If the process deviation from target can be held at 0.015 cm, what is the Taguchi loss?

26. Ruido Unlimited makes electronic soundboards for car stereos. Output voltage to a certain component on the board must be 10 ± 0.1 volts. Exceeding the limits results in an estimated loss of $50. Determine the Taguchi loss function.

27. An electronic component has a specification of 150 ± 4 ohms. Scrapping the component results in an $80 loss.
    a. What is the value of k in the Taguchi loss function?
    b. If the process is centered on the target specification with a standard deviation of 2 ohms, what is the expected loss per unit?

28. An automatic cookie machine must deposit a specified amount of 7.5 ± 0.1 grams (g) of dough for each cookie on a conveyor belt. If the machine either over- or underdeposits the mixture, it costs $0.04 to scrap the defective cookie.
    a. What is the value of k in the Taguchi loss function?
    b. If the process is centered on the target specification with a standard deviation of 0.05 g, what is the expected loss per unit?

29. A computer chip is designed so that the distance between two adjacent pins has a specification of 2.000 ± 0.002 millimeters (mm). The loss due to a defective chip is $4. A sample of 25 chips was drawn from the production process and the results, in mm, can be found in the C12dataset file for *Prob.12-29* on the student CD-ROM.
    a. Compute the value of k in the Taguchi loss function.
    b. What is the expected loss from this process based on the sample data?

30. The average time to handle a call in a call processing center has a specification of 6 ± 1.25 minutes. The loss due to a mishandled call is $12. A sample of 25 calls was drawn from the process and the results, in minutes, can be found in the C12dataset file for *Prob.12-30* on the student CD-ROM.
    a. Compute the value of k in the Taguchi loss function.
    b. What is the expected loss from this process based on the sample data?

31. In the production of transformers, any output voltage that exceeds ± 25 volts is unacceptable to the customer. Exceeding these limits results in an estimated loss of $200. However, the manufacturer can adjust the voltage in the plant by changing a resistor that costs $1.75.
    a. Determine the Taguchi loss function.
    b. Suppose the nominal specification is 120 volts. At what tolerance should the transformer be manufactured?

32. In the transformer business mentioned in the previous problem, managers gathered data from a customer focus group and found that any output voltage that exceeds ± 20 volts was unacceptable to the customer. Exceeding these limits

results in an estimated loss of $250. However, the manufacturer can still adjust the voltage in the plant by changing a resistor that costs $1.75.

a. Determine the Taguchi loss function.

b. Suppose the nominal specification remains at 120 volts. At what tolerance should the transformer be manufactured?

33. Two processes, P and Q, are used by a supplier to produce the same component, Z, which is a critical part in the engine of the Boring 778 airplane. The specification for Z calls for a dimension of 0.24 mm ± 0.03. The probabilities of achieving the dimensions for each process based on their inherent variability are shown in the table found in the *C12dataset* file for *Prob.12-33* on the student CD-ROM. If $k = 75,000$, what is the expected loss for each process? Which would be the best process to use, based on minimizing the expected loss?

34. A machining process has a required dimension on a part of 0.560 ± 0.015 inch. Twenty-five parts each were measured as found in the *C12dataset* file for *Prob.12-34* on the student CD-ROM. What is its capability for producing within acceptable limits?

35. Adjustments were made in the process discussed in Problem 34 and 25 more samples were taken. The results are given in the *C12dataset* file for *Prob.12-35* on the student CD-ROM. What can you observe about the process? What is its capability for producing within acceptable limits now?

36. From the data for Kermit Theatrical Products, construct a histogram and estimate the process capability. If the specifications are 24 ± 0.03, estimate the percentage of parts that will be nonconforming. Finally, compute C_p, C_{pu}, and C_{pl}. Samples for three parts were taken as shown in the *C12dataset* file for *Prob.12-36* on the student CD-ROM.

37. Samples for three parts made at River City Parts Co. were taken as shown in the *C12dataset* file for *Prob.12-37* on the student CD-ROM. Data set 1 is for part 1, data set 2 is for part 2, and data set 3 is for part 3.

a. Calculate the mean and standard deviations for each part and compare them to the following specification limits:

Part	Nominal	Tolerance
1	1.750	± 0.045
2	2.000	± 0.060
3	1.250	± 0.030

b. Will the production process permit an acceptable fit of all parts into a slot with a specification of 5 ± 0.081 at least 99.73 percent of the time?

38. Omega Technology Ltd. (OTL) is a small manufacturing company that produces various parts for tool manufacturers. One of OTL's production processes involves producing a Teflon® spacer plate that has a tolerance of 0.05 to 0.100 cm in thickness. On the recommendation of the quality assurance (QA) department and over objections of the plant manager, OTL just purchased some new equipment to make these parts. Recently, the production manager was receiving complaints from customers about high levels of nonconforming parts. He suspected the new equipment, but neither QA nor plant management would listen.

The manager discussed the issue with one of his production supervisors who mentioned that she had just collected some process data for a study that the quality assurance department was undertaking. The manager decided that he would prove his point by showing that the new equipment was not capable of meeting the specifications. The data provided by the supervisor are shown in the *C12 Dataset.xls* file for Problem 12.38 on the student CD-ROM. Perform a process capability study on these data and interpret your results.

39. Suppose that a process with a normally distributed output has a mean of 55.0 and a variance of 4.0.
   a. If the specifications are 55.0 ± 4.00, compute C_p, C_{pk}, and C_{pm}.
   b. Suppose the mean shifts to 53.0 but the variance remains unchanged. Recompute and interpret these process capability indexes.
   c. If the variance can be reduced to 40 percent of its original value, how do the process capability indices change (using the original mean of 55.0)?
40. A process has upper and lower tolerance limits of 5.60 and 5.20, respectively. If the customer requires a demonstrated C_p of 2.0, what must the process capability be? If both C_{pu} and C_{pl} must also be 2.0, determine the mean and standard deviation of the process, assuming a normal distribution of output.
41. Clearly demonstrate that Six Sigma requires $C_p = 2.0$ and $C_{pk} = 1.5$.

 ## PROJECTS, ETC.

1. Using whatever "market research" techniques are appropriate, define a set of customer attributes for
   a. Purchasing books at your college bookstore
   b. A college registration process
   c. A hotel room used for business
   d. A hotel room used for family leisure vacations
   For each case, determine a set of technical requirements and construct the relationship matrix for the House of Quality.
2. (This exercise would best be performed in a group.) Suppose that you were developing a small pizza restaurant with a dining area and local delivery. Develop a list of customer requirements and technical requirements and try to complete a House of Quality. What service standards might such an operation have?
3. Most children (and many adults) like to assemble and fly balsa-wood gliders. From your own experiences or from interviews with other students, define a set of customer requirements for a good glider. (Even better, buy one and test it to determine these requirements yourself.) If you were to design and manufacture such a product, how would you define a set of technical requirements for the design? Using your results, construct a relationship matrix for a House of Quality.
4. Fill in the following relationship matrix of a House of Quality for a screwdriver. By sampling your classmates, develop priorities for the customer attributes and use these and the relationships to identify key technical requirements to deploy.

	Price	Interchangeable bits	Steel shaft	Rubber grip	Ratchet capability	Plastic handle
Easy to use						
Does not rust						
Durable						
Comfortable						
Versatile						
Inexpensive						
Priority						

5. Discuss and prepare a report with examples on how DFMEA might be used in a service application rather than in a pure product design application.

6. Conduct an R&R study with a team of your fellow students to measure a set of sharpened pencils of various sizes. Use both an ordinary ruler and a metric ruler? What conclusions do you reach?

7. Visit several of the following metrology Web sites or find some new ones and summarize new ideas, concepts, or findings that are not discussed in this chapter.
   http://www.kinematics.com
   http://www.sandia.gov/psl
   http://www.metrology.org
   http://www.boulder.nist.gov
   http://www.nist.gov
   http://www.gecals.com

8. Visit a local machine shop, bakery, or similar factory to determine what type of measurements they perform, what instruments they use, how they use the data, and how they ensure the precision and accuracy of their instruments and gauges. Write a report of your findings.

CASES

I. HYDRAULIC LIFT CO.

The Hydraulic Lift Company (HLC) manufactures freight elevators and automotive lifts used in garages and service stations. Figure 12.28 shows a simplified diagram of a hydraulic lift. The check valve is an important component in the system. Its purpose is to control the flow of hydraulic oil from the oil reservoir to the cylinder when the elevator is rising. As the elevator descends, the rate at which oil flows from the cylinder back to the reservoir is also controlled by the check valve.

One of the most important parts of the check valve is the piston, which moves within the valve body as the valve is opened or closed. The quality manager at HLC noticed that scrap rates on the piston had been quite high over the past three years. Two models (part numbers 117227 and 117228) of check valve pistons are being manufactured. Because of extremely critical tolerances, these parts are among the most difficult ones produced in the machine shop.

A study to determine the magnitude of the problem revealed that approximately $2,200 per month worth of parts had been scrapped over the past three years (see Figure 12.29). This amount translates to about 14 percent of total production of the parts, a scrap rate that is considered unacceptable. About half of the defective items were

scrapped due to inability of the process to hold a 0.4990/0.4985-inch tolerance on the valve stem (see Figure 12.30). The machining operation used to shape the valve stem is performed on a grinding machine, which should have the capability of holding a tolerance within 0.001–0.002 inch under standard operating conditions. Manufacturing engineers and the quality manager decided to do a process capability study on one part (no. 117227) to gather statistical data on the stem problem and make a recommendation for improvements.

For the first step, an operator ran 100 parts using the standard production methods. Results of the study [see the histogram in Figure 12.31(a)] revealed that a machine problem existed. The data showed that a few parts were being produced outside the specifications. In addition, the strange shape of the histogram for dimensions within the specification limits prompted an investigation into the possibility of instability of the process. The study team observed that the operator was constantly adjusting the machine setting to try to hold to the specified tolerance.

As a check on machine capability, the team asked the operator to run 20 parts without adjusting the machine, which resulted in scrap-

Figure 12.28 Simplified Diagram of Hydraulic Lift

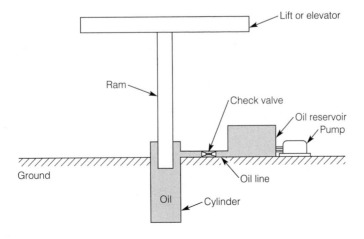

Figure 12.29 Average Scrap Cost per Month

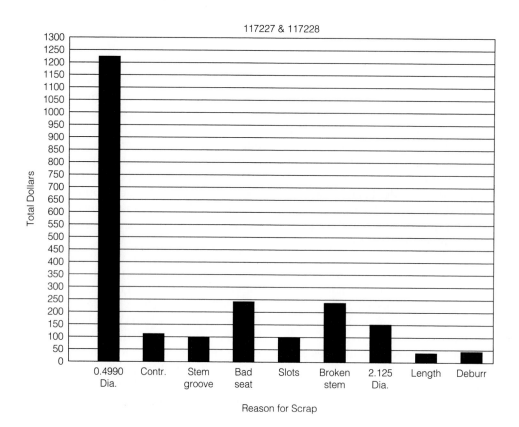

Figure 12.30 Part No. 117227 Check Valve

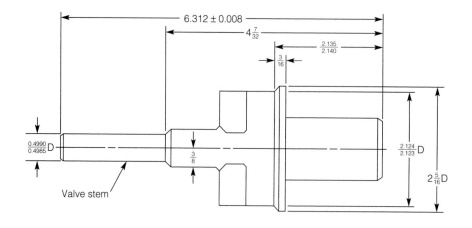

Figure 12.31 Process Capability for Hydraulic Lift Company

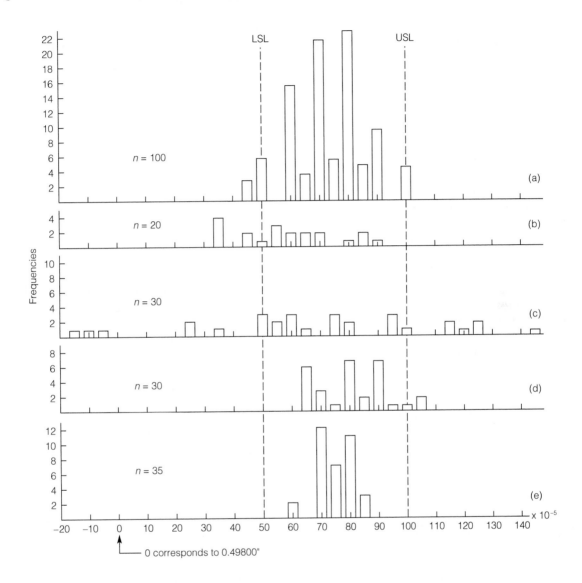

ping six of 20 parts, a 30 percent scrap rate [see Figure 12.31(b)]. This test verified that the machine needed some major adjustments.

The machine manufacturer was contacted and a technician was dispatched to the plant. A run of 30 parts was made to show how the machine operated. Twelve of the 30 pieces were defective, with the stem dimension out of tolerance [see Figure 12.31(c)]. The technician made the following adjustments:

- Installed new gaskets
- Cleaned machine, adding oil and coolant

- Loaded hand wheel bearing for more positive control
- Reset retard pressure on grind wheel
- Adjusted stone dresser mechanism
- Reset dwell time (time the grindstone stays on the workpiece after reaching final diameter)

The results of these adjustments were significant. Another 30 parts were run, with only two falling outside the tolerance limits [Figure 12.31(d)]. The team still did not consider the process to be fully satisfactory. The manufacturer's technician said that the grinder "ways" (channels on which the machine head travels) would have to be reground and that some parts in the machine would have to be replaced. This recommendation was made to management, who agreed to have the machine overhauled as required.

After the work was completed, a run of 35 parts was made. The results, shown in Figure 12.31(e), showed that all parts were well within tolerance limits. As a final step, operators and maintenance personnel were instructed on the proper use and care of the machine.

Discussion Questions

1. Using the histograms in Figure 12.31, estimate the process capability indexes for each situation.
2. What lessons can be learned in terms of performing process capability studies and interpreting the results?

II. BLOOMFIELD TOOL CO.

Bloomfield Tool Co. (BTC) is a small manufacturing company that produces precision tools to order. One of BTC's production processes involves producing a metal spacer plate that has a tolerance of 0.05 to 0.100 cm in thickness. Recently, the QA manager was receiving complaints from customers about high levels of nonconforming parts. He suspected problems in the gauges used to check outgoing parts were to blame, because they had not been sent out for calibration in some time. However, it was expensive to do, so he wanted to be sure that it was needed. He decided to do a gauge R&R test and selected two experienced inspectors to perform the test using 15 identical parts, whose dimensions had been verified. Table 12.9 shows data provided by the supervisor. Thus, data were from two operators, two gauges, and 15 parts that were measured twice, independently, by the two operators.

A reliability engineer pointed out that variations in the data could be traced to three causes: repeatability problems (equipment variation or EV), reproducibility variations (appraisal variation or AV), and process variation (part variation or PV). Thus, total variation (TV) could be seen as made up of repeatability and reproducibility (R&R) variation and PV. Team members had heard about EV, AV, and R&R in a training class on measurement, but realized that the last item was an obvious but important point that they had not previously considered. They were given the following formulas for computation of the PV and TV:

$$PV = R_p \times K_3$$

and

$$TV = \sqrt{(R\&R)^2 + (PV)^2}$$

Table 12.9 Data Set for R&R Study

Sample	Operator 1		Operator 2	
1	0.0650	0.0600	0.0650	0.0550
2	0.1000	0.1050	0.1050	0.0950
3	0.0850	0.0800	0.0820	0.0750
4	0.0850	0.0950	0.0820	0.0940
5	0.0550	0.0580	0.0485	0.0525
6	0.0875	0.0915	0.0945	0.0925
7	0.0920	0.0880	0.0990	0.0900
8	0.0850	0.0800	0.0750	0.0700
9	0.0890	0.0980	0.0920	0.0990
10	0.0600	0.0700	0.0550	0.0640
11	0.0680	0.0750	0.0670	0.0720
12	0.0545	0.0500	0.0525	0.0495
13	0.0800	0.0910	0.0870	0.0820
14	0.0700	0.0805	0.0865	0.0830
15	0.0750	0.0650	0.0650	0.0680

The R_p value is obtained by calculating the range of the sample averages in a gauge study. The K_3 value depends on the number of parts measured in the study. Some of these values are found in Table 12.10.

Discussion Questions

1. Calculate the R&R, process, and total variation for the data. Using the TV as the divisor, calculate the percentage of total variation that the EV, AV, R&R, and PV encompass. (*Note:* These variations are not directly related to one another, so the percentages

will not total to 100 percent.) What conclusions can you draw about the variations that were observed?

2. Based on your analysis, what recommendations could you make on how the measurement system could be improved?

3. What would you tell the production manager? *Note:* Readers who have need for professional software for performing extensive R&R studies or keeping track of gauge records and calibration may wish to look at R&Rpack and GAGEpack software developed and distributed by PQ Systems, Inc., PO Box 10, Dayton, OH 45475-0010.

Table 12.10 Numbers of Parts (n) and K_3 Factors

n	5	6	7	8	9	10	11	12	13	14	15
K_3	2.08	1.93	1.82	1.74	1.67	1.62	1.57	1.54	1.51	1.48	1.45

ENDNOTES

1. *Reliability Guidebook, The Japanese Standards Association* (Tokyo: Asian Productivity Organization, 1972), 4.

2. C. M. Creveling, J. L. Slutsky, and D. Antis, Jr., *Design for Six Sigma in Technology and Product Development* (Upper Saddle River, NJ, Prentice Hall, 2003).

3. L. P. Sullivan, "Quality Function Deployment: The Latent Potential of Phases III and IV," in A. Richard Shores (ed.), *A TQM Approach to Achieving Manufacturing Excellence* (Milwaukee, WI: ASQC Quality Press, 1990), 265–279.

4. Christina Hepner Brodie, "A Polaroid Notebook: Concept Engineering," *Center for Quality of Management Journal* 3, no. 2 (1994), 7–14.

5. Laura Horton and David Boger, "How Bose Corporation Applied Concept Engineering to a Service," *Center for Quality of Management Journal* 3, no. 2 (1994), 52–59.

6. Jennifer Reese, "Starbucks: Inside the Coffee Cult," *Fortune*, December 9, 1996, 190–200.

7. Susan Dillingham, "A Little Gross Stuff in Food Is OK by FDA," *Insight*, May 22, 1989, 25.

8. Alan Vonderhaar, "Audi's TT Coupe's Ever So Close," *Cincinnati Enquirer*, November 27, 1999, F1, F2.

9. Statement made by Belinda Collins before the

House Subcommittee on Technology, Committee on Science, June 29, 1995.

10. *ASQC Automotive Division Statistical Process Control Manual* (Milwaukee, WI: American Society for Quality Control, 1986).

11. This section is adopted from NIST Calibration Services, available at http://www.nist.gov.

12. Paul F. McCoy, "Using Performance Indexes to Monitor Production Processes," *Quality Progress* 24, no. 2 (February 1991), 49–55; see also Fred A. Spring, "The Cpm Index," *Quality Progress* 24, no. 2 (February 1991), 57–61.

13. Helmut Schneider, James Pruett, and Cliff Lagrange, "Uses of Process Capability Indices in the Supplier Certification Process," *Quality Engineering* 8, no. 2 (1995–1996), 225–235.

14. Mark L. Crossley, "Size Matters. How Good Is your Cpk, Really?" *Quality Digest*, May 2000, 71–72.

15. Appreciation is expressed to Christine Schyvinck, VP Operations, Shure, Inc., for providing this case (October 2000).

16. Adapted from R. Nat Natarajan, Ralph E. Martz, and Kyosuke Kurosaka, "Applying QFD to Internal Service System Design," *Quality Progress*, February 1999, 65–70. © 1999, American Society for Quality. Reprinted with permission.

BIBLIOGRAPHY

Boser, Robert B., and Cheryl L. Christ. "Whys, Whens, and Hows of Conducting a Process Capability Study." Presentation at the ASQC/ASA 35th Annual Fall Technical Conference, Lexington, Kentucky, 1991.

Gunter, Bert. "Process Capability Studies Part I: What Is a Process Capability Study?" *Quality Progress* 24, no. 2 (February 1991), 97–99.

Tomas, Sam. "Six Sigma: Motorola's Quest for Zero Defects." *APICS, The Performance Advantage*, July 1991, 36–41.

———. "What Is Motorola's Six Sigma Product Quality?" American Production and Inventory Control Society 1990 Conference Proceedings. Falls Church, VA: APICS, 27–31.

Tedaldi, Michael, Fred Seaglione, and Vincent Russotti. *A Beginner's Guide to Quality in Manufacturing.* Milwaukee, WI: ASQC Quality Press, 1992.

Zubairi, Mazhar M. "Statistical Process Control Management Issues." 1985 IIE Fall Conference Proceedings. Reprinted in Mehran Sepehri (ed.), *Quest for Quality: Managing the Total System.* Norcross, GA: Industrial Engineering & Management Press, 1987.

CHAPTER

13

TOOLS FOR PROCESS IMPROVEMENT

When Cincinnati City Manager Valerie Lemmie started her job in April 2002, she asked building inspectors whether the city had a "one-stop shop" for building permits. They said, "Sure. You stop here once, you stop there once, and you stop there once." What she found out was that a permit stops 473 times on its way from the initial application to the printer! After spending a week at City Hall and taking notes on every step of the process, a consultant hired to analyze the Department of Buildings and Inspections ended up with about 30 feet of flowcharts that depicted the building permit process. Although Ms. Lemmie conceded that improvement wouldn't be easy, an assistant noted that a lot of people wanted to know how they could do their jobs better. "They know everything that's wrong with it probably more than anyone else. And more than anyone else, they need to be part of the solution."[1]

Improving such a complex process takes a lot of work, as companies such as Armstrong and Xerox (see *Quality Profiles*) certainly understand. Having the right tools is important and can make the task considerably easier. We introduced basic concepts of process improvement in Chapter 7. However, the focus in that chapter was on the philosophy of improvement in the broader context of process management. In this chapter we focus on a variety of tools and techniques to help individuals and teams in process improvement projects. Most of these tools are included in basic Six Sigma Green Belt training.

PROCESS IMPROVEMENT METHODOLOGIES

Numerous methodologies for improvement have been proposed over the years. We already looked at one of them in the context of Six Sigma in Chapter 10: DMAIC. In this section we review some other popular approaches; most are simple variations of each other, but understanding them may provide new and unique insights into problem solving for process improvement.

The Deming Cycle

A part of the kaizen philosophy (see Chapter 7), is the use of the Deming cycle to guide and motivate improvement activities. The **Deming cycle** is a simple methodology for improvement that was strongly promoted by W. Edwards Deming. It was originally called the *Shewhart cycle* after its original founder, Walter Shewhart, but was renamed the Deming cycle by the Japanese in 1950. The Deming cycle is composed of four stages: *plan, do, study,* and *act* (PDSA) as illustrated in Figure 13.1. (The third stage—study—was formerly called *check,* and the Deming cycle was known as the *PDCA cycle.* Deming made the change in 1990. "Study" is more appropriate; with only a "check," one might miss something. However, many people still use "check.")

Figure 13.1 The Deming Cycle

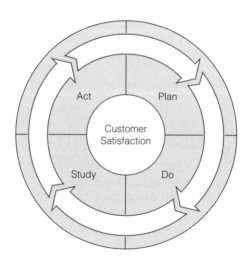

QUALITY PROFILES

ARMSTRONG WORLD INDUSTRIES BUILDING PRODUCTS OPERATIONS

AND XEROX BUSINESS SERVICES

ARMSTRONG WORLD INDUSTRIES

Armstrong World Industries Building Products Operations (BPO), headquartered in Lancaster, Pennsylvania, manufactures acoustical ceilings and wall panels and employs about 2,400 people, 85 percent of whom work at the operation's seven manufacturing plants in six states. All quality-focused changes, from redesigning jobs and operations to reorganizing its salesforce, are driven by thoroughly evaluated expectations of increases in customer value. More than half of the BPO workforce participates in the approximately 250 improvement teams operating at any given time. The team objectives range from correcting specific operational problems at a plant to improving key business processes across the organization. All quality improvement teams are required to develop specific action plans and set goals that will have a measurable impact on one of the company's key business drivers: customer satisfaction, sales growth, operating profit, asset management, and high-performance organization (human resource capabilities). Change is purposeful, guided by information and evaluations pointing the way to improvements that will make a major difference in customer value, employee value, and shareholder value. BPO enhanced its information gathering and analytical capabilities, and stepped up its benchmarking studies to better understand the dynamics of the market, competitors' performance, and its own business results. From these initiatives, scrap was cut by 38 percent, and manufacturing output per employee rose 39 percent between 1991 and 1995. From 1992 to 1994, notices of nonconformance sent to suppliers fell 32 percent and on-time delivery improved from 93 percent to 97.3 percent, while reducing the delivery window from 4 hours to 30 minutes.

Xerox Business Services (XBS) provides document outsourcing services and consulting, including on-site management of mailrooms and print shops and the creation, production, and management of documents. XBS puts heavy emphasis on benchmarking throughout its organization, gathering comparative information from companies that are large, small, tenured, new, inside, or outside their industry. XBS uses a process called Managing for Results, an integrated planning and management process that cascades action plans into measurable objectives for each manager, supervisor, and front-line associate. The entire process, the company says, is designed to "align goals from the customer's line of sight to the empowered employee and throughout the entire organization." Key performance measures are deployed to all teams and individuals in the company, and the process enables them to design work systems more rapidly and with greater flexibility. XBS also develops strategic initiatives based on its understanding of the division's strengths and weaknesses as well as its reading of opportunities and threats. This analysis draws on the division's extensive competitive intelligence, "voice of the customer," and "voice of the market" information systems. In monthly and quarterly reviews, the effectiveness of work processes is assessed against performance measures. The division invests more than $10 million annually for training, and it is continually searching for innovative learning approaches. Examples are mini-camps—designed to help employees contemplate and prepare for future changes in the way they work and in how XBS addresses evolving customer requirements—and each employee's personal learning plan that is regularly reviewed by assigned "coaches."

Source: Malcolm Baldrige National Quality Award, Profiles of Winners, National Institute of Standards and Technology, Department of Commerce.

The plan stage consists of studying the current situation and describing the process: its inputs, outputs, customers, and suppliers; understanding customer expectations; gathering data; identifying problems; testing theories of causes; and developing solutions and action plans. In the do stage, the plan is implemented on a trial basis, for example, in a laboratory, pilot production process, or with a small group of customers, to evaluate a proposed solution and provide objective data. Data from the experiment are collected and documented.

The study stage determines whether the trial plan is working correctly by evaluating the results, recording the learning, and determining whether any further issues or opportunities need be addressed. Often, the first solution must be modified or scrapped. New solutions are proposed and evaluated by returning to the do stage. In the last stage, act, the improvements become standardized and the final plan is implemented as a "current best practice" and communicated throughout the organization. This process then leads back to the plan stage for identification of other improvement opportunities.

The Deming cycle focuses on both short-term continuous improvement and long-term organizational learning.

Table 13.1 summarizes the steps in the Deming Cycle in more detail. The fundamental premise is that improvement comes from the application of knowledge.[2] This knowledge may be knowledge of engineering, management, or how a process operates that can make a job easier, more accurate, faster, less costly, safer, or better meet customer needs. Three fundamental questions to consider are:

- What are we trying to accomplish?
- What changes can we make that will result in improvement?
- How will we know that a change is an improvement?

Through a process of learning, knowledge is developed. With this philosophy, one can easily see why the Deming cycle has been an essential element of Japanese quality improvement programs.

The following example demonstrates how the Deming cycle can be applied in practice. The co-owners of a diner decided to do something about the long lines that occurred every day in their place of business.[3] After discussions with their employees, several important facts came to light:

- Customers waited in line for up to 15 minutes.
- Usually, tables were available.
- Many of their customers were regulars.
- People taking orders and preparing food were getting in each other's way.

To measure the improvement that might result from any change they made, they decided to collect data on the number of customers in line, the number of empty tables, and the time until a customer received the food ordered.

In the plan stage, the owners wanted to test a few changes. They decided on three changes:

1. Provide a way for customers to fax their orders in ahead of time (rent a fax machine for one month).
2. Construct a preparation table in the kitchen with ample room for fax orders.
3. Devote one of their two cash registers to handling fax orders.

Both the length of the line and the number of empty tables were measured every 15 minutes during the lunch hour by one of the owners. In addition, when the

Table 13.1 Detailed Steps in the Deming Cycle

Plan

1. Define the process: its start, end, and what it does.
2. Describe the process: list the key tasks performed and sequence of steps, people involved, equipment used, environmental conditions, work methods, and materials used.
3. Describe the players: external and internal customers and suppliers, and process operators.
4. Define customer expectations: what the customer wants, when, and where, for both external and internal customers.
5. Determine what historical data are available on process performance, or what data need to be collected to better understand the process.
6. Describe the perceived problems associated with the process; for instance, failure to meet customer expectations, excessive variation, long cycle times, and so on.
7. Identify the primary causes of the problems and their impacts on process performance.
8. Develop potential changes or solutions to the process, and evaluate how these changes or solutions will address the primary causes.
9. Select the most promising solution(s).

Do

1. Conduct a pilot study or experiment to test the impact of the potential solution(s).
2. Identify measures to understand how any changes or solutions are successful in addressing the perceived problems.

Study

1. Examine the results of the pilot study or experiment.
2. Determine whether process performance has improved.
3. Identify further experimentation that may be necessary.

Act

1. Select the best change or solution.
2. Develop an implementation plan: what needs to be done, who should be involved, and when the plan should be accomplished.
3. Standardize the solution, for example, by writing new standard operating procedures.
4. Establish a process to monitor and control process performance.

Source: Adapted from *Small Business Guidebook to Quality Management*, Office of the Secretary of Defense, Quality Management Office, Washington, DC (1998).

15-minute line check was done, the last person in line was noted, and the time until that person got served was measured.

In the do phase, the owners observed the results of the three measures for three weeks. In the study phase, they detected several improvements. Time in line went down from 15 minutes to an average of 5 minutes. The line length was cut to a peak average of 12 people, and the number of empty tables decreased slightly. In the act phase, the owners held a meeting with all employees to discuss the results. They decided to purchase the fax machine, prepare phone orders in the kitchen with the fax orders, and use both cash registers to handle walk-up and fax orders.

FADE

A variation of the Deming cycle and DMAIC used by a number of organizations, including the U.S. Coast Guard, is known by the acronym FADE: *focus, analyze, develop,* and *execute*. In the Focus stage, a team selects the problem to be addressed and defines it, characterizing the current state of the process, why change is needed, what the desired result should be, and the benefits of achieving that result. In the analyze stage, the team works to describe the process in detail, determine what data and information are needed, and develop a list of root causes for the problem. The develop stage focuses on creating a solution and implementation plan along with documentation to explain and justify recommendations to management who must allocate the resources. Finally, in the execute stage, the solution is implemented and a monitoring plan is established.

Juran's Breakthrough Sequence

According to Juran, all breakthroughs follow a commonsense sequence of discovery, organization, diagnosis, corrective action, and control, which he formalized as the "breakthrough sequence," and which can be summarized as follows:

- *Proof of the need*: Managers, especially top managers, need to be convinced that quality improvements are simply good economics. Through data collection efforts, information on poor quality, low productivity, or poor service can be translated into the language of money—the universal language of top management—to justify a request for resources to implement a quality improvement program.
- *Project identification*: All breakthroughs are achieved project-by-project, and in no other way. By taking a project approach, management provides a forum for converting an atmosphere of defensiveness or blame into one of constructive action. Participation in a project increases the likelihood that the participant will act on the results.
- *Organization for breakthrough*: Organization for improvement requires a clear responsibility for guiding the project. The responsibility for the project may be as broad as an entire division with formal committee structures or as narrow as a small group of workers at one production operation. These groups provide the definition and agreement as to the specific aims of the project, the authority to conduct experiments, and implementation strategies. The path from problem to solution consists of two journeys: one from symptom to cause (the diagnostic journey) and the other from cause to remedy (the remedial journey), which must be performed by different individuals with the appropriate skills.
- *Diagnostic journey*: Diagnosticians skilled in data collection, statistics, and other problem-solving tools are needed at this stage. Some projects will require full-time, specialized experts (such as Six Sigma Black Belts) while the workforce can perform others. Management-controllable and operator-controllable problems require different methods of diagnosis and remedy.
- *Remedial journey*: The remedial journey consists of several phases: choosing an alternative that optimizes total cost (similar to one of Deming's points), implementing remedial action, and dealing with resistance to change.
- *Holding the gains*: This final step involves establishing the new standards and procedures, training the workforce, and instituting controls to make sure that the breakthrough does not die over time.

Many companies have followed Juran's program religiously. A Xerox plant in Mitcheldean, England, for example, cut quality losses by 30 percent to 40 percent and won a national prize in Britain in 1984 for quality improvement using the Juran system.[4]

Creative Problem Solving

Solving quality problems often involves a high amount of creativity. In Japanese, the word *creativity* has a literal translation as "dangerous opportunity." In the Toyota production system, which has become the benchmark for world-class efficiency, a key concept is *soikufu*—creative thinking or inventive ideas, which means capitalizing on worker suggestions. The chairman of Toyota once observed, "One of the features of Japanese workers is that they use their brains as well as their hands. Our workers provide 1.5 million suggestions a year, and 95 percent of them are put to practical use. There is an almost tangible concern for improvement in the air at Toyota."[5]

An effective problem-solving process that can easily be adapted to quality improvement stems from creative problem-solving (CPS) concepts advocated by Osborn and by Parnes.[6] This strategy consists of the following steps:

- Understanding the "mess"
- Finding facts
- Identifying specific problems
- Generating ideas
- Developing solutions
- Implementation

Notice that the plan stage in the Deming cycle, for example, actually consists of the first five steps; the do, study, and act stages deal more with implementation. In Juran's program, the "diagnostic and remedial journeys" are essentially the same as this process. Thus, understanding these steps will help improve the application of other problem-solving models. For example, at Bethesda Hospitals of Cincinnati, Ohio, both the Juran and Deming approaches are integrated as shown in Figure 13.2.

How one approaches problem solving is not as critical as doing it in a systematic fashion, whether one uses the Deming cycle, FADE, Juran's approach, CPS, or some hybrid variation.

The left side of the figure incorporates the essential elements of Juran's diagnostic/remedial journeys. Once a solution is proposed, the Deming cycle is then used to evaluate the solution's effectiveness prior to implementation. Not every approach is appropriate for all organizations; one must be chosen or designed to fit the organization's culture and people.

BASIC TOOLS FOR PROCESS IMPROVEMENT

Six Sigma created a renewed focus on process improvement. Among the many tools that comprise the Six Sigma toolbox are seven simple tools: flowcharts, check sheets, histograms, Pareto diagrams, cause-and-effect diagrams, scatter diagrams, and control charts. The Japanese called them the **Seven QC** (quality control) **Tools**, and they have been used for decades to support quality improvement problem-solving efforts. Table 13.2 shows the primary applications of each tool in Six Sigma and creative problem-solving processes. You can easily see how they also apply in the Deming cycle or Juran's approach. They are designed simply so that workers at all levels can use them easily. We will briefly review each tool to explain its role in quality improvement.

Figure 13.2 Bethesda Hospital Process Improvement Model

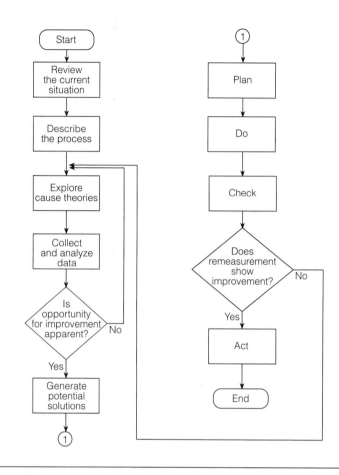

Source: Reprinted with permission of Bethesda Hospital, Inc., 619 Oak Street, Cincinnati, OH 45241.

Flowcharts

To clearly define a Six Sigma or any process improvement project, one must first understand the process that creates the outputs that internal or external customers receive. This understanding sets the foundation for identifying critical to quality (CTQ) issues, selecting measurements, and identifying root causes of problems, identifying non-value-added steps, and reducing variation.

Flowcharts are best developed by having the people involved in the process—employees, supervisors, managers, and customers—construct the flowchart. A facilitator provides objectivity in resolving conflicts. The facilitator can guide the discussion through questions such as "What happens next?" "Who makes the decision at this point?" and "What operation is

> *A **flowchart** or **process map** identifies the sequence of activities or the flow of materials and information in a process. Flowcharts help the people involved in the process understand it much better and more objectively by providing a picture of the steps needed to accomplish a task.*

Table 13.2 Application of the Seven QC Tools in Six Sigma

Tool	DMAIC Application	CPS Application
Flowcharts	Define, Control	Mess-finding
Check sheets	Measure, Analyze	Fact-finding
Histograms	Measure, Analyze	Problem-finding
Cause-and-effect diagrams	Analyze	Idea-finding
Pareto diagrams	Analyze	Problem-finding
Scatter diagrams	Analyze, Improve	Solution-finding
Control charts	Control	Implementation

performed at this point?" Quite often, the group does not universally agree on the answers to these questions due to misconceptions about the process itself or a lack of awareness of the "big picture." Flowcharts can easily be created using Microsoft Excel using the features found on the drawing toolbar.[7]

Flowcharts help all employees understand how they fit into a process and who are their suppliers and customers. This realization then leads to improved communication among all parties. By participating in the development of a flowchart, workers feel a sense of ownership in the process, and hence become more willing to work on improving it. If flowcharts are used in training employees, more consistency will be achieved. Flowcharts also help to pinpoint places where quality-related measurements should be taken. Once a flowchart is constructed, it can be used to identify quality problems as well as areas for productivity improvement. Questions such as "How does this operation affect the customer?" "Can we improve or even eliminate this operation?" or "Should we control a critical quality characteristic at this point?" trigger the identification of opportunities.

The AT&T customer-supplier model that we introduced in Chapter 4 provides a way of building a detailed process flowchart. Start with the outputs, or customer requirements, and move backward through the process to identify the key steps needed to produce each output; stop when the process reaches the supplier input stage. AT&T calls this technique **backward chaining**.[8] AT&T suggests the following steps:

1. Begin with the process output and ask, "What is the last essential subprocess that produces the output of the process?"
2. For that subprocess, ask, "What input does it need to produce the process output?" For each input, test its value to ensure that it is required.
3. For each input, identify its source. In many cases, the input will be the output of the previous subprocess. In some cases, the input may come from external suppliers.
4. Continue backward, one subprocess at a time, until each input comes from an external supplier.

This technique can be applied to each subprocess to create a more detailed process description.

Once a flowchart is constructed, several fundamental questions can be asked to analyze the process:

- Are the steps in the process arranged in logical sequence?
- Do all steps add value? Can some steps be eliminated and should others be added in order to improve quality or operational performance? Can some be combined? Should some be reordered?
- Are capacities of each step in balance; that is, do bottlenecks exist for which customers will incur excessive waiting time?
- What skills, equipment, and tools are required at each step of the process? Should some steps be automated?
- At which points in the system might errors occur that would result in customer dissatisfaction, and how might these errors be corrected?
- At which point or points should quality be measured?
- Where interaction with the customer occurs, what procedures and guidelines should employees follow to present a positive image?

Process mapping and analysis is a powerful tool. Using process mapping as a basis for improvement, Motorola reduced manufacturing time for pagers from 40 days to less than one hour. Citibank adopted this approach and reduced internal callbacks in its Private Bank group by 80 percent and the credit process time by 50 percent. Its Global Equipment Finance division, which provides financing and leasing services to Citibank customers, lowered the credit decision cycle from three days to one. Copeland Companies, subsidiaries of Travelers Life & Annuity, reduced the cycle time of processing statements from 28 days to 15 days.[9] The following example shows in more detail how Boise exploited process mapping.[10]

The Timber and Wood Products Division of Boise Cascade (now Boise) formed a team of 11 people with diverse backgrounds from manufacturing, administration, and marketing to improve a customer claims processing and tracking system that affected all areas and customers in its six divisions. Although external customer surveys indicated that the company was not doing badly, internal opinions of the operation were far more critical.

The first eye-opener came when the process was flowcharted and the group discovered that more than 70 steps were performed for each claim. Figure 13.3 shows the original flowchart from the marketing and sales department. Combined division tasks numbered in the hundreds for a single claim; the marketing and sales portion of the flowchart alone consisted of up to 20 separate tasks and seven decisions, which sometimes took months to complete. Most of these steps added no value to the settlement outcome. The flowchart accomplished much more than just plotting Boise's time and efforts; it also helped build team members' confidence in each other and foster mutual respect. When they saw how each member was able to chart his or her part of the process and state individual concerns, everyone's reason for being on the team was validated. The group eliminated 70 percent of the steps for small claims in the original flowchart, as shown in Figure 13.4.

Run Charts and Control Charts

A **run chart** is a line graph in which data are plotted over time. The vertical axis represents a measurement; the horizontal axis is the time scale. The daily newspaper usually includes several examples of run charts, such as the Dow Jones Industrial Average. They can be used to track such things as production volume, costs, and customer satisfaction indexes.

The first step in constructing a run chart is to identify the measurement or indicator to be monitored. In some situations, one might measure the quality characteristics for each individual unit of process output. For low-volume processes, such as

Figure 13.3 Original Flowchart from the Marketing and Sales Department

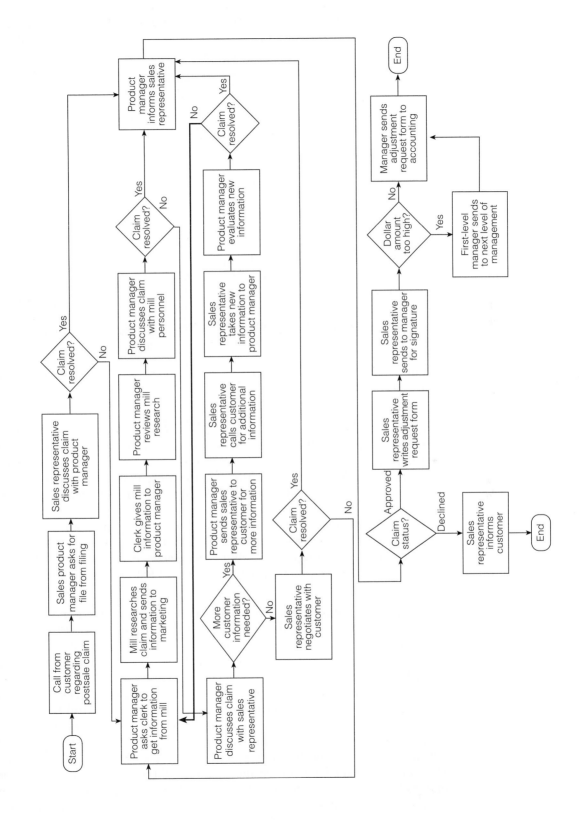

Figure 13.4 New Small Adjustment Request Form Process Flowchart for Marketing and Sales Department

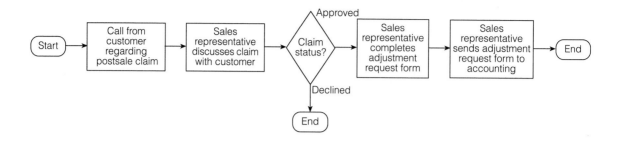

chemical production or surgeries, this approach would be appropriate. However, for high-volume production processes or services with large numbers of customers or transactions, it would be impractical. Instead, samples taken on a periodic basis provide the data for computing basic statistical measures such as the mean, range or standard deviation, proportion of items that do not conform to specifications, or number of nonconformances per unit.

> *Run charts show the performance and the variation of a process or some quality or productivity indicator over time in a graphical fashion that is easy to understand and interpret. They also identify process changes and trends over time and show the effects of corrective actions.*

Constructing the chart consists of the following steps:

Step 1. Collect the data. If samples are chosen, compute the relevant statistic for each sample, such as the average or proportion.

Step 2. Examine the range of the data. Scale the chart so that all data can be plotted on the vertical axis. Provide some additional room for new data as they are collected.

Step 3. Plot the points on the chart and connect them. Use graph paper if the chart is constructed by hand; a spreadsheet program is preferable.

Step 4. Compute the average of all plotted points and draw it as a horizontal line through the data. This line denoting the average is called the center line (CL) of the chart.

If the plotted points fluctuate in a stable pattern around the center line, with no large spikes, trends, or shifts, they indicate that the process is apparently under control. If unusual patterns exist, then the cause for lack of stability should be investigated and corrective action should be taken. Thus, run charts can identify messes caused by lack of control.

A **control chart** is simply a run chart to which two horizontal lines, called **control limits** are added: the **upper control limit (UCL)** and **lower control limit (LCL)**, as illustrated in Figure 13.5. Control charts were first proposed by Walter Shewhart at Bell Laboratories in the 1920s and were strongly advocated by Deming. Control limits are chosen statistically to provide a high probability (generally greater than 0.99) that points will fall between these limits if the process is in control. Control limits make it easier to interpret patterns in a run chart and draw conclusions about the state of control. These issues will be discussed in more detail in Chapter 14.

Figure 13.5 Structure of a Control Chart

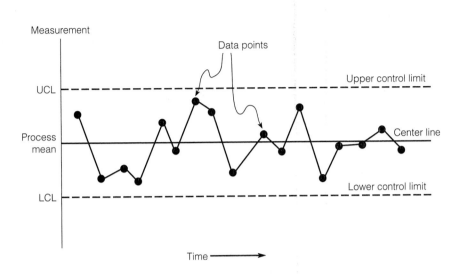

If sample values fall outside the control limits or if nonrandom patterns occur in the chart, then special causes may be affecting the process; the process is not stable. The process should be examined and corrective action taken as appropriate. If evaluation and correction are done in real time, then the chance of producing nonconforming product is minimized. Thus, as a problem-solving tool, control charts allow operators to identify quality problems as they occur. Of course, control charts alone cannot determine the source of the problem. Operators, supervisors, and engineers may have to resort to other problem-solving tools to seek the root cause.

Consider the following example.The Joint Commission Accreditation of Health Care Organizations (JCAHO) monitors and evaluates health care providers according to strict standards and guidelines. Improvement in the quality of care is a principal concern. Hospitals are required to identify and monitor important quality indicators that affect patient care and establish "thresholds for evaluation" (TFEs), which are levels at which special investigation of problems should occur. TFEs provide a means of focusing attention on nonrandom errors (that is, special causes of variation). A logical way to set TFEs is through control charts.

For instance, a hospital collects monthly data on the number of infections after surgeries. These data are shown in Table 13.3. Hospital administrators are concerned about whether the high percentages of infections (such as 1.76 percent in month 12) are caused by factors other than randomness. A control chart constructed from these data is shown in Figure 13.6. (Note that if the control limits are removed, it becomes a simple run chart.) The average percentage of infections is 55/7995 = 0.688 percent. Using formulas described in Chapter 14, the upper control limit is computed to be 2.35 percent. None of the data points fall above the upper control limit, indicating that the variation each month is due purely to chance and that the process is stable. To reduce the infection rate, management would have to attack the common causes in the process. The upper control limit would be a logical TFE to use, because any value beyond this limit is unlikely to occur by chance. Management can continue to use this chart to monitor future data.

Table 13.3 Monthly Data on Infections After Surgery

Month	Surgeries	Infections	Percent
1	208	1	0.48
2	225	3	1.33
3	201	3	1.49
4	236	1	0.42
5	220	3	1.36
6	244	1	0.41
7	247	1	0.40
8	245	1	0.41
9	250	1	0.40
10	227	0	0.00
11	234	2	0.85
12	227	4	1.76
13	213	2	0.94
14	212	1	0.47
15	193	2	1.04
16	182	0	0.00
17	140	1	0.71
18	230	1	0.43
19	187	1	0.53
20	252	2	0.79
21	201	1	0.50
22	226	0	0.00
23	222	2	0.90
24	212	2	0.94
25	219	1	0.46
26	223	2	0.90
27	191	1	0.52
28	222	0	0.00
29	231	3	1.30
30	239	1	0.42
31	217	2	0.92
32	241	1	0.41
33	220	3	1.36
34	278	1	0.36
35	255	3	1.18
36	225	1	0.44
	7,995	55	

Check Sheets

Check sheets are simple tools for data collection. Nearly any kind of form may be used to collect data. **Data sheets** use simple columnar or tabular forms to record data. However, to generate useful information from raw data, further processing generally is necessary.

Check sheets are special types of data collection forms in which the results may be interpreted on the form directly without additional processing.

In manufacturing, check sheets similar to Figure 13.7 are simple to use and easily interpreted by shop personnel. Including information such as specification limits

Figure 13.6 Control Chart for Surgery Infections

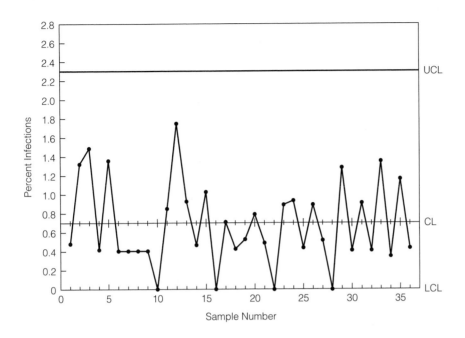

makes the number of nonconforming items easily observable and provides an imme-diate indication of the quality of the process. For example, in Figure 13.7 a significant proportion of dimensions are clearly out of specification, with a larger number on the high side than the low side.

A second type of check sheet for defective items is illustrated in Figure 13.8, which shows the type of defect and a tally in a resin production plant. Such a check sheet can be extended to include a time dimension so that data can be monitored and analyzed over time, and trends and patterns, if any, can be detected.

Figure 13.9 shows an example of a defect location check sheet. Kaoru Ishikawa relates how this check sheet was used to eliminate bubbles in laminated automobile windshield glass.[11] The location and form of bubbles were indicated on the check sheet; most of the bubbles occurred on the right side. Upon investigation, workers discovered that the pressure applied in laminating was off balance—the right side was receiving less pressure. The machine was adjusted, and the formation of bubbles was eliminated almost completely.

Histograms provide clues about the characteristics of the parent population from which a sample is taken. Patterns that would be difficult to see in an ordinary table of numbers become apparent.

Histograms

A **histogram** is a basic statistical tool that graphically shows the frequency or number of observations of a particular value or within a specified group. The check sheet in Figure 13.7, for example, was designed to provide the visual appeal of a histogram as the data are

Figure 13.7 Check Sheet for Data Collection

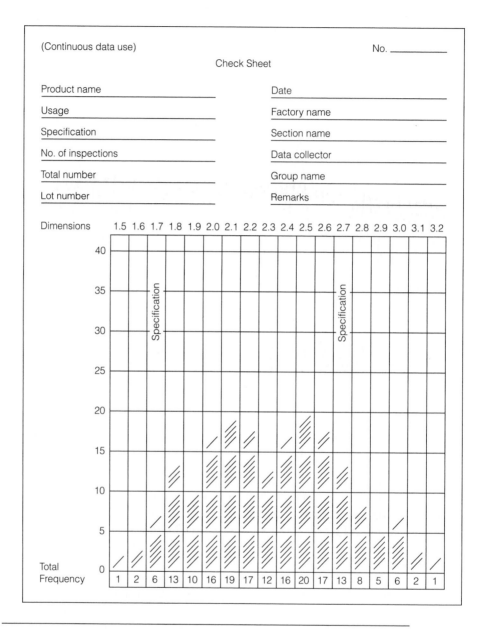

Source: K. Ishikawa, *Guide to Quality Control* (Tokyo: Asian Productivity Organization, 1982), 31.

tallied. For these data, one can easily determine the proportion of observations that fell outside the specification limits.

Some cautions should be heeded when interpreting histograms. First, the data should be representative of typical process conditions. If a new employee is now operating the equipment, or some aspect of the equipment, material, or method has changed, then new data should be collected. Second, the sample size should be large

Figure 13.8 Defective Item Check Sheet

Check Sheet

Product:

Manufacturing stage: final insp.

Type of defect: scar, incomplete, misshapen

Total no. inspected: 2530

Remarks: all items inspected

Date:

Factory:

Section:

Inspector's name:

Lot no.

Order no.

Type	Check	Subtotal
Surface scars	卌 卌 卌 卌 卌 卌 //	32
Cracks	卌 卌 卌 卌 ///	23
Incomplete	卌 卌 卌 卌 卌 卌 卌 卌 卌 ///	48
Misshapen	////	4
Others	卌 ///	8
	Grand total	115
Total rejects	卌 卌 卌 卌 卌 卌 卌 卌 卌 卌 卌 卌 卌 卌 卌 卌 卌 /	86

Source: K. Ishikawa, *Guide to Quality Control* (Tokyo: Asian Productivity Organization, 1982), 33.

enough to provide good conclusions; the larger, the better. Various guidelines exist, but a suggested minimum of at least 50 observations should be drawn. Finally, any conclusions drawn should be confirmed through further study and analysis.

Pareto Diagrams

Joseph Juran popularized the Pareto principle in 1950 after observing that a high proportion of quality issues resulted from only a few causes. He named this technique after Vilfredo Pareto (1848–1923), an Italian economist who determined that 85 percent of the wealth in Milan was owned by only 15 percent of the people. For instance, in analyzing costs in a paper mill, Juran found that 61 percent of total quality costs were attributable to one category—"broke," which is paper mill terminology for paper so defective that it is returned for reprocessing. In an analysis of 200 types of field failures of automotive engines, only five accounted for one-third of all failures; the top 25 accounted for two-thirds of the failures. In a textile mill, three of fifteen weavers were found to account

*A **Pareto distribution** is one in which the characteristics observed are ordered from largest frequency to smallest. A **Pareto diagram** is a histogram of the data from the largest frequency to the smallest.*

Figure 13.9 Defect Location Check Sheet

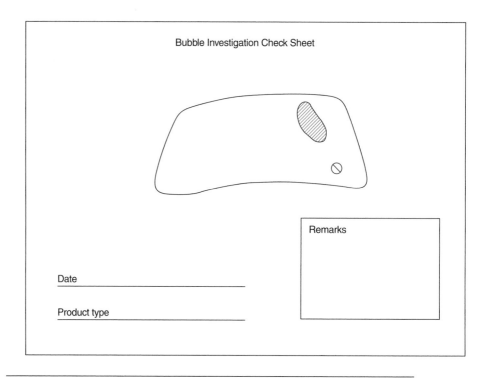

Source: K. Ishikawa, *Guide to Quality Control* (Tokyo: Asian Productivity Organization, 1982), 34.

for 74 percent of the defective cloth produced. Pareto analysis clearly separates the vital few from the trivial many and provides direction for selecting projects for improvement.

Pareto analysis is often used to analyze data collected in check sheets. One may also draw a cumulative frequency curve on the histogram, as shown in Figure 13.10. Such a visual aid clearly shows the relative magnitude of defects and can be used to identify opportunities for improvement. The most costly or significant problems stand out. Pareto diagrams can also show the results of improvement programs over time. They are less intimidating to employees who are fearful of statistics.

A good example of Pareto analysis is found at Rotor Clip Company, Inc., of Somerset, New Jersey, a major manufacturer of retaining rings and self-tightening hose clamps, and a believer in the use of simple quality improvement tools.[12] One application involved the use of a Pareto diagram to study rising premium freight charges for shipping retaining rings. The study covered three months in order to collect enough data to draw conclusions. The Pareto diagram is shown in Figure 13.11. The results were startling. The most frequent cause of higher freight charges was customer requests. The decision was made to continue the study to identify which customers consistently expedited their shipments and to work closely with them to find ways of reducing costs. The second largest contributor was the lack of available machine time. Once a die was installed in a stamping press, it ran until it produced the maximum number of parts (usually a million) before it was removed for routine mainte-

Figure 13.10 Pareto Diagram

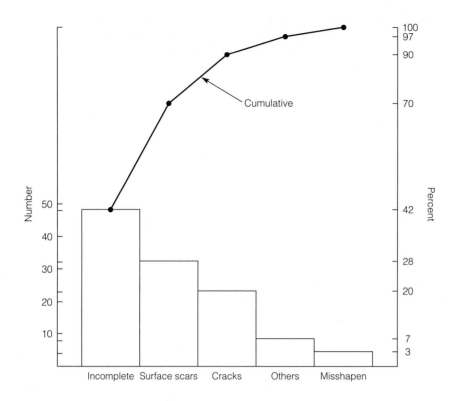

Figure 13.11 Pareto Diagram of Customer Calls

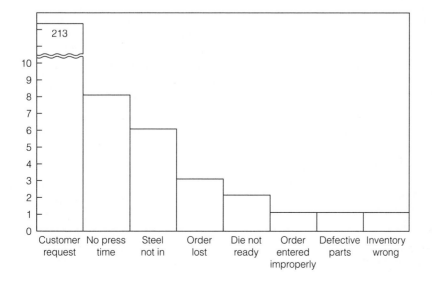

nance. Although this policy resulted in efficient utilization of tooling, it tied up the press and ultimately accounted for rush shipments. The policy was revised to limit die runs to fill orders more efficiently.

Pareto diagrams help analysts to progressively focus in on specific problems. Figure 13.12 shows one example. At each step, the Pareto diagram stratifies the data to more detailed levels (or it may require additional data collection), eventually isolating the most significant issues.

Cause-and-Effect Diagrams

Variation in process output and other quality problems can occur for a variety of reasons, such as materials, machines, methods, people, and measurement. The goal of problem solving is to identify the causes of problems in order to correct them. The cause-and-effect diagram is an important tool in this task; it assists the generation of ideas for problem causes and, in turn, serves as a basis for solution finding.

Kaoru Ishikawa introduced the cause-and-effect diagram in Japan, so it is also called an Ishikawa diagram. Because of its structure, it is often called a *fishbone diagram*. The general structure of a cause-and-effect diagram is shown in Figure 13.13. At the end of the horizontal line, a problem is listed. Each branch pointing into the main stem represents a possible cause. Branches pointing to the causes are contributors to those causes. The diagram identifies the most likely causes of a problem so that further data collection and analysis can be carried out.

> *A **cause-and-effect diagram** is a simple graphical method for presenting a chain of causes and effects and for sorting out causes and organizing relationships between variables.*

Cause-and-effect diagrams are constructed in a brainstorming type of atmosphere. Everyone can get involved and feel they are an important part of the problem-solving process. Usually small groups drawn from operations or management work with a trained and experienced facilitator. The facilitator guides attention to discussion of the problem and its causes, not opinions. As a group technique, the cause-and-effect method requires significant interaction between group members. The facilitator who listens carefully to the participants can capture the important ideas. A group can often be more effective by thinking of the problem broadly and considering environmental factors, political factors, employee issues, and even government policies, if appropriate.

To illustrate a cause-and-effect diagram, a major hospital was concerned about the length of time required to get a patient from the emergency department to an inpatient bed. Significant delays appeared to be caused by beds not being available. A quality improvement team tackled this problem by developing a cause-and-effect diagram. They identified four major causes: environmental services, emergency department, medical/surgery unit, and admitting. Figure 13.14 shows the diagram with several potential causes in each category. It served as a basis for further investigations of contributing factors and data analysis to find the root cause of the problem.

Scatter Diagrams

Scatter diagrams are the graphical component of regression analysis. Even though they do not provide rigorous statistical analysis, they often point to important relationships between variables, such as the percentage of an ingredient in an alloy and the hardness of the alloy. Typically, the variables in question represent possible causes and effects obtained from Ishikawa diagrams. For example, if a manufacturer suspects that the percentage of an ingredient in an alloy is causing quality problems

Figure 13.12 Use of Pareto Diagrams for Progressive Analysis

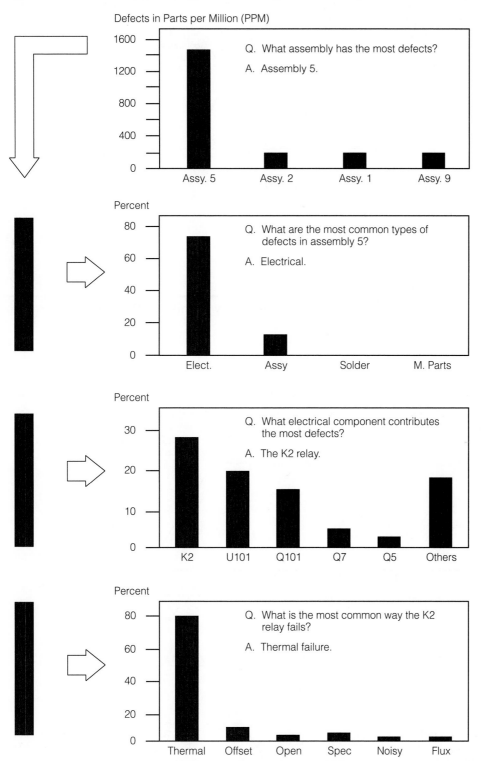

Source: Small Business Guidebook to Quality Management, Office of the Secretary of Defense, Quality Management Office, Washington, D.C.

Figure 13.13 General Structure of Cause-and-Effect Diagram

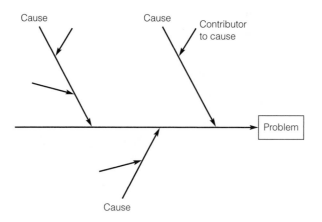

Figure 13.14 Cause-and-Effect Diagram for Hospital Emergency Admission Problem

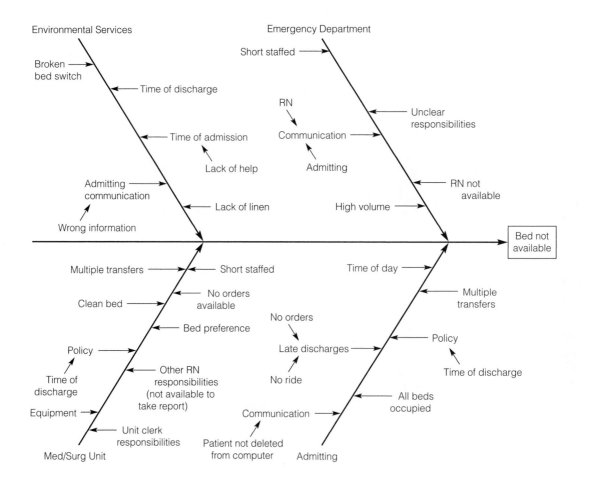

in meeting hardness specifications, an employee group might collect data from samples on the amount of ingredient and hardness and plot the data on a scatter diagram.

Statistical correlation analysis is used to interpret scatter diagrams. Figure 13.15 shows three types of correlation. If the correlation is positive, an increase in variable *x* is related to an increase in variable *y*; if the correlation is negative, an increase in *x* is related to a decrease in *y*; and if the correlation is close to zero, the variables have no linear relationship.

At Rotor Clip, which we highlighted earlier, the effect of advertising expenditures on the bottom line had been difficult to assess.[13] Management wanted to learn whether the number of advertising dollars spent correlated with the number of new customers gained in a given year. Advertising dollars spent by quarter were plotted against the number of new customers added for the same period for three consecutive years (see Figure 13.16). The positive correlation showed that heavy advertising

Quality Spotlight
Rotor Clip

Figure 13.15 Three Types of Correlation

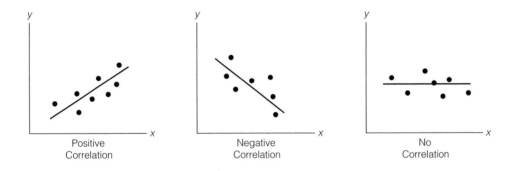

Figure 13.16 Scatter Diagram of New Customers versus Advertising Dollars

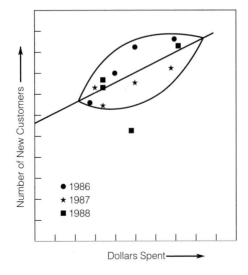

was related to new customers. The results were fairly consistent from year to year except for the second quarter of the third year, in which an outlier clearly stood out from the rest. Advertising checked the media schedule and discovered that experimental image ads dominated that particular period. This discovery prompted the advertising department to eliminate image ads from its schedule.

OTHER TOOLS FOR PROCESS IMPROVEMENT

A variety of tools, developed and refined over the years, support process improvement efforts. In this section, we review some of the more popular ones.

Kaizen Blitz

Blitz teams are generally comprised of employees from all areas involved in the process who understand it and can implement changes on the spot. Improvement is immediate, exciting, and satisfying for all those involved in the process.

*A **kaizen blitz** is an intense and rapid improvement process in which a team or a department throws all its resources into an improvement project over a short time period, as opposed to traditional kaizen applications, which are performed on a part-time basis.*

Some examples of using kaizen blitz at Magnivision include the following:[14]

- The molded lens department ran two shifts per day, using 13 employees, and after 40 percent rework, yielded 1,300 pieces per day. The production line was unbalanced and work piled up between stations, which added to quality problems as the work-in-process was often damaged. After a three-day blitz, the team reduced the production to one shift of six employees and a balanced line, reducing rework to 10 percent and increasing yield to 3,500 per day, saving more than $179,000.
- In Retail Services, a blitz team investigated problems that continually plagued employees, and discovered that many were related to the software system. Some of the same customer information had to be entered in multiple screens, sometimes the system took a long time to process information, and sometimes it was difficult to find specific information quickly. Neither the programmers nor the engineers were aware of these problems. By getting everyone together, some solutions were easily determined. Estimated savings were $125,000.

Poka-Yoke (Mistake-Proofing)

Human beings tend to make mistakes inadvertently.[15] Typical mistakes in production are omitted processing, processing errors, setup errors, missing parts, wrong parts, and adjustment errors. Such errors can arise from the following factors:

- Forgetfulness due to lack of concentration
- Misunderstanding because of the lack of familiarity with a process or procedures
- Poor identification associated with lack of proper attention
- Lack of experience
- Absentmindedness
- Delays in judgment when a process is automated
- Equipment malfunctions

Blaming workers not only discourages them and lowers morale, but also does not solve the problem.

The poka-yoke concept was developed and refined in the early 1960s by the late Shigeo Shingo, a Japanese manufacturing engineer who developed the Toyota produc-

Poka-yoke (POH-kah YOH-kay) is an approach for mistake-proofing processes using automatic devices or methods to avoid simple human error.

tion system.[16] Shingo visited a plant and observed that the plant was not using any type of measurement or statistical process control system for tracking defects. When asked why, the manager replied that they did not make any defects to track! His investigation led to the development of a mistake-proofing approach called Zero Quality Control, or ZQC. ZQC is driven by simple and inexpensive inspection processes, such as successive checking, in which operators inspect the work of the prior operation before continuing, and self-checking, in which operators assess the quality of their own work. Poka-yokes are designed to facilitate this process or remove the human element completely.

Poka-yoke is focused on two aspects: (1) prediction, or recognizing that a defect is about to occur and providing a warning, and (2) detection, or recognizing that a defect has occurred and stopping the process. Many applications of poka-yoke are deceptively simple, yet creative. Usually, they are inexpensive to implement. One of Shingo's first poka-yoke devices involved a process at the Yamada Electric plant in which workers assemble a switch having two push buttons supported by two springs.[17] Occasionally, the worker would forget to insert a spring under each button, which led to a costly and embarrassing repair at the customer's facility. In the old method, the worker would take two springs out of a large parts box and then assemble the switch. To prevent this mistake, the worker was instructed first to place two springs in a small dish in front of the parts box, and then assemble the switch. If a spring remains in the dish, the operator knows immediately that an error has occurred. The solution was simple, cheap, and provided immediate feedback to the operator.

Many other examples can be cited:

- Machines have limit switches connected to warning lights that tell the operator when parts are positioned improperly on the machine.
- A device on a drill counts the number of holes drilled in a work piece; a buzzer sounds if the work piece is removed before the correct number of holes has been drilled.
- Cassette covers are frequently scratched when the screwdriver slips out of the screw slot and slides against the plastic covers. The screw design shown in Figure 13.17 prevents the screwdriver from slipping.
- A metal roller is used to laminate two surfaces bonded with hot melted glue. The glue tends to stick to the roller and causes defects in the laminate surface. An investigation showed that if the roller were dampened, the glue would not stick. A secondary roller was added to dampen the steel roller during the process, preventing the glue from sticking.

Figure 13.17 A Poka-Yoke Example of Screw Redesign

Old Design

New Design

- One production step at Motorola involves putting alphabetic characters on a keyboard, and then checking to make sure each key is placed correctly. A group of workers designed a clear template with the letters positioned slightly off center. By holding the template over the keyboard, assemblers can quickly spot mistakes.
- Computer programs display a warning message if a file that has not been saved is to be closed.
- A 3.5-inch diskette is designed so that it cannot be inserted unless the disk is oriented correctly (try it!). These disks are not perfectly square, and the beveled right corner of the disk allows a stop in the disk drive to be pushed away if it is inserted correctly.
- Power lawn mowers now have a safety bar on the handle that must be engaged in order to start the engine.
- A proxy ballot for an investment fund will not fit into the return envelope unless a small strip is detached. The strip asks the respondent to check to see whether the ballot is signed and dated.

From this discussion and examples, we see three levels of mistake-proofing with increasing costs associated with them:

1. *Designing potential errors out of the product or process.* Clearly, this approach is the most powerful form of mistake-proofing because it eliminates any possibility that the error or defect might occur and has no direct cost in terms of time or rework and scrap.
2. *Identifying potential defects and stopping a process before the defect is produced.* Although this approach eliminates any cost associated with producing a defect, it does require the time associated with stopping a process and taking corrective action.
3. *Finding defects that enter or leave a process.* This approach eliminates wasted resources that would add value to nonconforming work, but clearly results in scrap or rework.

It is not always possible to achieve the highest level in designing or improving a process, but it is certainly advantageous to try.

Richard B. Chase and Douglas M. Stewart suggest that the same concepts can be applied to services.[18] The major differences are that service mistake-proofing must account for the customers' activities as well as those of the producer, and fail-safe methods must be set up for interactions conducted directly or by phone, mail, or other technologies, such as ATM. Chase and Stewart classify service poka-yokes by the type of error they are designed to prevent: server errors and customer errors. Server errors result from the task, treatment, or tangibles of the service. Customer errors occur during preparation, the service encounter, or during resolution.

Task errors include doing work incorrectly, work not requested, work in the wrong order, or working too slowly. Some examples of poka-yoke devices for task errors are computer prompts, color-coded cash register keys, measuring tools such as McDonald's french-fry scoop, and signaling devices. Hospitals use trays for surgical instruments that have indentations for each instrument, preventing the surgeon from leaving one of them in the patient.

Treatment errors arise in the contact between the server and the customer, such as lack of courteous behavior, and failure to acknowledge, listen, or react appropriately to the customer. A bank encourages eye contact by requiring tellers to record the customer's eye color on a checklist as they start the transaction. To promote friendliness at a fast-food restaurant, trainers provide the four specific cues for when to smile: when greeting the customer, when taking the order, when telling about the dessert special, and when giving the customer change. They encourage employees to observe whether the customer smiled back, a natural reinforcer for smiling.

Tangible errors are those in physical elements of the service, such as unclean facilities, dirty uniforms, inappropriate temperature, and document errors. Hotels wrap paper strips around towels to help the housekeeping staff identify clean linen and show which ones should be replaced. Spell-checkers in word processing software help reduce document misspellings (provided they are used!).

Customer errors in preparation include the failure to bring necessary materials to the encounter, to understand their role in the service transaction, and to engage the correct service. A computer manufacturer provides a flowchart to specify how to place a service call. By guiding the customers through three yes-or-no questions, the flowchart prompts them to have the necessary information before calling.

Customer errors during an encounter can be due to inattention, misunderstanding, or simply a memory lapse, and include failure to remember steps in the process or to follow instructions. Poka-yoke examples include height bars at amusement rides that indicate rider size requirements, beepers that signal customers to remove cards from ATM machines, and locks on airplane lavatory doors that must be closed to turn on the lights. Some cashiers at restaurants fold back the top edge of credit card receipts, holding together the restaurant's copies while revealing the customer's copy.

Customer errors at the resolution stage of a service encounter include failure to signal service inadequacies, to learn from experience, to adjust expectations, and to execute appropriate post-encounter actions. Hotels might enclose a small gift certificate to encourage guests to provide feedback. Strategically placed tray-return stands and trash receptacles remind customers to return trays in fast-food facilities.

Mistake-proofing a service process requires identifying when and where failures generally occur. Once a failure is identified, the source must be found. The final step is to prevent the mistake from occurring through source inspection, self-inspection, or sequential checks.

Process Simulation

Process simulation has been used routinely in business to address complex operational problems, so it is no wonder that it is a useful tool for Six Sigma applications, especially those involving customer service improvement, cycle time reduction, and reducing variability. Process simulation should be used when the process is highly complex and difficult to visualize, involves many decision points, or when the goal is to optimize the use of resources for a process.[19]

> *Process simulation* is an approach to building a logical model of a real process, and experimenting with the model to obtain insight about the behavior of the process or to evaluate the impact of changes in assumptions or potential improvements to it.

Building a process simulation model involves first describing how the process operates, normally using a process map. The process map includes all process steps, including logical decisions that route materials or information to different locations. Second, all key inputs such as how long it takes to perform each step of the process and resources needed must be identified. Typically the activity times in a process are uncertain and described by probability distributions, which normally makes it difficult to evaluate process performance and identify bottlenecks without simulation. The intent is for the model to duplicate the real process so that "what if?" questions can be easily evaluated without having to make time-consuming or costly changes to the real process. Once the model is developed, the simulation process repeatedly samples from the probability distributions of the input variables to create a distribution of potential outputs.

As an example, a common customer support process is the help desk or call center process responsible for answering and addressing customers' questions and complaints.[20] Typically, customer satisfaction ratings of the help desk are low. Although this process is common, it is difficult to analyze with conventional Six Sigma tools. The measure phase usually identifies "time to resolve an issue" and "quality of the issue resolution" as the two CTQs. When these factors are measured, performance is generally at less than a 1-sigma level, so significant improvement potential exists.

Help desks are much too complex to analyze using basic Six Sigma tools. Most help desks have two or three levels of support. When a call comes in, it often waits in a queue. When a level 1 person is available, he or she takes the call. If this person cannot resolve the issue, the call is forwarded to level 2. If the level 2 representative cannot resolve the call, it is forwarded to engineering or a similar support group. Between each of these levels, the call may wait in several more queues, or the customer may be asked to wait for a call back.

By developing a process simulation model, a Black Belt can validate the model against the real process by collecting data for model inputs, running the model, and statistically matching the results with data collected during the measure phase. Once the model is validated, analysis can begin. Most simulation packages provide operational output data for all the process steps, resource utilization data, and additional variables tracked throughout the process. When the data are collected, it becomes a straightforward task to analyze it statistically, identify bottlenecks, develop proposed solutions, and rerun the simulation to confirm the results.

To provide a simple illustration, suppose that in a phone support center, incoming calls arrive randomly with an average time between calls of about 5 minutes and a support representative evaluates the nature of each problem.[21] Each call may take anywhere between 30 seconds and 4 minutes, although most can be handled in about 2 minutes. The representative is able to resolve 75 percent of the calls immediately. However, 25 percent of the calls require that other support representatives do research and make a return call to the customer. The research, combined with the return call, requires on average 20 minutes, although this time may vary quite a bit, from as little as 5 minutes to more than 35 minutes. Figure 13.18 shows the process map for this situation, including the support representative resources.

It is difficult to perform a process simulation, even for such a simple process, without some type of commercial simulation software. For this example, we used a package called ProcessModel[22] which facilitates the simulation process by allowing the model to be built by simply "dragging and dropping" the process map symbols on the computer screen, entering the appropriate data input descriptions, and running the model. As the model runs, ProcessModel provides a visual animation of the process, allowing the user to see the buildup of calls at each support stage to gain insight into the system performance.

Standard output reports, such as the one shown in Figure 13.19, are generated automatically. By examining these results (see the circled entries in the figure), we see that support problems waited in the *Return Call inQ* activity an average of more than 496 minutes, and as many as 51 calls were waiting at any one time. Thus, this activity should be identified as a problem area suitable for process improvement efforts. In

Figure 13.18 Process Map for Help Desk Simulation Model

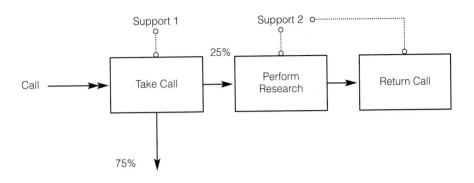

the RESOURCES section, we see that Support 1 was busy about half the time, while Support 2 was busy nearly 100 percent of the time. Any time human resource utilization is greater than 80 percent for extended periods, the system will most likely result in long waiting times and queue lengths, requiring more resources or changes in the assignment of resources. The simulation results suggest that better allocation of resources should improve performance. To reduce the customer waiting time we might add additional support representatives or cross-train and share the existing representatives. The simulation model can easily be modified to incorporate these changes and the impacts on the results can be evaluated. Clearly, trying to do this in the real process would be costly and disruptive, with no guarantee that it will work.

Simulation is a rich and complex topic. Many good books exist about process simulation and we encourage you to explore some of the references given in the bibliography.

ENGAGING THE WORKFORCE IN PROCESS IMPROVEMENT

People are key to process improvement. Good people create innovative ideas and find and solve process problems. Expert team members perform the Deming cycle or the Six Sigma DMAIC process. People initiate and implement process improvement projects. It is not so much a question of what things people need to know as it is a question of what things they need to know *how* to do. One team or one team member can make or break an improvement project or a Six Sigma initiative. People skills can be learned, but often take more time than is available for a single project; thus, they should be a routine part of every employee's educational program. Many of these issues, such as team leader roles, leadership development, team development, motivation, and job design, were discussed in Chapter 6.

> *Compared to the technical tools for gathering and analyzing data, the "soft skills"—those that involve people—such as project management and team facilitation, are more difficult to teach and learn.*

Some of the essential elements for effective process improvement from a people perspective are a *shared vision* and *behavioral skills*. A shared vision can unify a team and provide the motivation for successfully implementing the project. Developing one generally requires team discussions early on; unfortunately, inexperienced project

Figure 13.19 ProcessModel Simulation Results

Scenario	=	**Normal Run**
Replication	=	**1 of 1**
Simulation Time	=	**48 hr**

ACTIVITIES

Activity Name	Scheduled Hours	Capacity	Total Entries	Average Minutes Per Entry	Average Contents	Maximum Contents	Current Contents	% Util
Take Call inQ	40	999	504	1.01	0.21	5	0	0.02
Take Call	40	1	504	2.17	0.45	1	0	45.62
Perform Research inQ	40	999	114	112.50	5.34	11	4	0.53
Perform Research	40	10	110	19.92	0.91	1	1	9.13
Return Call inQ	40	999	109	496.78	22.56	51	51	2.26
Return Call	40	1	58	3.00	0.07	1	0	7.25

ACTIVITY STATES BY PERCENTAGE (Multiple Capacity)

Activity Name	Scheduled Hours	% Empty	% Partially Occupied	% Full
Take Call inQ	40	84.85	15.15	0.00
Perform Research inQ	40	10.50	89.50	0.00
Perform Research	40	8.67	91.33	0.00
Return Call inQ	40	2.06	97.94	0.00

ACTIVITY STATES BY PERCENTAGE (Single Capacity)

Activity Name	Scheduled Hours	% Operation	% Idle	% Waiting	% Blocked
Take Call	40	45.62	54.38	0.00	0.00
Return Call	40	7.25	92.75	0.00	0.00

RESOURCES

Resource Name	Units	Scheduled Hours	Number of Times Used	Average Minutes Per Usage	% Util
Support 1	1	48	504	2.17	45.62
Support 2	1	48	168	14.08	98.58

RESOURCE STATES BY PERCENTAGE

Resource Name	Scheduled Hours	% In Use	% Idle	% Down
Support 1	40	45.62	54.38	0.00
Support 2	40	98.58	1.42	0.00

ENTITY SUMMARY (Times in Scoreboard time units)

Entity Name	Qty Processed	Average Cycle Time (Minutes)	Average VA Time (Minutes)	Average Cost
Call	398	4.19	2.18	0.43
HardCall	58	596.99	24.99	004

Figure 13.19 ProcessModel Simulation Results *(continued)*

VARIABLES

Variable Name	Total Changes	Average Minutes Per Change	Minimum Value	Maximum Value	Current Value	Average Value
Avg BVA Time Entity	1	0.00	0	0	0	0
Avg BVA Time Call	391	6.10	0	0	0	0
Avg BVA Time HardCall	59	39.04	0	0	0	0

leaders frequently bypass these discussions in an effort to get the project underway. People who are technically oriented often neglect behavioral skills, thinking that such skills are unnecessary in order to solve technical problems. Behavioral skills require both knowledge and practice. Part of Deming's foundation for "profound knowledge" (Chapter 3) was the requirement to study, learn, and use psychology to improve quality.

Skills for Team Leaders

As we discussed, team members often assume the role of project leaders and project managers and yet must defer to superior knowledge of other team members and take on roles as followers. In an insightful book on team-based project management, James Lewis observed that people skills needed by project managers could also be easily applied to team members.[23] These skills include the following:

- Conflict management and resolution
- Team management
- Leadership skills
- Decision making
- Communication
- Negotiation
- Cross-cultural training

Conflict management involves dealing proactively with disagreements that may occur when two or more technical experts get together. Team management involves ensuring that project members remain focused on the goals, time frame, and costs of their part of the project. Leadership skills require that the project leader guide the work of the team, including team development, while managing upward to the project champion and outward to other project teams and team leaders. Decision making requires that good decisions be made in a timely fashion. Communication channels must be established and maintained throughout the course of the project. Negotiation is needed in order to secure the resources required for successful project completion. Cross-cultural training may involve team members of other nationalities, or it may simply involve people from different functional areas with divergent points of view. In either case, it is extremely important for team members to be able to listen and learn about different perspectives on shared project goals from team and nonteam people who may have widely differing thoughts about issues under consideration.

Skills for Team Members

Perhaps the two areas of greatest importance in team functioning for process improvement project team members are meetings and shared decision making. Meetings are important because they consume considerable valuable time of team members. Shared decision making is important because most individuals in organizations have more practice in receiving direction from a supervisor, or making an individual decision in their own workplace. Shared decisions are new territory for many individuals.

Peter Scholtes provides some rules for effective meetings[24]:

- Use agendas.
- Have a facilitator.
- Take minutes.
- Draft the next agenda.
- Evaluate the meeting.
- Adhere to the "100-mile" rule.

Scholtes suggests the use of detailed agendas that include topics, a sentence about the importance of each, who will present them, the estimated time for each topic, and the type of item, such as discussion, decision, or information topics. A facilitator can keep the discussion on time and on target, prevent anyone from dominating or being overlooked, and help bring the discussion to a close. A scribe who takes minutes can record subjects, decisions, and who will be responsible for actions taken. Drafting the next agenda at the end of the meeting serves to set a plan of action for going forward. Evaluating the meeting incorporates a continuous improvement step. Adhering to the "100-mile" rule requires a commitment to focus on the meeting so clearly that "no one should be called from the meeting unless it is so important that the disruption would occur even if the meeting was 100 miles away from the workplace."[25]

Decision-making techniques abound in quality improvement literature. One of the most powerful is called the nominal group technique (NGT), developed to provide a way to prioritize and focus on important project objectives in the project definition stage.[26] One of the major advantages of the technique is that it balances the power of each individual involved in the decision process. Key steps in the process include the following:

1. Request that all participants (usually 5–10 persons) write or say which problem or issue they feel is most important.
2. Record all problems or issues.
3. Develop a master list of problems or issues.
4. Generate and distribute to each participant a form that numbers the problems or issues in no particular order.
5. Request that each participant rank the top five problems or issues by assigning five points to their most important perceived problem and one point to the least important of their top five.
6. Tally the results by adding the points for each problem or issue.
7. The problem or issue with the highest number is the most important one for the team as a whole.
8. Discuss the results and generate a final ranked list for process improvement action planning.[27]

This approach provides a more democratic way of making decisions and helps individuals to feel that they have contributed to the process.

QUALITY IN PRACTICE

PROCESS IMPROVEMENT ON THE FREE-THROW LINE[28]

Timothy Clark observed that in basketball games, his son Andrew's free-throw percentage averaged between 45 and 50 percent. Andrew's process was simple: Go to the free throw line, bounce the ball four times, aim, and shoot. To confirm these observations, Andrew shot five sets of 10 free throws with an average of 42 percent, showing little variation among the five sets. Timothy developed a cause-and-effect diagram (Figure 13.20) to identify the principal causes. After analyzing the diagram and observing his son's process, he believed that the main causes were not standing in the same place on the free-throw line every time and having an inconsistent focal point. They developed a new process in which Andrew stood at the center of the line and focused on the middle of the front part of the rim. The new process resulted in a 36 percent improvement in practice (Figure 13.21). Toward the end of the 1994 season, he improved his average to 69 percent in the last three games.

During the 1995 season, Andrew averaged 60 percent. A control chart (Figure 13.22) showed that the process was quite stable. In the summer of 1995, Andrew attended a basketball camp where he was advised to change his shooting technique. This process reduced his shooting percentage during the 1996 season to 50 percent. However, his father helped him to reinstall his old process, and his percentage returned to its former level, also improving his confidence.

Key Issues for Discussion

1. How does this application conform to Deming's PDSA cycle?
2. Design a check sheet that might be useful to collect data for this analysis. How might Pareto diagrams be used to enhance the analysis?

Figure 13.20 Free-Throwing Cause-and-Effect Diagram

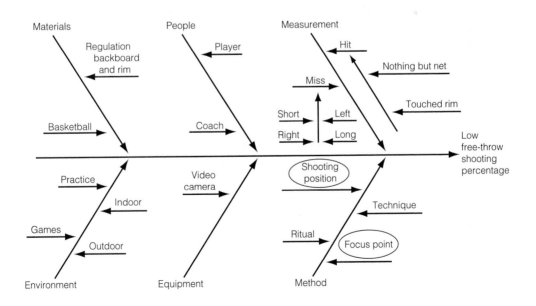

Source: Adapted from Timothy Clark and Andrew Clark, "Continuous Improvement at the Free-Throw Line," *Quality Progress,* October 1997, 78–80. © 1997, American Society for Quality. Reprinted with permission.

Figure 13.21 Free-Throwing Shots Made Before and After Implementing the Improvement

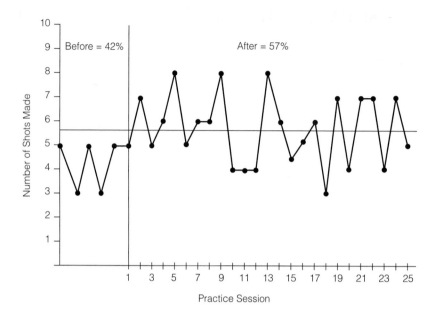

Source: Adapted from Timothy Clark and Andrew Clark, "Continuous Improvement at the Free-Throw Line," *Quality Progress,* October 1997, 78–80. © 1997. American Society for Quality. Reprinted with permission.

Figure 13.22 Determining Whether the Free-Throw Process Is Stable

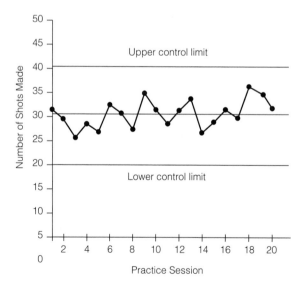

Source: Adapted from Timothy Clark and Andrew Clark, "Continuous Improvement at the Free-Throw Line," *Quality Progress,* October 1997, 78–80. © 1997. American Society for Quality. Reprinted with permission.

QUALITY IN PRACTICE

IMPROVING PATIENT SERVICES AT MIDDLETOWN REGIONAL HOSPITAL[29]

Middletown Regional Hospital (MRH) is a licensed 310-bed acute-care hospital located in Middletown, Ohio, a southwestern Ohio city about 35 miles from Cincinnati. The parent, MRHS Corporation, includes a major hospital and 20 off-site locations. MRH employs approximately 1,700 people across a four-county area and provides all major medical services with the exception of open-heart surgery.

CEO Douglas W. McNeill led MRH to become a quality-driven organization. This drive for continuous improvement can be seen from the top management all the way down to the front-line employees. Dedication to quality is also evident in the mission, vision, and value statements. Every department at MRH is required to develop performance improvement goals and indicators annually. All employees are trained annually in tools and approaches developed by the Quality Management Department. Because of these efforts, the hospital received a number of quality awards and recognitions, including winning the first Codman Award, presented by the Joint Commission on Accreditation of Healthcare Organizations (JCAHO) for quality in a health care organization, and being named one of the 100 top hospitals in the United States.

An important part of ensuring smooth-running daily operations at MRH is Maintenance and Environmental Services, whose director is Jim Faze. This division consists of two departments—the 20-person Maintenance Department, which is responsible for the power plant, grounds, and the general maintenance of the facility for the main campus and the 20 off-site locations; and the Environmental Services (EVS) Department, which employs 56 people and is responsible for linen, waste management, and cleaning services for the 650,000 sqare foot main facility. To focus on improving services to its internal and external customers, EVS developed a customer service monitoring system (CSMS) with three distinct parts: the Press Ganey Customer Survey, written customer comments that MRH receives from the survey, and a seven-step quality improvement process.

Patients fill out the Press Ganey Customer Satisfaction Survey after receiving services. This survey asks a full range of questions relating to all aspects of care the patient received while at any facility. The survey is divided into four major service sectors: Inpatient Services, Ambulatory Services, Outpatient Surgery, and Emergency Services. A direct question about the cleanliness of the hospital is asked for all sectors except Emergency Services. Results of the questionnaire are ranked against all hospitals nationwide in the database for each sector. The data are also sorted by geographic region and hospital size for additional benchmarking results. Approximately 450 hospitals use this survey, enhancing its value as a benchmarking tool. MRH receives the report quarterly.

The second portion of the CSMS consists of written customer comments from the survey. These comments are forwarded to the Guest Relations Department and then to the specific departments for action. MRH receives both positive and negative comments from this source. EVS formally praises employees with positive comments and retrains those who receive negative comments.

The third element of the CSMS is improvement. Any time a major problem is encountered, MRH associates have been taught to apply a seven-step process, which was developed and implemented by an external management consultant group, and is taught and reinforced during the annual employee training sessions. The steps of this process are:

1. Activate organizational awareness.
2. Seek environmental transformation.
3. Identify and define the process.
4. Determine measurements.
5. Collect data using statistical process control (SPC).
6. Analyze and make recommendations.
7. Remeasure to assess improvement.

One problem EVS recognized was that "A significant gap exists between the current level of perceived customer satisfaction and the management goal, as measured by the Press Ganey Customer Satisfaction Survey. The objective is to find ways to eliminate the gap between the current level of 69th percentile ranking and the management goal of 85th percentile."

At the time of this study, MRH had been using the Press Ganey Customer Satisfaction Survey for eleven quarters. One question pertained to the cleanliness of the facility; thus, the key issue for EVS was "How clean was the facility?" Two factors created difficulties in attacking this problem. First, MRH's management only monitored the percentile ranking in the Press Ganey Survey for each division, but no one had the responsibility for completely analyzing all of the survey data. The second factor was the speed at which MRH received the data. MRH and the EVS department had no opportunity for service recovery because the patients were no longer at the facility when MRH received their complaints.

The return rates on the customer surveys had remained fairly constant at 24 percent over the past three years. Return rates for the hospital's three service sectors were: 26 percent for Inpatient Services, 30 percent for Ambulatory Services, and 16 percent for Outpatient Surgery. The raw data for this question can be found in Table 1 in the Chapter 13 database on the student CD-ROM. Three key outcomes were measured: the percentile rank, the mean score analysis, and correlation coefficients. The percentile ranking was favored historically by upper management. It is simply the ranking against all the other hospital facilities involved in the nationwide survey. This information was tracked by Faze on a quarterly basis, charted, and forwarded to upper management. Previously, nothing was done at the departmental level to analyze the data and use it for improvement. An x-bar & R chart for the percentile rank for the department over the past 11 quarters can be seen in the database (in Table 1) and shows stable, consistent results.

The mean and range scores had also stayed very consistent over the past 11 quarters. It is important to understand the relationship between the mean score and the percentile ranking when analyzing the Press Ganey data. One might expect that a consistent mean score would be correlated with the percentile ranking. The %Rank vs. Mean graph in the database shows a line chart for the relationship between the mean scores and the percentile rank for the last 11 quarters. It is obvious that no direct correlation appears between these two sets of data. A higher mean score does not necessarily coincide with a high percentile rank.

A related measure from the Press Ganey Survey is the correlation coefficient, which measures the relative importance of a specific question to the overall score. The higher a question's relative correlation, the more likely that the overall satisfaction score for the survey will go up when this question's score goes up. Similarly, an item with a high correlation coefficient will bring down the overall satisfaction score if the individual question score goes down. Essentially, it is an indicator of the importance of the service in a given area to the customer. The correlations over time for EVS are shown in the x-bar & R chart for the correlation coefficients. Customer concerns show the relatively high degree of interest and concern relating to measures of cleanliness in a hospital setting. The chart shows a process that is stable. However, revealing information was discovered about correlation coefficient differences among the three service areas. The correlation coefficients for the Ambulatory Services and the Outpatient Surgery are much higher than for Inpatient Services. This result shows that the cleanliness question has less of an impact on the overall score of the inpatient section than in Outpatient Services.

Over a two-year period, EVS teams tried three different approaches to improving the survey scores: implementing a computerized cleaning assignment system, tracking and addressing responses to comments received on customer surveys, and developing and deploying a daily room checklist to be filled out by housekeepers. The computerized cleaning assignment system helped improve the Press Ganey scores early in the process, but had more of an impact on the internal customers. The survey comments suggested that customers did not know what services to expect on a daily basis. MRH formed a team that developed tent cards similar to the ones used in the hotel industry. The tent card serves to let customers know what their room should look like when they arrive, what daily services they can expect, and a phone number to contact EVS if their expectations are not being met. The name of the housekeeper and encouragement to contact him/her about any cleaning issues is also on the card. This approach reduced the number of negative written comments MRH receives. EVS uses the daily room checklist to provide documentation on what services have been performed and to hold housekeepers accountable to get the work done right the first time.

Management and associates in EVS at MRH continue to search for ways to continually improve service levels in their quest to reach the elusive 85th percentile level that is management's long-term goal.

Key Issues for Discussion

1. How do MRH's Total Quality Improvement Implementation System steps compare to the Deming Cycle and the DMAIC improvement steps?

2. What quality improvement tools have been used by EVS to address the problem?
3. What other insights can you get from analysis of the charts on the CD-ROM?
4. What have the three initiatives contributed in the efforts to solve the stated problem?
5. What else would you recommend in order to close the gap between perceived quality and the quality levels that EVS and MRH management wants to provide?

REVIEW QUESTIONS

1. Contrast the different process improvement methodologies described in this chapter. How are they alike, and how do they differ?
2. What is the Deming cycle? Explain the four steps.
3. Why do messes arise in organizations?
4. Describe the key issues that organizations face in the fact-finding phase of the CPS process.
5. Describe some techniques used to generate ideas.
6. What issues must be addressed in the solution-finding and implementation phases of the CPS process?
7. List and explain the Original Seven QC Tools. In what phases of the CPS process might each be most useful?
8. What types of questions might one ask to identify opportunities for improvement with a process flowchart?
9. Describe a control chart. How does it differ from a run chart?
10. Describe different types of check sheets that are useful in quality improvement.
11. Explain the difference between a histogram and a Pareto diagram. Do they apply to the same types of data?
12. Describe the structure of a cause-and-effect diagram.
13. How do scatter diagrams assist in finding solutions to quality problems?
14. Why do people make inadvertent mistakes? How does poka-yoke help prevent such mistakes?
15. What are the components of a process simulation? In what types of problem solving is it most useful?
16. Describe the types of errors that service poka-yokes are designed to prevent.
17. List and describe the tools needed for running an effective meeting.
18. What are the steps required to perform the nominal group technique (NGT)?

DISCUSSION QUESTIONS

1. Table 13.4 shows the Pepsi-Cola Company's three-step method for customer-valued process improvement. Discuss its differences and similarities to the Deming cycle.

Table 13.4 Pepsi-Cola Process Improvement Methodology

Steps	Actions
1. Start with the customer	a. Understand and prioritize customer needs b. Establish customer measures and success criteria c. Select a process with most impact on customer needs
2. Understand ourselves and plan improvements	a. Analyze the current process involving the performers in each step b. Design improved process c. Establish process measures
3. Do it	a. Pilot-test improved process b. Implement improved process c. Stabilize process d. Go to Step 1 (continuously improve)

Source: Courtesy of Pepsi-Cola Co. Reprinted with permission of The Forum Corporation.

2. What types of defects or errors might the following organizations measure and improve as part of a Six Sigma initiative?
   a. A metropolitan bus company
   b. A local department store
   c. An electric power company
   d. Walt Disney World or a regional amusement park, such as Paramount or Six Flags
   e. Your college or university
3. Discuss what would be the most appropriate tool to use to attack each of these quality issues:
   a. A copy machine suffers frequent paper jams and users are often confused as to how to fix the problem.
   b. The publication team for an engineering department wants to improve the accuracy of its user documentation but is unsure of why documents aren't error-free.
   c. An office manager has experienced numerous problems with a laser printer: double-spaced lines, garbled text, lost text, and blank pages. She is trying to figure out which is the most significant problem.
   d. A military agency wants to evaluate the weight of personnel at a certain facility.
   e. A bank needs to determine how many teller positions, drive-through stations, and ATM machines it needs for a new branch bank in a certain busy location. Its information includes the average numbers and types of customers served by other similar facilities, as well as demographic information to suggest the level of customer traffic in the new facility.

    f. A contracting agency wants to investigate why they had so many changes in their contracts. They believe that the number of changes may be related to the dollar value of the original contract or the days between the request for proposal and the contract award.

    g. A travel agency is interested in gaining a better understanding of how call volume varies by time of year in order to adjust staffing schedules.

4. The following two summaries of quality improvement projects performed by employee teams at Siemens Energy and Automation and Lucas Sumitomo Brakes, Inc., were presented in the 1997 Ohio Manufacturers' Association Case Studies in Team Excellence competition. Discuss how each example can be viewed in the context of (1) the Deming cycle, and (2) the creative problem solving process.

Siemens Energy and Automation: Makin' Waves[30]

The Makin' Waves team is a Continuous Improvement team from the Siemens facility located in Urbana, Ohio. The Urbana facility is a supplier plant to the Siemens plant in Bellefontaine. We supply molded plastic, stamping, and plating support to the Bellefontaine plant. The Makin' Waves team is from the Plastics Department. Our team has been functioning for four years and has completed many highly successful projects. The team consists of two press operators, one product repairperson, one janitor, and one Quality Assurance person, all from the Plastics Department. We also included a supervisor from the E-Frame circuit breaker line in Bellefontaine who was added at the beginning of this project as a representative of our stakeholders and to provide valuable input.

Our team began this project by looking into ideas for a project from the Corrective Action System and the Value Improvement Program. Our project started out as a way to reduce the negative effect caused by the poor appearance of the E-Frame breaker. Upon investigating the problem we dis-covered that we could actually eliminate the operation that was causing the negative appearance. We decided to make our project the elimination of the washing operation station in the production of the E-Frame plastic case.

The E-Frame breaker case is molded in a compression press. The problem begins during the trimming and filing processes that are done after the part is removed from the mold. The plastic contains fiberglass, which becomes a fine dust that adheres to the part. To eliminate the dust, the parts are put through a washing operation. This process uses a conveyor system to carry the parts through a water spray cleaning system. The problem with this process is that the finish comes out looking spotty and with some fiberglass particles still adhering to the parts themselves.

Our customers on the E-Frame breaker line had written Corrective Actions against this procedure because of the poor appearance and the dust still being present on the parts. They were experiencing problems with the fiberglass and had to wear gloves to protect their hands.

Through data collection we realized that this operation takes 6,831 labor-hours a year at a cost of over $96,000. Yet after the washing process the parts still were not clean and had a negative appearance that was not acceptable. We took the top five part numbers and charted the clean versus the dirty parts. We found that 97 percent of the parts did not meet customer standards and that our customers had to add a rework operation to keep the E-Frame line going!

We set a goal to eliminate the washing operation by May 1997. In order to have this happen we needed to find a better process to take its place. We did a fishbone analysis to outline the causes of the problem, and followed up with a root cause analysis to eliminate any causes that did not pertain.

We brainstormed for possible solutions, producing five possible alternatives to the washing operation. They were:

- *Constant air flow*
- *Shop vacuum*
- *Deflashing parts*
- *Ionizer (mouse trap)*
- *Air hose at press*

We tested and evaluated each solution, working with both the operators in the Plastics department and our customers on the breaker line. As a result of our evaluation, we found that an air hose at the press was the best solution. We instructed the operators that after the parts were filed, they should be blown free of all fiber particles. Because they were not being washed with water, this would eliminate the spotty appearance of the parts. We set up direct communication with our customers to make sure that this process was eliminating the problem permanently. Their feedback showed that they were satisfied with the new process and that there was not a problem with either the fiberglass or the appearance of the parts. We then took the findings and recommended that the washing operation be eliminated and replaced by an air hose at the press. We communicated to Quality Assurance that the job instructions should be updated to include our new process so that supervisors and operators would be trained on the new process at the end of their safety meetings. We then went to the scheduler and had the washing process eliminated from the system. After this was accomplished and there was still favorable feedback from the customers, we pulled the plug on the washing operation altogether.

Our goal as a team was to eliminate the washing operation and we accomplished this goal. There were other benefits attached to the project:

- *$98,000 cost reduction in labor and maintenance*
- *Additional 136 square feet of valuable floor space freed up*
- *Improved delivery to customer*
- *Improved teamwork between customer and supplier*
- *Open communication with customer*
- *Elimination of a rework operation*
- *Improved quality to the consumer*
- *Improved safety and health of operators*

Lucas Sumitomo Brakes, Inc.: Easy Money [31]

Lucas Sumitomo Brakes, Inc., has been manufacturing front disc brake calipers at its plant in Lebanon, Ohio, since 1989. As a result of this manufacturing facility's success and worldwide reputation for quality, an expansion into manufacturing anti-lock braking system (ABS) components took place in early 1996. This expansion, and the subsequent start-up of production, created new challenges for the company and its employees.

The company's basic philosophy is that employees are involved in the development and growth of the company and are encouraged to focus on the continuous improvement of processes to meet company goals. As soon as the ABS unit began production, some significant problem areas appeared, one of which was the large amount of downtime throughout the factory. In keeping with the company philosophy, the employees in the Maintenance Department formed a Continuous Improvement Team to address the downtime issue, and moved quickly to gather data. For a period of three months, each time a call for maintenance assistance was answered within the factory, team members completed a Maintenance Response Report that indicated the machine associated with the downtime, the duration of the downtime, and the root cause of the production delay. The information from these reports was entered into a computer database, and a Pareto chart was generated that indicated downtime by machine. This chart clarified that machines located on the Housing Machining Lines accounted for the majority of factory downtime; more specifically, two identical high-pressure washing machines were causing approximately 80 percent of the Machining Line downtime. The team established a goal of reducing downtime associated with the high-pressure washers by 40 percent in the short term, and by 70 percent over the long term.

Using the data collected, the team members brainstormed possible causes for the excessive washer downtime. The results pointed to three major recurring problems that, according to the data taken from the Maintenance Response Reports, accounted for approximately 99 percent of the downtime. These are:

- *Proximity switch replacement and adjustments*
- *Repairing or replacing jig clamps or dryer clamps*
- *High pressure drops within the machine associated with the erosion of O-rings inside the rotary joints*

Utilizing more brainstorming sessions, the fishbone diagram technique, and asking the five Whys (see Chapter 10), the team identified some possible solutions to these recurring problems. As a result, it was able to present specific ideas for improvement to Engineering and Manufacturing, which enabled these departments to assist in communicating with the machine manufacturer, give the project the support that was needed to implement the countermeasures identified by the team, and allow for scheduling of Machine Line downtime to perform trials, which were essential during a time when the Machine Lines were running production six days a week to meet customers' schedules in a just-in-time system. With this support, the team implemented the following corrective actions related to the problems associated with high-pressure washer downtime:

- *The proximity switches and wires were relocated outside the washing machines to eliminate melted switches, and to prevent switches from being destroyed by the high-pressure water blast.*
- *High-temperature-resistant O-rings and seals were installed in the machines, and air tubing was changed to a larger size to eliminate machine-clamping problems.*
- *A preventive maintenance program was implemented to rebuild rotary joints during scheduled downtime to eliminate unscheduled downtime due to worn O-rings inside the rotary joints.*

Following implementation of these improvements, the team members tracked downtime associated with the washing machines for a period of three months, and found that the results exceeded their expectations. A 45 percent decrease in downtime associated with the problems identified by the team was achieved, and average downtime per month was improved from 507 minutes to 276 minutes, saving more than a week of production time each year. Following these improvements, the team moved on to focus on other areas of high downtime within the factory, and washer downtime associated with the improvements made has continued to improve as production levels have increased.

5. Maintaining accuracy of books on the shelves in a college library is an important task. Consider the following problems that are often observed.

a. Books are not placed in the correct shelf position, which includes those books that have been checked out and returned, as well as those taken off the shelves for use within the library by patrons.

b. New or returned books are not checked in and consequently, the online catalog does not show their availability.

What procedures or poka-yokes might you suggest for mitigating these problems? You might wish to talk to some librarians or administrators at your college library to see how they address such problems.

PROBLEMS

1. A flowchart for a fast-food drive-through window is shown in Figure 13.23. Determine the important quality characteristics inherent in this process and suggest possible improvements.

2. A catalog order-filling process for personalized printed products can be described as follows:[32] Telephone orders are taken over a 12-hour period each day. Orders are collected from each person at the end of the day and checked for errors by the supervisor of the phone department, usually the following morning. The supervisor does not send each one-day batch of orders to the data processing department until after 1:00 P.M. In the next step—data processing—orders are invoiced in the one-day batches. Then they are printed and matched back to the original orders. At this point, if the order is from a new customer, it is sent to the person who did the customer verification and setup of new customer accounts. This process must be completed before the order can be invoiced. The next step— order verification and proofreading—occurs after invoicing is completed. The orders, with invoices attached, are given to a person who verifies that all required information is present and correct to permit typesetting. If the verifier has any questions, they are checked by computer or by calling the customer. Finally, the completed orders are sent to the typesetting department of the print shop.

a. Develop a flowchart for this process.

b. Identify opportunities for improving the quality of service in this situation.

3. An independent outplacement service helps unemployed executives find jobs. One of the major activities of the service is preparing resumes. Three word processors work at the service typing resumes and cover letters. Together they handle about 120 individual clients. Turnaround time for typing is expected to be 24 hours. The word-processing operation begins with clients placing work in the assigned word processor's bin. When the word processor picks up the work (in batches), it is logged in using a time clock stamp, and the work is typed and printed. After the batch is completed, the word processor returns the documents to the clients' bins, logs in the time delivered, and picks up new work. A supervisor tries to balance the workload for the three word processors. Lately, many of the clients have been complaining about errors in their documents— misspellings, missing lines, wrong formatting, and so on. The supervisor has told the word processors to be more careful, but the errors still persist.

a. Develop a cause-and-effect diagram that might clarify the source of errors.

b. What tools might the supervisor use to study ways to reduce the number of errors?

Figure 13.23 Flowchart for a Fast-Food Drive-Through Window (Problem 1)

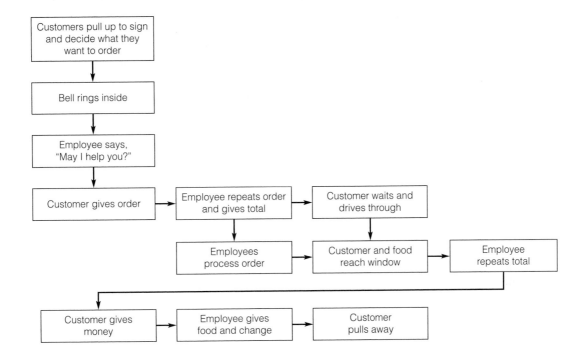

4. The times required for trainees in an electronics course to assemble a component used in a computer were measured. These are shown in the *C13dataset* file for *Prob. 13-4* on the student CD-ROM. Construct a histogram to graphically show the data. What recommendations for improvement would you give the course instructor, based on your findings?

5. A Six Sigma analyst in a bank suspected that errors in counting and manually strapping cash into bundles were related to the number of weeks that employees had been employed on that job. The data found in the *C13dataset* file for *Prob. 13-5* on the student CD-ROM were gathered from the process. What do you conclude from your analysis? What do you recommend?

6. The data found in the *C13dataset* file for *Prob. 13-6* on the student CD-ROM were gathered from a process used to make plastic gears for a computer printer. The gears were designed to be 2.5 ± 0.05 centimeters (cm) in diameter. Construct a histogram based on the data given. What can you observe about the shape of the distribution? What would you recommend to the production manager, based on your analysis?

7. The times required to prepare standard-size packages for shipping were measured. These data are shown in the *C13dataset* file for *Prob. 13-7* on the student CD-ROM. Construct a scatter diagram for these data. What recommendations for improvement would you give the section leader, based on your findings?

8. In a manufacturing process, the production rate (parts/hour) was thought to affect the number of defectives found during a subsequent inspection. To test this theory, the production rate was varied and the numbers of defects were collected for the same batch sizes. The results can be found in the *C13dataset* file for

Prob. 13-8 on the student CD-ROM. Construct a scatter diagram for these data. What conclusions can you reach?

9. Ace Printing Company realized that they were losing customers and orders due to various delays and errors. In order to get to the root cause of the problem, they decided to track problems that might be contributing to customer dissatisfaction. The following list of the problems found shows their frequencies of occurrence over a six-month period. What technique might you use to graphically show the causes of customer dissatisfaction? What recommendations could you make to reduce errors and increase customer satisfaction?

Error/Delay Cause	Frequency
Customer change delays	15
Lack of press time	180
Design department delays	55
Paper not in stock	75
Lack of proper order information	24
Lost order	11
Press setup delays	240

10. Rick Hensley owns an automotive dealership. Service is a major part of the operation. Rick and his service team spent considerable time in analyzing the service process and developed a flowchart, shown in Figure 13.24, that describes the typical activities in servicing a customer's automobile. Rick wants to ensure that customers receive superior service and are highly satisfied; thus, he wants to establish poka-yokes for any possible failures that may occur. Your assignment is to identify any possible failure in the service process that may be detrimental to customer satisfaction and suggest poka-yokes to eliminate these failures.

11. Figure 13.25 shows a medication administration process in a hospital. The administrative staff of the hospital is concerned about frequent medication errors. After examining this flowchart, discuss possible sources of errors, the types of individuals responsible (e.g., physicians, nurses, pharmacists, other), and poka-yokes that might be used to mitigate these errors.

12. Analysis of customer complaints for a large dot-com apparel house revealed the following:

Billing errors	537
Shipping errors	2,460
Electronic charge errors	650
Long delay	5,372
Delivery error	752

Construct a Pareto diagram for these data. What conclusions would you reach?

13. The number of defects found in 25 samples of 100 Gamma Candy Company lemon drops taken on a daily basis from a production line over a five-week period is given here (by rows). Plot these data on a run chart, computing the average value (center line), but ignoring the control limits. Do you suspect that any special causes are present? Why?

0	5	4	4	3	1	0	0	3	6
14	12	1	7	6	6	5	7	6	3
3	2	2	4	6					

Figure 13.24 Automobile Service Flowchart (Problem 10)

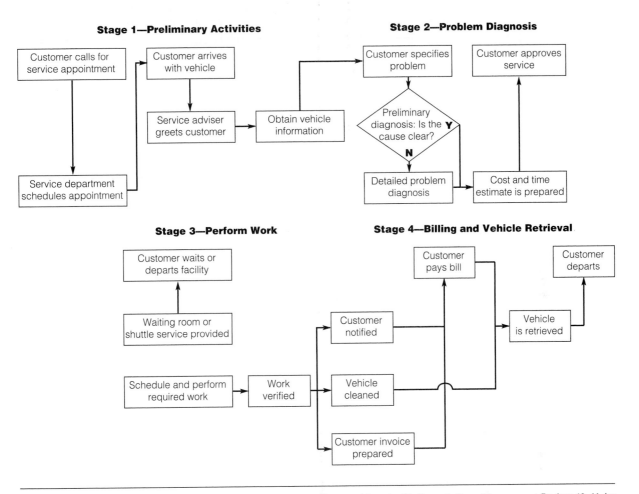

14. A pharmaceutical company that manufactures individual syringes is conducting a process capability study (see Chapter 11). The data shown in the *C13dataset* file for *Prob. 13-14* on the student CD-ROM represent the lengths of 35 consecutive samples.[33] Plot these data on a run chart. Do the data appear to come from a stable system so that a process capability study may be conducted appropriately?

15. The Monterey Fiesta Mexican Restaurant is trying to determine whether its popular Pan Con Mucho Sabor breadsticks are correlated with the sales of margaritas. It has data on sales of breadstick baskets and margaritas for 25 weeks, shown in the *C13dataset* file for *Prob. 13-15* on the student CD-ROM. Use the correlation utility, along with a scatter diagram, in Microsoft Excel to analyze these data. What do they indicate?

Figure 13.25 Medical Administration Process (Problem 11)

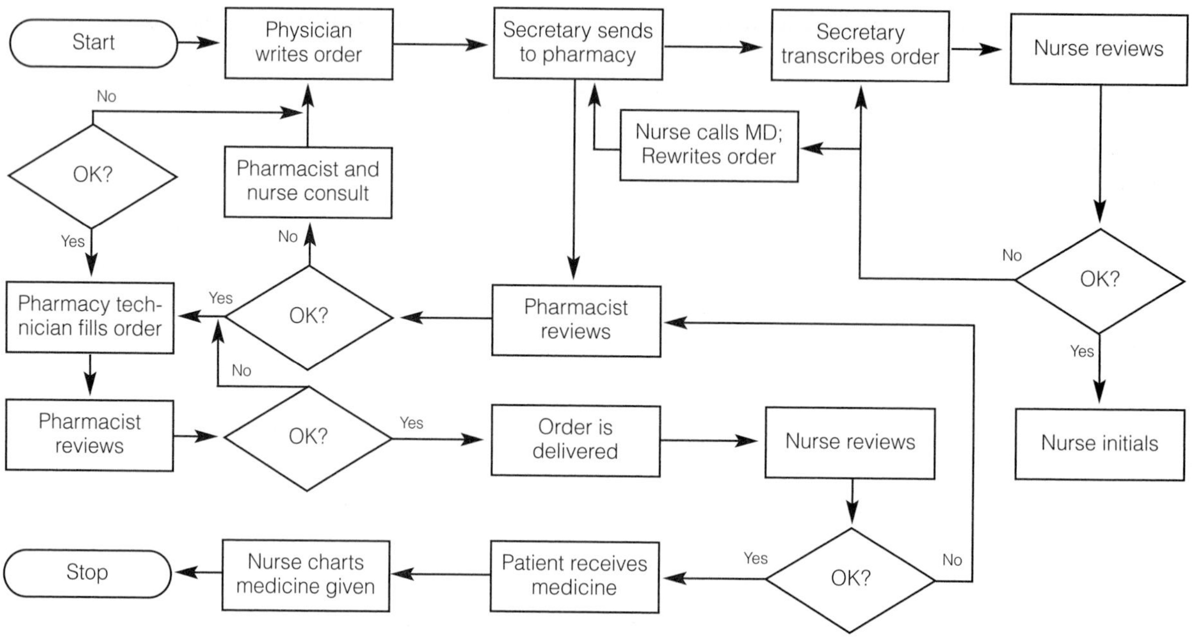

Source: Ellen Williams and Ray Tailey, "The Use of Failure Mode Effect and Criticality Analysis in a Medication Error Subcommittee," *ASQC Health Care Division Newsletter,* Winter 1996, 4.

Projects, Etc.

1. Research several companies to identify the type of problem-solving approach they use in their improvement efforts. Compare and contrast their approaches. Which, if any, of the approaches described in the chapter are they most similar to?
2. Work with your school administrators to identify an important quality-related problem they face. Outline a plan for improvement. If time permits, apply some of the problem-solving tools to collect data, identify the root cause, and generate ideas for solving the problem or improving the situation.
3. Develop a flowchart of the process you use to study for an exam. How might you improve this process?
4. Describe a personal problem you face and how you might use the Deming cycle and the Seven QC Tools to address it.
5. In small teams, develop cause-and-effect diagrams for the following problems:
   a. Poor exam grade
   b. No job offers
   c. Late for work or school
6. Work with teachers at a local high school or grade school to identify some students who are having difficulties in school. Apply quality tools to help find the source of the problems and create an improvement plan.

7. Identify several sources of errors as a student or in your personal life. Develop some poka-yokes that might prevent them.
8. Interview a plant manager or quality professional at one or more local companies to see whether they use any poka-yoke approaches to mistake-proof their operations.
9. Check out the Web site http://www.freequality.org. It contains descriptions and examples of the use of quality improvement tools. Find some that have not been discussed in this chapter and develop a short tutorial for using them.
10. Examine the ProcessModel output for the help desk example. Are the results compatible with the assumptions given about the process? For example, what percentages of calls actually go to the second support person? Are the simulated times close to the stated input values?
11. Search the Internet for John Grout's Poka-Yoke Web site. Read several of the interesting articles available there and write a report on the information you discover.
12. Meet with key decision makers in your fraternity, sorority, or other organization for which strategic issues need to be considered and prioritized. Research nominal group technique beyond the scope of this text to have a clear idea of how to proceed. Apply it to your organization's planning and report on the results.

 # CASES

Additional cases are available in the Bonus Materials Folder on the CD-ROM.

I. READILUNCH RESTAURANT

Carole Read, the owner of the Readilunch Restaurant, a downtown, quick service restaurant, was concerned about the loss of several regular customers. She measured the number of empty lunch tables from 11 A.M. until 2 P.M. over a four-week period. To better understand the reasons for the loss of customers, long lines, and dissatisfied patrons, Carol talked to several regular customers. She found that they liked the food and atmosphere of the restaurant, but felt that there were opportunities for improvement based on the lack of capability to quickly handle take-out orders (they had to be phoned in, not faxed), excessive time spent waiting for tables, inefficient service, surly waiters on certain days, and long lines at the cash register. She puzzled over how to sort out possible causes that led to these perceived problems. Carol also decided to design a check sheet to systematically gather data and determine which of these problems were the most significant.

Note: Data for the check sheet information gathered for "Vacant Tables" and for "Customer Concerns" can be found in the *C13dataset.xls* file under the Readilunch 1 and Readilunch 2 tabs on the student CD-ROM.

Discussion Questions

1. Plot the average number of empty tables on a run chart, computing the average value (center line), but ignoring the control limits. What do these data show?
2. Use one of the seven Tools to come up with possible causes to explain customer dissatisfaction, based on the reasons described in the case.
3. Analyze the check sheet data on the student CD-ROM. What conclusions do you reach?
4. What do you recommend that Carol do to overcome these problems?

II. National Furniture

National Furniture is a large retail design and furniture store. The store often orders special merchandise at the request of its customers. However, the store recently experienced problems with the on-time delivery of these special orders. Sometimes the orders were never received, resulting in irate customers.

The process of fulfilling a special order begins with the sales associate who records the customer information and obtains approval from a manager to process the order. The sales associate puts the order form in a bin for the office manager to fax to the special order department at the regional office. When the office manager faxes the special order forms from the bin, she files them in a notebook. If a problem arises with the order, the manager receives notification, and contacts the sales associate who took the order to decide what needs to be done next. Typical problems that are often observed include sales associates not filling out the order form completely or entering a request date that is impossible to fulfill. Sometimes the sales associate does not put the form in the proper bin, so the form never gets faxed. Other times, sales associates are asked to obtain more information from the customer, but fail to call the cus-

tomer back, or do not inform the office associate to refax the form after getting additional information from the customer.

At the regional office, the special order department receives the fax from the store, reviews it, and informs the store if additional information is needed. When all the information is complete, they process the order. Sometimes they lose or misplace the form after it arrives on the fax machine, order the wrong merchandise, or fail to notify the store when additional information is needed or when the merchandise should be expected to arrive.

Discussion Questions

1. Develop a process map for special orders. What steps might you suggest to improve this process?
2. Construct a cause-and-effect diagram for identifying reasons why special orders are not received on time.
3. Discuss the relationship between the process map and the cause-and-effect diagram. How can they be used together to attack this problem?

III. Janson Medical Clinic

The Janson Medical Clinic recently conducted a patient satisfaction survey of 100 patients. Using a scale of 1–5, with 1 being "very dissatisfied" and 5 being "very satisfied," the clinic compiled a check sheet for responses that were either 1 or 2, indicating dissatisfaction with the performance attributes. This check sheet is shown in Table 13.5.

Doctors have extremely busy schedules. They have surgeries to perform, and many are teaching faculty at the local medical school. Many surgeries are emergencies or take longer than expected, resulting in delays of getting back to the clinic.

In the clinic, one or two telephone receptionists answer calls for three different departments, which include 20 or more doctors. Their job is basically to schedule appointments, provide directions, and transfer calls to the proper secretaries, which generally requires putting the patient on hold. Often, the receptionist must take a handwritten message and personally deliver it to the

secretary because the secretary's phone line is busy. However, the receptionist cannot leave her desk without someone else to cover the phones.

A student intern examined the processes for answering phone calls and registering patients. The flowcharts she developed are shown in Figures 13.26 and 13.27.

Discussion Questions

1. Construct a Pareto diagram for dissatisfaction. What conclusions do you reach?
2. Select the top three sources of patient dissatisfaction and propose cause-and-effect diagrams for the possible reasons behind them.
3. Propose some process improvements to the flowcharts in Figure 13.26 and develop redesigned processes along with new flowcharts. How will your suggestions address the sources of dissatisfaction in Table 13.5?

Table 13.5 Check Sheet of Dissatisfied Responses

Making an Appointment
      Ease of getting through on the phone—10
      Friendliness of the telephone receptionist—5
      Convenience of office hours—7
      Ease of getting a convenient appointment—12

Check-in/Check-out
      Courtesy and helpfulness of the receptionist—7
      Amount of time to register—1
      Length of wait to see a physician—13
      Comfort of registration waiting area—4

Care and Treatment
      Respect shown by nurses/assistants—0
      Responsiveness to phone calls related to care—5
      How well the physician listened—3
      Respect shown by the physician—2
      Confidence in the physician's ability—1
      Explanation of medical condition and treatment—2

Figure 13.26 Current Process for Answering Phone Calls

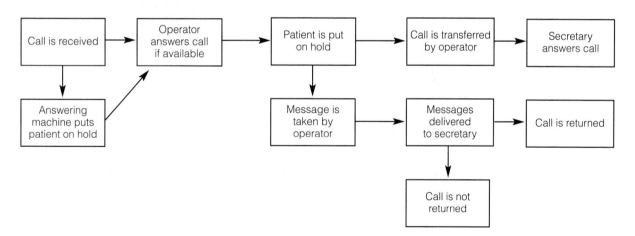

Figure 13.27 Current Patient Registration Process

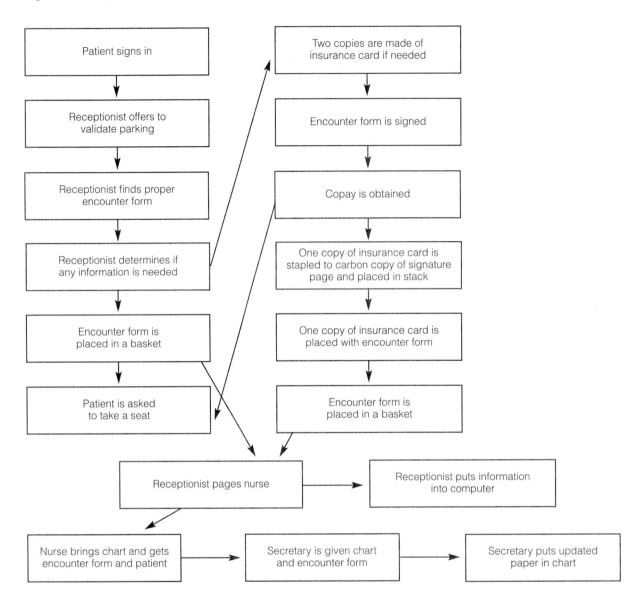

ENDNOTES

1. Gregory Korte, "473 Steps," *The Cincinnati Enquirer,* October 30, 2002, A1, A10.

2. Gerald Langley, Kevin Nolan, and Thomas Nolan, "The Foundation of Improvement," Sixth Annual International Deming User's Group Conference, Cincinnati, OH (August 1992).

3. Langley et al. (see note 2).

4. Jeremy Main, "Under the Spell of the Quality Gurus," *Fortune,* August 18, 1986, 31.

5. Masaaki Imai, *Kaizen: The Key to Japan's Competitive Success* (New York: McGraw-Hill, 1986), 15.

6. A. F. Osborn, *Applied Imagination,* 3rd ed. (New

York: Scribner's, 1963); S. J. Parnes, R. B. Noller, and A. M. Biondi (eds.), *Guide to Creative Action* (New York: Scribner's, 1977).

7. Daniel R. Heiser and Paul Schikora, "Flow-charting with Excel," *Quality Management Journal* 8, no. 3 (2001), 26–35.

8. AT&T Quality Steering Committee, *Reengineering Handbook,* AT&T Bell Laboratories (1991), 45.

9. Rochelle Rucker, "Six Sigma at Citibank," available at http://www.insidequality.wego.net.

10. Adapted from Dwight Kirscht and Jennifer M. Tunnell, "Boise Cascade Stakes a Claim on Quality," *Quality Progress* 26, no. 11 (November 1993), 91–96. With permission of Dwight M. Kirscht, Timber and Wood Products Division, Boise Cascade Corporation.

11. Kaoru Ishikawa, *Guide to Quality Control,* 2nd rev. ed. (Tokyo: Asian Productivity Organization, 1986). Available from UNIPUB/Quality Resources, One Water Street, White Plains, NY 10601.

12. Adapted from Bruce Rudin, "Simple Tools Solve Complex Problems." Reprinted with permission from *Quality,* April 1990, 50–51; a publication of Hitchcock Publishing, a Capital Cities/ABC, Inc.

13. Adapted from Rudin (see note 12).

14. Eleanor Chilson, "Kaizen Blitzes at Magnivision: $809,270 Cost Savings," *Quality Management Forum* 29, no. 1 (Winter 2003).

15. For an interesting, albeit academic discussion of the psychology of human error and its relationship to mistake-proofing, see Douglas M. Stewart and Richard B. Chase, "The Impact of Human Error on Delivering Service Quality," *Production and Operations Management* 8, no. 3 (Fall 1999), 240–263; and Douglas M. Stewart and John R. Grout, "The Human Side of Mistake Proofing," *Production and Operations Management* 10, no. 4 (Winter 2001), 440–459.

16. From *Poka-Yoke: Improving Product Quality by Preventing Defects.* Edited by NKS/Factory Magazine, English translation copyright ©1988 by Productivity Press, Inc., P.O. Box 3007, Cambridge, MA 02140, 800-394-6868. Reprinted by permission.

17. Harry Robinson, "Using Poka-Yoke Techniques for Early Defect Detection," Paper presented at the Sixth International Conference on Software Testing and Analysis and Review (STAR '97).

18. Excerpts reprinted from Richard B. Chase and Douglas M. Stewart, "Make Your Service Fail-Safe," *Sloan Management Review* 35, no. 3 (Spring 1994), 35–44. © 1994 by the Sloan Management Review Association. All rights reserved.

19. Steve Fleming and E. Lowry Manson, "Six Sigma and Process Simulation," *Quality Digest,* March 2002.

20. Fleming and Manson (see note 19).

21. This example is adapted from a tutorial for ProcessModel, a commercial simulation package (see note 22). ProcessModel, Inc. 32 West Center, Suite 209, Provo, UT 84601.

22. ProcessModel, Inc. 32 West Center, Suite 209, Provo, UT 84601.

23. James P. Lewis, *Team-Based Project Management* (New York: Amacom, 1998).

24. Peter R. Scholtes, *The Team Handbook,* 3rd ed. Madison, WI: Oriel, Inc., 2003, 4-2 through 4-5.

25. Scholtes (see note 24), 4–5.

26. Andre L. Delbecq, Andre H. Van de Ven, and David H. Gustafson, *Group Techniques for Program Planning* (Glenview, IL Scott Foresman and Co., 1975).

27. John E. Bauer, Grace L. Duffy, and Russell T. Westcott (eds.), *The Quality Improvement Handbook* (Milwaukee, WI: ASQ Quality Press, 2002), 108–109.

28. Adapted from Timothy Clark and Andrew Clark, "Continuous Improvement on the Free-Throw Line," *Quality Progress,* October 1997, 78–80. © 1997 American Society for Quality. Reprinted with permission.

29. Appreciation is expressed to one of the author's students, Jim Faze, who wrote the paper on which this case is based, as part of the requirements for MGT 640, Total Quality Management, 2001, at Northern Kentucky University.

30. Courtesy of Siemens Energy and Automation Distribution Products Division.

31. Courtesy of Lucas Sumitomo Brakes, Inc., and "Easy Money" team members Ron Gogan, Darren Brown, Jeff Carroll, Mike Watkins, Denis Muse, Marte Wolfensperzjer, and Sean Miller.

32. Adapted from Ronald G. Conant, "JIT in a Mail Order Operation Reduces Processing Time from Four Days to Four Hours," *Industrial Engineering* 20, no. 9 (September 1988), 34–37.

33. Leroy A. Franklin and Samar N. Mukherjee, "An SPC Case Study on Stabilizing Syringe Lengths," *Quality Engineering* 12, no. 1 (1999–2000), 65–71.

BIBLIOGRAPHY

AT&T Quality Steering Committee. Batting 1000. AT&T Bell Laboratories, 1992.

———. *Process Quality Management & Improvement Guidelines.* AT&T Bell Laboratories, 1987.

Box, G. E. P., and S. Bisgaard. "The Scientific Context of Quality Improvement." *Quality Progress* 20, no. 6 (June 1987), 54–61.

Brassard, Michael. *The Memory Jogger Plus+.* Methuen, MA: GOAL/QPC, 1989.

Evans, James R., and David L. Olson. *Introduction to*

Simulation and Risk Analysis. Upper Saddle River, NJ: Prentice Hall, 2002.

Gitlow, H., S. Gitlow, A. Oppenheim, and R. Oppenheim. *Tools and Methods for the Improvement of Quality.* Homewood, IL: Irwin, 1989.

Godfrey, Blan. "Future Trends: Expansion of Quality Management Concepts, Methods and Tools to All Industries." *Quality Observer* 6, no. 9 (September 1997), 40–43, 46.

Harrington, H. James, and Kerim Tumay. *Simulation Modeling Methods.* New York: McGraw-Hill, 2000.

Hradesky, John L. *Productivity and Quality Improvement.* New York: McGraw-Hill, 1988.

The Inc Team. *The Team Memory Jogger.* Madison, WI: Brian Joyner and Associates, Goal/QPC, 1995.

Tomas, Sam. "Six Sigma: Motorola's Quest for Zero Defects." *APICS, The Performance Advantage* (July 1991), 36–41.

———. "What Is Motorola's Six Sigma Product Quality?" *American Production and Inventory Control Society 1990 Conference Proceedings.* Falls Church, VA: APICS, 27–31.

14

STATISTICAL PROCESS CONTROL

Deming's funnel experiment, described in Chapter 11, demonstrates that failure to distinguish between common causes and special causes of variation can actually increase the variation in a process. This problem often results from the mistaken belief that whenever process output is off target, some adjustment must be made. Knowing when to leave a process alone is an important step in maintaining control over a process. Equally important is knowing when to take action to prevent the production of nonconforming product.

Statistical process control (SPC) is a methodology for monitoring a process to identify special causes of variation and signaling the need to take corrective action when it is appropriate. When special causes are present, the process is deemed to be *out of control*. If the variation in the process is due to common causes alone, the process is said to be *in statistical control*. A practical definition of statistical control is that both the process averages and variances are constant over time.[1]

SPC relies on *control charts*, one of the basic quality improvement tools that we briefly introduced in Chapter 13. SPC is a proven technique for improving quality and productivity. Many customers require their suppliers to provide evidence of statistical process control. Thus, SPC provides a means by which a firm may demonstrate its quality capability, an activity necessary for survival in today's highly competitive markets. Because SPC requires processes to show measurable variation, it is ineffective for quality levels approaching six sigma. However, SPC is quite effective for companies in the early stages of quality efforts.

Although control charts were first developed and used in a manufacturing context, they are easily applied to service organizations. Table 14.1 lists just a few of the many potential applications of control charts for services. The key is in defining the appropriate quality measures to monitor. Most service processes can be improved through the appropriate application of control charts.

In this chapter we describe how to develop and use statistical process control to monitor manufacturing and service processes. The Bonus Materials folder for this chapter provides an explanation of the statistical details for understanding the theory underlying control charts.

Table 14.1 Control Chart Applications in Service Organizations

Organization	Quality Measure
Hospital	Lab test accuracy Insurance claim accuracy On-time delivery of meals and medication
Bank	Check-processing accuracy
Insurance company	Claims-processing response time Billing accuracy
Post Office	Sorting accuracy Time of delivery Percentage of express mail delivered on time
Ambulance	Response time
Police Department	Incidence of crime in a precinct Number of traffic citations
Hotel	Proportion of rooms satisfactorily cleaned Checkout time Number of complaints received
Transportation	Proportion of freight cars correctly routed Dollar amount of damage per claim
Auto service	Percentage of time work completed as promised Number of parts out of stock

QUALITY PROFILES

TRIDENT PRECISION MANUFACTURING, INC. AND OPERATIONS MANAGEMENT

INTERNATIONAL, INC.

Founded in 1979 with only three people, privately held Trident manufactures precision sheet metal components, electromechanical assemblies, and custom products, mostly in the office-equipment, medical supply, computer, and defense industries with a workforce of about 170. Trident's human resource strategies emphasize training, involvement through teams, empowerment, and reward and recognition. Since 1989, Trident has invested 4.4 percent of its payroll in training and education, two to three times the average for all U.S. industry and an especially large amount for a small firm.

All goals, however, contribute to achieving Trident's overarching aim of total customer satisfaction. Each improvement project begins with a thorough analysis of how to meet or exceed customer requirements in four critical areas: quality, cost, delivery, and service. Metrics are designed to ensure that progress toward the customer-targeted improvements can be evaluated. The company's data collection system provides all personnel with a current record of the company's progress toward its goals. The senior executive team also reviews performance data in each department daily and weekly. Once each month, this team aggregates the data for the entire company and reports on progress toward goals set for each of the five key business drivers.

Beyond tracking its operational and financial performance, Trident also analyzes data collected from a variety of other internal and external sources. These sources include semiannual surveys of customers, suppliers, and employees; benchmarking studies; discussions with customers; employee forums; market reports; quarterly quality audits; and an independently conducted annual assessment of the company's competitive position within its industry. Defect rates have fallen so much that Trident offers a full guarantee against defects in its custom products. Trident was a 1996 recipient of the Baldrige Award.

Headquartered in Greenwood Village, Colorado, Operations Management International, Inc. (OMI), operates and maintains more than 160 public and private sector wastewater and water treatment facilities in 29 states and facilities in Brazil, Canada, Egypt, Israel, Malaysia, New Zealand, Philippines, and Thailand. OMI's primary services are processing raw wastewater to produce clean, environmentally safe effluent and processing raw groundwater and surface water to produce clean, safe drinking water. OMI's "E3" motto, "Exceed our customers' expectations, empower our employees, enhance the environment," is the foundation for its Quality as a Business Strategy leadership system. Key enablers are the company's Linkage of Process Model, which defines relationships among processes, and its Family of Measures, a balanced scorecard of 20 integrated metrics. These measures of operational performance correspond to OMI's four strategic objectives—customer focus, business growth, innovation, and market leadership.

Improvement initiatives in the company's strategic plan are selected and crafted so that each initiative contributes significantly to achieving one or more strategic objectives and key customer requirements. In 2000, OMI had 26 improvement initiatives under way, each one assigned to a team led by a high-level executive. All teams write charters that state their purpose, objectives, and timeline for completion. A team charter also specifies which of OMI's more than 150 critical processes are involved, the metrics that will be used for evaluation, costs, required resources, and other information vital to the success of the initiative. Charters provide team members and company executives with the means for a quick and thorough analysis of progress toward planned goals. OMI received a 2000 Baldrige Award.

Source: Malcolm Baldrige National Quality Award, Profiles of Winners, National Institute of Standards and Technology, Department of Commerce.

QUALITY CONTROL MEASUREMENTS

Quality control measurements and indicators fall into one of two categories. An **attribute** is a performance characteristic that is either present or absent in the product or service under consideration. For example, a dimension is either within tolerance or out of tolerance, an order is complete or incomplete, or an invoice can have one, two, three, or any number of errors. Thus, attributes data are discrete and tell whether the characteristic conforms to specifications. Attributes can be measured by visual inspection, such as assessing whether the correct zip code was used in shipping an order; or by comparing a dimension to specifications, such as whether the diameter of a shaft falls within specification limits of 1.60 ± 0.01 inch. Attribute measurements are typically expressed as proportions or rates, for example, the fraction of nonconformances in a group of items, number of defects per unit, or rate of errors per opportunity. The second type of performance characteristic is called a **variable**. Variables data are continuous (e.g., length or weight). Variables measurements are concerned with the *degree* of conformance to specifications. Thus, rather than determining whether the diameter of a shaft simply meets a specification of 1.60 ± 0.01 inch, a measure of the actual value of the diameter is recorded. Variable measurements are generally expressed with such statistics as averages and standard deviations. Table 14.1 provides additional examples of both attributes and variables measurements.

Collecting attribute data is usually easier than collecting variable data because the assessment can usually be done more quickly by a simple inspection or count, whereas variable data require the use of some type of measuring instrument.

In a statistical sense, attributes inspection is less efficient than variables inspection; that is, it does not provide as much information. This means that attributes inspection requires a larger sample than variables inspection to obtain the same amount of statistical information about the quality of the product. This difference can become significant when inspection of each item is time-consuming or expensive. Most quality characteristics in services are attributes, which is perhaps one reason why service organizations have been slow to adopt measurement-based quality management approaches.

CAPABILITY AND CONTROL

Consider Table 14.2, which shows measurements of a quality characteristic for 30 samples from a manufacturing process with specifications 0.75 ± 0.25. Each row corresponds to a sample size of 5 taken every 15 minutes. The mean of each sample is also given in the last column. A frequency distribution and histogram of these data is shown in Figure 14.1. The data form a relatively symmetric distribution with a mean of 0.762 and standard deviation 0.0738. Using these values, we find that $C_{pk} = 1.075$, indicating that the process capability is at least marginally acceptable.

Because the data were taken over an extended period of time, we cannot determine whether the process remained stable. In a histogram, the dimension of time is not considered. Thus, histograms do not allow you to distinguish between common and special causes of variation. It is unclear whether any special causes of variation are influencing the capability index. If we plot the mean of each sample against the time at which the sample was taken (because the time increments between samples are equal, the sample number is an appropriate surrogate for time), we obtain the run chart shown in Figure 14.2. It indicates that the mean has shifted up at about sample 17. In fact, the process average for the first 16 samples is only 0.738 while the average

Table 14.2 Quality Measurements for Thirty Samples

Sample	Observations						Mean
	A	B	C	D	E	F	H
1	0.682	0.689	0.776	0.798	0.714		0.732
2	0.787	0.860	0.601	0.746	0.779		0.755
3	0.780	0.667	0.838	0.785	0.723		0.759
4	0.591	0.727	0.812	0.775	0.730		0.727
5	0.693	0.708	0.790	0.758	0.671		0.724
6	0.749	0.714	0.738	0.719	0.606		0.705
7	0.791	0.713	0.689	0.877	0.603		0.735
8	0.744	0.779	0.660	0.737	0.822		0.748
9	0.769	0.773	0.641	0.644	0.725		0.710
10	0.718	0.671	0.708	0.850	0.712		0.732
11	0.787	0.821	0.764	0.658	0.708		0.748
12	0.622	0.802	0.818	0.872	0.727		0.768
13	0.657	0.822	0.893	0.544	0.750		0.733
14	0.806	0.749	0.859	0.801	0.701		0.783
15	0.660	0.681	0.644	0.747	0.728		0.692
16	0.816	0.817	0.768	0.716	0.649		0.753
17	0.826	0.777	0.721	0.770	0.809		0.781
18	0.828	0.829	0.865	0.778	0.872		0.834
19	0.805	0.719	0.612	0.938	0.807		0.776
20	0.802	0.756	0.786	0.815	0.801		0.792
21	0.876	0.803	0.701	0.789	0.672		0.768
22	0.855	0.783	0.722	0.856	0.751		0.793
23	0.762	0.705	0.804	0.805	0.809		0.777
24	0.703	0.837	0.759	0.975	0.732		0.801
25	0.737	0.723	0.776	0.748	0.732		0.743
26	0.748	0.686	0.856	0.811	0.838		0.788
27	0.826	0.803	0.764	0.823	0.886		0.820
28	0.728	0.721	0.820	0.772	0.639		0.736
29	0.803	0.892	0.740	0.816	0.770		0.804
30	0.774	0.837	0.872	0.849	0.818		0.830

Process capability calculations make little sense if the process is not in statistical control because the data are confounded by special causes that do not represent the inherent capability of the process.

for the remaining samples is 0.789. Therefore, although the overall average is close to the target specification, at no time was the actual process average centered near the target. We should conclude that this process is not in statistical control, and we should not pay much attention to the process capability calculations.

Control and capability are two different concepts. As shown in Figure 14.3, a process may be capable or not capable, or in control or out of control, independently of each other. Clearly, we would like every process to be both capable and in control. If a process is neither capable nor in control, we must first get it in a state of control by removing special causes of variation, and then attack the common causes to improve its capability. If a process is capable but not in control (as the previous example illustrated), we should work to get it back in control.

Figure 14.1 Frequency Distribution and Histogram

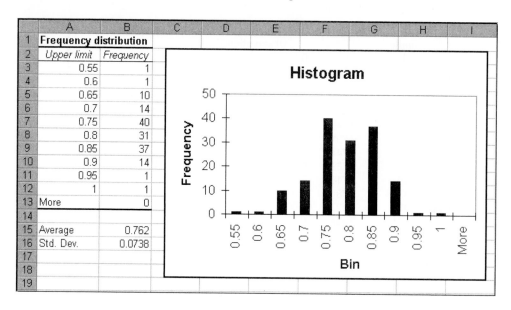

Figure 14.2 Run Chart of Sample Means

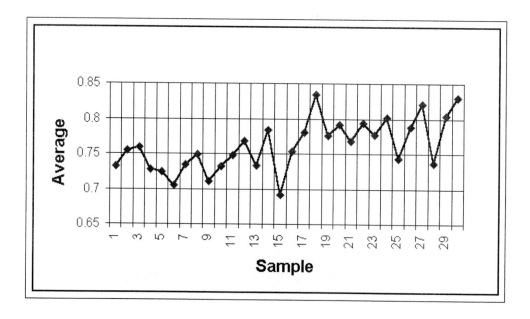

Figure 14.3 Capability versus Control (Arrows indicate the direction of appropriate management action)

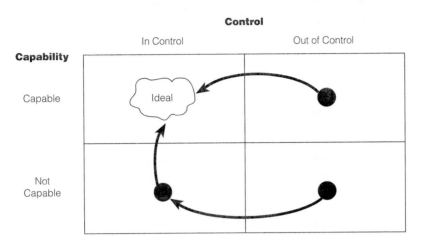

SPC METHODOLOGY

Control charts, like the other basic tools for quality improvement, are relatively simple to use. Control charts have three basic applications: (1) to establish a state of statistical control, (2) to monitor a process and signal when the process goes out of control, and (3) to determine process capability. The following is a summary of the steps required to develop and use control charts. Steps 1 through 4 focus on establishing a state of statistical control; in step 5, the charts are used for ongoing monitoring; and finally, in step 6, the data are used for process capability analysis.

1. Preparation
   a. Choose the variable or attribute to be measured.
   b. Determine the basis, size, and frequency of sampling.
   c. Set up the control chart.
2. Data collection
   a. Record the data.
   b. Calculate relevant statistics: averages, ranges, proportions, and so on.
   c. Plot the statistics on the chart.
3. Determination of trial control limits
   a. Draw the center line (process average) on the chart.
   b. Compute the upper and lower control limits.
4. Analysis and interpretation
   a. Investigate the chart for lack of control.
   b. Eliminate out-of-control points.
   c. Recompute control limits if necessary.
5. Use as a problem-solving tool
   a. Continue data collection and plotting.
   b. Identify out-of-control situations and take corrective action.
6. Determination of process capability using the control chart data

In the remainder of this chapter we discuss the construction, interpretation, and use of control charts following this methodology. Although many different charts are described, they differ only in the type of measurement for which the chart is used; the methodology previously described applies to each of them.

CONTROL CHARTS FOR VARIABLES DATA

Variables data are those that are measured along a continuous scale. Examples of variables data are length, weight, time, and distance. The charts most commonly used for variables data are the $\bar{x}$-chart ("x-bar" chart) and the R-chart (range chart). The $\bar{x}$-chart is used to monitor the centering of the process, and the R-chart is used to monitor the variation in the process. The range is used as a measure of variation simply for convenience, particularly when workers on the factory floor perform control chart calculations by hand. For large samples and when data are analyzed by computer programs, the standard deviation is a better measure of variability (discussed later in this chapter).

Constructing $\bar{x}$- and R-Charts and Establishing Statistical Control

The first step in developing $\bar{x}$- and R-charts is to gather data. Usually, about 25 to 30 samples are collected. Samples between size 3 and 10 are generally used, with 5 being the most common. The number of samples is indicated by k, and n denotes the sample size. For each sample i, the mean (denoted $\bar{x}_i$) and the range (R_i) are computed. These values are then plotted on their respective control charts. Next, the *overall mean* and *average range* calculations are made. These values specify the center lines for the $\bar{x}$- and R-charts, respectively. The overall mean (denoted $\bar{\bar{x}}$) is the average of the sample means $\bar{x}_i$:

$$\bar{\bar{x}} = \frac{\sum_{i=1}^{k} \bar{x}_i}{k}$$

The average range ($\bar{R}$) is similarly computed, using the formula:

$$\bar{R} = \frac{\sum_{i=1}^{k} R_i}{k}$$

The average range and average mean are used to compute upper and lower control limits (UCL and LCL) for the R- and $\bar{x}$-charts. Control limits are easily calculated using the following formulas:

$$\text{UCL}_R = D_4\bar{R} \qquad \text{UCL}_{\bar{x}} = \bar{\bar{x}} + A_2\bar{R}$$

$$\text{LCL}_R = D_3\bar{R} \qquad \text{LCL}_{\bar{x}} = \bar{\bar{x}} - A_2\bar{R}$$

where the constants D_3, D_4, and A_2 depend on the sample size and can be found in Appendix B.

The control limits represent the range between which all points are expected to fall if the process is in statistical control. If any points fall outside the control limits or if any unusual patterns are observed, then some special cause has probably affected the process. The process should be studied to determine the cause. If special causes are present, then they are *not* representative of the true state of statistical control, and the calculations of the center line and control limits will be biased. The corresponding data points should be eliminated, and new values for $\bar{\bar{x}}$, $\bar{R}$, and the control limits should be computed.

In determining whether a process is in statistical control, the R-chart is always analyzed first. Because the control limits in the $\bar{x}$-chart depend on the average range, special causes in the R-chart may produce unusual patterns in the $\bar{x}$-chart, even when the centering of the process is in control. (An example of such distorted patterns is given later in this chapter.) Once statistical control is established for the R-chart, attention may turn to the $\bar{x}$-chart.

Figure 14.4 shows a typical data sheet used for recording data and drawing control charts, which is available from the American Society for Quality (ASQ). This form provides space for descriptive information about the process, recording of sample observations and computed statistics, and drawing the control charts. On the back of this form is a worksheet (see Figure 14.5) for computing control limits and process capability information. The construction and analysis of control charts is best seen in an example. The thickness of silicon wafers used in the production of semiconductors must be carefully controlled. The tolerance of one such product is specified as ±0.0050 inches. In one production facility, three wafers were selected each hour and the thickness measured carefully to within one ten-thousandth of an inch. Figure 14.6 on page 698 shows the results obtained for 25 samples. For example, the mean of the first sample is

$$\bar{x}_1 = \frac{41 + 70 + 22}{3} = \frac{113}{3} = 44$$

The range of sample 1 is 70 − 22 = 48. (*Note:* Calculations are rounded to the nearest integer for simplicity.)

The calculations of the average range, overall mean, and control limits are shown in Figure 14.7 on page 699. The average range is the sum of the sample ranges (676) divided by the number of samples (25); the overall mean is the sum of the sample averages (1,221) divided by the number of samples (25). Because the sample size is 3, the factors used in computing the control limits are $A_2 = 1.023$ and $D_4 = 2.574$. (For sample sizes of 6 or less, factor $D_3 = 0$; therefore, the lower control limit on the range chart is zero.) The center lines and control limits are drawn on the chart in Figure 14.8 on page 700.

Examining the range chart first, it appears that the process is in control. All points lie within the control limits and no unusual patterns exist. In the $\bar{x}$-chart, however, sample 17 lies above the upper control limit. On investigation, some defective material had been used. This data point should be eliminated from the control chart calculations. Figure 14.9 on page 701 shows the calculations after sample 17 was removed. The revised center lines and control limits are shown in Figure 14.10 on page 702. Customarily, out-of-control points are noted on the chart. The resulting chart appears to be in control.

When a process is in statistical control, the points on a control chart fluctuate randomly between the control limits with no recognizable pattern.

Interpreting Patterns in Control Charts

The following list provides a set of general rules for examining a process to determine whether it is in control:

Figure 14.4 ASQ Control Chart Data Sheet

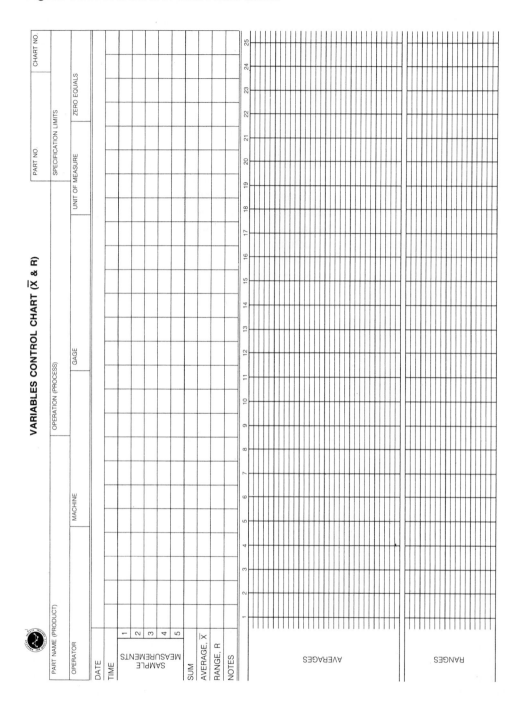

Figure 14.5 ASQ Control Chart Calculation Worksheet

CALCULATION WORKSHEET

CONTROL LIMITS

SUBGROUPS
  INCLUDED _____

$\bar{R} = \dfrac{\Sigma R}{k} =$ _____ = _____ =

$\bar{\bar{X}} = \dfrac{\Sigma \bar{X}}{k} =$ _____ = _____ =

OR

$\bar{X}'$ (MIDSPEC. OR STD.) = =

$A_2\bar{R} =$ x   = _____   x   = _____

$UCL_{\bar{x}} = \bar{\bar{X}} + A_2\bar{R}$ =   =

$LCL_{\bar{x}} = \bar{\bar{X}} - A_2\bar{R}$ =   =

$UCL_R = D_4\bar{R} =$ x   =   x   =

LIMITS FOR INDIVIDUALS

COMPARE WITH SPECIFICATION OR
TOLERANCE LIMITS

$\bar{\bar{X}}$ =

$\dfrac{3}{d_2}\bar{R} =$ x   = _____

$UL_x = \bar{\bar{X}} + \dfrac{3}{d_2}\bar{R}$ =

$LL_x = \bar{\bar{X}} - \dfrac{3}{d_2}\bar{R}$ =

US   =

LS   = _____

US − LS   =

$6\sigma = \dfrac{6}{d_2}\bar{R}$ =

MODIFIED CONTROL LIMITS FOR AVERAGES

BASED ON SPECIFICATION LIMITS AND PROCESS CAPABILITY.
APPLICABLE ONLY IF: US − LS > 6σ.

US   =   LS   =

$A_M\bar{R} =$ x   = _____ $A_M\bar{R}$ = _____

$URL_{\bar{x}} = US - A_M\bar{R}$ = $LRL_{\bar{x}} = LS + A_M\bar{R}$ =

FACTORS FOR CONTROL LIMITS

n	A_2	D_4	d_2	$\dfrac{3}{d_2}$	A_M
2	1.880	3.268	1.128	2.659	0.779
3	1.023	2.574	1.693	1.772	0.749
4	0.729	2.282	2.059	1.457	0.728
5	0.577	2.114	2.326	1.290	0.713
6	0.483	2.004	2.534	1.184	0.701

Source: Reprinted with permission of ASQ.

1. No points are outside control limits.
2. The number of points above and below the center line is about the same.
3. The points seem to fall randomly above and below the center line.
4. Most points, but not all, are near the center line, and only a few are close to the control limits.

The underlying assumption behind these rules is that the distribution of sample means is normal. This assumption follows from the central limit theorem of statistics, which states that the distribution of sample means approaches a normal distribution as the sample size increases regardless of the original distribution. Of course, for small sample sizes, the distribution of the original data must be reasonably normal for this assumption to hold. The upper and lower control limits are computed to be three standard deviations from the overall mean. Thus, the probability that any sample mean falls outside the control limits is small. This probability is the origin of rule 1.

Because the normal distribution is symmetric, about the same number of points fall above as below the center line. Also, since the mean of the normal distribution is the median, about half the points fall on either side of the center line. Finally, about 68 percent of a normal distribution falls within one standard deviation of the mean; thus, most—but not all—points should be close to the center line. These characteristics will hold provided that the mean and variance of the original data have not changed during the time the data were collected; that is, the process is stable.

Several types of unusual patterns arise in control charts, which are reviewed here along with an indication of the typical causes of such patterns.[2]

Figure 14.6 Silicon Wafer Thickness Data

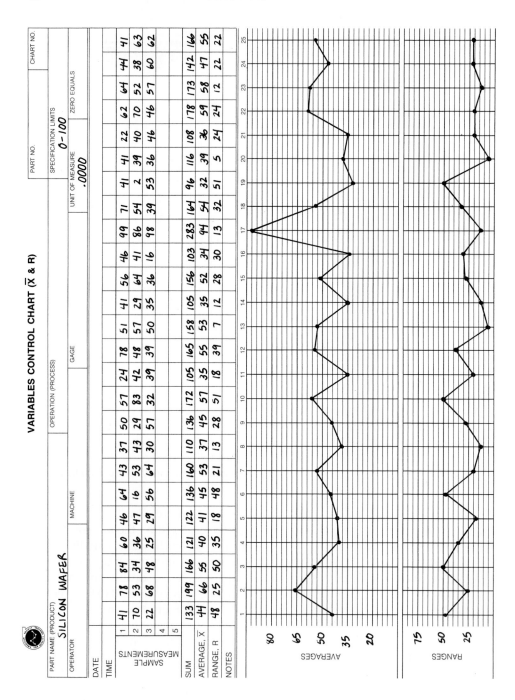

Figure 14.7 Control Limit Calculations

CALCULATION WORKSHEET

CONTROL LIMITS		LIMITS FOR INDIVIDUALS

SUBGROUPS INCLUDED __ALL__

$\bar{R} = \dfrac{\Sigma R}{k} = \dfrac{676}{25}$ = 27 _____ =

$\bar{\bar{X}} = \dfrac{\Sigma \bar{X}}{k} = \dfrac{1221}{25}$ = 48.8 _____ =

OR

$\bar{X}'$ (MIDSPEC. OR STD.)   = 50   =

$A_2\bar{R} = 1.023 \times 27$ = 27.6   x   = _____

$UCL_{\bar{X}} = \bar{\bar{X}} + A_2\bar{R}$ = 76.4   =

$LCL_{\bar{X}} = \bar{\bar{X}} - A_2\bar{R}$ = 21.2   =

$UCL_R = D_4\bar{R} = 2.574 \times 27$ = 69.5   x   =

LIMITS FOR INDIVIDUALS
COMPARE WITH SPECIFICATION OR TOLERANCE LIMITS

$\bar{\bar{X}}$ =

$\dfrac{3}{d_2}\bar{R} =$ x   = _____

$UL_x = \bar{\bar{X}} + \dfrac{3}{d_2}\bar{R}$ =

$LL_x = \bar{\bar{X}} - \dfrac{3}{d_2}\bar{R}$ =

US   =

LS   =

US − LS   =

$6\sigma = \dfrac{6}{d_2}\bar{R}$ =

MODIFIED CONTROL LIMITS FOR AVERAGES	FACTORS FOR CONTROL LIMITS

BASED ON SPECIFICATION LIMITS AND PROCESS CAPABILITY.
APPLICABLE ONLY IF: US − LS > 6σ.

US   =   LS   =

$A_M\bar{R} =$ x   = _____ $A_M\bar{R}$ = _____

$URL_{\bar{X}} = US - A_M\bar{R}$ = $LRL_{\bar{X}} = LS + A_M\bar{R}$ =

n	A_2	D_4	d_2	$\dfrac{3}{d_2}$	A_M
2	1.880	3.268	1.128	2.659	0.779
3	1.023	2.574	1.693	1.772	0.749
4	0.729	2.282	2.059	1.457	0.728
5	0.577	2.114	2.326	1.290	0.713
6	0.483	2.004	2.534	1.184	0.701

One Point Outside Control Limits A single point outside the control limits (see Figure 14.11 on page 703) is usually produced by a special cause. Often, the R-chart provides a similar indication. Once in a great while, however, such points are a normal part of the process and occur simply by chance.

A common reason for a point falling outside a control limit is an error in the calculation of $\bar{x}$ or R for the sample. You should always check your calculations whenever this occurs. Other possible causes are a sudden power surge, a broken tool, measurement error, or an incomplete or omitted operation in the process.

Sudden Shift in the Process Average An unusual number of consecutive points falling on one side of the center line (see Figure 14.12 on page 703) is usually an indication that the process average has suddenly shifted. Typically, this occurrence is the result of an external influence that has affected the process, which would be considered a special cause. In both the $\bar{x}$- and R-charts, possible causes might be a new operator, a new inspector, a new machine setting, or a change in the setup or method.

If the shift is up in the R-chart, the process has become less uniform. Typical causes are carelessness of operators, poor or inadequate maintenance, or possibly a fixture in need of repair. If the shift is down in the R-chart, the uniformity of the process has improved. This shift might be the result of improved workmanship or better machines or materials. As mentioned, every effort should be made to determine the reason for the improvement and to maintain it.

Three rules of thumb are used for early detection of process shifts. A simple rule is that if eight consecutive points fall on one side of the center line, one could conclude that the mean has shifted. Second, divide the region between the center line and each control limit into three equal parts. Then if (1) two of three consecutive points fall in the outer

Figure 14.8 Initial Control Chart

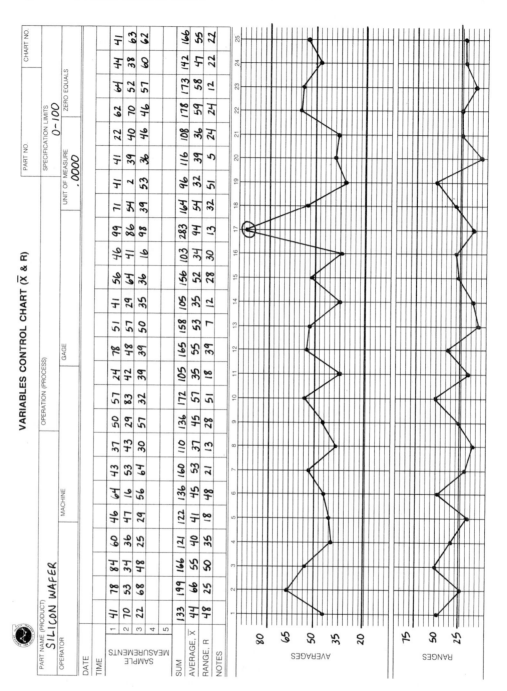

Figure 14.9 Revised Control Chart Calculations

CALCULATION WORKSHEET

CONTROL LIMITS

SUBGROUPS
INCLUDED __ALL__   __#17 REMOVED__

$\bar{R} = \dfrac{\Sigma R}{k} = \dfrac{676}{25} = 27$ $\dfrac{663}{24} = 27.6$

$\bar{\bar{X}} = \dfrac{\Sigma \bar{X}}{k} = \dfrac{1221}{25} = 48.8$ $\dfrac{1127}{24} = 47.0$

OR

$\bar{\bar{X}}'$ (MIDSPEC. OR STD.) $= 50$ $= 50$

$A_2\bar{R} = 1.023 \times 27 = 27.6$ $1.023 \times 27.6 = 28.2$

$UCL_{\bar{X}} = \bar{\bar{X}} + A_2\bar{R} = 76.4$ $= 75.2$

$LCL_{\bar{X}} = \bar{\bar{X}} - A_2\bar{R} = 21.2$ $= 18.8$

$UCL_R = D_4\bar{R} = 2.574 \times 27 = 69.5$ $2.574 \times 27.6 = 71.0$

LIMITS FOR INDIVIDUALS

COMPARE WITH SPECIFICATION OR
TOLERANCE LIMITS

$\bar{\bar{X}}$ =

$\dfrac{3}{d_2} \bar{R} = \quad \times \quad =$ _____

$UL_x = \bar{\bar{X}} + \dfrac{3}{d_2}\bar{R}$ =

$LL_x = \bar{\bar{X}} - \dfrac{3}{d_2}\bar{R}$ =

US =

LS =

US − LS =

$6\sigma = \dfrac{6}{d_2}\bar{R}$ =

MODIFIED CONTROL LIMITS FOR AVERAGES

BASED ON SPECIFICATION LIMITS AND PROCESS CAPABILITY.
APPLICABLE ONLY IF: US − LS > 6σ.

US   =   LS   =

$A_M\bar{R}$ =   ×   = _____ $A_M\bar{R}$ = _____

$URL_{\bar{X}} = US − A_M\bar{R}$ = $LRL_{\bar{X}} = LS + A_M\bar{R}$ =

FACTORS FOR CONTROL LIMITS

n	A_2	D_4	d_2	$\dfrac{3}{d_2}$	A_M
2	1.880	3.268	1.128	2.659	0.779
3	1.023	2.574	1.693	1.772	0.749
4	0.729	2.282	2.059	1.457	0.728
5	0.577	2.114	2.326	1.290	0.713
6	0.483	2.004	2.534	1.184	0.701

one-third region between the center line and one of the control limits or (2) four of five consecutive points fall within the outer two-thirds region, one would also conclude that the process has gone out of control. Examples are illustrated in Figure 14.13 on page 704.

Cycles Cycles are short, repeated patterns in the chart, alternating high peaks and low valleys (see Figure 14.14 on page 705). These patterns are the result of causes that come and go on a regular basis. In the $\bar{x}$-chart, cycles may be the result of operator rotation or fatigue at the end of a shift, different gauges used by different inspectors, seasonal effects such as temperature or humidity, or differences between day and night shifts. In the R-chart, cycles can occur from maintenance schedules, rotation of fixtures or gauges, differences between shifts, or operator fatigue.

Trends A trend is the result of some cause that gradually affects the quality characteristics of the product and causes the points on a control chart to gradually move up or down from the center line (see Figure 14.15 on page 705). As a new group of operators gains experience on the job, for example, or as maintenance of equipment improves over time, a trend may occur. In the $\bar{x}$-chart, trends may be the result of improving operator skills, dirt or chip buildup in fixtures, tool wear, changes in temperature or humidity, or aging of equipment. In the R-chart, an increasing trend may be due to a gradual decline in material quality, operator fatigue, gradual loosening of a fixture or a tool, or dulling of a tool. A decreasing trend often is the result of improved operator skill or work methods, better materials, or improved or more frequent maintenance.

Figure 14.10 Revised Control Chart

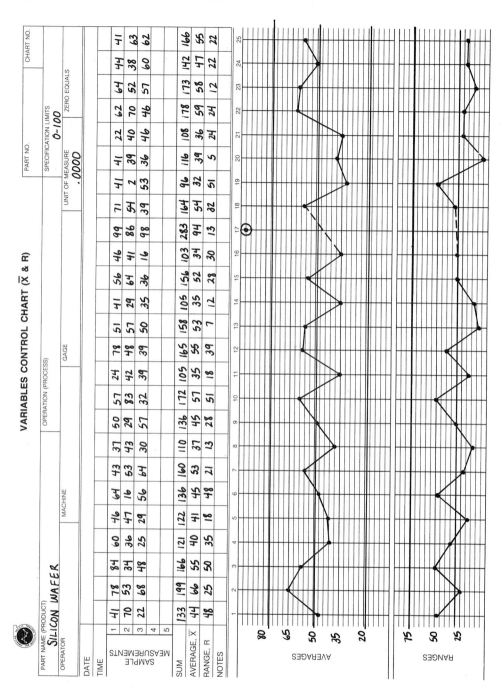

Figure 14.11 Single Point Outside Control Limits

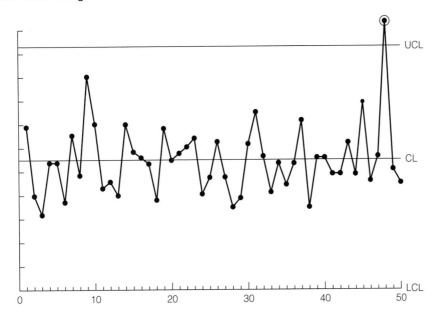

Figure 14.12 Shift in Process Average

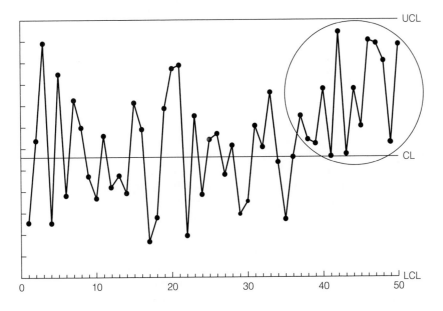

Figure 14.13 Examples of Out-of-Control Processes

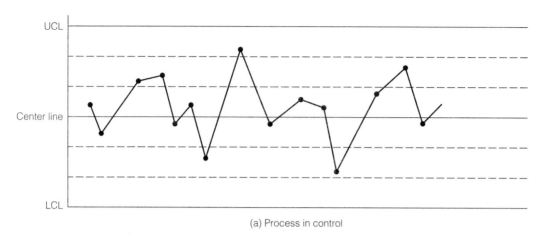

(a) Process in control

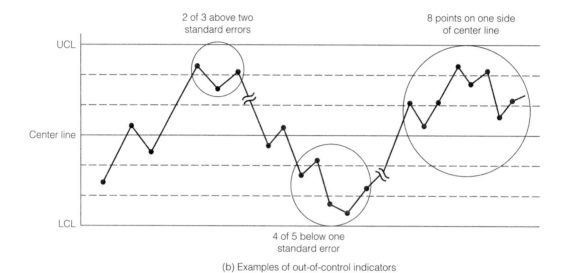

(b) Examples of out-of-control indicators

Hugging the Center Line Hugging the center line occurs when nearly all the points fall close to the center line (see Figure 14.16). In the control chart, it appears that the control limits are too wide. A common cause of hugging the center line is that the sample includes one item systematically taken from each of several machines, spindles, operators, and so on. A simple example will serve to illustrate this pattern. Suppose that one machine produces parts whose diameters average 7.508 with variation of only a few thousandths; a second machine produces parts whose diameters average 7.502, again with only a small variation. Taken together, parts from both machines would yield a range of variation that would probably be between 7.500 and 7.510, and average about 7.505. Now suppose that one part from *each* machine is sampled, and a sample average computed to plot on an $\bar{x}$-chart. The sample averages will

Figure 14.14 Cycles

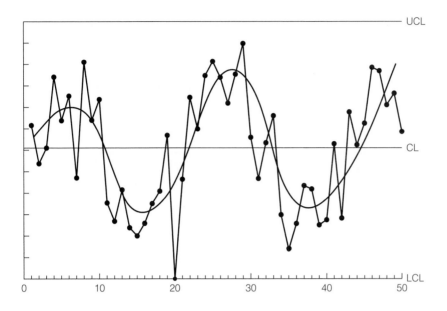

Figure 14.15 Gradual Trend

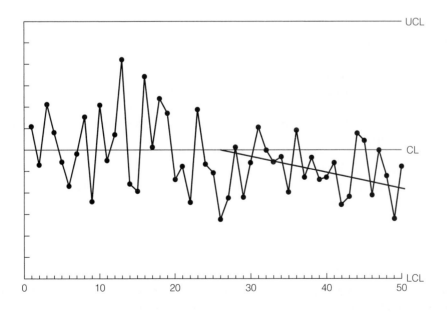

Figure 14.16 Hugging the Center Line

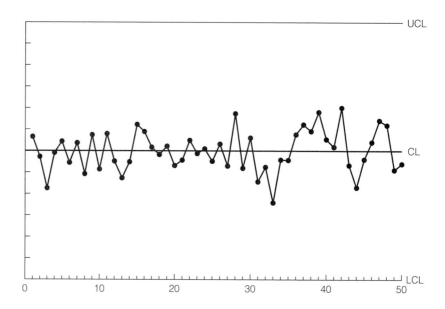

consistently be around 7.505, because one will always be high and the second will always be low. Even though a large variation will occur in the parts taken as a whole, the sample averages will not reflect this variation. In such a case, a control chart should be constructed for *each* machine, spindle, operator, and so on.

An often overlooked cause for this pattern is miscalculation of the control limits, perhaps by using the wrong factor from the table, or misplacing the decimal point in the computations.

Hugging the Control Limits This pattern shows up when many points are near the control limits with few in between (see Figure 14.17). It is often called a mixture and is actually a combination of two different patterns on the same chart. A mixture can be split into two separate patterns, as Figure 14.18 illustrates.

A mixture pattern can result when different lots of material are used in one process, or when parts are produced by different machines but fed into a common inspection group.

Instability Instability is characterized by unnatural and erratic fluctuations on both sides of the chart over a period of time (see Figure 14.19). Points will often lie outside both the upper and lower control limits without a consistent pattern. Assignable causes may be more difficult to identify in this case than with specific patterns. A frequent cause of instability is overadjustment of a machine, or the same reasons that cause hugging the control limits.

As suggested earlier, the R-chart should be analyzed before the $\bar{x}$-chart, because some out-of-control conditions in the R-chart may *cause* out-of-control conditions in the $\bar{x}$-chart. Figure 14.20 on page 709 gives an example of this situation. The range (a)

Figure 14.17 Hugging the Control Limits

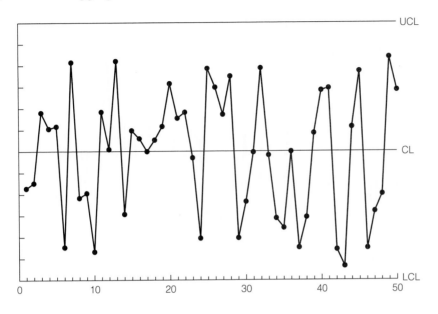

Figure 14.18 Illustration of Mixture

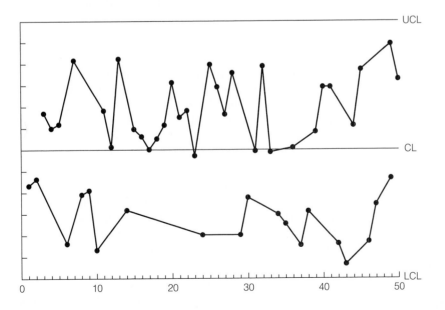

Figure 14.19 Instability

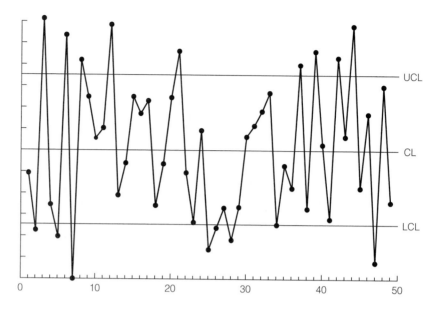

shows a drastic trend downward. If you examine the $\bar{x}$-chart in Figure 14.20(b), you will notice that the last several points seem to be hugging the center line. As the variability in the process decreases, all the sample observations will be closer to the true population mean, and therefore their average, $\bar{x}$, will not vary much from sample to sample. If this reduction in the variation can be identified and controlled, then new control limits should be computed for both charts.

Process Monitoring and Control

After a process is determined to be in control, the charts should be used on a daily basis to monitor performance, identify any special causes that might arise, and make corrections only as necessary. Unnecessary adjustments to a process result in nonproductive labor, reduced production, and increased variability of output.

> *Control charts indicate when to take action, and more importantly, when to leave a process alone.*

It is more productive if the employees who run a process take the samples and chart the data. In this way, they can react quickly to changes in the process and make adjustments immediately. For greatest effectiveness, training of employees is essential. Many companies conduct in-house training programs to teach operators and supervisors the elementary methods of statistical quality control. Not only does this training provide the mathematical and technical skills that are required, but it also gives them increased quality consciousness.

Improvements in conformance typically follow the introduction of control charts in any process, particularly when the process is labor intensive. Apparently, management involvement in employees' work often produces positive behavioral modifications (as first demonstrated in the famous Hawthorne studies). Under such circumstances, and

Figure 14.20(a) Trend Down in Range . . .

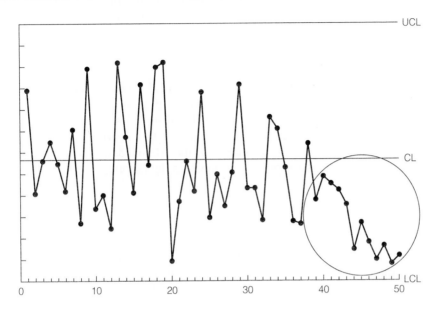

Figure 14.20(b) . . . Causes Smaller Variation in $\bar{x}$

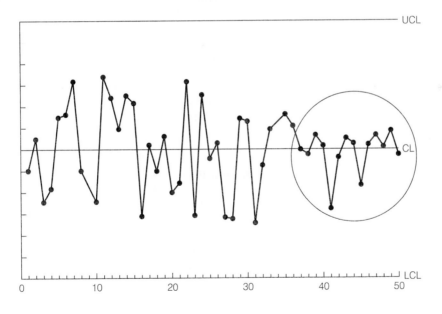

as good practice, management and employees should revise the control limits periodically and determine a new process capability as improvements take place.

Control charts are designed to be used by employees in their work areas rather than by inspectors or quality control personnel. Under the philosophy of statistical process control, the burden of quality rests with the employees themselves. The use of control charts allows them to react quickly to special causes of variation. The range is used in place of the standard deviation for the very reason that it allows users to easily make the necessary computations to plot points on a control chart. Only simple calculations are required.

Estimating Process Capability

After a process has been brought to a state of statistical control by eliminating special causes of variation, the data may be used to estimate process capability. This approach is not as accurate as that described in Chapter 11 because it uses the average range rather than the estimated standard deviation of the original data. Nevertheless, it is a quick and useful method, provided that the distribution of the original data is reasonably normal.

Under the normality assumption, the standard deviation of the original data can be estimated as follows:

$$\hat{\sigma} = \bar{R}/d_2$$

where d_2 is a constant that depends on the sample size and is also given in Appendix B. Process capability is therefore given by $6\hat{\sigma}$. The natural variation of individual measurements is given by $\bar{\bar{x}} \pm 3\sigma$. The back of the ASQ control chart form (Figure 14.21) provides a work sheet for performing the calculations.

In Figure 14.21, the calculations for the silicon wafer example discussed earlier are shown in the "Limits for Individuals" section of the form. For a sample of size 3, $d_2 = 1.693$. In Figure 14.21, UL_x and LL_x represent the upper and lower limit on individual observations, based on $3\hat{\sigma}$ limits. Thus, the scaled thickness is expected to vary between −1.9 and 95.9. The zero point of the data is the lower specification, meaning that the thickness is expected to vary from 0.0019 below the lower specifica-

---

Figure 14.21 Process Capability Calculations

tion to 0.0959 above the lower specification. The process capability index (see Chapter 12) is

$$C_p = 100/97.8 = 1.02$$

However, the lower and upper capability indexes are

$$C_{pl} = (47 - 0)/48.9 = 0.96$$

$$C_{pu} = (100 - 47)/48.9 = 1.08$$

This analysis suggests that both the centering and the variation must be improved.

If the individual observations are normally distributed, then the probability of being out of specification can be computed. In the preceding example, assume that the data are normal. The mean is 47 and the standard deviation is 97.8/6 = 16.3. Figure 14.22 shows the calculations for specification limits of 0 and 100. In Appendix A, the area between 0 and the mean (47) is 0.4980. Thus 0.2 percent of the output would be expected to fall below the lower specification. The area to the right of 100 is approximately zero. Therefore all the output can be expected to meet the upper specification.

A word of caution deserves emphasis here. Control limits are often confused with specification limits. Specification dimensions are usually stated in relation to individual parts for "hard" goods, such as automotive hardware. However, in other applications, such as in chemical processes, specifications are stated in terms of average characteristics. Thus, control charts might mislead one into thinking that if all sample averages fall within the control limits, all output will be conforming. This assumption is not true. A sample average may fall within the upper and lower control limits even though some of the individual observations are out of specification. Because $\sigma_{\bar{x}} = \sigma/\sqrt{n}$, control limits are narrower than the natural variation in the process and do not represent process capability.

Control limits relate to averages of samples, while specification limits relate to individual measurements.

Figure 14.22 Process Capability Probability Computations

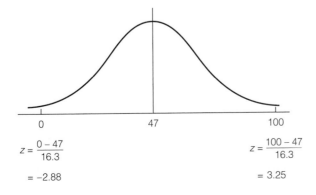

Modified Control Limits

The calculation worksheet on the back of the ASQ control chart form has one additional section entitled "Modified Control Limits for Averages." Modified control limits often are used when process capability is good. For example, suppose that the process capability is 60 percent of tolerance ($C_p = 1.67$) and that the mean can be controlled by a simple adjustment. A company may quickly discover the impracticality of investigating every isolated point that falls outside the usual control limits because the output is probably well within specifications. In such cases, the usual control limits may be replaced with the following:

$$\text{URL}_x = \text{US} - A_m \bar{R}$$

$$\text{LRL}_x = \text{LS} + A_m \bar{R}$$

where URL_x is the upper reject level, LRL_x is the lower reject level, and US and LS are the upper and lower specifications, respectively. Factors for A_m are found on the worksheet. These modified control limits allow for more variation than the ordinary control limits and still provide high confidence that the product produced is within specifications. Even though the ASQ chart states that these modified limits apply only if the tolerance is greater than 6σ, experts suggest that process capability should be at least 60 to 75 percent of tolerance. If the mean must be controlled closely, a conventional $\bar{x}$-chart should be used even if the process capability is good. Also, if the standard deviation of the process is likely to shift, modified control limits are not appropriate.

Figure 14.23 shows the completed worksheet for the silicon wafer thickness example. Because the sample size is 3, $A_m = 0.749$. Therefore, the modified limits are

$$\text{URL}_x = \text{US} - A_m \bar{R} = 100 - 0.749(27.6) = 79.3$$

$$\text{LRL}_x = \text{LS} + A_m \bar{R} = 0 + 0.749(27.6) = 20.7$$

Observe that if the process is centered on the nominal, these control limits are looser than the ordinary control limits. In this example, the centering would first have to be corrected from its current estimated value of 47.0.

Excel Spreadsheet Templates

Figure 14.24 shows an Excel template and solution for the silicon wafer example. The template includes an automatic plot of the $\bar{x}$- and R-charts and calculation of process capability indexes. Some scaling of the chart display ranges may be necessary for certain problems. The spreadsheet (XBAR&R.XLS) is available on the CD-ROM accompanying this book, as are all other Excel applications in this chapter.

Please note the following:

- The recalculation option for the spreadsheets is set to manual. Therefore, to recalculate any spreadsheet after making changes, press the F9 key or set the recalculation option to automatic in the *Calculation* tab from the *Tools/Options* menu.
- To rescale the vertical axis in a chart, to widen the range of the plotted data for instance, double-click on the *y*-axis, and select the *Scale* tab in the dialog box that appears. Change the "min" and "max" parameters as appropriate.
- When deleting special cause data and recomputing control limits, be sure to update the number of samples used in the calculations to compute the statistics.

Figure 14.23 Modified Control Limit Calculations

CALCULATION WORKSHEET

CONTROL LIMITS		LIMITS FOR INDIVIDUALS

SUBGROUPS INCLUDED **ALL**   **#17 REMOVED**

$\bar{R} = \frac{\Sigma R}{k} = \frac{676}{25}$ = 27 $\frac{663}{24}$ = 27.6

$\bar{\bar{X}} = \frac{\Sigma \bar{X}}{k} = \frac{1221}{25}$ = 48.8 $\frac{1127}{24}$ = 47.0

OR

$\bar{X}'$ (MIDSPEC. OR STD.) = 50   = 50

$A_2\bar{R} = 1.023 \times 27$ = 27.6 1.023×27.6 = 28.2

$UCL_{\bar{x}} = \bar{\bar{X}} + A_2\bar{R}$ = 76.4   = 75.2

$LCL_{\bar{x}} = \bar{\bar{X}} - A_2\bar{R}$ = 21.2   = 18.8

$UCL_R = D_4\bar{R} = 2.574 \times 27$ = 69.5 2.574×27.6 = 71.0

LIMITS FOR INDIVIDUALS — COMPARE WITH SPECIFICATION OR TOLERANCE LIMITS

$\bar{X}$ = 47.0

$\frac{3}{d_2}\bar{R} = 1.772 \times 27.6$ = 48.9

$UL_x = \bar{X} + \frac{3}{d_2}\bar{R}$ = 95.9

$LL_x = \bar{X} - \frac{3}{d_2}\bar{R}$ = -1.9

US = 100

LS = 0

US − LS = 100

$6\sigma = \frac{6}{d_2}\bar{R}$ = 97.8

MODIFIED CONTROL LIMITS FOR AVERAGES

BASED ON SPECIFICATION LIMITS AND PROCESS CAPABILITY. APPLICABLE ONLY IF: US − LS > 6σ.

US = 100   LS = 0

$A_M\bar{R} = .749 \times 27.6$ = 20.7 $A_M\bar{R}$ = 20.7

$URL_{\bar{x}} = US - A_M\bar{R}$ = 79.3 $LRL_{\bar{x}} = LS + A_M\bar{R}$ = 20.7

FACTORS FOR CONTROL LIMITS

n	A_2	D_4	d_2	$\frac{3}{d_2}$	A_M
2	1.880	3.268	1.128	2.659	0.779
3	1.023	2.574	1.693	1.772	0.749
4	0.729	2.282	2.059	1.457	0.728
5	0.577	2.114	2.326	1.290	0.713
6	0.483	2.004	2.534	1.184	0.701

- When a sample is deleted from a data set in the templates, do not enter zero for the data; instead, leave the cells blank. The charts are set up to interpolate between nonmissing data points in the *Tools/Options/Chart* tab.

SPECIAL CONTROL CHARTS FOR VARIABLES DATA

Several alternatives to the popular $\bar{x}$- and R-charts for process control of variables measurements are available. This section discusses some of these alternatives.

$\bar{x}$- and s-Charts

The sample standard deviation is a more sensitive and better indicator of process variability than the range, especially for larger sample sizes. Thus, when tight control of variability is required, s should be used.

An alternative to using the R-chart along with the $\bar{x}$-chart is to compute and plot the standard deviation s of each sample. The range has traditionally been used because it involves less computational effort and is easier for shop-floor personnel to understand, making it advantageous. With the availability of modern calculators and personal computers, the computational burden of computing s is reduced or eliminated, and s has thus become a viable alternative to R.

The sample standard deviation is computed as

$$s = \sqrt{\frac{\sum_{i=1}^{n} (x_i - \bar{x})^2}{n-1}}$$

Figure 14.24a Excel Spreadsheet and $\bar{x}$- and R-Charts for the Silicon Wafer Example (XBAR&R.XLS)

X-bar and R-Chart

This spreadsheet is designed for up to 30 samples, each of a constant sample size from 2 to 10. Enter data ONLY in yellow-shaded cells.

Enter the number of samples in cell D6 and the sample size in cell D7. Then enter your data in the grid below.

Click on sheet tabs for a display of the control charts. Specification limits may be entered in cells N7 and N8 for process capability.

Number of samples (<= 50)	24
Sample size (2 - 10)	3

Grand Average	47.083333	A2 1.02	D3 0	D4 2.57	d2 1.69
Average Range	27.625				

Process Capability Calculations

Upper specification	100	Six sigma	97.9
Lower specification	0	Cp	1.02
		Cpu	1.08
		CpI	0.96
		Cpk	0.96

DATA

	1	2	3	4	5	6	7	8	9	10	11	12	13	14	15	16	17	18	19	20	21	22	23	24	25
1	41	78	84	60	46	64	43	37	50	57	24	78	51	41	56	46		71	41	41	22	62	64	44	41
2	70	53	34	36	47	16	53	43	29	83	42	48	57	29	64	41		54	2	39	40	70	52	38	63
3	22	68	48	25	29	56	64	30	57	32	39	39	50	35	36	16		39	53	36	46	46	57	60	62
4																									
5																									
6																									
7																									
8																									
9																									
10																									
Average	44.33	66.33	55.33	40.33	40.67	45.33	53.33	36.67	45.33	57.33	35	55	52.67	35	52	34.33	#N/A	54.67	32	38.67	36	59.33	57.67	47.33	55.33
LCLx-bar	18.82	18.82	18.82	18.82	18.82	18.82	18.82	18.82	18.82	18.82	18.82	18.82	18.82	18.82	18.82	18.82	18.82	18.82	18.82	18.82	18.82	18.82	18.82	18.82	18.82
Center	47.08	47.08	47.08	47.08	47.08	47.08	47.08	47.08	47.08	47.08	47.08	47.08	47.08	47.08	47.08	47.08	47.08	47.08	47.08	47.08	47.08	47.08	47.08	47.08	47.08
UCLx-bar	75.34	75.34	75.34	75.34	75.34	75.34	75.34	75.34	75.34	75.34	75.34	75.34	75.34	75.34	75.34	75.34	75.34	75.34	75.34	75.34	75.34	75.34	75.34	75.34	75.34
Range	48	25	50	35	18	48	21	13	28	51	18	39	7	12	28	30	#N/A	32	51	5	24	24	12	22	22
LCLrange	0	0	0	0	0	0	0	0	0	0	0	0	0	0	0	0	0	0	0	0	0	0	0	0	0
Center	27.63	27.63	27.63	27.63	27.63	27.63	27.63	27.63	27.63	27.63	27.63	27.63	27.63	27.63	27.63	27.63	27.63	27.63	27.63	27.63	27.63	27.63	27.63	27.63	27.63
UCLrange	71.11	71.11	71.11	71.11	71.11	71.11	71.11	71.11	71.11	71.11	71.11	71.11	71.11	71.11	71.11	71.11	71.11	71.11	71.11	71.11	71.11	71.11	71.11	71.11	71.11

To construct an *s*-chart, compute the standard deviation for each sample. Next, compute the average standard deviation $\bar{s}$ by averaging the sample standard deviations over all samples. (Notice that this computation is analogous to computing $\bar{R}$.) Control limits for the *s*-chart are given by

$$UCL_s = B_4\bar{s}$$

$$LCL_s = B_3\bar{s}$$

where B_3 and B_4 are constants found in Appendix B.

Figure 14.24b $\bar{x}$-Chart for the Silicon Wafer Example

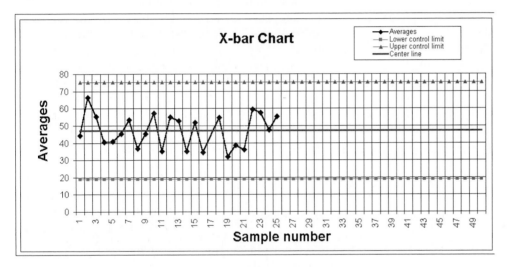

Figure 14.24c *R*-Chart for the Silicon Wafer Example

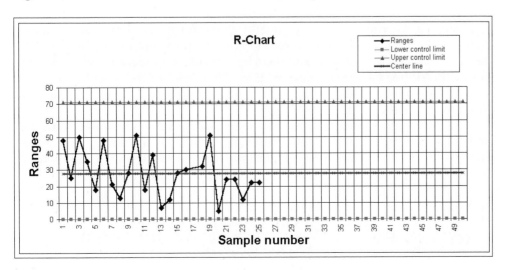

For the associated $\bar{x}$-chart, the control limits derived from the overall standard deviation are

$$UCL_{\bar{x}} = \bar{\bar{x}} + A_3\bar{s}$$

$$LCL_{\bar{x}} = \bar{\bar{x}} - A_3\bar{s}$$

where A_3 is a constant found in Appendix B.

Observe that the formulas for the control limits are equivalent to those for $\bar{x}$- and R-charts except that the constants differ.

Constructing $\bar{x}$- and s-Charts To illustrate the use of the $\bar{x}$- and s-charts, consider the data given in Figure 14.25. These data represent measurements of deviations from a nominal specification for some machined part. Samples of size 10 are used; for each sample, the mean and standard deviation have been computed.

The average (overall) mean is computed to be $\bar{\bar{x}} = 0.108$, and the average standard deviation is $\bar{s} = 1.791$. For samples of size 10, $B_3 = 0.284$, $B_4 = 1.716$, and $A_3 = 0.975$. Control limits for the s-chart are

$$LCL_s = 0.284(1.791) = 0.509$$

$$UCL_s = 1.716(1.791) = 3.073$$

For the $\bar{x}$-chart, the control limits are

$$LCL_{\bar{x}} = 0.108 - 0.975(1.791) = -1.638$$

$$UCL_{\bar{x}} = 0.108 + 0.975(1.791) = 1.854$$

The $\bar{x}$- and s-charts are shown in Figure 14.26. This evidence indicates the process is not in control, and an investigation as to the reasons for the variation, particularly in the $\bar{x}$-chart, is warranted.

Charts for Individuals

With the development of automated inspection for many processes, manufacturers can now easily inspect and measure quality characteristics on every item produced. Hence, the sample size for process control is $n = 1$, and a control chart for *individual measurements*—also called an *x-chart*—can be used. Other examples in which x-charts are useful include accounting data such as shipments, orders, absences, and accidents; production records of temperature, humidity, voltage, or pressure; and the results of physical or chemical analyses.

With individual measurements, the process standard deviation can be estimated and 3σ control limits used. As shown earlier, $\bar{R}/d_2$ provides an estimate of the process standard deviation. Thus, an x-chart for individual measurements would have 3σ control limits defined by

$$UCL_x = \bar{x} + 3\bar{R}/d_2$$

$$LCL_x = \bar{x} - 3\bar{R}/d_2$$

Figure 14.25 Data and Calculations for $\bar{x}$- and s-Charts (XBAR&S.XLS)

	A	B	C	D	E	F	G	H	I	J	K	L	M	N	O	P	Q	R	S	T	U	V	W	X	Y	Z
1	**X-bar and s-Chart**																									
2	This spreadsheet is designed for up to 50 samples, each of a constant sample size from 2 to 10. Enter data ONLY in yellow-shaded cells.																									
3	Enter the number of samples in cell D6 and the sample size in cell D7. Then enter your data in the grid below.																									
4	Click on sheet tabs for a display of the control charts (some rescaling may be needed). Specification limits may be entered in cells N7 and N8 for process capability.																									
5																										
6	**Number of samples (<= 50)**			25						Process Capability Calculations						**Six sigma**	2.71									
7	**Sample size (2 - 10)**			10						**Upper specification**						**Cp**										
8										**Lower specification**						**Cpu**										
9	**Grand Average**		0.108		A3	B3	B4	d2								**Cpl**										
10	**Avg. std. dev.**		1.7905259		0.98	0.28	1.72	3.08								**Cpk**										
11																										
12	DATA	1	2	3	4	5	6	7	8	9	10	11	12	13	14	15	16	17	18	19	20	21	22	23	24	25
13	1	1	9	0	1	-3	-6	-3	0	2	0	-3	-12	-6	-3	-1	-1	-2	0	0	1	1	-1	0	1	2
14	2	8	4	8	1	-1	2	-1	-2	0	0	-2	2	-3	-5	-1	-2	2	4	3	2	2	0	0	0	2
15	3	6	0	0	0	0	0	0	-3	-1	-2	2	0	0	5	-1	-2	-1	0	-3	1	2	2	-1	0	1
16	4	9	3	0	2	-4	0	-2	-1	-1	-1	-1	-4	0	0	-2	0	0	0	3	1	1	-1	0	1	2
17	5	7	0	3	1	0	2	-1	-2	-3	-1	1	-1	-8	-5	-1	-4	-1	0	3	-3	2	2	1	1	-1
18	6	9	0	1	1	1	-1	-1	1	0	0	-2	4	-4	1	0	0	-1	3	1	2	2	2	0	2	2
19	7	2	3	2	2	0	2	-3	-3	1	-1	-2	2	-6	5	-2	-2	2	0	0	1	1	-1	0	0	2
20	8	7	4	0	0	-2	0	0	0	-3	-2	-1	-3	-1	-4	-1	-4	-1	0	1	-2	1	0	0	0	1
21	9	9	8	2	0	0	-3	-2	-3	-1	-2	1	-4	-1	-1	0	-1	1	1	2	3	1	0	-1	-1	-1
22	10	7	3	3	1	-2	0	-2	-2	0	0	1	0	-2	-5	-1	0	-2	0	-2	0	2	-1	0	0	2
23	**Average**	6.5	3.4	1.9	0.9	-1.1	-0.4	-1.5	-1.5	-0.6	-0.9	-0.6	-1.6	-3.1	-1.2	-1	-1.6	-0.3	0.8	0.8	0.6	1.5	0.2	-0.1	0.4	1.2
24	**LCLx-bar**	-1.64	-1.64	-1.64	-1.64	-1.64	-1.64	-1.64	-1.64	-1.64	-1.64	-1.64	-1.64	-1.64	-1.64	-1.64	-1.64	-1.64	-1.64	-1.64	-1.64	-1.64	-1.64	-1.64	-1.64	-1.64
25	**Center**	0.108	0.108	0.108	0.108	0.108	0.108	0.108	0.108	0.108	0.108	0.108	0.108	0.108	0.108	0.108	0.108	0.108	0.108	0.108	0.108	0.108	0.108	0.108	0.108	0.108
26	**UCLx-bar**	1.854	1.854	1.854	1.854	1.854	1.854	1.854	1.854	1.854	1.854	1.854	1.854	1.854	1.854	1.854	1.854	1.854	1.854	1.854	1.854	1.854	1.854	1.854	1.854	1.854
27																										
28	**Std. Dev.**	2.838	3.134	2.47	0.738	1.595	2.503	1.08	1.434	1.578	0.876	1.713	4.526	2.807	3.91	0.667	1.506	1.494	1.476	2.098	1.838	0.527	1.317	0.568	0.843	1.229
29	**LCLs**	-1.64	-1.64	-1.64	-1.64	-1.64	-1.64	-1.64	-1.64	-1.64	-1.64	-1.64	-1.64	-1.64	-1.64	-1.64	-1.64	-1.64	-1.64	-1.64	-1.64	-1.64	-1.64	-1.64	-1.64	-1.64
30	**Center**	1.791	1.791	1.791	1.791	1.791	1.791	1.791	1.791	1.791	1.791	1.791	1.791	1.791	1.791	1.791	1.791	1.791	1.791	1.791	1.791	1.791	1.791	1.791	1.791	1.791
31	**UCLs**	3.073	3.073	3.073	3.073	3.073	3.073	3.073	3.073	3.073	3.073	3.073	3.073	3.073	3.073	3.073	3.073	3.073	3.073	3.073	3.073	3.073	3.073	3.073	3.073	3.073

Figure 14.26(a) $\bar{x}$-Chart for the Machined Part Example

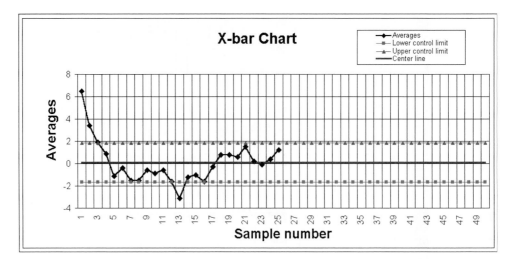

Samples of size 1, however, do not furnish enough information for process variability measurement. Process variability can be determined by using a moving average of ranges, or a *moving range*, of n successive observations. For example, a moving range for $n = 2$ is computed by finding the absolute difference between two successive observations. The number of observations used in the moving range determines the constant d_2; hence, for $n = 2$, from Appendix B, $d_2 = 1.128$. In a similar fashion, larger values of n can be used to compute moving ranges. The moving range chart has control limits defined by

Figure 14.26(b) s-Chart for the Machined Part Example

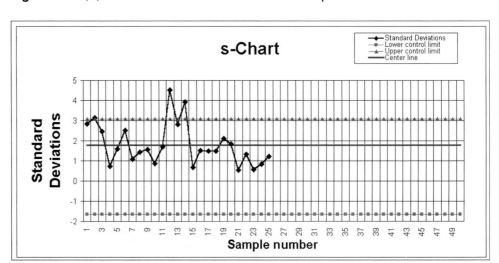

$$UCL_R = D_4\bar{R}$$

$$LCL_R = D_3\bar{R}$$

which is comparable to the ordinary range chart.

Constructing an *x*-Chart with Moving Ranges. Consider a set of observations measuring the percentage of cobalt in a chemical process as given in Figure 14.27. The moving range is computed as shown by taking absolute values of successive ranges and using the constants in Appendix B. For example, the first moving range is the difference between the first two observations:

$$|3.75 - 3.80| = 0.05$$

Figure 14.27 Data and Calculations for the Chemical Process Example (X&MR.XLS)

	A	B	C	D	E	F	G	H	I	J	K	L	M
1	X and Moving Range Chart												
2	This spreadsheet is designed for up to 50 observations and a moving range from 2 to 5. Enter data ONLY in yellow-shaded cells.												
3	Enter the number of samples in cell D6 and the sample size in cell D7. Then enter your data in the grid below.												
4	Click on sheet tabs to display the control charts (some rescaling may be needed).												
5													
6	Number of samples (<= 50)			25									
7	Sample size for moving range(2 - 5)			2									
8													
9	Grand Average		3.498	D3		D4		d2					
10	Average Range		0.352083333	0		3.267	1.13						
11													
12						Moving							
13	Observation	Value	LCLx	CLx	UCLx	Range	LCLr	CLr	UCLr				
14	1	3.75	2.562	3.498	4.4344								
15	2	3.8	2.562	3.498	4.4344	0.05	0	0.35	1.15				
16	3	3.7	2.562	3.498	4.4344	0.1	0	0.35	1.15				
17	4	3.2	2.562	3.498	4.4344	0.5	0	0.35	1.15				
18	5	3.5	2.562	3.498	4.4344	0.3	0	0.35	1.15				
19	6	3.05	2.562	3.498	4.4344	0.45	0	0.35	1.15				
20	7	3.5	2.562	3.498	4.4344	0.45	0	0.35	1.15				
21	8	3.25	2.562	3.498	4.4344	0.25	0	0.35	1.15				
22	9	3.6	2.562	3.498	4.4344	0.35	0	0.35	1.15				
23	10	3.1	2.562	3.498	4.4344	0.5	0	0.35	1.15				
24	11	4	2.562	3.498	4.4344	0.9	0	0.35	1.15				
25	12	4	2.562	3.498	4.4344	0	0	0.35	1.15				
26	13	3.5	2.562	3.498	4.4344	0.5	0	0.35	1.15				
27	14	3	2.562	3.498	4.4344	0.5	0	0.35	1.15				
28	15	3.8	2.562	3.498	4.4344	0.8	0	0.35	1.15				
29	16	3.4	2.562	3.498	4.4344	0.4	0	0.35	1.15				
30	17	3.6	2.562	3.498	4.4344	0.2	0	0.35	1.15				
31	18	3.1	2.562	3.498	4.4344	0.5	0	0.35	1.15				
32	19	3.55	2.562	3.498	4.4344	0.45	0	0.35	1.15				
33	20	3.65	2.562	3.498	4.4344	0.1	0	0.35	1.15				
34	21	3.45	2.562	3.498	4.4344	0.2	0	0.35	1.15				
35	22	3.3	2.562	3.498	4.4344	0.15	0	0.35	1.15				
36	23	3.75	2.562	3.498	4.4344	0.45	0	0.35	1.15				
37	24	3.5	2.562	3.498	4.4344	0.25	0	0.35	1.15				
38	25	3.4	2.562	3.498	4.4344	0.1	0	0.35	1.15				

The second moving range is computed as

$$|3.80 - 3.70| = 0.10$$

From these data we find that

$$LCL_R = 0$$

$$UCL_R = (3.267)(0.352) = 1.15$$

The moving range chart, shown in Figure 14.28(a), indicates that the process is in control.

Next, the x-chart is constructed for the individual measurements:

$$LCL_x = 3.498 - 3(0.352)/1.128 = 2.56$$

$$UCL_x = 3.498 + 3(0.352)/1.128 = 4.43$$

The process, shown in Figure 14.28(b), appears to be in control.

Some caution is necessary when interpreting patterns on the moving range chart. Points beyond control limits indicate assignable causes. Successive ranges, however, are correlated, and they may cause patterns or trends in the chart that are not indicative of out-of-control situations. On the x-chart, individual observations are assumed to be uncorrelated; hence, patterns and trends should be investigated.

> *Control charts for individuals offer the advantage of being able to draw specifications on the chart for direct comparison with the control limits.*

In addition, charts for individuals are less sensitive to many of the conditions that can be detected by $\bar{x}$- and R-charts; for example, the process must vary a lot before a shift in the mean is detected. Also, short cycles and trends may appear on these charts and not on an $\bar{x}$- or R-chart. Finally, the assumption of normality of observations is more critical than for $\bar{x}$- and R-charts; when the normality assumption does not hold, greater chance for error is present.

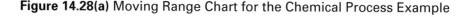

Figure 14.28(a) Moving Range Chart for the Chemical Process Example

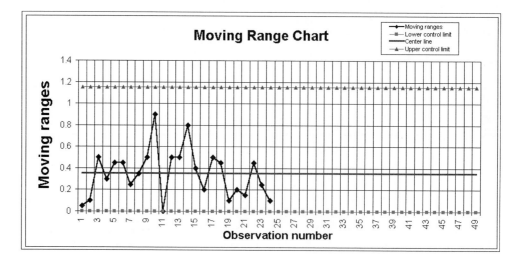

Figure 14.28(b) x–Chart for the Chemical Process Example

CONTROL CHARTS FOR ATTRIBUTES

Attributes data assume only two values—good or bad, pass or fail, and so on. Attributes usually cannot be measured, but they can be observed and counted and are useful in many practical situations. For instance, in printing packages for consumer products, color quality can be rated as acceptable or not acceptable, or a sheet of cardboard either is damaged or is not. Usually, attributes data are easy to collect, often by visual inspection. Many accounting records, such as percent scrapped, are readily available. However, one drawback in using attributes data is that large samples are necessary to obtain valid statistical results.

Several different types of control charts are used for attributes data. One of the most common is the p-chart. Other types of attributes charts are also used. One distinction that we must make is between the terms *defects* and *defectives*. A **defect** is a single nonconforming quality characteristic of an item. An item may have several defects. The term **defective** refers to items having one or more defects. Because certain attributes charts are used for defectives while others are used for defects, one must understand the difference. The term *nonconforming* is often used instead of *defective*.

Fraction Nonconforming (p) Chart

A **p-chart** monitors the proportion of nonconforming items produced in a lot. Often it is also called a **fraction nonconforming** or **fraction defective chart**. As with variables data, a p-chart is constructed by first gathering 25 to 30 samples of the attribute being measured. The size of each sample should be large enough to have several nonconforming items. If the probability of finding a nonconforming item is small, a sample size of 100 or more items is usually necessary. Samples are chosen over time periods so that any special causes that are identified can be investigated.

Let us suppose that k samples, each of size n, are selected. If y represents the number nonconforming in a particular sample, the proportion nonconforming is y/n.

Let p_i be the fraction nonconforming in the ith sample; the average fraction noncon-forming for the group of k samples then is

$$\bar{p} = \frac{p_1 + p_2 + \ldots + p_k}{k}$$

This statistic reflects the average performance of the process. One would expect a high percentage of samples to have a fraction nonconforming within three standard deviations of $\bar{p}$. An estimate of the standard deviation is given by

$$s_{\bar{p}} = \sqrt{\frac{\bar{p}(1 - \bar{p})}{n}}$$

Therefore, upper and lower control limits are given by

$$UCL_p = \bar{p} + 3s_{\bar{p}}$$

$$LCL_p = \bar{p} - 3s_{\bar{p}}$$

If LCL_p is less than zero, a value of zero is used.

Analysis of a p-chart is similar to that of an $\bar{x}$- or R-chart. Points outside the con-trol limits signify an out-of-control situation. Patterns and trends should also be sought to identify special causes. However, a point on a p-chart below the lower con-trol limit or the development of a trend below the center line indicates that the process might have improved, based on an ideal of zero defectives. Caution is advised before such conclusions are drawn, because errors may have been made in computation.

Constructing a p-Chart The operators of automated sorting machines in a post office must read the ZIP code on a letter and divert the letter to the proper carrier route. Over one month's time, 25 samples of 100 letters were chosen, and the number of errors was recorded. This information is summarized in Figure 14.29. The fraction nonconforming is found by dividing the number of errors by 100. The average frac-tion nonconforming, $\bar{p}$, is determined to be

$$\bar{p} = \frac{0.03 + 0.01 + \ldots + 0.01}{25} = 0.022$$

The standard deviation is computed as

$$s_{\bar{p}} = \sqrt{\frac{0.022(1 - 0.022)}{100}} = 0.01467$$

Thus, the upper control limit, UCL_p, is $0.022 + 3(0.01467) = 0.066$, and the lower control limit, LCL_p, is $0.022 - 3(0.01467) = -0.022$. Because this later figure is negative, zero is used. The control chart for this example is shown in Figure 14.30. The sorting process appears to be in control. Any values found above the upper control limit or evidence of an upward trend might indicate the need for more experience or training of the operators.

Figure 14.29 Data and Calculations for the ZIP Code Reader Example (P-CHART.XLS)

Fraction Nonconforming (p) Chart

This spreadsheet is designed for up to 50 samples. Enter data ONLY in yellow-shaded cells.

Click on the sheet tab to display the control chart (some rescaling may be needed).

| Average (p-bar) | 0.022 |
| Avg. sample size | 100 |

								Approximate Control Limits Using Average Sample Size Calculations		
Sample	Value	Sample Size	Fraction Nonconforming	Standard Deviation	LCLp	CL	UCLp	LCLp	CL	UCLp
1	3	100	0.0300	0.01467	0	0.022	0.066	0	0.022	0.066
2	1	100	0.0100	0.01467	0	0.022	0.066	0	0.022	0.066
3	0	100	0.0000	0.01467	0	0.022	0.066	0	0.022	0.066
4	0	100	0.0000	0.01467	0	0.022	0.066	0	0.022	0.066
5	2	100	0.0200	0.01467	0	0.022	0.066	0	0.022	0.066
6	5	100	0.0500	0.01467	0	0.022	0.066	0	0.022	0.066
7	3	100	0.0300	0.01467	0	0.022	0.066	0	0.022	0.066
8	6	100	0.0600	0.01467	0	0.022	0.066	0	0.022	0.066
9	1	100	0.0100	0.01467	0	0.022	0.066	0	0.022	0.066
10	4	100	0.0400	0.01467	0	0.022	0.066	0	0.022	0.066
11	0	100	0.0000	0.01467	0	0.022	0.066	0	0.022	0.066
12	2	100	0.0200	0.01467	0	0.022	0.066	0	0.022	0.066
13	1	100	0.0100	0.01467	0	0.022	0.066	0	0.022	0.066
14	3	100	0.0300	0.01467	0	0.022	0.066	0	0.022	0.066
15	4	100	0.0400	0.01467	0	0.022	0.066	0	0.022	0.066
16	1	100	0.0100	0.01467	0	0.022	0.066	0	0.022	0.066
17	1	100	0.0100	0.01467	0	0.022	0.066	0	0.022	0.066
18	2	100	0.0200	0.01467	0	0.022	0.066	0	0.022	0.066
19	5	100	0.0500	0.01467	0	0.022	0.066	0	0.022	0.066
20	2	100	0.0200	0.01467	0	0.022	0.066	0	0.022	0.066
21	3	100	0.0300	0.01467	0	0.022	0.066	0	0.022	0.066
22	4	100	0.0400	0.01467	0	0.022	0.066	0	0.022	0.066
23	1	100	0.0100	0.01467	0	0.022	0.066	0	0.022	0.066
24	0	100	0.0000	0.01467	0	0.022	0.066	0	0.022	0.066
25	1	100	0.0100	0.01467	0	0.022	0.066	0	0.022	0.066

Variable Sample Size

Often 100 percent inspection is performed on process output during fixed sampling periods; however, the number of units produced in each sampling period may vary. In this case, the *p*-chart would have a variable sample size. One way of handling this

Figure 14.30 *p*-Chart for the ZIP Code Reader Example

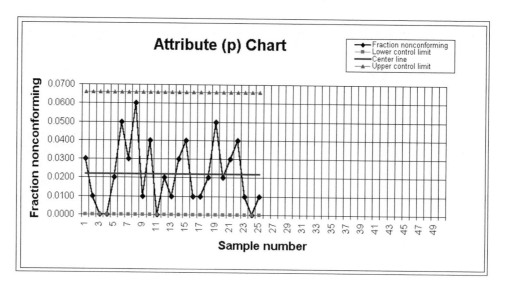

variation is to compute a standard deviation for each individual sample. Thus, if the number of observations in the *i*th sample is n_i, control limits are given by

$$\bar{p} \pm 3 \sqrt{\frac{\bar{p}(1-\bar{p})}{n_i}}$$

where $\bar{p} = \dfrac{\Sigma \text{ number nonconforming}}{\Sigma n_i}$

The data given in Figure 14.31 represent 20 samples with varying sample sizes. The value of $\bar{p}$ is computed as

$$\bar{p} = \frac{18 + 20 + 14 + \ldots + 18}{137 + 158 + 92 + \ldots + 160} = \frac{271}{2,980} = 0.0909$$

The control limits for sample 1 are

$$\text{LCL}_p = .0909 - 3 \sqrt{\frac{.0909\,(1 - .0909)}{137}} = 0.017$$

$$\text{UCL}_p = .0909 + 3 \sqrt{\frac{.0909\,(1 - .0909)}{137}} = 0.165$$

Figure 14.31 Data and Calculations for the Variable Sample Size Example
(P-CHART.XLS)

	A	B	C	D	E	F	G	H	I	J	K	L	M
1	**Fraction Nonconforming (p) Chart**												
2	This spreadsheet is designed for up to 50 samples. Enter data ONLY in yellow-shaded cells.												
3	Click on the sheet tab to display the control chart (some rescaling may be needed).												
4													
5	**Average (p-bar)**		0.090939597										
6	**Avg. sample size**		149										
7										**Approximate Control Limits Using**			
8			**Sample**	**Fraction**	**Standard**					**Average Sample Size Calculations**			
9	**Sample**	**Value**	**Size**	**Nonconforming**	**Deviation**	**LCLp**	**CL**	**UCLp**		**LCLp**	**CL**	**UCLp**	
10	1	18	137	0.1314	0.02456	0.017	0.091	0.165		0.02028	0.09094	0.1616	
11	2	20	158	0.1266	0.02287	0.022	0.091	0.160		0.02028	0.09094	0.1616	
12	3	14	92	0.1522	0.02998	0.001	0.091	0.181		0.02028	0.09094	0.1616	
13	4	6	122	0.0492	0.02603	0.013	0.091	0.169		0.02028	0.09094	0.1616	
14	5	11	86	0.1279	0.03100	0.000	0.091	0.184		0.02028	0.09094	0.1616	
15	6	22	187	0.1176	0.02103	0.028	0.091	0.154		0.02028	0.09094	0.1616	
16	7	6	156	0.0385	0.02302	0.022	0.091	0.160		0.02028	0.09094	0.1616	
17	8	9	117	0.0769	0.02658	0.011	0.091	0.171		0.02028	0.09094	0.1616	
18	9	14	110	0.1273	0.02741	0.009	0.091	0.173		0.02028	0.09094	0.1616	
19	10	12	142	0.0845	0.02413	0.019	0.091	0.163		0.02028	0.09094	0.1616	
20	11	8	140	0.0571	0.02430	0.018	0.091	0.164		0.02028	0.09094	0.1616	
21	12	13	179	0.0726	0.02149	0.026	0.091	0.155		0.02028	0.09094	0.1616	
22	13	5	196	0.0255	0.02054	0.029	0.091	0.153		0.02028	0.09094	0.1616	
23	14	15	163	0.0920	0.02252	0.023	0.091	0.159		0.02028	0.09094	0.1616	
24	15	25	140	0.1786	0.02430	0.018	0.091	0.164		0.02028	0.09094	0.1616	
25	16	12	135	0.0889	0.02475	0.017	0.091	0.165		0.02028	0.09094	0.1616	
26	17	16	186	0.0860	0.02108	0.028	0.091	0.154		0.02028	0.09094	0.1616	
27	18	12	193	0.0622	0.02070	0.029	0.091	0.153		0.02028	0.09094	0.1616	
28	19	15	181	0.0829	0.02137	0.027	0.091	0.155		0.02028	0.09094	0.1616	
29	20	18	160	0.1125	0.02273	0.023	0.091	0.159		0.02028	0.09094	0.1616	

Because the sample sizes vary, the control limits are different for each sample. The *p*-chart is shown in Figure 14.32(a). Note that points 13 and 15 are outside the control limits.

An alternative approach is to use the average sample size, $\bar{n}$, to compute approximate control limits. Using the average sample size, the control limits are computed as

$$\text{UCL}_p = \bar{p} + 3 \sqrt{\frac{\bar{p}(1-\bar{p})}{\bar{n}}}$$

and

$$\text{LCL}_p = \bar{p} - 3 \sqrt{\frac{\bar{p}(1-\bar{p})}{\bar{n}}}$$

Figure 14.32(a) *p*-Chart for the Variable Sample Size Example (Actual Sample Sizes

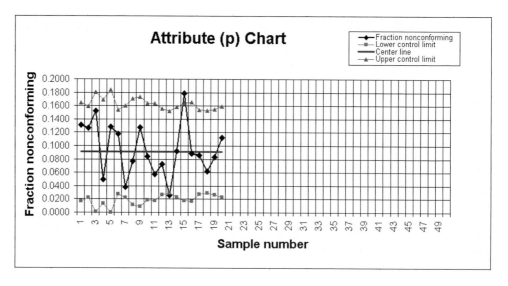

Figure 14.32(b) *p*-Chart for the Variable Sample Size Example (Average Sample Size

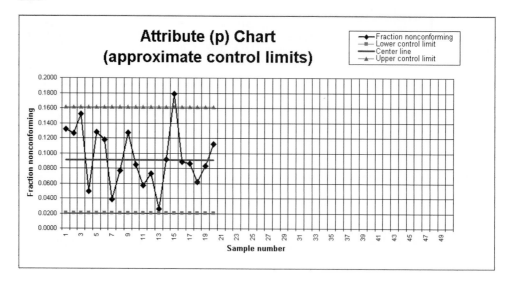

These result in an approximation to the true control limits. For the data in Figure 14.31, the average sample size is $\bar{n} = 2{,}980/20 = 149$. Using this value, the upper control limit is calculated to be 0.1616, and the lower control limit is .0202. However, this approach has several disadvantages. Because the control limits are only approximate, points that are actually out of control may not appear to be so on this chart. Second, runs or nonrandom patterns are difficult to interpret because the standard deviation differs between samples as a result of the variable sample sizes. Hence, this approach should be used with caution. Figure 14.32(b) shows the control chart for this example with approximate control limits using the average sample size. Note the difference in sample 13; this chart shows that it is in control, whereas the true control limits show that this point is out of control.

As a general guideline, use the average sample size method when the sample sizes fall within 25 percent of the average. For this example, 25 percent of 149 is 37.25. Thus, the average could be used for sample sizes between 112 and 186. This guideline would exclude samples 3, 6, 9, 11, 13, and 18, whose control limits should be computed exactly. If the calculations are performed on a computer, sample size is not an issue.

np-Charts for Number Nonconforming

In the *p*-chart, the fraction nonconforming of the *i*th sample is given by

$$p_i = y_i/n$$

where y_i is the number found nonconforming and n is the sample size. Multiplying both sides of the equation $p_i = y_i/n$ by n, yields

$$y_i = np_i$$

That is, the number nonconforming is equal to the sample size times the proportion nonconforming. Instead of using a chart for the fraction nonconforming, an equivalent alternative—a chart for the *number* of nonconforming items—is useful. Such a control chart is called an ***np*-chart**.

The *np*-chart is a control chart for the number of nonconforming items in a sample. To use the *np*-chart, the size of each sample *must be constant*. Suppose that two samples of sizes 10 and 15 each have four nonconforming items. Clearly, the fraction nonconforming in each sample is different, which would be reflected in a *p*-chart. An *np*-chart, however, would indicate no difference between samples. Thus, equal sample sizes are necessary to have a common base for measurement. Equal sample sizes are not required for *p*-charts, because the fraction nonconforming is invariant to the sample size.

The *np*-chart is a useful alternative to the *p*-chart because it is often easier to understand for production personnel—the *number* of nonconforming items is more meaningful than a fraction. Also, it requires only a count, making the computations simpler.

The control limits for the *np*-chart, like those for the *p*-chart, are based on the binomial probability distribution. The center line is the average number of nonconforming items per sample as denoted by $n\bar{p}$, which is calculated by taking k samples of size n, summing the number of nonconforming items y_i in each sample, and dividing by k. That is,

$$n\bar{p} = \frac{y_1 + y_2 + \ldots + y_k}{k}$$

An estimate of the standard deviation is

$$s_{n\bar{p}} = \sqrt{n\bar{p}(1-\bar{p})}$$

where $\bar{p} = (n\bar{p})/n$. Using 3σ limits as before, the control limits are specified by

$$UCL_{n\bar{p}} = n\bar{p} + 3\sqrt{n\bar{p}(1-\bar{p})}$$

$$LCL_{n\bar{p}} = n\bar{p} - 3\sqrt{n\bar{p}(1-\bar{p})}$$

The data for the post office example discussed earlier is given in Figure 14.33. The average number of errors found is:

$$n\bar{p} = \frac{3 + 1 + \ldots + 0 + 1}{25} = 2.2$$

To find the standard deviation, we first compute

$$\bar{p} = \frac{2.2}{100} = 0.022$$

Figure 14.33 Data and Calculations for the Post Office Example (NP-CHART.XLS)

	A	B	C	D	E
1	Number Nonconforming (np) Chart				
2	This spreadsheet is designed for up to 50 samples. Enter data ONLY in yellow-shaded cells.				
3	Each sample must have a constant sample size; enter this in cell C6.				
4	Click on the sheet tab to display the control chart (some rescaling may be needed).				
5					
6	Sample size		100		
7					
8	Average (np-bar)		2.2		
9	Standard deviation		1.466833324		
10					
11		Number			
12	Sample	Nonconforming	LCLnp	CL	UCLnp
13	1	3	0	2.2	6.6005
14	2	1	0	2.2	6.6005
15	3	0	0	2.2	6.6005
16	4	0	0	2.2	6.6005
17	5	2	0	2.2	6.6005
18	6	5	0	2.2	6.6005
19	7	3	0	2.2	6.6005
20	8	6	0	2.2	6.6005
21	9	1	0	2.2	6.6005
22	10	4	0	2.2	6.6005
23	11	0	0	2.2	6.6005
24	12	2	0	2.2	6.6005
25	13	1	0	2.2	6.6005
26	14	3	0	2.2	6.6005
27	15	4	0	2.2	6.6005
28	16	1	0	2.2	6.6005
29	17	1	0	2.2	6.6005
30	18	2	0	2.2	6.6005
31	19	5	0	2.2	6.6005
32	20	2	0	2.2	6.6005
33	21	3	0	2.2	6.6005
34	22	4	0	2.2	6.6005
35	23	1	0	2.2	6.6005
36	24	0	0	2.2	6.6005
37	25	1	0	2.2	6.6005

Then,

$$s_{n\bar{p}} = \sqrt{2.2(1 - .022)}$$

$$= \sqrt{2.2(0.978)}$$

$$= \sqrt{2.1516} = 1.4668$$

The control limits are then computed as

$$\text{UCL}_{n\bar{p}} = 2.2 + 3(1.4668) = 6.6$$

$$\text{LCL}_{n\bar{p}} = 2.2 - 3(1.4668) = -2.20$$

Because the lower control limit is less than zero, a value of 0 is used. The control chart for this example is given in Figure 14.34.

Charts for Defects

Recall that a *defect* is a single nonconforming characteristic of an item, while a *defective* refers to an item that has one or more defects. In some situations, quality assurance personnel may be interested not only in whether an item is defective but also in how many defects it has. For example, in complex assemblies such as electronics, the number of defects is just as important as whether the product is defective. Two charts can be applied in such situations. The *c*-**chart** is used to control the total number of defects per unit when subgroup size is constant. If subgroup sizes are variable, a *u*-**chart** is used to control the average number of defects per unit.

The *c*-chart is based on the Poisson probability distribution. To construct a *c*-chart, first estimate the average number of defects per unit, $\bar{c}$, by taking at least 25 samples of

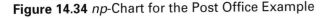

Figure 14.34 *np*-Chart for the Post Office Example

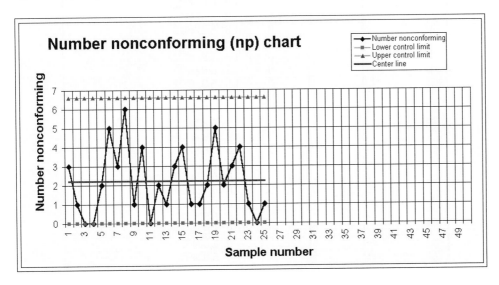

equal size, counting the number of defects per sample, and finding the average. The standard deviation of the Poisson distribution is the square root of the mean and yields

$$s_c = \sqrt{\bar{c}}$$

Thus, 3σ control limits are given by

$$UCL_c = \bar{c} + 3\sqrt{\bar{c}}$$

$$LCL_c = \bar{c} - 3\sqrt{\bar{c}}$$

Figure 14.35 shows the number of machine failures over a 25-day period. The total number of failures is 45; therefore, the average number of failures per day is

$$\bar{c} = 45/25 = 1.8$$

Figure 14.35 Data and Calculations for the Machine Failures Example (C-CHART.XLS)

	A	B	C	D	E	F	G	H
1	**Average Number of Defects (c) Chart**							
2	This spreadsheet is designed for up to 50 samples. Enter data ONLY in yellow-shaded cells.							
3	Click on the sheet tab to display the control chart (some rescaling may be needed).							
4								
5	Average (c-bar)		1.8					
6	Standard deviation		1.341640786					
7								
8		Number						
9	Sample	of Defects	LCLc	CL	UCLc			
10	1	2	0	1.8	5.824922			
11	2	3	0	1.8	5.824922			
12	3	0	0	1.8	5.824922			
13	4	1	0	1.8	5.824922			
14	5	3	0	1.8	5.824922			
15	6	5	0	1.8	5.824922			
16	7	3	0	1.8	5.824922			
17	8	1	0	1.8	5.824922			
18	9	2	0	1.8	5.824922			
19	10	2	0	1.8	5.824922			
20	11	0	0	1.8	5.824922			
21	12	1	0	1.8	5.824922			
22	13	0	0	1.8	5.824922			
23	14	2	0	1.8	5.824922			
24	15	4	0	1.8	5.824922			
25	16	1	0	1.8	5.824922			
26	17	2	0	1.8	5.824922			
27	18	0	0	1.8	5.824922			
28	19	3	0	1.8	5.824922			
29	20	2	0	1.8	5.824922			
30	21	1	0	1.8	5.824922			
31	22	4	0	1.8	5.824922			
32	23	0	0	1.8	5.824922			
33	24	0	0	1.8	5.824922			
34	25	3	0	1.8	5.824922			

Control limits for a c-chart are therefore given by

$$UCL_c = 1.8 + 3\sqrt{1.8} = 5.82$$

$$LCL_c = 1.8 - 3\sqrt{1.8} = -2.22, \text{ or zero}$$

The chart is shown in Figure 14.36 and appears to be in control. Such a chart can be used for continued control or for monitoring the effectiveness of a quality improvement program.

As long as the subgroup size is constant, a c-chart is appropriate. In many cases, however, the subgroup size is not constant or the nature of the production process does not yield discrete, measurable units. For example, suppose that in an auto assembly plant, several different models are produced that vary in surface area. The number of defects will not then be a valid comparison among different models. Other applications, such as the production of textiles, photographic film, or paper, have no convenient set of items to measure. In such cases, a standard unit of measurement is used, such as defects per square foot or defects per square inch. The control chart for these situations is the u-chart.

The variable u represents the average number of defects per unit of measurement, that is $u = c/n$, where n is the size of the subgroup (such as square feet). The center line $\bar{u}$ for k samples each of size n_i is computed as follows:

$$\bar{u} = \frac{c_1 + c_2 + \ldots + c_k}{n_1 + n_2 + \ldots + n_k}$$

The standard deviation of the ith sample is estimated by

$$s_u = \sqrt{\bar{u}/n_i}$$

Figure 14.36 c-Chart for the Machine Failures Example

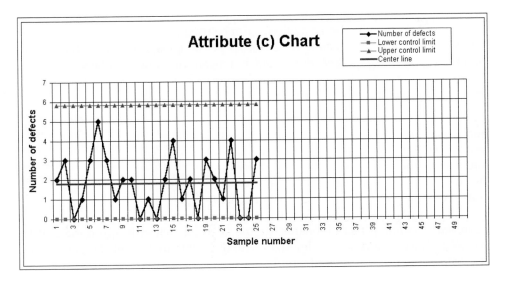

The control limits, based on three standard deviations for the ith sample, are then

$$UCL_u = \bar{u} + 3\sqrt{\bar{u}/n_i}$$

$$LCL_u = \bar{u} - 3\sqrt{\bar{u}/n_i}$$

Note that if the size of the subgroups varies, so will the control limits. This result is similar to the p-chart with variable sample sizes. In general, whenever the sample size n varies, the control limits will also vary.

Because the sample size varies each day in the following example, a u-chart is appropriate. A catalog distributor ships a variety of orders each day. The packing slips often contain errors such as wrong purchase order numbers, wrong quantities, or incorrect sizes. Figure 14.37 shows the error data collected during August.

To construct the u-chart, first compute the number of errors per slip as shown in column 3. The average number of errors per slip, $\bar{u}$, is found by dividing the total number of errors (217) by the total number of packing slips (2,843):

$$\bar{u} = 217/2,843 = .076$$

The standard deviation for a particular sample size n_i is therefore

$$s_u = \sqrt{.076/n_i}$$

The control limits are shown in the spreadsheet. As with a p-chart, individual control limits will vary with the sample size. The control chart is shown in Figure 14.38. One point (#2) appears to be out of control.

One application of c-charts and u-charts is in a quality rating system. When some defects are considered to be more serious than others, they can be rated, or categorized, into different classes. For instance,

A – very serious
B – serious
C – moderately serious
D – not serious

Each category can be weighted using a point scale, such as 100 for A, 50 for B, 10 for C, and 1 for D.[3] These points, or demerits, can be used as the basis for a c- or u-chart that would measure total demerits or demerits per unit, respectively. Such charts are often used for internal quality control and as a means of rating suppliers.

Choosing Between c- and u-Charts

The key issue in selecting between c- and u-charts to consider is *whether the sampling unit is constant*. For example, suppose that an electronics manufacturer produces circuit boards. The boards may contain various defects, such as faulty components and missing connections. Because the sampling unit—the circuit board—

Confusion often exists over which chart is appropriate for a specific application, because the c- and u-charts apply to situations in which the quality characteristics inspected do not necessarily come from discrete units.

is constant (assuming that all boards are the same), a c-chart is appropriate. If the process produces boards of varying sizes with different numbers of components and connections, then a u-chart would apply.

Figure 14.37 Data and Calculations for the Packing Slip Errors Example
(U-CHART.XLS)

	A	B	C	D	E	F	G	H	I
1	**Average Number of Defects Per Unit (u) Chart**								
2	This spreadsheet is designed for up to 75 samples. Enter data ONLY in yellow-shaded cells.								
3	Click on the sheet tab to display the control chart (some rescaling may be needed).								
4									
5	**Average (u-bar)**		0.076327823						
6									
7			**Sample**						
8		**Number**	**Unit**	**Defects**	**Standard**				
9	**Sample**	**of Defects**	**Size**	**per unit**	**Deviation**	**LCLu**	**CL**	**UCLu**	
10	1	8	92	0.0870	0.02880	0	0.076	0.163	
11	2	15	69	0.2174	0.03326	0	0.076	0.176	
12	3	6	86	0.0698	0.02979	0	0.076	0.166	
13	4	13	85	0.1529	0.02997	0	0.076	0.166	
14	5	5	123	0.0407	0.02491	0.002	0.076	0.151	
15	6	5	87	0.0575	0.02962	0	0.076	0.165	
16	7	3	74	0.0405	0.03212	0	0.076	0.173	
17	8	8	83	0.0964	0.03033	0	0.076	0.167	
18	9	4	103	0.0388	0.02722	0	0.076	0.158	
19	10	6	60	0.1000	0.03567	0	0.076	0.183	
20	11	7	136	0.0515	0.02369	0.005	0.076	0.147	
21	12	4	80	0.0500	0.03089	0	0.076	0.169	
22	13	2	70	0.0286	0.03302	0	0.076	0.175	
23	14	11	73	0.1507	0.03234	0	0.076	0.173	
24	15	13	89	0.1461	0.02929	0	0.076	0.164	
25	16	6	129	0.0465	0.02432	0.003	0.076	0.149	
26	17	6	78	0.0769	0.03128	0	0.076	0.170	
27	18	3	88	0.0341	0.02945	0	0.076	0.165	
28	19	8	76	0.1053	0.03169	0	0.076	0.171	
29	20	9	101	0.0891	0.02749	0	0.076	0.159	
30	21	8	92	0.0870	0.02880	0	0.076	0.163	
31	22	2	70	0.0286	0.03302	0	0.076	0.175	
32	23	9	54	0.1667	0.03760	0	0.076	0.189	
33	24	5	83	0.0602	0.03033	0	0.076	0.167	
34	25	13	165	0.0788	0.02151	0.012	0.076	0.141	
35	26	5	137	0.0365	0.02360	0.006	0.076	0.147	
36	27	8	79	0.1013	0.03108	0	0.076	0.170	
37	28	6	76	0.0789	0.03169	0	0.076	0.171	
38	29	7	147	0.0476	0.02279	0.008	0.076	0.145	
39	30	4	80	0.0500	0.03089	0	0.076	0.169	

As another example, consider a telemarketing firm that wants to track the number of calls needed to make one sale. In this case, the firm has no physical sampling unit. However, an analogy can be made with the circuit boards. The sale corresponds to the circuit board, and the number of calls to the number of defects. In both examples, the number of occurrences in relationship to a constant entity is being measured. Thus, a c-chart is appropriate.

Figure 14.38 *u*-Chart for the Packing Slip Errors Example

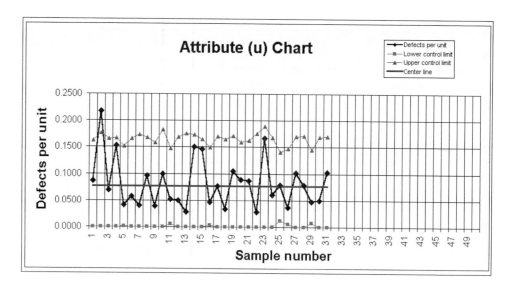

SUMMARY OF CONTROL CHART CONSTRUCTION

Table 14.3 summarizes the formulas used for constructing the different types of control charts discussed thus far. The Bonus Materials folder on the CD-ROM contains a discussion of some advanced types of control charts used in special situations. Figure 14.39 provides a summary of guidelines for chart selection.

A wide variety of commercial software is available to implement SPC. For example, one of the more recent packages is *CHARTrunner 2000*, product of PQ Systems (http://www.pqsystems.com). *CHARTrunner* generates SPC charts and per-

Table 14.3 Summary of Control Chart Formulas

Type of Chart	LCL	CL	UCL
$\bar{x}$ (with R)	$\bar{\bar{x}} - A_2\bar{R}$	$\bar{\bar{x}}$	$\bar{\bar{x}} + A_2\bar{R}$
R	$D_3\bar{R}$	$\bar{R}$	$D_4\bar{R}$
p	$\bar{p} - 3\sqrt{\bar{p}(1-\bar{p})/n}$	$\bar{p}$	$\bar{p} + 3\sqrt{\bar{p}(1-\bar{p})/n}$
$\bar{x}$ (with s)	$\bar{\bar{x}} - A_3\bar{s}$	$\bar{\bar{x}}$	$\bar{\bar{x}} + A_3\bar{s}$
s	$B_3\bar{s}$	$\bar{s}$	$B_4\bar{s}$
x	$\bar{x} - 3\bar{R}/d_2$	$\bar{x}$	$\bar{x} + 3\bar{R}/d_2$
np	$n\bar{p} - 3\sqrt{n\bar{p}(1-\bar{p})}$	$n\bar{p}$	$n\bar{p} + 3\sqrt{n\bar{p}(1-\bar{p})}$
c	$\bar{c} - 3\sqrt{\bar{c}}$	$\bar{c}$	$\bar{c} + 3\sqrt{\bar{c}}$
u	$\bar{u} - 3\sqrt{\bar{u}/n}$	$\bar{u}$	$\bar{u} + 3\sqrt{\bar{u}/n}$

Figure 14.39 Control Chart Selection

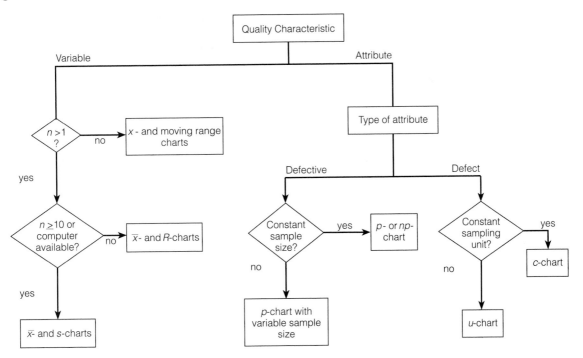

forms statistical analyses using data that are collected, stored, and managed by other applications such as Microsoft Access or Excel, SQL Server, Oracle, text files, and many others. It generates control charts, as well as histograms, process capability results, Pareto charts, scatter diagrams, and others; performs curve fitting and linear regression; and allows users to customize out-of-control tests, select colors for sigma zones, display multiple sets of control limits, and save charts as image files. Annual software surveys can be found in such professional publications as *Quality Progress* (http:// www.asq.org) and *Quality Digest* (http://www.qualitydigest.com).

DESIGNING CONTROL CHARTS

Designers of control charts must consider four issues: (1) the basis for sampling, (2) the sample size, (3) the frequency of sampling, and (4) the location of the control limits.

Basis for Sampling

The purpose of a control chart is to identify the variation in a system that may change over time. In one case, a hospital was monitoring the waiting time in its emergency room. In constructing a control chart, five patients were chosen randomly over the course of each shift. In this example, it is unlikely that process conditions would remain stable over an entire working shift. Thus, little useful information was provided in the chart. First, any change in the process average during a shift would not be reflected in the data, and second, a change in the process level would cause points on the R-chart to be out of control, even if no change in the variability of the process actually occurred.

A good sampling method should have the property that, if assignable causes are present, the chance of observing differences between samples is high, while the chance of observing differences within a sample is low. Samples that satisfy these criteria are called **rational subgroups**.

> *In determining the method of sampling, samples should be chosen to be as homogeneous as possible so that each sample reflects the system of common causes or assignable causes that may be present at that point in time.*

One approach to constructing rational subgroups is to use consecutive measurements over a short period of time. Consecutive measurements minimize the chance of variability within the sample while allowing variation between samples to be detected. This approach is useful when control charts are used to detect shifts in process level. One must also be careful not to overlap production shifts, different batches of material, and so on, when selecting the basis for sampling. Thus, the method of selecting samples should be chosen carefully so as not to bias the results.

Sample Size

Sample size is a second critical design issue. A small sample size is desirable to minimize the opportunity for within-sample variation due to special causes. This issue is important because each sample should be representative of the state of control at one point in time. In addition, the cost of sampling should be kept low. The time an employee spends taking the sample measurements and plotting a control chart represents nonproductive time (in a strict accounting sense only!). On the other hand, control limits are based on the assumption of a normal distribution of the sample means. If the process is not normal, this assumption is valid only for large samples. Large samples also allow smaller changes in process characteristics to be detected with higher probability.

> *In practice, samples of about five have been found to work well in detecting process shifts of two standard deviations or larger. To detect smaller shifts in the process mean, larger sample sizes of 15 to 25 must be used.*

Figure 14.40 shows the probability of detecting a shift in the mean in the next sample (that is, the probability of seeing the next point outside the 3σ control limit when the process has shifted some number of standard deviations) as a function of the sample size for an $\bar{x}$-chart. Thus, if a process has shifted 1.5 standard deviations, a sample size of 5 provides only a 64 percent chance of detection. For a 90 percent chance of detecting this particular process shift, a sample of at least 8 is needed.

For attributes data, too small a sample size can make a p-chart meaningless. Even though many guidelines such as "use at least 100 observations" have been suggested, the proper sample size should be determined statistically, particularly when the true portion of nonconformances is small. If p is small, n should be large enough to have a high probability of detecting at least one nonconformance. For example, if $p = .01$, then to have at least a 95 percent chance of finding at least one nonconformance, the sample size must be at least 300. Other approaches for determining attribute data sample sizes include choosing n large enough to provide a 50 percent chance of detecting a process shift of some specified amount, or choosing n so that the control chart will have a positive lower control limit. The reader is referred to the book by Montgomery in the bibliography for details on these calculations.

Figure 14.40 Probability of Detecting a Shift in Mean

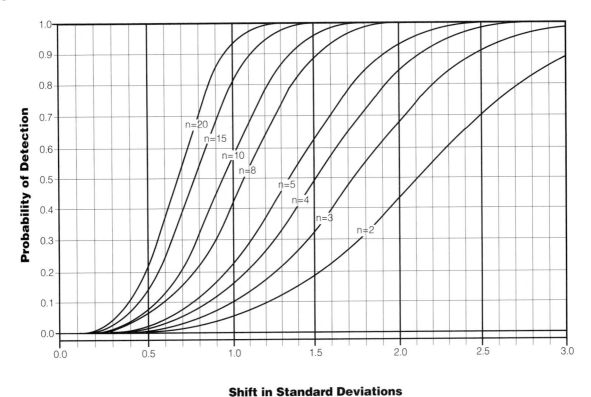

Source: Adapted from Lyle Dockendorf, "Choosing Appropriate Sample Subgroup Sizes for Control Charts," *Quality Progress* 25, no. 10 (October 1992), 160.

Sampling Frequency

The third design issue is the sampling frequency. Taking large samples on a frequent basis is desirable but clearly not economical. No hard-and-fast rules exist for the frequency of sampling. Samples should be close enough to provide an opportunity to detect changes in process characteristics as soon as possible and reduce the chances of producing a large amount of nonconforming output. However, they should not be so close that the cost of sampling outweighs the benefits that can be realized. This decision depends on the individual application and production volume.

Location of Control Limits

A Type I error occurs when an incorrect conclusion is reached that a *special cause is present when in fact one does not exist* and results in the cost of trying to find a nonexistent problem. A Type II error occurs when *special causes are present but are not signaled in the control chart* because points fall within the control limits by chance. Because nonconforming products have a greater chance to be produced, a cost will eventually be incurred as a result. The size of a Type I error depends only on the control limits that are used; the wider the limits, the less chance of a point falling outside the limits, and consequently the smaller is the chance of making a Type I error. A Type II error, however, depends on the width of the control limits, the degree to which the process is out of control, and the sample size. For a fixed sample size, wider control limits increase the risk of making a Type II error.

The location of control limits is closely related to the risk involved in making an incorrect assessment about the state of control.

The traditional approach of using 3σ limits implicitly assumes that the cost of a Type I error is large relative to that of a Type II error; that is, a Type I error is essentially minimized. This situation will not always be the case, however. Much research has been performed on economic design of control charts.[4] Cost models attempt to find the best combination of design parameters (center line, control limits, sample size, and sampling interval) that minimize expected cost or maximize expected profit.

Certain costs are associated with making both Type I and Type II errors. A Type I error results in unnecessary investigation for an assignable cause, including costs of lost production time and special testing. A Type II error can be more significant. If an out-of-control process is not recognized, defectives that are produced may result in higher costs of scrap and rework in later stages of production or after the finished good reaches the customer. Unfortunately, the cost of a Type II error is nearly impossible to estimate because it depends on the number of nonconforming items—a quantity that is unknown.

The costs associated with Type I and Type II errors conflict as control limits change. The tighter the control limits, the greater is the probability that a sample will indicate that the process is out of control. Hence, the cost of a Type I error increases as control limits are reduced. On the other hand, tighter control limits will reduce the cost of a Type II error, because out-of-control states will be more easily identified and the amount of defective output will be reduced.

The costs associated with sampling and testing may include lost productive time when the process owner takes sample measurements, performs calculations, and plots the points on the control chart. If the testing is destructive, the value of lost units would also be included. Thus, larger sample sizes and more frequent sampling result in higher costs.

The sample size and frequency also affect the costs of Type I and Type II errors. As the sample size or frequency is increased, both Type I and Type II errors are reduced, because better information is provided for decision making. Table 14.4 summarizes this discussion of the three-way interaction of costs. In the economic design of control charts we must consider these simultaneously. Most models for such decisions can become quite complex and are beyond the scope of this text.

As a practical matter, one often uses judgment about the nature of operations and the costs involved in making these decisions. Raymond Mayer suggests the following guidelines:

1. If the cost of investigating an operation to identify the cause of an apparent out-of-control condition is high, a Type I error becomes important, and wider control limits should be adopted. Conversely, if that cost is low, narrower limits should be selected.
2. If the cost of the defective output generated by an operation is substantial, a Type II error is serious, and narrower control limits should be used. Otherwise, wider limits should be selected.

Table 14.4 Economic Decisions for Control Chart Construction

Source of Cost	Sample Size	Sampling Frequency	Control Limits
Type I error	large	high	wide
Type II error	large	high	narrow
Sampling and testing	small	low	—

3. If the cost of a Type I error and the cost of a Type II error for a given activity are both significant, wide control limits should be chosen, and consideration should be given to reducing the risk of a Type II error by increasing the sample size. Also, more frequent samples should be taken to reduce the duration of any out-of-control condition that might occur.

4. If past experience with an operation indicates that an out-of-control condition arises quite frequently, narrower control limits should be favored because of the large number of opportunities for making a Type II error. In the event that the probability of an out-of-control condition is small, wider limits are preferred.[5]

SPC, ISO 9000:2000, AND SIX SIGMA

ISO 9000:2000 places increased emphasis on the use of statistical methods compared with the previous version.[6] For example, the standards require "applicable methods, including statistical techniques" be identified and used for monitoring and measuring products and processes, and that through monitoring and measurement, the organization can demonstrate the ability of processes to meet requirements and that product requirements have been met. A new ISO standard, 11462-1, provides guidance for organizations wishing to use SPC to meet these requirements. The standard addresses the folowing elements:

- *Definition of SPC goals.* Such goals might include reducing variation around target values and compensating for process variation to ensure product conformity, reducing costs, indicating how the process is likely to behave in the future, and quantifying process capability.
- *Conditions for a successful SPC system.* These conditions include integration with a formal quality management system, management support, use of information for data-driven decisions and management reviews, and ensuring the competence of those who will be using the tools.
- *Elements of the SPC system.* These address the processes an organization should implement and actions it should take to ensure that a successful SPC system includes both operational and support activities. These elements can be organized into a Plan-Do-Study-Act framework, and include a process documentation and control plan, definition of process targets and limits, data collection, measuring equipment, data recording and analysis, process control, short- and long-term process capability assessment, communication of results, and process improvement implementation and project management activities.

This standard can provide useful assistance for organizations that are beginning to develop a formal SPC approach.

Controlling Six Sigma Processes[7]

SPC is a useful methodology for processes that operate at a low sigma level, for example 3-sigma or less. However, when the rate of defects is extremely low, standard control charts are not effective. For example, in using a p-chart for a process with a high sigma level, few defectives will be discovered even with large sample sizes. For instance, if $p = 0.001$, a sample size of 500 will only have an expected number of $500(.001) = 0.5$ defects. Hence, most samples will have only zero or one defect, and the chart will provide little useful information for control. Using much larger sample sizes would only delay the timeliness of information and increase the chances that the process may have changed during the sampling interval. Small sample sizes will typically result in a conclusion that any observed defect indicates an out-of-control condition, thus, implying that a controlled process will have zero defects, which may be impractical. In addition, conventional SPC charts will have higher frequencies of false alarms and make it difficult to evaluate process improvements. These issues are important for Six Sigma Green Belts and Black Belts to understand.

One way of handling this situation is to use variable data rather than attribute data; however, this approach may be prohibitive from a cost or physical standpoint. An alternative for attribute data is to construct a **cumulative count of conforming (CCC) chart** to monitor the total number of conforming items until a defective item is found. The control limits for this type of chart are

$$LCL = \ln(1 - \alpha/2)/\ln(1 - p)$$

$$CL = \ln(0.5)/\ln(1 - p)$$

$$UCL = \ln(\alpha/2)/\ln(1 - p)$$

where α is the risk of a false alarm, for example, 0.0027, the value traditionally used for standard control charts. This level can be adjusted for different processes, depending on their criticality and costs of adjustments. A value that exceeds UCL indicates the process has likely improved; a value lower than LCL indicates deterioration of the process. Other advanced techniques are also available.

PRE-CONTROL[8]

Pre-control is a technique useful in operations such as machining, where quality characteristics are easily monitored and can be adjusted. It is valuable for monitoring process capability over time. A major advantage of pre-control is its direct relationship to specifications, which requires no recording, calculating, or plotting of data.

The idea behind pre-control is to divide the tolerance range into zones by setting two *pre-control lines* halfway between the center of the specification and the tolerance limits (see Figure 14.41). The center zone, called the *green zone*, comprises one-half of the total tolerance. Between the pre-control lines and the tolerance limits are the *yellow zones*. Outside the tolerance limits are the *red zones*.

Pre-control is applied as follows. As a manufacturing run is initiated, five consecutive parts must fall within the green zone. If not, the production setup must be reevaluated before the full production run can be started. Once regular operations commence, two parts are sampled; if the first falls within the green zone, production continues, which eliminates the need to measure the second part. If the first part falls in a yellow zone, the second part is inspected. If the second part falls in the green zone, production can continue; if not, production should stop and a special

Figure 14.41 Pre-Control Ranges

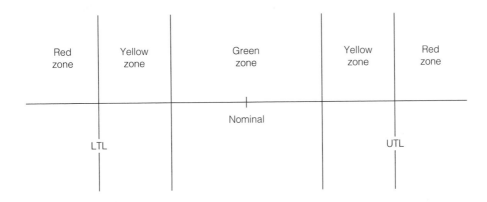

cause should be investigated. If any part falls in a red zone, then action should be taken.

The rationale behind pre-control can be explained using basic statistical arguments. Suppose that the process capability is equal to the tolerance spread (see Figure 14.42). The area of each yellow zone is approximately 0.07, while that of the red zone is less than 0.01. The probability of two consecutive parts falling in a yellow zone is $(0.07)(0.07) = 0.0049$ if the process mean has not shifted. If $C_p > 1$, this probability is even less. Such an outcome would more than likely indicate a special cause. If both parts fall in the same yellow zone, you would conclude that the mean has shifted; if in different yellow zones, you would conclude that the variation has increased.

The frequency of sampling is often determined by dividing the time period between two successive out-of-control signals by six. Thus, if the process deteriorates, sampling frequency is increased; if it improves, the frequency is decreased. For example, the force necessary to break a wire used in electrical circuitry has a specification of 3 gm–7 gm. Thus, the pre-control zones are

Range	Zone
<3	Red
3–4	Yellow
4–6	Green
6–7	Yellow
>7	Red

Figure 14.42 Basis for Pre-Control Rules

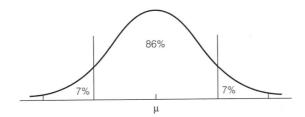

The following samples were collected:

Sample	First Measurement	Second Measurement
1	4.7	
2	4.5	
3	4.4	
4	4.2	
5	4.2	
6	4.0	
7	4.0	
8	3.7	3.6
9	6.5	3.5

For samples 1 through 7, the first measurement falls in the green zone; thus no further action need be taken. For sample 8, however, the first measurement falls in a yellow zone. The second measurement also falls in a yellow zone. The process should be stopped for investigation of a shift in the mean.

At the next time of inspection, both pieces also fall in a yellow zone. In this case, the probable cause is a shift in variation. Again, the process should be stopped for investigation.

If managers or operators are interested in detecting process shifts even though the product output falls within specifications, pre-control should not be used because it will not detect such shifts.

> *Pre-control is not an adequate substitute for control charts and should only be used when process capability is no greater than 88 percent of the tolerance, or equivalently, when C_p is at least 1.14. If the process mean tends to drift, then C_p should be higher.*

Quality in Practice

Applying SPC to Pharmaceutical Product Manufacturing[9]

A Midwest pharmaceutical company manufactures (in two stages) individual syringes with a self-contained, single dose of an injectable drug. In the first stage, sterile liquid drug is filled into glass syringes and sealed with a rubber stopper. The remaining stage involves insertion of the cartridge into plastic syringes and the electrical "tacking" of the containment cap at a precisely determined length of the syringe. A cap that is "tacked" at a shorter than desired length (less than 4.920 inches) leads to pressure on the cartridge stopper and, hence, partial or complete activation of the syringe. Such syringes must then be scrapped. If the cap is "tacked" at a longer than desired length (4.980 inches or longer), the tacking is incomplete or inadequate, which can lead to cap loss and potentially a cartridge loss in shipment and handling. Such syringes can be reworked manually to

attach the cap at a lower position. However, this process requires a 100 percent inspection of the tacked syringes and results in increased cost for the items. This final production step seemed to be producing more and more scrap and reworked syringes over successive weeks. At this point, statistical consultants became involved in an attempt to solve this problem and recommended SPC for the purpose of improving the tacking operation. The length was targeted as a critical variable to be monitored by $\bar{x}$- and R-charts, which eventually led to identifying the root cause of the problem. The actual case history contains instances in which desired procedures were not always followed. As such, this case illustrates well the properties, problems, pitfalls, and peculiarities in applying such charts, as well as the necessity of having well-trained quality specialists involved.

Operators of the final stage of this syringe assembly process were trained in the basics of process capability studies and control charting techniques. In an attempt to judge the capability of the process, the responsible technician was called in to adjust the tacking machine and to position and secure it at what seemed to be its best possible position. Then, 35 consecutive samples were taken (see Table 14.5), and a capability study was undertaken.

The process had a sample mean of $\bar{x} = 4.954$ inches, which was close to the nominal aim (or target) of 4.950 inches with a sample standard deviation of $s = 0.0083$ inches. Upper and lower specifications of 4.980 and 4.920 inches, respectively, gave an estimated $C_{pk} = 1.03$. Thus, it was determined that the process was minimally capable and could indeed produce the length desired.

To establish the control charts, the operators collected 15 samples each of size 5 taken every 15 minutes. The $\bar{x}$- and R-charts are shown in Figure 14.43. These charts show that the process is already out of statistical control in both charts. Proper application of SPC procedures would have indicated that special causes should be identified and new control limits constructed. Unfortunately, the operators from this shift did not plot these points but only used the control limits they obtained to evaluate future measurements. The operators from this first shift continued to collect samples of size 5 every 15 minutes, but due to their unfamiliarity with charting, they never plotted these 15 new points either. At 4:00 P.M. of the same day, a new shift arrived and operators did plot this second set of 15 points using the control limits obtained from the first set of 15 points as

---

Table 14.5 Initial 35 Consecutive Samples Taken for the Capability Study

4.95888	4.95533	4.94294	4.95422	4.96679	4.94487	4.95775	4.95710
4.96543	4.95603	4.95210	4.95311	4.95385	4.96014	4.95252	4.96633
4.96255	4.95287	4.93541	4.94840	4.96114	4.93901	4.95966	4.93667
4.95941	4.94539	4.96238	4.94337	4.95550	4.95482	4.96230	4.96175
4.96016	4.94626	4.95904					

Figure 14.43 Initial $\bar{x}$- and R-Charts of the First 15 Samples

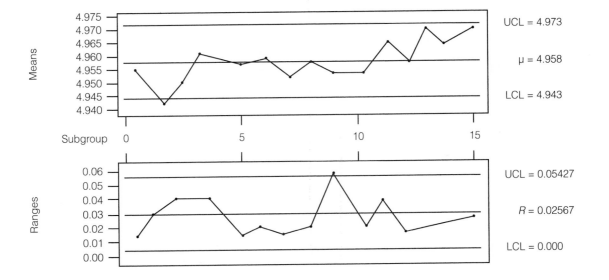

shown in Figure 14.44. These charts show clearly that the centering was out of statistical control, with the average length far greater than desired. This conclusion was substantiated by operators noticing that the caps were not being tacked properly. The maintenance technician was immediately called in to adjust the machine properly.

After the first adjustment by the technician, the plot of the next sample taken 15 minutes later was already beyond the upper control limit for the $\bar{x}$-chart. Thus, the syringes were still too long, although the technician affirmed that he had set the height lower just 15 minutes earlier. The technician was recalled to readjust the machine. The second try was no better, and so the technician was called a third time to adjust the machine. This third try was successful in the sense that the length seemed to be reduced enough to have both the $\bar{x}$ and R values inside their control limits.

This second shift operators continued sampling and collected 15 additional samples of size 5, at 15-minute intervals. They plotted these results (see Figure 14.45), but because no values were beyond the control limits, they took no action. It was at this point that the statistical consultants reviewed what had transpired. They not only determined that the *original* 15 points used to

define the $\bar{x}$- and R-charts were themselves showing a process not under statistical control, but that the last 15 points also showed a process not under statistical control. The second shift workers had failed to notice the string of 15 points of the $\bar{x}$-chart all above the center line and failed to conclude that the center was "not where you wanted it." If they had, they would have once again called the technician to adjust the machine to lower the length of the syringes.

Fortunately, however, the consultants examined the R-chart as well as the $\bar{x}$-chart. Again, the last 14 points of R were all on one side of the center line, indicating a lack of statistical control. Careful examination of both charts revealed that the points of R were below the center and were indicating that the overall variation had been reduced by what the maintenance technician had done. Yet, in reading the $\bar{x}$-chart (after examining the R-chart), the length of the syringes seemed to have increased. The consultants contacted both the operators and the technician in order to try to find out what had happened to cause this confusing "good and bad" thing to occur. The maintenance technician's story was most revealing.

The maintenance technician said that for his first two (unsuccessful) attempts when he was told

Figure 14.44 $\bar{x}$- and R-Charts, the Next 17 Samples

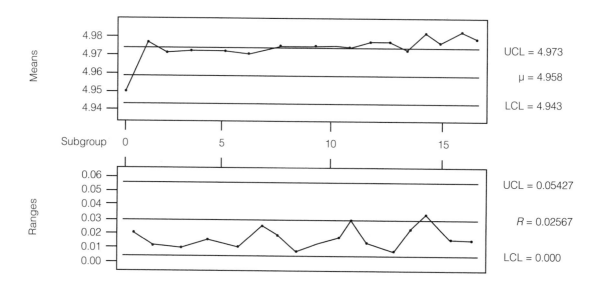

Figure 14.45 $\bar{x}$- and R-Charts for the Last 15 Samples

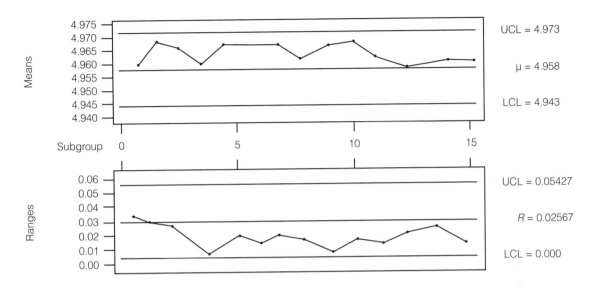

to adjust the process center (length of syringe) down, he moved the height adjustment stop down on its threaded shaft. However, he found it was difficult to tighten the locknut for this adjustment stop. The third time (the successful one), being frustrated that the thread of the shaft was too battered at the lower end of the stud, he actually moved the adjustment stop *up* even though he was asked to make the syringe lengths shorter. He thought this would result in still longer syringes being produced, but at least the locknut would hold. When he was told by the shift that the process was now producing the proper length syringes and that the operators were satisfied, he was mystified. He left wondering how a machine adjusted upward (toward longer lengths) could wind up producing shorter-length syringes!

The consultants realized the dramatic improvement (shortening) of the process variation told the important story. When the maintenance technician set the length of the adjustment cap where he was supposed to (lower), the threads were so worn as to make it impossible to hold the locknut in place. Thus, the vibration from the running machine (within about 15 minutes) loosened the locknut and adjustment cap quickly, resulting in drifts off center, producing syringes of erratic lengths. However, when the maintenance techni-

cian set the adjustment cap higher (which would make syringes longer), the threads there were good enough for the locknut to hold the cap in place. The lengths, indeed, were a little longer than what was targeted, but the variation had been so dramatically reduced that the overall effect was one of making acceptable syringes; that is, the syringes were a tiny bit longer than desired but very consistent in their length so no plotted points were beyond the upper control limit for the $\bar{x}$-chart.

The operators were satisfied with this situation because now the plotted points of the syringe lengths came under the upper control limit of the $\bar{x}$-chart, which convinced them that they were making syringes to the proper length. The consultants recommended to the managers that the threaded stud on which the adjustment stop moved be replaced. The repair work needed a special part that was fairly expensive and necessitated some downtime for the manufacturing process; nevertheless, on the strength of the control chart data and the explanation of the maintenance technician's and consultant's stories, the recommendation was implemented. Upon replacement of the threaded stud, waste and rework from the final step dropped to virtually zero over the period of many weeks.

Key Issues for Discussion

1. Using the data for the initial process capability study sample given in Table 14.5, compute the process capability indexes and construct a histogram for these data.

2. Explain why it was incorrect that the operators did not plot the initial data, find special causes, and compute new control limits. What might have happened had they done it this way?

3. What lessons can be learned from this case?

QUALITY PROFILES

USING A *U*-CHART IN A RECEIVING PROCESS[10]

CBT, Co. is a distributor of electrical automation and power transmission products. The company began to implement a total quality management process in early 1990. One manager was eager to collect data about the organization's receiving process because of a decrease in the organization's on-time deliveries. The manager suspected that the data entry person in the purchasing department was not entering data in the computer in a timely fashion; consequently, packages could not be properly processed for subsequent shipping to the customer. A preliminary analysis indicated that the manager's notion was inaccurate. In fact, the manager was able to see that the data entry person was doing an excellent job. The analysis showed that handling packages that were destined for a branch operation in the same fashion as other packages created significant delays. A simple process change of placing a branch designation letter in front of the purchase order number told the receiving clerk to place those packages on a separate skid for delivery to the branch.

However, this analysis revealed a variety of other problems. Generally, anywhere from 65 to 110 packing slips were processed each day. These were found to contain many errors in addition to the wrong destination designation that contributed to the delays. Errors included

- Wrong purchase order
- Wrong quantity
- Purchase order not on the system
- Original order not on the system
- Parts do not match
- Purchase order was entered incorrectly
- Double shipment
- Wrong parts
- No purchase order

Many packing slips contained multiple errors. Table 14.6 shows the number of packing slips and total errors during early 1992. A *u*-chart was constructed for each day to track the number of packing slip errors—defects—found. A *u*-chart was used because the sample size varied each day. Thus, the statistic monitored was the number of errors per packing slip. Figure 14.46 shows the *u*-chart that was constructed for this period. (This change in the branch designation took place on January 24, resulting in significant improvement, as shown on the chart.)

Although the chart shows that the process is in control (since the branch designation change), the average error rate of more than 9 percent still was not considered acceptable. After consolidating the types of errors into five categories, a Pareto analysis was performed. This analysis showed the following:

Category	Percentage
Purchase order error	35
Quantity error	22
No purchase order on system	17
Original order not on system	16
Parts error	10

The analysis is illustrated in Figure 14.47.

The first two categories accounted for more than half of the errors. The remedy for these problems was to develop a training module on proper purchasing methods to ensure that vendors knew the correct information needed on the purchase orders. The third category—no purchase order on the computer system—caused receiving personnel to stage the orders until an investigation could find the necessary information. Because of this

Table 14.6 CBT, Co. Packing Slip Error Counts

Date	Packing Slips	Errors	Date	Packing Slips	Errors
21 Jan	87	15	4 Mar	92	8
22 Jan	79	13	5 Mar	69	13
23 Jan	92	23	6 Mar	86	6
24 Jan	84	3	9 Mar	85	13
27 Jan	73	7	10 Mar	101	5
28 Jan	67	11	11 Mar	87	5
29 Jan	73	8	12 Mar	71	3
30 Jan	91	8	13 Mar	83	8
31 Jan	94	11	16 Mar	103	4
3 Feb	83	12	17 Mar	82	6
4 Feb	89	12	18 Mar	90	7
5 Feb	88	6	19 Mar	80	4
6 Feb	69	11	20 Mar	70	4
7 Feb	74	8	23 Mar	73	11
10 Feb	67	4	24 Mar	89	13
11 Feb	83	10	25 Mar	91	6
12 Feb	79	8	26 Mar	78	6
13 Feb	75	8	27 Mar	88	6
14 Feb	69	3	30 Mar	76	8
17 Feb	87	8	31 Mar	101	9
18 Feb	99	13	1 Apr	92	8
19 Feb	101	13	2 Apr	70	2
20 Feb	76	7	3 Apr	72	11
21 Feb	90	4	6 Apr	83	5
24 Feb	92	7	7 Apr	69	6
25 Feb	80	4	8 Apr	79	3
26 Feb	81	5	9 Apr	79	8
27 Feb	105	8	10 Apr	76	6
28 Feb	80	8	13 Apr	92	7
2 Mar	82	5	14 Apr	80	4
3 Mar	75	3	15 Apr	78	8

problem the company realized it needed to revamp the original order-writing process. Specifically, both the order-writing and purchase order activities needed to be improved.

An analysis of the control chart in Figure 14.46 shows that the average error rate has gradually improved. To a large extent, this improvement was due to the recognition of the problems and enhanced communication among the constituents. While the full training program had not been implemented at the time this case was written, the company believed that a significant reduction in

the error rate would result once the training was completed.

Key Issues for Discussion

1. Verify the computation of the center line and control limits in Figure 14.46.
2. What information might a separate chart for each error category provide? Would you recommend spending the time and effort to make these additional computations?

Figure 14.46 *u*-Chart for CBT, Co. Packing Slip Errors

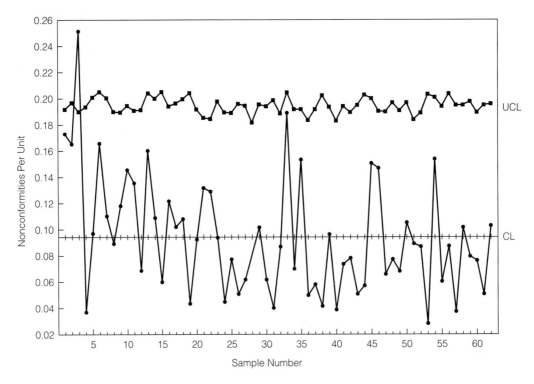

Figure 14.47 Pareto Analysis of Packing Slip Errors

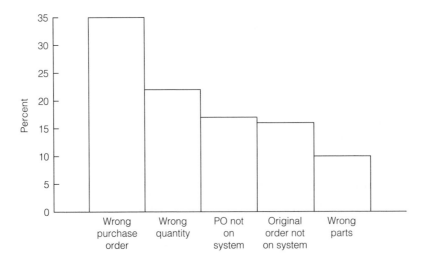

REVIEW QUESTIONS

1. Define *statistical process control* and discuss its advantages.
2. What does the term *in statistical control* mean? Explain the difference between capability and control.
3. What are the disadvantages of simply using histograms to study process capability?
4. Discuss the three primary applications of control charts.
5. Describe the difference between variables and attributes data. What types of control charts are used for each?
6. Briefly describe the methodology of constructing and using control charts.
7. What does one look for in interpreting control charts? Explain the possible causes of different out-of-control indicators.
8. How should control charts be used by shop-floor personnel?
9. What are modified control limits? Under what conditions should they be used?
10. How are variables control charts used to determine process capability?
11. Describe the difference between *control limits* and *specification limits*.
12. Why is the *s*-chart sometimes used in place of the *R*-chart?
13. Describe some situations in which a chart for individual measurements would be used.
14. Explain the concept of a moving range. Why is a moving range chart difficult to interpret?
15. Explain the difference between *defects* and *defectives*.
16. Briefly describe the process of constructing a *p*-chart. What are the key differences compared with an $\bar{x}$-chart?
17. Does an *np*-chart provide any different information than a *p*-chart? Why would an *np*-chart be used?
18. Explain the difference between a *c*-chart and a *u*-chart.
19. Discuss how to use charts for defects in a quality rating system.
20. Describe the rules for determining the appropriate control chart to use in any given situation.
21. What types of charts would be appropriate for the applications listed in Table 14.1?
22. Discuss the concept of rational subgroups.
23. What trade-offs are involved in selecting the sample size for a control chart?
24. Explain the economic trade-offs to consider when determining the sampling frequency to use in a control chart.
25. Discuss the implications of control limit location in terms of Type I and Type II errors.
26. Describe approaches for applying SPC to short production runs.
27. Explain the situations for which EWMA and CuSum charts might be preferred to more traditional control charts (see Bonus Materials).

Note: Data sets for many problems in this chapter are available in the Excel workbook *Chapter14Data.xls* on the CD-ROM that accompanies this text. Click on the appropriate worksheet tab as noted in the problem (e.g., *Prob. 14-1*) to access the data. The Excel templates for control charts used in this chapter are also available in a separate folder on the CD-ROM.

1. Mount Hope Hospital is working on improving waiting time in order to give customers better service in their waiting rooms. Forty samples of size 5 were taken at random times from their main waiting room. These data can be found in the worksheet *Prob. 14-1*.
   a. Compute the mean and range of each sample and plot them on control charts.
   b. Does the process appear to be in statistical control? Why or why not?
2. Thirty samples of size 3 were taken from a Wilmer Machine Shop machining process over a 15-hour period. These data can be found in the worksheet *Prob. 14-2*.
   a. Compute the mean and standard deviation of the data.
   b. Compute the mean and range of each sample and plot them on control charts. Does the process appear to be in statistical control? Why or why not?
3. The data in worksheet *Prob. 14-3* list electrical resistance measure values for 50 samples of size 5 that were taken from Babbage Chips, Inc.'s computer chip-making process over a 25-hour period.
   a. Compute the mean and standard deviation of the data.
   b. Calculate the control limits and construct the $\bar{x}$ and R charts, using the first 30 samples. Is the process under control at that point?
   c. After calculating the control limits, the last 20 samples were collected. When plotted using the control limits calculated earlier, does the process appear to be in statistical control? Why or why not? What should be done if it is not under control?
4. Thirty samples of size 6 yielded $\bar{x} = 400$ and $R = 30$. Compute control limits for $\bar{x}$- and R charts and estimate the standard deviation of the process.
5. Twenty-five samples of size 5 resulted in $\bar{x} = 8.0$ and $\bar{R} = 2.0$. Compute control limits for $\bar{x}$- and $\bar{R}$-charts and estimate the standard deviation of the process.
6. Using the data listed in the worksheet *Prob. 14-6*, construct $\bar{x}$- and R charts. The sample size used is $n = 4$.
7. In testing the voltage of a component used in a microcomputer for the Hertz Company, the data listed in the worksheet *Prob. 14-7* were obtained. Construct $\bar{x}$- and R charts for these data. Determine whether the process is in control. If not, eliminate any assignable causes and compute revised limits.
8. Use the sample data from the Inky-U Printing Company, listed in the worksheet *Prob. 14-8* for a sample size of $n = 4$.
   a. Construct $\bar{x}$- and R charts.
   b. After the process was determined to be under control, process monitoring began, using the control limits established in part (a). The results of 20 more samples are shown in the worksheet. Does a problem with the process appear? If so, when should the process have been stopped, and steps taken to correct it?

9. Beta Sales Corp. is trying to improve the sales forecasting ability of its five sales regions. The data in the worksheet for *Prob. 14-9* represent the difference between actual sales and forecasted sales in millions of dollars. Construct $\bar{x}$- and R charts for the data in the worksheet *Prob.14-9*. What conclusions do you reach, if positive variances are considered good and negative variances are looked on as opportunities for improvement?

10. General Hydraulics, Inc., is a manufacturer of hydraulic machine tools. It has had a history of leakage trouble resulting from a certain critical fitting. Twenty-five samples of machined parts were selected, one per shift, and the diameter of the fitting was measured.
    a. Construct $\bar{x}$- and R charts for the data listed in the worksheet *Prob.14-10*.
    b. If the regular machine operator was absent when samples 4, 8, 14, and 22 were taken, how will the results in part (a) be affected?
    c. A second table in the worksheet represents measurements taken during the next 10 shifts. What information does this table provide to the quality control manager?

11. Fujiyama Electronics, Inc. has been having difficulties with circuit boards purchased from an outside supplier. Unacceptable variability occurs between two drilled holes that are supposed to be 5 cm apart on the circuit boards. Thirty samples of 4 boards each were taken from shipments sent by the supplier as shown in the data listed in the worksheet *Prob. 14-11*.
    a. Construct $\bar{x}$- and R charts for these data.
    b. If the supplier's plant quality manager admitted that they were experiencing quality problems for shipments 18, 19, and 21, how would that affect your control chart? Show this adjustment on revised $\bar{x}$- and R charts for these data.
    c. Ten more observations were taken, as shown in the second table in the worksheet. Using the revised $\bar{x}$- and R charts from part (b), comment on what the chart shows after extending it with the new data.

12. Discuss the interpretation of each of the following control charts:

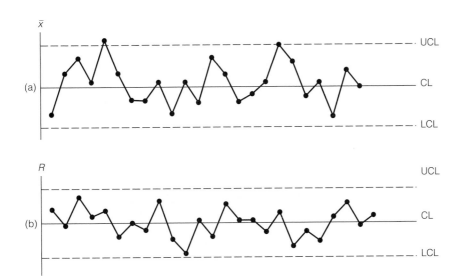

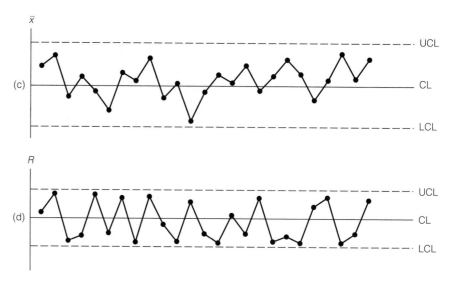

13. For each of the following control charts, assume that the process has been operating in statistical control for some time. What conclusions should the operators reach at this point?

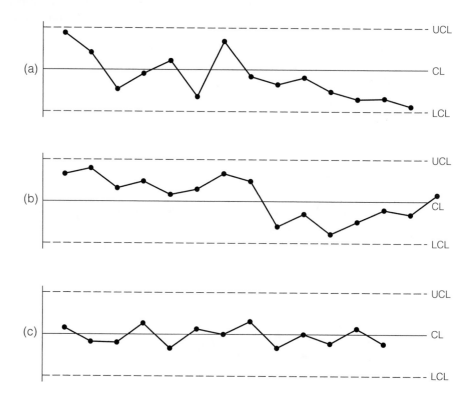

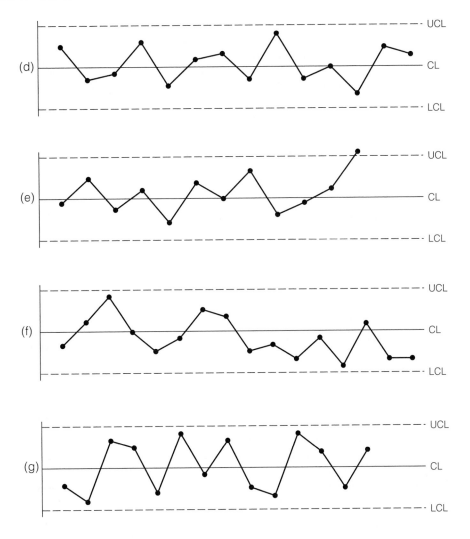

14. Consider the data for the time required to begin loading the homepage in an Internet browser for Slowbay's Web site. Fifteen samples of size 5 are shown in the worksheet *Prob.14-14*. Specifications are 0.076 ± 0.009.
   a. Compute control limits for an x-chart (chart for individuals) using the statistic $\bar{R} / d_2$ as an estimate of the standard deviation and using the actual standard deviation for the data. Why might they be different?
   b. Construct the $\bar{x}$- and R charts and an x-chart for individuals using the data. Interpret the results.
   c. Estimate the process capability by using the estimated sample standard deviation, available on the $\bar{x}$- and R chart spreadsheet templates on the student CD-ROM.
15. Ricardo's Widgets makes a critical part for a popular brand of cell phones. Consider the data for 15 samples of size 4 of a key dimension for the part, shown in the worksheet *Prob.14-15*. Specifications are 0.110 ± 0.015.

754

Part 3   Six Sigma and the Technical System

a. Compute control limits for an x-chart using the statistic $\bar{R}/d_2$ as an estimate of the standard deviation and using the actual standard deviation for the data. Why are they different?
b. Construct the $\bar{x}$- and R charts and a chart for "individuals" using the data. Interpret the results.
c. Estimate the process capability by using the actual sample standard deviation.

16. Squawk Boxes, Inc., a speaker manufacturer, has a process that is normally distributed and has the following sample means and ranges for eight samples of size 5. Determine process capability limits. If specifications are determined to be 50 ± 25, what percentage would be out of specifications?

Sample	1	2	3	4	5	6	7	8
$\bar{x}$	51.6	45.1	49.3	55.9	46.5	58.1	54.3	53.6
R	13.1	24.5	19.4	12.4	15.3	19.9	9.8	26.9

17. PCDrives has a manufacturing process that is normally distributed and has the following sample means and ranges for eight samples of size 5. Determine process capability limits. If specifications are determined to be 70 ± 25, what percentage will be out of specification?

Sample	1	2	3	4	5	6	7	8
$\bar{x}$	77.4	60.2	63.5	72.7	54.4	80.4	70.8	74.6
R	18.3	20.1	22.6	27.5	15.3	17.9	26.8	30.6

18. Suppose that in Problem 7, after it was revised, the upper specification limit became USL = 475, and the lower specification limit became LSL = 325. Compute the process capability and the modified control limits.

19. Suppose that in Problem 11, after it was revised, the upper specification limit became USL = 6.75, and the lower specification limit became LSL = 3.25. Compute the process capability and the modified control limits.

20. The Bell Vader Company, which produces heavy-duty electrical motors, machines a part called an end cap. To meet competitive pressures, the company began to apply statistical quality control to its processes. Because each motor produced by the company uses two end caps that could cost as much as $200 each, the company sees the importance of bringing the process under control. The table in the worksheet *Prob. 14-20* shows data collected to construct a control chart.
a. Compute control limits and construct and analyze the $\bar{x}$- and R charts for this process. What conclusions can you reach about the state of statistical control?
b. Using the control chart, estimate the process capability. The specification limits for the end cap are 3.9375 to 3.9380. Note that the data are coded, so 75 = 3.9375, 77 = 3.9377, and so on. Determine what percentage of end caps would be expected to fall outside specifications. What conclusions and recommendations can you make?

21. An injection molding machine at the Moby Molding Co. used to make plastic bottles has four molding heads. The outside diameter of the bottle is an important measure of process performance. The table in the worksheet *Prob.14-21*

shows the results of 30 samples in which the data are coded by subtracting the actual value from the nominal dimension. Construct $\bar{x}$- and R charts and discuss the results.

22. Suppose that the 40 sample means and standard deviations are observed on a measure of feed quality at the Bluegrass Horse Farm for samples of size 5, as shown in the worksheet *Prob.14-22*. Construct $\bar{x}$- and s-charts for these data.

23. The sample means and standard deviations gathered in a calibration project by Precision Measuring Co. are observed for samples of size 10, as shown in the worksheet *Prob.14-23*. Construct $\bar{x}$- and s-charts for these data.

24. Construct $\bar{x}$- and s-charts for the data given in Table 14.2 in the chapter.

25. Construct $\bar{x}$- and s-charts for the data for the Wilmer Machine Co. given in Problem 2.

26. Construct $\bar{x}$- and s-charts for the data from the Babbage Chips in Problem 3.

27. Construct $\bar{x}$- and s-charts for the data from the Hertz Company in Problem 7.

28. R. A. Smith Packaging Machinery Company is trying to adjust a new machine designed to fill one-pound containers. They took 25 readings of the ounces filled, as shown in the worksheet *Prob.14-28*. Construct charts for individuals using both two-period and three-period moving ranges for the observations (in sequential order).

29. Assume that the data in Problem 14, the SlowBay Web site, represent individual measurements instead of samples. Construct charts for individuals and ranges using a five-sample moving range.

30. Twenty-five samples of 50 orders each at the Dixie Ice Co. were inspected, and 56 items were found to be defective. Compute control limits for a p-chart.

31. Thirty samples of 75 items each were inspected at the Yummy Candy Company and 75 were found to be defective. Compute control limits for a p-chart for this process.

32. The fraction defective of automotive pistons made by the Hasty Piston Co. is given in the worksheet *Prob.14-32* for 20 samples. Two hundred units are inspected each day. Construct a p-chart and interpret the results.

33. The fraction defective for a folding process in a Quality Printing plant is given in the worksheet *Prob. 14-33* for 25 samples. Fifty units are inspected each shift.
    a. Construct a p-chart and interpret the results.
    b. After the process was determined to be under control, process monitoring began, using the established control limits. The results of 25 more samples are shown in the second part of the worksheet. Is there a problem with the process? If so, when should the process have been stopped, and steps taken to correct it?

34. Samples of size 125 have been randomly selected during each shift of 25 shifts in a production process at Lean Manufacturing, Inc. The data are given in the worksheet *Prob.14-34*. Construct a p-chart and determine whether the process is in control. If not, eliminate any data points that appear to be due to assignable causes and construct a new chart.

35. One hundred insurance claim forms are inspected daily at Full Life Insurance Co. over 25 working days, and the number of forms with errors have been recorded in the worksheet *Prob. 14-35*. Construct a p-chart. If any points occur outside the control limits, assume that assignable causes have been determined. Then construct a revised chart.

36. Edgewater Hospital surveys all outgoing patients by means of a patient satisfaction questionnaire. The number of patients surveyed each month varies.

Control charts that monitor the proportion of unsatisfied patients for key questions are constructed and studied. Construct a *p*-chart for the data in the worksheet *Prob.14-36*, which represent responses to a question on satisfaction with hospital meals.

37. AtYourService.com, an Internet service provider (ISP), is concerned that the level of access of customers is decreasing, due to heavier use. The proportion of peak period time when a customer is likely to receive busy signals is considered a good measure of service level. The percentage of times a customer receives a busy signal during peak periods varies. Using a sampling process, the ISP set up control charts to monitor the service level, based on proportion of busy signals received. Construct the *p*-chart using on the sample data in the table in the worksheet *Prob.14-37*. What does the chart show? Is the service level good or bad, in your opinion?

38. Construct an *np*-chart for the data in Problem 34. What does the chart show?

39. Construct an *np*-chart for the data in Problem 35. What does the chart show?

40. Construct a *c*-chart for a situation involving 30 samples and having a total of 340 defects and interpret the results.

41. Construct a *c*-chart for a situation involving 40 samples and having a total of 1,000 defects and interpret the results.

42. Smoothsoft, Inc., a software developer, measured the number of defects per 1,000 lines of code in software modules being developed by the company. Construct a *c*-chart for data in the table in the worksheet *Prob. 14- 42* and interpret the results.

43. Consider the sample data for defects per pizza in a new store being opened by Rob's Pizza Palaces in the worksheet *Prob.14-43*. Construct a *c*-chart for these data. What does the chart show?

44. Tom Pyzdek, a noted quality consultant, presented data on falls at the Great Falls Hospital (fictitious name), for patients[11] as shown in the table in the worksheet *Prob. 14-44*. Note that the "sample size" is in 100s of Patient Care Days (PCDs). Develop a run chart, a frequency histogram, and a *u*-chart for these data. What insights do you get from each chart? What would you advise the administration of the hospital to do about falls?

45. Find 3σ control limits for a *c*-chart with an average number of defects equal to 18.

46. Find 3σ control limits for a *u*-chart with $u = 16$ and $n = 4$. What do the limits show?

47. Determine, using Figure 14.40, the appropriate sample size for detecting:
    a. A 1-sigma shift in the mean with a 0.80 probability.
    b. A 2-sigma shift with 0.95 probability
    c. A 2.5-sigma shift with 0.90 probability

For problems 48 through 51, see the Advanced Control Charts Section on the Bonus Materials folder on the CD-ROM.

48. Develop a stabilized control chart for the silicon wafer example (Figure 14.6). What does the chart show?

49. Develop a stabilized control chart for the post office example (Figure 14.29). What does the chart show?

50. Using a value of $\alpha = 0.4$, construct an EWMA chart for the data shown in the worksheet *Prob. 14-50* as applied to the means of the samples. What does the chart show?

51. Repeat problem 50 for a value of a = 0.8. What does the chart show, now?

For problems 52 through 54, see the Statistical Foundations of Control Charts Section in the Bonus Materials folder on the CD-ROM.

52 If control limits for a project are based on 2.5 standard deviations, what percentage of observations will be expected to fall beyond the limits?

53. What are the probability limits corresponding to a Type I error of $\alpha = 0.10$?

54. What is the probability of observing 11 consecutive points on one side of the center line if the process is in control? 10 of 11 points? 9 of 11 points? How many points out of 11 on one side of the center would indicate lack of control?

CASES

I. LA VENTANA WINDOW COMPANY

The La Ventana Window Company (LVWC) manufactures original equipment and replacement windows for residential building and remodeling applications. LVWC landed a major contract as a supplier to Southwestern Vista Homes (SVH), a builder of residential communities in several major cities throughout the southwestern United States. Because of the large volume of demand, LVWC expanded its manufacturing operations to two shifts. Soon, they were working six days per week and hired additional workers and added on to their facility.

Not long after La Ventana began shipping windows to Southwestern, it received some complaints about narrow, misfitting gaps between the upper and lower window sashes. This information alarmed Jim Dean, CEO of La Ventana. He had sold his door business in a cold midwestern city when he decided that he wanted to retire to the desert Southwest. He had played all the golf that he could during the first six months, but then realized that he needed more of a challenge than the game could provide. That was when he started La Ventana, using his experience in manufacturing products for the residential construction market, which was expanding with the amount of construction going on in the Southwest.

LVWC, under Jim's leadership, soon built a reputation as a high-quality manufacturer, which was the principal reason that it was selected as a supplier to SVH. The company based its manufacturing capability on its well-trained and dedicated employees, so it never felt the need to consider formal process control approaches. In view of the recent complaints, Jim suspected that the rapid expansion to a full two-shift operation, the pressures to produce higher volumes, and the push to meet just-in-time delivery requests were causing a breakdown in their quality.

On the recommendation of the plant manager, Jim hired a quality consultant to train the shift supervisors and selected line workers in statistical process control methods. As a trial project, the plant manager wants to evaluate the capability of a critical cutting operation that he suspects might be the source of the gap problem. The nominal specification for this cutting operation is 25.500 inches with a tolerance of 0.030 inch. Thus, the upper and lower specifications are LSL = 25.470 inch and USL = 25.530 inch. The consultant suggested inspecting five consecutive window panels, per operator, in the middle of each shift over a 15-day period and recording the dimension of the cut. The table in the worksheet *LVWC Case* in the workbook *C14Data.xls* (on CD-ROM), shows 15 days' data collected for each shift, by operator.

Discussion Questions

1. Interpret the data in the *LVWC Case* worksheet in the Excel workbook *C14Data.xls*, establish a state of statistical control, and evaluate the capability of the process to meet specifications. Consider the following questions: What do the initial control charts tell you? Do any out-of-control conditions exist? If the process is not in control, what might be

the likely causes, based on the information that is available? What is the process capability? What do the process capability indexes tell the company? Is LVWC facing a serious problem that it needs to address? How might the company eliminate the problems found by SVH?

2. The plant manager implemented the recommendations that resulted from the initial study. Because of the success in using control charts, LVWC made a decision to continue using them on the cutting operation. After establishing control, additional samples were taken over the next 20 shifts, shown in second part of the table in the *LVWC Case* worksheet. Evaluate whether the process remains in control, and suggest any actions that should be taken. Consider the following issues: Does any evidence suggest that the process has changed relative to the established control limits? If any out-of-control patterns are suspected, what might be the cause? What should the company investigate?

II. MURPHY TRUCKING, INC.

Murphy Trucking, Inc. (MTI), supplies contract transportation services to many different manufacturing firms. One of its principal customers, Crawford Consumer Products (CCP), is actively improving quality by using the Malcolm Baldrige National Quality Award criteria. In an effort to improve supplier quality, Crawford Consumer Products mandated, last year, that all suppliers provide factual evidence of quality improvement efforts that lead to highly capable processes.

As part of its supplier development program, CCP held a seminar for all its suppliers to outline this initiative and provide initial assistance. The executive officers of MTI participated in this seminar and recognized that MTI was seriously lacking in its quality improvement efforts. More importantly, Jeff Blaine, who was the purchasing manager at CCP, told them privately that many errors had been found in MTI's shipping documents. CCP would not continue to tolerate this high number of errors; and if no improvements were made, it would seek transportation services elsewhere. Rick Murphy, president and CEO of MTI, was concerned.

During an off-site meeting, Murphy and other MTI executives developed a comprehensive blueprint to help MTI develop a total quality focus. One of the key objectives was to establish an SPC effort to gain control of key customer-focused processes and establish priorities for improvement.

The Billing Study After Process Improvement
In a good-faith attempt to respond to CCP's feedback, MTI turned its attention to its billing input errors and worked on them over the following six months. To gain some understanding of the situation, MTI conducted an initial (base case) study by sampling 20 bills of lading, each day, over a 20-day period. Initial results were dismal, with defective bills averaging a horrible 60 percent!

After process improvement and an intensive effort to train shipping clerks not to make errors, the company was ready to make another study to determine what progress had been made. The first set of tables in the *MTI-Base* worksheet in the Excel workbook *C14Data.xls* shows the results of the initial study. The worksheet *MTI-Rev* shows the results of the second study, after improvements were made. Both studies revealed that field employees were correcting the errors as they found them. In both cases, rework was costing the company almost $2 per error, but the number of errors had been substantially reduced between the two studies. However, field employees still were not always catching the errors, which led to field service and other problems.

Discussion Questions

1. At this point, MTI is unsure of how to interpret these results. You have been hired as a consultant by the executive committee to analyze these data and provide additional recommendations for integrating SPC concepts into MTI's quality system. Using the results from the base case data, determine the performance, that is, the process capability, in a qualitative and quantitative sense, of the billing input. What is the average rate of defective bills? Is the process in control? What error rates might the company expect

in the future? What general conclusions do you reach?

2. Perform the same statistical analysis with the second set of data. How do the results differ? What is the average rate of defective bills? Is the process in control? What error rates might the company expect in the future? What general conclusions do you reach?

The Billing Study, Part II The revelations from the initial study had been startling. The results from the second study were encouraging, but not yet where the company wanted to be. Rick Murphy personally led a group problem-solving session to address the root causes of the current error rate. During this session, the group members constructed a cause-and-effect diagram to help determine the causes of incorrect bills of lading.

Eight categories of causes were identified:

1. Incomplete shipper name or address
2. Incomplete consignee name or address
3. Missing container type
4. Incomplete description of freight
5. Weight not shown on bill of lading
6. Improper destination code
7. Incomplete driver's signature information
8. Inaccurate piece count

Using Deming's plan-do-study-act process, the group at Murphy designed a plan to examine all bills of lading over a 25-day period and count the number of errors in each of these categories. They repeated the study six months later to determine

what progress, if any, had been made in error reduction. The second table in the *MTI Base* worksheet and the second table in the worksheet *MTI-Rev* shows the data for these studies. Rick Murphy thought that the *p*-chart developed in the first study and reapplied to the second study provided significant information about the process; however, he was curious to find out whether another method could tell them more about the nature of the defects they were encountering.

Discussion Questions (cont.)

3. After developing *p*-charts for the first and second studies, you decide to analyze the data to determine whether the system is in control by constructing another appropriate control chart (other than a *p*-chart) that could better tell you about the nature of the defects. You also decide that it would be wise to construct a Pareto diagram to gain additional insight into the problem, and suggest recommendations to reduce billing errors.

4. Complete your analysis by using the three charts from each of the two studies to advise Rick and his managers at Murphy on the next steps. How do the results differ from the first to the second study? Is the process in control? What error categories have improved? Which ones might the company need to work on immediately in order to bring about further improvements? What general conclusions do you reach?

III. Day Industries[12]

Day Industries is a medium-sized paint manufacturer. The process of making paint consists of four major steps: weigh-up, premix, milling, and letdown. In the weigh-up stage, the ingredients are added to a tank one at a time according to the formula. Next, the batch is mixed on a dispersion mixer; this premix stage takes about 30–60 minutes. Then the batch is pumped into an agitated vessel that contains a milling medium (small steel or titanium dioxide balls of consistent size), which reduces it to a specified particle size. Finally, the paint is removed from the mill and allowed to cool, then tested. Solvent is lost during the milling stage because of elevated temperatures; in the let-

down stage, solvent is added to lower the viscosity to proper levels.

Viscosity, percent weight solids, and weight per gallon are all important quality characteristics because they determine the dry thickness, how well it applies to a surface, and corrosion properties. For a particular type of paint used by automotive companies to prevent corrosion, specifications are

Viscosity: 60–80
Weight solids: 60–65 percent
Weight per gallon: 12.6–13.5

The Excel file *Day Industries.xls* contains data for a series of batches that were produced. Using appropriate SPC charts or other statistical tools, evaluate how well the process is in control and its capa-

bility to meet requirements. Express your results in a report to the plant manager.

ENDNOTES

1. Robert W. Hoyer and Wayne C. Ellis, "A Graphical Exploration of SPC, Part 1," *Quality Progress* 29, no. 5 (May 1996), 65–73.

2. This discussion is adapted from James R. Evans, *Statistical Process Control for Quality Improvement: A Training Guide to Learning SPC* (Englewood Cliffs, NJ: Prentice Hall, 1991). Reprinted with permission of Prentice Hall, Upper Saddle River, NJ.

3. H. F. Dodge and M. N. Torrey, "A Check Inspection and Demerit Weighting Plan," *Industrial Quality Control* 13, no. 1 (July 1956), 5–12.

4. D. C. Montgomery, "The Economic Design of Control Charts: A Review and Literature Survey," *Journal of Quality Technology* 12, no. 2 (1980), 75–87.

5. Raymond R. Mayer, "Selecting Control Limits," *Quality Progress* 16, no 9, (1983), 24–26.

6. John E. West, "Do You Know Your SPC?" *Quality Digest*, July 2001, 51–56.

7. T.N. Goh and M. Xie, "Statistical Control of a Six Sigma Process," *Quality Engineering* 15, no. 4 (2003), 587–592.

8. Robert W. Traver, "Pre-Control: A Good Alternative to x- R-Charts," *Quality Progress* 18, no. 9 (September 1985).

9. Adapted from LeRoy A. Franklin and Samar N. Mukherjee, "An SPC Case Study on Stabilizing Syringe Lengths," *Quality Engineering* 12, no. 1 (1999–2000), 65–71. Reprinted from *Quality Engineering*, courtesy of Marcel Dekker, Inc.

10. We are grateful to Rick Casey for supplying this application.

11. Thomas Pyzdek, "Preventing Hospital Falls," *Quality Digest*, May 1999, 26–27.

12. Our thanks go to a former student, Jeffrey Day, for providing this case application.

BIBLIOGRAPHY

American National Standard, Definitions, Symbols, Formulas, and Tables for Control Charts. ANSI/ASQC A1-1987. American Society for Quality Control, 310 W. Wisconsin Ave., Milwaukee, WI 53203.

Brown, Bradford S. "Control Charts: The Promise and the Performance." Presentation at the ASQC/ASA 35th Annual Fall Technical Conference, Lexington, Kentucky, 1991.

Grant, Eugene, L., and Richard S. Leavenworth. *Statistical Quality Control*, 7th ed. New York: McGraw-Hill, 1996.

Ledolter, J., and A. Swersey. "An Evaluation of Pre-Control." *Journal of Quality Technology* 29, no. 2 (April 1997), 163–171.

Montgomery, D. C. *Introduction to Statistical Quality Control*, 4th ed. New York: John Wiley & Sons, 2000.

Nelson, Lloyd S. "Control Charts for Individual Measurements." *Journal of Quality Technology* 14, no. 3 (July 1982), 172–173.

Pyzdek, Thomas. *Pyzdek's Guide to SPC, Volume Two—Applications and Special Topics.* Milwaukee, WI: ASQ Quality Press, 1992.

Rosander, A. C. *Applications of Quality Control in the Service Industries.* New York: Marcel Dekker and ASQ Quality Press, 1985.

Squires, Frank H. "What Do Quality Control Charts Control?" *Quality,* November 1982, 63.

Vance, Lonnie C. "A Bibliography of Statistical Quality Control Chart Techniques, 1970–1980," *Journal of Quality Technology* 15, no. 12 (April 1983).

Wadsworth, Harrison M., Kenneth S. Stephens, and A. Blanton Godfrey. *Modern Methods for Quality Control and Improvement*, 2nd ed. New York: John Wiley & Sons, 2002.

APPENDIXES

APPENDIX A

AREAS FOR THE STANDARD
NORMAL DISTRIBUTION

Entries in the table give the area under the curve between the mean and z standard deviations above the mean. For example, for $z = 1.25$ the area under the curve between the mean and z is 0.3944.

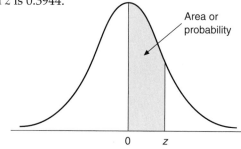

z	0.00	0.01	0.02	0.03	0.04	0.05	0.06	0.07	0.08	0.09
0.0	0.0000	0.0040	0.0080	0.0120	0.0160	0.0199	0.0239	0.0279	0.0319	0.0359
0.1	0.0398	0.0438	0.0478	0.0517	0.0557	0.0596	0.0636	0.0675	0.0714	0.0753
0.2	0.0793	0.0832	0.0871	0.0910	0.0948	0.0987	0.1026	0.1064	0.1103	0.1141
0.3	0.1179	0.1217	0.1255	0.1293	0.1331	0.1368	0.1406	0.1443	0.1480	0.1517
0.4	0.1554	0.1591	0.1628	0.1664	0.1700	0.1736	0.1772	0.1808	0.1844	0.1879
0.5	0.1915	0.1950	0.1985	0.2019	0.2054	0.2088	0.2123	0.2157	0.2190	0.2224
0.6	0.2257	0.2291	0.2324	0.2357	0.2389	0.2422	0.2454	0.2486	0.2518	0.2549
0.7	0.2580	0.2612	0.2642	0.2673	0.2704	0.2734	0.2764	0.2794	0.2823	0.2852
0.8	0.2881	0.2910	0.2939	0.2967	0.2995	0.3023	0.3051	0.3078	0.3106	0.3133
0.9	0.3159	0.3186	0.3212	0.3238	0.3264	0.3289	0.3315	0.3340	0.3365	0.3389
1.0	0.3413	0.3438	0.3461	0.3485	0.3508	0.3531	0.3554	0.3577	0.3599	0.3621
1.1	0.3643	0.3665	0.3686	0.3708	0.3729	0.3749	0.3770	0.3790	0.3810	0.3830
1.2	0.3849	0.3869	0.3888	0.3907	0.3925	0.3944	0.3962	0.3980	0.3997	0.4015
1.3	0.4032	0.4049	0.4066	0.4082	0.4099	0.4115	0.4131	0.4147	0.4162	0.4177
1.4	0.4192	0.4207	0.4222	0.4236	0.4251	0.4265	0.4279	0.4292	0.4306	0.4319
1.5	0.4332	0.4345	0.4357	0.4370	0.4382	0.4394	0.4406	0.4418	0.4429	0.4441
1.6	0.4452	0.4463	0.4474	0.4484	0.4495	0.4505	0.4515	0.4525	0.4535	0.4545
1.7	0.4554	0.4564	0.4573	0.4582	0.4591	0.4599	0.4608	0.4616	0.4625	0.4633
1.8	0.4641	0.4649	0.4656	0.4664	0.4671	0.4678	0.4686	0.4693	0.4699	0.4706
1.9	0.4713	0.4719	0.4726	0.4732	0.4738	0.4744	0.4750	0.4756	0.4761	0.4767
2.0	0.4772	0.4778	0.4783	0.4788	0.4793	0.4798	0.4803	0.4808	0.4812	0.4817
2.1	0.4821	0.4826	0.4830	0.4834	0.4838	0.4842	0.4846	0.4850	0.4854	0.4857
2.2	0.4861	0.4864	0.4868	0.4871	0.4875	0.4878	0.4881	0.4884	0.4887	0.4890
2.3	0.4893	0.4896	0.4898	0.4901	0.4904	0.4906	0.4909	0.4911	0.4913	0.4916
2.4	0.4918	0.4920	0.4922	0.4925	0.4927	0.4929	0.4931	0.4932	0.4934	0.4936
2.5	0.4938	0.4940	0.4941	0.4943	0.4945	0.4946	0.4948	0.4949	0.4951	0.4952
2.6	0.4953	0.4955	0.4956	0.4957	0.4959	0.4960	0.4961	0.4962	0.4963	0.4964
2.7	0.4965	0.4966	0.4967	0.4968	0.4969	0.4970	0.4971	0.4972	0.4973	0.4974
2.8	0.4974	0.4975	0.4976	0.4977	0.4977	0.4978	0.4979	0.4979	0.4980	0.4981
2.9	0.4981	0.4982	0.4982	0.4983	0.4984	0.4984	0.4985	0.4985	0.4986	0.4986
3.0	0.4986	0.4987	0.4987	0.4988	0.4988	0.4989	0.4989	0.4989	0.4990	0.4990

APPENDIX B

FACTORS FOR CONTROL CHARTS

	x-charts				s-Charts				R-charts					
n	A	A_2	A_3	c_4	B_3	B_4	B_5	B_6	d_2	d_3	D_1	D_2	D_3	D_4
2	2.121	1.880	2.659	0.7979	0	3.267	0	2.606	1.128	0.853	0	3.686	0	3.267
3	1.732	1.023	1.954	0.8862	0	2.568	0	2.276	1.693	0.888	0	4.358	0	2.574
4	1.500	0.729	1.628	0.9213	0	2.266	0	2.088	2.059	0.880	0	4.698	0	2.282
5	1.342	0.577	1.427	0.9400	0	2.089	0	1.964	2.326	0.864	0	4.918	0	2.114
6	1.225	0.483	1.287	0.9515	0.030	1.970	0.029	1.874	2.534	0.848	0	5.078	0	2.004
7	1.134	0.419	1.182	0.9594	0.118	1.882	0.113	1.806	2.704	0.833	0.204	5.204	0.076	1.924
8	1.061	0.373	1.099	0.9650	0.185	1.815	0.179	1.751	2.847	0.820	0.388	5.306	0.136	1.864
9	1.000	0.337	1.032	0.969	0.239	1.761	0.232	1.707	2.970	0.808	0.547	5.393	0.184	1.816
10	0.949	0.308	0.975	0.9727	0.284	1.716	0.276	1.669	3.078	0.797	0.687	5.469	0.223	1.777
11	0.905	0.285	0.927	0.9754	0.321	1.679	0.313	1.637	3.173	0.787	0.811	5.535	0.256	1.744
12	0.866	0.266	0.886	0.9776	0.354	1.646	0.346	1.610	3.258	0.778	0.922	5.594	0.283	1.717
13	0.832	0.249	0.850	0.9794	0.382	1.618	0.374	1.585	3.336	0.770	1.025	5.647	0.307	1.693
14	0.802	0.235	0.817	0.9810	0.406	1.594	0.399	1.563	3.407	0.763	1.118	5.696	0.328	1.672
15	0.775	0.223	0.789	0.9823	0.428	1.572	0.421	1.544	3.472	0.756	1.203	5.741	0.347	1.653
16	0.750	0.212	0.763	0.9835	0.448	1.552	0.440	1.526	3.532	0.750	1.282	5.782	0.363	1.637
17	0.728	0.203	0.739	0.9845	0.466	1.534	0.458	1.511	3.588	0.744	1.356	5.820	0.378	1.622
18	0.707	0.194	0.718	0.9854	0.482	1.518	0.475	1.496	3.640	0.739	1.424	5.856	0.391	1.608
19	0.688	0.187	0.698	0.9862	0.497	1.503	0.490	1.483	3.689	0.734	1.487	5.891	0.403	1.597
20	0.671	0.180	0.680	0.9869	0.510	1.490	0.504	1.470	3.735	0.729	1.549	5.921	0.415	1.585
21	0.655	0.173	0.663	0.9876	0.523	1.477	0.516	1.459	3.778	0.724	1.605	5.951	0.425	1.575
22	0.640	0.167	0.647	0.9882	0.534	1.466	0.528	1.448	3.819	0.720	1.659	5.979	0.434	1.566
23	0.626	0.162	0.633	0.9887	0.545	1.455	0.539	1.438	3.858	0.716	1.710	6.006	0.443	1.557
24	0.612	0.157	0.619	0.9892	0.555	1.445	0.549	1.429	3.895	0.712	1.759	6.031	0.451	1.548
25	0.600	0.153	0.606	0.9896	0.565	1.435	0.559	1.420	3.931	0.708	1.806	6.056	0.459	1.541

Source: Adapted from Table 27 of ASTM STP 15D ASTM *Manual on Presentation of Data and Control Chart Analysis.* © 1976 American Society for Testing and Materials, Philadelphia, PA.

APPENDIX C

 RANDOM DIGITS

63271	59986	71744	51102	15141	80714	58683	93108	13554	79945
88547	09896	95436	79115	08303	01041	20030	63754	08459	28364
55957	57243	83865	09911	19761	66535	40102	26646	60147	15702
46276	87453	44790	67122	45573	84358	21625	16999	13385	22782
55363	07449	34835	15290	76616	67191	12777	21861	68689	03263
69393	92785	49902	58447	42048	30378	87618	26933	40640	16281
13186	29431	88190	04588	38733	81290	89541	70290	40113	08243
17726	28652	56836	78351	47327	18518	92222	55201	27340	10493
36520	64465	05550	30157	82242	29520	69753	72602	23756	54935
81628	36100	39254	56835	37636	02421	98063	89641	64953	99337
84649	48968	75215	75498	49539	74240	03466	49292	36401	45525
63291	11618	12613	75055	43915	26488	41116	64531	56827	30825
70502	53225	03655	05915	37140	57051	48393	91322	25653	06543
06426	24771	59935	49801	11082	66762	94477	02494	88215	27191
20711	55609	29430	70165	45406	78484	31639	52009	18873	96927
41990	70538	77191	25860	55204	73417	83920	69468	74972	38712
72452	36618	76298	26678	89334	33938	95567	29380	75906	91807
37042	40318	57099	10528	09925	89773	41335	96244	29002	46453
53766	52875	15987	46962	67342	77592	57651	95508	80033	69828
90585	58955	53122	16025	84299	53310	67380	84249	25348	04332
32001	96293	37203	64516	51530	37069	40261	61374	05815	06714
62606	64324	46354	72157	67248	20135	49804	09226	64419	29457
10078	28073	85389	50324	14500	15562	64165	06125	71353	77669
91561	46145	24177	15294	10061	98124	75732	00815	83452	97355
13091	98112	53959	79607	52244	63303	10413	63839	74762	50289
73864	83014	72457	22682	03033	61714	88173	90835	00634	85169
66668	25467	48894	51043	02365	91726	09365	63167	95264	45643
84745	41042	29493	01836	09044	51926	43630	63470	76508	14194
48068	26805	94595	47907	13357	38412	33318	26098	82782	42851
54310	96175	97594	88616	42035	38093	36745	56702	40644	83514
14877	33095	10924	58013	61439	21882	42059	24177	58739	60170
78295	23179	02771	43464	59061	71411	05697	67194	30495	21157
67524	02865	39593	54278	04237	92441	26602	63835	38032	94770
58268	57219	68124	73455	83236	08710	04284	55005	84171	42596
97158	28672	50685	01181	24262	19427	52106	34308	73685	74246
04230	16831	69085	30802	65559	09205	71829	06489	85650	38707
94879	56606	30401	02602	57658	70091	54986	41394	60437	03195
71446	15232	66715	26385	91518	70566	02888	79941	39684	54315
32886	05644	79316	09819	00813	88407	17461	73925	53037	91904
62048	33711	25290	21526	02223	75947	66466	06232	10913	75336

Source: Reprinted from page 44 of *A Million Digits With 100,000 Normal Deviates,* by the Rand Corporation. New York: The Free Press, 1955. © 1955 by The Rand Corporation. Used by permission.

APPENDIX D

 ## BINOMIAL PROBABILITIES

Entries in the table give the probability of x successes in n trials of a binomial experiment, where p is the probability of a success on one trial. For example, with six trials and $p = 0.40$, the probability of two successes is 0.3110.

						p					
n	x	0.05	0.10	0.15	0.20	0.25	0.30	0.35	0.40	0.45	0.50
1	0	0.9500	0.9000	0.8500	0.8000	0.7500	0.7000	0.6500	0.6000	0.5500	0.5000
	1	0.0500	0.1000	0.1500	0.2000	0.2500	0.3000	0.3500	0.4000	0.4500	0.5000
2	0	0.9025	0.8100	0.7225	0.6400	0.5625	0.4900	0.4225	0.3600	0.3025	0.2500
	1	0.0950	0.1800	0.2550	0.3200	0.3750	0.4200	0.4550	0.4800	0.4950	0.5000
	2	0.0025	0.0100	0.0225	0.0400	0.0625	0.0900	0.1225	0.1600	0.2025	0.2500
3	0	0.8574	0.7290	0.6141	0.5120	0.4219	0.3430	0.2746	0.2160	0.1664	0.1250
	1	0.1354	0.2430	0.3251	0.3840	0.4219	0.4410	0.4436	0.4320	0.4084	0.3750
	2	0.0071	0.0270	0.0574	0.0960	0.1406	0.1890	0.2389	0.2880	0.3341	0.3750
	3	0.0001	0.0010	0.0034	0.0080	0.0156	0.0270	0.0429	0.0640	0.0911	0.1250
4	0	0.8145	0.6561	0.5220	0.4096	0.3164	0.2401	0.1785	0.1296	0.0915	0.0625
	1	0.1715	0.2916	0.3685	0.4096	0.4219	0.4116	0.3845	0.3456	0.2995	0.2500
	2	0.0135	0.0486	0.0975	0.1536	0.2109	0.2646	0.3105	0.3456	0.3675	0.3750
	3	0.0005	0.0036	0.0115	0.0256	0.0469	0.0756	0.1115	0.1536	0.2005	0.2500
	4	0.0000	0.0001	0.0005	0.0016	0.0039	0.0081	0.0150	0.0256	0.0410	0.0625
5	0	0.7738	0.5905	0.4437	0.3277	0.2373	0.1681	0.1160	0.0778	0.0503	0.0312
	1	0.2036	0.3280	0.3915	0.4096	0.3955	0.3602	0.3124	0.2592	0.2059	0.1562
	2	0.0214	0.0729	0.1382	0.2048	0.2637	0.3087	0.3364	0.3456	0.3369	0.3125
	3	0.0011	0.0081	0.0244	0.0512	0.0879	0.1323	0.1811	0.2304	0.2757	0.3125
	4	0.0000	0.0004	0.0022	0.0064	0.0146	0.0284	0.0488	0.0768	0.1128	0.1562
	5	0.0000	0.0000	0.0001	0.0003	0.0010	0.0024	0.0053	0.0102	0.0185	0.0312
6	0	0.7351	0.5314	0.3771	0.2621	0.1780	0.1176	0.0754	0.0467	0.0277	0.0156
	1	0.2321	0.3543	0.3993	0.3932	0.3560	0.3025	0.2437	0.1866	0.1359	0.0938
	2	0.0305	0.0984	0.1762	0.2458	0.2966	0.3241	0.3280	0.3110	0.2780	0.2344
	3	0.0021	0.0146	0.0415	0.0819	0.1318	0.1852	0.2355	0.2765	0.3032	0.3125
	4	0.0001	0.0012	0.0055	0.0154	0.0330	0.0595	0.0951	0.1382	0.1861	0.2344
	5	0.0000	0.0001	0.0004	0.0015	0.0044	0.0102	0.0205	0.0369	0.0609	0.0938
	6	0.0000	0.0000	0.0000	0.0001	0.0002	0.0007	0.0018	0.0041	0.0083	0.0156
7	0	0.6983	0.4783	0.3206	0.2097	0.1335	0.0824	0.0490	0.0280	0.0152	0.0078
	1	0.2573	0.3720	0.3960	0.3670	0.3115	0.2471	0.1848	0.1306	0.0872	0.0547
	2	0.0406	0.1240	0.2097	0.2753	0.3115	0.3177	0.2985	0.2613	0.2140	0.1641
	3	0.0036	0.0230	0.0617	0.1147	0.1730	0.2269	0.2679	0.2903	0.2918	0.2734
	4	0.0002	0.0026	0.0109	0.0287	0.0577	0.0972	0.1442	0.1935	0.2388	0.2734
	5	0.0000	0.0002	0.0012	0.0043	0.0115	0.0250	0.0466	0.0774	0.1172	0.1641
	6	0.0000	0.0000	0.0001	0.0004	0.0013	0.0036	0.0084	0.0172	0.0320	0.0547
	7	0.0000	0.0000	0.0000	0.0000	0.0001	0.0002	0.0006	0.0016	0.0037	0.0078
8	0	0.6634	0.4305	0.2725	0.1678	0.1001	0.0576	0.0319	0.0168	0.0084	0.0039
	1	0.2793	0.3826	0.3847	0.3355	0.2670	0.1977	0.1373	0.0896	0.0548	0.0312
	2	0.0515	0.1488	0.2376	0.2936	0.3115	0.2965	0.2587	0.2090	0.1569	0.1094
	3	0.0054	0.0331	0.0839	0.1468	0.2076	0.2541	0.2786	0.2787	0.2568	0.2188
	4	0.0004	0.0046	0.0185	0.0459	0.0865	0.1361	0.1875	0.2322	0.2627	0.2734
	5	0.0000	0.0004	0.0026	0.0092	0.0231	0.0467	0.0808	0.1239	0.1719	0.2188
	6	0.0000	0.0000	0.0002	0.0011	0.0038	0.0100	0.0217	0.0413	0.0703	0.1094
	7	0.0000	0.0000	0.0000	0.0001	0.0004	0.0012	0.0033	0.0079	0.0164	0.0312
	8	0.0000	0.0000	0.0000	0.0000	0.0000	0.0001	0.0002	0.0007	0.0017	0.0039

		p									
n	x	0.05	0.10	0.15	0.20	0.25	0.30	0.35	0.40	0.45	0.50
9	0	0.6302	0.3874	0.2316	0.1342	0.0751	0.0404	0.0207	0.0101	0.0046	0.0020
	1	0.2985	0.3874	0.3679	0.3020	0.2253	0.1556	0.1004	0.0605	0.0339	0.0176
	2	0.0629	0.1722	0.2597	0.3020	0.3003	0.2668	0.2162	0.1612	0.1110	0.0703
	3	0.0077	0.0446	0.1069	0.1762	0.2336	0.2668	0.2716	0.2508	0.2119	0.1641
	4	0.0006	0.0074	0.0283	0.0661	0.1168	0.1715	0.2194	0.2508	0.2600	0.2461
	5	0.0000	0.0008	0.0050	0.0165	0.0389	0.0735	0.1181	0.1672	0.2128	0.2461
	6	0.0000	0.0001	0.0006	0.0028	0.0087	0.0210	0.0424	0.0743	0.1160	0.1641
	7	0.0000	0.0000	0.0000	0.0003	0.0012	0.0039	0.0098	0.0212	0.0407	0.0703
	8	0.0000	0.0000	0.0000	0.0000	0.0001	0.0004	0.0013	0.0035	0.0083	0.0176
	9	0.0000	0.0000	0.0000	0.0000	0.0000	0.0000	0.0001	0.0003	0.0008	0.0020
10	0	0.5987	0.3487	0.1969	0.1074	0.0563	0.0282	0.0135	0.0060	0.0025	0.0010
	1	0.3151	0.3874	0.3474	0.2684	0.1877	0.1211	0.0725	0.0403	0.0207	0.0098
	2	0.0746	0.1937	0.2759	0.3020	0.2816	0.2335	0.1757	0.1209	0.0763	0.0439
	3	0.0105	0.0574	0.1298	0.2013	0.2503	0.2668	0.2522	0.2150	0.1665	0.1172
	4	0.0010	0.0112	0.0401	0.0881	0.1460	0.2001	0.2377	0.2508	0.2384	0.2051
	5	0.0001	0.0015	0.0085	0.0264	0.0584	0.1029	0.1536	0.2007	0.2340	0.2461
	6	0.0000	0.0001	0.0012	0.0055	0.0162	0.0368	0.0689	0.1115	0.1596	0.2051
	7	0.0000	0.0000	0.0001	0.0008	0.0031	0.0090	0.0212	0.0425	0.0746	0.1172
	8	0.0000	0.0000	0.0000	0.0001	0.0004	0.0014	0.0043	0.0106	0.0229	0.0439
	9	0.0000	0.0000	0.0000	0.0000	0.0000	0.0001	0.0005	0.0016	0.0042	0.0098
	10	0.0000	0.0000	0.0000	0.0000	0.0000	0.0000	0.0000	0.0001	0.0003	0.0010
11	0	0.5688	0.3138	0.1673	0.0859	0.0422	0.0198	0.0088	0.0036	0.0014	0.0005
	1	0.3293	0.3835	0.3248	0.2362	0.1549	0.0932	0.0518	0.0266	0.0125	0.0054
	2	0.0867	0.2131	0.2866	0.2953	0.2581	0.1998	0.1395	0.0887	0.0513	0.0269
	3	0.0137	0.0710	0.1517	0.2215	0.2581	0.2568	0.2254	0.1774	0.1259	0.0806
	4	0.0014	0.0158	0.0536	0.1107	0.1721	0.2201	0.2428	0.2365	0.2060	0.1611
	5	0.0001	0.0025	0.0132	0.0388	0.0803	0.1321	0.1830	0.2207	0.2360	0.2256
	6	0.0000	0.0003	0.0023	0.0097	0.0268	0.0566	0.0985	0.1471	0.1931	0.2256
	7	0.0000	0.0000	0.0003	0.0017	0.0064	0.0173	0.0379	0.0701	0.1128	0.1611
	8	0.0000	0.0000	0.0000	0.0002	0.0011	0.0037	0.0102	0.0234	0.0462	0.0806
	9	0.0000	0.0000	0.0000	0.0000	0.0001	0.0005	0.0018	0.0052	0.0126	0.0269
	10	0.0000	0.0000	0.0000	0.0000	0.0000	0.0000	0.0002	0.0007	0.0021	0.0054
	11	0.0000	0.0000	0.0000	0.0000	0.0000	0.0000	0.0000	0.0000	0.0002	0.0005
12	0	0.5404	0.2824	0.1422	0.0687	0.0317	0.0138	0.0057	0.0022	0.0008	0.0002
	1	0.3413	0.3766	0.3012	0.2062	0.1267	0.0712	0.0368	0.0174	0.0075	0.0029
	2	0.0988	0.2301	0.2924	0.2835	0.2323	0.1678	0.1088	0.0639	0.0339	0.0161
	3	0.0173	0.0853	0.1720	0.2362	0.2581	0.2397	0.1954	0.1419	0.0923	0.0537
	4	0.0021	0.0213	0.0683	0.1329	0.1936	0.2311	0.2367	0.2128	0.1700	0.1208
	5	0.0002	0.0038	0.0193	0.0532	0.1032	0.1585	0.2039	0.2270	0.2225	0.1934
	6	0.0000	0.0005	0.0040	0.0155	0.0401	0.0792	0.1281	0.1766	0.2124	0.2256
	7	0.0000	0.0000	0.0006	0.0033	0.0115	0.0291	0.0591	0.1009	0.1489	0.1934
	8	0.0000	0.0000	0.0001	0.0005	0.0024	0.0078	0.0199	0.0420	0.0762	0.1208
	9	0.0000	0.0000	0.0000	0.0001	0.0004	0.0015	0.0048	0.0125	0.0277	0.0537
	10	0.0000	0.0000	0.0000	0.0000	0.0000	0.0002	0.0008	0.0025	0.0068	0.0161
	11	0.0000	0.0000	0.0000	0.0000	0.0000	0.0000	0.0001	0.0003	0.0010	0.0029
	12	0.0000	0.0000	0.0000	0.0000	0.0000	0.0000	0.0000	0.0000	0.0001	0.0002
13	0	0.5133	0.2542	0.1209	0.0550	0.0238	0.0097	0.0037	0.0013	0.0004	0.0001
	1	0.3512	0.3672	0.2774	0.1787	0.1029	0.0540	0.0259	0.0113	0.0045	0.0016
	2	0.1109	0.2448	0.2937	0.2680	0.2059	0.1388	0.0836	0.0453	0.0220	0.0095
	3	0.0214	0.0997	0.1900	0.2457	0.2517	0.2181	0.1651	0.1107	0.0660	0.0349
	4	0.0028	0.0277	0.0838	0.1535	0.2097	0.2337	0.2222	0.1845	0.1350	0.0873
	5	0.0003	0.0055	0.0266	0.0691	0.1258	0.1803	0.2154	0.2214	0.1989	0.1571
	6	0.0000	0.0008	0.0063	0.0230	0.0559	0.1030	0.1546	0.1968	0.2169	0.2095
	7	0.0000	0.0001	0.0011	0.0058	0.0186	0.0442	0.0833	0.1312	0.1775	0.2095

n	x	\multicolumn{10}{c}{p}
		0.05	0.10	0.15	0.20	0.25	0.30	0.35	0.40	0.45	0.50
	8	0.0000	0.0000	0.0001	0.0011	0.0047	0.0142	0.0336	0.0656	0.1089	0.1571
	9	0.0000	0.0000	0.0000	0.0001	0.0009	0.0034	0.0101	0.0243	0.0495	0.0873
	10	0.0000	0.0000	0.0000	0.0000	0.0001	0.0006	0.0022	0.0065	0.0162	0.0349
	11	0.0000	0.0000	0.0000	0.0000	0.0000	0.0001	0.0003	0.0012	0.0036	0.0095
	12	0.0000	0.0000	0.0000	0.0000	0.0000	0.0000	0.0000	0.0001	0.0005	0.0016
	13	0.0000	0.0000	0.0000	0.0000	0.0000	0.0000	0.0000	0.0000	0.0000	0.0001
14	0	0.4877	0.2288	0.1028	0.0440	0.0178	0.0068	0.0024	0.0008	0.0002	0.0001
	1	0.3593	0.3559	0.2539	0.1539	0.0832	0.0407	0.0181	0.0073	0.0027	0.0009
	2	0.1229	0.2570	0.2912	0.2501	0.1802	0.1134	0.0634	0.0317	0.0141	0.0056
	3	0.0259	0.1142	0.2056	0.2501	0.2402	0.1943	0.1366	0.0845	0.0462	0.0222
	4	0.0037	0.0349	0.0998	0.1720	0.2202	0.2290	0.2022	0.1549	0.1040	0.0611
	5	0.0004	0.0078	0.0352	0.0860	0.1468	0.1963	0.2178	0.2066	0.1701	0.1222
	6	0.0000	0.0013	0.0093	0.0322	0.0734	0.1262	0.1759	0.2066	0.2088	0.1833
	7	0.0000	0.0002	0.0019	0.0092	0.0280	0.0618	0.1082	0.1574	0.1952	0.2095
	8	0.0000	0.0000	0.0003	0.0020	0.0082	0.0232	0.0510	0.0918	0.1398	0.1833
	9	0.0000	0.0000	0.0000	0.0003	0.0018	0.0066	0.0183	0.0408	0.0762	0.1222
	10	0.0000	0.0000	0.0000	0.0000	0.0003	0.0014	0.0049	0.0136	0.0312	0.0611
	11	0.0000	0.0000	0.0000	0.0000	0.0000	0.0002	0.0010	0.0033	0.0093	0.0222
	12	0.0000	0.0000	0.0000	0.0000	0.0000	0.0000	0.0001	0.0005	0.0019	0.0056
	13	0.0000	0.0000	0.0000	0.0000	0.0000	0.0000	0.0000	0.0001	0.0002	0.0009
	14	0.0000	0.0000	0.0000	0.0000	0.0000	0.0000	0.0000	0.0000	0.0000	0.0001
15	0	0.4633	0.2059	0.0874	0.0352	0.0134	0.0047	0.0016	0.0005	0.0001	0.0000
	1	0.3658	0.3432	0.2312	0.1319	0.0668	0.0305	0.0126	0.0047	0.0016	0.0005
	2	0.1348	0.2669	0.2856	0.2309	0.1559	0.0916	0.0476	0.0219	0.0090	0.0032
	3	0.0307	0.1285	0.2184	0.2501	0.2252	0.1700	0.1110	0.0634	0.0318	0.0139
	4	0.0049	0.0428	0.1156	0.1876	0.2252	0.2186	0.1792	0.1268	0.0780	0.0417
	5	0.0006	0.0105	0.0449	0.1032	0.1651	0.2061	0.2123	0.1859	0.1404	0.0916
	6	0.0000	0.0019	0.0132	0.0430	0.0917	0.1472	0.1906	0.2066	0.1914	0.1527
	7	0.0000	0.0003	0.0030	0.0138	0.0393	0.0811	0.1319	0.1711	0.2013	0.1964
	8	0.0000	0.0000	0.0005	0.0035	0.0131	0.0348	0.0710	0.1181	0.1647	0.1964
	9	0.0000	0.0000	0.0001	0.0007	0.0034	0.0116	0.0298	0.0612	0.1048	0.1527
	10	0.0000	0.0000	0.0000	0.0001	0.0007	0.0030	0.0096	0.0245	0.0515	0.0916
	11	0.0000	0.0000	0.0000	0.0000	0.0001	0.0006	0.0024	0.0074	0.0191	0.0417
	12	0.0000	0.0000	0.0000	0.0000	0.0000	0.0001	0.0004	0.0016	0.0052	0.0139
	13	0.0000	0.0000	0.0000	0.0000	0.0000	0.0000	0.0001	0.0003	0.0010	0.0032
	14	0.0000	0.0000	0.0000	0.0000	0.0000	0.0000	0.0000	0.0000	0.0001	0.0005
	15	0.0000	0.0000	0.0000	0.0000	0.0000	0.0000	0.0000	0.0000	0.0000	0.0000
16	0	0.4401	0.1853	0.0743	0.0281	0.0100	0.0033	0.0010	0.0003	0.0001	0.0000
	1	0.3706	0.3294	0.2097	0.1126	0.0535	0.0228	0.0087	0.0030	0.0009	0.0002
	2	0.1463	0.2745	0.2775	0.2111	0.1336	0.0732	0.0353	0.0150	0.0056	0.0018
	3	0.0359	0.1423	0.2285	0.2463	0.2079	0.1465	0.0888	0.0468	0.0215	0.0085
	4	0.0061	0.0514	0.1311	0.2001	0.2252	0.2040	0.1553	0.1014	0.0572	0.0278
	5	0.0008	0.0137	0.0555	0.1201	0.1802	0.2099	0.2008	0.1623	0.1123	0.0667
	6	0.0001	0.0028	0.0180	0.0550	0.1101	0.1649	0.1982	0.1983	0.1684	0.1222
	7	0.0000	0.0004	0.0045	0.0197	0.0524	0.1010	0.1524	0.1889	0.1969	0.1746
	8	0.0000	0.0001	0.0009	0.0055	0.0197	0.0487	0.0923	0.1417	0.1812	0.1964
	9	0.0000	0.0000	0.0001	0.0012	0.0058	0.0185	0.0442	0.0840	0.1318	0.1746
	10	0.0000	0.0000	0.0000	0.0002	0.0014	0.0056	0.0167	0.0392	0.0755	0.1222
	11	0.0000	0.0000	0.0000	0.0000	0.0002	0.0013	0.0049	0.0142	0.0337	0.0667
	12	0.0000	0.0000	0.0000	0.0000	0.0000	0.0002	0.0011	0.0040	0.0115	0.0278
	13	0.0000	0.0000	0.0000	0.0000	0.0000	0.0000	0.0002	0.0008	0.0029	0.0085
	14	0.0000	0.0000	0.0000	0.0000	0.0000	0.0000	0.0000	0.0001	0.0005	0.0018
	15	0.0000	0.0000	0.0000	0.0000	0.0000	0.0000	0.0000	0.0000	0.0001	0.0002
	16	0.0000	0.0000	0.0000	0.0000	0.0000	0.0000	0.0000	0.0000	0.0000	0.0000

						p					
n	x	0.05	0.10	0.15	0.20	0.25	0.30	0.35	0.40	0.45	0.50
17	0	0.4181	0.1668	0.0631	0.0225	0.0075	0.0023	0.0007	0.0002	0.0000	0.0000
	1	0.3741	0.3150	0.1893	0.0957	0.0426	0.0169	0.0060	0.0019	0.0005	0.0001
	2	0.1575	0.2800	0.2673	0.1914	0.1136	0.0581	0.0260	0.0102	0.0035	0.0010
	3	0.0415	0.1556	0.2359	0.2393	0.1893	0.1245	0.0701	0.0341	0.0144	0.0052
	4	0.0076	0.0605	0.1457	0.2093	0.2209	0.1868	0.1320	0.0796	0.0411	0.0182
	5	0.0010	0.0175	0.0668	0.1361	0.1914	0.2081	0.1849	0.1379	0.0875	0.0472
	6	0.0001	0.0039	0.0236	0.0680	0.1276	0.1784	0.1991	0.1839	0.1432	0.0944
	7	0.0000	0.0007	0.0065	0.0267	0.0668	0.1201	0.1685	0.1927	0.1841	0.1484
	8	0.0000	0.0001	0.0014	0.0084	0.0279	0.0644	0.1134	0.1606	0.1883	0.1855
	9	0.0000	0.0000	0.0003	0.0021	0.0093	0.0276	0.0611	0.1070	0.1540	0.1855
	10	0.0000	0.0000	0.0000	0.0004	0.0025	0.0095	0.0263	0.0571	0.1008	0.1484
	11	0.0000	0.0000	0.0000	0.0001	0.0005	0.0026	0.0090	0.0242	0.0525	0.0944
	12	0.0000	0.0000	0.0000	0.0000	0.0001	0.0006	0.0024	0.0081	0.0215	0.0472
	13	0.0000	0.0000	0.0000	0.0000	0.0000	0.0001	0.0005	0.0021	0.0068	0.0182
	14	0.0000	0.0000	0.0000	0.0000	0.0000	0.0000	0.0001	0.0004	0.0016	0.0052
	15	0.0000	0.0000	0.0000	0.0000	0.0000	0.0000	0.0000	0.0001	0.0003	0.0010
	16	0.0000	0.0000	0.0000	0.0000	0.0000	0.0000	0.0000	0.0000	0.0000	0.0001
	17	0.0000	0.0000	0.0000	0.0000	0.0000	0.0000	0.0000	0.0000	0.0000	0.0000
18	0	0.3972	0.1501	0.0536	0.0180	0.0056	0.0016	0.0004	0.0001	0.0000	0.0000
	1	0.3763	0.3002	0.1704	0.0811	0.0338	0.0126	0.0042	0.0012	0.0003	0.0001
	2	0.1683	0.2835	0.2556	0.1723	0.0958	0.0458	0.0190	0.0069	0.0022	0.0006
	3	0.0473	0.1680	0.2406	0.2297	0.1704	0.1046	0.0547	0.0246	0.0095	0.0031
	4	0.0093	0.0700	0.1592	0.2153	0.2130	0.1681	0.1104	0.0614	0.0291	0.0117
	5	0.0014	0.0218	0.0787	0.1507	0.1988	0.2017	0.1664	0.1146	0.0666	0.0327
	6	0.0002	0.0052	0.0301	0.0816	0.1436	0.1873	0.1941	0.1655	0.1181	0.0708
	7	0.0000	0.0010	0.0091	0.0350	0.0820	0.1376	0.1792	0.1892	0.1657	0.1214
	8	0.0000	0.0002	0.0022	0.0120	0.0376	0.0811	0.1327	0.1734	0.1864	0.1669
	9	0.0000	0.0000	0.0004	0.0033	0.0139	0.0386	0.0794	0.1284	0.1694	0.1855
	10	0.0000	0.0000	0.0001	0.0008	0.0042	0.0149	0.0385	0.0771	0.1248	0.1669
	11	0.0000	0.0000	0.0000	0.0001	0.0010	0.0046	0.0151	0.0374	0.0742	0.1214
	12	0.0000	0.0000	0.0000	0.0000	0.0002	0.0012	0.0047	0.0145	0.0354	0.0708
	13	0.0000	0.0000	0.0000	0.0000	0.0000	0.0002	0.0012	0.0045	0.0134	0.0327
	14	0.0000	0.0000	0.0000	0.0000	0.0000	0.0000	0.0002	0.0011	0.0039	0.0117
	15	0.0000	0.0000	0.0000	0.0000	0.0000	0.0000	0.0000	0.0002	0.0009	0.0031
	16	0.0000	0.0000	0.0000	0.0000	0.0000	0.0000	0.0000	0.0000	0.0001	0.0006
	17	0.0000	0.0000	0.0000	0.0000	0.0000	0.0000	0.0000	0.0000	0.0000	0.0001
	18	0.0000	0.0000	0.0000	0.0000	0.0000	0.0000	0.0000	0.0000	0.0000	0.0000
19	0	0.3774	0.1351	0.0456	0.0144	0.0042	0.0011	0.0003	0.0001	0.0002	0.0000
	1	0.3774	0.2852	0.1529	0.0685	0.0268	0.0093	0.0029	0.0008	0.0002	0.0000
	2	0.1787	0.2852	0.2428	0.1540	0.0803	0.0358	0.0138	0.0046	0.0013	0.0003
	3	0.0533	0.1796	0.2428	0.2182	0.1517	0.0869	0.0422	0.0175	0.0062	0.0018
	4	0.0112	0.0798	0.1714	0.2182	0.2023	0.1491	0.0909	0.0467	0.0203	0.0074
	5	0.0018	0.0266	0.0907	0.1636	0.2023	0.1916	0.1468	0.0933	0.0497	0.0222
	6	0.0002	0.0069	0.0374	0.0955	0.1574	0.1916	0.1844	0.1451	0.0949	0.0518
	7	0.0000	0.0014	0.0122	0.0443	0.0974	0.1525	0.1844	0.1797	0.1443	0.0961
	8	0.0000	0.0002	0.0032	0.0166	0.0487	0.0981	0.1489	0.1797	0.1771	0.1442
	9	0.0000	0.0000	0.0007	0.0051	0.0198	0.0514	0.0980	0.1464	0.1771	0.1762
	10	0.0000	0.0000	0.0001	0.0013	0.0066	0.0220	0.0528	0.0976	0.1449	0.1762
	11	0.0000	0.0000	0.0000	0.0003	0.0018	0.0077	0.0233	0.0532	0.0970	0.1442
	12	0.0000	0.0000	0.0000	0.0000	0.0004	0.0022	0.0083	0.0237	0.0529	0.0961
	13	0.0000	0.0000	0.0000	0.0000	0.0001	0.0005	0.0024	0.0085	0.0233	0.0518
	14	0.0000	0.0000	0.0000	0.0000	0.0000	0.0001	0.0006	0.0024	0.0082	0.0222
	15	0.0000	0.0000	0.0000	0.0000	0.0000	0.0000	0.0001	0.0005	0.0022	0.0074
	16	0.0000	0.0000	0.0000	0.0000	0.0000	0.0000	0.0000	0.0001	0.0005	0.0018

n	x	p									
		0.05	0.10	0.15	0.20	0.25	0.30	0.35	0.40	0.45	0.50
	17	0.0000	0.0000	0.0000	0.0000	0.0000	0.0000	0.0000	0.0000	0.0001	0.0003
	18	0.0000	0.0000	0.0000	0.0000	0.0000	0.0000	0.0000	0.0000	0.0000	0.0000
	19	0.0000	0.0000	0.0000	0.0000	0.0000	0.0000	0.0000	0.0000	0.0000	0.0000
20	0	0.3585	0.1216	0.0388	0.0115	0.0032	0.0008	0.0002	0.0000	0.0000	0.0000
	1	0.3774	0.2702	0.1368	0.0576	0.0211	0.0068	0.0020	0.0005	0.0001	0.0000
	2	0.1887	0.2852	0.2293	0.1369	0.0669	0.0278	0.0100	0.0031	0.0008	0.0002
	3	0.0596	0.1901	0.2428	0.2054	0.1339	0.0716	0.0323	0.0123	0.0040	0.0011
	4	0.0133	0.0898	0.1821	0.2182	0.1897	0.1304	0.0738	0.0350	0.0139	0.0046
	5	0.0022	0.0319	0.1028	0.1746	0.2023	0.1789	0.1272	0.0746	0.0365	0.0148
	6	0.0003	0.0089	0.0454	0.1091	0.1686	0.1916	0.1712	0.1244	0.0746	0.0370
	7	0.0000	0.0020	0.0160	0.0545	0.1124	0.1643	0.1844	0.1659	0.1221	0.0739
	8	0.0000	0.0004	0.0046	0.0222	0.0609	0.1144	0.1614	0.1797	0.1623	0.1201
	9	0.0000	0.0001	0.0011	0.0074	0.0271	0.0654	0.1158	0.1597	0.1771	0.1602
	10	0.0000	0.0000	0.0002	0.0020	0.0099	0.0308	0.0686	0.1171	0.1593	0.1762
	11	0.0000	0.0000	0.0000	0.0005	0.0030	0.0120	0.0336	0.0710	0.1185	0.1602
	12	0.0000	0.0000	0.0000	0.0001	0.0008	0.0039	0.0136	0.0355	0.0727	0.1201
	13	0.0000	0.0000	0.0000	0.0000	0.0002	0.0010	0.0045	0.0146	0.0366	0.0739
	14	0.0000	0.0000	0.0000	0.0000	0.0000	0.0002	0.0012	0.0049	0.0150	0.0370
	15	0.0000	0.0000	0.0000	0.0000	0.0000	0.0000	0.0003	0.0013	0.0049	0.0148
	16	0.0000	0.0000	0.0000	0.0000	0.0000	0.0000	0.0000	0.0003	0.0013	0.0046
	17	0.0000	0.0000	0.0000	0.0000	0.0000	0.0000	0.0000	0.0000	0.0002	0.0011
	18	0.0000	0.0000	0.0000	0.0000	0.0000	0.0000	0.0000	0.0000	0.0000	0.0002
	19	0.0000	0.0000	0.0000	0.0000	0.0000	0.0000	0.0000	0.0000	0.0000	0.0000
	20	0.0000	0.0000	0.0000	0.0000	0.0000	0.0000	0.0000	0.0000	0.0000	0.0000

Source: Reprinted from *Handbook of Probability and Statistics with Tables,* 2nd ed., by R. S. Burington and D. C. May. New York: McGraw-Hill Book Company, Inc., 1970, by permission of the authors' trustee.

APPENDIX E

POISSON PROBABILITIES

Entries in the table give the probability of x occurrences for a Poisson process with a mean μ. For example, when $\mu = 2.5$, the probability of four occurrences is 0.1336.

					μ					
x	0.1	0.2	0.3	0.4	0.5	0.6	0.7	0.8	0.9	1.0
0	0.9048	0.8187	0.7408	0.6703	0.6065	0.5488	0.4966	0.4493	0.4066	0.3679
1	0.0905	0.1637	0.2222	0.2681	0.3033	0.3293	0.3476	0.3595	0.3659	0.3679
2	0.0045	0.0164	0.0333	0.0536	0.0758	0.0988	0.1217	0.1438	0.1647	0.1839
3	0.0002	0.0011	0.0033	0.0072	0.0126	0.0198	0.0284	0.0383	0.0494	0.0613
4	0.0000	0.0001	0.0002	0.0007	0.0016	0.0030	0.0050	0.0077	0.0111	0.0153
5	0.0000	0.0000	0.0000	0.0001	0.0002	0.0004	0.0007	0.0012	0.0020	0.0031
6	0.0000	0.0000	0.0000	0.0000	0.0000	0.0000	0.0001	0.0002	0.0003	0.0005
7	0.0000	0.0000	0.0000	0.0000	0.0000	0.0000	0.0000	0.0000	0.0000	0.0001

					μ					
x	1.1	1.2	1.3	1.4	1.5	1.6	1.7	1.8	1.9	2.0
0	0.3329	0.3012	0.2725	0.2466	0.2231	0.2019	0.1827	0.1653	0.1496	0.1353
1	0.3662	0.3614	0.3543	0.3452	0.3347	0.3230	0.3106	0.2975	0.2842	0.2707
2	0.2014	0.2169	0.2303	0.2417	0.2510	0.2584	0.2640	0.2678	0.2700	0.2707
3	0.0738	0.0867	0.0998	0.1128	0.1255	0.1378	0.1496	0.1607	0.1710	0.1804
4	0.0203	0.0260	0.0324	0.0395	0.0471	0.0551	0.0636	0.0723	0.0812	0.0902
5	0.0045	0.0062	0.0084	0.0111	0.0141	0.0176	0.0216	0.0260	0.0309	0.0361
6	0.0008	0.0012	0.0018	0.0026	0.0035	0.0047	0.0061	0.0078	0.0098	0.0120
7	0.0001	0.0002	0.0003	0.0005	0.0008	0.0011	0.0015	0.0020	0.0027	0.0034
8	0.0000	0.0000	0.0001	0.0001	0.0001	0.0002	0.0003	0.0005	0.0006	0.0009
9	0.0000	0.0000	0.0000	0.0000	0.0000	0.0000	0.0001	0.0001	0.0001	0.0002

					μ					
x	2.1	2.2	2.3	2.4	2.5	2.6	2.7	2.8	2.9	3.0
0	0.1225	0.1108	0.1003	0.0907	0.0821	0.0743	0.0672	0.0608	0.0550	0.0498
1	0.2572	0.2438	0.2306	0.2177	0.2052	0.1931	0.1815	0.1703	0.1596	0.1494
2	0.2700	0.2681	0.2652	0.2613	0.2565	0.2510	0.2450	0.2384	0.2314	0.2240
3	0.1890	0.1966	0.2033	0.2090	0.2138	0.2176	0.2205	0.2225	0.2237	0.2240
4	0.0992	0.1082	0.1169	0.1254	0.1336	0.1414	0.1488	0.1557	0.1622	0.1680
5	0.0417	0.0476	0.0538	0.0602	0.0668	0.0735	0.0804	0.0872	0.0940	0.1008
6	0.0146	0.0174	0.0206	0.0241	0.0278	0.0319	0.0362	0.0407	0.0455	0.0540
7	0.0044	0.0055	0.0068	0.0083	0.0099	0.0118	0.0139	0.0163	0.0188	0.0216
8	0.0011	0.0015	0.0019	0.0025	0.0031	0.0038	0.0047	0.0057	0.0068	0.0081
9	0.0003	0.0004	0.0005	0.0007	0.0009	0.0011	0.0014	0.0018	0.0022	0.0027
10	0.0001	0.0001	0.0001	0.0002	0.0002	0.0003	0.0004	0.0005	0.0006	0.0008
11	0.0000	0.0000	0.0000	0.0000	0.0000	0.0001	0.0001	0.0001	0.0002	0.0002
12	0.0000	0.0000	0.0000	0.0000	0.0000	0.0000	0.0000	0.0000	0.0000	0.0001

					μ					
x	3.1	3.2	3.3	3.4	3.5	3.6	3.7	3.8	3.9	4.0
0	0.0450	0.0408	0.0369	0.0344	0.0302	0.0273	0.0247	0.0224	0.0202	0.0183
1	0.1397	0.1304	0.1217	0.1135	0.1057	0.0984	0.0915	0.0850	0.0789	0.0733
2	0.2165	0.2087	0.2008	0.1929	0.1850	0.1771	0.1692	0.1615	0.1539	0.1465
3	0.2237	0.2226	0.2209	0.2186	0.2158	0.2125	0.2087	0.2046	0.2001	0.1954
4	0.1734	0.1781	0.1823	0.1858	0.1888	0.1912	0.1931	0.1944	0.1951	0.1954

					μ					
x	3.1	3.2	3.3	3.4	3.5	3.6	3.7	3.8	3.9	4.0
5	0.1075	0.1140	0.1203	0.1264	0.1322	0.1377	0.1429	0.1477	0.1522	0.1563
6	0.0555	0.0608	0.0662	0.0716	0.0771	0.0826	0.0881	0.0936	0.0989	0.1042
7	0.0246	0.0278	0.0312	0.0348	0.0385	0.0425	0.0466	0.0508	0.0551	0.0595
8	0.0095	0.0111	0.0129	0.0148	0.0169	0.0191	0.0215	0.0241	0.0269	0.0298
9	0.0093	0.0040	0.0047	0.0056	0.0066	0.0076	0.0089	0.0102	0.0116	0.0132
10	0.0010	0.0013	0.0016	0.0019	0.0023	0.0028	0.0033	0.0039	0.0045	0.0053
11	0.0003	0.0004	0.0005	0.0006	0.0007	0.0009	0.0011	0.0013	0.0016	0.0019
12	0.0001	0.0001	0.0001	0.0002	0.0002	0.0003	0.0003	0.0004	0.0005	0.0006
13	0.0000	0.0000	0.0000	0.0000	0.0001	0.0001	0.0001	0.0001	0.0002	0.0002
14	0.0000	0.0000	0.0000	0.0000	0.0000	0.0000	0.0000	0.0000	0.0000	0.0001

					μ					
x	4.1	4.2	4.3	4.4	4.5	4.6	4.7	4.8	4.9	5.0
0	0.0166	0.0150	0.0136	0.0123	0.0111	0.0101	0.0091	0.0082	0.0074	0.0067
1	0.0679	0.0630	0.0583	0.0540	0.0500	0.0462	0.0427	0.0395	0.0365	0.0337
2	0.1393	0.1323	0.1254	0.1188	0.1125	0.1063	0.1005	0.0948	0.0894	0.0842
3	0.1904	0.1852	0.1798	0.1743	0.1687	0.1631	0.1574	0.1517	0.1460	0.1404
4	0.1951	0.1944	0.1933	0.1917	0.1898	0.1875	0.1849	0.1820	0.1789	0.1755
5	0.1600	0.1633	0.1662	0.1687	0.1708	0.1725	0.1738	0.1747	0.1753	0.1755
6	0.1093	0.1143	0.1191	0.1237	0.1281	0.1323	0.1362	0.1398	0.1432	0.1462
7	0.0640	0.0686	0.0732	0.0778	0.0824	0.0869	0.0914	0.0959	0.1002	0.1044
8	0.0328	0.0360	0.0393	0.0428	0.0463	0.0500	0.0537	0.0575	0.0614	0.0653
9	0.0150	0.0163	0.0188	0.0209	0.0232	0.0255	0.0280	0.0307	0.0334	0.0363
10	0.0061	0.0071	0.0081	0.0092	0.0104	0.0118	0.0132	0.0147	0.0164	0.0181
11	0.0023	0.0027	0.0032	0.0037	0.0043	0.0049	0.0056	0.0064	0.0073	0.0082
12	0.0008	0.0009	0.0011	0.0014	0.0016	0.0019	0.0022	0.0026	0.0030	0.0034
13	0.0002	0.0003	0.0004	0.0005	0.0006	0.0007	0.0008	0.0009	0.0011	0.0013
14	0.0001	0.0001	0.0001	0.0001	0.0002	0.0002	0.0003	0.0003	0.0004	0.0005
15	0.0000	0.0000	0.0000	0.0000	0.0001	0.0001	0.0001	0.0001	0.0001	0.0002

					μ					
x	5.1	5.2	5.3	5.4	5.5	5.6	5.7	5.8	5.9	6.0
0	0.0061	0.0055	0.0050	0.0045	0.0041	0.0037	0.0033	0.0030	0.0027	0.0025
1	0.0311	0.0287	0.0265	0.0244	0.0225	0.0207	0.0191	0.0176	0.0162	0.0149
2	0.0793	0.0746	0.0701	0.0659	0.0618	0.0580	0.0544	0.0509	0.0477	0.0446
3	0.1348	0.1293	0.1239	0.1185	0.1133	0.1082	0.1033	0.0985	0.0938	0.0892
4	0.1719	0.1681	0.1641	0.1600	0.1558	0.1515	0.1472	0.1428	0.1383	0.1339
5	0.1753	0.1748	0.1740	0.1728	0.1714	0.1697	0.1678	0.1656	0.1632	0.1606
6	0.1490	0.1515	0.1537	0.1555	0.1571	0.1584	0.1594	0.1601	0.1605	0.1606
7	0.1086	0.1125	0.1163	0.1200	0.1234	0.1267	0.1298	0.1326	0.1353	0.1377
8	0.0692	0.0731	0.0771	0.0810	0.0849	0.0887	0.0925	0.0962	0.0998	0.1033
9	0.0392	0.0423	0.0454	0.0486	0.0519	0.0552	0.0586	0.0620	0.0654	0.0688
10	0.0200	0.0220	0.0241	0.0262	0.0285	0.0309	0.0334	0.0359	0.0386	0.0413
11	0.0093	0.0104	0.0116	0.0129	0.0143	0.0157	0.0173	0.0190	0.0207	0.0225
12	0.0039	0.0045	0.0051	0.0058	0.0065	0.0073	0.0082	0.0092	0.0102	0.0113
13	0.0015	0.0018	0.0021	0.0024	0.0028	0.0032	0.0036	0.0041	0.0046	0.0052
14	0.0006	0.0007	0.0008	0.0009	0.0011	0.0013	0.0015	0.0017	0.0019	0.0022
15	0.0002	0.0002	0.0003	0.0003	0.0004	0.0005	0.0006	0.0007	0.0008	0.0009
16	0.0001	0.0001	0.0001	0.0001	0.0001	0.0002	0.0002	0.0002	0.0003	0.0003
17	0.0000	0.0000	0.0000	0.0000	0.0000	0.0001	0.0001	0.0001	0.0001	0.0001

x	6.1	6.2	6.3	6.4	μ 6.5	6.6	6.7	6.8	6.9	7.0
0	0.0022	0.0020	0.0018	0.0017	0.0015	0.0014	0.0012	0.0011	0.0010	0.0009
1	0.0137	0.0126	0.0116	0.0106	0.0098	0.0090	0.0082	0.0076	0.0070	0.0064
2	0.0417	0.0390	0.0364	0.0340	0.0318	0.0296	0.0276	0.0258	0.0240	0.0223
3	0.0848	0.0806	0.0765	0.0726	0.0688	0.0652	0.0617	0.0584	0.0552	0.0521
4	0.1294	0.1249	0.1205	0.1162	0.1118	0.1076	0.1034	0.0992	0.0952	0.0912
5	0.1579	0.1549	0.1519	0.1487	0.1454	0.1420	0.1385	0.1349	0.1314	0.1277
6	0.1605	0.1601	0.1595	0.1586	0.1575	0.1562	0.1546	0.1529	0.1511	0.1490
7	0.1399	0.1418	0.1435	0.1450	0.1462	0.1472	0.1480	0.1486	0.1489	0.1490
8	0.1066	0.1099	0.1130	0.1160	0.1188	0.1215	0.1240	0.1263	0.1284	0.1304
9	0.0723	0.0757	0.0791	0.0825	0.0858	0.0891	0.0923	0.0954	0.0985	0.1014
10	0.0441	0.0469	0.0498	0.0528	0.0558	0.0588	0.0618	0.0649	0.0679	0.0710
11	0.0245	0.0265	0.0285	0.0307	0.0330	0.0353	0.0377	0.0401	0.0426	0.0452
12	0.0124	0.0137	0.0150	0.0164	0.0179	0.0194	0.0210	0.0227	0.0245	0.0264
13	0.0058	0.0065	0.0073	0.0081	0.0089	0.0098	0.0108	0.0119	0.0130	0.0142
14	0.0025	0.0029	0.0033	0.0037	0.0041	0.0046	0.0052	0.0058	0.0064	0.0071
15	0.0010	0.0012	0.0014	0.0016	0.0018	0.0020	0.0023	0.0026	0.0029	0.0033
16	0.0004	0.0005	0.0005	0.0006	0.0007	0.0008	0.0010	0.0011	0.0013	0.0014
17	0.0001	0.0002	0.0002	0.0002	0.0003	0.0003	0.0004	0.0004	0.0005	0.0006
18	0.0000	0.0001	0.0001	0.0001	0.0001	0.0001	0.0001	0.0002	0.0002	0.0002
19	0.0000	0.0000	0.0000	0.0000	0.0000	0.0000	0.0000	0.0001	0.0001	0.0001

x	7.1	7.2	7.3	7.4	μ 7.5	7.6	7.7	7.8	7.9	8.0
0	0.0008	0.0007	0.0007	0.0006	0.0006	0.0005	0.0005	0.0004	0.0004	0.0003
1	0.0059	0.0054	0.0049	0.0045	0.0041	0.0038	0.0035	0.0032	0.0029	0.0027
2	0.0208	0.0194	0.0180	0.0167	0.0156	0.0145	0.0134	0.0125	0.0116	0.0107
3	0.0492	0.0464	0.0438	0.0413	0.0389	0.0366	0.0345	0.0324	0.0305	0.0286
4	0.0874	0.0836	0.0799	0.0764	0.0729	0.0696	0.0663	0.0632	0.0602	0.0573
5	0.1241	0.1204	0.1167	0.1130	0.1094	0.1057	0.1021	0.0986	0.0951	0.0916
6	0.1468	0.1445	0.1420	0.1394	0.1367	0.1339	0.1311	0.1282	0.1252	0.1221
7	0.1489	0.1486	0.1481	0.1474	0.1465	0.1454	0.1442	0.1428	0.1413	0.1396
8	0.1321	0.1337	0.1351	0.1363	0.1373	0.1382	0.1388	0.1392	0.1395	0.1396
9	0.1042	0.1070	0.1096	0.1121	0.1144	0.1167	0.1187	0.1207	0.1224	0.1241
10	0.0740	0.0770	0.0800	0.0829	0.0858	0.0887	0.0914	0.0941	0.0967	0.0993
11	0.0478	0.0504	0.0531	0.0558	0.0585	0.0613	0.0640	0.0667	0.0695	0.0722
12	0.0283	0.0303	0.0323	0.0344	0.0366	0.0388	0.0411	0.0434	0.0457	0.0481
13	0.0154	0.0168	0.0181	0.0196	0.0211	0.0227	0.0243	0.0260	0.0278	0.0296
14	0.0078	0.0086	0.0095	0.0104	0.0113	0.0123	0.0134	0.0145	0.0157	0.0169
15	0.0037	0.0041	0.0046	0.0051	0.0057	0.0062	0.0069	0.0075	0.0083	0.0090
16	0.0016	0.0019	0.0021	0.0024	0.0026	0.0030	0.0033	0.0037	0.0041	0.0045
17	0.0007	0.0008	0.0009	0.0010	0.0012	0.0013	0.0015	0.0017	0.0019	0.0021
18	0.0003	0.0003	0.0004	0.0004	0.0005	0.0006	0.0006	0.0007	0.0008	0.0009
19	0.0001	0.0001	0.0001	0.0002	0.0002	0.0002	0.0003	0.0003	0.0003	0.0004
20	0.0000	0.0000	0.0001	0.0001	0.0001	0.0001	0.0001	0.0001	0.0001	0.0002
21	0.0000	0.0000	0.0000	0.0000	0.0000	0.0000	0.0000	0.0000	0.0001	0.0001

x	8.1	8.2	8.3	8.4	μ 8.5	8.6	8.7	8.8	8.9	9.0
0	0.0003	0.0003	0.0002	0.0002	0.0002	0.0002	0.0002	0.0002	0.0001	0.0001
1	0.0025	0.0023	0.0021	0.0019	0.0017	0.0016	0.0014	0.0013	0.0012	0.0011
2	0.0100	0.0092	0.0086	0.0079	0.0074	0.0068	0.0063	0.0058	0.0054	0.0050
3	0.0269	0.0252	0.0237	0.0222	0.0208	0.0195	0.0183	0.0171	0.1060	0.0150
4	0.0544	0.0517	0.0491	0.0466	0.0443	0.0420	0.0398	0.0377	0.0357	0.0337

					μ					
x	8.1	8.2	8.3	8.4	8.5	8.6	8.7	8.8	8.9	9.0
5	0.0882	0.0849	0.0816	0.0784	0.0752	0.0722	0.0692	0.0663	0.0635	0.0607
6	0.1191	0.1160	0.1128	0.1097	0.1066	0.1034	0.1003	0.0972	0.0941	0.0911
7	0.1378	0.1358	0.1338	0.1317	0.1294	0.1271	0.1247	0.1222	0.1197	0.1171
8	0.1395	0.1392	0.1388	0.1382	0.1375	0.1366	0.1356	0.1344	0.1332	0.1318
9	0.1256	0.1269	0.1280	0.1290	0.1299	0.1306	0.1311	0.1315	0.1317	0.1318
10	0.1017	0.1040	0.1063	0.1084	0.1104	0.1123	0.1140	0.1157	0.1172	0.1186
11	0.0749	0.0776	0.0802	0.0828	0.0853	0.0878	0.0902	0.0925	0.0948	0.0970
12	0.0505	0.0530	0.0555	0.0579	0.0604	0.0629	0.0654	0.0679	0.0703	0.0728
13	0.0315	0.0334	0.0354	0.0374	0.0395	0.0416	0.0438	0.0459	0.0481	0.0504
14	0.0182	0.0196	0.0210	0.0225	0.0240	0.0256	0.0272	0.0289	0.0306	0.0324
15	0.0098	0.0107	0.0116	0.0126	0.0136	0.0147	0.0158	0.0169	0.0182	0.0194
16	0.0050	0.0055	0.0060	0.0066	0.0072	0.0079	0.0086	0.0093	0.0101	0.0109
17	0.0024	0.0026	0.0029	0.0033	0.0036	0.0040	0.0044	0.0048	0.0053	0.0058
18	0.0011	0.0012	0.0014	0.0015	0.0017	0.0019	0.0021	0.0024	0.0026	0.0029
19	0.0005	0.0005	0.0006	0.0007	0.0008	0.0009	0.0010	0.0011	0.0012	0.0014
20	0.0002	0.0002	0.0002	0.0003	0.0003	0.0004	0.0004	0.0005	0.0005	0.0006
21	0.0001	0.0001	0.0001	0.0001	0.0001	0.0002	0.0002	0.0002	0.0002	0.0003
22	0.0000	0.0000	0.0000	0.0000	0.0001	0.0001	0.0001	0.0001	0.0001	0.000

					μ					
x	9.1	9.2	9.3	9.4	9.5	9.6	9.7	9.8	9.9	10
0	0.0001	0.0001	0.0001	0.0001	0.0001	0.0001	0.0001	0.0001	0.0001	0.0000
1	0.0010	0.0009	0.0009	0.0008	0.0007	0.0007	0.0006	0.0005	0.0005	0.0005
2	0.0046	0.0043	0.0040	0.0037	0.0034	0.0031	0.0029	0.0027	0.0025	0.0023
3	0.0140	0.0131	0.0123	0.0115	0.0107	0.0100	0.0093	0.0087	0.0081	0.0076
4	0.0319	0.0302	0.0285	0.0269	0.0254	0.0240	0.0226	0.0213	0.0201	0.0189
5	0.0581	0.0555	0.0530	0.0506	0.0483	0.0460	0.0439	0.0418	0.0398	0.0378
6	0.0881	0.0851	0.0822	0.0793	0.0764	0.0736	0.0709	0.0682	0.0656	0.0631
7	0.1145	0.1118	0.1091	0.1064	0.1037	0.1010	0.0982	0.0955	0.0928	0.0901
8	0.1302	0.1286	0.1269	0.1251	0.1232	0.1212	0.1191	0.1170	0.1148	0.1126
9	0.1317	0.1315	0.1311	0.1306	0.1300	0.1293	0.1284	0.1274	0.1263	0.1251
10	0.1198	0.1210	0.1219	0.1228	0.1235	0.1241	0.1245	0.1249	0.1250	0.1251
11	0.0991	0.1012	0.1031	0.1049	0.1067	0.1083	0.1098	0.1112	0.1125	0.1137
12	0.0752	0.0776	0.0799	0.0822	0.0844	0.0866	0.0888	0.0908	0.0928	0.0948
13	0.0526	0.0549	0.0572	0.0594	0.0617	0.0640	0.0662	0.0685	0.0707	0.0729
14	0.0342	0.0361	0.0380	0.0399	0.0419	0.0439	0.0459	0.0479	0.0500	0.0521
15	0.0208	0.0221	0.0235	0.0250	0.0265	0.0281	0.0297	0.0313	0.0330	0.0347
16	0.0118	0.0127	0.0137	0.0147	0.0157	0.0168	0.0180	0.0192	0.0204	0.0217
17	0.0063	0.0069	0.0075	0.0081	0.0088	0.0095	0.0103	0.0111	0.0119	0.0128
18	0.0032	0.0035	0.0039	0.0042	0.0046	0.0051	0.0055	0.0060	0.0065	0.0071
19	0.0015	0.0017	0.0019	0.0021	0.0023	0.0026	0.0028	0.0031	0.0034	0.0037
20	0.0007	0.0008	0.0009	0.0010	0.0011	0.0012	0.0014	0.0015	0.0017	0.0019
21	0.0003	0.0003	0.0004	0.0004	0.0005	0.0006	0.0006	0.0007	0.0008	0.0009
22	0.0001	0.0001	0.0002	0.0002	0.0002	0.0002	0.0003	0.0003	0.0004	0.0004
23	0.0000	0.0001	0.0001	0.0001	0.0001	0.0001	0.0001	0.0001	0.0002	0.0002
24	0.0000	0.0000	0.0000	0.0000	0.0000	0.0000	0.0000	0.0001	0.0001	0.0001

x	μ 11	12	13	14	15	16	17	18	19	20
0	0.0000	0.0000	0.0000	0.0000	0.0000	0.0000	0.0000	0.0000	0.0000	0.0000
1	0.0002	0.0001	0.0000	0.0000	0.0000	0.0000	0.0000	0.0000	0.0000	0.0000
2	0.0010	0.0004	0.0002	0.0001	0.0000	0.0000	0.0000	0.0000	0.0000	0.0000
3	0.0037	0.0018	0.0008	0.0004	0.0002	0.0001	0.0000	0.0000	0.0000	0.0000
4	0.0102	0.0053	0.0027	0.0013	0.0006	0.0003	0.0001	0.0001	0.0000	0.0000
5	0.0224	0.0127	0.0070	0.0037	0.0019	0.0010	0.0005	0.0002	0.0001	0.0001
6	0.0411	0.0255	0.0152	0.0087	0.0048	0.0026	0.0014	0.0007	0.0004	0.0002
7	0.0646	0.0437	0.0281	0.0174	0.0104	0.0060	0.0034	0.0018	0.0010	0.0005
8	0.0888	0.0655	0.0457	0.0304	0.0194	0.0120	0.0072	0.0042	0.0024	0.0013
9	0.1085	0.0874	0.0661	0.0473	0.0324	0.0213	0.0135	0.0083	0.0050	0.0029
10	0.1194	0.1048	0.0859	0.0663	0.0486	0.0341	0.0230	0.0150	0.0095	0.0058
11	0.1194	0.1144	0.1015	0.0844	0.0663	0.0496	0.0355	0.0245	0.0164	0.0106
12	0.1094	0.1144	0.1099	0.0984	0.0829	0.0661	0.0504	0.0368	0.0259	0.0176
13	0.0926	0.1056	0.1099	0.1060	0.0956	0.0814	0.0658	0.0509	0.0378	0.0271
14	0.0728	0.0905	0.1021	0.1060	0.1024	0.0930	0.0800	0.0655	0.0514	0.0387
15	0.0534	0.0724	0.0885	0.0989	0.1024	0.0992	0.0906	0.0786	0.0650	0.0516
16	0.0367	0.0543	0.0719	0.0866	0.0960	0.0992	0.0963	0.0884	0.0772	0.0646
17	0.0237	0.0383	0.0550	0.0713	0.0847	0.0934	0.0963	0.0936	0.0863	0.0760
18	0.0145	0.0256	0.0397	0.0554	0.0706	0.0830	0.0909	0.0936	0.0911	0.0844
19	0.0084	0.0161	0.0272	0.0409	0.0557	0.0699	0.0814	0.0887	0.0911	0.0888
20	0.0046	0.0097	0.0177	0.0286	0.0418	0.0559	0.0692	0.0798	0.0866	0.0888
21	0.0024	0.0055	0.0109	0.0191	0.0299	0.0426	0.0560	0.0684	0.0783	0.0846
22	0.0012	0.0030	0.0065	0.0121	0.0204	0.0310	0.0433	0.0560	0.0676	0.0769
23	0.0006	0.0016	0.0037	0.0074	0.0133	0.0216	0.0320	0.0438	0.0559	0.0669
24	0.0003	0.0008	0.0020	0.0043	0.0083	0.0144	0.0226	0.0328	0.0442	0.0557
25	0.0001	0.0004	0.0010	0.0024	0.0050	0.0092	0.0154	0.0237	0.0336	0.0446
26	0.0000	0.0002	0.0005	0.0013	0.0029	0.0057	0.0101	0.0164	0.0246	0.0343
27	0.0000	0.0001	0.0002	0.0007	0.0016	0.0034	0.0063	0.0109	0.0173	0.0254
28	0.0000	0.0000	0.0001	0.0003	0.0009	0.0019	0.0038	0.0070	0.0117	0.0181
29	0.0000	0.0000	0.0001	0.0002	0.0004	0.0011	0.0023	0.0044	0.0077	0.0125
30	0.0000	0.0000	0.0000	0.0001	0.0002	0.0006	0.0013	0.0026	0.0049	0.0083
31	0.0000	0.0000	0.0000	0.0000	0.0001	0.0003	0.0007	0.0015	0.0030	0.0054
32	0.0000	0.0000	0.0000	0.0000	0.0001	0.0001	0.0004	0.0009	0.0018	0.0034
33	0.0000	0.0000	0.0000	0.0000	0.0000	0.0001	0.0002	0.0005	0.0010	0.0020
34	0.0000	0.0000	0.0000	0.0000	0.0000	0.0000	0.0001	0.0002	0.0006	0.0012
35	0.0000	0.0000	0.0000	0.0000	0.0000	0.0000	0.0000	0.0001	0.0003	0.0007
36	0.0000	0.0000	0.0000	0.0000	0.0000	0.0000	0.0000	0.0001	0.0002	0.0004
37	0.0000	0.0000	0.0000	0.0000	0.0000	0.0000	0.0000	0.0000	0.0001	0.0002
38	0.0000	0.0000	0.0000	0.0000	0.0000	0.0000	0.0000	0.0000	0.0000	0.0001
39	0.0000	0.0000	0.0000	0.0000	0.0000	0.0000	0.0000	0.0000	0.0000	0.0001

Source: Reprinted from Handbook of Probability and Statistics with Tables, 2nd ed., by R. S. Burington and D. C. May. New York: McGraw-Hill Book Company, Inc., 1970, by permission of the authors' trustees.

Appendix F

Values of e^{-iN}

To find $e^{-1.5}$, choose $N = 15$ and $i = .10$.

						i						
N	.01	.02	.03	.04	.05	.06	.07	.08	.09	.10	.11	.12
1	0.990	0.980	0.970	0.961	0.951	0.942	0.932	0.923	0.914	0.905	0.896	0.887
2	0.980	0.961	0.942	0.923	0.905	0.887	0.869	0.852	0.835	0.819	0.803	0.787
3	0.970	0.942	0.914	0.887	0.861	0.835	0.811	0.787	0.763	0.741	0.719	0.698
4	0.961	0.923	0.887	0.852	0.819	0.787	0.756	0.726	0.698	0.670	0.644	0.619
5	0.951	0.905	0.861	0.819	0.779	0.741	0.705	0.670	0.638	0.607	0.577	0.549
6	0.942	0.887	0.835	0.787	0.741	0.698	0.657	0.619	0.583	0.549	0.517	0.487
7	0.932	0.869	0.811	0.756	0.705	0.657	0.613	0.571	0.533	0.497	0.463	0.432
8	0.923	0.852	0.787	0.726	0.670	0.619	0.571	0.527	0.487	0.449	0.415	0.383
9	0.914	0.835	0.763	0.698	0.638	0.583	0.533	0.487	0.445	0.407	0.372	0.340
10	0.905	0.819	0.741	0.670	0.607	0.549	0.497	0.449	0.407	0.368	0.333	0.301
11	0.896	0.803	0.719	0.644	0.577	0.517	0.463	0.415	0.372	0.333	0.298	0.267
12	0.887	0.787	0.698	0.619	0.549	0.487	0.432	0.383	0.340	0.301	0.267	0.237
13	0.878	0.771	0.677	0.595	0.522	0.458	0.403	0.353	0.310	0.273	0.239	0.210
14	0.869	0.756	0.657	0.571	0.497	0.432	0.375	0.326	0.284	0.247	0.214	0.186
15	0.861	0.741	0.638	0.549	0.472	0.407	0.350	0.301	0.259	0.223	0.192	0.165
16	0.852	0.726	0.619	0.527	0.449	0.383	0.326	0.278	0.237	0.202	0.172	0.147
17	0.844	0.712	0.600	0.507	0.427	0.361	0.304	0.257	0.217	0.183	0.154	0.130
18	0.835	0.698	0.583	0.487	0.407	0.340	0.284	0.237	0.198	0.165	0.138	0.115
19	0.827	0.684	0.566	0.468	0.387	0.320	0.264	0.219	0.181	0.150	0.124	0.102
20	0.819	0.670	0.549	0.449	0.368	0.301	0.247	0.202	0.165	0.135	0.111	0.091
21	0.811	0.657	0.533	0.432	0.350	0.284	0.230	0.186	0.151	0.122	0.099	0.080
22	0.803	0.644	0.517	0.415	0.333	0.267	0.214	0.172	0.138	0.111	0.089	0.071
23	0.795	0.631	0.502	0.399	0.317	0.252	0.200	0.159	0.126	0.100	0.080	0.063
24	0.787	0.619	0.487	0.383	0.301	0.237	0.186	0.147	0.115	0.091	0.071	0.056
25	0.779	0.607	0.472	0.368	0.287	0.223	0.174	0.135	0.105	0.082	0.064	0.050
26	0.771	0.595	0.458	0.353	0.273	0.210	0.162	0.125	0.096	0.074	0.057	0.044
27	0.763	0.583	0.445	0.340	0.259	0.198	0.151	0.115	0.088	0.067	0.051	0.039
28	0.756	0.571	0.432	0.326	0.247	0.186	0.141	0.106	0.080	0.061	0.046	0.035
29	0.748	0.560	0.419	0.313	0.235	0.176	0.131	0.098	0.074	0.055	0.041	0.031
30	0.741	0.549	0.407	0.301	0.223	0.165	0.122	0.091	0.067	0.050	0.037	0.027

N	13	.14	.15	.16	.17	.18	.19	.20	.21	.22	.23	.24
1	0.878	0.869	0.861	0.852	0.844	0.835	0.827	0.819	0.811	0.803	0.795	0.787
2	0.771	0.756	0.741	0.726	0.712	0.698	0.684	0.670	0.657	0.644	0.631	0.619
3	0.677	0.657	0.638	0.619	0.600	0.583	0.566	0.549	0.533	0.517	0.502	0.487
4	0.595	0.571	0.549	0.527	0.507	0.487	0.468	0.499	0.432	0.415	0.399	0.383
5	0.522	0.497	0.472	0.449	0.427	0.407	0.387	0.368	0.350	0.333	0.317	0.301
6	0.458	0.432	0.407	0.383	0.361	0.340	0.320	0.301	0.284	0.267	0.252	0.237
7	0.403	0.375	0.350	0.326	0.304	0.284	0.264	0.247	0.230	0.214	0.200	0.186
8	0.353	0.326	0.301	0.278	0.257	0.237	0.219	0.202	0.186	0.172	0.159	0.147
9	0.310	0.284	0.259	0.237	0.217	0.198	0.181	0.165	0.151	0.138	0.126	0.115
10	0.273	0.247	0.223	0.202	0.183	0.165	0.150	0.135	0.122	0.111	0.100	0.091
11	0.239	0.214	0.192	0.172	0.154	0.138	0.124	0.111	0.099	0.089	0.080	0.071
12	0.210	0.186	0.165	0.147	0.130	0.115	0.102	0.091	0.080	0.071	0.063	0.056
13	0.185	0.162	0.142	0.125	0.110	0.096	0.085	0.074	0.065	0.057	0.050	0.044
14	0.162	0.141	0.122	0.106	0.093	0.080	0.070	0.061	0.053	0.046	0.040	0.035
15	0.142	0.122	0.105	0.091	0.078	0.067	0.058	0.050	0.043	0.037	0.032	0.027
16	0.125	0.106	0.091	0.077	0.066	0.056	0.048	0.041	0.035	0.030	0.025	0.021
17	0.110	0.093	0.078	0.066	0.056	0.047	0.040	0.033	0.028	0.024	0.020	0.017
18	0.096	0.080	0.067	0.056	0.047	0.039	0.033	0.027	0.023	0.019	0.016	0.013
19	0.085	0.070	0.058	0.048	0.040	0.033	0.027	0.022	0.018	0.015	0.013	0.010
20	0.074	0.061	0.050	0.041	0.033	0.027	0.022	0.018	0.015	0.012	0.010	0.008
21	0.065	0.053	0.043	0.035	0.028	0.023	0.018	0.015	0.012	0.010	0.008	0.006
22	0.057	0.046	0.037	0.030	0.024	0.019	0.015	0.012	0.010	0.008	0.006	0.005
23	0.050	0.040	0.032	0.025	0.020	0.016	0.013	0.010	0.008	0.006	0.005	0.004
24	0.044	0.035	0.027	0.021	0.017	0.013	0.010	0.008	0.006	0.005	0.004	0.003
25	0.039	0.030	0.024	0.018	0.014	0.011	0.009	0.007	0.005	0.004	0.003	0.002
26	0.034	0.026	0.020	0.016	0.012	0.009	0.007	0.006	0.004	0.003	0.003	0.002
27	0.030	0.023	0.017	0.013	0.010	0.008	0.006	0.005	0.003	0.003	0.002	0.002
28	0.026	0.020	0.015	0.011	0.009	0.006	0.005	0.004	0.003	0.002	0.002	0.001
29	0.023	0.017	0.013	0.010	0.007	0.005	0.004	0.003	0.002	0.002	0.001	0.001
30	0.020	0.015	0.011	0.008	0.006	0.005	0.003	0.002	0.002	0.001	0.001	0.001

SOLUTIONS TO EVEN-NUMBERED PROBLEMS

CHAPTER 8

2. The values for percentages of sales attributable to quality costs are the index base for the three products A, B, and C, and their cost categories. However, because no time-phased data per product were provided, no trend can be established for various product indexes. Comparison of the data shows that both internal and external failure costs appear to be much too high for product A, appraisal costs appear to be high for product B in comparison with prevention cost, and both internal failure and appraisal costs appear to be high for product C. However, product C does have a much lower total cost of quality as a percent of total sales. Managers of all product lines should put more emphasis on prevention and attempt to reduce costs in other categories. Also, they should determine what methods are being used in product C to keep the cost of quality low. A spreadsheet should be constructed to show these relationships.

4. The composite index for quality costs for Midwest Sales shows a steady decrease in total quality cost down to $0.16/total sales dollars. Internal failure rates were reduced substantially, from $468.20 in the first quarter to $166.40 in the fourth quarter. External failure rates also showed substantial improvement since the first quarter, dropping from $280.80 to $128.60 in the fourth quarter. Increases in prevention and appraisal expenditures apparently led to improvements in failure costs. The overall index fell by one-third (8 percentage points). Management should maintain or increase the level of prevention and appraisal in an effort to reduce quality costs, especially failure costs. A graph can be constructed from the data in the following table.

Total Sales and Quarterly Quality Costs ($ thousands)

	1	2	3	4
Total sales	$4,120.00	$4,206.00	$4,454.00	$4,106.00
External failure	280.80	208.20	142.80	128.60
Internal failure	468.20	372.40	284.40	166.40
Appraisal	194.20	227.70	274.40	266.20
Prevention	28.40	29.20	50.20	80.20
Total Quality Cost	$971.60	$837.50	$751.80	$641.40

Index of Quality Costs as a % of Sales

	1 Qtr.	2 Qtr.	3 Qtr.	4 Qtr.
External failure	6.82%	4.95%	3.21%	3.13%
Internal failure	11.36	8.85	6.39	4.05
Appraisal	4.71	5.41	6.16	6.48
Prevention	0.69	0.69	1.13	1.95
Total Quality Cost	23.58%	19.91%	16.88%	15.62%
Total Sales/Base Sales	100%	102.09%	108.11%	99.66%

6. The following table shows that total quality costs as a percent of sales ranges from very high to moderate between products. Internal and external failure costs are large for product A, because little appraisal or prevention is done. For product B, defects are being screened out, causing much higher appraisal costs, in total and as a percent of quality costs. However, this method does reduce overall quality costs as a percent of sales (20%) somewhat. Product C attained a good balance among quality cost categories, although a larger percentage of prevention costs might prove to be advantageous. A graph can be constructed from these data.

Sales and Quality Costs ($ millions)

Total Sales	$2.500	$1.800	$2.600			
% Quality Costs	30%	20%	25%			
	Product A	Product B	Product C	Product A	Product B	Product C
External failure	$0.315	$0.072	$0.098	42%	20%	15%
Internal failure	0.338	0.090	0.260	45	25	30
Appraisal	0.090	0.187	0.228	12	52	40
Prevention	0.008	0.011	0.065	1	3	15
Total Quality Cost	$0.750	$0.360	$0.650			

8. The spreadsheet data for the Great Plates Printing Company show that the company may be spending too much on appraisal and internal failure costs and too little on prevention. Improvement efforts should concentrate on the categories of proofreading, press downtime, and correction of typos. A pie chart may be constructed from these data.

Great Plates Printing Company	**Quality Costs ($1,000s)**
External failure	$ 28
Internal failure	615
Appraisal	592
Prevention	71
Total Quality Cost	$1,306

	Percentage of Costs (%)
External failure	2.14%
Internal failure	47.09
Appraisal	45.33
Prevention	5.44
Total Quality Cost	100.00%

10. For the Edison Bank, a detailed report might be prepared by an internal or external quality consultant to the bank as follows:

		Quality Cost Categories	
Cost Elements	**Costs**	**Subtotal**	**Proportion**
APPRAISAL			
1. Run credit checks	$2,675.01		
Loan Payment & Loan Payoffs			
1. Receive, inspect, and process documents (2 items)	1,024.99		
		$3,700.00	

Cost Elements	Quality Cost Categories		
	Costs	Subtotal	Proportion
Inspection			
2. Review documents	3,000.63		
4. Prepare tickler file, etc.	155.75		
5. Review all output	2,243.62		
		$5,400.00	
Total Appraisal Cost		$9,100.00	0.569
PREVENTION			
10. Conduct training	1,500.00		
Total Prevention Cost		$1,500.00	0.094
INTERNAL FAILURE COSTS			
Scrap and Rework			
3. Make document corrections	1,032.65		
6. Correct rejects	425.00		
7. Reconcile incomplete collateral reports	78.34		
9. Compensate for system downtime	519.01		
		$2,055.00	
Loan Payment or Payoff			
2. Respond to inquiries—no coupon	829.65		
2. Research payoff problems	15.35	$ 845.00	
Total Internal Failure Cost		$2,900.00	0.181
EXTERNAL FAILURE COSTS			
8. Handle dealer problem calls, etc.	2,500.00		
		$2,500.00	0.156
Total Costs		$16,000.00	

Analysis:
As one would hope, the external failure costs for the bank are not extremely high at $2,500.00. However, they do represent 15.6 percent of the total quality costs. The process of working with dealers should be investigated to determine whether it can be simplified, better communications established, and problems avoided in the future.

The highest cost category is in appraisal costs at $ 9,100.00 and 56.9 percent of total quality costs. If the categories of "document review" and "review all output" can be reduced without compromising the quality of the lending procedure, these costs could be greatly improved.

The largest internal failure costs are being incurred in the document correction and "Respond to inquiries—no coupon areas" A fairly substantial cost of quality also comes from the "Compensate for system downtime" category. These areas should be investigated to determine whether procedures can be improved in order to reduce costs.

In the prevention area, it appears that not much attention is being given to the need for this activity, since only 9.4 percent of quality costs are for prevention. If training could be given in quality improvement techniques, as well as time spent on quality planning and improvement, then the other cost categories might be reduced with only a modest increase in prevention costs.

12. See the following table for Pareto analysis. A spreadsheet with a Pareto chart should be constructed from these data.

Oakton Paper Co.
Quality Costs and Percentages

	Percent	Cumulative %	Cost
Rejected paper	56.82%	56.82%	$375,000
Customer complaints	15.91	72.73	105,000
Odd lot	10.61	83.33	70,000
High material costs	5.91	89.24	39,000
Downtime	4.24	93.48	28,000
Excess inspection	3.18	96.67	21,000
Testing costs	2.12	98.79	14,000
Quality Imprv. Tmg.	1.21	100.00	8,000
Total Costs			$660,000

Conclusion: Oakton Paper Co. is experiencing problems in two major categories: rejected paper and customer complaints. These categories, which could be related to each other, account for 72.7 percent of their quality costs. Rejected paper suggests a possible technical problem in the chemistry of the materials or paper machine adjustments. If customers perceive that the paper does not meet their requirements, then the causes need to be determined as well. Thus, it may be recommended that two improvement teams be formed, but that they coordinate closely to work on these areas. After these problems have been eliminated, then work could begin on addressing the next two defect areas.

14. Summary data for National Computer Repairs, Inc. are shown. A spreadsheet with a Pareto chart should be constructed from these data.

National Computer Repairs, Inc.
Quality Costs and Percentages

	Percent	Cumulative %	Cost
Customer returns	40.00%	40.00%	$120,000
Workstation downtime	16.67	56.67	50,000
Rework costs	16.67	73.33	50,000
Inspection—out	11.67	85.00	35,000
Training/improvement	10.00	95.00	30,000
Inspection—in	5.00	100.00	15,000
Total Costs			$300,000

The data show that two categories of customer returns and workstation downtime total 56.7 percent of the defects. These two are possibly related and may indicate "short staffing" and lack of training of setup personnel. Only 10 percent of total quality cost is allocated to prevention (training/improvement). Steps should be taken to analyze root causes for these problem areas in order to correct them as quickly as possible.

16. Because nothing is mentioned here about the Herzberg Company using discounted present value, simplified calculating methods, not considering the time value of the money invested, are used in the following solutions:

a) Lost profits = ($20/sale × 900,000)/5 = $3,600,000 per year

b) Recovered profits = .10 × $3,600,000 = $360,000

So, return on quality for each year is $360,000/$300,000 = 120, or 1.20% return. This result means that the investment will pay for itself in approximately 10 months of savings each year.

CHAPTER 10

2. To calculate the dpmo, we use 13/35 to get the number of defects per unit (DPUs). However, 60 opportunities per aircraft checked must be taken into consideration, as shown, in order to calculate dpmo.

dpmo = (18/35)(1,000,000/60) = 8571.4, which is less than 4 sigma with off-centering of 1.5 sigma.

4. No indication is given of how many opportunities for defects occur per component, so assume that the defect rate is 1 per 1,000 units produced. Therefore, only 750 defective items (0.001 × 750,000) were produced. Calculate dpmo as follows:

dpmo = (1/1000)(1,000,000) = 1,000, which is slightly better than 4.5 sigma with off-centering of 1.5 sigma.

CHAPTER 11

2. One of the advantages of using Excel spreadsheets is that a great deal of analysis can be done easily. The summary statistics follow. A histogram may be constructed by using Excel's Data Analysis tools (found under the "Tools" heading on the spreadsheet). For best results in constructing the histogram, it is suggested that you set up their own "bins" so as to provide 7 to 10 approximately equal-sized class intervals for the data. Note that if the program finds that the classes shown in the bins do not extend over the upper or lower range of the data, it will automatically compensate by adding a "Less" or "More" category for the outliers.

Column 1	
Mean	3.5910
Standard Error	0.0809
Median	3.6500
Mode	3.6000
Standard Deviation	0.8088
Sample Variance	0.6542
Kurtosis	−0.2919
Skewness	−0.2404
Range	3.6000
Minimum	1.7000
Maximum	5.3000
Sum	359.1000
Count	100.0000
Confidence Level (95.0%)	0.1605

The conclusion that can be reached from looking at the summary statistics and the histogram (not shown) is that these data are fairly normally distributed, with some slight skewing to the left.

4.

Descriptive Statistics	
Column 1	
Mean	38.6700
Standard Error	0.0456
Median	38.7000
Mode	38.4000
Standard Deviation	0.4556
Sample Variance	0.2076
Range	2.6000
Minimum	37.3000
Maximum	39.9000
Sum	3867.0000
Count	100.0000

The conclusion that can be reached from looking at the summary statistics and the histogram (that must be constructed "by hand" or by using the Excel spreadsheet) is that these data are fairly normally distributed, with some slight skewing to the right.

6. For cans of New Orleans Punch the mean, $\mu = 15.8$; the standard deviation, $\sigma = 0.10$

$$z = \frac{x - \mu}{\sigma} = \frac{16 - 15.8}{0.10} = 2.0$$

$$P(x > 16) = 0.5000 - P\,(0 < z < 2.0)$$

$$P(z > 16) = 0.5000 - 0.4772 = 0.0228$$

(Results are based on the Standard Normal Table in Appendix A.)

8. (Results are based on the Standard Normal Distribution Table in Appendix A.) Given the standard deviation for OutBack Beer of $\sigma = 5$ ml,

$$z = -1.64 = \frac{535 - \mu}{5}\,; \therefore \mu = 543.2\ \text{ml}$$

10. The mean, $\mu = 12.1$; the standard deviation, $\sigma = 0.05$

$$P(x < 12.0) = 0.5000 - P\,(12.0 < x < 12.1)$$

$$z = \frac{x - \mu}{\sigma} = \frac{12.0 - 12.1}{0.05} = -2.0$$

(Results are based on the Standard Normal Distribution Table in Appendix A.)

$$P\,(z < 12.0) = 0.5000 - 0.4772 = 0.0228$$

Thus, 2.28% will have less than 12 oz.

$P(x > 12.1) = 0.5000$ or, expressed another way:

$$z = \frac{x - \mu}{\sigma} = \frac{12.1 - 12.1}{0.05} = 0$$

$P(x > 12.1) = 0.5000 - P(0 < z < 0) = 0.5000 - 0 = 0.5000$

Thus, 50.0% will have more than 12.1 oz.

12. An older statistics book from the library may have to be consulted in order to find background information on the formulas used for grouped statistics in solving this problem. See the following table and use class midpoints estimated from the given cells. (Note that the data have been resorted in descending order to conform to the format in the Excel statistical package.)

Class	mp (x)	f	fx	fx^2
1	37.35	1	37.35	1395.023
2	37.65	3	112.95	4252.568
3	37.95	8	303.60	11521.620
4	38.25	26	994.50	38039.625
5	38.55	29	1117.95	43096.973
6	38.85	15	582.75	22639.838
7	39.15	13	508.95	19925.393
8	39.45	4	157.80	6225.210
9	39.75	1	39.75	1580.063
		100	3,855.60	148,676.313

a. $\bar{x} = \dfrac{\Sigma fx}{n} = \dfrac{3,855.6}{100} = 38.556$ (vs. 38.632 from the actual data in problem 11-3)

$s = \sqrt{\dfrac{\Sigma fx^2}{n-1} - \dfrac{\Sigma (fx)^2/n}{n-1}} = \sqrt{\dfrac{148,676.313}{99} - \dfrac{(3,855.6)^2/100}{99}} = 0.4472$ (versus .4436 from the data in problem 11-3)

b. The conclusion that can be reached from looking at the summary statistics and a histogram (not shown) is that these data are fairly normally distributed, with some slight skewing to the right. More detailed data can be found by constructing a spreadsheet and histogram from these data.

c. A normal probability plot shows that the data are approximately normally distributed, with an R-square value of 0.939.

14. Specification for answer time is:
H_0: Mean response time: $\mu_1 \leq 0.10$
H_1: Mean response time: $\mu_1 > 0.10$
$\bar{x}_1 = 0.1023$; $s_1 = 0.0183$

and the t-test is:

$$t_1 = \frac{\bar{x} - 0.10}{s/\sqrt{n}} = \frac{0.1023 - 0.10}{0.0183/\sqrt{30}} = \frac{0.0023}{0.0033} = 0.697, \, t_{29,\,.05} = 1.699$$

Specification for service time is:

H_0: Mean service time: $\mu_2 \leq 0.50$
H_1: Mean service time: $\mu_2 > 0.50$
$\bar{x}_2 = 0.5290$; $s_2 = 0.0902$

and the t-test is:

$$t_2 = \frac{\bar{x} - 0.50}{s/\sqrt{n}} = \frac{0.529 - 0.50}{0.0902/\sqrt{30}} = \frac{0.029}{0.0165} = 1.761, \, t_{29,\,.05} = 1.699$$

Because $t_{29,\,.05} = 1.699$, we cannot reject the null hypothesis for t_1 but we can reject the hypothesis for t_2. Therefore, there is no statistical evidence that the mean response time exceeds 0.10 for the answer component, but the statistical evidence does support the service component.

Note: **Problems 16 and 18 are related to materials on sample size determination contained in the Bonus Materials on the student CD-ROM.**

16. The size of the population is irrelevant to this problem, although it is good to know that it is sizable. Therefore, make the following calculations:

$n = (z_{\alpha/2})^2 \, p \, (1 - p)/E^2 = (1.96)^2 \, (0.07)(0.93)/(0.02)^2 = 625.22$; use 626

18. Using the formula $n = (z_{\alpha/2})^2 \, p \, (1 - p)/E^2$, we can solve for $z_{\alpha/2}$ as follows:

$800 = (z_{\alpha/2})^2 \, (0.10)(0.90)/(0.02)^2$

$800 = (z_{\alpha/2})^2 \, (225)$

$(z_{\alpha/2})^2 = 800/225$

$(z_{\alpha/2})^2 = \sqrt{3.556} = 1.886$; use 1.87

From the Standard Normal Distribution table in Appendix A, we find a probability of 0.4693 for $z = 1.87$. Because it is only one tail of the distribution, we multiply the area by 2 to get the confidence level of 0.9386. Thus, the management engineer can only be almost 94 percent confident of her results based on this sample size.

20. Calculations of the main effects are as follows:

Signal
High $(18 + 12 + 16 + 10)/\,4 = 14$
Low $(8 + 11 + 7 + 14)/\,4 = 10$
High – Low $= 4$

Material
Gold $= (18 + 12 + 8 + 11)/\,4 = 12.25$
Silicon $= (16 + 10 + 7 + 14)/\,4 = 11.75$
Gold – Silicon $= 12.25 - 11.75 = 0.5$

Temperature
Low = (18 + 16 + 8 + 7)/ 4 = 12.25
High = (12 + 10 + 11 + 14)/ 4 = 11.75
Low – High = 12.25 – 11.75 = 0.5

The main effects of the "signal" far outweigh the effects of material and temperature, indicating that these factors are insignificant. Therefore, interaction effects will be negligible.

CHAPTER 12

2. With the new data given for Bob's customers, a partial House of Quality for the design of the burger itself can be built (see the following outline). Note that the relationships between customer requirements (flavor, health, value) and associated technical requirements (% fat, calories, sodium, price) of the burger design will be strong.

   The interrelationships of the roof may be sketched in. For example, they would show a strong interrelationship between fat and calories.

PARTIAL HOUSE OF QUALITY MATRIX

Bob's Big Burgers

		Price	Size	Calories	Sodium	% Fat	Importance 1 2 3 4 5	Compet. Eval. 1 2 3 4 5	Selling Pts. 1 2 3 4 5
Taste	Moistness								
	Flavor								
Visual	Visually Appealing								
Healthy	Nutritious								
Value	Good Value								
Competitive Evaluation: Grabby's Queenburger Sandy's									
Targets									
Deployment									

● = Very strong relationship

○ = Strong relationship

▲ = Weak relationship

Bob's Big Burgers' technical requirements must be placed on a more equal basis, which would best be shown as units/ounce, except for the percent fat value. These values could be entered in a table with labels, shown as follows.

Company	Price/oz.	Calories/oz.	Sodium/oz.	% Fat
Grabby's				
Queenburger				
Sandy's				

This analysis suggests that Bob's should try to increase its size and visual appeal, while reducing the cost per ounce. At the same time, it should build on the strength of the nutrition trend keeping the sodium and percent fat low, as did Grabby's, and slightly reducing the number of calories per ounce to be more competitive. If Bob's can design a flavorful, healthy, 7 oz. burger and sell it at an attractive price (say, $1.85 or less), it should be a very profitable undertaking.

4. With the new data given for Fingerspring's potential customers, a partial House of Quality for the design of the PDA can be built as suggested by the form as outlined here. Take note of the strong relationships between customer requirements and associated technical requirements of the PDA design.

The interrelationships of the roof may be sketched in. For example, they would show a strong interrelationship between size and weight.

PARTIAL HOUSE OF QUALITY MATRIX

For Fingerspring's PDA Case

		Cost	Size (in.)	Wt. (oz.)	Featr. (num.)	Opr. Prog.	Bat. Life	Opr. Cost	Importance 1 2 3 4 5	Compet. Eval. 1 2 3 4 5	Selling Pts. 1 2 3 4 5
Reliable	Keeps operating										
Compact	Fits pocket										
	Not heavy										
Features	Calendar, contact mgt., etc.										
Ease of use	Intuitive operations										
Value	Good value										
Competitive Evaluation: Fingerspring Springbok Greenspring											
Targets											
Deployment											

This analysis suggests that Fingerspring should try to position itself between Springbok and Greenspring in price and features. It should build on the strength of the customer's reliability concern, keeping battery life up near 35 hours and using a proven operating program, such as PalmOS. Enough features (10) should be offered to be competitive. If Fingerspring can design a high-value PDA and sell it at an attractive price (say, $350 or less), it should be a very profitable undertaking.

6. Based on the cumulative failure rate curve:

From $0 - 30$, slope $= 29/30 = 0.967$
From $30 - 60$, slope $= (35 - 29)/(60 - 30) = 0.200$
From $60 - 90$, slope $= (65 - 35)/(90 - 60) = 1.000$
From $0 - 100$, slope $= 90/100 = 0.9$

8. a. $P(x > 56{,}000) = 0.5 - P\ (50{,}000 < x < 56{,}000)$

$$P(50{,}000 < x < 56{,}000) = P\left(z < \frac{56{,}000 - 50{,}000}{3{,}000}\right) = P(0 < z < 2.0) = 0.4772$$

Therefore, $P(x > 56{,}000) = 0.5 - 0.4772 = 0.0228$ should survive beyond 56,000 miles.

b. $P(x < 47{,}000) = P\left(z < \dfrac{47{,}000 - 50{,}000}{3{,}000}\right) = P(z < -1.00) = 0.5 - P(47{,}000 < x < 50{,}000) = 0.5 - 0.3413 = 0.1587$

c. The distribution for part a looks approximately as follows:

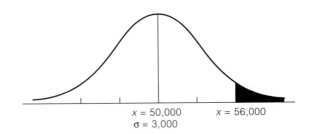

$x = 50{,}000$ $x = 56{,}000$
$\sigma = 3{,}000$

d. Let x_w be the limit of the warranty period.

$$P(x < x_w) = 0.10;\ z = -2.33,\ \text{for } z = \frac{x - 50{,}000}{3{,}000} = -2.33,$$

$x_w = 43{,}010$ miles for the warranty limit.

10. The reliability function is $R(T) = 1 - F(T) = e^{-\lambda T}$

$\lambda = 0.002;\ R(T) = P(x < 400) = 1 - e^{-0.002\ (400)} = 1 - 0.449 = 0.551$

12. Mean days between breakdowns $\bar{x} = 180$, $s = 10$, using 365 days per year.

For no preventive maintenance: $365/180 = 2.028$ breakdowns per year

2.028 breakdowns/year $\times$ $750{,}000$/breakdown $= \$1{,}521{,}000$

For a 1% chance of breakdown, let x be time between maintenance:

$\dfrac{x - 180}{10} = -2.33,\ x = 156.7$ days

$365/156.7 = 2.329$ maintenance checks per year

$$2.329 \times \$500{,}000/\text{check} \;=\; \$1{,}164{,}500.00$$
$$+\; 0.01 \times 2.329 \times \$750{,}000 \;=\; \underline{\qquad 17{,}467.50}$$

Total $\$1{,}181{,}967.50$

For a 0.5% chance of breakdown, let x be time between maintenance:

$$\frac{x-180}{10} = -2.58, \; x = 154.2 \text{ days}$$

$365/154.2 = 2.367$ maintenance checks

$$2.367 \times \$500{,}000/\text{check} \;=\; \$1{,}183{,}500.00$$
$$+\; 0.005 \times 2.367 \times \$750{,}000 \;=\; \underline{\qquad 8{,}876.25}$$

Total $\$1{,}192{,}376.25$

Therefore, we may conclude that preventive maintenance is worthwhile.

14. The reliability of the parallel R_{cc} shown in the diagram above the problem is calculated as follows:

$$R_{cc} = 1 - (1 - 0.90)^2 = 0.99$$
$$R_a R_b R_{cc} R_d = (0.96)(0.98)(0.99)(0.99) = 0.922$$

16. a. $R_a R_b R_c = (0.80)(0.90)(0.98) = 0.706$

    b. $R_{aa} R_{bb} R_{cc} = [1 - (1 - 0.80)^2][1 - (1 - 0.90)^2][1 - (1 - 0.98)^2] =$
    $(0.96)(0.99)(0.9996) = 0.950$

18. Spreadsheets should be constructed in order to calculate and analyze frequency statistics, histograms, etc.

    Accuracy of: Accuracy of:
    Scale A   Scale B

$$100 \times \frac{\text{Abs}\,[113.96 - 114]}{114} = 0.035\% \qquad 100 \times \frac{\text{Abs}\,[115.92 - 114]}{114} = 1.685\%$$

Scale A is more accurate.

The frequency distribution, taken from the Excel printout, shows that Scale B is more precise than Scale A.

Scale B is a better instrument, because it is likely that it can be adjusted to center on the nominal value of 0.

SCALE A FREQUENCY TABLE FOR PROBLEM 12-18(a)				
	Upper Cell Boundaries	Frequencies	Standard Statistical Measures	
Cell 7	116.00	2	Mean	113.96
Cell 6	115.33	6	Median	114
Cell 5	114.67	0	Mode	114
Cell 4	114.00	9	Standard deviation	1.14
Cell 3	113.33	5	Variance	1.29
Cell 2	112.67	0	Max	116
Cell 1	112.00	3	Min	112
			Range	4

SCALE B FREQUENCY TABLE FOR PROBLEM 12-18(b)				
	Upper Cell Boundaries	Frequencies	Standard Statistical Measures	
Cell 5	118.00	2	Mean	115.92
Cell 4	117.33	5	Median	116
Cell 3	116.00	10	Mode	116
Cell 2	115.33	5	Standard deviation	1.12
Cell 1	114.00	3	Variance	1.24
			Max	118
			Min	114
			Range	4

20. Note that the range in sample 7 exceeded the control limit of 0.302 for the first operator. This point could have been due to a misreading of the gauge. If so, this sample should be thrown out, another one taken, and the values recomputed. Detailed spreadsheet data can be obtained by inputs to the R&R spreadsheet template on the student CD-ROM. Spreadsheet results are as follows:

			Tolerance analysis
Average range	0.117	Repeatability (EV) 0.3579	89.47%
X-bar range	0.058	Reproducibility (AV) 0.1423187	35.58%
		Repeatability and Reproducibility (R&R) 0.3851275	96.28%
		Control limit for individual ranges 0.30272	

Note: Any ranges beyond this limit may be the result of assignable causes. Identify and correct. Discard values and recompute statistics.

22. The Taguchi loss function is $L(x) = k(x - T)^2$
$25 = k (0.05)^2$
$k = 10,000$
$\therefore L(x) = k(x - T)^2 = 10,000 (x - T)^2$

24. The Taguchi loss function is $L(x) = k(x - T)^2$

a. $17.50 = k(0.05)^2$
$k = 7,000$
$\therefore L(x) = k(x - T)^2 = 7,000 (x - T)^2$

b. $L(x) = 7,000 (x - T)^2$
$\therefore L(0.020) = 7,000(0.020)^2 = 2.80

26. The Taguchi loss function is $L(x) = k(x - T)^2$
$50 = k(0.1)^2$
$k = 5,000$
$\therefore L(x) = k(x - T)^2 = 5,000k (x - T)^2$

28. For a specification of 7.5 ± 0.1 grams:

a. $L(x) = k(x - T)^2$
$0.04 = k(0.1)^2$
$k = 4

b. For σ = 0.05
   $EL(x) = k(\sigma^2 + D^2) = 4(0.05^2 + 0^2) = \$0.01$

30. For a specification of 6 ± 1.25 minutes and a $12 scrap cost:
    $\bar{x} = 6.016;\ D = 6.016 - 6.00 = 0.016$
    σ = 0.8957

   a. $L(x) = k(x - T)^2$
      $\$12 = k(1.25)^2;\ \therefore k = 7.68$

   b. $E[L(x) = k(\sigma^2 + D^2)] = 7.68(0.8957^2 + 0.016^2) = \$6.163$

32. a. The Taguchi loss function is $L(x) = k(x - T)^2$
       $250 = k(20)^2$
       $k = 0.625$

       So, $L(x) = 0.625(x - T)^2$

   b. $\$1.75 = 0.625(x - 120)^2$
      $2.80 = (x - 120)^2$

      $(x - T)_{\text{Tolerance}} = \sqrt{2.80} = 1.673$ volts
      ∴ $x = 121.673$

34. For sample statistics of $\bar{x} = 0.5750;$ σ = 0.0065

    $C_p = \dfrac{UTL - LTL}{6\sigma} = \dfrac{0.575 - 0.545}{6(0.0065)} = 0.769;$ not capable, unsatisfactory

36. Summary statistics are shown. A histogram should be constructed for further analysis using a spreadsheet.

Column 1	
Mean	24.0014
Standard Error	0.00097
Median	24.001
Mode	24.000
Standard Deviation	0.00967
Sample Variance	9.4E-05
Kurtosis	0.53132
Skewness	0.05271
Range	0.058
Minimum	23.971
Maximum	24.029
Confidence Level (95.0%)	0.00192

Bin	Frequency
23.971	1
23.977	0
23.983	0
23.988	7
23.994	14
24.000	26
24.006	20
24.012	19
24.017	7
24.023	5
More	1

For sample statistics of $\bar{x} = 24.0014$; $s = 0.0097$

Specification limits for the process are $23.97 \le \mu \le 24.03$

$z = \dfrac{24.0300 - 24.0014}{0.0097} = 2.95$; $P(z > 2.94) = (0.5 - 0.4984) = 0.0016$ that items will exceed upper limit

$z = \dfrac{23.9700 - 24.0014}{0.0097} = -3.24$; $P(z < -3.24) = 0.00$ that items will exceed lower limit

Therefore, the percent outside is 0.0016, or 0.16%.

$C_p = \dfrac{\text{UTL} - \text{LTL}}{6s} = \dfrac{24.030 - 23.970}{6(0.0097)} = 1.031$

$C_{pu} = \dfrac{\text{UTL} - \bar{x}}{3s} = \dfrac{24.030 - 24.0014}{3(0.0097)} = 0.983$

$C_{pl} = \dfrac{\bar{x} - \text{LTL}}{3s} = \dfrac{24.0014 - 23.970}{3(0.0097)} = 1.079$

The process capability indexes are slightly out of tolerance for the upper index, and within minimum limits for the lower and overall index. These results indicate that the process may be minimally adequate if it can be centered on the nominal dimension of 24. However, the ideal situation would be to launch process improvement studies so that the capability indexes could be at least doubled.

38. Omega Parts Ltd.'s process capability results from the Excel spreadsheet software are shown.

Average	0.0764
Standard Deviation	0.0104

C_p	0.8019
C_{pl}	0.8468
C_{pu}	0.7569
C_{pk}	0.7569

These data show that the process has a rather low overall capability, with $C_p = 0.8019$, and a total of 1.71% of the values falling outside of the specification limits of 0.05–0.10.

Process statistics: $\bar{x} = 0.0764$, $\mu = 0.0104$

$z = \dfrac{0.10 - 0.0764}{0.0104} = 2.27$; $P(z > 2.27) = (0.5 - 0.4884) = 0.0116$ that the part will exceed upper limit

$z = \dfrac{0.05 - 0.0764}{0.0104} = -2.54$; $P(z < -2.54) = (0.5 - 0.4945) = 0.0055$ that the part will exceed lower limit

Therefore, the percent outside is: 0.0171, or 1.71%

40. $C_p = \dfrac{UTL - LTL}{6\sigma} = 2.0 = \dfrac{5.60 - 5.20}{6\sigma} = \dfrac{0.4}{6\sigma}$; therefore, $\sigma = 0.033$

$C_{pu} = \dfrac{UTL - \bar{x}}{3\sigma} = \dfrac{5.60 - \bar{x}}{3\sigma} = 2.0$; therefore, we get $\bar{x} = 5.4$

$C_{pl} = \dfrac{\bar{x} - LTL}{3\sigma} = \dfrac{\bar{x} - 5.20}{3\sigma} = 2.0$; therefore, we get $\bar{x} = 5.4$

CHAPTER 13

2. A flowchart should be developed to show the process. The most serious problem from the standpoint of customer service is the potential for a 12-hour delay before an order reaches the supervisor for error checking, and another 3–4 hours may be required before entry into the computer. Obviously, too much checking and handling of the order occurred, and much of it was many hours after the customer and order information had originally been taken. Suggestions for improvement include processing small batches of orders (perhaps within 1–2 hours, or less); building in error checking, perhaps through direct entry of telephone orders into the computer; and many others.

4. Construction of a histogram will show that the assembly time for the computer component is concentrated in the two periods from 9 up to 14 minutes and from 15 up to 18 minutes, which shows a bi-modal distribution. The highest frequency is for 16 minutes. Many students (more than 50 percent) appear to be much slower than the average (14.15 minutes) in the class. Other conclusions should follow.

6. A histogram shows that, although the data are fairly uniformly distributed, 14 points are above the upper specification limit of 2.55 cm and 3 points are below the lower specification limit of 2.45 cm. It is likely that the process needs to be improved, with the first step being the removal of any special causes.

8. The scatter diagram shows an interesting and counter intuitive result. As the production rate increases, the defect rate decreases. Reasons should be advanced for these results.

10. For the Hensley automobile dealership problem, a comprehensive analysis is required. Chase and Stewart point out that ". . . poke-yokes are either *warnings* that signal the existence of a problem or *controls* that stop production until the problem is resolved." The following are only suggestions of the type of poke-yokes that are relevant in services.

Classification of Errors	Poka-Yoke "Fix" Examples
Task	Color-coded tags on vehicle roof to identify service order/advisor
Treatment	Smile, greeting with, "Hello, Ms. Smith, welcome to Hensley."
Tangible	Clean uniforms; waiting areas clean, with rugs, fresh coffee
Preparation	Appointment reminder calls; customer bring warranty paperwork
Encounter	Staple correct (legible) copy (not company's copy) of credit card receipt to customer's bill
Resolution	Customer satisfaction card given to customer when keys returned

12. From the following table, which can be used to construct a Pareto diagram, we can conclude that 55 percent of the problems are with long delays and another 25.2 percent are due to shipping errors, for a total in the top two categories of 80.2 percent. These categories should be improved first.

Dot.Com Apparel House
Quality Errors and Percentages

	Percent	Cumulative %	Frequency
Long delays	54.98%	54.98%	5,372
Shipping errors	25.18	80.16	2,460
Delivery errors	7.69	87.85	752
Electronic charge errors	6.65	94.50	650
Billing errors	5.50	100.00	537
Total			9,771

14. The data on the syringes can be graphed and will show a suspicious pattern that indicates the process may be unstable. Ten values from samples 20 to 29 are alternating above and below the average, indicating that some instability may be found in the system and should be carefully investigated.

CHAPTER 14

2. a. Descriptive statistics for Wilmer Machine Co., based on all 50 samples, are shown. The histogram (not shown) will exhibit the "classic" bell curve shape.

Descriptive Statistics for Problem 14-2	
Mean	3.526
Standard Error	0.044
Median	3.565
Mode	3.610
Standard Deviation	0.417
Sample Variance	0.174
Kurtosis	−0.383
Skewness	0.163
Range	1.790
Minimum	2.690
Maximum	4.480
Sum	317.340
Count	90.000

Bin	Frequency
2.69	1
2.89	6
3.09	7
3.29	12
3.49	12
3.68	26
3.88	8
4.08	7
4.28	5
More	5

b. Results from 30 samples of 3 when plotted on $\bar{x}$- and R-charts, show that the R-chart is apparently in control for the Wilmer Machine Co. However, on the chart, means for samples 11–18 fall below the center line (violating the rule that fewer than eight consecutive points should on the same side of the mean). Assignable causes should be determined and eliminated, and control limits should be recalculated.

4. For the center lines, $CL_{\bar{x}} : \bar{\bar{x}} = 400; CL_R : \bar{R} = 30$

Control limits for the $\bar{x}$-chart are $\bar{\bar{x}} \pm A_2\bar{R}$
$UCL_{\bar{x}} = \bar{\bar{x}} + A_2\bar{R} = 400 + (0.483)30 = 414.49$
$LCL_{\bar{x}} = \bar{\bar{x}} - A_2\bar{R} = 400 - (0.483)30 = 385.51$

For the R-chart: $UCL_R = D_4\bar{R} = (2.004)30 = 60.12$
$\qquad\qquad\quad LCL_R = D_3\bar{R} = 0$

Estimated $\sigma = \bar{R}/d_2 = 30/2.534 = 11.839$

6. When plotted on $\bar{x}$- and R-charts, the following results are found:

For the center lines, $CL_{\bar{x}} : \bar{\bar{x}} = 95.378; CL_R : \bar{R} = 0.667$

Control limits for the $\bar{x}$-chart are:
$\bar{\bar{x}} \pm A_2\bar{R} = 95.378 \pm (0.729)0.667 = 94.891$ to 95.864

For the R-chart: $UCL_R = D_4\bar{R} = (2.282)0.667 = 1.522$
$\qquad\qquad\quad LCL_R = D_3\bar{R} = 0$

See control charts as constructed. Note that points 17, 23, and 27 are outside the lower control limit. It is obvious from the $\bar{x}$-chart and the R-chart (point 26) that this process is not in control. It must be brought under control before control charts can be used.

8. a. For the Inky-U Printing Co., and based on $\bar{x}$- and R-chart results:

For the center lines, $CL_{\bar{x}} : \bar{\bar{x}} = 46.496;\ CL_R : \bar{R} = 1.653$

Control limits for the $\bar{x}$-chart are:
$\bar{\bar{x}} \pm A_2\bar{R} = 46.496 \pm (0.729)1.653 = 45.291$ to 47.701

For the R-chart: $UCL_R = D_4\bar{R} = (2.282)1.653 = 3.772$
$\qquad\qquad LCL_R = D_3\bar{R} = 0$

Although some unusual patterns appear in both charts, none give a strictly out of control signal. Sample-to-sample variation in the $\bar{x}$-chart seems to decrease after about the tenth sample. Samples 8–12 of the R-chart show an unusual high-to-low pattern also.

b. The additional samples show Inky-U's process gradually going out of control. This shift becomes noticeable with samples 35–43 all appearing above the center line. In addition, the R-chart goes out of control at sample 38. The process should have been stopped at sample 38 and action taken to correct the special causes of the problem.

10. Based on spreadsheets of $\bar{x}$- and R-charts (*Note:* Three runs will have to be made.):

We can see from the original R-chart for General Hydraulics, Inc., that samples 4, 8, and 22 are out of control on their ranges. Although sample 14 is not out of control limits on the current chart, it will no doubt be so in the next iteration, so it should be removed also.

a. For the center lines, $CL_{\bar{x}} : \bar{\bar{x}} = 10.587;\ CL_R : \bar{R} = 0.438$

Control limits for the $\bar{x}$-chart are:
$\bar{\bar{x}} \pm A_2\bar{R} = 10.585 \pm 0.729(0.438) = 10.268$ to 10.906

For the R-chart: $UCL_R = D_4\bar{R} = 2.282(0.438) = 1.000$
$\qquad\qquad LCL_R = D_3\bar{R} = 0$

b. After dropping the four previously mentioned points:

For the **revised** $\bar{x}$-chart:
The new center lines, $CL_{\bar{x}} : \bar{\bar{x}} = 10.587;\ CL_R : \bar{R} = 0.336$
$\bar{\bar{x}} \pm A_2\bar{R} = 10.587 \pm 0.729(0.336) = 10.342$ to 10.832

For the **revised** R-chart: $UCL_R = D_4\bar{R} = 2.282(0.336) = 0.767$
$\qquad\qquad\qquad\qquad\quad LCL_R = D_3\bar{R} = 0$

c. The additional data show that General Hydraulics' process is still operating within control limits. However, new sample number 5 is just under the upper control limit of the $\bar{x}$-chart.

12. Analysis of these control charts show the following:
    a. Two points outside upper control limit.
    b. Process is in control.
    c. Mean shift upward in second half of control chart.
    d. Points hugging upper and lower control limits.

14. After constructing a control chart for "individuals," (see templates on the student CD-ROM), we find:

    a. For the center lines, $CL_{\bar{x}}: \bar{x} = 0.0762$; $CL_R: \bar{R} = 0.0023$

    Estimated $\sigma = \bar{R}/d_2 = 0.0023/1.128 = 0.00204$; actual $\sigma = 0.00204$
    $\pm 3\sigma_{est} = 0.0762 \pm 3(0.00204) = 0.0701$ to 0.0823;
    $\pm 3\sigma_{actual} = 0.0762 \pm 3(0.00204) = 0.0701$ to 0.0823

    These limits apply to *individual items* only. In this case, a "perfect" estimate of the standard deviation was based on the moving range, using 2. An estimate so accurate will not happen in every case because $\sigma = \bar{R}/d_2$ is only an estimator for the population standard deviation. Individual items can only be plotted on $\bar{x}$-charts.

    b. To understand how $\bar{x}$-chart and R-chart results differ in comparison with the preceding charts for individuals, charts (not shown) can be caluculated with these limits:

    For the $\bar{x}$-chart:
    $\bar{\bar{x}} \pm A_2\bar{R} = 0.0762 \pm 0.577(0.0049) = 0.0734$ to 0.0790

    For the R-chart: $UCL_R = D_4\bar{R} = 2.114(0.0049) = 0.0103$ (ignore rounding error)
    $$LCL_R = D_3\bar{R} = 0$$

    Of course, these limits apply to sample groups of five items each.

    c. The comparisons of process capability using the estimated σ value are shown on the following table. Note that C_p, C_{pl}, C_{pu}, and C_{pk} from the spreadsheet are based on estimated values using $\sigma = \bar{R}/d_2 = 0.0049/2.236 = 0.00219$.

Nominal specification	0.076
Upper tolerance limit	0.085
Lower tolerance limit	0.067

| Average | 0.0762 |
| Standard Deviation | 0.0049 |

C_p	1.4338
C_{pl}	1.3998
C_{pu}	1.4678
C_{pk}	1.3998

Actual $\sigma = 0.00204$, as calculated previously, would make a slight difference in process capability calculations.

16. Process capability can be determined based on the following:

For the center lines, $CL_{\bar{x}}: \bar{\bar{x}} = 51.80$; $CL_R: \bar{R} = 17.66$

Control limits for the $\bar{x}$-chart are:
$\bar{\bar{x}} \pm A_2\bar{R} = 51.80 \pm 0.577(17.66) = 41.61$ to 61.99

For the R-chart: $UCL_R = D_4\bar{R} = 2.114(17.66) = 37.33$
$\qquad\qquad\quad LCL_R = D_3\bar{R} = 0$

These limits apply to sample groups of five items each.

Estimated $\sigma = \bar{R}/d_2 = 17.66/2.326 = 7.59$

A process capability analysis is only justified if the process is in control. The fact that the process is thought to be normally distributed does not establish that it is in control. The $\bar{x}$- and R-charts, when plotted, do show that the process is in control.

Nominal specification	50
Upper tolerance limit	75
Lower tolerance limit	25

Average	51.80
Standard Deviation	17.66

C_p	1.098
C_{pl}	1.176
C_{pu}	1.018
C_{pk}	1.018

The capability indexes show that the capability is adequate.

18. With data from Problem 7 and USL = 475 and LSL = 325, note that the spreadsheet template for process capability uses an **estimated** standard deviation of $\sigma = \bar{R}/d_2 = 30.957 / 1.693 = 18.285$. As shown on the spreadsheet:

$C_p = 1.367$
$C_{pl} = 1.362$
$C_{pu} = 1.372$
$C_{pk} = 1.372$

When the **actual** standard deviation of: $\sigma = 18.807$ has been calculated, we obtain modified values for C_p, C_{pl}, C_{pu}, and C_{pk}:

Nominal specification	400
Upper tolerance limit	475
Lower tolerance limit	325

Average	400.290
Standard Deviation	18.807

C_p	1.329
C_{pl}	1.334
C_{pu}	1.324
C_{pk}	1.324

0% outside indicates that the process is well within specification limits.

The modified control limits are:

$URL_x = US - A_m\bar{R} = 475 - (0.749)(30.957) = 451.813$
$LRL_x = LS + A_m\bar{R} = 325 + (0.749)(30.957) = 348.187$

20. Based on the $\bar{x}$- and R-charts that are constructed:

a. Note that coded data should be used on the control chart. For example, 75 represents 3.9375. Parameters for the charts will be calculated in coded form and "translated" at the end of the problem.

For the center lines, $CL_{\bar{x}} : \bar{\bar{x}} = 77.435$ (actual = 3.93774); $CL_R : \bar{R} = 3.300$ (actual = 0.00033)

Control limits for the $\bar{x}$-chart are:
$\bar{\bar{x}} \pm A_2\bar{R} = 77.435 \pm 0.577(3.300) = 75.531$ to 79.339

For the R-chart: $UCL_R = D_4\bar{R} = 2.114(3.300) = 6.976$
$\qquad\qquad\qquad LCL_R = D_3\bar{R} = 0$

Although the tendency is for the data to hug the center line, the control charts establish that the process is in control.

b. These limits apply to sample groups of five items each.
% outside calculations are based on specification limits for individual items.

Estimated $\sigma = \bar{R}/d_2 = 3.300/2.326 = 1.419$

$\therefore C_p = \dfrac{UTL - LTL}{6\sigma} = \dfrac{80 - 75}{6(1.419)} = 0.5873$; very poor capability

The % outside calculation is performed as follows.

Percent outside specification limits (actual = 3.9375 to 3.9380)

% below LSL: $z = \dfrac{LSL - \bar{\bar{x}}}{\sigma}$

$z = \dfrac{3.93750 - 3.93774}{0.000142} = -1.69$; $P(z < -1.69) = (0.5 - 0.4545) = 0.0455$ that items will exceed lower limit

% above USL: $z = \dfrac{USL - \bar{\bar{x}}}{\sigma}$

$z = \dfrac{3.9380 - 3.93774}{0.000142} = 1.831$; $P(z > 1.831) = (0.5 - 0.4664) = 0.0336$ that items will exceed upper limit

Therefore, the total % outside is calculated as 7.9%.

Obviously, the problem lies in the fact that the process is not capable of producing good end caps that consistently fall within specification limits. Even though the process is under control, the Bell Vader Company needs to analyze the process to determine what may be done to make it capable. This investigation should look at current materials, equipment, methods, and any other pertinent areas. The process needs to be improved or new equipment purchased in order to improve capability and reduce costs.

22. Based on results from $\bar{x}$- and s-charts:

For the center line, $CL_{\bar{x}} : x = 2.124$; $CL_s : \bar{s} = 0.114$

Control limits for the $\bar{x}$-chart are:
$\bar{\bar{x}} \pm A_3\bar{s} = 2.124 \pm 1.427(0.114) = 1.961$ to 2.287

For the s-chart: $UCL_s = B_4\bar{s} = 2.089(0.114) = 0.238$
$LCL_s = B_3\bar{s} = 0$

Both the $\bar{x}$- and s-charts when constructed, show that the data are hugging their center lines. Therefore, the process appears to be out of control, and causes must be determined and corrected.

24. Based on results from $\bar{x}$- and s-charts:

a. For the center line, $CL_{\bar{x}} : x = 0.762$; $CL_s : \bar{s} = 0.066$

Control limits for the $\bar{x}$-chart are:

$\bar{\bar{x}} \pm A_3\bar{s} = 0.762 \pm 1.427(0.066) = 0.667$ to 0.856

For the s-chart: $UCL_s = B_4\bar{s} = 2.089(0.066) = 0.138$
$LCL_s = B_3\bar{s} = 0$

The $\bar{x}$-chart when constructed, shows an out-of-control condition, with the first 11 points below the center line. Causes must be investigated and the process must be brought under control before $\bar{x}$- and s-charts can be used for process monitoring.

26. Based on results from $\bar{x}$- and s-charts:

For the center line, $CL_{\bar{x}} : \bar{\bar{x}} = 9.170$; $CL_s : \bar{s} = 1.046$

Control limits for the $\bar{x}-$ $-$ s-charts:

$\bar{\bar{x}} \pm A_3\bar{s} = 9.170 \pm 1.427(1.046) = 7.677$ to 10.662

For the $\bar{s}$-chart: $UCL_s = B_4\bar{s} = 2.089(1.046) = 2.185$

$\phantom{For the \bar{s}-chart: }LCL_s = B_3\bar{s} = 0$

As in problem 14-3a, results from 30 samples of 5 show that both the $\bar{x}$- and $\bar{s}$-charts are apparently in control. However, on the $\bar{x}$-chart, samples 12–23 have an unusual pattern. Although it may not be statistically significant, these points could be seen as having 7 or 8 points "hugging" the center line. This pattern bears watching to see if it recurs.

28. For Smith Packaging Machinery Company, when an $\bar{x}$-chart is constructed it will show the following:

   a. For the x-chart for individuals and two-period moving range calculations:

   $\bar{x}\text{-} = 12.004,\ \bar{R} = 4.017$

   Control limits on $\bar{x}$:

   $\text{UCL}_{\bar{x}} = \bar{x} + 3(\bar{R}/d_2) = 12.004 + 3(4.017)/1.128 = 22.688$
   $\text{LCL}_{\bar{x}} = \bar{x} - 3(\bar{R}/d_2) = 12.004 - 3(4.017)/1.128 = 1.320$

   Control limits on $\bar{R}$: $\text{UCL}_R = D_4\bar{R} = 3.267(4.017) = 13.124$
   $\qquad\qquad\qquad\qquad \text{LCL}_R = D_3\bar{R} = 0(4.017) = 0$

   x values and ranges are all within control limits.

   b. Three-period moving range calculations are:

   $\bar{x} = 12.004;\ \bar{R} = 7.148$

   Control limits on $\bar{x}$: $\text{UCL}_{\bar{x}} = \bar{x} + 3\ (\bar{R}/d_2) = 12.004 + 3(7.148)/1.693 = 24.670$
   $\qquad\qquad\qquad\qquad \text{LCL}_{\bar{x}} = \bar{x} - 3\ (\bar{R}/d_2) = 12.004 - 3(7.148)/1.693 = -0.662$

   Control limits on $\bar{R}$: $\text{UCL}_R = D_4\bar{R} = 2.574(7.148) = 18.399$
   $\qquad\qquad\qquad\qquad \text{LCL}_R = D_3\bar{R} = 0(7.148) = 0$

30. Control limits for Dixie Ice Company orders can be calculated using:

   $$\bar{p} = \frac{p_1 + p_2 + p_3 + \ldots\, p_k}{k}$$

   So, $\text{CL}_{\bar{p}} = 56/1{,}250 = 0.045$

   $s_p = \sqrt{[\bar{p}(1 - \bar{p})]/n}$

   $s_p = \sqrt{(0.045)(0.955)/50} = 0.0293$

   Control limits:

   $\text{UCL}_p = \bar{p} + 3s_p$

   $\text{UCL}_p = 0.045 - 3(0.0293) = 0.1329$

   $\text{LCL}_p = \bar{p} - 3s_p$

   $\text{LCL}_p = 0.045 + 3(0.0293) = -0.234$, use 0

32. Data and p-charts, when constructed for Hasty Piston Company, reveal the following:

a. Initially, $CL_{\bar{p}} = 0.13$ (from p-chart template on the Student CD-ROM).

$$s_p = \sqrt{[\bar{p}(1 - \bar{p})]/n}$$

$$s_p = \sqrt{[(0.13)(0.87)]/200} = 0.0238$$

Control limits:

$$UCL_p = \bar{p} + 3s_p$$

$$UCL_p = 0.13 + 3(0.0238) = 0.2014$$
$$LCL_p = \bar{p} - 3s_p$$

$$LCL_p = 0.13 - 3(0.0238) = 0.0586$$

Initial data and the control chart show that a point is out of control.

b. Hasty Piston Company (continued)

Revised $CL_p = 0.1247$ (after sample 12, with a fraction defective of 0.23, was removed).

$$s_p = \sqrt{[(\bar{p}(1 - \bar{p})]/n} = \sqrt{[(0.1247)(0.8753)]/200} = 0.0234$$

Control limits:

$$UCL_p = \bar{p} + 3s_p$$

$$UCL_p = 0.1247 + 3(0.0234) = 0.1948$$

$$LCL_p = \bar{p} - 3s_p$$

$$LCL_p = 0.1247 - 3(0.0234) = 0.0546$$

See data and the revised control chart when constructed, after sample 12 was removed.

34. a. The p-chart must be constructed, using the available spreadsheet template.

Based on the average number of defects per sample, the average proportion can be calculated as:

$$CL_{\bar{p}} = 28.88/125 = 0.2310$$

$$s_p = \sqrt{[(\bar{p}(1 - \bar{p})]/n} = \sqrt{[(0.2310)(0.7690)]/125} = 0.0377$$

Control limits:

$$UCL_p = \bar{p} + 3s_p = 0.2310 + 3(0.0377) = 0.3441$$

$$\text{LCL}_p = \bar{p} - 3s_p = 0.2310 - 3(0.0377) = 0.1179$$

The initial p-chart when constructed shows that it is highly likely that this process is not in control and that major changes need to be made. However, we can approximate our results by throwing out all points 43 and over and revising the chart.

b. Revised p statistics:

$$\text{CL}_{\bar{p}} = 22.45/125 = 0.1796$$
$$s_p = \sqrt{[(\bar{p}(1 - \bar{p})]/n} = \sqrt{[(0.1796)(0.8204)]/125} = 0.0343$$

Control limits:

$$\text{UCL}_p = \bar{p} + 3s_p = 0.1796 + 3(0.0343) = 0.2825$$

$$\text{LCL}_p = \bar{p} - 3s_p = 0.1796 - 3(0.0343) = 0.0767$$

Once again, the control chart shows several points out of control. Throw out all points 35 and over and revise again.

c. The final revised statistics show:

$$\text{CL}_p = 18.56/125 = 0.1485$$

$$s_p = \sqrt{[(\bar{p}(1 - \bar{p})]/n} = \sqrt{[(0.01485)(0.8515)]/125} = 0.0318$$

Control limits:

$$\text{UCL}_p = \bar{p} + 3s_p = 0.1485 + 3(0.0318) = 0.2439$$

$$\text{LCL}_p = \bar{p} - 3s_p = 0.1485 - 3(0.0389) = 0.0531$$

36. Note that the values obtained for Edgewater Hospital's data with a hand calculator will differ slightly from those obtained from the Excel spreadsheets, due to rounding differences. p-chart spreadsheets should be constructed to see the differences.

Initial Calculation:

a. The average sample size = 441.4, so the "approximate" control limits, based on total defects over total items sampled, are:

$$\text{CL}_p = 265/8,828 = 0.030,$$

$$s_p = \sqrt{[(\bar{p}(1 - \bar{p})]/n} = \sqrt{[(0.03)(0.97)]/441.4} = 0.0081$$

$$\text{UCL}_p = \bar{p} + 3s_p = 0.030 + 3(0.0081) = 0.0543$$

$$\text{LCL}_p = \bar{p} - 3s_p = 0.0305 - 3(0.0082) = 0.0057$$

Points 12 and 19 are outside the limits on the control chart when constructed. After deleting these points, we get:

b. The revised average sample size = 444.33

$$CL_{\bar{p}} = 216 / 7,998 = 0.027$$

$$s_p = \sqrt{[(\bar{p}(1 - \bar{p})]/n} = \sqrt{[(0.027)(0.973)]/444.33} = 0.0077$$

$$UCL_p = \bar{p} + 3s_p = 0.027 + 3(0.0077) = 0.0501$$

$$LCL_p = \bar{p} - 3s_p = 0.027 - 3(0.0077) = 0.0039$$

The process is now considered to be under control.

38. Using data from problem 34, we get results for the *np* chart when constructed that are similar to the *p*-chart:

Initial calculations:

$$CL_{n\bar{p}} = n\bar{p} = 125(0.2310) = 28.88$$
$$s_{n\bar{p}} = \sqrt{[n(\bar{p})(1 - \bar{p})]} = \sqrt{125(0.231)(0.769)} = 4.712$$

Control limits:

$$UCL_{n\bar{p}} = n\bar{p} + 3s_{n\bar{p}} = 28.88 + 3(4.712) = 43.016$$
$$LCL_{n\bar{p}} = n\bar{p} - 3s_{n\bar{p}} = 28.88 - 3(4.712) = 14.744$$

As in the previous results for problem 34, values for 9 out-of-limits samples had to be eliminated, leaving 16 usable data points. After eliminating the unusable points, we get revised control limits shown as follows:

Final revised:

$$CL_{n\bar{p}} = n\bar{p} = 125(0.1485) = 18.56$$

$$s_{n\bar{p}} = \sqrt{[n(\bar{p})(1 - \bar{p})]} = \sqrt{125(0.1485)(0.8515)} = 3.976$$

Control limits:

$$UCL_{n\bar{p}} = n\bar{p} + 3s_{n\bar{p}} = 18.56 + 3(3.976) = 30.488$$
$$LCL_{n\bar{p}} = n\bar{p} - 3s_{n\bar{p}} = 18.56 - 3(3.976) = 6.632$$

40. Center line for the *c*-chart: $\bar{c} = 340/30 = 11.33$

$$\bar{c} \pm 3\sqrt{\bar{c}} = 11.33 \pm 3\sqrt{11.33} = 11.33 \pm 10.1 = 1.23 \text{ to } 21.33$$

42. For the *c*-chart (using the template on the student CD-ROM):

Number defective = 147; number of samples = 25

Center line for the c-chart: $\bar{c}$ = 147/25 = 5.88

$\bar{c} \pm 3\sqrt{\bar{c}} = 5.88 \pm 3\sqrt{5.88} = 5.88 \pm 7.28 = 0$ to 13.16

44. The run chart, frequency distribution, and u-chart should be constructed and will all provide different insights on the problem. The run chart shows as many as 6 falls were recorded in four different months at the hospital.
A frequency histogram when constructed shows that the most common number of monthly falls was four per month. The run chart, in conjunction with the histogram, shows the months in which a certain number of falls happened.

The u-chart will show what the rate of falls was, based on the number of patient care days (PCDs), a variable "sample size." These data permit an analyst to develop a control chart with variable control limits. The chart shows that the process was under control, although it doesn't mean that falls were at an acceptable level! The acceptable level of patient falls is 0. Therefore, the hospital administration should be encouraged to use these data to analyze and find the root causes of falls and make every effort to reduce the frequency to 0.

46. For the u-chart conditions: number of samples = 4, number of defectives = 16.

Center line for the u-chart: $\bar{u}$ = 16/4 = 4

$\bar{u} \pm 3\sqrt{\bar{u}/n} = 4 \pm 3 = 4 \pm 3 = 1$ to 7

This calculation provides the control limits on one sample with a size of 4.

48. The stabilized control charts for $\bar{x}$ and R show the same out-of-control condition for the Silicon Wafer example as discussed earlier in the chapter. If only the first x-chart is constructed, it shows sample 17 out-of-control, as in the body of the chapter. It would be a simple matter to remove sample 17, which created the out-of-control condition, since control limits on the stabilized chart remain constant for a given sample size. Note that slightly different values for the control chart averages are calculated versus those in the text problem, due to rounding the data in the original problem to whole number values.

To verify calculations, for example, the first data point is:

$\bar{\bar{x}}$ = 48.973; $\bar{R}$ = 27.040; CL_x = 0; CL_R = 1

$UCL_{\bar{x}} = A_2 = 1.023$

$LCL_{\bar{x}} = -A_2 = -1.023$

$UCL_R = D_4 = 2.574$

$LCL_R = D_3 = 0$

Note that the limits on $\bar{x}$ are not multiplied by 3, which is the estimated *process* range variation, not the sample range variation. The following example shows how the transformed values for the first sample were obtained.

$$z_{\bar{x}} = \frac{\bar{x} - \bar{\bar{x}}}{\bar{R}} = \frac{44.333 - 48.973}{27.040} = -0.172$$

$$z = \frac{R}{\bar{R}} = \frac{48}{27.04} = 1.775$$

50. The control chart for the EMWA versus observed values must be constructed. With an $\alpha = 0.4$, we see that the process is under control, but the EMWA estimate does not closely anticipate the next observed value. The conclusion is that a better "forecast" of future values might be obtained for volatile values such as these if a larger α value were used to give greater weight to more recent values.

The following final problems relate to concepts found in the Bonus Materials on the student CD-ROM.

52. For $z = \pm 2.75$, $P(z > 2.75) = P(z < -2.75)$
From the normal probability table: $0.5000 - 0.4970 = 0.003$; therefore, the % outside $= 100 \times 2(0.003) = 0.6\%$

54. Using the binomial formula:

$$P(\text{acceptance}) = \overset{n}{\Sigma} f(x) \text{ and } f^n(x) = (x)\, p^x (1 - p)^{n-x}$$

11 in a row $= (0.5)^{11} = 0.049\%$

10 of 11 $= \binom{11}{10}(0.5)^{10}\,(0.5)^1 = 11(0.5)^{11} = 0.539\%$

9 of 11 $= \binom{11}{9}(0.5)^9(0.5)^2 = 55(0.5)^{11} = 2.695\%$

8 of 11 $= \binom{11}{8}(0.5)^8(0.5)^3 = 165(0.5)^{11} = 8.085\%$

7 of 11 $= \binom{11}{7}(0.5)^7(0.5)^4 = 330(0.5)^{11} = 16.17\%$

$\therefore$ 9 out of 11 (or more) points are statistically significant ($p < 0.05$).

INDEX